International Relations Since 1945

International Relations Since 1945

A Global History

John W. Young and John Kent

THIRD EDITION

OXFORD
UNIVERSITY PRESS

OXFORD
UNIVERSITY PRESS

Great Clarendon Street, Oxford, OX2 6DP,
United Kingdom

Oxford University Press is a department of the University of Oxford.
It furthers the University's objective of excellence in research, scholarship,
and education by publishing worldwide. Oxford is a registered trade mark of
Oxford University Press in the UK and in certain other countries.

First edition 2003
Second edition 2013

Impression: 1

Published in the United States of America by Oxford University Press
198 Madison Avenue, New York, NY 10016, United States of America

British Library Cataloguing in Publication Data
Data available

Library of Congress Control Number: 2019940875

ISBN 978–0–19–880761–2

Printed in Great Britain by
Bell & Bain Ltd., Glasgow

Preface to the Third Edition

For the third edition, we have again largely adhered to the approach taken in the first and second editions, while expanding on what we said about world events in the twenty-first century, and incorporating coverage of the latest developments in the history of international relations by adding the new Part VIII on the period since 2011. As in the second edition, we have fully revised the text, trimming back some material, while strengthening interpretative material on some points.

Preface to the First Edition

This book provides a general account of the nature and development of the post-war international system with the origins, nature, and end of the Cold War at its centre. The approach is a historical one but one which hopes to offer something of value to general International Relations students interested in the development and interpretation of the post-1945 international system from a sounder empirical foundation. In particular, the book seeks to examine Cold War controversies in a way which will stimulate debate and produce some reinterpretations. It implicitly challenges the importance of realism and suggests that realism is an unsuitable tool for understanding and explaining the Cold War and its end because it ignores the importance of domestic influences on foreign policy. The book makes no claim to contribute to historical sociology, but it does attempt to suggest that domestic affairs, ideologies, and culture have significant connections to international events and are influences on the events described and analysed here. In particular, that it is inappropriate to consider the post-war international system in isolation from the nature of the domestic state, the role of elites, and their use of ideas and ideologies.

Although world politics will be examined throughout from an essentially historical perspective rather than in terms of any particular theory of international relations, the aim is not simply to tell what happened but to provide overall analysis and broad interpretations of events. Theories rest more securely on detailed empirical understanding, and good historical methodology does not neglect theoretical concepts or fail to deal with causation. Yet we recognise that it may not be possible to explain fully the causes of the changes in the international system after 1945, either in general or specific terms.

Given the work available on the post-1945 period, we set out specifically to provide a book which incorporates some new ways of synthesizing complicated material and which also adds new and controversial interpretations for consideration, while attempting to define the Cold War more precisely. For those teachers eager to get students thinking for themselves and contributing ideas to seminars and tutorials, this should be a provocative book which outlines different ideas, as well as providing basic information. As such, it should offer something to students seeking to discover and reflect on new interpretations, rather than simply discovering the facts and the so-called 'correct' explanations. Special attention is placed on new interpretations of the Cold War and its various phases, while trying to link its development to a number of military and economic themes. Not least because a feature of the Cold War on both sides of the Iron Curtain has been the expenditure of vast resources on making people think in particular ways about many aspects of international relations; new interpretations of the Cold War's development are especially needed now it has ended. It is only by reflecting more fundamentally about the ascribed nature of the Cold War that we can begin to understand just why it ended so dramatically.

By placing more emphasis on controversies and challenging some conventional interpretations, the book hopes to offer a basis for debate and discussion in courses associated with the nature and development of the post-Second World War international system. A more analytical overview defining key issues precedes the more detailed coverage in the six chronological sections. This is intended to reinforce some of the key questions for debate which are also featured in much of the main text. Where there is repetition of interpretation, it is hoped that students will benefit from being able to consider again some of the key issues raised. Both general and more specifically focused chronologies are included, along with considerable cross-referencing. Where terms are used which may be unfamiliar and require explanation, we hope to have provided this. Interpretations are not usually presented as definitive, and the intention is often to present alternative views, especially where detailed evidence cannot be produced. Text boxes will be found throughout, especially in the earlier sections, to provide details of important documents, interesting meetings and memoranda, summaries of debates, or interpretations and brief biographies of key figures. They will also be used to provide glimpses of the kind of ideas which are unusual, less well known, and hopefully interesting and revealing.

As with the interpretations, there will be some variety in the way specific themes are treated in different chronological periods which inevitably produce different issues and more or less debate. The variety should again serve to encourage the use of a general text as a means of thinking about the post-war world while discovering what happened. Some aspects of it will be covered in more detail than others, and the constraints of space inevitably require that some topics which others might deem important will not be featured at all. The changes in the international economic order, the importance of the end of the European and Soviet empires, and links between the developed and less developed worlds will be touched on. And we hope to provide glimpses of all areas of the world and of the effects of international changes in and after the Cold War which have for many years been felt in both global and regional contexts.

We would like to express our thanks in helping to prepare this manuscript for publication to Lindsey Kent and Martine Langer, and especially to Janet Smith for her extensive and excellent typing, and to Helen Adams for having to confront a very demanding manuscript.

New to this Edition

- A new final part on the 'Age of Uncertainty' brings readers up to date with key IR events and developments from 2011 to 2018.
- Three brand-new chapters explore the war in Syria, Brexit, and President Trump, and the rise of challenges to the West in Europe and Asia.
- The text has been thoroughly updated to reflect developments of different discourses, such as the UK's strategy for Middle East defence during the early Cold War.
- Additional maps are included to help students visualize the conflicts and territories in the Middle East region.

Outline Contents

Detailed Contents

List of Abbreviations

ABM	Anti-Ballistic Missile
ADIZ	Air Defence Identification Zone
AFPL	(Burmese) Anti-Fascist People's Freedom League
AIIB	Asian Investment Bank
ALCM	Air-Launched Cruise Missile
ANC	African National Congress (South Africa)
ANF	Atlantic Nuclear Force
ANSOM	(French) National Archives Overseas Section
ANZUS	Australian–New Zealand–US Alliance
APEC	Asia–Pacific Economic Co-operation
ARAMCO	Arabian–American Oil Company
ARENA	(El Salvador) National Republican Alliance
ARM	Adjustable-Rate Mortgage
ARVN	Army of the Republic of Vietnam
ASEAN	Association of South-East Asian Nations
AWACS	Airborne Warning and Control System
BRI	Belt and Road Initiative (China)
CAP	Common Agricultural Policy (of EEC)
CARICOM	Caribbean Community
CBW	Chemical and Biological Weapons
CCP	Chinese Communist Party
CDO	Collateralized Debt Obligations
CDS	Credit Default Swap
CDU	(German) Christian Democratic Union
CENTO	Central Treaty Organization
CFCs	Chloro-Fluoro-Carbons
CFE	Conventional Forces in Europe Treaty
CFM	Council of Foreign Ministers
CFSP	(EU) Common Foreign and Security Policy
CIA	(American) Central Intelligence Agency
CIS	Commonwealth of Independent States (in former USSR)
CK	*Compagnie du Katanga*
COCOM	Co-ordinating Committee (on East–West trade)
COMECON	Council for Mutual Economic Aid
Cominform	Communist Information Bureau
COS	Chiefs of Staff
CPA	Coalition Provisional Authority (Iraq)
CPP	(Gold Coast) Convention People's Party
CPSU	Communist Party of the Soviet Union
CSCE	Conference on Security and Co-operation in Europe
CSK	*Comité Spécial du Katanga*
CTBT	Comprehensive Test Ban Treaty
DBPO	Documents on British Policy Overseas
DEFCON	(US) Defence Condition
DMZ	De-Militarized Zone
EC	European Community
EDC	European Defence Community
ECOWAS	Economic Community of West African States
ECSC	European Coal and Steel Community
EEC	European Economic Community
EFSF	European Financial Stability Facility
EFTA	European Free Trade Association
EMU	Economic and Monetary Union
ERM	(EC) Exchange Rate Mechanism
ETILAF	Syrian National Coalition of Syrian Revolution and Opposition Forces
EU	European Union
Euratom	European Atomic Energy Authority
Ex Comm	Executive Committee of the NSC
FALSG	Foreign Affairs Leading Small Group (China)
FATA	Federally Administered Tribal Areas
FBI	(US) Federal Bureau of Investigation
FBS	Forward Based Systems (of nuclear weapons in Europe)
FDI	Foreign Direct Investment
FIDES	(French) Funds for Economic and Social Investment
FLN	(Algerian) National Liberation Front
FLSN	(Nicaraguan) National Sandinista Liberation Front
FNLA	Front for the National Liberation of Angola
FPR	Rwandan Popular Front
FRELIMO	Front for the Liberation of Mozambique
FRUS	Foreign Relations of the United States
FSA	Free Syrian Army
FSB	Federal Security Service (Russian Federation)

FTAA	Free Trade Area of the Americas
G-7	Group of Seven leading economic powers
G-8	Group of Eight
GATT	General Agreement on Tariffs and Trade
GDP	Gross Domestic Product
GDR	(East) German Democratic Republic
GLCM	Ground-Launched Cruise Missile
GNP	Gross National Product
GSE	Government Sponsored Enterprise
IAEA	International Atomic Energy Agency
IBRD	International Bank of Reconstruction and Development
ICBM	Inter-Continental Ballistic Missile
IDF	Israeli Defence Force
IED	Improvised Explosive Device
IFOR	Implementation Force (NATO)
IGC	(EC and EU) Inter-Governmental Conference
IMF	International Monetary Fund
INDCS	Intended Nationally Determined Contributions
INF	Intermediate-Range Nuclear Forces
IRBM	Intermediate-Range Ballistic Missile
ISAF	International Security Assistance Force
ISI	Islamic State in Iraq
ISIS	Islamic State in Iraq and al-Sham (Syria)
ISSG	International Syria Support Group
JCOS	Joint Chiefs of Staff
KGB	(Soviet) State Security Committee (1954–91)
KHAD	Afghan secret police
KI	(Soviet) Small Committee of Information
KLA	Kosovan Liberation Army
KMT	Kuomintang (Chinese Nationalist Party)
KPD	German Communist Party
LCC	Local Co-ordination Committee (Syria)
LDC	Less Developed Country
LNM	Lebanese National Movement
MACV	Military Assistance Command, Vietnam
MAD	Mutual Assured Destruction
MBFR	Mutual Balanced Force Reduction (talks)
MBS	Mortgage-Backed Securities
MEC	Middle East Command
MEDO	Middle East Defence Organization
MERCUSOR	Common Market of the South (South America)
MGB	(Soviet) Ministry for State Security (1946–54)
MI5	(British) counter-intelligence and counter-subversion service
MIRV	Multiple Independent Re-entry Vehicle
MLF	(NATO) Multilateral Force
MNC	Multi-National Company
MOAB	Massive Ordnance Air Blast

MPLA	Popular Movement for the Liberation of Angola
MRBM	Medium-Range Ballistic Missile
MX	(US) Missile Experimental
NA	(UK) National Archives
NAFTA	North American Free Trade Area
NARA	US National Archives and Records Administration
NATO	North Atlantic Treaty Organization
NDF	National Defence Force (Syria)
NGO	Non-Governmental Organization
NIE	(US) National Intelligence Estimate
NKVD	Soviet Secret Police Apparatus (1934–46)
NLF	(South Vietnam) National Liberation Front
NPT	Non-Proliferation Treaty
NSA	(US) National Security Agency
NSA	(US) National Security Advisor
NSC	(US) National Security Council
NVA	North Vietnamese Army
OAS	Organization of American States
OAU	Organization of African Unity
OBOR	One Belt One Road (China)
OECD	Organisation for Economic Co-operation and Development
OEEC	Organisation of European Economic Co-operation
OPC	(US) Office of Policy Co-ordination
OPEC	Organization of Petroleum Exporting Countries
ORHA	Office of Reconstruction and Humanitarian Assistance
OSCE	Organization for Security and Co-operation in Europe
PAIGC	African Independence Party of Guinea and Cape Verde
PAP	(Singapore) People's Action Party
PCF	French Communist Party
PD	(US) Presidential Directive
PDA	Democratic Party of Angola
PDG	Guinea Democratic Party
PDPA	People's Democratic Party of Afghanistan
PFLP	Popular Front for the Liberation of Palestine
PKI	Indonesian Communist Party
PKK	Kurdistan Workers' Party
PLA	People's Liberation Army
PLF	Palestine Liberation Front
PLO	Palestine Liberation Organization
PMF	Popular Mobilization Force (Iraq)
PNA	Palestinian National Authority
PRC	People's Republic of China
PRO	Public Record Office

RCC	Revolutionary Command Council
RDA	African Democratic Rally
RENAMO	Mozambique National Resistance
RRR	Required Reserve Ratio
RSA	Non-UK Sterling Area
SAC	(US) Strategic Air Command
SALT	Strategic Arms Limitation Talks and Treaty
SAVAK	Iranian Secret Police
SCAP	Supreme Commander Allied Powers (Japan)
SDI	(US) Strategic Defense Initiative
SEATO	Southeast Asian Treaty Organization
SED	East German Communist Party
SHAPE	Supreme Headquarters Allied Powers Europe
SILF	Syrian Islamic Liberation Front
SIPRI	Stockholm International Peace Research Institute
SLBM	Submarine-Launched Ballistic Missile
SLCM	Sea-Launched Cruise Missile
SLF	Syrian Liberation Front
SNC	Syrian National Council
SPD	(German) Social Democratic Party
SPV	Special Purpose Vehicle
START	Strategic Arms Reduction Treaty
SWAPO	South-West African People's Organization
TARP	Troubled Asset Relief Program
TBT	Test Ban Treaty
TTP	Tehrik-i-Taliban Pakistan
UAR	United Arab Republic
UDSR	(French) Social Democratic Resistance Union
UGCC	United Gold Coast Convention
UK	United Kingdom
UKIP	UK Independence Party
UMHK	*Union Minière du Haut Katanga*
UN	United Nations
UNCTAD	United Nations Conference on Trade and Development
UNESCO	United Nations Educational, Scientific and Cultural Organization
UNIFIL	UN Interim Force in Lebanon
UNITA	National Union for the Total Independence of Angola
UNLU	(Palestinian) United National Leadership of the Uprising
UNO	(Nicaraguan) National Opposition Union
UNOSOM	UN Operation in Somalia
UNPROFOR	UN Protection Force (former Yugoslavia)
UNSCOM	UN Special Commission charged with the elimination of Iraq's CBW and ballistic missiles, and monitoring their sites to prevent the rebuilding of such capabilities
UNSCOP	UN Special Committee on Palestine
UPA	Union of Angolan Peoples
UPNA	Union of Peoples of Northern Angola
US	United States
USMCA	US–Mexico–Canada Agreement
USSR	Union of Soviet Socialist Republics
VPN	Virtual Private Network
WMD	Weapons of Mass Destruction
WTO	World Trade Organization

List of Maps

How to Use the Online Resources

www.oup.com/he/young-kent3e

The book is supported by online resources designed to help students take their learning further.

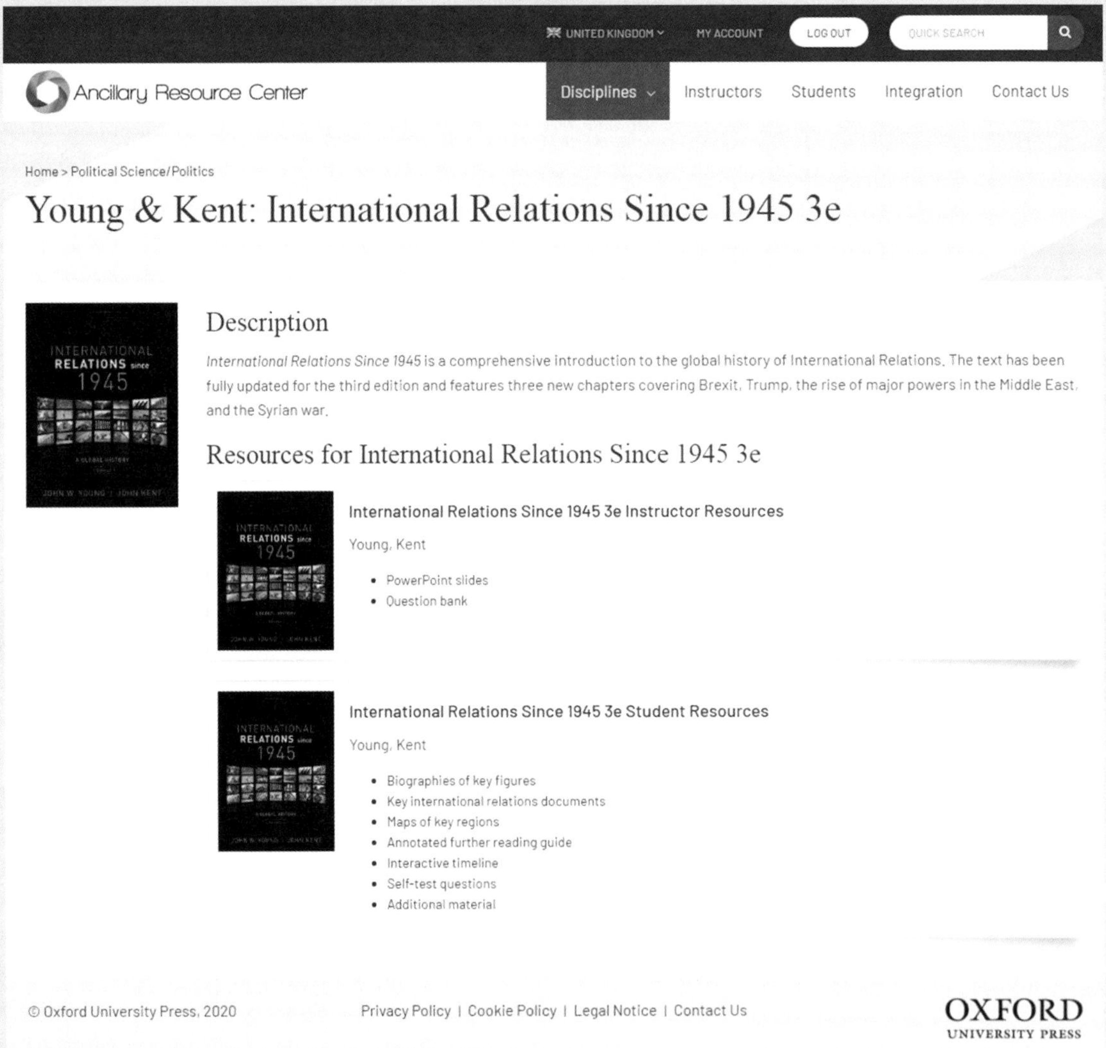

FOR STUDENTS:

Accessible to all, with no registration or password required, these resources help you get the most from your textbook.

Biographies of key figures

A series of short biographies, arranged alphabetically, focuses on important individuals who helped shape the course of post-war international relations.

Key international relations documents

Web links, organized by chapter, direct you to key international relations documents from the Cold War onwards.

Self-test questions

Self-test multiple-choice questions for each chapter allow you to assess your grasp of key concepts, theories, and ideas as you progress through your course. Answers are submitted online, and you receive your marks and feedback immediately.

Annotated further reading guide

An annotated reading guide directs you to the latest sources of information.

Interactive timeline

An interactive timeline guides you through key events in the history of international relations. Click on the date you want, and you can read about the key events in that year.

Maps of key regions

Maps show you the key regions discussed in the text.

Additional material

Extra material for students is available to take your learning further, including a financial glossary, extracts, and additional biographies.

FOR LECTURERS:

These password-protected resources are available only to lecturers.

PowerPoint slides

Adaptable PowerPoint slides for use as the basis for lecture presentations, or as hand-outs in class.

Question bank

General essay questions and questions relating to each part of the book allow you to test your students and provide valuable exam practice.

Introduction: Understanding the Cold War

The history of international politics since 1945 was dominated, down to the 1990s by the origins, development, and sudden end of the Cold War. Although defined in different ways, the Cold War fundamentally distinguished the post-Second World War period from the earlier years of the twentieth century in political and socio-economic terms and in its rapid technological changes. The change it produced, following the most destructive interstate global conflict in history, fundamentally altered the international system. But there were other international developments emerging in the Cold War which provided a link to the post-Cold War period. These included the growing importance of the mass media, the role of international organizations, the growth of transnational non-governmental organizations (NGOs), and the impact of globalization, which together served to erode the power and significance of sovereign states. Some of these developments arguably had positive consequences even if, as with the anticipated 'new world order', they did not fully fulfil their aims or expectations. Other developments had unforeseen and negative consequences in much of the post-Cold War Western world, dominated by 'new' types of armed conflict and increasingly dysfunctional economic relationships. In addition, the growing managerialism that imposed more and more authoritarian regulations on aspects of every-day life in the developed world resonated unhappily with the bureaucratic diktats of the defeated Cold War adversary.

The end of the Cold War produced drastic international changes but some similarities with the old order it replaced and an overview of the Cold War, and the new system it represented remains necessary, if controversial, for an understanding of the post-Cold War era with its continuities and changes. The book aims to highlight these interpretative challenges by taking a more detailed look at the Cold War's various phases over the first five sections of the book. The post-Cold War years can only be understood in a preliminary way by adopting the same mix of overview and detailed analysis of a much altered and less stable international system. The aim is also to present some alternative interpretations that may assist different reflections on the important links between international influences and domestic policies on foreign policy in a less state centric more interconnected world.

The Antecedents of the 1945 International System

The new post-war system that emerged in 1945 was now, for the first time in modern history, dominated by two extra-European powers. Relations between the European states had been destabilized by the unification of Germany in 1871. Prior to this, a balance of power within the continent had preserved stability only as long as the manpower and resources of Germany were not united. The problem of Germany after unification could not be solved without the intervention of non-European powers—the US and the Soviet Union (partly a European and partly an Asian power). Europe could no longer resolve its own problems and assistance from outside was required to overcome Germany in the last two years of the First World War, when the US became involved. American reluctance to shoulder the burdens of maintaining peace in the inter-war years became the key element which permitted the re-emergence of a powerful Germany. Containing the German threat post-1919 required the kind of commitment that the US was not prepared to make until the 1940s. The role of the US, as either a hegemonic power or as a key global player in a bipolar world, was by then a dramatic new feature of international politics after 1945. It had only one obvious challenger in the form of the Soviet Union, whose land-based empire extended into Asia, but whose victory in the great land battles against the Third Reich provided the opportunity for it to play an important if not dominant European role.

It is easy to portray the decline of European nation states as a direct result of two European wars and the enormous shift in the global balance of economic and military power. After the violent power struggles of 1939-45, the divisions in Europe became part of a global struggle in which the continent's position was fundamentally altered. Whatever the significance of Europe in terms of the peace settlement and the rise of international tensions, the continent was now only one part of a new global power political equation. Disagreements soon began to appear, as the victors in the war struggled to come to terms with a new global system of power and influence that was far from being a predominantly European one. One purpose of this book is to try and portray a Cold War developing out of the Second World War *not* because there were post-war differences in and over Europe, but because the world *as a whole* had radically changed.

The onset of the Cold War conflict has been given a number of different historical roots and chronological starting points. The development of two large land-based empires, particularly in the nineteenth century, could have paved the way for what some see as an inevitable clash. The economic and human resources they possessed were likely to produce growing international power and influence and a greater sense of rivalry. This certainly fits with a 'realist' explanation of international relations, but it ignores the ideological conflict between communism and capitalism, which is thus subordinated to geopolitical rivalries and a competition for resources. Yet the two land-based empires with rival ideologies had coexisted since 1917 and the relations which developed after 1945 were clearly different from those existing before the First and Second World Wars. Whatever the role of geo-politics and ideology—and both are important—the timing of the Cold War was connected to radical changes in the global power balance produced by the Second World War *and* to a new sense of ideological rivalry. In Western Europe, elite fears of domestic instability and the destruction of the social and economic status quo which the Second World War produced were particularly important.

General theories do not serve to explain the *timing* of the Cold War and, for those not primarily focused on power, realism serves no purpose, as it takes no account of ideas or ideologies. The Cold War's origins for them are better located in communist success in the Russian Revolution and the irreconcilable ideological conflict it produced. As better communications made the transmission of ideas on a global basis easier and cheaper, the conflict between two ideological state systems assumed global proportions. The Cold War was therefore about competing ideologies that, for the first time, threatened the social and economic status quo on which national ruling elites in capitalist countries depended. Thus, domestic interests and the pursuit of ideological goals superseded the old international rivalries and alliances that had been geared to the competing interests of all sovereign states. In such an analysis, the domestic social and economic systems and their political philosophies assume significance in shaping the global conflict, and explanations of the Cold War must define the relationships between power political and ideological requirements. Economic development and the maintenance or prevention of social mobility in Latin America, Africa, as well as in the developed states of Europe, then become crucial in the origins and development of the conflict.

Realism

The Realist school of international relations theorists was born out of the failure of liberal thinkers in the inter-war period to attach sufficient weight to the importance of power as a determinant of international relations—and, in particular, to Adolf Hitler's aggressive desire to maximize the territorial expansion and military power of the Third Reich. In contrast to liberals, who put their faith in international cooperation and the importance of states working together, realists, noting the lack of any single international authority and the anarchical nature of the international system, point to the necessity of survival through self-help. States are seen as competing with one another to achieve security from external threats, which can be achieved only through relative gains in military and economic power. As states pursue this goal, they are defined by realists as unitary actors, competing to maximize their power in ways determined by the nature of the international system. Hence, there is little or no linkage between domestic and foreign policy with the latter determined exclusively by external considerations. Regarding the Cold War, realists see it as a power political competition between two competing power systems led by the US and the USSR, with their development of new and more powerful weapons. Hence, the ideological and domestic considerations are not seen as important determinants of the Cold War.

The Origins of the Cold War

The initial failure to agree on how to resolve the rivalries which arose, in part, from the wartime shift in the global balance of economic and military power, owed much to domestic economic and political forces. It was not simply the existence of rival ideologies that caused problems, but the fact that the challenge to the pre-war social order in much of Western Europe was strengthened by the war itself, and by forces for change it had unleashed. By the end of the Second World War, it was clear that states would have to assume responsibilities for more than the maintenance of territorial integrity and the external pursuit of economic and military interests. Citizens throughout the globe expected improvements in their social and economic welfare, and that governments would promote these goals. Demands for social reform, with better conditions for the lower classes, had been feared and foreseen by those appeasers who sought to avoid war, like the British Prime Minister, Neville Chamberlain. By 1945, the USSR, their wartime ally in the East, had been strengthened by the war and threatened revolution rather than reform. For the first time since the French Revolution, a movement for radical social change was accompanied and supported by a powerful state. The Cold War was in fact a battle for the domestic and international survival of states, social elites, and ways of life. In such circumstances, students should be aware how much elites on both sides have been prepared to invest in distorting the truth. In terms of strengthening their position and attracting mass support, it has always been vital to blame their opponents for instigating the conflict and to portray the actions of their own states as defensive and reactive. This has led to all sorts of distortions and misunderstandings of the nature of the global struggle and the ways in which regional conflicts have been linked to it.

The quest for international power and influence both contributed to the breakdown of the victorious wartime alliance in 1945 and assumed greater importance in the disagreements over the new world order, because of the combination of the domestic and the international. Global status and prestige could influence the balance of domestic forces, and the appeal of radical ideologies, more so than in the inter-war years. Power politics and ideologies were always interlinked. While Europe may have been seen as the most valuable region where these were played out, it was as much the failure to agree on how to allocate power, influence, and responsibility on a global basis between three main areas (Asia, Europe, and the Middle East) that was central to the power-political disagreements in 1945.

The Decline of Europe and Global Economic Relations

The end of a Europe-dominated world was indicated during the war by the, albeit temporary, loss of many parts of its empire. The European states system had been central to great power relations in the first half of the century (and, indeed, long before that) as well as to the development of international relations theory. After 1945, it was the nature of Europe's relationship to the broader global balance of power that was crucial. Whatever the significance of the continent in terms of the rise of international tensions, it was now only one part of a new power political equation. The ending of European control over large areas of the globe, often referred to as decolonization, was one indication of the increasing shift of the focus of international politics. Large numbers of newly independent states were to change the nature of the newly-formed United Nations and focus attention on the relationship between the industrialized world and less developed areas (which relied on the production for export of raw materials and foodstuffs). At the same time, new regional power configurations had to be considered in Asia, Africa, and the Middle East; these assumed significance for the global Cold War, because some were seen as increasingly significant in global terms.

The decolonization debate was based on the relative importance of 'nationalist' challenges to colonial rule, the European policies of colonial reform which confronted them, and the international developments influencing all parties. The rise of what are generally deemed to be 'nationalist movements' began in nineteenth-century India, but did not emerge in parts of Black Africa until after the Second World War. Whether they were nationalist in terms of civic or ethnic nationalism is a matter of debate. It is true that the Western-educated elites, who tended to dominate political movements in the colonies, sought to build popular mass-based parties in support of independence. Yet, some would argue that the lack of a civic tradition and a sense of belonging to a wider society[1] in many African cultures weakened any sense of identification with newly-created states based on externally-imposed boundaries. Furthermore, while nationalist parties sought to transcend ethnic divisions and attract support on policies and issues, in both Africa and Asia, parties tended to divide on ethnic or religious grounds, particularly with the approach or attainment of independence. This lack of a civic or political culture has led some to conclude that nationalism in the era of decolonization constituted a set of elite groups whose supporters were united by anti-colonialism, but then divided by competition over who should wield power with the achievement of independence. Others have seen the failure of nationalist movements to create successful post-independence states as rooted in the divisive nature of colonial rule and the corruption and weakness of some African and Asian elites.

Important questions emerged about the economic and trade relations between these areas, with newly independent states emerging in the twenty years after the war and the developed world, including the former imperial powers. The debate about the structural nature of these relations remains unresolved. Some see economic problems being created in the developing nations, because of the alleged failure to give free rein to market forces. Others claim that capitalism in the developed world operates to the increasing detriment of the less developed world, through its control over raw material prices and investment capital flows. At the same time, the terms of trade of the rich countries improved at the expense of the poor ones. Whether this was linked to the effect of colonialism is another unresolved, but highly charged, debate about global economic relations, one subsumed within controversies over the nature and effect of globalization and the emergence of problems which require global cooperation to solve. In the post-Cold War world, environmental pollution and climate change, along with international crime and disease, are phenomena outside the control of individual nation states and can be seen as eroding their power.

The end of European rule over much of the world was accompanied by political and economic changes within Europe. It was these changes that indicated the weakening of the nation state and its exclusive role in international relations. The European colonial powers began to construct economic and institutional links between themselves, which undermined sovereignty and began the process of defining a common European approach to international and domestic affairs. The current study discusses these European developments, which began with economic integration in Western Europe, and the expanding international economy, but focuses more on the nature of the new regional conflicts and the role of the US and USSR in influencing them. European integration and the increasing 'transnational' contacts between elites, with loyalties not centred solely on the nation state, seemed for some to signify the beginning of a new era in international affairs, again with a legacy from the Second World War. Equally important is the continued existence of global inequality and the extreme poverty experienced by millions of people in the less developed world. The debates about economic development are briefly touched upon in parts of the book, to indicate that world politics do not simply take place between the rich nations with the power to dominate international affairs. With the 2008 near collapse of the post-Cold War international capitalist economy, under the growing weight of the neo-liberal consensus, new forms of instability resulted from the forces unleashed by the failures of communism.

Bipolarity or Hegemony?

The post-1945 world is normally defined as 'bipolar' because of the disparity between the military capabilities and economic resources of the world's two most powerful states and the lesser powers, and because of the alignment of many states with one of the opposing ideological blocs before 1989. After 1990, it became possible to talk of a 'unipolar' world, simply because the US now seemed much more powerful than any other state, in both military and economic terms. Yet the concept of bipolarity does require some qualification. At the end of the Second World War, only Britain and the US had the ability to act militarily in large areas of the world, but only the US had escaped the problems caused by the devastation of war and only the US had the economic strength to dominate the global economy and its institutions. Thus, it is possible to argue that the world after 1945 can already be seen in terms of the exercise of hegemonic power by the US. After emerging from a relatively isolationist position and its regional dominance in the western hemisphere, the US arguably began to extend that dominance to many other areas of the globe and the Cold War was not defined by a bipolar world but by the attempts to preserve or terminate US hegemony.

The original US desire to end isolationism was based on a belief in a set of universal values, which American wartime planners hoped to see established on a global basis. Non-discriminatory trade, the end of power political arrangements, the removal of imperial trade blocs, and the political values of self-determination and democratic government were felt necessary for the preservation of peace; they were also seen as important for the successful development of capitalism and the maintenance of national prosperity. These ideals and traditions helped define and justify the goals of post-1945 American foreign policy, in ways which would otherwise be more meaningfully interpreted as a quest for hegemony. US wartime planners put forward ideas that claimed to favour a principled world order, based on universal values that have been seen as benign and beneficial, especially when placed alongside the more brutal regimes which emerged under the ideological auspices of fascism and communism. Yet the exercise of American power was not far below the surface. The blend of international concerns and national self-assertion became a potent ideological mix as what was best for the world was juxtaposed with what was best for America.

The challenge of the Soviet Union was, from the start, portrayed as a dynamic force, driven by a mix of crusading Marxist ideology linked to global expansionism, which the US sought to resist in the name of universal values, rather than specific interests associated with the preservation of its hegemony. It may be more plausible to see the Soviet challenge as born, not from an assertive ideological triumphalism, but from a sense of weakness and a desire to achieve bipolarity and equality. And the US must also be judged in the context of a triumphalist ideology, which it sought—and continues to seek—to extend far beyond American shores. Yet seeing two hegemonic powers battling it out for primacy, with the outcome of such an equal contest uncertain until the last, is a highly questionable portrayal of the post-1945 world, and one possible explanation of why the Cold War's end surprised so many with its suddenness. The disparity between the two powers' capabilities was at times considerable and, if one interprets the Cold War world as a series of challenges to American hegemony, it is possible to find greater continuity between the Cold War and the post-Cold War periods.

In analysing the world of the two Cold War protagonists, there is also a need to take account of the emergence of the non-aligned movement, the impact of a powerful, communist China, and the tendency of newly independent states to try and manipulate the superpowers to help secure their own regional goals. All such things run counter to simplistic notions of bipolarity and from the end of the 1960s onwards, as the Soviets mounted a military challenge, the dominance of the two so-called superpowers was consistently eroded. Even before that, the control and influence exerted by the US and the USSR over their respective blocs faced a number of challenges within those blocs, which form another important feature of the Cold War world. Nevertheless, it was a world in which domestic interests, as well as foreign policy goals, often dictated support for one of the two main rivals – and one where the need to attract global support for the values and social and economic systems each held dear assumed unprecedented international importance.

Cold War, as Distinct from Hot War, and the Role of Armaments

Central to the concern of 'hot war' arising from alleged military threats was the role of nuclear weapons, which revolutionized thinking about war. One problem, which was never solved, was to try and integrate the use of nuclear weapons into a rational military strategy which did not risk large-scale national destruction. As strategists wrestled with this dilemma, military power became less useful as a means of forcing smaller states to comply with the wishes of the great powers. Combined with the Cold War need to win over international opinion this placed greater emphasis on prestige, status, the appearance of strength, and the preservation of credibility. While economic resources and key strategic areas remained of some significance, particularly in the 1940s and early 1950s, competition in areas of no economic or strategic importance became a feature of Cold War international politics and the ideological battle for credibility.

At the same time, it was necessary to find ways of fighting the Cold War which did not run too great a risk of developing into hot war. This distinction, between measures short of international armed conflict (Cold War) and preparations to fight a 'hot war' (international armed conflict), is an important one to bear in mind, particularly when analysing the nature of, and reasons for, the arms race. Yet the Cold

War cannot be fully isolated from military conflict, because the deployment of armed forces was deemed necessary to deal with internal conflicts, or to prevent the emergence of unfriendly governments. Also, the militarization of an essentially ideological threat was perceived as vital for the mobilization of popular support for the Cold War struggle. To do this, governments were prepared to exaggerate or invent an actual and immediate military threat, when what they really feared was an ideological challenge or a potential, long-term military danger. This was particularly significant in the later 1940s, when the Soviet leadership had most reason to fear the greater material wealth of the US, and when the American, and particularly Western European, elites had most reason to fear the strength of left-wing political movements, whose credibility had been enhanced by active resistance to fascism during the war and who promised radical social reform afterwards.

Western military alliances, such as NATO, SEATO, and the Baghdad Pact, were important manifestations of the Cold War. Yet, they have been seen from the start as military alliances geared to 'hot war', when they were actually far more important as political symbols of a will to resist communism, just as the Warsaw Pact in the East symbolized the resistance to capitalism and particularly to German capitalism. NATO was not an alliance preparing to attack the USSR, or even one seen as capable of winning a conventional war in defence of Western Europe; nor was the Warsaw Pact an organization geared to the expansion of Soviet power through the use of military force. Yet, they were both portrayed as such. The fact was that threat perception in the military sense did not drive force deployments or the level of armaments. More specifically, the strategic need to defend a particular area did not lead to consideration of the ways in which this could be done effectively by military means. Nor did the requirements of Western European defence, for example, produce the force levels needed to guarantee security, or the rationale for foreign-policy-makers to act on. Rather, it was political considerations, especially the need to keep Western Europe together as part of a liberal-capitalist unit, which dictated the development of military strategy. The latter was then used to provide and justify the rationale for the political needs which had produced the strategy in the first place. The result was that the actual military requirements to carry out the strategy were never met in any of the three Western military alliances mentioned above.

In such a situation, the role of armaments and the concept of security in particular have to be carefully considered in a Cold War context. Negotiations and discussions on arms levels formed a constant feature of Soviet–American relations and they consumed a vast amount of resources. Nuclear weapons and the strategies behind their development and possible use, were continually in the public eye. They had, and have, an obvious deterrent role (although the exact nature of such a role is debatable). In many ways, armaments can be seen in the context of global conflict as predominantly symbolic of the role of the military and of the technological dynamism characteristic of the contrasting economic systems. Arms negotiations became protracted and technically complex, but were often designed to secure advantages which, like the weapons themselves, would serve the appearance of greater strength. Equally, the political pressure from public opinion for governments to become involved in them was intense. The need to prevent hot war was a continuing feature of the Cold War and the need to appear committed to disarmament, peace, and stability a vital component of the 'battle for hearts and minds', even if the timing and nature of the process was up for debate and the commitment to it not always genuine.

The Nature of the Cold War World

The military threat and danger presented by the Cold War have generally been exaggerated, both at the time and in the literature. The military threat was, and has been often proclaimed as, the crucial element in the origins and development of the conflict, even though power has arguably become more associated with prestige and influence. The control of resources and the development of military capabilities, in practical terms, have perhaps become less important in the nuclear age especially in relation to a global war that is increasingly hard to contemplate. Instead, the Cold War brought a perceived need for states to control their citizens and ensure that their perceptions of the outside world reinforced the legitimacy of either a totalitarian communist or a democratic capitalist state. In this new situation, the very existence of an ideological rival was for a time seen as an unacceptable threat. The refusal to accept the long-term existence of rival sovereign states was a feature of the early period of Cold War, which strengthened or helped produce highly secret government agencies. Intelligence organizations also began to play more significant roles in overseas espionage and subversion. They were designed to operate covertly and to subvert or overthrow hostile or potentially hostile regimes in ways which could be denied by the governments ostensibly controlling them.

At the same time, propaganda became more extensive and significant in relation to domestic as well as foreign affairs. More effort was devoted to providing 'information' to citizens and to ensuring that 'subversives' were marginalized or eliminated. It was important, for example, for the Soviet dictator Joseph Stalin to try and convince his citizens that domestic opponents of his brutal and tyrannical regime were imperialist spies who deserved exile or death. At the same time, it was important for Western governments, not only to play on the horrors of the Soviet regime, but to present it as a threat in ways which would win support for a policy of confrontation and the pursuit of ambitious foreign policy goals. As a result, there is a need to examine if such dangers were exaggerated in both quantitative and qualitative terms largely in order to achieve maximum domestic effect.

The Use of Terminology in Western Interpretations of the Cold War

The initial increase in rivalries and tensions in and after 1945 produced a new international vocabulary, which itself was a feature of a particular Cold War mindset. In the West, many of these words display a subtle condemnation of the ideological opponent and reinforce a world-view in which Cold War confrontation stems from the activities of the communist states, rather than from their counterparts in the capitalist world. Moreover, this itself produces justifications for policies which assume a fundamental sense of righteousness in international as well as domestic terms. To produce an objective international analysis of the Cold War, it is necessary to question some of the standard Cold War terminology used in the West and to relate the conflict to the more traditional goals of great powers. At the same time, one must look more closely at the changes that occurred in the Cold War international system and their links to domestic forces and ideational influences. Thus, the two rival systems can be assessed more objectively and without the ascription of blame to the ideological opponent. When blame is given to one side, it is often done as part of fighting, rather than explaining, the Cold War.

The use of the word 'security' by both sides provided Cold War justifications for actions and policies that would previously have been interpreted differently. It has come to mean much more than protection from invasion and the avoidance of war. The fine dividing line between 'security' and imperial expansion needs to be carefully considered in relation to the Soviet Empire in Asia and to its satellites in Eastern and Central Europe. More importantly, the American use of the term 'national security' involves the merging of several older concepts into a radically new one, which underpinned much of Western Cold War rhetoric after 1947. Essential to this is the belief that any state controlling large resources in geographical areas unacceptable to the US presents a threat to American 'national security'. This means that, rather than having to deal with a specific military danger in a vital area (as Germany presented to Britain's maritime trade routes before the First World War), Washington's 'national security' is threatened by a more general global menace. In part, this reflects a shrinking world, in which more rapid aircraft and the arrival of the missile age have brought the global community closer together. Without unrestricted access to the world's resources, the US could be forced to impose domestic controls over raw materials and production which would threaten free enterprise, the American way of life, and thus 'national security'. Also, the adoption of communist or capitalist ideologies by newly independent states, or changes from one system to the other in any part of the globe, would have implications for Western or Soviet credibility and, in conventional Cold War terms, constitute a threat to 'national security'. In the pre-Cold War era, attempts to control access to important overseas resources and the installation of, or influence over, a particular foreign government would normally have been referred to as 'imperialism', not as a threat to national security.

Another feature of historical and social science writing in the West is the way in which phrases such as 'Soviet expansion(ism)' and 'Soviet behaviour' flow freely from the pages of many books on international politics after 1945. In the US, the Soviet Union came to be regarded as a revolutionary state not prepared to accept the norms governing international relations. The attribution of traits reflecting abnormal human actions is used to demonize an enemy to whom rational analysis could not then be applied.

The term 'American expansion', which was arguably far more extensive than that achieved by the Soviets after the War, is harder to find, while the US and its Western European allies are rarely deemed to suffer from international behavioural problems. In addition, although the Soviet Union expected additional post-war rewards from its wartime efforts, what it did secure came directly from the war. It acquired territory and satellites not from post-war expansion, but from the unscrupulous 1939 Ribbentrop-Molotov pact on eastern Europe and, after 1941, from the accepted military need to defeat Germany. Many general works on international politics imply that the Soviets 'behaved' in expansionist ways which aroused Allied disapproval after the war; but, during the war, the main Allied fear was of the Soviets *not* expanding and defeating the Germans.

Of course, a relative lack of evidence from Soviet archives, despite greater access to them in recent decades, means it is difficult to make definitive judgements about Moscow's goals and ambitions. It is quite clear that, not only did the Soviet Union have imperialist ambitions to expand its power and influence, but also its treatment of its own citizens and of those under Soviet occupation was appalling. Nevertheless, it should not be assumed that the US and Britain were simply reacting to Russian 'behaviour' in occupied Europe or to ambitious Soviet diplomacy. Nor should it be assumed that Washington and London were lacking in expansionist goals themselves. Both countries, like the Soviets, planned to extend their influence after 1945 and gain new military bases from which to project their power on an increasingly global basis. Indeed, the US military planned to acquire bases in Western Europe, the Middle East, North Africa, South, South-East and East Asia, including China, as well as island bases in the Atlantic and Pacific Oceans.

One way around the problem of Cold War terminology is to view all the great powers, particularly the wartime 'Big Three' (Britain, the Soviet Union, and the US), as seeking to maintain or enhance their influence. This projection of power and influence into new areas is one way of broadly defining imperialism and it is no bad thing for students of international politics to approach the post-war world from the perspective of imperial rivalries. This removes the need to consider ideological differences as a cause of the initial breakdown of cooperation and only requires that they be considered, along with the other changes brought about after the war, as defining elements of a Cold War world that later emerged from the initial international competition for control and influence in the 1945–6 period.

The use of the word 'containment' is another misleading term in standard Western historiography, because it is often applied to American policy throughout the Cold War period. In fact, while 'containment' can be deemed to contribute to the first stage of any offensive strategy, the idea that it was a consistent US policy employed as the ultimate response to Soviet power throughout the period is misleading. US policy went through several stages related to changing perceptions of how best to deal with the Soviet challenge. The period 1946-48 may be seen as a defensive response but, from 1948 until at least the mid-1950s, if not the early 1960s, the US moved to an offensive strategy designed to destroy the Soviet satellite empire rather than contain it.

Phases of the Cold War

The chronological divisions in the book correspond to changes in the nature of the Cold War or in Soviet–American relations (and the two things are not synonymous), as well as events since the Cold War. The first phase, up to 1953, was when the Cold War developed from the tensions and mistrust arising out of early attempts to agree on the nature of the post-war order and conclude peace treaties with Germany's allies. In the first and very intense phase of the Cold War, from 1947 to 1953, the ideological commitment of the Soviet Union and the capitalist states to differing economic and political systems was reinforced by the demands of post-war reconstruction. Survival in the short term was deemed to depend either on the success of Western democracy and free enterprise or on the maintenance of totalitarian, communist controls. In addition, the ability directly to control and exploit certain areas of the globe was seen as vital by both British and Soviet policy-makers, who both initially feared that the adoption of US principles was a recipe for maintaining or increasing American power and influence at their expense. Thus, there emerged a mix of old-fashioned imperialism and new ideological imperatives. The former helped prevent cooperation while the latter subsequently gave an entirely new meaning to imperial and interstate rivalries. It was a period in which confrontation, fuelled by competing, universal ideologies, then developed to such an extent that some on both sides saw the other's long-term existence as an unacceptable threat. However, there was a fear of another war and a reluctance to prepare for one on both sides, with the Western powers privately convinced that the Soviets would not deliberately start a major conflict (even though they did not reveal this publicly). War was only deemed possible through accident or miscalculation. In effect, this meant the extension of control or influence by one side without any realization that it would be so unacceptable to the other side that war would be preferable. In the West, the Cold War was nevertheless deemed to be winnable by means short of hot war.

By the early 1950s, Cold War fighting was perhaps at its most aggressive. In the West, German rearmament (deemed most likely to provoke armed Soviet aggression) was planned and attempts were made to devise more aggressive means of undermining Soviet control within its satellite empire, including psychological and economic warfare. In the East, Stalin finally agreed to endorse and support a North Korean attack on South Korea. Western Cold War strategists then had to consider the implications of fighting a limited war. Along with the death of Stalin in 1953, Winston Churchill's idea of encouraging more Western contacts with the Soviet bloc as a means of sapping the strength and appeal of communism, led to what became known as a 'thaw' in East–West relations. However, the 'thaw' was an attempt to stabilize relations and avoid armed conflict rather than a 'thaw' in the Cold War of propaganda and subversion. The need to avoid armed conflict increased steadily once the US and the Soviet Union exploded their first thermonuclear weapons in 1952 and 1953. The hydrogen bomb was thousands of times more powerful than the atomic bomb. It made the prospect of global war more fearsome and eventually made the pursuit of peace and arms agreements more necessary. More urgent consideration had now to be given to ways of preventing the aggressive fighting of the Cold War from leading to a hot war. The fears that an offensive strategy might lead to a thermonuclear confrontation eventually contributed to the modification of the American policy of undermining, and ultimately destroying, the Soviet system (often referred to as 'roll-back' or 'liberation'), as did the realization that changes would be difficult to achieve without a major war.

The Soviets had ostensibly also accepted the idea of peaceful coexistence in the mid-1950s, but ideological competition remained acute. In fact, in some ways, the Cold War was extended after the death of Stalin because of his successors' heightened interest in Asia, Africa, and regions of the less developed world. This increased the importance of competition for hearts and minds in these largely neglected areas and took the Cold War into a new era. Soviet–American Cold War competition now extended to all parts of the globe. By the end of the 1950s, this competition for influence between the communist and capitalist world was further intensified by the emergence of the newly independent nations, in Africa and Asia, and the importance of the future alignment of those non-self-governing territories earmarked for independence. The issue now was less the control of important resources or political stability, as initially it had been in Europe, than the need to claim ideological successes in terms of the progress of socialism or capitalist democracy. This did not remove the need for the power and status of the Soviet and American states to be enhanced. Rather, it meant that the success of one protagonist, whether in terms of greater influence in Africa, Europe, or even outer space, was an integral part of great power competition.

However, the 1960s saw the competition to preserve or gain ideological allies come near to military confrontation in Cuba in 1962. The Cuban missile crisis, when some US policy-makers were prepared to attack Soviet missiles, was a head-to-head Soviet–American confrontation that contributed to what some have argued was the end of the first Cold War. The risk of hot war was such that both sides were now prepared to accept long-term peaceful coexistence. Fighting the Cold War to eliminate their rival's control over its sphere of influence, to undermine their position as a great power, arguably ceased to be the ultimate aim of the superpowers. What mattered was a more traditional competition for greater global influence. In these circumstances, the arms race, conducted under the banner of deterring war, became even more of a battle for status and influence rather than serious preparation for global war.

However, in the 1960s, when the Soviets began for the first time to approach nuclear parity with their American rivals, the nature of the apparently bipolar world began to change. Washington faced serious challenges to its economic and military supremacy, while the growing split between the Soviets and their communist Chinese allies became a permanent rupture and resulted in border clashes. The Americans, having embarked on a massive programme of military expansion at the start of the decade, found themselves in a less advantageous position at the end of it. For the first time, their military supremacy was threatened by the expansion of Soviet nuclear arms and the development of an ocean-going navy which further increased perceptions of the Soviet Union as a world power equal to the US. American economic dominance was also challenged from within the Western world, particularly by the rapidly expanding German and Japanese economies and by the French attempt, under Charles de Gaulle, to win greater independence from the American-dominated international economic order. From 1963 onwards, international politics thus became a more general competitive battleground with alliances and regional power blocs assuming greater importance in a less bipolar world.

The emergence of a more multipolar world in the 1970s meant that new ways of attempting to manage Soviet–American relations within the changed international system had to be found. China's emergence, and the growing economic strength of Western Europe and Japan, presented new challenges to US hegemony. As the hegemonic power was defeated in Vietnam, new social forces appeared to be challenging the supremacy of democratic capitalism within the Western world. In the 1970s, faced with this new situation and with economic problems exacerbated by the oil price rises, greater efforts were made to maintain international stability. Détente offered the prospect of regulating the Cold War by agreement. For the Americans, it could prevent further erosion of their military superiority and maintain their general credibility which was being damaged by the continuation of the Vietnam War. Henry Kissinger, Nixon's National Security Adviser and later Secretary of State, was eager to take up the challenge to American power from an increasingly multipolar world by using détente. Traditional power-political goals were incorporated into a process of easing East-West tension over nuclear armaments that risked hot war, while retaining maximum American influence and preventing further communist successes in the Cold War. The Soviets were also attracted to détente, because it offered economic benefits and the prospect of encouraging revolutionary change in the Third World, with less risk of a hostile Western response.

Yet at the end of the 1970s—a decade of revolutionary change in many parts of the less developed world—the conflicting expectations of détente produced Soviet–American dissatisfaction and led to a return to greater confrontation. Sometimes referred to as a 'Second Cold War', the period 1979–85 saw tensions in Europe over the deployment of more advanced nuclear missiles and continuing crises in the less developed world which involved one or both superpowers. This produced another major Cold War confrontation, despite the more multipolar world. The rise of a more socially conservative and individualist Right in the West was matched in the mid-1980s by the emergence of a new generation of leaders in the Soviet Union, who were prepared to embark on a programme of radical reform and foreign policy reorientation. It was precisely when these forces were both encouraging international confrontation and redefining economic and social policy that the Cold War ended or, perhaps more accurately, was ignored or transcended by a new Soviet leader, Mikhail Gorbachev. While designed to preserve the basis of a reformed Soviet state with reduced influence over the constituent parts of its Empire, reform unleashed forces that Gorbachev initially did not want to control and by 1991 could not. The result was that the collapse of communism in East-Central Europe was followed by the disintegration of the USSR, which Gorbachev had neither sought nor expected. In a similar way, the forces which produced the economic crash and the 'war on terror' in the first decade of the new millennium have had unforeseen and uncontrollable consequences which have significantly altered the post-Cold War world.

1. John D Hargreaves *Decolonisation in Africa* 74–9.

PART I

The Origins and Development of the Cold War, 1945–53

The debate on the nature and origins of the early Cold War has had an enormous impact on the way historians and social scientists have interpreted the nature of the international system in the years up to 1991. Realists seeking confirmation of their emphasis on power, represented through economic and military strength, have maintained that the Cold War, with its associated expansion of weapons, vindicated their ideas. Yet the realist refusal to associate domestic factors with foreign policy and to consider ideology, domestic, social, and economic factors as key features of the Cold War have left an enormous void in many attempts to understand the conflict and its origins. The latter can only be fully understood if the linkage between power politics and the social and economic upheavals of war, which threatened a revolutionary change in the dominant capitalist status quo, is understood in historical terms.

Historiographical Debate

The origins of the Cold War remain a matter of long-standing historical dispute and the arguments, generally not mutually exclusive, are linked to ideas about the nature of the Cold War international system. Was it a bipolar world whose systemic characteristics dictated the power struggle between the two protagonists? Was it a world dominated by exogenous concerns about interstate rivalries or was it a world in which internal battles over economic power and political influence had a significant effect on external ideological and power-political rivalries?

Initial attempts to explain the Cold War in the West focused on the actions of the Soviet Union as the key factor in producing confrontation. These so-called 'orthodox' or 'traditional' theories assume that alleged Soviet aggression, or more usually, alleged Soviet expansionism, dictated American reactions. In essence, the Cold War became a battle for global power and influence because Stalin and/or the Soviet system made cooperation impossible. The reason for this in orthodox accounts rests with the paranoid and ruthless leader of an expansionist, ideologically driven Soviet state. Stalin and Soviet communism had to be confronted and contained by Western capitalist states for the sake of international peace and the survival of liberal democratic values. Or, in other Western Cold War words, an allegedly expansionist Soviet Union threatened the so-called national security of the US and Western Europe, requiring an economic and military response. The historical focus on security from external threats links with realist explanations of superpower rivalry, in which power and security have a more significant explanatory role than ideology or the internal make-up of capitalist and communist states.

In the 1960s, the crude orthodox approach was challenged by 'revisionist' historians, focusing less on the international state system and the struggle to gain greater power and influence than on the alleged requirements of international (and, in 1945, largely American) capitalism. Revisionists interpret the foreign policy of the US as designed to meet the expansionist requirements of capitalism. The Soviets therefore sought security in the form of resisting the expansion of capitalism into areas that would threaten Soviet communism. For the revisionists, blame for the Cold War lies with aggressive US policies to which the Soviets had to respond. Rather than Soviet expansionism creating American insecurity, then, the US commitment to the expansion of capitalism created Soviet insecurity.

Since the challenge by revisionists, other Cold War historians and political scientists, who allegedly reject the stark interpretations of the opposing schools, have been labelled 'post-revisionists'. This term can refer to a number of very different authors but is commonly based on interpretations that allegedly adopt a more balanced and research-orientated approach. Thus, ascribing responsibility exclusively to one side is often avoided and criticism of both powers is generally made on the basis of archival evidence. While this approach can embody attempts to reach consensus, and an acknowledgement that both superpowers may have misperceived the policies of the other, it should also be remembered that some post-revisionists still attribute blame to the Soviet Union rather than to the US, or to both powers equally. In addition, a significant part of the Cold War took the form of a massive state-influenced campaign on both sides of the Iron Curtain to justify military policies and expenditures in order to gain popular support for them. Thus, despite the greater sophistication of the various arguments and emphases of the post-revisionists in the 1980s and 1990s, they themselves may still have been justifying the Cold War, rather than explaining it.

The leading exponent of post-revisionism, John Lewis Gaddis, has claimed that the best ideas from both schools are subsumed in an emerging post-revisionist consensus. In addition to the emphasis on national security, one of Gaddis's books, *The Long Peace*, sees the alleged Cold War bipolar system as a basis for stability and gives support to the neo-realist approach in general, and to the work of Kenneth Waltz in particular. Here security concerns and the nature of the international system are portrayed as explanatory tools for understanding the nature of the early Cold War. While accepting that US policy-makers may have exaggerated the Soviet threat and failed to appreciate the impact of their own policies, Gaddis nevertheless portrays the US as reacting to an expansionist Soviet state in justifiable ways. The essential responsibility for the Cold War lies with Stalin, whose policies created the need for defensive resistance. This is despite the fact that the geopolitical position of the US had always provided it with more security than any other great power, at least in the years before intercontinental missiles. The reaction to this by Warren Kimball has been to dismiss the Gaddis version of post-revisionism as 'orthodoxy with archives'.

Other post-revisionist historians who share the emphasis on security issues have taken a different line to Gaddis's ascription of blame to Stalin. Post-revisionists less inclined to justify American policy, most notably Melvyn Leffler, still locate Cold War explanations primarily within a national security framework of power politics. Yet from Leffler's work it is not clear that US policy can be justified simply as a response to the Soviets. The quest for what he terms a 'preponderance of power' sometimes involved excessive efforts to project US power and influence. At best, therefore, this was an overreaction to Soviet policies. However, it also involved the formulation and implementation of policies, defined in terms of American goals and interests that existed independently of Soviet aims and ambitions. Thus, to some extent Leffler moves away from portraying a reactive, defensive strategy of national security to describing a more expansionist US strategy based on American global interests. These interests remain largely defined in terms of state power and supposed threats to the American exercise of this power, within a framework of international relations clearly dominated by military might, geopolitics, and control of economic resources. This is another example of the way post-revisionism can be compatible with realist theory.

It has been suggested, by Howard Jones and Randolph Woods, that national security concerns provide the basis for a post-revisionist consensus on the origins of the Cold War in general and the reasons for US policy in particular. This has been criticized on a number of grounds and has led to a debate on the role of ideology and ideas in foreign policy, as opposed to state concerns about power, survival, competition, and, in Cold War parlance, security. Anders Stephanson has noted that, in line with realist thinking, security removes ideology and class as explanations of, and influences on, foreign policy. In addition, there are vital questions to ask about security, in terms of for whom it exists and for what purpose. In the West, does it mean security for elite groups in the US, security for the western hemisphere, or security for American capitalism and its foreign markets? Emily Rosenberg has questioned the very meaning of 'national security', as it is itself a product of the Cold War, and its increasingly broad usage can serve the needs of 'advocates of almost everything and anything'. Randall and Woods define it as 'the relation between domestic and foreign elements affecting a country's safety and to include the social, economic, political and military considerations that influence strategy'. The implication is that external policy is geared to securing all aspects of social, economic, and political life on the basis of resisting threats to values or interest groups as well as threats to territory and physical safety. Such ideas prepare the ground for conceptions of common national interests in the face of external powers who may not pose a direct military threat, but who do represent an ideological danger, particularly to elite groups on both sides of the Iron Curtain.

More generally, the attempts to build a Cold War consensus on 'national security' issues sidestep the ideological and domestic conflicts which were central to the Cold War's origins and nature. They serve the realist cause by disconnecting foreign policy from domestic issues and by emphasizing state/national concerns about security and military power. Finally, such ideas disguise *descriptions* of Cold War thinking and strategies to win the conflict (building a domestic consensus on resisting the 'other' by portraying it as a military threat) as *explanations* of the Cold War. As Emily Rosenberg notes, some historians make the same 'discursive turn that Cold War policy-makers themselves made: conflating a wide variety of contexts and complexities into a symbolically powerful but increasingly diffuse phrase—national security'. The subordination of internal forces, in the sense that their dynamics are not of significance in determining—as opposed to justifying—foreign policy, is a key feature of realist and orthodox accounts of the Cold War's origins and nature.

Other historians have rejected the basic national security approach and the idea of a bipolar systemic analysis as central to a Cold War dominated by issues of power and security. Anders Stephanson has challenged the idea that the Cold War was essentially systemic in nature. The concept of a bipolar world from 1945 to the collapse of the Soviet Union dictated by a relative equilibrium of forces is, in his view, erroneous. It ignores the distinctive time periods, which reflect the changing character of the Cold War and the shifting nature of the threat to the internal social and economic order, particularly in Europe. Thus, the elimination of dissidents within the Soviet bloc and the McCarthyist persecution within the US cannot 'be reduced in origins and development, to geopolitics and strategy'.[1] Nor can determined efforts to overthrow governments throughout the world be explained solely in terms of strategy or economic resources.

Ideology thus becomes an important element in the Cold War, but in ways which are more complex than most Cold War accounts assume. In orthodox terms, and as seen by some policy-makers at the time, the ideology of Soviet communism promoted worldwide revolution which in foreign policy terms became a quest for Soviet world domination. More sophisticated explanations look at the general ways in which ideas are employed by elites to serve domestic political purposes. In more specific Cold War terms, this means examining how ideology, linked to foreign policy success or failure, can have a damaging impact on the internal social and political order which maintains the privileged position of elite groups. Thus, foreign policy goals reflect elite ambitions in the form of state preoccupations with power and expansion as linked to status rather than security. Domestic goals reflect elite needs to preserve the socio-economic order that secures their own position and ensures its acceptance through the portrayal of ideological challenges as external threats. This provides a key to an understanding of the early Cold War more as a political battle for domestic dominance than a military conflict over national security. This is certainly how elites in Britain and America perceived it at the time, even if the conflict was, and still is, often justified in terms of security and its military requirements.

There are, of course, always connections between foreign economic policy, geopolitics, territorial security, and ideology in any analysis of the Cold War. Those who question the alleged post-revisionist national security consensus and the explanatory value of 'national security' simply place more emphasis on economics and ideology. Or, in theoretical terms, they attach greater significance to internal non-state actors, their connections with the state, and the linkages between domestic affairs and foreign policy. Thus, corporatism is a post-revisionist approach which places less emphasis on power politics / security and more on the need to ensure the spread of liberal capitalism as a means to secure a stable world order. In the model put forward by Michael Hogan, corporatism embodies capitalist cooperation between government, non-governmental organizations, and business corporations in an attempt to establish a 'corporative world order'. Thus, there was an economic need to rebuild Western Europe, which served private interests as well as producing overall benefits for the US economy. This need dovetailed with, and provided the basis for, maintaining and preserving the socio-economic status quo in democratic capitalist states, which was under acute electoral threat in Western Europe in the immediate post-war years. It also complemented a broader global strategy of building a new economic world order on the expansion of multilateral trade, which required the reconstruction of Western Europe and the elimination of imperial and communist economic blocs.

For those post-revisionists concerned with the relations between public and private interests, and between foreign economic policy and military strategy, alleged external threats served more to justify than to explain policies linked to the domestic needs of the state and the position of its ruling elites. It seems that the Cold War developed when there was a conjunction of external and internal threats to the stability of capitalist states and their communist rivals, which had not existed to the same extent in the inter-war years. In Western Europe, the experiences of the Second World War produced more awareness of class divisions and privilege from which the Left gained new strength. Significant social reform, as predicted by appeasers like Neville Chamberlain, was now unavoidable, but post-war economic difficulties might open the door to more radical challenges to the capitalist status quo. In the East, the Soviet regime had been weakened by the destruction of the Second World War, in which traditional ideas about the nation had again proved more powerful than the ideology of communism in rallying the people. Consideration of these issues and their links to foreign policy is important if the nature of the early Cold War is to be fully understood.

More difficult to determine is the degree of responsibility for the Cold War, given the extent to which explanations of the conflict have been put forward as part of the strategy of fighting and winning the Cold War, rather than as determinants of policy or as analyses of the nature of the struggle. In this situation where all governments were involved in overt and covert propaganda campaigns, often aimed primarily at their own citizens, it is difficult to disentangle the genuine perceptions of policy-makers from the perceptions they wanted the public to have in order to succeed in their various Cold War aims. How far, for example, did the military measures adopted reflect genuine fears of attack or how far were they put forward in order to unite domestic opinion against an ideological and political challenge to elite values and interests?

Attempts to allocate blame by portraying the policies of one state as essentially free from the desire to maintain and expand power, and as geared only to countering the aggressive intentions of others, are not convincing. Far better to start from the position that all major states sought to expand their power and influence in proactive as well as reactive ways, for whatever combination of reasons. The Cold War was not essentially a reaction by one side to the actions of the other; its origins need explaining in terms of conflicting ambitions and the differing perceptions of what kind of post-war order was necessary to reconcile such ambitions and interests with order and stability. In addition, foreign policy in the immediate post-war years has to be connected to the dynamics of internal and external socio-economic relations. The issue then becomes how the external quest for power and the internal attempt to preserve the social and economic status quo combined to produce a unique Cold War era in international relations. In other words, how and why did the desires for two very different domestic political and economic orders prove internationally irreconcilable? In this context, aims and perceptions have to be explained and these historical details linked to broader theories locating the Cold War, within an interpretative international relations framework.

The Causes and Nature of the Early Cold War

The Power Political Issue of Confrontation Replacing Cooperation

The first stage of any effort to explain why three great victorious powers (all initially committed to the maintenance of cooperation in order to prevent a future global conflict) embarked on the Cold War is to define the different stages by which attempts at cooperation and compromise were replaced by confrontation and conflict. These stages are vital to any understanding of how and why the determination to ensure that recently defeated enemies should never again have the power to disturb world peace was replaced by an equal determination, on the part of one bloc, to rebuild them in opposition to a former ally. In essence, the prime commitment to cooperation was replaced in the first three months of 1946 (although the British had reached this stage by September 1945) by an emphasis on confrontation, followed by the definition of requirements which had to be accepted by the other parties if continued cooperation were to succeed.

Initially, in 1945, power politics dominated the disagreements, but ideology became increasingly more evident in the development of the conflict in 1946 and 1947. By the beginning of 1948, confrontation and hostility were accepted, and a new phase of Cold War conflict began. Yet both sides still justified actions and policies directed against ideological enemies in terms of traditional interstate threats and geo-political challenges.

The Impact of the Second World War

The world from which the Cold War was born was one in which popular expectations of social reform and international cooperation were high in the wake of the Second World War. Leaders in the allied states doubted whether such goals could be easily fulfilled, partly because of the enormous difficulties of economic reconstruction and the failure to fashion a peaceful world order in 1919. Moreover, there was no consensus as to how international peace and stability could best be preserved. In addition, the lessons of the past and the needs of the present were seen differently in the Soviet Union, Western Europe, and the US. In part, these differences can be explained by short-term self-interest, particularly in those countries which had suffered most from the war. In terms of insecurity and potential threats, it is necessary to consider the contrasting impact of the war on the allies. The Soviet Union suffered enormous economic losses. Its industries were moved eastwards and its population was reduced by up to 29 million in a war of extermination on the Eastern European front. Britain too was weakened economically, although it had neither the huge armed forces nor the massive problems of reconstruction which characterized the Soviet Union in 1945. The Soviet Union was desperate for economic aid and the British, eager to regain great power status, were determined not to sacrifice the short-term needs of recovery for the sake of free trade and international economic cooperation. Only the US could wield formidable military and economic strength, and this must be considered in any objective assessment of tensions stemming from supposed concerns about power and threats to security.

Reconciling Vital Interests and Idealistic Rhetoric

However, rather than so-called national security problems it was the failure to reconcile the maintenance of expanding vital interests with the preservation of the vital interests of others that was the initial source of disagreement and tension in 1945. The Soviet Union certainly had the greater territorial ambitions, but tensions also stemmed from the failure to implement the new principles of international political and economic cooperation which were expounded most forcefully in the US. In the 1940s, the principle

BOX 1.1

Post-Revisionism and the Geopolitics/Revisionist Debate on the Origins of the Cold War

Those post-revisionist writers who reject the orthodox idea that American policy was essentially reacting to Soviet actions also reject the revisionist idea that American policy was deliberately geared to confronting the Soviets. Instead, they have sought to focus on factors such as geopolitics, cultural traits, and elite perceptions, on psychology, bureaucratic politics, security requirements, misunderstandings, and misperceptions, none of which are mutually exclusive.

Geopolitics. At its most basic level, this view is linked to the pre-1917 development of two great land-based empires in Eurasia and the western hemisphere. Inevitably, these two exploitative land-based systems would come into conflict. Another explanation, based on the post-1945 period is the clash of three imperial powers, who sought to expand their influence but were unable to agree on a cooperative strategy for so doing. Thus, ideology is largely removed from the analytical framework and issues of power and security are, in the realist tradition, central to the conflict. However, the different geopolitical situations of the great powers and the different traditions and socio-economic systems provided different perspectives on 'security'.

Security. The emphasis many writers place on 'security' (or, in the US after 1947, 'national security') often fails to distinguish between security and imperial requirements. In the Soviet case, territorial vulnerability, the fear of another war of extermination, and more twentieth-century attacks from the West were undoubtedly real, but whether they justified the kind of repressive measures taken against the Soviet population and the peoples of Eastern and Central Europe is more questionable. In the US, 'national security' clearly came to involve factors other than military power and territorial defence. Even if the extension of a Soviet-controlled Eurasian empire constituted a threat to the US, did it justify the acquisition of a vast array of military bases and the determination to project a 'preponderance' of power? The US drive for 'security' on a global basis ironically ignored the more limited Soviet security/imperial requirements, largely confined to areas neighbouring the Soviet Union, and emphasized the universal, revolutionary rhetoric of Marxism-Leninism. Was this a misperception or a calculated strategy to protect state and elite interests?

In the West, the most commonly used Cold War terms are 'national security' and 'containment', with threats to the former from an expansionist Soviet Union allegedly leading to the latter. The importance of both terms as explanations of the Cold War have recently been questioned. National security has become so broad in its usage that it can be used to justify virtually any internal or external policies pursued by the US government, whether related to national or sectional interests. Moreover, its emphasis on the Soviet threat excludes many of the economic and social requirements of elite groups whose interests were most threatened by left-wing ideologies in the West or by opposition to communism in the East. Thus, two questions arise. How important were the influences of internal economic and

BOX 1.1 (continued)

political factors in producing external policy in the US and the Soviet Union, and were the alleged requirements of security policy, defined in terms of military power and inter-state struggles for influence, justified as defensive measures prompted by genuine fears? Barton Bernstein has argued that to use national security as an explanation of the Cold War makes more sense in relation to Soviet policy than it does to that of the US. Indeed, given the relative geopolitical positions of the two powers it is the US that has historically been secure and the Soviet Union that has been vulnerable. Moreover, given the ability of the US to project all forms of military power in 1945 (including the only nuclear weapons), and the superior American economic strength, it does seem odd that the quest for national security has been attributed more to the US than to a Soviets. After all, the Soviet state had been subjected to three twentieth-century invasions, has suffered from human and economic devastation on an almost unimaginable scale, and initially lacked atomic weapons.

of mutually beneficial international goals proclaimed by many American policy-makers did not square with their own practices, let alone gain universal acceptance. Despite much American rhetoric, idealism did not override American self-interest, even though it became an important element in US domestic politics.

The Cold War may, therefore, have been born out of the failure by both sides to reconcile old practices with new principles. The West needed to proclaim the end of power politics, but if such policies were still pursued, such hypocrisy had to be concealed from domestic opinion for political reasons. One way to do this was to attack Soviet power-political ambitions in Europe while pretending that Britain and the US had no such goals in the Middle East or the Pacific. Thus, even if an imperialist deal with the Soviet Union, based on vital interests, had been acceptable on a global basis to Stalin, it would not have been acceptable in the West.

Ideology and Legitimate Expansion

Such explanations of the Cold War have never satisfied most historians in the West. For them, conceptions of competing national interests, of conflicting rhetoric and practice, of equally crusading ideologies, or different understandings of democracy and security are less important than the allegedly in-built motivation of a communist state assuming the mantle of a traditional imperialist power. They do not see post-war leaders having to reconcile competing power-political ambitions—Soviet control of Eastern Europe, the maintenance and extension of exclusive British influence in the Middle East, or the acquisition of new US bases and control of Japan to ensure domination of the Pacific—but rather as facing the same situation as in the 1930s. Then the issue was not how to reconcile great power differences, but whether it would have been better to resist an inherently expansionist German power sooner rather than later. Viewed from this perspective, the Cold War could be attributed to the West's lack of realization that Stalin had unlimited ambitions, albeit with no timetable for achieving them, and its consequent failure to confront the Soviet dictator soon enough.[2]

Fundamental to these explanations is the belief that Western ambitions were legitimate and limited whereas, because of the ideological and repressive nature of the Soviet regime, its ambitions were neither. While there can be no doubt that the Soviets did have imperialist ambitions after 1945, the question is the extent to which, in foreign policy terms, they were fundamentally different from those that Britain and the US saw as essential to their post-war roles as great powers. To portray them in terms of an unlimited drive for global domination by Moscow means excluding the possibility that some (such as the demand for a trusteeship in Tripolitania in North Africa) may have been put forward in order to win acceptance of limited gains elsewhere, in areas more important to the Soviets. It also means ignoring the substantial evidence that Stalin, like his Western counterparts, and unlike Hitler, was not only extremely cautious but initially committed to the maintenance of great power cooperation and the concessions this would require. So, he was prepared to compromise over the nature of the United Nations (UN) and to accept the position of Greece as lying in the Western sphere of influence. And the main motivation for this cooperation was the self-interested need to prevent the revival of a strong Germany. More importantly it means accepting that the US did not have a crusading ideology whose aim was to shape the world in ways which would reconcile ideological principles with the expansion and success of American political and economic interests. Given the substantial, detailed evidence of the specific ways in which American post-war planners intended to create a world dominated by US values and interests, and while there is as yet no evidence of similar Soviet planning, the idea of a one-sided Soviet effort to gear a crusading ideology to world domination remains difficult to swallow.

Regional or Global Origins of the Cold War

Those who take the line of unlimited Soviet ambitions, which forced the West to confront Stalin, tend to focus more on European issues and on the aims of the Soviet Union and the US within a new bipolar framework. For some, Britain and France allegedly played subordinate roles to the dominant forces of Soviet–American rivalry, roots of which have been traced back before the 1917 revolution. In this clash between the two land-based empires of the western hemisphere and Eurasia, European problems served to arouse or exacerbate Soviet–American disagreements. It was in Europe that the Soviet Union carried out its most repressive and exploitative acts, in defiance of the Yalta agreements on Liberated Europe, which sought broadly based provisional governments and free elections. This focus on Eastern Europe has normally been accompanied by an ideological condemnation of the ruthless and undemocratic nature of Soviet power. In emphasizing European developments, historians have ensured that areas of vital interest to the Soviet Union became the centre of attention. The post-war aims and ambitions of Britain and the US in areas of vital interest to them (the Middle East and Pacific, for example) receive relatively less attention and the imperialist mantle of repression is placed squarely and solely on the Soviets. A full understanding of the Cold War's origins requires a closer examination of the Middle East and Pacific regions and the interaction between great power goals outside Europe, and the Soviet attempts to maintain and strengthen their control within it.

The efforts of the Western powers to preserve areas of exclusive influence outside Europe may have been seen by Soviet leaders as comparable to their determination to have an exclusive sphere of influence over the territories adjoining the Soviet Union. We can be more certain that while many Americans, then and in subsequent historical accounts, have seen Soviet imperialism as part of an ideological crusade for global domination, their Soviet counterparts have seen US power and ideology in precisely the same light. Messages from the Soviet embassy in Washington in 1946–7 portrayed America as keen to ensure global domination based on a crusading capitalist ideology and economic hegemony. In addition, it was believed that the Americans were even prepared to embark on global war to bring it about. These perceptions, an almost mirror image of the threat presented by the other superpower, had clearly developed by 1947, despite the perceived interests of both sides in maintaining cooperation. The most plausible power-political explanation of the Cold War lies in the failure to reconcile great power imperialist goals, *in areas outside Europe as well as within it*. The implications of this failure became more serious because of ideological concerns and the possible challenges to the domestic status quo that all elites faced in the wake of the Second World War's upheavals.

The Early Cold War's Portrayal and its Domestic Factors

Both sides faced a situation which was unique in the previous history of international relations since the French Revolution. Internal opposition threatened the socio-economic dominance of European ruling elites through a political ideology with mass appeal, which was more dangerous because it was backed by a powerful state. In the East, Stalin could contemplate, in the light of invasion and external intervention in the Russian Civil War, the threat presented by capitalist powers hostile to communism or the Soviet Union or both. External enemies could unite national sentiments and pre-empt opposition to oppression more effectively if they were presented as military and territorial threats. In the West, communism was now linked to the victorious and most powerful continental European state that was prepared to confront the Western Allies with its own imperial demands. It was now a more potent ideological threat because of the post-1941 increase in support for the Left in much of Western Europe, which was driven by its important role in resistance movements and by the increased demand for significant social reform. Again, it was far safer to present this as a military danger to the nation than an ideological threat to elites, even if it meant transforming wartime friends into post-war enemies. The military focus, portrayed in terms of containing a military or imperialist threat, has been subsequently emphasized but the problems and challenges of reconstruction and the preservation of the political and economic status quo were now even more important in defining the developing Cold War.[3]

Defining US Policy

Territorial security was much less of a direct concern for American policy-makers. The Soviets in 1945 had no powerful surface fleet to threaten US naval supremacy. American aims have been frequently explained in terms of the invented concept of 'national security' and in terms of a defensive reaction defined as 'containment' which has been associated with the diplomat George Kennan. National security came to encompass much more than the need to defend the boundaries or home waters of the state and has been used to explain US policy in terms of the geopolitical and strategic nature of the Soviet threat. Based on the fear, as in the Second World War, of one single power dominating the European land mass, the possibility of a hostile power dominating Eurasia was allegedly a much bigger threat to US national security than the prospect of a German-dominated Europe. Cold War hostilities are then explained in terms, not of a failure of three powers to accept a new power-political world order, but of America containing Soviet expansionism to preserve national security. Thus, economic and ideological factors are reduced in importance which is difficult to justify in 1947.

BOX 1.2

The Debate on the Role of Ideology and Perceptions on the Origins of the Cold War

Ideology has generally figured in the debate on the Cold War in terms of policy-makers assessing its influence on the policies of the opponent. Communism was perceived as innately hostile to capitalism just as the contradictions of capitalism were deemed in Moscow to produce war and conflict. Were these the most important influences of ideology or did ideology play a different role in the origins of the Cold War? And was ideology linked to misperception rather than misrepresentation.

Perception and Misperception. The importance of misperceiving the aims of the opponent and particularly of misperceiving ideology's influence on policy has featured strongly in the accounts of those post-revisionists who believe the Cold War could have been avoided. For such authors, the US view of Marxism-Leninism producing policies aimed at world domination misperceives the role of Soviet ideology and ignores such factors as differences within Soviet political elites and the historical traditions which shaped Russia's geopolitical fears and ambitions. The Soviet analysis of capitalist contradictions exaggerates the inevitability of US actions and ignores the various influences on US policy decisions. It also distorts the relations of capitalist powers by assuming rivalries and divisions arising from the contradictions of capitalism. Ideology is therefore connected to misperceptions of its influence on the foreign policy of the other, but it is normally assumed that as only the Soviets had a crusading ideology the issue is the impact of communism on foreign policy and US (mis)perceptions of this. In the West, the unstated assumption has been that liberal, democratic, free-market capitalism is not a crusading ideology or an ideological determinant of foreign policy. The focus is therefore on how the ideology of communism influences (mis)perceptions of Soviet foreign policy rather than on how the West's own ideology influences (mis)perceptions of Soviet foreign policy. Moreover, such assessments ignore the ideological influences which shaped US and Soviet elites' perceptions of the role their own state was to play and the extent to which these influenced (mis) perceptions or misrepresentations of the other's policies and actions. Ideology may well be most important in producing a particular conception of the kind of world role the perceiver's own state should play. This, in turn, produces a perception of what is required from the other, and when the other fails to play the required role ideology can serve as an explanation for this. Few studies have looked at the possible impact of a Western crusading ideology and the links to Western policy or on Soviet (mis)perceptions of this. Perceptions of one's own role may determine expectations of the other's role and the actions or ideology of the other may not shape perceptions of the other's policy as much as considerations of one's own world role with its ideological justifications. Hence the importance of each side's crusading ideology, and its ideological relationship to foreign policy and the real world may be linked more to Cold War misrepresentations than misperceptions. Moreover, these misrepresentations may have formed a vital part of a coordinated propaganda campaign to persuade the masses that the Cold War was more to do with power and military capabilities than it was to do with ideology. In the West, ideology is thus relegated to the simple question of freedom versus tyranny posed in political terms, with the fundamental nature of the social and economic order played down and divorced from the Cold War.

Acceptance of an Ideological Cold War

By the end of 1947, imperial ambitions and geopolitical rivalries were accompanied by a greater sense of ideological differences, which reflected genuine fears about domestic stability and the nature of the international economic order. If the period prior to the first quarter of 1946 was dominated by the desire for cooperation, but with growing tension that resulted from the failure to reconcile or compromise over imperial rivalries, 1946 and especially 1947 were dominated by ideological confrontation. This led to the real onset of Cold War by the beginning of 1948.

In early 1947, tensions increased, with the Truman Doctrine in March, and the economic problems brought by the winter hardships in many parts of Europe. The Truman Doctrine, by promising aid to Turkey, as well as Greece, was an early indication that, if it was a question of preventing the spread of communism, then Washington was willing to deal with authoritarian states. However, it was the Marshall Plan, launched in June, that subordinated rhetoric to the economic reality of whether capitalism or communism could survive in Europe. The Soviets saw in the Marshall Plan an economic threat to communist ideology and to their need to dominate Eastern Europe. In reality, the Americans were initially more concerned with keeping Western Europe within the democratic camp, while serving the interests of the US economy, than with attracting the countries of Eastern Europe into an American economic bloc. By alleviating the economic difficulties that could have been portrayed as the failure of democratic capitalism, the spread of communism in Western Europe could be prevented. But by including Eastern Europe in the offer of benefits to those prepared to accept the expansion of nondiscriminatory trade and economic integration, Soviet fears were heightened. Therefore, the Marshall Plan signalled the creation of a divided Europe in which the consolidation of confrontational capitalist and communist blocs became a priority on both sides.

The German Problem

The confrontation which developed during 1947 was formalized by the failure of the Council of Foreign Ministers, meeting in London in December, to reach agreement on the German peace treaty. The more that suspicion and confrontation developed in 1945–7, the more difficult it became to reach a decision on the future of Germany. As past German actions and future military potential were considered in an atmosphere of confrontation, both sides came to realize that a divided Germany offered the safest bet. The risk of

BOX 1.3

Biography: Joseph Vissarionovich Stalin (1879–1953)

Born in Gori, Georgia, Joseph Djugashvili, who later adopted the name Stalin, joined the Social Democratic Party in 1898 and the Bolsheviks in 1903. He founded Pravda in 1911 and was the Bolshevik leader in the Duma until exiled to Siberia in 1913. On his return after the October revolution of 1917, he became Commissar for Nationalities and General Secretary of the Communist Party in 1922, a position he held until his death. It was this position and the patronage it provided that enabled him to succeed Lenin as Chairman of the Politburo on Lenin's death in 1924. Stalin then changed his ideological stance in order to defeat all his rivals, including Trotsky, and become the all-powerful leader of the party and the government in 1927. At enormous human cost, Stalin embarked on the modernization of the Soviet Union, transforming it into a major industrial power by the Second World War. Millions died in the process with the collectivization of agriculture and the inefficient expropriation of rural surpluses for urban development. Stalin also moved to eliminate all potential rivals within the party and the military through show trials, and he created a regime of fear and terror in which families and neighbours were prepared to denounce each other to the secret police. In 1939, in a futile attempt to ward off an attack by Hitler and to secure territory in Poland, he signed an agreement with the Nazi leader. Reluctant to accept he had been duped when the Germans attacked in 1941, Stalin then embarked on a brutal war of survival in which millions died because of the extermination policies of the invaders or because of the sacrifices demanded by Stalin. After the war, he secured Soviet predominance in much of Eastern Europe, developed atomic weapons, and encouraged a 'personality cult' around himself. Preferring to work and hold meetings at night, he continued as the undisputed, but highly suspicious head of a brutal and tyrannical regime until his death from a stroke in March 1953.

a revived, united Germany allying with the opposing bloc was too great. Germany had too much potential, in terms of its industrial strength, large population, and central geographical position in Europe, to be left to the other side. However, there were economic difficulties inherent in a divided Germany that was unable to use its agricultural surpluses in the East to provide for the industrial population in the West. To avoid expenditure on foreign exchange, it was inevitable that the British and the Americans would support the revival of West German industry and attempt to limit the Soviet desire for reparations. Thus, a combination of power-political concerns and the economic needs of reconstruction placed Germany at the centre of the confrontation. However, because the final breakdown of the attempts to find an acceptable German solution did not occur until the end of 1947, it is hard to ascribe a causal role to the German question in the origins, as opposed to the development, of the Cold War. This is all the more significant when it is realized that initially there was a general assumption that self-interest in preventing the revival of Germany would facilitate agreement. At the same time, the economic difficulties and potential sacrifices created further antagonism and made it more likely that German industry would have to be rebuilt, which in turn would create further insecurity. The Berlin crisis of 1948–9 was born in this context. It was a crisis which is often deemed to herald the birth of the North Atlantic Treaty Organization (NATO) and another phase in the Cold War where the preparations for military conflict loomed much larger. However, this depends on the type of analysis of the Cold War, and in particular of the nature of its development, that is adopted.

The Myth of Containment?

In the West, the early Cold War has been described and justified in terms of the development of 'containment', on which Western strategy was allegedly based. However, there is a number of basic problems associated with this idea, particularly regarding the stages through which Western policies passed. A frequently encountered sketch of these developments, before and after 1947, is that in Europe a more or less expansionist and militaristic Soviet Union was eager to increase the pressure on the free world. This was allegedly indicated by the expansionist takeover of Eastern Europe, the 1947 actions of Western communist parties in calling widespread strikes, and by the dangerous 1948–9 Berlin Blockade, which necessitated a firm Western response. Thus, the militarization of containment, through the creation of a military alliance, NATO, was required to deter an aggressive Soviet attack on Western Europe. Then, in 1949 the focus of the Cold War allegedly moved to Asia, with the success of the communists in seizing power in China and the growing left-wing insurgencies in Indo-China, and Malaya. As the Americans began to consider these new challenges in the spring of 1950 with the production of a lengthy National Security Council Memorandum (NSC 68), the communist threat culminated in armed aggression in Korea. The Korean War of 1950–3 allegedly produced further modifications of containment. Not only did the war serve to prove the aggressive intentions of the Soviet Union, but it also signified that the Cold War had become a global conflict with an active military dimension that required rearmament on a gigantic scale. Most notably it required the arming of the recent German enemy to contain Soviet expansionism and ensure the defence of freedom in Western Europe.

The first problem with such a scenario is that the Soviets had in fact not expanded into areas outside their control after 1945. They simply kept control of the areas occupied during the war, while attempting expansion at the expense of Turkey and Iran in 1945–6. They drew back there out of fear of provoking hostilities with America, but Soviet ambitions justifiably aroused mistrust in the West. Second, there is the issue of whether US policy by 1948 can accurately be described as one of containment. Of course, in order to defeat an enemy, one would need to adopt an initial strategy of containment before a more aggressive strategy could be implemented. And, preventing the spread of Soviet control or influence from areas like Western Europe, to which the US attached particular significance, was an important consideration in 1946 and 1947.

However, from the end of 1947 the US also aimed at the destruction of the Soviet satellite empire in Eastern Europe, not simply at containing it. Indeed, the crusading American ideology had no place for the existence of communism, and Kennan himself, despite being labelled as the architect of containment, had not envisaged long-term coexistence with the Soviet Union. Thus, as the Soviets directed communists in Western Europe to undermine bourgeois governments there, so Washington began its campaign, not just to contain communism, but to weaken the Soviet hold on Eastern Europe. New agencies were created within the US government, beginning with the Office of Policy Coordination, whose aim was to prepare for undermining the Soviet system by weakening Soviet control over its satellites in Eastern Europe. It was already not just a question of containing Soviet power, but of reducing it. Most activities of American agencies within Eastern Europe generally remain classified, but they were the other side of the 1948 coin of assisting Western Europe. The strategy was more than just containment and reflected Kennan's earlier beliefs that coexistence between capitalism and communism was impossible: one or the other must be destroyed. We do not know so much about the aggressive aims of the Soviets in destabilizing the democratic capitalist world, but in Marxist doctrine the existence of bourgeois governments can be accepted as part of the ultimate transition to communism. Yet it seems more accurate to portray the Cold War in 1948 not in terms of coexistence or containment, but as a determined effort by both sides to develop offensive means of weakening the other in order to achieve outright victory, as in any military conflict where coexistence is ruled out. The idea of containment, then, serves more to indicate how, during the Cold War, the means of explaining and fighting it were subordinated in the West to the need to justify it and to build support for the attempts to win it. More than an attempt to explain American policy and long-term strategy, the idea of containment became a part of the Cold War struggle itself.

Bloc Consolidation

Whatever the nature of the two sides' strategies in 1948, there can be no doubt that one consequence was the attempt, in various ways, to consolidate influence or control over their respective blocs in Eastern and Western Europe. The Soviet Union began this process with a ruthless policy of economic exploitation based on the extraction of raw materials and machinery from Eastern Europe to serve the needs of Soviet reconstruction. Whether Moscow's influence was gradually extended from an initial position in which Stalin was determined never to allow any communist parties independence, or whether he was reacting more to growing concerns about Western policies, there can be no doubt of the result. One by one, Romania, Bulgaria, Poland, Hungary, and Czechoslovakia were, by 1948, denied the right to choose their own governments or even pursue their own form of socialist development. The fact that, in Yugoslavia, Marshal Tito was reluctantly allowed to develop his own form of communism only reinforced Stalin's determination to clamp down on any deviation from Moscow's control elsewhere in the region. As the attempts of both sides to subvert the other began in earnest, control and influence over the respective blocs became more important for the future of the European continent.

In the West, American influence and US dominance of the economic and political reconstruction of Western Europe has been deemed 'Empire by invitation' or 'Empire by inspiration'.[4] Certainly, there was a desire on the part of European elites to achieve stability and reconstruction, even if it meant accepting American terms. Suppressing the Left was both a short- and long-term goal, given its strength in much of post-war Western Europe. At the same time, short-term US assistance offered the prospect of eventually charting a more independent domestic and foreign policy course between raw, free-market American capitalism and the harsh and oppressive practices of Soviet communism. In the event, by 1949 the Western bloc was established voluntarily under US dominance as a permanent feature for the foreseeable future. More importantly, because the ideological competition was part of a broader battle over the nature and success of European economies and societies, Western European economic recovery was vital. It was firmly believed that such recovery was dependent not just on American aid to overcome the dollar gap but on a revived West German economy contributing to the recovery of Western Europe as a whole. As in other areas, there was a clear link between economic and political requirements. Fears of an economically powerful Germany, which were widespread in Western Europe and generally underrepresented in Cold War historiography, meant that the incorporation of Germany into a cohesive Western bloc was essential as part of a policy of containment. Indeed, containment can be seen as a more accurate description of the goals of Western policy to Germany in 1948 than the goals of Western policy to the Soviet Union.

The Cold War and European Integration

In 1948, the first moves to closer European cooperation coincided with the implementation of the Western European Recovery Program, talks on military alliances, and the attempts of both sides to undermine the opposing bloc. Like the process of decolonization, which was beginning to gather pace outside the European continent, European integration was linked to the dynamics of the Cold War as well as to the prevention of any further threat from Germany. Behind the process lay the vision of integrationists like France's Jean Monnet, who had a broad political agenda for the development of European integration, as well as a narrower economic agenda defined by the national needs of French recovery. Yet, Monnet's political vision of a more united Europe was always driven by the need to pursue Franco-German reconciliation within a framework that limited Germany's ability again on a path of confrontational nationalism.

The debate over the goals and achievements of European economic cooperation and integration has focused on whether this meant abandoning or strengthening the nation state. On the one hand, in the eyes of Alan Milward, the French in particular have been perceived as driven by nationalism and the process of integration interpreted as the salvation rather than the demise of the nation state in Europe.[5] On the other hand, liberal institutionalists like Joseph Nye and Robert Keohane do not see the creation of institutions like the European Coal and Steel Community as mere tools of the nation state but as significant in their own right and capable of producing greater international cooperation. Similarly, functionalists, in the tradition of David Mitrany and Ernst Haas, see European integration as promoting a transfer of allegiance away from the nation state by European elites and then the mass of the population.

In the early days of integration, the minds of both these groups were certainly focused more on the practical problems of recovery and German containment than on changing the nature of the international system. By 1946, the idea of a divided Germany had its attractions, particularly for those in the West, even though the Russians made a number of proposals for a neutral, but united Germany. The most famous of these occurred in March 1952 and debate has subsequently raged over whether Stalin's proposal was a serious one or one merely designed to prevent a rearmed Western Germany becoming a more important American partner. In a sense, some of the arguments are not mutually exclusive. On the one hand is the idea that Stalin was always driven by the idea of creating a united but communist Germany which would form part of the Eastern bloc. All his proposals for a united Germany therefore had that goal in mind, which was why it was important to prevent an economically revived West Germany from being incorporated into the capitalist bloc. Thus, talking to Stalin on such matters was deemed to be disadvantageous to the West given Stalin's allegedly spurious appeals to the German people, which would only arouse sympathy and undermine Western solidarity. On the other hand, Stalin may have genuinely been seeking a settlement, without aiming to dominate a united Germany, in ways which would bring greater German stability. It seems clear from Soviet sources that Stalin hoped to use the 12 March 1952 note as a means to thwart German disarmament, but that does not necessarily mean he was motivated by a quest for gain as opposed to genuine fears about a rearmed West Germany. In the latter case, he would be sharing the same fears as many in the West and his attempts to mitigate them were to be geared to modelling East Germany more on Soviet lines.

The Militarization of the Cold War

It was the Berlin Blockade that allegedly made a major contribution to the creation of NATO. A strong response to Soviet actions was seen as necessary by Western governments for the sake of credibility, but explained and justified in terms of the risk of war and the need to resist Soviet expansion. Here was the point, it is claimed, when the military dangers presented by the Soviet Union became clearer, presaging the limited warfare that the Soviets were to authorize in Korea two years later. Not normally mentioned are the first American moves in 1948 in what was to become a significant campaign to undermine Soviet control over Eastern Europe. Nor is it often mentioned that military opinion in Britain and the US in 1948 deemed it unlikely that the Soviets would deliberately start a major war. In other words, the US and British military believed that there was no immediate military threat to Western Europe (even if it was always possible that war might start through some miscalculation). Their assessments were borne out by another example of Stalin's cautious nature and his fear of a direct clash with the US, when the blockade was terminated in humiliating circumstances in 1949.

The reasons for creating what became NATO were not primarily geared to hostile Soviet actions in Berlin, nor to perceptions of an imminent Soviet military attack in Europe. In the West, while Soviet moves over Berlin were seen as increasing the risk of war by miscalculation, NATO was essentially conceived to meet political, not military, threats and requirements. Indeed, the military role for NATO in operational terms has always been subordinated to its political importance. The fear in 1948–9 was of further communist political successes, and NATO's creation was seen as a political boost to the morale of the people of Western Europe. Put another way, it was better to present the threat in military terms to encourage popular resistance to left-wing ideologies expounded by political parties, some of which were effectively dominated by a foreign power. NATO had little chance in the immediate future of providing a military defence of Europe but its political impact could be considerable. Unlike the military, the public and academics would come to accept that the Soviets were geared to attacking Western Europe, rather than spreading communism or increasing Soviet power and influence peacefully. This deception was a vital part of Cold War strategy in the West. It developed against a post-war background of what has been described as an exaggeration of Soviet military strength in order to maximize the need for strong American armed forces.[6]

In the Soviet Union, the creation of a confrontational military bloc also influenced the domestic aspects of Stalin's Cold War strategy. Paranoid and insecure, imagining internal and external threats to his personal power, the Soviet leader, although he would have known from spies within the British government that NATO was not planning to attack the Soviets, could, as in the West, use an invented short-term military threat for domestic purposes. Imperialist spies could be linked to armed aggressors seeking to destroy the Soviet Union and thus provide the excuse for the brutal elimination of political rivals and opponents alike. In a sense, by 1948–9 the three former allies were manipulating public perceptions of the external world for domestic as well as foreign policy reasons, and the US and the Soviet Union were consolidating influence or control over their respective European spheres.

The European Projection of Global Power: Imperialism, Colonialism, and the Impact of Decolonization

The Second World War had an enormous and wide-ranging transformative effect on many elements of the international system, not least on the position of Europe's colonies. It placed European rule firmly on the retreat, particularly after the colonial powers had either suffered overall military defeat, or had experienced defeat in Asian areas of the world, which had destroyed the belief in the innate superiority of the white man. As a result, and with the rhetoric surrounding the war for freedom from Nazi rule, there were those, particularly on the western side of the Atlantic, but including some in Europe, who realized that the days of colonial control were numbered.

In the case of Britain, imperialism and empire after the Second World War were essentially about the restoration and continued projection of power in the world, whether it be in the form of economic or military power or in the softer forms of cultural and political power, or, often more importantly, power as status in the form of the prestige accompanying its projection on a global stage. Hence the contemporary and long-lasting elite conceptions of a Britain in the future remaining as a 'world power', despite its relative decline in military capabilities. The different imperial power structures deriving from European societies seeking to expand their control over distant areas of the world in the nineteenth and early twentieth centuries had in part involved the possession of colonies and their contribution in the British case to their Empire or Commonwealth. Due to the impending war, the terminology used to refer to the imperial structure had been subjected to new ideas and pressures even before the war's dramatic impact had been felt by 1945.

The post-war quest for independence by people seeking to escape from colonial control, albeit if influenced and sometimes orchestrated by European powers, has somewhat incongruously been referred to as 'decolonization'. Not only does this imply that the proactive driving forces behind this process were the European powers in possession of colonies, which at best is only partially true, but it has encouraged the conflation and confusion that has led to 'colonialism' and 'imperialism' being used synonymously with empire by policy-makers at the time, especially in the US, and subsequently by some academics. India, for example, was for many years a key component of the British Empire but was never a colony, and was thus never part of the administrative apparatus of British colonial rule or decolonization. Part of the subcontinent was never under formal British rule and consisted of the princely states, which continued to be subjected to traditional rulers and their laws and practices under the watchful eye of a British resident. The other part was under British officials whose actions and administrative practices were linked to the India Office in London and not to any liberal, decolonizing Colonial Office, which, compared to the very separate and distinct Foreign Office, had specific priorities and practices arising from their different approaches to British overseas responsibilities. The geographic distinctions within and between European colonial possessions contained a variety of unique social and ethnic cultures that were subjected to the different political and administrative practices employed by the colonial powers, who had imposed some form of control or colonialism when expanding their overseas imperial interests. The range of societies and cultures exposed to different forms of external influences has added to the confusion over colonialism and imperialism, as well as over decolonization and empire.

In the British case, there were several distinct forms of overseas possessions, with different administrative structures imposed on territories where economic and political control and influence provided benefits for the ruling elites in Britain. The colonial element of the British Empire had a clearly defined institutional structure of governance embodying formal political and administrative control, albeit often exercised in Asia and Africa through local indigenous rulers in a system known as indirect rule, which was similar but less formal than British rule in India. The broader imperial element over both colonies and other non-self-governing states, like India, involved the exercise and maintenance of British power and influence projected in a global context. The aim of Britain in 1945 was to use its imperial position and the benefits it provided to regain its position as a world power on a par with its two wartime allies. This, as in some areas of the world, like the Middle East, did not generally involve colonies, and the key components of control and influence were similar to those featured in the later debate around the existence of an American empire, which did not require any imposition of formal rule. This has produced arguments about the relevance or not of an informal empire's existence, but leaving that aside, it has meant that decolonization after 1945 has been confused and conflated with the comparative global decline of British imperialism's military and economic power that was a distinctive (and much resisted) process operating separately from, if connected to, the transfer of political authority in, and power over, colonial territories.

With or without any specific use or exercise of military force, imperialism required the development of a system of empire defence and military planning. After its pre-war failure and disasters, followed by Britain's limited wartime successes in the years before the Soviets and Americans entered the conflict, the insufficiency of the British Empire's economic and military resources in a global conflict were exposed. Comparing its reduced and considerably smaller resources with its main allies after the war did not, however, result in a reduction of British imperial ambitions. Indeed, until 1949, the government's aim was to re-establish the Empire, with new European ties, as a world power equal to the US and the Soviet Union. Though imperial defence had been superseded after the war by the 'defence of the Commonwealth', protecting the Empire's resources was then replaced by the formulation of global strategy based on similar imperial concepts. By 1950, this global strategy and its planned implementation with even more limited resources had become disconnected from concrete and viable military operational planning.

Since then, such vague and abstract concepts as 'strategy' and 'strategic importance' have often become used, like 'security', with considerably less link to concrete reality, in ways in which they might be defined and realized. In effect, they have been, and still are, used to justify and provide more substance to the policies of maintaining prestige and international influence inherent in the post-war British quest for world power status. The components of the latter were also changing because of the new ideas the changing distribution of power produced by the war and its impact on the native inhabitants of European colonies. For British imperialists who preferred to focus on the non-colonial aspects of empire, pretending that strategic values and considerations were embodied in military deployments and meaningful operational plans was to become increasingly significant after the war, as the relative decline of British economic and military power became more obvious. This pretence was designed to camouflage the relative and absolute international reduction in substantive, or 'hard', British power in the world, and was at the heart of the generally unsuccessful post-1945 attempts to connect British defence strategy with foreign policy. As the aims and objectives of foreign policy diverged from those of defence policy, the latter remained based on an imperial strategy, with operational plans that could not be implemented because of the lack of available military resources. The loss of prestige and status that this decline of British 'hard' power threatened was always of more significance for the Empire than the changing status of colonies once the transfer of power in the latter got underway.

Unlike decolonization, this more 'imperial' aspect of the end of empire proved very hard to accept on both sides of the political spectrum. It has been particularly troublesome for the right of the British Conservative party and continues to form a key undercurrent of the British attitude towards European integration. The debates on Britain's overseas role, which started from a 1945 position of using Britain's desired leadership position in Western Europe, were initially focused on the power and resources Britain could draw from the Empire/Commonwealth. Over time, the issue has become whether or not having an important foot on both sides of the Atlantic, as a significant world power, allows Britain to exercise more authority and retain more importance internationally. The idea that Britain should be the crucial element through which influence flows from one side of the Atlantic to the other reflects its past as an imperial power, which its governing elites after the war perceived as making it distinct from, and superior to, most of Britain's European allies. Hard power, measured in imperial military terms, continued to be represented outside Europe after 1945 by bases used by British troops, ships, and aircraft. It was often accompanied by the economic dominance provided by the extraction of Asian and African resources, and was always more important than colonialism's political control. As the US was beginning to demonstrate, military and economic power could be developed and enhanced without political control. Nevertheless, the Second World War had terminated Britain's remaining economic and military advantages in global hard power compared to the US, and even to the land-based, and much less economic and militarily powerful Soviet Union.

Yet, as one senior official noted in the early 1950s, as he focused on what was to become, for the elites making overseas policy, an increasingly crucial element in trying to maintain Britain's position as a world power:

> Thinking over our difficulties in Egypt it seems to me that the essential difficulty arises from the very obvious fact that we lack power . . . But the basic and fundamental aim of British policy is to build up our lost power. Once we despair of doing so, we shall never attain this aim. Power, of course is not to be measured in terms alone of money and troops: a third ingredient is prestige, or in other words what the rest of the world thinks of us.
>
> Here the dilemma arises. We are not physically strong enough to carry out policies needed if we are to retain our position in the world; if we show weakness our position in the world diminishes with repercussions on our world-wide position . . . Ideally we should persuade the Americans of the disaster which such a policy would entail for us and them, and seek their backing, moral, financial and if possible, military, in carrying out a strong policy in Egypt.[7]

Yet, the true importance of British prestige and status as a world power has often been ignored or downplayed in an imperial context. In discussions around imperialism and colonialism in the era of decolonization, the processes by which they were both transformed, through radically different processes, in the end of empire are still often neglected. The different elements of imperialism and colonialism, as with the different manifestations of power, are still often conflated in the understanding of decolonization. To provide an overall interpretation to explain the developments that produced the transfer of power, in such disparate dependent territories as India, the Windward Islands, Algeria, Kenya, Fiji, the Belgian Congo, and Angola, is a difficult, if not impossible task. The circumstances in each former colony reflected differences in everything from geography to the structures of European rule. Moreover, the perceptions and policies of the imperialists concerned primarily with foreign policy and those prioritizing colonial policy in the metropoles, often reflected different ideas about the significance of empire and colonialism. In addition, both sets of officials in London, Paris, Brussels, and Lisbon sometimes had views which differed from those of officials in the colonial capitals, who in turn tended to see things differently from service officers many miles from the centre.

Yet, had the issue simply been the nature of the administrative, judicial, or cooperative arrangements between parts of Europe and large areas of the non-European world, then transferring power would not have been so burdened by conflicts and disputes. Nor would it have become so closely entwined with the developing Cold War if the only issues were how best to control or influence some of the poorest and most inhospitable places on the planet. It was precisely because European colonies reflected metropolitan perceptions of national roles as great powers, on occasions with specific economic and military benefits (usually portrayed as responsibilities), that the transformations during and after the Second World War helped produce some violent conflicts between colonial rulers and their subjects. Specific economic benefits to European nations from their empires, or to some leading wealthy individuals and corporations within them, when added to particular military requirements, did involve significant amounts of prestige and status. They provide a further complicating imperial element to add to the transfer of political and administrative control in the decolonization process.

The important political transformations in the control of British dependent territories had first begun much earlier than for other European possessions, with the Durham report of 1839, which introduced the idea of limited self-government for Canada. Internal affairs were to be the responsibility of a legislature and ministers chosen by Canadians under a British governor general, not officials appointed by London. This was gradually extended to the 'white' overseas territories of New Zealand, Australia, South Africa, Eire, and Newfoundland. The onset of the First World War, which ended with the 'Dominions' separately signing the peace treaties, then led to the 1926 Imperial Conference declaration that these 'dominions' were 'autonomous communities within the British Empire, equal in status, and no way subordinate to one another . . . as freely associated members of the British Commonwealth of Nations'. The Statute of Westminster of 1931 formally established these 'white' territories (apart from Newfoundland) internationally as separate states with complete legislative authority. Thus, when the cataclysmic results of the Second World War had their dramatic impact on the international system, and on the states and people within it, the British, unlike the other European imperial powers, had begun a process of moving former colonial dependencies towards self-government. When the impact of a war for freedom had spawned revolutionary ideas of self-government and independence, with all peoples deemed able to choose the form of government under which they should live, the writing was on the wall for many European possessions in Asia, and even, if more faintly, for those in Africa that were under colonial rule.

With the wartime US administration of Franklin D. Roosevelt leading the anti-colonial charge, diehard imperialists such as Winston Churchill were forced reluctantly to accept substantial changes as they struggled in vain to preserve the integrity and power of the entire British Empire or Commonwealth. Roosevelt sought to build policies that combined American idealism with a practical overall strategy for the pursuit of the war effort and the promotion of post-war US interests, through the joint Anglo-American adoption of the Atlantic Charter in 1941. Hence, Churchill was forced to argue that his Atlantic Charter commitment requiring 'people to choose the form of government under which they should live' applied only to those people liberated from Nazi rule and not to those governed by Britain.

The theoretical framework behind the twentieth-century control exercised over British overseas territories outside the white Dominions, and originally based on the idea of indirect rule, had to be applied through officials under a colonial governor. The governor was a Crown appointee, who headed the secretariat in the capitals of the British territories and the officers or district commissioners of the colonial service in the interior. These colonial service members, distinct from officials in the Colonial Office in London, were usually out in rural areas and acting through indigenous chiefs or leaders who were reliant on local laws and customs. The District Commissioners in the remote areas often found themselves in conflict with the 'secretariat wallahs' in the colonial capitals. Equally, differences appeared between Colonial Office officials in London and colonial governors, which had to be reconciled without clearly defined lines of authority. Many colonial peoples did not share the same degree of economic development that had been changing the face of many parts of twentieth-century Europe. They were thus open to the now perennial charge of failing in the process of 'modernizing' their alleged primitive and backward societies. This in turn could be used to justify British imperialism and the continuation of colonial rule, disingenuously or not, as a selfless pursuit or burden, which was necessary in order to prepare African or Asian people to stand on their own two feet in the new post-1945 world. This modification of the theories of British rule, which had long been circulating in and around the Colonial Office in the inter-war years, had also affected the theoretical development of the economic relationships between Britain and its colonies. The idea of colonial subjects imposing a duty on British colonial power had been enshrined in the League of Nations Mandated territories after 1918. These British mandates embodied responsibilities towards people in more 'advanced' overseas dependencies who lacked independence. The exercise of such responsibilities in the colonies of the defeated states was transferred to the Trusteeship Council of the new post-war United Nations to supervise their preparation by new colonial masters to meet the political and economic requirements of modern self-governing states. The development of those territories not allegedly blessed with British rule thus became a part of the rationale of maintaining British colonialism. In the short term, it would lead the colonial dependencies through decolonization to self-government, and in the long term to the more significant goal of independence.

The idea of British colonial economic development as part of preparing dependencies 'to stand on their own two feet' had initially been conceived in interwar legislation as using the Empire for Britain's benefit by securing better access to overseas resources. The 1929 Colonial Development Act publicized the idea of raw materials from the Empire helping Britain's industries to alleviate the effect of the Depression. By 1945, the war had transformed the way colonies were perceived, with the 1945 Colonial Development Act reversing the developmental objectives with metropolitan money going to assist the colonies. The British Treasury would provide capital, to benefit colonial producers and create or improve social and technical services. A less altruistic interpretation, allowing for the growing importance of wartime propaganda, sees the 1945 Colonial Development and Welfare Act originating primarily from the need to rally support against fascism. By contrasting the portrayal of a liberal colonial power and its planned economic benefits with the offerings of the Axis powers, crucial support for the war would be promoted. The state, and even the colonial state, could then hopefully be seen as a progressive, even beneficial force. However genuine the rhetoric from the Colonial Office, it was soon superseded after the war by the more pressing need to manufacture British goods, or to obtain primary products and raw materials from the Empire, that could be exported to the US to overcome the shortage of dollars. With the dominance of the US economy's production of consumer goods, dollars were essential for purchasing the imports to end wartime austerity and rebalance the global economy. Thus, in the short term the rhetoric of Britain providing imports and financial aid for the benefit of the colonies was transformed into the reality of the colonies providing foodstuffs and raw material to be exported to the dollar zone for the benefit of Britain. It was an economic example of the clear distinction, as the world of decolonization beckoned, between imperial requirements and policies developed to meet the needs of the colonies.

Unfortunately, the French rationale for the exercise of colonial control had never derived in theory or historical experience from a process by which states, subject to rule by French officials in Paris, moved towards self-government and independence. The French and Portuguese dealing with their overseas possessions found such concepts as independence and self-government for those they regarded as inferior or backward people as completely anathema. French colonial policy, and to a lesser extent that of Portugal, centred on *assimilation,* a process by which colonial subjects were assimilated into the French republic *une et indivisible*. People in French colonies, as they developed and became French 'citizens', would thus eventually assume the same rights and cultural experiences as citizens of metropolitan France. This idea was formally embodied in the French Union, created in 1946 to provide the framework by which France and its overseas territories became part of the same constitutional structure of a republic *une et indivisible.* It would thus justify the process of eliminating colonialism by introducing the great principles of *liberté, équalité,* and *fraternité.* The problem was that neither on a constitutional nor on an individual basis could French colonial subjects (*sujets*) all become French citizens by assimilating equal rights, as they vastly outnumbered the inhabitants of metropolitan France. Thus, in the one and indivisible Fourth Republic divisions were inevitable as overseas French citizens could not and would not achieve full political equality within any empire framework or union. Hence, the rhetoric of *assimilation* had been somewhat modified to *association* even before the creation of the French Union. A further anomaly existed because Algeria had become, in terms of its governance, a part of France, and as such it was administered as a French *département* by the Ministry of the Interior and not by the French Colonial Office. With the 1946 creation of the French Union, the Colonial Office became the Ministry of Overseas France and thus was aligned more closely with the rhetoric that France no longer had colonies but territories of overseas France which, as members of the French Union, were part of the single republic.

There were other distinguishing features of French rule which set it apart from British practices. In order to propagate French culture and values, the use of indigenous languages was banned as far as possible in native education in French colonies. But *assimilation/association* was more in evidence in the conduct of French colonial service officials. Whereas some British District Commissioners, members of the secretariat, and during the war the military officers stationed in the colonies, often had Asian or African mistresses, these liaisons were kept secret as far as possible, whereas their French equivalents, often from more mixed (i.e. lower) social backgrounds, conducted open relationships with native women. The economic position of the French Empire was defined by *mise en valeur* and was thus similar to the post-1918 British idea of development. It became for the Ministry of Overseas France, as for the British Colonial Office, essential after the war to inject a more progressive, even altruistic, element into the colonialism of a power that had collaborated with the Germans. The British had the 1945 Colonial Development Act to provide the means by which metropolitan resources could be used for the benefit of the colonial economies, while the French had the 1946 *Fonds d'Investissement pour le Développement Économique et Sociale* (FIDES). The demands of European Recovery and the American determination to link Marshall Aid to the weakening of imperial economic blocs were soon to ensure that the implementation of colonial development was cloaked in what would be seen in today's terminology as a large amount of 'spin'. Somewhat paradoxically, the French spent more metropolitan money than the British on the colonies. This was partly connected to the first French provisional government under the wartime leader of the Free French, General Charles de Gaulle, having to attempt to rebuild the damage done to French prestige and status internationally by the Vichy regime's capitulation to, and collaboration with, Hitler's Germany. An obvious way of doing this was through those parts of the French African Empire, which alone had remained loyal to the 'soul of France'. As a result, in January 1944, French Equatorial Africa had staged the Brazzaville Conference, in French Congo, of colonial governors and administrators to herald the idea of colonial reform. The focus was on development and welfare, with the exclusion of any idea of independence or self-government.

In the Portuguese territories, there was little evidence of organized anti-colonialism which needed to be appeased by economic development or social welfare provision. At the start of the 1950s, neither Angola nor Mozambique had any significant extractive industries to encourage collective organizations in general or Trades Unions in particular, but significant means of repression were available to the Portuguese authorities through, for example, the continued use of forced labour by the colonial state. As will be seen, the French had also used repressive practices which the war and its propaganda had made outmoded (see Chapter 3, B) and, Brazzaville notwithstanding, the nature of French imperial exploitation had always been closer to the unadorned reality of the subjugation and exploitation provided by European rule in Africa. The causes of the repression that some colonies endured were often economic in nature. Oil in the Middle East, particularly from Iraq and Iran, had always benefitted the British Treasury through the unfairness of the concessions agreements. Neither they nor the Trucial States in the Persian Gulf were colonies under the Colonial Office; what mattered after the war was not whether they were protectorates or colonies but whether they were members of the sterling area and able to provide oil priced in sterling rather than dollars. The ties and non-self-governing status of the European Middle Eastern and North African dependencies, or subordinate states and protectorates not under colonial rule, were primarily economic for those possessing oil. Whatever the nature of their quest for political freedom and independence, their dependency had grown from the exploitative economic seeds planted by earlier forms of imperialism, which by the 1950s had blossomed due to the developing world's links with the international economy. In some of these territories, as with those in other areas of the globe not rich in oil, the political freedom gained by decolonization was generally not matched by the gaining of economic freedom.

Whether this was due to some form of neo-colonialism is a matter of dispute, but international capital's development from the end of the Korean War with the drop in primary produce prices was beginning to handicap the economic progress of the poorer nations and non-self-governing territories. Whatever disadvantages 'the market' was providing for the less developed nations, colonies or not, those dependent on tropical produce, which could not be easily and cheaply stored, were affected by being less able to influence world market prices. The importance of the financial sector, as opposed to the manufacturing sector in the developed world economies and its profitability for the owners of capital in the developed world had yet to be realized by replacing the significant economic gains that colonialism had provided.

Nowhere were these gains more in evidence than in the Belgian Congo, where the Belgians, like the Portuguese with their white settlers, had treated their African subjects to little or nothing in the way of education, welfare, or development assistance. Originally the Free State of the Belgian King Leopold, the Congo was integrated into the Belgian colonial state in 1908 to reduce the level of international criticism of the terrible exploitation of African labour. With an injection of British and Belgian capital, King Leopold was able to ensure that a more respectable colonial framework was created, to continue some degree of exploitation and provide benefits for the metropole and European investors. Significant in the Congo was the blend of private companies and public institutions, controlled or influenced in Leopoldville and Brussels, to ensure that financial gains flowed to European investors. These gains were not simply from shares in the main operating company but from the concessionary rights, originally held by Leopold, and the interconnected web of holding companies present in the special circumstances provided by the Belgian colonial state. In the Congo, which may have been the exception rather than the rule, the key imperial features and its benefactors did not primarily come from trade and business but from finance and its connection to the colonial state's role in controlling the allocation and use of hard currency earned from exporting the Congo's raw materials.

In economic terms, the impact of the benefits or burdens of European colonialism, and for which actors, remains controversial. The French Empire at the beginning of the twentieth century, and well after the First World War, had been an important market that enabled French businesses, notably manufacturing, clothing, and metal products, to compensate for the limited internal market, which was constrained by low urban wages and significant peasant producers in the rural areas. It gave metropolitan producers, with overpriced goods that were unable to compete on world markets, privileged access to protected colonial markets. It could also be argued that French colonial producers benefited from produce prices which in the franc zone were fixed above world market prices. Jacques Marseille has argued that the economics of the French imperial trading bloc influenced the timing of decolonization. In the 1950s particularly, the value provided by the Empire was no longer compatible with the needs of French capital and the development of the French economy.[8] As the French economy changed in the 1950s with the modernization of French industry reducing the numbers of small producers who were dependent on the markets of Overseas France, so the resistance to ending French rule was weakened.

Portugal also adopted a system of imperial preference, which maintained close economic ties with its overseas possessions, and this trade was certainly important for the Portuguese economy. Moreover, in Portugal's African colonies, where many Portuguese settlers sought to escape the high levels of unemployment back home, as in French Algeria, racial tensions were high as white settlers competed with Black Africans for menial employment. The situation was made worse by the post-war continuation of forced labour, which the British and French no longer used for such tasks as road-building. As long as there were no significant opportunities available to the dominant peasant producers by growing cash crops such as coffee for the world market, the lid could be kept on any unrest outside Luanda.

In the rest of colonial Africa, development was of limited effect. The hopes of the British Colonial Office, that economic measures could be taken to assist African producers in achieving higher and more stable prices for their tropical produce, were dashed by 1947. The demands of the imperial state for post-war recovery centred on increasing colonial production, without any compensation in the form of increased imports of consumer goods. The latter were in short supply as wartime industry in Britain struggled to revert to peacetime production. The priority given to metropolitan consumers meant, at the very least, the short-term exploitation of colonial producers with materials like rubber that earned dollars to help overcome the 'dollar gap' and assist an ailing metropolitan economy. These pressures were never fully removed in this period and the chances of making a significant impact in a vast African continent lacking in infrastructure were always remote. Despite the acceptance by some policy-makers of the principle of colonial development for the colonies, it remained of marginal importance both from the point of view of benefiting the metropole and for producing significant changes in the colonies.

Moreover, as the urgency of economic requirements was reduced in the early 1950s, international pressures on colonial rule began to grow. In the 1930s, the British response to disturbances in some colonies, most notably in the West Indies and Palestine, was clearly influenced by the impending war and the greater need to avoid international criticism of British colonialism. After the Second World War, international pressures came from the anti-colonialism of Britain's two main wartime allies, particularly the US, with its potentially damaging consequences. However, this American criticism was almost immediately reduced as the war ended, owing initially to the demand of the American military for an extensive network of overseas bases, particularly in the Pacific and East Asia. The benefits accrued from hard power in military and economic terms had quickly become evident once the war ended. They would start to override or supersede the competing and often contradictory adoption of colonial policies embodied in British decolonization that were unleashed by the wartime changes and sometimes confusingly linked to imperial objectives.

At the end of the war, accepting the long-term decolonization goal of self-government for most colonies, however reluctantly, could be stomached more readily than independence or an end to imperialism by those elites on the political right. Imperialism, with its projection of British power in the world, seriously affected elite perceptions of Britain's importance as a significant world power, which they were committed to sustain. In a sense, as imperial needs increased and global power and status had to be rebuilt after the war, colonial policy, unlike foreign policy or military strategy, was generally regarded as less important for how metropolitan elites in Britain perceived the different components of their state's power.

For the French clinging on to their colonies at the end of the war, the desire to end colonialism was most evident in Asia in the three colonies (Tonkin, Annam, and Cochin China) of Vietnam, which during the war were occupied by the Japanese and declared independence in March 1945. How this was to be reconciled with the French Union was the cause of the breakdown of negotiations with the Vietnamese nationalists which led to a military conflict in 1946 (see Chapter 3, A). In the face of indigenous opposition, the French argued that with the policy of assimilation there could no longer be any colonies or authentic nationalist movements. Protests against colonial rule were seen simply as manifestations of external forces at work, whether they be communist-inspired or a consequence of American imperialism. This remained the case for the period in question, which by its end in 1953 was producing more North African challenges to French rule; it was only the British and the Dutch who were prepared to grant independence before 1953. For the British, this went with a determination to maintain the prestige and status of a world power inherent in an imperial presence, which would be unaffected or increased by the decolonization process that had begun transferring political power in its Asian non-self-governing territories. The post-Vichy fourth French Republic governments were also conscious of a need to rebuild French prestige, but there were important divisions in the higher echelons of French society. Some of the French elite remained committed to the French Union and portraying French imperialism under a new guise as advocated by the Ministry of Overseas France. Others, including the Quai d'Orsay, were less convinced that the Union's justification could be sold to international critics of colonialism, not least in the United Nations.

The new organization, with its Trusteeship Council, was well placed, especially with new Asian states becoming independent in the 1940s, to air grievances about the continuation of colonialism, especially of the French variety. Keeping their possessions away from UN meddling in colonial affairs with General Assembly resolutions became an important Anglo-French aim. To some extent, the nature of the international environment can be used to explain why in 1947 power was transferred in India, but not in what are often regarded as less important parts of the British Empire. In 1945–6, before the growing international tensions fully gave way to confrontation and Cold War, the spirit of internationalism, characterized by the commitment to freedom for which the war had allegedly been fought, ran through the newly established United Nations into all corners of the globe. The expression of that spirit and plans for its international implementation dominated the immediate post-war years, in which the key decisions on India's future were taken in a window of opportunity. Britain's status in the international community could be enhanced by embracing that principle of freedom and offering it to Indian subjects as well as to those deprived of it by Nazi rule.

Other explanations for the transfer of power in India have focused exclusively on the strength of the Indian nationalist movements which, it is claimed, forced the British hand. Subsequently, it can therefore be argued that, with the 'jewel' in the British Crown abandoned, it was inevitable that the rest of the dependencies would achieve independence as and when nationalist movements were strong enough to demand it. This does not explain why the British were so keen to resist Egyptian demands that would produce a loss of influence in the Middle East; nor why there was resistance in London to the transfer of power in parts of Black Africa. To some extent, explanations for this can be located in the different circumstances in the colonies, including their economic viability, political awareness, and educational development, but also such things as their racial mix, particularly when there was a significant white-settler minority. Thus, in many ways, it can be argued that India was ripe for independence when most parts of the British Empire were not. Another argument, which ignores the influence of international factors, is that by the end of the Second World War India was much less important to the British economy and was therefore abandoned because it had outlived its usefulness. Finally, the fact that Prime Minister Clement Attlee had an intimate involvement with India through his work on the Simon Commission (which drew up the devolved 1935 Constitution), and a personal commitment to Indian independence, has been portrayed as another significant metropolitan produced factor.

What the above have in common is that, to a greater or lesser extent, they made it easier to concede to the demands of the nationalists, and for Attlee to convince his reluctant colleagues of the need to leave India. The international situation, or rather elite perceptions of the kind of important international role they wanted Britain to play within it, had a similar and short-lived effect. The fact that Labour opponents of the Prime Minister's India policy (which included his close confidant as foreign secretary, Ernest Bevin) could offer no practical alternative to Indian independence was another crucial factor. In 1945–6, before the growing international tensions fully gave way to confrontation and Cold War, the spirit of internationalism, characterized by the commitment to freedom, for which the war had allegedly been fought, ran through the newly established United Nations and into all corners of the globe. The expression of that spirit and plans for its implementation dominated the immediate post-war years with very different results for British perceptions of the importance of the Middle East in comparison to India.

Interestingly, it was the Prime Minister and his foreign secretary who were again the protagonists in the 1945–6 disagreements and discussions on maintaining imperialism, or modifying it by retreating from power in the Middle East. On this occasion, Bevin, backed by the military expertise of the Chiefs of Staff, was to triumph through inventing an imminent threat from a Soviet communist regime already pre-defined as the enemy. Always the overriding fear of the military, even during the war, they argued that to deal with a Soviet communist threat, British imperialism, or the strategic position of the Commonwealth, had to be maintained by an exclusive British presence in the Middle East. This was well before the military and intelligence communities had begun to assess Soviet actions and to quantify the actual and specific nature of the threat. Attlee, conscious of the cost of defending Britain's Middle Eastern position, was arguing that such exclusive British responsibilities should be replaced by arrangements of an international character for what was the largest military base in the world in the Suez Canal zone in Egypt. Nothing could make the distinction between the imperialist and decolonizing elements of British overseas policy any clearer than these discussions.

Despite the forward-looking approach of the Prime Minister, the fundamentally imperialist approach of Bevin and the military, who were determined to prevent empire being replaced by some idealistic internationalism, won the day. Clement Attlee was a committed socialist and someone who embraced internationalism as a new addition to the post-war international order. Attlee did not see it as something which would supersede traditional approaches to power, and replace empire and interstate rivalry, but as something which would modify them and which therefore should be taken into account. It could be used effectively by Britain as a tool for crafting a more peaceful and affordable world role, which still appeared possible in 1946. Such ideas have proved easy to misrepresent and easier to dismiss once the Cold War world was established at the end of 1947.

It was certainly Bevin and the military who dominated the British response to the 1945 Egyptian request to evacuate the Suez base through an early renegotiation of the 1936 Anglo-Egyptian treaty due to expire in 1956. This was eventually to lay bare the incompatible approaches to Middle East policy and military strategy of the Foreign Office and the chiefs of staff. As the Foreign Office developed its third world force of Europe and its overseas possessions for the regaining of lost British power, its imperialism also came into conflict with the more realistic decolonization policies of the Colonial Office, especially in tropical Africa. An African tour by the Chief of the Imperial General Staff, Bernard Montgomery, led him to produce a paper for Bevin extolling the military manpower and abundant natural resources of the continent, which he claimed could be used to meet the needs of the British Empire. When circulated by the Foreign Secretary, Andrew Cohen, the head of the Africa division of the Colonial Office had to draft a paper pointing out the African illusions which Montgomery was labouring under.[9] As members of a relatively junior government department, some staff in the Colonial Office had already become increasingly frustrated with living in the shadow of the Foreign Office and its reluctance to accept the changes brought by the war. Well before Montgomery's 1947 African tour, one official had noted, on discussions about colonial cooperation with the French in West Africa, that Britain had to do what the Africans would accept, 'a point which cannot be made too strongly to the Foreign Office who seem to live in the middle of the 19th century on this and other matters'.[10]

The establishment of the United Nations and the influence of its Latin American, Middle Eastern, and Asian members, who had a strong anti-colonialist agenda, created a number of dilemmas. It was not simply a question of avoiding NATO divisions over empire which could jeopardize American strategic requirements. The broader Cold War dilemma stemmed from the disadvantages of fighting a Cold War for democratic freedom, with large areas of the Western world denied this right. The Soviets could point to the Western idea of freedom in the context of formal subjugation making colonialism a serious handicap in the propaganda battle. It therefore appeared to make sense to terminate colonial rule as soon as possible. If this did not happen, unrest would mount and the conditions would be ripe for communist exploitation even if growing numbers of colonial people did not look to the Soviets for support in their battle for independence. Unfortunately, if the European powers granted independence too soon, without adequate preparation, then the new states would be unstable and open to subversion if they proved unable to provide law and order and a stable political environment. From a Western Cold War perspective, there were dangers in transferring power too soon as well as in delaying it.

The question of timing was a key one, and remains so, for any understanding of the transfers of power which ended formal European rule. If anti-colonial movements were the sine qua non in producing change, is it plausible to say that they determined the timing of the transfers of power? Did the colonial powers change their policies or speed them up simply because they grew more aware of the strength of indigenous opposition to their continued presence? Or was the international situation important in determining precisely when power was transferred? And how important were considerations of preserving economic interests as opposed to establishing new collaborators who would look to their colonial masters for advice and guidance? Were Cold War considerations vital in efforts to ensure that preparations were made to transfer power at appropriate times to those elites whose allegiances would be to the Western rather than to the communist world, and who were deemed likely to provide the necessary stability in viable new states?

Some ideas on these and other questions arising from the complex process of decolonization will be suggested in the following sections, focused more on particular regions. Playing on the colonial stage in the other British overseas theatre was the start of a decolonization drama where a more subdued enactment of progressive policies was using soft power by cooperating with colonial peoples through a process of facilitating the end of empire. It was hoped that, by acting in tune with the spirit of self-government and the freely expressed wishes of colonial peoples, long-lasting benefits and kudos would be secured by ending imperialism and using liberal and progressive policies to gain status.

Once India was independent (see Chapter 3, A), the idea that Britain would gain kudos from transferring power as part of her quest to regain her international status as one of the Big Three powers was less plausible. Moreover, the glib assumption that Britain would recover economically from the war was under threat from the harsh winter of 1947 and the growing dollar gap. Empire thus came to be seen not only in the different light of the Cold War, but as something which would have to be employed to regain British economic strength and great power status. Thus, Colonial Office efforts to develop the colonies in ways which would prepare them for self-government now coincided with attempts by the Treasury and the Board of Trade, backed by the Foreign Office, to increase colonial production. Produce and raw materials could then help British industry and consumers or be sold to the dollar area. As a result, the second colonial occupation, as it has been termed, also involved increasing exploitation, through production without economic incentives, which in turn would influence anti-colonial movements and the nature of the British response to them. Increased exploitation was difficult to reconcile with increased cooperation with the peoples of the changing colonial world, the Cold War notwithstanding.

Moreover, on stage in the imperial theatre of declining empire, despite the growing pressure from newly independent states and non-self-governing territories (not just colonies), there were actors determined to avoid any overseas retreat from power. It meant that no compensation was to be had from abandoning overseas responsibilities where elements of hard military or economic power remained in place. In the British case, it was assumed that such concrete manifestations reflected the prestige and influence that an imperial role had always been perceived as generating. In this imperialist drama, the benefits of hard economic power or the maintenance of a military presence, with or without formal political control, were still required to convert empire into world power status through global strategy.

From 1947 until 1953, it is clear imperial forces were winning the battle with decolonization in Europe, but events beyond European control in the Empire would prevent total victory. Empire was at the heart of the divisions within Britain and France, albeit of a different nature, between the colonial and foreign offices. It was also to produce conflicting positions over global strategy between the British Foreign Office and the military and with their trans-Atlantic allies (see Chapter 3, C). Cold War requirements were then mixed up with an imperial legacy and often used to justify the maintenance of empire. In the Middle East, the nature of the Soviet threat was seriously misrepresented by the British to gain acceptance of a continued military presence, ostensibly to defend the region. Inadequate though it was to defend anything but the Egyptian base and its prestige, it took the Suez Crisis to dispel the illusions about the British Empire in the Middle East and its military capabilities.

Ideology and Power Politics in East Asia

It has been suggested that the tensions that developed in the Grand Alliance in 1945 stemmed from disagreements over power and influence on a global basis, with the Middle East and East Asia contributing as much as Europe to the failure to agree on the distribution of formal and informal influence. As such, the idea of a Cold War developing separately in Asia is a misperception despite the fact that the establishment of a new, unified China in October 1949 was the result of the particular circumstances that produced a communist victory over the Nationalists in the civil war. In order to understand Soviet and American reactions to this, one has to take into account the regional circumstances and the way in which East Asian events interacted with broader international considerations. Such interactions have to be seen in terms of the Cold War's ideological nature and in terms of the impact on the regional power balance. They cannot simply be defined by analyses of Soviet–American relations based on the assumption that a gain for one was a loss for the other—a so-called 'zero-sum game'. China's emergence in particular was a threat to both powers and both were uncertain about how best to respond.

The more powerful Mao Zedong and communist China became, the more they became a threat to Stalin, who had ambitions to achieve in East Asia, particularly with regard to a warm-water port and the extension of Soviet influence. The success of Mao effectively put a brake on these ambitions, especially the agreement which, with American help, Stalin had foisted upon Chiang Kai-shek's Chinese Nationalist regime. Arguably, Stalin's ambitions would have been achieved more easily with American support. It was logical for the Soviet leader to assume that the price would be paid by the Nationalists, with whom ideological sympathy was lacking, and therefore power-political goals would be easier to achieve at their expense. An ideologically friendly regime, while it might enhance the global communist movement, would not be so easy to reconcile with Stalin's power-political goals.

The conflict in Korea and the communist takeover in China were far more than an extension of a European confrontation into a more global one centred on Soviet–American rivalry. They involved a mixture of ambitions with purely Asian elements as well as the confrontation between the capitalist and communist worlds. The Chinese communist success was long seen as inevitable by those in the West with knowledge of the region, but this did not remove old Chinese fears and ambitions in East Asia. On the other hand, power politics did not mean that Mao would turn to the Americans. Just as the prospect of the US saving China was a forlorn hope, so was the prospect of Mao, disillusioned with Stalin, turning to Washington. Whatever Mao's disillusion and suspicion of the Soviets or his ideological affinities with Moscow, there was the American attitude to the Nationalists to consider. This major obstacle required a massive shift in American policy to surmount and to take into account the importance for Mao of unifying China. This fundamental Chinese communist goal was far more important than ideology or long-term regional ambitions. It would long constrain Sino-American relations and rule out any Sino-American cooperation.[11]

In a sense, given the closer links with the Chinese communists, the Korean War, for the Soviets, was part of the attempt to reconcile ideological support with Stalin's particular ambitions in East Asia. As has been argued by Shen Zhihua, this could be achieved by returning the port of Darien and replacing it with warm-water ports in Korea once the peninsula was united under communist control. Unfortunately for Stalin, his fears of taking on the Americans made him disinclined to risk such actions, and until early 1950 he refused to accede to the North Korean leader Kim Il Sung's requests to support a proposed invasion of the South. Only when the Chinese were on board, and it seemed the Americans were unwilling to fight for an area they deemed strategically unimportant, did Stalin finally give Kim Il Sung the green light. It was a grave miscalculation on Stalin's part and another example of his lack of understanding of the West, manifesting itself in serious consequences for the Soviets, who emerged the only real losers from the war, despite playing a back seat and only providing trained military personnel and equipment.

The Korean War can be characterized and assessed in contrasting ways. It was a war which enhanced the status of the United Nations and which saw a firm stand being taken against armed aggression on the part of the North, a war which saw a further extension of Soviet–American hostility and which clearly played a major role in the global conflict and added a new armed dimension. The Korean War can thus be seen as a Cold War which became hot but which was limited to a regional conflict. This indicated the fears in the communist camp about the military power of the US, and the fact that those in the latter country who favoured an extension of the war were finally defeated with Truman's sacking of General MacArthur in April 1951. The aggression perpetuated by the North Koreans brought no reward, yet the Chinese gained in status enormously, because of their proven capabilities against the Americans in a military stalemate. The Americans managed to prevent the loss of South Korea and, as they perceived it, the loss of credibility for their leadership and defence of the free world. They also concluded that communist aggression in Korea was instigated by Stalin, which led them to dramatically overstate the scale and ambitions of the Soviet Union and the closeness of its ties with China. Stalin was the loser because the Americans acted on this exaggerated perception and reinforced their commitment to the kind of aggressive Cold War actions that he feared. It was therefore a war which intensified the Cold War in the short term and reinforced Stalin's paranoid perceptions while bringing him no power political gains.

Visit the online resources that accompany this book to test your understanding and take your learning further: www.oup.com/he/young-kent3e.

NOTES

1. H. Jones and R. B. Woods et al., 'The Origins of the Cold War: A Symposium', *Diplomatic History*, 2 (1993), and commentaries by Rosenberg, Stephanson and Bernstein, 251–311.
2. John Lewis Gaddis, *We Now Know: Rethinking Cold War History* (Clarendon Press, New York, 1997), 31.
3. V. Zubok and C. Pleshakov, *Inside the Kremlin's Cold War: From Stalin to Khrushchev* (Harvard University Press, Cambridge, 1996), 102–3.
4. By Geir Lundestad and John Lewis Gaddis, respectively.
5. Argued in Alan Milward, *The European Rescue of the Nation-State* (2nd edn, Routledge, New York, 1992).
6. M. Evangelista, 'The "Soviet Threat": Intentions, Capabilities and Context', *Diplomatic History*, 3 (1998).
7. The National Archives (TNA), Kew, FO371/96920, Minute by Dixon, 23 January 1952.
8. Jacques Marseille, *Empire colonial et Capitalisme Français* (Albin Michel, Paris, 1989), 350, 368.
9. TNA, DO35/2380, Memorandum by CIGS, 19 December 1947.
10. TNA, FO371/60002, Minute by Robinson, 1946.
11. O. A. Westad, 'Losses, Chances and Myths: The US and the Creation of the Sino-Soviet Alliance, 1946–1950', *Diplomatic History*, 2 (1997).

PART I CHRONOLOGY

The origins and development of the Cold War, 1944–53

1944	
October	Percentages Agreement between Stalin and Churchill over Greece, Romania, Hungary, Yugoslavia, and Bulgaria.
1945	
January	USSR requests American loan.
February	Yalta conference of Big Three leaders.
	Ceasefire in Greek Civil War.
March	British Foreign Office discusses value of a tougher stance against and showdown with the Soviets.
	Some Anglo-American concern over Soviet installation of puppet Romanian government (27 Feb.) and failure to broaden Lublin governments in Poland in breach of Yalta agreement.
	Soviets denounce Turkish treaty and refuse to sign another one unless Turkey returns provinces of Kars and Ardahan.
April	President Roosevelt dies.
	Truman confronts Molotov over Soviet failure to stick to all the Yalta agreements.
May	German surrender ends the war in Europe.
May–June	Hopkins mission to Moscow succeeds in securing agreement on Poland, with Stalin broadening the Polish government.
June	Soviets inform Turkey of their desire for bases in the Straits of the Dardanelles.
	State Department report on international communism concludes it poses a serious challenge to the US.

PART I CHRONOLOGY (continued)

	UN Charter agreed at San Francisco.
	Soviet request for a say in the international administration of Tangier.
	James Byrnes becomes US Secretary of State.
	George Kennan reports that the end of the Comintern has not weakened Moscow's control over international communism.
July	Potsdam conference of Big Three leaders.
	British Foreign Office debates value of concentrating on protecting vital interests in the Mediterranean, Middle East, and Germany at the expense of endeavouring to retain a say in areas such as Poland and Romania, where no interests are at stake.
6 August	Atomic bomb dropped on Hiroshima.
8 August	USSR declares war on Japan.
9 August	Atomic bomb dropped on Nagasaki.
14 August	Japanese cease fighting.
September	54 per cent of US public opinion trusts Soviets to cooperate.
September–October	London Council of Foreign Ministers (UK, US, China, France, and USSR attend).
November	Communists are defeated in Hungarian elections.
	Marshall leaves for China to mediate between communists and Nationalists.
	44 per cent of US public opinion trusts Soviets to cooperate.
December	Ethridge report on Soviet policy in Romania and Bulgaria concludes that to concede Soviet sphere of influence in Eastern Europe would be to invite its extension.
16–26 December	Moscow Council of Foreign Ministers.
1946	
January	UN meeting where Iran complains about alleged Soviet interference in its internal affairs.
	Truman tells Byrnes he is tired of babying the Soviets.
	Secret Yalta agreement on Soviet acquisition of South Sakhalin and the Kurile Islands made public in the US.
February	US warship sent to Istanbul to signal support for Turkey.
9 February	Stalin speech calling for new five-year plan to prepare for the inevitable conflict between communism and capitalism.
February	35 per cent of US public opinion trusts the Soviets to cooperate.
	Reports on Soviet spy ring providing information on US atomic bomb.
22 February	Kennan's Long Telegram from Moscow.
March	Soviets fail to withdraw troops from Iran in accordance with agreement.
5 March	Churchill's Fulton speech describing an Iron Curtain across Europe from Stettin in the Baltic to Trieste in the Adriatic.
March	US sends a note complaining of the Soviet troops present in Iran, which violated the Soviet–Iranian treaty.
	70 per cent of Americans disapprove of Soviet actions.
April	Soviets agree to withdraw troops from Iran in May.

(continued...)

PART I CHRONOLOGY (continued)

	Fighting begins again in Manchuria between Chinese Nationalists and communists.
April–May	First Paris Council of Foreign Ministers takes place.
June–July	Second Paris Council of Foreign Ministers takes place.
July–October	Paris Peace Conference (all Allied nations attend).
November–December	New York Council of Foreign Ministers takes place.
December	The Bi-Zone agreement fuses US and British occupation zones in Germany.
1947	
January	Polish elections are rigged.
12 March	Truman makes his Doctrine speech.
March–April	Moscow Council of Foreign Ministers on Germany.
June	The Marshall Plan is launched.
July	Kennan's Mr X article in *Foreign Affairs*.
August	Elections in Hungary are rigged.
September	Rio Treaty of Latin American states signed.
November	UN partition plan for Palestine.
1948	
February	Communist coup in Czechoslovakia.
March	Brussels Treaty signed.
May	British leave Palestine and Israel established.
June	The Berlin blockade begins as the Soviets block the surface access to West Berlin.
	Yugoslavia is expelled from Cominform.
1949	
April	The North Atlantic Treaty is signed.
May	Berlin blockade ends.
August	Soviets explode their first atomic bomb.
September	The Chinese People's Republic is proclaimed by Mao Zedong.
1950	
January	Acheson speech withdraws Korea from US defensive perimeter.
	Stalin decides to authorize North Korean plan to attack South Korea.
February	The Sino-Soviet Alliance is signed.
April	The National Security Council memorandum number 68 (NSC 68) proposes a large arms build-up.
May	Schuman Plan launched for a European Coal and Steel Community.
June	North Korean forces invade South Korea.
October	Pleven plan for a European army launched.
November	The Chinese intervene by using force in Korea.
1951	
June	Establishment of Psychological Strategy Board.
July	Ceasefire talks concerning Korea begin.

PART I CHRONOLOGY (continued)

September	US Japanese defence treaty is signed.
November	An agreement on the ceasefire line is reached in Armistice Talks in Korea.
1952	
May	The occupation of West Germany ends.
November	US explodes first hydrogen bomb.

Take your learning further by viewing the interactive version of this timeline:
www.oup.com/he/young-kent3e

1

Tensions in the Grand Alliance and Growing Confrontation, 1945–7

Chapter contents

A. The Yalta Conference

The Context

The Yalta Conference of February 1945 was the second of the three wartime summits between the leaders of Britain, the US, and the Soviet Union. Unlike the first meeting between Churchill, Roosevelt, and Stalin at Tehran in the autumn of 1943, a significant part of the proceedings in Crimea involved discussions on the post-war settlement. Yet the military situation was bound to overshadow the Conference. The conduct of operations in various parts of the globe could not be divorced from the attempts of the Big Three allies to maintain or increase influence. As the talks took place, the Soviet armies had crossed the Vistula and reached the Oder–Neisse river, while in the West, although the December 1944 German offensive in the Ardennes had been repulsed, Allied armies were not making the progress expected when the invasion of France began in June 1944.

By 1945, a number of military decisions and developments had helped produce mutual suspicion. The Soviets had long been concerned about the delay in establishing the second front in Western Europe. Roosevelt (see Box 1.1) and Churchill (see Box 1.3) were aware that the Soviet military position in Europe was extremely strong and that in the lands east of Germany little influence could be brought to bear. There were fears that the Russians might eventually occupy the whole of Germany, which would increase the influence that the Soviet Union could exert on the peace process. At the same time, it was realized that without cooperation with the Soviets and the continuation of the offensive in the East, the defeat of Germany would be difficult and costly. There was a common interest

BOX 1.1

Biography: Franklin Delano Roosevelt (1882–1945)

Born in New York, FDR attended Harvard University and Columbia University Law School and qualified as a lawyer in 1907. In 1910, he was elected to the New York state senate and came up against the infamous Tammany Hall political machine. Roosevelt's political instincts were such that he survived the encounter and after a spell as assistant secretary to the Navy in Woodrow Wilson's administration he ran unsuccessfully as vice-presidential candidate in democrat James Cox's bid for the White House in 1920. The following year FDR contracted polio and remained partially paralysed as a result. Nevertheless, he returned to public life in 1928, when he was elected governor of New York. In 1932, he was elected president and served a unique three successive terms in the White House. His programme of reform to counter the economic and social problems of the Depression, known as the New Deal, was a landmark in government intervention in the US and was bitterly resented by the right. FDR, however, remained an immensely popular president whose 'fireside radio chats' charmed the American public and added to his enormous political abilities. Always preferring to use personal relations rather than political principles to retain his hold on the levers of power, FDR remains an enigma whose beliefs are difficult to define. In foreign affairs, while keen to play a leading role in international conferences and the affairs of Latin America, he was nervous of the public's reaction to any US involvement in alliances that would remove America's freedom to act. This kind of isolation helped keep the US out of the Second World War until the Japanese attacked Pearl Harbor in December 1941. Significantly, FDR agreed with Churchill that wartime military strategy should give priority to the defeat of Germany. Roosevelt, who has been accused of selling out to the Soviets at Yalta, died suddenly in April 1945 from a stroke. There has been much speculation as to whether cooperation with Stalin would have continued had he remained alive.

in securing Germany's unconditional surrender and in maintaining post-war cooperation to prevent a re-emergence of the German threat. But there was also a concern in both East and West that a separate peace could have unfortunate consequences by enabling German forces to be focused on a single front.

As the Red Army advanced westward, Stalin appeared determined to eliminate, as far as possible, those organized groups opposed to the Soviet Union and/or to the ideology of communism. In keeping with the ruthless and inhumane character of the Stalinist regime, this applied not only to the former enemy states but also to Poland, which had always fought on the Allied side. The most glaring example of Stalin's desire to eliminate potential sources of opposition, even if they were anti-German, occurred in Warsaw. In August 1944, members of the Polish resistance, known as the Home Army, rose against the Germans in an effort to seize the city before the arrival of the Red Army. The rebellion was ruthlessly put down by the Germans, as Soviet forces refused to cross the Vistula to assist the rebels, despite Anglo-American requests. This sign that Stalin supported the German destruction of independently minded or anti-Soviet Poles was matched at the start of 1945 by the deportations in Romania, the other nation with long-standing territorial disputes with Russia; these were also designed to make control from Moscow easier. It was never likely that the Soviets would even agree to semi-independent governments for their two most important regional enemies.

Roosevelt and Churchill were fully aware of the appalling nature of the Soviet regime and, if anything, had fallen over backwards to avoid condemnation of some of Stalin's wartime actions. It is easy to argue that the domestic policy of totalitarian regimes and the evil nature of men prepared, like Stalin, to send thousands of their fellow citizens to their deaths precludes effective international cooperation. Yet there is no evidence at the end of 1944 that the British or Americans saw this as a barrier to future cooperation with Moscow. The Russians were bound to be interested in cooperating to control Germany. To do this would require the maintenance of Allied cooperation and the formalization of a new international order dedicated to the preservation of peace. One key question was whether this could be achieved if the Soviets insisted on a tightly controlled sphere of influence containing Poland and Romania and possibly other parts of Eastern and Central Europe.

The US, Soviet, and British Approach to Yalta

Roosevelt had always been a supporter of the kind of world order and international cooperation advocated by President Woodrow Wilson. At the end of the First World War, Wilson had failed to win the approval of the American Congress for US participation in the League of Nations and this had fatally damaged the new organization. For Roosevelt, it was vitally important not to repeat the same mistake in 1945. A prime goal for the President when he went to Yalta was therefore to win his allies' support for the kind of world order and international organization that would be acceptable to Congress and public opinion in the US.

In addition to these requirements and general principles, Roosevelt, like the other leaders, had also to consider vital US defence and economic interests which were deemed essential for US influence and prosperity. The US had always had what was seen as a sphere of influence in Latin America, although the State Department was keen to emphasize the difference between the US position in the western hemisphere and the Soviet position that eventually emerged in Eastern and Central Europe. Charles Bohlen of the State Department, claimed the US right 'to have a guiding voice in a certain limited sphere of the foreign relations' of Latin America, but that the US did 'not attempt on the basis of that right to dictate their internal national life or to restrict their intercourse with foreign nations except in a limited sphere', which he defined as 'the politico-strategic sphere of their foreign relations'.[1]

While maintaining US influence and vital interests, Roosevelt had to establish a basis for cooperation with two other powers that did not share American views on the underlying principles of a new world order. In so doing, he had to convince opinion in the US that any post-war settlement was in line with American ideals and justify to international opinion the continuation of exclusive US influence in Latin America. At the same time, he had to take account of the military and political realities of the situation in early 1945. In the Pacific, where the Japanese were still fighting, the US was clearly the controlling Allied influence, but in Europe the Soviets had done most of the fighting against the German armies and were therefore likely to exercise dominance. The US had no vital economic or political interests in much of Central and Eastern Europe, and the issue was simply whether the post-war arrangements there would conform to American principles of democracy and non-discriminatory trading blocs. Here the only card the Americans had to play was the Soviet need for support in the containment of Germany, which might ensure that Russian desires to expand their power and influence would be limited. Roosevelt had to deal with this problem while maintaining the cooperation needed to establish an international organization that could preserve peace. Despite the dominant economic and military position which the US had obtained on a global basis (the Soviet Union had no significant navy and no real ability to project power beyond the areas adjacent to its borders), the President had a difficult task. The difficulties would have been there irrespective of the political or ideological stance of America's allies.

It is more difficult to assess Soviet ideas on the nature of the settlement and the new international order or the problems they had in realizing them. Historians, like many Western policy-makers who had to fight the Cold War, have sometimes attributed unlimited expansionist goals to Stalin and other Soviet leaders. For some, Stalin had a clearly worked-out plan to take control of Eastern and Central Europe, with the possible extension of such dominance to Western Europe if little resistance were met. Other historians have emphasized the important security requirements of a Soviet state whose short history had continually borne witness to frequent foreign invasions.[2] Recent research in Soviet archives, while still at an early stage, has helped cast doubts on such simple interpretations. From Stalin's statements at Tehran, it was clear that he favoured a world order based on spheres of influence, with each of the three great powers being responsible for peace and security within their respective spheres. It was also clear from the Soviet leader's unprincipled cooperation with the Nazis that his ambitions/security requirements in Eastern and Central Europe were considerable (see Chapter 2, B). Restoration of the borders of the old Tsarist empire and full access to the warm waters of the Mediterranean were also important Soviet goals. The latter could be secured by ending the restrictions on Soviet shipping passing through the Straits of the Dardanelles which had been imposed by the 1936 Montreux Convention. Such ambitions would likely have been present even under a capitalist Russian regime, and to some extent the peacemakers had to consider whether such aims were acceptable within the framework of the new world order. More generally, a desire to increase the world standing of the Soviet Union, given the importance of the Russian war effort to the Allied cause, was another unsurprising Soviet aim which had to be reckoned with.

With regard to Soviet desires for spheres of influence, the extent of the domination imposed on the lesser states was an important issue, given the ideological differences between the Soviets and the Western Allies. In the wake of the Tehran meeting and subsequent events in Poland, it should have been clear that Stalin was not going to accept a Polish regime which had the political freedom to oppose the Soviet Union.[3] It was likely that the Poles would only be independent in the cultural and linguistic sense. A free and democratic Poland, in the Western sense of the term, was not going to be achievable, given the long-standing hostility between the Russians and many sections of the Polish population. This was bound to cause problems in both London and Washington, despite the fact that neither the British nor the Americans had any vital interests in Poland. Many Poles had fought in the British armed forces and there would certainly be awkward questions in Parliament if the Poles were subjected to Russian domination. In the US, not only would the establishment of Soviet control over Poland be at odds with the principle of all peoples being allowed to choose the form of government under which they lived, but it would particularly affect the substantial Polish-American community.

The British went to Yalta as the weakest of the three allies but with an equal determination to protect what they saw as vital interests. As an imperial power with formal control over subject peoples, they had something in common with the Russians, despite the different nature of the controls pertaining in the Soviet Empire. The British Empire had certainly aroused hostility among sections of the American government during the war. Its existence clashed with American principles in the same way as the Soviet Empire and was more threatening to US economic interests. Yet the British shared the same ideology and political system as the US and were committed to the same kind of new economic order once British post-war recovery had been achieved.

British post-war planning was torn between acceptance of a set of principles and a system of cooperation based on spheres of influence. The former might threaten the future of the British Empire, but would ensure the support of the world's leading economic and military power. The latter would be more conducive to the maintenance of formal empire and the prevention of German domination of Europe, but might threaten the unusually close Anglo-American cooperation established during the war. British policymakers went some way towards the latter in October 1944 with the spheres-of-influence deal arranged by Churchill and Stalin in Moscow. In order to gain freedom of action in Greece, Churchill had proposed giving the Soviets the same licence in Romania on the basis of 90 per cent influence for both powers in their respective spheres. In addition, influence in Bulgaria would be divided 75–25 in the Soviets' favour with Hungary and Yugoslavia each shared on a 50 per cent basis. In essence, this kind of arrangement was designed to maintain Anglo-Soviet cooperation in Europe: Churchill did not see any need in late 1944 to construct, as the military desired, a British-led Western European bloc, with a view to containing the Russians. As it turned out, the Yalta Conference was to undermine Churchill's arrangements and claims that Yalta divided Europe are not compatible with the records of the conference.

The Conference Proceedings

The atmosphere at Yalta, the first crucial inter-allied meeting primarily on the post-war world, was one of hope that a new era of peace and cooperation could be fashioned from the rubble of war; the participants were also conscious of their responsibilities in the face of such an enormous task. There was no Anglo-American alliance, partly because Roosevelt had no desire to confront the Soviet Union. The President was also disinclined to support an unreformed British imperial system, which was a threat to US economic interests. Although it has been suggested that Roosevelt, whose health was failing, was duped by Stalin at Yalta, it appears that the President was fully aware of the problems of peacemaking. It would be difficult, if not impossible, to reconcile Stalin's requirements with the appearance of a new world order. US principles were never likely to override the Red Army's domination of Eastern and Central Europe, but this problem dictated Roosevelt's tactics in Crimea. It led the President to attempt to fool American opinion, at least until Congress had accepted the new United Nations organization, by pretending that the Yalta agreements embodied American principles.

One element of Roosevelt's plan at Yalta involved James Byrnes, a leading Southern democrat. Byrnes was excluded from certain sessions and sent home before the conclusion of the conference in order that he could quite genuinely portray a version of events that was incomplete but in line with American expectations. Meanwhile, Roosevelt was free to make agreements which suited great power interests and military realities rather than American principles. Byrnes was instrumental in leading the American public to believe that Yalta marked the end of old-fashioned power politics and the beginning of international cooperation based on American principles. On his return from Yalta, Roosevelt himself attempted to reinforce the message by telling Congress that: 'The Crimean Conference ought to spell the end of the system of unilateral action, the exclusive alliance, the spheres of influence, the balance of power and all the other expedients that have been tried for centuries, and have always failed.'[4]

By contrast, some historians have portrayed Yalta as an American betrayal of moral principles, which were sacrificed by an acceptance of a Soviet sphere of influence in Eastern Europe that effectively divided the continent. Both interpretations are wide of the mark. Yalta marked the first attempt to reconcile principles with power politics and to devise arrangements that protected vital Allied interests. One historian has noted that, 'Because FDR could not concede portions of Eastern Europe to Stalin or deny them to him he would in effect do both—the former through implicit understandings, the latter through the promulgation of principles that were interpreted differently by the Soviets and by the American people.'[5] In light of this, few specific agreements were finalized, much remained to be clarified, and little progress was made on the more difficult issues.

The most important, if not the most difficult issue, was the future of Germany. Germany had already been divided into zones of occupation by the three main Allies (with a fourth zone carved out for France late in the day), and would be governed by an Allied Control Council. But there was disagreement on whether Germany should remain a single state. A united Germany would again be in a position to wield economic and military power, which could not be contained by its neighbours in the West or the small states to the East. On the other hand, the dismemberment of Germany into a number of separate states, or the detachment of important economic areas, would run the risk of arousing the kind of German resentment that Hitler had exploited in the inter-war years. The feeling at Tehran had been in favour of dismemberment but nothing had been decided. At Yalta, the principle was accepted by all three Allies, but the method was deferred for further study and, despite the existence of separate occupation zones, Germany was to be treated as a single administrative unit by the Control Council. Similarly, the question of German reparations was referred to a commission in Moscow, directives to which would be given by the foreign ministers who would report back to the conference. What *was* decided (without consulting the inhabitants) was the position of Poland's eastern frontier. Poland would cede territory to the Soviet Union by following the Curzon Line with a digression from it in some regions of 5–8 kilometres in favour of Poland.[6] Poland would then gain German territory in the west as compensation for the territory lost in the east. Crucially, the western frontier on the Oder–Neisse river was not finally agreed upon. The Soviet proposal clearly referred to the Western Neisse rather than the Eastern Neisse, a difference that was to prove significant later.

With the future of Germany and its boundaries still undecided, the other European issue was the treatment of Germany's allies and the governance of other areas liberated from German control. In Greece, the British had been the arbiters between the competing political factions, while in Italy, a former German ally, the British and the Americans had decided to give control to the military commanders on the spot. This was exercised through an Allied Control Council, thereby excluding the Soviets, who had no military commanders in Italy, where a right-wing government under Badoglio was left in place. In Poland, Stalin had imposed a provisional government, the Lublin Committee, which excluded representatives of the Polish resistance (including local communists) and members of the London-based government-in-exile. In addition, the Soviets had supervised the installation of a communist-dominated Popular Front government in Bulgaria.

At Yalta, the discussions focused on the arrangements to be made for the provisional governments in the liberated areas and for the people eventually to choose, in line with the Atlantic Charter, the form of government under which they would live. The outcome was a formal agreement, the Declaration on Liberated Europe (see also Box 1.2), supplemented by an additional agreement on the formation of a Polish provisional government. The latter seemed necessary, given the particular interest in Poland as an ally for whom Britain had gone to war and over which Stalin had previously come to an arrangement with Hitler.

The Declaration on Liberated Europe made specific reference to the Atlantic Charter and required the signatories to 'form interim governmental authorities broadly representative of all democratic elements in

BOX 1.2

Key Development: Extracts from the Yalta Conference, 6th Plenary Meeting, 9 February 1945

THE PRESIDENT said he would like to add one word. He felt that the elections was [*sic*] the crux of the whole matter, and since it was true, as Marshal Stalin had said, not only at home but also abroad, he would like to have some assurance for the six million Poles in the US that these elections would be freely held, and he was sure if such assurance were present that elections would be held by the Poles there would be no doubt as to the sincerity of the agreement reached here . . .

THE PRESIDENT pointed out that the Declaration [on Liberated Europe] would of course apply to any areas or countries where needed as well as Poland.

THE PRIME MINISTER said he did not dissent from the President's proposed Declaration as long as it was clearly understood that the reference to the Atlantic Charter* did not apply to the British Empire. He said he had already made plain in the House of Commons that as far as the British Empire was concerned the principles already applied. He said he had given Mr Willkie [*sic*] [Wendell Wilkie, Republican presidential candidate 1940 and author of *One World*] a copy of his statement on the subject.

THE PRESIDENT inquired if that was what had killed Mr Willkie [*sic*].

* Declaration on war aims issued by Churchill and Roosevelt in 1941 affirming the right of peoples to choose their form of government.

Source: FRUS, 1945, *The Conferences of Malta and Yalta* (Dept. of State, Washington, DC, 1955, 848).

the population and pledged to the earliest possible establishment through free elections of governments responsive to the will of the people . . . and to facilitate where possible the holding of such elections'. The agreement on Poland was that the Lublin government should be 'reorganized on a broader democratic basis with the inclusion of democratic leaders from Poland itself and from Poles abroad'. Perhaps even more surprisingly Stalin informed Churchill and Roosevelt that elections would be held in Poland in a month provided there were no military disasters.[7] This agreement on applying the principles of the Atlantic Charter in Europe was accompanied by an agreement to break them in Asia. In return for Soviet entry into the war with Japan, it was agreed that, again without consulting the inhabitants, the Soviet Union would receive Southern Sakahlin and the Kurile Islands from the Japanese. Here was the mix of power politics and high-minded rhetoric which lay at the heart of Yalta and subsequent attempts to reconcile two conflicting approaches to the new world order.

Yalta did see some progress towards Roosevelt's beloved United Nations Organization. Stalin's acceptance of American views on voting procedures produced agreement on the calling of a conference at San Francisco. It would prepare a charter for a general international organization for the maintenance of peace and security based on a Security Council of five permanent members (Britain, China, France, the Soviet Union, and the US). This concession by Stalin matched a number of others he made, including: the acceptance of the Western request for French membership of the German Control Council, the commitment (particularly in Poland) to representative government and free elections in Europe, and the postponement of the reparations issue along with the issue of revising the Montreux Convention. No wonder that the British believed that Stalin had never been so obliging. In fact, the issues discussed at Yalta were related much more to the vital interests of the Soviet Union than they were to the interests of Britain or the US. In return for his concessions, although not part of an explicit bargain, Stalin had received territory on the Polish border, in Bukovina (from Romania) and in East Asia. Part of this territory agreed at Yalta was in return for committing Soviet forces to the war against Japan and the rest was territory the British had long felt was rightly part of the Soviet Union. Subsequent dissatisfaction with Yalta came because of the large number of unresolved issues and, as was to be revealed, the fact that Stalin failed to abide by the Yalta agreements whenever their rhetoric clashed with the interests of the Soviet state, whether defined in terms of security or imperial ambitions.

B. From Yalta to Potsdam

From the point of view of the British and the Soviets, the Yalta agreements were at odds with the agreements reached in October 1944 at Moscow regarding the exercise of British and Soviet influence in parts of Eastern and South-Eastern Europe. When, on 27 February 1945, the Soviets intervened in Romania to install a puppet regime under cover of a 'democratic front' government, the British could either regard this as a breach of Yalta or the implementation of the percentages agreement. It was an act that bypassed the Allied Control Council and confirmed that, as in Italy, the occupying power was going to exercise effective control. If Britain were to dispute this, it would mean that the Soviets might challenge the exercise of British control in Greece. Romania did not thus become an issue in the early spring, unlike Poland, which had not been a subject of the Anglo-Soviet deal.

In the US at the beginning of March, Roosevelt was proclaiming that Yalta had reversed the trend to a spheres-of-influence arrangement and provided hope for a free, independent, and prosperous Poland. It began to look as if Poland might provide an initial test case, of whether the Soviets would abide by the rhetoric of the Yalta declarations or impose controls on parts of Central and Eastern Europe in line with an exclusive spheres-of-influence arrangement.

Stalin may have believed that a gesture to Western opinion would be sufficient to maintain the great power cooperation to which all three allies attached importance. Roosevelt may have believed that he could convince the American people that accepting the realities of military power and political influence was all part of a new, idealistic world order. That was never tested, owing to the President's death in April 1945, and it is not possible to determine whether or not Roosevelt was set on a collision course with Stalin over the Soviet leader's initial refusal to abide by the Yalta agreements on Poland. Roosevelt's successor, the former Vice-President Harry Truman (see Box 1.4), had little or no knowledge of foreign affairs. He also lacked Roosevelt's chameleon-like character, which could represent different things to different people, and his political sleight of hand, which enabled him to keep abreast of public opinion and to manipulate supporters and opponents alike.

In stark contrast to Roosevelt, Truman's inexperience led him to give more weight to advisers within the State Department for whom his predecessor had little time. Thus, the influence of those more inclined to confront the Soviet Union as an ideological opponent began to grow. Truman was more inclined to join the British in challenging the Soviets over Yalta. On 23 April, he told the Soviet foreign minister in a famous confrontation that the Russians should stick to their agreements and, with the German surrender in May, Lend-Lease aid to Moscow (which had supplied the Soviets with arms and materials during the war) was terminated. Yet Truman too was torn between an inclination to confront the Soviets and a desire to maintain cooperation and good relations. At the end of May, the new president sent a close confidant of Roosevelt's, Harry Hopkins, to Moscow in an attempt to get agreement with Stalin over Poland. In defiance of what was said at Yalta, Stalin had neither held elections nor broadened the provisional government, but

BOX 1.3

Biography: Winston Churchill (1874–1965)

Son of Sir Randolph Churchill, a one-time Conservative Cabinet minister, and an American mother, Winston was committed to a world characterized by cooperation between English-speaking peoples. He saw military service in the Sudan and India, and was a journalist in the Boer War, before being elected to Parliament as a Conservative in 1900. Opposed to the party leadership, he joined the Liberals in 1904 and served as President of the Board of Trade, Home Secretary, First Lord of the Admiralty, and Minister for Munitions before the end of the First World War. When the war ended, he became Colonial Secretary but lost his seat in 1922. In 1924, he effectively rejoined the Conservatives and returned to Parliament serving as Chancellor of the Exchequer, alienating many workers with his stance over the 1926 General Strike. In 1931, he resigned from the Shadow Cabinet over his opposition to Indian self-government and, in the later 1930s, became chief critic of the government's appeasement of Nazi Germany. In 1939, he was again appointed to the Admiralty, until a Conservative revolt led to him becoming Prime Minister of a coalition government in 1940. An unconventional but brilliant wartime leader, Churchill aroused fear and respect in large measure. Despite some unrealistic ideas, he galvanized the war effort in all its aspects and, unlike some members of his party, realized the importance of cooperation with the Soviets and the necessity of involving the Americans in the war if Hitler was to be defeated. Defeated in the election of 1945, he returned victorious in 1951 and served as prime minister again until 1955.

in response to the Hopkins mission (26 May–6 June) on 21 June the Soviet leader gave four non-Lublin Poles ministerial office. The letter of Yalta was now adhered to in terms of the composition of the Polish government and, although the actual impact was negligible, for the Americans the problems of Poland no longer assumed centre stage. The Western democracies could hardly insist on elections in Eastern Europe when they had been unable to hold any in Western Europe.

However, it was not only in Europe that there was a clash between US principles and the Yalta agreements on the one hand, and Soviet desires to expand influence and control through spheres-of-influence arrangements on the other. The area of contention that emerged after the Hopkins mission was the Mediterranean, where the British and Soviet empires had long competed for influence. Having given up exclusive control (but not effective domination) in Poland, the Soviets began to press for greater involvement in what had previously been an area of exclusive British influence. In June 1945, the Soviets expressed a desire to share in the international administration of Tangier, an important port in North-West Africa, and informed the Turks of their desire to have bases in the Straits of the Dardanelles. In the run-up to the Potsdam Conference, the focus was not, as at Yalta, largely on Germany and those European areas of greatest concern to the Soviets, but on other regions where British vital interests, as well as American principles, were at stake.

The Potsdam Proceedings

At Potsdam, where Churchill was replaced towards the end of the conference by the newly elected Labour Prime Minister, Clement Attlee, there was more discussion of specific questions such as the resumption of diplomatic relations with the provisional governments of Germany's allies. Consequently, more difficulties emerged. Sometimes the British and Americans agreed and sometimes the Americans and the Soviets agreed, but the British and the Soviets almost always disagreed. The diplomatic conflict was initially an Anglo-Soviet one.[8] Significantly, Stalin pointed out that while Britain and the US were refusing to resume diplomatic relations with the non-elected governments of the former German satellites in the East, they had re-established relations with the unelected government in Italy. He was also unhappy about the lack of action against the extreme right-wing regime of General Franco in Spain.

The Western allies were naturally disturbed by the unilateral Soviet actions in East-Central Europe. The wartime brutality, economic devastation, and mass murder perpetuated by the Germans were followed by the reprisals of a Soviet regime whose recent history was steeped in atrocities and repression. The Russians were beginning the post-war economic subjugation of the Eastern European economies to Soviet recovery and removing industrial plant, notably oil equipment, from Romania. More significant was the

BOX 1.4

Biography: Harry S. Truman (1884–1972)

The son of a Missouri farmer, Truman served in France during the First World War before starting a clothing business in Kansas City. After his business failed, Truman entered politics in 1922 under the auspices of Kansas Party boss Thomas J. Prendergast and was chosen by him to stand for the Senate in 1934. On election, Truman became a committed New Dealer and achieved fame as head of a Committee to investigate waste in military expenditure in 1940. Roosevelt manipulated his vice-presidential nomination as a compromise candidate between Henry Wallace, a northern liberal and James Byrnes, a southern conservative. On succeeding to the presidency, Truman had little or no knowledge of foreign affairs and his greater reliance on the State Department officials shunned by Roosevelt has led some to conclude that Truman followed a more hard-line policy towards the Soviets. Certainly, this was the case by 1946, and the greater emphasis on confrontation produced the Truman Doctrine of March 1947. As a down-to-earth president with a tendency to 'shoot from the hip', Truman's Cold War policies in Europe with the Marshall Plan and the Berlin airlift are seen as great successes, in contrast to his China policies, which failed to prevent the loss of China to communism. Truman's unexpected electoral victory in 1948 was overshadowed by the triumph of Mao Zedong's forces, and his domestic Fair Deal programme of social reform was largely blocked by Congress. His determination to prevent a communist triumph in Korea led to the involvement of US forces in a drawn-out bloody conflict with the Chinese, which made him increasingly unpopular at home. But he remained committed to confronting the Soviets in both Europe and Asia.

unilateral Soviet action in handing over to the Polish government responsibility for the administration of the newly acquired territory in the West up to the boundaries of the Western Neisse river.

Although this was a contentious issue at Potsdam and stored up trouble for the future, Allied disagreements in the second half of 1945 centred neither on Germany nor Poland. In order to avoid an open breach, differences on Germany were papered over with a firm agreement on reparations and on the principles of deNazification, decentralization, and disarmament in governing Germany under Allied control. Decisions on the frontier between Germany and Poland were postponed until the final peace settlement, but it was accepted by all three powers that the territory up to the Western Neisse should in the meantime be administered as part of Poland. This added to the problems of transferring populations, and with these lands effectively removed from Germany it would not be possible, as initially assumed, to use their agricultural production to feed Germans. The administration of Germany as a single economic unit—a principle continued at Potsdam—would have to be done with a smaller food supply for the inhabitants of Germany's cities. In the event, this was to force the British to pay for the importation of wheat to feed the starving inhabitants of their occupation zone, which contained Germany's prime industrial region, the Ruhr.

No agreements could be reached on a number of other issues in addition to the acceptance of provisional governments in Romania and Bulgaria. The Soviets claimed a trusteeship, or involvement in a joint trusteeship, over Tripolitania, the western part of the former Italian colony of Libya; this aroused British fears about Soviet ambitions in the Mediterranean, which was seen as a vital part of Britain's imperial communications. Decisions on trusteeship and the fate of the Italian colonies (in Libya and the Horn of Africa) were to be taken by a Council of Foreign Ministers (CFM), which was to be established to draw up peace treaties with Germany and its allies. The future of Tangier was to be considered by representatives of the three governments at a special conference. The third Mediterranean issue also failed to produce full agreement. It was accepted that the Montreux Convention should be revised, but Soviet claims for bases in the Straits, put forward on the grounds that the British had a base in Egypt in order to protect the Suez Canal, another important international waterway, were rejected. The British maintained that, because of the supreme importance of the Middle East and the Eastern Mediterranean to their empire, they could not accept an increase in Soviet influence in the region or allow their responsibilities for its defence to be replaced by arrangements of an international character.

The Potsdam Conference was longer and more troublesome than Yalta. Although all the participants remained keen to reach agreement, there were more disputes, more problems with detail, and more areas of the world were discussed. While there was still no united Anglo-American front, it was clear that, for the Soviets and the British, concerns about their post-war positions were going to make confrontation difficult to avoid. Soviet economic recovery was not going to be helped directly by America, the only solvent capitalist power. It could only be secured indirectly through the exploitation of the Soviet zone in Germany and the lands to the east of it. This in turn was likely to produce difficulties and require sacrifices by the Western allies if Germany were to be treated as a single economic unit.

The problems of reconciling American principles embodied in the rhetoric of Yalta with Soviet spheres of influence and territorial adjustments, epitomized in the secret Yalta deal on the Far East, remained. They were complicated by the British determination to preserve what they regarded as an exclusive sphere of influence in the Eastern Mediterranean and the Middle East. British officials debated whether it would be desirable to accept a Soviet sphere in areas of Eastern Europe in return for Soviet recognition of a British sphere in the Mediterranean and Middle East. These issues pertaining to the great powers' vital interests, prestige, and status were to become more acute at the first CFM held in London in September 1945 when US vital interests were first seriously challenged. By then, the impact of the first atomic explosion, which took place during the Potsdam Conference, was a new factor in Allied relations.

C. Atomic Diplomacy and Council of Foreign Ministers Meetings, 1945

The first atomic test took place in the deserts of New Mexico on 16 July 1945. It was followed by the dropping of an atomic bomb on the Japanese city of Hiroshima on 6 August, with a second bomb dropped three days later on Nagasaki. Accusations have been levelled against the Truman administration that the bombs were dropped for political rather than military reasons. The surrender of Japan, it is alleged, would have taken place anyway because of the terrible destructive power of the conventional carpet bombing being undertaken by the US Air Force. The Japanese economy was in tatters and an invasion of Japan was not planned to take place until November—so that the dropping of the atom bombs did not save many American lives. Therefore, it is argued, Truman dropped the bombs in order to impress the Soviet Union with the destructive power of the US. Yet the fear of large-scale losses if the US had to invade Japan was clearly present in the minds of US policy-makers. On the other hand,[9] it is certainly likely that Truman's secretary of state, James Byrnes, believed at Potsdam and at the London CFM that the bomb would enable the US to pressure its allies into greater compliance with American post-war aims. It has also been suggested that the timing of the atomic attack on Japan was influenced by the Yalta agreement on the Far East, according to which the Soviets had to enter the war against Japan by 8 August. If Japan surrendered before the Soviets entered the war, then there would be no grounds for implementing Roosevelt's old-fashioned territorial deal by which the Soviets acquired Southern Sakahlin and the Kurile Islands. Even if the Soviets did enter the war, an early Japanese surrender would reduce the impact the Red Army could make in the Far East and thereby reduce future Soviet influence.

There were both political and military arguments for the use of the bomb, but if the Americans were influenced by a desire to strengthen their diplomatic hand it proved, at best, ineffective. With Stalin an overtly suspicious, paranoid character, and all Soviet leaders inevitably insecure in the wake of the German assault, a US monopoly of the bomb was only likely to create more distrust. This distrust could feed on ideological differences, geopolitical rivalries, and the increasing problem, more in evidence at Potsdam than at Yalta, of universal acceptance of what each of the Allies regarded as their vital interests. These interests were reflected in general approaches to the post-war settlement and in the particular aspects of it which, along with Germany's future, they regarded as most important to their world roles.

The first indication of the US approach to an area it regarded as vital to American interests came when Japan offered to surrender on 11 August. In Germany as in other parts of Europe, Allied Control Councils had been set up to provide at least for the nominal involvement of the Big Three (and in Germany's case, France). In Japan, the US, which had fought the Pacific War without British participation in an Allied Command, initially refused to consider an Allied occupation agreement for Japan. This was a key area for the Americans because of Japan's industrial power, its strategic position in relation to access to the Pacific, and its large, highly educated population. Determined to secure a dominant post-war position there, they were reluctant to consider even the token involvement of the British or the Russians. A willingness to reject cooperation in order to protect what were seen as vital interests was shared by all members of the alliance. The more it was done, the more mistrust was created, which in turn reinforced the tendency to seek security on a unilateral basis rather than through compromise and cooperation.

The London and Moscow CFMs

From Potsdam onwards, while it is not possible to make any confident judgements on Soviet strategy, the British were no longer prepared to compromise for fear of jeopardizing their vital interests. This British concern was heightened by the growing consciousness of their weakness in economic and political terms compared to their Allies. To make concessions and compromises would threaten their position as one of the three great powers, particularly if it increased the influence and importance of the Soviet Union. The Americans had not yet moved away from attempting to resolve issues through tripartite arrangements, but the British now believed their interests would be best protected by gaining the support of the US in a common front against the Soviets. This was especially important with regard to the Mediterranean.

These problems became more evident at the first meeting of the CFM, which broke up in disagreement and revealed the first significant failure of post-war Allied cooperation. The CFM met under the terms and conditions laid down at Potsdam. It was to consist of the representatives of Britain, China, France, the Soviet Union, and the US and was charged with drawing up the peace treaties with Germany's allies (Italy, Romania, Bulgaria, Hungary, and Finland) and preparing a peace settlement for a future German government. In discussing a particular peace treaty, the Council would be composed of members of those states which had signed the surrender agreement with the enemy state in question. The exception was Italy, where France was to be regarded as a signatory of the surrender terms. In order to exclude China from European affairs, other members would only be invited to take part when matters that directly concerned them were under discussion. But, at the first meeting, the British Foreign Secretary, Ernest Bevin, requested a change to enable all powers to be present and to participate in the discussions, but with only the signatories to the surrender terms having voting rights.

This having been agreed, there followed a wrangle over the agenda, with the Americans not wanting to discuss Japan and the British not wanting to discuss Greece. If Romania was going to be on the agenda, the Soviet Foreign Minister, Vyacheslav Molotov, could see no reason why the situation in Japan and Greece should not be addressed, although under the terms of the Potsdam agreement they were outside the Council's remit. The French, who now entered high-level Great Power discussions for the first time since 1940, also wanted to discuss Germany, intending to press for territorial changes on Germany's western border. But the Big Three, who had discussed Germany quite fully at Potsdam, wished to leave discussions on the German peace treaty until other less complex treaties were signed. Unhappy at this situation, the French were to veto all measures by the Allied Control Council to treat Germany as a single unit and this called into question an important element of the Potsdam agreements. After this inauspicious start, Italy was the first state to be dealt with and the first item on the agenda was the future of the Italian colonies. Libya was seen as vital by the British, who occupied most of the colony. They wanted not only the trusteeship of Cyrenaica (Eastern Libya) but to establish a new military base there and prevent the Soviet Union from being involved in the trusteeship arrangements for Tripolitania (Western Libya). After lengthy discussions, during which no progress was made, the issue was passed to the foreign ministers' deputies and eventually to the United Nations. It was finally resolved with the independence of Libya in 1952. The conference then turned to Finland and Romania, which the Soviets saw as vital interests. Again, no progress was made, with the Americans refusing to recognize the Romanian government as being broadly representative of all democratic elements.

If spheres of influence were ruled out and the Yalta agreements adhered to, it was perfectly understandable for the Americans, British, and French to complain about Soviet actions in Romania. However, if that was the case, then there was no sound argument for excluding the Soviets from Japan or from a trusteeship of an Italian colony. Soviet diplomacy seemed to have little room for manoeuvre. In this situation, Molotov claimed that progress had been too slow and raised a procedural issue on which the Council broke down: the Soviets would no longer attend the Council unless the Potsdam agreements on Council procedure, which would exclude the French from discussing most peace treaties, were reverted to. From the Soviet point of view, they had been outmanoeuvred, having agreed to change the Potsdam agreement in one case while the British and Americans were determined to stick by it in others.

The breakdown of the London Council revealed the determination of all the Allies to pursue their own power-political interests even if they involved confrontation. The commitment to cooperation, whether out of principle or self-interest, was weakening and priority was being given to protecting vital interests. Trust was being eroded and suspicions were developing. Crucially, the idea that the Allies could accept an international framework which met all their requirements and ambitions as great powers was proving unrealistic. The diplomatic battleground which was to become a Cold War was thus being laid out in power-political terms.

However, the attempts at cooperation did not end at the London Council and some Western concessions were to be forthcoming, largely at the instigation of James Byrnes. American opinion had been upset by the London failure and Byrnes may have decided that the attempts to pressure the Soviets under the shadow of the atomic bomb had not worked and that it would still be possible to make progress with a more conciliatory stance. He instigated another Council in Moscow, confined to the Big Three, and offered the prospects of international cooperation over the use of atomic energy. Bevin was not keen on such a meeting, preferring to build an Anglo-American front to convince the Soviets to modify their stance. He had now rejected any deal with the Soviets on spheres of influence, because it would be damaging to Britain's international position: exclusion from large areas of East-Central Europe was deemed by the Foreign Office to be incompatible with great power status, even if Britain's vital interests in the Middle East and Mediterranean were secured. The British foreign secretary argued that the Soviets had no need for a substantial European sphere of influence to offset the

British position in the Mediterranean and Middle East because the Soviets had gained other territory as a result of the war. Byrnes, however, was keen to compromise with the Soviets, whatever the British view.

The Moscow Council in effect witnessed the last serious attempt at compromise between the Big Three, but one which did not fundamentally alter power-political realities. It thus proved possible, as in Poland, to achieve an agreement on the broadening of the provisional governments. In Romania, a joint commission was to arrange for the inclusion of additional ministers, which was duly done in February 1946. Bulgaria was trickier because elections had been held in the autumn of 1945 that were not regarded in the West as entirely free. The agreement therefore was to advise the Bulgarian government to include some members of the opposition. In return, the US accepted an Allied Control Council for Japan. When the conference ended, a proposal was also accepted for a UN Commission on the international control of atomic energy and on the resumption of peace negotiations in the full CFM. The desire for compromise had prevented the collapse of cooperation but by the end of 1945 the atmosphere was very different from Yalta.

The London and Moscow CFMs clearly revealed that the issues which divided the Big Three, and which would lie at the heart of the Cold War, were of a global nature. Each power had vital interests to preserve: the US in Latin America and the Far East, the Soviets in Eastern Europe, and the British in the Mediterranean and Middle East. The principles and practices which were to be applied to the post-war world affected those interests which were linked to perceptions of global power and influence. The alliance experienced tensions because it proved difficult to reconcile vital interests within an agreed international framework. Principles and power politics were clashing and undermining cooperation; this was to assume much greater significance than previous great power rivalries because of the importance of ideology at the end of the Second World War.

At the end of 1945, the Soviets clearly saw the British as more antagonistic than the Americans, despite the American position on the Romanian and Bulgarian governments. Cooperation with the Americans could be combined with attempting to drive a wedge between the two capitalist powers, a process which Marxist ideology deemed in any case to be inevitable. Molotov complained bitterly about British actions in Greece and reasserted Soviet claims for bases in the Straits and for the return of two Turkish provinces (Kars and Ardahan), which had once been part of the Russian Empire. From the Soviet point of view, it was vital for them to move forward with post-war economic recovery, and while the Americans agreed to assist the British, they were not prepared to treat the Soviets, or indeed the French, in the same way. This was one factor which was to encourage assertive, unilateral action rather than tripartite cooperation. There was also the Soviet concern that, backed by the atomic bomb, the Americans were attempting to dictate the post-war settlement. The Soviets may have put forward claims for involvement in Tripolitania and Turkey in order to convince their Allies that a spheres-of- influence deal would be desirable. They may have been seeking recognition of their newly acquired importance as a great power, or they may have been determined to extend their influence outside Eastern and Central Europe in an attempt to undermine British vital interests and hasten conflict within the capitalist world. Whatever Soviet aims may have been, and despite the American concessions in Moscow, their realization through cooperation was going to be difficult.

From the American perspective, the Soviets were failing to carry out the Yalta agreements that had been sold as the embodiment of a new world order in which old-fashioned power politics were to be removed. Already, by the autumn of 1945 serious questions were being raised in the US following the Soviet occupation of Southern Sakhalin and the Kuriles in line with the Yalta agreements. Senators and members of Congress were questioning the Democrats' role in appeasing the Soviets through the abandonment of American principles. James Byrnes was called to account before a Senate investigatory committee. Both Republicans and Democrats were concerned about policies they regarded as too soft on communism. At the end of November, ambassador Patrick Hurley, an eccentric Republican right-winger, resigned over policy to China, calling the diplomats on his staff 'communist supporters'. Opinion polls were indicating that more and more Americans were less sympathetic to cooperation with the Soviets and supportive of a more assertive policy. The Soviets had reneged on some of the Yalta agreements and criticism of their ruthless and self-serving actions in Eastern Europe was mounting. Although Washington had no vital interests there, an American mission under Mark

Ethridge was sent to determine the facts in Romania and Bulgaria. The report was critical of Soviet actions and argued that representative government was necessary if peace was to be secured. Spheres of influence would invite further conflict and encourage Soviet ambitions.

Truman had to confront his growing domestic difficulties from a weak position because of his lack of experience in foreign affairs. In addition, he was in the unfortunate position of being a former protégé of his Secretary of State. He had tried the tough approach with the ending of Lend-Lease and harsh criticism of Soviet bad faith and he had tried the conciliatory approach through the Hopkins mission. His decisions on which line to take after Potsdam were not helped by Byrnes's tendency to keep him in the dark about diplomatic moves, in particular about the concessions made at Moscow. With the criticism of the US role at Moscow mounting, Truman declared in early 1946 that he was 'tired of babying the Soviets'.

BOX 1.5

Key Developments: The New Global Institutions of 1945

The United Nations (UN) Charter was issued on 26 June 1945, by 50 states, at the end of the San Francisco conference and it came into effect on 24 October 1945. In 1952, a permanent headquarters was opened for the UN in New York. The five great powers (the US, USSR, China, Britain, and France) became permanent members of the new **Security Council**, which could be convened quickly to discuss international crises and was supported in its work by a non-voting Secretary General. The Council had eleven members in all (fifteen from 1965), with non-permanent members being elected every two years. But the attempt to give a special role for the 'Big Five' included them obtaining the right to veto Security Council resolutions, which severely harmed the UN's ability to tackle problems. It was originally hoped the veto power would be used sparingly, but Moscow wielded it regularly down to the mid-1960s, when the growing number of newly independent states in the UN meant it could find more allies on issues—so that, in the later decades of the Cold War it tended to be Western powers who used the veto.

More broadly, the UN's recognition of the sovereignty of its members made it difficult to enforce joint decisions or principles like human rights. The whole membership meets between September and December each year in the **General Assembly** and it has some important powers, including electing the non-permanent members of the Security Council, the fifteen judges who sit on the International Court (and will rule on disputes, but only if asked to do so), and members of other UN subsidiary bodies. The last are a vast range, from the International Children's Emergency Fund (UNICEF, founded in 1946) and World Health Organization (founded in 1948), to the International Labour Organization (originally founded under the League) and International Postal Union (first founded in 1874). The General Assembly receives reports from other bodies, sets up sub-committees to consider issues (including the codification of diplomatic law), and holds debates, but the last often include long, dull, even irrelevant speeches and any recommendations are only binding on those that accept them, just as judgements of the International Court cannot be enforced except on a voluntary basis.

There were also three important bodies formed in 1945, after a conference at Bretton Woods, designed to ensure a stable, thriving environment for international trade. One major need was to rebuild war-shattered economies, hence the creation, in Washington in 1946, of the International Bank of Reconstruction and Development (IBRD), to make loans to governments, as well as to provide information and financial services. Over time, as Europe recovered, it became less focused on post-war recovery and more on ensuring economic improvements in the less-developed world. In 1960, another body, the International Development Association, was created to aid the world's poorest states. Together, the Association and the IBRD became the most important institutions of the **World Bank**. The Bank is funded by the member states and by raising capital on the financial markets; voting powers are weighted, roughly in line with the size of a member's economy. The second major institution was the **International Monetary Fund** (IMF), also based in Washington, with the same membership as the IBRD and a similar system of weighted votes, but with the aim of ensuring monetary stability, especially by monitoring economic trends, providing support for those in balance of payments difficulties, and advising members on policies to pursue (though it has been accused of slanting these in favour of Western states). The third major institution was the **General Agreement on Tariffs and Trade** (GATT), signed in October 1947, with the aim of reducing barriers to commerce, setting trade rules, and settling disputes. It negotiated a series of 'rounds' of barrier reduction, like the Kennedy Round of 1962–7, which was estimated to boost international trade by $40 billion. After the Cold War, former Eastern bloc countries began to join the major international economic institutions and, in 1995, GATT was transformed into the **World Trade Organization** (WTO), joined by China in 2001 and Russia in 2012.

The President appeared ready to embark on a more confrontational approach as public opinion became less willing to trust the Soviets. It was in early 1946 that a crisis in Iran was to provide a basis for a confrontation that, for the first time, was firmly to unite the British and the Americans in open opposition to Soviet ambitions.

D. Growing Confrontation: The Near East and Mediterranean

The Iranian Crisis

As President Truman tired of babying the Soviets, a crisis was developing in Iran, which had been jointly occupied by the USSR and Britain since 1942 and had served as a supply route from the West to Russia. From the Western perspective, this crisis confirmed the perception of the Soviet Union as an ambitious imperialist power. The Iranians were increasingly unhappy about the Soviet occupation of northern Iran, which they feared would encourage separatism in the border province of Azerbaijan and lead to pressure for oil concessions to Moscow. Like the British, who occupied the southern part of the country, the Soviets were required, under the terms of the 1942 treaty, to end their occupation six months after the termination of hostilities. Based on the Japanese surrender, this would be on 2 March 1946. Before then, however, the Iranians complained to the UN about Soviet interference in their internal affairs.

The British were keen to provide support and encouragement to the Iranians. They hoped to demonstrate to the Americans the need to resist a Soviet threat to an independent state, which also presented a threat to Britain's own imperial position in the Middle East and the Mediterranean. Soviet imperialism in Iran was justified in Stalin's eyes because of the alleged danger of Iranian sabotage of the Baku oilfields, and by the fact that the British were refusing to withdraw troops from Greece and were occupying Egypt with more troops than permitted by the Anglo-Egyptian treaty. The fact that the British refused to discuss the Greek situation at the Moscow Conference in December 1945 may have reinforced the Soviet desire to retain the influence stemming from a military presence in Iran.

When the Soviets broke the 1942 agreement in March 1946, by not withdrawing their troops from Iran, both the British and the Americans urged the Iranians to renew their complaint to the UN Security Council. The Soviet Union was thus placed in an unfavourable international light. Moreover, it had succeeded in uniting the British and the Americans against Soviet imperialism in a region where, unlike in Eastern and Central Europe, Soviet influence was bound to threaten Britain's imperial position. Stalin's ambitions had led the Americans, who had been genuinely suspicious of British imperialism, to support a common stance against the Soviet Union in a clash of rival imperialisms. This diplomatic blunder became more evident when the Soviets backed down in the face of British and American opposition and agreed to withdraw from Iran on 20 March. The reasons for this Soviet retreat remain unclear. The prospect of confrontation with a more powerful adversary possessing atomic weapons may have been a factor, as may have Stalin's fear of destroying future prospects of cooperation. Alternatively, Stalin may have assumed that his ambitions in Iran, including the securing of oil concessions, could be achieved at less cost through the creation of a separate state in Azerbaijan, which the Russians were actively encouraging. Either way it was clear that the Soviets were averse to a serious international confrontation with the British and the Americans.

The Turkish Crisis, 1946

In early 1946, Soviet ambitions presented another challenge to the Western powers. As in Iran, the issue centred not on those European areas, which the Soviets had inevitably come to dominate as part of the effort to defeat Germany, but on areas outside Europe. Nothing had been heard from the Soviets since the summer of 1945 about their claims for bases in the Straits and the return of the former Russian provinces of Kars and Ardahan. Western concerns about Turkey therefore focused on the presence of Soviet troops in Bulgaria and the Trans-Caucasus, but as 1946 began there were fears in the US of a possible Soviet attempt to use military force to seize the Straits. The Soviet press was unremittingly hostile to Turkey and as a gesture of support, in February 1946, the US sent the battleship *Missouri* to return the body of the Turkish ambassador.

The situation remained tense throughout the spring as conflicting reports of Soviet troop movements were received in Washington. It is clear that Stalin, by a combination of military and non-military means, was seeking to exert pressure on the Turks before in August 1946 calling for a revision of Montreux and joint Soviet–Turkish defence of the Straits. This prompted a determined stand by the Truman administration, which, while accepting the need for the revision of Montreux, warned against Soviet aggression against Turkey.

In Cold War terms, Washington's determination to assist Turkey (probably communicated to the Russians by the British spy Donald Maclean) was a reflection and reinforcement of a developing strategy, usually referred to as containment, which involved greater determination to confront the Soviets. Politically, it was important to avoid further expansion of Soviet influence. Militarily, it was believed that the Soviets could be stopped without risking a major conflict, because Stalin was not in a position to wage a war in 1946. It was therefore necessary to make clear the importance attached by the American government to defending Turkey from Soviet encroachment. If the Soviets were convinced that their attempts to make gains in the Near East would be resisted, then it was likely, as proved to be the case with both Turkey and Iran, that the status quo would be maintained and the Soviets would back down. Therefore, the issue was the prevention of Soviet expansion into areas not already dominated by the Russians as a result of the war. Unfortunately, this was not a line that could easily be sold to the Western public, who were more concerned about predominantly European issues and who therefore had to be convinced that the Soviet Union expanded after, not during, the war.

E. Containment, Confrontation, and the Truman Doctrine, 1946–7

During the Iranian crisis in the first two months of 1946, other developments revealed the increasingly confrontational approach adopted by the three former allies. In January and February, Soviet attacks on British policy became more hostile. The idea that cooperation was impossible with capitalist powers was reinforced in Stalin's address to the Supreme Soviet on 9 February, which claimed that economic competition under capitalism made war inevitable. The response of the British Foreign Office was to create the Russia Committee to examine how best to reply to what was seen as a Soviet propaganda offensive. Britain and the Soviet Union, like the Truman administration, were beginning to put confrontation, propaganda, and the protection of vital interests before cooperation and compromise.

Developments in Washington centred on the famous Long Telegram sent from Moscow by George Kennan two weeks after Stalin's speech. By then, opinion polls showed that the numbers of Americans who believed in the possibility of cooperation with the Soviet Union had fallen, from the 54 per cent of September 1945 to 34 per cent. Kennan had been a long-time critic of Roosevelt's policy of cooperation with the Soviet Union because he believed the nature of the Soviet system demanded a hostile approach to the outside world. In other words, Soviet foreign policy would essentially be dictated, not by external developments, but by ideological imperatives geared to promoting what Moscow believed would be the inevitable collapse of capitalism.

As early as February 1945, Kennan had urged the division of Europe into spheres of influence based on a line beyond which the expansion of Soviet power would not be permitted. Now, one year later, Kennan urged firm action on the part of the Western powers to confront and contain a Soviet state deemed ideologically averse to cooperation with the capitalist West. Kennan believed containment was necessary because cooperation with a state ideologically committed to the destruction of capitalist democracy was impossible. Thus, at the beginning of March 1946, US domestic opinion, Soviet defiance of its treaty agreements in Iran, and an extensive analysis of Soviet attitudes to the West all pointed America towards a policy of greater confrontation. In the British embassy in Moscow, Frank Roberts, who had always favoured a spheres-of-influence deal in 1945, now became concerned about the implications of any such arrangements. With the Soviets more and more interested in areas outside Europe, especially the Mediterranean and Middle East, any concessions there, even to legitimate Soviet aims, would be interpreted as a severe setback to Britain throughout the Arab world. Roberts saw prestige and security considerations intermingling in the Middle East and Soviet security could not be achieved without damaging British or American interests.[10] In early 1946, both Kennan and Roberts saw advantages in containment through confrontation rather than a spheres-of-influence deal involving concessions to the Soviets. For the Truman administration, while attempts at cooperation were not to be abandoned in 1946, from now on, cooperation was only desirable on American terms. US policy to the Soviets was now in line with that advocated by the British in 1945 and again it was Middle Eastern rather than European issues which had had the most important influence on policy.

Kennan's idea on the implementation of containment was based on securing the world's important industrial areas. The advance of Soviet communism at the expense of capitalism could be prevented if this could be achieved. Kennan, like most policy-makers in the US, was not afraid of the Soviet Union deliberately starting a global war. What most concerned the Americans and the British was the spread of Soviet influence and control on the basis of communist political successes. Churchill, who reinforced the moves to confrontation/containment in early March 1946 with his Iron Curtain speech in Fulton Missouri, emphasized this point. While criticizing the nature and extent of Soviet actions in Eastern and Central Europe, the former British prime minister, in Truman's presence, referred to the Soviet desire to achieve the fruits of war while avoiding military conflict.

The condemnation of Soviet actions in Central and Eastern Europe was linked to the growing realization of the ruthless nature of the persecution and economic exploitation they entailed. A satellite empire had not yet been fully consolidated, since the strict Soviet controls that would eventually be imposed were not in evidence outside Romania. The prospect of such an empire presented a threat to the British position, as a great power with European-wide interests, and to American perceptions of the new European order. Yet, fear of the extension of Soviet military power and/or political influence into areas such as the Mediterranean and Middle East remained more important in 1946 than developments in Eastern Europe, as it would constitute Soviet post-war expansion rather than wartime gains. However, by April, when the next session of the CFM met in Paris, Soviet demands were reduced when Molotov supported the French idea of returning the Italian colonies to Italy as compensation for its proposed loss of Trieste. Again, the Soviets appeared willing to bargain in the Mediterranean, while the British were adamant that no concessions should be contemplated that might threaten their vital interests and great power status. It still proved impossible to reach agreement at the first session of the Paris Council prior to the formal opening of the actual Paris Peace Conference. A second Council had to meet in Paris and a further one in New York before peace treaties with Germany's allies could be finalized at the end of 1946.

British interests continued to revolve around the Mediterranean and Middle East where, over the issue of the Dardanelles, they now had American support. The Soviets were aware that in that region Britain believed it had vital interests and were prepared to back down. In areas of Central and Eastern Europe, however, where the Soviets believed they had vital interests, there was to be no retreat in the face of Anglo-American pressure. This growing confrontation was exacerbated by the failure to secure agreement on future international controls over the use of atomic energy. In March 1946, the Acheson-Lilienthal proposal provided for a transition period to international control during which the US would retain its advantageous position as the only power with nuclear weapons. The American proposals seemed to be based on a determination to preserve the dominant US position until international arrangements were in place, which would prevent the Soviets securing any advantage. Moscow's position was that existing stocks of weapons should be dealt with as a precursor to future controls. In 1946, suspicion and mistrust were gathering pace even though there were still some signs of a willingness to compromise on both sides. In 1947, this willingness was to disappear and confrontation was eventually to lead to the end of efforts at cooperation.

One element in this scenario was the importance of propaganda. If both sides were, in effect, to insist that the maintenance of cooperation could only be on their terms, it was important to convince the rest of the world that the other side was to blame if cooperation proved impossible. So, when the attempts to produce a post-war settlement at the Paris Peace Conference became public, the propaganda battle was joined in earnest and by the end of 1947 was to become of much greater significance in the conduct of the Cold War. For both Washington and Moscow, 1947 was to be a crucial year, when fears of losing control over their respective European areas of influence reached such an extent that priority was accorded to the consolidation of Europe into two opposing blocs. The key events in the abandonment of cooperation and the start of an unremitting propaganda campaign were the failure to reach agreement on the future of Germany and the discussions on the Marshall Plan to provide American economic aid to Europe. They were to lead to an extension of Soviet control in Eastern Europe and to the modification of the doctrine of containment in the US.

The Truman Doctrine

Often portrayed as the defining moment for the American strategy of containment, Truman's famous speech, delivered in March 1947, can also be seen as a substantial modification of a previously defensive doctrine, which eventually opened the door to all kinds of proactive US actions throughout the globe. Its origins lay in the general sense of economic crisis in Europe which developed during the winter of 1946–7, but also in the specific problems faced by Turkey and Greece. While the Soviets had been unsuccessfully endeavouring to intimidate the former in 1945, Stalin had largely ignored Greece, despite the initial opportunity presented by a large communist-dominated left-wing opposition and a civil war. The conflict which began in 1944 and led to armed British intervention was renewed in 1946, when the Left reacted to the persecution of opposition groups by the British-backed government, and was to continue until 1949. The lack of Soviet interference prior to 1947 reflected a desire to appease the British and uphold the percentages agreement, which would increase the prospects for continued cooperation on the basis of agreed spheres of influence. Nevertheless, the cost of the British efforts to contain the conflict and create long-term stability was becoming too high to bear by the end of 1946.

The difficulties facing Greece and other areas of Western Europe were part of the general problem of post-war reconstruction, made more difficult by the failure to cooperate over the economic future of Germany. The Soviet desire to maximize the exploitation of all of Eastern Europe, ended the pre-war East–West trade in agricultural produce. The problem was made worse by the Soviets handing over to Polish administration the agricultural lands between the Eastern and Western Neisse. Thus, there was less food to feed the Germans in the West than the British and Americans had anticipated. A poor harvest in 1946 was followed by a desperately harsh winter, when it became clear that the post-war US loans to individual countries in Western Europe would not meet the needs of recovery. Fears of an economic collapse were exacerbated by the probability that already-strong communist movements in the West would seize the opportunity presented by the apparent failure of capitalism. The link between economic hardship and greater opportunities for the spread of communism was to remain central to the world view of Western elites for many years after 1945.

If economic hardship was to be mitigated, two immediate problems had to be confronted. One was the general imbalance in world markets resulting from the wartime disruption of previous global trade patterns and the consequent dominance of the US as a supplier of industrial goods and foodstuffs. The other was the economic revival of Germany, which was deemed necessary for the recovery of the rest of Western Europe. With German production levels only a third of what they had been in 1936, and with no food supplies from the territory in the east now controlled by Poland, basic foodstuffs were having to be imported into the Western zones. This not only exacerbated the trade imbalance and contributed to a serious 'dollar gap'[11] by the end of 1946, but also imposed further economic hardship on the occupying powers. These problems contributed to the British decision, communicated to Washington in February 1947, to end their economic and military assistance to Greece and Turkey.

Washington was then faced with a number of difficulties. The future of the capitalist world economy was in doubt and with it the capacity of the US to ensure that the economic expansion of the wartime years was maintained. If there was a serious trade imbalance, a worldwide recession could ensue, as many countries would not have the dollars to purchase American goods and foodstuffs. The serious crisis in Europe, particularly Germany, would threaten the successful implementation of George Kennan's strategy of preserving important areas of economic strength for the capitalist, as opposed to the communist, world. Finally, Turkey and Greece would be left more exposed to Soviet pressure and interference if British assistance was not replaced. One way in which all these problems could be tackled was the provision of US economic aid on a large scale. Unfortunately, these problems came to a head just after a Republican Congress had been elected and was committed to a policy of tax-cutting and retrenchment.

On the international front, although some progress had been made with the treaties with Germany's allies, tensions continued to grow as confrontation made compromise unlikely. These tensions and problems made it more difficult to draw up a German peace treaty, which had yet to be tackled in detail by the CFM. The West, because of the economic difficulties in running their zones, was already moving towards the division of Germany and the consolidation of the Western zones (see Chapter 2, D). It was an option which offered the largest economic advantages and the smallest geopolitical risks. Both sides were fully aware that, if cooperation could not be maintained, it was far better to extend control over their own spheres in Germany than to risk a united Germany coming under the influence of a potentially hostile power or bloc.

From the American perspective, if Germany was to be divided there was little prospect of eventually securing the kind of European settlement in line with their ideals. The Soviets had indicated in 1945, as before, that there was little chance of democratic governments in the Western sense emerging in Romania, Bulgaria, or Poland. What was now at issue were the future prospects of Western Germany and Western Europe, which might fall prey to a political ideology that would threaten the socio-economic system on which Western elites depended. Consolidating influence and control in the West therefore became more important than applying principles in the East. In these circumstances, the disadvantages of escalating confrontation were much less than the risks of standing aside from the specific crises in Greece and Turkey and the more general crisis in Western Europe. Similar considerations about the risk of not taking action in parts of Eastern Europe were likely to have influenced Stalin in 1947. By then, a more determined stance against communism also offered domestic political benefits for the Truman administration, because the more the threat was played up, the more likely it was that Congress would provide the money to aid Western Europe.

The result was a speech by Truman on 12 March 1947 which universalized the conflict then confronting the free world in Greece and Turkey. In the Greek case, a civil war was represented as part of a global struggle. Moreover, the speech portrayed the struggle in a general manner without specifying whether it emanated from the military threat of a rival state, a political ideology connected to a rival great power, or an economic threat to American business. Unlike any previous conflict in history between competing states, dynastic rivals, or other forms of government, according to Truman, the US was engaged in a world-wide battle between two different ways of life. What became known as the Truman Doctrine proclaimed that:

> One way of life is based on the will of the majority, and is distinguished by free institutions, representative government, free elections, guarantees of individual liberty, freedom of speech and religion and freedom from political oppression. The second way of life is based upon the will of a minority forcibly imposed upon the majority. It relies upon terror and oppression, a controlled press and radio, fixed elections and the suppression of personal freedoms.

The US therefore had 'to support free peoples who are resisting attempted subjugation by armed minorities or by outside pressures'.

The Truman Doctrine was not a response to an unforeseen or new situation, as the US had already sent $260 million dollars of aid to Greece in 1946. Moreover, concern over Greece increased after the Truman Doctrine, because of Yugoslav involvement and the greater Soviet commitment to support communist subversion in the West from the autumn of 1947. It was more a calculated attempt to instil fear into the American population and their representatives in order to procure aid on a much larger scale.[12] In this aim, it was astonishingly successful in the short term, but it sowed the seeds of a policy which would have unfortunate long-term consequences. By implying that the US had unlimited responsibilities to assist all those who were allegedly resisting a challenge to the American way of life, the Truman Doctrine opened the door to intervention in any civil war. As long as one of the participants could be portrayed as sympathetic to communism, then an internal conflict would become part of a global struggle against the Soviets and require US involvement. In addition, threats to the American way of life could emanate from within the US and the invocation of such threats, however far-fetched and imaginary, could be exploited for political benefit. In the long term, the US would pay a heavy price abroad for the development of an ideology of global dimensions which defined security in extremely broad terms. In the short term, the impact of the Truman Doctrine was much more significant within the US than it was on Soviet foreign policy. Stalin seemed unperturbed by the US president's proclamation. Actions rather than words always meant more to Stalin, and the forthcoming Moscow Conference still offered the prospect of an advantageous agreement on Germany. It was not until the Moscow Conference proved fruitless and the Americans produced the Marshall Plan to aid Europe as a whole, that Soviet policy underwent a decisive shift which effectively meant the abandonment of cooperation. It was to be replaced not just by confrontation and a significant tightening of Soviet political control over Eastern Europe, but by increasing efforts to weaken the Western hold over the other half of the continent. Particular attention was to be given to preventing the rebuilding of the Western zones of Germany as part of an anti-Soviet bloc. Similarly, by the end of the year the US, having devised a strategy for aiding the recovery of Western Europe in line with American economic interests, had begun the construction of a national security state. This was to be followed by policies to weaken the Soviet position in its sphere of influence in Eastern Europe. Whether such strategies can best be seen as the beginning or the end of containment remains a debatable Cold War question.

Visit the online resources that accompany this book to test your understanding and take your learning further: www.oup.com/he/young-kent3e

NOTES

1. US National Archives, Charles Papers, Box 4, memorandum 18 Oct. 1945. Cited in W. LaFeber, *Inevitable Revolutions. The United States and Central America* (New York, W.W. Norton, 1984), 89.
2. The distinction between genuine military security requirements and the requirements of expansionist imperial states is often impossible to make. To approach such matters objectively, it is safest to assume that all great powers are seeking to maximize their power and influence through territorial means or by direct or indirect control over the governments of less powerful states.
3. See Foreign Relations of the United States (FRUS), 1943, *The Conferences at Cairo and Tehran* (Dept. of State, Washington, DC, 1961).
4. *New York Times*, 3 March 1945.
5. B. Kuniholm, *The Origins of the Cold War in the Near East* (Princeton University Press, Princeton, 1980), 129.
6. The Curzon line was drawn up on general ethnic lines, with some inevitable exceptions, by Lord Curzon and the French prime minister, Clemenceau, after the First World War.
7. FRUS, 1945, *The Conferences at Malta and Yalta* (Dept. of State, Washington, DC, 1955), 781.
8. Fraser J. Harbutt, *The Iron Curtain: Churchill, America, and the Origins of the Cold War* (Oxford University Press, New York, 1986), 115.
9. R. L. Messer, *The End of an Alliance: James F. Byrnes, Roosevelt, Truman and the Origins of the Cold War* (University of North Carolina Press, Chapel Hill, 1982), 127.
10. Robert's views can be found in FO 371/47882, Roberts to Warner, 13 May 1945; FO 371/47856, Roberts to FO, 28 September 1945; FO371/52327, Roberts to Bevin 16 January 1946.
11. The 'dollar gap' was the result of a devastated Europe being unable to produce sufficient goods to sell to America to gain the currency to purchase much-needed imports.
12. W. LaFeber, *America, Russia and the Cold War 1945–2000* (9th edn, McGraw-Hill, New York, 2002), 52–3.

2

Two Worlds East and West, 1945–8

Chapter contents

By the end of 1947, the establishment of two opposing blocs was largely in place. Whether this was essentially an ideological, economic, or military confrontation is still a matter of contention. Moreover, historical understanding of this confrontation was made more difficult by the Cold War itself. It produced worst-case assumptions of the threats each side faced and claims that only one side had reason to be concerned. The evidence suggests that *both* sides had reason to be concerned and that in private these concerns were often genuine, but they were not predominantly military ones. The historical explanation of the emergence of the two blocs needs to be removed from the linear, aggressive action/defensive response model that ultimately produced military confrontation. If we want fully to understand the ambitions and, particularly after 1947, the concerns of both sides, we need to look beyond arms build-ups and the military dimension of power politics.

Traditional concepts of power in the economic and military sense were combined with ideologies based on liberal or socialist values. These were in tune with the deeper currents and traditions of elite culture, including the general preservation of domestic status, not just the specific economic interests which helped realize and preserve it. In this sense, Soviet elites lacked the historical memories of their Western counterparts and a clear conception of how the world could be moulded to reflect both their country's status and their own values and privileges. For elites in the West who felt threatened in 1947, a way of life at home was firmly linked, particularly in the US, to an international order embodying values as well as power.

At the heart of these values in 1947 was the establishment of a liberal order, which would involve the global dominance of a capitalist economy based on multilateral trade. If this failed, a liberal international order would not win mass acceptance. With Western

Europe unable to generate the means to recover, a free and unregulated market economy was more likely to create chaos than prosperity. Action was therefore required by Washington, not just in American economic interests, but in the interest of a new international liberal order, which had been planned for by the US in universal terms even before the attack on Pearl Harbor. Crucially, events propelled the US into a position to link its power with a crusading ideology at the appropriate historical moment. In the Soviet Union, the events of the 1940s, particularly the wartime devastation, inclined elites to concentrate less on the global and the universal than on the domestic and the regional. In ideology, as in most other fields, the Soviets were on the back foot, and while the Marshall Plan could offer both ideological and practical advantages, the Soviets could offer nothing of the latter.

A. The Marshall Plan and the Western Economic System

The Origins of the Marshall Plan

The Marshall Plan was, without doubt, a key turning point in the development of the two blocs and the origins of the Cold War, although some historians see it more as a watershed than others. On the political level, it was both a cause and a consequence of growing fears and tensions. On the economic level, its origins can be traced to long-held American perceptions of the kind of international economy that would bring prosperity and avoid war. Significant consequences stemmed from the threat it presented to Soviet status and influence and to the maintenance of a rival socio-economic system to capitalism. This unprecedented aid package, which provided about $17 billion to Western Europe in 1948–52, sought to ward off the threat of communism in Western Europe and to ensure that the post-war American economy was not sent into recession by unfavourable economic conditions. The Marshall Plan was thus partially geared to the requirements of US businesses and to the problems facing the American economy, which had expanded dramatically during the Second World War.

The American planners, who began their attempts to define a new international order even before the US entered the war, were clearly influenced by ideas that war in general developed from unfair economic competition. Both Cordell Hull, the US Secretary of State until late 1944 and Sumner Welles, Roosevelt's key foreign policy adviser until the autumn of 1943, believed that state power should not be used to exercise control over resources. Imperial trading blocs were deemed to lead to military confrontations and war. Hull and Welles were not advocates of free trade but of the elimination of discriminatory tariffs and quotas which allowed some nations privileged access to markets and resources. They sought ways to promote greater commercial access to all areas of the globe and to facilitate multilateral trade. During the war, at Bretton Woods in New Hampshire in July 1944, a system was put in place to do just that. The Bretton Woods agreements were endorsed by forty-four nations and led to the establishment of the International Bank for Reconstruction and Development (World Bank) and the International Monetary Fund (IMF). The former was designed to provide reconstruction loans and to promote private investment, while the latter was designed to prevent currency difficulties hampering international trade. If a nation found itself suffering from temporary balance-of-payments difficulties, the IMF would provide the requisite currency loans, which would encourage and facilitate multilateral rather than bilateral trade. The system was effectively underpinned by the strength of the dollar, which was exchangeable for gold, and by the economic power of the US, which, as the main provider of funds, was able to dominate both institutions. The World Bank has always had an American president and one-third of the World Bank's money and one-third of the votes in both institutions are exercised by the US.[1]

Despite this, the World Bank and the IMF, like the Marshall Plan, were not without opponents in the US. All were seen as embodying the New Deal ideology of government controls and interference. It was the influence of what the leading Marshall Plan historian has called the 'New Deal coalition', which was central to American attempts to define a new economic order at home and abroad. 'A bloc of capital-intensive firms and their allies amongst labour, farm, financial and professional groups' desired a new, world economic system. This would be founded on 'self-governing economic groups integrated by institutional coordinators and normal market mechanisms, led by cooperating public and private elites, nourished by limited but positive government power, and geared to an economic growth in which all could share'.[2] These ideals and interest groups tied the Bretton Woods system to American efforts to rebuild Western Europe.

They would have influenced US policy irrespective of the existence or ideology of the Soviet Union.

However, the ideological challenge mounted by the Soviets, especially if presented as a more sinister military threat, was a useful weapon for those wishing to use American economic power to create an integrated market for European goods that would serve the interests of US exporters. The fear that the American recovery from the Depression of the 1930s would be thwarted if new world markets were not secured was a real, if largely groundless, one. The vast expansion of the US economy, in which the trade surplus at the end of the war was greater than the total of US exports in the Depression, fuelled these fears. When it became obvious by the end of 1946 that the European dollar shortage had not been solved by the initial American loans, short-term self-interest reinforced the long-term goals of remodelling Western European economies as part of a new international economic order.

Whether the primary aim of the Marshall Plan was to enable the American economy to dominate Western Europe as part of a multilateral trading system, whether it was geared to the long-held views of specific interest groups on a new economic world order, or whether it was a reaction to growing fears about the spread of communism, all such aims and concerns were mutually reinforcing. Republican opponents of the New Deal were more likely to swallow the government expenditure involved if the Marshall Plan had a political goal, vividly represented in the Truman Doctrine, of defeating Soviet communism. Fighting communism and Soviet ambitions were more likely to be supported if American exporters and the US economy in general would benefit as a result.

Whatever the motivation, it has been argued that Western Europe did not need large-scale American aid and that certain countries were well on the road to recovery.[3] The American drive for European integration may have contained elements of self-interest and economic imperialism. However, any US attempt to consolidate Western Europe under its auspices at least offered something to attract European governments into a voluntary association. In contrast, the further consolidation of a Soviet sphere in Eastern Europe, which followed the Marshall Plan, offered economic asset-stripping and political repression as a means of preserving Soviet dominance. It was only later that Soviet imperialism achieved the unique distinction of an empire in which many inhabitants of the periphery were generally better off than their metropolitan equivalents.

The Implementation of the Marshall Plan and its Consequences

A US plan to provide economic aid to Europe was announced by the American Secretary of State, George Marshall, in a speech on 5 June 1947. It was followed by a conference in Paris later in the month of the British, French, and Soviet foreign ministers. It was expected in Washington that the Europeans would take the initiative in coordinating a more specific response to Marshall's general proposal. The Soviets attended because they saw the prospect of capital for much needed reconstruction and initially encouraged Eastern European countries to respond positively. There were, however, those in the Soviet government who saw the Plan as an attempt to undermine their position in Germany and Eastern Europe. Confronted with firm British and French intentions (which they never fully carried out) to produce a combined set of aid requirements rather than a series of country-based proposals, Molotov became more convinced that the main American aim was the creation of an anti-Soviet bloc, including the revived Western zones of Germany. As a result, and much to the relief of the Truman administration, the Soviets walked out of the Paris meeting and subsequently exerted sufficient pressure on Eastern European countries for them not to become involved. The Plan was never designed by the US to encompass all of Europe *and* the Soviet Union, but for domestic political reasons it would have been difficult to deny particular countries the opportunity to participate. Had the offer been taken up by the Soviet bloc, it is unlikely that Congress could have been persuaded to vote the necessary funds. As it was, the British and French convened a conference in Paris over the summer that was attended by sixteen Western European states and had framed a recovery plan by September. After considerable discussion in Congress, an aid package was approved in March 1948, when the Economic Cooperation Act was passed.

The Cold War consequences of the Marshall Plan were momentous. It reflected the American belief that the economic rebuilding of Western Europe, which required an economic contribution from Western Germany, was more important than attempting to maintain cooperation with the Soviets. Exactly the same conclusions were drawn in Moscow, where it was assumed that the Plan was designed to draw Western and Eastern Europe into the American economic orbit, thereby isolating the Soviet Union and creating a revived, united Germany. Stalin believed that even limited cooperation with the West was now impossible because the Marshall Plan was seen as a serious threat. Unlike the restrained Soviet response to the Truman Doctrine, after which the Soviets had agreed to American proposals to speed the work of a commission to form an interim German government, there was a very different reaction.[4] The response was to end cooperation in the commission and prepare to strengthen the Soviet hold over Eastern Europe. By February 1948, this extended to Czechoslovakia, the only country in which Western-style democracy had been preserved in the inter-war years.

According to one historian, the Soviet response to the Marshall Plan was essentially defensive. Soviet leaders saw their war-devastated country as weak, and were therefore unwilling to embark on a confrontation with the West.[5] It may well have been the case that this confrontation was inevitable, given the obstacles to agreement on the future of Europe, and that at some point the Soviet attempt to preserve token coalition governments in Eastern Europe for the sake of appearances would have ended and rigid controls been imposed from Moscow (see Chapter 2, B). Nevertheless, it was the Marshall Plan that influenced the timing of these developments. In July, the Molotov Plan, a series of bilateral agreements linking the Soviet Union with Eastern European countries, became the economic response to Marshall's offer and the forerunner of the Council for Mutual Economic Assistance (COMECON), established in 1949.

The political response was coordinated at a meeting of communist leaders at Szlarska Poreba in September 1947. Here the Communist Information Bureau (Cominform) was established to provide Moscow with the institutional means to control foreign communist parties and formally to end cooperation with other non-fascist parties. The chief Soviet ideologist, Andrei Zhdanov, spoke of the creation of two camps, and although there was one last attempt at cooperation at the London Council of Foreign Ministers (CFM) in November–December 1947, the Marshall Plan was the decisive catalyst for the division of Europe. Both sides had concluded that it was more important to maintain their preferred economic and political systems in one half of a divided Europe than to cooperate in creating a united Europe that would risk a reunited Germany siding with their ideological rival.

A satisfactory resolution of the German problem was another goal of the Marshall Plan and European economic integration. Tying the western zones of Germany into a system of economic cooperation would help prevent the revival of German economic power (see Chapters 2, D and 4, C). Although the Organization of European Economic Cooperation (OEEC), which was established in March 1948 to deal with Marshall Aid, was not a supranational body, it was the first stage of a process that ultimately aimed to revive the German economy while limiting German economic independence. The OEEC lacked the power to make policy independently of the sixteen national governments it represented, but it provided institutional evidence of the West's commitment to European economic recovery.

For the US administration, the Marshall Plan at one stroke offered a way to bring the long-held New Deal vision of a new international economic order a step nearer realization, a way to reduce the security risks of German recovery, and a way to make it more difficult for communists to take control of Western European governments. For the Soviet Politburo, the Marshall Plan was seen as an American attempt 'to restore the economy of Germany and Japan provided it is subordinated to the interests of American capital'. As a result, Germany would be linked to the 'forces of capitalist encirclement'. In the US, George Kennan published an article in *Foreign Affairs* in July 1947 (under the absurd pseudonym 'Mr X'), which claimed that Stalin was determined to overthrow all Western governments, and that the only counter to this would be the 'adroit and vigilant application of counterforce at a series of constantly shifting geographical and political points'.[6]

It is difficult to assess how far these interpretations stemmed from genuine fears or from a perceived propaganda need to maximize the threat of the other side. The rooting out of Stalin's internal opponents could be justified on the grounds that they were linked to Western imperialist forces encircling the Soviet Union. In the West by the end of the decade, the Truman administration was under fire for not rooting out alleged communist sympathizers, particularly those in the government service. By early 1950, Senator Joe McCarthy of Wisconsin was conducting a campaign of hate and vilification based on lies and accusations that would not have been out of place in Stalin's regime. McCarthyism was to lead to a loss of livelihood for a number of American officials and to an atmosphere in the US in which any contact with left-wing ideologies or governments was deemed unacceptable. Even moderate US opinion tended to regard Marxist-based political opposition to capitalism as undermining the security of the state. Overseas, in parts of the French and British empires after 1947 (see Chapter 3, A and B), as in Soviet controlled Eastern Europe, the alleged aims of the new enemy were used to justify repressive measures to maintain internal stability or to win support for the status quo. And this stability was seen to be important precisely because the attempts by both sides to maintain it were interpreted as an attempt to undermine the other's ability to do so in its areas of control. This is what national security (or old and new imperialisms), the Truman Doctrine, the Marshall Plan, and the Cominform had produced by the end of 1947.

B. The Soviet Takeover of Eastern and Central Europe

The origins of Soviet policy towards Eastern Europe can be traced back to before the Second World War, but its nature and motivation remain intense sources of controversy. At the heart of the debate is the extent to which Stalin sought, remorselessly, to extend Soviet controls as part of a grand scheme for European or even world domination. Views on this are bound to influence explanations of the Cold War, for the more determined and coherent Stalin's ambitions were, the more justifiable it becomes to see Western actions as a response to Soviet ambitions or, to employ the most common term, Soviet expansionism. Those who favour such explanations can point to the Nazi–Soviet pact of 1939 and the subsequent Soviet occupation of Eastern Poland and seizure of Northern Bukovina (part of Romania). These actions were followed by attempts to win Nazi approval for further territorial gains and influence. Stalin vainly endeavoured to secure greater influence over Finland, to make Bulgaria part of a Russian security zone, to acquire military bases in the Dardanelles, to establish a Russo-Danish condominium over the Baltic Straits, and to annex southern Bukovina, while securing a special interest in Hungary, Yugoslavia, and Greece.

Such goals bear some resemblance to the kind of situation created at the end of the war by Soviet arms, but in 1940 they were the product of desperate Soviet diplomacy in the face of gathering German power. What Stalin would have liked, what he could obtain, and what he saw as bargaining counters, have always to be carefully distinguished as elements of Soviet foreign policy throughout the 1940s. The lack of evidence and the contradictory policies also make it difficult to assess what Soviet aims actually were. The Soviet exploitation of German and Eastern European resources did not bode well if the aim was to enhance the appeal of Soviet communism. If the aim was to impose the Soviet model of political control and economic development, this was not initially attempted in all areas occupied by the Red Army and was not systematically imposed at any time during Stalin's rule. It may well have been that Stalin was proceeding cautiously in order to avoid taking on too much, too soon. On the other hand, the Soviet leader may have had limited ambitions in Eastern Europe in the expectation that these could be reconciled with Allied cooperation over the containment of Germany.

The motivation for Stalin's Eastern European policies is a further source of controversy. Were they born out of traditional Russian imperialism, out of Marxist-Leninism, which predicted the inevitable collapse of capitalism and the triumph of communism, or out of the specific needs of the Soviet state? Whatever the role of ideology, it can hardly be denied that the Soviet Union still remained an essentially imperialist power, seeking to enhance its power and influence. Yet it should not be forgotten that all great powers, including the Western allies, have had similar imperial goals. Their precise nature, and of course the means of their implementation, varied according to the type of regime and its geopolitical situation. It is also the case that prior to 1942 the Soviet Union faced more serious threats to its territorial security than either Britain or the US. Its enemies in Europe were not only the Germans, who had twice attacked in the twentieth century. There were also the Poles and the Romanians, long embroiled in territorial disputes with Moscow, and under German pressure the Hungarians, who had all recently been engaged in hostilities against the Soviets. On the other hand, it is clearly inappropriate to attempt to justify Soviet policy purely as a response to security needs. Stalin's ambitions extended to the restoration of those parts of the Russian empire lost in the First World War and the Russo-Japanese war of 1904–5. The Soviet leader also sought to extend Soviet influence into Iran and into areas such as the Eastern Mediterranean from which hitherto it had largely been excluded. Soviet foreign policy at the end of the

Second World War was geared very much to a crude pursuit of control and influence, and only after Stalin's death in 1953 to more sophisticated attempts at achieving greater status as a world power.

Much of this has subsequently been justified in terms of Soviet security needs. Territorial security in the traditional sense of protection against military aggression was something that must have played heavily on Stalin's mind. However, it cannot justify or explain all Soviet actions in Europe, let alone those in Asia and the Middle East. Nor can the control of Eastern European communist parties imposed by Moscow. Security and imperialism can be very similar concepts, and the same issues apply to defining US goals and policies, about which much more evidence is available.

Stalin's own personality remains a key factor in any analysis of Soviet actions, not least because foreign policy was always his policy rather than that of the Soviet foreign ministry or the Communist Party. A brutal and secretive leader whose personal habits reflected a deeply disturbed personality, Stalin and his murderous regime have sometimes been portrayed as incapable of conducting a cooperative foreign policy. It seems unlikely, however, from Western records of meetings with the Soviet leader that he was unwilling to compromise, or that he was irrational and unable to make judgements about Soviet interests in Eastern Europe or elsewhere. Nor was he regarded during the war by Western leaders as someone with whom a cooperative relationship was impossible.

The Pattern at the End of the War

In 1944–5, as the Red Army moved closer to Berlin, there was no evidence of Stalin deploying Soviet forces with an eye to the post-war settlement, other than allowing the Germans to eliminate anti-Soviet elements in Poland. Priority was given to the most expeditious way of defeating the Germans, at least until after the Yalta Conference in the spring of 1945, when it has been suggested that Soviet policy then began to change.[7] What may have influenced this was the British response to the Soviet-sponsored coup in Romania, which breached the Yalta agreements. Stalin's failure to include in the Polish provisional government democratic elements from abroad or to hold the elections he had promised within about one month (see Chapter 1, A) also flew in the face of the Yalta agreements.[8] Yet Yalta itself contradicted the 1944 percentages agreements.

The Romanian coup was the only Soviet-imposed government in Eastern Europe after Yalta and before the end of the war. Having led the efforts to remove the pro-German Romanian government in 1944, King Michael was faced in February 1945 with Soviet demands for a communist government. The decision had been taken by the Red Army to move Romanian units out of Bucharest in January 1945, prior to the Yalta Conference. On 27 February, with Soviet tanks in the streets of Bucharest, King Michael, on Andrei Vyshinski's insistence, appointed a Cabinet subservient to Moscow, although four of its members were non-communists. As British protests, more over Poland than Romania, were voiced, Stalin became increasingly fearful that a separate peace, if not collaboration with the Germans, was being sought. To the Russians, it was difficult to explain why German troops fought a desperate rearguard action in Czechoslovakia while offering only token resistance on the Rhine. Thus, it has been claimed that in April and May the Soviets began to view military operations with an eye to future bargaining counters in preparation for what was termed the strategies of occupation.[9]

It seems that Stalin had not, however, abandoned his commitment to cooperation with the West. Rather, in keeping with his character, he was increasingly suspicious and uncertain. While Zhdanov argued for encouraging socialism in Eastern Europe, other senior ministers, such as Georgi Malenkov, were more concerned with grabbing what was possible from Germany and Eastern Europe, then retreating into isolation, without becoming too concerned about cooperation with the West or Eastern European socialism. Whether cooperation remained Stalin's priority would depend on the extent to which any such cooperation satisfied Soviet interests. Unfortunately, it is impossible to be sure which Soviet interests Stalin regarded as vital and worth ending cooperation for. Maxim Litvinov defined the maximum aims in 1944 in terms of a Soviet sphere of influence including Sweden, Finland, Poland, Hungary, Czechoslovakia, Romania, and the Slav Balkan countries. A minimum set of aims would clearly have included Poland and Romania, both containing traditional Russian enemies, and more than in a traditional sphere of influence the latter countries would have required tight controls in order to ensure the necessary pro-Soviet regimes.

The imposition of Soviet control over Eastern Europe made little progress in 1945. In November, free elections in Hungary, in which the Communist Party won only 17 per cent of the vote, were followed by elections in Bulgaria, which were suspect but not rigged as blatantly as some later ones in areas less favourably disposed to the Russians. The unilateral search for the best means of maintaining Soviet interests in Eastern Europe, including Soviet security, may not have begun until early 1946[10] or even later. As 1946 began, the Polish elections were postponed, while elections in Czechoslovakia proved favourable to the communists, who gained 38 per cent of the vote. On the other hand, the elections in Romania in November 1946 were rigged. Disagreement rages on the significance of all this. Was Stalin playing for time to deter Western intervention if moves were made to impose communist rule throughout Eastern and Central Europe? Did Stalin believe that it was possible for communists to be freely voted into power? Did he still believe that cooperation with the West was desirable to contain Germany and therefore strict Soviet control would have to be minimized?

The communists throughout the region were certainly aware of the likely need to undermine opposition parties if their position was to be strengthened. In 1946, efforts were made in Hungary to weaken the opponents of communism. Yet there was clearly no imposition of total Soviet control over most of East-Central Europe in the face of majority opposition until 1947. The tightening of Soviet control began in Poland before the Truman Doctrine and the Marshall Plan, with the rigged elections of January 1947. However, it was the latter which increased the need, from a Soviet perspective, to preserve the communist system and maintain Soviet domination of the region. Nothing had yet happened before the late spring of 1947, brutality and exploitation notwithstanding, which would not have been clear to perceptive Western officials in 1943 and 1944—namely that the Soviets would not permit anti-Soviet political movements in Poland and Romania.

It was the defeat of Germany by the Red Army which put the Soviets in a position to control Eastern Europe and the issue after 1945 was less whether there would be further European expansion than whether there would be any contraction. With regard to political domination of provisional governments, even in Romania there was no certainty before 1947 that the Soviet economic and political model would be fully imposed. In Hungary and Czechoslovakia, Stalin had clearly not implemented a policy of strict Soviet control by the end of 1946, and even in Poland there were still opposition elements that had not yet been crushed. Indeed, Vojtech Mastny has argued that Stalin had no real desire for a tightly controlled system in Eastern let alone Western Europe. Rather than having a formally divided Europe, with half under communist domination, a Europe made pliable by internal conflict may have been the Soviet leader's preferred option.[11] Ideologically, communist leaders had to believe in the eventual demise of capitalism; therefore Stalin's natural preference could have been a system of political inefficiency and economic chaos for most of Europe, which would lead to that demise. Communist parties in both Eastern and Western Europe could contribute to this instability, which would serve an ideological purpose as well as satisfying the interests of the Soviet state, not least by preventing the re-emergence of a powerful Germany.

Such a scenario offered the prospect of maintaining cooperation with the British and the Americans, and avoiding the kind of confrontation in Europe that Stalin had engendered over Turkey and Iran before hurriedly backing down. Before 1947, there was always a need for Stalin to balance his heightened ambitions against the advantages of maintaining some form of cooperation with the West. The latter could not only solve the problem of German revival but also offer the possibility of economic assistance to help Soviet recovery. It is possible that the Soviet abandonment of any hope of cooperation with the West came as early as 1946. The strongest evidence indicates, however, that this important shift came between the failure of the Moscow CFM on the future of Germany in March 1947 and the Paris meeting on Marshall Aid for Europe, in June of the same year. Prior to Moscow, Stalin retained the hope that he could extract concessions over German reparations, which was a more important consideration than the rhetoric of the Truman Doctrine. After the failure of the Moscow CFM and after reflecting on the Marshall Plan, there seemed no advantage for the Soviets in maintaining cooperation. The Marshall Plan was seen as an attempt to build a Western economic bloc in opposition to the Soviet Union and as a scheme to bring Eastern Europe into the orbit of American capitalism. It therefore became vital for the Soviets to prevent this and to secure control over their half of a divided Europe.

The Extension of the Soviet System in Eastern Europe

Soviet interference with the political process in Eastern Europe had been considerable, but far from uniform, prior to the genesis of the Marshall Plan in the spring of 1947, after which it became much more repressive, with the exclusion of all non-communist parties and the imposition of the Soviet system without any consideration of local needs or wishes. Yet it remains uncertain as to the extent to which fear of Western interference embodied in the Marshall Plan affected the nature and timing of Stalinist rule in Eastern Europe, as steps towards this were taken both before and after June 1947. In Romania, the non-communist minority members of the government who had been installed as part of the Moscow Council agreement of January 1946 had been removed by fraudulent elections in November that year. But it was a year later, following the Marshall Plan and the creation of Cominform, that all opposition parties were finally repressed. In Hungary, some allegedly undesirable non-communists had been removed from the government in May 1947. Then in August, rigged elections, which still gave non-communist groups 35 per cent of the vote, were followed by the exclusion of all such groups from power. Hungary therefore followed Romania, Bulgaria, and Poland down the road of one-party governments subordinate to Moscow and committed to the imposition of the Stalinist approach to economic development. However, it was not until 1948 that the most significant events for the future of the Soviet bloc were to come in Czechoslovakia and Yugoslavia.

In the former, it appears possible that, until the events of 1947, Stalin was happy to let the Czechoslovaks develop their own socialist model in their own time. The fear after 1947 was that Czechoslovakia would ally itself with the West or that the West would interfere in the country, thereby threatening Soviet dominance. The coup, which took place at the end of February 1948 and installed a communist government under Klement Gottwald, was precipitated by elections scheduled to take place in the spring of 1948 in which the communists were likely to fare badly.[12] It is not clear whether Stalin was the instigator of the coup, or whether the initiative came from within the Czech communist party and was welcomed by Stalin. However, it raised the prospect of communist governments coming to power without the Red Army playing a direct role and in countries with a significant democratic past. Czechoslovakia thus symbolized the worst fears of Western governments, who were primarily concerned about the spread of communism by political means rather than the expansion of Soviet power by military means. Indeed, the State Department, as far as foreign policy was concerned, had already assigned Czechoslovakia a role as a Soviet satellite. However, the need to unite Western Europe against communism, which was now more closely directed by Moscow, contributed to an attempt, if not to promote a war scare, at least to portray what was viewed as a short-term political danger as an immediate military one.[13] Also, events in 1948 raised unpleasant memories of the 1938 Munich Crisis, when the Western powers had bowed to Nazi demands on Czechoslovakia.

The Tito–Stalin Split

Yugoslavia, like Czechoslovakia, had been relatively free of direct control from Moscow, not least because the liberating role of the Yugoslav resistance reduced the Red Army's influence. With Stalin's and Zhdanov's belief that Washington now sought to extend capitalism to Eastern Europe, the relative autonomy of Yugoslavia was seen as a greater threat in Moscow. Ironically, but with significance for any understanding of the role of ideology as opposed to state interests in Stalin's foreign policy, the Yugoslavs were the leading proponents of Zhdanov's revolutionary line. Tito was the Cominform's strongest supporter, one who, in ideological terms, was 'following Stalin out of conviction rather than fear'.[14]

Now that Stalin was determined to control what was perceived as a communist Eastern Europe, any lack of subservience on Tito's part was deemed a threat in itself. The threat loomed larger because there were a number of power-political differences to sour Soviet–Yugoslav relations and override ideological convictions. Tito had clashed with Stalin over military strategy during the war, and in the immediate post-war period Tito resented Stalin's refusal to give firm backing to Yugoslavia in its dispute with Italy over Trieste. By December 1947, when treaties were signed between Yugoslavia and Bulgaria, Romania, and Hungary respectively, Stalin feared that Yugoslavia could become a rival for the allegiance of Eastern European states. Such fears were confirmed by the announcement in January 1948 of a customs union between Bulgaria and Yugoslavia. Talks between Tito and Bulgaria's Dmitrov were geared to the formation of a Balkan federation which could even be extended to states outside the Balkans. The Yugoslavs and the Bulgarians were therefore informed that 'relations between people's democracies which exceeded the interests of the Soviet government and which did not have its approval . . . were inadmissable' and that the Soviet Union had the right to interfere in the internal affairs of the people's democracies.[15]

This was particularly galling to Tito, who had been persuaded to establish joint Soviet–Yugoslav economic enterprises on disadvantageous terms. The Yugoslav leader now faced continued economic exploitation by Moscow, more interference in Yugoslav Party affairs, and demands for special privileges for Soviet personnel. As a particularly strong personality, with a high self-regard, Tito was not prepared to accept Soviet economic or political domination. Rather than follow the Bulgarian leader to Moscow to accept a dressing down from Stalin, Tito only sent representatives. In March, Stalin therefore withdrew Soviet economic experts from Yugoslavia. With backing from the majority of the Yugoslav central committee, Tito was able to resist Stalin's efforts to orchestrate an internal pro-Soviet coup. On 28 June 1948, four days after the Berlin blockade (see Chapter 2, D) began in earnest, a special Cominform meeting expelled Yugoslavia. So began the final consolidation of the Soviet bloc.

As problems appeared to threaten Stalin's control, the necessity to install loyal followers and prevent the emergence of other Titos increased. Trade and friendship agreements between Yugoslavia and the other communist states were cancelled as part of the strategy of punishing Tito. Such actions served to open the door to economic and military cooperation between Yugoslavia and the West, and the Yugoslav regime was to survive. Elsewhere in Eastern Europe the Tito–Stalin split was followed by purges of alleged 'deviators' from the Soviet revolutionary path. In all the communist countries of the Eastern bloc except East Germany, arrests and show trials took place. Some ministers were executed, while others such as the Polish leader, Gomulka, faced imprisonment.[16] Yet as Stalinist tactics were succeeding in creating an atmosphere of terror and in imposing rigid controls over a Soviet satellite empire (with the exception of Yugoslavia), they were failing to resolve the German question to Moscow's satisfaction (see Chapter 2, D).

C. The Struggle for Influence in East Asia

A central argument of this text is that the Cold War was born out of a global conflict over the nature of the post-war international order, which was conceived, particularly in the West, as embodying principles which would enable power, domestically and internationally, to be exercised and preserved. It was not a conflict born out of actions and reactions in Europe which then spread to Asia or which can be portrayed predominantly in power-political terms without reference to principles and the ideologies which produced and justified them. Therefore, as Western concern over the economic condition of the defeated enemy in Europe became acute in 1947, so did concern about the economic condition of Japan in Asia. In both cases, there were fears that a failure to rehabilitate the two countries would play into the hands of the opponents of capitalism. It was not just that the worsening economic conditions would produce unrest, but that the failure to rebuild the important German and Japanese economies would prevent regional recovery and undermine the global vision of a new liberal order. Moreover, failure would vindicate Soviet ideology as it predicted that the contradictions of capitalism would produce conflict and divisions in the West. Such expectations on the part of Stalin and other communist leaders were to be proved wrong in both Europe and East Asia.

Japan and the Reverse Course

In Japan, the Americans, having abandoned their 1945 attempt to exclude their wartime allies from any formal role in the occupation of Japan, had to rely on all effective authority being exercised by the military commander. Thus, the situation in Italy and Eastern Europe was repeated in Japan except that the American commander, General Douglas MacArthur, considered himself to be more than capable of running Japan single-handedly. Strong-willed and not amenable to control or even advice, MacArthur as Supreme Commander Allied Powers (SCAP) began a programme of decentralization and the break-up of large economic groupings (*zaibatsus*), while purging those associated with the aggressive policies of expansion and war. In line with the American system of federalism and anti-trust laws, MacArthur believed he was reforming Japan in ways which would involve reparations and the destruction of a society which did not conform to the American model. While this might have succeeded in the long term, in the short term it did little or nothing to solve the pressing problems of preventing Japanese economic collapse. As in Germany, the war had destroyed the regional patterns of trade and by 1946 there were to be increasing signs of acute hardship amongst a population whose economic viability was soon to become more important than their social or economic structures.

MacArthur was, however, disinclined to be deflected from his chosen course when in 1946 the State Department, as in Germany, became concerned about the dangers of economic hardship. In early 1947, SCAP ordered the purge of business executives who could be linked to ultranationalist groups or who had supported military aggression. MacArthur was attacking the industrial-banking system without concern for the means by which the economy could attract foreign investment and earn the means to import food and avoid inflation and shortages. Moreover, in Japan the cost to the US of preventing hardship by supplying food and other essentials would be even greater than in Europe unless the Japanese themselves could make a contribution. In the middle of 1948, the non-military cost of supplying food, fuel, and medicine had almost reached $1 billion.[17] The State Department argued, at the moment the Truman Doctrine was launched, that a 'positive economic programme' must quickly 'create a viable Japanese economy' which would be 'self-sustaining' by 1950.[18]

In the spring of 1947, criticism of MacArthur's policies was intensified by George Kennan's appointment to the newly created Policy Planning Staff in the State Department. Kennan saw the main problems as political, economic, and psychological, rather than military in both Europe and Japan. He also conceived the Soviet ideological challenge in global terms in 1947. In other words, it was not just important to keep communism from gaining control and influence in Europe but in all areas, including Japan, which had developed strong industrial economies. Kennan linked these economic and political factors to a concept of a non-military balance of power in Eurasia, with a rebuilt Japan and Germany countering Soviet power but not threatening Western interests. Rebuilding Germany and Japan would 'immunize them and their regions against communism'.[19] He had support for a change of course and the abandonment of MacArthur's policies from an increasing number of sources, including former President Herbert Hoover and the War Department. Opposition to MacArthur was strengthened with the establishment of the Department of Defence in July 1947, which made it more difficult for MacArthur to portray himself as above the individual services. A more concerted effort was now to be made to produce what became known as the 'reverse course' in Japan that would end reparations and the decentralization programme with its attacks on the *zaibatsus*.

In the summer of 1947, the State Department produced a paper on Japanese recovery which contained similar ideas to those in the Marshall Plan and which aimed to provide $500 million to produce Japanese self-sufficiency by 1950. In September 1947, General William Draper, the recently appointed Under Secretary, visited Japan and took on the role of coordinating the State-Army assault on MacArthur. The crunch came in the first two months of 1948 when the State-War-Navy Coordinating Committee[20] approved a Japanese recovery programme, thereby accepting the State Department line. But then came proposals from Tokyo earmarking over 300 companies for possible dissolution. Kennan regarded this as a greater threat to Japan than Soviet military strength and departed for Tokyo determined to persuade MacArthur of the need to use the economic potential of Japan in the Cold War, rather than undermine it by a post-war reform programme.[21] As in Europe, what had been earmarked for destruction now had to be utilized in a new battle for salvation.

Kennan's visit coincided with that of Draper, who had been lobbying Congress to win support for a Japanese recovery programme. Kennan produced arguments for reversing course which portrayed Japan as more important than China in the struggle against Soviet communism. Draper got support from businessmen whom he brought to Tokyo and put the economic arguments in regional terms. The Japanese situation was portrayed as a regional problem that jeopardized the future of multilateral trade in Asia and, with it, the creation of an open international economic system. Even if Japan could successfully rebuild its manufacturing export sector, markets in Asia remained problematic. A full-scale civil war was underway in China and cheap sources of raw materials were no longer available because of the collapse of the pre-war Japanese empire. Japanese self-sufficiency would have to depend on access to Asian raw materials and markets with less dependency on obtaining them from the dollar zone. These were the official conclusions of the report drawn up by Draper and his aides which was followed by the Army under-secretary's establishment of a Deconcentration Review Board to make final recommendations to MacArthur on the policies to be adopted with regard to Japanese business and financial institutions.

By June, Congress had voted funds for the economic recovery of Japan as part of a programme laid out in June 1948, in National Security Council (NSC) memorandum 13, which proposed terminating the reform programme and seeking stability by siding with business against organized labour. Japan, like Europe, was being rebuilt rather than reformed in order to integrate it into an American-dominated economic world order, with the cooperation of traditional elites, in opposition to Soviet communism. Its recovery was to be accompanied by attempts to link Japan with other Asian economies, most notably South Korea, which had previously been a victim of Japanese imperialism. The fact that Japan's war machine was seen as having been run by the country's most able businessmen now mattered little.[22]

Thus, Japan moved further to the Right in 1948 as China moved further to the Left, with the prospect of a communist victory in the Civil War appearing increasingly likely. A new Japanese government was formed by the conservative Democratic Liberal Party leader, Yoshida Shigeru, and at the end of 1948 President Truman issued a new stabilization directive and appointed Joseph Dodge as a special emissary charged with overseeing the Japanese economy. MacArthur, who had suffered a crushing defeat in the Republican primaries, was no longer the powerful political force he had been in the immediate postwar years. The Kennan–Draper policy could now be implemented along with renewed efforts to integrate Japan successfully into an Asian regional economy as outlined in NSC 48. With China about to fall to communism, this assumed greater importance, but it was not until the disturbing events of 1950 that its success would be achieved.

The Emergence of Communist China

China entered the Sino-Japanese War in 1937 without a central government and having suffered a long period of internal weakness and chaos after the collapse of the Manchu dynasty. In the nineteenth and twentieth centuries, its independence was continually compromised, with the great powers interfering in Chinese affairs and winning extraterritorial privileges. The failure of the Boxer rebellion in 1900 indicated the futility of attempting to resist without using external alliances as a means of regaining greater independence. Michael Hunt has argued that China was torn between the need for support from friends and the dependence that this could produce. The conflict between dependency and autonomy was deeply embedded in the Chinese psyche and remained there after the Second World War, when China became one of the victorious allies.[23]

It was not, however, a unified or powerful China which emerged from the war in 1945. Sun Yat-sen had led a united nationalist party into the inter-war period, but divisions had appeared in 1927 as the split with the communists was formalized. Following the collapse of the united front during the next decade, the nationalist leader Chiang Kai-shek failed to establish a central government over all of China and found himself facing Japanese attacks on Chinese territory. Chiang had abandoned any attempt to win over the masses and preferred to bargain for support with local strongmen and warlords. Fighting the Japanese enemy led to a brief reconciliation with the communists, but when the Sino-Japanese War began in earnest in 1937, this further reduced the prospects of Chiang creating a united China.

The wartime problems stemmed from the Japanese invasion and their takeover of China's coastal cities, which provided a significant amount of government revenue through customs duties. Deprived of this resource, Chiang's Kuomintang (KMT, or Nationalist Party) had resorted to printing money, which created high inflation and discontent amongst government employees and manual workers. Things became more serious when the Japanese left and the KMT proved to be incapable of providing an effective, corruption-free administration. With labour unrest and student demonstrations taking place, even the KMT's traditional supporters were alienated when the administration acceded to workers' wage demands. In the rural areas not controlled by the communists, the KMT foolishly re-imposed the land tax in 1946 and caused further hostility by compulsory purchases of grain at below market prices. In addition, their poorly paid troops were ill-disciplined and aroused resentment both during and after the conflict with Japan.

The experiences of recent Chinese history were imprinted on the mind of the communist leader Mao

BOX 2.1

Bibliography: Mao Zedong (1893–1976)

Born in Shaoshan, Hunan province, Mao enlisted in 1911 for the revolutionary army in Hunan during the first rebellion against the Manchu dynasty. Influenced by the nationalistic ideas of Sun Yat-sen, Mao converted to Marxism and became involved in political activity as a student at Peking University. In 1921, he co-founded the Chinese Communist Party. He also organized communist guerrilla army units as part of the revolutionary forces between 1924 and 1925. Mao was appointed chief of propaganda and publicity under Sun Yat-sen and he also supported a united front with the Kuomintang (Nationalist Party) under Chang Kai-shek until 1927, when the two parties split and he was dismissed from office. Mao, now leader of the communists, retreated to south-eastern China, where he established the Chinese Soviet Republic in a section of Kiangsi province. In 1934, Kuomintang troops forced Mao to leave Kiangsi and he led his army on the 'long march' of 6,000 miles to Shensi in northern China. During the Second World War an alliance was negotiated between the communists and the Kuomintang against the Japanese, during which time Mao wrote major works on Marxist-Leninism. In 1945, the Civil War resumed and resulted in eventual victory for the communists. In 1949, Mao became leader of the newly established People's Republic of China. During the 1950s Mao abandoned the Soviet economic model and began to introduce his own reforms to rejuvenate the economy. In 1958, he initiated the Great Leap Forward. However, these new policies disrupted Chinese industry and opposition mounted, and in 1959 Mao resigned as leader of the republic but continued to influence policy as leader of the Communist Party. He launched the Cultural Revolution of 1966–9, during which revolutionary attitudes were encouraged, officials dismissed, and all aspects of culture destroyed. Schools and universities were closed and students were organized into Red Guards who attacked nonconformists and destroyed property. Mao's thoughts in the 'Little Red Book' provided a doctrine for the mass of Chinese people, inspiring a cult based on his own personality that lasted until his death.

Zedong (see Box 2.1) who, in the 1930s, began a struggle to unite the country under a single central authority and carve out a more independent and prestigious role for China in international affairs. They were to influence Mao's perception of how the international community could both strengthen and weaken his domestic position as he sought to re-establish China as a regional power. Like any other revolutionary movement, the Chinese communists were in need of domestic legitimacy, but the Cold War situation in 1949 would complicate this and significantly influence international reactions to the new state. In part, this was connected to the nature of the achievement of Mao. He ensured that for the urban middle classes and rural peasants who were equally opposed to the KMT in the years after 1945 the communists were the only viable alternative. While the urban middle classes were thoroughly disillusioned with Chiang Kai-shek, they had little positive commitment to a communist regime. Mao was conscious of the need to preserve this fragile alliance, which could require external help to overcome the enormous problems left by the demands of the war and the corruption and incompetence of the KMT administration. The weaknesses of the KMT clearly contributed to the communist victory, but the military and political strategies of Mao's forces were also significant.

In 1945, few expected the communist forces that were outnumbered by five to one to emerge victorious, and Stalin was particularly doubtful of such an eventuality. In part, this was because, with Soviet influence in East Asia very much in mind, Stalin had gained concessions from the nationalists, albeit with British and American support, regarding the warm-water port of Lushun and the control over the Chinese Eastern Railway. As a result, it is argued, Stalin was prepared to restrict communist activities in Manchuria when the Soviets entered the war against Japan in August 1945, and even to try and expel them from Manchurian cities. At the time of the Soviet involvement in the war against Japan, Stalin was more interested in possible territorial and economic gains than he was in the prospects of a communist revolution in China. This was one of the reasons why he was initially reluctant to offer aid to Mao and preferred to avoid a confrontation with the Americans over China. In 1945 and 1946, when cooperation with the Americans seemed possible and desirable, ideology was not a sufficient incentive for Stalin to give full backing to Mao. Moreover, Stalin, as in Europe, was suspicious of communists who might show independence from Moscow, and Mao's revolution had always been free of Moscow's control. This could sow the seeds of rivalry in East Asia, especially if China began to play a more important regional role.

In the West, the orthodox Cold War tendency has been to play down the impact of power politics and history as influences on Stalin's and Mao Zedong's foreign policy and emphasize Marxism-Leninism and global revolution as the dominant influences shaping Chinese and Soviet approaches to the external world. It may be more meaningful to see the ideological forces as justifying rather than determining foreign policy, which retained at least some of the traditional Chinese and Russian imperial influences. These gave priority to the pursuit of power and influence for the state and its rulers, and for a quest for domestic legitimacy through international means.

As the Civil War intensified in 1945, and with US and Soviet forces in China, the Americans initially attempted to reconcile the nationalists and the communists through the Marshall Mission. Led by General George Marshall, the initiative seemed to produce results in the form of a ceasefire in February 1946 but it had collapsed by April. By then, the Soviets were withdrawing from Manchuria, leaving behind considerable quantities of confiscated Japanese arms, which were seized by the communists. One month later, the communists, in the rural areas they controlled, shifted from a policy of rent reduction to a more radical one of land reform. Their policies in terms of winning support from the peasants were sensible and flexible. As they moved south and faced counter-attacks by the KMT, they would revert to rent reduction in areas where control was difficult, realizing that land reform could not be implemented without effective military control. All that was necessary at this stage was the overthrow of existing rural elites.[24]

In 1946, Stalin could feel confident enough to begin small-scale military aid to the communists, if only to mitigate future recriminations. Cautious as ever, he was unwilling to make a bigger commitment out of fear of an American military response. Nevertheless, for Mao this was a crucial turning point as it was the first concrete sign of the support which he desired from the Soviets. Research indicates that Mao was more desirous of close relations with the Soviets than had previously been thought. While it is true that there was little reason for Mao to trust Stalin, especially as Stalin was still attempting to maintain links with Chiang Kai-shek in 1946, he had even less reason to turn towards the Americans. Mao was preoccupied with what he perceived as the long-term hostility of the US to the communist revolution in China. He saw the prospects of renewed US intervention as a significant possibility, if only in the form of encouraging resistance on the part of the urban bourgeoisie to his attempts to forge a new China through the heat of revolution. Consequently, he needed backing from Stalin. It has been argued that in 1946 Mao had the basis of the Soviet alliance he had been seeking in place.[25] The Chinese communists were given free rein in Manchuria as the Soviet forces withdrew, and the contacts were certainly closer than has generally been assumed in the West.[26] For Mao, the fact that the Soviets gave the communists an increasing amount of military assistance and civilian aid as time progressed was more important than Stalin's subsequent attempts to reopen contacts with the nationalists.[27]

As the KMT continued to display incompetence and corruption, more members of the Truman administration became convinced that aid to the KMT would not rescue an increasingly unpopular organization which, by 1948, was clearly losing the war. Spreading forces too thinly had made the KMT army vulnerable to more concentrated communist deployments, and in 1948 Marshall, now secretary of state, had finally decided that the communists were going to win. By the end of that year, Stalin too was convinced that victory for Mao was in sight and that the US was unlikely to prevent it. Soviet attention now moved more towards influencing future relations with the Chinese Communist Party (CCP) within an East Asian context. One option was to act as a mediator in the final days of the conflict in order to win international acclaim as a peacemaker and to make the Chinese communists more beholden to Moscow. In the event, Mao was having none of it but remained determined to look to the Soviets for fear of malign American influence in China, although it was not until 1950 that a firm alliance was concluded.

D. The Division of Germany

The German question was perhaps the most important single problem facing the Allies at the end of the war. It was not, however, the source of immediate conflict in 1945, when issues about it were either resolved or more usually postponed. Talks on a German peace treaty, always seen as the most difficult to achieve, were delayed until 1947 after treaties with Germany's allies were concluded. It was more the case that, as wider Cold War tensions increased during 1946–7, they made an acceptable German peace settlement harder to achieve. Since Germany itself was such a significant issue, this in turn produced more tension and more unilateral actions in the Eastern and Western zones. The initial agreements on Germany resulted partly from the importance both sides attached to containing the principal enemy state of the Second World War. The fact that there might be different views on how to do this did not imply that failure to reach a final agreement was impossible. Yet, as the costs of various options became clearer, who should pay for them formed one irresolvable problem. To that extent, the Cold War role of Germany had an economic dimension linked to ideology as well as to the strategic interests of the great powers. In particular, the Soviet Union had reasons to be deeply concerned about such a potentially powerful state at the heart of Europe.

During the war, a number of conflicting ideas had arisen about how finally to prevent a resurgence of German militarism. The US Morgenthau Plan effectively proposed a pastoral state deprived of the industrial capacity to make war. From the Soviet point of view, the best way to ensure that a capitalist Germany was prevented from making war on its Eastern boundaries was to create a communist state. Given that it had been agreed during the war to establish an Allied Control Council, this was not an option in the short term. There was also the possibility of the dismemberment of Germany and of demilitarizing the country with international controls, to prevent its industrial capacity being used to produce military equipment. All this would require cooperation and joint control, which might have been why Stalin was not averse at the end of the war to American troops remaining in Europe. Finally, there was the issue of German reparations, which the Soviets, who had suffered most from German aggression, were desperately keen to impose.

From the Western perspective, it was important to prevent the revival of German militarism within a powerful centralized state. How best to do this was seen as more problematic, given that excessively harsh treatment (as some believed the Germans had received at the end of the First World War) was likely to foster resentment; this in turn could produce a determination to overturn any post-war settlement. There was a further consideration, which soon became important to the West, and that was Germany's role in European recovery. Stalin was not only unperturbed by the prospect of starving Germans, but had no interest in the revival of European capitalism, especially as this would require German resources, particularly coal. For the West, capitalism's ability to produce European prosperity was an important consideration, and for that Germany's role was crucial. The cost of preventing starvation in Germany also required some form of controlled German recovery, in which the Soviets had less interest.

The future treatment of the country, and the particular issues of dismemberment and reparations, had been broached at Yalta (see Chapter 1, A). There, it had been decided to 'take such steps including the complete disarmament, demilitarization, and dismemberment of Germany' as was deemed necessary for peace and security.[28] The specific issue of dismemberment, strongly favoured by the Soviets, was to be considered by a committee. On reparations, it was agreed by the Soviets and Americans that a commission would examine this on the basis of a figure of $20 billion, half of which would go to the Soviet Union. When the leaders next met at Potsdam, decentralization had replaced dismemberment as the accompaniment of disarmament and demilitarization, but during the period of occupation Germany was to be administered as a single economic unit. The occupying powers were to extract reparations from their own zones, but in addition the Soviets would be entitled to receive from the Western zones '10 per cent of industrial capital equipment as is unnecessary for the German peace economy', and '15 per cent of such usable and complete industrial capital equipment. . . as is unnecessary for the German peace economy' in return for an equivalent value of food and raw materials.[29]

The potential for conflict in such complex arrangements was enormous. For a start, there was a conflict between zonal reparations and Germany's administration as a single economic unit. This problem was made worse by the fact that the Russians gave over a sizeable part of the agricultural lands of Eastern Germany to the Poles. This increased the food shortages within Germany, making it more necessary to bring in food from outside, which in turn required German industries to be brought back into production to pay for it. The Russians remained determined that German industry and coal should primarily be used for reparations, even though they had handed over the German coalfields in Silesia to the Poles. The Western Allies were disturbed that they were expected to pay for the loss to Germany of dismantled industry, coal, and one-quarter of its agricultural land. The deputy American military governor, General Lucius Clay, emphasized the need to increase productive capacity in the Western zones even before the Potsdam meeting. The Western desire to use and develop German industrial resources was bound to increase in importance and to disturb the Soviets. If the people of a united Germany were to be fed, there would be costs to be met either by importing food or by increased industrial production and reduced dismantling for reparations.

These short-term economic costs had more serious political implications once it became clear, by early 1946, that the arguments on the Mediterranean, Eastern Europe, and Japan had produced confrontational speeches and increased tension. If control over Bulgaria and Libya were such difficult issues to agree on, how would control over Germany be resolved? If it was a battle between two rival economic and political systems, which one would prevail in a united Germany? If economic hardship could not be averted by increased production, was that not likely to increase support for communism? If it was averted, would that not only strengthen capitalism but raise the spectre of German revival?

For General Clay, the practical difficulties in the Allied Control Council stemmed in early 1946 more from the French than from the Soviets. The French demanded the right to take reparations from their own zone and the restitution of goods taken by the Germans during the war (something the Soviets were not interested in because of their 'scorched earth' policy on the Eastern front). Paris was determined to keep Germany weak, but in contrast to other powers, wanted to do this by severing areas from Western Germany (including the industrial Ruhr) and decentralizing the country. While there were Soviet–American arguments over the level of German industrial production, the nature of a German import–export programme and reparations from current production, the French were determined to sabotage any form of central planning. One vital issue was the standard of living to be accorded to the German population. The Americans were keen to bring it up to the European average, which understandably upset the Russians, whose post-war living standards were well below that average. It took until March 1946 to agree on a Level of Industry plan, but the Russians stalled on an export–import programme, claiming this was a zonal issue that could not be addressed by the Control Council before reparations had been settled and a trade surplus produced. The Russians, who had higher productivity levels in the east in both agriculture and industry, realized that they would be making economic sacrifices over imports and exports and were in effect postponing indefinitely a single import–export programme. With the Eastern zone the most self-sufficient, there were grounds for the Soviets to believe that a single import–export programme would result in them subsidizing the Western zones. On 3 May 1946, General Clay therefore suspended reparations deliveries from the Western zones, believing that zonal reparations had to be linked to a single export–import programme.[30]

At the same time, the Russians alienated the West by extending controls over their zone, including in April 1946 the forced merger of the Social Democratic Party with the German Communist Party (KPD). This move could have been part of Soviet preparations for the communization of all Germany, an indication of Soviet ambitions rather than Soviet security concerns, although a communist Germany would have been the best security option. It was in an endeavour to allay Soviet fears that a few days later on 29 April the Secretary of State, James Byrnes, had proposed a demilitarization treaty for Germany. The Soviets, whose priority remained dismantling for reparations and reparations from current production, rejected the idea. In Washington, it was assumed that this indicated the Soviets were interested in more than just security.

However, there is an alternative explanation stemming from Soviet ideology and fears. German Nazism, as other forms of fascism was, in communist eyes, a structural feature of capitalism. To prevent it re-emerging, fundamental changes in the German economy and society were needed. Demilitarization was not enough. Moreover, for security reasons it would be better, from the Soviet point of view, to ensure that the factories were dismantled to limit German war potential than to sign a disarmament treaty. For suspicious Soviet leaders, if the West were reluctant to dismantle German industry to the extent desired by Moscow, it would be important, as Molotov told Byrnes, to have inspections to ensure that disarmament measures were being enforced. Otherwise, German resources could ultimately be used against the Soviets. If the Americans were prepared to allow inspections, then the rebuilding of German industry would be less of a threat; and disarmament agreements would be more appropriate after the occupation had ended. Also, this would enable the Soviets to have a role in the more important industrial areas of Western Germany. None of this could be done by a demilitarization treaty and nor would the alternative of division provide the Soviets with any influence over the resources of the Ruhr.[31]

The value of a united or a divided Germany to the respective allies was related to security *and* economic requirements. The dismantling of German industry was linked not only to how much industrial production would enable the needs of the population to be met, but also to security and reparations. In 1946, there were advantages to the Soviets in a united Germany, whether one interprets their motives as defensive or expansionist (influence over the Ruhr and changes in, or controls over, German capitalism and society). For some Americans, like George Kennan, who discounted Soviet fears of Germany against the aggressive designs of communism and Russian imperialism, Stalin would succeed in his aim of creating a communist Germany if the country remained united. As early as March 1946, Kennan already believed it would therefore be preferable to integrate the Western zones into a Western bloc. In contrast, Clay and his associates in Germany did not believe in Soviet aggression and pointed out that the Russians had 'been meticulous in their observance of Potsdam'. There were thus clear divisions within the US administration over the desirability of a divided Germany which emerged in 1946.[32]

Whether or not Stalin had a long-term aim of dominating Germany, there were a number of possible benefits from posing as champions of German unity, which the Soviets continued to do in the summer of 1946. The British, on the other hand, who were faced with the largest zonal costs and who had little to gain but much to lose from a united Germany, were beginning to favour permanent division by May 1946. This would either enable them to exploit the Ruhr's resources more for their own benefit or ensure that the Ruhr was merged with the other Western zones to alleviate British costs. One reason for British support of a zonal merger, which the Americans favoured in July 1946, was to relieve the economic burdens of occupation. It was becoming more evident that for the West, German recovery, in whatever ultimate form, was an integral part of European recovery and therefore, as Byrnes outlined in his Stuttgart speech in September 1946, Germany would not be bled dry or dismembered.

The issue of European, as opposed to German, recovery was increasingly to be at the centre of the disagreements. With the growing need for a European recovery programme in 1947, it made the implementation of the relatively harsh Potsdam agreement more difficult for some Americans to swallow. By the time the next step towards division was taken, with the creation of the Bi-zone (the fusion of the British and American zones) in January 1947, Byrnes, it is claimed, had abandoned the idea of a united Germany out of fear it would fall prey to Soviet influence.[33] However, as the pro-'containment' group of officials in Washington favoured integrating the Western zones of Germany into a Western bloc, the Soviets made substantial concessions, which suggested that they were not primarily motivated by the desire to produce a Soviet-controlled Germany.

In October 1946, the Kolpakov proposal offered an upwards revision of the level of German industry and, once the Control Council had set the levels of current production reparations taking into account the capital removal, to institute a balanced export–import programme. That same month, the East Germans went to the polls in free elections and inflicted major losses on the Soviet-sponsored SED. The idea of communist successes through political integration would therefore depend on subversion, not elections, but the Soviets seemed to be backing away from this and emphasizing economic requirements. This gave credence to the idea, held by Clay, that it would be possible to gain influence in the Soviet zone as part of the price the Soviets were prepared to pay for the maintenance of acceptable cooperation in determining the economic future of all Germany. In particular, Clay believed that in exchange for reparations from current production the Soviets might permit democracy to develop in East Germany.[34]

In the run-up to the March CFM in Moscow, which began talks on a German peace treaty, the key issue was reparations from current production. Could this be used to secure agreement on Germany? Or would it be preferable to exclude the idea and use the resources of the Western zones for the rebuilding of Western Germany and Western Europe? Some in Washington were opposed to the former strategy and argued that a German settlement with the Soviets might not be in America's best interests. Others simply assumed that a united Germany would inevitably become communist. By the start of 1947, the British were keen to push ahead with the Bi-zone in order to produce self-sufficiency there. In Washington, even before the Moscow Council, the importance of European recovery as a means of countering communism and assisting the American and Western European economies meant that German resources in the Western zones were increasingly earmarked for that end. By March 1947, as the Moscow Council got underway, for Marshall, the Potsdam agreement to limit German industrial production to meeting German subsistence needs was no longer appropriate. Nor, for the same reasons, would it be desirable to accept reparations from current production, even though the Soviets were now prepared to accept a combined import–export programme. The bottom line was that for the US, German reparations for the Soviets had to be sacrificed in order to meet the needs of Western European recovery, which particularly required German coal, and the avoidance of starvation and unrest in Western Germany. The only compensation would be a disarmament treaty. The Soviets, on the other hand, wanted the economic benefits of reparations from current production while, for reasons of security and influence, maintaining joint controls over German industrial production. To achieve this, they were apparently prepared to accept a German Constitution based on the Weimar Republic model, with reduced executive powers and nationwide elections to decide the future governmental structure. Stalin may ultimately have been hoping for a united communist Germany at the expense of Allied cooperation, but the British and the Americans were already committed to the division of Germany in the interests of European recovery. In that sense, whether Stalin was seeking to control a communist Germany, embark on world revolution, or achieve security from right-wing German aggression made little difference. Western concessions to the Soviets would hamper German and Western European recovery, boost communism, and weaken the American and British economies.[35]

By the time the CFM met again in London in November 1947, the State Department was affirming that there were no terms under which the US would accept Germany's economic unification.[36] As in other areas of Cold War policy in the West, the approach to the German question was based on perceptions of economic and political advantages, not simply on responding to what the Soviets were doing. Even before the March 1947 meeting, many British and American policy-makers were determined to proceed with the integration of the Western zones of Germany into the Western European capitalist economy. After London, this could go ahead without further constraints and it led, in September 1949, to the creation of a West German state.

The Berlin Blockade

In February 1948, the Western powers convened a conference in London to run until June 1948 to discuss zonal policy in Germany, including control of the Ruhr, with a view to establishing a West German state. The decision to exclude the Soviets came after Stalin's objections to the currency reforms, which had been broached in the Control Council. The London Conference, with its published proposal on 6 March to incorporate the Western zones within the European recovery programme, led the Soviet Control Council representative, Marshal Sokolovsky, to walk out two weeks later. From this point on, Stalin produced a mix of coercion and diplomacy, in an endeavour to prevent the formation of a West German state strengthened by Marshall aid. The initial coercion took the form of restricting the movement of Allied personnel entering Berlin by rail and road from 1 April. The diplomacy included offers to discuss the disputed German issues on a Soviet–American basis, together with an attempt to encourage French doubts about the creation of a West German state. By June, as it seemed that a new currency would be introduced in the Western zones, the Soviets walked out of the Berlin *Kommandatura*. The following day, when the new currency was introduced in the Western zones of Germany but not in Berlin, the Soviet response was to close all surface routes into West Berlin on 24 June.

It could have been a desperate Soviet act to prevent the creation of a potentially threatening West German state or a calculated attempt to drive the West out of Berlin. More likely, perhaps, it was Stalin's attempt to prevent the former and to reopen talks on the future of Germany as a whole. If the Western Allies could be forced to reopen talks on Germany, the possibility of an economically strong West German state might be averted. Whatever interpretation is favoured, if the blockade failed to prevent a new German state, it would at least enhance the prospects of a Soviet-controlled East German state. In the West, this form of Soviet intimidation was seen as a challenge which had to be met, and an airlift was mounted to get supplies into the city of Berlin. Stalin offered to lift the blockade in August 1948 in return for a Council of Foreign Ministers on the future of Germany, and in January 1949 to end it if the establishment of a West German state was postponed. In the event, beating the blockade became a major operation which lasted 324 days and airlifted 13,000 tonnes of supplies per day.

Western leaders were determined to show resolve when, with European communist parties subverting elected governments, the morale of a war-weary European public might have fallen. An ability to retain credibility and resist pressure was important in resisting communism. On the other hand, if the crisis escalated a war-weary public might not have seen the value of an armed clash with a power that had been a key ally only three years earlier. The airlift challenged the Soviets to start a military conflict by shooting down the planes, but that was something Stalin was unprepared to contemplate in 1948. Consequently, the means chosen by the Soviet leader to try and stop the rebuilding of a capitalist western Germany led to humiliation and to further measures which proved disadvantageous to the Soviet Union.

The Berlin crisis was in many ways a symbolic crisis in a city which came to epitomize Cold War tensions until 1989. It has been regarded as an important cause of the militarization of the Cold War and the formation of NATO, although it is more plausible to see the crisis as a justification for, rather than a cause of, the formation of a Western military alliance. The crisis itself has also been interpreted as another indication of aggressive Soviet moves designed to win control of a communist Germany, but it probably stemmed from Soviet fears of a capitalist Germany being used as part of an anti-Soviet bloc. What is certain is that Stalin's ill-conceived actions, the risks they entailed, and the hardships they produced in Berlin, provided justification for those in the West who *were* seeking to construct an anti-Soviet bloc.

The airlift was ultimately successful as the Berlin blockade was lifted in May 1949, but Western resolve to see it through without concessions was not always firm. Both British and American representatives proposed compromise and a retreat from the London Conference proposals. Ultimately, those who saw the importance of Berlin as a symbol of Western resistance to communism prevailed. They feared a retreat from Berlin would drain confidence in the American commitment to Europe and lead to a withdrawal from Germany as a whole.[37] Thus, Berlin became an island of resistance to communism and a symbol of Western determination, not to defend Europe militarily against the Soviets (West Berlin was always indefensible), but to prevent the spread of communism as a political force. In addition, the crisis gave the West Germans confidence in American support and led opinion in the West to become more sympathetic to Germans only three years after the end of the Second World War. The adoption of communism was now less likely in Western Europe and Stalin's blunder had undermined Moscow's influence. This was the crux of what had become a Cold War and it explains the true significance of Berlin. Berlin was more important politically in terms of its resistance to Soviet attempts to extend communism or weaken capitalism than it was militarily in producing a Western alliance. The latter developed for reasons that were evident before the 1948–9 crisis over Berlin and were linked to a mix of fear and ambition concerning the political and economic future of Western Europe and to the links to non-European areas (see Chapter 4, B). None of this could be explained to the Western public for whom it was now easier and more advantageous to depict the Cold War, not primarily as a political or economic conflict, but as a military confrontation.

Visit the online resources that accompany this book to test your understanding and take your learning further: www.oup.com/he/young kent3e

NOTES

1. Thomas G. Paterson and J. Garry Clifford, *America Ascendant US Foreign Relations since 1939* (D. C. Heath & Co., Lexington, 1995), 34.
2. M. J. Hogan, *The Marshall Plan. America, Britain and the Reconstruction of Western Europe 1947–1952* (Cambridge University Press, Cambridge, 1987), 2–3, 427.
3. Alan Milward, *The Reconstruction of Western Europe, 1945–1951* (Methuen, London, 1984), 483, and Milward, 'Was the Marshall Plan Really Necessary', *Diplomatic History*, 2 (1989).

4. Scott D. Parrish. 'New Evidence on the Soviet Rejection of the Marshall Plan, 1947', *Cold War International History Project*, Working Paper no. 9 (1994).
5. Ibid.
6. W. LaFeber, *America, Russia and the Cold War, 1945–2000* (9th edn, McGraw-Hill, New York, 2002), 63–4, 69. Citing *Foreign Affairs*, 1947 and a telegram from the Moscow embassy to Washington, 26 May 1947 in the Papers of Joseph Jones, Truman Library.
7. Caroline Kennedy-Pipe, *Stalin's Cold War. Soviet Strategies in Europe 1943–1956* (Manchester University Press, Manchester, 1995), 59–66.
8. The time period was not in the protocols but had been stated by Stalin at the 5th Plenary Meeting at Yalta. FRUS, 1945, *Conferences of Malta and Yalta* (Dept. of State, Washington, DC, 1955), 79407.
9. Caroline Kennedy-Pipe, *Stalin's Cold War. Soviet Strategies in Europe 1943–1956* (Manchester University Press, Manchester, 1995), 60.
10. V. Zubok and C. Pleshakov, *Inside the Kremlin's Cold War from Stalin to Khrushchev* (Harvard University Press, Cambridge, 1996), 54.
11. V. Mastny, *The Cold War and Soviet Insecurity: The Stalin Years* (Oxford University Press, New York, 1996), 20.
12. Caroline Kennedy-Pipe, *Stalin's Cold War. Soviet Strategies in Europe 1943–1956* (Manchester University Press, Manchester, 1995), 123.
13. Several historians, including Caroline Kennedy-Pipe and Walter LaFeber, have claimed that the West promoted a war scare in 1948.
14. V. Mastny, *The Cold War and Soviet Insecurity: The Stalin Years* (Oxford University Press, New York, 1996), 45.
15. W. Loth, *The Division of the World 1941–1955* (Routledge, London, 1988), 169. Citing Milovan Djilas, *Gespräche with Stalin* (Hart Davis, London, 1962), 217–20.
16. Ibid., 170–1.
17. M. Schaller, *The American Occupation of Japan* (Oxford University Press, New York, 1985), 82–5.
18. Foreign Relations of the United States (FRUS), 1947, VI, 159,184. Cited in W. LaFeber, *The Clash: A History of US–Japan Relations* (W.W. Norton & Co., New York, 1997), 270–1.
19. W. LaFeber, *The Clash: A History of US–Japan Relations* (W.W. Norton & Co., New York, 1997), 273.
20. A wartime body which continued its endeavours to coordinate policy in areas of interest to the State Department and the Services.
21. M. Schaller, *The American Occupation of Japan* (Oxford University Press, New York, 1985), 109–25.
22. W. LaFeber, *The Clash: A History of US–Japan Relations* (W.W. Norton & Co., New York, 1997), 272; M. Schaller, *The American Occupation of Japan* (Oxford University Press, New York, 1985), 132–3.
23. Michael H. Hunt, *The Genesis of Chinese Communist Foreign Policy* (Columbia University Press, New York, 1996), ch. 1.
24. Suzanne Pepper, *Civil War in China: The Political Struggle 1945–1949* (2nd edn, University of California Press, Berkeley, 1999), 423–5.
25. On the above points, see O. A. Westad, 'Losses, Chances and Myths: the US and the Creation of the Sino-Soviet Alliance, 1946–1950', *Diplomatic History*, 2 (1997).
26. Chen Jian, 'The Myth of America's Lost Chance in China', *Diplomatic History*, 2 (1997).
27. O. A. Westad, 'Losses, Chances and Myths: the US and the Creation of the Sino-Soviet Alliance, 1946–1950', *Diplomatic History*, 2 (1997).
28. FRUS, 1945, *The Conferences of Malta and Yalta* (Dept. of State, Washington, DC, 1955).
29. FRUS, 1945, *The Conference of Berlin* (State Dept., Washington, DC, 1960), 1485–6.

30. Carolyn Eisenberg, *Drawing the Line: The American Decision to Divide Germany* (Cambridge University Press, New York, 1996), 210–12, 230.

31. Ibid., 228–30, 298.

32. Ibid., 224–5, citing Kennan Papers, Kennan to Secretary of State, 6 March 1946; RG 59 State Department Office of European Affairs, Box 146, Murphy to Matthews, 3 April 1946 and Matthews to Murphy 18 April 1946.

33. W. Loth, *The Division of the World 1941–1955* (Routledge, London, 1988), 124.

34. Carolyn Eisenberg, *Drawing the Line: The American Decision to Divide Germany* (Cambridge University Press, New York, 1996), 249–50, 252–4, 288.

35. Ibid., 291, 293, 314–15, 352–3.

36. FO 371/624207, FO to Lord Strang, 22 October 1947. Cited in Carolyn Eisenberg, *Drawing the Line: The American Decision to Divide Germany* (Cambridge University Press, New York, 1996), 353.

37. W. Loth, *The Division of the World 1941–1955* (Routledge, London, 1988), 244–5.

3

Empire, Cold War, and Decolonization, 1945–53

Chapter contents

A. Asia

The changes that took place within the European empires during the early years of the Cold War constituted another crucial element of the new international order after the Second World War. Often referred to as decolonization—even though colonies were not the only components of empires—these changes formed part of the broader shift in the global balance of power, with the war marking the end of the European-dominated system of nation states. It was followed by the decline of the major European powers, with international dominance lying for a quarter of a century with the US, challenged only by the Soviet Union. For many policy-makers in the European capitals, the loss of their overseas possessions was not simply about ending the formal administrative and judicial arrangements that constituted colonial rule. It was also about adjusting to the Cold War and the new forces of anti-colonialism in ways which would enhance their positions as great powers.

The challenges to colonial rule in the Indian subcontinent came from a mass-based anti-colonial movement. The Congress Party had emerged by the end of the First World War and the British had responded with a mix of concessions and repression. The economic changes, which influenced the nature and development of anti-British movements in India, also had an impact in Africa. British rule everywhere depended to an enormous extent on the collaboration of important social groups. The economic changes brought by the Second World War and production for the war effort added new difficulties to some already unstable situations. Moreover, the war brought a radically new political challenge to European colonialism. While its impact was not always immediate, and certainly not uniform, its importance as a precursor of political change is difficult to exaggerate.

In the first place, by 1942 the disastrous defeats suffered by the British, French, and Dutch in South-East Asia at the hands of a non-white people, the Japanese, dealt a massive international blow to the standing of European colonialism. If, as was the case, the indigenous people did not resist the Japanese invasion, the benefits of colonial rule had to be questioned. This was particularly so for the British, who were increasingly keen to point to the alleged value of colonial rule in nurturing and encouraging the advancement of native societies. The worst British military defeat of modern times, at Singapore in 1942, must be placed in the context of their position as rulers in South-East Asia. The indigenous inhabitants were generally not prepared to fight to preserve British colonialism and were generally indifferent as to who should rule them. The European defeats at the hands of the Japanese destroyed the myth of white supremacy, which had always underpinned colonial rule. In the second place, the Second World War was fought by the Allies as a war for freedom from Nazi oppression. The occupation of conquered territory by the Nazis was something that could not be tolerated. This was not just because of the inhumane nature of the new regimes, but because it denied people what was increasingly perceived as their legitimate right of self-determination. The publicity surrounding the Anglo-American signing of the Atlantic Charter in 1941, with its statement of the right of all peoples to choose their own governments, was a significant blow to colonialism. The war for freedom and for a new world order became exactly that, although its precise effects manifested themselves in different ways from what many at the time expected.

To comprehend the nature of the subsequent large-scale termination of colonial rule remains a complex undertaking, and explanations for the timing of the transformations are particularly difficult. Why was power transferred quickly in Sri Lanka but not in Malaya? Why was India given up when efforts were made to cling to influence in Egypt and to maintain control in East Africa? Why were so many territories granted independence in the early 1960s? Obviously, a key factor was the strength of those anti-colonial movements that were demanding the transfer of power and the establishment, often in very difficult economic circumstances, of independent nation states. The colonial powers had always to respond to these demands. Yet, at the same time, they devised policies to place relationships with their overseas possessions on new footings and, however much these were influenced by the colonial peoples' demands, they clearly affected the nature and timing of independence. Furthermore, these policies and the reaction to anti-colonial movements were to some extent determined by the nature of the Cold War and by broader perceptions of the European powers' own roles in the international system.

India

Organized political opposition to British rule in India had begun in the nineteenth century with the founding of the Congress Party in 1888. Congress was the first political organization to pose a threat to the continuation of British rule in the non-white Empire. Although dominated by educated, westernized Indians, Congress had become a broad-based mass party by the end of the First World War. It was then open to both Hindus and Muslims and could accommodate the radical, non-violent protests of Gandhi. The latter's emphasis on traditional, as opposed to Western values, was a marked contrast with the English-educated intellectual Jawaharlal Nehru (see Box 3.1), who became the party's leader in 1929 and the first Indian prime minister on independence in 1947. The inclusive nature of the Indian National Congress Party would not survive the Second World War and the religious divisions which were to scar India in the late 1940s were already significant in the 1930s.

The British have to assume some responsibility for the increasing conflict and bitterness which began to affect Hindu and Muslim communities that had happily coexisted for hundreds of years. The key point in the politicization of religious differences came with the enactment of the Government of India Act in 1935. The Act applied to those Indian provinces directly administered by the British and was designed to take the sting out of the opposition to British rule by devolving local power to the provinces while maintaining effective national control at the centre. The measure was never likely to quench the desire for independence and it enormously complicated the process of achieving it. After 1935, political power in the provinces was up for grabs and this, alongside the attempts to secure representation for both Hindus and Muslims, provided the reason for greater competition and conflict between the two communities. It eventually encouraged Congress to become a Hindu Party, as the various Muslim political groupings came to be effectively dominated by Mohammed Ali Jinnah's Muslim League.

The Second World War reinforced the politicization of these religious differences as the Muslim League grew in importance, assisted by the British. The latter perceived the Muslims as more reliable wartime partners in the wake of Gandhi's 'Quit India' campaign of civil disobedience. Both parties in Britain's wartime coalition saw this attempt to force the British to leave as a major threat to the war effort. In 1942, most of the leading members of the Congress movement were imprisoned. With the way clear for the Muslim League to strengthen its position as a political force, and therefore as a participant in any transfer of power, problems began to mount for any attempt to move India closer to independence.

By 1945, there was little doubt that India would soon become independent, despite the fact that die-hard imperialists in the Conservative and Labour parties had an emotive aversion to such a step. The issue was simply when and how. During the war, India had been offered Dominion status largely because of its importance to the war effort. In addition, the new Labour Prime Minister, Clement Attlee, was a long-time advocate of Indian independence. As a member of the Simon Commission, which looked at constitutional change in the 1930s and was responsible for the 1935 Government of India Act, Attlee had advocated Indian independence then and was the author of the Commission's minority report. The war could only have reinforced his support for Indian independence, although neither Attlee nor the Labour Party had any clear plans as to how this was to be achieved, except that the Indians should somehow be made to decide their own future.

Unfortunately, a Constitutional Assembly to do just this raised a number of difficulties. The position of the princely states, ruled indirectly by the British through the medium of 'residents' at the royal courts, was now overshadowed by the political/religious divisions in India. In order to ensure that Muslims and Hindus were fairly represented in any Constituent Assembly to determine an independent India's future, how was such a body to be elected? With Jinnah determined on a separate Muslim state, it was difficult to see a way forward to a united India. In 1946, a Cabinet mission was despatched to India to negotiate with Congress and the Muslim League on the basis of the provinces combining into three groups, one for Hindu majority provinces, one for Muslim majority ones, and one for Bengal and Assam. These groups would thus provide a third tier of government, which would be placed between the provinces and the central administration and that would still deal with foreign affairs and defence.

Unfortunately, both sides feared that accepting such a proposal would weaken their position in the constitutional battle. In the wake of the failure of the Cabinet mission, communal tensions between Muslims and Hindus erupted into large-scale violence in August 1946. The number of deaths in Calcutta ran into the thousands and, to make matters worse, there were growing doubts about the desirability of withdrawal within the government. In February 1947, in an attempt to put pressure on the Indians to agree on the mechanism by which to achieve independence, Attlee made a firm commitment of British withdrawal by June 1948.

At the forefront of those averse to Indian independence were the military, who were keen to retain bases in what was to become Pakistan. They were supported by the foreign secretary, Ernest Bevin, for broader

BOX 3.1

Biography: Jawaharlal Nehru (1889–1964)

Born in Allahabad, Nehru began his education in England at Harrow School and later attended Trinity College, Cambridge. He then qualified as a barrister at the Inner Temple, London. After his return to India in 1912, Nehru became involved in the India nationalist movement. He joined the Indian National Congress, led by Mahatma Gandhi, after the massacre at Amritsar in 1919. In 1929, Nehru was elected leader of the Congress Party, succeeding his father (Pandit) Motilal Nehru. Despite being imprisoned nine times by the British during the 1930s, Nehru worked closely with Gandhi in the campaign for Indian independence, even entering into negotiations with the British authorities. In 1947, when India and Pakistan became separate nations, Nehru was elected as India's first Prime Minister. An early act of Nehru in his new office was his decision to keep India as an independent republic within the continent, which helped it to evolve into a multiracial society of equals. He was also responsible for India's foreign policy, based on non-alignment. Nehru was popular with his people and remained in office until his death at the age of 74. His daughter, Indira Gandhi, was elected Prime Minister in 1966.

reasons of foreign policy and Britain's international standing. In essence, these were related to the problems of re-establishing Britain as a great world power, but the development of the Cold War by 1947 was also a factor. When the decision to plan for Britain's departure was taken, there were still expectations that a new world order guided by the spirit of internationalism and based on the cooperation of independent states in the UN would emerge. Even in February 1947, the Cold War had not been fully accepted and there was still the possibility that the proclamation of Indian independence would be seen in a positive way as a great power contribution to the new international order.

By then, there was an urgent need to convince the Indians to work together by giving a date on which Britain would withdraw, hence the statement of 18 February 1947. Yet the situation in India was so troublesome and the cost of attempting to resolve it by the continuation of British rule so enormous that avoiding future involvement with India's problems was a key consideration. Even so, in January 1947 Bevin urged the Prime Minister to resist pressure for withdrawal from India, fearing the consequences for Britain's position as a great world power and the subsequent loss of electoral support. Attlee, however, pointed to the lack of any viable plans to remain in India and appointed Mountbatten as the viceroy charged with securing Indian independence.

By the time Mountbatten arrived in the subcontinent in March 1947, the withdrawal date of June 1948 appeared too much like a costly dragging of British feet. Ignoring the desirability both of defence agreements before independence and of a united India, Mountbatten brought the date for the transfer of power forward to August 1947. While this helped to secure agreement between Congress and the Muslim League, it did so on the basis of two separate independent states. Congress accepted partition out of fear of even greater divisions that would lead to the Balkanization of the subcontinent. So, the independence of India was created in an unseemly rush and managed by a British plenipotentiary rather than ministers or officials in London. It brought the British little credit because population transfers between India and Pakistan were accompanied by large-scale bloodshed. Yet for all parties there was the saving grace that the creation of two new states within the British Commonwealth had spared everyone from something much less acceptable. In that respect, the transfer of power in India had revealed an important rationale for the end of empire which was to figure in future European decolonization.

Ceylon, Burma, and Indo-China

The loss of what was generally perceived as the 'jewel' in the British imperial crown helped produce the transfer of power in the rest of south Asia. During the war, both Burma and Ceylon had been promised self-government in a short space of time. For Ceylon in particular, having conceded independence for India, there seemed little reason to resist demands from moderate leaders for similar treatment when a defence agreement and membership of the Commonwealth were part of the package. Moreover, the elections of September 1946 confirmed Senanyake's United National Party as the leading political force, but in the face of a strong challenge from the communists. In 1947, strikes and disturbances in the wake of the elections only reinforced the British desire to work with the moderates in strengthening their position. There was thus every reason for the British to cooperate in the achievement of independence. Such a strategy offered the best prospects of replacing British control with British influence and avoiding the coming to power of radical leaders as the Cold War became an accepted fact of international life. Ceylon duly became the independent state of Sri Lanka in February 1948.

Burma was more problematic, and here it was less a question of working out a process with nationalist leaders than accepting the inevitable, however unpleasant. As in India, British weakness in the face of Burmese opposition was significant in determining the timing of the transfer of power. Burmese leaders were generally more distrustful of their British rulers than their Sri Lankan counterparts and Aung San, the most influential, who was head of the Anti-Fascist People's Freedom League (AFPL), could call on the Burmese 'national army', which had been created under Japanese rule. Aung San was determined to gain control of the administration without delay and to avoid any return of the old socio-economic order, based on British commercial interests and Indian migrant labour. Reluctantly, the British accepted the rapid speed of constitutional change, despite the fact that the Burmese were refusing to join the Commonwealth. The means to resist Burmese demands were simply not there and an additional concern in 1947 was the strength of the Burmese Communist Party. With the old order destroyed in all its aspects, there was no middle way for the British to pursue in Burma between armed resistance to political change or a rapid unconditional retreat from power, which was completed by January 1948.

While the British chose the path of retreat in Burma and India, the French chose to fight in Indo-China. These contrasting choices owed much to the perceptions of policy-makers in London and Paris, as well as to the situation on the ground and the strength of the opposition to colonial rule. Whereas in India a strong political movement seeking independence was already in existence before the onset of the great Depression and the Second World War, in Indo-China, Malaya, and Indonesia it was the dramatic social and economic changes in the 1930s and early 1940s that helped produce significant challenges to the continuation of European rule. Whether the extent of the change in socio-economic relations made it more likely that the colonial power would refuse to fight, as in Burma, or to embark on a bloody conflict, as in Indo-China, is a moot point.

Indo-China proved to be the longest and bloodiest of the conflicts born out of the quest for independence in Asia, and regional divisions exacerbated the subsequent struggle to control Vietnam. Tonkin, later to be known as North Vietnam, was a predominantly rural society of smallholding peasants, increasingly exploited on a sharecropping basis by absentee landlords. As population pressures mounted, those who escaped to the plantations of the south in Cochin China found themselves victims of an unregulated labour market. In South Vietnam, where the pattern of landholding was more varied, the existence of French and Chinese plantation owners provided another focus for Vietnamese discontent. When the Second World War began, the level of rural discontent in many parts of Vietnam made the situation ripe for the development of a mass-based movement opposed to foreign rule.

The leader of such a movement, created in 1941 and known as the Viet Minh, was Ho Chi Minh (see Box 3.2), a charismatic communist figure with experience of both China and the Soviet Union. Emphasizing the nationalist characteristics of the organization, Ho maintained communist control and established strongholds in many parts of Vietnam during the war. The Japanese left a puppet French Vichy administration in control until March 1945, which further eroded the legitimacy of the French regime in the eyes of many Vietnamese peasants, who retained a strong sense of hierarchy and authority. Food shortages added to the loss of French acceptability as rulers and produced growing internal support for the Viet Minh. Externally, Ho Chi Minh and his supporters received encouragement from the wartime Roosevelt administration and the Office of Strategic Services, the predecessor of the Central Intelligence Agency, because they were initially viewed predominantly as an anti-colonial nationalist movement. More significant were the military supplies that Ho and his forces were able to obtain from the Chinese. Thus, in the North the Viet Minh had established a viable government in Hanoi by August 1945. In the South, where the British, with some assistance from their former Japanese enemies, began to re-establish control in September, the situation was rather different. French settlers and the provisional French government in Paris had no intention of allowing a nationalist movement to control a united Vietnam. As the French began to pour forces into Indo-China, the stage was set for confrontation, despite the weakening of colonialism that the war had brought.

The weak French position did, however, contribute to the attempts to negotiate an agreement with Ho Chi Minh in 1946. The discussions took place as the constitution of the Fourth Republic was being drawn up. Central to the new republic's constitution was the Union Française (French Union) which, in imperial terms, was designed to reconcile the irreconcilable. It was made up of the indivisible French Republic, which along with metropolitan France included what was termed Overseas Territories and a number of Associated States, like those in Indo-China, which would achieve internal autonomy. Colonialism was therefore, in theory, abolished because within the republic 'one and indivisible', its individual citizens would eventually all be assimilated as equals with the same rights as metropolitan Frenchmen. Associated states would, the French claimed, willingly accept their new constitutional position. One contradiction was that if all the citizens of the French Empire were equal within a single republic, then those of metropolitan France would be outnumbered and the former Empire's subservience would be ended. Hence the structure of the Union, while proclaiming equality, had to ensure the dominance of metropolitan France, 'freely consented to', not least through the power granted to the French president as head of the Union Française. Another contradiction emerged in Indo-China where the essence of the problem was that Ho Chi Minh, while prepared to consent freely to

BOX 3.2

Biography: Ho Chi Minh (1890–1969)

Born in Kim-lien, North Vietnam, Ho Chi Minh was educated at a Franco-Annamite school. He worked as a teacher and a seaman before moving to England in 1915 and France in 1917. He became a founder member of the French Communist Party in 1920. Three years later Ho Chi Minh moved to Moscow and studied at the East University. In 1924, he travelled to China as a translator with the Soviet consulate in Canton and began to organize the Vietnamese nationalist movement. However, in 1927 Ho Chi Minh returned to Moscow after the split between the Chinese Nationalists and the communists. In 1930, he founded the Indo-Chinese Communist Party. He then escaped to Moscow in 1932, after being arrested as a revolutionary by the French, only to return to China five years later. In 1941, he formed the communist-dominated Vietnam League for Independence, the Viet Minh.

During the Second World War, he organized the Viet Minh in guerrilla raids against the Japanese. In 1945, Ho entered Hanoi and declared Vietnam an independent republic, with himself as president. But when the French returned, they refused to accept Vietnamese independence and a military struggle followed between 1946 and 1954, until the French were defeated at Dien Bien Phu. At the Geneva conference of 1954, Ho accepted the division of Vietnam along the 17th parallel and became President of the North. He supported the Viet Cong guerrillas who fought against South Vietnam and the US during the Second Indo-China War. When the South's capital, Saigon, fell to the North Vietnamese Army in 1975, it was renamed Ho Chi Minh City in his honour.

membership of some form of union, would only do so on the basis of an independent state first having the freedom to consent. For the French, the indivisibility of the French Union meant that no state could exist independently outside the Union and subsequently join on the lines of the British Commonwealth. On this barrier the talks broke down, while in Indo-China the determination of the French military and the settlers to reimpose control soon led to confrontation. In November 1946, the French bombardment of Haiphong marked the beginning of what was to become a protracted military struggle for control over a united Vietnam.

By 1947, the Viet Minh had become a guerrilla force and the French were seeking viable collaborators whom they could use to attract support away from Ho Chi Minh and his campaign for independence. The first figure to play such a role was the titular emperor Bao Dai who, despite his Catholic religion, did have some credibility as a supporter of Vietnamese nationalism. The problem was that, if the French were to increase his standing, they would have to offer the kind of meaningful concessions on independence that they had refused to offer to Ho Chi Minh. Catholic or communist made no difference to this fundamental issue, although the French were subsequently to emphasize the importance of combating the latter, particularly to the Americans. What mattered to the French was the impact of the loss of Vietnam to their position as a global power. It was a position constructed on the basis of a French Union which embodied the formal end of colonialism, but retained French domination under a new guise and refused to consider either independence or self-government. Unlike the British case, the constraints and contradictions it embodied made political concessions in the overseas territories to even the most pro-Western indigenous leaders extremely difficult to make.

B. Africa

French West Africa

In order to win African support for the Fourth Republic at the end of the war, the French, given the political constraints imposed by the Union Française, chose to rely on social and economic reform combined with greater representation in Paris for increased numbers of Africans. Those Africans who were deemed to have the required attributes of French civilization could qualify for the same rights as metropolitan Frenchmen and send significantly more representatives to the French Parliament. This still meant, however, that even educated Africans with full voting rights could wield no effective power in Paris or the local capitals. In French West Africa, prior to 1956, the right to vote did not enable Africans to elect members of local representative bodies with any executive or administrative functions. In Paris, the effective domination of the legislative assembly was difficult enough for metropolitan parties, let alone a limited number of African representatives. The growing African realization of this fact during the late 1940s was to change the focus of African political parties. It was also, eventually, to contribute significantly to the acceptance by the Ministry of Overseas France that neither social and economic reform, nor the ending of some of the worst abuses of pre-war French colonialism, would satisfy the demands of Africans. Meaningful political change would eventually be needed if the French were to continue to exert influence in Africa.

The impact of social and economic changes in the post-war African colonies should not, however, be dismissed entirely. The French in particular spent large sums of money under the Fonds d'Investissement Economiques et Socials (FIDES) programme, especially in the 1950s. If the effects were minimal, it was largely due to the nature and scale of the African developmental problem. Geography and demography, along with the linkages to the international capitalist economy, which were established before as well as during colonialism, and which were far from dependent on the continuation of European rule, made significant economic progress difficult to achieve. The principle of metropolitan taxpayers contributing to the benefit of colonial subjects through the development of the colonial economies was nevertheless accepted by both the British and the French by the end of the Second World War. Unfortunately, in the immediate post-war period the practice was to a large extent compromised by the economic needs of European recovery.

In the French case, it was the conference of colonial governors which met in Brazzaville in January 1944 that produced the commitment to provide public money for social and economic development. Africans were also to be wooed by the ending of forced labour and the *indegénat*, a system of justice whereby the French colonial authorities could imprison Africans without trial. Political reforms which might lead to independence were firmly excluded, although the tradition of assimilation[1] was questioned at Brazzaville, where there was some support for decentralization. In the end, these issues were left to the drafters of the new constitution to resolve and here the interests of metropolitan France were clearly paramount. The wartime importance of French Equatorial and later West Africa as a base for the Gaullist opponents of Vichy did not produce a desire to provide political benefits to Africans in Africa. There was to be no form of independence or equality in the foreseeable future and there were no Africans at Brazzaville even for consultation. Imperial questions of France's world role meant that France's African territories and the majority of their inhabitants would only receive greater freedom and status within a political structure, one still dominated by metropolitan France.

This was in contrast not only to British actions in South Asia, but also to the thrust of their West African policy, which was galvanized by events in the Gold Coast that began in 1948 with serious disturbances in Accra. As the war drew to a close, the French had sought to cooperate with the British over colonial policy in West Africa, partly so that in technical matters mutual benefits for Africans might occur, but primarily to keep out what they saw as American imperialism and the involvement of international bodies. Such proposed bodies would operate on a regional basis and would be accountable to the new United Nations. The French hoped that, by an association with the British, such bodies could be pre-empted. In the event, nothing came of the proposed regional commissions under international auspices, but the French, and to a lesser extent the British, became concerned to avoid any UN involvement in the affairs of non-self-governing territories, other than the former Mandates which were now placed under Trusteeship.

By the beginning of the 1950s, international pressures through the UN were on the increase and the very basis of the French Union was under threat in Africa from new internal and external forces. With the Cold War after 1947, those concerned with maintaining France's international standing could portray the nationalist challenges more as ones directed by the forces of international communism. These were certainly influential in Indo-China but were much weaker in Black Africa and the Magreb (North Africa). However, the fact that the Rassemblement Démocratique Africain (RDA), an interterritorial political grouping established in 1946, was associated with the French Communist Party (PCF) clearly offered the possibility of communist advances. Africans had initially been attracted to the communists prior to May 1947 when they were part of the coalition government. After that date, when the communists left the French government and adopted a strategy of subversion rather than cooperation, the threat they presented was more menacing. This coincided with serious disturbances in Madagascar, which began in

March 1947 and which remained out of control until July.[2] They were partly inspired by a general process in much of the French Empire stemming from reactions to reform and the nationalist/communist challenge. In broad terms, as the process of reform began, French settlers and merchant firms, fearing their economic and political interests threatened, began to react to changes in the colonies and the metropole. They and those focused on the general issue of French status in the post-war world were given a fresh impetus by the Cold War, which in turn was to produce a reaction in Africa. In Madagascar, this reaction was expressed in attacks on settlers by indigenous groups based on the wartime growth of secret societies. By August, the socialist Minister of Overseas France, Marius Moutet, wondered, after reading some intelligence reports on Africa, whether the problems were 'premonitory symptoms of a vast disintegration in our Overseas Territories, which is tending, following Indo-China and Madagascar to create new fronts of agitation and conflict'.[3] As the Cold War became firmly linked to disturbances in the colonies and the possible disintegration of France's overseas territories, the need for French resistance was strengthened. Support could be garnered on a mix of international and colonial fronts for repressive policies in Black Africa. In the Ivory Coast, where the RDA was strong, the French attempted to smash the party in 1949 and a series of violent incidents provoked or encouraged by the administration occurred between the RDA and its local African opponents. Strikes and boycotts created a serious situation, which led to the banning, in February 1950, of RDA meetings throughout French Africa. However, the dangers inherent in this policy of confrontation, which contrasted with the British response to the disturbances in Accra, were soon obvious.

The French were now dealing with a major war in Indo-China that was increasingly dependent on American assistance. When René Pleven, one of the architects of the Brazzaville reforms, became Prime Minister in July 1950, it was clear that the French lacked the ability to cope with a multitude of conflicts through the use of force. Pleven therefore sought, as in 1944, to mollify African opinion, which was now more politicized, and to isolate the communists by a combination of social and now political reforms based on electoral changes. François Mitterrand was sent to persuade the Ivory Coast leader of the RDA, Félix Houphouet-Boigny, to break with the PCF and affiliate to his Union Démocratique et Sociale de la Résistance (UDSR) party. Measures against the colour bar were introduced, along with greater African involvement in elections, but while the French had extended the hand of collaboration, it contained nothing of substance.[4] The problem remained that whoever was elected by whom, African deputies in the French Parliament remained essentially as supplicants to, or dependent on, French political parties. In Black Africa, progress towards self-government or even *s'administrer euxmêmes* remained dead in the water as long as local assemblies were given no administrative or legislative powers and remained merely advisory bodies.

International pressures now stemmed more from the UN and from the greater American interest in Black Africa, which was apparent from early 1950 with the conference in Lourenço Marques of consular and diplomatic representatives. It was followed by the reorganization of the State Department, which allowed for the creation of regional bureaux. Conflicts, as in Indo-China might be avoided and opportunities denied to communists if the French were to move more towards the kind of political concessions made by the British in their West African territories of Nigeria and the Gold Coast. To some extent this view was shared by the French Foreign Ministry (the Quai d'Orsay) in the early 1950s, who had a very different view from the Ministry of Overseas France on how to deal with African political movements and build up resistance to communism. In essence, by 1951 the Quai d'Orsay was in favour of greater cooperation with Britain on colonial matters concerned with political change. The ultimate aim was to create a West African Federation, which would be one of a number of federations linking European colonial territories with France and Britain in a new and close association. In part, this stemmed from the Quai's disillusionment with the French Union, which they believed was unacceptable to international opinion and less attractive to Africans than the British policy of granting self-government. Cooperating with the British in a West African federation would involve granting greater autonomy to French territories, together with Anglo-French joint policies on constitutional change and the problem of anti-colonial/anti-Western movements.[5] Regionalism and autonomy would provide an alternative attraction to nationalism and the centralism associated with assimilation. The Ministry of Overseas France was firmly opposed to such suggestions and it was to be several more years before the concept of a 'republic one and indivisible' ceased to be a barrier to moves to granting powers to local bodies in French West Africa.

British West Africa

The British granting of local powers to elected African representatives began in the 1940s and accelerated after the war. It was a process which involved social and economic development as well as political change, but it was influenced by broader imperial and international requirements. In this mix of conflicting intergovernmental pressures, Britain's post-war economic needs ran counter to the desire to use political concessions to attract pro-Western Africans who would cooperate in the process of handing over power. Again, there was a blend of Cold War goals to ensure that left-wing, 'irresponsible' Africans were excluded and traditional desires to maintain British as well as Western influence under a new guise could be met. The ultimate aim was to use new links with the colonies to reflect and preserve the world power status that was deemed the sine qua non by British elites. More specifically, in Africa the aim was the 'substitution of a relationship of friendly association for that of benevolent domination' in order that Britain could emerge as a 'leader of free associates rather than a commander of a band of subordinates'. To achieve this, it was necessary to devise machinery to 'substitute links of consultation for links of control' to avoid 'the very real danger of the ultimate dissolution of the colonial part of the British Commonwealth'.[6] The Colonial Office therefore became committed to taking initiatives to control and manage the process of political and constitutional change, but after the riots in Accra the British were always playing catch up in terms of pre-empting African protests. Political concessions never bought the hoped-for time that was believed necessary to provide greater social and economic benefits for Britain's African subjects.

The riots in the Gold Coast stemmed from economic dissatisfaction with the post-war regime, as much as from a desire for independence from Britain. Having lost out in the battle to benefit colonial producers, the Colonial Office had to rely on political means to appease African dissatisfaction. In a sense, the concessions stimulated further African political awareness and indicated that the best way of securing more economic benefits would be to escape external controls through the achievement of independence. A process of constitutional change designed to head off nationalist demands began and, in 1946, a new constitution was introduced essentially to give the Legislative Council an unofficial majority of Africans. By then, Africans had been appointed as assistant district officers in the colonial administration and town councils with elected majorities established in Accra, Cape Coast, and Sekondi. The reforms had at first been welcomed but then resented. By 1947, cocoa growers were being badly hit by swollen shoot disease and food prices in the rural areas were affected by low rainfall, while the loss of the wartime American air-staging base in Accra had increased unemployment.[7] Import prices had also been rising, as the British throughout the empire restricted imports to the colonies to preserve dollar resources for the United Kingdom itself.

That same year, the United Gold Coast Convention Party was founded, demanding 'self-government in the shortest possible time'. Discontent was on the verge of combining with organized anti-colonialism when the riots erupted in Accra in February 1948. Coming at a crucial time in the Cold War, and when the Colonial Office assumption was that anti-colonial forces were being contained and pre-empted, the scale of the disturbances caused a mixture of shock and outrage. New security measures involving the British counter-intelligence service, MI5, and the Gold Coast police reflected the belief that the riots, while inspired by social and economic discontent, must have been organized by communists or those who were influenced by communism. A commission of inquiry was soon set up, which reported within four months. Rather than identifying the communist problem, the Watson Report, although exceeding its remit, was extremely critical of the colonial government, and was described by one historian as 'one of the most important documents produced in the colonial period of not only Ghanaian history but also of modern African history'.[8] From then on, even though the British believed they could control developments, they were often taken by surprise by events which outstripped their expectations. The British failed to appreciate the growth of political consciousness and its translation into a movement for national independence. If, unlike in India, the British were not desperately seeking an avenue of escape, the pace of their retreat in the Gold Coast, however cooperative, was much more rapid than they expected.

The constitutional criticisms of the Watson Report were addressed by a British-appointed committee, composed entirely of Africans, who were expected to produce the necessary constitutional remedies. The Coussey Committee included members of the United Gold Coast Convention (UGCC) party who were deemed sufficiently 'responsible' to cooperate on, essentially, British terms in the transfer of power. The thrust of the recommendations was generally in line with Colonial Office thinking as, unlike their French counterparts, British officials were prepared to accept the transfer of power and the self-government that went with it. The issues were how, when, and to whom.

The British hope was that the Coussey proposals would enable them to control the pace of change. In 1948, a Committee on Youth Organization had been established within the UGCC by Kwame Nkrumah (see Box 3.3), an American-educated former schoolteacher. Nkrumah was a radical nationalist with left-wing beliefs and associations who was sometimes unfairly depicted as a communist detainee but who was less inclined to accept the gradualism with which the Colonial Office wished to approach self-government. In June 1949, Nkrumah formed his Committee into the Convention People's Party, which soon wrested the initiative from the British and the UGCC. Campaigning on the slogan of 'Self-Government Now', Nkrumah, to British surprise, quickly built support and established a political machine, which was more dynamic and had greater mass appeal than that of the UGCC. The reforms which were introduced included ministerial government and a legislative assembly with representatives from the whole of the Gold Coast. But they were measures which were seen as limiting the kind of radicalism Nkrumah represented. Crucially, ministers were responsible to the executive council and therefore to the governor who retained reserve powers over the whole constitution. It was a long way from 'Self-Government Now'.

In January 1950, Nkrumah launched 'Positive Action' in the form of a general strike but the colonial government prevented any serious violence and most of the leaders of the protest, including Nkrumah, were arrested, charged, and convicted. If there were expectations that this was another stage in containing radicalism and ensuring that the elections in early 1951 would be won by moderates, they were again to be mistaken. One leading member of the CPP, K. A. Gbedemah, had remained at large and was able to maintain the party organization. When municipal elections were held later in 1950, the CPP swept the board. As the registration for the assembly elections got underway, it became clear that the CPP was better equipped to assist in this process than the chiefs. When the CPP repeated their electoral success in 1951, even managing to gain twenty-nine seats from the collegiate electoral system, it was clear that Britain had to reckon with a mass-based political party demanding independence.

The next stage of the transfer of power was facilitated by the approach of the post-Accra riots governor, Charles Arden-Clarke, who had never believed in the idea that the Cold War involved African communists hiding under every bush. He was also aware that neither a commitment to democracy, nor to the retention of British influence, could be secured with the leader of the largest political party in gaol. Nkrumah was therefore released and persuaded to cooperate with Arden-Clarke and the British in transferring power to himself and the CPP. In the Gold Coast, this was to be a straightforward democratic process and the Africanization of government at all levels continued apace.

The smooth transfer of power was still dependent to some extent on the close cooperation between Nkrumah and the governor, which would avoid conflict and hopefully establish the kind of good

BOX 3.3

Biography: Kwame Nkrumah (1909?–72)

Born in Nekroful, Western Gold Coast (now Ghana) and educated at Catholic mission schools, Nkrumah trained to be a teacher in Accra in 1926. Later he travelled to the US and took degrees at Lincoln and Pennsylvania universities. Nkrumah then moved to London in 1945 and studied law. He was active in the West African Students' Union, and when he returned to the Gold Coast in 1947, he became leader of the UGCC. After being forced to resign in 1949 over his 'Positive Action' campaign, which included widespread agitation and civil disobedience, Nkrumah formed his own political party called the Convention People's Party (CPP). In 1950, he was imprisoned by the British as a subversive but was released in 1951 following a landslide victory by the CPP. He was elected the first Prime Minister of the Gold Coast in 1952 and five years later the Gold Coast became the first black African colony to achieve independence and took the name of Ghana. Nkrumah declared Ghana a republic in 1960 and decreed himself president for life in 1964 and banned all opposition parties. In 1966, he was deposed while on a visit in Peking and the Ghanaian people reacted with jubilation. He died in exile.

post-independence relations that the British valued as a means of preserving influence. Arden-Clarke was able to persuade Oliver Lyttelton, the new colonial secretary under the 1951 Churchill government, of the value of this strategy, even though there were many in the Conservative Party who fought shy of the idea of independence. Thus, Britain kept control of foreign and defence policy, along with the police, while in 1952 Nkrumah assumed the title of prime minister as the executive council became the Cabinet. In 1953, the British accepted that the legislative assembly should be directly elected and after fresh elections in June 1954 the CPP again emerged victorious.

The only cloud on the horizon was the emergence in Ashanti of an opposition party seeking independence on the basis of a federal system. Eventually, Nkrumah and the CPP were forced to undergo another electoral trial before the Gold Coast became independent in March 1957. In a sense, the importance of the process in the Gold Coast seemed a model success but although Ghana joined the Commonwealth it contained the seeds of failure that were to sprout in other areas of British Africa. The model was applied, as much out of necessity as choice in Nigeria, which also received a new Constitution in 1946 in order to remain in step with the Gold Coast. The same process of Britain reacting to events, perhaps in ways which accelerated the development of anti-colonialism, was to be evident in Nigeria.

East and Central Africa

In 1952, a rebellion broke out among the Kikuyu people of Kenya which was to bedevil the transfer of power in a colony that had to confront the interests of white settlers. The latter were more in evidence in Central Africa, where in 1953 the British created the 'Central African Federation' that ultimately presented an even bigger problem. It was not resolved until 1980. The Federation contained the territories of Nyasaland and Northern and Southern Rhodesia, but the latter had achieved an anomalous position under the Crown in 1923 as a self-governing territory. This enabled its settlers to benefit from the allocation of most of the land to white farmers, while promoting pass laws and colour bars that discriminated against non-whites. After the war, the Colonial Office feared that the Rhodesian settlers might turn to the exponents of a similar and even more pernicious and exploitative system in South Africa. Broader imperial concerns about the spread of South African economic power and influence also provided an incentive for the creation of an economically strong federation. Whites in Northern Rhodesia would be united with their more numerous equivalents in the south, providing an alternative to joining with the Union of South Africa. Pressure for federation came from their leader, Roy Welensky, who had risen through the trade union ranks and from the old-fashioned reactionary, Godfrey Huggins, Prime Minister of Southern Rhodesia, and later Lord Malvern. In 1960, he continued to believe the African was a 'decent fellow' provided things were explained to him, but that, 'he is being carried away by people who have been to Britain and America and have come back with left wing-ideas in their heads'.[9] What was established with ease in 1953 was to prove far more difficult to unravel in the early 1960s. It had to confront the problems and dilemmas of a multiracial society which were largely absent from West Africa.

By the time the problems became urgent in the late 1950s, there was more pressure from external sources to respond to the alleged needs of a changing Cold War world. These needs reflected the importance of regional and global requirements as opposed to the needs of individual colonies. In essence, this meant transferring power to the right people at the right time generally on the basis of negative, short-term goals (out of fear of more instability or outside interference) and the formality of Commonwealth membership. The Colonial Office's hope of building Western-orientated states, with sound economic prospects, education, and welfare, was even more difficult to attain. In East and Central Africa, settlers were able to influence governments in the colonial capitals as well as in London. As a result, there was to be less opportunity for establishing a basis for cooperation and compromise over the nature and timing of the end of British rule. Racial problems had already contributed to a guerrilla war in 1952 in Kenya and were eventually to become a key factor in the abrupt ending of British rule in Central Africa.

C. The Middle East

The Middle East, perhaps more than any other region has suffered from a multitude of conflicts and rivalry. Imperialism and the struggles against it have formed part of a post-war landscape that has also witnessed disputes over oil and water, superpower competition for influence, inter-Arab rivalry, and the conflict over Palestine and the fate of its peoples. It is an area which, particularly in the immediate post-war world, had a geopolitical and strategic significance because of its position at the meeting of three continents and the scene of large-scale battles between European powers. Yet colonialism in its purest form was largely absent by the end of the Second World War. French influence was no longer significant, and apart from the mandated territory and the colonies of Aden and Cyprus, British rule did not formally exist. Even in the Gulf in 1945, responsibility remained that of the India Office until 1947, while the Anglo-Egyptian condominium of the Sudan was the responsibility of the Foreign Office.

What existed in the region, dominated by the British, were less formal means of projecting and symbolizing power. In the inter-war years, this informal empire had involved considerable power and influence. In the 1920s, Britain exercised its mandatory responsibilities in Iraq by bombing its peoples; in Egypt, before 1945, it overthrew governments by both direct and indirect means, and was able to manipulate the king, the notables, and the nationalist party of the pashas, the Wafd, to maintain significant influence over the government. Informal empire was no longer able to operate in such ways after the war as British power declined, yet the importance of the region to the British increased (see Box 3.4).

This did not involve a process of decolonization but the abandonment of an ability to project power which was seen at the time, if not since, as a much more significant retreat than the abandonment of India or the moves towards self-government in South Asia and Africa. What was at issue in the Middle East was not nation-building nor the exercise of paternalism, but the future of the British Empire as a world system and the kind of world role Britain should play. Here there was no prospect of replacing control with influence, even if British domination had been more benevolent. It was a question of acknowledging to the world that Britain no longer had the power to exercise dominance in the Middle East and for that there was no substitute; no Commonwealth finesse could disguise this impotence and, if it was accepted, the implications were perceived as disastrous for Britain's status and prestige as a world power. British elites, always keen to maintain an international position, which reflected their superior social status at home, could not willingly accept such a loss of power. Therefore, it became vital to maintain the symbols of power in the hope that what little real power did remain would be buttressed by the Americans.

Palestine

Before that, a British failure occurred in Palestine which was reminiscent of the retreat from India, but without an agreement to go with the bloodshed. Palestine had become a major problem in the wake of the Balfour Declaration of 1917 and the establishment of the mandate six years later. The Palestine question was complicated by disputes over what constitutes Palestine, as the administrative units of the Roman and Ottoman empires had different boundaries from those established by the European powers after the defeat of Turkey in the First World War. Yet at one level the issue was very simple: a dispute over land between two people who believe their claims are justified. The Balfour Declaration gave British support to the establishment of a Jewish 'national home' in Palestine and the mandate confirmed this on the understanding that it was not prejudicial to the welfare of the native inhabitants. There was of course no inherent reason why two people could not coexist side by side within the same territory, but the Zionist movement which had developed since the end of the nineteenth century wanted the establishment of a Jewish *state* rather than the creation of a Jewish *homeland*. Almost immediately, this

BOX 3.4

The Post-War Importance of Maintaining the Vital Middle Eastern Interests of the British Empire

'the Middle East is therefore a region of life and death consequence for Britain and the British empire in four ways'

(a) as an indispensable channel of communications between the empire's western, eastern and southern territories;

(b) as a strategic centre, control of which would enable an enemy to disrupt and destroy a considerable part of the British imperial system and to deprive Britain herself of many supports and resources essential to her status and influence as a major power;

(c) as the empire's main reservoir of mineral oil;

(d) as a region in which British political method must make good if the British way of life is to survive.

Source: (CAB 66/67, CP(45)55 War Cabinet Memo by Sir E. Grigg 2 July 1945).

produced difficulties, as by 1920 Jewish immigration into Palestine had increased nearly five-fold and in 1921 Palestinian Arabs took to the streets of Jaffa in protest. The British subsequently made a number of efforts to deal with the rights of Arabs and Jews in Palestine and the issues arising from significant Jewish immigration. They were attempts to reconcile the irreconcilable.

A serious outbreak of communal violence in 1929 led to two commissions under Sir William Shaw and Sir John Hope-Simpson, which examined the causes of the riots and the problems they presented. The conclusions were that the attacks stemmed from 'Arab feelings of animosity and hostility to the Jews consequent upon the disappointment of their political and national aspirations and fear for their economic future'. The latter was understandable, given Hope-Simpson's assessment that there was 'no margin of land available for agricultural settlement by new immigrants'. However, the British could only ban further immigration at the expense of the commitment to a Jewish national home and so the fundamental contradiction of the Palestine mandate was to remain. In the wake of the Arab revolt of 1936, which required significant numbers of British troops to put down, the Peel Commission in 1937 recommended the partition of Palestine. However, this solution was unacceptable to the Arabs and as the Second World War approached the prospect of further disturbances, which would require the deployment of troops, led the British government to abandon the idea. As a further gesture to the Arab world, the British also imposed Jewish immigration quotas of 10,000 per year for five years plus 25,000 refugees. This coincided with the rise of Nazi persecution and genocide, which many European Jews were to experience as a result.[10]

The British were therefore in a tricky situation as the war drew to a close and boat-loads of refugees made desperate attempts to obtain sanctuary in Palestine. Their attempts to escape from it were based less on a solution acceptable to both parties (which did not exist) than on getting the US to assist in determining and then imposing one, which would be least hated. An Anglo-American Committee of Inquiry was set up in 1945. In 1946, it proposed the establishment of a bi-national state still under the supervision of the mandatory power and the entry of 100,000 Jews. The British government was not happy with the immigration proposal, nor with being left with sole responsibility for Palestine. Further discussions by British and American officials to resolve these issues produced the Morrison–Grady report, which placed a new emphasis on partition: separate and autonomous political units would be created under international supervision. As the solutions of partition or a bi-national state were debated within the British government, the American President, Harry Truman, decided to make a statement in support of the immediate entry of 100,000 Jews. This would affect decisions on the actual divisions in Palestine which had not yet been determined and effectively killed off the idea of Anglo-American cooperation in a solution to the Palestine problem. In the autumn of 1946, the British brought Zionist representatives together with those from Arab states in a final attempt to reach a settlement, but the effort proved counter-productive in that Arab leaders competed with each other to champion the Palestinian cause, making any compromise even more unlikely.

Meanwhile, the situation on the ground was continuing to worsen from the British point of view. Although the Arab Mufti of Jerusalem supported the Germans, the British were reluctant to create distinct Jewish forces for the war effort. Their concerns about their position in the broader Middle East created strong support for policies which were acceptable to Arab leaders and delayed the formation of a separate Jewish army, thereby hampering the creation of well-trained Jewish forces, except those who were incorporated individually into the British Army. The war in that sense increased the incentives to establish a Jewish organization which would be placed to wage a campaign against Palestinian Arabs, so as to establish a Jewish state. It also encouraged the development of underground Jewish forces in the Hagana, which had been created in 1920. Given the lack of Palestinian unity and the persistence of different political groupings, the British were the only organized force in the way of Zionist ambitions at the end of the war and some Jews were prepared to use all means to remove them. As a result, Arab nationalism and the Palestinian revolt were now accompanied by an anti-British Jewish campaign from 1942 onwards. Between 1944 and 1946 the Stern Gang and the Irgun, Jewish terrorist groups, carried out a number of operations against British forces. With the involvement of two future Israeli prime ministers, they also assassinated the Minister of State in the Middle East, Lord Moyne, and blew up the British military headquarters at the King David Hotel in Jerusalem, killing ninety-one people, including Jewish and Arab civilians.

BOX 3.5

Biography: David Ben-Gurion (1886–1973)

Born in Plonsk, Poland, Ben-Gurion attended local Jewish schools in Poland before emigrating to Palestine in 1906. He worked as a farm labourer and became an active Zionist. At the universities of Salonika and Constantinople, he studied law but was forced to leave Turkey in 1915 because of his Zionist activities. During the First World War, he fought against the Turks in Palestine. Ben-Gurion became Secretary General of the Jewish Labour Federation from 1921 to 1930, when he was elected leader of the Mapai Party. In 1935, he was appointed chairman of the Jewish Agency, the executive body of the World Zionist Organization. When the state of Israel was proclaimed in 1948, he became the first prime minister and minister for defence. He held these positions until 1953 and then again from 1955 to 1963, when he retired. He briefly returned to politics from 1965 to 1967 to lead the breakaway Labour (Rafi) Party, but resigned his seat in Parliament in 1970.

With violence on the increase by 1947 the British were reluctant to try and hold the ring in Palestine, even though in 1946 the military had argued that its retention was vital for their position in the region. Consequently, in February 1947, in the same month that Attlee announced the date of the British withdrawal from India, the government agreed to place the Palestine problem in the hands of the United Nations. The UN set up a Special Committee on Palestine (UNSCOP), which in August 1947 duly came out in favour of the partition of Palestine and the creation of a Jewish state. The partition solution was accepted by the Zionists and endorsed by the UN General Assembly in November 1947. It was a settlement which gave the Jews 56 per cent of the land when they constituted less than one-third of the population. The Arabs had never accepted the principle that they should give up their land to save significant numbers of Jewish refugees from the Holocaust, especially when the vast areas of Europe and North America were reluctant to share any of the burden. Neither were the British prepared to take up the burden of implementing the UN-devised settlement and, in the wake of the partition plan, London announced in September that all British forces would be withdrawn by May 1948.

The hanging of murdered and booby-trapped British soldiers had caused bitter feelings in post-war Britain, but the reasons for the withdrawal were more complex. They were partly financial, partly inherent in the realization that there was no settlement that both parties could accept, and partly because Britain's position could be maintained through a military presence in Egypt. In addition, there was a sense that Palestine was going to continue to be a source of trouble and it might therefore pay the British to wash their hands of the matter. It was believed that, if a Jewish state were established, blame would be focused on the Americans, with the British able to claim to the Arab world that they had done their best to work out a solution. Once partition was agreed, they could claim, on the back of an abstention in the UN, that they had not supported partition. By then refusing to be involved with its imposition, they would preserve some kudos in the Arab world. In that sense, it was not the first stage of a planned retreat from the Middle East but the mark of a renewed commitment to stay, and to attempt to get Arab support for that presence.

However, that support was far from guaranteed. Already in 1945, the Egyptians had requested that the British withdraw in peacetime from Egypt. Concerned as always with their military position within the region as a whole, the British military agreed to do so in the spring of 1946, when they still assumed it would be possible to retain Palestine. Unfortunately, an agreement was never ratified, because the rest of 1946 was taken up with arguments over the conditions under which the base would be maintained and reoccupied in times of conflict. By 1947, the position in Palestine was rather different and that year saw Britain facing the prospect of a military withdrawal. The military then claimed that large numbers of troops were necessary in Egypt in peacetime in order to defend the Middle East, which by 1951 was to bring them into serious conflict with the Egyptians.

With the UN acceptance of the partition in Palestine, conditions there deteriorated rapidly. British forces were no longer concerned with efforts to maintain law and order, as they were preoccupied with a safe and dignified withdrawal by May 1948. From November 1947 onwards, Palestine became the location for a civil war as Arabs and Jews battled for position and strategic advantage. Initial Arab attacks on Jews in Haifa, Tel Aviv, and other cities and the formation of a Palestinian force to resist partition, were followed by an attempted siege of Jerusalem. As spring broke, however, Jewish forces broke out and by March 1948 had gained control of the areas allocated to the Jews by the UN and began to seize Arab territory in Palestine. By the time the state of Israel was established on the departure of the British on 14 May 1948, the Palestine army was in disarray and many thousands of Arabs fled their homes. The following day Israel was attacked by the armed forces of Egypt, Jordan, Syria, and Iraq, thereby beginning the first Arab–Israeli war which, in three phases was to last until early 1949.

The first phase ended in June 1948 with a truce that was broken briefly in July. By September, the UN mediator, Sweden's Count Bernadotte, had produced a plan for the repartition of Palestine. He proposed to attach Arab Palestine to Transjordan, but the Arabs refused again to accept the principle of partition and a Jewish state. The Israelis were also unhappy because the Negev, which had enormous symbolic importance to some Jews, was now given to the Arabs. The peace process was abruptly halted by terrorists from the Stern Gang, who assassinated the peacemaker in September 1948. To all intents and purposes, the first Arab–Israeli war ended with the Egyptian–Israeli armistice in February 1949, by which time Israel had extended its share of territory by one-third.

After the Lausanne Conference in 1949, when both sides accepted the UN partition as a framework for discussion, Britain, France, and the US signed the tripartite declaration in May 1950, which was an attempt to prevent further armed conflict. The declaration indicated their opposition to the use of force, restricted the sale of arms to the region, and promised consultation over the action to take if either side breached the armistice lines. The Cold War now had a new dimension in the Middle East, because the Soviet Union had been an important backer of Israel and enabled it to receive vital arms supplies. The Russians had previously tried to gain greater influence in the Middle East on the basis of specific demands on Turkey and Iran. Now they supported Israel because the British in particular were seen as firmly linked to the Arab world. Soviet–Israeli links were broken when the Korean War broke out and Israel sided firmly with the West, but Soviet influence presented a prospect that would worry their policy-makers for years to come. As Western support for Israel became firmer, there was always the risk that the Soviets would be able to establish close links with the Arab states, which would greatly enhance their regional influence.

Clinging on to Empire: Egypt, the Cold War, and Middle Eastern Defence

Thus, the Cold War in the Middle East became a battle for influence rather than a battle to prevent Soviet territorial or military gains in the form of bases. As in Europe, however, this political and ideological battle for hearts and minds was connected to, but in reality separate from, the military issue of defence. As in Europe, when strategic defence plans were first formulated in 1946 for the Empire / Commonwealth, they were far from compatible with the ideas of the Foreign Office on what was needed politically and diplomatically to re-establish Britain's status as a global power. While the Foreign Office looked to Britain as the post-war leader of Europe, and to combining that relationship with the resources of the colonies and dominions, the emphasis of the military remained solely focused on the overall significance of the Empire (not merely colonies). For military leaders, the substantive embodiment of Britain's global power would not be alliances with the weak and ineffective Western Europeans who had rapidly caved in to the Germans in 1940, and would therefore be likely to do so again in the next war against the real enemy of Soviet communism. The defeat of the Nazis had not been produced with help from Western Europe, which might need to be abandoned as it had been in 1940, even though the near continent was important for the defending the UK (one of four main support areas). In the next war against the Soviets, the security and resources of the US and the western hemisphere nations, along with those of the dominions and African colonies (the other three main support areas) would be crucial. The next war could be won if the areas of strategic importance were also defended along with the main support areas. Even though, in 1946, Western Europe was seen as helping defend the UK itself, the most important strategic area for the military was the Middle Eastern empire with its mix of colonies, protectorates, and even technically independent states. Although many officials and Conservative politicians also saw the maintenance of an exclusive British sphere of influence in the Middle East as the crucial imperial element of British power,[11] it was the military priorities of empire that dominated the first post-war strategic defence plans.[12] In short, the region was of 'life and death consequence for Britain' and the 'British political method must make good, if the British way of life is to survive'.[13]

As British political control and influence was weakening and about to disappear in some areas of the world (through decolonization), in the Middle East imperial influence would definitely have to be retained.

The imperial DNA that flowed through military leaders' blood had been produced by their formative experiences in deployments outside Europe, and from the Asian/Middle Eastern rivalry with Russia, which was easily translated by the navy and the air force into fears about the growing Soviet political and military influence as the war ended. Even the army, because of its training and past rejections of continental commitments, tended to look to the Empire for its traditions and ways of increasing Britain's post-war military importance. After the fighting in two World Wars had provided some substance to that imperialist idea, British military triumphs had become more easily associated with the campaigns in the Middle East and on the Mediterranean shores of Africa than with Europe.

With a military presence still deemed particularly significant, in addition to the huge base in the Suez Canal Zone obtained by virtue of a 1936 treaty with Egypt, in the Levant there was the military personnel and equipment present in Palestine, Jordan, and Iraq and the colony of Cyprus. The Egyptians, in the negotiations on the future use of the base that had broken down in 1946, regarded the presence of troops on their soil in peacetime as the element of British imperialism from which they were keenest to escape. In a situation where the real reason for a military presence is to defend a given territory against a concrete threat, the natural response would be to take the British intelligence assessments of what forces the enemy was likely to be able to bring to bear on the target area and then decide how best it could be defended, with the quantities of men and equipment needed for a successful defence and, as the Americans, untainted by experiences of empire were to do, first decide what geographical areas had to be defended and then define a strategy for how best to defend them. The British started from the geographic areas their past imperial needs had provided in order to define a strategy of what should be defended. Unfortunately, when the Cabinet committee discussions on the strategic position of the British Commonwealth and the importance of the Middle East came to involve the operations from the Egyptian base and the forces required in peace and war, the Egyptian wish to revise the British peacetime presence had been made clear. Summing up, the Prime Minister said, 'our whole position in the Middle East required re-examination to determine our exact strategic requirements in the Middle East with particular reference to what in the Middle East it would be essential for us to defend in a possible future war, to determine what would be our wartime requirements to defend these essentials and what would be our peacetime minimum military requirements on which we could expand in war'.[14]

It was impossible to disagree with Attlee's succinct summary, but carrying out his suggestion was not something that the Chiefs of Staff (COS) were willing or able to do in 1946. In situations where the essential rationale is the imperialism inherent in the projection of power in the world, involving the subjugation and constraints imposed on foreign indigenous peoples, the specifics of any such rationales are undesirable. Moreover, no planning for Middle East defence had yet produced even an emergency defence plan and the COS preferred to concentrate on why Middle East defence was so important for the Empire and Britain's whole defence strategy. However, it was left to the Foreign Secretary, Ernest Bevin, to claim that the maintenance of Britain's position in the Mediterranean, through its bases and facilities, was vital to its continuance as a great power.[15] The imperial essence of this was the refusal to consider any total or immediate withdrawal of forces from the Egyptian base. Moreover, the fact that the amount of British military personnel present was, and was to remain, considerably exceeding the numbers permitted by the terms of the 1936 treaty for the use of the base, made the imperialist element clear.

In 1947, the strategic commitment to the defence of the crucial Middle Eastern region[16] required by the COS, and supported by the foreign secretary over the doubts and alternative suggestions of the prime minister, was finally accepted. This only increased the importance of the Egyptian base and the reluctance of the military to evacuate it fully. By the summer, the COS had asked the Joint Planning Staff to 'examine our peacetime requirements in the Middle East', as requested by the prime minister, yet the planners' response also avoided mentioning any detailed specifics. It did, however, bring up an added reason for retaining a peacetime presence in Egypt based on the region's importance. What was needed in the Middle East 'to maintain our position in peace' (that is, British imperial influence) and to 'do our utmost to defend it on war' was now dependent on the Suez base. In particular, the peacetime requirements were those forces necessary to 'establish ourselves and operate effectively from Egypt on the *threat* of war'.[17] Here was a stepping up of British demands in the face of Egyptian opposition, not a retreat or a transfer of power. The issue was whether this was caused more by imperial requirements than by the need to defend the region in order contain a significant Soviet threat.

In the face of Egyptian demands, any troop reduction in accordance with the Anglo-Egyptian treaty would create practical difficulties of where they would go, following the decision to abandon Palestine that May. The Palestine withdrawal, in the face of Jewish terrorism, also encouraged seeking compensation for the apparent weakening of Britain's regional position in the Middle East, if not in retaining a Suez presence in Egypt then by, for example, getting control (through a UN trusteeship) over Cyrenaica. The Egyptian problem over the base was already resulting in the Foreign Office considering whether something should be done to replace King Farouk's minority government.[18] More significantly for any linkage, or comparative causal importance, between maintaining the prestige of the Empire and dealing with the Soviet threat, in the summer of 1947 the Commanders-in-Chief Middle East decided that 'the time had come' to start a study of Middle East strategy in the event of war with Russia. In other words, this was some considerable time after the senior military leaders in London had been producing papers on the strategic position of the Commonwealth in the next global war, which since before D-Day in June 1944 they had assumed would be against Russia. These papers had emphasized the significance of defending the Middle East, and now the importance of maintaining an Egyptian base for implementing it became more significant, with the Egyptian objections and their growing hostility to a British peacetime presence.[19] Yet crucially the COS did not believe in the autumn of 1947 that Russia was ready to undertake an offensive war.[20] Hence the military had continued not to respond to Attlee's request until the military requirements for defending the region had been assessed.

Another factor to consider was the attitude of the American government, as the failure to secure an Anglo-Egyptian agreement and the continued breach of the 1936 treaty terms by Britain meant Egypt was about to take the whole problem to the UN. With the US taking over the British responsibilities in Greece and Turkey, in a sense the need to remain in Egypt was even more crucial for the British Empire in the Mediterranean and Middle East. The State Department had always defined US policy in the 1940s in terms of supporting Britain as the leading Western power in the Middle East, despite its imperialism. The Americans in 1947, when talks on defence were held at the Pentagon in the autumn, also accepted the importance that London attached to the defence of the Middle East. In military terms, American aircraft and troops were still planning to join with the British in attempting to defend the region within one month of war breaking out. The US Air Force was certainly interested in having a base in Egypt available on the outbreak of war, and Foreign Secretary Bevin saw hopes of US aid if the importance of Britain's role in Egypt could be demonstrated.[21] He had already made it clear to the Americans that he was opposed to a combined Anglo-American policy for the Middle East 'as the area was primarily of strategic and economic interest to the United Kingdom'.[22] This continued assertion of British supremacy provided by its imperial presence was in marked contrast to the beliefs of the Prime Minister, who could not see 'how the fact of us needing a Commonwealth base in the Middle East gives us any ground for demanding that the base be in Egypt, a sovereign state'.[23] It was an early indication of the need of the more imperially inclined leaders to justify a British military presence by containing the Soviet threat. Defending the Middle East would certainly fulfil this, but unfortunately once the military had assessed the forces needed for such anti-Soviet operations, they were to be found wanting.

The British imperial presence was being retained despite the reluctance of the Prime Minister, but British imperialism was now more firmly connected to resuming a role as a great world power in the very different post-war circumstances. This in turn was linked to a military presence in the Middle East, specifically in Egypt, which had been the largest base in the world. The changes which were undermining other components of empire did not have the same impact on the military, who remained committed to imposing their requirements on Egypt, ostensibly because of the need to defend the Middle East. As the Egyptians prepared to appeal to the UN over the British refusal to evacuate the Suez base or to abide by the 1936 treaty agreement, a further source of imperial embarrassment for the British at the dawn of decolonization and the granting of Indian independence was the economics of their relations with Egypt. With the local currency having been provided by the Egyptians in the war to pay British troops in the base through an Anglo-Egyptian financial agreement, this money was offset against sterling to be drawn upon once the war was over—the sterling balances. With the Americans insisting on convertibility as the price for the loan negotiated for the UK as the war ended, the British were soon faced with unsustainable demands on their foreign currency reserves, which required the drawing of the balances to be both limited and delayed in a specific agreement with Egypt.

As far as military strategy for 'hot war' was concerned, October 1948 finally saw the completion of the emergency plan to defend the Middle East, which served mainly to justify retaining a British imperial presence. Plan Sandown took a line from Tel Aviv to Ramallah as the main defence fall-back line. Not only did this not defend the Middle East, nor its oil, but as the Americans quickly pointed out, it did not even defend Israel. The Commanders-in-Chief, Middle East, however saw another problem and 'called attention to the most serious weaknesses of the plan, namely the vulnerability of Egypt to air attack and the inadequacy of fighter and ground attack aircraft'.[24] The British were insisting on retaining peacetime base facilities in Egypt ostensibly in order to defend the Middle East, while in practical operational terms, the military facilities in Suez were essentially only needed to defend the base in Egypt, which in itself was certainly not guaranteed, given the limited air squadrons available in 1948. Resources for increasingly expensive equipment would continue to be reduced in the 1950s despite the Korean War rearmament drive. Yet the reality was that Britain required a base in Egypt, as a symbol of power and prestige, and the military plans were not primarily to defend the Middle East against the Soviets, who were never assessed as presenting an immediate threat rather than a more distant possibility.

To make matters worse for the imperial-great-world-power outcome of the Middle Eastern focus of the British military, the strategic thinking of their US counterparts radically changed in 1949. The new US strategic concept, following the creation of NATO, involved a strategic offensive in Western Eurasia based firstly on allocating forces for the defence of the UK as an offensive base, secondly on forces for the western Mediterranean and thirdly on forces for the Cairo/Suez area. They would operate on a Morocco–Spain–France axis that involved a commitment to defend a bridgehead in southern Spain. With the consequent need to build up reinforcements in North Africa, the Americans were no longer prepared to commit forces to the defence of the Middle East in the early days of war, which they now deemed a sole British responsibility.[25] This was very much connected to the reservations even the United States Air Force were now having about using Suez, an imperial facility, as an important base for launching the strategic nuclear offensive against the Soviet Union.[26] Once the US plan was properly examined, the British COS criticized it because the deployment of US forces would not be adequate by D+6 months to 'achieve our political objective of preventing Europe being overrun'. A secondary factor was that it would mean that all three objectives of British defence policy (defence of the UK, the maintenance of sea communications, and a firm hold on the Middle East) would be unobtainable unless the US strategic air force was deployed tactically and the US naval force kept control of the Mediterranean. Neither of these conditions was likely to happen, and even if they did, it was thought that the British 'hold on the Middle East will be precarious'.[27]

After the change in US strategic thinking on global war preparations and new intelligence assessments of an increased Soviet military threat to the Middle East (albeit that it would arrive later), problems on this scale led to the British Defence Coordinating Committee, Middle East, reviewing the strategic problem in the region for the COS, while plan Speedway (the latest British emergency plan for global war) had to be revised. The report was grim reading for the imperialist thinkers still hoping to defend the Empire/Commonwealth by prioritizing the defence of the Middle East.[28] With reduced American assistance for the region, the British nevertheless accepted that it would no longer have priority over Western Europe for reinforcement. A refocus away from the Middle East to give Europe greater importance was slowly developing in the new decade, with Western Europe now being incorporated by the military planners into the defence of the UK. How much this was caused by the American military shift is a matter for debate, but the determination to maintain an imperial legacy remained firmly in place, with no reduction in the importance of the Middle East. Having to consider providing for the defence of both regions simply increased the unrealizable demands on the use of military resources. The British operational ability successfully to implement a strategy to defend one region in cooperation with its allies, notably the Americans, was clearly lacking, whether Western Europe or the Middle East was given priority.

The problems appeared worse in June 1950, when the first strategic review since 1947, now labelled defence policy and global strategy was completed, to reflect Britain's position as both a Commonwealth and Western Alliance member.[29] Essentially, the strategic significance of the empire embodied in the vital importance of defending the Middle East remained unchanged as one of the vital three pillars, with Egypt the key area, as its base was deemed indispensable. Along with Western Europe, the Far East, and sea communications, the defence priorities were outlined in the paper, with the hoped-for Commonwealth contributions simply noted. A concluding section on 'First priorities' then gave strategic precedence to cold war over hot war. Speedway's replacement, the emergency plan for global war, Galloper, did indicate the lack of fighter aircraft needed in the Middle East for an air defence system to protect the Suez base, but more importantly now needed for the defence of the UK. However, the planners rejected the idea that bombers and fighters from overseas should be repositioned in the UK, even though the Americans had abandoned the idea of launching their strategic bombers from the Middle East.[30] Yet the Americans did agree with the British that the Middle East was of great strategic importance, and with the new European demands it was important for the more imperially minded military that no reductions in Britain's future role in the region occurred. With this in mind, the Joint Planners reviewed British Middle East strategy. However, the initial draft was criticized by the COS for failing to examine the steps necessary to plan for a more forward defensive position than the Tel-Aviv-Ramallah line.[31] But the American Joint Chiefs of Staff (JCOS) criticized the initial British plan by stating the obvious: that it did not defend the Middle East nor its oil resources, but only the base in Egypt. Even worse, the British were at odds with the Egyptians over their right to be in the base only in order to defend it.

The detailed criticisms by the Americans over how the defence of the Middle East should be carried out and by whom were more extensive than simply stating what the strategy failed to do. Although Middle Eastern oil had recently become more important for peacetime economies and for the wartime potential of the Western powers, Britain's building on its imperial foundations in the Suez base and not defending it was only part of what the Americans saw as the problem. They provided a detailed response to the British paper on Middle East strategy, which was 'not in consonance with US strategy'.[32] There were nine general points of disagreement and some 40 specific comments on points of detail. The main thrust was that the 'Inner Ring or any lesser line [Lebanon-Jordan or Tel Aviv-Ramallah] is not an acceptable basis for Anglo-American strategy'.[33] The US believed that the Outer Ring was needed to defend the oil and make use of Turkey's resources and its strategic situation (see Figure 3.1).

Turkey, unlike Egypt, unfortunately did not contribute to Britain's Middle Eastern position (what the rest of the world thought of it), which only five years earlier had been deemed 'a matter of life and death for the British empire' and required the maintenance of a 'special position in the area'. Moreover, Turkey's acceptance (following its application to join NATO) to consult in NATO planning for the Eastern Mediterranean, which the British Commanders-in-Chief were not involved in, emphasized another Anglo-American difference arising from the imperial/European dichotomy.

The maintenance of British imperial requirements inherent in its special Middle Eastern position versus the development of NATO with its new European military focus was epitomized in the naval command arrangements in the Mediterranean. These were to handicap the attempts to form a Middle East Command (MEC) or Middle East Defence Organization (MEDO), as reinforcements for the Middle East depended on the Mediterranean being kept open. After the war, the Mediterranean was still divided into two areas (Eastern and Western) with different operational aims, and separate British and American Mediterranean commanders after the creation of NATO. The Americans argued, after the 1949 strategic planning shift, that a naval supreme commander in the Mediterranean should primarily be acting to support NATO ground forces in southern Europe and be responsible to Supreme Headquarters Allied Powers Europe (SHAPE), whose head, after his December appointment, was General Eisenhower. However, the British military could not accept that an imperial command in the key military area for them should be subordinate to an American, nor primarily focused on assisting the defence of Europe. Admiral Robert Carney, after talking with the British, was more forthright in rejecting what amounted to a duplication of naval resources. The British had emphasized the 'touchy' nature of the political situation and the need to protect their government and placate public opinion by giving them a supreme Mediterranean naval commander responsible to the NATO Standing Group. Carney rejected such political assumptions and stressed the military effectiveness and the comparative economic and military contributions. He argued that a supreme commander would in effect give the British naval control in Italy, Greece, and Turkey, all of whom owed their military strength to the US, and all of whom preferred a US supreme commander and regarded British overlordship as distasteful.[34]

The discussions with the Americans, despite their vacillating over what forces would be available and precisely when they would be able to commit them, had produced agreement on the importance of defending the Middle East, but conflicting views on how to do it. At the same time, 1950 had seen some important changes in Egypt which would affect Britain's imperial presence. After talks on the Suez base had stopped with the fall of Ismail Sidqi in December 1946, the new Egyptian Prime Minister, Mahmud Nuqrashi, made the British agreement to evacuate a pre-condition for resuming negotiations. On his assassination by the Muslim Brotherhood in December 1948, the Foreign Office consideration of how to get around the military's insistence that the Egyptian base was essential to defend the Middle East became more relevant. Unable to satisfy the Egyptians by sufficiently modifying the military requirements, the situation was becoming critical in 1951 as the Wafd (the Egyptian nationalist party of the more affluent Egyptian merchants) had been returned to power in 1950. On the one hand, there was growing concern over the lack of fighter aircraft and an integrated air defence system for the base, with even the military now arguing that for the base to function effectively the cooperation and goodwill of the Egyptians was essential.[35] On the other hand, to get this without altering the imperial mind-set, and its associated belief that the base was militarily essential for what could not be defended, and accept evacuation in peacetime, did not appear feasible. Hence, with no renewal agreement being in place when the treaty expired in December 1956, more confrontation would be likely. The British had only offered a phased withdrawal, but with civilians and RAF air defence personnel left in place, neither the Americans nor the British Ambassador in Cairo felt that was enough to secure an agreement.[36]

In the summer of 1951, the nationalization of the Anglo-Iranian Oil Company (discussed in detail below) was being implemented. Negotiations over compensation broke down in July, which heightened US fears about the consequences of British imperialism. The Americans were now extremely concerned by what the State Department termed a 'collision course' in Egypt with grave consequences for the US because of the 'rigid attitude of His Majesty's government'. If this were to happen it would be in US interests 'to escape any share of the odium. Only by so doing could they hope to retain any influence with Egypt or the Arab world as a whole.'[37] This divergence between British imperialism and the US acceptance of new Middle Eastern realities also arose from the continuing differences over command arrangements in the Mediterranean. With the Americans keen to use Turkish land and naval forces to assist in the battle for southern Europe under a NATO command, and the British wanting to use them for the Middle East with a British naval commander also supporting NATO's southern flank and operations in the Balkans,[38] the US proposed two naval commands but with Turkey linked to NATO's southern command. This was unacceptable to the British because it would leave the British commander in the Eastern Mediterranean as a subsidiary command outside NATO,[39] and thus arose the idea of a separate Middle East Command (MEC) which might also include the Egyptians. The British COS accepted this US idea with Egyptian equality as members of a MEC, under a supreme commander, but not the idea of total military evacuation (the *sine qua non* for the Egyptian Foreign Minister Salah al-Din).[40] Responsibility for keeping the Mediterranean open for the supply of reinforcements was thus left up in the air, but before any Middle East Command proposals could be presented to the Egyptians, a bill to abrogate the 1936 treaty was put before parliament and in October the collision was underway. Moreover, the British general election later in October brought a Conservative government back to power, with the nineteenth-century empire views of its aging leader, Winston Churchill. Churchill found the terminology of 'Commonwealth' an unacceptable replacement for 'Empire', and regarded any retreat from imperial power, or 'scuttle' as he termed it, complexly anathema. He had supporters in the Cabinet and was in contact with some diehard imperialists in the parliamentary party in both houses.

Immediately after abrogation, the new government had to deal with disturbances in the Suez Canal Zone, with strikes and buildings damaged in an attempt to force the British to leave.[41] By December, the strikes

Figure 3.1: Map showing the four British defence lines in the Middle East

Source: Adapted from The National Archives

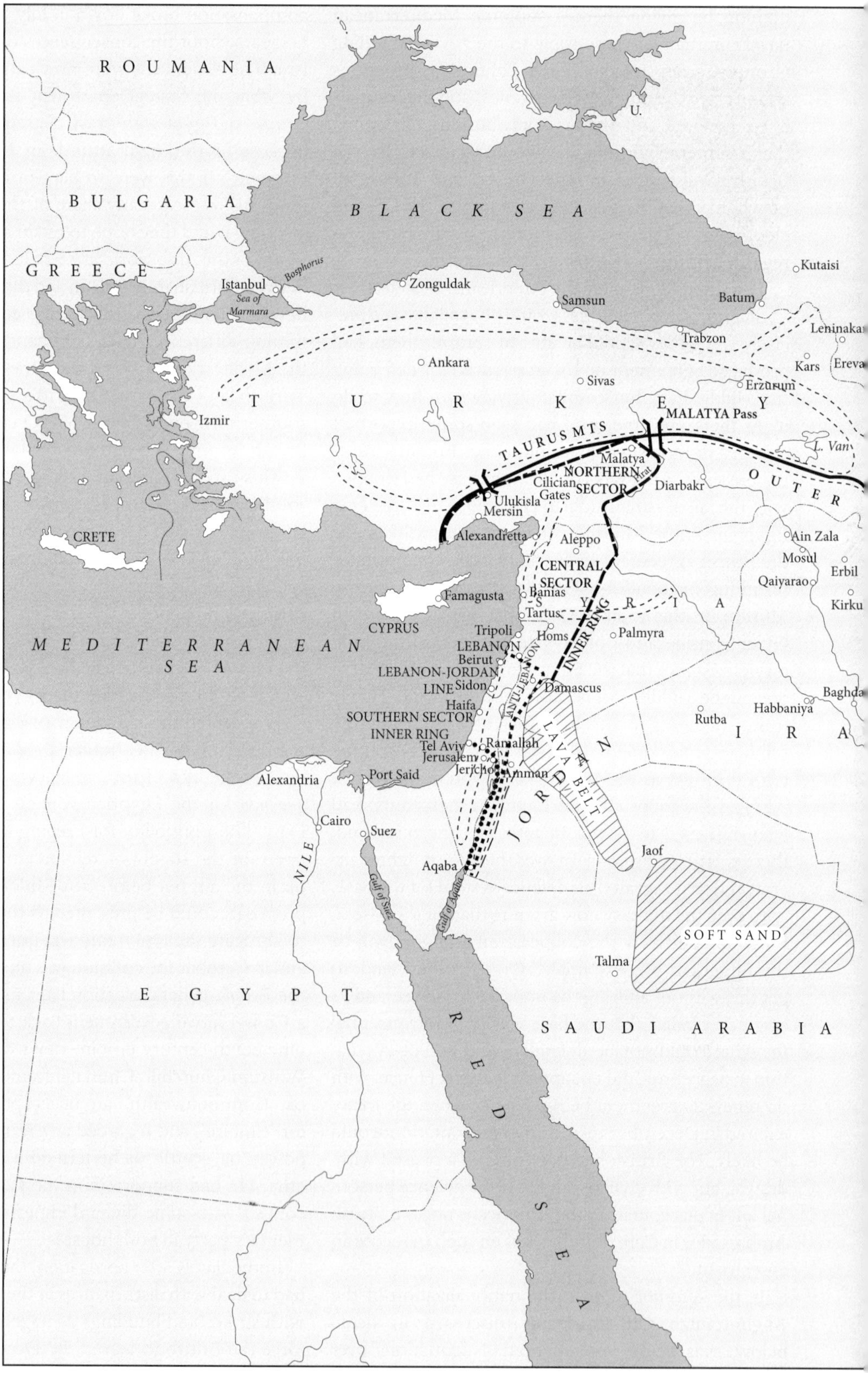

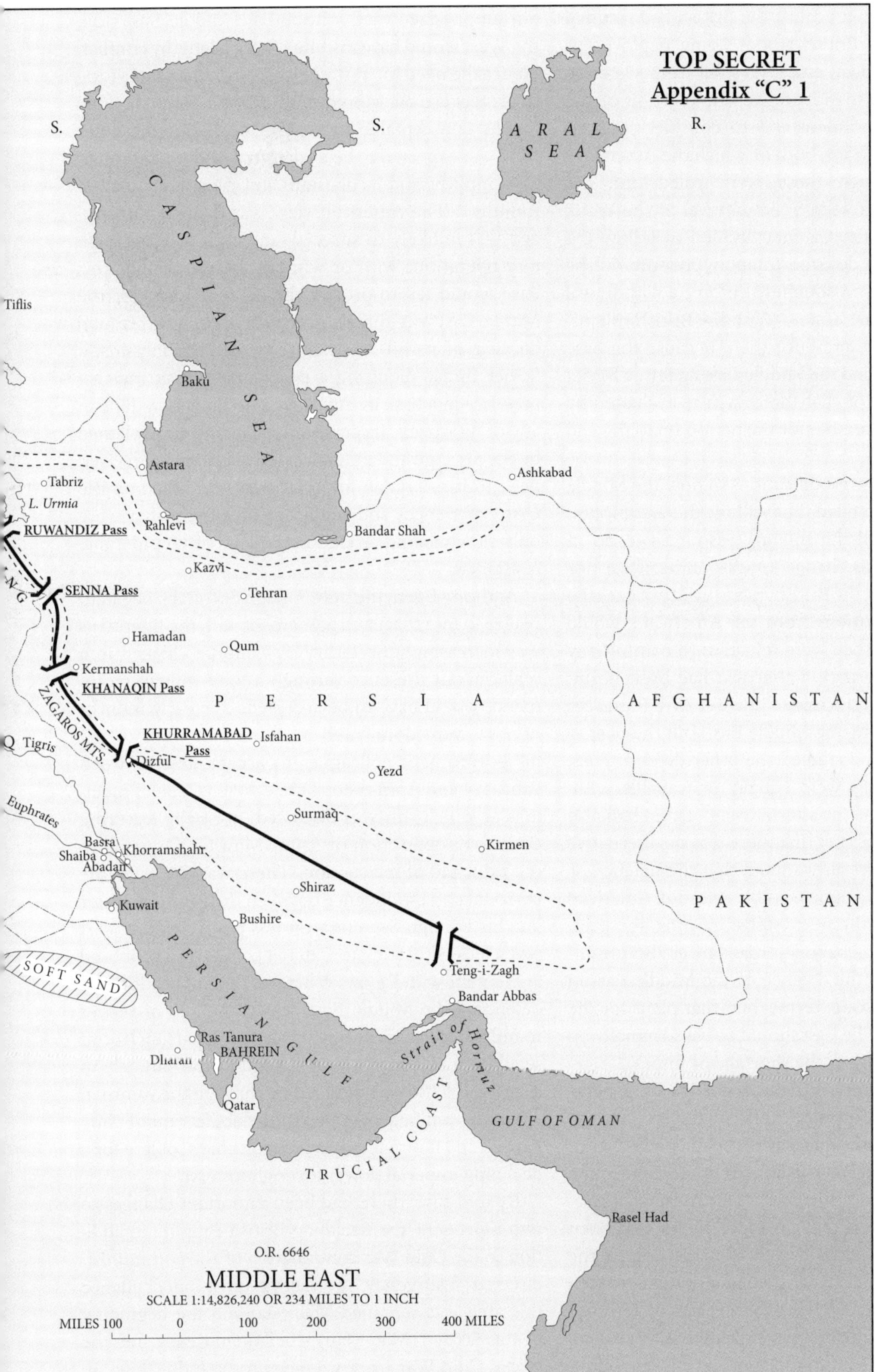
TOP SECRET
Appendix "C" 1
S.
S.
R.
ARAL SEA
CASPIAN SEA
Tiflis
Baku
Astara
Ashkabad
Tabriz
L. Urmia
RUWANDIZ Pass
Pahlevi
Bandar Shah
Kazvi
SENNA Pass
Tehran
Hamadan
Qum
Kermanshah
KHANAQIN Pass
ZAGAROS MTS.
PERSIA
AFGHANISTAN
Tigris
KHURRAMABAD Pass
Isfahan
Dizful
Yezd
Euphrates
Surmaq
Kirmen
Basra
Shaiba
Khorramshahr
Abadan
Shiraz
Kuwait
PAKISTAN
Bushire
SOFT SAND
Teng-i-Zagh
Bandar Abbas
PERSIAN GULF
Strait of Hormuz
Ras Tanura
BAHREIN
Dharan
Qatar
TRUCIAL COAST
GULF OF OMAN
Rasel Had
O.R. 6646
MIDDLE EAST
SCALE 1:14,826,240 OR 234 MILES TO 1 INCH
MILES 100 0 100 200 300 400 MILES

and incitement to act against the British had resulted in another 29,000 British troops being deployed as the number of civilian employees fell from 58,000 to 2,000. With the base inoperative, the reaction of the Conservative government was to consider countermeasures and sanctions, both of which the Americans opposed.[42] Although these were ruled out, the Embassy worked to secure the removal of the Wafd, while in London the Cabinet decided to follow the previous Cabinet's decision to apply pressure on the Egyptians if they ever sought to enforce a withdrawal from the Suez Canal Zone.[43] With the British still justifying a peacetime presence there because the base was needed to defend the Middle East against a Soviet threat, the nature of that threat was re-evaluated by the military in December for the period up to the end of 1954.[44]

There were some modifications to how the Middle East would be defended, but still on the assumption that only they had the military resources to do it. The reasons for this change appear neither clear nor rational. Given that the British military did not have the resources, contributions from the Americans would be important, yet they were reluctant to commit any forces in the initial period after war had broken out. Following the US criticism of the Tel Aviv-Ramallah line as not defending the Middle East, but the base in Egypt, the COS had studied the other defence lines, for which resources were equally unavailable without selecting any of the alternatives.[45] Bevin had also explained to the Cabinet that there was no alternative to the base in Egypt in war, and that the defence of the Middle East was not possible without American assistance.[46] Over the next twelve months, the planners identified the Lebanon–Jordan line as also unsuitable 'as a basis for the defence of the Middle East in the Medium and Long Terms' but 'that plans for the defence of the Middle East should be based initially on this position because of the shortage of forces'.[47]

Two months later and with a change of government, the British Chiefs of Staff concluded that 'the Inner Ring represents the only acceptable allied strategy that we are likely to be able to implement in the period [1951–4] under review'.[48] This somewhat irrational change, given that no more forces had been available for the Middle East, was made despite the American Joint Chiefs having ruled it out in a written submission to their British counterparts in October 1950 and meeting with them in November of that year. They agreed on the importance of the base in Egypt, but emphasized that, without the Middle East's oil, the West would have insufficient for a lengthy conflict. Hence the need for a strategy based on the Outer Ring to protect the oil. Moreover, the British force shortfall for the unacceptable strategy of defending the Inner Ring was expected to be 1.5 divisions and 160 aircraft at D+4 months and 3.5 divisions and 320 aircraft at D+6 months.[49] The American view was that such a strategy was unlikely to succeed, and even if it did, military operations with or without the use of the Suez base would fail to protect the oil. The idea that the Middle East was important (which many have claimed because of its oil) and had to be defended against a Soviet threat requiring a peacetime British military presence in a base in Egypt, was no longer credible in any of its aspects. Its persistence can only be explained by the prestige and influence derived from a perceived need to maintain an imperial presence, based on the past experiences and traditions of empire that were only slowly being eroded in the face of considerable resistance.

Anthony Eden, the new Foreign Secretary, began to realize in 1952 that as an agreement with the Egyptians was increasingly necessary, evacuation, cloaked in a replacement presence through a joint military command, would have to be accepted. The early months of 1952 were dominated by Eden's attempts to get his government colleagues to accept this. Between February and April there were a dozen Cabinet meetings at which this was discussed, normally featuring the strong opposition of Prime Minister Churchill to the principle of evacuation. There was the extensive personal correspondence between the Prime Minister and his Foreign Secretary on this point, with at least seven letters reacting to Cabinet papers on a proposed agreement with Egypt. Whatever the implications for defending the Middle East, it was the loss of power to influence events in Egypt that the departing troops would entail which Churchill found too difficult to swallow.[50] The issue dragged on through the summer, when the military coup led to the abdication of King Farouk and it remained an unresolvable problem for a declining imperial power throughout 1953.

By mid-1952, there had been important changes to two aspects of the declining British Empire, in addition to the Cold War continuation of the communist-directed insurgency in Malaya (post-independence this area was renamed Malaysia) and the beginning of the Kikuyu (Mau Mau) rebellion in Kenya. Yet, the global Cold War front was seen to be Indo-China, in which there was 'a very serious gap' created by the lack of the Cold War 'ramparts of the Atlantic Treaty and the European Recovery Programme'.[51] The first change was the pressure on government military expenditure on empire following the Korean War rearmament drive, which exposed a lack of capacity in the economy to produce the desired arms. The summer months saw the arguments about the cuts in 'Rab' Butler's 1953 defence budget develop. Butler was seeking to reduce expenditure and pointed out that the armed forces formed 10 per cent of the working population, while Britain was already losing civilian contracts to the Germans and Japanese.[52]

The dispute was to go before Cabinet in November, but the cuts first aroused concerns in the Foreign Office because of the implications for Britain's position as a global power. Eden produced a paper for the Cabinet on 'British Overseas Obligations', especially those in the Empire / Commonwealth that were 'inherited from several hundred years as a great Power'. It highlighted the dilemmas, which remain with us today, in the minds of the significant world power advocates, given that 'the essence of a sound foreign policy is to ensure that a country's strength is equal to its obligations'. Determining how the obligations can be reduced or transferred to the Americans or even shared with others, such as the Europeans, 'without impairing too seriously the world position of the UK' had to be the first task. If it was then determined that a lofty imperial position in the world was 'beyond the capacity of existing resources', a stark choice would be faced by UK citizens between giving up 'some of the advantages which a high standard of living confers upon them, or, by relaxing their grip on the outside world, see their country sink to the level of a second class power'. The paper then pointed out the 'very strong arguments' against completely abandoning major commitments (as in Egypt) in the present state of world tension. With the Cold War again connected to an imperial, world role, other disadvantages would flow from giving up commitments that 'would affect the national status of the UK'. They would reduce its value as an ally and undermine 'the cohesion of the Commonwealth and the special relationship of the United Kingdom with the United States and its European partners'. In addition, the British world position brought with it 'concurrent and beneficial results of an economic and financial nature. Finally, there is the general effect of the loss of prestige' which, like the financial and economic benefits, was not specified, although 'the effects of a failure of will and relaxation of grip in our overseas commitments are incalculable. But once the prestige of a country has started to slide there is no knowing where it will stop.'[53]

Two days later, the Defence Committee considered the new global strategy paper, which the military claimed was based on a review of the 'general strategic situation' and 'a policy in the field of imperial and foreign affairs' that had been 'constantly reaffirmed in public'. To carry out such a policy a compromise figure after cuts, 'with due regard for the economic difficulties of the country', left a defence budget of £1,645,000,000. The June 1952 defence and global strategy paper was an early reflection of the financial constraints following rearmament for the Korean War. The lessons the military had drawn from that conflict could now therefore be incorporated, and the military situations in the South East Asian and Middle Eastern empires compared and evaluated. The need to gear military deployments to the most crucial aspects of warfare by prioritizing their different requirements was important, as the cost of advanced equipment was continuing to escalate. The paper therefore emphasized that the priority was winning the Cold War, in order to prevent Russia and China infiltrating the free world and bringing about its disintegration.

> The present concept of Allied policy is to restore the economic strength of the Free World and by rendering aid to the backward countries to lessen their vulnerability to communism, to create a stable and self-confident spirit in the world, to form alliances against aggression and to build up military strength by rearmament, so enabling aggression to be halted and communism to be contained.[54]

If the actions to win the cold war were not successful, then Britain could find itself having to engage in hot war, as the Korean conflict had now demonstrated.

After the second strategic priority of the 'deterrents against war', which in its nuclear elements was entirely in US hands, came the last and least significant global strategy priority of 'preparations for war', which meant war in Europe and the Middle East for the British. In the latter area, there was 'at present . . . no direct threat of Soviet military aggression' but poverty and disorder there could encourage the growth of communism. Yet there was also the perceived need for military strength to avoid the spread of Russian influence, which an excessive reduction of British military forces was deemed to make more likely. As far as the NATO assessment of the forces needed to defend Western Europe, initially completed in 1950, was concerned, the figure was 96 divisions and 9,000 aircraft. This was completely impractical and could not be sustained by any combination of peacetime capitalist economies. While the Atlantic Council and the Military Committee had accepted these figures (with Britain to supply 10 divisions), they were being mulled over after the Lisbon Conference by the Standing Group in the light of 'certain new weapons and techniques'. Thus, there was a prospect of the use of nuclear weapons in both theatres being able to reduce the demands on the RAF and the 11 regular army divisions.

Two weeks later, the COS were not only faced with the welcome prospect of the US Strategic Air Command being used tactically against advancing Russian forces in the Middle East, but having to consider the second post-global strategy change. This came from a Joint Planning Staff paper on the possible altering of British military strategy in the Middle Eastern Empire. The existing unrealistic strategy of defending the region on the Inner Ring would be replaced by a more forward strategy. That would take Turkey, now a NATO member, into account, with its separate provision of ground troops defending the eastern frontier of their country. The British Levant–Iraq Forward Strategy based on defending the three passes into Northern Iraq would be more in line with the US strategy of defending Middle Eastern oil, but still retain a base in Egypt to operate from. Hence the now largely imaginary British influence there that the military and the diehard imperialists believed in would remain. The Forward Strategy was, however, not recommended by the Joint Planners, despite its apparent advantages, because it was not deemed feasible until Britain had overcome its logistical difficulties. These arose from the poor relations with Egypt affecting the use of the base, a lack of motorized transport, the likely Iraqi objections to the granting of peacetime storage facilities, the weakness in the Turkish command structure, and the fact that, until D+6 months, the reduced forces provided by the global strategy paper would be a meagre one division and 160 aircraft.[55]

Along with the military rejection of this risky Iraqi–Levant strategy went a revised concept of Soviet Middle Eastern goals and how they would seek to obtain them, by diverting Allied forces from Europe while denying oil to the West.[56] The late summer also brought renewed pressure for further defence cuts from the Treasury. The Chancellor of the Exchequer remained unhappy with the so-called compromise figure, because it retained 850,000 in the armed forces with more than 1,000,000 civilian administrators. The military opposed these further cuts, just as Churchill, another key Empire figure, was emphasizing, in another letter to Eden, his non-acceptance of the principle of 'evacuation' from Egypt. With no MEC in sight this opposition came when the Egyptian Prime Minister and Wafd leader, Nahas Pasha, was putting pressure on the Suez Canal Company.[57] The Egyptian company responsible for the international waterway of the Suez Canal, but managed and operated from Paris, with the UK government as the majority shareholder, retained 93 per cent of its profits made from a waterway in sovereign Egyptian territory. The British government thus received substantial revenues that constituted another form of imperialism, which Nahas was unhappy about, and it was another element of the final Middle Eastern Empire *dénouement* in 1956 being put in place on the Egyptian stage. As the British military once again faced the implications of not having Egyptian cooperation, but now also without a usable base, they finally accepted that an agreement with Egypt was the only option. Unfortunately, as they were unable to contemplate the retreat that complete peacetime evacuation constituted, they insisted on terms which effectively ruled out what they had accepted.[58] Nevertheless, the prospect of operating without a base in Egypt was very much on the table just when more defence cuts and revisiting the decision to reject a Forward Strategy were also being considered. All had implications for empire and the projection of global power.

The COS were adamant that reductions in defence expenditure beyond what was set out in the global strategy paper were 'totally unacceptable on military grounds', and that Britain's contribution to the now proposed Middle East Defence Organization (less controversial than the Middle Eastern Command) would be a mere token, exposing the inadequate British contribution to Middle East defence.[59] Interestingly, as the issue was about to be discussed in Cabinet, their opposition was expressed in a slightly different form, with arguments from the June Foreign Office paper on Britain's overseas obligations. It was based on the political rationale for an 'imperial and foreign policy' that would maintain 'Britain's vital interests in those areas of the world threatened by the cold war interests of Russia and China'. This would have to be buttressed by providing, with friends and allies, 'forces equipped to modern standards' to deter aggression and 'make reasonable provision for the security of the UK and our other interests throughout the world'. The quote about choosing between giving up a high standard of living or seeing their country sink to the status of a second class power was provided *verbatim*.[60] When the Cabinet discussed it, Butler accepted a figure of £1,610,000,000 for the cuts on condition that there was a radical review of the pattern of the defence effort with due regard to strategic needs and economic and financial factors.[61] But the pattern had been set, whereby military cuts could not be accepted because of the strategic needs, unless political decisions were first taken about which commitments were to be given up. As these were always harder to take due to the involvement of world power status and prestige, British forces and their equipment have generally been spread too thinly in many places far from Europe.

The radical defence review authorized by the Cabinet came with further consideration of the Forward Strategy that the Commanders-in-Chief in the Middle East had actually favoured,[62] but as part of determining the best strategy 'if the Egyptian base were not available to us'. Now, after the treaty abrogation and with the base effectively inoperable, the Planners reversed their July position of rejecting the Forward Strategy as the military claim that the Egyptian base, with a peacetime presence, was essential to defend the Middle East was abandoned. The COS then recommended the new strategy, which would require the presence of an armoured brigade group in North East Iraq by D+15, after a discussion on 14 November. It was not, however, a case of better late than never. As before, when the military first accepted in August that the cooperation of the Egyptians was necessary for the defence of the Middle East, 'the right political atmosphere' would have to be engendered. But the MEDO, in its first stage conceived as only a planning organization, was not making progress as there no agreement on the approach that should be made to the Arab states in order to get them to join.[63] Moreover, when the COS discussed the position of the base, it was agreed that 'the only possible basis for the main Middle East base *in war* was militarily Egypt'.[64] In that sense, the requirement to show British power in the face of Egyptian nationalist demands remained.

This small, but significant change was made before the latest round of negotiations with the Egyptians and the UK military's new negotiating position, prepared by the Joint Planning Staff, were discussed at the highest level by the military and political elites. There were four options up for consideration (A, B, C, and D), which were discussed by the British Defence Coordinating Committee (Middle East) after the Cabinet had looked at the Middle East situation as part of an overall review of foreign affairs. The disagreements with the Egyptians had also been over the King's titular position in the Sudan and the future of the Suez base given the abrogated treaty, which the British were now more in breach of than ever. Now, the abdication of the King removed the barrier and opened the door to Sudanese elections and the self-determination that the British had long been advocating. That 'colonial' part of empire, with its element of being prepared to decolonize, was about to be juxtaposed specifically in time and place with the 'imperial' part of empire, that was determined to stay and maintain the prestige elements of power, including in the form of military symbols.

At the same Cabinet which authorized Eden's proposals for getting Cairo's agreement on an electoral commission for the Sudan with fully equal Egyptian membership, Churchill stated that Britain had no intention of being forced out of the Suez Canal Zone until some satisfactory alternative arrangement to MEDO had been made[65]—not any longer for the defence of the Middle East, but for the protection of the international waterway. Another Suez brick was in the wall before anything went before the defence committee or the men on the spot. Case A, which involved the largest number of British troops (5,000) remaining under a MEDO, seemed to be favoured and all cases involved the base being handed back to the Egyptians. The BDCC believed a fully functioning base in Egypt by M+180 was essential and that any agreement with Egypt without an effective Middle East strategy was of no military interest, whatever the political or economic reasons for it. They emphasized the importance of obtaining American support in negotiations with the Egyptians and put their fingers on several key points. Would an agreement favourable to the Egyptians be perceived by the other Arab states as a sign of British weakness and would other Arab politicians need to have evidence of 'physical power' to see value in an association with Britain? With no hint of irony, Sir Thomas Rapp (head of the British Middle East Office in Cairo), querying the costs of leaving Egypt and some of the assumptions behind the Forward Strategy, stated that it might be 'militarily desirable in some circumstances to prepare military plans on doubtful assumptions'.[66] In the same vein of irony, General Robertson told the Ambassador Sir Ralph Stevenson that what he would object most strongly to was being told to make a plan to defend the Middle East when the basis for a sensible plan no longer existed.[67]

Somewhat surprisingly, when discussing the Defence Committee paper amongst themselves, the COS decided that accepting something between B and C (3,000 RAF personnel or a smaller number in civilian clothes without turning over stores and equipment) would be preferable to sitting it out until the treaty expired in 1956.[68] As in all cases, the airfields, communications, power stations, and amenities would be turned over to the Egyptians within a MEDO and an agreed rate of withdrawal would apply to the bulk of British forces, now numbering 81,000. The pill would be sugared by economic and military aid to Egypt. The Cabinet discussed this after a US delegation spent a week in London consulting. There was an agreement, endorsed by the Americans, to work jointly for a base agreement as close to Case A as possible, with a phased evacuation accompanied by an Egyptian agreement to participate in a regional defence organization and to 'retain sufficient technical aid' to make possible the immediate reactivation of the base possible in the event of war. All elements of the proposed agreement would be interdependent, with no withdrawal beginning until after talks on the important Middle East Defence arrangements had begun. This British sticking point was again left to confront the equally long-lasting Egyptian sticking point that until the British agreed to evacuate, no other arrangements could be made. Furthermore, the Chief of the Imperial General Staff now objected in Cabinet that, as Case A was the minimum requirement 'to ensure effective joint defence of the Middle East', without it there would be too long a time between the outbreak of war and British recovery of an effective full use of the base.[69]

Eden had to bring the question back to Cabinet again with a more forceful paper that ignored the growing Treasury concerns, perhaps often present in any declining imperial power, that a range of new ideas and strategies was being bandied about without any adequate consideration of the costs they would incur.[70] At the same time, Eden faced conflicting pressures from within the Foreign Office and from right-wing Conservative supporters of empire. For Ambassador Stevenson, 'sitting it out' without an agreement would mean the loss of influence in Egypt with damage to British economic interests and the withdrawal of US support. As a result, a settlement with Egypt on less than is militarily justifiable was the only option. Britain's Cold War position in Egypt was threatened by 'Communist infiltration and inflamed nationalism'. Therefore, Stevenson did not believe that a show of strength with a continuing military presence in Egypt would be of any value. It would certainly not produce a more positive perception of Britain in the other Arab states.[71] A very different perception was provided by a recent guest of the Ambassador and Lady Stevenson and director of the Suez Canal Company in a memorandum on the need to stand firm and remain in Egypt. Lord Maurice Hankey, a former chairman of the inter-war Committee on Imperial Defence and government minister with more than fifty years' experience of Suez Canal problems, spoke with General Mohammed Neguib, the nominal head of the Egyptian 'Free Officers', who had seized power in 1952. Hankey, having just spent a month in Egypt was convinced Britain was 'heading straight for a disaster far more serious than the evacuation of Abadan . . . and calculated to shatter what remains of British prestige throughout the world'. After outlining the Canal's importance and stating, 'if we cannot hold the Suez Canal the jugular vein of world and Empire shipping what can we hold', Hankey then used a couple of short League of Empire Loyalist epigrams to appeal to Eden to stand firm in Egypt.[72]

When the issue of the stance to be taken in talks with the Egyptians was brought back to Cabinet,[73] Eden essentially took the Foreign Office line. In a very strong paper, rebuffing the imperialists and drafted in the African Department, the Foreign Secretary pointed out that 'we cannot hope to maintain our position in the Middle East by the methods of the last century. However little we like it we must face that fact.' Another fact to be faced was that 'Our strategic purposes in the Middle East can no longer be served by arrangements which local nationalism will regard as military occupation by foreign troops.' Part of the Foreign Office was becoming more like parts of the Colonial Office and invoking decolonization principles to preserve influence by enabling the Egyptian people to play a part in defending their country, or at least to have a 'determining voice in the disposition of the defence forces for the area'. The benefits of such a tactic appeared to have been demonstrated four days earlier, although the concessions were primarily by Egypt, when the military government signed an agreement abandoning claims to sovereignty over the Sudan and which, in no more than three years from the resulting establishment of self-government, would lead to full independence. But, because in Egypt projection of power in the world was at stake, Eden's paper fell on very stony ground. As it turned out, the unreceptive ground was irrelevant, as it has already been made clear that such a position on evacuation would not be acceptable to the new Egyptian government, any more than to the old one. In fact, as noted by the Foreign Office, the Ambassador in Cairo had repeatedly urged that a statement should be made in advance of any negotiations announcing the intention to withdraw the troops from the base.[74] In the discussion in Cabinet, Case A and the presence in uniform of a small number of British troops were raised again. Now they were needed to ensure the base was readily available in a future war and to safeguard free passage through the Canal.[75] This was something else, like defending the Middle East, which troops were actually in no position to do, given the ease with which block-ships could be sunk.

The radical review and the acceptance of the Forward Strategy had now meant that the base was still required by the military, although the speed of getting reinforcements to the Middle East was equally crucial. In 1952, it appeared that fewer were now needed early on after the outbreak of war as the speed of the Soviet advance on the Levant would also be slower. What was most interesting in the Joint Planners' report was that in a year of increasing military cutbacks, deployments, more than had been previously envisaged, would be focused on the Cold War rather than hot war. The result would be two different force deployments, with hot war requiring the immediate deployment of at least one division to delay Soviet forces entering Iraq, before falling back to the Inner Ring. Cold War needs could be met with an essentially mobile force, of one infantry brigade group in Cyprus and one armoured and one infantry brigade group from the troops earmarked for Libya as Egypt was evacuated. As usual, the additional costs and savings were not factored in, but the 'imperial paradox' when fighting the Cold War was clearly in evidence. On the one hand, once the troops were withdrawn from Egypt and replaced by mobile forces, the 'present pretext for Egyptian hostility towards us' would be removed, but on the other 'the removal of all British forces from Arab territory in peacetime would have a prejudicial effect on Arab confidence in us'.[76]

The problems in this Joint Planning Staff proposal were much fewer than the problems with the base negotiations, which were destined to get nowhere again, as replacing the symbols of power and domination with significant cooperation could not supersede the imperial mind sets. In a mildly critical minute of the draft Cabinet paper for understating the problems of remaining in Egypt without an agreement, the Assistant Secretary heading the African Department, Roger Allen, pointed out the damage already done. Apart from the difficulty in operating the base, Anglo-Egyptian trade worth £40 million per annum had come to a standstill and the US was supplanting Britain in Egypt and the Middle East by appearing to the Arabs as a mediator. Yet the future looked far bleaker, with the prospect of large-scale guerrilla warfare having to be faced.

> The truth of the matter is that we are at present keeping 80,000 men in the Canal Zone for no purpose except to maintain themselves. It is their presence which creates the need for them to be there. This is at a time when it is vitally important that we should reduce our forces. We are no longer able to impose our will by force upon the countries of the Middle East, and therefore we should not fall between two stools as we are at present. It is useless to maintain our troops simply to be shot at.

His supervising undersecretary, in agreeing with the more junior African Department officials, maintained that Britain, by keeping its troops in Egypt, was making the worst of both worlds. Unable to impose its will on the Egyptians, Britain was also losing the ability to influence the Americans and others 'by normal means'.[77]

With the initial military emphasis on hot war, plans to defend the Middle East were primarily designed to defend the appearance of power perceived to emanate from the existing British presence in Egypt. They were not produced by a belief that an attack was likely, alongside an assessment of what should be defended and with what. It was the ideology of imperialism and the aspiration to project power in the world, whatever the reduction in military strength, which made the base into a symbol of British power. That symbol was justified as more than a facade by deeming it necessary for defending the Middle East, something it was actually never able to do. With its actual power reduced by the war, the British could not translate the imperialism of the inter-war years into actions that went beyond the symbolism of the base. As the Cold War developed, it was argued that a military presence was necessary to quell internal unrest and to promote confidence by convincing the indigenous people that they would be protected from the Soviet threat. The argument was disingenuous in several ways. In addition to the lack of British capability, it was unlikely to convince Arabs or Jews of the need to defend the region from an external threat when they saw the real threat as emanating from within it. Another point was that the Cold War required winning over the peoples of the Middle East to Western values, as the Americans began to realize, especially after the Iranian oil nationalization crisis had revealed the limitations of British imperialism. The imperial chickens were coming home to roost and the outmoded British presence in Egypt was becoming more of a threat to stability than a promoter of it. With the problems of early 1953, and the imperial/colonial dichotomy illustrated in the Middle East, the American Secretary of State, John Foster Dulles, embarked on a tour of the region to try and understand the benefits and drawbacks of depending on the British. What he found produced a turning point in American foreign policy and its approach to British imperialism in the Middle East.

The Iranian Crisis and the Coup in Egypt

In March 1951, the Iranian Parliament passed a decree preparing the way for the nationalization of the Anglo-Iranian Oil Company which was implemented in May by the party of Mohammed Mossadeq, the only bourgeois nationalist party in Iran. Mossadeq was striking at the greatest symbol of foreign domination, because the Anglo-Iranian Oil Company ran the biggest refinery in the world at Abadan. Accepting the principle of nationalization, the issue for the British was the arrangements for compensation, as demonstrations and picketing in Abadan prevented the company from operating. The growth of Middle Eastern oil production, in response to increasing demand from the internal combustion engine in 1950 had produced a new agreement between the Saudi monarchy and the Arabian–American Oil Company (ARAMCO), which had effectively been running Saudi Arabia for the royal family. This '50–50' arrangement replaced the royalty payments with what amounted to an equal profit-sharing arrangement. The massive reduction in profits this threatened was acceptable because the US Treasury and Inland Revenue Service allowed ARAMCO to offset the new payments to the Saudi regime against taxation. For the more cash-restrained UK government, this loss of revenue would not be acceptable, which effectively prevented the Anglo-Iranian Oil Company (BP) from following suit. The Americans were interested in the outcome of the crisis and in July had sent a team under Ambassador at Large Averell to Tehran, ostensibly to act as mediator.

By October, the issues of personnel and management within the newly nationalized company were still not resolved and resulted in the expulsion of British workers from Abadan. This 'scuttle' was regarded as a deep British humiliation by Churchill's Conservative government, which came to power in the same month, eager to persuade the Americans that Mossadeq and his supporters were anti-Western. Attacks on Britain were said to be damaging to the Western cause; the irresponsible nationalism of Mossadeq was likely to produce the kind of instability that would be exploited by the Communist Party. As the British sought support in the overthrow of Mossadeq, the members of the Truman administration were reluctant to accept the picture that the British were painting. For them, Mossadeq represented a progressive form of nationalism which was needed to create a more modern and democratic Middle East no longer subject to European, as opposed to American, imperialism.

More importantly, the State Department came to believe that, because Britain no longer had the power to impose itself on the region and dictate to the Arab states in the Cold War, Washington would have to take a greater interest in the Middle East. It was assumed that this would involve developing their own policies in conjunction with the British but, by 1951, that was becoming difficult to do. Seeing the corruption and inefficiency which characterized the rule of King Farouk in Egypt and the landowning notables who formed the palace cliques, the Central Intelligence Agency (CIA) had begun to foster contacts with young Egyptian officers who, it was hoped, would end the corruption of the monarchy and bourgeois nationalists on whom the British continued to rely. Once these 'Free Officers', led by Gamal Abdul Nasser, overthrew Farouk in July 1952, the Americans were particularly keen to play the role of mediators in the conflict between Britain and Egypt over the future of the Suez military base. With the British expecting US support to get an agreement out of the Egyptians allowing them to continue using the base, the Americans struggled to keep a foot in both camps. The next phase in the Middle East battleground began in June 1953, when the new Secretary of State, John Foster Dulles, visited the region. In addition to the conflict between the Arab states and Israel, which involved cross-border incidents and an Arab blockade, there was the Anglo-Iranian dispute which was diverting attention from resolving the Arab–Israeli dispute. Dulles returned shocked by the extent of anti-British feeling in the region and convinced that Washington must take the initiative in the Middle East, even if it meant pursuing policies which the British were unwilling to back.

This was to contribute to the subsequent disaster which befell the British in the Suez Crisis of 1956, but in the short term new American policies led to cooperation over Iran. Dulles, as part of the new Cold War American initiatives, sought to inaugurate a Middle East regional defence grouping. Unlike previous British-backed attempts, it would not be based on Egypt but on the so-called 'northern tier' of countries from Turkey down through Iraq, Iran, and Pakistan. It would aim to prevent Soviet expansion into the Gulf, although in reality such geopolitical ideas made little strategic sense. Apart from the lack of direct US military involvement in the Middle East and the lack of British and indigenous forces, the natural defence line of the Zagros Mountains ran through rather than between Iran and Iraq. This may have influenced American thinking, in as much as it made it more difficult to ensure Iranian involvement and it was, therefore, important to have a ruler there who could be relied upon to put US interests first. As a result, as H. W. Brands has suggested,[78] the Americans now changed their position on Iran. Mossadeq, whatever his value in relation to nationalism and anti-communism, could not be relied on; whereas the Shah, the Iranian monarch, would be happier to play the role defined for him by the Americans. Thus, the CIA cooperated with Britain's MI6 to create the conditions for a coup to restore the Shah to power, which took place in July 1953. As a result, the possibility of a modern, secular, political movement that might unify Iran was sacrificed for the uncertain prospect of a defence grouping that actually carried little strategic benefit—and had a lot of political disadvantages to offset any Cold War gains.

One of the main tensions resulting from fighting a global Cold War while tackling challenges created by regional instability and conflict was that measures deemed likely to assist in the Cold War could contribute to regional conflicts. This was particularly true in the Middle East, where the Soviet desire for more influence was made clear in 1945–6. Economic or political concessions were regarded as completely unacceptable by the British, who were able to persuade the Americans that Soviet imperialism was more threatening to the Middle East than their own. But, ironically, as the global Cold War got underway in 1948, the Middle East was the scene of a 'hot war' in Palestine, linked to the retreat of British power. If, as suggested by Ronald Hyam, decolonization was merely a footnote to the Cold War,[79] there can be no doubt that, in the Middle East, the mix of Cold War, regional conflicts, and the commitment to maintaining imperial interests provided a deadly concoction of irreconcilable aims. Decolonization may well have become a Cold War footnote, but if it had featured more prominently in the main Middle Eastern text, the benefits might have been considerable.

Visit the online resources that accompany this book to test your understanding and take your learning further: www.oup.com/he/young-kent3e

NOTES

1. The policy of assimilating Africans into French culture and political life.
2. John D. Hargreaves, *Decolonization in Africa* (2nd edn, Longman, New York, 1996), 98–9.
3. Ibid. Citing Archives National Section d'Outre-Mer (ANSOM), *Affaires Politiques* 2255/1, Moutet to Ramadier, 1 August 1947.
4. John D. Hargreaves, *Decolonization in Africa* (2nd edn, Longman, New York, 1996), 154–5.
5. CO 537/7148, minute by Sir J. M. Martin, note by C. P. Hope, 15 November 1951.
6. FO 371/67589, Report of the Committee on the Conference of African Governors.

7. Richard Rathbone (ed.), *British Documents on the End of Empire, series B, vol. 1, Ghana 1941–1957, pt 1, 1941–1952* (Stationery Office, London, 1992), 384–7.
8. Ibid.
9. US National Archives (NA) RG59, CDF, 745c.00, Box 1690, Consul General, Salisbury to State Dept., 27 May 1960.
10. Mark A. Tessler, *A History of the Israeli–Palestinian Conflict* (Indiana University Press, Bloomington, 1994), 230–46.
11. See, for example, CAB66/65, WP(45)256, War Cabinet Memorandum, 'Defence of the Middle East', 13 April 1945, stating that the Middle East was 'one of the most strategic areas in the world . . . which is a matter of life and death to the British Empire . . . For this reason alone we cannot afford to resign our special position in the area.' Printed in John Kent (ed.), *British Documents on the End of Empire, Series B, vol. 4, Egypt and the Defence of the Middle East, Part I, 1945–1949 (*hereafter *BDEEP/B4/1)* (The Stationery Office, London, 1998), 6–9.
12. Memorandum for Cabinet Defence Committee, 2 April 1946, and discussions in CAB 131/1, DO(46)10, 5 April 1946, *BDEEP/B4/I*, 94–104.
13. War Cabinet Memorandum, 'Imperial Security in the Middle East', 2 July 1945, *BDEEP4/1*, 20–34.
14. Cabinet Defence Committee minutes, 27 May 1946, *BDEEP/B4/1*, 125–9.
15. Cabinet Defence Committee minutes, 5 April 1946, *BDEEP/B4/1*, 102–4.
16. Defence Committee memorandum, 7 March 1947 *BDEEP/B4/1*, 220–2.
17. Report by Joint Planning Staff, 'Military Requirements in Egypt' 6 August 1947, *BDEEP/B4/1*, 238–41 (emphasis added).
18. FO371/62967, Sargent to Bevin, 15 March 1947, *BDEEP/B4/1*, 224–5; FO141/1173, Sargent Minute, 5 May 1947, *BDEEP/B4/1*, 230–5.
19. DEFE5/11, Study by the Commanders-in-Chief ME, 13 May 1948, *BDEEP/B4/1*, 277–80.
20. The National Archives (TNA), Kew, DEFE4/8, COS(47)134, 31 October 1947.
21. TNA/T236/1274, Playfair minute, 19 May 1947.
22. DEFE4/8, COS(47)144, 21 November 1947, *BDEEP/B4/1*, 251–4.
23. TNA/PREM8/837, Attlee minute, 10 August 1947.
24. DEFE4/16, Report by Joint Planning Staff, 7 October 1948, *BDEEP/B4/1*, 290–6.
25. DEFE4/23, COS(49)113, 3 August 1949, *BDEEP4/1*, 349–53. On Anglo-American differences, see David Devereux, *The Formation of British Defence towards the Middle East 1948–56* (Macmillan, Basingstoke, 1990), 38–42.
26. US National Archives and Records Administration (NARA), College Park, RG218, Box 21, JSPC 883/1, 'Military Viewpoints Regarding the Eastern Mediterranean Area', 12 July 1948.
27. DEFE4/24, COS(49)131, 8 September 1949, *BDEEP/B4/1*, 362–3.
28. DEFE5/20, COS(50)141 Annex, 28 April 1950, *BDEEP/B4/1*, 19–25.
29. CAB 131/9, DO(50)45 7 June 1950 Printed in *BDEEP B 4 Pt II* (The Stationery Office, London, 1998), 33–51.
30. For reaction to the new strategic situation see DEFE4/29, COS(50)39, 13 March 1950, and DEFE4/30, COS(50)63, 24 April 1950.
31. DEFE5/24, COS(50)363 Annex, 15 September 1950, *BDEEP/B4/1*, 77–100.
32. DEFE5/25, COS(50)416, 19 October 1950, *BDEEP/B4/1*, 116–121.
33. Ibid.
34. NARA/RG218 Records of the Joint Chiefs of Staff, Chairman's File, 092.2 Box 3, Carney to Eisenhower, 8 March 1951.
35. DEFE5/20, COS(50)141 Annex, 28 April 1950, *BDEEP/B4/1*, 19–25.
36. CAB129/45, CP(51)95, 30 March 1951, *BDEEP/B4/1*, 167–71.

37. FO371/90135, Franks to FO, 10 August 1951, *BDEEP/B4/1*, 206–7.
38. TNA/DEFE4/41, COS(51)54, 28 March 1951.
39. TNA/DEFE6/7, JP(51)61 Annex, 27 Mach 1951.
40. TNA/DEFE5/33, COS(51)537 Annex, 18 September 1951.
41. Mike Mason '"The Decisive Volley": The Battle for Ismailia and the Decline of British Influence in Egypt', *Journal of Imperial and Commonwealth History,* 19 (1991), 45–64.
42. FO371/90148, Stevenson to FO, 1 December 1951, *BDEEP/B4/1*, 265–6.
43. CAB128/20, CM(51)57, 1 August 1951, *BDEEP/B4/1*, 203–4.
44. DEFE5/35, COS(51)755 Annex, 18 December 1951, *BDEEP/B4/1*, 290–305.
45. DEFE5/24, COS(50)363, 15 September 1950, *BDEEP/B4/1*, 77–100.
46. TNA/CAB129/371, CP(49)209, 19 October 1949.
47. TNA/DEFE4/39, COS(51)13 Annex, 17 January 1951.
48. DEFE5/35, COS(51)755 Annex, 18 December1951, *BDEEP/B4/1*, 290–305.
49. DEFE5/24, COS(50)363, 15 September 1950, *BDEEP/B4/1*, 77–100.
50. See *BDEEP/B4/1*, documents between 326 and 379.
51. CAB131/9, DO(50)45, 7 June 1950, *BDEEP/B4/1*, 33–51.
52. TNA/CAB129/56, C(52)390, 5 November, and C(52)394, 6 November 1952.
53. TNA/CAB 129/53, C(52)202, 15 June 1952.
54. CAB131/12, D(52)26, 17 June 1952, *BDEEP/B4/1*, 398–429.
55. DEFE4/55, COS(52)98 Annex, 8 July, *BDEEP/B4/1*, 433–5.
56. DEFE5/41, COS(52)519 Annex, 18 September 1952, *BDEEP/B4/1*, 33–51.
57. FO371/96977, Churchill to Eden, 19 August 1952 and CAB129/54, C(52)267, 28 July 1952, *BDEEP/B4/1*, 438–44.
58. DEFE4/38, COS (52)121, 26 August 1952, *BDEEP/B4/1*, 448.
59. DEFE4/56, COS(52)135 Appendix, 23 September 1952, *BDEEP/B4/1*, 464–7.
60. DEFE5/42, COS(52) 618 Annexes, 7 November 1952, *BDEEP/B4/1*, 486–94.
61. TNA/CAB128/25, CC(52)94, 7 November 1952.
62. DEFE5/41, COS(52)519, 18 September 1952, and WO216/559, Brownjohn to Robertson, 19 September 1952, *BDEEP/B4/1*, 457–64.
63. The sponsoring states of MEDO were the UK, US, France, Australia, New Zealand, South Africa, and Turkey.
64. TNA/DEFE4/57, COS(52)157, 14 November 1952, and JP(52)129 Annex 1, 12 December 1952.
65. CAB128/25, CC(52)102, *BDEEP/B4/1*, 514–15.
66. FO141/1462, Rapp to Stevenson, 6 December 1952, *BDEEP/B4/1*, 516–17.
67. FO141/1464, Draft minutes of BDCC(ME) meeting, 8 December 1952, *BDEEP/B4/1*, 522.
68. DEFE4/58, COS(52)168, 9 December 1952, *BDEEP/B4/1*, 523–4.
69. CAB129/58, C(53)17, 14 January, and CAB128/26/2, CC(53)2, 14 January 1953, *BDEEP/B4/1*, 536–48.
70. T225/318, Flett Minute, 14 December 1952, and T225/319, Humphreys-Davies Minute, 16 February 1953, *BDEEP/B4/1*, 526–7 and 565–6.
71. FO141/1464, Stevenson to FO, 10 December 1952, *BDEEP/B4/1*, 524–5.
72. FO371/102763, Hankey to Eden, 11 February 1953, *BDEEP/B4/1*, 552–9.

73. CAB129/59, C(53)65, 16 February 1953, *BDEEP/B4/1*, 563–4.

74. FO371/102796, Allen Memorandum, 16 February 1953, *BDEEP/B4/1*, 561–3.

75. TNA/CAB128/26/2, CC(53)12, 17 February 1953.

76. DEFE 11/87, JP(53)24, 5 February 1953, *BDEEP/B4/1*, 549–52.

77. FO371/102796, Minutes by Allen and Bowker, *BDEEP/B4/1*, 559–60.

78. H. W. Brands, 'The Cairo-Tehran Connection in Anglo-American Rivalry in the Middle East, 1951–1953', *International History Review*, 3 (1989).

79. R. Hyam, unpublished paper given at Institute of Commonwealth Studies, London, 1997.

Key to abbreviations used above:

BDEEP	British Documents on the End of Empire
CAB	Cabinet Office
CO	Colonial Office
DEFE	Ministry of Defence
FO	Foreign Office
NARA	National Archives and Records Administration (US)
TNA	The National Archives (UK)

4

The Cold War Intensifies: Containment Superseded, 1948–53

Chapter contents

A. Covert Operations and the Origins of Cold War Fighting

By 1948, the dominant relationship between the Soviet Union, the US, and Britain had moved from one of cooperation to confrontation, and then to hostility and conflict. In this situation, the Cold War required a clearly defined strategy for fighting it. Western interpretations of this strategy have largely been based on the idea of containment, especially about the *form* of containment that should be adopted. Did it require military strength and a 'preponderance' of power, or should it concentrate on economic success, with the provision of full employment, growth, and consumer goods? Should it focus on the important economic areas of the world, or should it be a truly global struggle? But there is an alternative idea that, as confrontation gradually replaced cooperation from 1946, containment too was superseded by a Cold War aimed at destroying the enemy, or fatally undermining its strength. Of course, containment implies an expansionist power (in orthodox interpretations, the Soviet Union), which provokes a defensive response (the US and its European allies). Yet, as with the origins of the Cold War, fighting the conflict after 1948 needs to be seen more in terms of competing powers, each prepared to go beyond preserving the status quo.

One murky area is that of covert operations and propaganda, aspects of policy geared to aggressive subversion rather than defensive containment. The Soviets had numerous agents in the West during the inter-war years, reflecting their civil war experiences in which fear of the capitalist West was rooted. Fear was easily converted into paranoia by Stalin, who saw most things in terms of threats to his personal position of power, and who, even in the post-1945 period, may have been less concerned with undermining the capitalist system, than with preserving the Soviet state from its enemies. His paranoia required that every effort be made to discover internal and external enemies, and if possible, to eradicate them. Soviet intelligence activities at home and abroad in the inter-war years were geared to the detection and elimination of these 'enemies of the people'. In Britain, in the 1930s, a small number of recruits successfully infiltrated the British diplomatic and intelligence services. During the war, Stalin devoted considerable resources to spying on his allies, with 221 agents in the US, and he was never free from the paranoid suspicion that the British and the Americans would be prepared to do a deal with the Germans.

The use of espionage certainly had the potential to deliver real offensive advantages. The Soviet secret services had the advantage of knowing the British position prior to negotiations at some wartime conferences and about British attitudes to the Soviets in the 1940s, as well as the nature of British and American operations against the Soviet Union.[1] But it is impossible to tell exactly what information went to Stalin and there are doubts about how effectively the Soviets exploited the amount of information coming in. Papers of Britain's Post-Hostilities Planning Committee, reflecting military hostility to the Soviet Union, were sent to Moscow, but whether this encouraged Soviet suspicion and resentment remains a matter for speculation.[2] And espionage always carried real dangers. When the war ended, some agents that were operating in the West were compromised by an American code-breaking success known as Venona. Along with defectors' testimonies, Venona enabled some agents to be identified and the extent of the Soviet espionage system to be revealed. This exposure of Soviet espionage cast doubt about Stalin's desire to cooperate and was used to portray Moscow in a negative light from 1946 onwards.[3]

Of course, espionage was not one-sided. Throughout the war, Britain's MI5, responsible for counter-subversion, maintained extensive surveillance on communists in Britain.[4] The intelligence agency MI6 had always seen Bolsheviks as a major enemy, while Churchill's Special Operations Executive, which led subversion against the Axis powers during the war, kept some operatives in place afterwards who occasionally contributed—even before the end of 1947—to measures taken against the Soviet regime. Similarly, confrontation had also already begun in the propaganda field. In 1945, Russian diplomatic representatives claimed the 'Anglo-Americans have not curtailed but enhanced their propaganda apparatus' and redirected it to the 'ideological struggle against the USSR'. In turn, organizations in Moscow debated how propaganda could be improved to counter the West's 'global and reckless ideological offensive'. This led repeated assertions of the need for Soviet propaganda to be more 'offensive' and 'penetrating', although the idea of a vast and well-organized Soviet propaganda offensive at this time clearly needs revising.[5]

Once the Cold War began at the end of 1947, a significant campaign of psychological warfare was mounted by Washington and London, which involved more than espionage and propaganda. 'Instead it encompassed any initiative which might affect the position of a foreign regime.'[6] The West had the major advantage of a socio-economic and political system which was based largely on elements of popular support. As a result, there was less opportunity for communist agents to work with disaffected national minorities or opponents of a harsh repressive regime, but greater prospects for gathering information and recruiting sympathizers. In contrast, Soviet oppression made it harder for spies to operate within the Soviet Union. However, groups opposed to Russian communism had already made secret contacts with Western operatives. In December 1946, some of the 25,000 Ukrainian guerrillas assassinated the head of the Odessa MGB (the predecessor of the KGB). What precise role the West played in this remains obscure, but we do know that responsibility for managing Ukrainian exiles lay with the British Secret Service until 1953, when the Central Intelligence Agency (CIA) took over.[7] On the Soviet side, support for communist parties in the West had been geared to electoral success until September 1947. After that, support for the French and Italian communists remained a cause of concern in Britain and the US, but Moscow also demanded extra-parliamentary action, with strike action and sabotage. By mid-1948, the communists' popularity was being countered by the vast resources that the CIA could deploy to influence elections, with telling effect in Italy, where the Christian Democrats emerged in first place.

Truman's National Security Council (NSC) first attempted to devise an overall Cold War fighting strategy in March 1948.[8] NSC 7, 'The Position of the US with Respect to Soviet Directed World Communism', called for a worldwide counter-offensive against Soviet-directed world communism, concluding that:

> The defeat of the forces of Soviet-directed world communism is vital to the security of the US. This objective cannot be achieved by a defensive policy. The US should therefore take the lead in organizing a worldwide counter-offensive aimed at mobilizing and strengthening our own and anti-communist forces in the non-Soviet world, and at undermining the strength of the communist forces in the Soviet world.

At 'the appropriate time' this was to include 'a coordinated programme to support underground resistance movements in countries behind the iron curtain, including the USSR'.[9] Although details of the covert operation by Western intelligence services are sparse, it is clear that America's Cold War strategy involved more than containment. It sought to undermine the Soviet satellite-empire in Eastern Europe, a process sometimes known as 'roll-back' or 'liberation'—although such ideas are usually associated with US policy in the 1950s. True, there are those who would oppose this interpretation. John Lewis Gaddis points out that doubts were expressed about NSC 7 in the State Department. This is correct. But the Joint Chiefs of Staff endorsed it and the State Department's one criticism was that the memorandum and its recommendations, most of which were deemed worthy of support, lacked an overarching, general theme. This criticism, from one assistant secretary, was based on the lack of any measures to 'eliminate communism at its roots': if the right kind of economic and political programmes were put in place, there would be no need to suppress communist activities in the West because they would have no impact.[10] It was an important point, but separate from action to undermine communism in Eastern Europe.[11]

When NSC 20/4 replaced NSC 7 in November 1948, the State Department's Policy Planning Staff, set up in 1947 under Kennan, drew up the new memorandum. It argued that Moscow would seek to achieve world domination by 'seizing every opportunity presented by weakness and instability in other states and exploiting to the utmost the techniques of infiltration and propaganda, as well as the coercive power of preponderant military strength'. It was not felt 'that the Soviet government is . . . planning any deliberate armed action calculated to involve the US'; rather Moscow would 'achieve its aims primarily by political means, accompanied by military intimidation'. In this light, the US should 'encourage and promote the gradual retraction of undue Russian power and influence from the present perimeter areas around traditional Russian boundaries and the emergence of the satellite countries as independent of the USSR'.[12] This reinforced the need for measures that were offensive in nature and which, according to Kennan, should constitute 'Organized Political Warfare', meaning 'the employment of all the means at a nation's command, short of war, to achieve its national objectives'. The machinery which this required was deemed to be a 'covert operations directorate within the government'. What emerged was the Office of Special Projects, which was supervised by the Secretaries of State and Defence (rather than the CIA taking a lead) and which would be responsible for operations:

> Conducted or sponsored by this government against hostile foreign states or groups or in support of friendly foreign states or groups but which are so planned and executed that any US government responsibility for them is not evident to unauthorized persons and that, if uncovered, the US government can plausibly disclaim any responsibility for them. Specifically, such operations shall include any covert activities related to: propaganda; economic warfare; preventive direct action, including sabotage, anti-sabotage, demolition, and evacuation measures; subversion against hostile states, including assistance to underground resistance movements, guerrillas and refugee liberation groups, and support of indigenous anti-Communist elements in threatened countries of the Free World.[13]

The Office of Special Projects soon became the Office of Policy Coordination (OPC), responsible for all US covert operations behind the Iron Curtain. It is hard to see how this could be seen as containment. Although it did not seek the overthrow of the Soviet regime, it did seek to roll back Soviet power by all means short of war. From a staff of 302 with a budget of $4.7 million in 1949, the OPC had expanded by 1952 to 2,812 personnel with 3,142 contract staff and a budget of $82 million.

By 1948, many in the US administration were convinced that they were fighting a war. Not a hot war perhaps, but a crucial contest in which there could be only one winner. The Soviet Union presented a power-political and an ideological threat of great potency, a combination not seen since the French Revolution. Moreover, it threatened capitalist democracy and the new international order, planning for which had occupied so much attention in the wartime US.

This has been described as a liberal order, which the US was prompted to bring about after 1945 as a consequence of hegemony.[14] Once this order was seen to be threatened, the inauguration of political warfare became necessary. As suggested in the Introduction above, there was now a situation of competition for the survival or destruction of two incompatible world orders. The US was involved in an ideological crusade to impose an economic or political order, rather than simply to contain a Soviet one, as many accounts claim. This interpretation counters the standard orthodox and post-revisionist justification of Washington's role in the first two decades of the Cold War, without giving support to the revisionist emphasis on economics (the importance of the latter notwithstanding) or attributing blame to the US. Support for this interpretation has been provided by one of the most insightful Cold War historians, Scott Lucas, who quotes the following, from correspondence sent to the Psychological Strategy Board:[15] 'Though it seems to be widely believed inside the Government as well as by the public that our policy is simply "containment", it may be doubted whether it is or has been, except for public consumption.'[16]

B. Armaments and Militarization

The first steps to rearm the West came at a time when US and British military experts felt it unlikely that Stalin would deliberately begin a major war. The initial steps were political in nature and designed to create military alliances for political purposes. Furthering the Cold War in this way was, however, not the whole story. The first alliances in Europe—the Anglo-French Treaty of Dunkirk of March 1947 (which still saw Germany as the key menace to peace) and the Brussels Treaty a year later between Britain, France, Belgium, the Netherlands, and Luxembourg—had their roots in European concerns which were separate from the Cold War. The attempt to create a 'Third Force', able to stand up to the superpowers, and the desire to contain Germany, instigated a process of European integration which became tangled with, and taken over by, Cold War demands. The second stage of the process stemmed from a US strategy paper, NSC 68 (see Boxes 4.1 and 4.2), and involved the significant expansion of armed forces. NSC 68 was not a response to the aggression in Korea: it came from the internal debate about fighting the Cold War which began in 1948 and was to continue after the Korean War. While that war made this policy more acceptable to public opinion and legislatures on both sides of the Atlantic, it did not provide the original rationale for Western rearmament, any more than the Berlin crisis provided the original rationale for the North Atlantic Treaty Organization (NATO).

The Third World Power Idea

The involvement of the US in a European military alliance has generally been described by politicians as the key provider of deterrence and security, which they deemed necessary because of the developing Soviet threat to Western Europe. In reality, NATO's origins and its role in the Cold War were complex. As with other features of East–West relations, NATO was born out of a mix of fear and ambition and, in Cold War terms, was designed to serve political, more than military, goals. The broader value of a Western military alliance, linked only partially to the military threat of the Soviet Union, initially reflected different priorities in Washington, Paris, and London. For the Truman administration, having made an economic commitment to Europe, it seemed logical to make a military commitment, if only to defend a significant investment. In Europe, there was not only the communist danger to consider, but also how best to control an economically strong West German state. Concern was understandably most evident in Paris, although there were those in the Foreign Office in London who were worried about, and distrustful, of Germany.

For Britain, the move towards a Western alliance initially formed part of a broader scheme for economic cooperation aimed at the creation of a British-led 'Third Force' in Western Europe, an idea first discussed during the war. This was very different from NATO and showed that a US–European alliance was far from inevitable. By late 1947, sophisticated ideas were being discussed in London for maintaining British influence in the future. By combining the manpower and resources of Western Europe, the Middle East, and the African continent with those of the British Commonwealth, the Foreign Office hoped that this would provide the necessary economic strength (especially after the Marshall Plan put European economies on their feet) for a British-led bloc to stand on equal terms with the US and the Soviet Union. It was believed that the resources of the colonies and the Commonwealth would also be necessary, because

BOX 4.1

NSC 68 (extract)

US Intentions and Capabilities—Actual and Potential

Political and Psychological

Our overall policy at the present time may be described as one designed to foster a world environment in which the American system can survive and flourish. It therefore rejects the concept of isolation and affirms the necessity of our positive participation in the world community.

This broad intention embraces two subsidiary policies. One is a policy which we would probably pursue even if there was no Soviet threat. It is a policy of attempting to develop a healthy international community. The other is the policy of 'containing' the Soviet system. These two policies are closely interrelated and interact on one another. Nevertheless, the distinction between them is basically valid and contributes to a clearer understanding of what we are trying to do.

The policy of trying to develop a healthy international community is the long-term constructive effort we are engaged in. It was this policy which gave rise to our vigorous sponsorship of the UN. It is of course the principal reason for our long continuing endeavours to create and now develop the Inter-American system. It, as much as containment, underlay our efforts to rehabilitate Western Europe. Most of our international economic activities can likewise be explained in terms of this policy.

In a world of polarized power, the policies designed to develop a healthy international community are more than ever necessary to our own strength. As for the policy of 'containment', it is one which seeks by all means short of war to (1) block further expansion of Soviet power, (2) expose the falsities of Soviet pretensions, (3) induce a retraction of the Kremlin's control and influence, and (4) in general, so foster the seeds of destruction of the Soviet system that the Kremlin is brought at last to the point of modifying its behaviour to conform to generally accepted international standards. It was and continues to be cardinal in this policy that we possess superior overall power (1) as an ultimate guarantee of our national security and (2) as an indispensable backdrop to the conduct of the policy of 'containment'. Without superior aggregate military strength, in being and readily mobilizable—a policy of 'containment'—which in effect is a policy of calculated and gradual coercion—is no more than a policy of bluff.

Source: FRUS, 1950, I (State Dept., Washington, DC, 1977) NSC 68, 14 April 1950, 252–3.

Europe could not manufacture enough goods to sell to the dollar zone in order to finance the purchase of imports that Western Europe needed. Raw materials and primary produce, particularly from Africa, would provide exports to the western hemisphere and substitutes for imports from America. For the Foreign Secretary, Ernest Bevin, a 'spiritual union' would be created, in which the anti-communist forces of social democracy, backed by the US, could provide an alternative ideological focus to Soviet communism and America's unrestrained capitalism. More importantly, it would enable Britain to remain a world power as one of the Big Three by assuming leadership of this Third Force.

Serious problems became apparent with a British-led grouping, however, not least because of divisions within London. For example, the Foreign Office advocated the creation of a European Customs Union, which Britain would join.[17] However, they met opposition from the Treasury and the Board of Trade, who saw this as potentially damaging to British interests (especially if Commonwealth markets had to be shared with other Europeans) and unlikely to help tackle the 'dollar gap' (since all West European states had a trade deficit with the US). Military cooperation with Western Europe seemed to offer better prospects for mutual European benefits but, given Britain's relative lack of military resources, this made an American involvement essential. Also, fears of communist agents within the French government and hopes of recreating an exclusive Anglo-American military relationship, such as had existed in the war, made military chiefs less keen on purely European cooperation than the Foreign Office.

There were also those in the State Department who were attracted by the idea of an anti-communist Third Force, as a February 1948 memorandum revealed:

> Some form of political, military, and economic union in Europe will be necessary if the free nations of Europe are to hold their own against the people of the east united under Moscow rule … The only way in which a European union, embracing Britain but excluding eastern Europe, could become economically healthy would be to develop the closest sort of trading relationships either with this hemisphere or with Africa.[18]

If it were to provide for permanent European recovery and the resolution of the dollar-gap problem, then it could serve American interests without incurring continued costs to the US taxpayer. Furthermore, at the end of the last Council of Foreign Ministers meeting, in London in December 1947, Secretary of State Marshall had said that the West Europeans should get some form of European cooperation established, for the Americans to support *before* the nature of that support or involvement could be defined. The US wanted to see a willingness on the part of the West Europeans to protect themselves, before committing American resources further. The fact that it was an election year, and that massive resources were already being committed to the Marshall Aid Programme, also made Washington reluctant to rush into a military alliance in 1948.

Early in the year Bevin worked to create what he now called a 'Western Union', with the signing of the Brussels Treaty on 17 March. The Brussels Treaty was not simply designed to create a security organization, though it did include that. It had important economic clauses, inspired by ideas on future economic integration, as well as providing an indication that military issues were now a consideration. Clearly, the timing of the signature was influenced by the Czech coup and a sudden feeling of West European vulnerability as divisions grew with the Soviets. However, the main short-term fear was a political one, concerned with maintaining West European confidence, rather than the need to face any imminent military threat. It is also noteworthy that the pact referred to Germany as a potential menace. To what extent Bevin was following Marshall's advice, and creating a European security organization that Washington might later support, is also debatable. There is evidence that his hope was still to create a British-led group, even if it cooperated closely with the US. But as the months passed, enthusiasm for this concept waned, even in the Foreign Office. Assessments showed that an independent economic bloc was not viable and that, if Europe failed to recover, Britain could be dragged down by the devastated economies of Western Europe if it tied its future to theirs too closely. Eventually, a major financial crisis in October 1949, which led to a devaluation of the pound and required considerable US support, led the Cabinet to decide in favour of a special place in the American-dominated alliance. In any case, by then, such a solution had been partly established through the creation of NATO. The Third World Power concept was dead and Britain retreated from European economic cooperation.

The Creation of NATO

The reasons for creating what became known as NATO were not primarily geared to hostile Soviet actions in Berlin, nor to perceptions of an imminent Soviet military attack in Europe. What mattered was how an alliance could build the confidence to strengthen the political will to resist communism. Reluctance to accept a mere 'paper' treaty, rather than military aid or a joint military strategy as the basis for agreement, came from the French not the Americans. Britain's main contribution to the creation of NATO was to persuade the French that only through the political gains of signing a paper treaty in the short term would they get an American commitment to provide the defence resources for Western Europe in the long term. The military situation was such that, in March 1948, neither the British nor the Americans had an emergency war plan that set out how to employ existing forces if war should break out. Now that Europeans had signed the Brussels Pact, it became necessary to examine military strategy for future cooperation involving the Americans; and, with the Berlin crisis, there seemed a greater possibility of war 'by accident'.[19] The first emergency plans, produced in the summer of 1948, suggested that neither European nor US forces could halt the Red Army if it marched westwards.[20] But, obviously, such a pessimistic course could not be revealed to the public. It clashed with the political aim of bolstering European confidence, so as to encourage cooperation and resistance to communism. It was hoped that a military alliance, even a paper one, as long as it was backed by US power, could inspire confidence as part of a political Cold War strategy. The fact that the Soviets were not expected to attack meant that the lack of an effective Western military defence strategy did not really matter.

By mid-1948, there was general agreement on some military arrangement linking America to Western Europe, but not on its precise nature. Once it became clear that the Americans preferred to concentrate on a broad, Atlantic pact (partly because of short-lived fears of Soviet pressure on Norway, which suggested that Stalin might try to pick off West European countries one by one), this received priority. Political and constitutional obstacles in the US were removed in June, when the formerly isolationist senator, Arthur Vandenberg, sponsored a resolution in support of regional pacts. In July, talks began between the US, the Brussels Pact, and Canada in Washington. By September 1948, the French had given up on their initial hopes of large-scale US military aid to the Brussels Pact. After that, delays to the treaty were largely due to the US presidential election and discussion of exactly which states to include, the preference eventually being to cast the net widely. Aside from the Brussels Pact, America, and Canada, the alliance included Italy, Norway, Denmark, Iceland, and Portugal. The last two were included largely because they could provide air bases for the US to reinforce Europe in the event of war. It was further evidence of the US desire to prioritize anti-communism over liberalism that Portugal became a member despite having been ruled by a dictatorship since the 1920s.

The Atlantic Pact was formally signed on 4 April 1949 and was clearly directed against the Soviet Union. The West now portrayed an ideological conflict over the political and economic shape of the post-war world, as a military effort to defend strategically important territory. The irony was not just that the idea of such power blocs had been rejected in the immediate aftermath of the war, but that the Soviets appear to have had no desire to attack Western Europe at the time. Western military experts did not expect the USSR to be in a position to launch a war until about the mid-1950s, when the country had recovered from the last one. Indeed, there is evidence that the Western powers did not want to spend money on defence if this militated against another Cold War aim, the need for economic stability. After a NATO council meeting in Lisbon in February 1952, where it was proposed to create a force of 96 divisions, fears grew that this would create major economic and social dislocation. As a result, the force levels were effectively abandoned. Yet that same year the alliance stretched the area it had to defend even further, by extending membership to Greece and Turkey.

Military Considerations for Hot War

Since 1945, all the victor states had demobilized. The US had a monopoly, but limited numbers, of atomic weapons (with 13 in 1947 and 56 in 1948) and had reduced its forces from 10 million in 1945 to 1.4 million in 1947. The Soviets reduced theirs from 12 million to 2.8 million in the same period and only carried out their first atomic test in August 1949.[21] At the same time, they were taking up railway lines in Eastern Europe because of the shortage of steel in the Soviet Union. In early 1947, their 'Plan for the active defence of the territory of the Soviet Union' envisioned three main tasks for the armed forces. The first was to repel aggression and maintain the integrity of the frontiers agreed at the end of the war. The second task, for the Soviet air force, was to repel an air offensive, including one involving nuclear weapons. The third role, for the navy, was to repel a sea-borne assault and to operate in coastal waters in support of Soviet land forces. As in previous campaigns, these defensive operations to halt an invasion of Soviet territory would pave the way for a counter-offensive, but the details of the planned offensive operations have not yet been disclosed. The Soviet posture in Europe after the war, concludes one historian who has examined Soviet sources, 'was the posture of a state determined to consolidate its power on the territory it now occupied, rather than expand that territory'.[22] The militarization of the Cold War began at a time when neither side expected the other deliberately to start a major conflict.

The explosion of the first atomic weapons in summer 1945 clearly had momentous implications for the future nature of warfare. However, the implications were slow to produce new military ideas and the concept of deterrence was not immediately embraced in Western military circles. In fact, while civilian strategists like Bernard Brodie began to think through the implications of weapons that might make war too horrible to contemplate, military thinkers remained either uncertain about the role of atomic weapons or perceived them as merely an extension of conventional strategic bombing. Nor did the Americans believe that atomic weapons would prove decisive. In late 1948, a study of the likely outcome of dropping all their existing atomic bombs on the Soviets concluded that while it would result in 2.7 million deaths and the destruction of between 30 and 40 per cent of Soviet industrial capacity, it would not defeat the Soviet Union, nor prevent Soviet forces advancing into Western Europe or the Middle East. There were those, like Air Force General Curtis LeMay, the head of the Strategic Air Command (which controlled US nuclear bombs) in 1948, who saw nuclear weapons as the ultimate means of ensuring the supremacy of air power. For LeMay, nuclear devastation was an extension of war fighting by the kind of carpet-bombing he had employed against Japan in the Second World War. Total destruction was the way LeMay believed wars would be won in future.[23] Yet not everyone in the US air force accepted the indiscriminate nuclear targeting of cities that LeMay had in mind. In the early 1950s, there were major disputes within the American services about the role of nuclear weapons which, because of the resource implications, paralysed the drawing up of detailed global war plans on an inter-service basis.

Nuclear weapons did not immediately change the approach to war fighting or instantly inaugurate an age dominated by deterrence. It was a change that came gradually and one that was given more impetus by the development of the more powerful hydrogen bomb, than by the first atomic weapons. The hydrogen bomb, first tested by the US in November 1952 and by the Soviets in August 1953, used the fusion of atoms, not just their fission or break-up, to release energy thousands of times more powerful than the atomic bomb. The threat to civilization itself was now real, but it did not prevent the efforts to incorporate nuclear weapons into an active military role, as well as into a more passive one in the form of deterrence. The remark by Foreign Secretary Bevin, in 1947, that Britain must have an atomic bomb with 'the bloody Union Jack flying on top of it'—an aim it achieved five years later—was a sign that nuclear weapons were more of an asset in terms of status than as practical weaponry.

C. The Cold War and Integration in Europe

When European leaders surveyed the situation in Europe at the end of 1947, they faced a number of challenges. There was the dollar shortage, which it was hoped the Marshall Plan would address, providing the impetus for European economic recovery. There was the problem of rebuilding Germany so that it could contribute to economic revival without becoming a threat to peace once more. There was the need to prevent communist parties from becoming more popular and perhaps forcing their way back into power. Precise motives for seeking European integration in the various capitals stemmed from different national priorities: the political need to resist communism was strongest in France and Italy, for example. It has already been seen how Bevin, at least for a time, hoped to use influence in Europe to maximize Britain's importance in the world role. An interest in 'federalism', which might have led rapidly to the creation of a European state, was evidently restricted to a minority and it is still far from clear whether European integration represented an erosion of the nation state or merely its adaptation to a new role. On the one hand, the French in particular have been seen as driven by national self-interest and the process of integration has been interpreted as the salvation of the nation state in Europe, after its failures in the Second World War.[24] On the other hand, liberal institutionalists, like Joseph Nye and Robert Keohane, see European institutions as significant in their own right and capable of producing greater international cooperation. Similarly, functionalists in the tradition of David Mitrany and Ernst Haas see European integration as promoting a transfer of allegiance away from the nation state.

After mid-1948, the French government, though not necessarily the French public, was reconciled to the economic rebuilding of West Germany and the probable creation of a West German state. The concern was over how to achieve this without the risks that might flow from an independent, economically powerful West Germany. The answer seemed to lie in integrating Germany into a greater European whole, with 'supranational' bodies—bodies that involved some surrender of national sovereignty—to curtail German independence. Thus, while the British saw Europe as part of a solution to their global weakness, the French gave more emphasis to concerns nearer home. In September 1948, the French proposed that the Ministerial Council of the Brussels Treaty should study the idea of a European parliament, with the result, a year later, of the Council of Europe. This had a wider membership than the Brussels Treaty and included an Assembly, but the last was merely a consultative body, and real power rested with ministers on an intergovernmental level. The Council of Europe, though it proved invaluable in encouraging respect for human rights in Europe over the following decades, therefore lacked a supranational element. But it was also significant for showing that France was now taking a lead in European integration, as British interest in ideas for a third force (already discussed) waned.

The first moves to closer European cooperation coincided with the implementation of the Marshall Plan (through the European Recovery Programme of

1948–52) and talks on military alliances, both processes which involved a strong element of European cooperation. Like the process of decolonization, European integration was linked to the dynamics of the Cold War. Washington strongly supported the idea, believing it would strengthen capitalism if a large, single market were created on US lines. The CIA bankrolled pro-federalist groups. In Western Europe itself, old fears about Germany combined with, and to some extent were softened by, new fears about Soviet communism. The recipe for dealing with the communist threat, by strengthening capitalism through the Marshall Plan, could be neatly combined with cementing West Germany into a prosperous European economic and military bloc, which simultaneously put limits on German independence. The first stage of the process began in earnest with the Schuman Plan, launched in 1950, just before the Korean War broke out, and was implemented in 1952, when the European Coal and Steel Community (ECSC) was created. Behind this lay the vision of Jean Monnet, head of the French reconstruction plan, with a broad, political agenda for the development of European integration, as well as a narrower, economic agenda defined by the needs of French recovery.

The Schuman Plan and the European Coal and Steel Community

It was Monnet who devised the ECSC proposal, which was announced by the French Foreign Minister, Robert Schuman, on 8 May 1950. Schuman had been born in Luxembourg to a family from Lorraine, which had been part of Germany between 1871 and 1919. This background made him ideally suited to the appeal of European institutions as a way to reconcile France and Germany, even if they were also geared to French national interests. The Schuman Plan would bring Franco-German reconciliation in a way that bound Germany to its Western neighbours and served the needs of the French coal and steel industry. The more closely the German economy was integrated into the Western European, the less likely that it would be aggressive and nationalistic, especially if coal and steel industries were involved, because these were the backbone of a mid-twentieth-century industrial economy, as well as essential to weapons manufacture. West German steel production was much larger than the French and had significant cost advantages over it. Coal costs were higher in France, which in the post-war years was heavily dependent on supplies from the Ruhr, in north-west Germany. Price negotiations were therefore necessary if French industry was not to be disadvantaged—or unless the entire Franco-German coal and steel production was controlled by a single authority. In announcing his proposals for such a high authority, Schuman pointed out that this would 'create the first concrete foundation for a European federation which is so indispensable for the preservation of peace'. The threat to peace which the Germans represented would be reduced by federal controls, while the threat to peace which the Soviets represented would be reduced by the Western European nations uniting together.

While the French saw important economic and political advantages in the Plan, the British saw significant dangers. London was keen to support the efforts of its European allies in the early 1950s, but also keen to maintain its independence as a great power and not inclined, therefore, to become part of any supranational organization. The impact of the proposed Coal and Steel Community on Britain's nationalized industries was not seen as favourable, nor was greater economic cooperation after 1948 seen as bringing benefits, partly because most British trade was with the world beyond Europe. Significantly, however, German leaders saw political advantages in European integration and, in June 1950, proved ready to support the Schuman Plan, even as Britain rejected membership. The German chancellor, Konrad Adenauer, who assumed office in August 1949, was a staunch liberal democrat, a past opponent of communism and Nazism, who wanted to tie his country closely to the West, removing any chance of a return to dictatorship and militarism. He even proved willing to defer reunification with East Germany in order to anchor West Germany into a process of European integration. He also saw cooperation with France (which, hitherto, had been suspicious of German revival) as a way of hastening the removal of occupation controls.

Franco-German goals could be achieved through the Schuman Plan without British involvement and, although Monnet might have preferred them to join in discussions on the Schuman Plan, he was not prepared for them to delay progress. The French therefore issued invitations to discussions in Paris on the basis that acceptance required also accepting the principle of supranationality. The British were reluctant to do this: they wanted to know, in advance, what degree of control over their own coal and steel industries they would have to surrender. It was not so much the principle of giving up sovereignty that the British rejected as the open-ended commitment in advance. Attempts were made to find a formula to enable Britain to participate, but none could be found and the French—whose priority, after all, was to secure German participation in the scheme—imposed a deadline on talks. The loss of sovereignty was essential for the French, in order to tie down Germany, and not a principle they could compromise. The significance of British exclusion from the ECSC, which was established in 1952, with a strong High Authority under Monnet, remains a matter of debate. It has been described as 'missing the bus' on European integration. For twenty years, Britain was left in a detached position, when in 1948 Bevin had hoped to lead a European bloc. But the decision was not a matter of oversight; rather, London wished to avoid being seen as primarily a European power and had real fears, both about Europe's economic prospects and the need to preserve its global trade, based around the Empire-Commonwealth and Sterling Area. For France, in contrast, the Schuman Plan proved the cornerstone for a new relevance in the world, based on leadership of European integration. But the new path could prove an uncertain one, as the next supranational initiative showed.

The Pleven Plan and the European Defence Community

Although the military dimensions of the Brussels Pact and NATO had been less important than the political cooperation they embodied, the military wished to add some military clout to the Western defence. They wanted sufficient conventional forces to defend against a future attack, when the Soviets had recovered from the war. Even before the Korean War, both London and Washington concluded that some military contribution from West Germany would be necessary. At the same time, they were aware of the opposition this would produce, only four years after the defeat of Nazism. In late 1949, the British military began arguing for an armed German 'gendarmerie', but faced Foreign Office opposition. The French were likely to oppose such a development and the Soviets might be so hostile that they could launch a preventive war. The British military, however, could argue that a gendarmerie was simply the equivalent to the East German *Bereitschaften*, which the Soviets had already formed and was more a miniature army than a police force. In May 1950, Bevin approved the creation of a gendarmerie of 25,000 men, a proposal that fitted in with current thinking from Konrad Adenauer, who shared Britain's desire to defend Germany as far east as possible.[25]

The following month the Korean War broke out and the prospect of hot war loomed larger. Events in East Asia gave the German rearmament question a new importance, partly because North Korea's invasion of the South suggested that an East German attack on West Germany might be possible. By September, the American secretary of state, Dean Acheson, had been won over and he proposed the creation of a West German army to Bevin and Schuman. To win support for this, he offered a 'package deal', with a greater American military commitment to European defence, including the appointment of a US supreme commander for NATO. The British accepted this idea in principle, although they were increasingly cooler to the idea of German rearmament now that the Korean War had raised the stakes, by making a European hot war seem possible. The French were at first totally opposed to Acheson's scheme, but Monnet feared that this stance could offend Germany and bring about the collapse of the Schuman Plan. He therefore hastily developed a supranational blueprint for involving German forces in Western European defence. This time, the proposal was announced by the Prime Minister, René Pleven. The Pleven Plan was not for a German army integrated into NATO but for the creation of a European army into which German and other forces would be integrated, thereby removing the spectre of independent German forces with their own general staff. The plan posed a threat to NATO cohesion and to basic British military values and traditions. Even though their commitment to the importance of the Middle East was being eroded because of the attention given to Europe, they still lacked enthusiasm for a continental commitment and cooperation with European partners who were regarded as somewhat inferior. Economic and power-political interests remained important considerations for Britain and other European states, but these have tended to be underestimated by historians concentrating on the alleged security problem which they claim arose from the Cold War and the Soviet threat to Western Europe.

D. NSC 68, Rearmament, and the Cold War Offensive Controversy

The rearmament issue was closely connected to security and to the future development of the Cold War as involving a nuclear confrontation which began with the Soviet testing of an atomic bomb in 1949. The linking of the two separate issues of preparing for a possible hot war in the future and fighting the Cold War in the present now became more closely connected in the minds of some American policy-makers. In hot war terms, the Soviet bomb presented greater risks for the West because they would be more fearful of using atomic weapons. In the short term, the threat of retaliation would be faced only by the Europeans but there was a medium-term threat to the US. As Paul Nitze, a member of Kennan's Policy Planning Staff in the State Department pointed out, the fact that there might be no resort to nuclear weapons made conventional forces much more important. Consequently, in order to devote resources to increasing conventional forces in Western Europe it might be necessary to lower, rather than raise, civilian standards of living there.[26]

These kinds of ideas were to give a boost to advocates of West German rearmament but they were at odds with a key component of Cold War strategy. The Marshall Plan involved the reconstruction of Western Europe in order to remove the conditions of poverty and austerity which were deemed to give root to communism. For those like George Kennan who had argued for containment in this way between 1946 and 1948, rearmament and the militarization of the Cold War made no sense. However, once communism had been contained in Eastern Europe by 1948 and seemed unlikely to spread westwards, Kennan had also advocated the Cold War strategy of liberation of the Soviet satellites in order to win the Cold War by the rolling back of communism. Now if this Cold War fighting was to act as a provocation to the Soviets, their reluctance to risk a hot war rather than capitulate would actually be increased if the West rearmed to gain a clear preponderance of power.

Rearming for Cold War—NSC 68

The whole American approach to the Cold War was debated in 1949 and the famous NSC 68 memorandum was the culmination of that debate, which signalled a victory for the aggressive Cold War fighters and re-armers. A leading advocate of this group was Paul Nitze, even though he continued to believe that 'a total war started deliberately by the Soviets is a tertiary risk'.[27] The question was not whether the US should prepare for such an eventuality but how it should prepare for the prevention of hot war while fighting an offensive Cold War. For some, the answer was that hot war could only or best be avoided by winning the Cold War, which meant the fall of the Soviet government and the collapse of its satellite empire, which was what covert operations were seen by many of their advocates as designed to achieve.

Although Western support for Ukrainian rebels and anti-communist groups in Romania and Bulgaria began in 1946, by 1949 covert operations involved significant support for armed rebels and dissidents in the Soviet bloc, the infiltration of agents, the development of underground resistance, and the facilitation of guerrilla operations in strategic areas. Unmarked American aircraft were used to send supplies, dollars, and gold into the Baltic states, Czechoslovakia, Romania, and Yugoslavia, and Ukraine. Propaganda was broadcast through the voice of America and Radio Free Europe.[28] As outlined in a secret annex to NSC 68, there was a substantial attempt to implement what was termed 'The Ring Plan'. Powerful transmitters were to surround the Soviet satellites in order to prevent the Russians jamming the propaganda broadcast by American radio stations. Ukraine, Poland, and Hungary were the three main targets.[29]

The efforts to promote psychological warfare and subversion were not, however, confined to Europe. The success of the Chinese communists created new opportunities for the US to use the troops of the defeated Chinese nationalists in order to fight an aggressive Cold War in Asia. These efforts to assist armed incursions by the nationalists into mainland China took several forms and became increasingly important with Chinese involvement in the Korean War in 1950. General Li Mi, the Chinese nationalist warlord from Yunnan province, had retreated into Burma after the communist victory. In 1951, supported by the CIA through its running of front companies such as Civil Air Transport, Western Enterprises in Taiwan, and the Sea Supply Company in Thailand, Mi Li attempted an invasion of Yunnan which was repeated the following year with around 10,000 troops. The force advanced 60 miles into China before being repulsed. At the same time, in the early 1950s, the CIA was parachuting nationalists into communist China to build up opposition in the remote areas and to conduct sabotage missions on important installations.[30]

It is most unlikely that the Chinese and the Russians saw such actions as the implementation of containment rather than an attempt to destroy communism and to bring their subjects under the umbrella of capitalism. Could the Cold War then be described as an attempt to bring down communist regimes and liberate their subjects? Richard Aldrich, in a brilliantly researched book, has argued that within a year of coming to power in 1953 the Republican administration under President Dwight D. Eisenhower abandoned liberation but he never makes clear when liberation began. This is part of the controversy of whether the problem can be avoided by legitimately describing liberation and the overthrow of the Soviet government or its satellite regimes as part of containment.

In addition, there are different interpretations of the ultimate purpose of the new offensive Cold War policy of the US. The central issue is whether the Americans were keen to use their support for dissidents and rebels to overthrow the regimes in Moscow and Beijing and thereby win the Cold War, or whether their aims were less ambitious and more limited. A number of reasons have been put forward to justify the latter explanation. The British Russia Committee thought the goal of these policies was the stirring up of trouble in the Soviet Empire and George Kennan argued that covert operations were to maintain pressure on the Soviets in order to make them less likely to probe Western weak spots. William Donovan, head of the Office of Strategic Services, the wartime equivalent of the CIA, was clear that the aim of Cold War fighting was not liberation but 'keeping the communists off balance'. It has also been suggested that covert operations were a means of 'venting frustration against the intractability of Cold War problems and a means of finding ideological expression, rather than realistic plans to overturn communist rule'; or were 'a form of ideological aggression, the only honest expression of America as a freedom-loving nation'.[31]

On the other hand, when the Foreign Office became concerned at some of the American operations, because of a fear of hot war, they argued that instead of encouraging risings and revolts more specific operations should be launched against particular targets.[32] This clearly points to the difference between a policy of 'pinpricks' to keep the Soviets preoccupied and a policy designed to seriously threaten regimes behind the Iron Curtain. Lloyd Berkner, the director of Project Troy,[33] told Secretary of State Dean Acheson that 'it is possible to organize an aggressive political war of sufficient effectiveness to bring the Soviet Union to its knees in a relatively short time without resorting to widespread military action'. And the guidelines for Radio Free Europe defined its purpose as contributing 'to the liberation of nations imprisoned behind the Iron Curtain by sustaining their morale and stimulating in them a spirit of non-cooperation with the Soviet-dominated regimes'. According to its handbook, speakers should assert that there was 'no possibility of an enduring peace anywhere in the world until the Moscow-dominated regimes have been overthrown'. Kennan in 1948 had advocated not merely the liberation of the satellites but attempts to change boundaries and thereby break up the Soviet Union by encouraging minority groups to split. Moreover, a member of the Psychological Strategy Board, which was established in 1951 in a vain attempt to coordinate all activity related to the fighting of the Cold War, called for an all-out psychological counter-offensive. This was deemed to require less of an official change of policy than a frank recognition of what is really explicit in existing policy objectives, that is:

(a) abandoning 'containment' and openly espousing 'liberation';

(b) scrapping—not necessarily in public but in our strategic planning—the passive wishful thinking of 'coexistence' and adopting a positive approach that acknowledges the vital necessity of overthrowing the Kremlin regime;

(c) discarding our present strategy of fighting a defensive delaying action in the Cold War while we prepare to defend ourselves in a hot one, and substitute, therefore, a fully planned and phased global strategy of offensive underground fighting.

Others would go further in their suggestions, and consultants advising the Psychological Strategy Board proposed in November 1951 that:

US power and interests require continuation of the present hostilities in Korea, either on an active or standby basis until such time as the Japanese can be infiltrated on to the Asian land base. This concept requires control of a resurgent rearmed Japan with a major drive towards the Manchurian complex.

In Europe, the US was to work with Western Europeans, including the West Germans, to bring about 'the break-up of the USSR into separate national component states so that, in effect, the emissaries of the Grand Dukes of Moscovy are sent back to Moscow'.[34]

These different views do indicate that American policy-makers had different perceptions of what the goals of Cold War fighting should be, of what they actually were, and of what their consequences might involve. It thus makes it difficult to define precisely when liberation replaced containment because of these differences over the desirability of an offensive strategy and what it involved. What can be said is that the military on both sides of the Atlantic were generally more in favour of trying to win the Cold War than officials in the Foreign Office or the State Department. In the US, this was reflected in the bureaucratic wrangling, which, according to the CIA, meant it was impossible 'to arrive at a definitive answer for the fundamental question of whether it is possible to live with the Kremlin or whether it must be destroyed'. In Britain, Air Vice-Marshal Slessor had argued as early as the beginning of 1948 that the way to avoid hot war was to win the Cold War. By the end of the year, the desirability of winning the Cold War was endorsed by the Chief of the Air Staff Lord Tedder, who defined it as the overthrowing of the Soviet regime within five years.[35] Once the Korean War had begun, the British Chiefs of Staff were to argue that an offensive strategy of fighting the Cold War was even more necessary. If the West failed to win the Cold War, they would be increasingly embroiled in limited hot wars like Korea, which Britain's defence budget could ill afford to bear. As yet, nothing has been found in the limited number of archival resources available in the former Soviet Union to indicate any discussions about the desirability of destroying Western regimes by winning the Cold War. It may be that it was never considered feasible and that some historians researching Russian archives are right in their assessment that the emphasis in the Kremlin was on building up the Soviet bloc rather than undermining the Americans in Western Europe.[36]

Some in the American military were considering not only how to destroy the Kremlin by Cold War but also the possibility of doing so by resorting to hot war. To a large extent, this reflected the views of those who believed that there could be no coexistence with the Soviets. Either Moscow would start a war once they were ready, or else they would force the West to take military action to prevent the spread of communism. For those thinking along those lines, especially in the US air force, war with the Soviet Union was inevitable in the not too distant future, and the issue was when it would be best to fight it. In 1951, the British Director of Naval Intelligence noted that 'there is a clear danger of the USA becoming involved in a preventive war against Russia, however firmly their NATO allies object'.[37] Obviously, like the consequences of Cold War fighting, this was very much linked to a rearmament drive, which would provide for clear American military superiority in the light of the post-Soviet atom bomb danger that the Russian conventional forces would become relatively stronger.

The commitment to rearmament was clearly a feature of NSC 68 and the reasons for it can be linked to allegedly far-sighted people understanding the nature of the growing Soviet menace soon to be confirmed by Moscow-supported North Korean aggression. Yet NSC 68 was not just about rearmament, and its origins can also be traced to ideas about American perceptions of how best to achieve US goals in the East–West conflict, which were related more to the very existence of communist states than to a response to particular Chinese and Soviet actions. It was the general threat that was highlighted at the start of NSC 68 and portrayed in universal terms. The issues involved the 'fulfilment or destruction' not only of the American Republic, whose 'fundamental purpose is to assure the integrity and vitality of our free society' but of 'civilisation itself'. The Soviets were deemed to have universal goals aimed at domination of the world, or civilization (the free American society), in a negation of freedom through a 'quest for total power over all men'. Consequently:

> In a shrinking world which now faces the threat of atomic warfare, it is not an adequate objective merely to check the Kremlin design, for the absence of war among nations is becoming less and less tolerable. This fact imposes on us, in our own interests, the responsibility of world leadership. It demands that we make the attempt, and accept the risks inherent in it, to bring about order and justice by means consistent with the principles of freedom and democracy.

Here was reflected a perception of the temporary nature of peace and a desire to avoid a military stalemate and pursue American hegemony. Yet in an apparent compromise between the drive for Cold War victory and liberation on the one hand and containment or coexistence on the other,

> [I]t might be possible to create a situation which will induce the Soviet Union to accommodate itself, with or without the conscious abandonment of its design, to coexistence on tolerable terms with the non-Soviet world ... The objectives outlined in NSC 20/4 ... Are fully consistent with the objectives stated in this paper and they remain valid. The growing intensity of the conflict which has been imposed on us, however, requires the changes of emphasis and the additions that are apparent. Coupled with the probable fission bomb capability and possible thermonuclear capability of the Soviet Union, the intensifying struggle requires us to face the fact that we can expect no lasting abatement of the crisis unless and until a change occurs in the nature of the Soviet system.[38]

Central to NSC 68 therefore was consideration of how best to destroy the Soviet satellite empire and ultimately to win the Cold War. The Soviet Union itself could be transformed or destroyed, and the appeal of a free and healthy capitalist society could be relied on to contain the spread of communism. The reality was that the Soviets did not and could not use the kind of covert actions and support for rebel groups to endeavour to undermine the West, and many still have believed that such a situation was likely to lead to an undesirable hot war. The Soviets could only manipulate Western communist parties to endeavour to bring about change and therefore would need to rely on military force. In this situation, it made sense to go for massive rearmament to deter the Soviets from resorting to war either as a means of dominating the globe or as a reaction to their imminent demise brought on by a successful Western strategy of fighting the Cold War.

NSC 68 made clear the importance of the connection between rearmament and a more proactive and offensive fighting of the Cold War, rather than simply preparing for a Soviet hot war offensive. 'If such a course of increasing our military power is adopted now, the US would have the capability of eliminating the disparity between its military strength and the exigencies of the situation we face; eventually of gaining the initiative in the "cold" war and of materially delaying if not stopping the Soviet offensives in war itself.' And there was a third pillar to the NSC 68 strategy derived from the idea that rearmament would make the US appear resolute and determined, which would encourage its friends in Europe. Without the sense of purpose provided by the mobilization of greater military power, the free world for some unexplained reason would become demoralized. It was an interesting feature of the early Cold War that both sides were appealing for support for a particular ideology and way of life and both had doubts about their ability to attract such support without other Cold War measures.[39]

Time and again NSC 68 would come back to the connection between winning the Cold War and using rearmament to reduce the risk of hot war.

> The risk of having no better choice than to capitulate or precipitate a global war at any number of pressure points is bad enough in itself, but it is multiplied by the weakness it imparts to our position in the Cold War. Instead of appearing strong and resolute we are continually at the verge of appearing and being alternately irresolute and desperate; yet it is the Cold War which we must win, because both the Kremlin design, and our fundamental purpose give it the first priority.

For those assuming that the Soviets would attack when they believed they could win, rearmament would buy time for the fighting of the Cold War to at least produce some results.

> Such a build up of strength could safeguard and increase our retaliatory power, and thus might put off for some time the date when the Soviet Union could calculate that a surprise blow would be advantageous. This would provide additional time for the effects of our policies to produce a modification of the Soviet system.

Without the build-up of strength, the writers of NSC envisaged that (without producing any evidence other than the Soviet atom bomb) the balance of strength would continue to change to the advantage of the Russians. The American possession of nuclear weapons, while it could 'open the road to victory in a long conflict, it is not sufficient by itself to advance the position of the US in the cold war'. Consequently, 'a build-up of the military capabilities of the US and the free world is a precondition to the achievement of the objectives outlined in this report and to the protection of the US against disaster'.[40] Whether disaster would be less likely with some different objectives was not considered.

What was considered was persevering with what were deemed the existing programmes, war, isolation, or a military build-up as part of meeting Cold War objectives. The first scenario was criticized because the:

military capabilities, actual and potential, of the US and the rest of the free world, together with the apparent determination of the free world to resist further Soviet expansion, have not induced the Kremlin to relax its pressures generally or to give up the initiative in the cold war. On the contrary the Soviet Union has consistently pursued a bold foreign policy modified only when its probing revealed a determination and an ability of the free world to resist encroachment upon it.

Crucially, the resistance of encroachment was not deemed sufficient, as 'a continuation of present trends will mean that the US and especially other free countries will tend to shift to the defensive, or to follow a dangerous policy of bluff, because the maintenance of a firm initiative in the Cold War is closely related to aggregate strength in being and readily available'. Nor were economic programmes designed to remove the causes of communism regarded as sufficient. Finally, NSC 68, while ruling out negotiation at the present time, suggested that without a build-up of American military strength any attempt to negotiate a general settlement on US terms would probably be long drawn-out and ineffective.[41] In a sense, NSC 68 had rejected the very concept of containment but was struggling to define an acceptable way to move beyond that and specify the precise nature and objectives of roll-back and Cold War victory.

Isolation, as an alternative to the present policies, was ruled out because the abandonment of the European allies was deemed likely to result in the Soviet domination of most of Eurasia. And many Americans 'would feel a deep sense of responsibility and guilt for having abandoned their former friends and allies'. More importantly, with the resources of Eurasia the Soviet's relative military capabilities would increase and the US government would find itself facing a number of unpalatable options. There would be those advocating 'peace' on Soviet terms while others 'would seek to defend the US by creating a regimented system which would permit the assignment of a tremendous part of our resources to defence. Under such a state of affairs our national morale would be corrupted and the integrity and vitality of our system subverted.'[42]

The prospect of war which some favoured was rejected on the grounds that it would not be supported by the American people, and would give the US enormous problems in re-establishing some sort of order. Even a victory would bring the US:

little if at all closer to victory in the fundamental ideological conflict ... and that the only sure victory lies in the frustration of the Kremlin design by the steady development of the moral and material strength of the free world and its projection into the Soviet world in such a way as to bring about an internal change in the Soviet system ... A more rapid build-up of political, economic, and military strength and thereby of confidence in the free world than is now contemplated is the only course which is consistent with progress toward achieving our political purpose. The frustration of the Kremlin's design requires the free world to develop a successfully functioning political and economic system and a vigorous political offensive against the Soviet Union. These, in turn, require an adequate military shield under which they can develop.

In other words, a military victory was of little value in securing a way of life and the global triumph of capitalism and democracy over alternative economic and political systems.[43]

Rearming for Hot War, Questioning NSC 68

NSC 68 and its rearmament strategy, like NATO, were initially designed more to create the conditions for a strong foreign policy geared to fighting the Cold War and strengthening allies than to providing the resources for a military victory over the Soviet Union.

The immediate objectives—to the achievement of which such a build-up of strength is a necessary but not sufficient condition—are a renewed initiative in the Cold War and a situation to which the Kremlin would find it expedient to accommodate itself, first by relaxing tensions and pressures and then by gradual withdrawal.[44]

Yet the Kremlin had not embarked on any new initiatives. Rather the triumph of communism in China, combined with the Soviet atomic bomb, had created a fear that the American way of life, while secure in Western Europe, would not be universally emulated. The power of the Soviet Union was seen as sufficiently dangerous, despite its wartime losses, to detract from American achievements and as the source of a way of life which could become universal, by imposition if not emulation. Ultimately, therefore, the successes of communism would have to be reversed and NSC 68 was a clarion call for more military power that would enable cold warfare to triumph without a global conflict even though it was unclear how this triumph

BOX 4.2

NSC 68: An Extract

NSC 68 is based on the assumption that the military power of the USSR and its satellites is increasing in relation to that of the US and its allies. In view of the vast preponderance of US and allied assets in every respect except that of manpower, that assumption needs more documentation than is contained in NSC 68. In particular, no attention seems to have been given to the question of the possible drain which recent developments may have placed on Soviet military strength. Tightening of controls at home and in particular in the satellites would tie down military manpower and equipment. The furnishing of military technicians to China in any number would constitute an important drain on the USSR whose supply is relatively limited. Put another way, it is hard to accept a conclusion that the USSR is approaching a straight-out military superiority over us when, for example, (1) our air force is vastly superior qualitatively, is greatly superior numerically in the bombers, trained crews and other facilities necessary for offensive warfare; (2) our supply of fission bombs is much greater than that of the USSR, as is our thermonuclear potential; (3) our navy is so much stronger than that of the USSR that they should not be mentioned in the same breath; (4) the economic health and military potential of our allies is, with our help, growing daily; and (5) while we have treaties of alliance with and are furnishing arms to countries bordering the USSR, the USSR has none with countries within thousands of miles of us.

Source: FRUS, 1950 (State Dept., Washington, DC, 1977); Comments by the Bureau of the Budget on NSC 68, 8 May 1950.

would be achieved. The global conflict was something the Soviet Union, according to NSC 68, might now contemplate within the next four to five years, when it would possess sufficient capability to deliver a significant surprise atomic attack. As with the Cold War situation, this too required greater military strength for defence and deterrence rather than the offensive covert measures generally referred to in NSC 20/4 and reaffirmed in NSC 68. The needs of hot war began to assume greater importance after the outbreak of the Korean War, which convinced some in the US that Moscow was now prepared to risk a major conflict to achieve its goals.

The planned military expansion set out in NSC 68/4 and approved after the outbreak of the Korean War was on an unprecedented scale. The force goals for the 1952 financial year were 18 divisions, 397 combat vessels, and 95 air wings, compared with the previously planned goals for 1954 of 10 divisions, 281 naval vessels, and 58 air wings. In all, the numbers of military personnel were to double to 3,211,000. By the beginning of the summer of 1951, the US army had 18 divisions, the navy 342 combat ships, and the air force 87 wings.[45] Ironically, just as the military build-up was taking place, the US armed services were so riven by rivalry that they were unable to agree how these forces should be used if the Soviets were to launch a surprise attack within the next twelve months. This rivalry bedevilled the planning process, which had always suffered from the fact that war plans, for example a plan for a strategic offensive, could be drawn up by the individual services for a particular year and would then have to be incorporated into a joint planning process. The initial process could constitute outline plans as well as those geared to existing circumstances or long- and medium-term plans. In the wake of difficulties over agreement to approve the 1951–2 joint emergency plan (for fighting a war within twelve months with existing resources), related to the agreed outline plan, Truman attempted to systematize the planning process.

From the summer of 1952, long-, medium-, and short-term objectives would be defined for a ten-year period as a Joint Long Range Strategic Exercise, a Joint Strategic Objectives Plan, and a Joint Capabilities Plan, with the latter covering the forthcoming year. The Strategic Objectives Plan was to cover three different types or phases of conflict ranging from the peacetime conflict short of global war to the emergency phase of general war and the additional forces needed for a mobilization base along with the US and allied requirements in the first four years of general war. Objective and Capability plans would dictate priorities for resources and mobilization, which, in turn, would influence the relative importance of the services' roles. In this context, the main differences were over the importance of the strategic nuclear offensive with the army and the navy rejecting the overwhelming importance which the air force wished to attach to it. The result was that it took until March 1953 to draft a Joint Capabilities Plan, which the Joint Strategic Plans Committee spent three months arguing over without agreement. By the time the Joint Chiefs of Staff began debating it, the time period it was supposed to apply to had ended. The Joint Operations Plans ran into even greater difficulties, and if global war had occurred there would have been no combined plan for dealing with it.[46]

The fact that an enormous programme of military expansion was implemented owed less to the cogent arguments of the military strategists and the drafters of NSC 68 than to the outbreak of the Korean War, which increased the sense of insecurity in Washington. The fact was that NSC 68 rested on a number of general and questionable assessments that were disputed by other members of the administration and remain unproven to this day. The first, which was questioned by a leading State Department Soviet expert, Charles Bohlen, concerned Soviet aims. Bohlen took issue, not with the idea of rearmament, but with the depiction of the Soviets as hell bent on world domination. If that were the case, then war would be inevitable unless the Soviet regime was brought down. Here was the crux of the argument before and after NSC 68. The acceptance of the Soviets as determined on world domination ruled out the possibility of coexistence and the only issue, if that were the case, was whether the Soviet Union should be destroyed by cold or hot war. Bohlen, however, was to become an advocate of containment and coexistence and was therefore repeatedly to challenge some of the NSC 68 assessments of the goals of the Soviet regime. In 1952, he became responsible for coordinating the first major attempt at re-evaluating the goals of the Soviet Union and the implications for the national security of the US in the Cold War.

In the meantime, there were critics of other dubious assumptions contained in NSC 68. The Bureau of the Budget took exception to the idea that the Cold War was a conflict over the future of civilization between the 'slave world' and the 'free world'. While the Soviet Union, it argued, could properly be called a slave state, it was not true that the US and its friends constituted a free world. There were those living under the corrupt Quirino government in the Philippines and those in Indo-China who could not be termed free, and vast numbers of people who were in neither Cold War camp. The fact was that this simplistic and inaccurate approach to freedom obscured the important point that many people were attracted to communism precisely because they were experiencing despotic and/or corrupt governments.[47]

Despite these important question marks about the assumptions underlying NSC 68, the Korean War made it difficult to question the conclusion not only that more rearmament was necessary but also that a new phase in Moscow's quest for world domination had begun. When changes in the world situation in the light of the Korean War were examined in NSC 114, the conclusion was that the Soviet willingness to accept the risk of global war was greater than envisaged in NSC 68. Moreover, Moscow was now deemed to be preparing the Russian people for war with the US in order to achieve global domination. Whereas in April 1950 it was assumed that 1954 was the year when this would be most likely, by August 1951 it was argued in NSC 114 that this time of maximum danger already existed and would continue to do so until rearmament was complete.[48]

Bohlen continued to take issue with this interpretation of Soviet strategy as, like Kennan and the US ambassador in Moscow, he believed that the Soviets had no desire to start a global war. This did not mean that Bohlen and others in the State Department were averse to some degree of rearmament; it meant that they did not view rearmament as part of a crusade against an enemy that was committed to world domination and prepared to go to war to bring it about because of its revolutionary ideology. They tended to see Soviet ambitions as limited ones that had to be checked, which in a sense was a reversion to something like containment without any aggressive US Cold War attempts at roll-back that required greater strength to deter the Soviets from acting to prevent their demise. For Bohlen,

> In the eyes of Soviet rulers, they are in a constant state of warfare with all non-Soviet powers and organizations. However, the chief purpose of the Soviet Union is not the worldwide extension of communism to which all other considerations are subordinated, but rather the reverse. The world revolutionary movement is, since the inception of Stalin's dictatorship in Russia, the servant and not the master of the Soviet Union. Ever since his accession to power the guiding thought of the Stalinist Group has been that under no circumstances and for no revolutionary gains must the Soviet state be involved in risks to the maintenance of Soviet power in Russia. The process of imperialistic expansion will always take place when opportunities for such expansion exist without serious risk to the maintenance of Soviet power in Russia, but will not be undertaken if, in the eyes of the Kremlin, the acquisition of any positions for communism involves a serious risk to the Soviet system.

> Soviet actions since the end of the Second World War confirm in every respect the accuracy of this judgement. For at least six years after 1945, it was believed that it was within the power of the Soviet Union to acquire by overt force virtually all of continental Western Europe and the Middle East, since there was no force even remotely comparable to that which the Soviets could bring to bear in those areas. The reason why the Soviet Union has not capitalized on these opportunities is clearly the fear of world war or rather war with the US which would inevitably risk the continued existence of the system in Russia. The case of the armed aggression in Korea, according to available evidence, is not a departure from traditional Soviet caution in this respect but appears to have been based on a very profound miscalculation on the part of the Kremlin as to what US reaction would be.[49]

E. The Growing Importance of Communist China and the Conflict in Korea

It has been suggested (see Chapter 2, C) that the idea of a Cold War developing separately in Asia is a misperception despite the fact that the establishment of a new, unified China in October 1949 was the result of the particular circumstances that produced a communist victory over the nationalists in the Chinese civil war (see Chapter 2, C). In order to understand Soviet and American reactions to this, one has to take into account the regional circumstances and the way in which East Asian events interacted with broader international considerations in the 1940s. Such interactions have to be seen in terms of the Cold War's ideological nature and in terms of the impact on the regional power balance. The latter cannot simply be incorporated into analyses of Soviet–American relations based on the assumption that a gain for one was a loss for the other. To some extent, communist China's emergence was a threat to both powers and both were uncertain about how best to respond.

'Who Lost China?'

In the West, both at the time and in the historiography, controversy has arisen over how the emergence of another communist state was allowed to happen. Was there any possibility of preventing the alliance between the Soviet Union and communist China, which was formalized through the Sino-Soviet Treaty of February 1950? These issues became part of an American debate, which centred on the allocation of blame for the communist victory and played a key role in US politics. Based on the theme of 'Who lost China?' it contributed to the witch-hunts in the early 1950s of Senator Joseph McCarthy that led to many people being accused of communist sympathies. The degree of intolerance and persecution which this represented is a matter of debate but many lost their jobs and careers on the basis of false allegations that stoked up anti-communism and contributed to the Cold War crusade in the US.

The idea that somebody in the US could have lost such a vast and populous country as China is an extraordinary example of the American-centric world view. It assumes that in the wake of developments in, or actions by, foreign states, the US could have done something to improve what in this instance was a Cold War situation. And it goes counter to the views of all US policy-makers who believed by 1948, if not before, that nothing could be done to prevent a communist success, not least because of the incompetence and corruption of the Nationalist forces. The idea of the US being able to play a decisive role against the communists in a country where there was substantial mass support for their political and economic programme is now generally rejected. The rejection has been helped by the experiences in Vietnam where, with the lack of a viable indigenous alternative to the communists, no amount of money could prevent the latter's success, even when backed by the use of considerable military force.

This idea that the world can be shaped by American actions underlies the more interesting academic debate about what the US could have done once the communist victory in China was assured. 'The Last Chance' debate concerns the possibility of whether the US threw away an opportunity in 1949 for establishing better relations with China and preventing the 'lean to one side' embodied in the Sino-Soviet alliance of February 1950. It implies that the opportunity was lost because of the state of US domestic politics, with Republicans criticizing the Truman administration for being soft on communism. Proponents of the missed opportunity interpretation argue that China was in need of aid for reconstruction after the devastation of the war with Japan and the four-year civil war which followed it. Therefore, economic assistance and trade links could have mitigated the ideological ties with the Soviet Union and encouraged divisions between them. Even if Mao was not inclined to turn to the US, there may have been a prospect of him preserving some links to avoid any possible dependence on the Soviet Union.

Along with this incentive there went the assumed Chinese communist dislike and suspicion of Stalin's reluctance to give unequivocal support to Mao. This was evident in the inter-war years when Stalin sought to reconcile the communists and nationalists and after the war as Stalin showed a reluctance to abandon Chiang Kai-shek. In part, this was because, with Soviet influence in East Asia very much in mind, Stalin had gained concessions from the nationalists, albeit with British and American support, regarding the warm-water port of Lushun and the control over the Chinese Eastern Railway. At the same time as these were secured in the Yalta agreements of 1945, Stalin remained doubtful about the communists' prospects for ultimate, military victory. As a result, it is argued, Stalin was prepared to restrict communist activities in Manchuria when the Soviets entered the war against Japan in August 1945 and even to try and expel them from Manchurian cities.

While it is true that there was little reason for Mao to trust Stalin, there was less reason for him to trust the Americans and the thesis which rejects the idea of a lost American opportunity has been supported by new evidence from Chinese and Soviet sources. As early as the summer of 1946, when Stalin's attempts to maintain links with Chiang Kai-shek had collapsed, it has been argued that Mao had the basis of the Soviet alliance he had been seeking in place.[50] The communists were not only given free rein in Manchuria but active support, and the contacts were certainly closer during the subsequent period than has generally been assumed in the West.[51] For Mao, the fact that the Soviets gave the communists an increasing amount of military assistance and civilian aid was more important than Stalin's subsequent attempts to reopen contacts with the nationalists and to pressure him to seek a negotiated settlement. Moreover, Mao was preoccupied with the long-term hostility of the US to the communist revolution in China. He saw the prospects of renewed US intervention as a significant possibility, if only in the form of encouraging resistance on the part of the urban bourgeoisie to his attempts to forge a new China through an ideological campaign to maintain a revolutionary momentum. As a consequence, by 1948 Mao was speaking of squeezing out Western diplomats and firmly committed to seeking a Soviet alliance, whatever its flaws. Even though there is some evidence that the US sought to build some links with China, such links were never a possibility. Only by abandoning Chiang Kai-shek and treating the communists as equals could the door to China be even partially opened.[52] This, more than any chance of a partial rapprochement, was what was ruled out by US domestic politics and the 'Who Lost China?' lobby.

Stalin, the Establishment of Communist China, and the Origins of the Korean War

If Mao was committed to building cooperation with Stalin to meet his domestic, if not his international requirements, the question arises as to Stalin's attitudes to Mao and the emergence of a communist state on the Soviet Union's eastern border. Why was the Soviet leader reluctant to embrace a like-minded revolutionary? There were, of course, differences between Mao's vision of a revolutionary communist state and Stalin's. However, the motives for Stalin's China policies can also be explained by his concern with the implications of a strong China for Soviet leadership of the international communist movement, and more importantly for Soviet influence in East Asia. In addition, because the Cold War was a global issue, Soviet–American relations in one part of the world were affected by events in another. After the Council of Foreign Ministers in September, perhaps options were best left open for preserving the Soviet gains from Yalta and more generally the idea of the Soviet Union playing a role in the resolution of the civil war. In both cases, an outright victory or defeat for Mao Zedong would not be the most desirable option. As has been suggested in Eastern Europe, divisions may have been seen as desirable as a means of maximizing Stalin's ability to exploit the situation. Stalin in August 1945 may also have have been influenced by his expectation that cooperation with the British and Americans involved not supporting Mao strongly. On the other hand, when in 1948 all doubts about a communist victory in China were removed, it paid to move closer to Mao provided Soviet leadership and influence were not threatened.

In Mao's case, Michael Hunt has argued that China was torn between the need for support from friends and the dependence that this could produce.[53] This conflict between dependency and autonomy was deeply embedded in the Chinese psyche. These experiences from recent Chinese history were imprinted on the mind of the communist leader Mao Zedong as he began a struggle to unite China under a single central authority and carve out a more independent and prestigious role for China in international affairs. They were to influence Mao's perception of how the international community could both strengthen and weaken his domestic position as he sought to re-establish China as a regional power. Like any other revolutionary regime, the Chinese communist state was in need of domestic legitimacy, but the Cold War situation in 1949 would complicate this and significantly influence international reactions to the new state. In the West, the Cold War tendency has been to play down the impact of history and culture as influences on Mao Zedong's foreign policy and emphasize Marxist-Leninism and global revolution as the dominant influences shaping Chinese approaches to the external world. It may be more meaningful, as with the Soviet Union, to see the ideological forces as justifying rather than determining foreign policy, which retained at least some traditional Chinese and Russian imperial influences. These gave priority to the pursuit of power and influence for the state and its rulers and for the quest for domestic legitimacy through international means. On the other hand, Mao may have initially been inclined to turn more to Stalin out of fear and dislike of the Americans and to meet his domestic reconstruction needs. Yet this did not suppress power political rivalries between Moscow and Beijing and these need to be examined along with the ideological pressures of the Cold War.

It would not be surprising if the strengthening of the communist bloc, which the Americans saw as a Cold War reversal, was also perceived by Stalin as a reversal, if of a different type. Assuming the Cold War is distinct from traditional power-political rivalries, Stalin may have seen Mao's success more in terms of regional power politics than in terms of his Cold War conflict with the West. This argument is supported by the work of Shen Zhihua, in his interpretation of Stalin's Korean policy and in particular of Stalin's change of mind in January 1950, which led him to authorize and support a North Korean attack on the South which he had resisted in 1949.[54] From Stalin's point of view, there was a need to build up China and use her as an ally in the Cold War, but this would have a number of adverse regional consequences. It would mean a new treaty with the Chinese communists replacing Yalta and the loss of the port and railway concessions, which would deprive Stalin of a warm-water port in Asia. On the other hand, if North Korea controlled the whole peninsula, that could well provide Stalin with access to the warm-water port he desired. These former Russian imperialist goals were the advantages of a quick success, which was deemed likely if the US did not become involved. On the other hand, Stalin made it clear to the North Korean leader Kim Il Sung that Mao's agreement was an essential condition for his approval of the invasion and to Mao that the Soviets would not intervene directly in Korea. Therefore, if there was no quick success, provided the Chinese gave direct support, then the disadvantages would be offset by the Chinese inability to launch an invasion of Taiwan and by making China more dependent on Soviet assistance.

The prospect of direct confrontation with the US always haunted Stalin. It seems that the US Secretary of State Dean Acheson's speech of January 1950 in which Korea and Taiwan were excluded from the Asian-Pacific defence perimeter of the US led him to believe that a confrontation was unlikely in the wake of North Korean aggression. At the same time, Stalin may have been concerned by the prospect of another strong communist power in Asia. This would have threatened his control over international communism and created competition in parts of East Asia that were areas of traditional strategic concern to the Soviet Union. Thus, it may be that the emergence of China, the Korean War, and the rebuilding of Japan (see Chapter 2, C) were seen as regional problems as much as new aspects of the global confrontation with the US. Certainly, there is reason to believe that Stalin was attempting to balance these considerations with the aim of increasing Soviet influence in East Asia rather than in the hope of furthering a revolutionary ideology aiming at world domination. The Chinese Revolution and the Korean War may therefore constitute more complex international phenomena than when seen simply through the Cold War lens of the communist world versus the capitalist world.

However, bipolarity, where the focus is on the influences of the global conflict on regional and domestic events, remains the dominant image. A contrasting perception downplays the international dimension and seeks to locate the causes of the Korean War and the Chinese Revolution predominantly in the domestic circumstances of each country. A third interpretation assesses the interaction of the international and the domestic within a framework that was not exclusively defined by Soviet–American relations. It would take account of the regional situation and distinguish hot war from Cold War and the ideological struggle from the struggle to enhance and maintain traditional interests. The emphasis on international bipolarity as both cause and consequence tends to be accompanied by a belief that Soviet–American relations are all about power politics and military force and *are* the Cold War because they are accompanied by an ideological confrontation. A more sophisticated approach to regional dynamics may open up a greater understanding of the global Cold War.

The West and the Korean War

The events in China and Korea, whatever their domestic and international significance, have come to be seen in the West as landmarks in the development of a Cold War defined primarily and perhaps misleadingly by bipolar Soviet–American relations. In Western historiography, there are two accompanying assessments of the emergence of China and the conflict in Korea's significance in the developing Cold War. First, the events in East Asia allegedly embody the globalization of the Cold War inasmuch as containment was extended to Asia with the emergence of the Chinese communist threat and the Soviet-sponsored aggression in Korea. Second, they allegedly signify the militarization of the conflict as Korea indicated Stalin's intention to use force and limited war to realize his expansionist aims. As such, the Cold War was escalated to another level, requiring the kind of military response defined in NSC 68 and justifying the claims made when NATO was created that the free world was in imminent danger of military attack. Such interpretations justify the West as again simply responding to an aggressive Soviet Union and the portrayal of Stalin as determined to march towards new communist successes even at the expense of military conflict.

These standard interpretations may well contain some truth but they fail to consider a number of facts, as well as the evidence available from sources in the Soviet Union. A more aggressive American Cold War strategy was suggested before NSC 68, the communist triumph in China, and the Korean War. The latter had a double-edged impact on this proactive American policy. While it could serve to vindicate it, it also led to worries that an aggressive strategy aimed at undermining the Soviet satellites might increase the risk of hot war. Rearmament was advocated to reduce that risk. On the other hand, as the British military argued, if a more aggressive Cold War strategy was not pursued and the Cold War thereby won, the West could find itself facing more Koreas, which the British at least could ill afford. As far as the globalization of the conflict is concerned, it has been argued that the Cold War developed from disagreements about the nature of the post-Second World War global changes, not because of events in a particular region. While the Cold War can be portrayed as a series of events stemming from Soviet actions that had European and then worldwide implications, this argument based on reactions to Soviet initiatives is not convincing. It ignores the ambitions of the Western powers in areas of special concern to them outside Europe and the events in Indo-China and Malaya which occurred in 1946 and 1948. These had international implications but also domestic roots which preceded the Cold War.

The Korean War and its Internal Origins

The Korean War was an important Cold War watershed for a number of reasons. It massively increased tension, provided a new regional focus in Asia, which became the new danger area in Western eyes, and ensured that armaments and preparing for hot war began to figure more prominently in plans to deal with the Soviets. Its origins and development are still surrounded in controversy, despite the recent revelations from communist sources about the actions and thoughts of Stalin and Mao Zedong. The war provides a remarkable example of how internal conflicts can interact with the broader international situation to determine the nature and development of a military struggle. In particular, Korea provided an example of how a Cold War, which raged as a civil war from June 1950 until October of that year, developed into a regional hot one once the US, acting on behalf of the UN, then became engaged in a major war with China.

When the Second World War ended, Korea, as a territory under former Japanese control, was divided at the 38th parallel for occupation purposes between the Americans and the Soviets. Although a Joint Commission was set up at the Moscow Council of Foreign Ministers, leaders in both zones were not happy with the division and the drive for unification was to figure strongly in the political programmes of Korean political parties, who were split ideologically as well as geographically. In the North, the Soviets, whose zone comprised only one-third of the population, initially permitted all political groupings but restricted movement across the border, which would make the imposition of tighter controls easier if it was deemed necessary. In the South, the American commander refused to cooperate with the self-proclaimed Korean People's Republic and maintained the Japanese bureaucratic structure.

By early 1946, when Allied relations began to deteriorate, non-communist elements in the North were purged. The Soviets supported Korea being placed under trusteeship but the Americans campaigned against it with non-communists in the South, and the Joint Commission, having failed to produce proposals for the unification of Korea, was suspended in May 1946. Political turmoil and Soviet–American disagreement was accompanied in 1946 by bad economic conditions that produced riots and strikes in rural and urban areas in the South. There was support in Washington for building a non-communist coalition of moderates in the South but the man on the spot, General John Hodge, favoured the forces of the Right.

Polarization accompanied factionalism on the Korean peninsula, with the communists in the North attempting to build support in the South. Their leader, Kim Il Sung, was keen not only to reunite the peninsula but also to end the splits in the North. An invasion was one way of doing this, but its success proved to be more difficult than expected because of American intervention. The invasion was only launched because of Stalin's change of mind in early 1950 and the expectation that the US would not fight for Korea. Despite Soviet support in terms of equipment and trained personnel, the fact that the Americans were able to launch a counter-attack under UN auspices led to a bloody and destructive conflict. The counter-attack, spearheaded by a surprise landing behind enemy lines at Inchon, led to the re-crossing of the 38th parallel and the pushing back of the communist forces to the brink of defeat. The opportunity to reunify Korea under Western auspices appeared too good to miss, but after much consultation between Moscow and Beijing, and warnings to the Americans, the Chinese intervened on a large scale in November 1950.

The war had now become a fully fledged regional conflict as the opposing forces re-crossed the 38th parallel for the third time. Pressure began to mount for a negotiated peace, but the Chinese were determined that the talks should be on regional issues concerning peace and security, including the issue of Taiwan (Formosa). The British had been pressing for a negotiated settlement before Chinese intervention, not least because of the fear that the war would escalate into a global conflict involving the use of nuclear weapons. By the end of the year, some Americans, including the military commander General MacArthur, wanted to take the war to China either by blockading Chinese territory or by bombing the Chinese mainland. In the event, escalation by the Americans was avoided by Truman sacking General MacArthur and General Ridgeway preserving a foothold on the peninsula to prevent a Chinese victory. Once again, in 1951, the opposing forces battled up the Korean peninsula, until in June 1951 a stalemate was reached very close to the old dividing line on the 38th parallel.

The question was whether this stalemate could produce an armistice as what might have been a simple process dragged on in a lengthy and protracted wrangle for two years. Military pressure applied by the Americans in 1953 may have contributed to the ending of the conflict, as might the death of Stalin, who had his own reasons for keeping the Chinese and the Americans embroiled in a struggle. The fact that Eisenhower was threatening to escalate the war might have combined with Stalin's death to increase the communist desire to reach an agreement over an armistice. The difficulties arose primarily over the issue of prisoners of war. The Americans were reluctant to return to the communists those prisoners who did not wish to return to the oppressive societies they had come from, whereas the communists preferred the exchange and return of all prisoners. Elaborate efforts were made by both sides and through third parties to ensure that prisoners were persuaded to take the option of return or express a desire to stay. In the end, the problem was partly resolved by the establishment in May 1953 of a repatriation commission to supervise prisoners of war inside Korea to prevent intimidation during the time permitted for the exercise of a free choice. In addition, the five-member commission would allow representations to be made for non-repatriated prisoners for four months, which was shorter than the communists wanted but longer than the West would have liked.

In conclusion, the Korean War was a war that affected all aspects of Cold War and East–West relations. Propaganda and psychological warfare were promoted to fight the Cold War and win the propaganda battle over the repatriation of prisoners of war. A clear connection was made between Cold War and the fact that it could lead to regional military conflicts which made global war more likely. However, the lessons that were drawn both at the time and with hindsight have proved to be flawed. It was a war with domestic and international causes and consequences and to portray it simply as an internal struggle which developed into an international one is akin to seeing the Cold War as a European conflict which became a global one. The two were always intertwined. The West saw it not just as a test of how effectively they would resist communist aggression but how they could remain united in carrying out military action in a regional context that always threatened to become a global one. It was a war which set regional issues firmly within a global context and one in which the West for the first, but not the only time, confused Stalin's regional ambitions with ascribed global ones. Their determination to act firmly against the communist menace was now combined with some clear justification for military measures to deal with the Soviets and their new allies, and in the wake of NSC 68 for taking Cold War measures to avoid the outbreak of hot war.

As far as Stalin was concerned, the Korean War confirmed the idea suggested here (see Chapter 1, D) that in 1946 he was keen to extend Soviet power and influence along the same lines as Russian imperialism. Yet it also suggests that Stalin's imperialism was characterized by caution, fear, and paranoia rather than by revolutionary fervour and risk-taking. What was crucial was the need to avoid confrontation and military conflict with the US, which, nevertheless, it has been claimed, was likely to occur without American vigilance and rearmament. Stalin's ambitions were held in check by fear and caution until the beginning of 1950, when he saw the opportunity to benefit from Kim Il Sung's proposed aggression in Korea. However, it is unlikely that he sought simply to strike a Cold War blow against the US. His concerns were also with the regional power and influence that stemmed from old imperial ambitions and with his new requirements as the leader of international communism. As such, this was a reflection of all the wartime allies' concerns about old power-political requirements and their new post-war roles. When combined with the fears that new power alignments could threaten the domestic position of elites in new ways, the tensions became acute. The Cold War was the result of these ideological concerns but had to be painted as a military struggle in order to win the ideological battle and preserve the economic and social status quo, which was what, in 1948, the Cold War was primarily about. At least this was what distinguished it from a traditional battle between rival imperialisms. If the above analysis of Stalin's policies in East Asia is to be accepted, it may mean that although both sides were keen to give this conflict a predominantly military appearance, the West was the more concerned about imposing a particular ideology on to the rest of the world. Stalin, in East Asia and elsewhere, had the power-political concerns of the Soviet state foremost in his mind and thus neglected the international ideological battle. If so, this has important implications for interpretations of Soviet approaches to the Cold War conflict in general.

NOTES

1. Questions remain as to the impact this had on Soviet assessments.
2. Richard J. Aldrich, *The Hidden Hand Britain, America and Cold War Secret Intelligence* (John Murray, London, 2001), 110–11. See also J. Lewis, *Changing Direction: British Military Planning for Post-War Strategic Defence 1942–1947* (Sherwood, London, 1987); J. Kent, *British Imperial Strategy and the Origins of the Cold War 1944–1949* (Leicester University Press, Leicester, 1993).
3. On Soviet espionage, see Christopher Andrew and Vasili Mitrokhin, *The Mitrokhin Archive* (Allen Lane, London, 1999), 73–207.
4. Richard J. Aldrich, *The Hidden Hand Britain, America and Cold War Secret Intelligence* (John Murray, London, 2001), 41.
5. V. Pechatnov, 'Exercise in Frustration: Soviet Foreign Propaganda in the Early Cold War 1945–1947', *Cold War History*, 1 (2001).
6. Scott Lucas, *Freedom's War: The US Crusade against the Soviet Union 1945–56* (Manchester University Press, 1999), 47.

7. Richard J. Aldrich, *The Hidden Hand Britain, America and Cold War Secret Intelligence* (John Murray, London, 2001), 142–3.
8. See John L. Gaddis, *Strategies of Containment* (Oxford, Oxford University Press, 1982), Chs 2–3.
9. Foreign Relations of the US (FRUS), 1948, I, NSC 7, 30 March 1948, 548–9.
10. Ibid., I, Memorandum by Thorp (Assistant Secretary for Economic Affairs), 7 April 1948, 557–60.
11. John L. Gaddis, *Strategies of Containment* (Oxford, Oxford University Press, 1982), 155.
12. FRUS, 1948, I, NSC 20/4, 23 November 1948, 663–9.
13. Scott Lucas, *Freedom's War: The US Crusade against the Soviet Union 1945–56* (Manchester University Press, Manchester, 1999), 58–61.
14. Robert Latham, *Modernity, Security and the Making of Postwar International Order*, 36–41.
15. The Psychological Strategy Board was established by presidential directive on 4 April 1951.
16. Scott Lucas, *Freedom's War: The US Crusade against the Soviet Union 1945–56* (Manchester University Press, Manchester, 1999), 145.
17. The National Archives (TNA), Kew, FO371/62555, Minutes of December 1947 to January 1948.
18. FRUS, 1948, I, Report by the Policy Planning Staff, 24 February 1948, 510.
19. This appears to have meant that the Soviets might miscalculate what actions they could take without provoking a significant response from the West.
20. TNA, DEFE 4/11, COS (48) 37th, 17 March 1948.
21. David Holloway, *Stalin and the Bomb* (Yale University Press, New York, 1994), 152, 228; W. LaFeber, *America, Russia and the Cold War, 1945–2000* (9th edn, McGraw-Hill, New York, 2002), 49.
22. David Holloway, *Stalin and the Bomb* (Yale University Press, New York, 1994), 231–3.
23. Fred Kaplan, *The Wizards of Armageddon* (Simon & Schuster, New York, 1983), 43.
24. See Alan Milward, *The European Rescue of the Nation-State* (Routledge, London, 1992).
25. Spencer Mawby, *Containing the German Threat: Britain and the Arming of the Federal Republic* (Palgrave-Macmillan, Basingstoke, 1999), 20–35.
26. FRUS, 1949, 1, Minutes of the Policy Planning Staff, 11 October 1949, 402.
27. Ibid., 16 December 1949, 414.
28. Scott Lucas, *Freedom's War: The US Crusade against the Soviet Union 1945–56* (Manchester University Press, Manchester, 1999), 65–6, 134.
29. Richard J. Aldrich, *The Hidden Hand Britain, America and Cold War Secret Intelligence* (John Murray, London, 2001), 320.
30. Ibid., 296–8; Scott Lucas, *Freedom's War: The US Crusade against the Soviet Union 1945–56* (Manchester University Press, Manchester, 1999), 88.
31. Richard J. Aldrich, *The Hidden Hand Britain, America and Cold War Secret Intelligence* (John Murray, London, 2001), 173, 178, 294, 297.
32. Ibid., 324.
33. Troy was a 1951 project to look at how Soviet jamming of American propaganda broadcasts could be overcome, then to examine other ways of penetrating the Iron Curtain and developing a concept of political warfare.
34. Scott Lucas, *Freedom's War: The US Crusade against the Soviet Union 1945–56* (Manchester University Press, Manchester, 1999), 128, 146; G. Mitrovich, *Undermining the Kremlin: America's Strategy to Subvert the Soviet Bloc 1947–1956* (Cornell University Press, Ithaca, 2000), 20–34.
35. Scott Lucas, *Freedom's War: The US Crusade against the Soviet Union 1945–56* (Manchester University Press, Manchester, 1999), 144; Richard J. Aldrich, *The Hidden Hand Britain, America and Cold War Secret Intelligence* (John Murray, London, 2001), 145, 154.

36. V. Zubok and C. Pleshakov, *Inside the Kremlin's Cold War from Stalin to Khrushchev* (Harvard University Press, 1996), 130.

37. Richard J. Aldrich, *The Hidden Hand Britain, America and Cold War Secret Intelligence* (John Murray, London, 2001), 327.

38. FRUS 1950, 1, NSC 68, 14 April 1950, 238–42.

39. Ibid., 262, 255.

40. Ibid., 264, 267, 272, 277.

41. Ibid., 276–9.

42. Ibid., 280.

43. Ibid., 281–2.

44. Ibid., 284.

45. Robert R. Bowie and Richard H. Immerman, *Waging Peace: How Eisenhower Shaped an Enduring Cold War Strategy* (Oxford University Press, Oxford, 1998), 23.

46. See W. F. Poole and R. J. Watson, *The History of the Joint Chiefs of Staff, IV and V, 1950–1952 and 1953–1954* (Office of Joint History, Washington, DC, 1977 and 1986).

47. FRUS, 1950, 1, Schaub to NSC, 8 May 1950, 300–1.

48. FRUS, 1951, 1, NSC 114/1, 8 August 1951, 129–32.

49. FRUS, 1951, 1. Bohlen Memorandum, 22 August 1951.

50. O. A. Westad, 'Losses, Chances and Myths: the US and the Creation of the Sino-Soviet Alliance, 1946–1950', *Diplomatic History*, 2 (1997).

51. Chen Jian, 'The Myth of America's Lost Chance in China', *Diplomatic History*, 2 (1997).

52. Ibid.; O. A. Westad, 'Losses, Chances and Myths: the US and the Creation of the Sino-Soviet Alliance, 1946–1950', *Diplomatic History*, 2 (1997).

53. Michael Hunt, *The Genesis of Chinese Communist Foreign Policy* (Columbia University Press, New York, 1996), 26–7.

54. Shen Zhihua, 'Sino-Soviet Relations and the Origins of the Korean War', *Journal of Cold War Studies*, 2 (2000).

PART II

Cold War: Crises and Change, 1953–63

Soviet–American Approaches to Cold War and Peaceful Coexistence

The beginning of a new Cold War era, with the death of Stalin and a new Republican administration in Washington, has generally been analysed in terms of a quest for peace and of a 'thaw' in Cold War relations. One cause of debate is whether the new rulers in Moscow were genuinely prepared to introduce new policies and to change the foreign policy approach of the Soviet Union. Policy under Stalin was based on promoting a climate of Western hostility so that this could assist the regime's repression of dissent. The question was whether the death of Stalin would change this climate and lead to a new era of accommodation. In other words, was there any prospect of a real change in Soviet policy and a real possibility for accommodation, with agreement on issues such as Germany and the control of nuclear weapons?

The debate has been framed in the West with the usual onus on Soviet actions and policy. Therefore, issues tend to be defined in terms of whether the US missed an opportunity for real accommodation or whether the Kremlin's actions continued to reflect the ascribed goals of expansion and conflict, while employing different means to achieve them. As with other issues, the questions about Soviet motivation could be applied equally pertinently to American policy. Were the policies of Eisenhower, such as the 'atoms for peace' and 'open skies' initiatives, genuine attempts to reach accommodation with the Soviet Union? Or were they gestures to reassure Western opinion that the US was prepared to deal constructively with the Soviet Union? With the advent of the hydrogen bomb, it was clear that any resort to military conflict was now likely to have catastrophic consequences for the future of civilization, and public concerns about future war were to grow in the second half of the 1950s. We also know that there were those in the US administration who believed that it was not possible to reach agreement with Moscow. They believed that the Soviets would use any negotiating process to score propaganda points and raise false optimism in the West about the prospects for peace, in the hope that Washington would get the blame when this did not materialize. On the other hand, British premier Winston Churchill was set on trying to reach agreement with the Soviets and reduce Cold War tension through summit meetings, albeit as part of a grand exit from politics in the form of a peacemaking role.

The issue of whether the Soviets would genuinely participate in a process of détente has been defined within a Cold War framework which, as suggested in Part I, has tended to downplay both the offensive policy of the US and the extent to which it was defined, not by what the Soviets were doing, but by assessments of what they *might* do. When the extent of the American move away from containment is taken into account, and despite the opposition in 1952 to plans to subvert the Soviet regime and/or its control over the satellite regimes of Eastern Europe, the focus on peace initiatives becomes questionable. There are those who see the changes between 1953 and the Geneva summit of 1955 as constituting a 'thaw' in the Cold War. The issue of the extent to which the Soviets were genuine in trying to reduce tensions after Stalin's death, and how far Eisenhower's proposals were designed merely for propaganda purposes, are then transformed into the idea that the Cold War atmosphere was changing for the better.

The Changing Cold War

This concept of a 'thaw' in the Cold War depends on a definition of the conflict which encompasses all aspects of Soviet–American relations and does not distinguish between those policies aimed at the destruction of the Soviet bloc short of war and those policies designed to use diplomacy to lessen the chance of a major hot war. In Washington, the new administration contained a number of ardent supporters of psychological warfare, including covert operations to undermine the Soviet bloc. Moreover, the Eisenhower administration and the new Secretary of State, John Foster Dulles, became associated with ideas expressed publicly that communism could be rolled back, unlike during the Truman administration, which was criticized for not doing enough in the battle against the Soviets. At the same time, the Americans were becoming more concerned about the possibility of war and the vulnerability of the US to future Soviet attack with nuclear weapons. Similarly, with the Soviet Union, it is possible to distinguish between the encouragement given to communist parties to oppose Western governments by action outside the political process and the desire to seek accommodation and reduce the possible threat from American military might and a revived Germany. Thus, it is possible to see a 'thaw' not in the Cold War, but rather in the concerns to stabilize

Soviet–American relations and to mitigate the danger of Cold War becoming hot. Moreover, this Cold War could be intensified in the hope that the Soviet Union might collapse, while efforts were at the same time made to maintain an equilibrium that, along with greater American military strength, might reduce the risk of hot war. The post-Stalin period could therefore be interpreted as an intensification of the Cold War, while improving relations to reduce the risk of hot war breaking out if the Cold War was not won. Even with the impact of the hydrogen bomb, it took some time before the obvious point seemed to sink in that offensive Cold War policies would almost inevitably lead to greater risks of hot war in several important respects.

In addition, from the American point of view there were growing doubts about the effectiveness of subversive measures. These were seen as unlikely to have an impact on the USSR or its hold over the satellites without a major war, which would be increasingly destructive. On the other hand, there were those in the military who did not want to abandon the Cold War attempts at roll-back. The debate between the civilian and the military formed a growing division in the US, between advocates of coexistence and those in favour of the ultimate roll-back of the Soviet satellite empire or the transformation of the Soviet Union itself. Different Cold War measures would be needed for either strategy, but the US tried to keep both options open. Instead of going all out with an offensive Cold War strategy or accepting peaceful coexistence and the pursuit of US interests by trying to reach agreements with Moscow, Eisenhower avoided that choice. In the end, it faded away in the early 1960s as the USSR continued to exist and as Cold War attention moved away from Eastern Europe to the less developed world and the Cuban Missile Crisis provided more of an incentive for trying to reach agreements to avoid hot war.

Whatever the outcome of the debate on this question, there are three separate areas which need to be distinguished in order to provide a more meaningful analysis of the Cold War in this period. On the one hand, there are the specific points of disagreement between the United States and the Soviet Union, such as the failure to agree on peace treaties for Austria and Germany and the problem of reaching a settlement to the war in Korea. Linked to these is the more general attempt to put East–West relations on a better footing, whether it be through summit meetings or through proposals to grant overflying rights, so that military developments were not secret.

Another way in which the Cold War might be said to have intensified was the growing concern on both sides of the Iron Curtain about events in the colonial or less developed world. Stalin had little or no interest in areas of the world not adjacent to the USSR and had not attempted to compete with the West in such regions by, for example, providing economic or military aid. However, with the new regime of Malenkov, Khrushchev, and Bulganin, who were less stricken with the siege mentality of Stalin and keener to see the USSR compete as a superpower, the idea of competing with the West on a global basis held more attraction. In addition, Soviet attacks on Western imperialism and the continuation of colonialism would appeal not just to the peoples of Asia, Africa, and the Middle East who were still denied the freedom to choose the form of government under which they lived, but to those newly independent countries keen to oppose Western colonialism.

Cold War and Colonialism

The degree of Soviet hypocrisy on this could be hidden by the armed struggles against colonial rule that were taking place in Malaya, Kenya, Vietnam, and Algeria by 1954, along with disturbances in Egypt and Morocco. On the one hand, the demonstrations and armed rebellions could be portrayed by the colonial powers, Britain and France, as instigated by communists or as opening the door to communism and therefore as something for the Americans to oppose. On the other hand, the continued imposition of foreign rule against the wishes of so many people made the West appear guilty of hypocrisy in trumpeting the virtues of freedom and democracy, which were actually lacking in colonial situations as much as in the countries of the communist bloc. The US Secretary of State, John Foster Dulles, was keenly aware of the damage this did to the West's propaganda campaign against communism, as well as making it extremely difficult to balance the need to strengthen the Western alliance with the needs of increasing American and Western influence in the non-European world. Initially, Dulles tried to transcend these conflicting needs by shifting the NATO alliance away from the practical needs of military defence cooperation to the reasons why these were needed in the first place. At the end of 1953,

Dulles suggested a moral crusade against the 'root evil' of communism, which he claimed was a far bigger obstacle to freedom than Western colonialism. By no longer contrasting the military importance of NATO with the political importance of sympathy for those struggling against colonialism, as the US once had, the moral crusade against the enormity of the portrayed communist threat could unite the Western and non-Western worlds.

Unfortunately, the moral crusade meant little to those seeking political freedom and can only have encouraged those who worried about the implications of a world where everyone was roped into a conflict between two systems represented by military blocs. Even though the Warsaw Pact military alliance was not created until 1955, Dulles can only have encouraged those like India's leader, Nehru, who believed in non-alignment and the avoidance of blocs. The leaders of those countries who initiated the non-aligned movement in 1955, at a conference in Bandung, Indonesia, rejected any idea of crusades with the world divided into two groups. Bandung was an attempt to do just what Dulles was trying to avoid and associate non-alignment with the efforts to end colonialism.

Latin America and the Cold War

Dulles's initial failure to devise a means of removing the conflict between support for colonial powers and support for the Western bloc in opposition to communism was only part of a bigger failure of American policy outside Europe. In Latin America, which was now dominated economically and politically by the United States, fear of communism was growing. In Europe, 'the empire by invitation' which had produced enormous American influence was built on economic aid that Latin America never received. After the war, it soon became clear that Washington was going to extend a large measure of political as well as economic control over the region, but without the benefits given to Europe. Post-war American hegemony was more overt and less rewarding. The US involvement in the overthrow of the leftist Guatemalan government in 1954 has provoked a debate as to whether this was done out of Cold War concerns, or because of a need to protect American economic interests in the particular form of the United Fruit Company. What is certain is that the Eisenhower administration was not acting against the forces of communism, which barely existed in Guatemala or elsewhere in Latin America in the first half of the 1950s. Although there were communists associated with the Guatemalan leader, Jacob Arbenz, it was the belief that left-wing governments would prepare the way for communism that was crucial. The pressures exerted by the United Fruit Company, which had connections to the Dulles brothers, who were Secretary of State and Director of the Central Intelligence Agency, undoubtedly made the overthrow of Arbenz easier. However, it was the Cold War and Eisenhower's belief in the value of covert operations that probably proved more important. The early success in Guatemala followed that in Iran the previous year, but US attempts to mould the Third World to its economic and political requirements were not always to be successful. Even in Latin America, where the policy of the first Eisenhower administration to leave development and aid in the hands of the private sector began to change in 1958, the results were not good. They did not prevent the Cold War's key development in the western hemisphere, which was the emergence of a communist Cuba in the wake of Castro's successful 1959 revolution.

The Cuban revolution reflected the difficulties faced by Washington in reconciling capitalism with the need for welfare and development in those non-industrialized countries which lacked the resources that could command high world market prices. Such countries, especially those countries exporting tropical produce, were usually characterized in Latin America by gross inequality, corruption, and a landowning class whose economic interests were tied, as in pre-revolutionary Cuba, to the US economy. The dictatorial regime of General Batista had not tackled agrarian reform, modernization in the sugar industry, or low investment. Castro's attempts to do so soon fell foul of those middle-class supporters who had welcomed the overthrow of Batista along with the Eisenhower administration. As Castro's links to Moscow and communism became more influential, Washington began to take action to subvert the communist regime, and the Kennedy administration became obsessed with the removal of the Cuban dictator. How far the measures taken to bring down Castro can be linked to the Soviet decision in 1962 to deploy nuclear armed missiles is still being debated. The fact that Castro remained in power in Cuba and implemented health and education policies, which generally improved the lot of the population, was a source of concern to US governments after the revolution. The fear was that alternative paths of development, if they were successful, would be a boost to left-wing ideologies and to Soviet communism. Kennedy embarked on a significant attempt to use federal funds to promote the kind of liberal economic development that he associated with the American democratic system. The problem was that, without any form of social change or redistribution of wealth, the social and economic system was unlikely to be acceptable to a majority of the population. Kennedy's attempt to assist Latin America with what was known as the Alliance for Progress and provide an acceptable alternative to Castro were unsuccessful in promoting democracy or bringing broad-based development to the region.

Regional Defence Pacts and their Political and Military Roles

American policy was equally unsuccessful in producing positive results in areas of the world where either US economic interests were less prevalent or political control was deemed less of a requirement. In the Middle East and South-East Asia, which bordered on the Soviet Union, and where the negative achievement of preventing the spread of communism was the goal, the Eisenhower administration sought to build defence organizations like NATO which would encircle the Soviet Union and in theory prevent Soviet military expansion, which it was assumed lay behind the Korean War. More importantly they would, like NATO, be deemed to have a political effect in promoting the confidence to resist communism. The Southeast Asia Treaty Organization (SEATO) and the Baghdad Pact in the Middle East seemed to confirm that the US and other Western powers would come to the signatories' assistance if the Soviets were to use force to impose their political ideas. Both organizations remained militarily weak and the Baghdad Pact never came near to achieving the force levels that were deemed necessary to defend the Middle East.

In the Middle East, by 1953, Dulles had decided to pursue policies independent of the British, including the creation of the Baghdad Pact. Based on the 'Northern tier', which followed a line across Turkey and the Zagros mountains down through Iraq and Iran to the Persian Gulf, its political consequences were extremely destabilizing in both the Middle East and South Asia. With a membership of Pakistan, Iran, Iraq, Britain, and Turkey, the Baghdad Pact was probably the most useless and hated military organization of the Cold War. There was a shortfall of forces to meet a Soviet invasion and the pact only became plausible as a military organization when the British promised to use nuclear weapons to defend the Zagros passes. Unfortunately, these weapons could not be made available in the region until 1959. Militarily, the British thus invented a new meaning for deception plans based on deceiving your allies as well as your enemies. Politically, the Israelis disliked the pact because it allied an Arab state with a Western organization backed by the US and thereby reduced the likelihood of American aid and assistance. The Egyptians and Saudis disliked it, because it appeared to elevate their arch-enemies in Iraq towards leadership of the Arab world. Colonel Nasser, the Egyptian prime minister, particularly hated it, because his attempts to become the clear leader of the Arab world were linked to his success in 1954 in reaching an agreement by which the British were to remove their troops from the Suez base. The French hated it, because it signified the end of their last remaining influence in the Middle East. And even the Americans became lukewarm towards it after its creation in early 1955, because it re-injected anti-Western sentiments into the region and alienated Nasser, whom the Americans hoped would play the leading role in achieving an Arab–Israeli settlement. Moreover, because it placed Pakistan in an alliance backed by the US, it alienated the Indians, who were in dispute with their neighbour over the territory of Kashmir. Ultimately, it alienated the Pakistanis too, because it failed to give them the means to get help in their conflict with the Indians.

The Cold War in Asia and Africa

In South-East Asia, growing American involvement in the renewed Vietnam conflict after the Geneva settlement of 1954 was built on the perceived need to prevent the spread of communism. The motives for providing aid and military 'advisers' to South Vietnam during this period have been located in the so-called 'domino theory', whereby the fall of one part of the region would lead to the collapse of the other parts. Thus, even though Vietnam had little strategic or economic importance, the US had to prevent its takeover by the communist North, whether through the elections for a unified Vietnam (promised in the 1954 agreement which the US refused to sign) or through an armed rebellion. By the end of the 1950s, when the Chinese began assisting the insurgents in their campaign against the Saigon government, the Cold War had become a battle of wills in the developing world, where communist successes would undermine the prestige and credibility of the West. Would communism be able to surpass capitalism as the best means of development and progress, or would capitalism prove more able to satisfy the needs of non-Western people and offer them greater economic and technological benefits? This was the question that could only be answered by the allegiance and support of those in the world not yet associated with either bloc, who could still exercise a choice.

Africa was the continent where most nations still had choices to make once they achieved independence for the first time, hence the interest taken in the continent by both sides as the transfer of power moved closer in a large number of former colonies. The issue for the Americans became not so much how to reconcile the interests of the metropolitan powers and the unity of NATO with attracting support and allegiance from Africans, but how to ensure that power was transferred at the right time and to the right people. To delay might encourage the leaders of anti-colonial movements to become more radical and to turn to the Soviets for support. Or, it might lead to their replacement by new and more radical leaders not prepared to cooperate with the West. On the other hand, to transfer power too soon in Africa might produce unstable, non-viable regimes, which were prone to collapse and therefore seen as offering opportunities to communist parties or other radical left-wing groups. This was the dilemma for the British and eventually the French, if not the Portuguese, and the way in which American support came to be offered was on the basis of providing a specific commitment to self-government in return for US support in the United Nations, while efforts were made to arrange the appropriate moment for the transfer of power.

This approach, modelled on British policy for transferring power, eventually worked with the French in that it helped produce a commitment in 1953 for Moroccan self-government and thereby sounded the death-knell for the French Union. Yet it failed with the Portuguese in Angola. Portugal, under the right-wing dictator Salazar, was determined to hang on to Angola at all costs, even—as their foreign minister told the Americans— if it meant the start of a third world war. Once a rebellion in Angola broke out in February 1961, the issue became vital as over the border in the former Belgian Congo, which became an independent state (later Zaire) in June 1960, chaos reigned and the possibility of Soviet intervention loomed. To the east of the Congo, the British were faced with a delicate situation as the Central African Federation of Northern and Southern Rhodesia and Nyasaland was on the verge of breaking up. Thus, in Central Africa all the complexities of African decolonization were in evidence. The UN was involved, the Soviets were being asked to support the Congo's first Prime Minister, Patrice Lumumba, and the British policy of creating a multiracial society, through political representation being allocated to racial groups, rather than the will of the majority, was collapsing. Fighting and internal conflict became serious in the Congo as Moïse Tshombe established a breakaway kingdom in the mineral-rich province of Katanga. The intervention of Belgian troops further complicated a situation comprising a failed transfer of power, the problems of multiracialism, important European economic interests, the Cold War implications of Soviet involvement, the responsibilities of the UN, and the determination of the Kennedy administration to give support to Africans.

The first thing to be aware of in this extraordinary tangle of the Cold War with the end of empire and multiracialism, is that the Cold War did not simply involve Soviet–American competition over giving aid to some of the groups competing for control over the central government or those in Katanga seeking to escape from it. The issue was a broader one, particularly with regard to newly independent West African states. Kennedy was determined that Africa should be at the centre of American foreign policy, and the allegiance of the newly independent states, such as Nkrumah's Ghana, was deemed crucial. The concern within Africa about the possible collapse of the Congo, or the secession of Katanga, was based on a determination that the gaining of independence should not be seen as a failure; and, in particular, that Belgian or other European forces should not create what was expected to be a blatant form of neo-colonialism based on Katangan secession. If Lumumba, whose position was under threat from internal enemies and from the Central Intelligence Agency (CIA), who were working towards his assassination, could not unite the country and Katanga seceded, then the transfer of power would be seen as a failure. The role of Belgian troops and the assets of the Union Minière company in Katanga would be interpreted as economic neo-colonialism. On the other hand, to have a united Congo, courtesy of Soviet help to Lumumba, was another disaster for the West to avoid.

One of the lessons to emerge from the crisis was the extent to which Washington and the UN Secretary-General, Dag Hammarskjöld, shared the common goal of preventing Soviet involvement in the Congo. Over time, and well before Hammerskjöld's death in September 1961, there were disputes about the best means to achieve this but the fact that the UN worked closely with the American government is undeniable. Once Lumumba's murder became public knowledge in February 1961, the Americans had to provide a 'moderate' alternative for the leadership of an increasingly divided Congo. The struggle to win support for the former trade unionist, Cyrille Adoula, whose election as Congo premier was secured by American money in August 1961, meant defeating Lumumba's left-wing successor, Antoine Gizenga, and ending Katanga's secession. More importantly for US policy, it meant fighting British, Belgian, and French reluctance to involve the UN in the forcible termination of Tshombe's regime in Katanga. Not only were there links between European governments and the financial interests of the Union Minière du Haut Katanga and its associated companies, but neither the British nor the Belgians were keen to eject the anti-communist Tshombe in such a fluid and unpredictable situation. Interestingly, in ending Katangan secession, the Kennedy administration opted for a policy which would win African support in the Cold War. In avoiding the easy option of preferring the devil they knew who would be pro-European and anti-communist (Tshombe) to a devil with an uncertain future (Adoula), the Kennedy administration showed its commitment to a liberal Cold War political strategy, which was to be repeated in Angola after the 1961 revolt began. Sadly, as the dangers of African instability seemed to increase, as in other areas, Kennedy's successor, Lyndon Johnson, was to abandon the efforts to win over the less developed world by liberal policies and to rely on dictators, like the military leader Joseph Mobutu, who took over the Congo in 1965. African decolonization did not always equate with political freedom, let alone economic opportunity.

The End of European Empires

The end of French rule in Africa was almost as rapid as that of Belgian rule in the Congo. The Algerian War, which began in 1954, was obviously a key moment in post-war French history, not least because it led to the return of Charles de Gaulle as President of the new Fifth Republic in 1958. In the same year, de Gaulle established the French Community, which served to replace the defunct Fourth Republic's French Union and provided a new constitutional framework for the territories of Overseas France. This framework was more in line with the British Commonwealth, in terms of being a friendly association, than a manifestation of the French Republic 'one and indivisible'. To explain why this change took place is a matter of juggling the various changes that occurred from 1953 onwards. At the top of the list are pressures from the developing anti-French nationalist movements in North Africa. The Istiqlal in Morocco, the Neo-Destour in Tunisia, and the National Liberation Front (FLN) in Algeria were willing to use more violent means than their equivalents in French West and Equatorial Africa during the first half of the 1950s. Faced with riots, disturbances, and a full-scale war in Algeria, the French had little alternative. Yet there were other pressures from within France, given the foreign ministry's dislike of the French Union as an acceptable means of preserving influence over Overseas France, which may have influenced the Minister for Overseas France, Pierre-Henri Teitgen when, in 1955, he began to prepare for real devolution. The French equivalent of this British process involved constitutional change that required a *loi cadre*, or enabling law, which came into force in 1956.

Before then, however, the process of moving towards internal self-government was well advanced in Morocco and Tunisia, which were associated territories of the French Union. Again, it is easy to attribute this simply to the French conceding to the demands of the Istiqlal and the Neo-Destour. Yet the American role may have also been important. Given their economic interests and the existence of important US air bases in Morocco, it was clear that American concerns about French policy were at a much higher level than in Black Africa. Active American involvement had to take the form of a quest for stability that depended on preserving good relations with the nationalists and their allies in the Asian and Arab worlds, without alienating the French. After 1951, when riots occurred in Casablanca and efforts began to bring the North African situation before the UN General Assembly, American involvement may have prevented the French from refusing to devolve power in ways which would damage the interests of French settlers. US support in moderating UN resolutions may have led the French to contemplate bringing Morocco to self-government. Once the French had acknowledged this possibility, progress towards it could not be delayed and the ultimate fate of the French Union was sealed.

The deposition of the Sultan of Morocco in August 1953, where traditional leaders were more in favour of the French than the Istiqlal or the Sultan, and the Algerian revolt in 1954 made progress easier in Tunisia, where the principle of internal self-government was conceded that same year. Thus, by the time de Gaulle was faced with the problem of solving the Algerian mess, a pragmatic approach would not require principles to be conceded other than those emotive ones inherent in Algeria's constitutional position as part of France. De Gaulle had, of course, always given consideration to how French greatness could be best pursued on the international stage. It may be argued that de Gaulle had rapidly concluded that the drain of a bloody and bitter conflict in Algeria was the last thing that would rebuild French prestige and status as a leading world power. Moreover, that power in political and economic terms could only be exercised through an emphasis on a modern Europe centred on France, rather than on an outmoded collection of undeveloped colonial territories. Hence, the establishment of the French Community, a federal organization whose president, elected primarily by metropolitan Frenchmen would retain control over foreign and defence policy and certain aspects of economic policy. Membership was voluntary and although most African leaders accepted the argument on what today would be considered the advantages of an increasingly interdependent world, the people of Guinea chose independence. The French did what they could to make life difficult for the newly independent state, but when they failed to cajole Sékou Touré, the radical Guinean leader, the attractiveness of African independence received a massive boost. For de Gaulle, who was seeking to base European cooperation on a union of nation states, endeavouring to hold a reluctant group of African federalists together was singularly unattractive. Close bilateral links could be created, which would preserve French influence on the African continent more effectively.[1]

The British, having led the way with the Gold Coast, now found themselves having to catch up with the French as eleven French territories in Black Africa became independent in 1960. Difficulties for Britain were growing at the end of the decade as troubles in Nyasaland and Kenya added to the political problems of creating a federal structure in Nigeria, which was facing division and conflict. The final phase of Britain's African Empire was not finally given up after careful calculations about costs of resisting nationalists, or because of a strategic choice between Africa and Europe, but because it was the easiest way to resolve a growing list of problems. Plans that Britain had for transferring power were hardly ever implemented on the basis of social and economic infrastructure, multiracialism, or strategic requirements for bases. As particular plans ran into difficulty, whether in Africa or in smaller colonies like Malta and Cyprus, political change was concocted on an ad hoc basis that would encounter the least resistance. These plans could involve increasing British control, as in the Aden Protectorates, and not just relinquishing it by bowing to the inevitable. In many respects, Britain was slow to realize what was necessary, let alone inevitable, particularly in terms of timing. In places like the Central African Federation, white settler interests were still seen in 1959 as protectable under the guise of multiracialism. In the last moments of Empire, rather than transferring power reluctantly under pressure from Africans, the latter were suddenly pushing at an open door through which the British government was only too happy to go if only it could find a way to do so without bringing greater disasters upon itself.

The disasters that befell the French in South-East Asia and North Africa, in the form of long and bloody wars, were largely avoided by the British, whose conflicts were of a much smaller scale and significance, except in areas where most British control and influence was exercised informally. A major crisis erupted in 1956 in independent Egypt, which has been seen by some as a milestone in the history of British decolonization. In defiance of the US and Arab world, Britain invaded Suez in November in collusion with the French and the Israelis. This infamous moment in British history, when some members of the Eden government and the Foreign Office tried to hide from the world the true nature of the military aggression perpetrated against Egypt, has engendered controversy ever since.

There are those who maintain that the disgrace and humiliation experienced at Suez destroyed any claim that might have been made for the liberal, progressive nature of the British Empire. Moreover, the limited nature of the British ability to project power by using military force was exposed to the world. Without

Washington's backing, the British imperial lion was powerless and with the use of force now ruled out in 'colonial' situations the increasing pace of decolonization was inevitable. On the other hand, there are those who do not see Suez as a watershed in British imperial history. Suez was essentially about power and the end of British dominance in the Middle East, as expressed in the ability to deploy military forces in strategic positions overseas. They were to be used in global or regional conflicts as befitting the world-power status desired by British elites. The humiliation of no longer being able to use forces to depose independent governments had little to do with the formal transfer of power on a basis of cooperation. In terms of power, and particularly world-power status, Suez simply affected the means by which this was now to be exercised. Military power and the occupation of bases now became more symbolic and totally dependent on American support. Yet the pursuit of world-power status and the preservation of overseas commitments remained at the heart of British policy, at least between the fiasco at Suez and the retreat from East of Suez over a decade later.

Moreover, while the strategic importance of the Suez crisis was great in terms of the loss of overflying rights, the British continued to fight for their position in the Gulf and South Arabia by sending troops to Kuwait in 1961 and by trying to tighten their control over the Aden Protectorates in the 1950s. Even in the heart of the Middle East, the British sent troops to the region as part of an effort to react to the problems presented by the Iraqi revolution in 1958. The British pleaded for the Americans to allow them to send troops to Jordan, allegedly to stabilize the situation in the same way as the Americans were allegedly deploying forces to stabilize the situation in Lebanon. As a result, the British perception was very much that their continued involvement in the Middle East was important for their world status and as a means of protecting the region from Soviet influence. The latter was seen as increasingly likely as more radical Arab regimes came to power.

What was certain was that the US was now the dominant regional power in the Middle East, which was given formal expression through the Eisenhower Doctrine in January 1957, and which basically offered aid to countries threatened by the forces of international communism. The subsequent issue has been whether the stability of Middle Eastern states was threatened by international communism or whether, as in Lebanon in 1958, the instability was internally engendered. By then, the only significant external influence in the Middle East came from the US.

The Years of Crisis, 1958–62: Soviet Challenges to US Hegemony

The second half of the 1950s witnessed, for some, the true emergence of bipolarity when the old European empires were crumbling, China was suffering the internal convulsions of the Great Leap Forward and its economic disasters, and the economic strength of Western Europe and Japan was not yet in evidence. Others see merely the zenith of American hegemony as the Soviet Union's military and economic strength was well below that of the US. The debate over this challenge concerns the post-1956 degree of Soviet commitment to their proclaimed policy of peaceful coexistence and the seriousness of Khrushchev's attempt to bully the West over Berlin and Cuba.

The Russian leader made a number of claims about the success and future of socialism in the wake of Sputnik's launch. His provocative boasting was probably born from a feeling of weakness, but it helped feed the rhetoric of John F. Kennedy, who promised a more dynamic America both at home and abroad. The two leading powers both sought more and more adherents to their cause, as the global community expanded and more newly independent states joined the United Nations. The Cold War became acute as a result and a number of crises occurred in the early 1960s in Laos and Berlin, as well as the escalation of the Vietnam conflict, and culminated in the Cuban Missile Crisis. Their roots may be traced back to the late 1950s and to 1958 in particular, when the Soviets began their challenge to the Western position in Berlin soon after the Sino-American confrontation over the Chinese nationalist hold on a number of islands a few miles off the Chinese coast.

Clearly designed to intimidate, this breast-beating—and grandiose claims about the success of socialism in military and economic terms —did not translate into determined attempts to secure Soviet changes to the post-war order by force if necessary. Given the parlous state of the Soviet economy, the true nature of which was not fully understood at the time, and the clear Soviet inferiority in nuclear weapons, it is more convincing to see Khrushchev's policies as nothing more than bluff. Equally Mao Zedong's desire to unify

China was never posited on plans to tackle the military might of the US again, at least in a situation where US naval and air forces were likely to be decisive. This is not to say that the crises over Berlin, the Offshore Islands, and Cuba were mere communist gestures, as there were some specific aims for them to achieve. In Europe, the position of Berlin was increasingly causing problems to the Soviets and the East Germans, and a change in the status quo was both logical and necessary from Moscow's perspective. The need to strengthen a hold on a key component in the Eastern bloc was made more important by the need to prove that the proclaimed policy of peaceful coexistence could bring concrete benefits to Moscow. In the West, the German problem had been solved with the integration of the Federal Republic into NATO and the establishment of the European Economic Community (EEC). The unity of the Western bloc was only problematic from the American point of view in that it might become too much of a rival if the EEC's policies deviated too far from those serving US interests as well. The 1950s ended with Western unity preserved at the failed Paris summit, where the Soviets produced embarrassment by shooting down an American spy plane and proving that Eisenhower had lied about its true nature and mission.

However, divisions in the communist bloc were becoming serious as the Sino-Soviet split grew wider in the late 1950s. Some of Khrushchev's harsh words and threats of action against the West may have been designed to impress hardliners in Moscow. But it was also necessary to take the sting out of Chinese claims to be the true inheritors of revolutionary Marxism-Leninism. The Offshore Islands crisis indicated more differences between Moscow and Beijing. And the Cuban crisis was in part exacerbated by Khrushchev's fears of losing Castro and his own reputation as the leader of global communism. Preserving the Cuban revolution would serve to prove that the progress of revolutionary socialism could take place without the revolutionary wars that Mao still deemed necessary. For the Americans, bloc divisions were to become more of a problem with the challenge mounted by de Gaulle, which was to grow during the 1960s. But, in essence, victory for them in the early 1960s Cold War now meant preserving the status quo by resisting the communist challenge wherever it occurred, and their ideological friends never broke with them as the Chinese broke with the Russians.

The Soviet rift with the Chinese, which began in the wake of Khrushchev's rejection of Stalinism in 1956, has been linked to ideological differences, competition for geopolitical rivalries in East Asia, the quest for leadership of the communist world, the re-emergence of China as a leading Asian power, and the personalities of Mao and Khrushchev. The Sino-Soviet split was a shock to those who saw the communist challenge as monolithic, but it had little impact on American Cold War strategy in this period. Subversive operations were carried out against China as well as in Eastern Europe and, while the determination to subvert and destroy the Soviet Union waned in Eisenhower's second term, such activities were not abandoned. The focus was much less on destroying the Soviet Union than on preventing the spread of communism in the less developed world as part of a struggle for hearts and minds. Khrushchev and others could claim to offer a better way towards economic and national development free from the shackles of Western imperialism and exploitation by vaunting the socialist model, but people were fleeing from it in Berlin. Some had been taken in by such claims, as the Soviets sent the first satellite into space in 1957 and produced fears that socialist technology might outstrip the West; the sense of American insecurity had not gone away.

Part of this Soviet attempt to claim superiority was linked to military power and the development of nuclear weapons with intercontinental delivery systems, which promised to bring instant destruction on an opponent. The Soviets' desire to claim far greater military strength than they actually possessed could have been linked to fears that their inferiority would make them vulnerable to diplomatic pressure. Ironically, it was not their actual inferiority but their imagined superiority that was emphasized by the Democratic opponents of President Eisenhower. They claimed a missile gap in favour of the USSR, caused by the neglect of the Republican administration. The accusations about Eisenhower letting things slip and handing an advantage to the Soviets have been replicated in the subsequent historical controversy. Initially, historians portrayed Eisenhower as a lacklustre president lacking in assertiveness, who let things drift by neglecting to keep a firm grip on government. Later, Eisenhower revisionists claimed that in reality he was a 'hands-on' president, who calmly and carefully defended American interests without getting carried away by Soviet posturing and rushing into excessive and unnecessary military spending. Then there was a re-emergence of orthodoxy, portraying Eisenhower as an ineffective president, albeit one who considered his options carefully before deciding not to decide.

At the time, the arguments about missile gaps proved bad for both Eisenhower and Khrushchev, with the American president's age and apparent neglect of defence needs contributing to his party's defeat at the hands of the younger, and apparently more dynamic, John F. Kennedy. Problems began for Khrushchev when the Americans finally revealed the reality of Soviet weakness in missile development in 1961. Soviet prestige was badly dented and may have contributed to Khrushchev's decision to install missiles in Cuba in 1962 in an attempt at least to gain the appearance of overcoming the advantages enjoyed by Washington.

It is certainly important to view the development of the arms race in the 1950s and early 1960s in terms of the political advantages that the appearance of strength offered. The Cold War was less about the actual military balance, effective deterrence, or nuclear conflict than about the attractiveness or advantages of socialism and capitalism. The arms race was not the essence of the Cold War, or even central to its pursuit, but something which was linked to it and which thereby threatened international stability. The growing importance of nuclear weapons and armaments had stemmed from the perceived American need to have them in order to deter a military reaction to the aggressive fighting of the Cold War, as in NSC 68. Then, particularly after the hydrogen bomb, there developed on the one hand attempts to integrate nuclear weapons into the conventional conduct of warfare and diplomacy and, on the other hand, efforts to devise meaningful strategies of deterrence to avoid their use. These conflicting aims were to affect Soviet and American approaches to a number of crises particularly in the early 1960s. By then, the number of newly independent states had grown and the battles in the less developed world were increasingly being won by the West.

The result was an increasing Soviet attempt to challenge the US by a greater emphasis on world power status, and to hope that revolutionary movements would develop, building on the communist success in Cuba. Hence the need to exploit the impact of the Sputnik and to install missiles in Cuba when power in tangible terms, as opposed to its appearance, was weighted in favour of the US. The prospect of changes in the East–West status quo were much greater outside Europe, where the long-running crisis over Berlin reflected the Soviet desire to do precisely that—either by removing the Western powers from the city or achieving the recognition of East Germany. For the Soviets and for Khrushchev's own personal position, the need to achieve something from the proclaimed policy of peaceful coexistence that could at least appear to change the status quo became increasingly urgent as the 1960s began. It was not enough to preserve Soviet control of their area of influence by repression in Hungary or to forge links with what began as a broad-based revolutionary movement in Cuba. Credibility in global terms was now more of an issue, so that by 1962 the so-called long peace was increasingly unstable—because of instability outside Europe and challenges to the status quo within it. As the Cold War came to focus more on Asia and Africa and as the Americans, inspired by the rhetoric of the young President Kennedy, became more determined to resist the Soviet challenge everywhere, the risk of Cold War becoming hot war increased. Then came the crisis over Cuba and the subsequent realization that the risk of nuclear war had to be prevented from being gambled with again. As 1963 began, the Cold War might be said to have been entering a new phase.

Visit the online resources that accompany this book to test your understanding and take your learning further:
www.oup.com/he/young-kent3e

NOTE

1. John D. Hargreaves, *Decolonization in Africa* (2nd edn, Longman, New York, 1999), 189.

PART II CHRONOLOGY

Cold War: Crises and Change, 1953–63

1953

20 January	Eisenhower becomes President of the US.
5 March	Death of Stalin.
16 April	Eisenhower's 'Chance for Peace Speech'.
11 May	Churchill's call for a summit meeting with the new Soviet leaders.
17 June	Riots in East Germany.
27 July	An Armistice agreement ends the Korean war.
8 August	Soviets explode their first hydrogen bomb.
19–20 August	US-backed coup in Iran restores the Shah to power.
12 September	Khrushchev becomes First Secretary of the Communist Party of the Soviet Union.
8 December	Eisenhower makes his 'Atoms for Peace' speech.

1954

25 January–18 February	Berlin Foreign Ministers' Conference on Germany.
15 January	Dulles makes Massive Retaliation Speech.
7 April	Eisenhower statement on danger of 'falling dominoes' in South-East Asia.
26 April–21 July	Geneva Conference on Korea and Indo-China takes place.
7 May	The French are defeated in Vietnam at Dien Bien Phu.
19–27 June	The Central Intelligence Agency (CIA) backed coup takes place in Guatemala.
24 July	Soviet proposal for a European-wide security agreement, excluding the US.
30 August	French parliament refuses to ratify European Defence Community (EDC) treaty.
6–8 September	The South East Asia Treaty Organization (SEATO) is created at a conference in Manila.
28 September–3 October	London conference of Western powers agrees on German rearmament under certain controls.
19 October	Anglo-Egyptian agreement on future of the Suez base.
December	Chinese Offshore Islands Crisis begins, as Chinese communists begin shelling Jinmen.

1955

8 February	Khrushchev assumes sole effective leadership of USSR.
4 April	The Baghdad Pact is created.
18–24 April	Bandung conference of developing nations takes place.
25 April	First Chinese Offshore Islands Crisis ends.
8 May	West Germany joins NATO.
15 May	Austrian peace treaty signed.
11–14 May	Conference in Poland leads to the creation of the Warsaw Pact to counterbalance NATO.

PART II CHRONOLOGY (continued)

26 May–2 June	Khrushchev visits Tito in Yugoslavia.
11–25 June	Jawarahal Nehru visits the USSR.
16 July	South Vietnam's premier, Diem, cancels pan-Vietnamese elections.
18–24 July	Geneva Summit takes place (US, Britain, France, and the Soviet Union attend).
	Eisenhower's 'Open Skies' speech.
8–13 September	Chancellor Adenauer goes to Moscow.
27 October–16 November	Geneva Foreign Ministers' Conference takes place.
1956	
25 February	Khrushchev denounces Stalin at 20th Party Congress.
18 April	The Cominform is dissolved; Khrushchev begins visit to Britain.
28 June	'Poznan Rising' in Poland.
26 July	In Egypt, Nasser nationalizes the Suez Canal Company.
19–20 October	Khrushchev visits Poland and makes Gomulka leader, bringing decline in discontent.
22–24 October	Pro-reform demonstrations in Hungary lead to Imre Nagy becoming premier.
29 October–6 November	Suez Crisis.
2–4 November	Soviets suppress the Hungarian anti-communist revolt and imprison Nagy.
6 November	Eisenhower is re-elected President.
1957	
5 January	Eisenhower doctrine for the Middle East is enunciated.
25 March	Treaty of Rome establishes the European Economic Community.
3 July	Khrushchev defeats 'Anti-party' plot by Malenkov and others.
1 August	US and Canada begin a Distant Early Warning (DEW) system against nuclear attack.
26 August	USSR tests first intercontinental ballistic missile.
19 September	US carries out first underground nuclear test.
2 October	Rapacki plan launched for a nuclear-free zone in central Europe.
4 October	First spacecraft, Sputnik I, is launched by USSR.
14–16 November	Mao's visit to Moscow forms watershed in ending Sino-Soviet cooperation.
1958	
10 January	First US intercontinental missile launched.
31 January	First US spacecraft, Explorer I, launched.
8 February	French air force attack on Sakhiet, Tunisia.
Mid-May	Vice-President Nixon encounters strong anti-American feeling during a trip to Latin America.
29 May	French Fourth Republic collapses over Algerian problem; de Gaulle asked to form a government.
1 July	Talks begin in Geneva on a nuclear test ban.
14 July	Iraq coup overthrows monarchy.
15 July	US troops land in Lebanon to prop up government.
17 July	British troops sent to Jordan to support King Hussein.

(continued...)

PART II CHRONOLOGY (continued)

6 August–6 October	Second Chinese Offshore Islands Crisis.
10 November	Khrushchev delivers an ultimatum over Berlin, calling for it to become a free city.
1959	
2 January	Castro takes power in Cuba.
24 July	Nixon visits the USSR and takes part in the 'Kitchen Debate'.
15–27 September	Khrushchev visits the US.
1960	
1 February	Chinese refuse to attend communist conference in Moscow.
13 February	The French perform their first atomic bomb test.
1 May	An American U-2 spy plane is shot down over Soviet territory.
8 May	Cuba establishes diplomatic relations with USSR.
16 May	Khrushchev storms out of the abortive Paris summit.
30 June	Congo (later Zaire) becomes independent of Belgium.
11 July	Province of Katanga secedes from Congo under leadership of Moïse Tshombe.
12 October	Khrushchev bangs his shoe on the desk as another delegate addresses the UN.
19 October	US begins trade embargo against Cuba.
8 November	John F. Kennedy is elected President of the US.
1 December	Former premier Lumumba of Congo is captured by the army; later killed.
14 December	Organisation for Economic Co-operation and Development (OECD) is founded.
1961	
6 January	Khrushchev backs 'wars of national liberation'.
20 January	Kennedy is inaugurated as US President.
13 March	Alliance for Progress announced by Kennedy.
12 April	Soviets send Yuri Gagarin into space.
17–20 April	The Bay of Pigs invasion takes place.
3 May	Ceasefire between pro-US and pro-Soviet sides in Laos.
5 May	US sends Alan Shepard into space.
3–4 June	The Vienna Summit, involving Khrushchev and Kennedy, takes place.
31 July	Britain launches application to join EEC.
19–22 August	Berlin Wall is constructed.
17 September	UN Secretary-General Dag Hammarskjöld is killed in the Congo, when his aircraft crashes.
19 October	Emergency declared against 'Viet Cong' in South Vietnam.
27–29 October	Stand-off between Soviet and US tanks at Checkpoint Charlie in Berlin.
1962	
31 January	Cuba is excluded from the Organization of American States (OAS).
8 February	US sets up a Military Assistance Command in South Vietnam.
19 March	Ceasefire between Algerian National Liberation Front and French forces.

PART II CHRONOLOGY (continued)

3 July	Algeria becomes independent.
23 July	Laos becomes neutral after talks in Geneva.
10 October–21 November	Chinese invasion of India over border dispute.
14–28 October	Cuban Missile Crisis.
18–21 December	Kennedy–Macmillan Nassau conference agrees US will supply Polaris missiles to Britain.
28 December	UN forces in Katanga act to put an end to secession.

Take your learning further by viewing the interactive version of this timeline:
www.oup.com/he/young-kent3e

5

Soviet–American Relations: Avoiding Hot War and the Search for Stability

Chapter contents

Soviet–American relations in the wake of Stalin's death were generally more complex than standard accounts of the Cold War allow. There was the basic distinction between Cold War and hot war, and how to conduct them both. Fighting a major hot war was transformed by the destructive power of the hydrogen bomb. Fighting the Cold War thus became riskier because of the possibility of hot war breaking out, especially if the survival of the other side was under severe threat in a military or ideological sense. There were some ways in which the US and the USSR began a more concerted period of competition, as great powers seeking global influence or the destruction of the other's area of influence or control. The desire to prove that their domestic socio-economic and political systems were superior was linked to covert Cold War measures on an increasing scale as the period began. At the same time, particular problems and traditional disputes in and outside Europe had to be addressed by attempting to resolve them through diplomatic agreement. If only to appease public opinion by apparently reducing tension, such efforts could be used to reap Cold War propaganda benefits. Having inspired fear in their populations, it was incumbent on Western politicians to appear to be endeavouring to reach an overt modus vivendi with the Soviets when the destructive powers of the hydrogen bomb could threaten the very existence of human civilization. Efforts had therefore to be made to avert this and achieve some form of détente, either to reduce the danger of nuclear war or to cultivate an image of searching for peace more determinedly than the other side; or to attempt to gain a particular advantage through negotiating an agreement. The question of the genuineness of both sides' efforts to achieve disarmament and resolve troublesome disputes is an important one to consider in Cold War interpretations.

A. The German Question

The future position of Germany was vital to the future of Europe and a particular concern of the Soviet Union. Germany's industrial might, strategic position at the heart of Europe, and military potential made it a major potential prize in the Cold War contest. The Soviet attitude at the time of Stalin's death has often been explained in terms of imposing communist control over all of a united Germany. There is no doubt that Stalin would have considered such a possibility, but he may have concluded that the problems this presented were such that a better option would be to formalize the division of Germany. This would provide some measure of relief from the possibility of a revived, expansionist state bent on another conflict with the Soviet Union. On the other hand, there were two main worries inherent in such a scenario, both associated with the future of West Germany. The rapid economic reconstruction of a viable West German state under Western auspices was accompanied by the 1952 agreement, which was never in fact ratified, to create a European Defence Community incorporating a rearmed West Germany. The prospect of Germans in the West being rearmed, perhaps eventually even having access to nuclear weapons, made the situation far more dangerous from the Soviet point of view. Hence, it is reasonable to conclude that the Soviets had an interest in the possibility of a neutral and permanently disarmed Germany, whether it became capitalist or communist. The dilemmas of rearmament, or neutralization and division, or unity over maximizing security may well have accounted for the Kremlin's interest in proposals for the reunification of Germany if there were guarantees that no part of it would again figure as a potential armed aggressor.

The same basic dilemma was evident to Western leaders, but their fundamental concerns over Germany's future incorporated a clear strategy for dealing with the German problem. Initially, as with the Soviets, they saw advantages in the creation of a divided Germany, which reduced the potential risks of future German aggression. Western writers, focusing on the idea of a Cold War and the risk of an expansionist Soviet Union, have tended to underplay the continuing fears, throughout Europe, about a revived Germany. The extent to which this influenced policy on the German question has been neglected. One key element in the economic and military moves to integrate West Germany into Western Europe was to minimize this risk by controlling German power in a greater whole; but it was easier to control the Western half of Germany in this way, rather than to run the risk of recreating a strong, united Germany. It was a very different approach to control from that followed by the Soviets. Division of Germany for them, in the spring of 1953, still meant control and domination, not integration. Therefore, a united Germany could present a more attractive option, provided it produced security, than it did to the West, where integration rather than direct control was the prime means of containing Germany. The greater the emphasis (see Chapter 6, A) on reducing direct Soviet dictation over the internal policies of the Eastern bloc countries, the more this was so. As John Lewis Gaddis has pointed out, both sides wanted to rely upon, and yet contain, Germany.[1]

The Death of Stalin

When Stalin died, Western policy was defined through the response to the Stalin note of March 1952 and subsequent exchanges with Moscow over the unification and demilitarization of Germany. The Western position was, in essence, based on two principles. In the first place, reunification must not mean the denial of the right of a united Germany to join any alliance it chose; and, second, free elections, monitored by the United Nations, should precede unification. Clearly, such a process was likely to produce a liberal regime that opted to join NATO. Stalin's proposal may have been posited on the possibility of disrupting German rearmament, by winning the propaganda war and putting the Soviet Union in a favourable position to appeal to the German people to support unity under communism. The Western response, also disingenuous, was clearly designed to be rejected by Moscow without arousing too much criticism. Once Stalin was dead, the new regime under Georgi Malenkov put forward another proposal in April 1953 which was part of their so-called peace offensive (see Chapter 5, B). It has not been taken seriously by Western leaders or historians, who have portrayed it as something purely designed to disrupt the Western alliance. The new proposal called for the immediate formation of a provisional government for the whole of Germany, thus sidestepping the disagreement over whether to form a government before or after elections. It also reduced the risk of such elections producing results which threatened the Soviets with the loss of all Germany to the liberal-capitalist world. The fact that this proposal might have reflected a genuine desire for the neutralization of Germany and might be associated with the policies that came to be adopted for loosening controls over the Eastern bloc in the following three months, deserves more consideration. In particular, its links with the strategy advocated by the secret police chief, Lavrenti Beria, and its emphasis on security and economic needs, as opposed to ideology deserve more consideration, despite Beria's fall from grace and elimination in June 1953 (see Chapter 6, A).

Reunification or Rearmament

In the West, those prepared to take the possibility of German unification seriously were led by the British Prime Minister, Winston Churchill. Churchill regarded German reunification at some point in the future as inevitable and thus was prepared to consider the terms under which it might be implemented. Against this were Dulles, the US Secretary of State, and Eisenhower, who were focused on the economic and military strengthening of the Western bloc as the main requirement of German policy, just as West German Chancellor Adenauer, from a different perspective, saw reunification as something that should follow but not precede West Germany's full restoration to independent statehood through its incorporation into the Western world. When the US National Security Council (NSC) examined the problem in August 1953, they defined the goal of German policy as:

> Firm association of a united Germany, or, at a minimum the Federal Republic with the West, preferably through an integrated European community, to enable Germany to participate in the defence of the West and make the greatest contribution to the strength of the Free World, with the least danger of its becoming a threat.[2]

As Moscow began its efforts to strengthen the diplomatic status of the German Democratic Republic (GDR), the possibility of summit meetings, as desired by Churchill in 1953, receded and the prospects grew of division becoming more permanent. Eisenhower had reluctantly agreed to Churchill's contacts with Moscow partly because he feared the impact on Western public opinion if he appeared, in the age of the hydrogen bomb, as the obstacle to progress on resolving key issues such as the future of Germany or disarmament. The American President, however, saw any summits on Germany or other issues as first requiring Soviet concessions to prove that they were changing their approach to relations with the West. The Russians did not, however, respond positively to Churchill's ideas and their proposal for a Foreign Ministers' Conference instead led to a four-power meeting, in Berlin in January–February 1954, where the future of Germany was again discussed.

The West produced what became known as the Eden Plan, which represented a change from their 1952 position. It proposed that elections would now take place for an all-German constituent assembly supervised by the four powers. Decisions it took would be based on a majority vote and any future government would be given the right to take over the existing international obligations of the West German government. For the Soviets, Molotov responded by proposing that the elections should only take place after the withdrawal of occupation forces apart from those supervising the elections. From the propaganda perspective, the West was helped by the crushing of the East German revolt in the summer of 1953 (see Chapter 6, A) and Molotov's offer lacked sufficient appeal to compensate for the dislike and distrust of the Soviets. His last attempt at agreement was based on a security treaty for the whole of Europe, which would, of course, have the advantage from the Soviet perspective of excluding the Americans.[3] The Western allies, however, preferred to continue with the existing policy of incorporating a rearmed Federal Republic into an integrated Western Europe to counter future threats from both the Germans and the Soviets. In the event, the collapse of the European Defence Community—because of the French Assembly's refusal to ratify it in August 1954—appeared to undermine this strategy. But agreement was quickly reached on the incorporation of West Germany into NATO (see Chapter 6, B). The extent of the Soviet fear of a revived West Germany, and its importance in influencing their policy on reunification, may be gauged from the fact that the next Soviet proposal did not come until the very day the Treaties of Paris ratifying the new arrangements were signed in January 1955.

The Soviets now indicated their willingness to accept the Eden Plan for holding elections for the whole of Germany as a basis for discussion. It was shutting the stable door after the horse of German rearmament had definitely bolted. The next Soviet move, perhaps to emphasize their seriousness about the neutralization of Germany, offered Austria a state of armed neutrality without the condition that this would have to be linked to the resolution of the German question. In May 1955, the Austrian State Treaty was signed, followed by the withdrawal of Soviet troops. This too was probably a propaganda step aimed at the German problem: Moscow could now claim that there was no reason why the same thing could not happen in Germany. Indeed, from the Soviet point of view there would be great advantages in a peace treaty, with or without German reunification. Western recognition of a divided Germany would at least formalize the division of the country, and thereby consolidate East Germany's position in the Eastern bloc after the 1953 riots. Whether this was the secondary aim and German reunification the main aim will continue to arouse controversy.

The problems of 1953 and the failure to prevent the rearmament in the West indicate that Khrushchev's preference by 1955 was to consolidate the position of Walter Ulbricht and the East German state of which he was leader. The whole question was linked to the three issues of security and disarmament arrangements in Europe (see Chapter 5, B), to the nature of the Eastern bloc and Soviet controls (see Chapter 6, A), and to the general development of the Cold War (see Chapter 7, A and Chapter 5, C). Some Americans saw the latter as still requiring the weakening of the Soviet hold over Eastern Europe. But by 1955 the Soviet approach was beginning to be defined in terms of the peaceful coexistence of two European blocs. Certainly, for Moscow there was less reason to pursue a reunification policy after 1955, and even less after more problems in the Eastern bloc in 1956 (see Chapter 6, A). The importance of preserving the Soviet and Western blocs began to reduce the importance of proposals for German reunification and neutrality. Rather than the potential threat from a revived Germany being reduced by reunification and neutrality, it became tied to broader proposals for European security based on disarmament and neutral zones.

During this transition period, in 1955–6, the British proposed that reunification could be furthered by creating a zone between the blocs in which armaments would be limited. In response to Adenauer's concerns, this area was defined as lying to the east and west of the demarcation line between a united Germany and the Eastern bloc; it was thus never likely to be acceptable to Moscow.[4] In fact, it can only have reinforced the need for the Soviets to consolidate East Germany's position in the Eastern bloc, just as Adenauer did not want to rule out reunification through Western integration. Thus, on the one side of the Iron Curtain a treaty between the GDR and the Soviet Union in 1955 guaranteed the presence of Soviet troops on East German soil and, in 1956, the People's Army's (of East Germany) was incorporated into the military forces of the Eastern bloc. On the Western side, West Germany was part of NATO and the Hallstein Doctrine was formulated whereby the Federal Republic would not establish diplomatic relations with any state (the Soviet Union had a special position) that had formal ties to the GDR.

As the Soviet moves towards bloc consolidation increased, a summit conference took place in Geneva in July 1955, which attempted in vain to make progress

BOX 5.1

Biography: John Foster Dulles (1888–1959)

Dulles was born in 1888 in Washington, DC and was the grandson of two former secretaries of state. He was educated at Princeton and George Washington universities and at the Sorbonne. He joined a New York law firm after attaining acceptance to the bar, and specialized in international law. Dulles enjoyed an early career in diplomacy as he attended The Hague Conference in 1907 as secretary to his grandfather. He also performed the role of legal adviser to US delegates at the Versailles Peace Conference in 1919. In 1945, after having helped prepare the United Nations charter, Dulles became a consultant to the US delegation which took part in the San Francisco UN conference. He was also appointed by President Truman to negotiate the 1952 peace treaty with Japan. In 1953, he finally filled the role of secretary of state when appointed by President Eisenhower. His main goal in his new position was to better the position of the US in the Cold War, being a strong anti-communist who was against any negotiation with the Soviet Union. Dulles was also responsible for the policy of 'brinkmanship' due to confrontations with China and the Soviet Union. He famously described the possible US response to Soviet aggression as 'massive retaliation', which referred to the large-scale use of nuclear weapons. Dulles remained in power as secretary of state until his resignation on the grounds of ill health in April 1959. He died of cancer only six weeks later.

on Germany. This summit has traditionally been associated with détente, despite its notable lack of achievement. The signing of the Austrian Treaty in May 1955 marked a Soviet concession and thus made the conference difficult for the Eisenhower administration to continue to oppose. But the 'spirit of Geneva' lacked substance, even if it did focus attention on arms control from a broader European perspective, rather than as a means to bring about German reunification. In the West, progress was to continue towards integration, with West Germany restored to independent statehood in 1955 and becoming a founder member of the European Economic Community in 1957. Moscow then suddenly experienced a new set of major Eastern European challenges to its control born from the attempts to change the nature of Soviet domination (see Chapter 6, A).

B. The Progress of Arms Control and Peace Efforts

The impact of the hydrogen bomb cannot be exaggerated, either for strategies for hot war plans or for a Cold War 'fought by all means short of international armed conflict'. Even if many in government and in the military were opposed to the idea, there was bound to be pressure to reduce the risks of nuclear conflict. The role of nuclear weapons in the Cold War and disarmament talks, then, lay partly in convincing the public on both sides of the Iron Curtain that their side was engaged in a quest for peace, but hampered by the aggressive designs of the other. Yet, whether or not responses to these concerns with disarmament proposals were genuine and designed to secure an agreement, their advocates also had to consider ways

BOX 5.2

Biography: Nikita Sergeevich Khrushchev (1894–1971)

Khrushchev was born in 1894 in the province of Kursk. He later moved to Ukraine, where he trained as a metal fitter. Khrushchev first became involved in politics in 1917, when he represented miners at political meetings. In 1918, he became a communist, and a year later joined the Red Army. In 1921, his first wife died, and he returned from the front in 1922. He then became deputy director of the Ruchenkov mines as well as a student and political leader at Yuzovka Workers' Faculty. In 1925, he was appointed Party Secretary of Petrovsko-Marinsk District of Stalino (formerly Yuzovka) Region. A year later he made his first political speech at the Ukrainian Party Conference in Kharkov. He was then promoted to regional politics in 1926 and became the Deputy Chief of the Organizational Section of the Ukrainian Central Committee in Kharkov. His rapid rise through the political ranks continued when he was appointed to the Moscow City Party Committee and then promoted to be First Secretary of Red Presnya District in 1931. Three years later, Khrushchev became the first secretary on the Moscow City Party Committee. He took an active role in the construction of the Moscow metro. Also in 1934, he was elected to the Central Committee at the 17th Party Congress.

Khrushchev's rise continued as Stalin's career progressed and when he was made the First Secretary of the Ukrainian Central Committee, he announced that he would annihilate 'all agents of fascism, Trotskyites, Bukharinites, and all those despicable bourgeois nationalists on our free Ukrainian soil'. As a full member of the Politburo, Khrushchev supervised the occupation and Sovietization of Western (Polish) Ukraine from 1939 to 1940. In 1944, after Ukraine was liberated, he took up the position of Chairman of the Ukrainian Soviet of Ministers. After 1945, however, Khrushchev suffered some political setbacks. He was accused of not effectively ridding Ukraine of nationalist agitation and was removed as First Secretary. However, he was reinstated as First Secretary of Ukraine in 1948. In 1953, following the death of Stalin, Khrushchev was named as a possible First Secretary of the Supreme Soviet. In 1954, he toured the Soviet Union and also brought 32 million acres of previously uncultivated land in Kazakhstan and south-western Siberia into cultivation. By 1955, he had consolidated his power by ridding the Party of those opposed to him and, in 1956, he continued this process by creating a Central Committee bureau for the Russian Union Republic, which he headed and also filled with his supporters. He escaped an assassination attempt the same year. In the 'anti-party' plot of 1957, three members of the Party attempted to have Khrushchev dismissed. However, he refused to accept the vote, and had the Central Committee consider the matter and overturn it. In 1958, Khrushchev became Premier and party leader. He visited the US the following year and addressed the UN in New York in 1960. In 1961, he met Kennedy in Vienna during the Berlin Crisis. Khrushchev was responsible for erecting the Berlin wall during this period. In April 1962, Khrushchev decided to place missiles in Cuba, and precipitated the Cuban Missile Crisis. Following the end of the crisis, in which he withdrew the missiles, he signed a Nuclear Test Ban Treaty in 1963 but was overthrown in October 1964 and died in obscurity in 1971.

in which armaments might best be deployed and integrated into a military strategy for hot war.

It may be argued that the level of armaments generally has no decisive impact on the reasons for going to war, and that control or limitation has an equally small impact on the maintenance of peace. Weapons do not automatically produce conflict or tension. However, it was seen as desirable for public consumption at least to seek ways of using agreements on weapons to indicate the decreasing likelihood of war. At the same time, the simplistic idea that the Cold War reflected the likelihood of a military conflict developing from bloc confrontation, which was conditioned by levels of armaments, was convenient for governments to have the public believe. A more persuasive analysis focuses on how the covert means and ideological ends at the heart of the Cold War interacted with other elements of interstate relations and their power political requirements, including the role of armaments.

Peace Proposals

Eisenhower's arrival in the White House was swiftly followed by the death of Stalin and the Soviet 'peace offensive'. There was a need to respond and counter the expressed desire of the British Prime Minister, Winston Churchill, for détente with the Soviets. Another issue was the UN Disarmament Commission, established in 1951, the conclusions of which were to be dealt with at the 1953 General Assembly. The initial Eisenhower approach was to tie progress on disarmament and the control of nuclear energy to the way in which Soviet stances on important international concerns developed. However, pressure grew for the definition of a disarmament policy in 1953, even though many in the West claimed that the same aggressive policies were being followed by Moscow but that different means were being employed. As part of the so-called 'peace offensive', the Soviets announced that they were ready to settle all unresolved differences and suggested a new approach to disarmament involving a discussion of 'detailed proposals for an international control organ, which could put into effect and supervise a comprehensive disarmament program'. Eisenhower himself was clear that the US would now have to do something to demonstrate its desire for comprehensive disarmament, hence his 'Chance for Peace' Speech in April 1953.[5]

There was already a five-point programme for the 'reduction in the burden of armaments' in the British and the American submission to the UN Disarmament Commission and the speech was generally vague and non-specific. Its first part was directed to the situation in East Asia and the efforts to achieve an armistice in Korea; then it turned to the German and Austrian questions left by the post-war failure to agree on peace treaties. The speech has been interpreted positively as reflecting Eisenhower's genuine belief that the Soviets should 'choose between war and peace, fear and security and hunger and prosperity'. Yet, it has also been claimed that it was 'not intended to promote a starting point negotiation but had the opposite aim'.[6] Eisenhower noted that 'Every gun that is made, every warship launched, every rocket fired signifies in the final sense, a theft from those who hunger and are not fed, those who are cold and not clothed.' However, disarmament was consciously placed after the resolution of important problems, which would involve a change in Soviet policies. It was the creation through this of the right atmosphere which was deemed to be decisive in the efforts to reduce the risk of nuclear war. The President did not make any firm disarmament proposals, because he remained determined that the Soviet Union most show some sign that it was being more accommodating and changing its ways over Austria, a Korean settlement, Indo-China, or Malaya. Only then, he believed, could the control of nuclear energy and arms limitations be considered.[7]

The speech therefore provided very little of substance. This was partly because the administration could not agree on an approach to disarmament or the reduction of the nuclear threat. The State Department was supportive of an attempt to make progress in arms negotiations, while the Defence Department was opposed to holding such talks. The issues were discussed in the NSC as part of the 1953 attempt to redefine national security policy. The latter now, in essence, encompassed anything that might pose problems or dangers to the US and how best to alleviate such threats within the general Cold War context. One problem, which was to reoccur in nuclear disarmament talks for much of the Cold War, was the problem of inspection of military facilities. The Pentagon doubted whether any safe system of inspection to prevent cheating was feasible, whereas the State Department wanted such issues explored fully, on the grounds that some limited safeguards were less risky than no limitation of nuclear weapons. In 1954, the military were still arguing that 'Soviet bad faith, evasion, and outright violation would render any disarmament agreement sterile, except as a means to advance Soviet objectives.'[8] Eisenhower clearly rejected the idea that the US could always say 'No' to talks and so the crux of the issue came back to the conditions required to make it advisable to hold them, or impossible not to.[9]

The situation that Eisenhower experienced has been described as the 'Disarmament Dilemma' in that there were a number of reasons why disarmament could be detrimental to American interests, but it was impossible to say so and therefore something had to be done to show willing to push the process forward. Thus, a debate has emerged between those, notably Eisenhower revisionists, who see a president committed to disarmament and trying, through a series of speeches, to promote progress towards an effective means of preserving peace, and those who see the proposals being geared to a Cold War strategy of attempting to appear more committed to peace than the Soviets, but never really desiring an agreement with them. Interpretations range from those who put disarmament and reducing the nuclear danger at the top of Eisenhower's agenda, to those who regard it as something which Eisenhower had to avoid without giving that impression. In the latter case, it has been argued that Eisenhower subordinated his disarmament efforts to psychological warfare and the maintenance of Western strategic superiority. Their purpose was thus to discourage neutralism, satisfy Western opinion, discredit Soviet initiatives, and expose Soviet intransigence.[10] Rather than agreement, Eisenhower opted for a policy of half-heartedly attempting to win the Cold War by undermining the Soviet satellite empire, while failing to accept fully that this might promote hot war.

There is evidence for both arguments, just as there are reasons for taking Soviet proposals for German neutralization at face value or of dismissing them as attempts to divide the West. It is easy to point to American concerns, expressed privately, about the dangers of nuclear war and the need for some form of disarmament—for example, Eisenhower's conversation with Senator Knowland in 1956, when he said there would be no reason for staying here if he had to give up the objective of getting a disarmament agreement. He believed a decent disarmament treaty was an absolute must.[11] Eisenhower revisionists are particularly clear that he was therefore committed to disarmament and attached importance to American efforts for peace.[12] Yet a case can also be made for Eisenhower's reluctance to accept disarmament, and certainly the attempt to redefine national security policy produced unequivocal opposition to the idea. Whether based on a principled aversion to the holding of talks or on the need for the Soviet Union first to change its approach to international affairs, there was disquiet about disarmament (see Chapter 7, A).

Internationally, the settlement of the Korean War affected the claim that the Soviets first had to prove their behaviour was changing before meaningful talks could take place. But for some it was not enough. In any case, US interpretations of change could have been related to the US Cold War strategy of eliminating or altering the Soviet Union as a communist state in control of satellites in Eastern Europe (see Chapter 4, D and Chapter 7, A). Only then would talks be valuable. In September 1953, Dulles came out with the suggestion of linking disarmament to the creation of a broad zone of restricted armaments in Europe and to a Soviet withdrawal from Eastern Europe, accompanying a US withdrawal from the West. Withdrawal could well mean liberalization in the satellite states, which would effectively achieve US goals and at the same time could produce international control of nuclear weapons, to accompany an end to the revolutionary mission of the Soviet Communist Party. In such a scenario, disarmament again appeared to be linked to the end of the Soviet system. Other proponents in the NSC of an American initiative on a more modest scale pointed to the increased Allied pressure for disarmament proposals, especially after the Soviet testing of a hydrogen bomb in August 1953. They suggested something on the lines of a Chance for Peace proposal which did not introduce 'new major substantive proposals on disarmament'.[13]

The next attempt or gesture for peace and reconciliation came in December 1953 with Eisenhower's 'Atoms for Peace' speech. The Atoms for Peace idea involved the transfer of a certain amount of fissionable materials to an atomic energy agency where they would be used for peaceful purposes. The proposal was vague enough to avoid any basis for concrete disarmament discussions and has been described as 'deliberately not a disarmament proposal'. It emerged against the background of the administration's failure to agree on the way forward on such matters. The ratification by the French of the European Defence Community Treaty, which would integrate a rearmed West Germany into the Western bloc, was still in the balance and the concern still present that disarmament talks would encourage its failure.

Immediately after, and in the wake of the US New Look policy (see Chapter 5, C), the Soviets announced that Atoms for Peace did not address the two fundamental problems of acquiring the capacity to produce nuclear weapons and the actual use of them in war. The Soviet response was the idea of a 'no first use' agreement; they therefore proposed an agreement not to undertake the use of weapons of mass destruction. This move towards the possible renunciation of the use of nuclear weapons was rejected by the US in January 1954. Eisenhower remarked, 'In the present state of world affairs, it is impossible that any effective agreement toward [disarmament] could be worked out which could provide the necessary safeguards.' Nothing would undermine the New Look policy more than an agreement banning the first use of nuclear weapons. Dulles and Secretary of Defence Charles Wilson commented in the same NSC meeting that there had to be an 'opening up of the iron curtain'.[14] In other words, disarmament was not something that could bring about the end of the Cold War but something that could occur when the Cold War had ended. The Soviet response, in April 1954, was to reject any discussion on Atoms for Peace until the two powers had first agreed on renouncing the use of atomic weapons.[15]

Unfortunately, waiting for that day without some meaningful disarmament was rendered more difficult for the Americans by the contamination of a Japanese fishing vessel, ironically named 'Lucky Dragon', by nuclear fall-out from an American thermonuclear test, in March 1954. Renewed demands for a summit meeting were made by Churchill around this time, although this had to wait until his successor, Anthony Eden, came to power in April 1955. By then, more pressure was mounting on the US as a result of the French and British disarmament proposals and the signature of the Austrian peace treaty. Britain, France, and the US finally agreed on the desirability of a summit on 10 May, the same day as the Russians made detailed disarmament proposals, including the means of on-site inspection. The lack of any inspection had been one key reason for Eisenhower claiming that disarmament agreements might not be safe, given Soviet secrecy. Now, he changed course somewhat and asked in a press conference, 'Are we going to open up every one of our factories, every place that something might be going on that could be inimical to the interests of someone else?'[16]

Earlier in 1955, Eisenhower had received a report advocating a different type of inspection regime, in some ways more comprehensive, than the Soviets were to produce and this now became the basis of his Geneva 'Open Skies' speech. That speech of 21 July 1955 referred again to the dangers of disarmament without proper inspection and he therefore proposed the exchange of full information on military establishments, and the provision of facilities for aerial photography to the other country, thereby producing transparency on all military issues. Both the Soviets and the US Joint Chiefs of Staff were horrified and so initially was Dulles. If the proposal had been accepted by Moscow, it might have produced an important breakthrough in arms control and could thus be described as a reflection of the priority Eisenhower gave to disarmament. The Soviets have to take the blame for its failure. It is certainly the case that the Soviet commitment to disarmament was questionable. When Malenkov spoke in January 1955 about the hydrogen bomb making peaceful coexistence both necessary and possible, this was used against him shortly after by Khrushchev as part of the discrediting of Malenkov, which was necessary for his own rise to power. Such ideas were deemed to be detrimental to the 'proletarian revolution', but were promptly adopted by Khrushchev when he emerged as leader. Whatever the Soviets were, being strong on principles was not among them.

It does seem, however, that there are many reasons to suspect the Americans did not want disarmament or peaceful coexistence. Their Cold War strategy aimed at undermining the Soviet Empire, for instance, may have been more important than any perceptions about the untrustworthiness of Soviet leaders, especially given their reluctance to test the latter. The Open Skies Proposal can be seen as an attempt to benefit the US most, given that it already had an open society and the Soviets could thus acquire information there relatively easily. It was more difficult for US agents to gather information behind the Iron Curtain. Or, the speech could be interpreted as an attempt to legitimize the U-2 programme of illegal spy flights which was about to get underway. Perhaps the most meaningful conclusions to draw from the failure of disarmament by the mid-1950s, was that it was never accepted by the Americans as something which could create détente. They saw it as something which was irrelevant to the course of the Cold War or which was best produced by its end. For the Soviets, it might have had value in furthering revolution because it could reduce the prospects of American military intervention and create the impression of military equality, which Khrushchev pursued by other means in the second half of the decade.

European Disarmament and Arms Control

By the mid-1950s, the German question's link to disarmament was changing. In 1956, Adenauer developed the idea that rather than link reunification to German neutrality the latter should be linked to the withdrawal of all troops from Europe. This would sidestep in the short term the growing problem of East Germany's consolidation in the Eastern bloc (see Chapter 5, A) and was similar to a proposal made in 1957 by the Polish Foreign Minister, Adam Rapacki. Adenauer's proposal was put to Eisenhower in January 1957 and was more comprehensive than Rapacki's, which was put to the United Nations in October 1957. Rapacki's idea, endorsed by the Soviet government, was based on a zone free of nuclear weapons encompassing the two Germanies and Poland. Given the lengthy discussions on the Rapacki Plan, Soviet documents suggest it was less a genuine arms reduction plan than an attempt to undercut the West German government.[17] More particularly, it may have been influenced by Adenauer's decision about the dilemma he faced in 1956 over removing or acquiring weapons on German soil. If, because of the 'New Look' in 1953 and the American policy of less reliance on conventional forces it embodied (see Chapter 5, C), US troops were to be reduced in Europe, both political and military benefits might accrue to West Germany. The prospect of West Germany using the opportunity to acquire American battlefield nuclear weapons was raised. The prospect of any nuclear weapons in German hands was regarded with horror in Moscow. For West Germany, the dilemma over conventional forces was only resolved with the Berlin Crisis of 1958 and is discussed below (Chapter 7, B).

Another set of disarmament proposals came from France and Britain, in February 1955, calling for a total ban on the manufacture of nuclear weapons and reductions in all nuclear and conventional forces, with the establishment of a control organ to guarantee the agreed prohibitions and reductions. The Soviets then produced their programme for arms reduction and the banning of nuclear weapons to be implemented in stages according to a precise timetable, with an international body that would operate through the 'inspection of large ports, railroad junctions, highways and airports'. There was no outright rejection of inspection.[18]

The Geneva Summit Conference was held in mid-1955, despite Eisenhower's reluctance and Dulles's attempt to exclude disarmament from the agenda. There was little hope of substantive agreement. The Soviets might have been prepared to take a more cooperative line in order to gain time for the consolidation of East Germany's position or, as Dulles feared, seeking international prestige by demonstrating their equality with the West.[19] But the Kremlin was losing interest in a neutralized Germany, as the prospect of a rearmed and reunited Germany in NATO loomed larger. Disturbances in Eastern Europe (see Chapter 6, A) followed in 1956 and prevented contacts on disarmament. The East–West atmosphere worsened as the

BOX 5.3

Biography: Dwight D. Eisenhower (1890–1969)

Dwight D. Eisenhower was born in Texas in 1890, but grew up in Kansas. He joined the army and was a second-lieutenant, stationed in Texas when he married Mamie Geneva Doud in 1916. He enjoyed a successful army career, serving under General Pershing and Douglas MacArthur. In 1942, Eisenhower commanded the landing of Allied forces in North Africa. On D-Day in 1944, he was the supreme commander of the troops invading France. Following the war, he took up the post of President of Columbia University but left in 1951 in order to take up command of the newly assembled NATO forces. In 1952, he was persuaded by the Republican Party to run for president of the US and won a large victory. Eisenhower made a number of vague proposals for peace and control of atomic energy between 1953 and 1955. In 1955, he had a heart attack, but he was elected for his second term in 1956. Eisenhower was a believer in equal rights and was keen to desegregate the army and also enforce (albeit slowly) the Federal decision to desegregate schools. Some have portrayed him as a weak and indecisive president who lacked a firm grip on his administration, but he has been praised by others as bringing a steady but firm hand to government, without the rhetoric that has handicapped many other leaders. He left office in January 1961, and died after a long illness in 1969.

decade progressed. The Soviet achievement of putting a satellite, Sputnik I, into orbit in 1957 (see Chapter 5, C) and the 1958 Berlin Crisis were other disincentives to disarmament talks. The crisis provided the Europeans with the opportunity to install American medium-range missiles in Europe, although no members of NATO were given independent control over them. Khrushchev emphasized the importance of disarmament in his 1959 meeting with Eisenhower, but by then the President was approaching the end of his term. Yet, as tensions continued, there was a greater need to preserve the appearance of seeking peace, if only for the sake of public relations. Preparing for war and pursuing diplomacy were not contradictory, hence the Paris summit of 1960.

The Paris Summit and the U-2 Incident

The Paris summit proved an even bigger fiasco than the Geneva one and was effectively sunk by the U-2 incident and the reactions of both sides to it. The Soviets had been watching these high-altitude American spy planes flying 70,000 feet above them for nearly five years. When they finally managed to shoot one down the pilot, Gary Powers, allowed himself to be captured and Khrushchev decided to exploit this flagrant violation of Soviet airspace. Assuming that the pilot would not have allowed himself to be taken alive, the Americans claimed that the plane was a weather plane which had gone off course when flying near the Iranian border. The Soviets then produced the pilot and pictures of the crash site, which was thousands of miles from where the Americans claimed the plane had inexplicably entered Soviet airspace. Khrushchev insisted that Eisenhower apologize at Paris, but the President refused and the summit was abandoned in acrimony. It could be that neither side wanted the summit to succeed. Apart from the general reluctance to agree on concrete measures, Khrushchev, from motives of self-preservation, may have been keen to pander to the hardliners and opponents of peaceful coexistence, not least China's Mao Zedong. On the other hand, Khrushchev may have believed that Eisenhower knew little about the flights and was being manipulated by imperialists in the US administration. At all events, the summits of Geneva and Paris, like all the disarmament and peace proposals, achieved nothing, and Germany remained divided.

When Kennedy became president in January 1961, a new era began. There would be no more summits involving second-rate powers such as France and Britain. In order to give the impression of seizing the initiative and playing a more positive world role, the Americans began a massive rearmament programme, while arms control attention focused on a Test Ban Treaty. Abandoning tests would have the effect of making it difficult to develop new nuclear weapons, although it took the Cuban Missile Crisis to bring concrete results (see Chapter 9, A on the Test Ban Treaty and Chapter 7, D on the Missile Crisis) in the form of a Test Ban Treaty. Kennedy focused on the world of ideas and the changing nature of technology in the expectation that American achievements, not least the quest to put a man on the moon, would outshine the Soviet Sputnik. The rhetoric of the early 1960s was soon to have a destabilizing effect.

C. Cold War, Armaments, and Preparations for Hot War

The relationship of arms control to the use of weapons in hot war and to some aspects of fighting the Cold War now need to be examined. When Eisenhower became president, one key aspect of preparing for hot war was the role of nuclear weapons and how to integrate them into a strategy for so doing. The use of nuclear weapons, particularly in global war, was becoming unthinkable for many, especially in Europe, but for Eisenhower, with the lesson of the end of the Korean War (see Chapter 4, E) very fresh in his mind, there was a different conclusion to be drawn. Dulles, in particular, saw value in using the retaliatory threat they presented as a means of deterring the kind of aggression which had produced the Korean War in the first place. It may have been inaccurate that this costly war came to an end thanks to threats about using nuclear weapons, but a policy of massive retaliation through the nuclear threat now seemed a distinct option to Dulles. Eisenhower's inclination to look to nuclear weapons was reinforced by the savings they offered, compared to the costs of conventional forces. The implications of this were considerable, because Eisenhower was reluctant to accept some of the arguments of NSC 68. The substantial increase in armaments it proposed seemed to contain dangers for the US economy. Its desire to maintain high levels of defence expenditure was not welcomed by Eisenhower, because he feared that this could threaten the American way of life. In the worst-case scenario, the role of the state in an economy geared primarily to production for a possible war was likely to increase government controls and deprive Americans of the individual freedoms they had been used to. Alternatives therefore had to be found to acquiring the overwhelming all-round military strength allegedly required to deter the Soviet Union everywhere in the world. In that sense, the 'New Look' policy that emerged was a combination of attempts to redefine US national security taking account of military *and* economic needs. It emphasized the importance of defending a way of life as well as a territory, and, as such, figured in Cold War thinking and in particular in the role of covert operations and psychological warfare[20] (see Chapter 7, A).

How this would be done was closely related to the tasks of 'Project Solarium', which was set up to determine the best ways of dealing with the Soviet Union. In May 1953, a panel of military and civilian dignitaries was established to define the precise terms of reference under which three task forces would consider what was required to meet three alternative scenarios in the development of a Cold War strategy and its implications for hot war. One general requirement for all task forces would be the forces needed and the costs that would be incurred, although equally important were the various assessments of the nature of the Soviet threat. In subsequent discussions, Eisenhower ruled out policies which would be opposed by America's allies, or which would cost too much or increase the risk of general war by, for example, arguing that the US could survive a nuclear one. These discussions influenced the formulation of the New Look, which in policy-making terms was one element of US national security strategy because it determined the role of US military forces. While the precise circumstances in which nuclear weapons were to be used remained vague, with the New Look there was a much greater inclination to use them.

The New Look

Thrashed out in the autumn of 1953, the New Look was not intended to mean that because nuclear weapons would now be relied upon a conflict would involve the ultimate commitment of US nuclear strike forces. What it meant was that nuclear weapons were now an integral part of American military deployments and would enable the US to make conventional force reductions. Nuclear weapons used on the battlefield would thus be like any other weapon and serve to give the US an advantage as and when needed. This point was then developed by Dulles into what became known as 'massive retaliation', in a speech in January 1954. Rather than wait and react to any Soviet or communist aggression, Dulles argued that the best way to deter any such actions was to be willing to respond at a time and in a place of the West's own choosing. The forces of local allies would be backed by the nuclear power of the US.[21] The credibility of such an idea was always questionable as the idea of risking annihilation over a localized conflict was never likely to be convincing. The New Look was also designed to make the use of nuclear weapons more meaningful—crucially, making *threats* to use them more viable—as well as making the provision of conventional forces less costly by using covert operations. It would place particular emphasis on the roles of America's allies as vital players in any conflict. Implicit was the hope that, as the Americans provided the nuclear components in Western strategy, their European partners might become more involved in the provision of conventional forces.[22]

Thus, there was little change in the US acquisition of more nuclear weapons, or the development of a NATO strategy based on their first use, because of the advantage enjoyed at the time by the Eastern bloc's conventional forces. It was necessary for the Eisenhower administration to work out a strategy for the preparations for hot war in a situation where the Europeans did not believe that they could provide sufficient conventional forces for the defence of Western Europe. The connections between the use of nuclear weapons, conventional force strategy, and deterrence were to preoccupy Eisenhower during his first administration. It is understandable why historians who see Eisenhower as genuinely committed to a process of disarmament downplay the subsequent development of the New Look.

Whatever the President's views, there were those who regarded disarmament as largely irrelevant to the real problem of two opposing ideological blocs. More importantly, there were those who were still committed to policies aimed at undermining the Eastern bloc, or the Soviet Union, or both. For them, disarmament and cooperation ran counter to the ultimate goal of US Cold War policy and its undermining or destruction of the Soviet Union. There were also those who wanted to seize the opportunity presented by Stalin's death to further these Cold War goals, including the President's psychological warfare adviser, C. D. Jackson. He wanted a speech from Eisenhower to produce divisions between Soviet leaders and allies such as China, which would combine elements of a serious policy proposal with elements of Cold War psychological strategy. Dulles, for his part, simply believed that nothing could be achieved and that dealing with the Soviets would encounter delays, handicapping the efforts to incorporate West Germany into a united Western European bloc, hence the importance of an aggressive Cold War strategy, of the New Look, and massive retaliation.

Sputnik and the Gaither Report

In 1957, thinking about nuclear weapons was transformed with the Russian development of an intercontinental ballistic missile (ICBM), which could leave and re-enter the atmosphere, and therefore pass over the US or descend to earth there. Even though the Eisenhower administration had seen a massive expansion of American nuclear weapons, the reaction in the US was dramatic. Edward Teller, who was associated with the development of the H-bomb and who later became a nuclear expert, stated on television that the US 'had lost a battle more important and greater than Pearl Harbor'. There was a suggestion that the Russians would reach the moon within a week and an aide to Senator Lyndon B. Johnson wrote in a memorandum. 'It is unpleasant to feel that there is something floating around in the air which the Russians can put up and we can't ... It doesn't really matter whether the satellite has any military value. The important thing is that the Russians have left the earth and the race for control of the universe has started.'[23] In this kind of Cold War atmosphere, the politics of disarmament were unlikely to have much of an impact.

The situation was not improved by the establishment of a special presidential commission to examine the implication of the hydrogen bomb for civil defence measures—measures that some saw as essential to deter the enemy. Formally established on 8 May 1957, under H. Rowan Gaither, the committee of industrialists, academics, and engineers ended up with a remit broadened into considering the question of civil defence in a wider security context, especially that of maintaining 'second-strike capability', so as to be able to hit back at the Soviets even if they launched a surprise 'first strike'. By preparing a 'second-strike capability', the US would deter the very idea of launching a surprise attack. Assisted by researchers and an advisory panel composed largely of former government experts, the committee was effectively led by Robert Sprague, of the Sprague Electric Company. He had a number of conversations with Curtis Le May, the head of the Strategic Air Command (SAC), which was responsible for US nuclear bombers. Le May initially told him that B-52s would solve any problems and there would be no missile threat in his lifetime. A few weeks later, on 4 October, Sputnik I was launched. But Sprague was unhappy before then and returned to talk with Le May. As a result, a nuclear alert was staged and it emerged that it would take nearly six hours for nuclear bombers to be loaded and take off. Even if the bombers were on alert, the early warning detection of an incoming Soviet attack would not allow them to be loaded (although they could get off the ground unloaded). Le May was unruffled and told Sprague about the U-2 spy planes that were making frequent spying missions over the USSR, at altitudes so high that it was extremely difficult for them to be shot down by ground-to-air missiles. As a result, Le May claimed he would know when there was activity on Soviet bases and when he saw planes gathered for an attack he was 'going to knock the shit out of them before they take off the ground'.

This was not government policy and it is unlikely that Eisenhower knew about it, but it was indicative of military thinking, especially in the air force and SAC. The determining factor was that the most sensible thing to do was to fire nuclear weapons first and with as much force as possible—at least if the aim was to have any chance of partial survival, or to inflict the most damage on an enemy as a result of a nuclear exchange. If this was one disconcerting element in the US approach to hot war, then it was similar to the Soviet strategy of using massive force as the mainstay of strategy in a major conflict. There was another worry about US thinking in relation to preparing for hot war that had Cold War implications. In the wake of the Sputnik launch, one thing the Gaither Committee did favour was the installation of nuclear weapons in Europe, as part of a call for more rearmament in the face of what seemed a major Soviet military success. The drafting of the final Gaither Committee report, presented in November 1957, was entrusted to an academic James Baxter III, who called on Paul Nitze for advice and assistance. Nitze, it will be recalled, had been involved in the drafting of NSC 68 and its revision in NSC 141 (see Chapter 4, D). Its call for more arms to enable the US to fight the Cold War from a position of strength, that would deter hot war, had led to a massive increase in defence spending of nearly 300 per cent. Eisenhower had rejected NSC 141, and slightly reduced defence spending, a decision which was reinforced by the development of the New Look. Nitze was able to return to the charge through his significant contribution to the drafting of the Gaither report. The report claimed that the Soviets now had the material to produce 1,500 nuclear bombs and that their GNP was growing. The Soviet Union's long-range air force, intermediate range missiles, air defence system, and intercontinental rockets in which it 'probably surpasses us' were all described. These assets were deemed to be particularly dangerous, given the vulnerability of the SAC to surprise attack, especially when international tension was low.[24] We now know that the claims of Soviet strength were wide of the mark, but attention was again fixed on rearming and matching the Soviets when the US was in fact still way ahead, especially with regard to nuclear weapons.

Eisenhower may have been reluctant to listen to the calls for disarmament, but he was definitely loath to commit himself to more rearmament. If he is not to be praised for his commitment to reducing the risks of war with the Soviets, he must at least gain credit for not exaggerating them. Eisenhower refused to give in to pressure from those in Congress who began to claim that the US was falling behind in the nuclear race. He also reasoned that there could be no war without international tension first and therefore there need be no panic over warning times. The claims of a possible 'bomber gap', and then a 'missile gap', also failed to change Eisenhower's approach. In the run up to the 1960 election, the Democrats tried to make political capital out of the missile gap as it indicated weakness in the face of post-Sputnik Soviet strength. John F. Kennedy, who was running against Eisenhower's Vice-President, Richard Nixon, in 1960, hoped to win support by claiming that the Republicans had neglected American defence needs. 'We are facing a gap on which we are gambling with our survival' was one of his campaign lines.[25]

The various estimates made by the different intelligence organizations all saw the US falling behind, but the estimates of how far the Soviets were in front varied. The National Intelligence Estimate (NIE) of February 1960 was full of footnotes referring to service disagreements with the estimates. The NIE claimed the Soviets would have between 170 and 270 missiles by mid-1961 and between 450 and 650 by mid-1963. The higher number reflected the air force view, and the lower number that of the CIA. Army and navy estimates were about one-fifth to one-quarter of those figures. The difference in part stemmed from the estimates of how far the Soviets would increase the rate of production and from guesses about what lay in the Plesetsk region of northern Russia, which the U-2s had not reached. They can also be explained by the roles the respective services would have in dealing with the Soviet nuclear threat and the money that could be justified for such purposes in the defence budget.

As more became known from satellites, it appeared that, in 1961, the Soviets had 3.5 per cent of the NIE estimates and in 1960 may only have had three ICBMs. Kennedy was to emphasize the importance of Americans making a commitment and moving forward to tackle the danger. Eisenhower, on the other hand, was not prepared to use the danger of hot war to make commitments that were too costly and too threatening to the American way of life. Unlike Kennedy, he was prepared to play down the risk of nuclear war, whatever the political costs.

Visit the online resources that accompany this book to test your understanding and take your learning further: www.oup.com/he/young-kent3e

NOTES

1. John Lewis Gaddis, *We Now Know. Rethinking Cold War History* (Clarendon Press, Oxford, 1997), 135.
2. Foreign Relations of the US (FRUS), 1952–4, VII, NSC 160/1, 17 August 1953, 518. Cited in ibid., 132.
3. Wilfred Loth, *Overcoming the Cold War: A History of Détente* (Palgrave, New York, 2001), 26–8.
4. Ibid., 37.

5. Ibid., 179–82.
6. Robert Bowie and Richard H. Immerman, *Waging Peace: How Eisenhower Shaped an Enduring Cold War Strategy* (Oxford University Press, Oxford, 1998), 120; David Tal, 'Eisenhower's Disarmament Dilemma: From Chance for Peace to Open Skies Proposal', in *Diplomacy and Statecraft*, 2 (2001), 175–7, 182.
7. Stephen E. Ambrose, *Eisenhower the President 1952–1969, vol. 2* (Allen & Unwin, London, 1984), 94–5.
8. Robert Bowie and Richard H. Immerman, *Waging Peace: How Eisenhower Shaped an Enduring Cold War Strategy* (Oxford University Press, Oxford, 1998), 229. Citing FRUS, 1952–4, II, part II, 680–6.
9. Robert Bowie and Richard H. Immerman, *Waging Peace: How Eisenhower Shaped an Enduring Cold War Strategy* (Oxford University Press, Oxford, 1998), 227–30.
10. David Tal defines the dilemma in 'Eisenhower's Disarmament Dilemma: From Chance for Peace to Open Skies Proposal', in *Diplomacy and Statecraft*, 2 (2001), 175–7, 182; on disarmament's relationship to the needs of psychological warfare see Kenneth A. Osgood, 'Form before Substance: Eisenhower's Commitment to Psychological Warfare and Negotiations with the Enemy', *Diplomatic History*, 3 (2000).
11. Stephen E. Ambrose, *Eisenhower the President 1952–1969, vol. 2* (Allen & Unwin, London, 1984), 343.
12. In addition to Ambrose, see Robert Bowie and Richard H. Immerman, *Waging Peace: How Eisenhower Shaped an Enduring Cold War Strategy* (Oxford University Press, Oxford, 1998), 120 and S. Dockrill *Eisenhower's New Look National Security Policy* (Macmillan, Basingstoke, 1996), 132.
13. David Tal, 'Eisenhower's Disarmament Dilemma: From Chance for Peace to Open Skies Proposal', in *Diplomacy and Statecraft*, 2 (2001), 183–4; John Lewis Gaddis, *We Now Know. Rethinking Cold War History* (Clarendon Press, Oxford, 1997), 132.
14. David Tal, 'Eisenhower's Disarmament Dilemma: From Chance for Peace to Open Skies Proposal', in *Diplomacy and Statecraft*, 2 (2001), 185.
15. Ibid., 182–5.
16. Stephen E. Ambrose, *Eisenhower the President 1952–1969, vol. 2* (Allen & Unwin, London, 1984), 247.
17. John Lewis Gaddis, *We Now Know. Rethinking Cold War History* (Clarendon Press, Oxford, 1997), 138. Citing Beate Ihme-Tuchel, 'The Soviet Union and the Politics of the Rapacki Plan', CWIHP Conference Paper, Essen, (1994).
18. John Lewis Gaddis, *We Now Know. Rethinking Cold War History* (Clarendon Press, Oxford, 1997), 186.
19. Saki Dockrilll and Gunter Bischof (eds), 'Geneva: the Fleeting Opportunity for Détente', in *Cold War Respite* (Louisiana University Press, Baton Rouge, 2000).
20. Psychological warfare as described by Kenneth Osgood was 'Planned use of propaganda and other actions designed to influence the opinions, emotions, actions, attitudes and behavior of enemies, neutrals and friendly foreign groups to support the accomplishment of national aims and objectives' (Introduction), 13, in *Total Cold War* (University Press of Kansas, KS, 2006).
21. Fred Kaplan, *The Wizards of Armageddon* (Simon & Schuster, New York, 1983), 175.
22. Andreas Wenger, *Living with Peril Eisenhower Kennedy and Nuclear Weapons* (Rowman Littlefield, Lanham, 1997), 38–47; Robert R. Bowie and Richard H. Immerman, *Waging Peace* (Oxford University Press, Oxford, 1998), 125–36, 227–30.
23. Fred Kaplan, *The Wizards of Armageddon* (Simon & Schuster, New York, 1983), 135.
24. Ibid., 136–8, 141–2.
25. Richard Reeves, *President Kennedy* (Papermac, London, 1993), 58.

6

Maintaining the Spheres of Influence

Chapter contents

A. Eastern Europe

The Stalinist period of bloc consolidation had been based on a combination of terror and strict adherence to Soviet models of political and economic development. It was justified by Cold War concerns and the need to fight 'enemies', internal and external, that the Soviet Union allegedly faced. Moreover, the atmosphere of threat, danger, and sacrifice was accompanied in Eastern Europe by the economic exploitation and plunder of territory for the benefit of post-war Soviet recovery. With the death of Stalin and the assumption of power by the triumvirate of Beria, Khrushchev, and Malenkov, a fresh approach to domestic issues and to the nature of Soviet control over its European satellites soon emerged. The change was partly out of necessity and partly out of the desire to get away from the type of system associated with the Stalinist state. The apparent change produced a new Soviet approach to East–West relations, if not to the fighting of the Cold War by covert means, as well as having a dramatic impact in East Germany, Poland and, most significantly, in Hungary.

The New Leadership and the Crisis in East Germany

The full horror and paranoia of the latter days of Stalin's rule experienced by members of the party and governmental elite only gradually became evident. Yet it was something that the three leaders were very much conscious of and an important consideration in deciding to change Stalin's approach to domestic policy that, like most things in the Cold War, as this book argues, was intimately linked to foreign policy. One way to begin the process of change was to remove the central role that Stalin had played, by emphasizing the idea of joint leadership and undermining the cult of personality which Stalin had encouraged. Another was to reduce the degree of repressive interference carried out by the security services. This posed difficulties for Beria, who had been responsible for state security under Stalin. It was therefore easier for Beria to distance himself from Stalin by proposing foreign, rather than domestic, policy initiatives, and he therefore came up with a new policy towards Germany which was the key problem for the Soviets in Europe (see Chapter 5, A).

This, like other initiatives, failed to secure any fundamental changes in foreign policy, since the perceptions of the new Soviet leaders, stemming in part from the 'small Committee of Information' (KI), ultimately remained unchanged. The KI was an autonomous intelligence body affiliated to the Ministry of Foreign Affairs, which was imbued with Stalinist assumptions about the dangers presented by the West. It was the attempt to define new responses to such beliefs that led to the idea of change in Soviet foreign policy. What the new leadership wanted, above all, was to avoid giving any impression of Soviet weakness which might encourage more aggressive Western policies, including the campaign of subversion,[1] which had been waged against the Soviets since 1948. This may have required some commitment to better relations and preventing hot war but the ultimate goal was the interests of the Soviet Union in terms of defence (security) and, unlike under Stalin, its status as a superpower capable of competing on equal terms with the leading capitalist power.

This was the beginning of the attempt to introduce peaceful coexistence which, for the Soviets, involved the idea of competition between two equal powers representing two different socio-economic systems. Both Malenkov and Khrushchev may have seen things in terms of better relations with the West, which would reduce the Soviet fear of attack and overcome the sense of military and economic inferiority. The latter was seen to require reform of the domestic structures in order to provide for the people of the Soviet Union and its satellite empire in Eastern Europe, in the same way that American capitalism, through the Marshall Plan, had provided for the people of Western Europe. Khrushchev was to pursue both the foreign and domestic aspects of such a strategy more effectively than Malenkov, and certainly more effectively than Beria. Arguing for radical new projects like the 'Virgin Lands Scheme' for expanded agricultural production in Soviet Central Asia and against the 'anti-party' bureaucrats in the Soviet establishment, Khrushchev sought greater popular legitimacy which, as in the West, required success relative to the ideological adversary. Whether or not this was a means to achieve personal power more than an aversion to the horrors of Stalinism, Khrushchev succeeded, between 1953 and February 1955, in removing both of his rivals for power and assuming complete control.

Beria was the first to fall as a result of attempts to portray himself as a reformer with regard to the future of East and West Germany. According to Sudoplatov, then head of the First Directorate of the MGB (Ministry for State Security), which was incorporated into what officially became the KGB in March 1954 (the term KGB is often used to denote the security and intelligence apparatus of the whole Soviet era), Beria wanted to link solving the German question (see Chapter 5, A) to the solution to Soviet economic difficulties. He cited the following points for exploratory talks:

1. extending German reparations to the Soviet Union;
2. a reconstruction programme for Russia, Ukraine, White Russia, and the Baltic states; the costs were to be borne by Western sponsors, mainly the Germans.

New industrial works were to be built, as well as a large network of railroad lines and highways. Beria contemplated technical help, with German participation in the range of $10 million. As he argued, if the Soviets wanted to support the illusory construction of socialism in the GDR, they must invest no less than £20 billion within ten years, which would include deliveries of raw materials and food to East Germany and Poland. He wanted to be rid of that heavy burden. In its place, he sought a wide-ranging economic agreement with the West, which he wanted to have blessed by the UN after arranging things with America, England, and France.[2]

Beria thus wished for a treaty guaranteeing a neutral Germany in which the issue of socialism came second to the issue of Soviet economic recovery, even if the latter involved capitalist help. As Molotov recalled, for Beria, if Germany became a peaceful state, it mattered little whether it was socialist or not. The extent to which this turned the Soviet leadership against Beria or the extent to which they seized on this as a reason for his removal and death remains unclear. Whatever their views, the situation regarding the East Germans in 1952–3 does indicate the importance of power over ideology. In 1952, East Germany began to witness a programme of forced collectivization and industrialization, subsidized by the Soviet Union, which had an important ideological component. However, in early 1953, when it produced understandable reactions (with over 100,000 fleeing to West Germany, crossing from East to West Berlin, in the first four months of the year), things began to change.[3] The new leadership now had to address the possibility of an East German economic collapse in addition to the other concerns. Worse, in 1953 they faced the prospect of a revived, rearmed West Germany and in such a situation ideology eventually went out of the window.

Collectivization and industrialization were still favoured by the East German leader, Walter Ulbricht, and what to do about this situation seems to have caused some disagreement in Moscow. After a meeting on 27 May 1953, the Presidium did, however, condemn the forced construction of socialism and the intensified collectivization. The broad issue was how best to ensure some control over East Germany, while preventing a powerful West Germany attracting more and more people to the West or, even worse, incorporating the East into a rearmed capitalist state. As Beria's arguments were heard, Molotov argued for a relaxing of the military occupation in order to increase the popularity of the East German government.[4] If Beria, possibly with some support from Malenkov, was ready to give up the GDR for German neutralization and economic cooperation with the West, it shows the enormous differences from Stalin's regime, especially if Stalin, as late as March 1952, was committed to the creation of a communist Germany as part of the westward advance of the Soviet revolutionary state. The proposals discussed in 1953 now suggest a picture in which communist revolution and the expansion of Soviet power in Germany were definitely *not* at the top of the agenda, or even in the debate. The murderous nature of the Soviet regime would still be in evidence, albeit in a reduced form, but its concerns, if they had ever been anything else, were the maintenance of controls in Eastern Europe. The preservation of the East German state remained vital to some and emerged as the main requirement. But it was now to be achieved by means other than Stalinist controls and ideological development. Therefore, 1953 was an important milestone for considering how the Soviets viewed the maintenance of their control and influence east of the Iron Curtain.

The Soviet leadership opted to reduce Soviet subsidies, while the East Germans slowed the pace of change in order to attract more support within the GDR. The aim was to obtain more popular acceptance of the East German state by relaxing the kind of controls associated with Stalin. Such a policy might also bring dividends if Germany was reunified. Consequently, the politburo of the East German communists (technically the East German Socialist Unity Party) rescinded all measures against the existence of private farmers and artisans, along with new measures pertaining to cultural and religious freedoms. The alterations were justified on the basis of 'securing and expanding a mass movement for the creation of a unified, peace-loving, independent Germany'.[5] Yet they contained some obvious risks. To introduce economic measures which would impoverish and alienate people, and then to follow them by lifting some forms of economic and political repression, was a potentially explosive mix. Within a week of the announcements, workers in East Berlin and elsewhere took to the streets in open revolt. The uprisings were quelled throughout East Germany with the help of Soviet troops and tanks. They did, however, see the end of Beria and the salvation of Ulbricht, yet it was no clear victory for the hardliners in Moscow. The problems created by liberalization had to be compared to those created by forced collectivization and industrialization, and the new leadership faced a dilemma irrespective of the German problem. Was it now better to move towards liberalization or away from it? It was a key issue awaiting resolution.

Hungary and Poland

The troubles faced by the Soviets in 1953 were a taste of things to come and the crunch came after the 20th Party Congress in February 1956. Khrushchev's famous speech attacking Stalin heralded a series of events that indicated a definite change of approach by the Soviets under Khrushchev, and which was seen as an opportunity by many in Hungary and Poland. Apart from confessing to the crimes of Stalin and suggesting that conflict with capitalism was not inevitable, the speech claimed that Moscow could no longer tell communist parties in other countries what to do but should encourage them to adapt to local conditions. The change since Stalin, with the prospect of peaceful coexistence and greater independence, seemed to be confirmed by the disbanding of the Cominform in April and the unilateral reduction in Soviet troop numbers by over one million in May. It was reasonable to conclude that bloc ties were loosening and greater freedom and reduced militarization were on the way.

For Khrushchev, the worries that unrest of the East German variety would spread to the rest of the bloc, encouraged by American psychological warfare, had not disappeared. There were those in Moscow who were disinclined to pursue the more relaxed approach which Khrushchev favoured as they drew the opposite conclusions about the cause of dissent and its remedies. In Poland, the Communist Party leader Bierut died in 1956 and deStalinization was in progress, accompanied by the release of political prisoners. As news of Khrushchev's speech was leaked in the ensuing months, a series of strikes helped strengthen the demands for the return of Wladyslaw Gomulka, one of Stalin's leading victims. By August, Gomulka's rehabilitation was complete and the final step for his supporters was to bring him back to power in October on the back of massed rallies. In response, Soviet troops in Poland were put on alert and a Soviet tank division moved towards Warsaw, but the Soviets could not guarantee effective control over the Polish army. A worried Khrushchev flew to Warsaw on 19 October as Gomulka was about to be elected and halted the Soviet advance towards the capital. The Poles and Gomulka refused to back down, but Gomulka combined assurances that Poland would not leave the Warsaw Pact (the Eastern bloc's equivalent to NATO, formed in response to West Germany joining the Atlantic Pact) with threats of arming workers to resist. Khrushchev compromised, Gomulka was returned to power, and communism in Poland was given a more nationalist leader demanding a more equal relationship with Moscow.

Hungary was a different story, one where protests were more rooted in the mass of the population, including the workers. The demands were thus more threatening to the increasingly fragile nature of bloc solidarity in the East. In the wake of the East German riots, Prime Minister Imre Nagy had rejected greater concentration on heavy industry. He had placed more emphasis on the production of consumer goods and by 1955 had released a number of political prisoners. His departure from government meant that opposition to Prime Minister Rakosi, after Khrushchev's 20th party Congress speech, began to focus on Nagy's return. Student protest groups called for this, but unlike in Poland it was not just changes in the party hierarchy but in Hungarian politics and society that they demanded. The immediate withdrawal of Soviet troops from Hungary was a demand that reflected deep-rooted Hungarian resentments at control by Moscow, but the reformers also demanded the introduction of a multi-party system and free elections to the National Assembly. In addition, they wanted Rakosi and another leading figure in the Hungarian Workers' Party (the ruling Communist Party) to be put on trial for past crimes. The students in Budapest planned a massive demonstration in the capital for 23 October 1956 and won the backing of workers there, to the extent that the latter had to be persuaded not to call a political strike in support of the demonstration.[6] The protests in Hungary were based on a more radical and wide-ranging programme than in Poland, and were developing a much greater focus on political reform than those in East Germany. The role of workers was also to assume greater significance in trying to wrest control from the Workers' Party and place it directly in the hands of those in the factories. Hungarian workers on whose behalf the Communist Party allegedly acted were at the forefront of opposition in 1956.

The Budapest demonstration had grown in size during 23 October and unrest spread outside the capital, with four people shot dead in Debreccen. This brought home to the Soviets that the Hungarian crisis was becoming more serious than the Polish problem and a delegation from the Hungarian Workers' Party was summoned to Moscow. As Nagy returned to the Parliament building to speak, the decision was taken in Moscow to send in troops. Ironically, Nagy, who was sworn in as prime minister in the morning, was calling for the demonstrators to return home and allow the government to deal with Hungary's problems. But dealing with Hungary's problems on the basis of the 1953–5 reforms made by Nagy was not enough and his speech to the demonstrators damaged his credibility, reinforcing the support for radical change.

Soviet troops arrived in Budapest on the morning of 24 October with the task of turning the rebels over to the police, but their presence initially added fuel to the flames of nationalist protest and made the demonstration more favourable of national liberation. By the end of the morning, as the situation deteriorated and organized resistance groups began to form at key points in the city, the Soviet troops were ordered to open fire when attacked, while Hungarian troops proved unreliable. As the Soviet army began to establish control over Budapest, Nagy, whose return the Soviets were now backing, lost further credibility when he referred to the organized resistance as fascist, and martial law was declared. Armed resistance grew, with young workers playing a leading role, and the numbers of deaths at the hands of Soviet troops was well into three figures by 25 October. Two Soviet emissaries, Mikoyan and Suslov, began to call for compromise and a political solution as a means to win back the mass of the workers, by implying that bloody repression was undesirable.

By 28 October, it appeared that peace could be restored by the new government's proclamation of a general ceasefire and the introduction of some radical changes. The State Security Authority was dissolved and the government reorganized on a multi-party basis. Its new programme retained socialist control over the 'commanding heights' of the economy but announced a more nationalist-oriented foreign policy. The government in Moscow examined the options it faced in the light of the Polish situation, where it had opted for a less obedient, but more populist government rather than maintaining a puppet regime in the face of a possible revolt. In Hungary, the armed revolt was already happening with workers' groups to the fore, the Hungarian army in disarray, and the collapse of the old government system in the capital and the regions well advanced. On 28 October, the decision was made to support the Nagy government and comply with its demand for the withdrawal of Soviet troops. Therefore, the following day, tank units began leaving Budapest and the withdrawal was complete on 30 October. The Soviet newspaper *Pravda* then published a declaration outlining the need for more equality between the socialist countries of Europe. The inclination to reconsider the kind of controls Moscow exercised over the Eastern bloc continued at the Presidium meeting. Foreign Minister Shepilov talked about widespread anti-Soviet sentiments in Eastern Europe and, in order to overcome them, it was necessary to remove 'elements of direct control'. Significant evidence existed that events were leading to a revision of relations within the Eastern bloc.[7]

The following day, circumstances changed and the decision was taken to redeploy troops and use force. The reasons for this sudden shift have always been speculated on in terms of the local situation, the requirements of socialism, or the Soviet position in the region. Now that we have archival evidence, it seems that more attention needs to be given to the international context and the global rivalries. For the Soviets, a key element of the Cold War now involved a determined quest for greater equality with—or the surpassing of—the achievements of Western capitalism and the acquisition of global status. In the mid-1950s, the best means of doing this were being considered in two ways—the maintenance of the socialist bloc of states in Europe and also the development of Soviet relations with the non-European states and colonial territories of the Western powers. The cohesion of the satellite states and the position of Germany were central to the first issue, and particularly so, given the determination of the West to incorporate a rearmed West Germany into the anti-Soviet alliance. In addition, the decisions of the Truman and Eisenhower administrations to embark on measures designed at least to undermine the Soviet position must have been another influence. The second issue was how the Soviets could win kudos in the less developed world by playing on their own anti-imperialism, or at least their opposition to Western colonialism, in this instance by developing a more active role in the Middle East.

The importance of these international considerations for the Kremlin and its Hungarian policy lies in the fact that on 31 October, as the Soviet forces were leaving Budapest, British bombers began attacking Egypt, a possible Soviet ally and recipient of Czech arms. Their express but secret purpose of bringing down the Nasser regime was being implemented in collusion with the French and the Israelis who, on 29 October, had launched an unprovoked attack on Sinai (see Chapter 8, C). Moreover, by the end of the first week of the revolt in Hungary, it was clear that the Americans were not going to use force to assist the rebels there. Soviet control was not, therefore, under threat from American military intervention. The first action taken by the Soviet military supplied convincing proof of US inaction, but on 31 October, Eisenhower announced that the US was pursuing a policy of non-intervention in the affairs of other countries. This statement was addressed as much to the British, and their French and Israeli allies, as to anyone else, but it provided some final reassurance for Moscow. Khrushchev had initially expressed concerns on 28 October about the need to avoid getting into the same company as the British, who he believed were stirring up trouble in Egypt. However, the Soviets had little confidence in Egyptian resistance and were expecting the attack on Suez to result in a significant loss of Soviet influence in the Middle East, which might be combined with a loss of Soviet influence in Eastern Europe.[8] It was exactly the same scenario as in 1945 (see Chapter 1, D) when the Soviets were faced with the possibility of losing out in Eastern Europe while the British gained in the Middle East. As Khrushchev noted, 'If we withdraw from Hungary, it will inspire the British, French, and American imperialists. They will regard it as our weakness and go on the offensive . . . Then we will add

Hungary to Egypt. We have no other choice.' Soviet global influence was deemed to be on the line. The Chinese had also become concerned by 30 October. After initially being in favour of more equal relations between East European states and Moscow, they then became worried about a 'capitalist restoration' in Hungary.[9]

The emphasis on Eastern Europe and the idea that Soviet concern was about Hungary's proposed withdrawal from the Warsaw Pact, precipitating a wholesale crisis in the Eastern European states, now seems less credible.[10] The announcement of the Hungarian withdrawal from the Pact was made on 1 November, when Soviet forces had redeployed around Budapest. The decisions on the use of force were taken after meetings with other European Communist Party leaders in the last days of October and, therefore, before the Hungarian announcement on the Warsaw Pact, although the troops did not immediately move into Budapest. It was only the visit to Belgrade to consult the Yugoslavs, with whom a post-Stalin reconciliation had been made, that took place after the announcement. The reasons given by Khrushchev for the invasion were very similar to those motivating the British Prime Minister Anthony Eden in the attack on Suez—fear of communist advances in Egypt combined with concern about Britain's position in the region. The consequences were far more serious in Hungary, where the Soviets were battling for global status and facing an ideological struggle for influence against the advances of capitalism. As the British Cabinet voted to go ahead with the airborne landings in Egypt on 4 November, Soviet troops were in Budapest, where 25,000 people were killed and 200,000 fled.[11] The rebels fought alongside some regular Hungarian troops, but their resistance was ended by the following week. The relaxation of controls in Poland was therefore followed by a clampdown in Hungary.

Khrushchev's speech rejecting Stalinism and allowing different forms of socialism was rendered meaningless by a crisis which threatened to highlight apparent Soviet weakness. It coincided with events in the Middle East which threatened to reinforce Western imperialism. The possibility of the Soviet Union relaxing controls and eschewing the use of force was rendered less likely by the international conditions prevailing at the time. The Kremlin again resorted to repression and coercion, with little or no consideration for the consequent large-scale loss of life. For the Americans, the events in Hungary proved that the liberation concept inherent in the attempts to subvert the Eastern bloc were not going to lead to anything other than the death of local insurgents, unless considerable military forces were deployed. The aversion to this in the thermonuclear age was part of the re-evaluation of the aggressive Cold War strategy pursued in Washington in the first half of the decade.

B. Western Europe

The Western bloc, which arguably came to be dominated, if not controlled, by the US, was first conceived during the war in Britain as an organization which would assist in dealing with a future German threat. It later came to be seen as a counter to the communist challenge mounted by Moscow (see Chapter 4, B). By 1952, a European Coal and Steel Community (ECSC) and a European Defence Community (EDC) had been agreed which provided for closer Western European ties, at least among six countries (see Chapter 4, C), but an important setback to European integration occurred in 1954 with the refusal of the French National Assembly to ratify the EDC treaty. The setback was overcome in 1955 (see Chapter 5, A), the year that further steps were taken towards European economic integration and which were soon to create the European Economic Community (EEC). The progress towards integration within Europe was closely watched by Washington because of a number of important factors influencing its support for the movement. As Europe recovered, the prospect of a powerful economic bloc appeared to present a possible threat to American interests and the Kennedy administration began to seek more effective ways of 'influencing' European economic developments. Although American influence was exerted very differently from Soviet control, in essence both powers were to some extent concerned with ensuring that the members of the respective blocs followed their wishes. In the East, there were a number of popular revolts against Soviet domination, while, in the West, disquiet about American domination took the form of intergovernmental tensions. These were largely confined to economic policy and nuclear weapons—two things the US was particularly concerned to influence—and led by the French President, Charles de Gaulle.

Western European Union

The collapse of the EDC was produced by a number of factors. Aside from popular fears in France of a rearmed Germany, the French were reluctant to give up national control of some of their army in order to absorb a German army into a federal European force. The French were also influenced by the British refusal to become part of, rather than merely associated with, the EDC. From the French point of view, nationalists feared both the equality a European army gave to the Germans and the prospect of that equality being replaced by German domination, especially if the British were refusing to act as a possible counterweight. A lot of effort had been expended in trying to ensure the EDC's ratification, but it seemed that much less thought had been given to its possible failure. The exception was in Britain, where doubts about its success and viability had always been strong. The Americans were particularly annoyed with the collapse of the EDC, because the idea of the Europeans contributing more conventional forces to the defence of the continent was an integral part of the New Look (see Chapter 5, C). It was the British Foreign Secretary, Anthony Eden, who embarked on a tour of European capitals in order to get the framework of an agreement for a Western European Union in place. It had to meet the requirements of a rearmed West Germany, integrated into the Western alliance, without presenting the same kind of threat to the French as a European army. The agreement involved all the key parties, the British, French, and Germans making some concessions at a conference in London for the sake of taking Western unity further. The Brussels Treaty Organization was expanded by adding West Germany and Italy and it became the Western European Union, while West Germany was also admitted as a full member of NATO into which a West German army would be incorporated. Giving a rearmed West Germany equality in NATO had been rejected by the French at the time of the Pleven Plan in 1950 (see Chapter 4, C). Now there was a much greater fear of French isolation and the prospect of facing a US reassessment of its commitment to Western Europe. The French acceptance was made easier by the West German agreement not to manufacture its own atomic armaments or any other weapons of mass destruction, chemical or bacteriological. It was also helped by the British acceptance of a commitment to provide and maintain four divisions in Europe, along with the 2nd Tactical Air Force or its equivalent. The French desire to involve the British in a continental commitment was designed to reduce the threat from a rearmed West Germany. The whole agreement was embodied in the Treaty of Paris. From the Western point of view, the incorporation of the Federal Republic into the Western bloc had survived another setback and the German danger was therefore reduced.

The Messina Conference and the Spaak Committee

The economic integration of the Western bloc took another step forward with a conference at Messina in 1955, to get agreement on the next stage of the process. A key decision had to be made over whether economic integration would proceed on a piecemeal basis, or whether there would be a more comprehensive approach through the creation of a customs union or 'common market'. The success of the Western European Union had inspired the proponents of integration. Yet the failure of the more federal EDC had strengthened the British view that Western Europe's future should be based on intergovernmental cooperation in which Britain, basking in the glory of Eden's diplomatic successes, would have a key role to play. At Messina, the ECSC ministers confronted a memorandum from the Dutch putting the case for a full-blown customs union and a committee was established in Brussels, under the chairmanship of Belgium's Paul-Henri Spaak, to assess the merits of the sector-by-sector approach to integration (already seen in the ECSC and associated with Jean Monnet), and the 'common market' idea of the Dutch foreign minister, Jan Beyen.

With the setting up of the Spaak Committee, Britain was again confronted with a choice about Europe that, as before, affected perceptions of its role as a world power as opposed to a European one. The Six countries at Messina (Italy, France, Belgium, Luxembourg, West Germany, and the Netherlands) invited Britain, as an associate member of the ECSC, to send a representative to the Spaak Committee and join in the work as a member. The Six asked for no commitment to the supranational principle in advance, unlike in 1950 before the negotiations for the ECSC. The British government instinctively wanted, as in the past, to be associated with the European move towards the extension of the supranational ideal and the new prime minister, Anthony Eden, was a supporter of the idea that Britain should encourage the movement towards greater European integration. By continuing to support and associate Britain with such developments, Eden believed Britain would remain in a position to serve as a link between Western Europe and the US, while remaining a world power with important links to the Empire/Commonwealth. Harold Macmillan, the foreign secretary in 1955, saw things rather differently, in that he regarded the strengthening of economic ties between the states of Western Europe *without* Britain's involvement as a dangerous development. Western Europe could emerge as a powerful economic force, which the US might eventually treat as more significant than Britain. In other words, Britain had to do more than be associated with the European integration movement.

Macmillan was not, however, in favour of Britain becoming involved in a supranational Europe where its independence would be restricted. It was also the case that most British trade lay outside Europe, much of it still directed at the Empire/Commonwealth. The general lack of enthusiasm for anything which would detract from Britain's perceived status as a world power different from its Western European allies was reflected in the fact that Britain sent a representative to the Spaak Committee in the form of a lowly Board of Trade official, called Russell Bretherton. He was sent 'without prior commitment' and with a wish that consideration be given to the significance of existing intergovernmental organizations for cooperation, such as the Organization for European Economic Co-operation (OEEC).[12] In that sense, the British were making a half-hearted attempt to steer the discussions along lines away from supranationalism, but without any coherent alternative. The vision that Macmillan had articulated several years earlier was that of a confederal Europe. Such ideas, like many of Macmillan's, remained grandiose but vague, and apart from being something akin to the Commonwealth, with a ministerial committee and a consultative assembly, the concept of a confederated Europe offered no real alternative to the stark choice between a supranational Europe or an intergovernmental Europe.

Bretherton was initially able to report that there was little emphasis in the Spaak Committee on supranational authority, but it eventually became clear that if Britain were to remain a member of the committee it would be drawn into unacceptable decisions.[13] Bretherton therefore asked Spaak to draw up the final report without reference to Britain's position. Britain had avoided any possibility of being committed to a supranational outcome of the committee's deliberations. However, there was a growing belief in the idea that the establishment of a common market might be damaging to Britain's interests and that, rather than simply encouraging the development of a supranational Western Europe Britain should provide an alternative—one which was not hampered by the vagueness of Macmillan's confederal proposals. The idea was to be based on a free trade area, controlled by member governments, rather than a customs union, with supranational institutions, but the extent of support for Britain's approach and the enthusiasm for a common market was badly misjudged by Whitehall.

In the first place, the failure of the EDC was given too much emphasis in Britain and led too easily to the mistaken conclusion that the Germans in particular were against the idea of a common market. The idea that such a union would not work was particularly misplaced, as it was generally accepted that if a common market were established the long-term economic outcome would be disadvantageous for Britain if it were excluded. Hence the importance of the belief that this next stage in European integration would not work. It was true that the German economics minister, Ludwig Erhard, would have preferred the looser arrangements involved in a free trade area but Adenauer came out in favour of a common market. Moreover, the Americans were very much in favour of continued European integration and were to work hard for such an outcome by covert and overt means. How determined the British were to sabotage the work of the Six is a matter of debate, but the announcement that Britain would not join with them certainly came before the publication of the Spaak Committee's report.

It was at Venice, in May 1956, that the Spaak Committee's report was finally considered and it was agreed to draw up two treaties to establish a European Atomic Energy Authority (Euratom)—in effect, integrating a new energy sector of the European economies—and a European Economic Community (EEC), based around a customs union. There were a number of difficulties to be overcome, including the reconciliation of high French tariff barriers with the German and Dutch preference for low ones, an idea also favoured by the British for a future free trade area. The differences were eased by the British failure to produce their proposals for a free trade area, Plan G, until July 1956, and by the British and French fall-out over the ending of the Anglo–French–Israeli invasion of Egypt (see Chapter 8, C). Plan G incorporated a free trade area to be run through the OEEC, all of whose members were to be eligible, with the six EEC countries joining as a single bloc. In other words, it was not an alternative to the EEC, which even the British accepted would now be created, and can therefore be interpreted less as an attempt to frustrate the kind of economic integration born from Messina than an attempt to forge closer ties with the Six as Britain had originally envisaged at the start of the decade.[14]

In a way, the situation embodied the reluctance of British elites to compromise their perception of themselves as a leading force in the world. There is a case for arguing that such perceptions of status mattered more than the economic-commercial issues. But there were economic and commercial, as well as the more emotive, reasons indicating that Britain could not afford to be included either. The Commonwealth still accounted for over 40 per cent of Britain's trade and, while the focus was shifting more towards Europe and North America, the Commonwealth still offered advantages in the way of cheap food imports. The dilemma over the advantages of being out or in was also reflected in the creation of a free trade area, which would enable Britain to benefit from important low-cost food imports while gaining access to the European industrial market, where cheap food would allow British industrialists to pay their workers less and benefit from comparative cost advantages. Britain wanted the best of both worlds.

Sixes and Sevens and the First British Application

It can hardly have been a surprise that the Six were both distrustful and unenthusiastic about the creation of a European Free Trade Area, especially once their own difficulties had been resolved with the signing of the Treaties of Rome, in March 1957. For a time, it seemed that the French insistence on special arrangements being made for the overseas territories of the French Union, and another French dispute over social policies, would produce failure. However, the treaties were implemented in January 1958, eighteen months before the creation of the European Free Trade Area (EFTA) comprising Britain, Austria, Denmark, Norway, Portugal, Sweden, and Switzerland. Before the creation of the EEC and EFTA, Britain had proposed a 'Grand Design', outlined by Selwyn Lloyd, foreign secretary in Macmillan's post-1957 government. It was a proposal for joining the various European institutions which had developed in the Western bloc during the Cold War—the Western European Union, NATO, the ECSC, the EEC, and the Council of Europe—through representation in a single assembly. It was, of course, another recipe for strengthening intergovernmental links at the expense of supranational ones, but Europe was prepared for a future without Britain if necessary and London seemed slow to realize that it was no longer powerful enough to act as a restraining influence. There was a further problem in that, following the Anglo-American divisions over Suez and the attack on Egypt, Macmillan was determined to rebuild relations with Washington. While Washington was in favour of European integration, it was worried by the problem of British exclusion and by the dangers of creating two, competing economic blocs (the Six and the Seven) within the Western alliance.

Macmillan was certainly conscious that influence in Washington would be harder to achieve in terms of Britain's special position as a link to Europe if there was no way of reconciling a free trade area with the EEC. Attempts were certainly made within an OEEC framework but, with de Gaulle's return to power in 1958, French interests were now asserted more powerfully and the new French leader had no desire to open up French markets to OEEC states. If anything, as Miriam Camps argued, the talks between the Six and the FTA countries forced the EEC countries to define their own policies and speeded up their integration.[15] The British favoured a low-tariff system, with loose ties and maximum access to world markets, while the French wanted a common market surrounded by high tariffs to protect French industry. More generally, the British were concerned that their exclusion from a politico-economic bloc would, especially in the long term, harm British economic interests and result in the EEC becoming the key American partner within the Western alliance. 'The French feared that the EEC, carefully constructed to protect French political and economic interests, and to limit German power would be dissolved within a wider FTA.'[16] With Adenauer again prepared to support the basic French position, there was to be no agreement on links between the EEC and a free trade area in 1958, which forced Britain to become one of the seven members outside the EEC.

The Americans had no love for EFTA, which they regarded as economically and politically divisive, and

US support and encouragement were to become an important factor in Britain's decision to apply for EEC membership in 1961. The American attitude highlighted the growing British fear of being overtaken by the EEC with regard to its importance as a major actor in international affairs. At the end of 1959, just after the first meeting between Eisenhower and Khrushchev took place and just before the last summit meeting in which the British and French were to participate collapsed in acrimony, the EEC foreign ministers agreed to hold quarterly meetings to discuss international affairs. It is easy to point to the imminent loss of the colonial Empire as a further international consideration requiring a reordering of Britain's international priorities and a move to Europe. However, there are alternative explanations based more firmly on Macmillan's own personal predilections and assessments of Britain's difficulties in redefining its world role. There were also domestic factors, which, as in many instances, impinged on international considerations and policies. In the spring of 1960, economic problems seemed to reinforce a feeling of national unease, and the economy appeared unable to match the growth rates in much of Western Europe. Some in Whitehall began to argue that EEC membership would stimulate growth, attract US investment, and make the British economy more competitive. Internationally, the Congo crisis began in June 1960 as Britain's policy of multiracialism was under severe challenges in Central Africa (see Chapter 8, B and D). It began to look as if the last days of Empire would be filled with difficulties, if not major loss of life. Nor did the Commonwealth appear to offer an attractive way forward. The 1958 Commonwealth Economic Conference appeared to confirm that any prospects of making the organization into an effective economic or trading bloc stood no chance of success. The Americans were likely to look more and more to Europe, and less and less to Britain, if the success of the EEC and the relative failures of EFTA and the Commonwealth continued.

There were thus a great variety of reasons for Britain to join Europe and be more positive about economic integration. Yet Macmillan was first and foremost an Empire / Commonwealth man with considerable governmental experience of several aspects of Empire life. It might therefore be possible to argue that Europe and the application to join the Common Market were supported for extra-European reasons. The Americans were very much in favour of British entry, because they believed the EEC was then more likely to develop along lines favoured by the US as a low-tariff, lightly regulated organization, with Britain supporting such goals inside the organization. And, if the EEC could revive the British economy, then Britain could strengthen its Commonwealth ties through aid and economic development programmes which, in the existing circumstances, it could ill afford. If so, a strengthened Commonwealth could continue to bolster Britain's position as a global power, carry weight in Washington, and lessen the apparent risk of becoming just another European state as long as the EEC provided the means to achieve economic success. The idea of an old imperialist like Macmillan becoming converted to the idea of Europe helping Britain reinvigorate the Commonwealth is certainly no more implausible than the idea that Britain made a strategic choice between a shrinking empire with its decreasing trade importance and an expanding Europe with its economic potential and political importance. If that was such a clear-cut case, the great debates within Britain at the turn of the decade over the relative importance of NATO or defence commitments 'out of' the European area would not have been so prolonged within the corridors of power. And Britain would have easily strengthened its European forces rather than argue for the need to keep an East of Suez presence during most of the 1960s.

Nuclear Cooperation and the Multilateral Force

Much of the development within the Western bloc focused on the nature and extent of its members' roles within Europe. However, the guiding hand of Washington was always there, even if only to offer support and encouragement in the economic sphere, and it was certainly ever present in the area of nuclear cooperation. In part, this indicated a more controlling hand or at least the attempt to try and exercise one. In economic terms, the fact that, for instance, the US exported such a small amount of its total steel production led it to believe that there was little inherent in the creation of a strong Western European economic unit that would pose a threat. The Eisenhower administration consistently supported integration from the sidelines, but was more interested in the nuclear aspect of cooperation, which began with the establishment of Euratom by the Treaties of Rome. Under Kennedy, nuclear issues continued to be important and potentially more divisive in alliance terms. Within the American administration there was more of a split between the 'Europeanists', who wholeheartedly supported integration, and the 'Atlanticists', who preferred to reduce the importance of integration and accept a much broader and less regulated framework which would be more acceptable to Britain.

Initially, Euratom seemed to many on both sides of the Atlantic a more manageable project than the creation of a common market. The idea was that there should be common European ownership of all raw materials used in the production of nuclear energy. By emphasizing the peaceful use of energy, the French were enabled to go ahead with their production of nuclear weapons. And the Americans could be satisfied that they were not assisting European powers with their own weapons programmes. On the other hand, the launch of Sputnik justified the Eisenhower administration's move some way towards this with the amendment of the McMahon Act. Under the terms of the Act, passed in 1946, supplying nuclear technology or information to foreign parties was outlawed, but in 1957, the year Britain exploded its first hydrogen bomb, Eisenhower directed that the 'exchange of information on the design and production of warheads and the transfer of fissionable materials' be permitted with those nations that had made 'substantial progress' in nuclear weapons development.[17]

In effect, this meant Britain, but while the Eisenhower administration was seeking to provide help and ensure greater cooperation, it was done in a way that could preserve American control over European, including Britain's nuclear weapons. While fears grew under Kennedy that the Germans might develop their own nuclear programme, and the French faced pressure to submit to US desires to prevent national weapons programmes, the British position remained ambivalent. To a large extent, American policy reflected the Europeanist versus Atlanticist divisions in Washington and the key issue came to be the creation of a Multilateral Nuclear Force (MLF). There were those 'Europeanists' eager to integrate nuclear weapons in Europe into a European force in NATO outside national control. This would include British and future French warheads. The British abandonment of their missile programme in 1960 coincided with the first MLF ideas. The term itself contained an in-built ambiguity over whether any European MLF would be based on a 'pool' of national contributions or require the creation of a mixed manned force.

Kennedy himself was unclear about this and about the precise importance of an MLF. He was, however, committed to the principle of a more united Europe, perhaps because he believed it would be the best way to secure American influence. On the other hand, he did look favourably on the British as in a different or special position to the states of mainland Europe, even if he was prepared to use them to serve American interests. The question of US hegemony again has to be considered in this Western European context. Was it the case that policy in Washington was driven by the idea of maintaining influence and continued hegemonic control as Western Europe became more powerful economically and a possible nuclear rival? Was it a non-hegemonic relationship based on partnership or, as Macmillan would have had it, 'interdependence'? The question has to be asked in terms of relations with Britain and with the Six EEC states to determine the extent of shared US interests and a special relationship with Britain. By that is meant a relationship based on a common culture and language, which was significantly different from that with other members of the Alliance and influenced the American approach to Europe.

One example of the alleged special British relationship has been the nuclear cooperation between London and Washington, which culminated at the Nassau conference of 1962. Here the Kennedy administration agreed to supply the British with Polaris missiles that gave the appearance of preserving Britain's 'independent' nuclear deterrent. This was the end of a long-running saga involving a commitment, never formalized by Eisenhower, to supply an air-launched missile, Skybolt, to the British. With the Americans developing a sea-launched missile, Polaris, Macmillan tried and failed to establish Anglo-American cooperation and 'interdependence' in nuclear submarines and sea-launched missiles by trading the granting of base rights to the Americans at Holy Loch, Scotland for such 'interdependence'. The Americans regarded Holy Loch as the quid pro quo for Skybolt, but when the Skybolt programme was abandoned the British were left with nothing,[18] hence Macmillan's determination to remain a nuclear power by obtaining Polaris from the Americans, while blurring the nature of the commitment of a British Polaris force to an MLF. Polaris would have been made available to the French too, but de Gaulle was determined on an independent French deterrent and the French leader chafed at the prospect of US domination of Europe with exclusive control of nuclear weapons.

This is precisely how the aims of Kennedy's policy can be defined in relation to his Grand Design, which embodied the American president's ideas for the future of US–Western European relations. Britain would gain entry into the EEC, which was applied for in 1961, Europe would bear more of the defence burden, its nuclear aspirations would be channelled into the MLF, and US exports would be enhanced by the reduction of transatlantic tariff barriers. It was all designed to bolster the US position, which was becoming relatively weaker in economic terms with a growing US trade deficit—hence the idea of creating a willing but largely subservient partner. In specific terms, Adenauer was told that good relations with Washington depended on Britain in the EEC and the creation of the MLF, rather than on Franco-German nuclear cooperation. It has all been termed a quest for greater US influence in Western Europe and NATO with Britain, as one official put it, acting as America's lieutenant, but it was marketed under the auspices of a more equal Atlantic community.[19]

Fear of Britain as an American lieutenant was precisely what de Gaulle wanted to avoid as France began its own quest to shape Western Europe to its own advantage. Once de Gaulle realized that neither Britain nor America were keen to follow his idea of a tripartite global directorate for the Western alliance, he looked more to Western Europe and Germany to realize his plans of regaining France's position of leadership in the world, which he believed had not been attained since Waterloo. The first attempt, through the Fouchet Plan, involved the creation of a political community of the Six EEC nations forming an intergovernmental organization to coordinate foreign and defence policy. The Dutch, in particular, were opposed to a political union of such a type without Britain, whereas for de Gaulle, who vetoed Britain's entry into the EEC in 1963, the exclusion of the British and their American backers was vital to ensure French leadership in Europe.[20]

The Fouchet Plan had failed by 1962, but de Gaulle was later to pursue other means to challenge US leadership (see introduction to Part III) and permit France a more prominent European role. The unrealized aim was a change in the nature of inter-bloc relations as well as intra-Western European links. Kennedy's Grand Design was no more successful, and the MLF never got off the ground, so preserving the British illusion of an independent nuclear deterrent, even though the warheads and delivery systems were dependent on American know-how and equipment. Although the EEC did in fact develop broadly along the lines desired by the Americans, the degree of US influence remained less than many would have liked. The integrationists among the Kennedy 'Europeanists' were somewhat disappointed by the failure of Britain to join the EEC, which was to remain both a challenge and an opportunity to Washington, while for Europeans, not just de Gaulle, the US remained an essential support for the Continent but had to be prevented from becoming a determinant of the kind of Europe it would have to back. It is difficult to claim that the Americans 'controlled' Western Europe, but equally difficult to avoid the impression of them trying, albeit in rather uncoordinated ways, to do so without appearing to be engaged in such a quest.

C. Latin America

US relations with Latin America had long been characterized by intervention and a determination, evidenced as soon as the 1890s, to exclude other powers from the region. US marines in the years before and after the First World War were constantly landing in South and Central America to protect US economic interests and to attempt to produce stable regimes. When Roosevelt became president, he aimed to replace the use of military force with a 'Good Neighbour' policy, but the problems remained and US intervention was not entirely ruled out. Dictators like the Somozas in Nicaragua tended to wield force in a brutal manner and without any hint of democracy, yet still win support from Washington. In 1944, dictators were ousted in Guatemala and El Salvador, but the war for democracy did not bring elected governments to much of Latin America. Indeed, in 1949, when Uruguay proposed that the Organization of American States (OAS) consider action against those regimes who violated human rights, the idea was rejected by the US.[21] In terms of political freedoms, Latin America was more akin to Eastern Europe than the US sphere in the Western half of the Continent. The problem for many in Latin America lay in the lack of economic development in the region, which some thought had to be overcome if democracy were to take root, while others believed that democracy could provide the means to encourage economic development.

There were significant differences between countries such as Argentina and Uruguay, who produced primarily temperate-zone produce, and those, especially in Central America, who were reliant on tropical produce. Prices for the latter were far more volatile and the chances of agricultural improvements providing surpluses for investment in other economic activities, as in Europe, were much fewer. In Argentina, the standard of living of the lowest 20 per cent of the population was three times higher than in Brazil in the 1960s, where particular attention was given to externally promoted development, and foreign investment capital was encouraged with incentives and by wages being kept low.[22] Another handicap was faced by countries with high population densities, such as Guatemala, as compared to those like Nicaragua, where, on paper, fewer people should have led to easier access to land. In the event, this proved to be less important than the social relations which determined the use of, and access to, that land. Finally, in trade terms, dependency for some countries was reflected in trade with the US, which took up to 80 or 90 per cent of crops such as coffee produced in countries like Nicaragua. The producer country was inescapably dependent on the US for earnings from its exports, which formed a small fraction of US imports and which could be easily obtained elsewhere. An alternative to the large US market was not readily available for most Latin American producers.

Economic Development, US Policy, and the Early Cold War

At the heart of the debate about US policy lies the issue of development and the US role in hindering or supporting the diversification of many Latin American economies. Were the activities of US companies promoting wealth creation to benefit the local population, or extracting resources for the benefit of their shareholders and/or US consumers? What form of dependency dominated the economic relationship between the two parts of the western hemisphere, and how was this affected by the actions of the US government? In terms of the Cold War, the important question is whether policy in Washington was dictated primarily by the need to protect economic interests, or by the need to defeat communism. It is easy to link the two together, in the sense that free trade and respect for private property were associated with the development of free societies. Yet in Latin America, for much of the time, this did not involve the exercise of political freedom but the maximization of the opportunities for the wealthy and powerful to operate freely in economic terms.

At the end of the Second World War, all Latin American countries, apart from Mexico, still had in place colonial agrarian structures where the ownership of land, with the exception of Chile, dictated the basic institutions of social organization. As one State Department analysis had noted at the end of the 1940s: 'The economic development of these countries, adapted to the shifting market of the industrial countries of the Northern hemisphere and handicapped by a system of large landed estates, was so unbalanced as to prevent the emergence of an economically strong and politically conscious middle class.' During the Eisenhower and Kennedy administrations, it was certainly the case that the US would have been delighted to welcome a strong middle class on which to build a democratic capitalist society, and it tried various ways to encourage the economic development to achieve this. Unfortunately, these efforts proved a failure because the existing social structures were never tackled and the distribution of the economic surplus they produced was never altered. Change would not have accorded with the political and economic principles, which were based on very different economic conditions in North America and which the US government was fighting a Cold War to preserve.

In terms of the power-political relations between the US and its southern neighbours, the State Department, like the British with regard to the Middle East at the end of the war, wanted the UN kept out of the region, which they regarded as an exclusive US zone, or sphere of influence. The difference between Latin America and Eastern Europe was described thus: 'While we do claim the right to have a guiding voice in a certain limited sphere of the foreign relations of Latin America we do not attempt to dictate the internal national life or to restrict their intercourse with foreign nations except in that limited sphere.'[23] The importance of the region increased with the Korean War and the need for raw materials. George Kennan believed that US policy must be directed to their protection, to preventing the enemy gaining any military benefits from the region, and to preventing any mobilization of the region under a banner of anti-Americanism directed at the US.[24]

Dulles shared the concern about the loss of raw materials if revolutionary movements seized power, and Eisenhower saw dangers of changes in the region being exploited by communists. The first National

Security Council paper on inter-American affairs analysed everything in terms of the global struggle against communism, emphasizing US concern about respecting property rights and guaranteeing security, which would require consideration of unilateral intervention.[25] The development of the New Look formalized Eisenhower's preference for intervention in the form of covert operations, which could be developed from the activities being considered in Eastern Europe. What concerned the US in this area of large economic interests and important foreign policy requirements were often explained by policy-makers within a Cold War framework and associated with security. Yet, there was no real military threat and with regard to the distinction between the ideology of communism and Soviet power-political goals, there were only three countries in the whole of the region with which Moscow had diplomatic relations in 1952.[26] In addition, the post-war concerns in America about the possibility of European economic weakness or collapse did not apply in Latin America under Truman. Despite its problems, Truman did not provide government aid in the form of a Marshall Plan and, during Eisenhower's first term, the new president continued the policy of relying on private capital to serve the region's financial needs. If communism appeared, it could be dealt with by cheap, covert means.

The 1954 Coup in Guatemala

In 1944, the rich landowners, constituting around 2 per cent of the population, owned nearly three-quarters of the cultivatable land in Guatemala, most of which was left fallow, because it was more profitable for large landowners to limit production and maintain higher price levels. The election of President Arevalo began to change this and other iniquities in Guatemala. The franchise was extended and forced labour ended. In March 1951, a more radical impetus was given to the reform programme by Jacobo Arbenz, who was elected president in 1950 with 60 per cent of the vote. Arbenz introduced income tax, poured money into building ports and roads and, worryingly for American companies such as United Fruit, in 1952 he expropriated uncultivated tracts of land that were larger than 670 acres. Eighty-five per cent of the United Fruit Company's land was uncultivated and the compensation payment in the form of government bonds was disputed by them, as the figure decided on by the government was based on the company's tax valuation, which turned out to be considerably lower than the company's market valuation.

United Fruit looked to the American government for help as it had influential contacts in the Eisenhower administration. Both the Dulles brothers had represented the company (Allen Dulles was now Deputy Director of the Central Intelligence Agency until February 1953, when he became the head of the CIA and John Foster Dulles was Secretary of State). The alarm cry of communism in Guatemala was soon heard and encouraged by US officials in the region. Yet, while communists figured in the parliamentary coalition under Arbenz, they numbered only four out of fifty-one and none of them was in the Cabinet. According to US intelligence, there were only 500 Communist Party members in Guatemala in 1952, who had become 1,000 by 1953 when the new administration took office. The US commitment to covert operations could now be tested in terms of removing undesirable governments that were tainted with the communist brush. It would clearly be inaccurate to portray the Arbenz government as communist, rather than left-wing or reformist, but in this context, it was not that such governments were communist that was crucial for Dulles. The Secretary of State abhorred the Arbenz government, not because it was a communist regime controlled or largely influenced by Moscow, which it clearly was not, but because it could easily become so. Dulles believed that all left-wing Popular Front governments, as in Eastern Europe or in the pre-Second World War years in the West, faced an uphill struggle to avoid being taken over by the more ruthless communist parties. The government had thus already defined Latin American problems in global, not regional or country-specific terms. And those at the highest level did not fail to understand what constituted a communist government but were opposed to any left-wing regimes of a radical nature, because they might open the door to communism. How much this was influenced by the need to protect US economic interests remains an unresolved question.

By his own admission, Dulles had no evidence of Arbenz's links to Moscow but it was decided that action should be taken against his regime. The catalyst was provided by a shipment of Czech arms, in May 1954, and a small force, numbering no more than those in the Communist Party, was assembled by Colonel Castillo Armas. The following month, the CIA flew planes over the capital with leaflets, bombed shipping, and dropped explosive devices in the form of dynamite. As Armas marched towards the capital, the CIA's aim was to create the impression of a large force of rebels preparing to overthrow the government. Arbenz then made a fatal mistake, by distributing arms and trying to create a peasant militia, only to alienate the army. It was this which resulted in Arbenz's demise and Guatemala abandoned efforts at reform to face a period when the economy was dominated by foreign enterprises, operating without labour legislation. Death squads appeared and the United Fruit Company was able to acquire more land. It was brought about, according to Dulles, by the action taken against the evil designs of the Kremlin and their manipulation of Arbenz.[27] And the success of the attempts to overthrow Arbenz, along with the overthrow of Mossadeq in Iran, were to reinforce the American commitment to covert operations.

The Change of Policy under Eisenhower and the Initial Response to the Cuban Revolution

The end of democracy and reform in Guatemala did not mean that the Eisenhower administration became convinced that a successful Latin American policy had to be based on dictators rather than democrats, nor that the status quo had to be preserved at all costs. Eisenhower himself preferred democracy of a non-left-wing kind and he became more committed to its promotion in the second half of the decade, as dictators failed to provide stability and were more frequently opposed or overthrown by popular movements. In 1954, thirteen out of twenty Latin American countries were under the thumb of dictators, but as economic conditions deteriorated, with the terms of trade moving against Latin American countries and producers of primary produce and raw materials generally, things began to change. Ironically, the USSR under Khrushchev became more interested in the less developed world and in building aid and trade links with it, but Latin American consumers found Soviet goods singularly unattractive. The Soviet diplomatic presence in the region remained low key and, at the end of the 1950s, there were still representatives only in Argentina, Mexico, and Uruguay. There were contacts made between Latin America and Soviet satellites such as Bulgaria, but in general there was little 1950s interference in what the Soviets may have regarded as an American sphere of influence.

It was certainly more likely that problems which appeared had nothing to do with Soviet influence and everything to do with the economic conditions in the region. At all events, the situation led to a change in Eisenhower's thinking as dictators were overthrown and the Vice-President, Richard Nixon, narrowly escaped serious injury or worse, when he was mobbed on a 1958 visit to Venezuela. Between 1956 and 1960 ten dictators fell from power and, as early as 1957 Eisenhower, for the first time, asked Congress for more economic than military aid. Dictators apparently had not provided the hoped-for political and economic stability. Nor had the private sector, on which Eisenhower had earlier placed so much reliance, produced successful, self-sustaining development. In 1958, the US supported the establishment of a regional development bank as the economic turmoil produced the overthrow of one of America's leading, dictatorial friends, President Jimenez of Venezuela. Nixon attributed the stone-throwing demonstrators in Caracas to communist infiltration into the region, but his reaction to the experience was part of a US shift to a more state interventionist economic policy that culminated with John F. Kennedy's Alliance for Progress.

Significant elements of this were in place by 1960 and partly connected to the progress of the Cuban Revolution, which brought Fidel Castro to power in 1959 (see next section, 'The Bay of Pigs and the Alliance for Progress'). The economic problems were now reflected by the fact that, in 1960, Latin American interest payments were almost equal to the foreign loans and investments provided. Brazil made a trade-and-aid agreement with the Soviet Union the same year, so there was the danger that capitalism's increasing failure in the Latin American context could lead to the adoption of more radical solutions and closer links to Moscow. In order to pre-empt this, Eisenhower established a Social Progress Fund, while the Inter-American Development Bank was now to focus on loans to those who imposed progressive income taxes. The US even supported the more progressive regimes, like those of Frondizi in Argentina and Betancourt in Venezuela, who had earlier been frowned upon while dictators like Jimenez were seen as preferable. They were regimes which, in the words of the National Security Council (NSC), favoured 'rising living standards and a more equitable distribution of national income within the general framework of a free enterprise system'.[28]

Part of this concern came from what later drove John F. Kennedy in his obsessive campaign against

Fidel Castro. In essence, it was a fear that the Cuban Revolution might provide an example of alternative ways to develop under a different social and economic system. Castro came to power on the sugar-growing island of Cuba, where US investors controlled 40 per cent of the sugar production, by leading a popular uprising against the former US-backed dictator, Fulgencio Batista. The rebellion was initially supported by a broad-based coalition of reformers from the middle classes, as well as by peasants and workers. But Castro, and particularly his brother Raoul, had close links with Moscow and, in 1959, he legalized the Communist Party and began to move towards the establishment of a left-wing dictatorship. Farmland over 1,000 acres was expropriated in 1960 and he became more determined to abandon the US connection. But, as early as January of that year, Allen Dulles was calling for Castro's overthrow and, in March 1960, Eisenhower approved a covert operation to achieve this. Castro proceeded with his radical reform programme which, as he embraced nationalization, produced debates as to whether anti-Castro US actions actually encouraged this radicalization and ultimate ties with the Soviet Union. Only in December 1961 did Castro publicly announce his conversion to Marxism-Leninism, but his sympathies lay in that direction long before 1961 and, even if the Americans had not been so obsessed with the global communist challenge, the outcome in Cuba was likely to have been the same.

The Cuban Revolution produced someone who could be painted as a dictator of the wrong political kind, that is, left-wing. It reinforced Eisenhower's belief that communism had to be stopped; dictators like Batista were probably not the kind of leader to do it but the kind who produced revolutionaries like Castro. Eisenhower's policies provided the initial impetus for those with which the Kennedy administration became identified. These reflected an intense dislike of Castro and his ideas and a belief in a more interventionist approach, to produce the kind of political and economic conditions that would suit both US ideals and interests. Such policies laid out the contradictions between attempts to prevent another Castro and protect American interests, and attempts to bring about economic and political change. The latter might claim to be in tune with US ideals, but they threatened to damage American economic interests. Put another way, changes were needed in Latin America to ensure the kind of stability that did not depend on brutal dictators but, without brutal dictators, Castro's influence could spread along with Marxism-Leninism.

The Bay of Pigs and the Alliance for Progress

When John F. Kennedy became president, there was a belief in America and in his administration that all problems could be tackled by applying fresh new ideas and moving away from what seemed to be those of the old, outmoded Republican administration. In Latin America, Kennedy saw the problems of poverty and instability that had not been solved by Eisenhower. His belief that US government money could make a difference to the plight of the Latin American poor, producing development and stability, was enhanced by the growing difficulties he faced over Cuba.

Kennedy inherited a covert operational plan from the Eisenhower administration, which resembled the overthrow of Arbenz in Guatemala. A small force of exiles would land in Cuba in April 1961, gain support from the populace, and overthrow the regime. The President failed to realize the flaws in the operation, which were not pointed out to him by the military or the CIA. The chosen landing place was completely unsuitable and led into swamps, which were not easy for any invading force to escape through if under air attack. Intelligence was poor and secrecy not well kept, with the result that the belief that Castro's forces would take two days to respond proved wrong. To make matters worse, considerable numbers were lost in the initial invasion as some landing craft were sunk on reefs in the bay, while the Cuban air force sank two ships. The remaining force soon faced surrender if overt US intervention with increased air support was not forthcoming. Kennedy refused to deploy regular US air crews, to add to the small number of CIA pilots flying unmarked planes, and the debacle therefore ran its course. There was little support from the general population anyway and the idea that the people would defect to the US once an invasion had established itself was exposed as wishful thinking.[29] Both the miscalculations and Kennedy's refusal to authorize what would have amounted to a full-scale invasion of Cuba had lasting effects. The President became reluctant to accept advice from those he did not trust and grew more concerned about any appearance of weakness. Castro became, for Kennedy, a figure associated with his failure and therefore an enemy of supreme importance.

The response to the Bay of Pigs failure came in the form of a series of covert operations designed to help Cubans overthrow the Castro regime by using psychological warfare, sabotage, diplomacy, economic, and, if necessary, military action. The type of activities considered, under what became known as Operation Mongoose, were often extremely bizarre. The Pentagon suggested dropping one-way air tickets onto Cuba, using high-powered transmitters in Florida to override Cuban TV, putting chemical agents into fuel storage tanks, introducing corrosive materials to cause aircraft, boat, or vehicle accidents, and issuing fake photos of an obese Castro surrounded by food and beautiful women, with a caption referring to his different rations.[30]

The need to destroy Castro was accompanied by a need to ensure that there was some alternative attraction to the promises of Marxism-Leninism. In keeping with the general desire to demonstrate the benefits of capitalism and prove its superiority over communism, Kennedy sought to promote the development of Latin America through an ambitious programme of government aid. The Alliance for Progress, announced in March 1961, was what resulted. The hope was that dollars and freedom would prove more attractive than communism and Castro, who would be unable to provide what the US could offer. The new administration would bring to bear American drive and money, and produce their own form of revolution in Latin America. Unfortunately, in the long run, Kennedy did more than Castro to provide the kind of revolution he feared and Castro would have wanted.

One explanation for the failure of the Alliance for Progress was that Kennedy concentrated too much effort on the Castro side of the equation. Stopping Castro began to loom too large in his thinking. Thus, the aid and development programme became subordinated to the efforts to remove Castro and to the need to encourage measures that would quell any unrest which was deemed to be exploitable by Cuba. The result was expenditure on internal security and counter-insurgency measures in Latin America, which encouraged the military to promote repression rather than freedom and democracy. And there was more expenditure on security measures than on health and sanitation programmes. By October 1963, Kennedy's Assistant Secretary of State for Latin American affairs was admitting that the goals of development and democracy could not be attained in every country in the near future. The US had promised change through another democratic revolution while training the armies to prevent it.[31] And even that was to some extent a failure as in the wake of the Alliance for Progress there were seventeen coups in a nine-year period.

Another reason for the failure of the Alliance can be illustrated by Nicaragua, which in the 1980s was to produce exactly the kind of mass-based left-wing government Kennedy was keen to prevent. In many ways, Nicaragua can be seen as a good prospect for development as it had a low population density. Therefore, in theory, land should have been more readily available than in countries such as Guatemala, where the population density was much higher. The ownership of land was, of course, crucial and the fact was that most of the population lived on less than 5 per cent of the land. In 1962, when the Sandinistas—the National Sandinista Liberation Front (FLSN)—were founded in opposition to the American-backed General Anastasio Somoza, the US took 40 per cent of Nicaraguan exports and supplied 50 per cent of its imports.

What the Alliance for Progress did do was to achieve economic growth in this situation of dependency but, put starkly, it was growth without development. In the Nicaraguan case, the country used the injection of resources to export more cotton and more coffee as more land was brought into production and the country's GNP grew. In fact, exports rose by 20 per cent in the first half of the 1960s but, in order to achieve this, more peasants were thrown off their land and more recruits from a growing class of landless labourers joined the Sandinistas over the next 15 years. The Alliance for Progress failed to instigate land reform, and therefore simply made the old system and its enormous inequalities more effective. It was an alliance with the old land-holding elite, who received US money to increase production and maintain the existing social system without progress. The efforts to bring stability on occasions proved counter-productive and created more developmental problems than they solved. With coups again taking place on a regular basis and unrest increasing, this time the cure would be what was once seen as the problem—military dictators. The circle of unrest and brutal repression would begin again even if Americans were to become increasingly indifferent to it.

Visit the online resources that accompany this book to test your understanding and take your learning further: www.oup.com/he/young-kent3e

NOTES

1. Vladislav M. Zubok, CWIHP Working Paper 4, 'Soviet Intelligence and the Cold War: The "Small" Committee on Information, 1952–53' (1992), 11.
2. Wilfred Loth, *Overcoming the Cold War: A History of Détente* (Palgrave Macmillan, Basingstoke, 2002), 20. Citing Lev Besymenski, '1953—Beria will die DDR beseitigen', in *Die Zeit*, 15 October 1993.
3. John Lewis Gaddis, *We Now Know. Rethinking Cold War History* (Clarendon Press, Oxford, 1997), 130.
4. Vladislav Zubok and Constantine Pleshakov, *Inside the Kremlin's Cold War from Stalin to Khrushchev* (Harvard University Press, Cambridge, 1996), 160–1.
5. Wilfred Loth, *Overcoming the Cold War: A History of Détente* (Palgrave Macmillan, Basingstoke, 2002), 22–3.
6. Alexsandr Stykalin, 'The Hungarian Crisis of 1956: The Soviet Role in the Light of New Archival Documents', *Cold War History*, 1 (2001), 114, 118–20.
7. The above paragraphs are based on ibid., 121–34.
8. Ibid., 136.
9. Ibid., 137.
10. Caroline Kennedy-Pipe, *Russia and the World 1917–1991* (Arnold, London, 1998).
11. Raymond Pearson, *The Rise and Fall of the Soviet Empire* (Macmillan, Basingstoke, 1998).
12. John W. Young, *Britain and European Unity 1945–1999* (2nd edn, Macmillan, Basingstoke, 2000), 41.
13. Sean Greenwood, *Britain and European Co-operation since 1945* (Blackwell, Oxford, 1992), 65.
14. John W. Young, *Britain and European Unity 1945–1999* (2nd edn, Macmillan, Basingstoke, 2000), 46–8.
15. M. Camps, *Britain and the European Community, 1955–63* (Princeton University Press, Princeton, 1964), 508–9.
16. John W. Young, *Britain and European Unity 1945–1999* (2nd edn, Macmillan, Basingstoke, 2000), 53–60.
17. Pascaline Winand, *Eisenhower, Kennedy and the United States of Europe* (Macmillan, Basingstoke, 1993) 83–8, 211.
18. See Michael Middeke, 'Britain's Interdependence Policy and Anglo-American Co-operation on Nuclear and Conventional Force Provision, 1957–1964', Unpublished Ph.D. thesis, LSE, 1999, from where this argument is taken.
19. F. Costigliola, 'The Pursuit of Atlantic Community: Nuclear Arms, Dollars and Berlin', in T. G. Paterson (ed.), *Kennedy's Quest for Victory: American Foreign Policy, 1961–63* (Oxford University Press, New York, 1989), 24–56.
20. Jeffrey W. Vanke, 'An Impossible Union: Dutch Objections to the Fouchet Plan 1959–1962', *Cold War History*, 1 (2001).
21. Stephen G. Rabe, *Eisenhower and Latin America: The Foreign Policy of Anti-Communism* (Chapel Hill, London, 1988), 14.
22. C. Furtado, *The Economic Development of Latin America* (Cambridge University Press, Cambridge, 1976).
23. Walter LaFeber, *Inevitable Revolutions* (2nd edn, W.W. Norton, New York, 1993), 89.
24. Ibid., 107.
25. Foreign Relations of the US (FRUS), 1952–4 (Dept of State, Washington, DC, 1979), NSC 144/1, 18 March 1953.
26. Stephen G. Rabe, *Eisenhower and Latin America: The Foreign Policy of Anti-Communism* (Chapel Hill, London, 1988), 21.
27. Walter LaFeber, *Inevitable Revolutions* (2nd edn, W.W. Norton, New York, 1993).

28. Stephen G. Rabe, *The Most Dangerous Area in the World: John F. Kennedy Confronts Communist Revolution in Latin America* (Chapel Hill, London, 1999), 11.

29. Peter Wyden, *Bay of Pigs the Untold Story* (Cape, London, 1979), 327.

30. Mark J. White (ed.), *The Kennedys and Cuba: The Declassified Documentary History* (1999), 88–95, 100–5.

31. Stephen G. Rabe, 'Controlling Revolutions: Latin America, the Alliance for Progress and Cold War Anti-Communism', in T. J. Paterson (ed.), *Kennedy's Quest for Victory* (Oxford University Press, New York, 1983), 115.

7

Fighting the Cold War: The Offensive Strategies

Chapter contents

A. US Covert Operations and the Revised National Security Strategy

When the Eisenhower administration took office, it confronted the need to examine the effectiveness of the offensive Cold War strategy developed by the Truman administration and the machinery put in place to implement it, most notably the Psychological Strategy Board. However, there was also the questioning of NSC 68 and some of its assumptions, which had been begun by the State Department and Charles Bohlen in particular (see Chapter 4, D). NSC 68 and its proposals might no longer be accepted as effectively contributing to national security. Given also the President's concern over economic policy and the need to control defence expenditure to maintain the kind of low-tax, sound economy deemed to be essential to the American way of life, NSC 68 might require considerable revision. The other obvious concern was the danger of hot war, which increased the importance of a Cold War successfully destroying or weakening the Soviet Union, while simultaneously increasing the risks inherent in attempting to do so.

Operation Solarium and the Basis of a New Strategy

Stalin's death further encouraged the reassessment of Truman's Cold War/national security policy, with Nitze posing the question as to whether the US would find itself committed to the overthrow of the regime in the Kremlin, or else be willing to reach a diplomatic modus vivendi with it, which might be better than the present tensions and uncertainty. The first formal reassessment came with Robert Cutler's critical examination of Truman's aims, which was produced in mid-March. Its criticism was in many ways based on an unrepresentative account of Truman's policy, but it belittled its effectiveness and was contemptuous of its limited and defensive objectives. NSC 20/4 and NSC 68 were described as merely policies of coexistence, with the objective of a military build-up being only to deter the Soviets from hot war and live with them until they changed their ways.[1] This criticism was very much in accordance with the initial thinking of Eisenhower and Dulles who, after Stalin's death, saw inducing the disintegration of Soviet power as a means of ending the danger presented by Moscow. If psychological and other pressure were maintained, the Soviet Union would either collapse or be transformed into a harmless state.[2] The issue was clearly whether NSC 68 was good enough to deter the Soviets from hot war *and* to enable psychological pressure to wear down and eventually bring about the collapse, or transformation, of the communist regime—roll-back over the long term, in effect.

Those who believed in the value of making a determined effort to overthrow the Soviet regime because of the opportunity presented by Stalin's death, such as C. D. Jackson,[3] favoured a policy of 'rolling back' Soviet power, with much greater determination than under Truman. Jackson produced a psychological war plan, PSB D-43, whose objectives were 'to induce the Soviet armed forces to overthrow the Soviet regime at a propitious future time ... and to weaken Soviet power by psychological exploitation of the vulnerabilities of the Soviet armed forces'. The push for success in destroying the Soviet regime was encouraged by the East German revolt (see Chapter 6, A). Jackson produced another paper on the exploitation of satellite unrest in Eastern Europe which was approved as NSC 158 in June 1953. Its first objective was to 'nourish resistance to communist oppression throughout satellite Europe, short of mass rebellion in areas under Soviet military control, and without compromising its spontaneous nature'.[4]

The rapidity of the East German uprising and its end indicated one of the problems the Americans faced with such policies, but the issue of how to proceed further with undermining the Soviet Union or its satellites, while avoiding hot war, remained. Operation Solarium was in essence directed at this question, as part of a review of national security policy which would examine the key assumption of NSC 68—the need for rearmament to deter hot war, while the Cold War was fought in ways which would bring about the collapse or transformation of the Soviet satellites, or of the Soviet regime itself. As has been seen, Eisenhower had concerns about the H-bomb and about the cost of the rearmament programme, which was accompanied by an interest in covert operations (see Chapter 5, B and C). He was also ready to relax controls on trade with the Eastern bloc, which had been introduced since 1947 and which, since January 1950, were set by a secretive Western organization known as the Co-ordinating Committee (COCOM). Through a policy of 'economic warfare', the Truman administration hoped to prevent Soviet access to military materials and industrial equipment that could help manufacture weapons. After 1949, limits were placed on trade with China too, and in 1951 Truman approved the Battle Act, which allowed the US to cut financial aid to European countries that refused to conform with US-defined embargo items. Although this was never put into effect, European governments were increasingly critical of trade controls, because these made it difficult to expand trade with the Eastern bloc. Churchill also saw trade as a way to create division in the Eastern bloc and demonstrate the superiority of Western products, an argument that appealed to Eisenhower. In late 1953, Washington agreed to relax trade controls against the Soviet bloc somewhat, while maintaining them against China. There was a further relaxation in August 1954.

Operation Solarium consisted of three teams or task forces examining a set of assumptions pertaining to the mix of pursuing Cold War and avoiding hot war. Teams A and C considered alternatives for policy towards the Soviet Union as a whole in this context, while Team B looked at the relationship of US nuclear weapons to deterring Soviet aggression. Team A, as has been pointed out by Gregory Mitrovich, has commonly been considered as the 'containment' option, but was really aimed at the liberation of the satellites and changing Soviet behaviour. Along with Team C it reflected the divisions in the State Department about just how far to pursue an aggressive policy in order 'to induce the disintegration of Soviet power', as Dulles put it. The report of Task Force A thus proposed a dual strategy of 'roll-back' in Eastern Europe and some element, at least in the short term, of peaceful coexistence with a changed Soviet Union. Greater emphasis on the latter would be somewhat contradicted by the US taking the strategic offensive in the ideological Cold War conflict. Containment, unlike covert operations, was not in the picture, whereas concern to prevent a hot war definitely was.[5]

The fundamental difference between Task Force A and Task Force C was that, while A advocated roll-back of the Soviet satellite empire in Eastern Europe, but was prepared for possible coexistence with the Soviets, Task Force C aimed at the destruction of the Soviet Union itself and peaceful coexistence was rejected in the medium term.[6] It made clear that the US must face up to 'the lack of a national strategy to end the Cold War by winning it'. The general goals were the removal of the Iron Curtain, reducing the strength of any communist elements left in the USSR, and the overthrow of the Soviet leadership. More specifically, Task Force C proposed that the US should ensure that in five years the unification of Germany and Korea and a nationalist stronghold in mainland China were achieved. In the next phase, up to 1965, the satellite governments would be overthrown by an all-out political offensive. How all this could have been done without a major war remains unclear.[7]

The Cold War strategy defined by Task Force A was one that envisaged the possibility of coexistence if, or when, roll-back proved undesirable because of the difficulty of achieving it without resorting to hot war. The problem, which Eisenhower never fully came to terms with, was that aggressively fighting the Cold War risked disaster through hot war, yet accepting the continued existence of the Soviet Union could require such strong military forces over a long period, and such large defence expenditures, as to threaten the American way of life and ultimately lead to Cold War defeat. Aggressive moves against the communists were not therefore abandoned, but merely reduced in importance. And the choice between doing whatever it took to win the Cold War or accepting peaceful coexistence because the Cold War could not be won was consequently fudged.

The Search for a Post-Solarium National Security Policy

The fact that the emerging policy after Solarium came to contain more of Task Force A than C was an indication that acceptance of peaceful coexistence was coming closer. For one thing, the aim of destroying the Soviet Union was no longer to be the aim of US covert activities. The subsidiary goal of undermining the Soviet bloc seemed less dangerous, but not necessarily any more realistic, unless it provided for direct involvement by the US. As NSC 162/2 pointed out, while there were strains evident within the Eastern bloc, as evidenced by the June 1953 East German uprising (see Chapter 6, A), the Soviet ability to exercise control had not been appreciably reduced, and was unlikely to be so while Moscow maintained adequate military forces. Detachment of satellites was, therefore, not feasible except by war or Soviet acquiescence.[8]

Continuing doubts about the efficacy of an aggressive Cold War strategy were to produce disagreements between the Joint Chiefs and the more cautious State Department in the post-Solarium attempts to produce a new national security strategy to fight the Cold War. Initially, in forming a new policy, consideration was given to how to boost the strength of the free world while putting the Soviet bloc on the defensive, but what this would involve and at what risk remained vague. Consequently, the immediate impact of Solarium was to produce indecision and conflicting views about the future development of any national security strategy centred on fighting the Cold War. The outcome, as it emerged during the first half of Eisenhower's presidency, was to prove a key moment in the American approach to the Cold War, even though there was an absence of agreement or decisive presidential leadership. The eventual shift in emphasis came largely as a result of three other factors: the reassessment of Soviet capabilities with regard to hot war and which related in particular to the communist acquisition of nuclear weapons; the fact that, as more interest was taken in areas outside Europe, the success of a Cold War strategy came to be defined, less in terms of the eradication of communism in Eastern Europe through an aggressive strategy, and more in terms of preventing communism spreading to other areas of the world; and finally the concern, particularly in 1954 as divisions seemed to be appearing within the Western alliance (see Chapter 4, C on the problem of German rearmament), that the unity of the Western bloc would be difficult to maintain, unless diplomatic efforts to reach an agreement with the Soviets were made while avoiding aggressive acts that might provoke war.

However, despite the problems and reservations about the success of an aggressive strategy in Eastern Europe, American reluctance to accept the continued existence of the Soviet Union led to importance still being attached to the conduct of covert operations and psychological warfare, some of which were included in the formal paper on overall national security policy NSC 162/2. The paper referred to measures to impose pressure on the Soviet bloc, which should take account of the desirability of creating conditions to induce the Soviet leadership to be more receptive to negotiated settlements. Covert measures, in particular, should be taken to create and exploit problems for the USSR and eliminate its control over its satellites. Thus, although the aim of destroying the Soviet regime was removed as the goal of US policy, the means to achieve this still included similar measures and left scope for the kind of secret actions which were risky and provocative. The change was that the possibility of peaceful coexistence was now more acceptable and was likely to involve attempts at reaching negotiated settlements beneficial to the US.[9]

Effectively, Eisenhower was presented with two options (A and C) in the wake of Solarium and could not decide which to choose. The indecision was made worse by the growing realization that the Soviets had the H-bomb and would at some point in the future be likely to achieve nuclear parity. If under Truman, and especially in the wake of NSC 68, coexistence was not in the interests of the US, would not a pre-emptive strike in 1953–4 be better than waiting for parity or bankrupting the US? The question then reverted to that raised by Charles Bohlen, whether the Soviets aimed at world domination by all means including the use of force (see Chapter 4, D). If they did, as the military claimed, then there was no real choice other than the destruction of the Soviets, but if they did not, coexistence was an option. It was another dilemma which Eisenhower considered, but never decisively resolved. What was certain was the destruction of the assumptions behind NSC 68. If rearmament was to enable the US to fight an aggressive Cold War, to destroy or weaken the Soviets without risking hot war (because of the deterrence provided by America's overwhelming nuclear and conventional strength), this policy was no longer an option once the Soviets achieved thermonuclear capability.

Subversion and Intelligence Gathering

The contrast between, on the one hand, policies of diplomatic negotiation and peaceful coexistence and, on the other, covert actions to weaken the Soviet Union and its control over the satellites (subversion) was to remain a feature of US policy under Eisenhower. As Dulles and the State Department favoured the former, the military remained committed to more aggressive Cold War policies. The scope and value of covert operations and psychological operations remained part of US Cold War policy and helped produce a number of risky operations against the Soviet Union. If the Soviet Union had to be destroyed or its behaviour radically altered, there was no real need to limit the risk of war. Or, as fears of war grew (again, as in earlier periods, there was a belief that the Soviets were unlikely to deliberately start a war), more attention was paid to how the US would be best able to cope with Soviet capabilities in defensive and offensive hot war terms. The need to consider how best to assess and cope with Soviet hot war capabilities, combined with the underlying offensive and aggressive strategy in the Cold War of the US military, led to dangerous risk-taking. The former need also helped produce much more National Security Council (NSC) attention to such matters in its reviews of national security. By the time Kennedy radically changed the whole NSC approach and reduced its importance, it was dealing with such issues as civil defence, early warning, Soviet air defence systems, and relative nuclear and conventional capabilities, including joint war plans for hot war.

One of the most secretive US operations involving the clearest most direct risk of hot war was Operation Home Run, about which a lot less is known than the illegal overflying of Soviet airspace by U-2 spy planes. Staged from Greenland, fifty US bombers were sent into Soviet airspace carrying eavesdropping equipment and cameras as opposed to nuclear weapons. Most of northern Russia was penetrated over a period of seven or eight weeks in the spring of 1956, and 156 missions over Russian airspace were flown. Part of the aim was to acquire information about Russian radar, which may be considered in relation to the mysterious and disastrous overflight of the Korean civilian airliner, KAL 007, under President Reagan (see Chapter 16, A). US reconnaissance overflights of the Soviet Union began in 1954.[10] The US military were not just concerned about hot war intelligence; they also wanted to use air power and technological supremacy for Cold War purposes. They initially proposed Project Control in 1953, which was based on the political use of air power. The reconnaissance offensive could lead to the use of US nuclear weapons to resolve key problems with the USSR. In other words, US technological supremacy in the air could be used as a bargaining tool with the Soviets, for example, to urge the withdrawal from Eastern Europe. If concessions were not given by Moscow, and there were attempts to stop the reconnaissance planes, the US would respond with a nuclear attack.[11]

Whatever may have come of such a plan, Soviet espionage and subversion appear, from what we know, to have been of a very different kind in the 1950s to those of the US. Soviet spies operated in an environment where it was easier for agents to escape detection. Developing their agents to follow on from the wartime defectors to the cause of Soviet communism was now more difficult because of recruitment problems in the Cold War. Recruits would have to come from members of the Soviet intelligence services and become illegal entrants to the West. In the US, Venona (see Chapter 4, A) had revealed such knowledge of Soviet agents that the network in the US had to be almost entirely rebuilt. The essence of Soviet espionage and subversion was a legacy of Stalinist paranoia and wartime mistrust, which had produced a need to discover what the West was planning to do against the Soviet Union. Fears in the Cold War may have been better grounded in reality, but they were based on perceptions that the Soviets needed to know more about the nature of what was being planned against them. Hence, probably their most successful agent, apart from those recruited in the inter-war years, was the British George Blake,[12] who betrayed a large number of Western agents to his Soviet masters.

Counter-subversion for the Soviets and for Blake was also directed at the secret Western tunnel in Berlin. Approved in 1953, the tunnel was begun in the late summer of 1954 and completed in 1955; at 1,600 feet long, it ran from West Berlin underground into East Berlin, so that the West could intercept land-lines running from the Soviet military and intelligence HQ at Karlshorst. The Soviets learned of the planned tunnel through Blake in January 1954, but were unable to 'discover' it until 1956 for fear of compromising their British agent.[13] The Berlin tunnel and the Blake spy case came to symbolize some of the similarities and differences between Soviet espionage and subversion and the Western variety. Both sides were keen to use agents to provide knowledge of what the other side was doing, to compromise officials, and to prevent the efficient conduct of intelligence operations. The different features of the two societies (see Chapter 4, A) made it easier for the Soviets to use agents inside the US or Europe. This meant, in the 1950s, that the West used more devious means, like the Berlin tunnel, to obtain information on Soviet intelligence and military activities; and in the military case this made risky exercises to assess Soviet capabilities more likely (see next section, 'Defining an Overall Cold War National Security Strategy'). In the case of subversion, it meant that because the degree of underground resistance was less in the West, it was therefore more difficult for the communists to encourage the use of illegitimate means (uprisings) to overthrow the regime. The result was that while 'illegals' were sent by Moscow with the aim of disrupting Western governments' policies and obtaining secrets, the West was better able to use tactics based on encouraging insurrection of the people against the communist governments. Actions to disrupt economic planning, to highlight the relative lack of consumer goods with food and leaflet drops, to establish contacts with dissidents, and to continue broadcasting propaganda, were not part of Soviet subversion. This was irrespective of whether there were those individuals and agencies who linked their activities to a strategy based on the ultimate destruction of the other side. Here we must wait for evidence from the Soviet side that this was ever considered as part of a Cold War strategy, at the centre of which was the issue of eventual coexistence, for the Americans.

At the same time, what each side understood by subversion was also partly influenced by the different possibilities that were made available by the nature and location of the two opposing societies. Subversion to the Americans was not just action authorized and controlled by the Soviet state and its agents, aimed at the destruction or weakening of the US, but any left-wing communist political activity. Because such activities were, in theory at least, permitted in free societies, any such group, whether controlled or influenced by the Soviets or largely independent of them, was labelled subversive. Moreover, in some societies it was possible for groups to emerge which had different variants of interests and ideology, as in Vietnam, which by 1954 was the key US example of Soviet subversion. The confusion then and now arose over the analysis of these movements as both ideological and power political opponents controlled by Moscow, when some were not.

The advantage for the communists was the ease of encouragement of ideological opposition to capitalism that the existence of communist parties provided. It is arguable, however, that the Soviets were never fundamentally interested in ideology, but were aware of its importance to justify and explain actions which were always primarily geared to the power political goals of the Soviet state. Naturally, the old debate over whether Soviet expansion, world domination, the survival of the satellite Empire, the needs of state security, or the achievement and enhancement of world power status was the dominant goal remains crucial, as does the role of ideology in Soviet foreign policy. Yet the Americans arguably used ideology, not as a power-political state tool, but as a universal principle of international well-being. In other words, communist/socialist ideology was interpreted in the same way as, and often juxtaposed or confused with, the advancement of Soviet state power as a threat to US national security. Communist ideology was not a threat because it was seen as a tool of another state but because it was deemed a threat to international well-being and American interests and values. The result, in the 1950s, was that the US perceived threats on a broader front and propaganda became more important. Moreover, to a significant extent it was prepared to run greater risks to remove or counter them.

Defining an Overall Cold War National Security Strategy

While there was some reluctance to abandon an aggressive strategy, the voices of moderation continued to gather strength in late 1953 and in 1954. They were boosted by the destructive power of the H-bomb, the prospect of Soviet nuclear sufficiency or equality, and the futility of the immediate Cold War destruction of the enemy. In one sense, American policy-makers can be seen as attempting to justify and reconcile the two somewhat contradictory tracks in US policy and to modify NSC 162. By 1954, this modification was deemed necessary, because of the increasing likelihood of Soviet subversion, with North Vietnam lost to the West, the increased Soviet nuclear capability, and the growing signs of divisions between the Western allies. As NSC 5440 put it, in December 1954, the hostile policies of the Soviet Union could only be resolved in accordance with US security interests, either through the overthrow of the Soviet regime and its replacement by a government with no expansionist policies 'or any other objectives inconsistent with US security'. Or, the problem could be resolved by the modification of the Soviet system so that its leaders 'abandon expansionist policies and accept arrangements in accordance with US national security interests'.[14] Thus, covert measures could be continued with the aim of encouraging the modification of the Soviet regime, or the withdrawal from Eastern Europe and the end of Soviet expansion, which most Americans wrongly believed had caused, rather than encouraged, the events in Korea and Vietnam.

Dulles, to his credit, tried to define the limits to which the Operations Coordinating Board (the replacement for the Psychological Strategy Board in September 1953) could go in covert operations, by arguing in September 1954 that no actions should be taken which would impair a negotiated settlement.[15] The statement proved to be ironic in that it was the covert U-2 spy flights in 1960 which effectively sabotaged the Paris summit negotiations (see Chapter 5, B). Moreover, the crux of the controversy was over the acceptance or rejection of peaceful coexistence and negotiation as the best strategy for ending Soviet hostility. The debate was formalized in NSC 5440 in terms of the Joint Chiefs of Staff (JCS) and State Department views. The former argued that it was dangerous to try and solve problems with the Soviets through negotiations, and should therefore be rejected until Soviet behaviour changed. The latter sought, from a position of strength, to achieve a modus vivendi with Moscow.[16] Thus, the dilemma posed by the NSC committee in June 1954 under Robert Cutler remained unresolved. Cutler noted that:

> As it has been formulated, NSC policy towards the USSR has not provided a 'strategic concept' adequate for operational guidance in the exploitation of Soviet vulnerabilities ... There is no clear guidance in NSC policies for determining the balance and relationship between measures taken within the context of a policy of coexistence and measures to be taken within a context which postulates the destruction of the Soviet system and regime.[17]

The problem of linking subversion and covert operations to the destruction of the Soviet regime, with a policy based on coexistence and reducing the Soviet threat by negotiation was to remain during the Eisenhower administration. In 1954, the JCS continued to argue that for a change in Soviet attitudes to occur communists had to be convinced that their policies would produce countermeasures that would threaten their continued existence.[18] Dulles, however, believed that while he could sympathize with the military desire for a more dynamic Cold War policy, which he himself had called for in 1952, it was not easy to go beyond the point the Eisenhower administration had reached in translating policy into action. If strong pressure were applied to change the Soviet system, or to overthrow the Chinese communist regime, general war was likely. And, even if this did not occur, the problem of Soviet atomic plenty (which had ended the

NSC 68 strategy of being able to apply Cold War pressure from a position of hot war superiority) would remain. Finally, to continue with an aggressive Cold War policy was likely to destroy the unity of the free world.[19] When the next review of national security gave rise, in 1955, to NSC 5501, the outline national security strategy was defined as a choice between meeting the Soviet threat by 'destroying the power of the Soviet-communist bloc or modifying the policies of the Soviet government along lines more compatible with US security interests'. The means to implement this were not addressed; instead it was merely stated that: 'Either policy could include action to disrupt or neutralize the international Communist apparatus *in the free world*.'[20]

The emphasis on the 'free world' effectively meant counter-subversion not subverting or destroying the Soviet system but protecting the Western one. Yet it took more time before the aggressive Cold War policy disappeared. The basic reviews of national security policy in 1956, 1957, 1958, and 1959 (NSC 5602, NSC 5707, NSC 5810, NSC 5906 memoranda) changed little in terms of strategy and still contained sections on 'Means of Directly Influencing the Soviet bloc', including the exploitation of Soviet vulnerabilities as part of a Cold War strategy which encouraged bureaucratic and popular pressures inside the bloc. Thus, the scope was there for the continuation of measures originally designed as part of a strategy of undermining the Soviet Union or its satellites. However, negotiations and the exploitation of Soviet vulnerabilities now went hand in hand.

Throughout the 1950s, the contradictions in the two elements of Cold War strategy were not totally resolved in the context of national security strategy. What happened was that new things were added to it, again stemming from the attempts to define such a strategy in the wake of Solarium in 1953 and 1954. In the first place, more emphasis was given to hot war now that the Soviets were approaching nuclear plenty, meaning that, by the second half of the decade, they could deliver an immensely damaging strike on the US. More emphasis was placed on deterring this, and analysing ways in which it might be prevented by military and technological means. Second, the growing importance of the less developed world had enormous implications by the end of the decade. Rather than concentrating on destroying the Soviet bloc, it now became more necessary to strengthen the free world against the spread of communism. Aid and other measures to do this, including counter-subversion, had to be an integral part of such a strategy and under Kennedy the whole emphasis was placed there. Covert operations would no longer be organized as part of a general Cold War strategy of peaceful coexistence or roll-back, or both, as it had become for much of Eisenhower's administration.

The implications of this Cold War shift away from Europe, as fear of hot war grew and peaceful coexistence became something of a fact, as well as a more desirable State Department goal, have important implications for interpretations of US national security and Cold War strategy. The difference between policies geared to hot war and to those pertaining to all other forms of conflict, short of an international armed one, are again vital for coming to grips with the Cold War. Yet, understanding that the whole process was never fully centred on containment is even more important. The old idea of containing Soviet power in Europe in a Cold War, which then became, for the US, a global form of containment, needs challenging. In the 1950s, the issues were coexistence and negotiation with the communists or destroying or radically changing the Soviet regimes Moscow imposed on the Eastern bloc. As Dulles pointed out: if the US was going to accept coexistence, it would be important to determine which areas of the world it should hold. One can only 'contain' something which exists. Practising a policy of coexistence, as Secretary of the Treasury George Humphrey, pointed out in 1954, would be the result of abandoning roll-back. Containment was, arguably, more in evidence after roll-back was being abandoned than before it. The difficulties and doubtful success of a policy of removing the communist problem by weakening and/or removing the regime in Moscow were rightly seen as greater in the wake of Solarium. Coexistence and peaceful negotiations, arguably leading to containment, then became more attractive. Eisenhower never made the choice and the implementation of a policy never went beyond what Dulles had defined as the problem in 1954.

B. The Berlin Crises

Berlin was at the heart of the Cold War, the heart of the German question, and on several occasions became the focus of tension between the two blocs in Europe. The airlift of 1948–9 to preserve the Western position in the city, which was an island in East Germany

(GDR), had become a potent Cold War symbol. Berlin could be portrayed as a beacon of freedom in a land devoid of democracy, where communist aggressors were poised to strike once Western vigilance relaxed. It also symbolized the division of Germany, yet was a city that offered a gateway to the West for people who could move between the Soviet sector and the British, French, and American sectors. Thus, it became a focal point for East German citizens seeking a better life in the West.

In the early 1950s, the scale of the exodus was fast becoming a problem for the East German authorities and a massive disadvantage in propaganda terms, as people began to 'vote with their feet' on the success of communism. Nevertheless, the roots of the crises, which began in 1958 and 1961, were not simply communist designs on the city, because of a need to ease the political and economic difficulties faced by Walter Ulbricht's regime in the GDR. Nor was the American response simply based on a reaction to the crises provoked by Khrushchev. American policy was defined by two key considerations before the first crisis broke, at the Russian leader's instigation, in 1958. One was related to the pressure the Soviets could bring to bear on the US position by a repeat of the blockade strategy; the other was the pressure the US could put on the Soviets through covert operations and psychological warfare conducted from West Berlin.

The Background to the 1958 Crisis

The West was very aware of the virtual impossibility of defending West Berlin in the wake of a determined Soviet attack. The Eisenhower administration considered this and concluded by 1954 that the Western position was sufficiently important to retain even at the risk of general war. This raised the stakes, by changing Truman's policy of threatening war only when the Western position was unsustainable. Eisenhower saw that as too defensive and, while the defence of West Berlin was impossible, he wanted to use the US position in the city to wrest the Cold War initiative away from Moscow. The President believed West Berlin could be used to implement a 'dynamic programme of penetration to bring freedom to those who want it'.

The covert operations programme comprised disinformation and radio broadcasts to encourage Eastern Europeans to revolt against communist rule, even though its effectiveness had been put into question by the collapse of the East German uprising in the summer of 1953. By then, West Berlin had become the centre of anti-Soviet activities in Europe, including eavesdropping projects in a secret Berlin underground tunnel (see Chapter 7, A). One particularly embarrassing Western campaign for the East Germans and Soviets was the provision of food parcels. This forced the East Germans to impose restrictions on travel into West Berlin and to penalize East Berliners who were found to be participating in the programme. Eisenhower also adopted a more assertive Cold War policy with new defensive measures and believed that the blockade relief option, despite stockpiling in West Berlin, was no longer desirable. Whatever the increased difficulties of implementing a repeat of the 1948 airlift in response to a new blockade, there might come a time when the US, by finally threatening military action, would be placed on the back foot. There would then be the possibility of a humiliating climbdown, after losing a battle to save West Berlin without resorting to general war. Of course, the threat of general war was inevitable if the Soviets were determined enough, given the relative strengths of the opposing forces, but Eisenhower wanted to resort to the threat of military action at the *beginning* of any future crisis.[21]

Khrushchev was aware of East German weakness and, particularly after the incorporation of West Germany into the Western alliance, he became more committed to strengthening the GDR as a firm member of the Eastern bloc. The fear of losing a satellite to capitalism was accompanied by a desire to prevent any Eastern European state collapsing, especially in the second half of the decade. The failure to make any progress on a German settlement, which could be portrayed as a success, was also something that he became concerned about. After 1956, Khrushchev had embarked on a policy of peaceful coexistence and cut Soviet conventional forces considerably. If this continued to fail to bring results in the form of increased security and status for the Soviets, then domestic criticism would grow. Some analysts told Khrushchev that Adenauer could soon force Washington to support the 'implementation of German reunification on a bourgeois basis'. And there were other fears of a West German rapprochement with Poland which would force Russian troops back inside the Soviet borders. There was particular concern about the Germans getting their hands on nuclear weapons.[22] In addition, pressure on Khrushchev came from Ulbricht, who reminded him of the subversive activities of the Americans and the continued flow of East Germans to the West. Ulbricht urged Moscow to take measures which would enhance the international status of the largely unrecognized GDR. The East Germans were increasingly seeing the need to gain sovereignty over the whole of Berlin, which otherwise would remain an open sore inside the GDR.

In Berlin, as elsewhere, US subversion policy (see Chapter 7, A) moved to one of supporting passive resistance, rather than armed rebellion, in the Eastern bloc. The Americans also made it clear that they would not tolerate interference with Western access to the city and based their response to any such interference on 'immediate and forceful action to counter the Soviet challenge even though such countermeasures might lead to general war'. Berlin was also placed under the NATO nuclear umbrella, and, fearing that the Russians might relinquish some of their administrative officials to the East Germans, a decision was made in 1954 to accept GDR officials as representatives of the Soviet Union.[23] But the crux of the developing crisis was Soviet concerns over nuclear developments in West Germany and the increasing need to strengthen the East German state, while the US attached enormous symbolic importance to West Berlin as the centre of psychological warfare against the Eastern bloc.

The Crisis of 1958

The attempts to strengthen East Germany had led, in 1954, to a Soviet announcement that it regarded the GDR as a sovereign state and to Ulbricht's statement, the following year, that East Berlin was its capital and that he was prepared to restrict traffic between the zones. As economic conditions in West Berlin began to improve, the attractions of the Western sector only increased and Khrushchev's domestic credibility became increasingly threatened. Internationally, there was the impact of a massive increase in 1958 of the numbers of escaping East Germans. The victory of socialism, as an economic force, could not be reconciled with the growing desire to escape from its clutches in East Germany, in order to share in the economic success of capitalism. Nor could the security benefits of peaceful coexistence be squared with a West German state apparently on the verge of controlling nuclear weapons. In the spring of 1957, Adenauer did not deny to the Soviet ambassador that West Germany might become a nuclear power, and Heinrich Brentano, the West German foreign minister, asked why, if other West European powers had nuclear weapons, Germans should not too. Khrushchev suspended high-level contacts with the West Germans for a year as a result. In 1958, Ulbricht sent Khrushchev alarming reports about American nuclear weapons in Berlin and, at the end of the summer, the Soviet leader devised a way to strengthen his and East Germany's position. Berlin would be declared a free, demilitarized city and he would threaten to transfer control over West Berlin access routes to the East Germans. The ultimate aim was to use this threat to persuade the West to recognize the GDR, and with it the formal division of Germany, preferably with both states renouncing nuclear weapons. Khrushchev was confident he could reduce the rights of the West in Berlin, bit by bit, without giving a real justification for war.

On 10 November 1958, he therefore announced that the Soviet Union would transfer its Berlin occupation rights to the GDR so that the West would have to discuss all Berlin questions with the East Germans. He then informed the West Germans that talks in Bonn would only continue on the basis of the West Germans not acquiring nuclear weapons and acknowledging the GDR as a negotiating partner. Finally, on 27 November he presented a large memo to the Western powers demanding an agreement to transform Berlin into a free, demilitarized city and an understanding with the GDR, on unhindered travel between the city and the rest of the world. If no such agreement was reached within six months, the Soviet Union would make its own agreement with the GDR, giving the latter full sovereignty over East Berlin. This ultimatum occurred, coincidentally or not, at the same time in 1958 as German bomber units were trained so that they might have a nuclear capability, and at the same time that the construction of German nuclear storage facilities was completed.[24] The NATO powers rejected Khrushchev's demands the following month.[25]

In early 1959, Khrushchev tried to take the heat out of the stalemate by claiming that the speech was not intended to be an ultimatum, an assurance repeated to the British Prime Minister, Harold Macmillan, when he visited Moscow in February 1959. The Russian leader also accepted Eisenhower's suggestion for another foreign ministers' conference on the German question, which began in Geneva in May 1959. By then, the possibilities for agreement on disarmament had been exhausted (see Chapter 5, B and C) and the conference made no progress but it effectively ended the ultimatum. It also led to another formal process of meetings designed to reduce tension through more summits and other high-level discussions, but Khrushchev's motives for this have not been made clear. The most logical one seems a desire, born from a genuine fear, to reduce the German military threat. What particularly concerned Khrushchev was the possibility of West German forces being used against a weak East Germany, backed by the threat of nuclear weapons. When Khrushchev visited the US in September 1959, to meet Eisenhower, tensions over Berlin were further reduced as the American president seemed willing to discuss the partial withdrawal of US troops from West Berlin. Thus, Berlin for the moment was subsumed in the general round of meetings on bigger and broader issues and the crisis would not re-emerge in acute form until a new American president was in the White House.

The Crisis of 1961

The importance of Berlin was likely to render any agreement difficult, as the real question was whether the Soviets would take any military action to change the status quo and, if they did, would the Americans go to war in response. It was a cat-and-mouse game of bluff for the two protagonists which, in 1961, involved their respective allies much more than in 1958. It has been suggested that Ulbricht, not Khrushchev, drove the 1961 crisis because of the desperate situation in East Germany. Something had to be done, irrespective of Khrushchev's domestic problems or any Soviet desire to avoid confrontation with the US. For Ulbricht, the general questions of West Germany obtaining nuclear weapons and the creation of two neutral Germanies were also less important. Some 200,000 inhabitants of East Germany fled into West Berlin in 1960, many of them qualified professional people most needed by the country. The East German economy could not afford the salaries needed to retain them. When the two communist leaders met in the last months of 1960, they agreed on what their priorities would be in seeking a settlement that would solve East Germany's problem. Top of the list was West Berlin becoming a free city and the recognition of both Germanies in the form of a four-power peace treaty. If not, the communist aim was to get an interim four-power agreement pending the negotiation of a peace treaty based, for example, on the withdrawal of troops. Finally, there was the possibility of a separate peace treaty between the Soviet Union and its allies, which would give the East Germans control over the access routes to Berlin.[26]

The real problem was that there was no possible resolution of the situation that would satisfy both sides. From the communist perspective, the status quo had to change, whereas from the American perspective it was vital to preserve it. As 1961 came, the exodus from East Germany increased, as did the numbers of Westerners taking advantage of buying basic subsidized goods in the East at cheaper prices. The failed Paris summit of 1960 (see Chapter 5, B) also made peaceful coexistence less attractive and increased pressures for more confrontational policies. Thus, in January 1961, Khrushchev told the West German ambassador that the Berlin problem must be solved within a year.[27] The problem with the American determination to preserve the status quo remained—that a US conventional response to any Soviet actions was bound to be ineffectual, while the threat of nuclear war, simply because the Soviets signed a peace treaty with the GDR, seemed way out of proportion. On the other hand, the abandoning of American rights, or any real alteration of the West's position, was deemed likely to reduce international confidence in any form of US guarantee.

The scene was set for Berlin, and a German peace treaty to form an important part of the summit between Kennedy and Khrushchev, planned for June 1961, in Vienna. The meeting has become notorious for Khrushchev's attempts to bully the young, inexperienced president. There is no doubt that Kennedy was taken aback by Khrushchev's attempts at intimidation and his crude, stark portrayals of US–Soviet disagreements, but there was no caving in to Khrushchev's demands, especially on Berlin. The Soviet leader proposed his ideal solution, already agreed with Ulbricht, but Kennedy likened West Berlin to Western Europe, in an attempt to get across the importance that the US attached to Berlin. He told Khrushchev he was determined to avoid anything which would appear as a change in the global balance to the benefit of the communists. Khrushchev emphasized that the Soviets could not afford a long delay and if there were no agreement by the end of the year, they would sign a separate peace treaty with East Germany. The President repeated the importance the US attached to Berlin and to American occupation rights, which would be infringed if the status quo were changed. He hoped that the two states would not end up confronting each other in a situation where vital interests were at stake. The Soviet leader put the responsibility for choosing war on the Americans, if war was what they wanted over Berlin.[28]

The prospect of war was of particular concern to the British, who would have preferred a negotiated settlement, even if it involved changing the status quo. Surprisingly, for all his supposed dislike of American domination, de Gaulle was more firmly behind Kennedy in 1961. De Gaulle, who wanted to maintain close cooperation between France and West Germany as leaders of the European Economic Community, believed (correctly) that Khrushchev was bluffing. De Gaulle was in favour of facing the Soviets down at the risk of general war. When the Soviets made the ultimatum public on 10 June 1961, Kennedy pushed through a conventional arms build-up, with the aim of giving US forces more flexibility and announced the call-up of reservists. It was little more than a token gesture, but it forced Khrushchev, already under pressure from the military, to cancel his proposed cutbacks in the Red Army[29] and it was designed to indicate the seriousness of Western intent. As tension rose, the Americans began to examine exactly what had to be preserved in West Berlin at all costs. The bottom line was the freedom and survival of the Western sector, but how to ensure this except by deterring Soviet action was less clear. As Khrushchev told John McCloy, the President's disarmament adviser, a German peace treaty would be signed no matter what and as the Soviet leader increased the defence budget by one-third the game of cat and mouse reached its peak at the end of July. On 31 July, Kennedy himself acknowledged that Khrushchev would have to stop the refugee flow, with perhaps the building of a wall.[30]

Despite Ulbricht's June denial that a wall was anyone's intention, one had already been discussed on the basis of a well-prepared East German plan, which aimed to see if the US would start a major war to preserve West Berlin. In contrast to this potentially provocative step, the KGB chief, Shelepin, advocated a far-reaching programme of covert operations and psychological warfare, like those favoured by Eisenhower, but on a global scale. This would be something to tie American forces down in various parts of the world, while the attempts to secure a German peace treaty were pursued. The aim was to convince the Americans that, if they unleashed a military conflict, they could lose influence in many parts of the less developed world, as armed uprisings against reactionary pro-Western governments took place. When the Cuban Missile Crisis broke in 1962, Kennedy believed the Soviets might actually be aiming at concessions over Berlin (see Chapter 7, D). Shelepin also suggested

BOX 7.1

Biography: John F. Kennedy (29 May 1917–22 November 1963)

John F. Kennedy was born in Brookline, in the state of Massachusetts. He was educated at the University of Harvard and upon graduating in 1940 he joined the US navy. During his naval career, Kennedy became something of a hero in 1943 when, after a Japanese attack, he led many survivors to safety despite his own serious injuries. After the war, Kennedy became a Democratic Congressman for Massachusetts in November 1946. He entered the Senate in 1953 and, in September of that year, married Jacqueline Bouvier. In 1958 and 1959, Kennedy gave much of his time to labour reform legislation. In 1960, he became the first ballot nominee for president, which was the culmination of a career planned out for him by his ruthless and domineering father, Joe. John F. Kennedy, or Jack as he was known, won the presidential election by a narrow margin, following televised debates with Richard Nixon, and became the first Roman Catholic to enter the White House. At the age of 43, he was also the youngest man to take up the office. It was in his inaugural address that Kennedy's famous phrase was first used: 'Ask not what your country can do for you—ask what you can do for your country.' He was a president who eventually backed the cause of civil rights, and pledged to rid the country of persistent areas of poverty. He set up the Alliance for Progress in 1961, to attempt to alleviate much of the poverty in Latin American countries. The Peace Corps were also established by the administration in 1961. Then, in April 1961, Kennedy faced his first international challenge as president, when he allowed the unsuccessful Bay of Pigs invasion of Cuba to take place. The failure of the invasion was a major setback. In 1961–2, he also had to deal with the Soviet leader, Nikita Khrushchev, over the Berlin crisis. Then a crisis over Cuba also emerged in 1962, with the discovery that Soviet missiles had been positioned on the island. Kennedy was credited with US success during the ensuing 'Missile Crisis' and gained great international support. Tragically, on 22 November 1963, Kennedy was shot and killed by an assassin in Dallas, Texas.

a campaign of deception, exaggerating the size of the Soviet nuclear arsenal (see Chapter 5, C). The KGB was instructed to present more specific measures for consideration by the Presidium.[31]

For Berlin, the worst part of the crisis was over when, on 13 August, the two halves of Berlin were separated by barbed wire, followed a month later by the building of a wall. Ulbricht's problems were solved, the haemorrhage of skilled labour from East Germany came to an end and, although Soviet and American tanks confronted each other for a time across the sector boundary in Berlin, the possibility of war over the city suddenly no longer seemed likely. The Soviets had failed again to change the status quo and the Western alliance had held firm despite doubts from some of its members. But the West could do nothing to stop the wall being built, effectively accepting the Soviet sphere of influence in Eastern Europe.

C. The Offshore Islands Crises

The Formosa Situation

The numerous small islands in the Formosa Strait, between Mao's forces on mainland China and the forces of Chiang Kai-shek on the island of Formosa (now Taiwan), came close to producing a major war in the 1950s. They formed an essential element in the conflict between the US and communist China after the Korean War, as they could serve as a stepping stone for the nationalist Chinese to invade the Chinese mainland. On the other hand, the island groups of Jinmen (Quemoy), Mazu (Matsu), and Dachen could be used to put pressure on the nationalists and to weaken their hold on Formosa. The artillery shelling, which the communists began in 1954, was certainly tied to the issue of the 'two Chinas' and the battle over the right to control Formosa.

The Chinese island of Formosa had been taken by the Japanese in the Sino-Japanese War of 1895. During the Second World War, the Cairo Declaration signed by China, Britain, and the US stated that 'all the Chinese territories Japan has stolen from the Chinese, such as Manchuria, Formosa and the Pescadores, shall be returned to the republic of China'. This was reaffirmed at the Potsdam Conference, which resolved to implement the terms of the Cairo Declaration.[32] The US thus formally acknowledged that there should be one Chinese authority governing mainland China and the islands lost to the Japanese. The fact that, as a result of the Chinese civil war, the rump of the defeated nationalists was in possession of Formosa, and the communists in possession of the mainland, led the Americans to renege on their commitment as soon as this fact became evident in 1949. Truman placed the US 7th Fleet in the Strait of Formosa as the Korean War began, to prevent a communist Chinese invasion.

The offshore Chinese islands were very much on the mainland side of the Straits adjacent to the Chinese coast, and within artillery range, but were controlled by nationalist forces. The actions taken by the Chinese communists against the islands have been interpreted as part of the general communist attempts to test Western resolve, as part of the Chinese geo-strategic quest to become the dominant power in East Asia, as the attempt to complete the unification of China, or as the need to preclude an invasion from Formosa, which it was feared would be aided by American imperialists. The most probable explanation relates to Mao's determination to avoid the long-term potential threat from a rival seat of Chinese government, and the need to reduce the military difficulties of having islands within a few miles of the coast in the hands of Chiang's troops. Some interpretations depend on accepting a belief by American policy-makers that the communists in Beijing were the puppets of Moscow. Not only was this not the case, but we can be almost certain that in private US leaders did not believe it either. They were under more pressure in public to justify their policies in the face of political opponents; this frequently involved simplifications and stark portrayals of the unity of purpose which US enemies allegedly possessed. Hence the interference in China's internal conflict was influenced by domestic Cold War politics.

The Chinese Approach

The islands were vital for Chinese defence but above all else they, along with the Pescadores and Formosa, both islands of greater size and distance from the Chinese coast, were part of the emotive desire for the restoration of complete Chinese sovereignty. Mao saw American imperialism in terms of its efforts to undermine China, by interfering in the internal affairs of its civil war. His opposition to that imperialism was not yet fully formulated into a broader regional strategy, which was to be based on confronting the US and bringing conflict with the Soviet Union. In 1954–5, when the first Offshore Islands Crisis developed, it was the specifics of the Formosa question which preoccupied Mao. The fact that Washington had, since 1950, forced the postponement of communist attempts to reclaim Formosa by force, intervened in Chinese affairs, and provided military aid to Chiang Kai-shek was both annoying and disturbing for Mao. The importance of the Formosa issue was highlighted by the ceasefire in Korea in 1953, and by military manoeuvres between the American and Formosan forces. They were followed one month later, in September 1953, by an Agreement on Mutual Military Understanding. The fact that the US was now training and equipping Chiang's army, ensuring consultation over the movement of nationalist troops and then, in early 1954, discussing a Mutual Defence Treaty, seemed to foreshadow a military front in the Strait of Formosa, as Chiang built up troops on the offshore islands. By July 1954, Mao responded by launching a propaganda campaign, in which the importance of 'liberating' Formosa was emphasized, alongside the prevention of external interference in Chinese affairs.

The political offensive, related to sovereignty and outside interference more so than to the Cold War, was extended to the military sphere in August 1954, when the Central Committee of the Chinese Communist Party issued instructions for the shelling of Jinmen, which began on 3 September. It was unlikely that Mao had any intention of provoking the US, but he was seeking to focus world attention on what he believed was a situation in which imperialists were opposing China's determination to reclaim full sovereignty over its territory. The shelling of Jinmen would also 'puncture the arrogance' of the Kuomintang army and enable forces to be concentrated on parts of the coast, especially Zhejiang. Mao may well have been determined both to express resolve over, and to make some progress towards, regaining Formosa, or at least to reduce the threat from the nationalists and their imperialist backers. On the other hand, he may have been seeking to test US resolve or to probe for any possibility of settling the Formosan question in the communists' favour through diplomacy. Either way, the issue was becoming increasingly urgent with the moves towards greater military cooperation between Taipei and Washington.

There is evidence that in the months after the Korean War's end and the beginning of the shelling of Jinmen, the Chinese made considerable efforts to establish contacts with US diplomats and offer to negotiate on the Formosan issue. It is also likely that Mao did not see any inconsistency between the strategy of friendly approaches to the US in pursuit of negotiations and the strategy of using force against the offshore islands. If the US continued to pursue its fundamental policy of maintaining 'two Chinas', he was indicating a determination to resist and that relations could deteriorate significantly. Yet, he was also offering cooperation if the Americans were prepared to stop supporting Chiang.[33]

Mao was probably looking for ways to put pressure on Chiang and the Americans as part of an attempt to end the division of China. With the Korean War only over for a year, and with communist China still seeking to consolidate the revolution, there was little incentive to take on the US in another major conflict. The communist emphasis was on rebuilding the country economically and seeking national unity rather than regional influence. On the other hand, the links between the Americans and Chiang were very worrying. The prospect of regaining some at least of the offshore islands was another reason why Mao was keen to combine pressure and a show of force with the prospect of cooperation rather than war. This strategy made cooperation with the Soviets easy to maintain. Good relations with Moscow were still seen as important despite Mao's reservations, which had been heightened by his Korean War contacts with Stalin. Hence the first Offshore Islands Crisis brought little tension between Moscow and Beijing, as Khrushchev was largely informed of Chinese actions and had little reason to fear that Mao was prepared for a war with the US.

The American Approach

Much more information is available on the approaches of US policy-makers, and the difference of views between the military and civilian policy-makers. Interestingly, the crises expose the apparently different approaches of both Eisenhower and Dulles as they vacillated between moderation and extremism. This is, in part, related to the debate on Eisenhower revisionism (see Part II, Introduction) and whether Eisenhower exercised a calm, controlling influence over US policy or was a victim of indecision sometimes imposed on an irrational anti-communism. In part, it is also related to the different ways Americans could conceive of the crisis and which perceptions were most useful to emphasize as a way of undermining domestic critics of US foreign policy. Was the issue of 'two Chinas' fundamentally related to the international communist conspiracy, with its alleged commitment to expansion; or was it related to the more traditional US battle for influence in East Asia and the Western Pacific?

The domestic factor had traditionally been important in terms of America's China policy, and the roles of the 'China lobby' and the Republican Right. It may have been these domestic influences that produced the kind of description of the crisis that figured in Dulles's first public statement after the shelling had begun. The Secretary of State referred to the 'danger that stems from international communism and its insatiable ambition'. However, the records now available reveal not only a less stark US analysis in private, but also a tendency to see China's actions as part of its geopolitical ambitions in Asia. The US had itself long regarded influence in East Asia and the Pacific as an important component of American foreign policy, before the communist takeover in Beijing. Traditional Chinese ambitions were often mixed with US references to China as a dangerous and ambitious state, such as the analysis in NSC 5429 in December 1954. It was the mix of geopolitical rivalries with the ideological framework of the Cold War which is particularly relevant in Asia. Did the ideology force an exaggeration of the threat power-political challenges represented or did they help produce them? In the American case, it is difficult to believe that they did anything other than exacerbate hostility to China and to distort geostrategic perceptions. Hence, the judgement of Senator Wiley that 'we can defend the US in the Formosa Straits now, or we can defend it later in San Francisco Bay'.[34]

The divisions between US policy-makers and between the Americans and their allies over China were considerable. As Eisenhower noted in his memoirs:

> The administration heard the counsel of Attlee (liquidate Chiang), Eden (neutralize Jinmen and Mazu), [Democratic Senators] (abandon Jinmen and Mazu), Lewis Douglas (avoid entry into a civil war, on legal principles), Radford (fight for Dachen, bomb the mainland), Knowland (blockade the Chinese coast), and Rhee (join him and Chiang in a holy war of liberation).[35]

The main differences were between the military, who were keen to fight for the offshore islands, and Eisenhower and Dulles, who were not. Some civilians, notably outside the administration, were happy to support the Chairman of the Joint Chiefs of Staff, Admiral Radford, who was suspected by the US ambassador in Formosa of encouraging Chiang to step up his attacks on the mainland in response to the shelling. NSC 5429 of December 1954 also urged the provision of a commitment to defend all the offshore islands, as it portrayed Beijing as the key source of the challenges to American power and influence in Asia. Moreover, this strategy was part of the broader offensive Cold War strategy that was advocated, especially during the early years of the Eisenhower presidency. NSC 5429 favoured an expanded programme of 'psychological activities and the use of all feasible covert means against the communists'.[36]

One cause of concern was the possible role for nuclear weapons. The crisis was instrumental in producing presidential statements about the acceptance of the use of tactical nuclear weapons in the same way as conventional ones. Nevertheless, according to one historian, in early 1955 the US came closer to using nuclear weapons than at any other time under Eisenhower.[37] There is no doubt that the President was determined to fight for Formosa: the question was whether the communist pressure on the offshore islands constituted the build-up to an assault on Formosa or not. Eisenhower, as with other alleged 'falling dominoes', was initially keen to draw the line against communist successes, but then came to see the problems this would cause if the communists knew precisely what actions the US would resist by force. How could some islands be deemed more important than others? Would it be better to keep the communists guessing?

The fact that Eisenhower declined to respond, except in vague tones, has been used by Eisenhower revisionists to illustrate his calm, calculated, and responsible handling of a crisis in the face of communist provocation. By saying that he would only take action if the attacks on the offshore islands constituted a threat to Formosa, he produced the maximum deterrence and the minimum danger of global war. At the same time, he remained true to the policy of recognizing and supporting Chiang as the legitimate ruler of China. He could not ignore communist actions or abandon the offshore islands, for fear of undermining nationalist morale by creating the impression that the US was abandoning hope of restoring Chiang as ruler of mainland China. This kind of analysis largely depends on the need to deter the Chinese from starting a major war, or achieving significant gains through pressure and intimidation. If the Chinese were simply trying to produce talks on the future of Formosa, and not inclined to go to war over the islands or even

Formosa, then Eisenhower's strategy may have been irrelevant. On the other hand, Eisenhower can be portrayed as being locked into an unreasonable and dangerous policy which did not produce unfortunate consequences because of the lack of any serious Chinese wish to go to war. Thus, while there may be a good deal of truth in the revisionist Eisenhower assessment, it depends on the Western assumption about the threat of Chinese expansion (as in the Korean War) as opposed to the securing of islands close to the Chinese coast.

The First Offshore Islands Crisis

As has been noted, the shelling was related to Mao's attempts to encourage the full exercise of Beijing's sovereignty and the US attempts to prevent it by increasing support for Chiang Kai-shek's claim to exercise sovereignty over the whole of China. This only increased the US belief in the aggressive nature of communist regimes and focused attention on aiding the nationalists. As Admiral Radford urged the bombing of the mainland and the deployment of American forces on the offshore islands, Eisenhower informed the Joint Chiefs, in October 1954, that there would be no retaliation and no war with China unless Formosa was attacked. In that case, the US would deploy naval forces to assist in its defence and Congress would be consulted.[38]

As American military cooperation with the nationalists developed further and the prospect of a defence treaty loomed, Mao increased the tension and the stakes. While the attention was focused on Jinmen, the communists began shelling Dachen on 1 November and sank a Formosan destroyer off the Zhejiang coast. The short-term tactical aim was probably to seize Yijiangshan, an offshore base of the Dachen Islands, without a major confrontation with the US. On 23 November, the Chinese sentenced US airmen taken prisoner after being shot down in the Korean War to terms in jail, some on the basis of espionage charges. Not surprisingly, this brought no response in the form of offers to negotiate but rather the signing, on 2 December 1954, of a Mutual Defence Treaty between Formosa and the US.

Mao's response was to have Premier Zhou Enlai denounce the treaty and order the People's Liberation Army (PLA) to consider an opportune moment to seize Yijiangshan. On 10 January, the Chinese air force raided Dachen, and eight days later Yijiangshen was attacked by Chinese forces, who wiped out about 1,000 nationalist troops and threatened Dachen, which was now in range of PLA artillery fire. Eisenhower was thus forced to consider a suitable response, if the morale of the nationalists and their commitment to return to the mainland were to be maintained. The result was the 'Formosa Doctrine', asking Congress to authorize the use of American troops to defend Formosa, but not to defend Jinmen and Mazu, as Dulles preferred. The resolution went through the Senate on 28 January 1955 and, in effect, Eisenhower was given carte blanche to take military action to defend either Formosa or the Pescadores, but not to be involved with Dachen. In early February, however, the escalation of the crisis stopped. The US announced that the 7th Fleet would help the nationalist forces on Dachen evacuate and Mao issued orders not to fire on withdrawing troops with or without the presence of US naval forces. By April 1955, the crisis was effectively over, as talks were agreed to. There was thus no confrontation or renewed Sino-American war, but Mao had reaffirmed China's 'commitment to liberating Taiwan, reduced the KMT's dangerous strongholds along the coast and tested the resolve of the US'.[39] For their part, the Americans had preserved Chiang in Formosa and demonstrated their commitment to a 'two China' policy.

Sino-Soviet Relations and China's New Anti-Imperialist Strategy

In 1955, the Chinese made efforts to produce talks that would resolve the Formosa issue peacefully, most notably at the Afro-Asian conference at Bandung, in April 1955. In July, eleven Americans detained in China were released and talks then began at the ambassadorial level, which Beijing hoped would lead to higher-level conversations focused on the future of Formosa. This was exactly what the Americans did not want, preferring only to secure a guarantee from the communists that they would not use force against Chiang. The lengthy ambassadorial talks merely produced an agreement on the rights of citizens to return to their own countries. Mao was to become increasingly frustrated by the attempts to work with the Americans and to bring about the peaceful liberation of Formosa. Yet, in July 1956, Zhou Enlai proposed another period of cooperation between the communists and the nationalists as had taken place in the inter-war years. In 1957, Taipei dismissed the concept as a ploy which aimed at the seizure of Formosa and, from the autumn of 1957, the nationalist raids and sabotage on the Chinese coast intensified.[40]

The years 1956 and 1957 witnessed broad changes in the nature of Chinese foreign policy, which were reflected in another Offshore Islands Crisis in 1958. In part, this was produced by a belief that American imperialism was determined to interfere in Chinese affairs; in part, it stemmed from a different assessment of the Soviet Union that followed Khrushchev's denunciation of Stalin in February 1956; and, in part, it reflected Mao's analysis of the changing international situation. The turning point in relations with the Americans over Formosa came at the end of 1956. In August, Mao told the Eighth Party Congress that he was still willing to pursue friendly relations with Washington. But, as the American commitment to its 'two China' policy remained firm in 1957, in September of that year with a renewed threat from Chiang, Mao stated that China's policy towards Western countries was now 'to fight against them'.[41]

Mao's visit to Moscow in November 1957 has also been described by one historian as a watershed in Sino-Soviet relations and the last time that the Sino-Soviet alliance functioned well. The background to this was the collectivization, which began in 1955 and marked for Mao an intensification of socialist transformation. The denunciation of Stalin by Khrushchev, on which Mao had not been consulted, made the Chinese leader more committed to finding his own version of socialist development, accompanied by his own, Stalin-like personality cult. At the same time, the problems that Khrushchev had had to confront in Eastern Europe gave Mao food for thought about the policies of deStalinization pursued by the Soviet leader. The apparent successes of socialism in 1957, including the launch of the first Sputnik, led Mao to doubt the wisdom of the whole idea of peaceful coexistence, as socialism seemed to be emerging as a stronger force than capitalism. As Mao put it, the east wind was prevailing over the west wind and thus it should now be possible for the communist world to 'confront the Americans with confidence in their own strength and without fearing war'. Khrushchev on the other hand, wanted 'to redirect Soviet policy towards a relaxation of tension with the West'.[42]

By 1957, Mao had decided on a far more assertive foreign policy. It may have been motivated primarily by the need to confront the Americans over their determination to maintain a 'two China' policy. It may have been based on an ideological commitment to revolution, in which the growing strength of China was important both as a regional power and as a key member of the world communist movement. It may have been linked, essentially, to the perceived need to take the Chinese revolution further through the Great Leap Forward and a greater commitment to socialist transformation. Either way, the change had an impact on relations with the US and with the Soviet Union and produced a second Offshore Islands Crisis.

The Second Offshore Islands Crisis

The second Offshore Islands Crisis began with the shelling of Jinmen on 23 August 1958. Attitudes on all sides had hardened, as Mao was now committed to confrontation and Chiang more determined to cling to the hope of returning to the mainland with American help. Eisenhower and Dulles were keener to protect Formosa from what they saw as Chinese attempts to drive the US from Asia, in accordance with the well-known domino theory of one state falling to communism and precipitating a total collapse of the pro-Western position, hence their commitment to Chiang to assist in the defence of the islands, unlike in 1954–5. As early as December 1957, Dulles told the NSC that the defence of the offshore islands was now an integral part of the defence of Formosa (over 100 miles away) and that their loss to the communists could not be accepted.[43] The islands had now become a symbol to Dulles, as well as Chiang, because it was overall US military sea and air power which were important to the defence of Formosa, not islands adjacent to the Chinese coast.

Yet in this situation in 1958, the main American concerns were to maintain the morale of the nationalists and their determination to resist communism by not abandoning the prospect of returning to the mainland and preserving the territorial integrity of Formosa. As Dulles claimed, a few days before the shelling began, if the offshore islands were taken by the communists 'morale [on Formosa] would crumble and Chiang's control would be lost'. And as Eisenhower noted, 'the key point is the evaluation of morale, since physically the islands would not help the Chinese Communists against Formosa'. Initially, the Americans faced two major problems in the form of, first, restraining Chiang and preventing him from dragging them into a war with China; and, second, of convincing world and Western opinion that it was worth risking a major war to prevent communist China retaking islands some four miles from its coast. The first scenario was more likely to arise if Chiang attacked Chinese airfields on the mainland. If the communists retaliated, this would serve as the means by which he might secure the American support he needed to re-establish himself on mainland China. The second problem related to perceptions of what was at stake. The Americans saw everything in terms of assisting Chiang and maintaining the morale of the nationalists, which was vital for their 'two China' policy. But many saw the cause of defending the nationalist claim to the islands as being unjustifiable and Chiang as a dangerous, untrustworthy partner. Moreover, there was something contradictory in both trying to restrain Chiang and prevent American involvement in a war with China, and perhaps the Soviet Union, while maintaining a commitment to the very person most likely to bring this about. Sustaining the morale of the nationalists might eventually have come to mean endorsing the very offensive operations in which the Americans feared Chiang wanted to involve them.

The Chinese were now not only confronting the Americans, but also prepared to go against Moscow. Khrushchev had recently embarked on what became known as his 'peace offensive' towards the Americans and had visited Beijing in July 1958. Mao may still have been nervous of war with the US, but he had no time for peace offensives and did not tell Khrushchev that the shelling of Jinmen would soon begin. Instead, he concentrated on acquiring more Soviet aid and establishing closer military cooperation.[44] Khrushchev, while warning the Americans against an attack on China, was now prepared to be critical of Mao over his more aggressive approach to international relations. Khrushchev now believed in coexistence and in developing a more peaceful Cold War strategy. The Sino-Soviet split, which was now beginning, was to be characterized by moves to develop cooperation, juxtaposed with frequent disagreements and denunciations, as the international situation seemed to require one approach or the other.

One issue for the American president to face was the nature of a White House statement on the islands. With more importance attached to their defence, pressure for an unambiguous statement was greater than in 1954, but again Eisenhower refused to give a clear public commitment to the defence of Jinmen, as opposed to indicating a willingness to take military action. In private, a three-stage plan was devised in which the US would convoy ships resupplying nationalist forces. Then, if a major assault was mounted on any of the islands, the Americans would join in their defence; and, finally, if China extended the action to international waters, 'appropriate' action would be taken, which would almost certainly involve the use of tactical nuclear weapons favoured by the Joint Chiefs.[45]

Despite the more confrontational position taken by Mao in terms of the global struggle between communism and capitalism, it seems unlikely that he was prepared for a major confrontation with the US. Yet, the perceptions of the Americans did not indicate an appreciation of this possibility. The emphasis was on preventing or deterring the communist capture of the offshore islands, because it represented the alleged communist challenge aimed at driving the US from Asia, epitomized by the possible destruction of the pro-Western regime of Chiang Kai-shek. Moreover, this anti-communist stance over the importance of a few offshore Chinese islands was justified with reference to the Munich Crisis of 1938, even though neither Eisenhower nor Dulles were keen on a war with China. By September, Eisenhower was seeking a way out and considered an offer to Chiang to withdraw his forces, in exchange for an amphibious capability to make an assault on the mainland more feasible. The only bright spot was the effectiveness of the convoys which, by the end of the month, were bringing sufficient quantities of supplies to Jinmen.[46]

The stalemate at the end of September did not alter the American position of using direct military intervention in publicly unspecified circumstances to preserve Chiang and the 'two China' policy. In private, these circumstances were defined as preventing the offshore islands falling to the communists. Yet, the prospect of nuclear war remained equally unpalatable and Eisenhower, in particular, continued to look for ways out. This was made easier by the Chinese proclaiming a seven-day ceasefire on 6 October, provided the Americans agreed to stop convoying supplies, which they did. Dulles then pressurized Chiang to announce that the liberation of China would be achieved principally by the application of Sun Yat-sen's[47] three principles of nationalism, democracy, and social well-being, rather than by the use of force. As in 1954, talks offered by the Chinese at ambassadorial level were taken up by the US and the crisis was virtually over in October. Even though the communists resumed the bombardment on 25 October, this indicated the islands' importance as propaganda and political symbols rather than serious Chinese military intent. Tension was further reduced by Chiang agreeing to remove 15,000 men in November 1958.

The Aftermath

The Sino-American confrontation in 1958 also had an impact on Sino-Soviet relations. The lack of consultation with Moscow worried Khrushchev, not least because of the nuclear implications, while Mao believed the Soviets were lessening their commitment to the defence of China. Although Mao did not criticize Soviet policies towards the US in the immediate aftermath of the crisis in June 1959, the Soviets told the Chinese that they were abandoning the programme of nuclear cooperation. From this point on it has been argued, as the Great Leap Forward ran into difficulties, Mao began to see the Soviets as more of a handicap than a benefit in the development of China and the pursuit of revolutionary goals at home and abroad. Therefore, he began to distance China from the Soviet Union while still preserving the basic commitment to the alliance. Then came the border incidents with India in the summer of 1959, directed against the Soviet's main non-aligned contact, which could have produced a bigger rupture had it not been for Mao's weak domestic position. It was Mao's stronger position at the time of the Sino-Indian War in 1962 that finally produced an unbridgeable gap between the two former communist allies.[48]

The Sino-Soviet split featured ideological disputes which had implications for domestic and foreign policy, particularly with regard to relations with the Western world and non-aligned nations. The latter had implications for straightforward power-political influence especially in Asia, as well as for the development of Cold War policies. The relationship between domestic weakness and the commitment to a cooperative relationship with Moscow was evident in Chinese policy and the progress of the split. For the Soviets, the need to avoid being dragged into a confrontation with the Americans was a key factor in their relationship with Beijing. The Offshore Islands Crises could be seen from the Chinese perspective as originating in the civil war and the fundamental struggle to achieve a united China, to which Chiang presented a threat irrespective of ideological differences.

The role of the Cold War in American policy during the Offshore Islands Crises is clearer. Policy was unequivocally influenced more by Cold War considerations than traditional state goals expressed in terms of vital interests. The second crisis was extremely revealing of American attitudes, which were hard-line in political Cold War terms. There was a determination, for reasons of morale and credibility, to defy the communists, however absurd or trivial the economic and strategic issues at stake. At the same time, it is evident that leading policy-makers in the US were reluctant to risk a major war which might well involve the use of tactical nuclear weapons. Mao was also exercising restraint, despite his desire to confront the Americans, as he was still unprepared for a major military confrontation with the nuclear power of the US. The crisis should be compared to the Cuban Missile Crisis (see Chapter 7, D) for, despite the differences between the two events, the American conceptions of the geostrategic importance of the islands in relation to security provides an interesting example of how the US failed to consider the perceptions of the other side.

One interesting question is the role of national security. Then and now, the concept of US national security being dependent on the preservation of an alien military presence on an island four miles from China, and thousands of miles from the US, has been stated without any sense of the absurd. Nor do Western writers normally attempt any analysis of what might constitute Chinese national security by a comparison based on similar criteria. What can be stated, very simply, in terms of understanding the Cold War is that the islands, which the Americans were reluctantly prepared to defend with nuclear weapons, had no military or strategic significance. Their significance was as symbols representing the preservation of a political and ideological position that was under challenge. The particular policies followed by the US, on the basis of this general perception, required the preservation of the nationalists' position and their determination to return to the mainland. The irony was in providing them with support, while persuading them not to act. It is worth speculating as to whether, subconsciously or not, the development of the link to the preservation of the US position in Asia and the Western Pacific was to justify the importance attached to the islands' symbolism or whether it produced it.

D. The Cuban Missile Crisis

Origins

The crisis that resulted from Khrushchev's decision secretly to install intermediate and medium-range nuclear missiles in Cuba in 1962 has frequently been portrayed as the only time that the world stood on the 'brink' of a nuclear war between the superpowers. The latest research has tended to downplay the risk of war, but the crisis continues to engender controversy, despite detailed records of the American decision-making process becoming available. Explanations of why Khrushchev decided to risk the deployment of surface-to-surface missiles that could threaten cities in most of the US have varied, while many in America have retained a mix of outrage and incomprehension. Some analysts have located Khrushchev's motives in the situation in Cuba, where the Castro regime (see Box 7.1) appeared to be under threat from an American determination to bring it down by covert means, or even by an invasion. Others have seen Khrushchev's motives stemming from his penchant for bullying and intimidation, and his perception of Kennedy as a weak president of whom he could take advantage. A third explanation stems not from the local or the international situation, but from the domestic situation in the Soviet Union, which may have forced Khrushchev to be more adventurous in order to appease domestic critics. None of the interpretations are mutually exclusive and all may have acted as influences on the Soviet leader.

The first idea, that Khrushchev was concerned about the threat to Castro, is undoubtedly true to some extent. As the only country to have turned to communism in this period, Castro's symbolic importance to the credibility of the communist world was considerable and Khrushchev could ill afford the deposition of the Cuban leader. The damage to the Soviet claim to leadership of the alleged progressive socialist countries would be great, particularly as this was under threat from communist China in the early 1960s. Moreover, Khrushchev knew that the CIA was hatching a number of plots to take Castro's life and may well have been aware of US plans (unapproved) for an invasion of the island. However, if the Soviet leader was merely concerned with the defence of the Cuban revolution, it is difficult to see why medium-range and intermediate-range ballistic missiles (MRBMs and IRBMs) served a better defence than tactical nuclear weapons or even conventional forces.

The military/strategic value of these weapons remains a matter of dispute, as it did at the time when the Executive Committee (Ex Comm) was established to advise President Kennedy on how best to respond to the installation of the missiles. The American military saw them as giving the Soviets an important advantage, which changed the strategic balance in their favour. The Secretary of Defence, Robert McNamara, believed they had no real effect on the strategic balance, but gave the Soviets the appearance of a significant gain, a view which the President seemed largely to share. It is likely that Khrushchev was attracted by the idea of appearing to gain greater military strength relative to the US, particularly as he was desperately concerned to cover up the military and economic weakness of the USSR. Such things were crucial in terms of convincing the rest of the world that the Soviets, as demonstrated by the success of Sputnik, were in fact outstripping the US because of the superiority of socialism. Khrushchev was particularly concerned about apparent Soviet weakness in nuclear terms and the reality was less important than its perception. This was particularly the case for those Americans who had been arguing with the Democrats, in the 1960 election, that there was a 'missile gap' encapsulating Soviet superiority. There was, indeed, an enormous missile gap, but one in favour of the US, which was duly indicated by the U-2 spy flights and finally revealed by the Assistant Secretary of Defence, Roswell Gilpatric, in August 1961.

Khrushchev was almost certainly embarrassed by this revelation, even though it was done in a relatively unobtrusive manner. From his perspective, not only was it bad Cold War news for the world to learn how far the Soviet Union was behind America in missile production, but the Soviet leader was under considerable domestic pressure. Those who wanted a more hard-line assertive policy towards the West, which was certainly the line being taken by the Chinese, were keen to increase military expenditure and were generally unhappy about the adoption of peaceful coexistence with the West. In addition, Khrushchev, rather like Mikhail Gorbachev twenty-five years later, was keen to restructure the ailing Soviet economy, particularly the agricultural sector, by reducing military expenditure. His hope had been that by using Berlin as a pressure point on the West, he could gain concessions, which would be regarded as Soviet achievements and a justification for his foreign policy. Unfortunately, his Berlin policy had led to the passing of two Soviet deadlines without changes in the status quo in Berlin or in the position of East Germany.

In these circumstances, there was a desperate need for a successful Soviet initiative, which would silence domestic critics by enhancing the Soviet position as a great world power and leader of the communist movement. The temptation of attempting to score a nuclear success over the Americans was therefore enormous, even if it was more apparent than real. Moreover, Khrushchev could justify his Cuban policy by the fact that the Americans had similar, Jupiter missiles in position right on the Soviet doorstep in Turkey. On these grounds, it might have been reasonable to conclude that the Americans would find it hard to take a strong line in opposition to the arrivals of missiles in Cuba.

And then there was the idea of Kennedy as a weak and uncertain president lacking in experience and guile. Such perceptions could have been based on Kennedy's handling of the Bay of Pigs Crisis in 1961 (see Chapter 6, C), just months after he took office. Subsequently, Kennedy had seemed intimidated by Khrushchev at their summit meeting in Vienna in June 1961 and, rather than give unconditional support to the anti-communist forces engaged in a civil war in Laos, had sought a compromise. Why therefore should the American president react by confronting the Soviets over nuclear weapons in Cuba? After all, when, in July 1960, Khrushchev had spoken of Soviet missiles perhaps one day being used to defend Cuba, he had received no response, unlike over Berlin, where the US had always made its position clear.

The Crisis

The crisis began in earnest on 16 October 1962 when Kennedy and his advisers first saw U-2 pictures of Soviet missile sites on Cuba that had been taken two days before. However, the immediate origins of the crisis and the explanation of the installation's impact on the Americans goes back to April 1962, the date when Khrushchev decided on their deployment. The deployment was not only to be done in secret, but the Americans were subsequently lied to about Soviet intentions, which was naturally disturbing to the Kennedy administration. What made the situation worse were the leaks about the concerns of some, like the CIA director, John McCone, that produced a series of questions and accusations regarding the role of the Soviets in Cuba. It was only two days before the President examined the photos of the site that McGeorge Bundy had asserted that there was no likelihood of the Soviets acquiring a major offensive capability in Cuba. This was the last statement by the administration based on Khrushchev's denying the Soviets had any intention to install surface-to-surface missiles and equip Cuba as an offensive base, which the President had warned against.

When the reality was revealed, whatever US assessments of the strategic or symbolic importance, the sense of resentment was enhanced by an awareness of Khrushchev's deception. Unsurprisingly, Kennedy's initial reaction was along the lines that the US would have to do something in response. The determination to take some action was reinforced by Kennedy's sense of his own domestic position, and the belief that he was vulnerable to accusations of weakness in terms of anti-communism and American defences. The President, from the start, was also convinced that the crisis was connected to the situation in Berlin, where the Soviets held the military cards and could well be using the missiles in Cuba as a further means of putting pressure on the Americans in Berlin. At all events, the question now was what kind of response the US should make.

The essential requirement of any action was that it would lead to the removal of the missiles, even though Kennedy and McNamara believed their presence did not alter the strategic nuclear balance. One option was an air strike to take out the missiles, but the US air force would not guarantee 100 per cent success and this raised the question of whether the missiles had nuclear warheads in place. In the event, we now know that they *did* and such warheads could in fact have been fired at US cities. Decision-makers at the time, some of whom changed their minds over the days, were not, of course, to know this. Other military options were a nuclear attack on, or a full-scale invasion of, Cuba. Those members of the Ex Comm who had been in power during the days when the US enjoyed a nuclear monopoly tended to believe that the nuclear advantage held by the Americans in 1962 would enable them to get their demands met for the withdrawal of the weapons. Yet, if the Soviets refused, then some form of military action seemed inevitable. It was Robert McNamara on 18 October who came up with the idea of a quarantine on further Soviet shipments to Cuba, as a means of exerting pressure for the removal of the missiles.

Such action would have no basis in international law, but it would place the Soviets in a difficult position, where they might have to be the first to use force to beat the naval quarantine. When the first Ex Comm vote was taken, on 18 October, eleven members were in favour of the quarantine option, while six voted for an air strike. Three days later opinion had hardened, with nine members in favour of the air attack and only six for quarantine. By then, however, Kennedy had given up on the idea of an air strike, and when he addressed the American people on 22 October, it was to tell them that in order to halt the offensive military preparations in Cuba he had ordered a strict quarantine on the shipment of military equipment there. If necessary, further military action would be taken and the US armed forces had been instructed to prepare for any eventuality. He would regard any military attack on the US from Cuba as an attack by the Soviet Union, requiring a full retaliatory strike. The quarantine would begin on the morning of 24 October.

The US response was essentially dictated by the need not to look weak in the face of Khrushchev's challenge to the status quo in the western hemisphere. Accepting the missiles as a fait accompli would give the impression of growing Soviet strength and increasing American vulnerability, although, as Kennedy had said, it mattered little whether nuclear warheads were fired on the US from 50 or 500 miles. For domestic and Cold War reasons, Kennedy *had* to act. The method he initially chose was the most reasoned and restrained of the ones available to him. Khrushchev initially responded by denouncing the interference with vessels on the high seas as unjustified, and an action which constituted a threat to peace, but Kennedy had wrested the initiative away from the Soviet leader. When the crunch came, some Soviet ships stopped and one tanker carrying a non-military cargo was allowed through. However, the following morning Kennedy received another message from Khrushchev, accusing the President of banditry and pushing mankind to the brink of nuclear war. In it, he stated that the Soviet government could not give instructions to the captains of Soviet vessels to obey the instructions of American ships blockading Cuba.

As Khrushchev continued to refuse concessions on the missiles, the American press published a column by the journalist Walter Lippmann, in effect suggesting a trade-off between Soviet missiles in Cuba and American missiles in Turkey. Such a deal, while eminently sensible, had the disadvantage of appearing to give concessions to the Soviets. On the other hand, as Kennedy realized, to start a nuclear war for the sake of preserving some obsolete missiles in Turkey might not be the most popular action either. The world continued to wait, as ships bound for Cuba were intercepted on 26 October and the US navy forced six Soviet submarines to the surface, but there were no signs of the missiles being removed from Cuba. On 27 October, Kennedy received another letter from Khrushchev, in which the Soviet leader accused the US of threatening him with war, which he believed could only be done by lunatics or suicides. More importantly, Khrushchev suggested that if the US would guarantee not to invade Cuba and recall its navy, the question of armaments would disappear because if there was no threat, they would simply be a burden to maintain. Almost immediately, after the contents had been digested by the Ex Comm the White House received news of another letter from Khrushchev, this time a public one. The Soviet leader was now offering a deal: he would remove the missiles from Cuba if the US did the same for those in Turkey and pledged not to invade Cuba.

The US faced a new difficulty because if they accepted the public deal Khrushchev would have gained the removal of the missiles in Turkey. On the other hand, if the deal was rejected what could the US reasonably do if Khrushchev went ahead with developing the missile sites with material already in Cuba? Would it mean that an invasion of Cuba would have to be launched as the Joint Chiefs were suggesting? The President then came to two key decisions. The first was that the US could not invade Cuba to remove missiles that they could have had taken out by agreeing to remove obsolete weapons from Turkey. The second was to follow McGeorge Bundy's suggestion of replying to the first private letter from Khrushchev, rather than to the second public one. In other words, the basis of the public deal would be that the Soviets would remove the missiles if the US gave a guarantee not to invade Cuba. Khrushchev would not have gained anything at the expense of the Americans, but could save face by claiming to have protected Cuba from invasion.

This, in fact, formed the public basis of the agreement, although it was buttressed by a private commitment made to the Soviet ambassador by the President's brother, Attorney-General Robert Kennedy. This involved an assurance that the Jupiter missiles in Turkey would be withdrawn in the near future. Such a commitment could not be part of a public deal because of how it would reflect on the US, which emerged from the crisis having apparently been successful in resisting Khrushchev's brinkmanship. It appeared to have stood firm and prevented any advantages accruing to the Soviets, whether apparent or real. Yet, while Kennedy resisted the options which presented the greater threat to peace, he also engaged in brinkmanship in order to avoid the impression of weakness or conceding any advantage to the Soviets. In terms of credibility and the assertion of US nuclear power in the face of a Soviet challenge, Washington had preserved its superiority and made clear that Khrushchev's intimidation was essentially bluff and bluster.

The risks that were run, and indeed the reasons for running them, have probably both been overstated. At the end of the day, neither leader was likely to have ordered a major nuclear strike for the sake of what were more apparent than actual strategic benefits. Yet there were risks, and not just from those in Washington who were prepared to be more assertive than the President. There was the danger of local commanders seizing the initiative and dragging their superiors into a conflict they would have wanted at all costs to avoid. Not only did the US navy clash with the Soviets, but a local commander in Cuba, acting on his own authority, shot down an American U-2 on 25 October. In addition, General Tommy Power, the head of the Strategic Air Command, placed his forces on DEFCON 2 and prepared for immediate action without consulting the White House. The flaws in the decision-making process and the chain of command could have led to a nuclear clash because of the level of brinkmanship, and in spite of the politicians' desire to avoid any such conflict.

Consequences

The consequences of the Cuban Missile Crisis were felt at both local and international levels and had a profound impact on the future nature of the Cold War. The impression that a catastrophe had only just been avoided made the need to prevent the Cold War turning into a hot one all the more urgent. Arguably, the Cuban Missile Crisis made the US accept, for the first time, that no longer should American foreign policy aim at the eventual removal of the USSR, or even seek to prevent the Soviets being fully accepted as a great power. It was now more a question of learning to cope with a world in which the US was unable to exercise hegemony, adapting to a world in which capitalism had to coexist with communism. Peaceful coexistence certainly now meant more to both Moscow and Washington and efforts were made, like the hot-line communications link between the Kremlin and the White House, to prevent any more direct confrontations in which it was difficult for either side to back down. None of this made the winning of hearts and minds in the less developed world any less important, but now the battles had to be fought more carefully. For the Americans, there was a hope that in the future such less developed world confrontations could eventually be removed if the status quo was accepted by the communists, but this was never likely, given that the status quo would only serve to maintain American hegemony.

As to the practical reasons for the fears provoked by the Cuban Missile Crisis, namely the existence of growing numbers of nuclear weapons, it is tempting to argue that, after 1962, there began the process to control and limit them starting with the Test Ban Treaty in 1963 (see Chapter 9, A) and leading via the 1968 Non-Proliferation Treaty to SALT 1 in 1972 (see Chapter 12, B). However, other lessons were undoubtedly drawn at the time. For the Americans, the crisis reinforced the value of nuclear superiority, whereas for the Soviets, the need to achieve nuclear parity became a sine qua non of equality with the Americans, in order to avoid another humiliating climb-down. Thus, while, in the early 1960s, it was the Americans that led the way in producing more armaments, later in the decade the Soviets outpaced them in this field. More weapons, rather than fewer, remained the order of the day, even if this could be justified in the name of deterrence, which must at best remain questionable. Whether this was responsible for the disastrous long-term decline of the already weak Soviet economy is a moot point. More immediately, Khrushchev's position within the Soviet Communist Party and government was weakened, although his removal from power would take another two years and follow the Chinese acquisition of nuclear weapons.

With regard to the local situation, the effect was not what the Americans would have desired. In effect, they had placed the Cold War goal of appearing more powerful than the Soviet Union on a nuclear issue, above the Cold War goal of preventing the spread of left-wing revolutionary ideas in the western hemisphere. By guaranteeing not to remove Castro by overt means, they had limited their ability to cut off the source of communist propaganda and assistance. Of course, that did not stop some of the covert efforts to remove Castro under the Mongoose programme, but it could no longer be backed up with any overt involvement of US forces. As a result, while Castro was furious with Moscow for agreeing to the removal of the weapons, he probably emerged slightly more secure as a result.

BOX 7.2

Biography: Fidel Castro (1926–2016)

Castro was born in Biran in 1926. He went on to be educated at a Jesuit school and completed his legal studies at the University of Havana. Graduating with a law degree in 1950 he began work with the poor. In 1953, Castro attempted to overthrow the Cuban dictator, Batista. The attempt failed and Castro was imprisoned but his movement became known as the 26th of July Movement and achieved lasting recognition. Upon his release in 1955, Castro organized more guerrilla campaigns and after another unsuccessful revolt in 1956, Castro and his men fled into the Sierra Maestra mountains and began a three-year-long guerrilla campaign. In 1959, Castro finally overthrew Batista and became the leader of a socialist government. The US was quick to enforce economic sanctions and also instigated the Bay of Pigs invasion. This merely reinforced Castro's desire to look to the Soviet Union for help and support. Cuba's dependence on the Soviet Union eventually led to the Cuban Missile Crisis, as Khrushchev was able to install missile bases on Cuba. Castro later created a new Constitution in which he took the role of president and secretary general of the Communist Party, as well as commander-in-chief of the army. Castro refused to liberalize Cuban society and criticized the reforms of Mikhail Gorbachev. This resulted in an increasingly isolated position for Cuba in the international community, but the regime survived, nonetheless. Increasingly beset by illness, Fidel handed power over to his brother and fellow revolutionary, Raul, in 2009.

Whether the changes after the Cuban Missile Crisis were sufficient to warrant describing 1962 as the end of the first Cold War remains contentious, but the relations between the two superpowers certainly entered a new phase. Even if the idea of peaceful coexistence was now generally accepted within the US, the aftermath of the crisis was not the first time that the US and USSR can be regarded as having made an effort to improve relations. Nor was it the time when consideration was first given to the advantages of peaceful coexistence. The issue now was whether the existence of nuclear weapons, combined with the realization of the dangers of unrestricted competition, meant that new approaches to the Cold War *had* to be adopted. If so, these would have to be based on a greater acceptance of the other side as a power with whom coexistence was desirable.

Visit the online resources that accompany this book to test your understanding and take your learning further: www.oup.com/he/young-kent3e

NOTES

1. Gregory Mitrovich, *Undermining the Kremlin. America's Policy to Subvert the Soviet Bloc, 1947–1956* (Cornell University Press, Ithaca, 2000), 123, 127.
2. Foreign Relations of the US (FRUS), 1952–4, II, Pt II (Dept of State, Washington, DC, 1979), Record of Discussion at NSC Special Meeting, 31 March 1953, 266–7.
3. Former Head of the Psychology Strategy Board until its dissolution in September 1953 and a member of the Operations Coordinating Board.
4. Gregory Mitrovich, *Undermining the Kremlin. America's Policy to Subvert the Soviet Bloc, 1947–1956* (Cornell University Press, Ithaca, 2000), 128–9, 133.
5. Ibid., 134–40.
6. Mitrovich points out that this was not apparent from the sanitized version of the Task Force reports declassified in 1991 but emerged in a synopsis of the reports declassified in 1996.

7. US National Archives, Dept. of State Records Lot Files 66 D 148. Records pertaining to State Dept. participation in OCB and NSC 1947–63, box 129. Report by Task Force C 16 July 1953. Cited in Scott Lucas, *Freedom's War: The US Crusade against the Soviet Union 1945–1956* (Manchester University Press, Manchester, 1999), 179; Gregory Mitrovich, *Undermining the Kremlin. America's Policy to Subvert the Soviet Bloc, 1947–1956* (Cornell University Press, Ithaca, 2000), 141–2.
8. FRUS, 1952–4, II, Pt II (Dept of State, Washington, DC, 1979) NSC 162/2, 30 September 1953, 491–514.
9. Ibid.
10. James Bamford, *Body of Secrets* (Arrow, London, 2002), 35–8.
11. Scott Lucas, *Freedom's War: The US Crusade against the Soviet Union 1945–1956* (Manchester University Press, Manchester, 1999), 190.
12. Blake was an SIS agent whom the Soviets recruited in 1951 after the dismissal of the notorious spy Kim Philby. Blake betrayed Western agents in the Eastern bloc and alerted the Soviets to the Berlin tunnel.
13. Christopher Andrew and Vasili Mitrokhin, *The Mitrokhin Archive* (Allen Lane, Penguin Press, London, 1995), 521; David E. Murphy, Sergai A. Kondrashev, and George Bailey, *Battleground Berlin* (Yale University Press, New Haven, 1997), Ch. 11.
14. FRUS, 1952–4, II, Pt II (Dept. of State, Washington, DC, 1979) NSC 5440, 13 December 1954, 806–22.
15. Gregory Mitrovich, *Undermining the Kremlin. America's Policy to Subvert the Soviet Bloc, 1947–1956* (Cornell University Press, Ithaca, 2000), 147.
16. FRUS, 1952–4, II, Pt II (Dept. of State, Washington, DC, 1979) NSC 5440, 13 December 1954, 806–22.
17. Report on US Policy for the Exploitation of Soviet Vulnerabilities in Box 18 of the Papers of the Office of the Special Assistant for National Security Affairs, NSC Series 1952–61, Briefing Notes Subseries, White House Office Files, Dwight D. Eisenhower Library. Cited in Gregory Mitrovich, *Undermining the Kremlin. America's Policy to Subvert the Soviet Bloc, 1947–1956* (Cornell University Press, Ithaca, 2000), 161.
18. FRUS, 1952–4, II, Pt II (Dept. of State, Washington, DC, 1979), Memo by the JCS, 17 December 1954, 828–30.
19. Ibid.
20. FRUS, 1955–7, vol. XIX (Dept. of State, Washington, DC, 1985), NSC 5501, 7 January 1955, 24–9, emphasis added.
21. David G. Coleman, 'Eisenhower and the Berlin Problem 1953–54', *Journal of Cold War Studies*, 2 (2000), 13–17.
22. Vladislav Zubok and Constantine Pleshakov, *Inside the Kremlin's Cold War from Stalin to Khrushchev* (Harvard University Press, Cambridge, 1996), 195.
23. David G. Coleman, 'Eisenhower and the Berlin Problem 1953–54', *Journal of Cold War Studies*, 2 (2000), 25, 32, citing NSC 5401, 29 December 1954.
24. Marc Trachtenberg, *A Constructed Peace. The Making of the European Settlement 1945–1963* (Princeton University Press, Princeton, 1999), 253.
25. Wilfred Loth, *Overcoming the Cold War* (Palgrave Macmillan, Basingstoke, 2002), 47–50; Vladislav Zubok and Constantine Pleshakov, *Inside the Kremlin's Cold War from Stalin to Khrushchev* (Harvard University Press, Cambridge, 1996), 194–8.
26. John Lewis Gaddis, *We Now Know. Rethinking Cold War History* (Clarendon Press, New York, 1997), 143–4.
27. Michael R. Beschloss, *Kennedy v Khrushchev: The Crisis Years 1960–63* (Faber & Faber, Boston, 1991), 216, 221, 224.
28. Ibid.
29. Wilfred Loth, *Overcoming the Cold War* (Palgrave Macmillan, Basingstoke, 2002), 60–1.
30. Michael R. Beschloss, *Kennedy v Khrushchev: The Crisis Years 1960–63* (Faber & Faber, Boston, 1991), 223.
31. David E. Murphy, Sergei A. Kondrashev, and George Bailey, *Battleground Berlin CIA v. KGB in the Cold War* (Yale University Press, New Haven, 1997), 371–3; Vladislav Zubok and Constantine Pleshakov, *Inside the Kremlin's Cold War from Stalin to Khrushchev* (Harvard University Press, Cambridge, 1996), 253–5.

32. Cited in Gong Li, 'Tension across the Taiwan Strait in the 1950s: Chinese Strategy and Tactics', in Robert S. Ross and Jiang Changbin (eds), *Re-Examining the Cold War. US–China Diplomacy 1954–1973* (Harvard University Press, Cambridge, 2001), 142.

33. Zhang Bajia, 'The Changing International Scene and Chinese Policy towards the United States, 1954–1970', in Robert S. Ross and Jiang Changbin (eds), *Re-Examining the Cold War. US–China Diplomacy 1954–1973* (Harvard University Press, Cambridge, 2001), 50.

34. Ronald W. Pruessen, 'Over the Volcano. The United States and the Taiwan Strait Crisis, 1954–1955', in Robert S. Ross and Jiang Changbin (eds), *Re-Examining the Cold War. US–China Diplomacy 1954–1973* (Harvard University Press, Cambridge, 2001), 80; Stephen E. Ambrose, *Eisenhower the President 1952–1969* (Allen & Unwin, London, 1984), 239.

35. Cited in Stephen E. Ambrose, *Eisenhower the President 1952–1969* (Allen & Unwin, London, 1984), 244.

36. Ronald W. Pruessen, 'Over the Volcano. The United States and the Taiwan Strait Crisis, 1954–1955', in Robert S. Ross and Jiang Changbin (eds), *Re-Examining the Cold War. US–China Diplomacy 1954–1973* (Harvard University Press, Cambridge, 2001), 94–7.

37. Stephen E. Ambrose, *Eisenhower the President 1952–1969* (Allen & Unwin, London, 1984), 231.

38. Ibid., 213.

39. Gong Li, 'Tension across the Taiwan Strait in the 1950s: Chinese Strategy and Tactics', in Robert S. Ross and Jiang Changbin (eds), *Re-Examining the Cold War. US–China Diplomacy 1954–1973* (Harvard University Press, Cambridge, 2001), 148–51; Stephen E. Ambrose, *Eisenhower the President 1952–1969* (Allen & Unwin, London, 1984, 231.

40. Gong Li, 'Tension across the Taiwan Strait in the 1950s: Chinese Strategy and Tactics', in Robert S. Ross and Jiang Changbin (eds), *Re-Examining the Cold War. US–China Diplomacy 1954–1973* (Harvard University Press, Cambridge, 2001), 151–6.

41. Zhang Bajia, 'The Changing International Scene and Chinese Policy towards the United States, 1954–1970', in Robert S. Ross and Jiang Changbin (eds), *Re-Examining the Cold War. US–China Diplomacy 1954–1973* (Harvard University Press, Cambridge, 2001), 50–2.

42. Odd Arne Westad, in the Introduction to Odd Arne Westad (ed.), *Brothers in Arms: The Rise and Fall of the Sino-Soviet Alliance 1945–1963* (Stanford University Press, Stanford, 1998), 18–20.

43. Robert Accinelli, '"A Thorn in the Side of Peace": The Eisenhower Administration and the 1958 Offshore Islands Crisis', in Robert S. Ross and Jiang Changbin (eds), *Re-Examining the Cold War. US–China Diplomacy 1954–1973* (Harvard University Press, Cambridge, 2001), 112.

44. Odd Arne Westad, 'The Sino-Soviet Alliance and the United States', in Odd Arne Westad (ed.), *Brothers in Arms: The Rise and Fall of the Sino-Soviet Alliance 1945–1963* (Stanford University Press, Stanford, 1998), 176.

45. Robert Accinelli, '"A Thorn in the Side of Peace": The Eisenhower Administration and the 1958 Offshore Islands Crisis', in Robert S. Ross and Jiang Changbin (eds), *Re-Examining the Cold War. US–China Diplomacy 1954–1973* (Harvard University Press, Cambridge, 2001), 114, 118.

46. Ibid., 120–8.

47. Sun Yat-sen was the first Chinese nationalist leader, who died in 1925 and is often referred to as the father of modern China.

48. Odd Arne Westad (ed.), *Brothers in Arms: The Rise and Fall of the Sino-Soviet Alliance 1945–1963* (Stanford University Press, Stanford, 1998), 22, 28.

8

Collapsing Empires: The Cold War Battle for Hearts and Minds, 1953–63

Chapter contents

A. The End of the French Empire

The war between the French and the Vietnamese nationalists led by the communist Ho Chi Minh became a long and bloody affair, which received substantial American financial backing from May 1950. Despite US aid, it ended with the French defeat at Dien Bien Phu in May 1954. The Geneva Conference, which took place at the same time, saw agreement on the neutralization of an independent Laos and Cambodia, while Vietnam was divided in two along the seventeenth parallel, with French forces regrouping in the South before their eventual withdrawal and a communist government being set up in the North under Ho. The Americans were unhappy about the partial loss of a former French possession to communism. The division between North and South was not meant to last: under the terms of Geneva, all-Vietnamese elections were meant to reunite the country within two years. Such elections, however, were never held, mainly because their outcome was mostly likely to result in a victory for Ho. Instead, as French power disintegrated, Washington backed the South Vietnamese government of Ngo Dinh Diem in its refusal to deal with the North and became involved in a new and drawn-out post-colonial conflict.

In Africa, the French approached their empire after the Second World War in fundamentally different ways from the British. Black Africa had been the only part of the empire loyal to the 'true' French republic, and had enabled de Gaulle and the Free French to emerge as an important source of opposition to the collaborators in Vichy. Empire and its preservation was thus totally tied up with French greatness and world power status. Moreover, unlike in Britain, where those on the Left were thinking about which colonies might follow the Dominions, the Popular Front government in Paris during the 1930s saw reforms, not as leading the empire to self-government, but tying it closer to metropolitan France. This signified what was soon an important fact of French political life in the 1940s: that those on the Left as well as the Right were committed to an imperial future. Yet, by the early 1950s the French Union had ceased to attract Africans by its offer of associating them with the exercise of power in metropolitan France (see Chapter 3, B). The issue was thus becoming whether the French Union would survive, or whether and under what conditions the French would accept a transfer of power in Africa.

The Loss of French Indo-China and the Start of American Involvement in Vietnam

Ngo Dinh Diem was appointed prime minister of South Vietnam by the French-selected head of state, Emperor Bao Dai, in June 1954, when the days of French rule were numbered. Born in 1901, the son of a mandarin official, Diem had already served as a regional governor and, in 1932–3, as a government minister. But then he had retired to private life, exasperated by France's failure to reform its methods of colonial rule. Diem became increasingly reclusive but, in 1945–6, his anti-communist convictions were hardened when he was imprisoned for a time by the Viet Minh. In 1950 he went into exile, living for some time in the US, where his pious Catholicism helped him establish links with, among others, the Kennedy family. By late 1954 the US government, unhappy with the prospect of an all-communist Vietnam, saw Diem as a potential saviour. In particular, the Central Intelligence Agency (CIA) counter-insurgency expert, Edward G. Lansdale, fresh from defeating a rebellion by the communist 'Hukbalahup' movement in the Philippines, took it upon himself to groom Diem as an ally, while also providing the South with advice on covert military operations. Diem appealed to Americans, because his background made him both anti-French and anti-communist, so that he could pose as a defender of South Vietnamese independence from both colonial rule and Marxism-Leninism. The only serious doubt about him concerned his ability to face up to dissident elements. But, in March–May 1955, aided by Lansdale, he proved his worth on this front by ruthlessly securing control of Saigon, driving out armed groups who were opposed to him. In October 1955 he was able to depose Bao Dai and establish a republic, being approved as president by a 98 per cent majority in a rigged poll. To US satisfaction, he also refused to prepare for all-Vietnamese elections on the grounds that his government had not been party to the Geneva Accords.

Diem's overwhelming triumph in the 1955 referendum disguised the fact that South Vietnam was a complex society, in which his support was severely restricted, a legacy partly of French colonial tactics of 'divide and rule'. His military victory in May 1955 was essentially over three groups, each with its own private army: two were Buddhist sects, the Hoa Hao and the Cao Dai; the other—and the most serious threat—was a criminal group, the Binh Xuyen, who effectively ran the police force in the capital, Saigon. The victory gave Diem some respite from serious opposition, as did the withdrawal of the last French troops in September 1956. A 'mixture of monk and mandarin, he was honest, courageous and fervent in his fidelity to Vietnam's national cause' but he was also 'distrustful of everyone outside his family, he declined to delegate authority, nor was he able to build a constituency … beyond his fellow Catholics'.[1] Buddhist opposition to his Catholic-dominated regime continued and even intensified, as Northern Catholics fled to the South in the wake of Geneva and were shown favouritism in terms of landholdings and official appointments. Catholics were always a minority in the country, numbering up to one-and-a-half million, out of a total population of thirteen million, in the mid-1950s, and they were identified by many with French colonial rule. Other groups in the country, particularly ethnic minorities such as the Chinese, Cambodians, and Montagnards (the last living in the sparsely populated highland areas) were also alienated, in their case by Diem's practice of favouring the majority Viets. Neither did the President try to tackle the problems of government corruption, grasping landlords, and peasant debt, which had become widespread. Instead, as with religious and ethnic issues, he tended to compound problems, by relying on rich landlords (who controlled about three-quarters of the land) and government officials for support. In 1957 Lansdale left South Vietnam, disappointed that Diem had failed to reform the country on liberal democratic lines, which the US would have welcomed. Instead the President, personally aloof from his people, insisted on an authoritarian form of rule, appointed members of his family to leading positions, and especially relied for advice, not on American representatives, but his corrupt brother Nhu, who dreamt up the vague doctrine of 'personalism' as justification for a system dominated by one individual.

Despite the weaknesses of his regime, Diem seemed to succeed until 1959 in limiting the threat from the communist Viet Minh, and South Vietnam's position was far from hopeless. His determined campaign after 1956 to arrest or execute any suspected communists helped reduce their active numbers markedly, as well as claiming thousands of innocent lives. Alongside the defeat of the 'Huks' in the Philippines (1946–54) and of the Malayan communists (1948–60), South Vietnam seemed part of a pattern of Western victories against leftist subversion in South-East Asia. However, Diem never succeeded in completely destroying the Viet Minh and neither was the Vietnam situation without costs for the US, even if they avoided a direct commitment of troops there.

The Eisenhower administration had provided about $1 billion worth of military aid to South Vietnam by 1961, as well as a lesser amount of economic assistance, and the first American casualties occurred in July 1959, when two military advisers were killed. Furthermore, there were already signs that American involvement carried its own problems: Diem became ever more reliant on US money, the circulation of which created inflationary pressures and oiled the wheels of corruption among officials. The Army of the Republic of Vietnam (ARVN) was resentful of the patronizing and bullying approach of many Americans, and US advice took the form, not of anti-insurgency expertise (which was what was needed), but of help in creating a 150,000-strong conventional army that could meet an all-out North Vietnamese invasion (which never came). The ARVN was in any case poorly led, largely by Catholic officers promoted more for their loyalty to Diem than for ability, and was another element identified in the popular mind with French rule. Neither did its supposed loyalty prevent one group of officers from attempting a coup in November 1960, suggesting that not all was well, even at the heart of Diem's regime. This was doubly worrying because the ARVN was about to face a resuscitated communist campaign, backed by the North.

Ho Chi Minh and North Vietnam, 1954–61

Ho Chi Minh, who had led the Viet Minh to victory over the French, accepted the idea of elections at the 1954 Geneva Conference as the best way to remove French troops from the North. It was in northern Vietnam that the colonial war had been at its most intense, where the physical destruction was greatest, and where he wished to secure control first. But, supported by the USSR and China, he expected that North and South Vietnam would soon be united, especially since it seemed improbable in 1954 that anyone like Diem might emerge who could forge a separate state in the South. Reunification was an economic as well as a political imperative because the North had a higher population, yet the South had the most productive areas for growing the staple food, rice. In 1954–6, therefore, Ho pursued a peaceful strategy for securing the reunification of Vietnam, based on the fulfilment of the Geneva Accords, and concentrated on setting up a classless society and a centralized government in the North. The latter did not prove an easy task, and it was accompanied by considerable violence. He succeeded in collectivizing agriculture, but only by wiping out anyone suspected of being a 'landlord', a process which involved executing or imprisoning tens of thousands of people. Many were not real landlords at all (the real ones had often joined the refugee trail to the South), but fell victim to local feuds or the overenthusiasm of Ho's officials. Another practice was the extensive use of forced labour to help the reconstruction efforts. Small wonder that more than a million people fled to the South in the mid-1950s. In November 1956 such policies had become so unpopular that there was serious peasant unrest in Ho's native province of Nghe An.

The events in Nghe An were salutary in a number of ways: they led Ho's government to backtrack on certain policies, especially collectivization; they created the impression that life in the North was no better (and for some was far worse) than in the South; and they underlined the need to strengthen communist rule in the North before beginning any serious armed campaign to reunite the country, now that it was clear that peaceful reunification was unlikely. In any case, the ability of the Viet Minh to mount such a campaign was limited in 1956. Although they had numbered perhaps 100,000 in the South in 1954, and had controlled large swathes of the countryside, most communists had moved to the North in the wake of the General Accords and those who remained were mainly prepared for self-defence, not major offensive operations. One Viet Minh leader from the South was Ho's deputy, Le Duan, who was increasingly exasperated at the situation. A limited guerrilla war was revived in 1957, mainly marked by assassinations of government officials, but by 1959 there were perhaps as few as 5,000 active Viet Minh in the South, repressed by Diem's secret police and demoralized by the apparent lack of support from the North. There was still widespread sympathy for the communists among the peasantry, to whom they promised land reform, lower taxes, and an end to corrupt officialdom. But such support was latent, not active. Furthermore, despite religious, ethnic, and political opposition to Diem, this too was difficult for the communists to exploit. Buddhists, criminal gangs, and would-be liberals were naturally unsympathetic to Marxism.

Despite this unpromising situation, in January 1959 the 15th plenum of the Vietnamese Communist Party decided to back military action and revolutionary violence in the South, meeting Le Duan's pleas and hoping to expose the weakness of Diem's regime. In part, this was linked to the greater Chinese commitment to support revolutionary movements throughout Indo-China. Little was initially forthcoming in practical terms for the Vietnamese and their 'momentous decision did not lead immediately to war . . . attention was instead directed towards strategic and logistical preparation'.[2] The foundations of a supply route to the South—the 'Ho Chi Minh Trail'—were laid and Viet Minh attacks on local officials, government offices, and the army were intensified, so that some country areas again came under communist rule, especially in the Central Highlands. Only in 1960 did the Chinese begin to back the armed struggle in South Vietnam. One way in which Diem responded was to draw some peasants into fortified 'agrovilles', but these were hated by the peasantry, who were torn from their ancestral villages. In any case, the number of 'agrovilles' was limited: more significant in alienating the peasantry—the bulk of the population—from Diem was his destruction of village autonomy in creating a centralized state. Even the French had respected village rights. By September 1960 the North Vietnamese leadership was convinced that a revolution was in sight in the South, a conviction probably helped by Ho's success in creating a strong, united North Vietnam in the wake of the 1956 troubles. Ho's Politburo now presided over a stable, one-party state, financially supported by both the USSR and China, with a (largely) centrally planned economy that was approaching self-sufficiency. Industrial production was expanding, although from a very narrow base. The communists could also be confident that, in aiming above all at national reunification, they had one cause which appealed to most Vietnamese whilst paradoxically, by promising to respect ethnic minorities, they could win sympathy among the Chinese and Montagnard minorities.

On 20 December 1960 Ho's government finally confirmed the primacy of the armed struggle in the South over consolidation in the North, when it set up the National Liberation Front as a government-in-exile for the South, designed to win the widest possible political sympathy there, including non-communist groups, but under communist leadership. 'After six years of trying to reunify the country through political means alone, the (North Vietnamese leaders) accepted a combination of political and military struggle movements to overthrow the Diem regime.'[3] The NLF quickly expanded its number of recognized sympathizers in the South to over a quarter of a million, although only about 20,000 were Viet Minh activists and even fewer could be termed guerrillas. Also, in February 1961 it formally created a military wing, the People's Liberation Armed Forces, although Northern leaders hoped that it might be possible to undermine Diem and create a coalition government (as a step to communist domination) without a drawn-out, costly conflict. These important developments made Vietnam a challenging situation for the incoming American administration of John F. Kennedy.

Kennedy, the Viet Cong Menace, and the Fall of Diem, 1961–3

Kennedy arrived in office as a critic of the supposed weakness of the Eisenhower regime in the face of the communist menace, keen to resist the 'wars of national liberation' (about which Khrushchev first publicly spoke on 6 January 1961, promising Soviet support and specifically mentioning Vietnam) and already personally allied to his fellow Catholic, Ngo Dinh Diem. Viet Cong activity continued to intensify, and Kennedy immediately came under pressure to increase the 685 military advisers whom Eisenhower had despatched to South Vietnam. Despite the evident discontent with Diem and the genuine desire of Vietnamese nationalists for reunification, it was easy for Americans to see the NLF as a puppet movement of North Vietnam, itself seen as part of a monolithic communist menace which would spread throughout South-East Asia if it was not resisted. The crisis in Laos actually dominated US thinking about South-East Asia in 1961, however, and its peaceful outcome in 1962, when a neutralist coalition was formed, suggested that an armed Vietnamese conflict involving the US was not inevitable. Kennedy, with plenty of problems elsewhere in the world, was warned soon after coming into office in a report by Edward Lansdale about the weaknesses of the anti-communist position in South Vietnam. Diem's failure to reform, together with the unreliability of the ARVN, led the US to follow a dual policy of providing greater military assistance to South Vietnam while trying to win Diem over to the wisdom of change. Discussions of military requests to send US combat troops led to Kennedy opposing any mention of the possibility of such a policy and to subsequent speculation that he would never have got embroiled in the later conflict. The aim was to contain the communists militarily in the short term, while broadening political support for the South's government in the long term. By such means, Kennedy apparently hoped to prevent any communist advance without the need for direct US involvement, a policy which essentially built on Eisenhower's, albeit with a greater commitment of advisers and money.

By the end of 1961 there were 3,200 US military advisers in Vietnam and the Defence Department had effectively replaced the State Department as the prime factor in policy-making on Vietnam. A number of senior officials in the administration, including Walt Rostow (Deputy National Security Adviser) were becoming sympathetic to a deployment of American combat troops. Although Kennedy always ruled out the combat option, his support for Diem remained undiminished, despite the latter's continued failure to carry out land reform or legalize opposition groups. By late 1963 US personnel in South Vietnam had climbed to 16,000. The 1961 Bay of Pigs fiasco and the need to compromise on Laos, may have strengthened the desire to 'win' in Vietnam and such alternatives as negotiation with the communists, or making further aid to Diem conditional on reform were not properly considered. Arguably, the Americans were already becoming trapped in a situation where their anti-communism tied them to an unpopular regime fighting an unwinnable war. Even those who feared an escalation of the US commitment, like George Ball, the under-secretary of state, did not speak out strongly at this time. In any case, during 1962 over-optimistic reports from US representatives in Vietnam created the impression that the 'Viet Cong' (as the communists were now described by the Saigon government and the Americans) were being contained.

One development, backed by the US at this time and inspired by British policy against communists in Malaya, was the US 'strategic hamlets' programme which, like Diem's 'agrovilles', tried to move peasants away from communist influence. The programme at least showed a recognition of the need for a proper counter-insurgency programme, winning the peasantry to the government side, but it was carried out too hastily and proved as unpopular with the peasants as had the 'agrovilles', although its failure took some time to become evident. Even the celebrated battle of Ap Bac in January 1963, when 1,400 heavily armed ARVN troops were held at bay by about 350 Viet Cong, failed to destroy American optimism about the war and in 1963 Kennedy was hopeful that the US presence in Vietnam might soon be reduced. The weaknesses of Diem's position—his reliance on repression rather than reform, an ill-disciplined, badly led army and widespread alienation of the countryside—were not yet fully exposed by a Viet Cong movement which still numbered only several thousand guerrillas. Nor was the extent and nature of the South Vietnamese support for the communist-led resistance movement perceived accurately by American leaders, preoccupied as they were with communism as the explanation for anti-Western revolts.

US confidence in Diem was finally, fatally, questioned in mid-1963 not by any communist action but by dissatisfaction among the Buddhist majority. There were widespread disturbances in May following a new law which gave the national flag precedence over all other symbols, even religious banners carried during celebrations. Then, on 11 June 1963, in front of Saigon press cameras, one Buddhist priest burnt himself to death as a protest against Diem. Several similar cases followed, increasing doubts about Diem's leadership among the American media and further emphasizing his failure to reform. The situation was made worse by remarks from his sister-in-law, Madam Nhu, that she was quite happy to have monks 'barbecue' themselves. By mid-August, Diem felt so threatened that he introduced martial law, as well as raiding Buddhist pagodas in key cities, imprisoning hundreds. The US was shocked and, in Washington, the issue of replacing Diem was seriously considered. There was a major problem with any such step: he had no obvious successor. But, by late October his opponents in the army were confident that the US government would welcome his replacement. Certainly, the American ambassador, Henry Cabot Lodge, did not discourage this belief and on 1 November 1963 after trying to flee, Diem was captured by an army unit and murdered, along with the much despised Nhu. Kennedy, who had known that a coup was possible, but who did not want Diem dead, was stunned by the news.

Only three weeks later Kennedy too was assassinated, leaving the problems of South Vietnam to be tackled by his successor, Lyndon Johnson. The question of what Kennedy would have done about Vietnam, had he lived, is one which continues to exercise historians. Some are sympathetic. William Post, for example, believes that the President 'would not have bombed North Vietnam, and would not have committed US ground troops' in the way Johnson later did. But even this claim is qualified by the admission that there was an 'absence of clear direction to Kennedy's policy'.[4] The President had spoken privately on several occasions of his desire to reduce US personnel levels in South Vietnam; yet, on the very day he died, he was planning to give an address which confirmed his commitment to fighting communism in South-East Asia. The contradiction is probably best explained by Gary Hess, who argues that by late 1963 Kennedy 'was thinking on two levels: the commitment to South-Vietnam was integral to US national security, but the price of upholding it seemed less controllable'.[5] He did not live long enough to focus upon, or resolve this dilemma and, as another study of Kennedy's policy concludes, he 'bequeathed to Johnson a failing counter-insurgency programme and a deepened commitment to the war in South Vietnam'.[6] From this commitment Johnson would find no easy escape.

The Collapse of French Rule in Morocco and Tunisia

In North Africa, as in Indo-China, the French faced a number of nationalist movements that grew in strength after 1945 and were causing major problems by 1953–4. The existence of French settlers created additional political problems in dealing with them, even for those ministers who came to accept the idea of self-government, if not independence. The region, particularly Algeria, had significant numbers of French settlers along the coastal plain, many of whom were competing for menial jobs with the local population. In addition, while Morocco and Tunisia had originally been French protectorates that were the responsibility of the Quai d'Orsay (the French foreign ministry), Algeria provided a much bigger constitutional and emotive problem. Technically part of metropolitan France, like French *départements* it was the responsibility of the French Ministry of the Interior. This produced, amongst certain French elites, an absolute refusal to give up a part of French soil to nationalists, who began a campaign of violent resistance in November 1954. Thus, strong Gaullists and former members of the resistance, including Georges Bidault, who had been both prime minister and foreign minister under the post-war Fourth Republic, were prepared to abandon loyalty to de Gaulle and to the French state over the issue of Algeria.

The events in Sétif, Algeria in 1945, which involved a considerable loss of life—with over 100 settlers massacred, followed by large-scale reprisals—seriously damaged relations between the European and Muslim communities. When the hoped-for reforms never materialized, the already significant nationalist groups throughout North Africa became more and

BOX 8.1

Biography: Ngo Dinh Diem (1901–63)

Diem was born into an important Roman Catholic family in South Vietnam in 1901. In the years before the Second World War he was a civil servant. In 1954 Diem became the prime minister of South Vietnam, after having previously refused any position in Bao Dai's government. A year later he became the president of his country, after controlling the 1955 referendum which abolished the royal family. Washington supported Diem strongly, because of his combination of being anti-French, anti-communist, and pro-American. But there were problems within Vietnam owing to his favouring Roman Catholics over the Buddhist population. This, combined with his arbitrary and dictatorial rule, resulted in much dissatisfaction. Opposition to Diem had also increased by 1960 as his attempt to root out opponents in the civil war in the South became less effectual, with help to the rebels coming from the North. In 1963 Diem was murdered during a takeover by unhappy generals, in which the CIA was involved, and to which the American government gave tacit approval.

more disillusioned with French promises. As the 1950s began, the French were facing increasingly radical nationalists. In Algeria these were grouped in the Front de Libération National (FLN); in Morocco the nationalist focus was provided by the Istaqlal (Independence) Party, founded in 1943 and supported since 1947 by the Sultan of Morocco, Mohammed V; and in Tunisia the Neo-Destour (New Constitutional) Party was created as early as 1934 although, like many nationalist groups it first sought better links with France and easier access to French citizenship. Its leader was Habib Bourguiba who, after 1949, returned to Tunisia to lead the campaign for independence.

The French hope was to head off any political reform which would undermine the French Union or damage the privileged position of the French settlers. In Morocco, Sultan Mohammed V came to seek the renegotiation of the 1912 Treaty of Fez, which defined the protectorate status, to gain greater influence for himself, as opposed to the traditional pashas and caids, and then to end French controls. Troubles began when the proposed reforms of General Juin were revealed by 1951 to be a sham. The Istaqlal used demonstrations and riots, most notably in Casablanca in 1952, and attempted to exploit American and international concern to demand realistic reforms leading to self-government. In the face of these pressures and the inscription of Morocco on the UN Security Council agenda, the French position became increasingly difficult. Their attempts to introduce local assemblies with equal representation for settlers and the indigenous population were patently inadequate, though consistent with avoiding any commitment to the devolution of local power which would have implications for the future of the French Union. There were those in the Quai d'Orsay, who had never believed that the French Union would gain international acceptance; the writing was on the wall for the centralization it embodied from the early 1950s. The need for American support at the UN may well have been a decisive factor in influencing the eventual French acceptance of meaningful self-government by 1954.

Paying lip-service to political change, which would temporarily satisfy the Americans, had ultimately to be followed by meaningful actions to start the process of change. In Morocco this was more easily said than done, as in September 1953, when traditional dislike of the Sultan's commitment to the Istaqlal led to the armed followers of the reactionary leader, El Glaoui, preparing to overthrow the Sultan. The French, rather than be seen as lacking the will to maintain law and order, took action themselves and deposed Mohammed V.[7] As in many other cases, nationalist opposition to European rule was not uniform and this complication led to greater progress to self-government in cooperation with the French being made in Tunisia. Pierre Mendès-France, the new Radical prime minister in June 1954, was instrumental in this acceptance of self-government just as he sensed the impossibility of successfully continuing the war in Indo-China. In July 1954 he promised Tunisia full internal self-government, but by then the demand was for independence and control over foreign and defence policy. The French were now simply reacting to events. To make matters worse, an armed insurrection had broken out in Algeria in November 1954, and although by the following year El Glaoui was prepared to accept the return of Mohammed V in Morocco, there was no respite from French difficulties. After Minister of Overseas France, Pierre-Henri Teitgen, had begun its preparation in 1955, the passing of the enabling law (*loi cadre*), to permit the constitutional changes that rendered the French Union inoperable, was achieved in 1956. Tunisia and Morocco gained independence the same year and there was now the prospect of a meaningful process of transferring power in France's Black African territories. Algeria, however, was a very different situation.

Algeria

Algeria became an acute crisis for the French Republic and one which was to threaten the very basis of civilian government. Unlike the other territories in North Africa, the abandonment of Algeria was seen by many establishment figures as akin to the abandonment of Brittany or any other French *département*. The war itself had become a brutal, bloody affair with atrocities on both sides and emotions running high. In 1957 fierce fighting in the Muslim quarters of Algiers was accompanied by the extensive use of torture by the authorities. The French army could win control of the urban areas, albeit at significant cost, but it was in no position to extend that control into the mountainous rural regions, despite the deployment of 400,000 troops. The war also assumed an important international dimension, not least because Egypt's President Nasser was supplying the rebels and the French could not seal the Algerian borders. When the Tunisian border town of Sakiet was bombed in 1958, the French also incurred widespread international condemnation. As the burden of the war fell more heavily on metropolitan France and opposition to it grew, the army in Algeria became increasingly frustrated. Believing that they were winning the military battle and concerned with another loss of political will, they joined with a settler protest in May 1958, which resulted in the proclamation of a 'Committee of Public Safety' being established in Algiers. A military coup in Paris was becoming a real possibility when agreement was reached on the return of the French wartime hero Charles de Gaulle, with authority to reform the constitution.

In a famous outdoor speech, de Gaulle told a cheering mass of settlers, *'Je vous ai compris'*, but in fact he had understood what he believed were more important issues pertaining to the future of France. Always confident in his ability to both understand and personify France, de Gaulle looked to the continued transformation of the country with a view to playing a more important world role, not on the back of an increasingly burdensome empire, but through a reinvigorated Europe under French leadership. Moreover, he also understood that the Algerian settlers, when France last faced a crisis, had, to a man, supported the collaborationist regime of Marshal Pétain, not de Gaulle's Free French. There could be no reason for de Gaulle being reluctant to sacrifice the interests of such people to further the true interests of France, if this required escaping from the millstone of Algeria. Once this was accomplished, the economic modernization of France could continue and foreign policy refocused on Europe and building a partnership with West Germany, so as to escape US domination.

The Algerian imbroglio, like many other key elements in decolonization, became something from which de Gaulle had to find the best way out. It was not a question of planning a strategy, but of finding one which would be acceptable to nationalist leaders and to at least some of the French governing elite. In 1959 de Gaulle spoke of an Algerian Algeria as something in line with the self-government idea embodied in the *loi cadre*, but it was February 1961 before secret negotiations began with the FLN. One obstacle in the way of any agreement to end the fighting was the French army, or at least some of its former generals, who launched a failed coup in April 1961. Another was the French determination to obtain a special regime for the Sahara, in the south of the country, which was rich in oil and gas. In the end, it took over a year before French concessions secured an agreement, the Evian Accords, in which the settlers were to be given three years to choose whether or not to remain in an independent Algeria. If they left, their goods and capital could go with them while the French retained their atomic test site in the Sahara and the naval base at Mers el Kebir for limited periods. The war had cost hundreds of thousands of lives and nearly brought down the French government on two occasions. The loss, perceived by some as the loss of a part of France, was another seminal moment in French history with its bitter internal divisions at all levels of French society and politics.

Black Africa

By 1953 the divisions between French and British colonial policy in Black Africa were still starkly evident as the French idea was to avoid political change leading to self-government. The French Union continued to define the constitutional process, whereby French overseas territories were to be incorporated into the single and indivisible French Republic, and the Black African Empire's importance for metropolitan France's regaining world power was still generally accepted by both Right and Left. Divisions were soon to appear, with the Algerian war and colonial policy becoming an important distinguishing feature between parties of the Right.[8] In Black Africa, the wars in Indo-China and Algeria were not, however, to be repeated except in Cameroon, where the *Union des Peuples Camerounais* launched an armed struggle in 1956.

The prospect of fighting a major war in Black Africa seemed to be largely irrelevant by 1958, when de Gaulle was committed to the giving up of Algeria. Therefore, the struggle for independence in Africa was concluded quickly between the establishment of the French Community in 1958 and its dissolution two years later, when independence was largely conceded. From the French side, the years until de Gaulle's return to power began the process, formalized in 1956, whereby power was devolved at the local level to 'responsible' African leaders. For the Africans, obtaining this power was the inevitable result of their abandonment, in the early 1950s, of the policy of associating themselves with the power exercised in Paris by French politicians. By 1956 the French were effectively following the same path as the British, even if their expectations and planning remained somewhat different.

The *loi cadre* encouraged the development of territorially based political movements, and the weakening of the French regional and the semi-federal structures in place in French West and Equatorial Africa. Critics of the process refer to the 'Balkanization' of West Africa and the determination of the richer territories, like Ivory Coast, to divest themselves of any sacrifices inherent in regional structures with supranational powers. In fact, there were important changes undermining the very idea of African unity, which was embodied in the Organization of African Unity, established in 1963, even before the African states themselves had been formally created with the end of French colonial rule. It is true that from the French perspective the idea of centralization in the French Union was replaced by the goal of creating structures, which would tie the former overseas territories closer to France. Hence, the French were determined to include their African territories in the economic provisions of the Treaty of Rome, so that the creation of the European Common Market would not disadvantage them. The need, with the end of the French Empire, to distinguish the struggle for political independence from the achievement of economic independence was clear.[9] There are obviously links between the two and it has been argued that the economic changes in France enabled political changes to accompany economic developments in the empire.[10]

Jacques Marseille points to the importance of the modernization of French industry and claims that this process weakened the role of small businesses, who benefited from protected empire markets. Once greater competitiveness became more necessary, as French trade and industrial expansion took place, smaller, less efficient or cost-effective enterprises, traditionally empire supporters, were displaced by those with equivalent economic ideas to the political ideas on France's future being developed by de Gaulle.

For de Gaulle, the problems of Black Africa in 1958 were much less than those of Algeria. The Constitution of the Fifth Republic effectively committed Black African territories to a new federal structure, but on the principle of decentralization. Africans would elect leaders to the French Community whose president, de Gaulle, would retain responsibility for foreign and defence policy and large areas of economic policy. Leaders would emerge from the territorial assemblies constituted in 1957, after the *loi cadre*, and membership of the Community would be determined by the individual territories on the basis of plebiscites. Those in favour would be the recipients of continued French aid and assistance, while those choosing independence would be left to fend for themselves. While most countries were prepared to join, in Guinea, where the radical former trades unionist Sékou Touré had established a large following, the voters chose independence by a large majority. Once de Gaulle had tried and failed to prevent the establishment of a viable state by withdrawing French equipment and administrators, he realized that French ties could best be preserved by a series of bilateral agreements with suitable African leaders. Consequently, in 1960, most French African territories secured new constitutions as internationally sovereign states within the Community. As the French Community was, like its predecessor, never intended to be a community of equals, pressure for formal independence was bound to build up quickly. Between June and November 1960, seven new states came into being and the final vestiges of the Federation inherent in French West Africa also disappeared. What was left was a mix of French education and culture, military agreements based on the stationing of the modern-day equivalent of rapid reaction forces, and economic

BOX 8.2

Biography: Sékou Touré (1922–84)

Touré was born in 1922, the son of a Muslim peasant farmer. He completed his education at a French technical school and, following his expulsion, worked at a variety of different jobs. He first caught the attention of the public in his younger years during his time in the Labour Union, where he became Secretary General. He was very critical of colonialism but became Mayor of Conakry (the capital of Guinea) in 1956 and Guinea's deputy to the French national assembly. In 1958, when Guinea gained its independence under Touré, he became its first president. His leadership of the sole political party, the Parti Démocratique de Guinée (PDG) marked him as a radical Leftist. During his presidency, Touré received aid from the USSR but at the same time tried to improve relations with the Western world. He died in 1984 and a week later a military coup took over governance and banned the PDG.

assistance programmes.[11] The *loi cadre*, for good or ill, had failed to produce a Commonwealth and arguably left a different perspective to that of the British on the meaning of great power status.

B. The Crises in the Congo and Angola

The Zenith of the Cold War in Black Africa

The two crises which began in Central Africa in 1960 and 1961 illustrate the importance that was attached to the Cold War in Black Africa at the turn of the decade. They both involved the Americans in situations where the French and the British were playing minor roles—roles generally at odds with what the Americans desired. The situation in the Congo raised issues of neo-colonialism, important European economic interests, Soviet involvement, regional conflict with racial overtones, and the importance of Cold War issues for Africa as a whole. In Angola, Portuguese–American relations over the future direction of colonial policy combined with strategic issues, centred on the continued American use of the Portuguese airbase in the Azores. It was an unprecedented mix of Cold War and colonialism. As has already been seen, in the US the questioning of covert operations and propaganda directed at the Soviet bloc in Europe, combined with the increasing importance of the less developed world as European rule was ending, to shift the focus of Cold War attention more to Asia and Africa. The idea that the Cold War was a battle for hearts and minds was indicated by an examination of the Congo and Angolan issues, and their importance for many members of the Kennedy administration.

Kennedy, Cold War, Empire, and Neo-Colonialism

As the Kennedy administration assumed power in Washington, the world, and particularly the UN, was on the cusp of some dramatic developments. The international system dominated by the Cold War rivalry between communism and capitalism was affected by a decolonization process, welcoming significant numbers of newly independent African states as full members of the global community. What was at stake was whether they would adopt the values and beliefs of the Western or communist worlds, and this ideological battle for the hearts and minds of tropical African people therefore assumed greater importance. For a few short years the 'dark' continent, where colonial empires were generally retreating, became the heart of the Cold War strategy of the youthful new president. The ideas of key members of Kennedy's 'New Frontier' administration, referred to as the 'best and the brightest',[12] were replete with hope and expectation that would infect many African leaders whose countries at the start of 1961 had just gained, or were about to achieve, independence.

A crucial element of this was the expectation that capitalist development would provide for the needs of the masses in the less developed world, in similar ways that it had benefitted European and American workers. Aided by state intervention through socialism and the Marshall Plan, mixed capitalist economies had provided for European Recovery and the maintenance of US economic expansion. Walt Rostow, initially deputy to National Security Advisor McGeorge Bundy in the Kennedy administration, believed that capitalist development would go through five stages, with a 'take off' enabling the less developed economies to follow a path cleared by free trade and private enterprise and thus defeat communism. The new president had travelled extensively in the less developed world as a senator and congressman, courtesy of his father's vast wealth, and once in the White House made a point of meeting with new and emerging African nationalist leaders. Removing the political and economic restraints of colonialism became a crucial economic component of Kennedy's determined Cold War opposition to communism. Unfortunately, where white settler populations were combined with the finance capital that provided significant profits for European investors and shareholders, these elements provided obstacles to the hoped for new economic order. In the eyes of the Kennedy administration, such economic obstacles had to be removed, along with the restoration of the political rights denied by colonialism. Communism or socialism could only offer appealing alternatives to democratic capitalism if made attractive by European colonialism.

Unfortunately, ending European economic imperialism would create tensions with some of America's allies, which would threaten the Cold War cohesion of the Western alliance. These tensions became most evident in Central Africa, where the exploitative profits of finance capital were greatest and the timing of the transfer of power most problematic. They became acute in the Belgian colony of the Congo, which gained independence four months before Kennedy was elected president and from which the mineral-rich province of Katanga seceded days after independence. The merging of private and state operations, and their financial benefits, from King Leopold's time was epitomized by the colonial state and the *Comité Special du Katanga* (CSK) assuming joint responsibility for the costs and benefits of developing the Congo's resources. The CSK was a holding company not involved in extracting resources, as its assets in land (from Leopold) and concessions to exploit that land were granted to the *Union Minière du Haut Katanga* (UMHK) in return for shares. The CSK was managed by a board of six directors, four of whom were appointed by the Brussels Government and two from the private *Compagnie du Katanga* (CK). One Belgian and one British company (Tanganyika Concessions and the holding company *Société Générale de Belgique*) had then provided new capital when King Leopold's Free State was incorporated into the Belgian colony in 1908. The shares in private companies operating in the Congo which provided benefits to European managers and owners of capital, whether or not in the form of concessionary shares, were derived in part from the brutally acquired assets of Leopold's regime that had aroused much international criticism. They were to remain an element of British and European imperialism even when the Congo's decolonization process had been formally completed in 1960.

That transfer of power threatened to have particularly damaging implications for European interests in the Congo if it also included transferring economic power. The initial threat arose from the pre-independence election with the largest party headed by Patrice Lumumba, a radical left-wing African nationalist, assuming power despite efforts by the Belgian authorities to prevent it. It was not just the damage that could be produced by a left-wing African politician, but the fact that the involvement of the colonial state as a shareholder with voting rights in the holding and operating companies benefitting from the extraction of copper, notably the UMHK, created additional dangers for European elites. UMHK had four British board members who were also members of Tanganyika Concession's (TC) board. These men were influential within the Conservative Party to which TC was a leading financial donor.[13] The earnings of European capital in UMHK were significant, although the Foreign Office was unable to put a firm figure on it. The State Department, however, believed UMHK to average $15 million per month. Tanganyika Concessions owned shares in UMHK, but shareholders also received 40 per cent of the concessionary payments in the form of dividends until 1962.[14] Other concessionary payments went through the CSK and its share portfolio, including its shares in UMHK. Owned and operated by the state and the private *Compagnie du Katanga*—itself an associate of the *Société Génerale de Belgique*—just prior to independence, shareholders, largely the colonial state, agreed to dissolve the CSK.[15] One-third of its assets would go to the CK and two-thirds to the government of the Congo, whose elected head turned out to be Patrice Lumumba. With the secession, the CSK was expropriated by Moïse Tshombe's Katanga government.

If the central government was deprived of Katanga's resources by such overt neo-colonialism (which could not be supported overtly) and unable to control the allocation of the foreign exchange earned by copper exports, African leaders, UMHK, and its European managers and shareholders could all gain. When Katanga seceded days after independence, the transfer of political power to the newly independent state had not been accompanied by the transfer of economic power. Unlike the British South Africa Company, the Central African copper belt's other important producer in Northern Rhodesia, whose mineral rights were surrendered to the new African government on independence in 1964, in the Congo, where the recipient was a more left-wing government, this did not happen. Hence the UMHK and the secessionist state were able to retain a greater proportion of the foreign exchange earned, and to avoid the export duties payable to the legitimate independent government. The Katangan leader, Moïse Tshombe, also benefitted personally from neo-colonialism by the creation of a new currency and the 'disappearance' of deposits in the Central Bank of Congo and Ruanda-Burundi in Katanga.[16]

This blatant form of neo-colonialism, initially backed by Belgian troops in Katanga, was not welcomed by the new administration in Washington. With the credibility of the UN also at stake (despite Secretary Dag Hammarskjöld's obsessive fear of communism spreading to Africa through left-wing ideas), the Kennedy administration was determined to bring about the end of Katangan secession and secure the establishment of an effective central government in the new state. How this was to be done and by applying what form of pressure on Tshombe was to prove controversial. After the election in April 1961 of a coalition government in Belgium containing the socialist Paul-Henri Spaak as foreign minister, the main obstacle to the application of pressure on Tshombe and his Belgian and white Rhodesian mercenaries for the re-integration of Katanga came from the British Conservative government of Harold Macmillan and its foreign secretary from July 1960, Alec Douglas-Home. The latter was a dinner companion of Charles Waterhouse, the chairman of TC and UMHK board member, who was asking the Foreign Office to pressurize the Belgian government to follow the wishes of the *Société Générale* in supporting an independent Katanga.[17] Whatever the result of the lobbying of the Foreign Secretary and his department, the desired continuation of the economics of colonialism and preventing the financial threat to the Conservative Party and some of its leading members produced serious Anglo-American disagreements in 1962. Conversations between Kennedy and Macmillan could not reconcile the conflicting reactions to the Katanga secession. The Cold War need to ensure that Africans received the expected benefits of capitalist development freed from the economic chains of colonialism was too important for the anti-communist Kennedy to sacrifice, even on the high altar of relations with the UK.

In Washington, those who still saw Western Europe as the mainstay of the Cold War front and the important economic partner (or competitor) with the US, battled against others like Chester Bowles and the assistant secretary of state for African affairs, G. Mennen Williams, who believed that the US could not afford to alienate African opinion. It was certainly the case that, as in the 1940s and 1950s in Europe, there was an exaggeration of Africa's importance in both economic and political terms. It took a few years for the Americans to realize this, but it does not lessen the Kennedy administration's commitment to the less developed world or to the ideals of freedom and self-determination, even when other interests were at risk. Cynics might argue that progressive policies regarding Black Africans were easier to endorse and brought greater political dividends in the US than progressive policies towards Afro-Americans. Alternatively, it might be argued that there was no genuine concern for the welfare of Africans, but merely a sign that they were important pawns in the latest Cold War game. Either way, the fact that such policies were followed at all provides a contrast with many other American administrations.[18]

The Congo Crisis

The crisis in the Congo, which sprang from the way the Belgians transferred power to a large, unprepared colony lacking trained personnel and indigenous administrators, began on 8 July 1960, just over a week after independence. The lack of any provisions for political transition, or the effective functioning of public services without trained Belgian personnel, made the loss of discipline in the army and subsequent rioting more serious. Rivalries between different ethnic groups in Leopoldville province and Luluabourg added to the difficulties of maintaining order which, with the assaults on Europeans, was used by the Belgians as a reason to reinforce their troops in Katanga on 10 July. The initial crisis was compounded the following day when Katanga province, under Moïse Tshombe, proclaimed its independence from the government of Patrice Lumumba in the capital, Leopoldville. The Belgian presence led Lumumba to appeal first to the UN for assistance in what his government termed a state of war with Belgium, and then to the Soviets.

UN troops soon arrived in Leopoldville, but without a mandate to end the Katangan secession that Lumumba and his important African supporters, particularly Kwame Nkrumah in Ghana, saw as vital for a united Congo. In fact, UN Secretary General Dag Hammarskjöld began to liaise with Washington, not the Congo government, on the best way of dealing with the crisis, while keeping the Soviets out of the region. They could not, however, stop the supply of Soviet aid or remove the risk of direct Soviet military involvement or assistance. The longer the Belgian troops stayed, the greater the risk of increasing Soviet influence, as there was a danger that Belgian or other European forces would continue to assist what would be perceived as a blatant form of neo-colonialism based on Katangan secession. The issue was crucial for the newly independent African states and those colonies which were about to gain independence. Kennedy, if not Eisenhower, was determined that Africa should now be at the centre of American Cold War policy and the allegiance of the newly independent states, such as Nkrumah's Ghana, was deemed crucial. The concern within Africa and the Kennedy administration, about the possible collapse of the Congo or the continuing secession of Katanga was based on a determination that the gaining of independence should not be seen as a failure. If Lumumba could not unite the country and Katanga was allowed to secede, then the transfer of power would be seen as the ultimate failure. It might also encourage secession by other regions in other colonies and former colonies. On the other hand, the success of Lumumba was seen by the Americans as opening the door to pro-Soviet or other radical left-wing groups in Africa.

One obvious way to ease the difficulty was to eliminate Lumumba. On 5 September 1960 President Kasavubu, in a move of dubious constitutional legitimacy, dismissed Lumumba from his position as prime minister, but Lumumba then set up a rival government until, on 14 September, General Joseph Mobutu announced a temporary army takeover. Mobutu dismissed both government and Parliament, placing Lumumba under house arrest, in the light of the growing problems in the Congo. The number of UN troops in the Congo, including those from Ghana and Guinea who backed Lumumba, was now growing. The long-term issues were whether they would be used to end Katangan secession and restore the territorial integrity of the new state, and whether or not Lumumba would remain as the elected leader of a reunited Congo. The latter outcome was not acceptable to the Americans who, in September 1960, split with Nkrumah over this issue. When Nkrumah attended Khrushchev's speech in the UN, the Eisenhower administration portrayed the Ghanaian as pro-Soviet rather than pro-Lumumba. The reality was that, for Eisenhower, the idea of a radical African leader in the Congo was more than problematic and in fact completely beyond the pale. The new Kennedy administration did not have to deal with the uncomfortable fact of Lumumba being for many Africans the legitimate Congo leader, and was more able, with an eye to the future Cold War position of the West in Africa, to pursue a more pro-African independence policy. The short-term problem in the Congo was the maintenance of order and governmental authority as Lumumba's supporters, led by Antoine Gizenga, were firmly established in Stanleyville. Along with the capital in Leopoldville, and the Katangan capital Elizabethville, there were now three rival power centres, with an additional secessionist movement based in South Kasai and ethnic divisions and violence in most provinces.

As acrimonious disputes occurred in the General Assembly, and the UN Secretary General, Dag Hammerskjöld, worked closely with the Eisenhower administration to pre-empt Soviet involvement in the region, the divisions were made worse by Lumumba's escape and recapture. The problem was that the government in Leopoldville lacked the legitimacy that it could only get through the reconvening of Parliament. As Washington devised various plans for the liquidation of the Congo's first leader, in January 1961 Lumumba was moved to Katanga. At some point after the journey he was beaten to death by his captors, although his death was not announced until 13 February. The US was thus relieved of the Lumumba problem, but still had to find and legitimize a Congo leader who would be acceptable to African opinion. They settled on Cyrille Adoula, a former trades unionist, and when Parliament was reconvened, on 19 July 1961, CIA bribes effectively ensured that Adoula was elected prime minister.

The first priority for the new leader was to reunite the country, which above all required the ending of Katangan secession. Unfortunately, this was easier said than done, despite the support of the new Kennedy administration. For one thing, the Belgians, the French, and the British did not share American confidence in the future stability of a united Congo run from Leopoldville. Any regime containing Lumumba's supporters was seen as capable of again appealing to the Soviets and irresponsible enough to provide opportunities for the spread of radical left-wing ideas. A radical regime would affect significant European financial interests in the copper-rich Katanga, represented by the UMHK, in which the British company Tanganyika Concessions had a particular financial interest. The British were nervous of the political risk of alienating the right-wing Empire supporters in the Conservative Party, who were keen to preserve white-dominated regimes, particularly those in the Central African Federation (see Chapter 8, D), which had close links with Tshombe. Therefore, the last thing they wanted to see was a beacon of pro-Western anti-communism removed from power by UN forces, consisting largely of Asian and African troops operating with American logistic support. As time went on, the British became keener to escape from any responsibility for Central Africa which might involve them in a racial conflict. The Americans, with their determination to end Katangan secession, were seen as stirring up trouble that would threaten British economic interests and cause conflict involving the Central African Federation whose leader, Roy Welensky, was allowing arms to be supplied to Tshombe via Northern Rhodesia.

In September 1961 Adoula announced that Gizenga would become vice-premier in the Leopoldville government, and UN forces engaged Tshombe's troops and mercenaries in Elizabethville. A ceasefire was announced the following month, but by then the agreement between Adoula and Gizenga had collapsed and the former's supporters were becoming increasingly incensed by the Prime Minister's failure to end Katangan secession. The Americans were determined to bring the two governments together and reunite the former Congo territory. If they failed, and independence was seen to have failed, the aim of ensuring that power should be transferred peacefully to new African states as part of the Western world would have received a serious blow. The British were less concerned with that kind of successful outcome than with their large financial interests in the Congo, which would be threatened by a civil war that could spread to British territories, especially after a rebellion broke out in neighbouring Angola in the spring of 1961. In November, as renewed incidents took place between the white mercenaries and Tshombe's *gendarmerie* they were supporting and the UN troops, a second security council resolution was passed, reaffirming the February resolution specifically charging the UN with the task of securing the withdrawal and evacuation from the Congo of mercenaries.

Hammarskjöld was now dead, killed in a plane crash in Northern Rhodesia in September 1961, and his successor, Burma's U Thant, had to deal with Tshombe and Gizenga, who was waiting in Stanleyville as a potential radical successor to Lumumba. In this situation, the British feared that law and order could completely collapse if Tshombe was attacked by UN forces, while valuable economic assets could be lost and the white community endangered even if the fighting did not spread. They therefore preferred the preservation of Tshombe as a form of stability, rather than the use of UN force to remove him if negotiations ultimately failed between Adoula and Tshombe. However, in December 1961 the Kitona Accords brought success and agreement on the reincorporation of Katanga into the Congo state.

Unfortunately, Tshombe, playing for time, declined to take any steps to implement the agreement and the supporters of Adoula became more and more disillusioned. The Americans were increasingly concerned about Adoula being replaced by more radical Africans from Leopoldville or Stanleyville, with whom Tshombe was more than prepared to ally. As the UN representatives in the Congo became convinced that Tshombe would never voluntarily reintegrate Katanga into the Congo, discussions began in Washington as to the best means to apply pressure on Tshombe to demonstrate his willingness to implement the Kitona agreement. After a May tripartite Anglo-American-Belgian meeting on this had only served to reveal their divisions, the Americans, consulting with the Belgian Foreign Minister Paul-Henri Spaak, went ahead alone. The differences in Washington over how best to put pressure on Tshombe were evident, but the stages by which measures would be escalated if Tshombe did not voluntarily take action were agreed upon. The plan, drafted in the State Department, was presented to U Thant at the start of the summer. The Secretary General then endorsed it as the UN plan with minor amendments. The British were adamantly opposed to its idea of collecting tax revenue through customs posts in Katanga without Tshombe's agreement, and could not accept sanctions even though they imported little Katangan copper, because of the impact on the London Metal Exchange, where prices were manipulated to maintain the high price of Northern Rhodesian copper. Thus, they could only agree to part of the US/UN plan.

The need for international involvement resulted from the 'inability' of Washington to pressure the UMHK to pay its taxes to the legitimate Congo government and, as the French pointed out, the refusal of the Belgian government to require it to do so. According to the French Foreign Minister, Maurice Couve de Murville, everyone knew that the Belgian government controlled *Société Générale Belgique*, the holding company that had originally provided share capital for UMHK in the final years of Léopold's Congo Free State. At all events, George McGhee was sent to Katanga in October 1962, as an American diplomat welcomed by Tshombe, who could win his acceptance of the US/UN plan. The Kennedy administration was so determined to bring about Congo reunification that by December, although McGhee was making progress, the President was prepared to send a squadron of US fighter planes to the Congo which would at least convince Tshombe that the US were serious about securing the reintegration of Katanga. The despatch of the squadron was, however, ruled out by U Thant, who had adequate air support and was adamant that Hammarskjöld's policy of only accepting forces from the lesser powers should be maintained. Thus, as in all the operations of the UN military mission in the Congo, heavy equipment for its forces would simply be positioned by US transport planes where needed.

Although civilian representatives of the UN mission had long been convinced that some form of action was necessary to bring the secession to an end, the final military climax resulted from the keenness of the Katangan mercenaries to fire on UN troops, probably initially without Tshombe's instructions. Well-trained Indian troops were then able to seize control of the whole of Elizabethville. While the Americans stated their opposition to further fighting in Katanga, they were unable to influence events on the ground or even get reliable information on them. Indian UN troops marched on the Katangan mining towns of Jadotville and Kolwezi whose capture in January, including the UMHK installations, signalled the end of secession.

A reunited Congo symbolized the US commitment to African independence and the attempt to win the support of the emerging African states. Yet it came too late for the economic conditions of the independent state, emerging from the poisoned chalice left by the Belgians, to be rectified. The UN mission remained until 1964 but the number of troops was drastically reduced as the economic conditions, particularly for internal trade, further deteriorated. Thus, the benefits provided by the corrupt use of political office, including the issuing of import licences, became even more important. Even though the US took nation building in the Congo seriously, the resources to enable democratic capitalism to operate successfully were simply not there, whatever good will existed.

Although the credibility of the US and the UN had been preserved, the triumph was short-lived and as elsewhere, particularly in Latin America, the idealistic commitment of the Kennedy administration in the Cold War did not produce the desired long-lasting effects and was soon changed under the Johnson and Nixon administrations (see Chapter 11, A). In the Congo, which became Zaire in 1971, Tshombe returned as prime minister of the reunited state in 1964, largely to help counter the new rebellions, with the US now more a supporter than opponent of the Tshombe regime. Produced by the increasing economic dislocation in the Congo, separate revolts broke out in Kwilu and Kivu in 1963 and early 1964, aided by the departure of the reduced UN presence that had remained after the end of secession. The Conseil National de Libération, a divided group of radical Africans, was unable to unite the new rebellions with the successors to Gizenga's Stanleyville regime. Even Ché Guevara, who joined the rebels in Kivu, was unable to bring organization and discipline to the rebel forces. With the UN and its increasing numbers of newly independent Afro-Asian states unable to be so easily manipulated by the US, Washington's Congo policy changed. After seeking the removal of Tshombe's mercenaries from the Congo under Kennedy, the Americans, now under Lyndon Johnson, began paying for them to help against the opponents of the Tshombe regime, and airlifted Belgian paratroops into Stanleyville to release rebel held hostages.

It was only when General Mobutu returned to power in 1965, with a military coup backed by the Americans, that order began to return, not under the banner of freedom and independence, but through brutal repression under a military strongman. It was characteristic of changing American policy in the less developed world, where the importance of promoting support for the West was replaced by encouraging the imposition of pro-Western regimes, whether indigenous people liked them or not. In this situation, the Cold War became even more about preserving the values of capitalism than enabling the spread of democracy.

The Angolan Crisis

Over the border from the Congo, in north-western Angola, a rebellion broke out against Portuguese colonial rule in the spring of 1961 which has been associated with the Union of Angolan Peoples (UPA), established and led by Holden Roberto. Roberto had come to prominence though the Union of the Peoples of Northern Angola (UPNA), which was based on Bakongo nationalism and on the idea of restoring the old Kongo kingdom. The UPA was an attempt to establish a single Angolan nationalist movement to oust the Portuguese. It was, however, just one of the fifty or more Angolan political movements operating from Leopoldville when the Congo became independent in 1960. Those in the UPA seeking to make alliances with these other groups were initially opposed by Roberto, who was determined to establish himself as leader, a position he only achieved in 1961.[19] The fact that the UPA then, unlike its main rival, the Popular Movement for the Liberation of Angola (MPLA), became more committed to armed struggle, means it is easy to interpret the revolt in Northern Angola as stemming from the growth of nationalism, spearheaded by the UPA.[20] Actually, there is evidence from missionaries in the region that the outbreak of violence was more spontaneous and due less to political organization than to the economic grievances associated with peasants being removed for forced labour and unable to tend to their own crops, particularly coffee. In any event, it is likely that the UPA benefited from being able to politicize the rebels.

The anti-communist Roberto was a frequent visitor to the US and met with President Kennedy. His ideological opponents, the MPLA, did not initially favour violence until the revolt effectively forced their hand, and by the end of 1961 they too were established in Leopoldville, under the leadership of Mario de Andrade, the founder of the movement, and Viriato da Cruz. The fact was that the rebellion occurred only a few months after a key UN resolution of December 1960, supported by the US and influencing Portuguese perceptions of the rebellion. While it was eventually brutally suppressed and largely contained, the rebellion was never totally extinguished by Portugal. The UN resolution referred to colonialism as alien domination and a denial of human rights; it called for immediate steps to be taken to transfer power. It was followed by another in March 1961, calling for Portugal to introduce reforms and allow the exercise of the right of self-determination. The Portuguese therefore began to assume that it was the Americans who were responsible for the troubles in Angola and who were, thereby, providing opportunities for communism to advance.

The US State Department rightly concluded early on that, in order to avoid jeopardizing American standing with the African states and in the UN, it would be necessary to maintain a position that was unpalatable to the Portuguese. It was certainly unpalatable to the Portuguese Foreign Minister, Alberto Nogueira, who warned the Americans that, if their undermining of the Portuguese Empire continued, the communists could take over the whole of the Iberian peninsula. He also claimed that the Angolan Crisis was more important than Berlin and that, if necessary, the Portuguese were prepared to go to the bitter end and face a third world war, rather than give up their empire. The argument of the State Department's Africanists was that it would be important to champion African self-determination, even if Portugal withdrew from NATO—a good example of the extent to which Cold War considerations were Africa-based.

The point is particularly relevant to the question of the Azores base, which was used by the Americans under an agreement due to expire at the end of 1962. The fact was that the agreement was neither renewed, nor the Americans thrown out and, while there were changes in the way the Kennedy administration dealt with the Angolan issue at the UN, the essential nature of the policy remained unchanged. Public criticism to win Afro-Asian support accompanied private criticism and persuasive pressure. The problem was that the resolutions put forward at the UN became more radical and the US feared not just their effect on Portugal, but on their relations with more moderate Afro-Asian states. It thus became more reluctant to support them, especially when sanctions were involved. However, the commitment to Africans still remained and while Kennedy was aware of the importance the military attached to the Azores and was keen not to lose the base, it did not mean that there was a move to preserve better relations with Portugal at the expense of the commitment to African self-determination. As late as December 1963 the US was supporting resolutions calling for self-determination and no arms supply to Portugal.

The problem was that the Portuguese would not tolerate the concepts of independence and self-government and would not introduce political change in any meaningful form. The Kennedy administration, at the very highest levels of Secretary of State Dean Rusk, and even Kennedy himself, tried to change these attitudes in meetings with high-level Portuguese representatives, but failed. Thus, the revolt simmered beneath the surface in Angola and the anti-colonial movements continued without establishing a single unified movement. The MPLA, with its *mestiço* domination, was at odds with the Black African UPA, which in March 1962 merged with the Democratic Party of Angola (PDA), another largely Kikongo-speaking group, to form the National Liberation Front of Angola (FNLA). The purpose was to broaden the ethnic base and aspire to become a national party and, in April, an Angolan revolutionary government in exile (GRAE) was formed with an anti-communist message. Later in the year, in December 1962, Agostinho Neto became leader of the MPLA after escaping from prison in Portugal and the seeds of future conflict were sown. Although the MPLA tried to play down its socialist links until 1964,[21] there was now an ideological division in Angolan anti-colonialism which could be interpreted in Cold War terms. Ultimately, the Cold War achieved little for Angolans except in contributing to their divisions, despite the commitment of the Kennedy administration to promote African nationalism of a 'responsible' kind.

C. Crises in the Middle East

The mid-1950s in the Middle East produced a number of crises during the transition from the period of British domination to the era of superpower competition in which the Soviets posed a challenge to Western dominance in the area. Outside interference was a feature of the post-1953 period, which focused on the conflict between the Arabs and the new Jewish state of Israel. The second Arab–Israeli war in 1956 (the Suez Crisis), stemmed from a number of interconnected international, regional, and national problems. In essence, these involved the maintenance of power, which as one senior British official pointed out, in terms that could also apply to the Cold War, is to be measured not only in terms of money and military forces but in prestige. What the world thinks about the status of a great power is, in other words, extremely important. In the Middle East, by the middle of the decade, there was one power, Britain, which was clearly declining in hard power terms as measured by military and economic strength, and was desperate to preserve its power in terms of status and prestige. As the British saw it, this had to be done in the face of threats from both friends (notably the US) and enemies, whether the Soviet Union or emerging radical Arab states. This British determination to remain the leading external power was accompanied by regional rivalries, which embodied not just the Arab–Israeli dispute but also serious rivalries within the Arab world. Finally, there were the problems and conflicts within individual states in the Middle East. It was the combination of all three that produced the Suez Crisis.

Britain's Declining Power

The collapse of Britain's informal empire in the Middle East, which was the clear result of the Suez Crisis, has formed a central part of the debate on decolonization. Having abandoned its position in India and other parts of South Asia, as well as Palestine, it can be argued that Britain was also engaged in planning its withdrawal from the Middle East. It therefore ran into difficulties over the nature and timing of this process. Britain was allegedly seeking to preserve some degree of influence and to resist the spread of Soviet communism by selecting pro-Western leaders as its successors. Equally, it can be argued that the Middle East was radically different from Asia, in that the development of the Cold War and the growing need for oil made Britain reluctant to abandon the Middle East until the Suez Crisis made Britain's departure inevitable. Thus, Suez can fit the model of the planned transfer of power, with the occasional aberration, or the model of radical nationalists demanding the end of external control, whether exercised formally or informally.

However, Suez has been interpreted as a much more important milestone in the history of British imperialism and decolonization. The Suez Canal was probably the most well-known symbol of the British Empire and the vain efforts to retain control of it in 1956 signified for some Britain's imperial demise.[22] The decolonization of the rest of Britain's empire was inevitable after the 'lion's last roar' had been muffled on the banks of the Canal. Suez was a watershed because force had failed and Britain could no longer fight to hold its empire. Opponents of that view argue that Suez was not a watershed because it failed to change the fundamental goals of British policy overseas.[23] This argument rests, in part, on the assumption that Suez was not part of decolonization, in the sense that it did not involve the formal transfer of power. It is much more accurate to see Suez as the loss of influence that was supposed to remain *after* power had been transferred. In the Middle East, this was particularly important because of the region's geopolitical importance and its association, not with colonies, but with Britain's status as a great world power by virtue of its responsibility for the defence of the area. Thus, the policy of maintaining the status of a great world power remained unaltered by the Suez fiasco, which had little effect on decolonization except to undermine the idea of Britain as a liberal colonial power. What it did do was to reveal that Britain could only exercise influence and employ force in a regional context with the approval and support of the US.

The Regional Crises

The first crisis, which the British and the Americans began to address at the end of 1955, was the Arab–Israeli conflict, which was centred now on Egyptian organized raids of *fedayeen* into Israel. Originally, such raids were largely the result of local grievances over the position of the border but, by 1955, their organization by Egypt and the scale of the Israeli reprisals had made the situation more inflammatory. If the British, or even the Americans, were to pose as the region's protectors against the Soviet threat, they would need a united Middle East in which such internal conflicts were no longer more important than an external threat. This meant securing an Arab–Israeli peace settlement. The plan to do this, code-named Alpha, involved the creation of a link between Egypt and Jordan to symbolize Arab unity, the right of Palestinian refugees to return to their homes or to receive compensation, which would be financed by the West, and the provision of guarantees of Israeli security. The Egyptian leader, Colonel Gamal Abdel Nasser, was chosen by the US to convince the Arab world of the plan's desirability before the Americans would begin to put pressure on the Israelis to accept it.

There were some obvious difficulties in that the Israelis would have to give up the Negev (in the south of the country) and accept the right of refugees to return, albeit in a controlled fashion. No amount of American pressure was likely to do that, even without the Jewish lobby in the US. Moreover, even if Nasser was personally willing to accept the existence of an Israeli state, his chances of persuading other Arab leaders to do the same, while recognizing his leadership, were almost as low. To some extent, the idea of Arab nationalism and anti-imperialism which Nasser had promoted raised more Arab divisions. He had deposed a monarch in Egypt and his rivals for leadership in Iraq and Saudi Arabia were both conservative monarchs. Yet Nasser's radical Arab nationalism, while certain to upset the old Arab landowning elites, was also unacceptable to the masses if it was combined with the recognition of Israel.

In the Middle East after 1955, Nasser was to emerge as the key challenger to the idea that Britain had a special regional role as military protector, and it was Nasser, who in effect, challenged the British for the right to exert predominant influence in the Arab parts of the region. In 1954 the Anglo-Egyptian agreement on the withdrawal of British troops from the Suez Canal Zone was based on maintenance of the base in peacetime and on its reactivation in war, and offered the prospect of a new era of Anglo-Egyptian cooperation. However, such hopes were dashed in April 1955, with the creation of the Baghdad Pact, an extension of the Turco-Iraqi Pact which, by the end of the year, would incorporate Pakistan and Iran, as well as Britain. Almost immediately, the Baghdad Pact became a hated military alliance, symbolizing again British attempts at domination, even though this dislike was inversely proportional to the Pact's military value. Its main achievement was to sour Anglo-Egyptian relations and exacerbate the major conflicts which bedevilled the Middle East. First, it involved the Iraqis, who were the main challengers to Nasser's claim to leadership of the Arab world. Second, Nasser's standing after the 1954 agreement depended to a significant extent on his claims to be an anti-imperialist leader who had finally got rid of the peacetime British military presence in Egypt. He could hardly, therefore, welcome his main rival's almost immediate conclusion of a new defence agreement with the imperialist power

BOX 8.3

Biography: Gamal Abdel Nasser (1918–70)

This future Egyptian statesman was born in Alexandria in 1918. He completed his education at the Cairo Military Academy, which he joined in 1936. While there, Nasser contributed to the establishment of a nationalist movement known as the Free Officers or the El-Dhobatt El-Ahrar. Nasser fought and was wounded in the 1948–9 war against Israel. Following this conflict there was increased support for the Free Officers' Movement because of the King's corrupt involvement in the procurement of inadequate weapons. In 1952 Nasser led a military coup against the King Farouk regime. A new Egyptian republic was born and Nasser became minister of the interior under General Neguib. Neguib was always a figurehead and Nasser formally assumed power as president and prime minister in 1954. Nasser caught the world's attention by announcing the nationalization of the Suez Canal Company in 1956 after a covert Anglo-American attempt to undermine his regime. The Suez Crisis ensued, which only enhanced Nasser's popularity in the Arab world. Although he attempted many reforms, including land redistribution, expansion of public works schemes, and improving educational opportunities, his domestic policies were a failure. Nasser used Arab nationalism to win support in Egypt but lost the 1967 war against Israel. Nasser resigned for a short period following that defeat, but he returned to power until his sudden death from a heart attack in 1970, which left the Arab world in deep mourning.

from whose clutches Egypt had finally been delivered. The result was that Nasser embarked on a campaign to denounce the Pact and to prevent any other Arab members from joining. This, in turn, made it less likely that he would cooperate with the British and the Americans in implementing Operation Alpha. In late 1955 the British became keener to promote the Pact by getting other Arab states to join. In December they approached Jordan in order to isolate Nasser in the Arab world and emphasize British leadership of the defence organization deemed necessary for the Middle East. The Baghdad Pact was proclaimed as the vehicle for this, even though the shortfall in the forces in the region that London and Washington deemed necessary to do this was greater than the number of forces available. The British efforts to secure Jordanian accession led to riots and disturbances which threatened King Hussein's government and had to be abandoned in January 1956.

In the meantime, Nasser, fearing his domestic position would be undermined by an inability to defend Egypt from large-scale Israeli reprisals against *fedayeen* raids, had turned to the Soviets for arms in September 1955. This deal between Egypt and Czechoslovakia raised the spectre of growing Soviet influence in the Middle East and was likely to lead to questions about the value of the Baghdad Pact. It was falsely claimed that the region, from Turkey through Iraq and Iran to the Persian Gulf (the so-called 'northern tier'), could be protected by defending the passes through the Zagros mountains. In any case, what good was that if the Soviets were already in Egypt? A further element of concern stemmed from the fact that once the new arms were absorbed into the Egyptian armed forces in about a year's time, the military superiority which the British and Americans believed the Israelis enjoyed over the combined forces of the Arab states, would be lost. Consequently, it was feared in Britain that Israel would attack Egypt in the near future to avoid such an eventuality.

The defence issue could more readily be turned to British advantage in that they could claim that, rather than the reality of competing with Nasser for influence in the Middle East, they were in fact serving Western interests by leading the struggle against the Soviets. This theme, of portraying the preservation of Britain's imperial interests as part of fighting the Cold War, was one with which the Americans were already closely acquainted. And they regarded it understandably with a certain scepticism, as it could be argued that the unwelcome presence of British forces in the region actually contributed to the instability which the Soviets might be able to exploit. But that presence was a vital symbol of Britain's influence in a region where, if it was lost, the country's status as a world power would be at risk. Now that Britain had given up its peacetime presence in Egypt it was even more important to emphasize the crucial role its forces in Iraq and Jordan might play in defence terms. This was, in fact, why they had joined the Baghdad Pact in the first place, because it was through that organization that they would secure their continued peacetime presence in Iraq. The consequences of the other problem created by the Czech arms deal would only become apparent in 1956.

With the failure to get Arab Jordan into the Baghdad Pact, it began to look as if Nasser was winning the battle with Britain for influence in the Middle East. In this situation, and encouraged by British intelligence assessments, Prime Minister Eden began to see that the only way of saving face was by the removal of Nasser. Yet the Egyptian leader was still regarded as essential to the realization of Alpha and an Arab–Israeli agreement, which in turn was necessary for a united Middle East to focus on the threat of the USSR, for which a British military presence was ostensibly needed. It was the dismissal of General Glubb, who led the British-officered Arab Legion in Jordan, and the American realization that Nasser was not going to sell Alpha to Arab leaders, that gave credence to Eden's arguments in Washington. The result was an American plan, codenamed Omega, with which the British were to cooperate and which sought to remove Nasser by a combination of measures designed to weaken his internal position and isolate him in the Arab world.

A number of economic measures were to be taken against Egypt, including the withdrawal of the promised aid to build a dam on the River Nile at Aswan. Externally, the Americans would try to turn King Saud of Saudi Arabia against Nasser, and the CIA and MI6 would sponsor a coup, code-named Straggle, against the left-wing Syrian regime which was Nasser's other important Middle Eastern friend. However, once Nasser realized that British and American policy had become hostile to Egypt, he looked for a way to strike back which would increase his support in the Arab world. In the wake of the announcement, based on Omega, that US aid for building the prestigious Aswan Dam would be withdrawn, on 26 July Nasser decided that the nationalization of the Suez Canal Company would best serve his needs.

The Suez Crisis

The nationalization of the Suez Canal Company, which was largely owned by the French and British governments, was a massive blow to British prestige as the dominant regional power. It was, however, an Egyptian registered company and, as Nasser offered compensation, he was in fact acting perfectly legally and simply buying out the shareholders. It was, nevertheless, a hugely symbolic moment, encapsulating the decline of British influence and belittling Britain in the eyes of the world—that was too much for Eden to swallow. He immediately ordered the Chiefs of Staff to prepare plans for an invasion of Egypt. He also began a long series of efforts to convince the Americans that Nasser would now use the nationalized company's control of the Canal to strangle Britain's supply of Middle Eastern oil. Eisenhower and Dulles were not impressed, but extremely worried about the reactions in the Middle East and elsewhere to a naked show of force by the British. With Omega, the Americans had shown a willingness to seek Nasser's removal, but they were reluctant to jeopardize the West's position by an act of overt aggression for which there was no justification. Both Eisenhower and Dulles realized that they would need to persuade Eden against using force, but to confront the British by ruling out military options in all circumstances, including the closure of the Canal to international shipping, would be counterproductive: the British might resent American opposition, unless qualified, and be encouraged to use force. The strategy therefore became one of playing for time, by convincing the British that regaining control of the Canal could be achieved by peaceful methods or that military force required further action by Nasser. The longer the attempts at negotiation went on, the less likely it would be that force would be used. In the event, a London conference of users and signatories to the 1888 Suez Canal Convention (which established the canal as an international waterway and governing its use) reached a majority agreement, in August 1956, on the principles of a new international regime for the Canal. Nasser, however, refused to go along with the agreement, which did not specify how international control was to be exercised over a waterway that was part of sovereign Egyptian territory. With another American proposal to establish a Users' Group that would assert the rights given under the Suez Canal Convention, the issue again came down to whether the Egyptian company would oversee the Canal through an international supervisory board, or whether an international body would actually run the Canal. The crux of the matter for Eden was whether the international body operating the Canal would have the power to impose sanctions and humiliate Nasser. If it did, it would be unacceptable to the Egyptians. When the British took the issue to the UN, the two countries were, nevertheless, coming close to a deal because the power to humiliate could not easily be portrayed as an international requirement. It was then that Eden received some unexpected French visitors.

General Challe and General Gazier, who visited London on 26 October, produced a plan which would avoid any need for a settlement and thereby spare Eden from being pilloried by the right-wing, imperialist wing of the Tory Party for 'appeasing' Egypt during its annual conference. Eden had every reason to believe that his party would find it difficult to live with a settlement that did not provide for the humiliation of Nasser and reassert British prestige in the Middle East. The French generals had been in close contact with the Israelis, who were keen to destroy any possible advantage the Egyptians might gain from the Czech arms deal. The French were also eager to strike at Nasser, because he was supplying the rebels in Algeria fighting for independence from France. The plan put to Eden was that Israel would first attack Egypt. As they did so, Britain and France would issue an ultimatum to cease fighting and, when this was refused, would send forces to Egypt, allegedly to protect the Canal from the warring parties. This plan had the advantage of heading off any Israeli attack on Jordan, which Britain was committed to defend. It would have been a strange irony if, having accused Nasser of wishing to take over the Middle East on behalf of the Soviet Union, and having suffered from Egyptian propaganda against imperialism and the Baghdad Pact, Eden had ended up assisting Jordan alongside Nasser. On the other hand, to collude with the French and the Israelis was even more bizarre and based on the illusion that the collusion with the Israelis could be kept secret.

One immediate reason for Eden's actions may have been the feeling at the Tory Party conference, but the roots of Eden's decision go back before this. Eden himself later argued that the decision helped prevent the spread of Soviet influence in the Middle East, while the strategic importance of the region and the existence of large quantities of oil also made action necessary. However, the more emotive perceptions of the Prime Minister and some of his Cabinet colleagues and officials reflected a world view of Britain as a global power with exclusive responsibilities in the Middle East. These perceptions and belief systems were broadly comparable to the ways in which the US and USSR saw their credibility in terms of competing in a Cold War. To lose status was seen as disastrous and, while all sorts of reasons could be brought forth to justify this view, ultimately, it reflected a sense of prestige derived from emotive belief systems rather than interests. Reason was thus cast aside, and Eden's failure to take account of the true extent of American opposition to the use of force is one example of how rationality could be overridden. The idea of collusion being kept secret is another.

The final agreement was reached with the French and Israelis after a number of secret meetings at Sèvres in France: it involved an Israeli attack on 29 October, followed by a 24-hour ultimatum. This would demand a withdrawal to ten miles from each bank of the Canal which, when refused, would be followed by a British attack on Egyptian airfields after midnight on 30/31 October. The reason for this was the Israeli fear of Egyptian planes bombing their cities, but in the event the bombing was postponed until after all American citizens were evacuated from Cairo. Unfortunately, by the time the ultimatum was delivered the Israelis were still a long way from the Canal. In effect, it demanded that the aggressor advance into Egyptian territory while the victim of the aggression fell back. In addition, the latest British military plan called for an extended period of psychological warfare, including the bombing of important civilian installations. This was clearly incompatible with the type of quick operation that would have been over before international and, especially American, opinion had time to mobilize.

By early November, the UN passed two resolutions calling for a ceasefire and, on 4 November, the British were in the position of being morally unable to condemn the Soviet assault on the civilians of Budapest (see Chapter 6, A) while they themselves were bombing Cairo. A UN peacekeeping force was then agreed by the General Assembly and, as a result, further pressure mounted for military action to be halted. The emotive nature of the Suez Crisis is epitomized by the majority decision of the Cabinet on 4 November, when it was believed (incorrectly) that both the Egyptians and the Israelis had accepted a ceasefire. When asked whether to go ahead with the airborne landings, to postpone them, or to abandon them altogether, the Cabinet voted to go ahead. It was the final futile attempt to assert British power in the Middle East that had already evaporated. Twenty-four hours later, when the Canal was half in British hands, but useless as the Egyptians had sunk block ships in it, the British government called the fighting to a halt. As the Americans refused to consider any action to stop the run on the pound that took place because of the economic uncertainty, the British were facing a balance of payments crisis and criticism from the entire world apart from the Antipodean Dominions. The pressure from the Americans and the disapproval of the UN, where the Americans and Soviets were, for once, essentially in agreement, finally brought home to the British the disastrous consequences were they to continue. The collusion always suspected by the Americans was soon obvious, despite the British denials, and having lied to Parliament, Eden was forced to resign in January 1957, to be succeeded by the American-backed Harold Macmillan.

The Aftermath of Suez

For the British, Suez meant that they could no longer operate militarily in old imperial areas without the tacit support of the US. Eden's efforts to maintain a dominant regional role as the leading representative of the Western Alliance was a futile attempt to cling to a world role of significance. Britain would have to accept American leadership in the Middle East, as well as in East and South-East Asia, Latin America, and even Africa. However, this did not mean that Britain was suddenly willing to decolonize and abandon Africa. Unlike the French who, under de Gaulle were prepared to abandon an empire that was becoming increasingly costly and an impediment to the modernization of French agriculture and industry, the British did not suddenly decide to abandon their African empire. The quest to retain some world status, to distinguish Britain from the other European powers, was to remain an almost constant theme of British foreign policy. Indeed, Macmillan was to see it as a means of embodying Britain's 'special' position as America's leading partner.

The most obvious consequence of Suez was the reduction of British status in the Middle East, although the British continued to try and preserve what influence did remain. As with the loss of empire in general, Suez did not mark a decisive watershed in British Middle East policy. British influence was to decline over a further period of years as Nasser's success contributed to the rise of radical Arab nationalism, if not in a united and coherent form. However, from 1957 onwards it was the US that had to face that challenge under the Cold War umbrella. What amounted to a formal expression of US policy came in January 1957, with the Eisenhower Doctrine. The Doctrine stated that the US would provide military and economic aid to those nations who were prepared to resist the forces of international communism. It was misleading in terms of Middle Eastern problems, which did not centre on communism but on radical Arab movements. The Americans, because of the Cold War, believed some Arab states were likely to be taken over by Soviet communism or would generate the kind of instability that communists could exploit. It was to lead very quickly to American involvement in what were local Middle East problems that, however they were depicted, had nothing to do with communism or Soviet interference.

The Eisenhower Doctrine was the second in the line of anti-communist doctrines that many post-1945 American presidents would have. It led to US marines landing in Lebanon in 1958 while British troops were sent into Jordan, inspired less by fear of communism than by fear of the spread of Arab movements unfriendly to the West, and in particular by the overthrow and murder of the Iraqi king and his pro-Western prime minister Nuri Said. Many Arabs disliked both Western imperialism *and* Soviet communism, and it became a bone of contention between London and some in Washington as to whether the leaders of radical nationalism in Egypt and Iraq could become a useful counter to communism. Ultimately, it was the Americans who would carry the clout and the Eisenhower Doctrine symbolized the end of British domination more than a new element in the Cold War. Nasser was to remain relatively favoured by some in Washington, while totally anathema to all in London, but in the end, he was unable to unite the Arab world. Despite Egypt joining with Syria to form the United Arab Republic for three years between 1958 and 1961, the lure of controlling their own nation state proved too compelling for territorial civil and military elites. The rivalry between Egypt and Iraq was also to continue, despite the ending of their respective monarchies. Arab leaders remained more willing to use the nationalism of the masses to build support for their positions as head of particular groups competing for power than to promote political union, or even cooperation, despite the existence of the common Israeli threat.

BOX 8.4

The Non-Aligned Movement

The mid-1950s saw a reaction to the bipolarity of the Cold War world. Rather than allying with the US or the Soviet Union, or defining themselves passively as neutrals in the East–West rivalry, many states wished to assert the importance of their own interests. In December 1954 Pandit Nehru of India met with Yugoslavian President Josip Tito and they issued a statement in favour of 'non-alignment', saying that this was 'a positive, active and constructive policy seeking to lead to collective peace'. India was a member of the British Commonwealth, but also wanted to build co-operation with the USSR and India's Asian neighbour, China; while Tito was a communist leader who had broken free of Soviet domination in the late 1940s and established friendly relations with the West. Earlier, in April 1954, the Chinese foreign minister, Zhou Enlai, visiting India to discuss a trade deal, had agreed with Nehru's view that international relations should be based on equality, respect for the sovereignty, independence of others, non-interference in their internal affairs, and non-aggression. Nehru's five principles particularly appealed to newly independent states, who had no wish to replace colonial rule with superpower domination, and they are sometimes associated with the April 1955 Bandung conference, held in Indonesia, the first major summit meeting of less-developed countries. Actually, Bandung had a wider agenda than non-alignment, being critical of colonialism and racism, but the Bandung principles later became the basis of membership of the non-aligned movement. The first proper summit of non-aligned leaders took place in September 1961, in Belgrade. Although other summits followed, usually at intervals of three or four years, and the movement still exists—with about 120 members—it is a loose organization, both in terms of its structures (though it does have a secretariat, based at the UN) and the diversity of its membership (with radically differing ideologies).

D. The End of the British Empire in Africa

The British Empire in Black Africa also came to an end with a rush, if not quite such a precipitate one as its French and Belgian counterparts. The Gold Coast (later Ghana) had already been irrevocably set on the road to independence by 1954 and the Sudan soon followed, thereby effectively following in the footsteps of the Dominions. Central to any analysis of the end of the British Empire in the early 1960s is accounting for its timing and for the lack of any long-term planning in that timing. The basic principles may well have been lurking in the minds of policy-makers, and if there was any impact of initiatives in the colonies, they had more of an immediate effect on policy than on planning in the Colonial Office. If there was a key rationale behind the decisions that were taken in the latter half of the 1950s and the first half of the 1960s, it was based on the principle of whatever was necessary, or could be made acceptable, in order to transfer power while minimizing the international and domestic problems that would result from satisfying the demands of African political leaders.

Originally, the plan was to prepare each of the larger colonies for independence by assisting in the social, economic, and political development that would make them viable states. Despite the lack of resources, the British Colonial Office still professed to believe in this, but by the middle of the decade other factors were coming into play. The Foreign Office became increasingly worried that the task of keeping Africa loyal to the West could not be trusted to a Colonial Office concerned with the particular issues of a number of fragmented territories. A regional or continental policy would be more suitable to deal with Cold War needs. Then there was the broader difficulty of transferring power too slowly which, perhaps in the face of Colonial Office claims that some colonies were not ready for independence, might produce the radicalization of independence movements in British Africa. There was the example of the Mau Mau rebellion in Kenya (1952–9), even though it did not fit the Cold War model and was produced by the changing nature of land use, with people being excluded from using land traditionally available to them. Then there was the opposite problem of moving too fast to independence, which would create unstable states that could, of course, be deemed exploitable by Soviet communism.

Multiracialism and its Demise

What was worse was the existence, in East and Central Africa (in Kenya, Northern and Southern Rhodesia in particular), of significant minorities of white settlers. The problem was further complicated by the creation of the Central African Federation of the two Rhodesias and Nyasaland in 1953, largely in order to prevent the influence of South Africa spreading northwards under the banner of apartheid. In effect, this united a white-dominated Southern Rhodesia, having effective internal self-government and the dominant economy, with two colonies still under Colonial Office tutelage. In Kenya, where the Mau Mau rebellion continued to smoulder, there was no courting of Black African parties, as in West Africa, and by 1957 it was difficult to see how the British were going to find native collaborators. There was a particular problem in Kenya, where African leaders like Jomo Kenyatta, who were suspected of association with Mau Mau terrorism, could not be trusted by the British as 'responsible' leaders of African parties. The problem in the largest West African colony, Nigeria, was in keeping the disparate three main regions together in the establishment of a modern state—divide and rule, but unite and decolonize in order to move from control to influence. The Gold Coast model of working cooperatively with the leaders of the largest African Party in return for early independence, seemed inapplicable to many other territories. Problems of regional differences, or the politicization of ethnic diversity, were formidable obstacles to the creation of viable pro-Western nations in East, West, and Central Africa.

One solution that the British came up with was the idea of multiracialism, in which the idea of African majority rule with 'one man, one vote' would be superseded by the idea of racial groups working in separate electoral colleges to produce governments based on racial cooperation, although not of a proportional kind. It was designed to give representation on a 'community' or ethnic basis, which would clearly benefit the European and Indian minorities. It was encouraged by a mistaken belief that white settlers brought added expertise to African farming and crop cultivation, and by the need to try and reconcile the racial groups in Central Africa to make the Federation work. As the 1950s wore on, it became increasingly less likely that the British would be able to get away with the avoidance of one man one vote.

The Americans were much quicker to realize this, even though they had long worried about too rapid a transfer of power leaving badly prepared and unstable states prone to communism. In 1959 they saw that the British were slow and rather too complacent because they believed that the transfer of power could be delayed and major conflict avoided, whether by multiracialism or anything else. In essence, this concern was based on the British paper 'Africa: The Next Ten Years', an official report begun in early 1959 and presented in June of that year. The report explicitly defined the dilemma between moving too fast and moving too slowly, but as the Americans noted, there was a lack of concrete proposals for avoiding this conundrum. Instead, there was some criticism, which the Prime Minister endorsed, along the lines that Britain still wielded influence in Africa. It was a strange illusion, one which was to be tested in East and Central Africa by a series of events which questioned the idea of moulding Africa in line with British designs, and was to lead, by the end of 1960, to a much greater commitment to the abandonment of responsibilities as soon as was reasonably possible.[24]

In those territories away from the troubled racial mix in Kenya and the Central Africa Federation, early 1959 saw the continuation of what was still a medium-term goal to transfer power by the Colonial Office, albeit without any coherent or precise time frame. It was true that after the Suez Crisis doubts were cast, if largely ignored, about the continuance of Britain's world role but this goal was to be maintained in changed form and, in the long term, without colonies. Resources for defence expenditure were less in relative terms, economic problems continued to mount, and strategic conceptions changed as the Suez-induced air barrier across much of the Arab world refocused attention on the Persian Gulf and East African regions. It is arguable that, in the Gulf, attempts were made to strengthen British involvement in ways other than through mere retention of influence that was being sought in the largest West African territory, Nigeria, as it approached independence. In Nigeria, the goal was to bring the new nation together under the banner of independence, but the latter was desired more by the educated and Westernized people of the eastern and western regions than by the more populated, but less politically aware Muslim north. British policy aimed to concede independence, demanded by the southern provinces, through the creation of a federal entity which would include a 'modernized' north that was somewhat reluctant to embark on such a process. In one sense, Britain was attempting to create nationalism in the north in order to comply with the wishes of the 'nationalists' in the south for the sake of a larger, more powerful state. Post-colonial British influence would then be stronger than in a divided set of newly independent small provinces. The main concern of the British was that the backward north would refuse to participate in a unitary state geared to the demands of a Christian, capitalist elite in the south. The Willink Report and constitutional conference in 1957 had set a precedent in as much as resolving difficulties by offering independence was seen as a way to avoid further problems. If the different parties in Nigeria could agree on the nature of a federal government, independence could be granted, and the role of the colonial power was to encourage in the north what the south was clamouring for.[25] As the Cold War began to focus more on the less developed world in the second half of the decade, and Africa in particular by 1959–60, escaping difficult situations assumed greater importance and meant that less attention was paid to the preparation for independence, which had dominated Colonial Office thinking in the first post-war decade.

Progress was easier in the less developed territory of Tanganyika, where independence was not expected to be achieved rapidly and the danger of 'irresponsible' elements inheriting power was less of a consideration. The idea, put forward in 'Africa: The Next Ten Years', that Kenya would not achieve independence until at least 1970 was even more true of Tanganyika, although for different reasons. While there was a united nationalist party, the country was deemed to be educationally backward and therefore not ready for even internal self-government until 1970. The fact that events moved more quickly resulted from the crises which emerged in Central Africa from 1959 onwards, although the first sign came in 1958, with the Southern Rhodesian rejection of Garfield Todd's liberal commitment to African advancement. Much worse was to follow in 1959 and, eventually, it was to make a significant impact on the approach to the transfer of power. The realization of the internal and international difficulties and, more importantly, the dangers Britain faced in clinging on to power provided an incentive to speed up the process. Power was thus transferred more quickly than anticipated when 'Africa: The Next Ten Years' was first drafted in the crisis year of 1959. Transferring power rapidly was encouraged by the need to retain the initiative and control the basis of present and future cooperation and because, as a last resort, it increasingly seemed the only way of avoiding embroiling Britain in the kind of scenarios that were emerging in the Congo (see Chapter 8, B).

The riots that broke out in that country in January 1959 were accompanied by a state of emergency in Southern Rhodesia in February. Fears among the whites in the Federation of wide-ranging disturbances led to Southern Rhodesian troops being sent to Nyasaland, which further increased tensions and produced clashes in which around fifty Africans died. In March, a state of emergency was declared and Hastings Banda, the leader of the Nyasaland Congress Party, was arrested. This provoked further demonstrations, in which twenty Africans were shot dead. A Commission of Inquiry under Lord Devlin, a distinguished high court judge, was then established and the Devlin report, delivered in July 1959, was scathing in its criticism of the colonial administration. The latter was accused of reacting to the widespread growth of African political consciousness by the creation of a 'police state'.

On the same day as Banda's arrest, at a remote camp in Kenya where terrorist suspects were detained (without a formal conviction), a number of African prisoners refused to carry out their forced labour. In response, their guards carried out beatings and eleven were beaten to death, with twenty more badly injured. The deaths at Hola became part of an attempted cover-up based on stomach illnesses that unsurprisingly failed and questions were asked in the British Parliament. The veil of liberalism, always somewhat threadbare since Suez, was now being unceremoniously lifted from British colonialism. Multiracialism, clearly a difficult if not an impossible goal, was also dramatically seen to be worthless as a liberal veneer when the Southern Rhodesian government interned some 500 people, including a white missionary farmer, Guy Clutton Brook, whose case was taken up in Parliament by Barbara Castle, a Labour MP. Clutton Brook was described as 'subversive' by the native commissioner, who was unaware in the bush of the concept of multiracialism. Regarded as an 'odious and harmful influence', because he allowed Africans to eat at his table and even sleep in his own house, Brook was accused of neglecting to require them to stand up if a European entered the room.[26]

The End Comes Quickly

The failure of multiracialism, the granting of independence by the French (see Chapter 8, A), and the atrocities in East and Central Africa contributed to a growing desire to avoid yet more difficulties and ridicule by solving problems as rapidly as possible whenever the easiest way to do so seemed an early transfer of power. Where this could be done in ways uncomplicated by multiracialism, as in Tanganyika, it stemmed from a desire to retain the initiative, as was vainly hoped in the 1940s, if not to slow down the African drive for independence but to ensure that the process ran smoothly. In Tanganyika, Governor Richard Turnbull presented proposals for rapidly increasing the pace of political advancement in 1959. His plan was 'to tame Nyerere', the leading African politician, and prevent the 'wild men' coming into positions of power, as appeared to be the case in other parts of eastern and central Africa. Turnbull therefore immediately introduced an unofficial majority (African representatives as opposed to British officials) on the legislative council. He envisaged an African majority on the Council of Ministers by 1965, some five years earlier than planned and new Colonial Secretary Iain Macleod, who came to office in October 1959, was more easily reconciled to such a rapid transfer of power. In the event, the Cabinet moved even faster, won over by the perceived need to retain confidence in Britain and ensure 'peaceful development'. The result was independence in December 1961.

Kenya, with its significant minority of white settlers, was more difficult to keep on the narrow road of peaceful development, given settler opposition to African majority rule. It was even more difficult in the Central African Federation, where African politicians seeking political advancement in Northern Rhodesia and Nyasaland were up against the white-dominated Federation. When government in the newly independent Congo effectively collapsed in 1960, the problem appeared even worse, as Europeans were attacked. In both cases, the options of Britain not giving independence seemed to present more problems and presage African disturbances, and even racial violence, with Europeans rallying to the regime in Pretoria. In January 1960 Macleod devised a new constitution for Kenya, which, by extending the electoral roll, effectively guaranteed an African legislative majority, and an important watershed was crossed. The Americans, worried as 1959 began at British reluctance to embrace the inevitable quickly enough, now had renewed confidence in the implementation of the British transfer of power in Africa. Of course, the acceptance of African majority rule still left the problem of compensation for white farmers and the rehabilitation from jail of Jomo Kenyatta, the only effective claimant for leading Kenyans on a national basis. As with Nkrumah in the Gold Coast, Banda in Nyasaland, and others, the inside of a British-run jail was the precursor to national leadership. What produced the change for the British were perceptions of the difficulties of slowing down, never mind preventing, change. Rapid change was easier to accept because of the mounting strength of African political movements, combined with a growing fear of turning a difficult situation into something worse. In Kenya, it was fear of reviving the Mau Mau rebellion, which had largely ended in 1959, and the general breakdown of law and order in the middle of a Cold War for the hearts and minds of Africans. By December 1963 Kenya was independent.[27]

The real problem was speeding up change in the Central African Federation, where independence for Nyasaland and Northern Rhodesia could herald the break-up of the Federation. In the crisis summer of 1959, the government decided to appoint a commission of inquiry under Walter Monckton, the former critic of his government's handling of the Suez affair (see Chapter 8, C), in order to examine the Federation's constitutional future. The Monckton Commission began work in February 1960 and, in September, eight of its twenty-five members submitted an agreed report. The rest had reservations and the two African members submitted a minority report. With the recommendations including an African majority on the Northern Rhodesian legislative council and the conclusion that the Federation could not continue in its present form, Macleod decided to bite the bullet and attempt to move forward along these lines. Kenneth Kaunda, another African political leader released from jail in Northern Rhodesia, had acted to restrain his followers and channel their protests along peaceful lines. Yet, given the complications of the Federation and the white opposition to its break-up, forcefully led by the former Union leader, Roy Welensky, there were serious obstacles to change.

Back home, white settlers had considerable support within the Conservative Party, while many in the government were loath to abandon the Federation and risk sending Southern Rhodesia into the arms of the South Africans. Macleod may have hoped that moving forward to African majority rule was a way of preserving the Federation by placing it on a new footing. But the whole of 1961, before and after Macleod's departure from the Colonial Office, was taken up with wrangling over the future of the Federation and the precise arithmetic to be applied to the Northern Rhodesian Constitution. White opposition to Macleod's proposal for the minimum impact and maximum concealment of an African majority produced protests in Africa and the Conservative Party, but the real menace lay in the prospect of large-scale African violence if it was not implemented. From the collapse of the Federation's constitutional review conference in December 1960 to the final decision on the Northern Rhodesian Constitution in February 1962, with its African majority built in, deceit, recrimination, and bitterness grew on all sides. Responsibility for planning the final denouement in the Federation in the worst possible situation was given in April 1962 to R. A. Butler, as head of a new government department. Inevitably, it resulted in the secession of Northern Rhodesia and Nyasaland, which achieved independence in 1964 as Zambia and Malawi, after the dissolution of the Central African Federation in December 1963.[28]

The extremely rapid end to the process of transferring power requires some explanation. The more committed empire supporters on the Right had never entirely accepted the abandonment of British responsibilities, even when significant amounts of British prestige, associated with world power status, were not at risk. Even in 1960 there were diehards who could not easily contemplate Africans being given greater political responsibility for white men and who were still prepared to offer determined resistance. That this was overcome is easy to ascribe to the growing effectiveness of mass-based African parties and to the momentum for decolonization, as what one country had obtained could not easily be withheld from another. The implications, for example, of the French territories being offered independence had implications for British Africa. If one country in East Africa was given an African majority, how could this be withheld from another? Yet reactions to the events of 1959 onwards and the demands of African leaders were also influenced by other concerns which contributed to the speed of the process. The process occurred as European trade grew in importance, and trade between the developed countries in the North rose much more than that between the North and the Commonwealth countries in Africa and the southern hemisphere. Britain's application to join the EEC in 1961 may have reflected a sea change in global focus. Far more important, however, was the influence of the Cold War and the fear of chaos and conflict that it induced and magnified. The Cold War had increasingly become an ideological battle for hearts and minds outside Europe by the second half of the 1950s. The focus was on Africa at the end of the decade, where the Congo had revealed only too well how the problems inherent in European rule could develop into international crises. Fear encouraged the process by making the rapid transfer of power desirable, if it avoided the type of situation that had developed in Algeria and the Congo. The British colonial empire's rapid demise in Africa did not come about because of foresight, strategy, or even as a careful readjustment to African demands. Its rapid termination offered the best prospect of preventing significant local difficulties becoming unmanageable and threatening Britain and the West with Cold War disasters that could have far more serious implications than the abandonment of colonies.

Visit the online resources that accompany this book to test your understanding and take your learning further: www.oup.com/he/young-kent3e

NOTES

1. Stanley Karnow, *Vietnam: A History* (Guild Publishing, London, 1983), 213.
2. Gerard J. de Groot, *A Noble Cause? America and the Vietnam War* (Pearson, Harlow, 2000), 68.
3. Robert K. Brigham, *Guerrilla Diplomacy: The NLF's Foreign Relations and the Vietnam War* (Cornell University Press, Ithaca, 1998), 18.
4. William J. Rust, *Kennedy in Vietnam* (Da Capo, New York, 1985), 181.
5. Gary R. Hess, 'Kennedy's Vietnam options and decisions', in David L. Anderson (ed.), *Shadow on the White House: Presidents and the Vietnam War*, 1945–75 (University of Kansas Press, Lawrence, 1993), 82–3.
6. Lawrence J. Bassett and Stephen E. Pelz, 'The Failed Search for Victory: Vietnam and the Politics of War', in Thomas G. Paterson (ed.), *Kennedy's Quest for Victory: American Foreign Policy, 1961–3* (Oxford University Press, New York, 1989), 252.
7. We are indebted to Ryo Ikeda for this information.
8. M. Kahler, *Decolonisation in Britain and France* (Princeton University Press, Princeton, 1984), 355.
9. On the relationship between the two, see Tony Chafer, *The End of Empire in French West Africa: France's Successful Decolonization?* (Berg, Oxford, 2002), 1–21.
10. J. Marseille, *Empire Colonial et Capitalisme Français* (Albin Michel, Paris, 1984), 367–73.
11. John D. Hargreaves, *Decolonization in Africa* (2nd edn, Longman, Harlow, 1996), 186–90.
12. See David Halberstam, *The Best and the Brightest* (Random House, New York, 1972).
13. The Americans were told by Sir Brian Urquhart, a Foreign Office official assigned to work for the UN in the Congo, that the lack of British support over the Congo was due to the influence within the government of the Conservative party's chief financial backers who 'almost to a man' were the principals in Tanganyika Concessions (with four of them also board members of UMHK): John F Kennedy Library (JFKL), Boston, National Security File, Congo, Box 30, Tel. 3657, USUN to Secretary of State, 4 May 1962.
14. The *Compagnie du Katanga* received the other 20 per cent of the concessions.

15. The CSK had been established under Leopold in 1900, but two-thirds of it was owned by the colonial government. Another feature of colonialism in the Congo was that the operating companies extracting mineral resources from the concessionary lands deposited share-securities to the domainial authority, that is the company owning the concessions from King Leopold—in southern Katanga primarily the CSK. For Tanganyika concessions this meant, until 1962, benefits were transferred in the form of dividends to shareholders. The CSK collected such dividends on behalf of the Belgian Congo government and the shares went into the Congo Portfolio, which, before and after independence, was still controlled in Brussels. See John Kent, *America, the UN and Decolonisation: Cold War Conflict in the Congo* (London, Routledge, 2010), 81, fn. 116.

16. A redacted source had provided the Americans with Tshombe's Swiss bank account details, where he held 11 million Swiss francs and 43 million Belgian francs. Tshombe's bank account numbers were not given to the Americans, unlike those of the more left-wing leaders (Gizenga, Mulele, and Kalonji), JFKL, President's Office File (POF), Box 114, Brussels to Secretary of State, 13 March 1962.

17. The National Archives, Kew, FO371/146639, Minute by Boothby, 13 July 1962.

18. For a good account, see R. D. Mahoney, *JFK: Ordeal in Africa* (Oxford University Press, New York, 1983).

19. Fernando Andresen Guimarães, *The Origins of the Angolan Civil War* (St Martin's Press, New York, 1998), 49–52.

20. J. Marcum, *The Angolan Revolution: The Anatomy of an Explosion 1950–1962* (MIT Press, London, 1969), 130–54.

21. Fernando Andresen Guimarães, *The Origins of the Angolan Civil War* (St Martin's Press, New York, 1998), 60.

22. See Brian Lapping, *The End of Empire* (Granada, London, 1985) and the debate with Robert Holland in 'Did Suez hasten the End of Empire?', *Contemporary Record*, 1 (1987–8), 39.

23. See especially, *British Documents on the End of Empire*, BDEEP, Series B, 4, Pt I, *Egypt and the Defence of the Middle East 1945–1956*, John Kent (ed.), Introduction (Stationery Office, London, 1998).

24. Ronald Hyam and Wm Roger Louis (eds), BDEEP, Series A, 4, Pt I, Introduction, xxxvi–xxxvii.

25. John Darwin, *Britain and Decolonisation* (Macmillan, Basingstoke, 1988), 181–3.

26. Ronald Hyam and Wm Roger Louis (eds), BDEEP, Series A, 4, Pt I, Introduction, xlv.

27. Ibid., lii–liii.

28. Ibid., liii–lvi; John D. Hargreaves, *Decolonization in Africa* (2nd edn, Longman, Harlow, 1996), 217–18.

PART III

The Cold War of Peaceful Coexistence and the Rise of Multipolarity, 1963–71

The international system that existed in 1963 was in many ways unrecognizable from that which was in place after 1945, or even 1953. The failed attempts to agree on the principles, or the power-political arrangements, that should govern it had produced the Cold War and, with it, the possibility of armed conflict between rival blocs, culminating in the Cuban Missile Crisis. In addition, the creation of many new independent states in Asia and Africa had challenged, and altered, the global domination of the rival blocs. This was one factor in the emergence of a more multipolar world, which required a more complex approach to the maintenance and pursuit of interests for the superpowers. Another key factor was the split in the communist bloc, with differences emerging, not only between the USSR and China, but also within Soviet-dominated east-central Europe. In addition, East–West relations were dramatically affected by the development and spread of nuclear technology. Finally, in economic terms, the success of the Bretton Woods system and the unrivalled dominance of the dollar, were increasingly called into question by the early 1970s. These developments did not lead to the disintegration of the post-1945 global system, but they were an indication of long-term systemic shifts. The 1960s saw signs of a world in which power relationships were more complicated, states were more numerous, international institutions more important, East–West rivalry more tied into regional issues, and the cohesion of the opposing blocs called into question. If the late 1950s had marked a move away from attempts to destroy the other side, the years after 1962 witnessed the further acceptance of peaceful coexistence, leading to Richard Nixon's talk, in his 1969 inaugural address, of an 'era of negotiations'. These negotiations included strategic arms talks, the status of Berlin, and a relaxation of tension in Europe. Anders Stephanson has even suggested that the Cold War, as seen by its participants as a struggle for survival, was now over.[1]

The confrontation engendered by the Cuban Missile Crisis made both sides acutely aware of the dangers of Cold War competition leading to hot war. From the Soviet perspective, the lessons learned by 1963 centred on their relative lack of traditional military and economic power, compared to the US. Always more concerned with the stark realities of power, the new Soviet leadership that replaced Khrushchev in 1964 saw the need to avoid any future humiliation similar to the Cuban Crisis. In order to do this, it was believed vital to increase all-round Soviet strength to equal that of Washington. Before the crisis, it was Kennedy who launched a significant arms build-up; after it, the Soviets led the way, helped by the fact that the Americans got bogged down in Vietnam. In the end, enormous American military expenditure failed to deliver dividends in strategic terms, nor did it produce domestic or political benefits—far from it. It was partly because the US realized that the Soviets had achieved nuclear parity that Nixon was willing to take up détente.

Vietnam Issues

The Vietnam experience has been seen as deeply scarring for American society and as undermining the US role in the world, even though the suffering and devastation was essentially borne by the Vietnamese. Its causes and consequences still remain controversial despite the vast, ever-growing literature on the subject. The fact that the war originated in an anti-colonial movement with deep roots, which came to be largely controlled by a communist leadership, was one explanation of the inadequate US understanding of the struggle. The extent and nature of support for the communist-led resistance movement within South Vietnam was poorly perceived by American leaders. The nature of the revolt in South Vietnam has been interpreted as either essentially an indigenous movement or one provoked by external forces sent from the communist North. In reality, it was a combination of these. There is little doubt that the revolt was southern in origin. However, the issue is complicated by the number of insurgents who were originally natives of the North. The repression that followed in the South limited the scope of the uprising by the early 1960s and its extension was undoubtedly connected to greater support from the North, as well the increasing involvement of North Vietnamese regular armed forces. This, in turn, was part of a wider campaign to promote revolution which received support from China and the Soviet Union.

For American opponents of the war, Lyndon Johnson is often seen as the villain who led America to greater disasters and inevitable defeat by increasing the scale and costs of the conflict. Kennedy, on the other hand, refused to send in combat troops and, in the months before his death, may have thought about scaling down the number of US military 'advisers' to the South Vietnamese government with a view to eventual withdrawal. But even those sympathetic to US aims accuse Johnson of fighting the war with one hand tied behind his back, hoping to win at low cost. There is certainly substance to the charge of fighting a limited war, but the idea that the war was ultimately winnable if only more resources had been used is less convincing. For example, if American ground forces had been used to invade the North, then the likelihood of direct Chinese intervention would have greatly increased. The possibility of another Korean conflict between the US and China would have constituted a major escalation and could have led to a third world war. Even without that, Johnson was reluctant to commit more than 500,000 US troops because of the political and financial implications arising from such extra numbers.

Internationally, Vietnam was seen as part of America's campaign to prevent the spread of communism anywhere. It was also a further indication that, in order to prevent the spread of communism, Washington was willing to support corrupt, authoritarian regimes. It was not that the US had given up on its ideological support for liberal democracy where this could be established on a stable basis, as in Western Europe and Japan. But, in the less developed world attempts to liberalize often led to political instability and, if it was a choice between communism and dictatorship, the US would rely on the latter. Also, the need to demonstrate US credibility as a reliable ally had become much more important, at the time, than the Truman Doctrine. If the Soviet Union was now accepted as a permanent great power player on the international stage, it was vital to prevent any increase in its communist allies. The growth of the blocs, measured in terms of political allegiance to Washington or Moscow, was now even more important as a global issue. This increased competition for ideological loyalty had been created by the emergence of so many independent countries in the years up to the early 1960s. As this process was being completed, US troops were landing in Vietnam and the fate of Indo-China became the most important element in this Cold War battle.

The debate about why the US lost in Vietnam revolves around not only the extent of Johnson's military commitment, but also the tactics employed by US generals, the nature of Washington's decision-making, the weaknesses of the South Vietnamese regime, and the fundamental fact that, in order to triumph, the insurgents did not have to win any battles but merely to stay in the war. Both General de Gaulle and Ho Chi Minh were confident that the Americans would lose, with Ho emphasizing that, however long it took, the communist forces seeking to unite the country would stay and fight longer than the Americans. In other words, for the North and the insurgents in the South, victory would only require continuing the fight. There were other reasons for the difficulties Johnson got into in Vietnam. Undoubtedly, one turning point which illustrates the political importance of military campaigns was the impact of the Tet offensive in 1968. This psychological victory for the North made a massive dent in Johnson's credibility, even though American forces inflicted heavy losses on the Viet Cong. The media may also have created political problems for Johnson by reporting the offensive as it happened, without restriction. At home, discontent grew and the scale of protests was such that, when Richard Nixon became president in January 1969, it was impossible for the US to stay in the war but almost as difficult to get out. Nixon claimed to have a 'secret plan' to achieve this, but the best he could produce was the old idea of the 'Vietnamization' of the war, the failure of which had got America involved in the first place. To put pressure on the North to make peace, Nixon tried extending the war outside Vietnam and the increased use of airpower; hence the secret bombing, and subsequent invasion, of Cambodia. Yet bombing had never worked in the past and American intervention in Cambodia arguably prepared the way for the triumph of Pol Pot's murderous communist regime there. The extension of the Vietnam War had similar destructive effects in Laos. The domino theory had predicted that the fall of Vietnam would lead to communist regimes seizing power beyond. Events showed that American action, as much as inaction, could help the process by widening divisions and encouraging extremism.

Problems within Blocs

Central to the problems of preserving a global system based on competition and coexistence between two opposing groups was the rift between the two principal communist powers. First evident in 1957, this assumed the proportions of an unbridgeable gulf by 1963, and came near to large-scale military conflict by 1969.[2] The reasons for this split, which astonished many Western observers, have been linked to a great variety of causes, including the personal rift between Khrushchev and Mao (see Chapter 7, C for its origins) but the power-political implications were clearly significant (see Chapter 9, B). Power politics here refers to the growing competition between the USSR and China, not merely over leadership of the communist bloc, but also in international and regional affairs. The decade saw the growth and extension of each power's relations with states outside the communist bloc and culminated in the Chinese–American links that began in 1971. Connected to this were the growing ideological divisions over the meaning of Marxism-Leninism for internal and external policy. In the latter case, this essentially boiled down to a commitment to peaceful coexistence or revolutionary conflict.

The Soviet Union also had continuing problems maintaining unity within its European satellite empire. Having suffered a number of challenges to Soviet authority in the 1950s, the Kremlin tended to be sceptical about attempts at reform. But a new challenge in 1968 came from Czechoslovakia under Alexander Dubček. By then, both sides had learned lessons from the Hungarian reforms and their suppression by Soviet troops. Dubček tried to ease Soviet fears by keeping the reformers within the Communist Party and emphasizing his commitment to the Warsaw Pact. The Russians were more alert to the threat and planned military intervention well in advance, while warning Dubček of that danger. In terms of the ideological challenge to Soviet-style communism, they had more reason to be concerned even than in 1956. The Sino-Soviet split involved a Chinese challenge to Soviet ideology, which Mao presented as deviating from the true path of Marxism-Leninism. It was therefore no surprise that the Czech efforts to liberalize led the Soviets to embark on another round of forcible repression in Eastern Europe.

It also led, as part of the drive to preserve Soviet domination of the communist countries in Europe, to Leonid Brezhnev coming up with a justification based on the need to preserve the unity of the Soviet bloc. Known as the 'Brezhnev Doctrine' (see Box 9.2), its commitment to prevent the spread of capitalism was in part the reverse image of the Western determination to prevent the spread of communism. It underlined the continuing connection—whatever Mao claimed—between ideology and power politics in Soviet foreign policy. Brezhnev emphasized the 'limited sovereignty' that resulted from maintaining socialism in Europe and justified this in ideological terms. Yet the Doctrine was effectively geared to the maintenance of the Soviet satellite empire and Moscow's credibility in the global Cold War. Those leaders in Eastern Europe who achieved a degree of independence from Moscow were those who, paradoxically, avoided liberalization. Nicolae Ceauşescu's strategy in Romania was to carve out a more independent foreign policy from within the Warsaw Pact; Albania's was to move closer to China, while preserving a Stalinist political system.

Parallel challenges were mounted to US domination within the Western bloc, which was starting to run into economic difficulties. In the long term, the West was to prove far more stable than the East, having only one leading power (there was no equivalent to China), and because capitalism in Europe proved far more successful and adaptable than Soviet communism, despite the difficulties brought by the war in Vietnam. Nonetheless, Ceauşescu's growing independence in the East was reflected in the policies of the French leader, Charles de Gaulle, who embarked on an effort to enhance the role of Europe in general and France in particular through the modification of US dominance. This, it has been argued,[3] was not simply the French assertion of a new leadership role, in a Europe more independent of the US, but part of an attempt to weaken the two opposing blocs in order to build better relations with the East and create a more 'European' Europe. However, it soon became clear that there were limits to how far such a policy could go. A more independent Western Europe was largely ruled out by the West German refusal to abandon the Atlantic alliance and, albeit temporarily, by the 1968 Soviet invasion of Czechoslovakia, which revealed the lack of progress in the East.

The Politics of Nuclear Strategy

The attempts to change the nature of relationships within the Western bloc were related to the role and development of thermonuclear weapons. The Soviet rearmament effort, arguably, for the first time produced a truly bipolar world as their nuclear forces caught up, around 1969, with the US. Their ability to project power over greater distances, as with the creation of an ocean-going navy, also grew. Of course, there was a growing realization that the use of thermonuclear weapons on a major scale made war unwinnable, so that such weapons were in essence unusable: once the Soviets achieved nuclear parity with the US, there was a situation of 'mutual assured destruction'—any war would result in both sides being annihilated. However, the weapons themselves symbolized power and consequently there was a strong case for making them seem usable. Opponents of such weapons argued that the effort to devise situations and strategies of use was simply trying to rationalize the irrational. But supporters claimed that nuclear weapons, when linked with conventional weapons in a clearly defined military strategy, would enhance deterrence. By making the use of nuclear weapons—in a limited and more flexible way, short of global war—seem rational, an all-out exchange would become less likely as the deterrent became more credible, hence NATO's development of 'flexible response' within the parameters of mutually assured destruction. The idea was that limited escalation would produce responses short of all-out war, encouraging the opponent at some stage to abandon the conflict for fear of further punishment through escalation.

The US Strategic Air Command did not accept the idea either of limited war or of flexible response. General Tommy Power, the head of the Strategic Air Command, said after listening to an explanation of the new concept: 'Why do you want us to restrain ourselves? . . . The whole idea is to kill the bastards.'[4] To many, the only sensible way to use nuclear weapons was to use them all first in order to limit the retaliation that would inevitably come, but as the numbers of nuclear warheads expanded this was increasingly difficult. Moreover, the development of nuclear weapons was still influenced by interservice rivalry, with none of the services prepared to leave the deterrent solely to another, so that by the 1960s the US was developing deterrents for all three services to deploy.

Whatever the strategic doctrine or military rationale, the political importance of nuclear weapons remained and was at the heart of the transatlantic debate over the power relationships within the Western Alliance. Should not the Europeans have a say in the exercise of such powerful weapons? Here the central issues were the continued, delicate question of Germans being in control of nuclear weapons, the nature of American leadership, and the problematic question of some powers (like Britain and France) retaining 'independent' nuclear systems when an integrated flexible response was deemed necessary. For the Americans, the idea of a multilateral nuclear force (MLF) provided a solution to all three problems. The Germans could be treated as a more equal partner by being involved in a nuclear force (even if the weapons were supplied by the Americans) and might therefore never ask for national control over any nuclear weapons. NATO would be united in contributing to an alliance force and the appearance of American domination would be reduced. Both these aspects could contribute to the strengthening of the alliance. At the same time, for those in the US who were worried about European independence, Britain and France could be induced to commit their nuclear forces to the MLF. The last thing that the US wanted was a European power provoking a major nuclear exchange independently of the Americans. But partly because it did aim at undermining their independence, the French were always openly hostile to the MLF concept, and the British had no enthusiasm for it. The Soviets were deeply concerned about the prospect of Germany sharing in the control of NATO's nuclear arsenal, which made it more difficult to progress with global limits on nuclear weapons. Despite years of discussion, MLF proved impossible to implement. But its failure did pave the way for a Non-Proliferation Treaty, signed in 1968, and followed in 1969 by the beginning of nuclear disarmament talks between the superpowers.

A Less Divided Europe?

The different views about the nature of the Western Alliance were eased with the departure of General de Gaulle in 1969. By then, the German leader, Willy Brandt, had taken up the mantle to create a new, less confrontational Europe of opposing blocs through his *Ostpolitik*. There had been a number of contacts between Western leaders and the Soviets in the 1960s, NATO had accepted the principle of détente in the 1967 Harmel Report, and there was a growing realization on both sides of the Iron Curtain of the benefits these could bring. There was the need to reduce the risk of military conflict, to resolve the German issue, to establish a more independent role within both blocs, and to benefit from economic contacts. All these were especially important for West Germans, but the Soviets too were attracted by the idea of obtaining technology and other economic advantages from the West, and by implementing their long-standing idea of a European security system. Such a development would enable them to reduce the threat from Germany, while removing the influence of the US from Europe and possibly creating divisions within the Western camp.

None of this meant that the Cold War was being superseded or that the ideological requirements of either side were changing. As in the past, the new moves towards détente were in many ways part of a strategy in the West to gain a Cold War advantage and win the ideological battle. By opening up new contacts, the attractions of a more successful economic system, as manifested in the more plentiful array of consumer goods, could prove attractive in the East and wean its people towards Western capitalism. In 1970, Brandt signed a treaty with Moscow renouncing force and increasing economic links, but also recognizing the inviolability of European boundaries. *Ostpolitik* had definite limitations as far as the erosion of blocs was concerned. The four-power agreement which recognized the status quo in Berlin in 1971 was another indication of how new policies were not designed to make a clear break with the old concepts of a divided Europe. Political agreements on these lines would take a long time to have more than a limited effect and détente leading to the end of the Cold War was not something that was envisaged. The agreement in 1971 to hold a European Security Conference seemed only another sign of the desire to avoid hot war while the ideological battle continued apace.

Latin America

In the western hemisphere, the nature of the Cold War was particularly affected by the advent to power of Fidel Castro. At first, Kennedy tried to encourage economic development, but his policies soon ran into the sand. Poverty and inequality were increasing in Latin America but they were not easy to tackle and the US Congress was reluctant to pump in vast amounts of dollars. Without structural change, such as land reform, the injection of capital was only likely to exacerbate the problems created by the structural inequality. If large landowners were given incentives to expand production by planting more cash crops, it required the removal of more land from food production and the inevitable creation of more landless labourers. What was created, then, was not a new middle class attracted to democracy, but more landless labourers who were ready to support revolutionary movements. As such movements spread, it became riskier, in US eyes, to support liberal reformists than to rely on the military dictators who already dominated many Latin American states. Once again, stability and anti-communism were more important aims for Washington than experiments with democracy.

Political instability and concern about left-wing movements produced numerous twentieth-century American interventions in the region, the latest being that by Lyndon Johnson in the Dominican Republic in 1965 (see Chapter 11, A). As in the 1950s, the fear was not what the communists might do (there were no strong communist organizations outside Cuba), but how they might be created. The fact that a government or leader might pave the way for communists still concerned American policy-makers. There were the old implications for Cold War credibility and American economic interests which were more worrisome since Castro came to power and tried to export his revolution. This was the aspect of the Cuban threat which increasingly obsessed Washington. Security was, in concrete terms, nothing more than the threat of an odd gunboat unless, of course, as the Missile Crisis had shown, the Soviets were given the opportunity to install weapons. In Latin America, the concern about the instability from which radicalism grew was, like a pendulum, swinging the US back towards support for dictators while Johnson and Nixon were in the White House. Eisenhower and Kennedy had seen that dictators created opposition, which led to their overthrow and the risk of radicalism. These presidents therefore experimented with reform. But as the failure of the Alliance for Progress became evident, Johnson and Nixon saw attempts to promote change leading to instability and the need for dictators to ruthlessly suppress any radical discontent.

Conflicts in Asia

The British clash with Indonesia in 1963, known as the 'Konfrontasi' or Confrontation, was part colonial and part post-colonial in that it involved areas still subject to colonial rule and a number of independent states. The British became concerned to maintain their position in South-East Asia during the final years of their direct rule, with a view to a future position of influence and the retention of great power status.

By now, the strains on an overstretched military position which symbolized this status were increasingly severe. The centre of the dilemma in the early 1960s was Singapore, site of the most significant British military base east of Suez. Premier Harold Macmillan approved a scheme whereby the island colony would be incorporated into the pro-Western newly independent Malayan Federation, thereby avoiding the danger of radical Chinese influence and saving Britain much of the expense of operating the naval facilities at Singapore. Unfortunately, like most attempts to avoid hard choices involved in political decline, the scheme went wrong. It involved not just the incorporation of Singapore, but also that of territories in North Borneo, to ensure that the Chinese did not dominate the new federation of Malaysia. This alienated the Indonesians, who had designs on North Borneo and proceeded to embark on a propaganda campaign and armed border raids short of full-scale war. In one sense, this relieved Britain of the problem of providing token forces to support the Americans in Vietnam, as the British could claim that, by committing forces to protect Malaysia, they were making a contribution to the Western cause in Asia. In another sense, it imposed an increasingly heavy defence burden, which was exactly what Malaysia had been designed to reduce. It was only with the collapse of the anti-Western Sukarno regime in Indonesia that the Confrontation ended and, meanwhile, British economic problems persisted, forcing a major reduction in overseas defence expenditure. By mid-1967, the British were therefore forced to accept military withdrawal from East of Suez, despite the rising threat from China in the region and American problems in Vietnam.

Meanwhile, in the South Asian subcontinent the post-colonial problem of the disputed territory of Kashmir continued to cause difficulties between the independent states of India and Pakistan, culminating in war in 1965. The failure fully to understand the complexities of new regional rivalries in the context of the Cold War brought significant regional instability. By the time of the Indo-Pakistani war in 1965, it was no longer realistic to see regional crises as simply manifestations of a bipolar conflict. The foreign policy of many new states did not fit into a Cold War framework as they had more pressing internal or regional concerns, in this case the claim to Kashmir. Both aspects also characterized the clash between India and Pakistan in 1971, but this time the clash grew from the break-up of East and West Pakistan (with the creation of an independent Bangladesh out of the eastern section). On this occasion, the US came down on the side of Pakistan for reasons quite unconnected to the local conflict; reasons that, predictably, were shaped by the Cold War. The importance of the White House's new link to China, the fact that Pakistan was a member of Western alliance systems, and the need to challenge Soviet backing for India led President Nixon to send US naval forces to the Bay of Bengal. This was too late to avert a Pakistani defeat and led to criticism from within the US itself, where there was sympathy for India (a liberal democracy) and Bangladesh (which seemed to be fighting for freedom). But the leaders of both superpowers remained slow to realize that conflicts in the less developed world could not be fitted into bloc politics. This was despite acknowledgement of the emergence of a more multipolar world.

The Divided Middle East

The Middle East remained an extremely unstable region, dominated by the Arab–Israeli conflict. It was to produce a number of military conflicts in the 1960s stemming, as elsewhere, from the legacies of Western rule and the problems of colonial territories on the verge of independence. Inter-Arab rivalries developed to the extent of being referred to as an Arab Cold War[5] and continued to take several forms: the clash between conservative monarchists (as in Saudi Arabia) and radical republicans (as in Egypt); the rivalry over leadership of the Arab world (as between Iraq and Egypt); the battle between secular and religious ideologies; and links to the respective superpower rivals. On top of this was the Arab–Israeli conflict and the fact that in this period there emerged, for the first time, a Palestinian organization prepared to stand up for a purely Palestinian, rather than the Arab, cause.

In 1964, the completion of the Israeli scheme for conveying water from the River Jordan to the Negev was accompanied by a rival Arab scheme to divert the river, which in turn produced Israeli attacks that effectively prevented its implementation. Disputes between Israel and Syria also centred on rights to use the waters of the Sea of Galilee, land use along their border, and Syrian support for Palestinian guerrilla groups, the largest of which was Al Fatah led by Yasser

Arafat. Arafat had ceased working with the Palestinian Liberation Organization (PLO), the umbrella organization set up in 1964 to provide a uniquely Palestinian voice, at the end of that year because of its ties with Egypt, which, like Jordan, was opposed to guerrilla attacks on Israel. These groups operated mainly from Jordan and were designed to drag Israel into a war with the Arab states.

In February 1966, a more radical Ba'athist group led by General Jadid seized power in Damascus and took a more aggressive, hard-line stance against Israel. Lacking domestic support, the way to encourage this was seen to lie in a harsher response to Israeli actions. As Israeli–Syrian tension rose, Cairo and Damascus came closer together. A major air and land battle near the Sea of Galilee in August 1966 led to the signing of a defence pact between Egypt and Syria in November. More immediately, it produced Syrian threats to attack targets in Israel and suspicion and insecurity were obviously heightened within Israel. In November 1966, after the signing of the defence pact, an Israeli Defence Force invasion produced attacks on three Jordanian towns which killed fifteen Arab Legion soldiers. These reprisals for guerrilla attacks or border disputes had been taking place for over a decade but rarely on such a large scale. Another serious clash followed in April 1967, when six Syrian MiG jets were shot down. Then came the complex events of May 1967, which preceded the Israeli attack on its Arab neighbours. These are sources of intensely conflicting interpretations, which will be discussed more fully below. The central issues are whether the withdrawal of the UN peacekeeping force in Sinai, the subsequent Egyptian blockade of the Straits of Tiran, and the security position on the Golan Heights, as well as in the old city of Jerusalem, constituted legitimate grounds for an Israeli pre-emptive strike. If not, were Arab fears of possible Israeli aggression, as seen in its talk of marching on Damascus, justified? Finally, regarding the superpowers, what can explain the Soviet warning that Israeli troops were massing on the Syrian border?

The war destroyed the Soviet-supplied Egyptian air force, led to the continuing, illegal occupation of the West Bank, and to the unilateral annexation of East Jerusalem. It was probably the most significant act in the whole history of the Arab–Israeli conflict and the settlement, on the basis of 'land for peace', suggested by UN Resolution 242 remains the basis for individual settlements of Arab–Israeli differences. There was no quick peace in the wake of the 1967 war. Instead, in 1969, a war of attrition began across the Suez Canal, and in 1970 Israel launched massive raids against Cairo. The following year came the second of the American attempts to bring about a settlement in the form of the Rogers Plan, but land for peace could not come about while Israel refused to make the first move by giving up land and the Arabs refused to recognize the right of the State of Israel to exist in peace. Nor were the superpowers prepared to back off from support for their respective clients. Following the 1967 war, the Soviets moved to re-supply Egypt and Syria, while the US remained deeply committed to the security of Israel. The next Arab–Israeli war would provide a major threat to a process of détente between Washington and Moscow, underlining the fragility of that process.

Summary

After 1962, it seemed that, in some important respects and not least in Europe where it had begun, the Cold War had stabilized. The Soviets' building of the Berlin Wall in 1961, however dangerous in the immediate term, could be seen as sealing a breach in the 'Iron Curtain'. The Eastern bloc was now more secure and the dividing lines in Europe, across which NATO and Warsaw Pact forces faced each other, were more clearly defined. The Cuban Missile Crisis, extremely dangerous at the time, also had a positive aftermath, in that it made both sides face up to the possibility of Armageddon—a message that was only reinforced by the advent of mutual assured destruction. The result was that both sides proved ready to tolerate the other's existence, and the Test Ban Treaty was one early result. There were still potential problems in Europe. The Kremlin was deeply concerned by the prospect of a German 'finger on the nuclear trigger' via the MLF, but this proposal ran into the sand by the end of 1966, opening the way to the Non-Proliferation Treaty and Strategic Arms Limitation Talks. On different sides of the Iron Curtain, Ceauşescu and de Gaulle tried to assert their independence but there were limits to how far they could go. The two blocs maintained their basic cohesion. Yet, even as coexistence and détente became key terms in the global lexicon, the two sides adhered firmly to their respective ideologies. The

Soviets still clung to the belief in the eventual collapse of capitalism, indeed the very historical 'inevitability' of the process meant that they could wait for it come about. Similarly, on the Western side, it was hoped that trade and exchanges with the East would demonstrate the superiority of free enterprise and individual rights, thus undermining faith in Marxist-Leninism. Détente, in that sense, was a new, safer way of fighting the Cold War.

In the less developed world, however, the situation was much more complicated. Here the dividing lines between the two sides were far from clear and, as the Cuban case showed, the US might even be vulnerable in its own backyard, not least because, in the realm of ideas, radical reformers looked to communism, rather than liberalism, as a model. China, a special case perhaps thanks to its size, showed that severe ideological rifts were possible within blocs, that third powers could carve themselves a niche in the Cold War world, and that it might even be possible to bring about a significant realignment of alliances. The superpowers could not always shape the behaviour of states beyond Europe, states which had their own regional, political, and economic agendas. As colonial empires faded, newly independent states were determined to assert their own agendas. The non-aligned movement clearly demonstrated this and helped underline the idea that it was now a multipolar world. But the superpowers discovered that even friends and allies in the less developed world might draw them into unwelcome crises. The escalation of the Vietnam War in 1965 set back the chance of détente between Moscow and Washington by years. The 1967 Middle East War showed that regional conflicts might spring up quickly, forcing the superpowers to back their respective clients or suffer a loss of credibility, but there were exceptions. During the Nigerian Civil War of 1967–70, both Britain and the USSR backed the federal government, indeed competed to become its main support, while France aided the rebel enclave of 'Biafra' and America stood on the sidelines. But basically, in the less developed world, the zero-sum game still held good: the superpowers generally lined up on each side and a gain for one was a loss for the other. After Nixon became US President in 1969, he and his National Security Adviser, Henry Kissinger, hoped to manage these problems by a process of 'linkage': if the Soviets wanted strategic arms control and Western technology, then they must help preserve stability in the less developed world. But the Indo-Pakistani war showed that 'linkage' could not easily be achieved. Multipolarity and coexistence were not necessarily easy bedfellows in a world where ideological rivalry persisted.

Visit the online resources that accompany this book to test your understanding and take your learning further: www.oup.com/he/young-kent3e

NOTES

1. Anders Stephanson's commentary in 'Symposium: The Origins of the Cold War', *Diplomatic History*, 2 (1993).
2. Odd Arne Westad (ed.), *Brothers in Arms: The Rise and Fall of the Sino-Soviet Alliance, 1945–1963* (Stanford University Press, Stanford, 1998), 20–9.
3. F. Bozo, *Two Strategies for Europe: De Gaulle, the United States and the Atlantic Alliance* (Rowman & Littlefield, Lanham, 2001), xi–xiii.
4. Fred Kaplan, *The Wizards of Armageddon* (Simon & Schuster, New York, 1984), 246.
5. See Malcolm Kerr, *The Arab Cold War: Gamal 'Abd Al-Nasir and his Rivals, 1958–1970* (3rd edn, London, Oxford University Press, 1971).

PART III CHRONOLOGY

The Rise of Multipolarity, 1963–71

1963

20 June	'Hot line' agreement signed.
26 June	Kennedy's 'Ich bin ein Berliner' speech at the Berlin Wall.
5 August	Test Ban Treaty signed in Moscow.
1 November	Overthrow of President Diem of South Vietnam following months of instability.
22 November	President Kennedy assassinated in Texas.

1964

20 January	France recognizes Beijing government.
February–March	Fighting between Greek-Cypriot and Turkish-Cypriot communities leads to deployment of UN peacekeeping force.
2–4 August	Gulf of Tonkin incident leads Congress to sanction US action in Vietnam.
14 October	Khrushchev replaced by Brezhnev and Kosygin.
16 October	First Chinese atom bomb exploded.
3 November	Lyndon Johnson wins US election.

1965

20 January	Warsaw Pact calls for a European Security Conference to include Eastern and Western bloc.
7 February	US aircraft bomb North Vietnam while Soviet premier Kosygin is in Hanoi.
24 February	US begins 'Rolling Thunder' bombing campaign against North Vietnam.
8 March	Marines are first US ground combat troops deployed in Vietnam War.
28–29 April	Johnson sends Marines to forestall leftist drift in Dominican Republic.
August	Indo-Pakistani tension in disputed Kashmir leads to war.
22 September	Ceasefire in Indo-Pakistani War.
30 September	Coup in Indonesia followed by army crackdown on Communist Party.

1966

10 March	De Gaulle quits NATO military structure.
20 June–1 July	De Gaulle visits USSR.
July	Warsaw Pact calls for Pan-European security system.

1967

27 January	Outer Space Treaty signed, demilitarizing the moon and other bodies.
7 April	Israelis shoot down several Syrian aircraft in latest border tension.
5–10 June	Six Day Arab–Israeli war.
17 June	China tests hydrogen bomb.
23–25 June	Glassboro' meeting of Johnson and Kosygin.
18 September	US announces deployment of an anti-ballistic missile system.
22 November	UN Resolution 242, on Middle East, passed.
14 December	NATO adopts Harmel Report, opening way for talks with Warsaw Pact, and accepting strategy of 'flexible response'.

PART III CHRONOLOGY (continued)

1968

23 January	North Korea seizes USS Pueblo: not released until December.
30 January	Start of 'Tet' offensive by communists in Vietnam.
31 March	Johnson starts partial 'bombing halt' in Vietnam and leaves US presidential race.
April	Czechoslovakian Communist Party, under Dubček, begins to liberalize.
1 July	Non-Proliferation Treaty signed.
Late August	USSR leads invasion of Czechoslovakia by Warsaw Pact members to end liberalization.
5 November	Nixon wins US Presidency.
12 November	Brezhnev Doctrine speech.

1969

20 January	Nixon's inaugural address calls for an 'era of negotiations'.
2 March	Major Soviet–Chinese border clash on Damyansky island.
25 July	Nixon's 'Guam Doctrine' on Vietnam: will hand fighting over to South Vietnamese.
2–3 August	Nixon visits Romania.
17 November	SALT talks open between US and USSR in Helsinki.

1970

10 March	US announces that it will deploy a multiple independent re-entry vehicle.
19 March	First ever meeting of West and East German prime ministers.
18 March	Prince Sihanouk of Cambodia overthrown by Lon Nol.
April–June	US and South Vietnamese launch incursion into Cambodia.
7 August	Ceasefire agreed in Arab–Israeli 'war of attrition', which followed the 1967 war.
12 August	Soviet–West German Treaty signed.
September	Civil war in Jordan between royal government and Palestinians.
7 December	Polish–West German treaty signed.
December	Unrest in Poland leads to fall of Gomulka.

1971

February–March	South Vietnamese incursion into Laos.
15 July	Forthcoming visit of Nixon to China announced; to take place in February 1972.
15 August	US introduces trade restrictions and ends convertibility of dollars into gold.
3 September	Four-power agreement on Berlin signed.
20 October	Brandt of West Germany wins Nobel Peace Prize for Ostpolitik.
25 October	UN votes for communist Chinese membership.
November	Rising Indo-Pakistani tension over East Pakistan.
10 December	NATO agrees to Warsaw Pact proposal for a European Security Conference.
16 December	Ceasefire in Indo-Pakistani War over 'Bangladeshi' independence, four days after the first use of the US–Soviet 'hot line'.

Take your learning further by viewing the interactive version of this timeline: www.oup.com/he/young-kent3e

9

The Eastern and Western Blocs in the 1960s

Chapter contents

A. US–Soviet Relations from the Missile Crisis to Détente, 1963–71

Khrushchev, Kennedy, and the Test Ban Treaty

In the wake of the Cuban Missile Crisis, the Soviet leader, Nikita Khrushchev, felt far less confident than he had been a year earlier about dealing with American power. Apart from the Cuban setback, Soviet interests had not advanced much in the Congo or Laos; the building of the Berlin Wall had staunched the haemorrhage of the East German population to the West, but essentially left the German problem deadlocked; and Khrushchev was beset, within the communist bloc, by criticism from China. Kennedy, in contrast, could be more confident. The Bay of Pigs humiliation had been expunged, the Democrats fared well in the November Congressional elections and America's nuclear superiority had been demonstrated to the world. But Arthur Schlesinger, the President's in-house historian, believed Kennedy's 'feelings underwent a qualitative change after Cuba: a world in which nations threatened each other with nuclear weapons now seemed . . . an intolerable . . . world'.[1] Indeed, both superpower leaders seemed to be thinking the same way about the need for nuclear arms control after the recent crisis. On 19 December, Khrushchev wrote to Kennedy urging progress on the Test Ban Treaty, which had been discussed for five years without result. The need to reduce the possibility of hot war between the world's two great rivals was now at the centre of their agenda, leading to three significant agreements within a decade: the Test Ban Treaty (TBT) of 1963, the Non-Proliferation Treaty of 1968, and the first Strategic Arms Limitation Treaty of 1972. Indeed, the nuclear issue provided a consistent, constructive focus for US–Soviet discussions which had been absent since 1947.

However, the image of Kennedy and Khrushchev turning easily to a policy of détente after the psychological shock of seeming close to hot war is a simplistic one. Their relationship became less volatile and more rational perhaps, but they remained firm ideological opponents and there was no early rush into signing the TBT. Indeed, if anything, the early months of 1963 saw a retreat. Khrushchev's letter had hinted at a major breakthrough because, for the first time, he appeared ready to accept that a TBT be verified through on-site inspections. Previously, the Soviets had condemned inspections on their soil as an infringement of sovereignty, likely to be exploited by the West for espionage purposes. Yet Washington had always insisted that, if there were to be a ban on *underground* nuclear tests, it could only be properly enforced through inspections. (Atmospheric and underwater tests were easily detectable, but underground ones could be disguised, if small, or confused with other seismic activity.) Khrushchev was offering to allow only two or three inspections per year, however, and the Americans felt this inadequate. When Kennedy explained this, Khrushchev felt let down and by February 1963 the TBT talks had stalled.

By now, such failures to achieve results in arms talks were becoming a pattern. The environmental danger posed by atmospheric tests had been an international concern since at least 1954, when a Japanese fishing boat had been caught in the fallout from a Pacific test. Various anti-nuclear groups had sprung up, especially in Western Europe, notably Germany's 'Campaign against Nuclear Death' and Britain's 'Campaign for Nuclear Disarmament'. In March 1958, Khrushchev had evidently spotted the propaganda value of the issue and began a unilateral moratorium on all tests. The US matched this seven months later and talks on a test ban then began between the superpowers and the third nuclear power, Britain, in Geneva under UN auspices. The moratorium held until August 1961, when the Soviets began a new series of tests, but the Geneva talks made little progress, partly because of the verification problem. When the Kennedy administration, too, revived its test programme, the situation for a TBT seemed bleak, yet there were strong reasons to revive it in late 1962: not only to ease East–West tensions after the Missile Crisis and to satisfy world opinion, but also to begin a policy of non-proliferation. The prospect of a large number of countries obtaining nuclear weapons, increasing the dangers of a nuclear war, was a concern to both superpowers and a TBT might help to deter states from developing them. The deadlock on a treaty in early 1963 was not helped by Khrushchev's weakened domestic position following the Missile Crisis. Then, in April, his main critic, Deputy Premier Frol Kozlov, suddenly died.

In mid-1963, a series of events suggested an improvement in US–Soviet relations. On 9 June, at the American University in Washington, Kennedy gave a major address in which he denied any desire for a 'Pax Americana' and urged a genuine peace with the USSR, based on mutual understanding. A full translation of the speech was, unusually, printed by the Soviet daily *Izvestia*. Eleven days later the superpowers signed the 'hot line' agreement, establishing a teletype link between the Pentagon (later moved to the White House) and the Kremlin, to allow direct, rapid communication in times of crisis. On 2 July, Khrushchev, in a speech in Berlin, welcomed these recent moves and made a definitive offer of a TBT, which was then negotiated in Moscow between 15 and 25 July, with a US team, headed by veteran envoy Averell Harriman, and a British team, under Lord Hailsham. The TBT was formally signed by the three foreign ministers on 5 August. Finally, on 9 October the first US sale of grain to the USSR was announced. This series of developments created the impression of a 'new dawn' for East–West relations which, in retrospect, some Kennedy acolytes felt was brutally ended with his assassination in Dallas, Texas on 22 November. 'The breathing spell had become a pause, the pause was becoming a détente and no one could foresee what further changes lay ahead.'[2] Indeed, it was probably because of the improvement in relations that suspicion of Soviet involvement in the assassination was quickly discounted.

The extent of détente in 1963 is easy to exaggerate, however. As Michael Beschloss writes, Kennedy's pro-peace speech at the American University, 'though deeply felt, was as much the product of political calculation as any address (he) ever gave', designed to revive progress on the TBT, win public support, and placate Khrushchev after their New Year wrangle over verification.[3] As to the 'hot line' agreement, it was a useful, practical step but it was only to be used at the most critical moments. Even the TBT, though significant as a first step towards nuclear arms control and welcome for ending radiation releases into the atmosphere, had two vital flaws. First, because of the continuing disagreements over verification, it was not a comprehensive ban. It ended them in the atmosphere and underwater, where verification was easy, but not underground. Second, and even more harmful from the non-proliferation point of view, the treaty was not signed by the latest nuclear power, France, nor by the next likely nuclear power, China. Also, other problems persisted, not least Berlin. Kennedy had visited the city in June 1963, making his celebrated remark 'Ich bin ein Berliner', which only highlighted Western determination to remain there; in October, Soviet harassment of traffic into the city was revived and lasted several weeks. October also saw Khrushchev take offence at NATO discussions on a 'Multilateral Nuclear Force' (see Chapter 9, D), in which West Germany might share control of nuclear weapons. Kennedy and Khrushchev may have succeeded in reducing tensions after Cuba, therefore, but ideological differences and security suspicions continued. The Cold War remained at the centre of international affairs even if there was less chance of it leading to global catastrophe.

In the Shadow of Vietnam, 1964–8

Signs of détente did not end with Kennedy's assassination. Soviet pressure on Berlin eased once more; in April 1964 Khrushchev and the new American President, Lyndon Johnson, agreed to reduce their production of fissionable uranium in a further attempt to ease public fears of the nuclear danger; and on 1 June 1964 a consular agreement was signed which freed travel between the superpowers. But the pattern of relations was similar to Kennedy's last months, with simultaneous signs of suspicion. Johnson refused to be drawn into an early summit with Khrushchev, well aware of what had happened to Kennedy in Vienna in 1961. The Soviets remained agitated by the prospect of German access to nuclear weapons via a Multilateral Force (MLF). In the second half of 1964, both countries were preoccupied by domestic events. Johnson was elected president by a landslide in November but, less than three weeks earlier, on 14 October, Khrushchev had been ousted in a Kremlin coup. His unpredictability, the failure of his agricultural reforms, and foreign policy setbacks led to his replacement as Communist Party leader by Leonid Brezhnev (see Box 9.2), who proved far more cautious, even unadventurous, and prepared to share power with a team of ministers. In the international field, he relied heavily on his Foreign Minister, Andrei Gromyko, as well as the Prime Minister, Alexei Kosygin, who often handled relations with non-communist states in the 1960s.

Anatoly Dobrynin, the long-serving Soviet ambassador to Washington, has written that, in the 1960s, despite the less frantic atmosphere, 'peripheral issues kept interfering with the development of Soviet-American relations, creating tensions and putting off the settlement of really important problems'.[4] The most important 'peripheral issue' was the Vietnam War which, in 1965, saw the deployment of US combat forces and large-scale bombing of North Vietnam. The Soviets had little interest in letting the war intensify, but had little choice other than to back their fellow Marxists in the North, especially given China's attempt to outbid Moscow for the leadership of the communist world by supporting Hanoi. The MLF was less important as a bone of contention after Johnson ceased to promote it in late 1964, but West Germany did not accept its demise until late 1966. Other peripheral issues included the June 1967 Middle East War, when the superpowers backed opposing sides. The war overshadowed the only meeting Johnson had with a high-ranking Soviet leader, the so-called 'mini-summit' with Kosygin at Glassboro', New Jersey, on 23–4 June. The atmosphere here was friendly enough, with Johnson accepting an invitation to visit the USSR for a full summit with Brezhnev, but on all the substantive points the two seemed to differ. Kosygin criticized Israeli expansion against its Arab neighbours, urged American withdrawal from Vietnam, and was unwilling to discuss the USSR's deployment of a new weapons system, the 'Galosh', a type of anti-ballistic missile (ABM).

Despite such differences, the demise of the MLF helped restore forward momentum on nuclear arms control. On 27 January 1967, after nine months of talks, the US, USSR, and numerous other countries signed an Outer Space Treaty, demilitarizing the moon and other celestial bodies. The smooth negotiation of this treaty reflected the fact that the militarization of space was a remote possibility, but in 1968 talks began on a more immediately useful agreement to demilitarize the seabed. Most important, progress was possible on a Non-Proliferation Treaty (NPT) designed, as the TBT had partly been, to prevent ever more countries obtaining nuclear weapons. It was signed on 1 July 1968 (see Box 9.1). It had one of the same fundamental flaws as the TBT, in that many of the countries who were most likely to develop nuclear weapons, such as Israel and India, refused to put their names to it. But it also promised to lead to further progress on arms control: 'By its very nature . . . the Non-Proliferation Treaty discriminates against non-nuclear countries', conceded the US Secretary of State Dean Rusk, 'and non-nuclear countries understandably sought a quid pro quo.'[5] The quid quo pro which the superpowers offered was that they would seek to control their own nuclear capabilities through strategic arms limitation talks (SALT).

The US had first approached the USSR about controlling long-range nuclear weapons in December 1966, when Soviet deployment of the 'Galosh' ABM put Johnson under pressure to develop a similar system. ABMs were defensive, designed to shoot down offensive nuclear missiles, but they threatened to accelerate the arms race because both sides were likely to deploy more offensive missiles in order to overcome them. At first, the Soviets showed less urgency about strategic arms talks and there were clear differences between the two sides: while the Americans would have been happy to 'freeze' the size of nuclear arsenals, thus preserving their current superiority, Moscow wanted to create a more genuine balance of security, reducing the US lead. The NPT negotiations added some urgency to the issue and, a month later, the Soviets suggested that, to get SALT off to a strong start, Johnson and Brezhnev should hold a summit. But this proposal was immediately scotched when, within days, the Soviets led an invasion of Czechoslovakia (see Chapter 9, C). Lyndon Johnson became the only Cold War president never to meet his Soviet opposite number.

BOX 9.1

Non-Proliferation Treaty, 1 July 1968

The key provisions of the Treaty were as follows:

- Under Article 1, each nuclear power that signed undertook 'not to transfer . . . nuclear weapons . . . or control over such weapons . . . directly, or indirectly and not in any way to assist . . . any non-nuclear weapon State to manufacture or otherwise acquire nuclear weapons . . .'.
- Under Article 2, each non-nuclear power that signed undertook not to receive, manufacture, 'or otherwise acquire' nuclear weapons.
- Article 3 provided for safeguards against proliferation, with a verification system under the auspices of the International Atomic Energy Agency to be carried out in non-nuclear-weapon states.
- The peaceful use of atomic energy was to continue and a system was outlined which would allow non-nuclear-weapon states to gain benefits from the peaceful applications of nuclear explosions.
- Article 6 committed all signatories 'to pursue negotiations . . . relating to cessation of the nuclear arms race . . . and to nuclear disarmament . . .'. It was this provision which led on to Strategic Arms Limitation talks.

Détente Deferred, 1969–71

Richard Nixon's administration began with the bold assertion, in his inaugural address, that 'after a period of confrontation we are entering an era of negotiations'. Notwithstanding his reputation as an anti-communist, his presidency eventually became identified with a policy of East–West détente. Yet in the early period, the Nixon years were characterized by caution and uneven progress in relations with Moscow. The US felt vulnerable on the world stage because of the continuing Vietnam imbroglio, which called into question the whole idea that Washington could 'contain' communist expansion. Meanwhile, the USSR under Brezhnev avoided foreign adventures and concentrated on achieving nuclear parity with America, so as to prevent another humiliation like Cuba. By 1969, the Soviets had roughly equalled the number of US intercontinental ballistic missiles (ICBMs) and reached a situation known as 'Mutual Assured Destruction' (with its apt acronym, MAD): even if one superpower launched a sudden nuclear attack on the other (a 'first strike'), the second superpower would retain enough weapons to launch a devastating counterattack (or 'second strike'). There was now a 'balance of deterrence', making it impossible for Washington to meaningfully threaten nuclear war as it had done under Eisenhower. The 'unwinnable' war in Vietnam and the advent of MAD posed a difficult challenge to Nixon and his National Security Adviser, Henry Kissinger. On the one hand, there was a retrenchment of US policy through the Nixon Doctrine (see Chapter 10, D), which implied that countries threatened by communism must in future look primarily to defend themselves. On the other hand, the White House reacted firmly, some would say irrationally, when it felt US interests were being threatened: 'an important element in Nixon's diplomacy was to keep the other side off its guard by showing readiness to employ force in an unpredictable manner'.[6] In 1970, far from retreating precipitately from Vietnam, Nixon launched an incursion into neighbouring Cambodia, and in December 1971, when India went to war with America's ally Pakistan (see Chapter 11, B), Nixon despatched a fleet to the region. On the nuclear arms front, although the State Department would have liked to open SALT talks early, Nixon delayed doing so until November 1969.

Nixon and Kissinger *were* interested in reaching agreements with the USSR, but not simply to achieve a mere improvement in atmosphere or please popular opinion. For them, agreements such as SALT, or greater trade links, were to be used as part of a strategy to ensure Soviet good behaviour. In essence, this meant gaining acceptance of the status quo and ensuring that US interests were not threatened. The superpowers should show 'restraint' in their actions, not seeking unilateral advantages over each other; meetings between them should address 'concrete' problems; and, most importantly, there should be a 'linkage' between the different elements in their mutual relations. As Kissinger explained it, 'We proceeded from the premise that to separate issues into distinct compartments would encourage the Soviet leaders to believe that they could use cooperation in one area as a safety valve while striving for unilateral advantages elsewhere. This was unacceptable.'[7] The White House demonstrated how it would meet 'unacceptable' behaviour in what Kissinger called 'the autumn of crises' in 1970. The election of a Marxist, Salvador Allende, as President of Chile on 4 September led to a (failed) US bid to prevent his inauguration. In mid-September, the outbreak of civil war in Jordan led Nixon to toy with the idea of a counter-intervention by Israel (see Chapter 11, C), while the discovery of work on a submarine base at Cienfuegos, Cuba led to strong diplomatic protests. Cuba was a particularly delicate issue and Nixon could not afford to appear weaker than Kennedy had been in 1962. The Cienfuegos Crisis ended in compromise in early October, with an assurance from Soviet Ambassador Dobrynin that no submarine base would be built and a formal confirmation of Kennedy's promise not to invade the island.

Clearly, the White House still interpreted events largely in a 'zero-sum' manner, in which any gain for the USSR was a loss for the US. But, in America's less confident state, Nixon and Kissinger had to limit communist advances, not by nuclear threats and military action, but through active diplomacy and 'linkage'. The Soviets, for their part, never accepted linkage but rather developed the old logic of 'peaceful coexistence'. They saw anti-imperialist unrest in the less developed world as historically inevitable, and there to be exploited, while SALT and freer East–West trade were desirable in themselves, not as part of some linkage deal. Nonetheless, in May 1971, at the Communist Party Congress, Brezhnev—as well as securing his own primacy in the leadership—committed the USSR to a policy of relaxing tension. This would restrain the financially draining arms race, secure greater access to Western technology (which would invigorate economic growth), lessen the dangers of nuclear war, and confirm the Soviet grip on east-central Europe. A few months later, however, Brezhnev was given another reason to improve superpower relations when, in July, it was suddenly revealed that Nixon was to visit Beijing. America's 'Opening to China', after years of deteriorating Sino-Soviet relations, gave Nixon another means by which to pressure Moscow for concessions and led Brezhnev to try to outbid China for American cooperation. As a result, America, apparently crippled by the Vietnam War a few years before, now found itself courted by both major communist powers. On 12 October 1971, it was announced that, in addition, to visiting Beijing in February, Nixon would travel to Moscow, in May 1972, to sign the long-awaited SALT treaty.

B. The Superpowers and the Emergence of an Independent China

Khrushchev's Last Years, 1963–4

One of the most significant signs that the world was moving to a more complicated, 'multipolar' system, was the final breach between communist China and the USSR. Paradoxically, as the Soviets began to attain military parity with the US, the significance of bipolar equality was reduced through the Sino-Soviet split. In the 1950s, Western governments generally treated the communist bloc as a monolithic one, but by 1963 the differences between Beijing and Moscow were deep. It took almost a decade for policy-makers in Washington to realize the full significance of this. The US now had two ideological enemies with different approaches to international order. At first, Moscow seemed the more moderate opponent, prepared to advocate peaceful coexistence, while Beijing seemed bent on the spread of revolution, but by 1971, as Mao's 'cultural revolution' ran into the sand and war between the two communist giants seemed possible, it became possible to perceive of Sino-American cooperation against Moscow.

It is now clear that 1963 marked the effective completion of the 'Sino-Soviet split'. In December 1962, the Soviets provided ground-to-air missiles and in January 1963 they agreed to continue developing the Chinese air force. However, while the Kremlin believed that the Cuban Missile Crisis showed the wisdom of relaxing Cold War tensions, Mao felt that a determined revolutionary approach to the global struggle would bring the triumph of what he referred to as the 'east wind' over the 'west wind'. His domestic political strength, stemming from his June 1962 attack on Chinese advocates of peaceful coexistence, combined with the success of the October–November attack on India in the disputed border areas, increased his confidence about going alone. A July 1963 conference between Soviet and Chinese representatives broke up without a date for any future meetings being fixed.[8] The breakdown was followed by Mao's attempt to forge a completely independent policy, not only at home but also in foreign and defence policies, while continuing to act as a loyal defender of Marxist-Leninism. Indeed, one problem for the Kremlin was that Mao posed as being truer to the anti-imperialist struggle than Khrushchev. This presented particular difficulties within the Eastern bloc where China helped protect Albania, and its Stalinist dictator Enver Hoxha, from Soviet pressure to conform with the post-Stalinist order. Mao also encouraged Romania's attempts to distance itself from the USSR. The dispute quickly took on features of a religious schism, with each side claiming to be the only 'true believers'. Indeed, their ideological attacks on each other differed 'little from those applied against Western capitalism'.[9] The Chinese ridiculed Khrushchev's performance during the Cuban Missile Crisis and condemned the Test Ban Treaty as a selfish attempt by the superpowers to preserve their nuclear status, denying equality to others.

The Chinese were already developing their own atomic bomb, having been refused assistance from the Soviets—another cause of contention between the two. Such a weapon was successfully tested on 16 October 1964, only two days after the overthrow of Khrushchev, and did more than anything else to establish China's credentials as the world's third greatest power, which, with the largest population on earth and vast, untapped economic potential, might one day match the superpowers. China's self-assertion even stretched to pressure on Moscow to restore land taken by the Tsars in the 'unequal treaties' of the nineteenth century, an issue first raised in 1957. In February 1964, the USSR and China actually opened border discussions but they were suspended in October without agreement. The Chinese also tried to establish their own following in the less developed world. They had been invited to the first Afro-Asian Conference at Bandung in 1955, where anti-imperialism and non-alignment were seen as the basis on which an Afro-Asian identity might be constructed. Here, Chinese premier Zhou en Lai accepted the principles of coexistence as a means of getting greater international acceptance and an important Asian role. However, the increasing radicalism of Mao and the presence of the Soviet Union at the second Afro-Asian Conference in Cairo in 1957–8 did not make unity easy. Neither did China find it easy to extend its influence in the 1960s. The Chinese were not invited to the first conference of non-aligned states in December 1961. In 1963–4, Zhou did make a three-month tour of twelve, mainly African, 'third world' countries but its meagre results only confirmed the limits of China's attraction as an ally. It lacked the potential of either America or the USSR to provide large-scale economic aid or modern military equipment and those who wished to pursue anti-Western policy saw the Soviet Union as a more attractive sponsor. Only a few countries, notably Nyerere's Tanzania, showed much interest in identifying with China. The Egyptian leader, Nasser, was not even present in Cairo when Zhou arrived; the Tunisian President, Bourguiba, was openly critical of China's 1962 attack on India; and planned visits to certain destinations were hastily cancelled. China's explosion of an atomic bomb drew more international condemnation.

Yet for China, there was no going back to the Soviet fold, despite some signs of an easier relationship after Khrushchev was ousted. Zhou was sent to Moscow immediately afterwards, to celebrate the October Revolution at the Kremlin's invitation, but relations were frosty. True, this did not prevent one Politburo member suggesting to Zhou that, with Khrushchev ousted, it might also be appropriate for the Chinese to overthrow Mao! But Zhou made no secret of this proposal on his return to Beijing and it would become one more nail in the coffin of the Sino-Soviet alliance. The Sino-Soviet split went deeper than mere personality clashes. One Western commentator even described relations between Moscow and Peking as 'the New Cold War' and talked of 'nothing less than a complex, perhaps cataclysmic, process of fission within the Communist movement'.[10]

Foreign Policy and the 'Cultural Revolution', 1965–9

It was the fear that, at home, Maoism was losing its vigour which led in May 1966 to the launch of the 'Cultural Revolution'. Supposedly intended to wipe out all remaining bourgeois influences in society, the Revolution was spearheaded by youthful 'Red Guards', armed with advice and encouragement from Mao's 'Little Red Book'. Their enthusiasm, ruthlessness, and immaturity led them not only to terrorize ordinary Chinese, but also to target moderates in the communist leadership for condemnation and to launch investigations of officials at all levels. The main victim was Mao's deputy, Liu Shoaqi, who was purged from the party in 1966. By the end of 1967, national government was effectively breaking down. The Revolution also wreaked havoc with the country's foreign policy. In May 1967, Red Guards invaded the foreign ministry, destroying many of its records. Numerous ambassadors were recalled from abroad, including all from those African countries that Zhou had tried to court so assiduously a few years before. The foreign minister, Chen Yi, disappeared from public view for months.

As part of a new, revolutionary foreign policy, the Red Guards urged Chinese minorities in South-East Asia to overthrow their governments, stirred up anti-British feeling over the colony of Hong Kong and, during January–February 1967, besieged the Soviet embassy. Despite this, the mid-1960s were not without their successes for China. In Indonesia, the Communist Party may have been virtually wiped out by the army in 1965–6 (see Chapter 11, B); but in Vietnam the Chinese found a cause which allowed them to resist US 'imperialism', compete with the Soviets for influence, and demonstrate the continuing applicability of Maoist guerrilla tactics (see Chapter 10, C). In 1967, a showpiece aid deal was agreed with Tanzania and Zambia, to build a 1,200-mile railway line between the two. In 1967, too, China exploded its first hydrogen bomb, pointedly refusing to contemplate non-proliferation, while also developing long-range rockets to carry nuclear warheads. Given the near-anarchy created by the Red Guards, however, the superpowers reacted to China's growing nuclear capacity with great concern. The Johnson administration did nothing to exploit the Sino-Soviet split but instead treated China as a pariah: 'throughout Asia, China became the focus of (Secretary of State) Rusk's campaign against Communism. Russian ambitions had been checked in the early 1940s. Now Mao assumed the role of aggressor.'[11] For its part, the Kremlin developed the Galosh ABM system chiefly as a means to defend Moscow from a Chinese attack.

Throughout the Cultural Revolution, Sino-Soviet relations worsened. The two communist parties broke off relations in 1966 and there were already intermittent small-scale border incidents, especially over disputed islands in the Amur and Ussuri rivers. The worst clash to date came in January 1968, when four Chinese were killed. Meanwhile, the USSR gradually increased its forces on its 4,500-mile eastern border, from 12 divisions in 1961 to 17 in 1964, and 27 by 1969, with medium-range ballistic weapons in support. The tension intensified further in late 1968 because of the invasion of Czechoslovakia and Brezhnev's subsequent assertion that the USSR had the right to intervene in states where socialism was under threat. For China, this rekindled fears that Moscow was determined to dictate policy to all other communist countries and it put back Mao's hopes that Eastern Europe might be able to loosen the Soviet grip. He condemned the invasion of Czechoslovakia and even seems to have feared war with the USSR as the year ended. However, in line with their uncompromising foreign policy, the Chinese were determined to stand up to the Soviets and in March 1969 the Sino-Soviet relationship reached another critical point. On 2 March, after several weeks of mounting border tension, large-scale fighting occurred on Zhen Bao island (known as Damyansky island to the Russians) when Chinese troops ambushed a Soviet patrol, killing more than 20. It was an event which tellingly underlined the depths of Sino-Soviet division and eventually helped bring a rapprochement between China and the US. But that was far from being Mao's original intention. While he spoke publicly of preparing for war, privately he was keen to avoid the crisis running out of control. Chinese evidence suggests that 'although Beijing's policy-makers . . . had prepared to . . . teach the Soviets a bitter lesson, they had not intended to enter a major military conflict with Moscow'.[12]

The Beginnings of 'Triangular Diplomacy'

The Kremlin was stunned by the events of 2 March 1969 and, already convinced of Chinese irrationality, feared that the crisis could lead to war. Determined not to appear weak, the Soviets employed heavy artillery in another clash on Zhen Bao island on 15 March but again found the Chinese well prepared. Moscow followed this up on 21 March with an offer to talk. There was in fact a division in the Soviet government between hardliners, led by defence minister Andrei Grechko, who was ready to consider war, and moderates like premier Kosygin, who favoured negotiation. But the Chinese refused even to reply to Kosygin's offer of talks for several weeks and there was a further series of border incidents in April–May, with clashes now spreading to the Kazakhstan border. There was a particularly bitter exchange on the border on 13 August, when the Soviets wiped out a 30-man Chinese patrol. Neither side seemed ready to back down and in China too, now, there was a genuine fear of war as events moved far beyond what Mao originally intended. Later that month he mobilized China's border defences. Then, tension receded. Zhou and Kosygin met on 11 September in Beijing, in the aftermath of Ho Chi Minh's funeral, and both appeared ready to strike a deal, on the basis of respecting the status quo for the present. But when official talks opened on 20 October 1969, they made little progress and each side continued to condemn the other on ideological grounds. Grechko now advocated a pre-emptive strike against China's nuclear facilities and the Soviets even sounded out the US on its likely reaction to such a development (an approach which confirmed the growing belief in Washington that Sino-Soviet differences could be exploited in America's favour). But Brezhnev, backed by most of the Politburo, preferred a continued build-up of conventional forces linked to a diplomatic campaign to isolate China.

When Nixon entered the White House, relations with the USSR were much better than those with China. Beijing was still blamed for the drawn-out war in Korea, it was behind the communists in Vietnam, its Maoist ideology seemed utterly sinister, and its revolutionary diplomacy made it, apparently, impossible to negotiate with. Like the USSR, the US was building an ABM system, which Nixon named 'Safeguard', which would primarily be useful against a Chinese attack. Yet in 1967 Nixon had written, in a remarkably forward-thinking article in *Foreign Affairs*, that 'we simply cannot afford to leave China forever outside the family of nations',[13] and by June 1969 the White House believed that it might be possible to use improved Sino-American relations as a pressure point on the USSR. An improved Sino-American relationship also appealed to Mao and Zhou, who now believed China to be far more threatened by the USSR than by the US. As a communist power bordering on China, the Soviet Union was seen by Mao as a potential menace to Chinese domestic stability, whereas America, thanks to Vietnam, seemed to be losing the battle for influence in Asia. On 11 July 1969, a study of the international situation by a high-level group neatly summed up the fear that, 'The Soviet revisionists have made China their main enemy, imposing a more serious threat to our security than the US imperialists.'[14] The timing of this report supports the view that it was the summer 'war scare that—both in a strategic and a psychological sense—created the necessary conditions for the [Chinese] leaders to reconsider the . . . policy of confrontation with the United States'.[15] Yet Sino-American suspicions ran deep, they had no diplomatic relations and Kissinger was determined to move carefully. 'If we moved too slowly', he wrote 'we might feed Chinese suspicions of Soviet–American collusion . . . As for the Soviets, we considered the Chinese option useful to induce restraint; but we had to take care not to pursue it so impetuously as to provoke a Soviet pre-emptive attack on China.'[16]

Nixon first signalled his readiness to improve relations by relaxing trade and travel with China in July 1969. Diplomatic contacts proved possible via third parties, such as the Romanian and Pakistani governments, and via meetings between US and Chinese diplomats in Warsaw. The American incursion into Cambodia in spring 1970 set back relations and within both governments there were divisions about the wisdom of a rapprochement, but in April 1971 the possibility was publicly acknowledged when the Chinese invited an American table tennis team to Beijing. This 'ping-pong diplomacy' was followed by another relaxation of US trade with China and by intensive discussions on an idea the Chinese had raised some months before of Nixon sending an emissary to Beijing. The emissary selected was the national security adviser, Henry Kissinger, who travelled to Peking on 9 July, via Pakistan. A cover story, that he had fallen ill while visiting Pakistan, held throughout two days of talks with Zhou and it was on 15 July that the world learnt not only that Kissinger had made his journey but also that Nixon would be visiting Beijing in early 1972.

C. Unity and Division in Eastern Europe

Eastern Europe in the 1960s

Although the Kremlin had used armed force to restore communist control in Hungary in 1956, this did not restore the full unity of the Eastern bloc under Soviet domination. Certainly, East European leaders were reluctant in future to experiment with any radical reforms that might undermine the one-party state. Even Khrushchev himself backed off from the 'deStalinization' process, which had helped spark problems in Poland and Hungary; only around 1961 did he revive his attacks on Stalinism and tolerate a limited amount of intellectual diversity in the USSR. But, inspired in part by Mao's China, East European leaders were suspicious of Khrushchev and keen to establish a degree of equality for themselves within the bloc, so that they did not slavishly have to mirror every major turn in Soviet policy. Paradoxically, it was hard-line communists, rather than would-be reformers, who were often most successful at distancing themselves from Moscow's authority in the 1960s. At the extreme, Enver Hoxha, the Stalinist dictator of Albania was able to assert his independence in 1960, openly criticizing Khrushchev and relying on Chinese aid to compensate for the economic embargo which the Soviets tried to impose. In December 1961, Moscow severed relations with Albania, though it remained a nominal member of the Warsaw Pact until 1968. But Albania remained the poorest country in Europe, geographically cut off from the rest of the Soviet bloc by Yugoslavia, which maintained its own independent form of communism under Tito. The Kremlin showed no interest in terminating Hoxha's independence by force, while he showed no sign of tilting towards the West.

Other countries in Eastern Europe, larger than Albania and closer to the USSR, found it more difficult to pursue their own course, but a degree of autonomy was achieved, particularly by Romania. The key element here was, once again, that Romania's leaders followed a ruthless, authoritarian form of rule internally, while gradually asserting an independent foreign policy. Under Gheorghe Gheorghieu-Dej, Romania's Latin—as opposed to Slavic—identity was fostered; the withdrawal of the Red Army was secured in 1958; and all attempts by Khrushchev to integrate the East European economies were opposed. In 1961–3, the Soviet leader, partly in response to the European Economic Community's success in Western Europe, tried to encourage integration via the Council for Mutual Economic Aid (COMECON), the organization for economic cooperation set up by Stalin in 1949, but hitherto insignificant. However, Gheorghieu-Dej feared that such a policy would leave Romania as an agricultural state, while industrial production was concentrated in East Germany and Czechoslovakia. All that came from Khrushchev's schemes was the establishment of a COMECON bank, for settling mutual debts, in 1964. Supranational economic integration, on the lines of the European Community in the West, proved impossible. Gheorghieu-Dej's successor in 1965 was Nicolae Ceauşescu, under whom internal repression was accompanied by an ever-more assertive foreign policy. He broke Eastern bloc unity by recognizing West Germany in 1967, stood aside from the invasion of Czechoslovakia in 1968, and ended active involvement in the Warsaw Pact military command. Yet he remained a member of the Pact and his policies were interpreted, not as some maverick bid for complete independence of the Soviets, but as an eastern equivalent of Charles de Gaulle's policy of semi-detachment from NATO. In fact, de Gaulle (see Box 9.3) and Ceauşescu worked together in advocating a loosening of alliance structures, a lowering of Cold War tensions and—the essential corollary—greater freedom from superpower domination for the countries of Eastern and Western Europe.

The only Warsaw Pact member which experimented much with decentralization in the 1960s was Hungary, where the events of 1956 had not ended the belief that the oppression of Stalinism should be relaxed. János Kádár waited until 1961 before releasing some political prisoners and relaxing censorship, emulating Khrushchev's moves in the USSR at that time. In 1963, some private enterprise was reintroduced, in 1967 there was provision for a choice of candidates in election (though all had to be from the Communist Party), and in 1968 a 'New Economic Mechanism' was launched. This introduced competitive elements into industrial production, although all industry remained in state ownership, and the government continued to set economic targets. The purpose of such reforms was to try to raise the sluggish economic growth which all Eastern bloc countries encountered in the

1960s. By then, the inefficiencies of the Stalinist model of industrialization became clear: labour-intensive, responsive to government predictions rather than market demand, and overseen by a cumbersome planning machine, the communist economies were wasteful of resources, geared to heavy industrial production rather than manufacturing consumer goods, and shoddy in workmanship. But Kádár's reforms were viewed with suspicion throughout the bloc and this was only intensified by events in Czechoslovakia in 1968.

Czechoslovakia's 'Prague Spring'

Under the leadership of Antonin Novotny after 1953, Czechoslovakia was one of the most orthodox and stable countries in the Eastern bloc. But the harshness of the regime, the rigid planning system, and the stagnation of economic growth in the early 1960s brought criticism from some party members, led by a Slovak politician, Alexander Dubček. In January 1968, Dubček replaced Novotny as party leader and Czechoslovakia soon became of deep concern to the Kremlin. Dubček was in fact a loyal Marxist-Leninist, but he and his fellow reformers hoped to improve the Czechoslovak system by breaking with the Stalinist past, decentralizing decision-making, introducing market elements into the economy, and allowing non-communist organizations to form. Their first step to achieving this new system was to allow freer discussion of reform in Czechoslovakian society through a marked relaxation of censorship. This move, however, led to the publication of anti-communist views, spearheaded by *Literary Pages*, first issued on 29 February 1968, by a group that included the poet Václav Havel. On 6–7 March, at an Eastern bloc summit in Dresden, Brezhnev and other leaders expressed concern at Dubček's reform programme, pointing out the dangers of losing control of events. Yet, over the following few months open opposition to the regime, including frequent popular demonstrations, continued.

On 4–5 May, Dubček was berated by Brezhnev again, this time at a bilateral meeting in Moscow. It was in the wake of this meeting that Dubček decided to call a party congress, to be held in mid-September, where he would put his authority behind a moderate reform programme. But, in April, the Soviet military had already begun to plan for possible intervention in Czechoslovakia and on 8 May there was a meeting of Soviet, East German, Polish, Bulgarian, and Hungarian leaders, at which Brezhnev criticized Dubček as weak, inexperienced, and unreliable. Among the 'Group of Five', only Kádár tried to defend the Czechoslovakian leader, while Ulbricht (of East Germany) and Zhivkov (of Bulgaria) urged action to restore order, if necessary, by force. Within the Kremlin, too, there were divisions, with Kosygin, who visited Prague in mid-May, ready to deal with Dubček, but others increasingly concerned at events. The second group included the KGB, under Yuri Andropov, who feared for Soviet internal security and believed NATO could exploit the Czechoslovakian situation, and the military, led by Marshal Ustinov, who feared a breach in Warsaw Pact defences. Military manoeuvres to intimidate the Czechoslovakians were begun by the Warsaw Pact in late May but Dubček was not easily frightened, refusing to meet with Soviet leaders for several weeks. 'In many ways Dubček was naïve in his dealings with Russians', admits one of his biographers. 'Nevertheless throughout the summer, he played an extremely delicate . . . political game' based on the belief that the Soviets would not intervene.[17] He tried to minimize the justification for intervention by following an orthodox foreign policy: 'the Dubček government seized every opportunity to emphasize its loyalty to the Warsaw Pact'.[18] But on 27 June the non-communists published a manifesto urging the people to mobilize behind reform and now even Kádár gave up on supporting Dubček, who further harmed his standing in Moscow by turning to Yugoslavia and Romania for diplomatic support.

Another meeting of the 'Group of Five', in Warsaw in mid-July, demanded that the Czechoslovakians restore order and at the end of the month, when Dubček finally met Soviet leaders, Kosygin bluntly warned that military intervention was possible. On 3 August, they met again in Bratislava but still seemed far apart. Over the following weeks, plans were finalized for armed intervention, a course which the Politburo finally approved in mid-August. The invasion, launched on 20–1 August under the codename 'Operation Danube', was meant to be accompanied by a domestic coup against Dubček, led by conservatives. As one American diplomat speculated, 'That is perhaps why the invader came with the claim of having been invited to rescue the country.'[19] However, the domestic side of the operation was botched. Instead the Soviets were forced to arrest Dubček (who

BOX 9.2

Brezhnev Doctrine, 12 November 1968

Several weeks after the Soviet-led invasion of Czechoslovakia the Soviet communist leader, Leonid Brezhnev, attended the Fifth Congress of the Polish Communist Party and, on 12 November made a speech that included what became known in the West as the 'Brezhnev Doctrine'. The speech interpreted recent events as part of the continuing struggle between the communist and imperialist-capitalist systems, in which anti-communist elements had tried to subvert Czechoslovakia and detach it from the Eastern bloc. Brezhnev defended armed intervention as follows: 'when . . . forces hostile to socialism seek to revert the development of any socialist country towards the restoration of capitalism . . . this is no longer a problem of that country's people but . . . the concern of all socialist countries'.

Thus, action was necessary in Czechoslovakia to safeguard the unity and borders of what he called the 'Socialist Commonwealth', and he insisted that this did not infringe the country's sovereignty; rather, 'fraternal solidarity' had priority over national sovereignty in such a crisis. There was already a precedent for such action in Hungary in 1956 and Brezhnev was clear that the idea of 'limited sovereignty' would hold good in future, where the unity of the Soviet bloc was threatened. The doctrine was evidently interpreted according to circumstances: Yugoslavia and China had already broken free of Soviet domination; Albania left the Warsaw Pact in 1968; and Romania developed a form of independence from the USSR while remaining a Warsaw Pact member. But the invasion of Afghanistan in 1979 could partially be justified on the grounds of 'limited sovereignty' and the doctrine was only abandoned under Gorbachev in the late 1980s, when Afghanistan and Eastern Europe broke free of Soviet control.

remained in office until April 1969) and other leaders, taking them to Moscow for several days of talks, during which they were forced to agree to the country's 'normalization' as a loyal member of the Soviet bloc. 'Operation Danube' brought half a million troops into Czechoslovakia, a force intimidating enough to prevent any armed response and ensuring a low casualty rate of about 100 Czechoslovakians. The occupation *was* opposed, however, by a widespread passive resistance campaign. On 19 January 1969, a student, Jan Palach, burnt himself to death in Prague, as a protest against the return of totalitarianism. One significant feature of the Prague Spring was that the Communist Party itself had not only remained strong, but was joined by many would-be reformers. 'Throughout this period the Communist Party remained the primary organized political force, exercising control over . . . government and most of the mass associations.'[20] But Dubček's successor, Gustáv Husák, purged it of reformers and, by 1970, had ended all signs of dissent.

On the international stage, even among communist states there were critics of Operation Danube. Tito of Yugoslavia was concerned enough by events to draw away from the USSR and, in 1969, to restore diplomatic relations with China, after they had been broken for eleven years. Ceauşescu's fears of Soviet domination also deepened and in 1971 he became the first Warsaw Pact leader in more than a decade to visit China. The invasion also had a predictably detrimental impact on Soviet relations with the Western powers, who roundly condemned it. There was a double impact on détente: first because the US was reluctant to improve relations after such an event, hence Johnson's cancellation of his planned summit with Brezhnev (see Chapter 9, A); and second, because the Soviets themselves were unwilling to pursue détente while their alliance bloc appeared so divided. Nevertheless, as with Hungary in 1956, there was nothing practical that the Western powers could do to help Czechoslovakia short of risking war. Their actions against the USSR were therefore little more than gestures of disapproval and they quickly returned to their earlier efforts to promote détente. As a guidance telegram to British diplomats in late October 1968 argued, such a policy was not designed to make life easy for the Soviets, far from it. 'We recognize that in the longer term contact with Eastern Europe is the principal means by which we can hope to encourage liberal forces in these countries.'[21] In the long term, the beneficial impact of détente—linked to the detrimental impact of continuing Soviet domination—would destroy communism in Eastern Europe. However, in the immediate term, 'NATO's policy not only failed to prevent the Soviet invasion, but may even have encouraged it . . . by giving Soviet leaders a high degree of confidence that they could move into Czechoslovakia with a free hand.'[22]

D. Unity and Division in the Western Bloc

NATO in Travail

The years 1963–71 were a troubled period for NATO, marked by arguments over how to share nuclear weapons for European defence, by de Gaulle's decision to withdraw from the alliance's military-institutional structure and, later, by the Nixon administration's relative neglect of European concerns. Between February and August 1964, there was a grave danger that two NATO members, Turkey and Greece, might even go to war over Cyprus, when fighting between the Greek-Cypriot and Turkish-Cypriot communities broke out. In March, a UN peacekeeping force was deployed on the island. The mid-1960s were also overshadowed by growing concern over America's mounting involvement in Vietnam. Previously, not least under Kennedy, America's moral reputation among Europeans stood high, but Vietnam called its liberal credentials into question and even close allies, like the German and British governments, had to be wary of arousing public discontent by supporting President Johnson. Relations between America, Britain, and Germany were in any case disrupted in 1965–7, by arguments over the financial costs the first two faced for basing their military forces on German soil; and this developed into broader disagreements over 'burden-sharing' in the alliance. Finally, there were also divisions within the Atlantic alliance over the pace of détente.

In December 1962, at the Nassau conference, where Kennedy agreed to supply Polaris missiles to Britain, the US reaffirmed its support for a Multilateral Nuclear Force (MLF) in NATO, to be manned by several alliance countries. The MLF, which originated in ideas for nuclear sharing under the Eisenhower administration, was intended to overcome criticism of America's monopoly control of the Western deterrent and to forestall West German ambitions to own nuclear weapons. However, the fact that Germany would share in running the MLF provoked criticism both within the Western alliance and from the Eastern bloc. The USSR wanted to see the MLF abandoned before negotiating the Non-Proliferation Treaty. De Gaulle never liked the MLF, partly because it was linked to US ambitions to end the independent status of the French and British nuclear deterrents. For the same reason, the British were always lukewarm about it and, in late 1964, the incoming Labour government of Harold Wilson proposed an alternative scheme, the Atlantic Nuclear Force, which would maximize British independence. This threw negotiations back into limbo and Lyndon Johnson became less keen to push it onto his unwilling allies. A formal renunciation was impossible at this time, given Germany's continued commitment to it. But, during 1965, the US Defense Secretary, Robert McNamara, pressed an alternative, far less ambitious scheme for improved nuclear consultations in NATO. This led, in 1966, to a Nuclear Defence Affairs Committee being set up to discuss nuclear policy-making in the alliance. 'The attempt to establish . . . nuclear sharing on the basis . . . of allied ownership and control of nuclear weapons was effectively abandoned in favour of a consultative approach to . . . nuclear policy.'[23] It was an approach that left Washington largely unimpeded in its control of the West's nuclear arsenal. Under the new Committee was a seven-member Nuclear Planning Group, including the US, Britain, and Germany, which first met in April 1967 and which helped the Americans educate their allies about problems associated with nuclear weapons, while giving the European allies a share in planning for their use.

Meanwhile, NATO's focus of attention shifted to a different challenge. De Gaulle's announcement, on 10 March 1966, that France was leaving the organizational side of the alliance came as a blow to alliance confidence, even if an expected one. Given his desire to maximize French independence, his criticism of American 'domination' of Europe, and the fact that he had, in 1959, pulled French ships out of NATO's Mediterranean command, his withdrawal had long been predicted. He probably timed his action in 1966 because of his successful re-election as president four months earlier. He never actually ended France's commitment to the North Atlantic Treaty, which bound it to aid fellow members if they were attacked; nor did he categorically state that NATO could not use French soil in the event of war, but he raised the danger that France might pursue a defence policy out of step with other Western powers. France's withdrawal did cause administrative inconvenience, too, in that NATO headquarters had to be moved from Paris to a new site, just outside Brussels. Lyndon Johnson's response to de Gaulle's action was remarkably accepting: 'when a man asks you to leave his home, you don't argue, you just get your hat and go'.[24] But one reason for the President's low-key response was the need to avoid even deeper rifts in the Atlantic alliance, especially while America was so embroiled in Vietnam.

BOX 9.3

Biography: Charles de Gaulle (1890–1970)

Born into an intensely nationalist family, de Gaulle became a professional soldier and was one of the few French generals to appreciate the potential of armoured warfare in the 1930s. After the fall of France in 1940, when he briefly served as Under-Secretary of Defence, he refused to accept defeat and instead founded the 'Free French' movement in London. He had 'a certain idea of France', an almost spiritual concept which saw greatness as part of the nation's essence: since the collaborationist regime of Marshal Pétain was a denial of such greatness then he, de Gaulle, would stand up for true French interests and restore the country's status. In 1944, he became head of the French government, through force of will and the support of resistance groups. However, in January 1946 he suddenly resigned, having fallen out with other political leaders who were unwilling to see him establish a strong presidential form of government. De Gaulle believed they would soon be forced to recall him, but the Fourth Republic survived for 12 years. In 1947, he launched the right-wing 'Rally of the French People', but it failed to win the 1952 election and de Gaulle retired to his home at Colombey-les-Deux-Églises. He was only recalled to power in May 1958, when the Fourth Republic, dogged by unstable governments, entered a terminal crisis over the colonial war in Algeria. By 1962, de Gaulle had ended the war and meanwhile established the Fifth Republic, based on the strong, elected presidency that he had wanted in 1946. Able to appoint his own prime minister, and backed by a Gaullist political party, he took a particular interest in foreign and defence policies. In order to assert French greatness on the world stage, he developed the nuclear 'force de frappe'; tried to limit the centralizing policies of the European Community, while also vetoing British membership and retaining France's leading role in the organization; and distanced the country from what he saw as US domination, particularly by quitting NATO's organizational side in 1966 and, as a corollary, developed links to Eastern bloc states. Internal unrest shook his confidence in 1968, however, and with the franc on the brink of devaluation he resigned in 1969. He died suddenly the following year, leaving behind a more stable form of government, as well as an independent line in foreign policy that his successors found it prudent to continue.

The danger of a disintegration of NATO in 1966 seemed real, not only because of uncertainty about de Gaulle's next move, but also because of growing differences between America, Britain, and Germany—the trio now very much at the centre of alliance relationships—over so-called 'offset costs'. In 1965, the US had 392,000 personnel committed to NATO, mostly serving in Germany, while Britain had 51,000 troops there. By then, the West German economy was one of the strongest in the world and no one believed war in Europe to be imminent, while the US and Britain both faced balance-of-payment difficulties. The German government agreed in principle to try to 'offset' the Anglo-American costs by buying military equipment from them, but such purchases fell well short of what Britain, in particular, believed to be fair. A British balance-of-payments crisis in mid-1966 led the country to talk of reducing its NATO commitment and Johnson, fearing an 'unravelling' of the alliance, put pressure on both his allies to begin three-way talks with America on the problem. As with French withdrawal, this issue ultimately showed the resilience of NATO, however, because in May 1967 a trilateral agreement was reached which increased German military 'offset' purchases, minimized British costs, and allowed the US to reduce its commitments through a policy of 'dual-basing'—effectively, the rotation of units between bases in Germany and America. The agreements were not welcome to all members of the alliance. 'In particular, the Belgian ambassador, André de Staercke, was critical that the trilateral agreements confronted NATO . . . with faits accomplis.'[25] But another cause of Western division had been overcome.

The common interest of the US and Western Europe in defending the continent was confirmed by the December 1967 Atlantic Council meeting, which took two important decisions. First, it accepted that NATO should have a role in developing détente with the Eastern bloc. Second, it accepted a new defensive strategy, known as 'flexible response', which had been discussed for several years and which reflected the fact that the USSR could now match the US in nuclear weapons. It has been pointed out that a 'crucial factor' in getting agreement on this policy was 'de Gaulle's decision to withdraw France from the military functions of the alliance': before 1966 he had opposed attempts to define a new alliance strategy and had questioned the validity of America's nuclear guarantee.[26] 'Flexible response' accepted that it was no longer possible to threaten all-out nuclear war in the event of a Warsaw Pact attack. Instead, there would be a graduated escalation of conflict, beginning with a conventional effort and working through different levels of nuclear response, before there was a strategic nuclear exchange. In order to make 'flexible response' credible, however, and prevent an early use of nuclear weapons, the US military believed a larger number of conventional forces was required, and these simply could not be found. America itself, thanks largely to Vietnam, had reduced its NATO commitment to about 300,000 in 1968, while West European countries were reluctant to spend more money on defence. It was partly because of this that the Atlantic Council, meeting in Reykjavik in June 1968, proposed talks with the Warsaw Pact on Mutual Balanced Force Reductions.

The result was that, increasingly, NATO was plagued by arguments over 'burden-sharing'. The US, especially, pressed the case that, with West European economies having recovered from the war, its own share of NATO defences in Europe should be reduced. By 1971, US troop levels in NATO were actually down to 282,000 but in the Senate a group led by Mike Mansfield demanded more cuts. In May 1971, he introduced an amendment in Congress that would have halved the US presence. However, for the American government, this would have again risked a collapse of the alliance, and it would have weakened the West in dealing with the Soviets. President Nixon campaigned strongly against Mansfield and the amendment was defeated. Once again, a potential disaster had, in the end, been overcome. If anything, this latest crisis confirmed Nixon's belief that NATO could be treated as a secondary concern, not because it was insignificant but because, in the last analysis, America and Western Europe needed each other too much to drift apart.

The EEC from Veto to Enlargement

In January 1963, de Gaulle vetoed Britain's first application to join the EEC, which had been launched 18 months before. The application had always been surrounded by conditions on Britain's part, it had not been pressed vigorously, and it divided both the British Commonwealth and the main political parties. One historian has written that, 'had it been handled differently, Britain's . . . application should have reached a successful conclusion long before de Gaulle was . . . strong enough to intervene'.[27] However, there were signs that the negotiations would have succeeded except for de Gaulle's action, which he had probably intended for some time, though in the event it was prompted by Britain's decision to buy Polaris missiles from America. He argued that this proved Britain's commitment to the 'special relationship' with Washington in preference to Europe. Others saw the veto as proof of the General's desire to dominate in the EEC. He was able to accompany the veto with a Franco-German Treaty, which cemented his own 'special relationship' with Chancellor Konrad Adenauer, and which forced the other four Community members to accept the veto. Adenauer's readiness to back de Gaulle, even when the latter criticized the Atlantic alliance, upset other German politicians however, and during a debate in May, the Bundestag reasserted both the importance of the alliance and the desirability of British entry to the EEC. In October, the ageing Adenauer resigned, to be succeeded by his more Atlanticist deputy, Ludwig Erhard, and relations between de Gaulle and his European partners continued to worsen thereafter. In 1964, the French leader was upset by Erhard's interest in the MLF and by the failure to make progress on a Common Agricultural Policy (CAP) for the EEC, from which France hoped to gain. In 1965, he became increasingly concerned too by the centralizing tendencies of the EEC, which might undermine French independence. There were proposals to give the EEC its own budgetary resources and to increase the power of the European Parliament and Commission. Furthermore, under the Treaty of Rome, the EEC was due to begin making decisions by majority votes in 1966.

In July 1965, to try to prevent further centralization, de Gaulle launched the 'empty chair' crisis, a French boycott of Community bodies. This secured him an apparently significant concession in January 1966 when, in the so-called 'Luxembourg compromise', it was agreed that any EC member could veto decisions which harmed essential national interests. But it was not clear how this would operate in practice and the fact is that de Gaulle had been driven to negotiate by his continuing desire for the CAP. The compromise has been described as 'more of a statement of disagreement' than a long-term settlement.[28] As with NATO, where de Gaulle's anti-Americanism led him to withdraw from the military structure while his anti-communism led him to remain an alliance signatory, so with the EEC he was determined to maximize

French independence, yet simultaneously recognized that supranational cooperation could bring benefits like the CAP. In 1967, de Gaulle's position was still strong enough to allow him to veto a second British attempt at EEC entry. But, in May 1968, his position was shaken by domestic unrest. Faced with the prospect of devaluing the franc, de Gaulle chose to resign in April 1969, freeing the EEC to make swifter progress.

De Gaulle's successor, Georges Pompidou, was a Gaullist but he had good reasons to alter the General's European policy. In particular, Pompidou was fearful of increased German power and its readiness, under Willy Brandt (see Box 9.4) after September 1969, to pursue an independent foreign policy regarding Eastern Europe. The strengthening of EEC institutions seemed the best way to limit German ambitions and this policy might also benefit from British entry. 'Britain's membership would be a counterweight to growing German influence in the EEC.'[29] Pompidou also wanted, finally, to achieve a fully operational CAP. At a summit meeting of Community leaders in The Hague in December 1969, it was possible to agree both on the completion of the CAP and on enlargement talks with Britain, Denmark, Ireland, and Norway. These got underway in June 1970 and, in contrast to previous attempts, the British kept their entry conditions at a minimal level. A summit between Pompidou and Britain's premier, Edward Heath, provided the key breakthrough. Although Norway voted against membership in a referendum, the other three signed a Treaty of Accession in January 1972, to take effect a year later. This 'northern enlargement' was only one of the advances made by the EEC at the time. The decision to finance the CAP by giving the Community its own financial resources (in the form of income from tariffs and expenditure tax) strengthened the Commission's independence. In October 1970, the 'Werner Report' proposed greater monetary cooperation. And, the following month, EEC foreign ministers began to meet together to discuss common foreign policy issues, a practice known as European Political Cooperation. But there were already signs that such progress might yet be side-tracked by economic uncertainties.

The Western Economies in the 1960s

In the 1960s, the economic growth of the previous decade was generally sustained in the West, but at a decreasing rate, and this lower growth brought the spectre of inflation and social unrest. The Paris riots of May 1968 were an early warning sign, but one that had more to do with political alienation than economic worries. Italy, where the 'economic miracle' brought average growth rates of 7 per cent in 1958–63, experienced a 'hot autumn' of strikes and demonstrations in 1969. Even a strong economy like Germany saw inflation rise from 2 per cent in 1969 to nearly 5 per cent in 1971. In the US, fuelled by spending on Vietnam, inflation was already nearly 5 per cent when Lyndon Johnson left office and it continued to rise under Nixon, to almost 9 per cent in 1974. The one continuing success story among the advanced economies was Japan, where growth rates between 1950 and 1973 averaged over 9 per cent, turning it into the world's second largest manufacturer, after the US, helped by high savings rates and relatively low wages. Particular challenges were created for the West by balance-of-payments difficulties, which had a detrimental effect on monetary stability. The British pound, long undermined by the country's relatively poor economic performance, was devalued in 1967, and the French franc, weakened by the troubles of 1968, followed in 1969. By then, the US dollar, the backbone of the Bretton Woods system of fixed exchange rates, was also in trouble. America had faced increasing balance-of-payments problems since the late 1950s, as the European and Japanese economies became increasingly strong competitors and inflation took root. In August 1971, Nixon finally introduced a package of measures to limit imports and restrict wage/price increases, as well as ending the convertibility of dollars into gold. This 'Nixon Shock' heralded the end of Bretton Woods and the beginning of a decade of economic stagnation in the West.

The problems of the developed economies in the 1960s should not be exaggerated. Living standards continued to rise, consumer goods production was increasing apace, and welfare services were improving. A situation of full employment was maintained, even if unemployment was beginning to rise by 1970 (reaching 6 per cent in the US). A slowing of growth rates from the heady days of the late 1950s and early 1960s was probably inevitable. The rising social discontent in France, Italy, and elsewhere was caused less by fear of poverty than a desire to maintain the wage increases and improved working conditions that higher growth rates and full employment had allowed. The 'high growth rate was coming to an end as the technological catching up phase tapered off, so that a gap began to open . . . between the declining productivity increases and the continued high annual wage increases'.[30] The US might have lost its clear predominance in the world economy, which had been so evident in 1945, but in 1971 it still had a third of world manufacturing production and its industrial efficiency (measured by output per worker) was still twice that of Japan and Germany. The Western economies were also becoming more closely integrated in terms of trade and investment. About two-thirds of the trade of industrialized countries was with other industrialized countries. By the mid-1960s, America had over $50 billion invested abroad. Meanwhile, in the trade field, the 'Kennedy Round' of trade reductions, negotiated by General Agreement on Tariffs and Trade (GATT) between 1963 and 1967, cut tariffs by an average of 25 per cent. The fact that it concentrated on manufactured goods made it most beneficial to the developed Western countries and it was they who generally gained most from the continuing growth of global commerce in the 1960s. By 1971, world trade was five times its 1948 level, but it was concentrated in manufacture rather than in primary products, the price of which remained low—to the detriment of producers in the less developed world.

E. The Rise of European Détente

Motives for European Détente

Down to 1972, as the US and USSR moved fitfully towards détente, more certain progress was made in Europe. It has been stated that détente 'emerged first in Europe. The groundwork was laid by President de Gaulle . . . and then, on a more lasting basis, by the West German Ostpolitik.'[31] In fact, European détente can be said to have had an even longer pedigree. Winston Churchill had first urged an East–West summit to discuss Cold War tensions in 1950 while, in November 1954, France's prime minister, Pierre Mendès-France, had used his address to the UN General Assembly to urge East–West talks. There were good reasons why British and French leaders should go further than the US in their eagerness for détente. The West European great powers had a different diplomatic tradition that was less ideological in emphasis, and more ready to accept the current state of power politics. For both Western and Eastern Europeans, inevitable concern developed from their being so close to the dividing line between the two camps: in the event of war, much of Europe would be obliterated. Furthermore, a lowering of tensions was the surest way to improve the freedom of diplomatic manoeuvre Europeans had between the US and USSR, something which de Gaulle and Ceauşescu were especially keen to see.

But détente can also be seen as fighting the Cold War by means other than the diplomatic deadlock, commercial freeze, and nuclear threats which had cemented the unity of both blocs until about 1962. For the Soviets, prime motives for relaxing tensions in the 1960s 'included a desire to . . . exploit divisions in the Western camp, obtain Western capital and technology to spur the lagging Soviet economy, and . . . cover themselves in the West against the risks of . . . conflict with China in the East'.[32] To these may be added the hope of 'decoupling' the US from Western Europe defence through the pursuit of an all-European security system. In the West, while some leftists were ready to tolerate the continued existence of communism, most advocates of détente in government saw it as a way of undermining the Eastern bloc by peaceful means. By respecting the European status quo in the short term, the West would use trade, talks, and other contacts to break down barriers and suspicions with the East, proving the superiority of Western economic goods, infiltrating liberal ideas across the Iron Curtain, and so diluting the cohesion of the Soviet bloc. The logic was admirably set out in a British policy paper of March 1960, which stated that:

> We were working for a reduction of tension in Europe. If this was successful, it might create pressures inside the Communist camp which could, in due course, loosen the Russian grip on Eastern Europe. It was not a policy of appeasement but a means of carrying the offensive into the Communist camp. [33]

Such a policy hoped to 'dilute the Soviet challenge: as the Soviet people became . . . aware of the realities of the world outside, their expectations and interests came into tacit collision . . .', with realities of the centralized economic planning system at home. But this took time to have effect and 'meanwhile the imperial outreach of the Soviet Union continued', as seen in Czechoslovakia in 1968.[34]

Progress on Pan-European Contacts, 1966–71

Early in 1966 the State Department remained sceptical about the prospects for détente in general, suspicious of Soviet motives, and determined only to negotiate from a position of strength. However, pressure for détente was growing from a number of directions. One was the behaviour of de Gaulle who, since 1962, had not only blocked deeper integration of the EEC and criticized US policy, but had also, in January 1964, opened diplomatic relations with communist China. The same month he signed an agreement on economic, cultural, and scientific exchanges with the USSR. In June 1966, he visited the USSR. Already, in February 1965, de Gaulle had spoken of restoring the broad unity of Europe 'from the Atlantic to the Urals' and his meetings in Moscow, coming so soon after the exit from NATO, were designed both to underline French independence and to demonstrate the possibility of pan-European links. French power would now be maximized in a system of more independent European states, no longer dominated by Moscow and Washington. Yet, as with his EEC and transatlantic policies, de Gaulle's approach to détente lacked coherence. His determination to break the superpower domination of world affairs meant that some of his actions, including recognition of China, as well as his growing friendship with Ceauşescu, upset the Soviets. The idea that France alone could achieve much in drawing down the Iron Curtain was absurd, especially since de Gaulle always made clear that, in a major East–West crisis he would side with the other democracies.

De Gaulle was not the only West European leader to visit Moscow in 1966. The British Prime Minister, Harold Wilson, had been there in February, mainly to develop trade and technological exchanges. Commercial motives were also at the centre of increasing Italian interest in détente, with the Soviet president, Nicolae Podgorny, visiting Rome in January 1967. Such events did not arouse the same popular interest as de Gaulle's behaviour, largely because Britain and Italy were perceived as loyal Atlanticists. However, to the Johnson administration, it was increasingly clear that many West European governments, backed by their parliaments and popular opinion, were keen to develop East–West links. Furthermore, in the immediate aftermath of de Gaulle's visit, the Warsaw Pact met in Bucharest and renewed pressure, first begun in 1954 but not pressed much under Khrushchev, for a pan-European security system. As in 1954, the proposal was not put in a way that attracted Western interest: America and Canada were to be excluded from the new system—and thus 'decoupled' from West European defence—and NATO was to be wound up; the existing status quo in Europe was to be recognized, thus condoning Soviet domination of the East; and trade was to be freed from Western security controls. Yet, in December 1966 the North Atlantic Council responded to the increasing pressures for détente by asking a committee chaired by the Belgian Prime Minister, Pierre Harmel, to study the Alliance's options. A year later, the Council accepted the Harmel Report. 'Its lifeblood was the statement . . . that the Alliance had two functions: military security and a policy of détente, and that these were not contradictory but complementary.'[35] The approach was radically different to that of the Soviets, in that NATO would only pursue détente if it preserved Western security. But the Harmel Report potentially opened the way to East–West talks on an unprecedented range of political, military, and economic issues.

Little happened in the short term. The Soviets showed no enthusiasm for the Harmel Report, partly because it adhered to a policy of Western military strength. In June 1968, NATO followed it up with calls for pan-European talks on Mutual Balanced Force Reductions (MBFR), but these, too, held little interest for the Soviets, who would be expected to surrender their conventional superiority in Europe. A few months later, the invasion of Czechoslovakia proved a setback for détente and made NATO cautious when, in April 1969, the Warsaw Pact renewed its call for a pan-European security system. But, a year later memories of Czechoslovakia were fading and the Warsaw Pact made a key concession, at its June 1970 meeting, agreeing that the US and Canada could take part in a European security conference. As on superpower détente and the Sino-American rapprochement, there was a real sense of forward momentum in 1971. In May, Brezhnev agreed that MBFR talks might be useful. The timing of this move was important, coming as the Nixon administration was under pressure, from the Mansfield Amendment, to cut troop levels in Europe unilaterally. Brezhnev's announcement allowed Nixon to argue that multilateral talks, rather than unilateral cuts, were the best way to secure troop reductions. In December, the Atlantic Council reciprocated by agreeing in principle to a European security conference. This sense of progress was greatly helped by parallel advances on the future of Germany.

The Emergence of *Ostpolitik*, 1966–71

Between 1948 and 1961, the German problem, and more specifically the position of Berlin, had been the main East–West flashpoint in Europe. The Western powers had refused to recognize East Germany's existence; the Eastern bloc had condemned West Germany's economic and military resuscitation. However, the building of the Berlin Wall in 1961 was followed by a growing recognition on both sides that the division of Berlin and Germany would continue for years to come. Increasingly, newly independent states in the less developed world gave diplomatic recognition to East Germany, undermining West Germany's Hallstein Doctrine (under which it had no relations with governments who recognized East Germany). 'Instead of isolating the GDR from the rest of the world, [West Germany] faced the prospect of being isolated itself.'[36] Furthermore, 'in the 1960s, a majority of West Germans started to identify with the Federal Republic, based on the success story of the "economic miracle" and the country's political stability'.[37] After December 1966, the West German 'Grand Coalition' government of Kurt Kiesinger tentatively began a new policy, *Ostpolitik*, designed to improve relations with the Soviet bloc by abandoning the Hallstein Doctrine, opening up trade and offering agreements. This 'eastern policy' became identified with the Social Democratic foreign minister, Willy Brandt, who believed that the division of Germany could only be broken down through a gradual relaxation of tension, rather than the confrontational policies favoured by the Adenauer administration. The Soviets were initially sceptical and the East Germans wanted Western diplomatic recognition as a condition of any agreements. Brandt kept up the pressure. In a speech in Nuremberg in 1968, he made a significant concession by offering to compromise on Germany's borders, opening the way to territorial deals with Poland, Czechoslovakia, and the USSR. At the same time, he had to reassure his NATO allies that he had no intention of defecting from the alliance. In an article in *Foreign Affairs*, he was careful to 'reject any German foreign policy that lessens the solidarity of [NATO] or limits the decisive participation of the United States in safeguarding freedom in Europe'.[38]

In October 1969, Brandt became West German Chancellor and, within two months, signed the Non-Proliferation Treaty, ending Warsaw Pact fears of a German nuclear arsenal. Christian Democrats, who had hitherto dominated government in the Bonn Republic, had their doubts about *Ostpolitik* and, in the White House, Kissinger feared that Brandt's enthusiasm might open NATO to 'selective détente', whereby the Soviets would 'ease tensions with some allies while maintaining an intransigent position towards us'.[39] Such fears proved exaggerated. Within a year, on 12 August 1970, Brandt signed the Moscow Treaty with the USSR, which became the basis for later *Ostpolitik* agreements. It involved the renunciation of the use of force, increased financial-commercial ties and—the point which caused most controversy in Germany—recognized the inviolability of existing European borders. Brandt did not give up the ambition of eventual German reunification, he did not recognize the East German government, and he insisted that, before the Moscow Treaty could be ratified, there must be an agreement on Berlin that recognized West Berlin's links to West Germany. This breakthrough agreement, which helped remove fears of German revanchism (the desire to recover territories lost at the end of the Second World War) in the East, was followed by the Warsaw Treaty of 7 December with Poland, which confirmed the German–Polish border.

Talks over Berlin proved more difficult, partly because the Stalinist East German leader, Walter Ulbricht, was reluctant to deal with Bonn, and partly because, where Berlin was concerned, agreement was needed from the four occupation powers. West Germany, the US, USSR, Britain, and France began to discuss Berlin in March 1970 and Brandt was determined to get an agreement here before ratifying the Moscow and Warsaw treaties. His aim was to win concessions from the USSR on Berlin in return for his acceptance of Germany's post-1945 borders. Ulbricht's doubts meant progress at first. But in May 1971 he was replaced by Erich Honecker, who was ready to accept that times had changed. The Berlin agreement of 3 September 1971, between the four occupying powers, essentially recognized the existing status quo. It guaranteed Western access to the city (reducing the risk of another blockade like 1948–9) and gave both sides concessions on the question of political links between Berlin and Bonn. The Soviets recognized the legitimacy of such links but Brandt agreed to reduce West Germany's political role in Berlin and gave up on hopes of fully integrating the city into West Germany. This was a dramatic advance on the situation of a decade before, when the Berlin Wall had been erected. The new agreement helped pave the way both to wider détente in Europe and to a fuller settlement between the West and East German governments.

BOX 9.4

Biography: Willy Brandt (1913–92)

A German social democrat and firm opponent of Nazism, Brandt went to live in Norway during the Hitler years but returned soon afterwards and, in 1949, became a member of the first West German Parliament. He was one of a revisionist group who, in the 1950s, worked to make the Social Democratic Party (SPD) more electable by toning down its Marxist elements and shifting its foreign policy away from a readiness to deal with the USSR, to support for such Western organizations as NATO and the European Community. Brandt rose to world prominence as Mayor of West Berlin after 1957, in which position he saw out the crisis of 1958–9, when Khrushchev threatened to drive the Western powers out, and the raising of the Berlin Wall in 1961. His firmness under pressure, together with his liberal views and experience of running the West Berlin government, made him an obvious candidate for the SPD to put forward as chancellor. However, it was in the joint position of vice chancellor and foreign minister that he first entered national government in December 1966, as part of a 'Grand Coalition' with the Christian Democrats. Becoming Chancellor in October 1969, Brandt pursued a policy of improved relations with the Eastern bloc vigorously, making treaties with the USSR, Poland, and Czechoslovakia. More remarkably, he secured better access between the two Berlins and, controversially at home, proved ready to deal with East Germany under the formula of 'two states in one nation'. The high point of his premiership was the November 1972 election, which gave the SPD 46 per cent of the vote—outstripping the Christian Democrats for the only time in West German history. But in May 1974 he felt forced to resign, an East German spy having been discovered working on his staff. Brandt remained SPD party chairman for some years and maintained his international profile with the 1980 Brandt Report, which vainly pressed the case for tackling the world's North–South divide between rich and poor.

Visit the online resources that accompany this book to test your understanding and take your learning further: www.oup.com/he/young-kent3e

NOTES

1. Arthur M. Schlesinger, *A Thousand Days: John F. Kennedy in the White House* (Andre Deutsch, London, 1965), 762.
2. Theodore C. Sorensen, *Kennedy* (Hodder & Stoughton, London, 1965), 745.
3. Michael R. Beschloss, *The Crisis Years: Kennedy and Khrushchev, 1960–63* (HarperCollins, New York, 1991), 600.
4. Anatoly Dobrynin, *In Confidence* (Random House, New York, 1995), 122.
5. Dean Rusk, *As I Saw It* (Norton, New York, 1990), 343.
6. Peter G. Boyle, *American–Soviet Relations* (Routledge, London, 1993), 165.
7. Henry Kissinger, *The White House Years* (Weidenfeld & Nicolson, London, 1979), 129.
8. Odd Arne Westad (ed.), *Brothers in Arms: The Rise and Fall of the Sino-Soviet Alliance 1945–1963* (Stanford University Press, Stanford, 1998), 27–8.
9. Alfred D. Low, *The Sino-Soviet Dispute* (Associated University Presses, London, 1976), 343.
10. Edward Crankshaw, *The New Cold War* (Penguin, London, 1963), 153.
11. Thomas W. Zeiler, *Dean Rusk* (Scholarly Resources, Wilmington, 2000), 100–1.
12. Yang Kuisong, 'The Sino-Soviet Border Clash of 1969', *Cold War History*, 1 (August 2000), 48.
13. Richard Nixon, 'Asia after Vietnam', *Foreign Affairs*, 1 (October 1967), 111–25.
14. Chen Jian and David Wilson, 'New Evidence on the Sino-American Opening', *Cold War International History Project Bulletin*, 11 (Winter 1998), 166–7.
15. Yang Kuisong, 'The Sino-Soviet Border Clash of 1969', *Cold War History*, 1 (August 2000), 49.

16. Henry Kissinger, *The White House Years* (Little, Brown, New York, 1979), 177–8.
17. William Shawcross, *Dubček* (Hogarth Press, London, 1990), 138–9.
18. Philip Windsor and Adam Roberts, *Czechoslovakia, 1968* (Columbia University Press, New York, 1969), 19.
19. Kenneth K. Skoug, *Czechoslovakia's Lost Fight for Freedom* (Praeger, Westport, 1999), 141.
20. H. Gordon Skilling, *Czechoslovakia's Interrupted Revolution* (Princeton University Press, Princeton, 1976), 498.
21. *Documents on British Policy Overseas, Series III, vol. 1: Britain and the Soviet Union, 1968–72* (Stationery Office, London, 1997), 85.
22. James G. McGinn, 'The Politics of Collective Inaction: NATO's Response to the Prague Spring', *Journal of Cold War Studies*, 1/3 (Autumn, 1999), 136.
23. Paul Buteaux, *The Politics of Nuclear Consultation in NATO* (Cambridge University Press, Cambridge, 1983), 60.
24. Lyndon B. Johnson Library, oral history interview with John Leddy.
25. Helga Haftendorn, *NATO and the Nuclear Revolution, 1966–7* (Clarendon Press, Oxford, 1996), 290.
26. David Schwartz, *NATO's Nuclear Dilemmas* (Brookings, Washington, 1983), 187.
27. Piers Ludlow, 'A Mismanaged Application', in Anne Deighton and Alan Milward (eds), *Widening, Deepening, Acceleration: The EEC, 1957–63* (Bruylant, Brussels, 1999), 273.
28. Peter Stirk, *A History of European Integration since 1914* (Pinter, London, 1996), 175.
29. Martin Dedman, *The Origins and Development of the European Union, 1945–95* (Routledge, London, 1996), 119.
30. Sidney Pollard, *The International Economy since 1945* (Routledge, London, 1997), 108.
31. S. R. Ashton, *In Search of Détente* (Macmillan, London, 1989), 105.
32. A. W. De Porte, *Europe between the Superpowers* (Yale University Press, New Haven, 1986), 176.
33. The National Archives, Kew, CAB 134/1929, FP(20)1st, 23 March 1960.
34. Vladislav Zubok, 'Unwrapping the Enigma: The Soviet Challenge in the 1960s', in Diane Kunz (ed.), *The Diplomacy of the Crucial Decade* (Columbia University Press, New York, 1994), 173–4.
35. Helga Haftendorn, *NATO and the Nuclear Revolution, 1966–7* (Clarendon Press, Oxford, 1996), 374.
36. Josef Korbel, *Détente in Europe* (Princeton University Press, Princeton, 1972), 147.
37. Gottfried Niedhart, 'Ostpolitik', in Caroline Fink, Philipp Gassert, and Detlef Junker (eds), *1968: The World Transformed* (Cambridge University Press, Cambridge, 1998), 190.
38. Willy Brandt, 'German Policy towards the East', *Foreign Affairs*, 3 (April 1968), 477.
39. Henry Kissinger, *The White House Years* (Little, Brown & Co., Boston, 1979), 410.

10

The Vietnam War

Chapter contents

A. The Escalation of US Involvement, 1963–5

Continuing Instability in South Vietnam

Lyndon Johnson inherited the Vietnam conflict in difficult circumstances. He had not been elected president in his own right and so, perhaps, believed that he should carry on with Kennedy's policies. It was unclear what exactly Kennedy would have done in Vietnam, but Johnson retained his predecessor's foreign policy team and did not question the basic principle of America's foreign policy, which called for communism to be resisted, wherever and whenever it threatened. It would have been difficult for anyone, even a newly elected president, to go against the consensus in Washington that opposed the spread of communism; and, as Senate Democrat leader in the Eisenhower years, Johnson had always backed that consensus. With thousands of US military advisers in South Vietnam already, any precipitate retreat would amount to a public admission of defeat, and even Kennedy had only talked of making any such withdrawal *after* securing his re-election in November 1964. Johnson's preference, given his determined, self-confident personality and his disdain for anything that smacked of appeasement, would probably have been to pursue the war with greater vigour, ending Kennedy's ambiguity and trying to force a decisive victory. But in 1963–4 he too had to focus on the upcoming presidential election, which he desperately wanted to win. The election, he decided, was safest fought without any particular emphasis on the difficult struggle in South-East Asia.

As if Kennedy's death and the approaching US election were not challenge enough, Johnson also had to deal with a South Vietnamese political situation which, in the wake of President Diem's assassination, was wracked by instability, tempting the communists to believe that the war could soon be decided in their favour. In December 1963, the war in the South intensified, with improvements in the Ho Chi Minh trail allowing a greater supply effort from the North. Johnson has often been criticized as a leader unfamiliar with foreign policy issues. According to an early assessment of his presidency he 'entered the White House not only little concerned with the outer world but leery of it'.[1] His anti-communism was of a crude sort, he showed little understanding of the problems in the less developed world, and though he had visited South Vietnam as Vice-President, his attitude towards the Vietnamese was condescending and racist. Yet he had been canny enough to oppose the overthrow of Diem and it was not his fault that he had to pick up the pieces in its wake. The coup in Saigon might have got rid of an increasingly embarrassing and unpopular figure, but it did not necessarily guarantee a more popular replacement, nor did it mean that South Vietnam's internal problems were removed. True, Buddhist discontent lessened for a while, only reviving on a serious scale in March 1966. But the government remained corrupt, dominated by Catholics and unwilling to carry out reforms, such as land redistribution, which might have won peasant sympathy.

The fact was that the war was also a political struggle like the fight against colonialism and foreign interference from which it emerged. For many non-political Vietnamese, the French defeat at the hands of the Japanese destroyed their legitimacy and neither Bao Dai nor Diem or their successors could regain it. They were perceived, like the Americans, as aliens who, in addition, were corrupt and inefficient supporters of oppressive landlords who were opposed to the kind of reforms that would appeal to the peasant masses. Ultimately, however, the Americans were precluded from embracing the kind of reform programme that would build the support of the rural masses. Whatever the flaws in the conception and administration of such attempts to undermine communist support as the strategic hamlets programme, the ultimate need was radical land reform and redistribution. Whether referred to or not as 'communist', such concepts were beyond the pale for any American approach to private property. No amount of welfare, education, and development could compensate for that in the eyes of most Vietnamese peasants struggling with rents and inadequate land.

The military too, despite ever more US advice and supplies, continued to perform badly against the Viet Cong. As under Diem, army officers were promoted for political loyalty rather than ability and they refused to take risks with their units, for fear either of sustaining heavy losses if defeated, or of arousing the suspicion of superiors if successful. Wealthy Vietnamese often bribed their way out of military service, while the poor simply deserted. On paper, in 1964 the Army of the Republic of Vietnam (ARVN) numbered 500,000 men, but the desertion rate that year was about 50,000 and few of the rest saw serious action against the Viet Cong. Indeed, some ARVN units made tacit 'peace' agreements with the communists at local level. That same year Johnson increased the number of US advisers in the country by 7,000, a reflection of the growing belief that only an increased American effort could offset South Vietnamese failings.

Just as the Truman–Eisenhower reliance on the French to defeat the communists had ended in disappointment in 1954, and just as the Eisenhower–Kennedy faith in Diem had evaporated in 1963, so in 1964 Americans came to doubt whether any potential South Vietnamese leader could stem the Viet Cong tide. As a result, many of the President's advisers came to believe that the US must effectively fight the war with its own armed forces. Diem's immediate successor, General 'Big' Minh, was the head of an unelected military junta which quickly became factionalized. Worse than that in American eyes, Minh showed signs of wanting to negotiate with the communist-led National Liberation Front (NLF), perhaps striking a deal that would neutralize Vietnam in the Cold War. Neither was General Minh alone in believing that Saigon's best option was to seek a settlement with its enemies: Diem's brother, Nhu, had had similar ideas. In late January 1964, the Americans encouraged Minh's replacement with the vain, volatile General Nguyen Khanh, who dominated the South Vietnamese leadership in the following year, despite a bewildering series of changes in the government, as attempts were made to replace him or to force him to share power. Khanh somehow survived, despite his failure either to control the army factions, to win genuine popularity, or to prosecute the war with vigour. Indeed, he too showed signs of wanting to talk with the NLF before finally being expelled from office in February 1965. After that, there were several more months of instability before, in June 1965, the junta fell under the domination of a flamboyant new Prime Minister, Air Vice-Marshal Nguyen Cao Ky, who survived in office for two years before losing a power struggle with his deputy, General Nguyen Van Thieu, who was more trusted by Washington. Through all these changes of government, it was increasingly clear, in fact, that American requirements decided who held power in Saigon. Despite US claims to be protecting South Vietnamese 'independence', it was the US which effectively ensured that its allies abandoned all thought of neutralism and focused on opposing the Viet Cong, in a war where Americans took on a greater burden of fighting, in the air and on the ground.

The Gulf of Tonkin Resolution

In March 1964, the US Defense Secretary, Robert McNamara, visited South Vietnam, saw the growing frustration of the US military at South Vietnamese ineffectiveness, and reported to Johnson that increased American action was necessary to save the country from communism. The Joint Chiefs of Staff favoured a much tougher approach to the war, including large-scale use of bombing (in Laos as well as Vietnam) and covert operations against the North. The use of air power against North Vietnam, which was seen as lying behind the Viet Cong campaign in the South, was especially attractive to American planners. They had clear superiority in the air, could hope to destroy communist fuel, weapons, and communications through air attack, and an air campaign risked far less casualties than one on land. It was an obvious area in which the US might bring to bear its technological advantages over the communists. However, while Johnson allowed preparations for air strikes to be laid (with reconnaissance flights over possible targets) from May onwards, he was reluctant to bomb the North in an election year and possibly still hoped that a strengthening of southern resolve might make such action unnecessary. During the election, Johnson wanted to focus the electorate on his plans for a major social reform programme, the 'Great Society', which he dreamed would be more important than Roosevelt's 'New Deal'. Regarding Vietnam, he undertook simply to assist in opposing communism and even suggested that substantial numbers of American troops would never be sent to fight, Korean War-style, in Asia again. He left it to his Republican opponent, the extreme right-winger, Barry Goldwater, to alienate voters with a rabidly anti-communist, warmongering campaign. The reward was a landslide victory in the November election, which gave Johnson greater confidence about defining his own Vietnam policy in future.

Three months before the election, his ability to fight the Vietnam war as he pleased was strengthened by a brief clash with the North. On 2 August, North Vietnamese torpedo boats attacked an American vessel, the USS *Maddox*, operating in the Gulf of Tonkin, where US covert operations, intelligence gathering, and support of commando raids on North Vietnam had been taking place. Two days later American ships reported a further attack, but one that probably had never taken place. The sense of outrage in Washington, at what was seen as an unprovoked assault, was such that, on 7 August, a motion was introduced in the Senate allowing Johnson to take 'all necessary measures to repel any armed attack against the armed forces of the United States and to prevent further aggression'. Democrats were keen to support the President ahead of the upcoming election, Republicans did not want to appear less 'patriotic' than the Democrats, and so the 'Gulf of Tonkin' resolution was duly passed, with little real discussion, by 88 votes to 2. Not repealed until 1970, it effectively gave Johnson carte blanche to deal with the Vietnam conflict as he pleased. But at first it was not clear how he would exploit it. In the wake of the Gulf of Tonkin incident, US aircraft attacked the North for the first time, but only in limited, retaliatory raids, not the all-out bombing campaign which US military leaders favoured. With the presidential election only days away, Johnson even reacted mildly to a communist attack on Bien Hoa airbase, in which several Americans were killed. And, once elected, Johnson would have preferred to focus on the 'Great Society' programme, which itself demanded large sums of money that a war in Vietnam could only compromise. Yet the US commander in South Vietnam after June 1964, General William C. Westmoreland, had no doubt that, to avoid a communist victory, the US must take over the war from the unreliable ARVN and pursue a war of attrition using American units. The Viet Cong were now reckoned to have about 200,000 fighters; in the wake of the Gulf of Tonkin episode, infiltration from the North began to increase; and the attack on Bien Hoa had shown that they were prepared to target US forces directly. Until August 1964 Hanoi had doubted whether Johnson would expend large-scale resources for the sake of the crumbling

South, but now it was prepared for the possibility of a direct struggle with the Americans.

1965: Johnson's Decision to Escalate

In early 1965, American policy on Vietnam reached what McNamara and Bundy called 'the fork in the road', and two fateful decisions were made: first, to begin a long-term bombing campaign against the North; and second, to deploy US ground troops to fight in the South. Both options had been pressed by the military for several months, but McNamara himself later criticized the way in which America slipped into war: 'Why did we escalate rather than withdraw? Why did we fail to see the implications of our actions?'[2] In fact, there was some questioning of escalation in Washington. Indeed, there is evidence that, despite the criticism often levelled at him for being bent on war, Johnson 'reached widely for advisory . . . encounters',[3] and there were several Democratic Party senior figures who warned of the likely public backlash to escalation. There was also a leading figure in the administration, Under-Secretary of State George Ball, who preferred negotiation with Hanoi and stated, with regard to military escalation, in a memorandum of October 1964, that 'Once on the tiger's back we cannot be sure of picking the place to dismount.'[4] But Ball and the others were heavily outnumbered by those in the President's team who urged greater US involvement to save South Vietnam. In the wake of the November election, Johnson had set up a working group on how to proceed in Vietnam which did not even view withdrawal as an option, because defeat at the hands of the communists seemed unthinkable. Instead, three courses were considered. The first, continuing with current policies, seemed no better than withdrawal, given the South's poor performance in the war. The second, a rapid build-up against Hanoi, would mean a costly commitment of US resources at an early date, with the risk of provoking a violent Chinese response, which might lead to another Korean War—a war which had ended in a costly stalemate. The preferred option, therefore, was the third, a gradual application of pressure against the North to strangle its support for the Viet Cong. Such pressure would take the form of bombing but, since this might not break the North's resolve and might even provoke it to greater efforts, some of the Working Group also wanted to deploy US combat troops on the ground.

Johnson himself recognized the possible limitations of a bombing campaign and was troubled by the prospect of war but, faced by the continuing political instability in Saigon, he was increasingly prepared to accept the third option. Then, on 6 February 1965, a Viet Cong attack on Pleiku killed eight Americans, leading Johnson to approve retaliatory air attacks on the North, as he had after the Gulf of Tonkin episode. The Pleiku attack had probably been timed to coincide with a visit by the Soviet premier, Andrei Kosygin, to Hanoi; and the harsh US response, while Kosygin was still there, helped ensure Soviet sympathy for the North—an early demonstration that, if anything, bombing played into communist hands. Certainly, the very need to bomb the North implied that the communists were winning the struggle in the South. Nonetheless, Johnson's advisers believed that a permanent bombing campaign would blunt the North's war effort, as well as giving a boost to Southern morale. Another Viet Cong attack on 10 February, this time in Saigon, killed over twenty Americans and was answered by further retaliatory air attacks. More importantly, Johnson was now convinced that a permanent campaign, codenamed Operation Rolling Thunder, should begin. Delayed at first by poor weather, it went ahead on 2 March. The Joint Chiefs would have preferred a massive bombing campaign, to include Hanoi and the major North Vietnamese port, Haiphong, rather than the gradual build-up of pressure (initially limited in its target areas) favoured by Washington. Even so, Rolling Thunder, which went on until 1968 and eventually did strike targets around Hanoi and Haiphong, involved the use of B-52 aircraft which could each carry 30 tons of bombs, capable of levelling 1.5 square miles at a time.

The military could also be satisfied that, on 8 March, the first US ground troops arrived in South Vietnam, when 3,500 marines landed at Da Nang, already the location of a large American airbase. Some of Johnson's advisers were less certain about this step than they were about bombing, because of the risk of greater American casualties in an unconventional war for which they were not prepared. As with Rolling Thunder, however, the ground war unfolded in a gradual way for Americans: the marines were initially deployed only to defend air-bases, then in April they were allowed to extend operations to a radius of fifty miles and their numbers were increased, with the first regular army units arriving in May. Indeed, the gradual nature of escalation, both in the air and on the ground, was partly designed to prevent a war frenzy, or alternatively a major outcry against the war, at home. With a friendly Congress and an overwhelming election victory behind him, Johnson believed he could carry opinion with him in executing a limited war, and he still hoped to focus on his dream of a 'Great Society' rather than conflict overseas. Only in retrospect would it become clear that, with the launch of Rolling Thunder and the arrival of the marines, America was fatally committed to a quagmire war from which there was no easy escape. Yet, even at the time, 'informed observers knew that a key moment had come and a line had been crossed',[5] and it did not take long for the policy of escalation to run into problems, in Vietnam, at home in America, and internationally.

B. America versus North Vietnam, 1965–7

The Course of the War

In the wake of the first American troop commitments, it became easier for General Westmoreland to win support for offensive 'search and destroy' missions against the communists. The alternative approach, of concentrating on the defence and pacification of heavily populated areas on the coast and in towns, the so-called 'enclave strategy', was favoured by the Marines, but did not promise rapid results. The pattern of escalation continued along the lines of early 1964: the area of bombing over the North was gradually extended, with oil depots around Hanoi and Haiphong hit in June 1966 and the US air force eventually risking raids close to the Chinese border; the numbers of troops was also raised gradually, without any formal, dramatic announcement to the American people. Thus, on 27 July 1965, after an intensive debate among his advisers, Johnson announced that he was sending an additional 50,000 men to South Vietnam but kept quiet the fact that he had privately agreed to send 50,000 more than that (taking the total in Vietnam to 175,000). He also doubled the quota of draftees into the US armed forces to 35,000 but, in another example of his reluctance to risk controversy, refused to call up trained reserves because, while this might have produced a substantial, trained force more rapidly, it would also have meant forcing older men to fight. The President also gave the impression that US troops were merely supporting the ARVN, he made no stirring patriotic appeal, and he refused all calls to estimate the cost or duration of the conflict.

In early full-scale battles, Westmoreland's conventional warfare approach seemed successful. At Chu Lai in August, US marines killed about 600 Viet Cong for the loss of only 50 to themselves, an attrition rate which it seemed must ultimately force the communists to back down. Then, in October–November, in the Ia Drang valley of the Central Highlands, the regular North Vietnamese Army (NVA) lost over 1,500 compared to 300 American dead. The American use of helicopters, airlifted artillery, and B-52 bombers in the battle underlined their technological superiority. After this bloody encounter, however, the communists simply changed tactics, refusing to engage in large-scale clashes, harassing US forces when they were at company strength or less—and then only at close range (so that aircraft and artillery were harder to use)—and melting away in the face of 'search-and-destroy' missions, only to return to old haunts when the Americans had moved on. As one military historian notes, 'Ironically, one of the safest places for a US soldier to be in Vietnam was in one of Westmoreland's big battles, since they provided the best opportunity to minimize contact with the enemy.'[6] Visiting Vietnam in late November, McNamara reported that the North seemed to be matching the US escalation and that over half-a-million men might be needed there in the next few years, with no firm promise of victory. Communist numbers in South Vietnam in 1966 probably numbered about 50,000 NVA, 225,000 active Viet Cong (both guerrillas and regular troops), and a further 150,000 'local defence' forces, the last a kind of part-time militia.

The military conduct of the war can be criticized on a number of grounds. The reliance on the effectiveness of the South Vietnamese army, which was often devoid of the will to fight and the technical competence to do so, was never likely to bear fruit either at the beginning or the end of the conflict. Moreover, the tactics and strategy employed by the Americans were often counterproductive. In one general sense, the political need to win support in the countryside was undermined by the military actions. Ignorant of the customs of South Vietnamese peasants and their attachment to the local village, the Americans effectively destroyed the peasant way of life. They forced villagers away from their homes in the strategic hamlets programme and then deprived more than 3 million of them of any homes at all by accidental and

BOX 10.1

Lyndon Johnson and his Foreign Policy Advisers

When the assassination of John F. Kennedy brought Johnson (1908–73) to the Presidency, the latter had only limited experience in the foreign policy field. Since his early political life, in his home state of Texas, the new president had been far more interested in social reform programmes, being an ardent supporter of Franklin Roosevelt's 'New Deal'. Entering the House of Representatives in 1937 and the Senate in 1948, Johnson was an energetic, driven figure who, as Democratic leader in the Senate from 1953 to 1961, proved able to manipulate and dominate the other ambitious politicians around him. He also strongly backed the bipartisan consensus in favour of an anti-communist policy. Even a serious heart attack in 1955 could not force him out of political life and, as a well-known Southern politician, he was an obvious choice to strengthen the Kennedy ticket in the 1960 election. As Vice-President, Johnson visited South Vietnam, without gaining much of an understanding of local realities, and he chaired the National Security Council, but he had little enthusiasm for the latter body, considering it prone to 'leaks'. As president, he preferred to rely on so-called 'Tuesday luncheons': select meetings in the White House with those he trusted.

While never personally close to Kennedy, Johnson kept his predecessor's appointees in key positions in the foreign policy-making machine. Indeed, the Secretary of State, Dean Rusk (1908–94), served in this role throughout the Kennedy and Johnson administrations. Partly educated at Oxford University on a Rhodes Scholarship, Rusk had originally begun his career as a professor of international relations but, after war service, had worked in the State Department and by 1952 was well enough networked to become President of the Rockefeller Foundation. He had been one of several candidates recommended to Kennedy as Secretary of State and, partly because of his age (most of Kennedy's aides were in their forties) had not been personally close to the President. However, these very facts, combined with his Southern background, may have helped Rusk work with Johnson. Philosophical and deferential, Rusk was happy to let the Defense Department play the leading role on Vietnam policy but, as a convinced anti-communist, supported the escalation of the war, whose prosecution he continued to defend when in retirement.

Ironically, this could not be said of the Secretary of Defense for most of the 1960s, Robert McNamara (1916–2009). From California, educated at Berkeley and at Harvard Business School, McNamara's force of character and quick-mindedness helped him rise through the Ford Motor Company to be its president in 1960, before joining the Kennedy administration at the age of 44. In many ways, McNamara was also the ideal character to get on with Johnson, who valued his loyalty and energy. However, McNamara's interest in statistics, technology, and managerial techniques, while they helped him make the Defense Department's planning and budget systems more efficient, proved inappropriate for fighting the Vietnam War, where he was slow to understand the psychology and determination of the communists. By 1967, he was increasingly concerned about the way the conflict was going and in August admitted to a Senate inquiry that the US bombing of the North had achieved little. Three months later it was announced that he was moving to head the World Bank. In 1995, he published *In Retrospect*, critical of the escalation of the Vietnam War, which he had helped to direct 30 years before.

One novel feature of policy-making under Kennedy was the rise in significance of the National Security Adviser (NSA), as a presidential appointee (not subject to Congressional approval), based in the White House itself. Such a position had existed under Eisenhower, but mainly in the role of supporting the work of the National Security Council. Under Kennedy, the NSA, McGeorge Bundy (1919–96), became an important influence on presidential decision-making. Bundy came from a privileged Boston background, educated at Yale and Harvard, later teaching government at the latter. A self-controlled, laconic figure, he too shared a tough, anti-communist outlook and was retained by Johnson until February 1966, when disagreements over Vietnam, added to differences of personality, led him to return to academic life. His successor was his former deputy, Walt Rostow (b. 1916), from Russian immigrant stock, but another product of Yale and an academic background. A convinced 'hawk' on Vietnam, energetic, and self-confident, Rostow advocated a firm military policy in Vietnam, including large-scale bombing of the North and, like Rusk, continued to defend the war after returning to private life in 1969.

deliberate bombing, by the creation of fire zones, and by search-and-destroy missions.[7] If villagers were not political or supporting the insurgents before losing their homes, and sometimes their wives and children, they were certainly likely to become so and actively to oppose the Saigon government and their American backers afterwards.

Moreover, the communist Viet Cong would be difficult to distinguish from those not involved in the fighting and for much of the war would often engage American forces and then melt into the jungle. Efforts to search and destroy them measured in terms of a 'body count' were seen by the commander of US forces in Vietnam as the key to victory through the crushing of the Viet Cong. The body count of Americans, large as it was, tended to be very substantially lower than North Vietnamese losses and in that sense a 'success' of the search-and-destroy missions. It could therefore be argued, and certainly was at the time, that the Americans were winning the war. But, by making the issue manpower losses, this played to the insurgents' strengths, as they could find replacements more easily than the Americans and were immune to the kind of political consequences that body bags arriving at US airports inevitably produced. It also encouraged the kind of indiscriminate destruction of towns and village, along with many of their inhabitants, that the fear of an elusive enemy often produced. As one US army officer said about the almost complete destruction of the city of Ben Tre, occupied by the Viet Cong in 1968 and subjected to indiscriminate US air and naval bombardment: 'It became necessary to destroy the town in order to save it.'[8]

In 1966, the US military predicament became clearer. While the NVA remained the key threat in the Central Highlands, the far more densely populated Mekong Delta was largely the preserve of the Viet Cong. Tackling these two enemies, one a conventional army, the other a guerrilla force, meant that the US could not even make secure South Vietnam's short, northern border—ironically called the Demilitarized Zone—which the NVA crossed with impunity. Large-scale bombing neither destroyed the North's ability to wage war nor prevented sufficient arms and equipment coming down the Ho Chi Minh trail to maintain the war in the South, which it is estimated required only ten tons of supplies per day (many weapons being captured from the ARVN). US troops, the bulk of them young draftees, found it a difficult, demoralizing war to fight, far from home, in a hot climate, with no obvious 'front line', and under constant danger from surprise attacks, landmines, and booby traps. Communist tactics after the battle of Ia Drang valley proved very frustrating: only one in a hundred 'search-and-destroy' missions made contact with the enemy. And technological advantages provided no magic breakthrough but instead alienated the South Vietnamese people. The use of defoliants, in 'Operation Ranch Hand', caused environmental havoc to a fifth of the country in an attempt to remove the vegetation used by the communists as cover; the use of bombs and other explosives, together with the creation of 'free fire zones' (removing peasants from whole regions, so that the US and ARVN could concentrate on communist fighters, who remained) helped render over 4 million South Vietnamese homeless by 1968; and American attempts to measure communist deaths proved unreliable, partly because many peasants remained inside 'free fire zones' and, if they were killed, there was no way to tell them from guerrillas.

Nonetheless, in January 1967, Westmoreland was confident that, with estimated communist deaths running at twelve times the American figure, the war of attrition was working, even if he could not prove that Viet Cong numbers were in decline. That month he launched Operation Cedar Falls, in the Viet Cong-controlled 'Iron Triangle' north of Saigon. Bombs and artillery were followed up by the bulldozing of whole villages. Yet, by summer the Viet Cong were back in control of the area. Despite the evidence of such failing tactics, there was only a belated attempt to improve pacification techniques, the so-called Phoenix Programme, designed to win 'hearts and minds' and wipe out the Viet Cong by covert means, in mid-1967. The Thieu-Ky team remained the Americans' preferred government in Saigon despite periodic Buddhist unrest (especially in spring 1966) and despite winning only 35 per cent of the vote in elections in September 1967. The government was now seen to be completely dependent on Washington and little respected by most of its own people. Civilian leaders in Washington were increasingly frustrated with the military failure to break communist resolve; military leaders, for their part, were resentful at the political constraints put on their operations by the nature of 'limited war', with Johnson's gradual escalation of pressure against the North and the reluctance to bomb areas near the Chinese border. A school of thought has always claimed that, if the US had been tougher earlier, the war could have been won. For example, the wider air war might have been launched at an early date. As it was, by the time Rolling Thunder was extended, anti-aircraft defences had been improved over the North, so that US aircraft losses were high. One critical American analysis argues that, 'instead of seeing it was possible to fight and win a limited war in Asia . . . we allowed our fears to become a kind of self-deterrent and surrendered the initiative to our enemies'.[9] However, even at its most intense, and with all the North's large facilities and factories destroyed, bombing showed no sign of forcing Hanoi to back down. The rural economy survived and the North was never dependent on sophisticated technology. As to the war on the ground, 'looking at numbers . . . deployed, . . . their straining at the margins of the existing logistics infrastructure . . ., it is possible to argue that the . . . build-up . . . was as decisive as it could have been'.[10] An invasion of the North was considered but swiftly dismissed as it would almost certainly have brought China into the war, making the costs incalculable—and certainly not guaranteeing victory.

By 1967, Johnson was obsessed with Vietnam, monitoring daily operations in the White House Situation Room, and despairing of mounting divisions among his advisers. The continued problem of how to be sure of the situation on the ground, and how to decide between conflicting advice, was now opening up more serious divisions within the administration. As early as mid-1966, McNamara doubted the value of continued escalation and in 1967 went public with such criticisms. The President was also troubled that, despite his earlier attempts to underplay the significance of the war and concentrate on domestic reform, public opposition was becoming ever more vocal and the 'Great Society' programme stalling. March 1965 had seen the first university 'teach-in' against the war, reflecting doubts among the younger generation. In August 1965, a National Coordinating Committee was set up as an umbrella organization for the political, religious, and humanitarian groups opposed to the war and, in October 1967, the largest anti-war demonstration of all took place, when 100,000 marched on the Pentagon. By then, draft resistance was widespread. Meanwhile, in Congress, doubters led by Senator William Fulbright had forced special hearings on the war as early as February 1966. Yet in 1967 few in Congress were ready to advocate unilateral withdrawal, most media reports still accepted official versions of events in Vietnam, and two-thirds of American people still supported 'saving' Vietnam from communism, even if more than half were unhappy with the war's progress. Domestic opposition was, therefore, far from crippling the war effort, which Westmoreland in December 1967 believed was at a critical phase. Convinced that the communists had reached the 'crossover point', beyond which they were unable to compensate for their losses, he saw increased clashes with the NVA along the Laos border as evidence that a decisive struggle was imminent.

The Vain Search for Peace

From the start of direct American involvement, in early 1965, Johnson tried to disarm critics at home and abroad by posing as an advocate of peace talks. His first offer to negotiate came in a speech at Johns Hopkins University in April that year (see Box 10.1) and in mid-May he initiated the first 'bombing halt', a suspension of the Rolling Thunder campaign, designed to give the North a chance to talk. A longer 'bombing halt' was called between Christmas and the end of January 1966. Meanwhile, numerous potential intermediaries came forward, trying to broker a peace deal between Washington and Hanoi. There were various peace initiatives by the UN Secretary-General, U Thant; the British government, co-chair (along with the USSR) of the Geneva conference, made three bids to establish a dialogue with North Vietnam in 1965; and there were efforts by, among others, India, Canada, Sweden, Norway, and Romania. In October 1966, the US, and other countries fighting alongside it in Vietnam, met in Manila and made an offer to withdraw if the North did likewise. This was followed by a Polish attempt, codenamed 'Marigold', to bring Hanoi and Washington directly into contact. Then, in February 1967, came the 'Sunflower' initiative, arguably the most promising peace bid before 1968: another bombing halt was accompanied by talks between the British premier, Harold Wilson, and Soviet premier, Andrei Kosygin, in London. There was no breakthrough, however.

In his memoirs, Johnson inserted a ten-page list of the various negotiation attempts and insisted: 'I did everything I could to make one fact clear: that the United States sought only a peaceful settlement to the turmoil that . . . raged in Vietnam.' He had no doubt that the reason all efforts failed was that the North Vietnamese were 'never . . . ready . . . to negotiate seriously the terms of a fair peace settlement'.[11] Yet, in a seminal account of the war, the journalist Stanley Karnow, stated that during the 'Marigold initiative it was Johnson who had not been ready to talk—unless, of course, the enemy submitted to his terms'; whilst the 'Sunflower' initiative collapsed when Johnson toughened the US negotiating terms as talks were underway. Such failures showed that neither belligerent was ready 'to shift the conference table before they had improved their battlefield postures'.[12] In fact, Washington and Hanoi consistently talked past each other when it came to negotiating terms. Reflecting the view that the North was guilty of aggression, Johnson was only prepared to wind down the US war effort after Hanoi ended its infiltration of troops and supplies into the South; and he was determined that Saigon's independence be preserved. To Hanoi, however, South Vietnam was an American puppet state; the Viet Cong was fighting a legitimate struggle against a corrupt regime and in favour of the reunification which Vietnam should have won after the Geneva conference; and the Rolling Thunder campaign was itself an act of aggression.

There were differences on the communist side as the war escalated in 1965. In the Hanoi government, 'worried that American bombing threatened socialist construction in the North, some members wondered aloud if the southern insurgency was worth the high price', whilst Viet Cong leaders feared that the government would indeed 'put the long-term interests of the North before Southern liberation'.[13] In May, Johnson's first 'bombing halt' provoked considerable debate in Hanoi, with the NLF opposed to any negotiations ahead of a US withdrawal, but some northerners were ready to open a diplomatic dialogue with Washington. There was, in fact, an attempt to establish a link to the US government through Paris over the next few months. However, Johnson's continuing escalation of the war (especially with his increased troop commitments in July), and evidence that the US call for talks was insincere, gave ammunition to Le Duan and other hardliners. By August, the Paris channel had closed and in early 1966 Hanoi's line was firmly behind a military victory. Ho Chi Minh showed little interest in peace feelers before 1968, and Johnson's own much-trumpeted offers to negotiate were probably designed more as publicity exercises than genuine attempts to talk. The difference between the belligerents was highlighted in a further exchange of public statements in late 1967. On 29 September, in a speech at San Antonio, Johnson offered to halt the bombing in return for a firm promise of discussions and an end to further infiltration; but in December Hanoi replied that Rolling Thunder must end before discussions began. By then, each side was preparing for a military showdown.

International Factors

Another way in which Johnson tried to maintain domestic support for the war was by suggesting that the defence of South Vietnam was a general Western interest, and his peace offers were designed in part to secure international sympathy. Washington especially hoped that the members of the South-East Asia Treaty Organization (SEATO), founded in 1954 would join in defending Saigon. In fact, some members of the organization who felt particularly threatened by the spread of communism in Asia did take part: Australia and New Zealand sent troops in June 1965, followed by the Philippines in 1966 and Thailand in 1967. However, these contingents were too small to have any impact on the war and they were actually outnumbered by the 45,000 men contributed by a non-SEATO country, South Korea. The terms of SEATO did not oblige its

BOX 10.2

Two Approaches to Peace: The Johns Hopkins University Speech and North Vietnam's 'Four Points', 7 and 8 April 1965

President Johnson accompanied the escalation of the Vietnam War in the first half of 1965 with an address at Johns Hopkins University in Baltimore, in which he hoped to show a more positive side to US policy. The main points of the speech were:

- the US would resist Chinese communist expansion which threatened all Asia;
- America would also 'help South Vietnam defend its independence';
- but he was ready to enter 'unconditional discussions' on a peaceful settlement in Vietnam;
- and he offered a one-billion-dollar aid package to provide food, health, and education to help Vietnam develop after peace was achieved.

The following day the North Vietnamese Prime Minister, Pham Van Dong, replied with a four-point programme:

- the US bombing campaign against the North should stop;
- US forces should withdraw from South Vietnam;
- South Vietnam's political future should be decided 'in accordance with the programme of the National Liberation Front';
- and Vietnam should then be reunited peacefully.

Taken together, these statements showed the two sides to be far apart. America wanted an independent South Vietnam and an end to what it saw as communist 'aggression'. Hanoi wanted Vietnam's reunification and an end to what it saw as American interference in Vietnamese affairs.

members automatically to go to war in the event of communist expansion and some of them were distinctly unsympathetic to the US. In the mid-1960s, America's relations with Pakistan were troubled, partly because Pakistan had improved its relations with communist China following the Sino-Indian war of 1962. France, under the Anglophobe de Gaulle, and in the wake of its own departure from Vietnam, was critical of the US war effort: in August 1966 de Gaulle, on a visit to Cambodia, called on Johnson to withdraw. Even the British, usually America's closest Western ally, and one with political and commercial interests in Hong Kong and Malaysia, resisted pressure to commit troops to Vietnam. Britain, like other Western European countries, was troubled by the war which, as in America, became the focus of leftist criticism and youth protest. Even Laos and Cambodia, two South-East Asian states that SEATO claimed to protect, did nothing to help the US effort to defeat communism in the region. In Laos, the revived struggle between the Pathet Lao and the royal government, together with the country's position on the Ho Chi Minh trail, led the US to drop 3 million tons of bombs on it between 1964 and 1973. In Cambodia, also on the trail, the government of Prince Sihanouk subtly tried to maintain a neutralist policy. On the one hand, he broke diplomatic relations with the US in 1965 and allowed the communists to receive supplies through the chief port, Sihanoukville. On the other, he tried to limit communist numbers within Cambodia and, in 1968 tolerated US 'hot pursuit' of the Viet Cong over the border.

North Vietnam may have fought its war on the front line alone, but it had significant diplomatic, economic, and military assistance from the Eastern bloc, and indeed was able to exploit rivalry between the USSR and China to maximize the scale of this. The Chinese had been unenthusiastic about Hanoi's decision in 1959–60 to expand the guerrilla war in South Vietnam, believing it better, at that stage, to concentrate in the North on economic consolidation. But the Chinese provided a range of supplies, from ammunition, rifles, and artillery to radio sets, lorries, and uniforms, as well as agricultural produce, increasing deliveries as US involvement escalated. Mao's support for Hanoi was based both on a desire to counter American 'imperialism' and an eagerness to outbid the Soviets for North Vietnamese support. Ho Chi Minh was reluctant to take sides in the Sino-Soviet split but by 1964 felt he had little choice other than to rely mostly on China, since Moscow seemed more interested in improving East–West relations. In 1964, China strengthened its armed forces on the Vietnam border, and Johnson was probably correct in his belief that, if US military action went too far, Mao was prepared to defend North Vietnam. The Chinese were already intolerant of America's meddling near their borders (in Korea and Taiwan), were entering a new policy phase at home—the Cultural Revolution—and were keen to support Wars of National Liberation in the less developed world. Ho Chi Minh visited Beijing in April 1965 and over 300,000 Chinese troops were sent to North Vietnam over the following years, many of them engineers, helping to run installations, man anti-aircraft batteries, build airfields and roads, thereby freeing North Vietnamese troops to fight in the South. Mao and his colleagues 'were genuinely concerned about the American threat from Vietnam . . . and adopted significant measures in war preparations at home'—so that Johnson was right to fear Chinese direct intervention in the war if he invaded the North.[14] Even with their indirect involvement, over 1,000 Chinese troops were killed in Vietnam, before they left in 1970. By then, the Chinese were critical both of Hanoi's decision to launch the Tet offensive and its subsequent readiness to open peace negotiations with Washington. Mao was also offended by growing Soviet influence in Hanoi, whilst the North Vietnamese had always been wary of the danger of Chinese domination, a fear based on long historical experience.

The Soviet Union and its East European satellites did send military advisers and supplies to North Vietnam before 1965, but on a more limited scale than China and, until he lost power, Khrushchev was reluctant to antagonize the US by backing Hanoi too strongly. In November 1964, however, his successors decided that they must try to match Chinese influence, partly because Moscow saw itself as the leader of the communist world, partly because it seemed in order to act as a moderating influence on Ho and to prevent the war spreading. Andrei Kosygin's visit to Hanoi in February, coinciding as it did with US air-raids, confirmed the USSR in its determination to aid the North Vietnamese. Diplomatic and propaganda support for them was intensified and Moscow, at least in 1964–6, refused to become involved in any peace attempts. By 1968, Soviet aid to the North, in the form of arms, aircraft machinery, medicine, and raw materials, amounted to half of all aid to the country and outstripped Chinese assistance, thus reversing the

CHRONOLOGY

Vietnam—Escalating American Involvement, 1959–65

1959	
May	North Vietnamese ruling party agrees to support armed struggle in South Vietnam.
8 July	Two US military advisers killed in an attack by Viet Cong on Bien Hoa.
1960	
11 November	Failed attempt at a coup against Diem by army elements.
2 December	North Vietnam sponsors the creation of the National Liberation Front (NLF), a shadow government for South Vietnam.
1961	
28 January	Kennedy's incoming National Security Council decides to boost aid to South Vietnam.
16 May–23 July	Geneva conference reaches compromise settlement on political future of Laos: neutralist coalition formed.
3 November	General Maxwell Taylor recommends sending a limited number of US combat troops, but Kennedy rejects this idea.
1962	
6 February	US forms Military Assistance Command, Vietnam (MACV), reflecting the rise in US advisers to Vietnam to over 3000.
March	Launch of the 'strategic hamlets' programme to isolate South Vietnamese peasants from the Viet Cong.
1963	
2 January	Battle of Ap Bac, effectively a defeat for the South Vietnamese army.
11 June	A Buddhist priest, Thich Quang Duc, burns himself to death in Saigon, in protest at Diem's regime.
1 November	Diem and Nhu assassinated after an army coup; new government formed under General Duang Van ('Big') Minh.
22 November	Kennedy assassinated; succeeded by Lyndon Johnson.
1964	
16 January	Johnson approves covert operations in North Vietnam itself.
30 January	'Big' Minh replaced by General Nguyen Khanh.
June	US begins bombing communist 'Pathet Lao' bases in Laos in 'Operation Barrel Roll'.
2 August	US destroyer, *Maddox*, attacked by North Vietnamese torpedo boats in Gulf of Tonkin.
4 August	Claims of more attacks on US ships.
5 August	US aircraft launch limited raids on North Vietnam.
7 August	Gulf of Tonkin resolution: Congress gives Johnson a blank cheque to deal with Vietnam situation.
3 November	Johnson wins presidential election.
24 December	Viet Cong attack on US base in Saigon.
1965	
5 February	Soviet premier Kosygin visits Hanoi, underlining support for the North.
7 February	Viet Cong attacks a US base at Pleiku, killing eight.
8 February	US retaliatory air raids launched on North Vietnam, while Kosygin is still in Hanoi.

(continued...)

CHRONOLOGY (continued)

10 February	Twenty-three Americans killed in a Viet Cong attack on Qui Nhon; leads to more retaliatory air raids.
17 February	After months of internal unrest, General Khanh is overthrown.
24 February	Start of 'Operation Rolling Thunder': long-term bombing campaign by US of North Vietnam.
8 March	US marines land at Da Nang: first commitment of US ground troops.

situation of 1964. But this did not necessarily outweigh China's predominance, which was partially based on common values: 'The North Vietnamese leadership shared with its Chinese counterpart many ideological views, including the assessment of the world communist movement and the international situation.'[15] Also, the number of Soviet advisers, at about 1,000 (mainly in the air defence field), was much fewer than the Chinese. In 1968, the Soviets were able to outmanoeuvre China on the issue of negotiations, and helped bring Hanoi and Washington to the negotiating table. The North's preference, however, was to avoid becoming reliant on one ally, and to continue securing aid from both Moscow and Beijing which, together with East European support, was valued at about a billion dollars in 1968. Little wonder that Johnson's successor, Richard Nixon, saw improved relations with the USSR and China as one possible way to pressure the North into a settlement.

C. 'Tet' and its Implications, 1968

The 'Tet' Offensive

At the start of 1968, with half a million US troops in Vietnam and a presidential election beginning, Westmoreland's confidence that the war was going well had some basis. The Thieu regime seemed stable even if it was not popular; urban centres were securely under government control and heavy losses were being inflicted on the Viet Cong and the NVA. Westmoreland remained wedded to the belief that large-unit conventional warfare, rather than a drawn-out, 'pacification' effort, would wear down the communists and he saw an NVA build-up around Khe Sanh (near the Demilitarized Zone) as an opportunity to score a decisive victory. Suspecting that the NVA were planning the long-awaited conventional invasion of the South, he concentrated 50,000 troops around Khe Sanh. But, in line with a plan drawn up by General Giap six months before, Khe Sanh was a lure, designed to draw Westmoreland's attention while the Viet Cong guerrilla army prepared for a general offensive inside the South. The communist aim was to attack urban centres, undermining Thieu and demoralizing the Americans, perhaps even sparking a popular uprising that would sweep the NLF to power. The offensive went forward at the Vietnamese new year, Tet, on 30–1 January, when half the ARVN was on leave and a ceasefire was supposed to be in place. In a damning indictment of US and South Vietnamese intelligence, the communists achieved complete surprise, helped by the fact that, for the first time in the war, they concentrated their attacks on major towns and cities. Targets were hit all over the country and in Saigon even the American embassy compound was partially occupied for several hours.

The Tet offensive went on for weeks before dying down, with the former imperial capital, Hué, not being cleared of Viet Cong until 24 February. The dead in Hué numbered 500 Americans or ARVN, 5,000 communists, and 10,000 civilians, many of the last executed by the Viet Cong for working with the Thieu regime. Nationally too the 'kill ratio' between the communists and their opponents was now about 10:1, an attrition rate that still pleased Westmoreland, who could reasonably claim a military victory. He may have misjudged the significance of Khe Sanh, from which the NVA retreated once Tet was over, but the Viet Cong attack on urban centres proved disastrous for them. In the towns, the guerrilla army made a more obvious target than in the countryside, unable to melt so easily away, and losses to their front-line forces were probably around 35,000, a large proportion of their number. Significantly, in future, the NVA would bear a greater share than the decimated Viet Cong of the fighting in the South. Significant too was the fact that there had been no popular uprising against Thieu and that the ARVN did not crumble in the face of widespread initial setbacks. A second round of communist attacks on towns in early May inevitably proved less dramatic and a third round, 'Tet Three', in August, confirmed that the Viet Cong were far away from a decisive military victory. Indeed, one historian describes Tet as 'a colossal blunder which prolonged the war, causing unnecessary suffering on both sides'.[16]

Yet, if Tet proved a setback for the communists on the ground, in retrospect it is remembered primarily as an American defeat, the turning point in a war which was now recognized to be 'unwinnable' for Washington. As one communist general later admitted: 'In all honesty, we didn't achieve our main objective which was to spur uprisings throughout the South . . . As for making an impact in the United States, it had not been our intention—but it turned out to be a fortunate result.'[17] Indeed it did. The fact that the Viet Cong could launch such an audacious countrywide assault, seizing control of so many cities, and catching Westmoreland by surprise, after his recent assurances that victory was only a matter of time, came as a profound psychological shock to many Americans. The public and the press increasingly lost faith in official pronouncements on the war. Johnson's chances of re-election in November were almost immediately called into question when he only narrowly won the New Hampshire primary over an 'anti-war' opponent, Eugene McCarthy. Furthermore, claims that Tet was a defeat were simply not believed with any confidence. America's international problems were underlined by the seizure, a week before Tet, of a US navy ship, the *Pueblo*, by North Korea (the vessel was only released at the end of the year after a humiliating apology from Washington for its intelligence-gathering mission). Regarding Vietnam, Westmoreland now believed that he needed a further 206,000 troops, plus an intensified bombing campaign throughout Indo-China, in order to achieve victory. Yet he could not say how long it would take to achieve a victory and the new Defense Secretary, Clark Clifford, feared that the request would simply lead to higher costs and casualties. Few Americans advocated withdrawal, some even hawkishly advocated all-out war on the North, but the Defense Department now preferred to 'de-Americanize' the conflict, handing fighting back to the ARVN. A group of 'wise men', called together to give the President advice at this critical point, and comprising such foreign policy luminaries as Dean Acheson and George Ball, also recommended disengagement as the best course. And on 31 March Johnson made a national address which not only limited US bombing of the North to areas below the 19th parallel, but also offered peace negotiations and withdrew his candidacy from the upcoming election. Johnson preferred to let a new president tackle the Vietnam challenge. But his withdrawal from the race was the clearest indication to the world that America no longer expected an outright victory in Vietnam.

The War after Tet

Whilst each side could claim a victory of sorts after Tet, it was the case that 'the position of each was also significantly weakened and neither emerged with sufficient leverage to force a settlement'.[18] Some of Johnson's aides, such as his National Security Adviser, Walt Rostow, still believed it possible to put military pressure on Hanoi but, with the administration increasingly divided against itself, defining US military strategy was as difficult as ever. Johnson had been careful only *partially* to limit the bombing campaign in his 31 March speech but he called a complete bombing halt on 31 October, partly to help the election chances of his Vice-President, Hubert Humphrey. Troop figures continued to drift up, but by the time of the election it was widely accepted that they had reached their peak. However, with a greater emphasis on 'pacification' within South Vietnam and helped by Viet Cong losses during Tet, the US and ARVN forces were actually able to extend the area of government control. Despite Johnson's 31 March speech, US bombing in the South was as intense as ever.

The weakening of the Viet Cong, together with America's partial bombing halt, induced Hanoi to adopt a new tactic of 'fighting while talking', which mirrored what Johnson himself was now attempting. The North accepted the idea of talks on 3 April and the two sides opened peace negotiations in Paris on 13 May, with the veteran ambassador Averell Harriman leading the US delegation and Xuan Thuy the North. However, much of the discussion was then spent in trying to design a table at which both the South Vietnamese and NLF representatives could sit. The South Vietnamese, fearing that their independence could only be compromised by discussions, were reluctant to talk at all and certainly did not want to recognize the NLF. Even if this problem had been resolved earlier, it is doubtful whether the peace talks would have got far by the end of the year. For one thing, the two sides were still diametrically opposed on likely peace terms, with the US hoping for a withdrawal of their forces after a North Vietnamese withdrawal from South Vietnam and Thieu's survival in power, neither of which was acceptable to Hanoi. Another problem was that the North's 'fighting while talking' tactic probably meant that they had no intention of serious negotiations before the Viet Cong's 'Tet Three' offensive was over.

While the war in the South settled back into deadlock and the Paris peace negotiations made laborious progress, the clearest signs that events had decisively swung in the communists' favour were to be found in the United States. Anti-war protests grew, the media became highly sceptical about official statements on the conflict, and only about a third of Americans felt progress was being made in Vietnam. This still meant that there was a sizeable group in favour of fighting on, and the war actually remained quite popular among, for example, young, white males. But the very danger of a polarized society helped influence Johnson's decision to pull out of the election race. As he told an aide, the President felt he could have won the election, but the result 'would be too close for me to be able to govern. The nation would be polarized.'[19] Instead of allowing a popular alternative to step into power and reunite the country, however, the election soon became a nightmare, underlining the violence, racism, and political division in American society. On 4 April, the Black civil rights leader, Martin Luther King, was assassinated in Memphis; on 5 June, Robert Kennedy, brother of the late President, was shot dead, immediately after winning the Democrat Primary in California; and on 28 August, the Democratic Party convention in Chicago became the scene of rioting as the police tried to break up a demonstration. The nightmare only ended in November when the Republican Richard Nixon narrowly beat Humphrey to the presidency, with a third, populist candidate, Henry Wallace, winning 13.5 per cent of votes on a hard-line, pro-war ticket. The result only confirmed the confusion in America over Vietnam, and suggested that a majority favoured persevering with the struggle, even if they doubted it could be won.

Containment in Crisis: The Cost of the War for the US by 1968

Deepened political divisions associated with the war were not the only problem for America. By the end of the Johnson presidency, the burdens of conflict affected the US economy, its social cohesion, international standing, and self-confidence. Taken together these costs also called into question the whole policy of resisting communism, predicated as it was on America's ability to meet the communist challenge wherever it threatened. The most obvious costs were linked directly to the war itself: by the end of 1968 about 30,500 Americans had been killed (over 14,000 that year alone) and 536,000 were serving in South Vietnam; America had dropped well over a million tons of bombs on the South and about 650,000 tons on North Vietnam, without destroying the communists' ability to wage war, but with the loss of about 500 aircraft, whose crews often became prisoners of war; and the financial price tag of the war was now running at about $20 billion per year (eventually totalling $150 billion over the whole period of direct US involvement from 1965 to 1973). Anti-war demonstrators also protested against non-American casualties in the war. In 1968 alone, the US military reckoned it had killed about 180,000 Viet Cong and North Vietnamese, while 28,000 ARVN and almost 1,000 other allied troops had been killed. Civilian casualties were less easy to calculate but also ran into tens of thousands in the year of Tet. The casualty figures on the communist side were substantial but this in itself underlined a vital point: 'they were fighting a war to the death . . . the United States commitment fell far short of that', and this simple fact lay at the heart of the war's 'unwinnability' by 1968.[20]

The cost of the war to the Americans in economic terms was also clear by 1968, even if it was not the only reason for a worsening position. Inflationary pressures already existed in the shape of high consumer demand, low business investment and social spending. Interest rate rises helped keep inflation to less than 3 per cent, even in early 1967, but by late 1968 it was nearly 5 per cent and defence spending was undoubtedly a factor in causing this. Defence took up 7.9 per cent of GDP in 1966, 9 per cent in 1967, and 9.7 per cent in 1968. As well as paying for their own forces, Americans were maintaining a South Vietnamese army of 850,000 in 1968. In certain other respects, the shape of the US economy was surprisingly good: unemployment was only 3.5 per cent when Johnson left office, reflecting a healthy domestic economy, and the tax burden, at about 28 per cent, was about 5 per cent less than the advanced European economies. However, a reluctance to increase taxes to pay for the Vietnam War was one of the factors which contributed to inflation. Johnson himself fought off such increases for as long as he could, before asking Congress to approve a 6 per cent tax surcharge in January 1967, later raised to 10 per cent. Congress was reluctant to grant this, however, without corresponding cuts in government expenditure, so as to drive down demand in the economy, and a long tussle between the White House and Capitol Hill on these points was not resolved until June 1968, after Johnson agreed to wipe $6 billion off the budget. Meanwhile, these problems also affected confidence in the US abroad, especially after the devaluation of the British pound in November 1967, which sparked off months of monetary upheaval. Pressure on the dollar, linked to an outflow of gold from America, led to a critical situation in March 1968, the same month that Johnson shifted policy in Vietnam and chose to pull out of the presidential race.

The destruction of Johnson's own career was another cost of the Vietnam imbroglio. The man who had won a landslide victory in 1964 found his approval rating at below 50 per cent in mid-1966 and below 40 per cent a year later. But the war also affected Johnson and the presidency in two other significant respects. First, the need to restrain, then cut, domestic government expenditure to pay for Vietnam inevitably affected the Great Society programme. Numerous measures had been carried through, from medicine and urban renewal programmes to vocational training and environmental protection, but they were now underfunded. As to Johnson's hopes of tackling racial problems, they evaporated in the unrest that followed the assassination of Martin Luther King. Again, Vietnam did not create problems but, as with inflation, it added to existing social pressures and prevented them being tackled properly. Second, Vietnam called into question presidential domination of the foreign policy process, the so-called 'Imperial Presidency', as well as bipartisan support for countering the communist threat. After 1968, Congress was far more questioning about foreign policy, repealing the Gulf of Tonkin resolution in 1970 and eventually, in the 1973 War Powers Act, limiting the President's freedom to commit troops abroad.

Finally, linked to the foreign policy theme, Vietnam called into question America's international reputation, weakened its position in the Cold War, and provoked a crisis in its whole approach to world affairs. The country's moral standing, as a defender of democracy and freedom, was compromised by its use of carpet bombing, napalm, and defoliation, all in the defence of a corrupt, unelected regime. Allies, in Western Europe in particular, were critical of the US obsession with South-East Asia and the USSR was able to achieve effective nuclear parity with its superpower rival by 1968. This last development had been predicted for some time but it now came at the worst possible point, when America's ability to contain communism was being called into question.

BOX 10.3

Historiographical Debate: Was Vietnam 'LBJ's War'?

A key question about the escalation of US involvement in Vietnam in the mid-1960s is whether it was due to the personality and decisions of Lyndon Johnson, or to structural factors in America's approach to world affairs which made escalation inescapable. The conflict became known as 'LBJ's War', and student demonstrators at the time had little doubt where responsibility lay, chanting:

Hey, hey, L.B.J.,

How many kids did you kill today?

However, some historians have been sympathetic to Johnson's predicament. Thus, Gary Hess in *Vietnam and the United States* (Twayne, New York, 1990, 88), writes that having 'seen themselves in the previous two decades as the guardians of democracy in Greece, Berlin, Korea and elsewhere, Americans in 1965 saw the burdens of world leadership thrusting a new challenge' in Vietnam, which there was little alternative but to confront. More tellingly, Michael Hunt, in *Lyndon Johnson's War* (Hill & Wang, New York, 1996, 107) insists that the war reflected 'a firm Cold War consensus amounting almost to a religion . . . It was the product of a string of . . . Presidential decisions, of which Johnson's happened to be the last.' Structural factors working in favour of escalation included:

- America's liberal-democratic political culture and universalist ideology; with
- its antipathy to communism, which demanded that the communist threat be met worldwide and saw any retreat as a defeat;
- the commitment of previous presidents, since 1950, to 'save' Vietnam from communist domination, partly through fear of a 'domino effect' in South-East Asia if Vietnam fell;

(continued...)

BOX 10.3 (continued)

- Johnson's inheritance, as political heir to John F. Kennedy, who had increased the number of US advisers in South Vietnam from fewer than 1,000 to more than 16,000;
- growing fear of the People's Republic of China, which seemed a more revolutionary, fundamentalist communist menace than the USSR in Asia;
- the need to stand by any ally, demonstrating America's reliability to friends and enemies alike which was essential for the maintenance of Cold War credibility;
- the self-confidence, born of America's wealth, military might, and technological prowess, which suggested it could meet any threat successfully.

Despite these weighty influences, however, the fact is that other presidents since 1947 had tolerated communist advances where it seemed too costly to reverse them. Truman was blamed in 1949 for 'losing' China to communism; Eisenhower accepted the creation of a communist regime in North Vietnam in 1954; and Kennedy agreed, in 1962, not to overthrow Castro's government in Cuba by military force. In contrast to these, Johnson took a number of decisions which drew the US into a large-scale commitment in Vietnam that might have been avoided. As Larry Berman argues in another work entitled *Lyndon Johnson's War* (Norton, New York, 1989, 203), the President: 'chose to Americanize the war . . . to accept General Westmoreland's attrition strategy . . . to paint optimistic scenarios for the American public . . . to hide the anticipated enemy build-up prior to Tet'. Among the criticisms levelled at Johnson are that:

- he was a domineering individual who either failed to listen to alternative views or else he ignored them when they were put to him (by Under-Secretary of State George Ball, for example);
- he was unskilled in foreign and military affairs, showed little understanding of the Vietnamese, and vastly underestimated the determination of Hanoi to reunify Vietnam;
- he suggested in the 1964 election that he would not escalate the war, yet within months had both begun the 'Rolling Thunder' bombing campaign *and* sent ground troops to Vietnam;
- he continued to mislead the US public by avoiding a full explanation of the escalation, and as a result he forfeited public trust;
- he backed a corrupt, unrepresentative government in Saigon, without any serious attempt to induce it to reform; instead he relied on a destructive military campaign to maintain South Vietnam;
- he presided over an inefficient bureaucratic machine (typified by 'Tuesday luncheons' of key advisers in the White House) which never properly defined US political aims in the war.

Therefore, whatever general factors led Johnson to believe that South Vietnam must be preserved, the responsibility for fighting a 'limited war', relying on an attrition strategy and without a proper explanation to the American people, must lie with him. As Frederick Logevall writes in his detailed study of the years 1963–5, *Choosing War: The Lost Chance for Peace and the Escalation of War in Vietnam* (University of California Press, Berkeley, 1999, 394): 'while the responsibility for the outcome of the policy process rested with all those who participated in it, it rested chiefly with the President'.

D. Nixon's War in Vietnam, 1969–71

The Continuing Failure of Peace Talks

Inevitably, the Vietnam War was the most serious challenge facing Richard Nixon when he entered the White House. During the election campaign, he had claimed to have a 'secret plan' to resolve the conflict but once in power, no such plan was unveiled. It may be that he hoped to emulate Eisenhower (to whom he had been Vice-President), who had ended the Korean War in 1953 after threatening to use atomic weapons. Certainly, Nixon tried to demonstrate toughness to the communists. When they launched an offensive in February 1969, indicating that there would be no let-up in their own campaign, the President decided to launch a clandestine bombing campaign against the Ho Chi Minh trail in supposedly neutral Cambodia. Neither the North Vietnamese nor the Cambodians made any public complaint about this, helping to keep the raids secret for months: the former were flouting Cambodian neutrality themselves; the latter were happy to see communist numbers on their borders reduced. The bombing showed the President ready to widen the conflict and resort to extreme tactics, but did nothing to weaken Hanoi's resolve to replace Thieu and turn the Americans out of South Vietnam. Like Johnson before him, Nixon found there was no easy way to force the communists to the peace table on anything less than their terms, which for America

CHRONOLOGY

The Quagmire: America's 'Unwinnable' War in Vietnam, 1965–71

1965

7 April	Johnson lays out terms for Vietnam peace settlement in speech at Johns Hopkins University.
11 June	Nguyen Cao Ky, an air force officer, becomes South Vietnamese Prime Minister.
2 July	Johnson decides on large increase in US troop numbers to 125,000.
Mid-October	First anti-war demonstrations in America.
24 December	US initiates a 'bombing halt' over Christmas period, an attempt to encourage peace talks.

1966

29 June	US extends bombing to areas near Hanoi and Haiphong: widely condemned.
13 October	Johnson rejects idea of a new 'bombing halt' as possible first step to negotiations.

1967

February	Soviet premier Kosygin and British premier Harold Wilson fail to broker peace deal in London.
19–21 March	In a conference on Guam with South Vietnamese leaders, Johnson decides to maintain military pressure on North Vietnam.
3 September	Nyugen van Thieu, an army general, becomes South Vietnam's President.

1968

30–31 January	Launch of 'Tet' offensive: communist attacks on numerous cities and military installations.
22 March	General Westmoreland relieved as commander of US forces in Vietnam, confirming that Johnson will not escalate the war further.
31 March	Johnson announces partial bombing halt and withdraws from presidential election race.
13 May	Peace talks open between US and North Vietnam in Paris, but make no progress.
1 November	Complete bombing halt by US on North Vietnam.

1969

20 January	Inauguration of Richard Nixon.
18 March	US begins secret bombing of communist bases in Cambodia.
8 June	Nixon announces withdrawal of 25,000 men from Vietnam: beginning of slow process of withdrawal.
25 July	On Guam, Nixon launches 'Vietnamization': handing ground-fighting over to the South Vietnamese.

1970

18 March	Pro-American general, Lon Nol, overthrows Prince Sihanouk of Cambodia.
20 April	Nixon announces latest reductions in US force levels in Vietnam: another 150,000 to leave.
30 April–29 June	US and South Vietnamese forces attack communist 'sanctuaries' in Cambodia.
2 May	Large-scale US bombing of North Vietnam, suspended under Johnson, restarted by Nixon.
4 May	Four anti-war protestors shot at Kent State University.

1971

8 February–24 March	South Vietnamese attacks on Ho Chi Minh trail in Laos.
3 October	South Vietnamese presidential election, in which Thieu is the only candidate.

signified defeat. Even most Democrats hoped for peace terms based on a mutual withdrawal by both sides, linked to a negotiated political settlement within South Vietnam among the warring local groups. Secretary of State William Rogers, all too aware of domestic opposition to the war, favoured a similar compromise and the President took the view that, 'I would have to end the war as quickly as was honourably possible.'[21] But when, in May, Nixon offered an 'eight-point programme' which embodied a mutual *simultaneous* withdrawal (in contrast to Johnson's demand that the North withdraw first), the communists saw no need to respond. In July, Nixon's National Security Adviser, Henry Kissinger, did secretly meet North Vietnam's Xuan Thuy in Paris, but the best they could do was to agree to meet again.

Twelve rounds of secret talks took place down to September 1971 between Kissinger and either Xuan Thuy or Le Duc Tho. Regarding a peace deal, Nixon made one major concession in a speech in October 1970: urged on by US critics of the war, he offered the North a 'ceasefire in place'. The significance of this was that it would allow a ceasefire to occur before negotiations on a North Vietnamese withdrawal from South Vietnam took place. Nixon still hoped for a mutual withdrawal and he wanted the South Vietnamese to decide their own form of government; he was not offering to overthrow Thieu. But clearly the 'ceasefire in place' could seriously undermine the government in Saigon, since the North Vietnamese army might hold on to areas of the South after a ceasefire, when there would be intense international and popular pressure on the Americans to leave, regardless of the North's behaviour. Furthermore, in another concession, Kissinger assured Xuan Thuy that any US military withdrawal would be total. But a series of long, sometimes hopeful talks in Paris in 1971 ended in ultimate disappointment, with the North still keen to put an end to Thieu. He was 're-elected' President of South Vietnam, in October 1971 but since he was the only candidate in the election, the event was ridiculed by the North.

Nor did domestic events in the US help Nixon. Congressional criticism and popular demonstrations against the war (often numbering tens of thousands in 1969–70) went on; the November 1970 Congressional elections proved a setback for Republicans, making Nixon even more desperate to end the war before seeking re-election in 1972; and in June 1972 the White House was embarrassed by the leak of a substantial volume of official documents on Vietnam, the so-called 'Pentagon Papers'. Some critics even urged a simple, unilateral withdrawal from Vietnam. Such a course would have meant the blatant betrayal of an ally, harming American credibility worldwide, and it is easy to see why an arch anti-communist like Nixon dismissed it. As he told his Cabinet in September 1969, he did not want to be 'the first American President to lose a war'.[22] Yet at the other extreme, the choice of escalation of the war, perhaps an invasion of North Vietnam, or even the local use of atomic weapons, was denied him because of public opposition, international criticism, and the danger of Chinese entry into the conflict, which might then prove even more bloody and protracted. If the costs of hanging on in Vietnam were great, the cost of radical options like withdrawal or escalation could be greater.

The Guam Doctrine and Vietnamization

The Nixon administration did develop a strategy of sorts for fighting the Vietnam War, holding out the hope of a negotiated settlement in future whilst reducing the current cost of the war to America in lives and money. The new strategy centred on 'Vietnamization', a policy particularly identified with the Defense Secretary, Melvyn Laird, but which had its origins in the Johnson administration's hopes of 'De-Americanizing' the war and in earlier hopes of President Kennedy to avoid the sending of combat troops. Under Johnson, after March 1965, the US had increasingly taken on the primary role in South Vietnam of fighting the communists and the war had thereby become 'Americanized'. By 1968, this was seen as a mistake and the aim of 'Vietnamization' was to reverse the process, putting the onus of fighting back on the South Vietnamese themselves whilst decreasing US troop levels: 'reducing losses to American forces became the goal of US commanders. In so far as US troops did enter the field they accompanied the . . . [ARVN], offering instruction in rooting out guerrillas.'[23] The attractions of the policy were clear. A reduction in the US presence would please domestic opinion but resistance to the communists would go on. Yet there were also obvious flaws in 'Vietnamization'. It would take time to train, equip, and galvanize the South Vietnamese to fight for themselves, if indeed they would ever have the skill and morale to do so. Meanwhile, US troops could only be withdrawn gradually. Also, such withdrawals might simply encourage the communists to hold out for a complete victory. Certainly, Kissinger believed that Vietnamization, along with domestic opposition and the weakness of the Thieu regime, undermined his attempts to negotiate peace in Paris. If the North would not agree to a settlement when there were over 500,000 American troops in Vietnam, why should they agree when there were fewer than 100,000? 'Troop cuts poulticed public sores at home,' he later wrote, 'but they were evaporating Hanoi's need to bargain about our disengagement.'[24]

Despite these problems, Nixon and Thieu met at Midway and agreed to begin the US troop withdrawals. Shortly afterwards, on 25 July 1969, Nixon gave an important, yet apparently unplanned explanation to journalists of the new approach to international challenges, which his administration would pursue. This so-called 'Guam Doctrine' was related directly to 'Vietnamization', stating that in cases of non-nuclear aggression, 'we shall furnish military and economic assistance . . . but we shall look to the nation directly threatened to assume the primary responsibility of providing manpower for its defence'. These points dovetailed with the general policy of US retrenchment abroad after 1968, sometimes called the 'Nixon Doctrine' (see Box 10.4) and contrasted with the crusading tone of earlier presidents. In September 1969, Nixon announced more troop withdrawals, despite a lack of concessions from Hanoi, and further steps in 1970 took the total number of withdrawals above 150,000. But at the same time Nixon maintained US air support for South Vietnam, with regular bombing raids by B-52s. His strategy was not simply one of relying on a defensive posture, but of continuing to put military pressure on the North, a point further emphasized by the controversial invasion of Cambodia in spring 1970.

The Cambodia and Laos Operations

The Vietnam War had a major impact on neighbouring states and Nixon's bombing of Cambodia in 1969 had already shown how the war, though often described as limited and local, could spread. In early 1970, trouble in Laos intensified once more. The 1962 agreement to respect the country's neutrality had long been undermined by both sides, with the North Vietnamese using Laos as part of the Ho Chi Minh trail and the CIA possessing links to various anti-communist elements in Laos. February 1970 saw a communist offensive in Laos and further use of American B-52s to help the royal government to stop it. Then, in March, the neutralist Prince Sihanouk of Cambodia was overthrown by his Prime Minister, an army general named Lon Nol, who was known as a firm anti-communist. Sihanouk had long tried to play off the Americans and communists against each other, keeping contact with all sides, tolerating the use of Cambodian territory to supply the Viet Cong, yet not complaining about the US secret bombing of 1969. There were immediate suspicions that America had helped Lon Nol's coup but it did not necessarily help them. He too was now faced by communist threats, including Pol Pot's Khmer Rouge movement, an extremely violent, Maoist party, hitherto lacking much popularity.

Despite Lon Nol's appeals for help, the Americans lacked resources to fight a long campaign in Cambodia and were, of course, set on a policy of de-escalation in South-East Asia. Another round of US troop withdrawals was publicized on 20 April. Nonetheless, only ten days later, in a move that confused and surprised the US public, Nixon announced a cross-border attack into Cambodia. Nixon's initial aim had been to use a mainly South Vietnamese force to attack North Vietnamese sanctuaries in one border region of Cambodia, known as Parrot's Beak, but he soon decided to attack another area, Fishhook, in a joint US–South Vietnamese operation. It marked the last large-scale use of US ground forces in offensive operations during the war. Incursions were limited to thirty kilometres into Cambodia, the operation ended on 30 June, and it captured large amounts of communist supplies. But it proved costly in several ways. North Vietnamese troops simply retreated and avoided heavy losses; diplomatic efforts to improve relations with China were set back because Beijing opposed the operations (see Chapter 9, B); whilst, in America, Congressional opposition was revived and the Cooper-Church amendment was passed, which effectively prevented US ground forces launching any more operations outside South Vietnam. There was also another bout of anti-war demonstrations and in one protest, on 4 May, four students were shot dead by National Guardsmen at Kent State University. The President boasted about the falling number of American casualties in the war after the Cambodian operation and this fact certainly helped reduce the number of anti-war protests in 1971–2. But US losses were only falling as a natural result of Vietnamization: casualties among the South Vietnamese army were increasing. Meanwhile, in Cambodia, a fully fledged civil war began, with the Khmer Rouge, North Vietnam,

BOX 10.4

The Nixon Doctrine

The 'unwinnable' war in Vietnam called into question the whole US approach to the Cold War. Since the 1947 Truman Doctrine (see Chapter 1, E), America had been publicly committed to a policy of 'containment', ostensibly seeking to resist communist advances wherever they threatened. But the 1968 Tet offensive showed that a decisive defeat of the communists in Vietnam was impossible. This left the incoming Nixon administration in 1969 with a fundamental dilemma. Neither 'containment' nor roll-back seemed to be working in Vietnam, so what should they present as America's Cold War strategy in a multipolar world?

In contrast to earlier presidential doctrines, the 'Nixon Doctrine' was not stated in one single document, but was refined through several. In tone, it certainly represented a departure from the Truman Doctrine: retrenchment and a concentration on US interests replaced the crusading, globalistic declarations of the earlier document. It was on the island of Guam, on 25 July 1969, that Nixon first broadly outlined the ways in which America might avoid further Vietnams. These 'off-the-record' remarks were clarified in an address to the nation on 3 November, the essential points of which were that:

- America would adhere to its treaty commitments;
- it would 'provide a shield if a nuclear power threatens the freedom of a nation allied with us, or . . . whose survival we consider vital to our security . . .';
- in the event of non-nuclear threats, the US would provide military and economic aid 'as appropriate. But we shall look to the nation directly threatened to assume the primary responsibility of providing the manpower for its defence.'

But whilst the tone might be less forthright than Truman, the Nixon Doctrine was deliberately vague on details: it was not clear when nuclear weapons might be used, and even the use of US ground troops was not categorically ruled out. It was also, still, global in its implications, given that the US had allies in many regions, who might have to be defended, even if they were now treated more as partners than clients. America's Cold War policy might be less self-confident in the wake of Tet but, under Nixon, it still proclaimed ineffectively the containment of communist expansionism—but the reality with or without honour, was rather different in Vietnam.

and Prince Sihanouk forming an alliance to overthrow Lon Nol. 'Pol Pot could not have asked for a better recruiter than Nixon.'[25]

The mixed results of the Cambodia operation did not deter plans for another, similar bid to disrupt communist supply lines in early February 1971. This time the South Vietnamese army alone, though with US air support, launched an ambitious assault on the Ho Chi Minh trail, in Laos. At first, the operation seemed quite successful but the North Vietnamese responded by sending their best troops against the South Vietnamese and even used tanks. By mid-March, the South's forces were in retreat and question marks were raised about the success of Vietnamization. Thieu's army had fared badly without American troops alongside it. The 'offensive designed to prove that Vietnamization was working had turned into a rout . . . The images of ARVN troops hanging onto helicopter skids', as they tried to escape from Laos, had a 'devastating' effect on US popular opinion.[26] By December 1971, there were only 140,000 Americans in Vietnam, with few of those on combat duty, but Hanoi showed little interest in entering meaningful peace talks at this stage. One year away from the next presidential election, Nixon seemed no nearer to a Vietnam settlement than he had been in January 1969.

Visit the online resources that accompany this book to test your understanding and take your learning further: www.oup.com/he/young-kent3e

NOTES

1. Eric F. Goldman, *The Tragedy of Lyndon Johnson* (MacDonald, London, 1969), 378.
2. Robert S. McNamara, *In Retrospect* (Times Books, New York, 1995), 169.

3. David M. Barrett, *Uncertain Warriors: Lyndon Johnson and his Vietnam Advisers* (University Press of Kansas, Lawrence, 1993), 193.
4. Quoted in Marilyn B. Young, *The Vietnam Wars, 1945–90* (HarperCollins, New York, 1991), 127.
5. Frederick Logevall, *Choosing War* (University of California Press, Berkeley, 1999), 375.
6. Spencer C. Tucker, *Vietnam* (UCL Press, London, 1999), 131.
7. James S. Olson and Randy Roberts, *Where the Domino Fell: America and Vietnam, 1945–1995* (2nd edn, St Martin's Press, New York, 1996), 163–4.
8. Ibid.
9. Harry G. Summers, *On Strategy: Critical Analysis of the Vietnam War* (Dell, New York, 1982), 93.
10. John Prados, *The Hidden History of the Vietnam War* (Ivan R. Dee, Chicago, 1995), 110.
11. Lyndon B. Johnson, *The Vantage Point* (Weidenfeld & Nicolson, London, 1971), 249–50.
12. Stanley Karnow, *Vietnam: A History* (Guild Publishing, London, 1983), 494, 496.
13. Robert K. Brigham, *Guerrilla Diplomacy* (Cornell University Press, Ithaca, 1998), 41.
14. Qian Qichen, *China and the Vietnam Wars, 1950–75* (University of North Carolina Press, Chapel Hill, 2000), 155.
15. Ilya V. Gaiduk, 'The Soviet Union and Vietnam', in Peter Lowe (ed.), *The Vietnam War* (Macmillan, London, 1998), 145.
16. Gerard J. de Groot, *A Noble Cause? America and the Vietnam War* (Pearson, Harlow, 2000), 182.
17. Stanley Karnow, *Vietnam: A History* (Guild Publishing, London, 1983), 545.
18. George C. Herring, *America's Longest War* (Temple University Press, Philadelphia, 1986), 220.
19. Quoted in Gerard J. de Groot, *A Noble Cause? America and the Vietnam War* (Pearson, Harlow, 2000), 176.
20. James S. Olson and Randy Roberts, *Where the Domino Fell: America and Vietnam, 1945–1995* (2nd edn, St Martin's Press, New York, 1996), 284.
21. Richard Nixon, *RN: the Memoirs of Richard Nixon* (BCA, London, 1978), 349.
22. Melvin Small, *The Presidency of Richard Nixon* (University Press of Kansas, Lawrence, 1999), 74.
23. Robert D. Schulzinger, *Henry Kissinger* (Columbia University Press, New York, 1989), 34–5.
24. Henry Kissinger, *The White House Years* (Little, Brown & Co., Boston, 1979), 475.
25. Gerard J. de Groot, *A Noble Cause? America and the Vietnam War* (Pearson, Harlow, 2000), 223.
26. Stephen Ambrose, *Nixon, II: 1962–72* (Simon & Schuster, New York, 1989), 420.

11

Other Regional Conflicts

Chapter contents

A. Latin America: US Intervention in the Dominican Republic

Lyndon Johnson's decision to escalate the war in Vietnam may have been encouraged in spring 1965 by events in the Caribbean, where armed intervention by US Marines put a rapid end to a supposed communist menace in the Dominican Republic. After Castro came to power in Cuba, the significance of the Dominican Republic to American Cold War interests greatly increased: the Republic was less than 200 miles from Cuba, and even closer to US-controlled Puerto Rico. However, this very fact meant that the Eisenhower administration was cautious about endorsing the incumbent dictator, Rafael Trujillo, any longer. The Dominican Republic, with its large proportion of landless labourers working the plantations of a wealthy minority, seemed a potential hotbed of discontent. In 1960, Eisenhower decided that it was better to work for Trujillo's replacement, rather than risking an upsurge of revolutionary discontent. The Central Intelligence Agency (CIA) established links to Trujillo's opponents and diplomatic relations were severed in mid-1960. Trujillo was assassinated on 30 May 1961, but Washington was not directly involved in the act. Under US pressure, free elections were eventually held in December 1962, which brought about the victory of Juan Bosch, leader of the Dominican Revolutionary Party. But, once in power, Bosch showed little of the ability needed to transform the Republic into a stable democracy. He alienated landowners with his social reforms, he criticized US 'imperial' domination and, worse still in American eyes, was tolerant of communist organizations. In response, the US refused him significant economic aid and, in September 1963, condoned his overthrow in a military coup, which led to the presidency being handed to a businessman, Donald Reid Cabral. But he was heavily reliant on the military, never won much popularity, and was overthrown in a counter-coup on 24 April 1965.

With Cabral out of the way, a power struggle immediately developed between a pro-Bosch group and elements in the military. General Elias Wessin, who had led the 1963 coup against Bosch, launched air attacks on the pro-Bosch elements and tried to install such a junta under Colonel Pedro Benoit. On 28 April, the balance in the capital was still uncertain, and Benoit appealed to the US ambassador, John Martin, for help. In backing this request to Washington, Martin effectively came down in favour of military rule, at least in the short term, rather than the return of an elected president. On 29 April, 4,000 US marines landed in the Republic and by early May the number had mushroomed to 23,000. At first, this sudden, large-scale intervention was justified by the need to protect American citizens and restore order, but soon emphasis was being put on the potential communist menace, with the State Department naming fifty-eight communists supposedly at work within the Dominican Republic. On closer analysis, this list turned out to contain exiles, certain individuals in prison, and some double-counting, yet US public opinion welcomed the intervention. 'The US government's preoccupation with avoiding a "second Cuba" had structured the way American officials looked at the Dominican Republic . . . Dominican communists were seen as potential agents of extra-continental power, not as weak and fragmented groups of dissidents.'[1] In early May, Johnson followed the invasion up with a statement that America would not allow another Castro-style government in the Americas; a statement which became known as the 'Johnson Doctrine'. 'Hence, what began as a civil war ended as an international crisis linked to the US military intervention in Vietnam, US policy against Cuba and, later, to the declared US intention of saving democracy in the Dominican Republic.'[2] On 6 May, Johnson persuaded a meeting of the Organization of American States (OAS)—an organization he held in such contempt that he accused it of being unable to 'pour piss out of a boot if the instructions were written on the heel'[3]—to set up a peacekeeping force in the Republic. The OAS, despite doubts from a few members, secured a formal ceasefire in the capital and in September installed a moderate interim premier, Hector Garcia Godoy. Elections were held in May 1966 and won by Joaquin Balaguer, a former Trujillo supporter. Foreign troops withdrew a few months later. The Dominican intervention showed that the US remained ready to use its economic and military might to defend its ideological and economic interests in the Americas. 'The problem', as one academic writes, 'was that in dealing with crises of stability, the administration could focus only on the threat of Communist advantage and allowed democracy and development to slip from view.'[4]

B. South Asia: The Indo-Pakistan Wars of 1965 and 1971

The War of 1965

The separation of India and Pakistan in 1947, after independence from British rule (see Chapter 3, A), left deep animosity as well as complex border and property claims. The worst cause of tension was Kashmir, which was 80 per cent Muslim by population but whose ruler had opted to join India. War in 1948 had ended with the creation of an uneasy ceasefire across Kashmir: the UN initially planned to hold a plebiscite there, but it was never held. The Pakistani government claimed that in a plebiscite the Kashmiris would vote to join their fellow Muslims in Pakistan; but the Indian government was reluctant to settle the dispute in this way, partly because India was a multi-religious, non-secular state, even if Hindu-dominated. Over the following decade, the Indian leader, Jawaharlal Nehru, pursued a non-aligned policy, while making his country the largest recipient of Soviet aid outside the Eastern bloc itself. 'Nehru's intransigence regarding Kashmir, his courtship of China and his . . . Indian–Soviet friendship—chilled Indian–US relations . . .' and prevented these two democracies from working together.[5] In contrast, Pakistan, although it fell under the military rule of Ayub Khan in 1958, initially aligned itself with the West, being a member of both the Baghdad Pact and the Souteast Asian Treaty Organization (SEATO). It provided the US with base facilities, including an intelligence-gathering facility at Peshawar, but never received sufficient diplomatic strength to gain the upper hand in the Kashmir dispute.

Pakistani disillusionment continued to grow in the early 1960s. In May 1960, the U-2 incident (see Chapter 5, B) led Ayub Khan to fear that he had become over-reliant on America—the U-2 spy plane, which so enraged Khrushchev, had flown from a Pakistan airbase—and so he began to improve relations with the USSR and China. Then, the arrival of John F. Kennedy as President in 1961 led the US to court India as a large, liberal-democratic state in Asia which might limit Chinese power. But Kennedy's approach offended Ayub Khan without having any impact on Nehru's non-alignment. In December 1961, India's invasion of the Portuguese enclave of Goa, though it could be defended as an anti-colonial step (and thereby won sympathy in the less developed world), undermined Nehru's reputation as an enlightened, non-violent leader. It both offended Kennedy and aroused Pakistani fears of Indian aggression. Finally, the sudden, short-lived war between India and China in 1962 upset everyone's calculations and cemented links between Pakistan and China. What had developed was an increasingly unstable situation that was difficult for Washington to influence. The US, seeing a renewed chance to turn India into an ally against China, now provided Nehru with military aid. The Indians, stunned by the surprise invasion, became less self-confident in their foreign policy, while the Pakistani armed forces were more hopeful about defeating India in war. Yet, the Sino-Indian War also made it more difficult to resolve the Kashmir problem because the Indians now saw Kashmir, which bordered on China, as having a strategic significance.

In early 1965, India still adhered to its non-aligned policy, although Pakistan remained a member of SEATO and CENTO (the Central Treaty Organization, formed in 1959 after the collapse of the Baghdad Pact). The Indian premier was now Lal Bahadur Shastri, Nehru having died the previous May. India felt beleaguered abroad, with Chinese relations as bad as ever and the US pressing for negotiations on Kashmir which were likely to result in a Kashmiri vote to join Pakistan. Pakistan, on the other hand, had settled its own border disputes with China in 1963 and Ayub Khan even visited Beijing. This upset the Johnson administration, which was preoccupied by Cold War considerations and deeply antagonistic to China. Ayub Khan's obsession was increasingly with Kashmir; he was frustrated at the lack of diplomatic progress and even threatened to leave SEATO. In April 1965, largely in frustration at Ayub's closeness to China, Johnson abruptly cancelled a visit to Pakistan. Then, because he could hardly meet Shastri without doubling the offence to Ayub, the US President cancelled a planned visit to India as well. This simply underlined the bankruptcy of US attempts to fit Indo-Pakistani affairs into a Cold War mould, and severely reduced American influence in both countries during the critical events that followed. In April 1965, border clashes had already begun in the Rann of Kutch, a marshy area far removed from Kashmir and, since it was under water for half the year, it was not worth a serious struggle. The British, as leading members of the Commonwealth, of which India and Pakistan were both members, were agreed as arbitrators of this dispute in June (and a border deal was reached in 1968). But the Rann of Kutch episode, however limited in itself, led both sides to mass forces in Kashmir and encouraged the Pakistanis to feel confident about an armed clash.

From April 1965 onwards, tension in Kashmir was mounting, as the Pakistanis supported irregular forces in sabotage raids across the ceasefire line. In May, the arrest by the Indians of the local Muslim leader, Sheikh Abdullah, inflamed passions further. Then, at the end of August, full-scale war began, with both sides accusing the other of starting it. In early September, the Pakistanis seemed to be having the best of the conflict, with a drive into Indian-ruled territory in southern Kashmir. In fact, this soon stalled and Ayub seems to have planned to run the war down. However, around 6 September, the Indians struck back with an offensive towards Lahore, followed up by an attack much further south, on Gadra (not far from the Rann of Kutch), taking the Pakistanis by surprise: 'the most surprised person was Ayub' who had 'assumed that . . . the Indians would relax' once the violence died down in Kashmir.[6] By the middle of the month, the war was deadlocked, with Pakistan's confidence blunted and the Indians happy to have recovered from early setbacks. China was surprisingly quiescent during the war, and the US and Britain had suspended military supplies to both sides once the war began. This harmed Pakistan most, since India continued to receive Soviet supplies.

Pakistan argued that (in contrast to its own actions in disputed Kashmir) India had launched an attack across an internationally recognized border, an argument that seems to have won some sympathy in Britain, which issued a statement critical of India's conduct. For this reason, the British were not seen as a potential arbitrator in the conflict, as they had been in the case of the Rann of Kutch. Instead, when a UN-sponsored ceasefire took effect on 22 September, it was the USSR that took the lead in trying to broker an Indo-Pakistani settlement. American policy still seemed in disarray. 'Indians were outraged at the equation, implicit in the embargo of American weaponry to both sides, of their actions with those of Pakistan . . . In Pakistan . . . Ayub . . . lost no opportunity to . . . blame . . . Pakistan's frustrations on Washington.'[7] Soviet Premier Andrei Kosygin brokered a settlement between Ayub and Shastri at a conference in Tashkent in January 1966. However, this did little other than restore the status quo and Indo-Pakistani diplomatic relations. The vexed question of Kashmir was unresolved and Soviet influence made no great advance. But if America could be pleased with the re-establishment of peace, its influence was no longer decisive. Pakistan was still nominally tied to the West but on good terms with the Chinese, while the danger posed by close Indo-Soviet relations remained. Regional alliances in the context of the Cold War had proved to be a destabilizing factor, rather than a source of Western strength. The lesson that the conflict between two blocs could no longer be the defining priority of international relations was there to be learned.

The War of 1971

Shastri collapsed and died at the end of the Tashkent Conference, to be succeeded by Nehru's daughter, Indira Gandhi. She maintained her father's non-aligned policy, accepting the revival of US military aid in 1967 while criticizing Johnson over Vietnam. In Pakistan, Ayub was succeeded by another general, Yahya Khan, in 1969, a year after terminating the US lease on its Peshawar base. Pakistan's rulers were happy to see America recommence its military aid programme in 1970 but also determined to hang on to the Chinese alliance. This had harmed Pakistan's standing in Washington's eyes while Lyndon Johnson was in office, but the situation changed after Richard Nixon became President. Nixon never got on personally with Indira Gandhi. Furthermore, in great secrecy, he and his National Security Adviser, Henry Kissinger, came to rely on Pakistan as a line of contact for their 'Opening to China' (see Chapter 12, A). It was from Pakistan that Kissinger made his all-important visit to China in July 1971. By then, tension in South Asia was rising once more, not over Kashmir, but about a very different problem, the growing rift between the two halves of Pakistan, West and East.

In 1947, Pakistan had been formed from two Muslim-populated regions: Eastern Bengal and the so-called 'North-West Frontier', which were about a thousand miles apart. The East had the bulk of the population but was poorer and, because it was low-lying and subject to heavy monsoons, prone to floods. West Pakistan included the capital city, Islamabad, which dominated the armed forces and which had its own language, Urdu, accepted as the 'official' one. This caused increasing resentment in East Pakistan, compounded by the fact that 'Pakistani' foreign policy often seemed designed to defend specifically Western interests, based on West Pakistan's proximity to the USSR and China, and on its close interest in the Kashmir problem. East Pakistan was almost surrounded by Indian territory and virtually indefensible from an attack. In 1970, after more than a decade of military rule, Yahya Khan was planning a return to parliamentary government, hoping this would preserve national cohesion. However, severe cyclones and floods in November killed about 200,000 in Bengal and helped create a situation whereby, in elections the following month, most East Pakistanis voted for the Awami League of Mujibur Rahmann, known simply as Mujib, whose aim was to secure an autonomous 'Bangladesh'. Meanwhile, West Pakistan overwhelmingly voted in favour of Ali Bhutto's Pakistan People's Party, which favoured a more centralized government. This outcome threatened to tear the country apart, especially since the Awami League (thanks to the East's larger population) won a parliamentary majority, leading Bhutto to boycott the National Assembly in March 1971. This 'created an explosive situation and a point of no return'.[8] As a result, Yahya Khan decided to suspend the meeting of Parliament, to introduce martial law in East Pakistan (backed by 40,000 troops), and imprisoned Mujib without charge.

Far from solving Pakistan's problems, Yahya's tough actions worsened them. Mujib now demanded full independence; up to ten million East Pakistanis fled abroad to neighbouring India, putting the latter's food and aid resources under great strain; and Indira Gandhi was under increasing pressure to help 'Bangladesh' achieve independence. In April 1971, Indian-trained 'Mukti Bahini' resistance fighters began an armed campaign against the Pakistani army in East Pakistan. Western opinion tended to side with the Bangladeshis, who were seen as being subjected to military oppression, having already suffered a terrible natural disaster. The Indians also continued to have Eastern bloc support. Indeed, on 9 August, the USSR moved to consolidate its ties to India when Andrei Gromyko signed a 24-year friendship treaty in New Delhi. This mainly involved technical assistance but also provided for consultations should one of them be attacked. Nixon and Kissinger were surprised by this step and, in contrast to most Western opinion, became convinced that they must back West Pakistan, while encouraging Yahya to show moderation. The concessions Yahya made, however, such as opening talks with Awami moderates, proved too little, too late. Meanwhile, 'Indira Gandhi's goals became more precise . . . to win recognition for Bangladesh nationalism . . . [and] to make it clear that the continuing threats to Indian security posed by the crisis in Pakistan gave New Delhi the right to resolve the situation by any means it deemed effective.'[9] In November 1971, border incidents intensified with a massing of forces on the Indo-Pakistani border in both East and West.

As in 1965, both sides blamed each other for the outbreak of war, with the Indians accused of launching an invasion of East Pakistan and the Pakistanis accused of beginning large-scale hostilities with an attack in Kashmir and Western India. Whoever was most to blame, India always had the upper hand in the East. The Soviets, who continued to supply India with arms, vetoed a potentially embarrassing UN resolution in favour of a mutual withdrawal on 4 December. India recognized Bangladeshi independence two days later and by 10 December it was clear that Pakistan's forces in the East were overwhelmed. As in 1965, Chinese support for Pakistan was mainly verbal. Indeed, it was the US which did most to press India to end the war. In the so-called 'tilt' towards Pakistan, and despite public criticism in America, the White House now made fully apparent its support for Yahya Khan. A US naval task force was despatched towards the Bay of Bengal and, on 12 December, for the first time in the Nixon administration, the 'hot line' to Moscow was used to press for a ceasefire. Nixon and Kissinger wished to demonstrate to China that they could be relied upon in a crisis; and they were determined that India should not follow up its victory in the East, by defeating Pakistan in Kashmir as well, potentially putting the country's existence under threat. On 16–17 December, a ceasefire took hold on the borders of both West and East Pakistan. This ended fears of a full-scale war over Kashmir, for which neither side was properly prepared, given their concentration on the war in the East. There were now 70,000 Pakistani prisoners of war and diplomatic efforts were focused on their release, while the Bangladeshi state won international recognition, even if Chinese opposition kept it out of the UN until 1974.

Bangladesh was unable to establish a stable democracy, despite the high hopes of 1971. Mujibur became its first President but was killed during a military coup in 1975, after which long periods of military rule were interspersed with attempts to return to democratic government. In Pakistan, the 1971 defeat undermined the position of the military and led Yahya Khan to hand power to the popular Ali Bhutto, but the latter was overthrown by General Zia ul-Haq in 1977. After Zia's death in an air crash in 1988, there was an uneasy return to civilian government for several years, with the premiership twice falling to Bhutto's daughter, Benazir. Yet the army again seized power in 1999 under General Pervez Musharraf, who held power for nine years, before another uneasy return to civilian rule. Meanwhile, India survived as a democracy, despite considerable internal religious–ethnic divisions, the rise of Hindu militancy, and the assassinations of both Indira Gandhi (by her Sikh bodyguards in 1984) and her son, Rajiv (in 1991 by a Tamil group), who had also become Prime Minister. Despite periodic attempts at a rapprochement, Indo-Pakistani tension continued, focused on Kashmir. There were border clashes in 1985–6 and, from 1989 onwards, India faced intermittent unrest within Kashmir from Muslim groups. In mid-1999, Pakistan-backed incursions into Indian-controlled Kashmir were accompanied by further internal unrest. By that time, the dangers were heightened by the fact that, in 1998, both countries tested nuclear weapons in quick succession. In December 2001, Kashmiri militants were blamed for a deadly attack on the Indian Parliament, and there were renewed fears of war in mid-2002, following Pakistani tests of nuclear-capable missiles. Over the following years, attempts to improve relations were set back by sudden outbreaks of violence, the worst being an attack by Pakistan-based terrorists on the Indian city of Mumbai in November 2008, which killed 174 people. Although a slow thaw in relations followed, further problems were caused by a terror attack on an Indian air force base at Pathankot in January 2016 and upsurge of violence in Kashmir later that same year. Kashmir thus remained one of the world's potentially most destructive flashpoints.

C. The Middle East: The Arab–Israeli Six Day War

The Middle East in the Mid-1960s

In the early 1960s, Arab–Israeli enmities had been overshadowed by conflicts in the Arab world, and there was limited superpower concern over the region.

Israel, which had proved its military superiority in the wars of 1948 and 1956 (Chapters 3, C and 8, C), was the dominant regional power. Despite intermittent Palestinian guerrilla attacks and border clashes with Syria, a nuclear weapons programme was underway and the state seemed secure. The Arabs, on the other hand, appeared increasingly divided. The union of Egypt and Syria into the United Arab Republic had broken down, after less than four years, in September 1961. Iraq had fallen under radical leadership in 1958 but the government faced challenges from the Iraqi communists and supporters of Nasser's brand of Arab nationalism. In 1963, the secular, leftist-but-nationalist Ba'ath Party took power there; but deep-seated Iraqi–Egyptian rivalry for Arab leadership prevented the two countries working together. The final split between the Syrian and Iraqi sections of the party did not occur until 1966, but different factions in both countries meant that the Ba'ath provided no basis for the creation of Iraqi–Syrian unity. Arab radicals of all factions despised the conservative regimes in Jordan and Saudi Arabia, although they failed to undermine them: Jordan survived an attempt by Nasserites to overthrow King Hussein in early 1963; and internal differences among the Saudi royal family were resolved in 1964 when Feisal became King.

When Kennedy became President, the US tried to improve relations with Nasser as a step to building links with radical elements in the Arab world, thereby reducing the opportunities for the Soviets to gain more influence. However, America's links to Israel, Jordan, and Saudi Arabia put strict limits on such a policy. Moreover, in the 1960s, both superpowers increasingly armed their respective clients in the Arab–Israeli conflict. In 1962, Kennedy agreed to supply anti-aircraft missiles to Israel, in the mistaken hope that a more effective defence would no longer require them to develop nuclear weapons. In 1965, Kennedy's successor, Lyndon Johnson decided to supply the Israelis with advanced offensive weapons for the first time. With the Soviets supplying Egypt and Syria well before the 1967 war, 'the Middle East had already been . . . integrated into the existing bipolar world order',[10] raising the danger that any local conflict would assume much wider significance.

By the mid-1960s, tensions in the region had grown considerably. Most serious was the civil war in Yemen which broke out in September 1962, after radicals under Colonel Abdullah Sallal overthrew the traditionalist government of the Imam, Mohammed Al-Baar. Egypt backed the former, Saudi Arabia the latter. When Egyptian planes attacked the Saudis in 1963, Kennedy was forced to choose between the conservative or radical elements in the Arab world. Despite an attempt by Nasser and Feisal to reconcile their differences in 1965, neither side would give way, and the East–West split was largely replicated in the Middle East. The Western position was weakened in 1966 when Britain announced that, within two years, it would be pulling out of the neighbouring South Arabian Federation, which included the wealthy trading port of Aden. The British were being pressed to withdraw by nationalist groups in Aden, who carried out a terrorist campaign supported by Nasser and Sallal. Indeed, despite the fact that he had already been committed to a costly, deadlocked war for five years without result, Nasser's hopes of achieving victory once the British left, led him to commit 70,000 troops to the Yemen conflict by 1967.

Other disputes in the region had an Arab–Israeli significance, especially the Jordan waters dispute, a long-standing argument over how to exploit the River Jordan. It had flared up again because an Israeli plan to divert water for industrial and irrigation purposes was completed in 1964. In January that year Arab leaders gathered together in Cairo, at Nasser's invitation, and agreed on their own plan, which would bypass the Israeli construction. Now that the loss of water was deemed to threaten the existence of the Arab nation, they declared that they would together plan the forces that would ultimately lead to the destruction of the state of Israel. Work on the scheme in Syria then led in 1965 and 1966 to Israeli attacks to prevent its completion. This was one of the major points of dispute between the two countries, alongside guerrilla attacks within Israel.

The first Arab summit in 1964 was also important for promoting the creation of a political body to head the Palestinians, some of whom were still living within Israel, but many of whom were scattered in refugee camps, particularly in the Egyptian-controlled Gaza Strip and the Jordanian-controlled West Bank of the River Jordan. The Palestine Liberation Organization (PLO) was an Egyptian-backed umbrella organization, resulting from a meeting of 422 delegates in 1964 that resolved to liberate the Palestinian homeland and destroy the Jewish state. Initially led by Ahmed Shukeiri, the PLO soon suffered from internal conflict, often linked to criticism of its ties with Egypt. Radical Palestinian groups engaged in guerrilla attacks, such as the Palestine Liberation Front, resented the determination of the Egyptian and Jordanian governments to prevent such raids taking place from their territory. (After the Six Day War their leaders would come together under the PLO umbrella and with the Vengeance Youth formed the Popular Front for the Liberation of Palestine, which was led by George Habash.) At the end of 1964, another group, led by Yasser Arafat, which had contacts with the Palestine Liberation Front, left the PLO and began commando raids against Israel. Known as Al Fatah and formed in the late 1950s, it established a militia *al-Asifa* (the Storm) whose members received training in Syria. Many of these raids and those of other radical groups were launched from Jordan and their realistic aim was to provoke conflict between Israel and other Arab governments. They were followed by tough Israeli reprisals, culminating in November 1966 when the Israeli Defence Force (IDF) attacked the West Bank towns of Samu, Jimba, and Khirbet Karkay south of Hebron, causing 72 casualties. Although the reactions to this may be seen as the start of the road to war, the real problem was the deterioration in Israeli–Syrian relations, where the situation worsened with the seizure of power in February 1966 by a more radical Ba'ath group in Damascus. As the Israeli Foreign Minister, Abba Eban, later wrote, 'I regarded this Syrian terrorism as an early stage of malignancy. It could not be left alone.'[11]

The Six Day War

By 1966, the conflict between Israel and its Arab neighbours increasingly reflected the superpower rivalry for influence in the Middle East. Syria and Egypt were stockpiling arms from the USSR, encouraged by the US government's firm support for Israel. Khrushchev had visited Cairo in 1964, making Nasser a 'Hero of the Soviet Union', and his successors maintained their support. In the US, Kennedy's shift to Saudi Arabia in the conflict with Egypt over Yemen was followed by Johnson severing all aid to Egypt in 1966, giving up on Kennedy's attempts to improve US–Arab relations. In August 1966, Syrian and Israeli air and ground forces fought a fierce battle in the Galilee area, which contributed to the new regime drawing closer to Egypt and signing a defence pact in November 1966 that was followed by the Israeli attack on Jordan. In turn, Al Fatah raids into Israel were stepped up and the escalating cycle of violence continued into the following year. On 7 April 1967, there was a major border incident in which the Israeli air force attacked Syrian positions on the Golan Heights, shooting down several Soviet-supplied MiG jets. In mid-May, the Israelis threatened to strike at Damascus. While such statements were not supported by any evidence of troop build-ups, and a UN investigation found no evidence to substantiate these fears, Nasser received information from Soviet intelligence that around twelve Israeli brigades were concentrating on the Syrian border. The events in May mark the time when interpretations became diametrically opposed. (See Box 11.1 for radically different interpretations of the war.)

The Syrians were blamed by Israeli leaders for mounting a number of terrorist raids on the country. But at least one Jewish historian has argued that 'Israel's strategy of escalation on the Syrian front was probably the single most important factor in dragging the Middle East to war . . . despite the conventional wisdom . . . that singles out Syrian aggression as the principal cause.'[12] The Syrian government, unstable and nervous, continued to fear an attack. Nasser, anxious to be seen to back Syria and reluctant to lose face, mobilized his army on 14 May; and the Soviets, keen not to lose their allies, seemed prepared to support them. One major feature of superpower involvement in the Middle East during the Cold War was 'the difficulty that the superpowers encountered in controlling the behaviour of their clients. The local powers invariably had their own agenda and they employed various tactics . . . to mobilize their superpower ally behind this.'[13] In 1967, the USSR and US ended up backing their local clients even though there was little desire, in either Moscow or Washington, for an East–West confrontation.

Whenever concerns about Israel grew in the Arab world, Nasser had to consider his reputation as the leading Arab nationalist. The very fact that he had failed to triumph in Yemen increased the pressure in May 1967 for him to be seen to be supporting Syria. Nasser had two armoured divisions and 300 front-line aircraft, which was what the Israelis feared, and he was generally better equipped than in 1956. On the other hand, there was no logical reason for him to go to war when he had 70,000 men committed to the Yemen quagmire. Yet, given the military balance, there was a distinct advantage to be had by the side that struck first.

On 16 May, Nasser declared a state of emergency and asked the UN to withdraw the force which it had installed in Sinai after the 1956 war. Secretary-General U Thant was criticized for agreeing to the withdrawal and pulling UN troops out over the next week. They might, it was argued, have deterred a war if they had remained or if they had been positioned in Israel. But he felt he had no choice: opinion in the UN was divided on the Arab–Israeli issue, the troops were on Egyptian sovereign territory (Israel had refused to have them on its side of the border), and Nasser could easily have used force to remove them. The reality was that neither side was now prepared to have an effective peacekeeping force in place. The UN withdrawal gave Egypt control of the Straits of Tiran, on which Israel relied for access to the Red Sea (since Egypt would not allow Israeli ships through the Suez Canal), and around 23 May Nasser closed the Straits of Tiran to Israeli shipping, provoking international concern. In 1957, in order to secure Israel's withdrawal from Sinai following the recent war, America had promised to support Israel's right to send its own ships through

BOX 11.1

The Pro-Arab and Pro-Israeli Explanations of the Six Day War

The Israeli Version

Israelis point to the first Arab summit in January 1964 and say this strengthened the terrorists who were launching attacks on Israel. The first formal statement of the Arab states' intention to bring about the destruction of Israel was made in a joint statement at the summit and confirmed by the first Palestinian National Council in early 1964. Guerrilla attacks on Israel, conducted from Syria, emphasized the insecurity of Israeli farmers around the Sea of Galilee. Moreover, with a more radical Ba'athist government in Damascus from February 1966, the support and training given to Palestinian groups operating from Jordan increased. In August 1966, after a fierce skirmish when Israeli forces were attacked around the Sea of Galilee, growing Arab hostility led to Syrian threats to strike targets within Israel. Israel was under siege and its retaliatory raids were failing to provide a deterrent. Its insecurity was heightened in November 1966 by the Egyptian–Syrian mutual defence pact. In April 1967, when the Syrians began shelling Israeli settlements, the Israeli air force was called into action and clashed with its Syrian counterpart. It began to look as if Israel was about to face a major military challenge. On 13 May, the Soviets falsely claimed that Israeli troops were amassing on the Syrian frontier. When Nasser insisted on the withdrawal of UN peacekeeping forces from Sinai on 16 May, fears of a major attack appeared to be confirmed. Nasser was keen to respond to the Soviet information designed to lead to Cairo joining with Damascus in a combined assault on Israel. His determination to crush the Israelis was further demonstrated by his blockade of the Straits of Tiran on 23 May after the UN forces had left, which made an Israeli response unavoidable—hence the surprise Israeli attack on Egyptian and Syrian airfields.

The Arab Version

The Arab view of the war's origins is very different. It says that after 1965, having received offensive arms, the Israelis were determined both to crush Arab resistance to the illegal occupation of Palestine and to ensure that further expansion of the state of Israel took place. With these goals in mind, they sought the right moment to seize an opportunity to justify an attack on their Arab neighbours. Their military superiority would be total if an air strike was made in a surprise assault on Arab airfields, which would enable them to exploit the absence of 70,000 Egyptian troops in Yemen. In 1964, the Israelis were enabled to justify attacks on their neighbours in retaliation against Palestinian freedom fighters, which were far in excess of retaliatory raids and enabled Israeli Defence Forces to undertake operations in preparation for the more serious conflict that was being planned. The Israelis also began to attempt provocative settlements in the Demilitarized Zone bordering Syria. Clashes with Syria became more serious in 1966 as air and ground forces on both sides became involved. In particular, the Israelis tried to prevent Syrians accessing the waters of Lake Galilee from its northern shore, and attacked Arab workers trying to complete works that would regain the vital water of the River Jordan now being used for Israeli irrigation projects. Significant military battles were fought in August 1966 and April 1967. On the latter occasion, six Syrian MiG jets were shot down by Israeli fighters. Barely a month later, General Rabin announced that it was about time Israeli forces marched on Damascus. When the Soviets confirmed that Israeli troops were amassing on the Syrian border on 12 May, Nasser believed the danger to Syria was so acute that something had to be done to try and deter further Israeli aggression. In an effort to deter the Israelis by aiding the Syrians, which he could barely afford to do with his commitments in Yemen, Nasser asked for the UN forces to be partially withdrawn, thus exposing part of Israel to attack from Egypt. When the UN insisted that all of its forces or none would have to be withdrawn, Nasser reluctantly agreed to the former, then decided to try and regain the Arab position in the Straits of Tiran by closing them to Israel on 23 May. Had the Israelis also been keen to avoid war, they would have accepted the troops on the Israeli side of the border. The Arab world now tried to mobilize to deter an Israeli attack on Syria, but more hawks came into the government in Tel Aviv. The Arab efforts were therefore in vain, and the Israelis launched an unprovoked attack on 5 June.

the Straits in future. Now the Americans, who had insufficient forces near the Red Sea, told the Israelis to take no action while they attempted to form an international naval force to fulfil the undertaking, but the scheme came to nothing. The closure of the Straits of Tiran, restoring the 1956 *status quo ante* the Israeli attack on Egypt, marked the crucial watershed between war and peace.

On 27 May, the Israeli government, a coalition led by the distinctly unwarlike Levi Eshkol, voted 9–9 over whether to launch a pre-emptive strike. On 30 May, a dramatic turn of events stemming from King Hussein of Jordan's visit to Cairo produced a reconciliation between him and Nasser, which even placed the Jordanian army under Egyptian command in the event of war.[14] This step, taken out of fear, produced a classic illustration of the security dilemma in that it produced more fear in the adversary. Israeli contacts with the US government suddenly indicated a shift away from urging restraint to diplomatic backing for Israel at the UN and intervention if the Soviets became involved. They coincided with the formation of a national government including the former terrorist and future Prime Minister Menachem Begin, with Moshe Dayan as Defence Minister. With the military determined to launch an attack approved by the new Cabinet, on 5 June the Israelis struck. The key to the ensuing, rapid victory was the surprise destruction of the Arab air forces while they were largely still on the ground, which left the Israelis with a marked advantage in reconnaissance, aerial support of ground attacks, and the dropping of paratroops. The USSR must shoulder some of the blame for Arab failures because of their misleading intelligence, and failure to appreciate the consequences of attaching so much importance to assisting the regime in Syria.[15] By the morning of 8 June, on the Egyptian front, Israeli forces had reached the Suez Canal, while paratroop and naval forces had captured Sharm el-Sheikh at the bottom of the Straits of Tiran: all the Sinai peninsula was soon in Israeli hands. Meanwhile, 8 June also saw Israeli forces reach the River Jordan, having overrun the whole of the West Bank, including the Eastern half of Jerusalem. The victory was completed with an assault, on 9 June, on the Golan Heights, from which the Syrians withdrew the following afternoon.

The Security Council had called for a ceasefire on 6 June and it was accepted by Egypt, Jordan, and Syria on 9 June. Yet the Israeli assault continued, with the USSR threatening to review its relations with Tel Aviv and hinting at intervention.[16] As the US Sixth Fleet approached, the Washington–Moscow 'hot line' was used for the first time in a crisis. A ceasefire was then agreed, which left the Arab armed forces humiliated and the Israelis with new, more defensible military borders that were still short of the original Zionist ideas on the boundaries of a Jewish state. Nasser immediately offered to resign but popular acclamation kept him in power. It was 'the most spectacular military victory in Israel's history',[17] greater even than those of 1948 and 1956. The consequences of the war remain central to the future conflict and its resolution in that the Palestinian issue and the extension of Israeli settlement began to emerge as the crux of the dispute.

Aftermath: The 'War of Attrition'

In the immediate wake of their success, some observers hoped it would be possible to make a trade of 'land for peace' quite quickly: Israel would return all or most of the conquered territories in return for Arab recognition of its right to existence and to do so in peace. The closure of the Suez Canal, now the front line between Israel and Egypt, increased international pressures to find a solution. In July 1967, a joint Soviet–American UN proposal proved unacceptable to both sides. An Arab summit the following month agreed neither to recognize, nor to negotiate with, Israel, many Arab states broke off diplomatic relations with America, and there was a short-lived Arab oil boycott of Western pro-Israeli states (a precedent for more dramatic action the next time war occurred). In November, a 'land for peace' deal did form the essence of a UN Resolution (see Box 11.2), number 242, which became the basis of all future attempts to achieve an Arab–Israeli settlement. And there were some clandestine Israeli–Jordanian contacts, late in the year, to explore such possibilities. But peace proved impossible to achieve. Israel, believing it had acted in self-defence and backed by the US, was reluctant to abandon its conquests without the Arabs *first* guaranteeing the right of Israel to exist. Moreover, it did not wish to give up certain territories, not least East Jerusalem, which held great religious significance for both Muslims and Jews. For their part, the Arabs, backed by the USSR, held Israel guilty of launching an unprovoked attack and continued to refuse to recognize a Jewish state, on what they took to be Arab soil. Thanks to the war, about 250,000

Palestinians fled from the West Bank into Jordan, worsening the problem of refugees from lands that the Arabs considered to be 'occupied' by an enemy and increasing the PLO's moral standing in the Arab world. There was even a far-reaching attempt to settle differences within the Arab camp between radicals and conservatives, in that oil-rich Saudi Arabia and Kuwait agreed to provide financial aid to Egypt and Syria in return for Nasser's withdrawal from the Yemen conflict which, by 1970, was effectively resolved in the Saudis' favour. International opinion also grew more sympathetic to the Arabs in the late 1960s: 'Israel fought the Six Day War in a favourable climate of world opinion. Its extension of Israeli sovereignty to Arab Jerusalem, and the picture of poor Arab refugees crossing from the West Bank into Jordan . . . soon dispelled this.'[18]

Rather than achieving a peace settlement on the basis of Resolution 242, the next few years in Arab–Israeli relations were characterized by a 'war of attrition', between Egypt and Israel in particular. Arguably, it began in October 1967 with the Egyptian sinking of an Israeli ship, the *Eilat*. It came to include raids, often by Palestinian paramilitary groups, from Jordan, Syria, and Lebanon. In 1968, the Palestinians also began a series of aircraft hijackings which advertised their cause to the world. In 1968, Al Fatah, the largest of the Palestinian groups—boosted by the so-called Battle of Karameh (Honour), in which they inflicted significant casualties on the Israeli Defence Force (IDF)—effectively challenged the PLO leadership and transformed the organization into a political front uniting the guerrilla groups bar the Popular Front for the Liberation of Palestine (PFLP). The following year, they won control of the PLO executive committee and the process of unification under Fatah leadership was completed by 1970.[19]

BOX 11.2

UN Security Council Resolution 242 of 22 November 1967

Following long discussions about the Arab–Israeli conflict, the Security Council adopted a British-drafted resolution, the full text of which is given below. Resolution 242 was based around the idea of a 'land for peace' arrangement but was carefully worded to try to please all sides. Thus, the Israelis were asked to withdraw 'from territories occupied in the recent conflict' but not from *all* the territories—creating a fundamental ambiguity about what a 'land for peace' deal might include.

The Security Council

EXPRESSING its continuing concern with the grave situation in the Middle East.

EMPHASIZING the inadmissibility of the acquisition of territory by war and the need to work for a just and lasting peace in which every State in the area can live in security.

EMPHASIZING further that all Member States in their acceptance of the Charter of the United Nations have undertaken a commitment to act in accordance with Article 2 of the Charter.

1. AFFIRMS that the fulfilment of Charter principles requires the establishment of a just and lasting peace in the Middle East which should include the application of both the following principles:
   (i) Withdrawal of Israeli armed forces from territories occupied in the recent conflict;
   (ii) Termination of all claims or states of belligerency and respect for and acknowledgement of the sovereignty, territorial integrity and political independence of every State in the area and their right to live in peace within secure and recognized boundaries free from threats or acts of force;

2. AFFIRMS further the necessity
   (a) For guaranteeing freedom of navigation through international waterways in the area;
   (b) For achieving a just settlement of the refugee problem;
   (c) For guaranteeing the territorial inviolability and political independence of every State in the area, through measures including the establishment of demilitarized zones;

1. REQUESTS the Secretary-General to designate a Special Representative to proceed to the Middle East to establish and maintain contacts with the States concerned in order to promote agreement and assist efforts to achieve a peaceful and accepted settlement in accordance with the provisions and principles in this resolution;

2. REQUESTS the Secretary-General to report to the Security Council on the progress of the efforts of the Special Representatives as soon as possible.

Across the Suez Canal, the war of attrition initially took the form of limited-scale, punitive raids in the form of shelling, bombing, and commando operations, by one side on the other. Once the war was formally declared by Nasser in March 1969, it assumed new dimensions. In December 1969, the American Secretary of State, William Rogers, launched the 'Rogers Plan', which was designed to achieve a ceasefire as a prelude to 'land for peace' talks. Almost immediately, the Israelis rejected the plan and began actively to oppose it. In January 1970, the Israelis tried to use their air superiority to intimidate Egypt by inflicting unacceptable losses on the Egyptian hinterland, but Nasser simply secured better air defences from the Soviets, worsening Israel's aircraft losses. In June, Rogers launched Plan B, which was designed to secure a ceasefire, to gain acceptance of 242, and start negotiations. In August 1970, a ceasefire was finally agreed in the war of attrition on the basis of Rogers B, and for a brief moment peace talks seemed possible, spearheaded by the UN's special envoy Gunnar Jarring. However, once the Egyptians breached the standstill agreement in the ceasefire the Israelis withdrew from the talks. US President, Richard Nixon, let his Secretary of State take responsibility for an initiative that was always likely to fail. Indeed, he even contributed to it by making clear that the Israelis would not be pressured to accept the terms of the original Plan involving a settlement of the refugee problem as well as Israeli withdrawal. Moreover, in September the Arab position was harmed by a civil war in Jordan.

The Jordan Crisis of 1970

Although Jordan had joined in the 1967 war against Israel, the ruler, King Hussein, was a conservative in the Arab camp who retained close links with America and Britain. After the Six Day War, however, Jordan, which already had a substantial Palestinian population, had become the main base of the PLO, which favoured a more determined, anti-Israeli policy and hoped for Hussein's overthrow as a step to radicalizing the Jordanian government. On 1 September 1970, the latest of several assassination attempts on Hussein sparked off several days of fighting between the PLO and the King's army. This had just begun to die down when, between 6 and 9 September, an extremist group, the PFLP, hijacked four civilian airliners, flew three of them to Amman (Jordan's capital), and took hundreds of passengers—from an assortment of, mainly Western, nationalities—hostage. The hijackings ended without the widely feared bloodbath: the hijackers won the release of several Palestinian prisoners from Western Europe, the aircraft were blown up and, by the end of the month, all the hostages were released. But the hijack crisis led to a security crackdown on Palestinians living in Israel, to a US naval force being sent to the Lebanese coast, and to a decision by Hussein to force a showdown with the PLO in Jordan.

On 16 September, Hussein formed a military government in Amman, and the following day civil war broke out with the Palestinians. The royal army had the better of the fighting but on 19–20 September another critical point was reached when neighbouring Syria, sympathetic to the PLO, sent tanks over the border to attack the Jordanians. Hussein was in such difficulties that he told the US and British governments that air strikes were needed to halt the Syrian advance. The US, reluctant to intervene itself, then encouraged Israel to plan air raids in support of Hussein. This desperate solution—which in any case had little appeal to Hussein—proved unnecessary, however. Jordanian resistance stiffened; the USSR, fearful of a mounting crisis, urged Syria to back down; and on 23 September Syrian tanks were withdrawn, leaving the PLO to be defeated. For Palestinian radicals, the month became known as 'Black September'. Instead of overthrowing Hussein, he was now as safely in power as ever, and in 1971 the PLO was forced to switch its headquarters to nearby Lebanon. The Jordanian civil war had only served to highlight Arab divisions and weaknesses, with Syria forced into retreat and the humiliating prospect being raised of Israeli military assistance to an Arab government. To make matters worse, September 1970 ended with the sudden death, on the 28th, of Egypt's President, Gamal Abdel Nasser.

His successor, Anwar Sadat, at first seemed committed to existing policies, whilst the radical cause was strengthened by the coming to power in Syria of a ruthless, determined radical leader, Hafez al-Assad. In April 1971, an attempt to revitalize the Rogers Plan came to nothing. The two sides, armed by the superpowers, seemed as far apart as ever and Arab–Israeli tensions would continue to menace world peace. The Arabs were now in a desperate position after yet more humiliation and division as a result of the Six Day War and there seemed little prospect of persuading the protagonists to make a determined effort at peace.

Visit the online resources that accompany this book to test your understanding and take your learning further:
www.oup.com/he/young-kent3e

NOTES

1. Abraham Lowenthal, *The Dominican Intervention* (Johns Hopkins University Press, Baltimore, 1995), 153.
2. Frank Moya Pons, 'The Dominican Republic since 1930', in Leslie Bethell (ed.), *The Cambridge History of Latin America, VII* (Cambridge University Press, Cambridge, 1990), 527.
3. *New York Times*, 9 May 1965, quoted by Walter LaFeber in *Inevitable Revolutions* (Norton, New York, 2nd edn, 1993), 158.
4. Joseph S. Tulchin, 'US Relations with Latin America', in Warren Cohen and Nancy Tucker (eds), *Lyndon Johnson Confronts the World* (Cambridge University Press, New York, 1994), 233–4.
5. Stanley Wolpert, *Nehru* (Oxford University Press, Oxford, 1996), 466.
6. Altaf Gauhar, *Ayub Khan* (Oxford University Press, Karachi, 1996), 223.
7. H. W. Brands, *The Wages of Globalism* (Oxford University Press, New York, 1995), 139.
8. G. W. Choudhury, *The Last Days of United Pakistan* (Hurst, London, 1974), 231.
9. Surjit Mansingh, *India's Search for Power* (Sage, New Delhi, 1984), 223.
10. Bassam Tabi, *Conflict and War in the Middle East* (Macmillan, London, 1998), 68.
11. Abba Eban, *Personal Witness* (Putnam, New York, 1992), 353.
12. Avi Shlaim, *The Iron Wall: Israel and the Arab World* (Allen Lane, London, 2000), 235.
13. Yezid Sayigh and Avi Shlaim (eds), *The Cold War and the Middle East* (Clarendon Press, Oxford, 1997), 281; Edgar O'Ballance, *The Third Arab–Israeli War* (Faber, London, 1972), 278.
14. Mark Tessler, *A History of the Israeli–Palestinian Conflict* (Indiana University Press, Bloomington, 1994), 387–97.
15. Avi Shlaim, *The Iron Wall: Israel and the Arab World* (Allen Lane, London, 2000), 237.
16. Ibid., 248–9.
17. Ibid., 241.
18. Ritchie Ovendale, *The Origins of the Arab–Israeli Wars* (Longman, London, 1992), 208.
19. Mark Tessler, *A History of the Israeli–Palestinian Conflict* (Indiana University Press, Bloomington, 1994), 425–9.

PART IV
The Détente Era, 1972–80

The 'era of negotiations', which Richard Nixon had proclaimed in 1969, finally emerged three years later with his visits to Beijing and Moscow, the signature of a major nuclear arms agreement (the Strategic Arms Limitations Treaty, SALT I), promises of increased US–Soviet trade, and even an attempt to regulate superpower behaviour during crises. Between 1972 and 1975, the Soviet leader, Leonid Brezhnev, met Nixon and his successor, Gerald Ford, on five occasions, and there were advances, too, in Europe with a continent-wide agreement on security, signed in Helsinki in 1975. Yet even in 1973, there was a severe superpower confrontation—the worst since Cuba eleven years before—over the Middle East, and throughout the decade East–West relations were troubled by a series of regional problems in the less developed world, from Angola and the Horn of Africa to South-East Asia and Afghanistan. The attempt to stabilize East–West relations, which had begun in the 1960s with the Test Ban Treaty and the hot-line agreement, broke down into acrimony by 1979, and in 1980, following the Soviet invasion of Afghanistan, there was a return to Cold War confrontation.

The Nature of Détente

The 1970s were the era of détente (a French word meaning 'relaxation'), but there is great debate over what exactly détente signified. There was, in the early 1970s at least, an undoubted attempt to reach a broad range of agreements, from arms and borders to commerce and scientific research, as well as an effort to establish formal modes of behaviour, where previously such modes had been tentative and unwritten. Not only was the propaganda war between the two sides relaxed, and high-level meetings held, but also limits were put on nuclear arsenals, the division of Europe was mutually recognized, and a plethora of personal contacts built up. Yet, in contrast to the relaxation of tension in the late 1980s, the 1970s did not end in the disintegration of one bloc. Throughout the decade, both sides remained ideologically far apart, conventional arms reductions by NATO and the Warsaw Pact were impossible to achieve, and the superpowers continued their dangerous rivalry for influence in Asia and Africa. Why these processes occurred can be interpreted in a number of ways: as attempts to end the expensive military confrontation, or to manage the emergent multipolar balance of global power, or as attempts to preserve (or destroy) American hegemony.

One reason why the US and USSR may have felt able to pursue détente was that they believed they could safely enter agreements whilst balancing the power of the other. The Americans were still far superior to the Soviets in terms of industrial power, trade, and technology, even though the Soviets were out-producing them in some basic items such as coal and steel. The Soviets were now also in front of the Americans regarding numbers of missile launchers, but the US had many more nuclear warheads and a larger navy. While the Vietnam War sapped national confidence, inflation, economic decline relative to major trading rivals in Europe and Japan, and the 1973–4 Watergate scandal also hinted at American weakness. Yet NATO held together, even though it was troubled by France's continued distance from the alliance, arguments over arms expenditure, and political turmoil in some member states, especially Portugal and Italy. In Eastern Europe, the Warsaw Pact held together under Soviet domination and experienced no major upheavals. Even Ceauşescu did not defect from Moscow in the way Tito and Mao had earlier. The Soviets were aware of their inferiority in warhead numbers but, given the belief in Mutual Assured Destruction (MAD), that hardly seemed to matter. Moreover, their nuclear arsenal continued to be upgraded, with ever-larger intercontinental missiles and more accurate SS-20s in Europe. Under Andrei Grechko (Defence Minister in between 1967 and 1976), conventional armed forces also greatly expanded. A 'blue water' navy and improved air transport gave the Soviets the ability to act in the less developed world at a time when, thanks to Vietnam, the US was more restrained. The USSR had truly become a global power, yet it faced not only the Western challenge, but also the hostility of the Chinese, which could be exploited by the US. In short, both superpowers had problems and strengths which could be balanced or exploited through a process of détente.

It is worth asking how much had changed from the deep Cold War of the 1950s to the relaxation of tension in the 1970s. A multipolar world may have emerged in the 1960s, and China might be an important 'third power' in international affairs, but the strategic balance in the world was still very much bipolar and US–Soviet rivalry continued to impact on all parts of the globe. China's anti-Soviet policy was of great concern to the Kremlin, but China's nuclear arsenal was puny, it faced political turmoil in the mid-1970s, and it did not achieve a normalization of relations with America until the end of the decade. Therefore, it could be that détente was simply another phase of the old bipolar relationship. Yet multipolarity, Chinese power, relative US economic decline vis-à-vis the European Economic Community, and instability in the less developed world could all be seen as new challenges to an established order. So, while in retrospect the 1970s can be seen as continuing the bipolar, Cold War world (with more successful attempts than the mid-1950s to control nuclear weapons), at the time it seemed a new and uncertain world for both superpowers. If the idea of radical new challenges to the superpowers is accepted, then détente can be interpreted as driven by uncertainties that forced the adversaries together, in an attempt to manage the changed international environment. But each sought to do so while preserving or developing their leading position in world politics.

From a Western perspective, replacing confrontation with a more trusting relationship could reduce the dangers of nuclear war, lead to greater economic contacts with the East, and promote liberal values on a universal scale—a process which might undermine communism from within. In any case, the Vietnam imbroglio, the advent of MAD, and economic difficulties made Washington less able to contemplate a threatening policy such as Dulles had pursued. For Moscow, a number of concerns may have driven the desire for a relaxation of tension with America, including fear of China, the need for Western technology, or the desire to support wars of national liberation while avoiding nuclear war. The Soviets, with Brezhnev politically secure at home and the country militarily stronger abroad, may have felt able to act with greater boldness and confidence vis-à-vis Washington. As with Western hopes of undermining communism through liberal ideas, it is arguable that the Kremlin was preparing to win the Cold War in ideological terms, by demonstrating the success of its own system (which had achieved nuclear parity with the US) and seeing an expansion of Marxist regimes in the less developed world.

While both may have had a similar interest in détente, then, it is clear that their precise reasons for pursuing it differed and that a deep ideological rift remained. For the Americans, détente offered the possibility of Soviet cooperation in extracting them from Vietnam. As the declining hegemon, or the hegemon under threat, the US also had every reason to look beyond the old-style Cold War confrontation to the more long-term control of Soviet behaviour via cooperation. There were power-political and economic reasons for wooing the Soviets into an acceptance of the global status quo, which would preserve American dominance. In this scenario, the opening to China was seen by Henry Kissinger, President Nixon's National Security Adviser, as heralding the possibility of a return to old-fashioned balance-of-power politics, in which several great powers participated. Yet, when the Soviets acted forcefully, Kissinger continued to see the old Cold War bipolarity as the prime explanation for regional conflicts. This mix of old goals and new circumstances characterized the world of the early 1970s, partly because leading figures found it difficult to interpret the way the world was heading, surrounded as they were by dramatic developments in the nature of international relationships and by a highly uncertain economic environment.

The Collapse of the Bretton Woods System

Economics was perhaps the area where the US and the Soviet Union were most under challenge. The Vietnam War and the oil price increase associated with the 1973 Arab–Israel war created severe domestic differences in the US and the Western world. The strain on the American economy caused by the Vietnam War was serious when the 1970s began, with the US balance of payments in the red and the Bretton Woods system on the verge of collapse. Towards the end of his first term, Nixon made an extraordinary speech revealing American concerns, particularly about the new economic forces at work, even before the oil shocks. He referred to the 'five great economic superpowers' (the US, Russia, Japan, Western Europe, and China), 'four of whom challenge us on every front'. 'Because economic power will be the key to other kinds of power . . . in the last third of this century', and since domestic and foreign policies were so interlinked, Americans had to discipline themselves or face the 'decadence' that had brought ruin to Greece and Rome.[1]

What they did face in 1971 was first, the end of the Bretton Woods system of fixed (but flexible) exchange rates, with the end of the dollar's convertibility against gold on which it was based. Then, during the 1973 Middle East War, came a temporary embargo of oil exports from the Middle East and a dramatic increase in the price of oil. The Organization of Petroleum Exporting Countries (OPEC) had been fighting since the 1960s to secure higher prices and better returns for its thirteen members, seven of whom were Arab countries. The massive price rises hit the poorest countries hardest, produced enormous inflationary pressures, led Western banks, flooded with oil revenues, to be over-eager in lending to less developed countries, and posed large questions about the problems of the international economy.

Even in the 1960s difficulties were being experienced by newly independent countries in successfully developing their economies along standard Western lines. Diversification was proving difficult and the returns on the production of primary products, especially tropical ones, were falling. The terms of trade were moving against primary producers. It required the sale of more produce to purchase the same quantities of manufactured goods. As the Bretton Woods system passed into history, in the developed world a set of ideas based around the importance of 'market forces' began to gain credence. Problems were blamed on government intervention, which had brought social reform after 1945 and shifted the balance between workers and owners of capital in favour of the former. Now, it was claimed that the unbridled pursuit of wealth through the seizing of market opportunities would bring greater benefits to everyone. Even if the wealthy benefited more initially, this wealth would trickle down as the market rewarded all who were able to compete within it. If only the heavy hand of the state, often deemed to be deeply corrupt as well as incompetent, could be removed and even the kind of controls involved in fixed exchange rates terminated, then the world economy could recover. National governments merely had to act in accordance with enabling market forces to operate. Marx may have seen men as born free but everywhere in chains; neo-liberals saw market forces in the same light.

At the same time, other ideas challenged both the diagnosis of the world's economic problems and the cure. Particularly in the less developed world, problems were blamed on the workings of capitalism where any surplus/profit is not divided solely among the producers of that surplus. The profit/surplus allocated to shareholders as owners of capital was seen as maximizing their gains at the expense of those directly involved in the production process. Likewise, in the international context foreign investment and the operations of multinational companies were seen as essentially transferring resources away from those poorer countries and their producers. The latter, whether workers or peasants, lacked the ability to influence world market prices, unlike consumers and purchasers in the developed world, who could control or influence such prices. In other words, there were forces acting in the international economy system which, if not checked by state action (assuming any such action could be effective), would prevent development taking place in the less well-off countries. Variously attributing this to the legacy of colonialism, the competitive disadvantage from entering late into manufacturing, or to the extension of the global division of labour, dependency theorists and world system theorists saw the structure of the international economy as accentuating the divisions between the rich and the poor.

Neither interpretation of the problem is entirely accurate. Some countries outside Europe and North America did develop but other countries got poorer, and the issue is whether or not this can be explained primarily with reference to the specific circumstances of the particular country. The fact that the issue became more noticeable in the 1970s was connected to the growing shift in the balance of world trade as well as the general world economic problems. Whereas trade involving manufactures formed 17 per cent of world trade in the late 1940s, by the start of the 1970s it constituted 58 per cent, and the increasing strength of the developed world was behind the calls for a New International Economic Order. The concern with the less developed world culminated in the high-profile Brandt report in 1980 but then became buried by the growing dominance of neo-liberalism in the 1980s.

The communist bloc was certainly not free from the troubles afflicting the capitalist world. As the march of technology quickened and sophisticated consumer goods were in growing demand, the Soviet economy was finding it difficult to adapt or innovate. In the 1990s, it was revealed to have stagnated around 1975 and to have been about one-sixth the size of America's. Increasingly inefficient and unresponsive to consumer needs, the weakness of the Soviet economy meant that Moscow could not match America's generosity with financial aid and technological assistance to the less developed world even if it could provide education, arms, and raw materials to its allies. Surprisingly, the USSR became the world's largest oil producer in the 1970s, with much of it shipped to Eastern Europe. This illustrated how ideological belief, and the political need to maintain the unity of the Eastern bloc, could become a drain on the Soviet economy.

Differing Expectations of Détente

These problems and those faced by the Americans as a consequence of the Vietnam War gave both sides a similar economic rationale for détente, not least because of the cost-benefits of arms reductions. Despite this, the fundamental problem for détente was that each side interpreted it and its desired outcomes very differently. In particular, the expectations of détente's effect on the other side were also radically different. For the Soviets, it can be suggested that the overriding goal was the continuing quest to achieve greater recognition of their claim to equality with the US. Formal agreements such as SALT I, indicating that there was some form of parity between the two countries' arms levels, might certainly produce this. Involvement in the resolution of regional conflicts, as in the Middle East, would also provide recognition of a dual peacemaking role for both adversaries. It would involve a new and more prominent international role for the Soviets, but one reflecting their commitment to a peaceful world and the reduced hostility towards the Americans. The USSR and Warsaw Pact would balance the US and NATO in Europe and in the arms race, while events continued to unfold elsewhere in Moscow's favour. Brezhnev, who became closely identified with détente as he secured his political predominance in Moscow during 1971, was allegedly determined to put superpower relations on a stable, equal, peaceful basis while maintaining strong armed forces, weakening domestic opposition, and preserving support for Soviet leadership of international communism.

A less charitable interpretation is that the Soviets saw détente in realist terms, as another means of obtaining power and influence at the expense of the Americans, either by gaining an advantage in arms control or in the creation of communist satellites in the less developed world. The Soviets allegedly sought to win the ideological battle by aiding wars of national liberation and therefore they remained firmly committed to victory in the Cold War. Thus, in line with the precepts of 'peaceful coexistence', East–West competition would continue in ideological terms. This could be done because the USSR was still an attractive ally for less developed states. Even if few of them were conventionally Marxist-Leninist, they did wish to assert their independence of the West and to find an alternative economic model to capitalism. However economically inefficient, corrupt, and stagnant the Soviet system had become, and however divided the communist world, Marxist doctrine continued to influence Soviet foreign policy. A belief in class struggle, an urge to help fellow Marxists where possible, and a confidence in the historic inevitability of communist triumph still guided the Kremlin.

For the Americans in the early 1970s, under Nixon and Kissinger, détente and ideological competition were seen in precisely the opposite terms. Détente was clearly expected to stop the Soviets from supporting revolutionary movements and lead them to behave as a 'normal', non-revolutionary state. The USSR would be co-opted into creating stability in the less developed world. Those who interpret American policy in a favourable light believe Nixon and Kissinger were also determined that, in contrast to the mid-1950s, détente should involve more than an improved international atmosphere. Concrete agreements, of benefit to both sides, would help commit the Soviets to cooperation and the world would be a safer place through the establishment of arms control. Making the Soviets reasonable was based on the expectation that the Soviets would accept the American definition of 'reasonableness', in return for the US offer of aid and technology transfers. If it was made clear that Moscow could only expect to gain from détente under the principle of 'linkage', which Kissinger defined as the formal acceptance of greater equality of status for the Kremlin in return for the USSR restraining itself in the less developed world, then progress would be made. Improved Sino-American relations could be used as an additional lever against the Soviets, forcing them to respect the international order.

A more critical analysis of American aims would define them in terms of ambition and the maintenance of American hegemony, which perhaps were precursors of the future policy of post-Cold War administrations. Détente was the way of getting the Soviets and the Chinese to cooperate in the preservation of a world order run primarily for the advantage of the US, at a time when Vietnam put Washington's predominance under threat. The key aim was to manipulate these relations to maximize benefits for the Americans, in much the same way, critics argued, that Kissinger approached the SALT negotiations. The aim here, allegedly, was not the preservation of peace and global stability, but the maintenance of the American nuclear superiority by exploiting the development of multiple independent re-entry vehicle

(MIRV) missiles. Similarly, bad relations between the Soviets and Chinese could be exploited to induce Moscow at least to accept the American conception of linkage, which would increasingly come to demand more and more from the Soviets in line with American wishes. Ultimately, under President Carter after 1977, the very basis of Soviet domestic policy would be undermined as human rights became more of an issue in the continuation of American aid. In the less developed world, the aim of stopping Soviet support for revolution was, allegedly, to maintain influence for the benefit of Western world. This was not so much for economic benefits, but the ideological superiority that enhanced the status and influence of the US and the leading capitalist powers, who claimed to support freedom and democracy. For the Americans too, détente can be interpreted as simply another way of winning the Cold War. Moreover, the whole idea that the Soviets should cease supporting left-wing groups seeking to change the domestic status quo in Angola and Ethiopia smacked of hypocrisy. The Americans themselves were guilty of similar interference in Angola, Chile, and Indo-China. Conflicting views as to what détente should mean for the less developed world may well have been the most important factor in influencing its demise.

The Achievements of Détente?

Did the world become a safer and more stable place during and after the détente process? Undoubtedly, there seemed to be positives. The SALT treaties were important steps in arms control, although they did not formalize nuclear parity and American nuclear superiority was retained even if the Soviets had significantly closed the gap. The bad atmosphere created by propaganda and disinformation campaigns was significantly reduced. Increased trade, with the American provision of grain to the Soviet Union leading the way, began the opening up of the Eastern bloc through economic contacts. But it must be repeated that both sides viewed détente in different ways, so that it was difficult, if not impossible, for them to agree on where there were positive and negative results in the process. The Kremlin believed that East–West agreements, like SALT and Helsinki, were valuable in themselves, that both sides gained from arms control and European stability, and that America should support these policies without insisting on 'linkage'. In the less developed world, it was quite acceptable for ideological rivalry to continue. For Marxists, it was 'historically inevitable' that wars of national liberation would occur and that the balance of power should gradually shift against the 'Imperialists'. From the Soviet perspective, détente was successful in that it allowed communism to advance without risking general war. The important point was that regional crises should not raise the danger of nuclear war or threaten Soviet security. In that sense, détente for Moscow was a success. The Kremlin believed that by maintaining the Eastern bloc, securing nuclear parity, and winning allies in the less developed world, they had actually 'forced' Washington into détente. They were determined in fact to be formally recognized by America as an equal in world affairs. Such recognition would help win more allies abroad, demonstrate that the communist model of development could match capitalism, and ought also to give the USSR a voice in resolving the world's regional problems. In that sense, from the Soviet perspective, détente was a failure. Moreover, ultimately the greater access to consumer goods, the emphasis on human rights, and the commitment to cooperation may have paved the way for the changes in the Eastern bloc, which brought the collapse of communism and the end of the Cold War.

From the American perspective, détente showed that the Kremlin was not ready to accept US restraints on its behaviour and that it did not respect the principles of linkage. Success would have been making Moscow behave in an acceptable fashion compatible with American perceptions of world order and US influence. The establishment of a code of conduct in the 'basic principles' agreement, devised at the 1972 Moscow summit, was undoubtedly a success, but it remained vague, even if the Helsinki agreement reflected an agreement on American-type values. After that, from 1975 much of the burden of maintaining détente fell on the SALT II negotiations which, along with concerns that détente was undermining American power, ran into domestic opposition in the US which heightened a sense of failure. Perhaps the fact that the Americans expected more from changed Soviet behaviour was crucial in terms of détente's ultimate success or failure. Whereas the Soviets saw détente as allowing their goals to be realized without America changing its behaviour, the Americans required that cooperation embody a change in Soviet behaviour both at home and abroad. With Moscow seeing the capitalists as still seeking communism's destruction, the preservation of the USSR itself remained Moscow's priority. If the Americans were committed to better relations, then for Moscow all that was required was the acceptance of their support for wars of national liberation.

Overall, in the short term, it is difficult to detect any major benefits produced by détente. The prospect of the world becoming a less threatening place was to be followed by increased hostility after 1979. Robert Keohane, in his book *After Hegemony*, sees the 1970s as the end of American hegemony and the emergence of new forms of cooperation in the Western world. By focusing not so much on détente and the Cold War as on the new challenges of cooperation facing the Western world, Keohane sees the hand of progress and the benefits of cooperation being realized. Particularly, in economic terms, cooperation in a multipolar world might be more problematic because this new world signified the end of American hegemony. Yet the passing of US-dominated institutions such as those created at Bretton Woods, through which hegemony had been exercised, meant new opportunities in the 1970s. New institutions, now defined less as concrete organizations but as regimes, or abstract sets of expectations and common practices, could be the beginning of a new international order. In an age where cooperation began to replace confrontation, they arguably formed the background to a process which ended with the Soviet leadership wishing to adopt some of the ideas and practices of the Western world. Before that, however, there was to be the collapse of détente and the reversion to an old form of confrontation.

Crisis in the Less Developed World

Between 1962 and 1974, in Cold War terms, the West had clearly triumphed in the battle for the 'hearts and minds' of newly independent peoples, albeit at the cost of accepting numerous right-wing dictatorships rather than risking experiments with liberalization. Only in South Yemen was there a case of a revolutionary seizure of power, but between 1974 and 1980 left-wing or revolutionary movements came to power in fourteen countries if Angola, where the Popular Movement for the Liberation of Angola (MPLA) was the strongest but not the dominant force, is counted. Ethiopia, Cambodia, South Vietnam, Laos, Guinea-Bissau, Mozambique, Cape Verde, Sao Tomé, Angola, Afghanistan, Iran, Grenada, Nicaragua, and Zimbabwe all gained anti-Western regimes.[2] There are many different explanations for this, all connected to particular problems or dynamics within radically different geographical and cultural regions. The fact that the Soviet Union now had the capacity to airlift troops and equipment made the situation more dangerous, in that defeat for pro-Western groups seemed more possible. It was also more plausible to see a coordinated plan behind Soviet support for these left-wing movements in the form of creating satellites, which in turn would spread Soviet ideology and influence through proxy wars. Thus, Vietnam invaded Cambodia after the victory of the North and Cuba intervened in several African countries. For those, like Carter's National Security Adviser, Zbigniew Brzezinski, who interpreted these events as both Soviet-inspired and motivated by ideas of geopolitical expansion, Afghanistan and the Soviet invasion were the last act in a power-political game, which the US must respond to and win.

There were, of course, alternative explanations for these events and for the Soviet involvement. The Soviet Union may be seen as a reluctant participant in such costly conflicts but having, for ideological reasons, to provide some support for revolutionary movements. This alleged half-hearted commitment may have been strengthened by the need to make sure Beijing did not emerge as the sole supporter of revolution or opponent of imperialism. It seems unlikely that the Soviet Union had ambitious plans to create satellites through proxy wars, not least because Cuba, whose troops did intervene in Africa, was by no means the puppet of Moscow and acted for its own reasons rather than at the Kremlin's behest. One key question is whether the Soviets were the instigators of revolution, as part of a geopolitical plan or ideological commitment, or merely took the opportunity to embarrass the West in the Cold War. Conservatives, like Brezhnev, were reluctant to take risks, especially if they might lead to war but, in true Marxist-Leninist fashion, always committed to the ultimate triumph of the alleged victims of capitalism. The interesting point is the relative weight of ideology and power politics in the Kremlin's motivation. It is easy to say that the concern with protecting the interests of the Soviet state had always been paramount, but there were clear connections between the two. Protecting the ideas associated, correctly or not, with the Russian Revolution could be seen as requiring a powerful Soviet state. And the Cold War was seen by both sides as part of a global struggle for influence, where the triumph of revolutionary movements in the less developed world were seen as affecting the global balance of power. In that respect, the peoples of the less developed world can again be seen as central to détente's failure and to the Cold War itself.

The Collapse of Détente

At a general level, it was almost inevitable that the different interpretations of what détente was designed to achieve would lead each side to believe the other was taking unfair advantage. In a sense, the failure of the process indicates that one or both sides were being disingenuous. The fact that they attached more importance to the specific advantages they expected détente to bring them than to the general advantages to be gained from a relaxing of international tension is significant. The collapse may have been brought about by a series of specific crises, by the Soviet invasion of Afghanistan, or by the general fear that expectations would not be met and, that instead of advantages, détente would bring disadvantages. There was also the problem that, however reluctant the superpowers were to be dragged into particular conflicts, they were continually dragged in because of the policies of their clients and allies (as during the Middle East War of 1973), by miscalculations over the impact of certain decisions (such as the Soviets seem to have made over Afghanistan in 1979), and by the basic fact that they continued to hope for a world shaped in their own ideological image.

By the second half of the 1970s, especially in America, the value of détente was much questioned. There was talk in 1980 of a 'decade of neglect', in which the US had made needless concessions to Moscow and allowed the Soviets to make major advances in the nuclear arms race. It seemed to some, notably the Committee on the Present Danger, formed in 1976, that the Cold War had continued, albeit less intensely, and that the Soviets were still determined to further Marxism-Leninism and undermine the US. Détente, they argued, was just a cover for Soviet expansion. It had not helped the US extricate itself from Vietnam. America was allegedly abandoning its commitment to resist the evils of communism and neglecting its military responsibilities, to the extent that American power was now becoming inferior to that of the Soviets. In the second half of the 1970s, domestic pressures in the US were increasingly important in opposing 'détente'. In the USSR, where the opening of economic links to the West had not revived the Soviet economy, which if anything had got worse as growth rates continued to decline, and where allowing Jewish emigrants to leave had merely produced further pressures to deal with human rights issues, some opposition to détente was also in evidence.

The problems which undermined détente were a classic mix of domestic and international forces which came together in mid-1978. Soviet support for left-wing movements in Vietnam, Angola, and Ethiopia had angered the Americans, even though they too were active in conflicts in the less developed world. They had undermined the Marxist President Allende in Chile, for example. The US, like the USSR, continued to see the less developed world as an arena of superpower competition. Thus, the 'Nixon Doctrine' may have marked a rhetorical shift to a less globalistic, less adventurist foreign policy but it actually sought to continue old anti-Soviet policies, by placing more of the burden of resisting communism on to America's allies. The Kremlin actually believed that it acted with restraint in conflicts in the less developed world and it was confused by the growing popular criticism of détente in the US. Soviet exclusion from any part of the less developed world, even in a peacekeeping role, seemed to be the prime US aim.

American support for human rights and Soviet dissidents had angered the Kremlin, especially after Jimmy Carter became President in 1976. Carter had an idea of making human rights a major concern of US foreign policy and initially combined this with a focus on the North–South divide. Carter was also interested in the 'trilateral' relationship between America, Western Europe, and Japan. He had been the only southern representative on the Trilateral Commission, a group of private individuals concerned with the economic problems of the Western world and how these might be resolved through cooperation. But by 1978, East–West issues had assumed centre stage, perhaps more as a result of domestic differences within the Carter administration than of concerns over particular international developments. Of 'the many foreign policy debates within the Carter administration that over policy toward the Soviet Union was the most prolonged and intense'.[3]

It was the old problem of the relationship between the Cold War and regional or local conflicts. The Soviets believed the Americans were simply being unrealistic if they did not expect the anti-imperialist forces to gain the upper hand in Africa and Asia. And the Americans were no more realistic. Kissinger was never able to reconcile his emotive anti-communism with his intellectual *realpolitik* in assessing whether regional conflicts had to be analysed in terms of their effect on the Cold War, or as things caused by the Cold War. Under Carter, the problem was that Brzezinski, his National Security Adviser, was quite a hard-line anti-communist, whereas Cyrus Vance, the Secretary of State, was more of a pragmatist, willing to compromise, and able to see that the communists were not behind everything that produced instability in the world. Brzezinski and Vance engaged in a battle to win the President's support but by 1978 the former had essentially triumphed and Vance resigned in 1980. The second oil price rise shock of 1979 created renewed economic pressures in the Western world in the wake of the Iranian revolution and the holding of American hostages in Tehran. A sense of America lacking the will to act assertively and of becoming a victim of circumstance accompanied the fatal blow to détente, which came with the Soviet invasion of Afghanistan. Carter's response was to increase the US military build-up which had begun before the invasion and to announce the 'Carter Doctrine', which pledged the US to intervene, unilaterally if necessary, to prevent Soviet control of the Persian Gulf.

Carter was castigated in retrospect for having failed to stand up to the Soviets when their ambitions had (supposedly) been plain for all to see. But there were a number of problems with such arguments. For one thing, Carter did stand up for American interests. He modernized the armed forces, improved relations with China, and pressed for improved human rights in the communist bloc, before taking a tough response to the invasion of Afghanistan. Also, Soviet advances were not as great as Americans supposed: Angola and Ethiopia became pro-Soviet but they were poor, politically divided countries; the invasion of Afghanistan soon turned into a disaster; and defence expenditure and assistance to allies put pressures on an already inefficient Soviet economy. The Soviets disliked the attempt to 'interfere' in Soviet domestic affairs through Carter's emphasis on human rights, and in the later 1970s, Moscow blamed the US for undermining good relations.

There were always problems in managing détente and the policy was undermined by a wide range of factors. Disagreements over the very meaning of their new relationship were compounded by inevitable misperceptions and misunderstandings. The occasion for the final collapse of détente was the Soviet invasion of Afghanistan, but it was in decline long before that and its problems cannot be blamed only on one side. As with the origins of the Cold War, ideological and power-political issues, a lack of mutual understanding, and developments beyond superpower control led to the breakdown of trust and cooperation between them. Each side took decisions which troubled the other, and by 1980 it was clear that the détente era had not altered the basic structure of the Cold War, even within a changed international system. The US and USSR, with less control of an ever more complex world, were still seen as the predominant powers, unable to escape profound differences of belief and interest. The next phase in the Cold War, with the revival of a blunt American anti-communism, was to change that.

Visit the online resources that accompany this book to test your understanding and take your learning further: www.oup.com/he/young-kent3e.

NOTES

1. *Public Papers of the Presidents . . . Richard Nixon . . . 1971* (Washington, DC, 1972), 806–12. Cited in W. LaFeber, *America, Russia and the Cold War, 1945–2000* (9th edn, McGraw-Hill, New York, 2002), 279.
2. F. Halliday, *The Making of the Second Cold War* (2nd edn, Verso, London, 1986), 81–104.
3. Z. Brzezinski, *Power of Principle* (Farrar Straus Giroux, New York, 1983), 146.

PART IV CHRONOLOGY

The Détente Era, 1972–80

1972

21–28 February	Nixon's visit to China includes meetings with Mao Zedong.
30 March	North Vietnam launches offensive in Vietnam.
15–16 April	Breakthrough on SALT in 'tundra talks' between US and Soviets in Finland.
17–19 May	West German Bundestag ratifies 'Ostpolitik' treaties with USSR and Poland (signed in 1970).
22–26 May	Nixon–Brezhnev summit in Moscow.
17 June	Watergate break-in: Democratic Party HQ in Washington entered by a group linked to Nixon.
18 July	President Sadat of Egypt expels thousands of Soviet advisers.
1 August	US–North Vietnamese peace talks reopen.
3 September	US–Soviet–British–French agreement on future of Berlin.
7 November	Nixon defeats George McGovern in landslide election win.
18–30 December	'Christmas bombing' campaign by US against North Vietnam.
21 December	'Basic Treaty' on bilateral relations between East and West Germany.

1973

1 January	Britain, Ireland, and Denmark join the EEC, in its first enlargement.
27 January	Vietnam peace agreement is signed in Paris.
22 February	US and China agree to open 'liaison offices' in each other's capital.
30 March	Last US servicemen leave Vietnam.
23 April	Kissinger proposes a 'New Atlantic Charter'.
30 April	Watergate Crisis begins to intensify, with resignations of key White House staff.
18–24 June	Nixon–Brezhnev summit in Washington.
3 July	Thirty-five countries begin talks on European security in Helsinki.
15 August	US ends all military involvement in Cambodia.
12 September	President Allende of Chile toppled in a military coup.
6–29 October	Middle East War, including US forces being put on a high level of nuclear alert on 25–26 October.
18 October	Arab oil producers raise prices and introduce oil embargo against US.
30 October	'Mutual Balanced Force Reduction' talks open in Vienna between NATO and Warsaw Pact.
7 November	US Congress passes War Powers Act.

1974

25 April	Portuguese dictatorship overthrown by the military, leading to Leftist-dominated governments.
18 May	India explodes its first atomic bomb.
27 June–3 July	Nixon–Brezhnev summit in USSR.
8 August	Nixon resigns over Watergate scandal.
12 September	Emperor Haile Selassie overthrown by Marxist army officers.
23–24 November	Ford–Brezhnev summit in Vladivostok.

1975

14 January	US–Soviet trade deal collapses over Jackson–Vanik amendment.
16 April	Fall of Phnom Penh, capital of Cambodia, to Khmer Rouge.
25 April	Communists fare badly in Portuguese elections.

PART IV CHRONOLOGY (continued)

30 April	Fall of Saigon to Vietnamese communists.
10 June	Rockefeller Commission (sitting since January) reports that the CIA spied on US citizens.
30 July–1 August	Helsinki summit of US, Canada, and European states; signing of Helsinki Accords.
23 August	Vientiane, capital of Laos, falls to communist Pathet Lao.
11 November	Angolan independence from Portugal; three rival nationalist movements prevent transfer of power to unitary government.
1976	
11 February	Organization of African Unity accepts pro-Soviet MPLA as government of Angola.
15 March	Egypt ends its 1971 treaty with USSR.
13 April	Kissinger opposes a communist role in Italian government.
21 June	Christian Democrats only narrowly ahead of communists in Italian elections.
9 September	Death of Mao Zedong.
2 November	Democrat Jimmy Carter wins US presidential election.
1977	
17 February	Carter letter to dissident scientist, Andrei Sakharov, backs human rights in USSR.
27 February	USSR rejects Carter's hopes of a major change of direction in SALT II talks.
30 June	Carter cancels B-1 bomber.
5 July	Ali Bhutto, President of Pakistan, overthrown by military under General Zia ul-Haq.
July	Fighting breaks out between Ethiopia and Somalia over disputed Ogaden.
7 September	Treaties signed to transfer Panama Canal from US to Panamanian sovereignty.
4 October	'Follow-up' conference to Helsinki, on European security, opens in Belgrade (closes 9 March 1979).
18 October	Václav Havel and other 'Charter 77' members are sentenced to imprisonment in Prague.
13 November	Somalia ends its 1974 friendship treaty with USSR; Soviets and Cubans support Ethiopia in Ogaden War.
19–21 November	President Sadat of Egypt visits Israel and addresses its Parliament.
31 December	Cambodia breaks diplomatic relations with Vietnam due to border clashes.
1978	
13 March	Israel launches an invasion of southern Lebanon to drive back PLO forces.
Late March	Somali forces withdraw from Ogaden.
5 April	West Germany's Chancellor, Helmut Schmidt, agrees to deployment of controversial 'neutron bomb' in Europe.
7 April	Carter suspends production of neutron bomb.
28 April	President Daud of Afghanistan overthrown by communists led by Mohammed Taraki.
18 May	Soviet dissident Yuri Orlov imprisoned.
7 June	Carter warns Soviets they must choose between confrontation and détente.
5–17 September	Camp David Summit on Middle East peace, between Carter, Sadat, and Begin.
3 November	Vietnam and USSR sign a Friendship Treaty.
6 November	Martial law declared in Iran after mounting unrest.
5 December	Soviet–Afghan friendship treaty.
25 December	Vietnamese invasion of Cambodia.

(continued...)

PART IV CHRONOLOGY (continued)

1979

1 January	Normalization of Sino-American relations.
16 January	Shah of Iran goes into exile.
1 February	Ayatollah Khomeini returns to Iran.
17 February–15 March	Chinese invasion of North Vietnam, followed by withdrawal.
26 March	Egyptian–Israeli peace treaty signed in Washington.
15 April	New round of oil price increases led by Iran.
7 June	Carter decides to build 'MX' missile.
15–18 June	Vienna Summit of Carter and Brezhnev; SALT II treaty signed.
17 July	President Somoza of Nicaragua overthrown by Sandinistas.
31 August	US complains about Soviet troop presence in Cuba.
16 September	President Taraki of Afghanistan overthrown by Hafizullah Amin.
22 October	Shah of Iran arrives in US for medical treatment.
4 November	Occupation of American Embassy in Tehran.
10 December	NATO agrees to deploy intermediate range Cruise and Pershing missiles in Europe.
25 December	Soviet troops invade Afghanistan; replace President Amin with Babrak Karmal.

1980

4 January	Carter suspends ratification of SALT II.
23 January	'Carter Doctrine' speech on defence of Persian Gulf.
29 January	Meeting of Islamic states condemns Soviet invasion of Afghanistan.
25 April	Failed US attempt to rescue the Tehran hostages.
4 May	Death of President Tito of Yugoslavia.
5 September	Polish communist leader Edward Gierek resigns.
22 September	Launch of 'Solidarity' union by Gdansk shipworkers; legalized on 10 November.
22 September	Iraqis launch invasion of Iran.
4 November	Republican Ronald Reagan wins US presidential election.

Take your learning further by viewing the interactive version of this timeline: www.oup.com/he/young-kent3e

12

An Era of Negotiations, 1972–3

Chapter contents

A. 'Triangular Diplomacy' and the East Asian Balance

Sino-American Rapprochement

The most dramatic change in international diplomacy in the early 1970s was the rapprochement between Beijing and Washington. After two decades of enmity, it was announced on 15 July 1971 that Richard Nixon was to visit China. The 'Opening to China' fitted the Nixon–Kissinger hope of maintaining a favourable position vis-à-vis the Soviets despite America's problems in Vietnam. The Sino-Soviet border clashes of ten years earlier had exposed the bitterness of relations between the two leading communist states and, if Washington could improve relations with both, it might hope to play a pivotal role between them. The policy required careful execution, since the White House did not want to seem to 'threaten' the Soviets by moving towards the Chinese too quickly. Thus, on 16 July 1971, Kissinger publicly stated that the moves towards rapprochement with China were not 'in any way directed against any other countries, and especially not against the Soviet Union'.[1] The aim was not to take sides in the Sino-Soviet rivalry, but to obtain the advantages of cooperation with both. Most obviously, Moscow and Beijing might be prepared to put pressure on Hanoi to agree to a Vietnam peace settlement. Also, once America left Vietnam, as it seemed certain it would in the aftermath of the Tet offensive, it was important that China and the USSR should be dissuaded from an adventurist policy in East Asia. The potential of the Opening to allow a retrenchment of American commitment, whilst avoiding a drift into neo-isolation, was emphasized by the implications for the country's military planning. Previously, US planners had to cope with a so-called 'two-and-a-half war strategy', based on the supposition that any global conflict was likely to involve a regional war and all-out confrontation with the USSR and China. However, if a rapprochement with China were successful, resources could be concentrated on fighting the USSR, in a 'one-and-a-half war strategy'. This meant a much-reduced burden on the Pentagon's military planners, who could now, for example, focus the US nuclear targeting on the USSR. It is rather ironic, in light of this, that the Reagan administration later characterized the 1970s as a 'decade of neglect' in US defence policy. At a time when Western economies were in the doldrums, with low growth and high inflation, the Opening also promised investment and trade opportunities.

For China's leaders, Mao Zedong and premier Zhou Enlai, it made strategic sense to move closer to Washington in order to counter Soviet power, which now seemed more threatening to them than the US. 'For Mao, the decision to make common cause with China's old enemy, the United States, against the new enemy . . . in Moscow was a repetition of the Communists' strategy during the Second World War, when they joined forces with Chiang Kai-shek's nationalists against Japan.'[2] China had become increasingly independent of Soviet influence since 1956 and came close to armed conflict with its mighty neighbour in 1969. The Americans, on the other hand, seemed increasingly troubled, both politically and economically. In East Asia, the most vital region for China, the US had acknowledged the Vietnam War to be unwinnable, whereas the Soviets were expanding their Pacific Fleet and moving more army divisions to the Chinese border, even hinting at nuclear war with China. Despite its own nuclear arsenal, its entry into the space race and attempts to win influence in the less developed world, China could not actually be considered a global power. In 1972, it had only a few hundred nuclear weapons, mostly based on aircraft, its navy was paltry, and its economy technologically backward. But with the US and USSR now more evenly balanced, especially in nuclear terms, China could play a significant role as the third power in a system of 'triangular diplomacy' and, with its huge army, it was of clear importance in East Asian politics.

The Defence Minister, Lin Biao, designated Mao's successor in April 1969, was the main opponent of a rapprochement with America. In common with other military figures, he doubted the wisdom of offending the USSR and it has even been argued that his 'overweening political ambitions in late 1970 stimulated' Mao and Zhou 'to become more serious about a rapprochement with the United States'.[3] But he was overruled in August 1970. In April 1971, his close ally, Chen Boda, was purged from the leadership. Lin then apparently planned to assassinate Mao but was himself killed in September 1971 in an air crash, trying to flee to Moscow after the failed coup attempt. The following month the advantages of the new approach were seen when Beijing achieved a long-standing aim, taking over China's UN seat. Since 1949, America had stood in the way of this step. China also won diplomatic recognition from an ever-growing number of states in the early 1970s. Yet the rapprochement with America never quite went the way Mao hoped. He wanted Beijing and Washington to move close together and confront the USSR, in direct contrast to the hopes of Nixon and Kissinger of reducing tensions with both the major communist powers while the US recovered from the Vietnam trauma. 'China was disconcerted by the continued links between the United States and Taiwan and by America's refusal to establish full diplomatic relations. America's efforts in developing US–Soviet cooperation . . . aroused even greater dissatisfaction.'[4]

Reactions to the 'Opening' in Moscow and Tokyo

The Sino-American rapprochement provoked understandable concern in the USSR, which in October 1969 had warned the US not to exploit the growing divide in Sino-Soviet relations. When the rapprochement became public, the Soviets foresaw many potential problems for themselves. First, it was clear that Mao now had even less need to seek an accommodation with Moscow: talks on border disputes began in late 1969 but ended without agreement three years later, and renewed border clashes occurred in December 1972. Meanwhile, the number of Soviet units on the Chinese border continued to grow, from twenty-seven divisions in 1969 to forty-five in 1973. This, in turn, highlighted a second problem. Whereas for the Americans the 'Opening to China' eased the challenge facing war planners, for the Soviets it raised the spectre of a two-front conflict, against NATO in Europe and China in Asia. Thus, whereas for the US the strain on their strategic forces was easing, further helped by a reduced involvement in Vietnam after 1969, the Soviets' strategic challenges were increasing. Moscow was also concerned about the situation of its regional allies, Mongolia and North Vietnam, which bordered on China. North Vietnam, which was encouraged by China during 1972 to make peace with America, drew closer to the USSR in the early 1970s. This was in marked contrast to the situation a decade before, when Mao had encouraged Hanoi in its attempts to overthrow South Vietnam and the Soviets had been cautious. Differences between Hanoi and Beijing did not become fully apparent, however, until 1974, when China occupied part of the Paracel Islands, ownership of which was disputed by the two countries.

At a global level, there was also concern in Moscow that China could influence America to abandon détente. The Soviets, who considered themselves much more important than China in the global balance, were dismayed that Nixon did not keep them informed of his China policy. In June 1973, Leonid Brezhnev frankly admitted to Nixon that what worried Moscow most was the prospect of Sino-American military links. But it was precisely such doubts and fears, as well as Brezhnev's desire for a SALT deal, which allowed America to open up relations with Beijing whilst pursuing an unprecedented improvement in negotiations with Moscow. However much they disliked the rapprochement, the Soviets could not afford to drive America and China closer together.

America's alliances in East Asia—with Japan, South Korea, Thailand, and the Philippines—all continued in the long term but, in the aftermath of the announcement of Nixon's visit, there were doubts in all these countries about America's intentions. The Japanese, still heavily reliant on the US for security and already concerned over events in Vietnam, were especially hurt because the July 1971 'Nixon Shock' came without any prior warning. Indeed, relations between America and its key East Asian ally became quite poor at this time. The White House was trying to reduce Japanese textile exports to America and August 1971 saw a second 'Nixon Shock' when the President announced several measures which were likely to harm Japanese trade. Significantly, Japan adopted 'a more active and independent foreign policy despite still sheltering under the American security umbrella' after 1971.[5] Japan was, however, the prime example of how an initial sense of concern over the changed power relationship in 1971 gave way to new opportunities. Despite historic rivalry, radically different ideologies, and territorial disputes over various island groups, China and Japan had strong reasons to cooperate. The Chinese saw Japan as vital in containing the USSR; the Japanese had a vested interest in stability in East Asia after Vietnam and wanted access to Chinese markets. The replacement of the pro-Taiwanese Prime Minister, Eisaku Sato, by Kakuei Tanaka paved the way for the normalization of diplomatic relations in September 1972, and Japan soon became China's biggest trading partner. In 1972, there was also a boost for Japanese–American relations with the restoration of Okinawa to Japanese sovereignty (having been a US military base since the war).

The Beijing Summit and the Position of Taiwan

The years 1969–71 saw cautious steps on both sides towards a rapprochement, with numerous setbacks along the way, not least because of the American incursion into Cambodia in 1970. Pakistan, Romania, and France acted as intermediaries at times and some direct Sino-American contacts took place via their embassies in Warsaw. The positive 'diplomatic signals' became clearer in April 1971 when America greatly liberalized trade with China and the Chinese welcomed an American table tennis team. A secret visit by Kissinger to Beijing, in July 1971, provided an opportunity for discussions with Zhou Enlai on the global balance, Vietnam, and the position of Taiwan. The last issue was difficult because of America's protection of the Nationalist regime on the island. But the announcement of Nixon's visit, followed by Taiwan's departure from the UN (neither Beijing nor Taipei would accept a 'two-China' presence there), showed that the issue could not forestall the rapprochement. The Nixon–Kissinger commitment to the Opening was further emphasized by their actions during the December 1971 Indo-Pakistani War (see Chapter 11, B): with Pakistan a conduit to China, the White House felt it essential to offer its support, whatever the rights and wrongs of the local situation.

Nixon's visit to China went ahead on schedule on 21–28 February 1972 and included a meeting with Mao, although most of the negotiating was conducted by Zhou. It was a well-managed media event, which boosted Nixon's hopes of re-election later in the year, especially when it was followed three months later by another summit in Moscow (see Chapter 12, B). Even if, to Chinese satisfaction, Nixon had visited Beijing before Moscow, the concrete results of the event were few. As one account pointed out, the summit may have represented 'a magnificent victory for the Chinese nation' on one level, but since the Americans were still fighting in Vietnam, 'it would be hard to describe it as a socialist foreign policy'.[6] There was no major US–Chinese agreement signed and, as mentioned, there was no change in America's alliance system in East

Asia—although it might be argued that the purposes of these alliances had changed in that they were no longer anti-Chinese. Washington even continued to recognize Taiwan as the official Chinese government. Indeed, the Shanghai Communiqué, issued at the end of the visit, was remarkable for its statement of differing Chinese and American positions on Taiwan, which Beijing still hoped to reabsorb. But Nixon underlined the real purpose of the visit when he told the Chinese, 'We have great differences today. What brings us together is that we have common interests which transcend those differences.'[7] In particular, both countries wished to contain Soviet power, a point the Shanghai Communiqué underlined by stating their mutual opposition to any state which sought hegemony in the Asia-Pacific region. There was no formal Sino-American alliance, then, but the two countries would pursue 'parallelism', avoiding clashes with each other while resisting any gains for Soviet communism.

B. The Moscow Summit and SALT I

The first Nixon–Brezhnev summit, announced in October 1971 and held in Moscow the following May, symbolized the great strides in détente between the spring of 1971 and summer 1973. En route to Moscow an exuberant Kissinger declared: 'This has to be one of the great diplomatic coups of all times.'[8] It witnessed various agreements, including attempts to avert future superpower crises and promises of scientific cooperation, and the centrepiece was the SALT agreement on nuclear arms control. SALT confirmed the superpowers' desire to restrict the impact and spread of nuclear weapons, to maintain a supposedly secure balance based around 'Mutual Assured Destruction' (MAD), and to keep defence costs under control. Arms agreements seemed an obvious area in which to demonstrate the relaxation of tension between them and build trust. Yet neither side rushed into a SALT treaty or a summit (see Chapter 9, A). The Soviets had been sceptical about strategic arms talks until 1968 and Nixon did not agree to open conversations on the subject until November 1969. By early 1970, Nixon, anxious to boost his domestic popularity and win Soviet support for a Vietnam settlement, wanted to hold a summit conference, but only in mid-1971, as Brezhnev tightened his grip on the Kremlin, were the Soviets won over, leading to the October announcement that such a meeting would take place. Various crises, from the Jordanian civil war of 1970 to the 1971 Indo-Pakistani War, could have wrecked the summit plans, as could a badly managed 'Opening to China' by the US. At the last moment, the US feared that the summit would be cancelled owing to renewed violence in Vietnam, where a major communist offensive on 30 March was followed by America's mining of Haiphong harbour. Some in the Kremlin were indeed offended by this latest example of US 'imperialism', but Brezhnev argued that détente was of great long-term importance, that (thanks to Vietnam) the Soviet Union was in a strong position to deal with Washington, and that the summit itself promised major gains—not only SALT, but also a recognition of the USSR's equality of status as a superpower by America, something of enormous significance to the USSR's self-esteem and its standing in the world. The conference also blunted China's sense of triumph after the Beijing summit.

The SALT Negotiations

The SALT treaty was the result of a number of developments, including the development of rough nuclear parity, popular enthusiasm for arms control, and concern, both in the Kremlin and the US Congress, over the costs of nuclear arms, which were becoming ever more technologically advanced. Two developments in particular in the 1960s had threatened to upset the nuclear balance: the anti-ballistic missile (ABM) and the multiple independent re-entry vehicle (MIRV). The first threatened to provoke a new spiral in the arms race, because if either side developed an effective ABM it might also be tempted to launch a 'first strike' on its opponent; and the other side was likely to counter such a threat by building additional offensive missiles to overcome the ABMs. In March 1969, Nixon renamed the ABM shield 'Safeguard' and planned to use it to protect offensive missile sites in the American mid-West but it was only approved by Congress in August by one vote. These events gave both sides reason to seek an ABM treaty. The USSR wished to pre-empt US advances in the field, whilst the Nixon administration recognized that a treaty might be preferable to defeat at the hands of Congress.

The second development, MIRV, was a means of improving US strike capacity without increasing the number of inter-continental ballistic missiles (ICBMs) or submarine-launched ballistic missiles (SLBMs). The number of ICBMs and SLBMs was actually frozen by the Johnson administration in 1968, at 1,054 and 656 missiles respectively, but the purpose of this was to concentrate on improving such weapons rather than halting the arms race. MIRV testing had been announced in December 1967. Independently targetable warheads which could hit separate targets many miles apart allowed a marked increase in nuclear warheads but were cheaper than building new missiles. The Soviets—who concentrated in the 1960s on building ever-larger, but less advanced missiles, like the giant SS-9—were well behind in this area and finally agreed to SALT negotiations in June 1968. The invasion of Czechoslovakia in August prevented talks beginning but they remained a popular idea in the US State Department. The Nixon administration was determined not to rush into détente but it did soon accept the aim of 'sufficiency' in nuclear arms. As one arms control expert explained it: the 'nation only needed to maintain a force capable of inflicting a destructive level of damage on the USSR'.[9] It was hard to define precisely, yet made arms talks easier because it implied that the US need not match the Soviets in all categories of nuclear weapon. However, the administration's decision to proceed with the testing and, in 1970, deployment of MIRVs was arguably a fatal error, for once the US successfully tested such a system the Soviets were bound to wish to do the same, so as not to risk falling behind in the arms race in future. This made it virtually impossible to negotiate a limit on MIRVs. MIRV was 'a less convincing bargaining chip than the Safeguard ABM . . . because neither side [was] serious about limiting MIRVs' once one side had decided to develop them.[10] In that sense, SALT I was dead in the water before it was actually launched.

The SALT talks took place over several sessions from November 1969, oscillating between Helsinki and Vienna. The challenges were enormous. Each side's nuclear arsenal had a different make-up, with the US possessing a 'triad' of land-, sea-, and aircraft-based systems, whilst the Soviets mainly had land-based weapons, though their submarine capacity was growing. It was difficult to decide what actually represented 'equality' between them and the possibility of one side stealing a march was always present, even without MIRVs. This problem was compounded by the existence of British and French nuclear arsenals on the Western side and the existence of American 'forward-based systems' (FBS) in Europe, which could strike Soviet territory, but which the Americans were unwilling to include in strategic talks because of their limited range. The two sides also set out with opposite aims: the Soviets were keen to achieve an ABM treaty, and to offset US technological advances by preserving their own ability to expand their ICBM arsenal; the US was anxious to preserve its technological lead while restricting the growth of Soviet ICBM numbers. Soviet opposition to onsite verification of an arms deal was not, however, the barrier to agreement it had been in the past, because the Central Intelligence Agency (CIA) believed it possessed other means, such as satellite surveillance, to police any agreement. Some confusion was caused on the US side by the existence of an official negotiating team, from the Arms Control and Disarmament Agency, headed by Gerard Smith, and an unofficial, so-called 'backchannel', set up in 1969 between Kissinger, and Soviet ambassador, Anatoly Dobrynin. The 'back-channel' allowed the White House to control the tempo of the talks and brought the breakthrough agreement of May 1971, which finally excluded FBS from the talks and confirmed that there would be a freeze on ICBM—steps which pleased the US—but which also promised the USSR an ABM deal. This skeleton arrangement still left a lot of details undecided and it gravely upset Smith that Kissinger had struck a deal behind the back of the official negotiators: 'The delegation's trust in Washington authorities was never restored.'[11] Nonetheless, once the Moscow summit was announced the pace of negotiation increased. The April 1972 'Tundra Talks' in Lapland, which effectively finalized the ABM treaty, were followed by a visit from Kissinger to Moscow, where a high ceiling on Soviet SLBM numbers was agreed. A few final points were hammered out at the summit itself, at the cost of some ambiguity (not least over what constituted a 'heavy' missile, one of the categories of weapon SALT sought to control).

The Moscow Summit and its Limitations

The Moscow conference of 22–26 May 1972 proved to be one of the most successful East–West summits of the Cold War, partly because it was carefully stage-managed and well prepared in advance. Yet, given the last-minute threat posed by the communists' spring offensive in Vietnam, it has been said that, 'The importance of the conference . . . lay in the fact that it was held at all.'[12] For this confirmed that the new relationship with Washington was more important to Brezhnev than solidarity with his fellow Marxist-Leninists in Hanoi. Ten documents were signed, but they had largely been negotiated beforehand. Apart from SALT (see Box 12.1), these included greater cooperation on health and the environment, a joint Apollo-Soyuz space mission (which went ahead in mid-July 1975), improvements in the 'hot-line', an agreement to avoid accidents at sea, and steps to reduce the risk of accidental nuclear war. A Joint Commercial Commission was established which negotiated a trade deal between the two countries five months later, involving a settlement of war debts, a US commitment to give the Soviets 'most favoured nation' status (that is, equal to that of other major trading partners), and the opening of trade offices in each other's capital. For the Soviets, another important document was the 'Basic Principles Agreement' (based on an October 1971 arrangement between Brezhnev and France's Georges Pompidou), which laid down twelve principles for the conduct of superpower relations. These included the acceptance of peaceful coexistence and mutual equality, restraint during crises, avoiding confrontation, and refraining from the use of force.

Moscow was intended to be the first of a series of summits and further Nixon–Brezhnev meetings did occur, in America from 16 to 24 June 1973 (when the venue moved between Washington, Camp David, and San Clemente, California) and again in Moscow from 27 June to 3 July 1974. The 1973 conference saw more minor agreements, on cultural exchanges, agriculture, and transport, some discussion of a SALT II treaty and, most importantly, an Agreement on the Prevention of Nuclear War. The last developed the Basic Principles Agreement and was wanted most by the Soviets, who had long wanted the US, with its nuclear superiority, to promise it would not be the first side to use nuclear weapons in war. The Agreement was much diluted by the Americans, however, and promised no more than that the superpowers would consult together if nuclear war ever threatened to involve one of them. By June 1973, the Nixon administration was already overshadowed by the Watergate scandal, and this was even more the case with the 1974 summit which did, however, see an important ABM deal, cutting the number of missiles on each side to 100.

Moscow and the SALT treaty were celebrated by both sides in 1972, understandably so. Brezhnev used them to solidify his control of the Kremlin, removing opponents from the Politburo in 1973. He pointed to the Basic Principles Agreement as evidence that the US both accepted the USSR as an equal and was ready to embrace the long-standing Soviet concept of peaceful coexistence. Nixon and Kissinger, in an election year, were bound to hail Moscow as qualitatively different from previous summits—with concrete agreements, not just an improvement in the international atmosphere—and to praise SALT as a breakthrough in East–West relations. Alongside the Beijing summit, and signs of a Vietnam settlement, the Moscow summit made 1972 seem a world away from 1968, the previous election year. However, the positive side of the meeting was oversold, helping to breed dissatisfaction in future. Both sides were still determined to maintain strong defences and to treat the other as an ideological enemy. The Soviets still supported 'national liberation' movements in the less developed world and maintained the Brezhnev Doctrine; America had no intention of abandoning its NATO allies or its new relationship with China, and flaws were soon clear in some of the main agreements. However important the Basic Principles were to Brezhnev, the Americans never saw them as more than a broad 'code of conduct', one against which Soviet as well as US behaviour could be measured. It was unclear what the Principles would mean in practice and little thought was given to their enforcement. As to the commercial agreement, it did lead to a major trade expansion in 1972–3, alongside large US credits to the USSR. But this was soured in American eyes by the so-called 'Great Grain Robbery' when the Soviets, faced by a harvest failure, were sold large amounts of grain, pushing up US prices and costing American taxpayers large subsidies.

The most significant flaws, however, lay in SALT I, the greatest symbol of US–Soviet trust and equality. Criticism must be tempered by the fact that SALT was an interim measure, designed to lead to a SALT II deal within five years. Certainly, the ABM treaty was a precise arrangement, strictly limiting a whole category of weapons. But in a sense the ABM treaty was of limited importance because the technical problems and financial costs made ABMs difficult to build anyway. The Soviets never believed they could outmatch the US here and the Nixon administration, aware of Congressional and public opposition, seems to have used Soviet fears of 'Safeguard' simply as a 'bargaining chip' to get a better deal on offensive missiles. Whilst confirming, or paying lip-service, to MAD, the offensive missile agreement itself had many shortcomings. It controlled missile numbers, but the 'ceilings' were set at a high level and there was no control on the number of MIRVs, so that the quantity of warheads continued to increase. In 1972, the US still had a marked advantage in warhead numbers: the 1,054 American ICBMs actually had 1,474 warheads on them thanks to MIRVing, and there were over 3,000 warheads on the 656 SLBMs. In contrast, the Soviets, without MIRVs and with only about 1,500 ICBMs and 500 SLBMs, were still well below the SALT ceilings. The Soviets could eventually use the opportunity to expand warhead numbers which SALT I presented once they obtained MIRV technology. One especially critical account argued that there 'were no Soviet concessions during the Moscow summit . . . The only major concessions were made by Henry Kissinger.' It pointed out that the decision to allow the USSR more SLBMs was particularly puzzling. The US had long held superiority in SLBM numbers, so why had they not simply been frozen?[13] Another account felt that the Soviets could hardly have refused a deal because Kissinger 'made the terms palatable to the Soviets by permitting them to fulfil their planned programmes'—including the expansion of SLBM numbers.[14] It was certainly possible to defend the summit if one took a long-term perspective. 'For all the flaws . . . Nixon had achieved a symbolic breakthrough, namely that the two sides could set limits on their destructive capability.'[15] And the flaws could be dealt with in subsequent negotiations. However, many Congressional critics in the US soon decided there was cause for concern, because the Soviets *were* allowed to deploy more offensive missiles than America under the Treaty, they had much larger missiles, and they began to MIRV them in 1975 (after successfully testing a MIRV two years beforehand—much earlier than the US expected).

C. The Vietnam Settlement, 1972–3

Vietnam in Early 1972

Despite the gloom surrounding its policy in Vietnam in late 1971, the situation from America's viewpoint was not hopeless. US troop levels were about to fall below 100,000. This arguably weakened America's hand in negotiations, but anti-war protests at home had subsided. The incursion into Laos showed the South Vietnamese army probably could not launch successful offensive operations; but, when put on the defensive, they might fare better, especially since the Americans still provided large-scale air support. The 'Nixon Doctrine' reassured President Thieu that, while his forces must now bear the brunt of ground fighting, the US would not abandon its allies and Nixon himself had several times demonstrated his readiness to match tough rhetoric with strong action. Furthermore, American relations with both the USSR and China were improving, raising the possibility that those countries might press Hanoi to make peace. In fact, despite détente, the USSR seems to have done little to help the Americans escape from the Vietnam imbroglio. 'The Soviet Union was a reluctant player in the diplomatic settlement in Vietnam . . . despite

BOX 12.1

The SALT I Agreements, May 1972: main points

Two arms control agreement were signed.

1. *The Anti-Ballistic Missile (ABM) Treaty*:
   - restricted the US and USSR to two ABM missile fields each, one to protect their capital, one to protect an ICBM field;
   - placed a limit of one hundred on the number of missiles in each of the fields (that is, two hundred missiles in total for each superpower);
   - banned certain new ABM developments, including multiple warheads and space-based systems; limited the location of early-warning systems; was to be monitored by an Oversight Commission;
   - was of indefinite duration, but either side could withdraw after six months' notice.
2. *The 'Interim Agreement on Offensive Missiles'*:
   - subjected strategic offensive weapon launchers to the following, unequal 'ceilings':
     Intercontinental Ballistic Missiles (land-based): 1,054 for the US and 1,618 for the USSR;
     Submarine-launched Ballistic Missiles: 656 for the US and 740 for the USSR;
     Strategic bombers: 455 for the US and 140 for the USSR;
   - had a duration of five years, during which time a SALT II agreement was to be negotiated.

the efforts of the Nixon administration and its policy of linkage', the logic of which was that Moscow should seek to reduce conflicts in the less developed world in return for cooperation with Washington.[16] The Chinese were rather more helpful, however. In November 1971, during a meeting in Beijing, Mao Zedong told North Vietnam's Prime Minister, Pham Van Dong, that compromise was now the best course. The Chinese did not necessarily want Thieu to survive in the long term but, arguably, if the North could negotiate America's military withdrawal from Vietnam, Thieu's days would be numbered anyway; there was no need for Hanoi to continue pressing for a communist-influenced coalition government in South Vietnam as the price of peace with America. 'He was arguing for Nixon', one North Vietnamese diplomat complained. 'Mao was telling us to maintain the status quo.'[17]

In January 1972, Nixon published the fact that Kissinger had held twelve rounds of secret peace talks with North Vietnamese representatives and that the US position had been more conciliatory than that stated in public. Coming at the start of an election year, after Congressmen had attacked his failure to negotiate realistically, this was an astute move which caught Hanoi by surprise. The Beijing summit in February was another success for Nixon and an unwelcome event for North Vietnam, and of course the Soviets too were preparing a meeting with Nixon. Even if the Soviets did not put pressure on the North to make a settlement of the war, the Hanoi politburo may have feared that both its major patrons were now ready to give relations with America a higher priority than Vietnamese interests. Thus, it has been speculated, it was to try to undermine the budding US–Chinese and US–Soviet links, 'that the politburo decided finally on the spring offensive' of 1972.[18] Then again, it was predictable for other reasons that North Vietnam would launch a major attack on the South during 1972. The 'Tet' offensive of early 1968 had shown the rewards that such an attack could bring during an American election year, sapping morale and destroying the President's re-election bid, even if communist losses were formidable. Indeed, it was because the Viet Cong had lost so many fighters in 1968 that the North Vietnamese army were to shoulder most of the 1972 operations. The North perhaps hoped that Nixon would wish to settle the war before the election if possible and that military success would ensure that this was done on communist terms. 'At its maximum, the leadership hoped, the offensive might actually cause the collapse of the Saigon government; at the very least it promised a victory . . . which would undermine the policy of Vietnamization.'[19] The downside was that North Vietnamese forces would be fighting a more conventional war to which the Americans were more suited.

The Spring Offensive

The spring offensive began on 30 March, being designed in part to upset the forthcoming Moscow summit. Despite the widespread expectation of an offensive, its timing and execution came as a surprise to Saigon and Washington. Its timing was surprising because, just before the first attacks, Hanoi had been discussing another round of peace talks with the Americans. Its execution was a surprise because the North Vietnamese Defence Minister, General Vo Nguyen Giap, not only launched his primary assault across the narrow, well-defended Demilitarized Zone between the North and South, but also he used three-quarters of all the North's available forces to launch a series of conventional attacks, led by artillery bombardments and tanks, on Thieu's million-strong army. Not only were whole South Vietnamese divisions shattered in a four-pronged North Vietnamese attack, but on 1 May the communists also seized control of a major city, Quang Tri, and they threatened to capture the ancient royal capital of Hué. If it fell, it would prove a dire psychological blow to Saigon; even if it did not, there was always the danger that the National Liberation Front would set up a provisional government in Quang Tri.

The North's offensive threw the White House into panic for a time. 'Nixon was impaled on the horns of a dilemma. If he did not support the South Vietnamese with heavy bombing . . . a US ally might well be defeated. But if he did escalate the war . . . he would face the probable cancellation of the Moscow summit by the Soviets.'[20] Hanoi was mistaken, however, if it believed that Nixon wanted peace at any price before the election. In fact, in line with his previous penchant for toughness, he quickly decided to use all available US aircraft to blunt Giap's assault, then agreed to use B-52s to bomb targets in North Vietnam. It was the first time since 1968 that American heavy bombers had attacked the North and, from 15 April, the targets included the major cities of Hanoi and Haiphong. In the past, such attacks would have drawn a harsh response from Beijing and Moscow but on this occasion, in another worrying sign for Hanoi, there were few complaints. Although Soviet vessels were struck by US bombs in Haiphong harbour, plans for the Moscow summit continued. A secret meeting between Kissinger and North Vietnam's Le Duc Tho on 1 May confirmed that the North still wanted Thieu's removal as the price of peace, but this diplomatic impasse simply made the Americans more determined to deny Giap a military breakthrough. On 8 May, Nixon announced a blockade of North Vietnam, with the mining of Haiphong and other harbours. This was a dramatic step but it did not stop the Moscow summit going ahead. By late May, Giap had committed all his reserves to the spring offensive but the South Vietnamese held on to Hué and, in June, were able to counter-attack, retaking Quang Tri. The offensive had failed in its main purposes: the South Vietnamese army survived; the Moscow and Beijing summits made it likely Nixon would be re-elected even if there were no peace in Vietnam; and the Soviets, far from abandoning détente, now sent President Nikolai Podgorny to Hanoi with the latest American peace offer.

The Peace Accords

Despite Giap's failure, North Vietnam was hardly in a weak position when Le Duc Tho and Kissinger revived their peace talks in mid-July 1972. The USSR and China might favour compromise, but they were not going to break with Hanoi over it; the North Vietnamese army and Viet Cong still controlled large tracts of South Vietnam; despite the US blockade, war supplies continued to reach the North; and Nixon was still committed to withdrawal. In August, all US army combat missions in Vietnam ceased and only 30,000 American troops remained, none of them draftees. Furthermore, the Americans continued to offer concessions in the Paris talks. Most important, Kissinger had implicitly told the Soviets that, if a 'ceasefire in place' could be agreed the US would not demand the subsequent withdrawal of North Vietnamese units from the South. All that America wanted was that Thieu should remain in power after the ceasefire, to take part in a political settlement negotiated by the various South Vietnamese political groups. By late September, rather than insisting on a coalition government which excluded Thieu, the North was prepared to accept that his regime might continue for a time. In a series of meetings between 8 and 11 October, the outline of a peace settlement was hammered out, which Hanoi hoped could become a signed accord by the end of the month. They now wanted an agreement before Nixon's hand was strengthened by a successful re-election.

The proposed settlement gave something to both sides. The Americans would have their prisoners of war returned (an essential point for domestic opinion) and the Thieu regime would survive. The North Vietnamese won a 'ceasefire in place', a promise that all US forces would withdraw, and an imprecise political arrangement that might, through a process of reconciliation and elections, reunite Vietnam. But by late October the settlement was already breaking down, largely thanks to President Thieu. Despite the vital importance of any settlement to South Vietnam, he had been kept only partially informed of the US–North Vietnamese contacts and was furious about the draft agreement when Kissinger brought it to Saigon on 19 October. He particularly disliked the idea that, under a ceasefire in place, the North Vietnamese could hold on to areas they occupied in South Vietnam, and he was unimpressed by Kissinger's reassurance that the South had a 'fighting chance' of survival once the Americans left. Despite Kissinger's celebrated remark on 26 October, that 'we believe that peace is at hand', hope of signing the accords by the end of the month evaporated.[21] As expected, Nixon won a landslide re-election on 7 November. He then tried to win Thieu over to a settlement, partly through diplomatic pressure and partly by a massive supply of arms to South Vietnam, so as to leave it in the best military position after a ceasefire. He also secretly undertook to restart US aid to Saigon if Hanoi breached the ceasefire on a large scale. But this strengthening of Thieu's armed forces simply led the North to ask for changes in the draft accords and by the middle of December negotiations had stalled.

The stall in the Paris negotiations was followed by the so-called 'Christmas Bombing' of Hanoi, Haiphong, and other targets in North Vietnam, one of the most controversial of all Nixon's actions. 'It was the most devastating bombing campaign of the entire war.'[22] Having been told 'peace was at hand', public opinion was shocked by the round-the-clock raids of B-52s near heavily populated areas (although, thanks to the North's civil defence preparations, actual casualties were limited to a few thousand). The raids did bring Hanoi back to the negotiating table. Le Duc Tho and Kissinger met again on 8 January 1973 and initialled a peace agreement on the 23rd. Yet the 'bombing did not produce a settlement markedly different . . . from the October agreement', again raising the question of why the Christmas Bombing was necessary.[23] Several factors seem to have influenced Nixon. One, certainly, was a desire to resolve the Vietnam War before his second term began and while an acceptable agreement seemed possible. Bellicose action also fitted in with his established behaviour and showed that, even at the end of its disastrous Vietnam involvement, America was capable of firm action. Significantly, such bellicosity also helped reassure Thieu of American resolve and gave credibility to Nixon's promises that Washington would not tolerate a major communist breach of any settlement. 'The bombs . . . were not just aimed at targets a few thousand feet away; their real target in a sense was Saigon.'[24] But also, the President knew that he might not remain in such a strong position for long. His landslide re-election was a remarkable achievement. But, at the same time, a new Congress had been elected which was ill-disposed towards him and was expected to introduce a War Powers Act to limit the President's independence in foreign affairs. Ideally, Nixon needed to resolve the Vietnam War before Congress met in late January.

The ceasefire-in-place in Vietnam came into force on 27 January, preceded by a 'land-grabbing' exercise by Hanoi and Saigon. Within sixty days of that, all American forces were to be withdrawn and all prisoners-of-war were to be released. The conditions for US withdrawal were clear enough, but many other parts of the accords were flawed. Rumours persisted for decades afterwards that Hanoi held more prisoners than the 591 Americans actually freed, and this soured relations between the two countries. Neither North Vietnam nor America was supposed to resupply either side in the South with troops or weapons, but there was a provision for 'replacement' of materials which allowed for breaches in the conditions. An international commission, with representatives from the Eastern and Western blocs, was supposed to police the ceasefire but was never effective. As to the process of 'national reconciliation' which was supposed to take place in the South, it was a dead letter. And though the accords talked of elections being held, they did not set a date. Also, the ceasefire only applied to Vietnam, not to Cambodia or Laos, where the civil wars continued.

The Nixon administration defended the Paris accords as an honourable settlement. 'I believed . . . that the agreement could have worked', insisted Kissinger, 'it reflected a true equilibrium of the forces on the ground', and he blamed subsequent unforeseen developments for its collapse.[25] South Vietnam had not fallen to communism and, with American supplies and secret promises of support if the settlement broke down, Thieu might yet survive for many years. Some take the view that, 'Almost certainly, no better terms could have been secured.'[26] But critics pointed to the flaws in the settlement, the failure to achieve a political solution in South Vietnam, and the weakness of Thieu's regime, given the North Vietnamese army's continuing presence in the South. Nixon, it was argued, had simply won a 'decent interval' between US withdrawal and Thieu's inevitable fall. 'As it turned out, the main thing Nixon and Kissinger achieved was a "decent interval" . . . between America's withdrawal and the defeat of the government it had committed itself to defend.'[27] Except that, as it turned out in retrospect, the 'interval' was a rather indecent two years. America in January 1973 might be at peace but in Vietnam neither side respected the ceasefire, and in Cambodia the US air force continued to aid the Lon Nol regime until mid-August, when Congress insisted such assistance must end. Attempts to improve relations with Hanoi by offering billions of dollars in 'reconstruction aid' backfired at home, where it was condemned as a 'reparations' payment. Reparations, of course, are usually paid by defeated powers. Yet, even so, at the time the settlement seemed to crown eighteen months of remarkable achievement by the Nixon–Kissinger duo (see Box 12.2), building on the China 'Opening' and the Moscow summit, and reversing the sense of helplessness in foreign affairs that had beset America only four years before.

BOX 12.2

Biographies: Richard Nixon (1913–94) and Henry Kissinger (b. 1923)

The two men who dominated US foreign policy-making between 1969 and 1974 came from very different backgrounds. Nixon was born into a poor, pioneering, Quaker family in California. Educated as a lawyer, after wartime naval service he stood successfully for Congress in 1946. By 1950, when he entered the Senate, he had made his name as a strong anti-communist, notably in the Alger Hiss spy case. Nixon's anti-communism helped him become Eisenhower's running mate in the 1952 election, followed by eight years as Vice-President. His underhand tactics, and accusations that he had misappropriated funds in one election, earned him the nickname 'Tricky Dicky', and in 1960 he narrowly lost the presidential race to John Kennedy. Another setback in 1962, when he failed to become Governor of California, seemed to spell the end of his political career. However, his ambition and persistence, linked to upheaval brought by Vietnam, helped him re-emerge as the successful Republican candidate in the 1968 election.

In contrast, Kissinger was born into a middle-class, Jewish family in Germany and only came to America as a teenager in 1938, fleeing Nazi oppression. He became a naturalized American in 1943. Wartime service in Army Intelligence widened his ambitions and gave him a taste of responsibility. In 1947, when he returned to the US, he enrolled at Harvard and specialized in international relations. Becoming an academic, he won a name for himself writing *Nuclear Weapons and Foreign Policy* and, as Director of the Harvard International Seminar, made many political contacts. He worked for a time in both the Kennedy and Johnson administrations, but was himself a Republican. On the liberal wing of the party, Kissinger acted as foreign policy adviser to Nelson Rockefeller, a candidate for Republican presidential nominee in both the 1964 and 1968 presidential races.

Kissinger was asked to become Nixon's National Security Adviser, despite criticizing the latter during the 1968 election. On the surface, the right-wing professional politician and liberal-leaning immigrant academic looked an unlikely team. But Nixon was tempted by the idea of having a respected intellectual on his White House staff, while Kissinger relished the opportunity to play a leading policy role. They never became close friends but did establish a fruitful working relationship, underpinned by shared outlooks on such problems as China and Vietnam. Both had risen from unpromising backgrounds, neither was a traditional 'establishment' figure, and both had a fascination with the study of history. They were also firmly anti-communist, determined to be 'tough' abroad, and ready to use secret diplomacy, concentrated in the White House, to achieve their aims. During Nixon's first administration, the Secretary of State, William Rogers, had only a limited policy-making role. Inevitably, as President, it was Nixon who long had the upper hand in the relationship with Kissinger; and who also pressed first for some of their more innovative policies, not least the 'Opening to China'. It was Kissinger, however, who provided an intellectual underpinning for 'Nixingerism'. Kissinger controlled much of the advice the President received on foreign policy, and carried out many diplomatic initiatives personally, not least the Vietnam peace talks.

In September 1973, Kissinger combined the position of National Security Adviser with that of Secretary of State, a commanding position, further reinforced by Nixon's embroilment in the Watergate scandal, which brought the presidency to an end in August 1974. Kissinger continued in his dual-post under Gerald Ford—himself no expert on foreign policy—until November 1975, when he was replaced as National Security Adviser by a close ally, his former deputy, Brent Scowcroft. But during the 1976 presidential election it was evident that Kissinger's public reputation had fallen since its peak in 1973. The breakdown of the Vietnam peace settlement and disappointment with détente harmed the administration and the Democratic candidate, Jimmy Carter, pressed an idealistic, human rights-based foreign policy, very different to the amoral *realpolitik* of 'Nixingerism'. Over the following decades, Kissinger was able to play an occasional front role in policy-making, for example as head of a Commission on policy towards Latin America in 1983–4. But Nixon was fatally tainted by Watergate.

Visit the online resources that accompany this book to test your understanding and take your learning further: www.oup.com/he/young-kent3e

NOTES

1. Quoted in Marvin Kalb and Bernard Kalb, *Kissinger* (Hutchinson, London, 1974), 256.
2. Philip Short, *The Dragon and the Bear: Inside China and Russia Today* (Hodder & Stoughton, London, 1982), 480.
3. Dick Wilson, *Chou: The Story of Zhou Enlai* (Hutchinson, London, 1984), 272.
4. Roy Medvedev, *China and the Superpowers* (Blackwell, Oxford, 1986), 105.
5. Michael Yahuda, *The International Politics of the Asia-Pacific* (Routledge, London, 1996), 241.
6. John Gittings, 'The Statesman', in Dick Wilson (ed.), *Mao Tse-tung in the Scales of History* (Cambridge University Press, Cambridge, 1978), 264.
7. Quoted in Richard Nixon, *RN: The Memoirs of Richard Nixon* (Sidgwick & Jackson, London, 1978), 565.
8. Quoted in ibid., 609.
9. Gerard Smith, *Double Talk* (University Press of America, Lanham, 1980), 23–4.
10. John Newhouse, *Cold Dawn: The Story of SALT* (Pergamon-Brassey's International Defense Publishers, London, 1989), 30–1.
11. Gerard Smith, *Double Talk* (University Press of America, Lanham, 1980), 235.
12. John Newhouse, *Cold Dawn: The Story of SALT* (Pergamon-Brassey's International Defense Publishers, London, 1989), 272.
13. Seymour Hersh, *The Price of Power* (Summit, New York, 1983), 535.
14. Raymond Garthoff, *Détente and Confrontation* (Brookings Institution, Washington, 1985), 163.
15. Stephen Ambrose, *Nixon, II: The Triumph of a Politician* (Simon & Schuster, London, 1989), 548.
16. Ilya Gaiduk, *The Soviet Union and the Vietnam War* (I. R. Dee, Chicago, 1996), 222.
17. Quoted in Seymour Hersh, *The Price of Power* (Summit, New York, 1983), 442.
18. Jeffrey Kimball, *Nixon's Vietnam War* (University Press of Kansas, Lawrence, 1998), 284.
19. Marilyn Young, *The Vietnam Wars* (HarperCollins, New York, 1991), 269.
20. Jonathan Aitken, *Nixon: A Life* (Weidenfeld & Nicolson, Washington, 1993), 436.
21. Henry Kissinger, *The White House Years* (Weidenfeld & Nicolson, London, 1979), 1399.
22. Gary Hess, *Vietnam and the United States* (Twayne's Publishers, Boston, 1990), 133.
23. George Herring, *America's Longest War* (McGraw-Hill, New York, 1986), 255.
24. Walter Isaacson, *Kissinger* (Faber & Faber, New York, 1992), 470.
25. Henry Kissinger, *The White House Years* (Weidenfeld & Nicolson, London, 1979), 1470.
26. William Bundy, *A Tangled Web* (Hill & Wang, New York, 1998), 368.
27. Walter Isaacson, *Kissinger* (Faber & Faber, New York, 1992), 485.

13

'Stagflation' and the Trials of Détente, 1973–6

Chapter contents

A. The October 1973 Middle East War

Sadat and the Origins of the War

In the aftermath of Israel's victories in the 1967 Six Day War, a situation of 'no peace, no war' prevailed in the Middle East. Israel—having captured control of the Sinai Peninsula, the West Bank of the Jordan, and the Golan Heights—was in a strategically strong position with regard to its Arab neighbours, especially when backed by American military supplies and diplomatic support. Attempts in 1970–1 by the UN envoy, Gunnar Jarring, and the American Secretary of State, William Rogers, to make progress on a peace settlement came to nothing. The Israelis saw little reason to negotiate away their recent gains, especially when the Arabs refused to recognize Israel's right even to exist. The Arabs, in a position of weakness, could wield little influence over the Israelis or the superpowers. In September 1970, the sudden death of Nasser brought another military figure, Anwar Sadat, to power in Egypt, the most populous and powerful Arab state. His early forays in the international arena suggested confusion rather than any intelligent plan to regain the lost territories. Keen to maintain Egyptian leadership of the Arabs and consolidate his domestic support, he publicly threatened to make both 1971 and 1972 a 'year of decisions' in the Middle East, but failed to force a showdown with Israel. In May 1971, he signed a fifteen-year Friendship Treaty with the USSR, which already had over 12,000 men in Egypt (some of them operating surface-to-air missile sites and piloting war planes), and which now increased its military supplies. But at the same time, he purged a pro-Soviet group in the Cairo government and the following year, on 23 July 1972, expelled almost all the Soviet advisers, leaving only those manning the missile sites. For three months afterwards, the Soviets suspended arms supplies to Egypt. Sadat also secretly opened contacts with the White House in 1972 but the Americans, bemused by his erratic policy and eager to maintain the Israeli-dominated status quo, did not exploit his desire to talk.

It eventually became clear that Sadat's behaviour had more logic to it than it appeared. Indeed, he was capable of outmanoeuvring both superpowers. Basically, he was determined to strike an independent course. He believed the Soviets to be cautious, self-seeking allies who would not give Egypt the military help they needed to overcome the defeat of 1967. They armed Egypt, but treated it as a pawn in superpower diplomacy and they would not willingly back a military reconquest of Sinai. Their influence over Egyptian politics and the military had to be cut back, hence the expulsions of July 1972. 'As a result of the 1967 war the balance at local level had tilted strongly in favour of the Israelis, so the only option to Egypt was to lift the conflict onto the higher, international level, where the balance was more equal.'[1] Sadat's attempts to deal with the Americans reflected his appreciation that only they could induce the Israelis to make concessions. But it was increasingly clear that he must do something dramatic to force the superpowers—and world opinion—to end the diplomatic stalemate in the Middle East. He was particularly offended by the Soviets' pursuit of détente with the Americans in 1971–2 without consulting Egypt or their other allies. Significantly, the Middle East was barely mentioned at Nixon and Brezhnev's Moscow summit. In 1972, Sadat was determined to force the Middle East onto the international agenda by launching an attack, in league with Syria's Hafez al-Assad, on Israel. 'I began to prepare for the battle,' he later wrote, 'although I knew that the entire world . . . had interpreted my expulsion of the Soviet military experts as an indication that I wasn't going to fight.'[2] In doing so, he proved the point, seen often before in the Cold War, that whilst the East–West struggle might be the dominant factor in world affairs, there were limits to the influence of the superpowers. America and the Soviet Union could sometimes be put at the mercy of their allies and clients, who dragged them into unwanted confrontation. In October 1973, the Egyptian–Syrian attack provoked the most serious US–Soviet tension since the Cuban Missile Crisis and called détente into question.

Regional Conflict and Superpower Confrontation

The Middle East War began on 6 October with an Egyptian advance over the Suez Canal. As one Israeli leader later admitted, a 5 October meeting of the General Staff was told that 'the probability of war breaking out was regarded as "the lowest of the low"'.[3] Until the last moment, the Israeli and US intelligence services had not expected such an attack, and for good reason. Not only had Sadat mobilized for war twice before without result, but it was obvious that, given Israel's military superiority, Egypt and Syria must lose any conflict. What the Israelis and Americans failed to consider was that Sadat and Assad would launch a war they knew they would almost certainly lose. Victory was not the point of their action. The aim, rather, was to force Israel and the world to see that there must be negotiations about the lost territories. The Americans complained that the Soviets should have warned them of the attack, in the spirit of the Basic Principles. But the USSR itself was only told by the Syrians of the forthcoming campaign a few days before. True, the Soviets had, for months, been building up the Egyptian armed forces but Moscow had also denied the Egyptians the latest MIG-23s, encouraged the Arabs to seek peace, and had warned the Americans repeatedly that a dangerous situation was brewing in the region. Immediately before the Arab attack the Soviets very publicly evacuated their civilians from Egypt and Syria, but again the US and Israeli intelligence services failed to draw the correct conclusion. The Soviets could hardly give a categorical warning to America without seeming to betray their Arab allies and losing future influence with them. Israel only finally guessed what was happening a few hours before the attack and was further hampered in its response by the fact it was the Jewish festival of Yom Kippur, a national holiday.

The Arabs initially advanced on both fronts, expunging some of the memory of their dismal 1967 performance. 'The operation had been well planned, and was executed by the Arab soldiers with tenacity, courage and skill.'[4] In contrast to the Six Day War, not only did Egypt and Syria have the element of surprise, but they also neutralized the Israeli air force with surface-to-air missiles. The Arabs also discovered, at this time, the potency of oil supplies as a weapon against America and the West (see Chapter 13, B). Washington was initially too sanguine about an Israeli victory, starting an airlift of supplies on 9 October but at first using only aircraft of the Israeli airline, El Al. A full-scale US airlift only began on 13 October, three days after the Soviets had started a similar programme. But even the Soviets seem to have had little faith in Arab aims and, to Sadat's annoyance, did their utmost to urge a ceasefire in the first week. In the second week of the war, the tide moved in Israel's favour and on 15–16 October, a counteroffensive carried them back over the central part of the Suez Canal. They then struck south, threatening to surround the Egyptian Third Army, which was still on the Sinai side. Meanwhile in Syria, the Israelis reversed their initial retreats in the Golan Heights and advanced towards Damascus. On 16–19 October, the Soviet Premier, Andrei Kosygin, visited Cairo and persuaded Sadat to agree to a ceasefire, a move followed by US–Soviet attempts to secure such a step, with the new American Secretary of State, Henry Kissinger, visiting Moscow from 20–22 October. Now, however, it was the Israelis who upset the attempts at superpower cooperation. A ceasefire was agreed on 23 October but, unpopular with Israel's generals, it quickly broke down. With Egypt's Third Army now in dire peril, the war entered its most dangerous stage.

Increasingly desperate to save the Arabs from the humiliation and preserve their own influence in the Middle East, the Soviets threatened, in a message from Brezhnev to Nixon on 24 October, to intervene militarily to end the war. This step was intended to force the Americans to put pressure on Israel rather than as a serious proposition. But it caused consternation in Washington. Sadat was prepared for both superpowers to send peacekeeping forces to the region, but the US had no desire to legitimize a Soviet military presence there. Kissinger 'felt it was important to get the Israelis to obey the ceasefire, but he considered it even more important to keep Soviet forces out of the area'.[5] With Nixon increasingly beset by the Watergate scandal, it was Kissinger who played the leading role in Washington, eager both to minimize Moscow's influence in the Middle East and to become the chief mediator in the conflict, winning Arab confidence whilst preserving the Israeli alliance. Following Brezhnev's warning, American strategic forces were placed on a high level of alert, Moscow was warned on 25 October not to intervene in the conflict, and pressure was successfully put on Israel to agree to end their advance. Since the Third Army was now entirely surrounded, the Israeli generals could afford to be moderate, meeting the Egyptians on 27 October to discuss implementation of the ceasefire. The following day, Kissinger's success in making America the mediator in the conflict was confirmed when Egypt's Foreign Minister, Ismail Fahmy, visited Washington. 'His management of the October War', it has been said, 'occasioned for Henry Kissinger perhaps the greatest personal successes of his career.'[6] Largely left in control of US decision-making, he had used arms supplies to underscore Israeli dependence on Washington, yet he was also courted by the Arabs as the pivotal player in post-war diplomacy.

'Shuttle Diplomacy'

The 1973 war was followed by months of talks, centred around Kissinger's 'shuttle diplomacy', in which he visited the capitals of the Middle East several times, consolidating the ceasefire, making step-by-step progress on a wider political settlement, and side-lining Soviet influence. Israel had won the war but in a very different way to 1967, with certain weaknesses exposed: it was a small country, unable to fight a long war, reliant on US support, and vulnerable to surprise attack. More divided among themselves than in the past, many Israelis now believed it sensible to bargain away the lands won in 1967 in return for security and peace. As Kissinger himself put it, 'Israel was exhausted no matter what the military maps showed. Its people were yearning for peace as only can those who have never known it.'[7] For his part, Sadat was already disposed to deal with the Americans and distance himself from the Soviets. At the first meeting between Sadat and Kissinger, on 6 November, 'the fate of the Soviet Union in the Middle East was sealed'.[8] In order to win the return of Sinai, ease the burden of defence spending on the economy, and reopen the lucrative Suez Canal, the Egyptian leader was ready to offer Israel its long-desired promise of recognition. In doing so, he was also prepared to compromise the interests of the Palestinians, for whom the Arabs had hitherto tried to secure a homeland. This divided him from Assad, who remained opposed to recognizing Israel, worked closely with the Soviets, and kept open the option of future military action—even if, without Egyptian participation, an Arab attack on Israel was unlikely.

Kissinger's 'shuttle diplomacy' succeeded in November 1973 in confirming the ceasefire in Sinai, securing supplies for Egypt's beleaguered Third Army, and arranging a release of prisoners-of-war.

As yet, however, there was no proper military disengagement. 'Although nominally aiming at a general peace . . . Kissinger concentrated on a series of small local disengagement agreements.'[9] On 21–22 December, an ambitious conference was held in Geneva between Israel and some of the Arab states, under joint US–Soviet chairmanship, to discuss a comprehensive regional settlement, but it only confirmed the difficulties of achieving such an aim. The Israelis refused to recognize the Palestine Liberation Organization (PLO) as the representative of the Palestinian people; Syria attended with reluctance and showed no enthusiasm for a deal. Yet this political setback did not prevent progress on military disengagement. On the Syrian front, a separation of forces was concluded in May 1974, and the more complicated, mutual withdrawal of Egyptian and Israeli forces took place over several stages in 1974–5. These steps were accompanied by the re-establishment of US–Egyptian diplomatic relations in February 1974, by a triumphant visit from Nixon to the Middle East in June, and by grants of US economic aid to Egypt and Jordan. The Israeli agreement to pull back from Suez allowed the Canal to be reopened in September 1975, following eight years of closure, Egypt agreeing that Israeli goods could be transported through it.

Sadat's shift in diplomatic loyalties was confirmed by his cancellation, in March 1976, of his friendship treaty with Moscow. But the Soviets were not yet powerless in the Middle East. 'The Soviet reaction to the absence of significant success in its Middle East policy was an increasingly anti-American, pro-radical line in the region.'[10] They maintained links not only with Syria but also with radical regimes in Iraq and Libya, and in August 1974, they gave diplomatic recognition to the PLO. This, alongside the united Arab insistence (confirmed by the October 1974 Rabat conference) that the PLO was the only legitimate voice of the Palestinians, and the invitation the following month to the PLO leader, Yasser Arafat, to address the UN, added to Israel's continuing sense of insecurity and made it even more difficult to contemplate a comprehensive regional settlement. In 1975, a majority of states in the UN General Assembly even voted to condemn Zionism as a form of racism.

Whatever the problems, 'shuttle diplomacy' had helped secure de facto peace in the area; and however insecure the Israelis might feel, their American ally was confirmed as the principal factor in Middle East diplomacy. 'In September 1973, no one would have dared to prophesy that within two years America would be restored to more influence in the Arab world than it had had since 1948.'[11] Yet this had only been achieved at great cost to US–Soviet relations. In the 1973 war, the first real test of détente, the American public believed it had been treated badly by the Soviets. They had armed the Arabs, failed to warn Washington of the impending conflict, and even threatened military intervention. The fact that Moscow had shown restraint during most of the war and that the superpowers ultimately achieved a ceasefire, was forgotten, largely because of the frightening events of 24–25 October, when the Americans had exaggerated the Soviet menace, partly to induce Israel to end the war. Thereafter, the Soviets felt that America was exploiting the situation, seizing the diplomatic initiative in the Middle East and refusing to treat the USSR as an equal in the peace process. A recognition of equality was one of the most important prizes Brezhnev wanted to win from détente. Then again, the Soviets did not become disillusioned with détente because of these events, nor did they do much to maintain good relations with Sadat. Even with their radical allies in the Middle East, the Kremlin demonstrated restraint: Soviet arms supply policy was designed 'not to allow the Arab countries a configuration of their armed forces such that they would be tempted to go for an all-out offensive war'.[12] There would be no repeat of 1973. The October war was a serious blow to détente, but not its death knell.

Instability in Lebanon, 1973–5

The growing instability in Lebanon has been interpreted in a number of ways—from an Arab–Christian civil war to an element in East–West competition—many of which misread or oversimplify the situation. One retrospective study notes: 'the Lebanese conflict is indeed complex. No more so, however, than the war in Yugoslavia . . . In any event, it did not result from some mysterious thunderbolt out of a tranquil sky, but from internal and external historical processes whose protagonists, Lebanese, regional, and international are identifiable.'[13] The key issue is perhaps whether the civil war, which began in 1975, was really a product of internal divisions or a reflection of the divisions in the Middle East from which Lebanon could not escape. In many respects, its territory became a battlefield on which most of them were directly fought out.

Lebanon is a small, mountainous country with close historical links to its larger neighbour, Syria. But the ethnic and religious mix in Lebanon was extremely complex. In the mid-twentieth century, slightly more than half its population was Christian, divided into Orthodox, Catholics, and the predominant, wealthy Maronites. The Muslims included not only Shi'ites and Sunnis, but also the Druze, believers in an offshoot from the Shi'ite branch of Islam and a fiercely independent sect, with strong family ties. For many years, these groups had existed in a Lebanon economically dominated by their seaport capital, Beirut—an important trading and banking centre. However, the maintenance of the Lebanese state was threatened on a number of fronts: the ethno-religious Constitution imposed under French colonial rule, which increasingly failed to represent the population balance; the failure to link the poorer mountainous regions economically with the more prosperous coastal plain; and the interference of the Palestinians, Syrians, and Israelis. These problems for the state reinforced the tendency of people to give their loyalty to localities and ethno-religious groups rather than to the government. The Maronites had a majority in Parliament and, under the Constitution always took the presidency, while representatives of the Sunnis, Shi'ites, and Druze held other key appointments. Thus, the Sunnis took the premiership and the Shi'ites took the speakership of Parliament. Indeed, where 'Lebanon parted company with the Arab state system was in its non-authoritarian state and open society', but it has been argued that this very openness 'left it open to being torn apart and subject to outside intervention'.[14]

After the American armed intervention in 1958 (Chapter 8, C), the regime's stability was restored by the new President, General Shihab, who secured the support of both the Maronite right-wing (the Phalange) and the Druze. However, the balance was then undermined by two key developments: first, the Arab defeat in the 1967 war, which both deflated Arab nationalism and led to a radicalization of certain groups, most importantly the Palestinians; second, the emergence of new political forces, notably the impact of Palestinians in Beirut, the establishment of a Maronite coalition, and the creation of Kamal Jumblatt's Lebanese Nationalist Movement. These more formalized divisions again served to weaken Lebanon's cohesion and challenge central authority. Palestinians had been arriving in Lebanon in increasing numbers especially after 1967 and the PLO set up its headquarters in Beirut in 1970. Soon there were about 400,000 Palestinian refugees living in Lebanon, and their presence further shifted the population balance in favour of Arabs and Muslims. Some also created problems by using bases in the south to launch attacks on Israel, which struck back in kind by bombing Beirut and crossing into Lebanese territory for the first time in 1972. 'Thus the war that it did not take part in [1973] . . . had more dramatic consequences for Lebanon than for any other Arab country. In 1970, it became—and until 1982 would remain—the chosen terrain for the Palestinians' struggle to recover their lost homeland.'[15]

In 1973, President Suleiman Frangieh announced that he would never allow the Palestinians to create 'a state within a state' in Lebanon and there were violent clashes between the PLO and the government army. The PLO was confirmed by the Arab League, at its Rabat summit in 1974, as the true representative of the Palestinian people and its self-confidence began to grow as the weakness of the Lebanese state became more evident. The Maronites began to believe that the army would become increasingly hamstrung by the Muslim elements and began to prepare themselves to act more decisively against the PLO. In April–May 1975, an obscure argument over Muslim–Christian fishing rights led to clashes, and when the bodyguards of Bashir Gemayel were murdered revenge was taken on the Palestinians, who would play little part in the next phase of the conflict. But the civil war was underway, the government had collapsed, and battles were raging between militias of the various Lebanese factions. It 'was not just a military confrontation between two hostile groups, but a conflict of communities, ideologies, power politics, parochial interests and values'.[16] Within the region, the Israeli government adamantly refused to speak to the PLO, despite their growing recognition as the sole and legitimate representatives of the Palestinian people, the corollary being that King Hussein of Jordan could no longer represent them in any peace process. There were signs of moderation emanating from the Palestinian National Council, with its call for a political solution by stages rather than by armed struggle. However, Yitzhak Rabin, the new Israeli Prime Minister in 1974, believed that while taking risks for peace was justified, peace should be approached cautiously and moves towards it should be made slowly. He described the coming years as 'seven lean years' because of Arab oil power and superpower rivalries, which would hopefully be followed by 'seven fat years'.[17]

B. The Era of 'Stagflation'

Challenges to the Bretton Woods System

Beyond the Middle East, the most significant result of the October war was the sudden, steep increase in oil prices which helped produce a global situation of stagnant growth rates and high inflation, hence the term 'stagflation'. But, the economic doldrums of the mid-1970s also had longer-term origins and in one vital aspect—the end of currency stability in the Western world—the turning point had been reached a few years before. At the end of the Second World War, from the time of the Bretton Woods Conference, the Western powers had tried to create the conditions for a stable, expanding international economy in which trade was maximized and unemployment minimized. The International Monetary Fund (IMF) provided help for those with balance-of-payments problems, the World Bank gave funds to developing countries, and monetary stability was provided by a system of fixed exchange rates, in which countries valued their currency against the dollar, which itself was pegged against the value of gold. In the 1950s and well into the 1960s, this system seemed successful. Western economies experienced consistently high growth rates, especially in Germany, Japan, and Italy; the volume of world trade expanded; service industries (like transport, banking, insurance, and tourism) increased markedly and typically, in 1970, provided about a third of jobs; and there was a particular demand for new consumer goods, from radios and vacuum cleaners to refrigerators and televisions.

However, by the late 1960s, growth rates were becoming less impressive, partly because post-war population growth had tailed off. The US economy was especially troubled, having had a worsening trade balance since the late 1950s and facing the burden of the Vietnam War. The US found itself increasingly in a poorer financial and commercial position vis-à-vis Europe and Japan, the regions it had put on the road to recovery after 1945. While it invested capital overseas and used up its gold reserves, they increased their reserves substantially. The most formidable new industrial competitor was Japan, which overtook the British economy in size in 1962 and that of Germany in 1967. By 1972, Japan had a $4 billion trading surplus, much of it with the US, which accounted for about one-third of Japanese imports and exports. Between 1952 and 1970 the Japanese economy grew five times over, its people ready to deny themselves high wages and consumer goods in order to generate national wealth and full employment.

Such changes in world trading patterns caused resentment in the US. There was pressure on Japan from the late 1960s to expand its armed forces and its aid to the less developed world, so as to reduce the relative burden of these on the US. In the 1968 election, Richard Nixon promised Americans that he would reduce the imports of cheap Japanese textiles, something he achieved in an agreement of October 1971. Japan and NATO countries were also pressed to make 'offset purchases' of American military hardware, to help cover the cost of US forces based on their soil. Since these armed forces spent substantial sums locally, they effectively added to America's balance-of-payments problems as well as its defence budget, which by 1969 stood at $4.85 billion. America's allies resented the implication that they were not cooperating fully or contributing enough to Western defence when the US still controlled nuclear weapons in Europe. True, NATO countries spent an average of 5 per cent of national income on defence, while America spent 9 per cent, but much of the US defence budget was devoted to the Vietnam War: in 1964–5, before the war began in earnest, defence spending had been less than $3 billion.

From Fixed to Floating Exchange Rates

One casualty of the increasingly volatile commercial and financial situation, and particularly of America's relative decline compared to Western Europe and Japan, was the system of fixed exchange rates. The US was no longer prepared to prop up the global monetary system when its own position was being damaged by the effort involved. By 1970, America's inflation had reached 6 per cent (having been barely noticeable a decade before), interest rates had to be raised, and unemployment rose above 5 per cent. Nixon, hoping for re-election in two years' time, wanted to improve the country's economic competitiveness by lowering the value of the dollar. As gold and foreign currency reserves continued to deteriorate, a devaluation of the dollar was widely expected and instability already affected other currencies. In November 1967, Britain, which had held the value of sterling constant against the dollar for eighteen years, was forced to devalue, largely because of chronic balance-of-payments problems; in August 1969, a year after severe domestic unrest, France devalued the franc by 11 per cent; and in May 1971—in a sign of things to come—the Germans, who were under pressure to revalue because of their strong trading position, decided to 'float' the Deutschmark, allowing its value to be influenced by the market, rather than being fixed at a certain value against the dollar.

Nixon finally launched a 'New Economic Policy' on 15 August 1971. To the rest of the world it became known as the 'Nixon Shock'. It included wage and price controls intended to limit inflation, a temporary 10 per cent surcharge on imports to help trade figures, and the end of the dollar's convertibility into gold. The last measure effectively implied 'that the Bretton Woods system was no longer viable'[18] and led more countries to 'float' their currencies over the following months including, in August, Japan. There were grave doubts about whether a system of floating exchange rates could work. If currencies altered in value against each other on a daily basis, it was feared that trade would suffer. Exporters who set a price one day might find it an uncommercial one when it came to the delivery date. There were discussions among the leading industrial nations about creating a new system of fixed exchange rates, following a devaluation of the dollar and a revaluation of the Japanese yen. Such a currency realignment was achieved to some extent in the Smithsonian Agreement of December 1971, but the pressure on currencies continued in 1972. In March 1973, at a meeting in Paris, the G10 group of industrial powers effectively abandoned all attempts to save fixed exchange rates. Over the summer of 1973, the world discovered that the new system actually operated quite well. Dire warnings of a return to the 1930s, with a collapse of world trade and rocketing unemployment, were not fulfilled. So-called 'managed floating' now 'became the exchange rate policy of almost all industrial countries . . . It did not prevent some very severe disturbances but it continued to provide a moderately orderly framework and . . . a fair degree of responsiveness to market forces.'[19]

The Impact of OPEC

Western economic growth in the 1950s and 1960s relied in part on the supply of cheap fuel for industry and transport. Even when the Organization of Petroleum Exporting Countries (OPEC) was founded in September 1960 to protect producers' rights, an oil glut in the mid-1960s limited its potential power and preserved cheap access to oil for the developed world. Then the situation began to change. 'Around 1970 a shortage of oil developed, US production began to decline rapidly, estimates of reserves ceased to increase more rapidly than production and there was a sudden consciousness that oil was finite.'[20] Western economies were now heavily dependent on oil imports, making little effort at energy conservation. In 1968, the Arabs formed their own group within OPEC and, in September 1969, Colonel Muammar Gaddafi came to power in Libya, taking a strong line in support of higher prices. In 1971, OPEC agreed to press for higher prices from the producers and a bigger share in profits; and in 1972 the Arab oil producers already talked about limiting oil production as a way to push up prices.

Although Western countries were already concerned about future oil supplies and prices before October 1973, it was the Middle East War that revolutionized relations between the oil producers and their suppliers. On 16 October, OPEC unilaterally increased oil prices by two-thirds. Four days later the Arab oil producers, controlling about a third of world oil reserves, launched a complete embargo of supplies to those countries who had aided Israel, including America, Holland, Portugal, and South Africa. To American annoyance, West Germany would not allow the Israelis to be resupplied from bases on its soil; Spain would not let its airspace be used; and Britain cut off arms supplies to all Middle East countries, a step which harmed Israel in particular. There were limits to what the oil producers could do without completely alienating their customers and some Western countries were more vulnerable to pressure than others. Thus, America only imported about 5 per cent of its oil from the Middle East, while Holland was almost entirely dependent on Arab supplies. Certain oil producers, especially Saudi Arabia and (non-Arab) Iran were close allies of America. Nonetheless, the oil embargo against the US remained in force until March 1974 and by then oil prices had risen by about four times the level of the previous year.

The impact on the Western economies was startling. Measures to reduce oil consumption and develop alternative energy sources were hard to achieve and could not prevent substantial balance-of-trade problems, an alarming fall in industrial activity, and a new twist to inflation. Certain countries—Japan, for example—coped well with the challenge. 'On the eve of the war Japan was the world's second largest consumer of petroleum and . . . was dependent on outside sources for 99.7 per cent of its oil',

Box 13.1

The Era of 'Stagflation': OECD Figures for Growth and Inflation Rates in the Leading Western Economies

Table 13.1 Rates of Consumer Price Inflation in selected years (%)

	1965	1971	1973	1975	1977	1979	1985
France	2.7	5.4	7.4	11.7	9.5	10.6	5.8
Germany	3.2	5.2	7.0	5.9	3.7	4.0	2.1
Italy	4.5	4.8	10.8	16.9	17.1	14.8	9.2
Japan	6.7	6.4	11.6	11.7	8.2	3.7	2.0
UK	4.8	9.4	9.2	24.2	15.8	13.4	6.1
USA	1.6	4.3	6.2	9.1	6.5	11.2	3.5

Source: www.oecd.org

Table 13.2 Rates of Real GDP Growth in selected years (%)

	1971	1973	1975	1977	1980	1982	1985
France	5.3	6.3	-1.0	3.5	1.6	2.4	1.6
Germany[1]	3.1	4.8	-0.9	3.3	1.4	-0.4	2.3
Italy	1.9	6.5	-2.0	2.4	3.5	0.3	2.8
Japan	4.4	8.0	3.1	4.4	2.8	3.4	6.3
UK	3.5	6.5	-1.5	2.5	3.7	2.0	4.2
USA	3.3	5.6	-0.2	4.6	3.2	-1.9	4.1

Sources: www.oecd.org and [1]www.worldbank.org

four-fifths of which came from the Middle East.[21] But, after slipping into a trade deficit in 1973, it generally maintained an export surplus, began to invest large sums abroad and, most significantly, turned from energy-demanding industries to high-technology products such as televisions and computers. Germany too managed to keep inflation relatively low and expand exports. Others suffered markedly. In Italy inflation reached 19 per cent in 1974, and in Britain in 1974–5 it peaked at over 20 per cent.

Between 1974 and 1978 oil prices held steady and there was a slow recovery of economic stability in the West. In 1974, the American-led bid to create an International Energy Authority, to facilitate joint action by the Western powers, had little effect. But in 1975–6, at French instigation, the leading economies (America, Japan, Germany, France, Britain, Italy, and Canada) had more success in founding the G-7 annual summits. This showed that, whatever their differences during the 1973 war, Western Europe, America, and Japan were capable of concerted action. However, attempts to tackle the problems of less developed world states—other than the oil producers (who were now markedly better off)—proved less successful. The energy crisis deepened concern about the 'North–South' divide in the world and in 1974 developing countries called for the creation of a New International Economic Order (see Box 13.2), but little was achieved on this front.

There was, however, a general move by Western banks to increase loans to developing countries. Indeed, in 1976 nearly $10 billion was lent in this way, a five-fold increase on the 1972 level. This shift from government-led aid to private assistance with development was another by-product of the oil crisis. Western governments were

BOX 13.2

The Proposed New International Economic Order

The idea of a New International Economic Order originated in the work of Raoul Prebisch, who in 1964 as the Secretary-General of the United Nations Conference on Trade and Development (UNCTAD) wrote a report entitled 'Towards a New Trade Policy for Development'. The timing of the resolution put forward by a group of less developed countries (LDCs) and adopted by the UN General Assembly in December 1974 was influenced both by the success of OPEC and the failure of import substitution as a development strategy. It called for the formation of LDC producer associations, some stable linkage between produce prices and the prices of manufactured goods to stop the deterioration in the terms of trade experienced by LDCs, the right to nationalize foreign enterprises, and the drawing up of regulations to be applied to the activities of multinational corporations (MNCs). It was not based on the idea of the overthrow of the international capitalist system but on the reform of that system. Reform would give LDCs more control over their natural resources, better terms of trade, reductions in the cost of obtaining Western technology, greater access to Western markets, and more control in the decision-making of international economic institutions. By the mid-1980s, the attempt to establish a New International Economic Order had clearly failed. The failure can be attributed to the LDCs receiving no backing from the powerful OPEC countries, the increasing difficulties inherent in high oil prices and growing debts, and most of all to the refusal of the Western countries to make concessions that would lead to higher domestic food prices for their voters.

keen to restrict their expenditure in the mid-1970s and there were limits to the money banks could make from loans to the troubled Western economies. But the OPEC countries invested much of their new-found financial wealth, known as 'petrodollars', in the Western banking system, 'which in turn had to find borrowers and offered low rates of interest'.[22] The need for banks to maximize profits by returns on the available capital seemed to offer developing countries the cheap loans they needed in order to boost their own growth. Only in the early 1980s did the potential problem of lending vast sums to poor countries in the less developed world become apparent. For the Western powers, the 1970s ended on a pessimistic note when oil prices began to mushroom again, thanks to the fall of the Shah of Iran in December 1978. The decade's apparently never-ending economic malaise undermined Western morale and led Americans to ask whether they were in long-term decline. This in turn helped give the impression of a world where Soviet communism and Western capitalism were equally strong, when in actual fact US wealth and industrial capacity far outstripped that of the Soviet Union.

C. Political Problems in Europe

The economic difficulties of the late 1960s and 1970s helped create a climate of self-doubt in the Western alliance, and Western Europe in particular saw industrial, social, and political divisions greater than any since the slump of the 1930s. At the same time, the continued division of Europe, fears of nuclear war, and, thanks to Vietnam, moral doubts about US leadership led to a greater Western tolerance of communist policy in Eastern Europe and a readiness to embrace détente. The years of détente were years of disruption and change in many aspects of Cold War society, but the problems of the liberal, social reform consensus and its international economic order in place since 1945 did not lead to radical domestic change or to the end of international tension. Instead, they eventually produced the kind of conservatism with a hard, more ruthless edge that would eventually characterize the international policies of much of the Western world in the 1980s.

NATO and the 'Year of Europe'

Although it had survived France's withdrawal from the military command structure in 1966, by the 1970s the cohesion of the Atlantic alliance was again being called into question. European members had recovered economically from the Second Word War and were now major trading rivals of the US. As Vietnam grew more costly, Americans came to resent the perceived reluctance of West Europeans to pay more for their own defence. It was not that the alliance was about to disintegrate. Indeed, one reason why Nixon and Kissinger did not focus much attention on reforming NATO before 1973 was that the underlying reasons for the 'Atlantic Partnership' continued:

Europe gained a sense of security and political confidence behind which it could build material prosperity; America secured liberal-capitalist allies on the front line of the ideological struggle with Moscow. But NATO's problems were real and growing. The USSR's achievement of near strategic nuclear parity led Europeans to doubt whether a US president would really defend them in war. Europeans even feared the creation of a US–Soviet condominium, which would shape Europe according to superpower interests. Nixon's August 1971 economic measures, affecting trade and monetary policy, added to the growing sense of distrust. For its part, having fostered European unity in earlier decades, the US government under Nixon continued to fear the European Community as a rival trading bloc, with a population roughly equal to America's, once Britain, Denmark, and Ireland became members in January 1973.

The 'Year of Europe' was launched by Kissinger in a speech on 23 April 1973, in which he tried to underline the mutual benefits of the Atlantic alliance whilst proposing solutions to various problems. Unfortunately, the speech itself generated suspicion. Its timing suggested that Kissinger had decided to deal with European problems only because he had time on his hands after resolving more important problems, like Vietnam. The idea that America could choose when to launch a 'Year of Europe' was distasteful to West European countries, who saw themselves as America's equals in the alliance. 'Pompidou remarked that for France every year was a year of Europe.'[23] Kissinger's promise to support European unity, to continue the American military presence, and to safeguard European interests in the détente process were all very well. But his complaints about EC protectionism and the lack of burden-sharing were obviously designed for a US audience. The climax of the speech was the call for a 'New Atlantic Charter' to embrace Japan as well as NATO. But, especially for the French, a New Charter could be no more than a new justification of US domination. Thus Kissinger discovered that dealing 'with several sensitive allies, each with its own interests and public opinion to consider, was not remotely the same as dealing with a handful of leaders controlling totalitarian governments', such as produced his earlier diplomatic successes.[24] Then again, with the Watergate Crisis, the oil crisis, and an upcoming (if unforeseen) war in the Middle East, 'he could hardly have picked a worse twelve months' for his initiative.[25]

Within months, the 'Year of Europe' was a virtual dead letter. Instead, the October Middle East War became the occasion for a deep transatlantic rift. The French were pro-Arab from the outset; most NATO members refused to let their soil be used for America's supply of arms to Israel; and Europeans were gravely offended, in the last phase of the war, when US forces were put on a high level of alert without consultations in NATO. Europeans feared that Washington could have dragged them into a nuclear war in which they had no direct interest, whilst Americans publicly criticized the Europeans for following an anti-Israeli policy, influenced by the selfish desire to safeguard oil supplies from the Middle East. Kissinger's April 1973 speech did result, in June 1974, in NATO's Ottawa declaration, which restated the purposes of the alliance. However, it fell far short of a new Atlantic Charter, excluded Japan, and had little public impact. Kissinger himself described it as 'drained of . . . moral and psychological significance by a year of bickering'.[26]

The Eastern Bloc in the 1970s

In the aftermath of the Czechoslovakian crisis, the communist regimes of Eastern Europe returned to their attempts to make the Soviet economic and political model more effective. 'The Eastern European regimes were politically stable, secure beneath the Soviet umbrella . . . and the economies appeared to have staved off the "oil shock" from which the rest of the world had suffered.'[27] Whilst retaining central planning, there were efforts to simplify its cumbersome bureaucracy and deal with the problem of poor-quality goods. Hungary in particular, after 1968, experimented with a 'New Economic Mechanism' which, while preserving the essential elements of Soviet planning, sought to decentralize economic decisions, introduce an element of competition, and make factories work more profitably. But, 'with the exception . . . of Hungary, economic reform . . . remained a timid, faltering enterprise'.[28] East Germany, Bulgaria, and Czechoslovakia (the last under its new leader, Gustáv Husák) were slavishly loyal to the USSR. In East Germany, Erich Honecker even tightened up central planning in 1971, after a period of decentralization. In Romania, Nicolae Ceaușescu maintained central planning and signed a new friendship treaty with Moscow in 1970, while continuing to steer as independent a line as possible in foreign policy. Attempts to integrate the bloc more closely together, in emulation of the European Community, came to nothing. Under the 'Complex Programme' of 1970–1, the Council for Mutual Economic Aid (COMECON) developed joint projects and an investment bank, but these achieved very little and the extension of the organization to Cuba (1972) and Vietnam (1978) merely underlined its fundamental lack of cohesion.

One way in which Eastern European communists tried to overcome inefficient management, poor production levels, and a lack of competitiveness on world markets was to rely on technological inputs from the West. The desire for freer access to Western technology was a strong motivation for them to pursue détente in the 1970s. Eastern bloc leaders, like their colleagues in the Third World, also exploited the readiness of Western banks (at a time of 'stagflation' at home) to lend substantial sums for investment. However, the top-heavy, centralized planning systems were unable to adopt Western technology effectively and, with little success in boosting their export trade, their economies became indebted to Western banks. They also began to 'import' inflation from the West. Furthermore, the decade of détente carried with it a political cost. Western trade and tourism, and agreements such as those made at Helsinki, opened the East to disruptive influences. 'Increasingly the political legitimacy of the regimes of eastern Europe . . . came to rest on their socio-economic accomplishments . . . But as the economies began to deteriorate . . . even this source of legitimacy disappeared.'[29] Communist leaders were never ready to legitimize themselves by holding democratic elections, but their people were now more aware of Western economic success and political freedoms, whilst the Helsinki process put a new emphasis on the importance of human rights. The result was movements like Czechoslovakia's Charter 77, in which over 200 leading figures joined together to demand respect for human rights. This and similar, smaller groups elsewhere were extinguished by the secret police, but such a response only highlighted the lack of political freedom: 'the party's political monopoly . . . left society with no effective role in the system, except as passive objects of policy'.[30]

Western critics of détente argued that the process of East–West contacts itself shored up communist regimes and helped them escape serious unrest in the 1970s. But the crises in Hungary (1956) and Czechoslovakia (1968) had shown that, short of provoking nuclear war, the West was powerless to help those who rose up against Soviet domination. The logic espoused by many exponents of détente was to wean the East Europeans away from communism through contacts which would increase awareness of the economic benefits available in the West. Nixon was, of course, both a convinced anti-communist and an architect of détente, who used visits to Romania (1969) and Poland (1972) to demonstrate that East Europeans could develop their own links to the West. The extension by Washington of 'most-favoured nation' trade status to Romania (1975) and Hungary (1978) delivered a similar message, and the April 1976 'Sonnenfeldt Doctrine', named after a State Department official, set out the logic of encouraging greater autonomy in the communist bloc. The West's potential to disrupt the communist system was not, however, revealed until 1979–80, when the process of détente ended and the Cold War returned. By 1979, US, West European, and Japanese banks were owed nearly $70 billion by the Eastern bloc states, compared to $10 billion in 1971. Any idea that they could survive in isolation from the capitalist world had disappeared and the Soviets, whose own economy had become stagnant, were faced with a growing threat to their economic predominance in the Warsaw Pact. Indeed, by absorbing huge amounts of financial aid and subsidized raw materials, such as oil, the Eastern bloc had already become a serious liability to the Soviet economy. The return to the Cold War forced the East Europeans to reduce investments and consumption once more, having actually made only marginal economic improvements in the mid-1970s. 'Economic failure, common throughout the region, was openly acknowledged . . . in Poland and Hungary, where high levels of foreign debt could [not] be concealed.'[31]

The Community of the Nine

The 'northern enlargement' of the EC to Britain, Ireland, and Denmark in January 1973 created a market of about 250 million people and accounted for about 20 per cent of world trade. The expansion was accompanied by great expectations of new political and economic cooperation among the members, encouraged by their October 1972 summit meeting in Paris, which planned a full 'European Union' by 1980, including monetary union and joint action in new areas like social welfare, regional development, and the environment. However, 'apart from the Community's enlargement the two decades from the mid-1960s to the mid-1980s can be seen as a long period of stagnation'.[32] Economic and monetary union, the subject of the 1970 Werner Report (which might have led to a single currency), was a direct victim of 'stagflation'. The instability of the world's commercial and financial system, with high inflation and the move towards floating exchange rates, damaged any prospects of European currency stability.

The different economic experiences of countries like Germany and Britain in this period also made economic coordination between them more difficult. In April 1972, the nine EC members (including the three due to join in 1973) formed the 'snake', to try to preserve monetary stability by valuing their currencies within a certain percentage of the dollar. But Britain was almost immediately forced out, others followed, and within a few years the 'snake' was limited to a small number of countries, dominated by Germany. Only in 1978–9 was it possible to create a more stable European Monetary System, the main element of which was an Exchange Rate Mechanism (ERM), which kept member currencies within a certain percentage of a central rate. It too suffered instability in its early years, marked by several renegotiations of the central rate, but provided greater stability after 1983. By then, healthy growth rates had returned to Europe, global trade was expanding, and a stable ERM proved a valuable weapon against inflation. True, there were a few political successes for the EC in this period. In 1979, a Treaty of Accession was agreed with Greece, which became the tenth member in 1981, and the first direct elections to the European Parliament were eventually held in June 1979. But the Parliament itself had only limited powers. A more important development was, arguably, the inauguration in 1975 of regular summit meetings among leaders, but this emphasized the power of national governments in shaping the Community. The forward momentum of European integration only properly revived in the mid-1980s.

Discord in Southern Europe

A series of crises in southern Europe in the mid-1970s threatened to divide NATO. A possible communist-led government in Italy, a military coup in Portugal, and a Greek–Turkish crisis over Cyprus made the period 1974–6 one of great uncertainty in the region, although by 1979 the sense of crisis was overcome and, in fact, liberal democracy advanced, replacing right-wing regimes in Portugal, Greece, and Spain.

Communist parties in Western Europe all tried to widen their appeal in the wake of the 1968 Czechoslovakian crisis by distancing themselves from Moscow, accepting the existing political system, and even tolerating the existence of NATO. It was the Italian communists who proved more successful in pursuing a 'Eurocommunist' line. In 1973, their general secretary, Enrico Berlinguer, expressed a readiness to work with other parties in order to contain the extreme Right, preserve social reforms, and demonstrate that communists could be trusted in office. He hoped that a deal with the Christian Democrats could help 'unblock the political system', paving the way for a communist role in government, as well as 'preventing . . . economic difficulties from causing a dangerous drift toward an authoritarian right-wing regime'.[33] Given Italy's dire problems with strikes, inflation, and terrorism, some moderate Christian Democrats, including premier Aldo Moro (1974–6), believed that cooperation with the communists, in a 'historic compromise', made sense. It could preserve Italian unity through a difficult period. In a sense, the Christian Democrats 'had little choice. Their regime was collapsing around them, amid economic crisis, financial scandal [and] incipient terrorism' from the Red Brigades.[34] Although Moro was murdered in 1976, his successor Giulio Andreotti relied on communist support in Parliament, even agreeing a common programme with them in 1977. Such cooperation was helped by the communists' acceptance, in 1975, of NATO membership and by the closely fought 1976 election, when they won 34.5 per cent of the vote to the Christian Democrats' 40 per cent. The Italian Right and the Americans, however, were deeply concerned by such developments. In April 1976, Kissinger warned that the communists must not be brought into the Italian government and, in fact, a formal coalition was avoided by the Christian Democrats. In 1979, the communists ended their parliamentary support for the government and in the ensuing election their share of the vote fell to 30 per cent.

The dangers for NATO in Portugal in the mid-1970s appeared far worse. The country had been ruled by a right-wing dictatorship since 1932, first under Dr Antonio Salazar and then, after 1968, under Marcelo Caetano. The existence of such an authoritarian regime in a founder member of NATO called the alliance's democratic credentials into question. All opposition to Salazar was crushed, little was done to tackle illiteracy and poverty, and protectionist economic policies were followed, which limited economic growth and industrialization. Equally important however, Portugal tried to hold on to its empire in the face of colonial wars in Angola, Mozambique, and Portuguese Guinea, which proved increasingly 'unwinnable'. On 24–25 April 1974, the regime was suddenly overthrown by left-wing army officers who were determined to resolve the colonial wars and modernize the country. This 'Carnation Revolution' went off surprisingly peacefully but was followed by two years of political turmoil. Although a respected, conservative army general, Antonio de Spinola, was appointed President, many army officers had absorbed Marxist ideology and were determined to pursue radical policies. A civilian Cabinet was formed but its members lacked administrative experience and faced impossible demands for land reform, greater social spending, and nationalization, at a time (in the aftermath of the Middle East War) of inflation and fuel shortages. In July, a new Cabinet was formed under a left-wing colonel, Vasco Gonçalves, who allied with the communists, and in September a power struggle led to Spinola's resignation, leaving the far Left in the ascendant. Potentially, this could have led to a major international crisis: 'as seen from Washington, Portugal could become a focus of Marxist contagion in southern Europe at a time when Generalissimo Francisco Franco, the Spanish dictator, was nearing death, and the power of the Communist Party was growing in Italy'.[35] Apart from some financial assistance to the communists however, the USSR did not try to exploit the situation, apparently accepting that Portugal was firmly in the US sphere of influence. Kissinger publicly expressed concern over the threat of Portugal's loss to the alliance and a new, strong-minded US ambassador, Frank Carlucci, was appointed to Lisbon. Significantly, the Portuguese people themselves showed their desire for liberal politics in a general election in April 1975, when the communists won only 17 per cent of the vote. By the time a constitution was published in April 1976, stability had been restored. At the same time, instability was avoided in neighbouring Spain, despite the death in November 1975 of Franco. His successors, King Juan Carlos and Premier Adolfo Suárez, moved quickly to legalize opposition groups and elect a constitutional Assembly, which published a liberal constitution in October 1978. Spain too was then set on a course towards stable democracy.

In Cyprus, the delicate 1960 Constitutional settlement between the Greek- and Turkish-Cypriots had soon been called into question. As early as 1963, an attempt by President Makarios to reform it in the Greek Cypriots' favour led to Greek–Turkish intercommunal violence and a threat by the Turkish government to intervene. In 1967, when a group of colonels seized power in Athens, there was another bout of intercommunal violence, but it was only in 1974, with their regime unpopular at home, that the colonels decided to stir up trouble over Cyprus. On 15 July, dissatisfied with Makarios' policies, the colonels instigated a coup against him, but the operation was botched, the President escaped and Cyprus rapidly slipped into violence. On 20 July, a Turkish force landed in the north of the island, insisting on the right to defend the Turkish-Cypriot community. Powerless to prevent such a disastrous development, the Athens junta collapsed and a former Prime Minister, Constantine Karamanlis, returned to power, restoring Greece's pre-1967 constitution. Meanwhile, in Cyprus the situation grew worse. The failure to reach a compromise at talks in Geneva led the Turks to renew their attacks in the north, partitioning the island, with 37 per cent now under Turkish-Cypriot control. In protest over NATO's failure to halt the Turks, Karamanlis pulled Greece out of the alliance's military command until 1980 and the US Congress, sympathetic to Greece, suspended military aid to Turkey in 1975 for three years. Karamanlis and the Turkish Premier, Bulent Ecevit, met to discuss their differences in 1978, ending the immediate crisis, but the Turkish army remained in Cyprus and the Turkish-Cypriots set up their own 'Turkish Republic of North Cyprus' in 1983. There were numerous rounds of talks over the following years to consider a possible settlement, but it proved impossible to satisfy both the Greek-Cypriot desire for reunification under majority rule with the Turkish-Cypriot desire for security against Greek domination under such a system. Nonetheless, Greece and Turkey remained members of NATO which, in retrospect, could look back on the problems of southern Europe in the mid-1970s as evidence of its own resilience.

D. European Détente at its High Point

MBFR and the Persistence of Ostpolitik

Despite the economic and political problems that beset Western Europe in the mid-1970s, these years saw better East–West relations across the Iron Curtain. Superpower détente had begun to turn sour just as

European détente reached its height at the Helsinki Conference of 1975. By then, European détente was an established tradition, stretching back through de Gaulle in the 1960s to Churchill in the 1950s. Western European countries had a less ideologically driven foreign policy than the US and, being close to the dividing line between East and West, were more concerned about the likely results of a nuclear exchange between NATO and the Warsaw Pact; they also recognized that a lowering of tensions would bring rewards, not least in the commercial field. While pursuing détente, both sides were clearly trying to defend their own interests. The Western powers hoped to reduce Soviet conventional superiority while opening the communist system to liberal ideology and commerce; the Eastern powers to 'decouple' the US from European security while giving international legitimacy to the Soviet-led satellite bloc. NATO was well aware that the Soviets could exploit détente to 'drive wedges' between members of the Western alliance, but the Czechoslovakian crisis had confirmed that the Soviet position in Eastern Europe could not easily be broken down. The USSR was aware of the dangers that increased Western cultural and economic contacts might bring to the communist world but, faced by the Chinese menace in Asia, the Kremlin was anxious to stabilize Europe's borders and to gain some Western acknowledgement of its predominance in the East.

Before meaningful talks could begin, there had to be compromises and the key steps came in May 1971, when Leonid Brezhnev (see Box 13.3) agreed to Mutual Balanced Force Reduction (MBFR) talks on the military side; and in December 1971, when NATO accepted that a European Security Conference should meet. At their Moscow summit in May 1972, Brezhnev and Nixon agreed that both these developments should go ahead. Preparatory conversations on MBFR began in Vienna in January 1973 and formal talks began nine months later, but they proved highly complex and, lacking political commitment on the Soviet side, made no progress until they were replaced by talks on 'Conventional Forces in Europe' in the late 1980s (Chapter 20, D). Preparatory conversations on a European Security Conference began in Helsinki in November 1972 and the first round of Foreign Ministers' talks started in July 1973. Thirty-five states took part, including all Warsaw Pact and NATO members, together with neutral and non-aligned nations, Albania being the only European country not present. Ahead of the meetings the Soviets vainly tried to reduce the Eastern bloc's need for Western economic assistance by initiating a new ten-year COMECON plan. At the same time, the Americans were keen to demonstrate their lack of respect for the Brezhnev Doctrine, with visits by Nixon to Poland and his Secretary of State, William Rogers, to several East European states. Such behaviour emphasized that, whatever the improved atmosphere in Europe, ideological differences were deep, and two well-armed alliances continued to face each other.

Across the European divide, however, relations seemed more relaxed because of a continuing improvement in relations between West Germany and its Eastern neighbours, thanks to Chancellor Willy Brandt's *Ostpolitik*. In 1970, he had signed treaties with the USSR and Poland, accepting Germany's eastern borders and renouncing the use of force (see Chapter 9, E). These Moscow and Warsaw 'Eastern Treaties' were ratified on 17 May 1972, with the Christian Democrats abstaining. The Christian Democrats, who had dominated German government for two decades before 1969, had never reconciled themselves to a policy that seemed, in effect, to recognize Germany's division into two parts. To them, and to some of the centrist Free Democrats, *Ostpolitik* 'appeared to be an unconstitutional acceptance of the permanent division of Germany, given the explicit commitment in the Basic Law [Germany's Constitution] to work towards German reunification'.[36] However, the popularity of *Ostpolitik* was confirmed in the November 1972 elections, which gave the Social Democrats the best result they ever achieved in West German polls. Recognition of Brandt's achievement was also seen in the award of the 1972 Nobel Peace Prize and it has been argued that, given the advances in superpower détente, 'had the German government not been willing to take its initiatives in Ostpolitik at this time, the Federal Republic would have appeared as a recalcitrant Cold War relic, and its vital interests could have been bartered away by others'.[37] In May 1973, Brandt followed up the Soviet and Polish arrangements with a German–Czechoslovakian Treaty that invalidated the 1938 Munich Treaty and confirmed Czechoslovakian control of the Sudetenland, thus resolving German relations with another of its neighbours. By then, the focus of *Ostpolitik* had moved to the more controversial and difficult question of a deal with East Germany.

The September 1971 Berlin agreement, between the four occupation powers (the US, USSR, Britain, and France) had marked a first step towards an improved atmosphere between West and East Germany, who still did not recognize each other's existence. Brandt's concept of 'two Germanies in one nation' was meant to allow Germany's division into separate states to be accepted in the short term, while reassuring the German people that the hopes of eventual reunification had not been abandoned. Indeed, for Brandt the hope was that a relaxation of tension would lead to the eventual withering away of the division of Germany: the *Ostpolitik* treaties 'did not affect our claim to self-determination and national unity'; rather, 'we had to accept the status quo territorially in order to dislodge it politically' (a logic that was applicable to European détente more generally).[38] In December 1971 and May 1972, agreements were signed on improved communications between the two Germanies, whilst ratification of the Eastern Treaties paved the way to negotiations on a 'Basic Treaty' on East–West German relations. Significantly, this was signed on 22 December 1972, in the immediate wake of Brandt's election triumph. The Treaty embodied the ideal of 'two Germanies in one nation' by extending the diplomatic recognition that the West had hitherto always denied to the East. It allowed both countries to enter the United Nations in 1974 with the approval of both superpowers and, although it implied a short-term acceptance of Germany's division, it was ratified more easily than the Eastern Treaties. The division of Germany was now an accepted fact of European life. Predictably, many interpreted the Basic Treaty as 'an admission by Bonn that Germany's division was, if not permanent, at least an existing reality' but the West German government reiterated that 'Reunification is required under constitutional law . . . The treaty is no treaty of partition.'[39] Ironically, the success proved short-lived for Brandt. He resigned as Chancellor in April 1974, after an East German spy was exposed in his private office. But the policy of *Ostpolitik* was maintained by his successor, Helmut Schmidt.

The Helsinki Conference and its 'Final Act'

The multilateral summit of European states, plus the US and Canada, at Helsinki between 30 July and 1 August 1975, marked both the culmination of the talks on European security and the high point of European détente. In some ways, it could be seen as representing the comprehensive post-Second World War 'peace settlement' that the Cold War had hitherto prevented. On the other hand, it did little more than accept existing territorial realities and breed new controversies of its own. Both sides could feel that they had made significant gains from the 'Final Act' of the conference, which included a range of agreements divided across three 'baskets'. The first of these concerned security issues. This section stated the principles of respect for sovereignty and non-interference in the domestic affairs of others, as well as respect for human rights. Some elements could be taken to be critical of Soviet domination of Eastern Europe, but the Kremlin also later exploited the principle of non-interference to oppose Western criticism of the domestic policy of communist states. Most importantly, this 'basket' declared European borders to be inviolable. This was not the same as unchangeable (as the Warsaw Pact had wanted), but it did mean that any border changes had to be made by peaceful means. The Eastern bloc treated this as de facto acceptance of the post-war territorial settlement and for this reason it was criticized by some in America and Western Europe as condoning Soviet domination in the East. 'After all, Moscow had obtained what it had fought for since the 1950s: the recognition of post-war borders . . . and thus the legitimatization of its East European sphere of influence.'[40] But again, it needs to be borne in mind that on the territorial issue, Helsinki 'essentially did little more than confirm . . . what the West had already accepted'.[41] No one in their right mind believed that European borders could be forcibly changed anyway, whereas the possibility of peaceful change remained open, allowing the dramatic redrawing of the map that would come in 1989–91. The problem was that too many 'western commentators critical of the Final Act . . . uncritically [repeated] Soviet claims about ratification of the post-war territorial and political status quo' and failed to emphasize that 'the Western negotiators managed to secure language that sanctioned the possibility of peaceful change in Europe'.[42] The Western powers effectively separated territorial realities and the military balance from issues of political legitimacy, and intended that the legitimacy of the Soviet system should be undermined by the greater East–West contacts fostered by Baskets 2 and 3.

'Basket 2', arguably the least important, covered economic, commercial, cultural, scientific, environmental, and other forms of cooperation. Trade between Eastern and Western Europe saw especially strong growth in the 1970s, much more than that between the superpowers, and the US became concerned at the scale of West European reliance on trade with the East. But this could hardly be attributed to the Helsinki agreements in themselves, even if the Final Act did

BOX 13.3

Biography: Leonid Brezhnev (1906–82)

Born in the industrial town of Dneprodzerzhinsk in Ukraine, Brezhnev, himself the son of a steelworker, trained as a steel engineer before moving into full-time political work. At first, he concentrated on administrative work in Ukraine and focused on its industrial reconstruction after the war. But under Khrushchev, he successfully managed the Communist Party in Kazakhstan, joined the Politburo and, in 1960, rose to be Soviet President. It was partly through fear of being removed from the Politburo that he led the overthrow of Khrushchev in 1964. By then, Brezhnev was the consummate Kremlin insider: a competent, experienced bureaucrat, orthodox in his opinions, with a strong sense of duty, who had risen to high level despite his natural caution. His very lack of individualism or charisma made him attractive in the wake of Khrushchev's adventurism and, fulfilling the expectations of his supporters, in the 1960s he neither ran risks abroad nor espoused reformism at home. At first, in the position of General Secretary of the Communist Party, he shared power with the Premier, Alexei Kosygin, and others. But he was always the most influential figure in the leadership and by 1971 Kosygin was very much in his shadow. At home, he tried to improve living standards while cracking down harshly on all signs of dissidence. Abroad, he came to support a policy of relaxing tension with the West in the 1970s, while becoming ever more estranged from communist China. After 1975 Brezhnev was increasingly troubled by personal ill health, stalling industrial output, and heavy defence spending. His final years were overshadowed by the demise of détente, economic stagnation, and an ill-fated decision, in 1979, to invade Afghanistan.

seem to endorse the process. In any case, in the long term, as Churchill and others had always expected, it was the Eastern bloc that became vulnerable to 'ideological subversion' because of its everyday contacts with the liberal democracies, not least because of the communist regimes' cravings for Western loans and imports. Of greater importance on this front was 'Basket 3', which dealt with respect for human rights, exchanges of visits, and the free flow of information and ideas—something the West had been pressing for since the 1955 Geneva summit. The Soviets agreed to this in order to make gains on territorial security and trade in the other baskets, but the West hoped that the stress on individual freedom and human rights would encourage political evolution in the communist bloc, undermining the Brezhnev Doctrine. The Final Act gave encouragement to Eastern European anti-communists who soon began to establish 'monitoring groups' to test how far they could now push the authorities to acknowledge human rights.

Helsinki was followed by other meetings of the Conference on Security and Cooperation in Europe (CSCE), beginning with the Belgrade meeting in October 1977. Inevitably, both sides emphasized different aspects of the agreements—the West human rights, the East territorial stability—and criticism soon deepened in America among Democrats and the Republican Right. Later academic accounts could be similarly dismissive, arguing that Helsinki 'scarcely justified the high hopes placed in it' and that Soviet indifference to human rights in its aftermath 'encouraged the view that totalitarian states were not capable of reform from within'.[43] With the crushing of Yuri Orlov's 'Helsinki Monitoring Group' by the KGB in May 1976, the Soviets certainly exposed the limited impact of 'Basket 3' in the short term, and during the ensuing presidential election in America, there was severe criticism of President Gerald Ford for having signed the Helsinki Accords. One critic was the Democratic Senator, Henry Jackson, who argued that the President had 'sold out' to the Soviets. This led the State Department's Helmut Sonnenfeldt to counter that, in fact, the US was supporting the 'aspirations in eastern Europe for a more autonomous existence within the context of a strong Soviet geopolitical influence'.[44] But the logic of the 'Sonnenfeldt Doctrine' proved difficult to defend in 1976 and Jimmy Carter was able to exploit the issue against Ford in their head-to-head television debates. In Western Europe, the increased personal contacts, trade, and tourism brought by détente gave Helsinki somewhat greater popularity and, in the wake of the collapse of communism in 1989, it was easier to see that the 'Helsinki process' might have had a very important role in generating self-doubt within the Eastern bloc. High-quality Western imports, the realization that the West was not a relentless military threat, the recognition of the importance of individual rights—all these slowly served the purposes of 'ideological subversion' and called into question the value of the planned economy, high military expenditure, and the totalitarian state. In retrospect, it was possible to claim that 'the Helsinki process—particularly its human rights aspect—played a significant role in bringing about the dismantling of Communist rule in . . . Europe by undermining the legitimacy of these regimes'.[45]

E. Crises in the Less Developed World

Détente and the Less Developed World

As seen, the October 1973 Middle East War led to questioning in America about the value of détente, only eighteen months after the Moscow summit. The war also reflected the inability of the superpowers to control their 'clients' in developing countries and showed that, however much the US might wish to stabilize the less developed world, conflicts there would go on. Indeed, from 1973 to 1979 there was a series of crises in the less developed world—the October War, the fall of South Vietnam (1975), the civil war in Angola (1975–6), the Ogaden conflict (1977–8), and the Soviet invasion of Afghanistan—which did much to destroy superpower détente. To a growing number of Americans, the common element in these crises was the Soviet determination to advance the cause of Marxism-Leninism worldwide, something which Nixon and Kissinger had hoped détente would prevent. By the time Kissinger left office in 1976, disaffection with détente in America was considerable. Having defined a policy of 'linkage', under which the Kremlin could only expect the gains of cooperation (trade and arms control) in return for restraint in regional conflicts, it was increasingly difficult to justify the continuation of détente if Soviet support for 'wars of national liberation' went on.

The Soviets, however, had a different view of these problems. To them it seemed ridiculous to expect changes in the less developed world to cease. Its Marxist beliefs, however diluted by the 1970s, did lead Moscow to see wars of national liberation as 'inevitable'; and Brezhnev had always made clear that, in the Soviet interpretation of détente, superpower rivalry in the less developed world would continue. Besides, although Western interests generally seemed to be on the defensive in Africa and Asia in the 1970s, the Americans had their successes. In the Middle East, the US edged Russia out of the post-1973 peace process; in South-East Asia, the fall of Vietnam was not followed by the loss of Thailand, Malaysia, and Indonesia as had once been feared; and in East Asia America could always 'play the China card' against the Soviets (as occurred in 1978–9). Neither did Americans show restraint in the less developed world when their interests were at stake and they felt powerful enough to act. Unsurprisingly, given past policy in the western hemisphere, they were especially determined to prevent pro-Soviet influence spreading in Latin America.

Chile and Allende

The violent overthrow of Salvador Allende, the Marxist President of Chile, on 11 September 1973 has often been blamed on the US. In fact, despite numerous other revelations about America's Chilean policy and the activities there of the Central Intelligence Agency (CIA), 'there is no evidence of direct involvement in, or provocation of, the 1973 coup by the US government'.[46] Ultimately, the Chilean military, under Augusto Pinochet, were responsible for the coup. Kissinger insisted that 'Allende was brought down by his own incompetence and inflexibility. What happened, happened for Chilean reasons, not as a result of the acts of the United States.'[47] However, the US government and multinational companies who were affected by Allende's nationalization policies did much to undermine his position before the military acted and it was no secret that Washington would welcome his fall. Thus, it can be argued that 'even if Nixon and Kissinger were not working toward a coup, they were eager to have Allende discredited in order to bring about his defeat in the 1976 elections'.[48] And, 'through the CIA's covert operations in Chile, the application of vast economic pressures, and military assistance to the Chilean armed forces, the United States government did without question help to create a situation in which the anti-Allende coup became possible'.[49]

The CIA had first used covert propaganda and funding of his opponents to prevent Allende coming to power at the head of a 'Popular Front' coalition in 1964. The victor on that occasion was Eduardo Frei Montalva, a Christian Democrat whose attempts at moderate reform could not prevent rising inflation and rural poverty. At the next election in 1970, despite CIA attempts to prevent it, Allende narrowly won a three-cornered race and was duly installed as President. This created a dilemma for the US: Allende had been legally elected in a country which, in contrast to the rest of Latin America, had retained a stable liberal democracy since 1938; but this was the first time a Marxist had been freely elected as the president of a country, he was a friend of Fidel Castro and, despite the narrow election victory, began a radical programme of land reform and nationalization. This had a profound effect on society: 'All aspects of life became politicized, and politics became polarized—it was impossible not to be either for or against the government.'[50] The CIA continued to fund both his opponents and adverse press reports on Allende, whilst the US government successfully managed to cut off most external financial aid to Chile. This, alongside rising inflation and upheaval in the valuable copper market, caused severe economic problems, leading to strikes and a growing number of anti-Allende demonstrations. Allende's policies also alienated important groups in Chilean politics, including the Church, landowners, and of course the military, who eventually toppled him even though they had never taken a leading role in Chilean politics in the past.

The fall of Allende demonstrated that even success in a democratic election would not make Marxists acceptable to Washington. Press revelations about CIA involvement led to an embarrassing Congressional investigation into the Agency's activities in the late 1970s. And Pinochet's brutal regime was an embarrassment to the US through the 1980s. Successfully confirmed in office in a 1980 referendum, Pinochet failed a similar test in 1989 and resigned, though he remained an important force in the background. Under his elected successor, the centrist Patricio Aylwin, Chile experienced good growth rates, comparable to other parts of the 'Pacific Rim' in the early 1990s and a stable liberal democracy seemed to have returned.

The Fall of South Vietnam and Cambodia

The January 1973 peace settlement (Chapter 12, C) in Vietnam removed American forces from the country but never brought real 'peace' to the South, where the communists and the Thieu regime continued to struggle for power. During 1973–4, over 50,000 South Vietnamese, troops, and twice as many communists, as well as thousands of civilians, died in the continued fighting. Thieu refused to recognize the existence of the opposition National Liberation Front or to accept the losses of territory which the 1973 settlement implied. But his regime was dogged by high inflation, widespread corruption, and large-scale desertions (about 200,000 in 1973–4) from its army. With 1 million men and with American equipment, the army looked strong on paper but its morale and leadership remained poor. About one-third of South Vietnam's 17 million people were reduced to refugee status by 1975, many had moved from the countryside to overcrowded towns, and agriculture had been so devastated that the country had to import its staple food, rice. Meanwhile, with the fall of Nixon and the determination of Congress to avoid further involvement and expenditure in South-East Asia, there was increasingly little chance that America would fulfil Nixon's promises of helping Thieu if the communists reneged on the 1973 settlement. Hence Kissinger would later claim that any hope of enforcing the 1973 settlement or of saving Cambodia 'was torpedoed by the United States Congress and our domestic turmoil' over Watergate.[51] Others, however, reject such logic; 'given the public's antipathy toward Vietnam . . . it is doubtful if the United States could have regenerated a commitment to rescue Thieu's government. The Vietnamese Communists . . . were determined eventually to gain power in Saigon. And Thieu, inept and corrupt, was unable to stop them.'[52]

The North Vietnamese continued to probe the South's military weak points in 1973–4 but only in December 1974 did Hanoi decide to abandon the Paris agreements completely and seek Thieu's overthrow. 'A string of local victories gave those in favour of a bolder strategy an edge at a politburo meeting in December 1974, and a two year plan was drawn up' for conquering the South.[53] The Politburo was surprised by the easy advances in the Central Highlands in January 1975 and astonished by how quickly a further offensive, in March, broke the Thieu regime. Thieu himself made the disastrous decision to withdraw his forces from much of the country to the Saigon-Mekong delta area, where more than half the South's population was concentrated. Asked to conduct such a long and dangerous retreat, his demoralized army was soon routed. On 21 April, under US pressure and still refusing to contemplate a coalition government with the communists, he resigned, blaming Washington for the collapse. His successor, Duang Van ('Big') Minh, called a ceasefire nine days later and the way was clear for the communists to create a united, centralized Vietnam. Economic planning was introduced, land redistributed, Southern officials 're-educated' or executed, and Saigon renamed Ho Chi Minh city (after the nationalist leader who had died in 1969). Despite some attempts to establish diplomatic links in 1977–8, the Americans showed little desire to help Vietnam recover from three decades of destruction. Whilst complaining that the Vietnamese were not doing enough to find the few American troops still posted as 'missing in action', Washington froze Vietnamese assets, cut off all aid to the country (as well as to Laos and Cambodia), and reneged on earlier promises of financial assistance.

Meanwhile, in Cambodia there had never been the shadow of a peace agreement in 1973, although Congressional action meant that US military support for the Lon Nol government ceased in mid-August. The extremist Khmer Rouge were suspicious of Hanoi after its settlement with the Americans, rejected the idea of forming a coalition government with the royalist leader, Prince Sihanouk, and exploited rural poverty and US bombing to win local support. By January 1975, only the capital, Phnom Penh, remained in Lon Nol's hands and it fell to the Khmer Rouge on 17 April, just days before the fall of Saigon. The American government demonstrated the following month that it was not quite powerless in the region: when the Khmer Rouge seized a US merchant ship President Ford despatched the marines on a rescue mission which, though unnecessary (the ship was released as the mission began) proved popular at home. The new Cambodian regime, under Pol Pot, proceeded to empty Phnom Penh and conducted a campaign of genocide against upper- and middle-class groups in a ruthless attempt to turn the country into a Maoist rural utopia. By the end of 1978, about 2 million people had died in Pol Pot's 'killing fields', or of starvation and disease.

The image of communist success in South-East Asia was completed in December 1975 by the triumph of the Pathet Lao in Laos, a country which had been subjected to even more American bombing than Cambodia. (Laos had been bombed since 1964, Cambodia only since 1969.) But the old American fear that the fall of one 'domino' would lead to another proved baseless. Propped up by the US, the royalist government in Thailand survived and within a few years the regions' communists were at each other's throats, with Vietnam invading Cambodia in 1978 and China striking against Vietnam in 1979 (Chapter 14). The number of deaths in the post-war Indo-China wars by then ran into several millions, the exact total incalculable.

Angola: The End of Portugal's Empire

The April 1974 'Carnation Revolution' in Portugal, which toppled the Salazar dictatorship, was a military coup that led to the decision to grant independence to the colonies. The empire had been central to Salazar's vision of Portuguese greatness; it provided food and raw materials, and by 1968 half a million Portuguese had settled in the two main colonies, Angola (the wealthiest) and Mozambique. The process of independence proved simple enough for Mozambique and a third, smaller colony, Portuguese Guinea (which became Guinea-Bissau), largely because there was an obvious nationalist opposition group to whom Lisbon could transfer authority. But Angola was a very different case. The divisions between the two main anti-colonial movements in the north of Angola, which were associated with the outbreak of what may be seen as a spontaneous rebellion in March 1961 (see Chapter 8, B) had widened in the 1960s. The difference was that after Lyndon Johnson became President, the dominance of the National Front for the Liberation of Angola (FNLA), led by Holden Roberto, was completely undermined and the leading movement in the struggle to represent Angolan nationalism became the Popular Movement for the Liberation of Angola (MPLA). The latter movement had succeeded after 1964, partly by developing links with the Soviet Union and Cuba, after which it assumed a more Marxist position, and partly by winning support from the government in the neighbouring state of Congo-Brazzaville. This enabled Agostinho Neto, the MPLA leader from December 1962, to rebuild the organization from a headquarters in Brazzaville. The political fragmentation was made worse in 1966 by the formation of another major grouping, the National Union for the Total Liberation of Angola (UNITA), under Jonas Savimbi, who defected from the FLNA in 1964. The founding of UNITA gave a voice to the southern peoples of rural Angola who were generally regarded as less advanced than those in the North. Now there were three groups largely based on the Mbundu, Ovimbundu, and Bakongo people. In addition, the MPLA, in contrast to UNITA and the FLNA, was a *mestico-* (mixed race) dominated party with its strength in the capital, Luanda. This injected an urban and a racial element into what was to become a civil war, as the other two main parties were essentially Black African led.

Partly as a result of these divisions, 'the nationalists posed no critical threat to the Portuguese presence in Angola during the armed struggle'.[54] But then neither could the Portuguese regain complete control over the country, as they had been trying to do since 1961. There were also ideological differences between the increasingly Marxist MPLA and the more pro-Western groupings, and the Chinese injected the Sino-Soviet split into the Angolan issue in the 1970s. From the time a FNLA delegation met with Deng Xaioping in December 1973, China supplied military training and arms until October 1975. Clearly, once the government in Lisbon collapsed in 1974 and independence became inevitable, the Cold War then became an even more important channel for outside intervention. Yet, the American response to these events was confused. In contrast to the Kennedy administration, which saw the Cold War in Africa being won through links with pro-Western Africans who would need help in achieving independence, Kissinger saw things differently. He initially saw the Portuguese as able to resist radical African challenges. After the Carnation Revolution, he had to come to terms with the failure of his assessment but refused to work towards an Angolan coalition government with left-wing elements.

The Carnation Revolution had catapulted General Augusto Spinola to power, who was initially in favour of some grandiose overseas Portuguese federation, but more left-leaning politicians, including the Socialist Party leader, Mário Soares, forced him to concede the principle of independence in July 1974.[55] In Angola, when the dictatorship ended, 'the whole colonial administration fell with it. Soldiers . . . would no longer risk their lives defending a defunct ideology . . . Officials were simply no longer obeyed.'[56] With the collapse of Portuguese authority, international involvement now became more important as it was unclear to which of the factions power would be transferred. Indeed, when the Portuguese flag was finally lowered on 11 November 1975 the High Commissioner handed power to no one group but to the Angolan people as a whole.

The initial idea had been to get the three main parties working together as a coalition in the form of a transitional government before the formal transfer of power in November 1975. Talks between all the parties had led to the 15 January 1975 Alvor Accord, under which a government was to be formed, but the external supply of aid and arms was soon to transform three relatively small and lightly armed forces into major combatants. As early as July 1974, the CIA had begun making payments to the FNLA which, along with Chinese weapons, considerably boosted the effectiveness of Roberto's organization and allowed it to consolidate its position in Northern Angola. In January 1975, the US agreed through a subcommittee of the National Security Council to fund the FLNA to the tune of another $300,000. More dramatic was the subsequent Soviet and Cuban support for the MPLA which followed.[57] At that time, the FLNA with an army of 10–20,000 easily outnumbered the MPLA (about 8,000) and UNITA (reckoned to be about 6,000). Moreover, in 1973–4 the MPLA had seemed bitterly divided, as it had been in 1963: an 'Eastern Revolt' led by Daniel Chipenda threatened Neto's leadership and led to the ending of Soviet assistance just one month before the coup in Lisbon. The resumption of Soviet aid has been dated to between March and October 1974 and was to play a major role in the revival of the MPLA's fortunes in 1975, particularly after March of that year, when the movement began to receive major Soviet arms shipments, followed by Cuban military advisers.[58]

One important question concerning Soviet and Cuban support was whether the Cubans were acting as proxies of Moscow. The evidence now suggests that they had their own reasons for intervening independently in Angola, including an ideological commitment to international revolutionary solidarity. Castro and the Cubans had their own links with the MPLA and were almost certainly asked for help by Neto. 'Castro initiated Cuban armed support for the MPLA without Moscow's . . . knowledge.'[59] Kissinger's claim that Cuban intervention was part of a Soviet geopolitical threat is almost certainly a misperception. It is probably the case that, once independence was conceded by Portugal, the Soviets, Americans, and Cubans had all decided independently to intervene in some form or other, irrespective of the actions of the others. But the scale of the intervention may have been influenced by the activities of rival powers. The Soviets, with their commitment to wars of national liberation, had some claim, not only to undermine the Americans but also to outbid China for support. 'The real object of Moscow's rivalry in Angola was less Washington than Beijing.'[60] This line becomes plausible if large amounts of Soviet aid are taken to be in response to the arrival of Chinese advisers in Angola in May 1975, the same month the Cubans are alleged to have been deployed. On the other hand, if the arrival of significant Soviet aid is taken as March 1975, this may have been a response to discovering US funding of the FLNA.

The Cuban intervention coincided with Kissinger overruling those in the State Department who saw African factors, rather than Soviet geopolitical ambitions, at the root of the conflict. President Ford approved Kissinger's request for $32 million of aid (which actually turned out to be over $60 million) and $16 million of military equipment.[61] Then in August 1975 UNITA formally entered the fray in support of Roberto and was secretly supplied by the Americans the following month. It only remained for the South Africans to throw in their forces in an attempt to destroy the MPLA, preferably before power was to be formally transferred in November. In the face of this mounting threat, the Cuban presence was increased. In late September and early October, significant supplies and equipment arrived from Cuba by boat and they were soon needed. The South African invasion force, including Chipenda's eastern rebels, UNITA soldiers, a small Portuguese force, and about 2,000 men of the South African Defence force, was rapidly closing on Luanda from the south. Faced with the prospect of defeat, the MPLA turned again to the Cubans who, one week before independence, despatched a battalion of crack troops to assist in the defence of Luanda. The result was that the FLNA failed to take control of the city and eventually suffered a disastrous collapse, despite assistance from Zairean troops.

The US successfully pressed Caribbean countries not to allow Cuban transfer flights, but in January 1976 the Soviets began to airlift Cuban troops and by the end of the year it is estimated that there were nearly 10,000 in Angola. By then, the groups seeking to prevent the MPLA governing Angola faced further problems. In December 1975, the American press unearthed the fact that the government was engaged in a covert assistance programme for Angola. Almost immediately, with concerns about 'another Vietnam', the Senate passed the Clark amendment cutting off funds for covert operations in Angola. In February 1976, the MPLA government in Luanda was recognized by the Organisation of African Unity and, in April, it became a member of the United Nations. Many Americans were left doubting the wisdom of backing the FNLA in the first place, in a far-off country where few direct US interests existed. The American-backed FNLA failure in Angola in the face of Cuban and Soviet intervention has come to be seen as a key point in the decline of détente. Yet, Kissinger claims he never raised the issue with the Soviets until October 1975. His argument was that, until then, it was only a question of the strength of the MPLA being raised to equal that of the FLNA, rather than to supersede it. Effectively, the US thought its supporters could win if it channelled vast amounts of aid to them; the consequences for détente emerged when it began to appear that they might not. The troubles in Angola, which were part of a continuing, bloody conflict that went on for decades, were clearly exacerbated by the involvement of external forces. Whatever Kissinger may have claimed about their implications for détente, they revealed more than anything that the battle for the hearts and minds of newly independent people was as intense as ever. The Cuban and—as it was perceived—Soviet 'victory' in Angola added to the questions surrounding détente and further indicated that both superpowers were prepared to put their Cold War interests above mutual cooperation[62].

Visit the online resources that accompany this book to test your understanding and take your learning further: www.oup.com/he/young-kent3e

NOTES

1. Mohammed Heikal, *Sphinx and Commissar* (Collins, London, 1978), 243.
2. Anwar el-Sadat, *In Search of Identity* (Collins, London, 1978), 232.
3. Chaim Herzog, *The War of Atonement* (Weidenfeld & Nicolson, London, 1975), 51.
4. Ritchie Ovendale, *The Origins of the Arab–Israeli Wars* (3rd edn, Longman, London, 1999), 220.
5. Walter Isaacson, *Kissinger* (Faber & Faber, Boston, 1992), 529.
6. Gil Carl Alroy, *The Kissinger Experience: American Policy in the Middle East* (Horizon Press, New York, 1975), 85.
7. Henry Kissinger, *Years of Upheaval* (Weidenfeld & Nicolson, London, 1982), 560.
8. Mohammed Heikal, *Sphinx and Commissar* (Collins, London, 1978), 263.

9. M. E. Yapp, *The Near East since the First World War* (Longman, Harlow, 1996), 423.
10. Galia Golan, *Yom Kippur and After* (Cambridge University Press, Cambridge, 1977), 250.
11. Coral Bell, *The Diplomacy of Détente* (St Martin's Press, London, 1977), 96.
12. Amnon Sella, *Soviet Political and Military Conduct in the Middle East* (Macmillan, Basingstoke, 1981), 122–3.
13. Elizabeth Picard, *Lebanon: A Shattered Country* (Holmes & Meier, New York, 1996), x–xi.
14. Farid el Khazen, *The Breakdown of the State in Lebanon* (Harvard University Press, Cambridge, 2000), 388.
15. Elizabeth Picard, *Lebanon: A Shattered Country* (Holmes & Meier, New York, 1996), 81.
16. Farid el Khazen, *The Breakdown of the State in Lebanon* (Harvard University Press, Cambridge, 2000).
17. Avi Shlaim *The Iron Wall* (Penguin, London, 2002), 327.
18. Derek Urwin, *A Political History of Western Europe since 1945* (Longman, Harlow, 1997), 216.
19. William Ashworth, *A Short History of the International Economy since 1850* (Longman, London, 1987), 299–300.
20. M. E. Yapp, *The Near East since the First World War* (Longman, Harlow, 1996), 422.
21. Paul Bailey, *Postwar Japan* (Blackwell, Oxford, 1996), 132–3.
22. David Fieldhouse, *The West and the Third World* (Blackwell, Oxford, 1999), 229.
23. Frank Castigliola, *France and the United States* (Macmillan, New York, 1992), 174.
24. William Bundy, *A Tangled Web* (Hill & Wang, New York, 1998), 415.
25. Robert Schulzinger, *Henry Kissinger* (Columbia University Press, New York, 1989), 212.
26. Henry Kissinger, *Years of Upheaval* (Weidenfeld & Nicolson, London, 1982), 193.
27. Geoffrey and Nigel Swain, *Eastern Europe since 1945* (2nd edn, St Martin's Press, New York, 1998), 146.
28. Z. A. B. Zeman, *The Making and Breaking of Communist Europe* (2nd edn, Blackwell, Oxford, 1991), 268.
29. David Mason, *Revolution and Transition in East-Central Europe* (2nd edn, Westview Press, Boulder, 1996), 34.
30. George Schopflin, *Politics in Eastern Europe* (Blackwell, Oxford, 1993), 158.
31. Geoffrey and Nigel Swain, *Eastern Europe since 1945* (2nd edn, St Martin's Press, New York, 1998), 147.
32. John Pinder, *The Building of the European Union* (Oxford University Press, New York, 1998), 16.
33. Patrick McCarthy, *The Crisis of the Italian State* (Macmillan, Basingstoke, 1995), 106.
34. Martin Clark, *Modern Italy* (Longman, London, 1996), 387–8.
35. Tad Szulc, *The Illusion of Peace* (Viking Press, New York, 1978), 764.
36. Mary Fulbrook, *Germany 1918–90* (Blackwell, Oxford, 1991), 209.
37. Anthony Nichols, *The Bonn Republic* (Longman, London, 1997), 235.
38. Willy Brandt, *People and Politics* (Collins, London, 1978), 498.
39. Dennis Bark and David Gress, *Democracy and its Discontents* (Oxford, 1993), 221.
40. Klaus Larres, 'International Security and Relations', in Mary Fulbrook (ed.), *Europe since 1945* (Oxford University Press, Oxford, 2001), 220.
41. Derek Urwin, *A Political History of Western Europe since 1945* (Longman, Harlow, 1997), 208.
42. John van Oudenaren, *Détente in Europe* (Duke University Press, Durham, 1991), 327.
43. Philip Thody, *Europe since 1945* (Routledge, New York, 2000), 54.
44. Both quoted in Richard Stevenson, *The Rise and Fall of Détente* (Macmillan, Basingstoke, 1985), 173.
45. Clive Church and Gisela Hendriks, *Continuity and Change in Contemporary Europe* (Elgar, Aldershot, 1995), 137.
46. Paul Sigmund, *The Overthrow of Allende* (University of Pittsburgh Press, Pittsburgh, 1977), 286.

47. Henry Kissinger, *Years of Upheaval* (Weidenfeld & Nicolson, London, 1982), 374.

48. Edy Kaufman, *Crisis in Allende's Chile* (Praeger, New York, 1988), 11.

49. Tad Szulc, *The Illusion of Peace* (Viking Press, New York, 1978), 720.

50. Leslie Bethell, *Chile since Independence* (Cambridge University Press, Cambridge, 1993), 158.

51. Henry Kissinger, *Years of Upheaval* (Weidenfeld & Nicolson, London, 1982), 369.

52. Stanley Karnow, *Vietnam* (Viking Press, New York, 1985), 656–7.

53. Marilyn Young, *The Vietnam Wars* (HarperCollins, New York, 1991), 292.

54. Norrie MacQueen, *The Decolonization of Portuguese Africa* (Longman, London, 1997), 35.

55. Fernando Andresen Guimaraes, *The Origins of the Angolan Civil War* (Macmillan, Basingstoke, 1998), 89–92.

56. Malyn Newitt, *Portugal in Africa* (Hurst, London, 1981), 245.

57. Soviet caution reflected the caution of Leonid Brezhnev, who was pressured by Andropov to provide more support for revolutionary movements for essentially ideological reasons. We are indebted to Arne Westad for this information obtained from his research in Soviet archives, details of which can be found in his book, *The Global Cold War: Third World Interventions and the Making of our Times* (Cambridge University Press, 2005, New York).

58. Fernando Andresen Guimaraes, *The Origins of the Angolan Civil War* (Macmillan, Basingstoke, 1998), 98, 103.

59. Odd Arne Westad, 'Moscow and the Angolan Crisis', *Cold War International History Project Bulletin*, nos 8–9 (Winter, 1996–7), 21.

60. Norrie MacQueen, *The Decolonization of Portuguese Africa* (Longman, London, 1997), 194.

61. Fernando Andresen Guimaraes, *The Origins of the Angolan Civil War* (Macmillan, Basingstoke, 1998), 166, 176, 186, 190; Raymond L. Gartoff, *Détente and Confrontation* (Brookings Institution, Washington, 1985), 508–11.

62. J. Marcum, *The Angolan Revolution*, vol. 2, *Exile Politics and Guerrilla Warfare 1962–1976* (MIT Press, Cambridge, 1981), 269–71.

14

Détente in Decline, 1977–9

Chapter contents

A. Détente and the Carter Presidency

Questioning of Détente in America

In March 1976, as he set out on the presidential campaign, Gerald Ford decided that 'détente' had become so unpopular that the word should not even be used by his election team. In 1972, the Beijing and Moscow summits had been oversold to help Nixon's re-election and since then numerous events had bred scepticism about détente in the US. It suffered in part from being identified with Nixon, who was discredited by the Watergate scandal. But his downfall also removed the one leading right-wing politician who was both trusted in the Kremlin and able to reassure American conservatives that national interests were not compromised by talks with the Soviets. After 1973, conservatives increasingly questioned détente, felt that the Strategic Arms Limitation Treaty (SALT I) benefited the USSR most, and were disturbed by an apparent pattern of communist adventurism abroad, in the 1973 Middle East War, Angola, and South-East Asia. Kissinger's argument that the Soviets could be co-opted into an orderly, 'normal' pattern of behaviour through a process of détente was questioned by those who believed they saw a determined Soviet strategy to advance in the less developed world whilst seeking nuclear superiority. Richard Pipes, one of the most consistent academic critics of détente, considered that the Soviets had abandoned confrontation 'in favour of less risky, flanking movements carried out, preferably by proxy forces, by way of the less developed world', that they hoped to divide the West by relaxing tension, and that they pursued 'at the same time, a major rearmament programme for possible World War III by projecting a peaceful image to weaken the Western defence effort'.[1]

Liberals in the Democratic Party were also doubtful about détente and the amoral outlook of foreign policy under Nixon and Kissinger. After Vietnam, it was perhaps inevitable that the crusading, idealistic element in US policy—which had helped lead to the Vietnam War in the first place—would reassert itself. Whereas, on the Republican Right, such idealism took the form of patriotic anti-Communism, in the Democratic Party it tended towards liberal anti-totalitarianism. Both groups criticized the 1975 Helsinki agreements for their failure adequately to protect human rights in the Eastern bloc and for condoning Soviet domination of the region. They also criticized the USSR's failure to allow sufficient Jews to emigrate. The Democratic Senator, Henry Jackson, a presidential hopeful, began a campaign in 1972 which linked both criticisms of SALT and the emigration issue. In December 1974, Ford was forced to accept the Jackson–Vanik amendment, which made an expansion of US–Soviet trade (under their 1972 commercial agreement) conditional on greater Jewish emigration. On 7 January, Kissinger warned Ford that this would severely damage America's ability to influence Moscow through 'linkage': 'The Soviets have to keep détente going for political reasons, but our hold on them is gone. These economic projects would have gotten our hooks into them for years.'[2] Sure enough, Jackson–Vanik immediately backfired. On 10 January, the Soviets, unwilling to accept such 'interference' in their internal affairs, simply scrapped the trade deal. Then they cut back the number of emigrants: in 1973 about 35,000 Jews had been allowed to leave the USSR, a big increase on the few hundred who left in 1968, but in 1975 the number fell to only 13,000. Yet, whatever its direct outcome, Jackson's campaign succeeded in highlighting the strength of opposition, across the political spectrum, to détente. On the Republican Right, Reagan 'saw the issue as tailor-made for his campaign against the Washington establishment. Using Henry Kissinger as a foil, he could attack the Ford administration without attacking Ford.'[3]

The Soviet Union and the Interpretation of Détente

Disappointment with détente was not one-sided. Moscow argued that the Americans were undermining it with their own actions in the less developed world (notably the campaign against Chile's Salvador Allende), their refusal to give the USSR a full role in Middle East peacemaking, and their attempts (with Jackson–Vanik) to interfere in Soviet domestic politics. Defence Minister Marshall Grechko (1967–76) was fearful that military agreements with the US might compromise the strength of Soviet armed forces, even if he continued to recognize the political benefits of a decrease in tensions. But in contrast to America, real faith in détente did survive in Moscow. Soviet politics were, of course, much less volatile than America's. With no public opinion to measure and no free press, the Kremlin was better able than the White House to control the policy-making machine. Brezhnev, though in physical decline (he suffered strokes in 1975 and 1978), kept the Politburo favourable to détente, despite the increasing doubts of some members. Even though the SALT II talks stalled in 1975–6 and the US–Soviet trade deal was scrapped, there were no major foreign policy humiliations—such as America suffered in Vietnam—to cause a questioning of Brezhnev's policy. Any failures were compensated for by the success of Soviet allies in Angola and Vietnam, and by advances in European détente. Besides, the USSR always had a more flexible view of détente than the US, arguing that it should include elements of cooperation, such as nuclear arms control, but also allow for competition in the less developed world. Thus, at the 25th Soviet Communist Party Congress, in February–March 1976, Brezhnev spoke in favour both of détente and of wars of national liberation. As the Soviet Ambassador to Washington, Anatoly Dobrynin, put it:

> members of the Politburo lived in the certainty that a historical process was under way: the collapse of the old colonial empires and the general weakening of the capitalist system . . . For ideological reasons we should support this process whenever possible, but this did not mean that we deliberately were trying to undermine . . . American interests . . .[4]

One central problem with the détente process, of course, was that each superpower had different interests in pursuing it, different interpretations of how it should work, and different expectations about where it should lead. Neither side had ever intended to give up its ideology or dismantle its alliances. But, 'while both superpowers were engaged in a process of adjustment, they were adjusting to different vulnerabilities and responding to different concerns'.[5] Thus, whereas the Soviets expected to win equality of status with the US, to retain their hold on Eastern Europe, and to secure agreements on trade and SALT, whilst continuing to support wars of national liberation, Americans had other expectations. Faced by relative American decline, economic problems, and the costs of Vietnam, Nixon and Kissinger hoped to use 'linkage' to secure Soviet good behaviour and an acceptance of the existing world order, especially in the less developed world, in return for SALT and trade deals. But in a pluralist Western system, it was harder for US leaders to keep the American body politic united behind détente. Soviet advances in the less developed world, mounting problems in NATO, and Congressional opposition made it more important for Kissinger to demonstrate a tough approach to the Soviets where he could, in the Middle East or the SALT II talks for example; but this, in turn, harmed trust between the superpowers. To many Americans, it was quite clear that, through its interference in Africa and South-East Asia, the USSR had violated détente but, 'while it is possible to take issue with the premisses . . . of Soviet policy . . . it is harder to argue that they sought to delude the West about their understanding of . . . détente, or to speak of Soviet violation of détente',[6] because, again, their view of détente was, quite simply, not the same as America's.

Policy-making under Carter

Although he avoided major military involvement abroad, Carter's foreign policy has been criticized as incoherent, misguided, and at the mercy of events. One blunt judgement, from a major study of US foreign policy, is that he 'confused friends and enemies alike, provoking contempt at home and abroad'.[7] He came to power as a Washington outsider who exploited popular dissatisfaction with the Nixon–Ford era, tried to appear during the 1976 election as 'all things to all men', and promised more than he could deliver. He seemed a hard-working, well-intentioned, certainly intelligent and well-informed leader, inspired both by liberal idealism and evangelical Christianity. But he lacked an overall programme (equivalent, for example, to Johnson's 'Great Society'), became obsessed by policy details, and was unable to master Congress, making effective government very difficult. He was not even very popular in the Democratic Party and in 1980 the Republicans successfully tarred him with the image of retreat and decline. To be fair, he faced problems which would have tried any president. Inflation, the energy crisis, the Vietnam syndrome, a shift in popular support away from costly Federal spending programmes, and Congressional limits on presidential powers abroad were all bad enough. But Carter was also elected in the bicentenary year of American independence, when expectations of a new era of achievement were high. He certainly tried to rise to the occasion in his acceptance speech at the 1976 Democratic Convention, describing America as 'a pioneer in shaping more just and decent relations among people' and stating that this required 'nothing less than a sustained architectural effort to shape an international framework of peace within which our own ideals gradually can become a global reality'.[8] Three years after the War Powers Act, two years after Nixon's resignation, and one year after the fall of Saigon, Carter believed the US still had the capacity to shape the world in its own image. But what followed failed to live up to such ambitious rhetoric.

Carter's policy-making machine has received particular criticism, not least because of the tension between his Secretary of State, Cyrus Vance, and National Security Adviser, Zbigniew Brzezinski, who, in particular, differed over détente (see Box 14.1). Vance, known for his pragmatism and caution, shared Carter's desire to improve relations with less developed world states. But he was not the President's first choice for the State Department and gradually lost influence to Brzezinski, who had sat with Carter before 1977 on the 'Trilateral Commission', a group formed to improve relations between America, Western Europe, and Japan—the three pillars of the Western alliance who had seemed to drift apart in the Kissinger years. Given to outspoken statements and to toughness in crises, the Polish-born Brzezinski believed the Soviets must be resisted in the less developed world, and he was ready to work with Beijing against Moscow. Vance, in contrast, was keen to proceed with SALT II, reluctant to cooperate with China, and sceptical about the USSR's ability to shape conflicts in the less developed world. In Afghanistan after 1979, he was eventually proved correct in his belief that the Soviets could no more manipulate poor, predominantly rural societies than America had been able to do in Vietnam.

Carter himself sometimes seemed to view the Brzezinski–Vance relationship as one of creative tension. But the division among his aides often seemed to run out of control and did not help Carter escape his own frequent indecision. Rather than giving consistent direction to policy, he was a workaholic who often became preoccupied with the complexities of a particular issue, refused to delegate work despite the enormous pressures on his own timetable, and appeared to pursue several different tracks at once. Then again, it has been argued that, in trying

BOX 14.1

Carter, Vance, and Brzezinski

Whereas foreign policy under Nixon had been dominated by the President and Kissinger, under Carter there was a broader group of policy-makers, including the Secretary of Defense, Harold Brown, and ambassador to the UN, Andrew Young, but with the key characters being the Secretary of State, Cyrus Vance, and National Security Adviser, Zbigniew Brzezinski. Jimmy Carter himself had only limited experience of foreign affairs before entering the White House. Born in Plains, Georgia in 1925, he joined the Navy during the war and served in submarines between 1948 and 1953. He then took over the family peanut business and, in the 1960s, became active in Georgia politics. Nationally, he was a virtual unknown quantity when he entered the race for the presidency. A 'born again' Christian, politically liberal yet from America's 'deep south'—which had not provided a president for more than century—he won the Democratic nomination surprisingly easily, before beating the incumbent Gerald Ford. Carter laid great emphasis on human rights in his foreign policy and had some major successes, notably over Panama and Egyptian–Israeli relations. However, he suffered setbacks over Iran and the revival of the Cold War in 1979–80, as well as over the economy, where unemployment was rising. In the 1980 election, he was challenged by Edward Kennedy from within his own party, then beaten by Ronald Reagan. In contrast to many presidents, however, Carter continued to play an active international role after his defeat, championing human rights and taking part in peacemaking efforts under Bill Clinton, eventually winning the Nobel Prize.

One of the criticisms levelled at Carter was that he failed to prevent growing tension between Vance and Brzezinski. Both shared Carter's belief in an active US diplomacy in the wake of the Vietnam failure, continued engagement with détente, and an emphasis on human rights. But Brzezinski was more determinedly anti-Soviet, increasingly sceptical about détente, and ready to intimidate Moscow through the 'normalization' of relations with China. Brzezinski was an academic writer on international affairs, who was not American by birth. Born in Warsaw in 1928, the son of a Polish diplomat, he had been educated in Canada after the war, before studying for his PhD at Harvard in 1950–3 and taking American citizenship in 1958. He headed the prestigious Institute on Communist Affairs at Columbia University in the 1960s and acted as an adviser to both the Kennedy and Johnson administrations. He met Carter on the Trilateral Commission, set up in 1973 to improve US relations with Western Europe and Japan, Brzezinski being its Director.

Cyrus Vance was somewhat older than either Carter or Brzezinski, being born in West Virginia in 1917. He had a more traditionally 'establishment' background, having been educated at Yale Law School, and working for a New York law firm (1946–61) following wartime naval service. After 1957, he served as counsel to the Senate Armed Services Committee and, in 1961, he was brought into government by Kennedy, serving as Secretary of the Army. Under Johnson in 1964–7, Vance was Deputy Secretary of Defense, in which position he was involved in various diplomatic discussions. In 1968, having become a critic of the Vietnam War, he was part of the US team in the Paris peace talks that were opened with Hanoi. Vance thus brought considerable experience in diplomatic and defence matters to the Carter team and had a primary negotiating role over Panama, the Middle East, and SALT. By 1980, however, it was definitely Brzezinski's tough anti-communism that held the upper hand in Washington. Brzezinski also backed the ill-fated attempt to rescue US hostages in Iran that April, which Vance opposed, choosing to resign over the issue. In the 1980s, Brzezinski returned to academic life and Vance to law practice. But the latter, like Carter, did re-emerge as an international figure in the 1990s, notably trying to settle the Bosnian problem in 1992–3.

(in contrast to his successor, Ronald Reagan) to come to terms with a complicated world, he was 'championing a post-Cold War foreign policy before the Cold War was over'.[9] Confident that the US was far stronger than the USSR if it came to war but recognizing that the 'Vietnam Syndrome' virtually ruled out the use of military force, Carter and his team at first believed it sensible to restrain military spending and concentrate on such issues in East–West relations as arms control, trade, and human rights. Aware too that there was now a 'multipolar' world, beyond the domination of the superpowers, they were anxious to address the North–South divide, to improve relations with NATO and Japan, and to retreat from America's past support for right-wing dictators in the less developed world. Yet the administration's attempt to break free of America's long obsession with the Soviet communist menace always carried tensions within it. Carter's policy may actually have made some sense, but it was poorly articulated and executed. Carter himself, though determined to maintain détente on the arms control front, was a strong liberal and Christian, who had triumphed over Ford in 1976 by attacking Soviet domination of Eastern Europe and who talked of an 'absolute' commitment to human rights in his inaugural address.

His belief that détente could safely be combined with an attack on the Soviet's human rights record proved naive. As early as February 1977, Brezhnev, as confused as anyone about what the new President stood for, complained about a letter Carter wrote to the leading dissident scientist, Andrei Sakharov. By highlighting Soviet internal repression and increasing expenditure on such propaganda outlets as Radio Liberty and Radio Free Europe, Carter hoped both to restore a moral tone to foreign policy after the Nixon years and to satisfy the anti-détente lobby in the US. Brzezinski 'saw in human rights an opportunity to put the Soviet Union ideologically on the defensive'.[10] But Nixon had been little interested in the human rights issue and under Ford the so-called 'Sonnenfeldt Doctrine' had argued that the best way to change the Soviet system was to encourage gradual evolution to a less oppressive regime via cultural, scientific, and media contacts. Nor did Carter's more ideologically driven campaign have any immediate success. Instead, like the Jackson–Vanik amendment, it only angered the Soviets, who abhorred any meddling in their internal affairs. In 1978, harsh sentences were imposed on Yuri Orlov and other dissidents, some of whom were accused of working for the Central Intelligence Agency (CIA).

Repression in the USSR encouraged American critics of détente, whose leaders launched the 'Committee on the Present Danger' in November 1976. The Committee argued, in contrast to Carter and some of his advisers, that the USSR was an increasing threat to US interests, that the Soviets might soon overtake America in terms of military power, and that there must be a return to confrontational resistance. By appealing to familiar ideas in post-war foreign policy, claiming to be bipartisan, and exploiting Soviet actions in the less developed world, the Committee won increasing sympathy in the press and among the public. Carter's human rights emphasis, indeed, proved a poor focus for foreign policy. It appealed to the idealism of Americans perhaps, but the President himself knew that he lived in an imperfect world where foreign policy could not be executed according to a rigid morality. In the less developed world, America was reliant on any number of distasteful but pro-American and anti-communist regimes from the Shah's Iran to Ferdinand Marcos's Philippines. And it was also difficult to criticize the authoritarianism of communist China when Brzezenski was determined to 'play the China Card' against Moscow. As a result, the human rights policy was 'often ambiguous, sometimes proved divisive and held only a tenuous relationship to many of Carter's more pragmatic policies'.[11]

B. The Middle East: Lebanon and Camp David

The Lebanese Civil War

By the end of 1975, fighting and religious killings were seriously affecting the Lebanese capital, Beirut, and the Christians were expelling Muslims from quarters under their control. Kamal Jumblatt, leader of the Lebanese National Movement (LNM), which was allied to the Palestine Liberation Organization (PLO), now sought to seize control of Lebanon and establish a secular state, as the Christian Maronite position was weakening.[12] The fighting in Beirut aroused the concerns of the Israelis and Syrians, who were both fearful of a Jumblatt victory. Syria had long had a keen interest in developments within Lebanon, not least because the country contained the main opposition elements to its government. The Syrian president, Hafez al-Assad, had close connections with leading Maronite families, and the collapse of the Lebanese state presented him with new problems. The Syrians first sought to re-establish the old constitutional arrangements in modified form, which would have ended the Christian parliamentary majority in return for the Muslims no longer holding the majority of important offices. But a Constitutional Document, influenced by the Syrians, was rejected in February 1976 by the Muslims, largely because they were in a strong position on the ground. Consequently, Assad 'was filled with horror at the prospect of a radical, adventurist Lebanon on his flank, provoking Israel and alarming the West'.[13] Moreover, if the Druze and the PLO triumphed, the Maronites would likely be pushed firmly into the arms of the Israelis. Assad hoped to avoid this by military intervention in June 1976 on the side of the Maronites. Usually seen as a radical Arab leader, Assad was keen to pacify the situation on his borders, gain influence over PLO activities, and prevent a war with Israel breaking out. The Israelis for their part established direct contact with the Christian militias in 1976 but were divided over the extent to which they should involve themselves in the conflict.

By the summer of 1976, the Israelis were providing assistance to militias in the South but, on 15 October, Syria proclaimed a ceasefire and the following day an

Arab summit considered the situation in Lebanon and agreed that the Syrian forces would be transformed into an Arab Deterrent Force. The first phase of the Lebanese Civil War was effectively over. It had produced much loss of life in Beirut and, rather than solving Lebanon's problems, had made them worse. The army had broken up and the population had regrouped geographically to reflect confessional divisions more firmly. The political position of the PLO was stronger, even if its military position was weaker. 'It was now politically established and secure, recognized, and taken seriously in the world of international diplomacy, and in possession of a platform that many judged to be pragmatic [an independent Palestine state] and a basis for serious negotiation.'[14] Initially, the Syrians were keen to use their forces against the PLO to restore order. But the Israelis were suspicious of this and insisted on what became known as the 'red line' in southern Lebanon: this meant that the Syrians would not despatch forces south of the line from Sidon to the Lebanese–Syrian border. The problem was that PLO activists moved themselves to this very area, where they could do most harm to Israel. The quest for security was actually bringing greater danger.

In 1977, a bad situation became worse. Likud, a right-wing party determined to maintain the sacred land of Israel, was elected to power for the first time under Menachem Begin. And, when Egypt's President Sadat launched his peace initiative with Israel (discussed below) the consequence for Lebanon was to push the PLO and the Syrians back together again. The LNM began to fall apart and Jumblatt was assassinated in March 1977. The conflict was now beginning to focus on the PLO and the Israelis. The latter began to create and finance an ally in the South, Major Saa'd Hadad, a Greek Orthodox army officer, to weld the Christian militias together. In March 1978, there was a short-lived Israeli invasion of southern Lebanon. It was widely condemned and led to the establishment of a small UN 'Interim Force' in Lebanon (UNIFIL), but the situation continued to deteriorate. The PLO was no longer the only opponent of Israel there. Militant Shi'ites now looked for protection to AMAL, the armed wing of the Shi'ite 'Movement for the Dispossessed', established in the year of the Israeli invasion and funded by the Syrians. Meanwhile, in northern Lebanon traditional Maronite leaders, such as former President Camille Chamoun, lost influence to hard-line Phalangists, led by Bashir Gemayel. The Israeli intervention weakened the position of the Syrians perhaps, but their influence was being replaced by other, more radical forces.

Origins of the Egyptian–Israeli Agreement

The Israeli–Egyptian peace settlement, signed in Washington in March 1979—six months after a breakthrough summit at Camp David—was Carter's greatest foreign policy success as president and evidence that he was no luckless mediocrity. At the time it was signed, Brzezinski wrote of the 'electricity in the air, a sense of joy . . . for Carter, it was a spectacular and historic triumph'.[15] The complexities of Middle East politics fascinated the President who had a deep interest in the Bible, an idealistic commitment to peace, a desire to master details, and a reluctance to admit defeat. America also had a clear national interest in settling the Arab–Israeli dispute, partly to ease the pressure on oil prices and partly to avoid another regional war, which might involve the superpowers. Both Secretary of State Vance and National Security Adviser Brzezinski agreed on the need for action and shared Carter's open-mindedness about how a general settlement should be achieved.

The basic formula for an Arab–Israeli agreement was provided by United Nations Resolution 242, which broadly promised the Arabs the return of land conquered by Israel in return for a guarantee of Israel's right to exist. Under Nixon and Ford, US policy focused on achieving a military disengagement of the two sides rather than a general settlement. 'Kissinger's step-by-step diplomacy avoided the central issues of the Arab–Israeli conflict', not least the Palestinian problem and the territorial issues left by the 1967 War.[16] But, in early 1977, Brzezinski began to study possible ways to achieve a general settlement in stages, while Vance visited Israel and Arab capitals in order both to explore their views and reinforce US diplomatic links in the region. Then, when Israeli premier Yitzhak Rabin visited Washington in March, Carter managed to upset both the Arabs and Israelis. By speaking indelicately of Israel's need for defensible borders, he suggested that the 1967 frontiers would not be fully restored, but by talking of the need for a Palestinian 'homeland', he provoked controversy in Israel ahead of its May general election. Carter's first meeting with Sadat, in April, was rather more successful. The Egyptian President was keen to see America involve itself closely in the Arab–Israeli dispute. 'Developing the dialogue with Washington could translate into pressure on Israel to return territory, relieve Sadat of having to deal directly with Israel, and obtain financial and military assistance from the United States.'[17] He wanted Sinai to be returned to Egypt and was ready to be flexible on the issue of recognizing Israel. He also quickly developed a trust in Carter, describing him as 'true to himself and true to others. It is because he is so honest . . . that is why I have no difficulty in dealing with him.'[18] By mid-May, Carter had also seen King Hussein of Jordan and President Assad of Syria and believed rapid action on a general settlement was possible. He hoped the Israelis might concede a Palestinian homeland, however controversial, if the Arabs normalized their relations with Israel after accepting its right to exist.

But the Israeli election in May produced a shock. Rabin and the Labour Party, which had dominated Israeli politics since 1948, were replaced by a self-righteous former terrorist, Menachem Begin, and his hard-line Likud coalition. Likud was committed to retaining the West Bank and Gaza. 'In early encounters with Carter . . . Begin brought maps with which to illustrate his standard lecture on Judea and Samaria', as he called the West bank. 'History and religion were at the heart of his claim to these territories, not just security.'[19] The Americans were still keen to begin a peace conference in Geneva in 1977, but they recognized that it was impossible to dictate a settlement—even a balanced one—to the regional powers and it was soon decided to invite Begin to Washington to explore ideas with him. He came in July and, whilst ready to talk to the Arabs and consider a withdrawal from Sinai, he wanted to retain territory on the West Bank and objected to anything that suggested that an Arab Palestinian state could be created in Gaza and the West Bank. Despite these unpromising views, Vance made another tour of Arab capitals in August to pave the way for such a conference in Geneva. This tour was followed by a series of visits by Middle Eastern foreign ministers to Washington in September, but these only highlighted the scale of differences between the various countries. There was no agreement, for example, about how to represent the Palestinians in talks, as Israel would not recognize the Arab-backed PLO. Carter became increasingly indecisive and the road to Geneva appeared blocked.

Sadat's Peace Initiative

It was Sadat who broke the growing deadlock by abandoning hopes of a successful Geneva conference and adopting a radical alternative. On 9 November, he dramatically announced his readiness to address the Israeli Parliament and ten days later stood before it, saying 'that we accept to live with you in permanent peace based on justice', with self-determination for the Palestinians, secure borders for Israel, and the return of the 1967 conquests.[20] In private discussions, he still hoped Israel would make concessions on the Palestinians on the West Bank and Gaza, but agreed with Begin that the Geneva conference, if it ever met, would merely be ceremonial. Both men were ready to press on with bilateral Egyptian–Israeli talks. But Sadat was over-optimistic in believing that his peace gesture would win Israeli concessions on the Palestinian front, the US was sceptical about relying on an Egyptian–Israeli deal, and other Arab countries were furious about the Egyptian President's initiative. When Begin returned Sadat's visit, meeting the latter in Ismailia on 25 December, it was clear that the most Israel would do for Palestinians would be to offer a severely limited form of self-government. But another mission by Vance to the Middle East showed that Syria and Jordan would only tolerate Sadat's strategy if it won real political rights for Palestinians and led on to a general settlement, not just an Israeli–Egyptian one.

In early January 1978, Carter, reduced to a spectator after Sadat's 9 November initiative, made his own limited tour of the Middle East and, though still sceptical of the value of an Egyptian–Israeli deal, decided to become more directly involved in the bilateral peace process. Sadat welcomed America's involvement, because he believed this would increase the pressure on Begin to compromise. Sadat 'felt that the American role was essential, especially after his unproductive meeting with Begin in Ismailia . . . what Sadat now sought was an American proposal to break the deadlock' in the direct Egyptian–Israeli talks.[21] By the middle of the month, the Egyptian–Israeli talks had stalled, but a visit by Sadat to Washington in February showed that the Egyptian leader was ready to make more concessions. He was now prepared to make a bilateral deal, as Begin wanted, on the Sinai front, in return for some general principles being agreed on a wider settlement. Nonetheless, several months of further argument and strong American pressure on Israel failed to find an acceptable formula for a bilateral deal. The US, Egyptian, and Israeli Foreign Ministers met at Leeds Castle in England in mid-July but Israel was unwilling to concede the Egyptian desire for a statement of intent on withdrawal from all the occupied territories. It was the failure of this conference that led Carter, on 20 July, to decide that a summit should be held between himself, Sadat, and Begin.

BOX 14.2

The Egyptian–Israeli Peace Treaty of 26 March 1979

The Treaty of Peace was signed by Egypt's President Sadat, and Israeli premier Begin in Washington, with President Carter as witness. The preamble hoped that a narrow Egyptian–Israeli deal would prove 'an important step in the search for a comprehensive peace in the area' and it invited 'other Arab parties to this dispute to join the peace process'. One important reason why other Arab countries did not, in the immediate term, take up this invitation, was that the peace treaty did nothing concrete for the Palestinian cause. The best Sadat could achieve here was a letter, signed alongside the treaty, in which Begin undertook to open talks in the near future, with the objective of establishing a 'self-governing authority in the West Bank and Gaza', in line with the Camp David framework. The peace treaty included nine articles, but the essence of the agreement was contained in the first two paragraphs of Article 1:

The state of war between the parties will be terminated and peace will be established between them upon the exchange of instruments of ratification of this treaty.

Israel will withdraw all its armed forces and civilians from the Sinai, behind the international boundary between Egypt and mandated Palestine . . . and Egypt will resume the exercise of its full sovereignty over the Sinai.

The Israeli withdrawal was to be achieved in stages and, in another letter separate from the treaty, Sadat undertook to exchange ambassadors with Israel within a month after Israel had completed its withdrawal to an interim line. Each country recognized the other's sovereignty, territorial integrity, and right to live in peace. Special security arrangements were made for their mutual border and Israeli ships were guaranteed access through both the Suez Canal and Strait of Tiran—tension over which had helped spark the 1967 War.

Camp David and the Peace Treaty

Carter, Sadat, and Begin met at Camp David for twelve days, beginning on 5 September 1978. The Americans believed that such a long summit, in a secluded location, would allow both Israel and Egypt to clarify their positions and explore a solution, with Carter acting as a mediator. Both Sadat and Begin arrived in a determined mood and for a time the talks were deadlocked, but on 17 September two 'accords' were signed. The first concerned an Egyptian–Israel peace treaty, to be completed in three months, and its formula was unsurprising: in return for normal diplomatic relations (and therefore recognition of its right to exist) Israel would withdraw from the Sinai Peninsula within three years. The second was a much vaguer document on the West Bank, which revealed further retreats on Sadat's part. Israel made no promises about Palestinian independence, the special status of Jerusalem, or even on limiting Jewish settlements in the area, and the document was understood to be totally separate from the peace treaty—so that the treaty could proceed regardless of what happened to the West Bank and Gaza. There was little in the Camp David agreements for Arab states other than Egypt, therefore, and Sadat was now increasingly ostracized in the Arab world. There was in fact, from the outset, a deep divide between Egypt and Israel over what Camp David symbolized. 'Whereas the Egyptians saw [it] as the model for similar understandings with Jordan and Syria . . . Begin saw it as the precise opposite . . . the withdrawal from Sinai would be the end of the story.'[22] He was always determined to hold on to the West Bank.

The Camp David breakthrough was widely seen as being due to Carter's perseverance, skills as a mediator, and (in contrast to his March 1977 behaviour) realism about what might be achieved. But there were difficulties in carrying out the agreements in detail, and it proved impossible to draw up an Egyptian–Israeli peace treaty by December, as originally hoped. Whilst pressing for a treaty to be completed quickly, Begin not only refused to move on the issue of Palestinian rights, but also extended Jewish settlements on the West Bank. It seemed at times that the Camp David deal might unravel. However, the fall of the pro-American Shah of Iran in January 1979 (Chapter 15, B) provoked concern in Washington, Cairo, and Tel Aviv and led to the so-called 'Camp David II' conference of foreign ministers in late February, where both Egypt and Israel were ready to compromise. A personal visit by Carter to the two countries was followed, on 26 March, by the signature of an Egyptian–Israeli peace treaty in Washington. 'Despite six months of negotiation, recrimination, and threats of total breakdown, the final treaty contained no important departures from the Camp David framework.'[23] The Israeli withdrawal from Sinai could now proceed, Sadat promised to exchange ambassadors within a month, and America gave both sides military aid, totalling $4.5 billion, to cement the deal.

The peace treaty caused controversy on both sides. The Israelis had secured peace and normal diplomatic relations with their most powerful Arab neighbour, but withdrawal from the Sinai Peninsula involved the abandonment of oil wells and Jewish settlements there, which upset domestic opinion. There was also some concern in Israel over America's closer military relationship with Egypt and Carter's periodic sympathy for Palestinian rights. In August 1979, a meeting between America's UN ambassador, Andrew Young, and the PLO leader, Yasser Arafat, provoked outrage in Israel. 'The Israelis assumed that . . . Young's meeting signalled a major change in US policy.'[24] Young, who in fact had not consulted the State Department before the interview, was forced to resign. For Sadat, the Sinai was won back but, despite American hopes, even moderate Arabs refused to follow him on the path to peace. The Arab League expelled him, he became heavily reliant on American money, and he had won almost nothing for Palestinians. Furthermore, at home a 'perceptual gap developed within the Egyptian public between what Sadat said was possible and what actually materialized'.[25] Instead Begin, narrowly re-elected in 1981, increased Jewish settlements in the occupied territories, which in turn simply increased Arab loathing of Sadat. On 6 October 1981, he was assassinated by a radical Muslim group in the army, to be succeeded by Hosni Mubarak who, while maintaining peace with Israel, slowly rebuilt relations with the Arab world. As to Carter, he took much of the credit for the peace treaty and continued to exclude the USSR from the peace process, but it was far removed from the general Middle Eastern settlement for which he had originally hoped, and even before it was achieved the focus of concern in the Middle East had moved to Iran, where he faced his worst foreign policy humiliation.

C. Conflict in the Horn of Africa

Marxist Advances in Ethiopia

Hopes that superpower détente might revive after the trials of the mid-1970s were dashed in 1977–8, largely because of events in the Horn of Africa, where a war between Somalia and Ethiopia was again portrayed in the US as evidence of Soviet adventurism in the less developed world. Echoing events in Angola a few years before, the Ogaden War was another African conflict with complex local roots in which Cuban forces intervened decisively, this time on the Ethiopian side. Rather than being seen as a triumph for the Soviet cause, however, later evidence suggests that the conflict wrong-footed Moscow, whose ambitions in the Horn were strictly limited.

In the 1960s and early 1970s, it was Somalia which seemed closest to the communist camp, while Ethiopia, under Emperor Haile Selassie, had made a defence agreement with the US as early as 1953. Somalia, formed in 1960 from the former colonies of Italian and British Somaliland, controlled the strategically placed port of Berbera, positioned where the Red Sea opened into the Indian Ocean. In 1969, Siad Barre became the Somali President, declared a Socialist republic, and increasingly aligned his foreign policy with Moscow. A Somali–Soviet friendship treaty was signed in 1974 and military aid began to flow two years later. Meanwhile, in neighbouring Ethiopia, the ageing Haile Selassie was overthrown in a military coup in September 1974, his traditionalist regime replaced by a Marxist-influenced, authoritarian government controlled by the 'Dergue', a council of military officers. After a long and confusing power struggle, in which many original revolutionary leaders were killed, Colonel Mengistu Haile Mariam ruthlessly eliminated his opponents and seized the leadership of Ethiopia on 3 February 1977. Until then, the 'Dergue' had seen China or Yugoslavia, rather than the USSR, as possible models and allies, but an Ethiopian delegation visited Moscow in July 1976 and the Soviets were probably forewarned of Mengistu's coup.

After February 1977, Ethiopia moved quickly towards Moscow. The ruthless Mengistu distanced himself from China, ended the defence arrangements with the US (which had decided to cut military aid to Ethiopia), and welcomed Cuba's Fidel Castro to Addis Ababa. Although Mengistu had shown no pronounced Marxist commitment in the past, Castro was personally impressed by him and it seemed that the Eastern bloc now had complete control of the Horn of Africa. The Soviets were disturbed by Mengistu's capacity for violence, Ethiopia's economic turmoil, and the lack (until 1984) of a local Communist Party, but hoped to keep both Mengistu and Siad Barre jointly committed to a Marxist future. 'Both Mengistu and Siad Barre were stubborn and ambitious leaders who confronted the Kremlin with difficult choices, which it tried to avoid for as long as possible.'[26] After their success in the Angolan civil war, the USSR and Cuba increasingly saw Africa as a continent where they could limit both American and Chinese influence. Dobrynin writes that, 'having suffered no major international complications because of its interference in Angola, Moscow had no scruples about escalating its activities in other countries' in Africa. But he adds that, from 'the long-term geopolitical point of view, the developments in . . . Africa were unmistakably of local importance, and . . . Moscow regarded them as such'.[27] The Soviets also hoped to counter the US success in dominating the Middle East process, a success that was confirmed in 1977–8 by Carter's leading role in the Camp David peace process. 'Cuba's policy in Africa was guided by Cuban national interest and ideology'[28] rather than the dictates of Moscow.

The Ogaden War

In the Horn of Africa, as in other regional conflicts throughout the Cold War, the designs of a superpower fell foul of deep-seated local enmities, and commitments to client states simply embroiled one superpower in a conflict in which it had no vital interests. Barre had never given up Somali claims to the Ogaden desert region of southern Ethiopia, where a secessionist, pro-Somali movement (the Western Somali Liberation Front) was active throughout the 1970s. Both Mengistu and Barre were stubborn nationalists, but it was the latter who, in spring 1977, rejected Castro's proposal for an Ethiopian–Somali confederation. As the year went on, he also became increasingly concerned about Soviet–Cuban links to Addis Ababa. In May, the Soviets began arms supplies to Ethiopia and the Cubans sent a military mission there. In response, Barre took some aid from China and began to sound out America about assistance. For a time, this threw US policy into confusion: in July 1977 America, Britain, and France agreed in principle to supply arms, but as conflict escalated in the Horn of Africa the Western powers felt it inappropriate to fuel the tension, and in September the State Department publicly said there would be no arms deliveries. 'American interest in detaching Somalia from the Soviet Union was now more than counterbalanced by reluctance to support a blatant invasion of one country by another.'[29] Barre, whose military actions in the Ogaden at this time may have been encouraged by the hope of US arms, felt betrayed. Between July and September, his forces had overrun most of the Ogaden.

Yet if American policy was confused, Soviet actions seemed hopelessly contradictory as their policy of maintaining Somali–Ethiopian unity fell apart. At first, it was not clear which side they would support. Having provided Somalia with weapons and advisers, Moscow must have been aware of planning for the Ogaden invasion and they did not sever arms supplies to Barre until August. Vain attempts to reach a local settlement also seem to have persisted until then. Eventually, however, the Soviets came down on Ethiopia's side and began to provide her with massive arms supplies in late 1977, as the Somali offensive in the Ogaden stalled. Somalia might be militarily better prepared for war but Ethiopia was wealthier, larger in both area and population, and more centrally placed in North-Eastern Africa. Then again, only in August did the Kremlin finally decide to back Ethiopia. It was argued at the time that the 'inadequacy of other explanations for Soviet intervention forces one back to the residual explanation, opportunism: that the Russians will be happy to extend their influence . . . where it appears they can do so without appreciable risk'.[30] It is not an interpretation that has stood the test of time. Evidence from the former Eastern bloc suggests not the expansionism of a Marxist automaton, but a 'relatively benign Soviet Union confronted with a situation it neither anticipated nor desired'.[31] In propaganda terms, however, it was easier to defend a country which was the victim of aggression and Moscow believed Mengistu to be more trustworthy than Barre. The Cubans too were much better disposed to Mengistu than Barre, who was now blamed for dividing the Marxist camp.

Between November 1977—when Barre tore up his friendship treaty with Moscow—and February 1978, about 15,000 Cuban troops and 1,500 Soviet advisers were sent to Ethiopia, and by the end of March they had helped liberate all the Ogaden. The operation was carried out as quickly as possible, to reduce the risk of any outside interference, and the Ethiopian–Cuban forces were careful to call a halt once they reached the Somali border, for fear of upsetting African opinion (and being labelled as aggressors) if they crossed it. Although most Arab states backed the Somalis, most African countries tolerated the Cuban intervention in the Ogaden because local borders were respected. The lack of an invasion of Somalia also made it more difficult for the Americans to condemn Soviet and Cuban activities. But that did not stop the conflict having a detrimental impact on superpower relations and appearing to divide Carter's advisers. On 1 March, Brzezinski stated that Soviet behaviour could lead to problems with SALT II, but the following day Vance insisted, 'There is no linkage between the SALT negotiations and the situation in Ethiopia.'[32]

An 'Arc of Crisis'?

Although guerrilla activity rumbled on for years in the Ogaden, by March 1978 the Soviets and Cubans seemed to have turned the confusion and embarrassment of the previous summer into a decisive triumph. Mengistu's regime survived until 1991, by which time the Cold War had ended. Yet in some ways the confusion went on: whereas the Soviets also now helped Mengistu in his attempts to crush Eritrean separatism in north-eastern Ethiopia, the Cubans saw the Eritreans as pursuing a 'justified national liberation' struggle, a struggle which eventually resulted in success in May 1993. These differences also underline the fact that Castro was no mere Soviet cipher. Nonetheless, as in Angola, the Cubans proved reliable and successful allies for Moscow, but they acted on their own motives, anti-American and pro-revolutionary, and were proud of their own standing in the less developed world, a standing confirmed when Havana hosted the sixth summit of non-aligned countries in September 1979. To many in the US, however, the crude message of the Ogaden War was of a Soviet success, brought by violence and, thanks to Cuban help, without the need for direct Soviet involvement. The Angolan and Ogaden contests may have differed markedly—the first a civil war fought as colonial rule ended, the second an attempt by one country to take advantage of its troubled neighbour in a long-running border dispute—but Cuban armed intervention made them seem part of the same struggle for influence in the less developed world.

In fact, there was evidence of mutual superpower restraint during the war. The US had refused to arm the Somalis; the Soviets and Cubans had refused to violate Somali territory. There had even been an offer to the US from Moscow in January 1978 of joint mediation in the conflict but Washington had rejected this as likely to legitimize the Soviet–Cuban intervention. For American critics of Soviet policy, like Brzezinski, the Ogaden War was not the only problem. Rather, it followed earlier episodes, like Angola and the fall of Vietnam, and it was only the most important part of an 'arc of crisis'—a term first used by Brzezinski in December 1978—stretching from Africa, through the Middle East to Central Asia. 'An Arc of Crisis', he said, 'stretches along the shores of the Indian Ocean, with fragile social and political structures in a region of vital importance to us threatened with fragmentation. The resulting political chaos could well be filled by elements hostile to our values.'[33] Throughout this vast area, it was argued, there was evidence of Soviet trouble-making. In pro-Western Zaire, separatists in the Shaba region (formerly Katanga) had support from the Angolan government and, in May 1978, the US condemned Soviet and Cuban activities there, despite a lack of evidence that they were directly involved. In the late 1970s, a rebellion in Oman had the backing of pro-Soviet South Yemen. In South Yemen itself, in June 1978, an extremist coup coincided with the assassination of the President of North Yemen, at that time aligned with America's ally, Saudi Arabia. Unrest in Iran, political instability in Turkey, and growing Soviet influence in Afghanistan, added to the sense of Western concern.

In fact, all these conflicts had complicated local origins and it was simplistic to see all of them as part of an East–West rivalry: 'the events of the Arc of Crisis cannot be reduced to a simple picture of Soviet trouble-making . . . A straightforward adversary policy is not justified by the facts.'[34] It was easy to misread volatile local situations: the North Yemen government, for example, gladly accepted Saudi aid against South Yemen in 1978–9, but then decided to enter an arms deal with the Soviets, partly to prevent Saudi domination. The US and other Western powers were active enough themselves in many conflicts: France and Belgium helped prop up Zaire, whilst pro-American Iran aided Oman. Both superpowers used allies to advance their influence in the less developed world, both were often forced to back these allies in unpleasant struggles, and both tended to simplify local situations, blaming the other superpower for creating problems. But, in surveying the rivalry of the mid-1970s, Americans believed that they had made the main retreats in Angola, South-East Asia, and the Ogaden. The fact that the Kremlin, even while espousing détente, posed as a defender of national liberation struggles, seemed to confirm the image of a one-sided communist advance and, at the same time, the Soviets were developing the military capacity to act far afield, with airlifts of Cuban troops and an expanded, 'blue water' navy. The fact that the USSR had lost an ally (Somalia) in the Ogaden War was soon forgotten by Brzezinski, who was anxious to punish Moscow for its supposed adventurism. But for the moment his anti-Soviet tendencies were tempered by others in the administration.

In early 1978, Cyrus Vance, who pointed out that the Somalis were the aggressors in the Ogaden and that the Soviets had limited aims, joined Defense Secretary Harold Brown in resisting Brzezinski's pressure for a demonstration of US naval power in the region. The Secretary of State also rejected Brzezinski's claim that the SALT II talks had been 'buried in the sands of the Ogaden'.[35] For Vance, these two issues should not be linked: SALT remained valuable to the US in its own right. 'If the United States accepted the essentially competitive nature of the US–USSR relationship and . . . wanted a SALT agreement, it could not make the latter conditional on Soviet withdrawal from less developed world involvements.'[36] Brzezinski had greater success, however, when he set out to face the Soviets with a US–Chinese combination in the wake of the Ogaden War.

D. Sino-US 'Normalization' and the Sino-Vietnamese War

'Playing the China Card'

The aim of the Nixon–Kissinger 'Opening to China' had been to provide a counterweight to Soviet power, not to threaten the USSR. The Chinese were disappointed with the successes of détente in 1972–5, fearing that the Soviets would now concentrate their military forces in Asia. Yet Beijing continued its policy of improving relations, not only with America, but also with other pro-Western states in East Asia, such as Japan and Malaysia. The fall of Vietnam removed an old problem in Sino-American relations and intensified Sino-Soviet competition for influence in the region since the Vietnamese, historically fearful of Chinese domination, now looked to Moscow as a protector. True, the whole course of Chinese policy was thrown into doubt in 1976, with the deaths first of Zhou Enlai in January, then of Mao himself on 9 September. The option of returning to a radical Maoist path was, however, removed with the arrest of Mao's widow and other members of the so-called 'Gang of Four'. A power struggle then began between the Communist Party chairman, Hua Guofeng, and Deng Xiaoping. Previously number three in the party hierarchy (after Mao and Zhou), Deng had been ousted by the Gang of Four in April 1976 but was rehabilitated in July 1977 and established his predominance in government over the following year. He was suspicious of the Soviets and keen to modernize China through the decentralization of decision-making, production of consumer goods, and expanded trade with the West.

The Carter administration was ready from its outset to consider 'normalizing' relations with Beijing by exchanging formal diplomatic recognition. This was not just an important symbolic step, it would also show the USSR that Sino-American relations were continuing to improve and, significantly, it would involve the US in severing formal diplomatic relations with Taiwan (since the communists and Taiwanese both claimed to be the only legitimate Chinese government). When Cyrus Vance visited Beijing in August 1977, however, the problems with such a course were exposed. Whilst Vance was eager to maintain the policy of 'balance', talking to China and Russia, the Chinese were critical of the SALT II negotiations and wanted a tougher anti-Soviet policy. Also, as Vance told Carter, 'I do not believe that we should feel so compelled to establish diplomatic relations with Beijing that we jeopardize the well-being and security of the people of Taiwan.'[37] Events in the Ogaden (Chapter 14, C), however, made the US more anxious to deter Soviet intervention in the less developed world and Brzezinski became a strong advocate of 'playing the China card', in the global struggle for influence which he believed was intensifying between Washington and Moscow. 'I had . . . become quite preoccupied with Moscow's misuse of détente . . . especially through the Cuban military presence in Ethiopia', he later wrote. 'I believed that a strategic response was necessary.'[38] In May 1978, he made his own visit to Beijing, discussed the strategic threat posed by the USSR, made tough anti-Soviet statements, and even revealed some secrets to the Chinese about American security policies. The contrast between his visit and the earlier journey by the more cautious Vance could not have been greater. The Chinese warmly welcomed Brzezinski; the Soviets were deeply suspicious and continued to strengthen their defences, now deploying Backfire bombers in Asia. There was also renewed Sino-Soviet border tension. In consequence, on the Chinese side, plans 'for normalization . . . moved parallel to stepped-up preparations for military action on China's northern and southern borders' and Beijing's 'need to build a counterweight to Moscow forced a softening of its bargaining position vis-à-vis Washington'.[39] In particular, China proved ready to tolerate US arms sales to Taiwan beyond normalization.

Sino-American normalization was finally agreed on 16 December 1978 and took effect on New Year's Day, 1979, with embassies being officially opened in each capital on 1 March. The Soviets expressed concern at this process on several occasions but, as with the 'Opening to China' in 1971–2, tried not to make their distress too obvious. To Chinese annoyance, the SALT II talks continued but there was no doubt that, in contrast to the early 1970s, the improvement in Sino-American relations in 1978–9 was accompanied by a deterioration in Soviet–American détente. Whereas Nixon and Kissinger had been able to use Sino-Soviet antagonism to play off each communist power against the other, Carter and Brzezinski effectively adopted a one-sided policy that deepened US–Soviet divisions. 'The timing of Sino-American normalization was clearly a triumph for Brzezinski. He strengthened containment while outmaneuvring . . . Vance and his preferred sequence requiring that SALT take precedence.'[40] Certainly, closer links brought benefits to both America and China. In January–February 1979, Deng made a lengthy visit to Washington, discussing trade and investment, and in April the Chinese even allowed the US to use their soil for electronic intelligence gathering about Soviet nuclear missiles. An agreement in July (effective in January 1980) granted China 'most favoured nation' trading status in America. But at the same time the dangers of the new relationship were apparent, especially in East Asia, where the US was drawn into increasingly tolerating bellicose Chinese activity.

The East Asian Impact of Normalization

The improvement in Sino-American relations was accompanied by a similar process between two historic rivals, China and Japan. Talks on a Soviet–Japanese peace treaty, to settle problems left by the Second World War, came to nothing in the mid-1970s, largely because of Moscow's threatening tone and its rejection of Japanese territorial claims to certain islands which had been seized by the Soviets in 1945. The Soviets had probably expected that tough diplomacy would deter Japan from moving closer to China and Tokyo certainly hoped at first to avoid joining China and America in an overtly anti-Soviet combination. But the Soviet tactics backfired, causing grave offence in Japan which, on 12 August 1978, signed a friendship treaty with Beijing. Within 'the next five years, the relationship flourished until China became Japan's number two trading partner—just behind the United States'.[41] The 'growing friendship and economic partnership between the two giant Asian powers fuelled Moscow's anxiety about encirclement' and led the Soviets to strengthen their links to Vietnam.[42]

The 'normalization' process had a direct impact on two other US allies in the region, South Korea and, of course, Taiwan. Although South Korea had relied on the US for protection since 1950 and had sent 50,000 troops to fight in the Vietnam War, Carter had controversially promised, during the 1976 election, to withdraw US forces from the country. He retreated from this pledge once in office—Korea, like Taiwan, had strong supporters in Congress—but force levels were reduced and this helped improve relations with China. Taiwan was, unsurprisingly, an even more difficult issue, another country under American protection but which Beijing claimed as part of its own territory. Even here, however, the drive for improved Sino-American relations allowed problems to be overcome through a compromise which was painful to all sides. The Americans abrogated their defence treaty with Taiwan on 31 December 1979, withdrew US forces from the island, and ended their *de jure* diplomatic recognition of the Taipei government; but diplomatic contacts were effectively maintained via an 'American Institute' in the capital, American arms were sold to the country in April 1979, and Congress forced a Taiwan Relations Act on Carter, which stated that America would forcibly resist any invasion of the island by China. The Act reflected 'a suspicion that China had not given up its option on the use of force to regain Taiwan'.[43] The Chinese did not give up their claim to Taiwan, but said they would seek reunification by peaceful means.

When Deng visited Washington in early 1979, he made it publicly clear that China had been willing to compromise on Taiwan and other issues in order to form an anti-Soviet front. Although the SALT II talks were continuing and Carter was unwilling to join in any anti-Soviet tirades, Deng was critical of Moscow throughout and even threatened to attack her ally, Vietnam. His 'meeting with members of Congress who encouraged China to teach Vietnam a lesson, his visits to US defence industry corporations, and his generally masterful public relations campaign all suggested enhanced US-[Chinese] security cooperation vis-à-vis the Soviet Union and Vietnam'.[44] Relations between China and Vietnam had been worsening since the fall of Saigon in 1975. With the removal of American influence, old Sino-Vietnamese rivalry reasserted itself, fuelled by Vietnam's reliance on the USSR for military and economic aid. Instead of an expansion of communist influence outside Indo-China, as the US had earlier feared, the various communist regimes in the area began to fall out. In particular, China backed Pol Pot's Khmer Rouge government in Cambodia (then called Kampuchea), which was both Maoist and anti-Vietnamese. Despite a visit by Pol Pot to Hanoi in September 1977, Vietnamese–Cambodian border tensions mounted, with China arming the Khmer Rouge and Russia the Vietnamese. By 1978, Sino-Vietnamese border tension was also apparent and both those countries laid claim to the Spratly and Paracel islands in the China Sea. The Vietnamese initiated a campaign of discrimination against their million-strong Chinese minority, about one-quarter of whom fled across the border. Neither side showed any sign of compromise. While China improved its relations with America and Japan, the USSR allowed the Vietnamese into the Council for Mutual Economic Aid (COMECON) in June 1978 and signed a 25-year friendship treaty with them on 3 November. The treaty included a commitment to 'consult' each other if either was attacked.

The Vietnamese Invasion of Cambodia and Sino-Vietnamese War

On 25 December 1978, months of border incidents culminated in a full-scale Vietnamese invasion of Cambodia. Ideological differences had developed between the Vietnamese and Pol Pot, which were exacerbated by the latter's alliance with China. The capital, Phnom Penh, was taken on 7 January and a pro-Vietnamese regime established under the Presidency of former Khmer Rouge guerrilla, Heng Samring. The gruesome story of Pol Pot's policy of genocide in Cambodia was now fully revealed. His regime had killed about 2 million people (out of 7 million) over the previous three-and-a-half years. The Vietnamese invasion was treated in the West not as a 'humanitarian intervention' but as an act of aggression which could not be condoned, however distasteful the Khmer Rouge were. The civil war in Cambodia ran on through the 1980s. American aid helped Thailand cope with the refugee crisis on its border; Japan and most non-communist countries in South-East Asia condemned Hanoi; and China accused Vietnam of seeking to dominate all Indo-China.

Following Deng's return from his American visit the Chinese themselves invaded Vietnam on 17 February 1979. Their 300,000 troops destroyed four provincial capitals and devastated large areas, but did not fare well against Vietnam's experienced armed forces and withdrew within a month. They did however warn, in June, that there would be a second invasion if Vietnam should threaten Thailand. And they had certainly demonstrated their opposition to Vietnam's occupation of Cambodia. The US knew in advance of the Chinese attack but did not consult the Soviets about it, preferring to urge them to show restraint. There was no 'joint planning' of Sino-American policy at this time, but the term 'parallelism' began to be used about the fact that they often moved in unison and it has been said that by his timing of the war, 'Deng made it appear that the United States was a silent partner in the invasion, an attack on a Soviet ally'.[45] Such 'parallelism' only convinced the Soviets, however, that détente was becoming less valuable and, although the USSR and Vietnam found themselves virtually isolated in East Asian politics, they refused to be cowed. Vietnam now decided to allow the Soviets the use of air and naval facilities. It has also been argued that, 'The rapid pace of rapprochement between the United States and China, based as it was to a large extent on an anti-Soviet posture, was evidently one of a number of reasons why the Soviet Union decided to send its troops into Afghanistan.'[46]

E. The SALT II Treaty

By early 1979, following the Ogaden War and Sino-American normalization, the SALT process was the only real evidence that superpower détente remained alive. But rather than giving the process a new hope, the signature of a SALT II treaty in June 1979 was surrounded by doubt. Two years overdue and the product of many compromises, the treaty was immediately called into question in the US Senate, and its ratification was eventually suspended.

The Vladivostok Framework

Whatever its success as an arms restraint measure and evidence of improved superpower relations, the SALT I treaty (Chapter 12, B) on offensive missiles had only ever been an 'interim agreement', to be succeeded by a new arrangement within five years. It also had obvious omissions that a future treaty would have to tackle, not least the multi-independent re-entry vehicle (MIRV), which allowed missiles to be armed with several, individually targeted warheads. The SALT I talks had demonstrated the problems of achieving a balanced US–Soviet agreement. The Soviets were concerned that it did not cover American 'forward-based systems' (FBS) in Western Europe, which could hit the USSR; Americans were concerned that it left the USSR with more land-based and submarine-launched missiles. From the start Senator Henry Jackson, the leading critic of détente, pressed hard for SALT II to be based on equal numbers (or 'ceilings') of missiles on each side, to prevent the possibility of the Soviets gaining nuclear predominance. Within the Nixon administration, the Defense Department took a tough approach to the SALT II talks especially, between July 1973 and November 1975, under James Schlesinger. He was identified with the doctrine of 'extended deterrence', announced in January 1974, a vitally important step in nuclear strategy, which shifted US war planning from a reliance on massive missile strikes to a readiness to fight a 'limited nuclear' war. This might mean the targeting of Soviet missile silos and command centres in order to cripple their war-making ability without the need for nuclear Armageddon. Sometimes called the 'Schlesinger Doctrine', it theoretically gave US planning greater flexibility, but it also introduced the danger that US planners might believe they could successfully fight a nuclear war, thus making it more likely. New weapons planned by America included the Poseidon submarine-launched ballistic missile (SLBM), a powerful MIRVed replacement for Polaris, to be launched from Trident submarines.

Although the SALT II talks formally began in November 1972, progress was slow and not helped by Nixon's decision, partly influenced by Jackson's criticisms, to replace the whole US negotiating team in January 1973. After the President's position was undermined by the Watergate scandal, insufficient time was given by the Americans to SALT II, and the talks became bogged down for months on the issue of 'equal ceilings'. To the Soviets, still technologically behind America even if they had now developed MIRVs, it made no sense to concede equal numbers of missiles. 'Unequal ceilings' had been a main Soviet gain in SALT I, not to be surrendered lightly, especially given the existence, not only of FBS but also of the British, French, and Chinese deterrents, all targeted on the USSR. Kissinger may have been ready to concede unequal ceilings again in SALT II, hoping to use that treaty to consolidate the US lead in MIRVed weapons, but Schlesinger totally opposed such a deal being made and, once President Ford was in office, the Kremlin realized it must retreat. In their summit at Vladivostok on 23–24 November 1974, Ford and Brezhnev agreed a framework SALT II deal. Despite the doubts of the Soviet military, Brezhnev conceded an equal ceiling of 2,400 missiles or bombers on each side, 1,320 of which could be MIRVed. The USSR also agreed to exclude FBS.

Kissinger claimed that the Vladivostok deal left SALT 90 per cent complete and hoped a treaty might be signed in 1975. He also insisted that the deal protected US interests: 'Brezhnev had settled for the equal numbers across the board that the Pentagon had been urging . . . we had made no significant concession.'[47] But the remaining 10 per cent of the treaty included highly technical details and the negotiations continued to be dogged by weapons advances and, more importantly, US domestic politics. Senator Jackson 'ignored the point that his demand for equality had been met and instead began to castigate the administration for what had been left out of the treaty'.[48] One key problem was, whether—or how—to control a new American innovation, the low-flying (and hard to detect) 'cruise' missile. Another, vital to Jackson, was the new Soviet 'Backfire' bomber (which could fly to the US but only one way, and would need refuelling), which the Kremlin therefore treated as a non-strategic weapon. Jackson also pressed the case for limiting the size of Soviet missiles, arguing that 'heavy' launchers would be able to carry more multiple warheads than US missiles. Schlesinger was removed from the Defense Department in November 1975, during the so-called 'Halloween Massacre', but Kissinger was still unable to secure a SALT II deal when he visited Moscow two months later. Thereafter the Ford Presidency was absorbed in the 1976 presidential election.

Delays under Carter

Although Carter was keen to pursue arms control and his Secretary of State, Vance, saw SALT II as central to détente, the new administration almost immediately put the arms talks in jeopardy. Eager to distance himself from his Republican predecessors and keen to reduce nuclear weapons numbers as far as possible, Carter made a well-intentioned but naive attempt, in February 1977, to abandon the Vladivostok formula and press for much lower ceilings. If this strategy had worked, 'the administration would have answered the arms control critics of both the Right and Left. They would be taking a strong response to the Soviet threat while making a commitment for both superpowers to accept meaningful reductions in their strategic forces.'[49] But Brezhnev, who had recently made a speech at Tula supporting both détente and SALT, felt betrayed by Carter's move. The Soviets had spent years negotiating the Vladivostock formula and had no wish to restart the SALT II talks from scratch. When Vance visited Moscow in March, Gromyko told him, 'we are wholly opposed to tampering with the Vladivostok accords. They took too much effort from both our sides to achieve.'[50] The Soviets said that, on the positive side, they were ready to extend talks on military détente (working groups were established on such issues as anti-satellite weapons and a comprehensive test ban), but they rejected the new US negotiating position on SALT II outright. It took several months before the SALT II talks were put back on track. Only in September, when Andrei Gromyko visited Washington, did the Carter administration accept the Vladivostock formula in return for a promise of further arms cuts in a SALT III treaty.

Meanwhile, like Nixon and Ford before him, Carter faced growing domestic criticism of SALT. Congress only narrowly approved his nominee, Paul Warnke, as head of the US negotiating team in March. In June, the President's cancellation of the expensive B-1 bomber project was criticized as a blunder, because it could have been used as a 'bargaining chip' to obtain an equivalent Soviet concession. The Committee on the Present Danger began to warn that, if the Soviets continued to MIRV their heavy missiles, a 'window of vulnerability' would open up in the 1980s, when the US would find itself running second in the nuclear stakes. Actually, claims of a 'window of vulnerability' were as empty as claims, twenty years before, that a 'missile gap' was opening up between America and Russia. In focusing on the deployment of more accurate and MIRVed SS-18s and SS-19s by the USSR, the Committee on the Present Danger overlooked the modernization of US systems, with the development of cruise missiles and the deployment, in May 1977, of a new Minuteman intercontinental ballistic missile (ICBM). In pointing up Soviet talk of 'nuclear war fighting', American critics overlooked that, in the Schlesinger Doctrine (which Carter maintained and developed), the US was doing the same. In August 1977, Carter approved a presidential directive, PD-18, which 'represented a fairly major step toward prescribing a war-waging capability', even if 'for the purpose of reinforcing deterrence by providing a resort if deterrence should fail'.[51]

Until 1976 at least, the CIA was not over-concerned by Moscow's improving nuclear capability, and in 1977 the tone of their intelligence reports may only have changed owing to the prevailing political atmosphere in Washington. Later evidence showed that Soviet defence spending levelled off in 1976, never having been as great as the CIA estimated. In contrast, Carter was strengthening US defence by expanding conventional spending, modernizing America's nuclear arsenal, and beginning experiments with laser particle-beam weapons. Brezhnev's insistence that he wanted a fair SALT II treaty, solidifying nuclear parity not superiority, seems to have been honest enough. Having been the inferior power in the past, the Soviets were quite content with nuclear parity and feared being outrun in any new technological race with America. In 1977, America's SLBMs remained largely immune to a Soviet 'counterforce' attack (even if land-based weapons were vulnerable) and, besides, the US had about 8,500 nuclear warheads compared to the USSR's 4,000.[52] US critics of SALT were sometimes sincere, sometimes scaremongering, but what most seems to have concerned them was the issue of prestige. America's old superiority had gone and nuclear parity had apparently made the Soviets bolder in conflicts in the less developed world. In 1978, however, thanks to the Ogaden War, there was growing pressure within the Carter administration to 'link' progress on SALT II to Soviet behaviour in the less developed world, just as Nixon and Kissinger had tried to do around 1970. Brzezinski, though a consistent supporter of the SALT process, did not feel that the talks could be insulated from other areas of superpower relations. Vance, in contrast, was more ready to accept that détente included elements of competition as well as cooperation, and still argued that a SALT II treaty was valuable in itself: 'we should face the fact of competition with the Soviets, and we should not link Soviet behaviour in the less developed world to issues in which we had so fundamental an interest as SALT'.[53] In late 1978, he believed that SALT must be maintained in order to counteract the negative effect on Moscow of Sino-US normalization.

Carter found it difficult to choose between Vance and Brzezinski on the issue of 'linkage'. On 17 March 1978, he made a speech which pleased his critics by expressing concern over the Soviet arms build-up, promised to maintain strong US defences, and stated that any SALT deal must preserve the nuclear balance. On 7 June, at Annapolis, he warned that the Soviets must choose between 'confrontation or cooperation'. Yet he never categorically linked SALT II to events in the less developed world and he continued to insist that he was loyal to détente. The Soviets studied such declarations with concern. *Pravda* pointed out that the President was being contradictory and the Politburo, noting Carter's continuing attacks on their human rights record, 'had the impression that Carter was leaning toward a policy of confrontation rather than détente'.[54]

The Treaty and its Non-Ratification

Continuing his paradoxical approach to superpower relations, Carter saw no need for normalization to interfere with SALT II. Anxious not to cement the Sino-American relationship, the Soviets too decided to persevere with détente and a final treaty text was announced on 9 May. Less than one month later, however, in another example of his schizophrenia, Carter announced a further significant modernization of the US nuclear arsenal, the development of the Missile Experimental, popularly known as 'MX'. This was a 'heavy', MIRVed missile, designed to match the SS-18s and 19s and allow the US to attack Soviet missile silos. Two hundred were to be built and, in an extremely ambitious building project, announced in September, they were to be protected by being placed on underground railway tracks, with twenty-three possible silos from which each missile might emerge. Ironically, while satisfying some critics, MX was soon questioned on grounds of cost and necessity: it would be the largest US public construction project ever and at the same time the 'Trident II' submarine was being developed, also armed with MIRVed missiles but less vulnerable to Soviet attack.

SALT II was eventually signed at the only Carter–Brezhnev summit, in Vienna on 15–18 June 1979. By accepting 'equal ceilings' and controlling MIRVs, it marked a major departure from SALT I (see Box 14.3). But in contrast to the 1972 Moscow summit, there were no other major US–Soviet agreements. Instead, Carter again criticized the USSR on human rights, Brezhnev (who was clearly unwell) attacked US links to China, and both sides differed on the causes of conflicts in the less developed world. The Soviets ratified the treaty quickly, but in America it was already in serious trouble. 'In retrospect it is clear that the Carter administration did not do an adequate job preparing the ground . . . to ensure sufficient public and congressional support for the SALT II treaty.' Now, 'for the first time he had a public document to defend' whereas his opponents had 'one to attack'.[55] Many in the Senate were

BOX 14.3

The SALT II Agreement, June 1979: Key Points

- There was to be an equal 'ceiling' of 2,400 strategic nuclear weapon launchers or heavy bombers in the arsenal of both superpowers (reducing to 2,250 by 1985).
- Up to 1,320 of these launchers could either be Multi-Independent Re-entry Vehicles (MIRVs) or Air-launched Cruise Missiles (ALCMs).
- Up to 1,200 launchers could be MIRVs.
- Up to 820 of these MIRVs could be on Inter-Continental Ballistic Missiles (ICBMs).
- The USSR could only deploy 308 'heavy' missiles.
- Limits were placed on the number of warheads on a MIRVed missile.
- Limits were placed on the deployment of new types of missile.
- The agreement was to last until 1985.

In addition, the following related points were agreed at the June 1979 Vienna summit:

- An interim protocol to SALT II, to last until 1981, placed limits on Air-Launched Cruise Missiles (ALCMs) and Ground-Launched Cruise Missiles (GLCMs) with a range over 600 kilometres.
- The USSR gave a written guarantee that its 'Backfire' bomber would not be used as a strategic weapon.
- SALT II should be followed by a SALT III treaty, including reductions in weapons numbers and possible controls on intermediate-range weapons in Europe.;
- In the Vienna communiqué, the US and USSR undertook not to seek military superiority over each other.

absolutely convinced that the strategic balance was moving in Moscow's favour and that SALT was useless for halting this trend. The treaty was criticized for failing properly to control the size of Soviet missiles or the 'Backfire' bomber, and for having inadequate verification arrangements.

A brief crisis over Cuba in late August and early September underlined the fragility of détente. The Carter administration, keen to appear tough in its dealings with Moscow, claimed to have 'discovered' the existence of a 2,800-strong Soviet army brigade in Cuba and there were immediate demands from Congress and the US press that it be withdrawn. It soon emerged that the brigade had been there since 1962. Even so, to Cuban annoyance, the Soviets were anxious that the issue should not upset the prospects for SALT II and agreed to downgrade the brigade to a 'training unit'. Carter's toughness on Cuba helped him avoid amendments to SALT II in the Senate in late 1979 and in November the Senate Foreign Relations Committee actually recommended, by nine votes to six, that it be passed. But the danger of amendments soon re-emerged and ratification was suspended following the Soviet invasion of Afghanistan (Chapter 15, C).

Visit the online resources that accompany this book to test your understanding and take your learning further: www.oup.com/he/young-kent3e

NOTES

1. Richard Pipes, *US–Soviet Relations in the Era of Détente* (Westview Press, Boulder, 1981), xii.
2. Henry Kissinger, *Years of Renewal* (Simon & Schuster, New York, 1999), 307.
3. John Robert Greene, *The Presidency of Gerald R. Ford* (University of Kansas Press, Lawrence, 1995), 164.
4. Anatoly Dobrynin, *In Confidence* (Random House, New York, 1995), 408.
5. Mike Bowker and Phil Williams, *Superpower Détente: A Reappraisal* (Sage, London, 1988), 257.
6. Raymond Garthoff, *Détente and Confrontation* (rev. edn, Brookings Institute, Washington, 1994), 57.
7. William Cohen, *The Cambridge History of US Foreign Relations, IV* (Cambridge University Press, Cambridge, 1993), 208.
8. Jimmy Carter, *Why Not the Best?* (Bantam Books, Eastbourne, 1977), 190.
9. David Brinkley, 'The Rising Stock of Jimmy Carter', *Diplomatic History*, 4 (1996), 522.
10. Zbigniew Brzezinski, *Power and Principle: Memoirs of the National Security Adviser 1977–81* (Weidenfeld & Nicolson, London, 1983), 149.
11. David Skidmore, 'Carter and the Failure of Foreign Policy Reform', *Political Science Quarterly*, 4 (1993), 714.
12. Helena Cobban, *The Making of Modern Lebanon* (Hutchinson Education, London, 1985), Chs 2 and 3.
13. Patrick Seale, *Asad of Syria* (I.B. Tauris, London, 1988), 281.
14. Mark Tessler, *A History of the Israeli–Palestinian Conflict* (Indiana University Press, Bloomington, 1994), 499.
15. Zbigniew Brzezinski, *Power and Principle: Memoirs of the National Security Adviser 1977–81* (Weidenfeld & Nicolson, London, 1983), 288.
16. Ishaq Ghanayem and Alden Voth, *The Kissinger Legacy* (Praeger, New York, 1984), 174.
17. Kenneth Stein, *Heroic Diplomacy* (Routledge, New York, 1999), 9.
18. Anwar el-Sadat, *In Search of Identity* (Collins, London, 1978), 302.
19. William Quandt, *Camp David* (Brookings Institution, Washington, DC, 1986), 65.
20. Quoted in David Hirst and Irene Beeson, *Sadat* (Faber, London, 1981), 269.
21. William Quandt, *Camp David* (Brookings Institution, Washington, DC, 1986), 166–7.
22. Ezer Weizman, *The Battle for Peace* (Bantam, New York, 1981), 190–1.
23. Seth Tillman, *The US in the Middle East* (Indiana University Press, Bloomington, 1982), 32.
24. Steven Spiegel, *The Other Arab–Israeli Conflict* (University of Chicago Press, Chicago, 1985), 375.

25. Kenneth Stein, *Heroic Diplomacy* (Routledge, New York, 1999), 258.
26. Paul B. Henze, 'Moscow, Mengistu and the Horn', *Cold War International History Project (CWIHP) Bulletin*, 8–9 (Winter 1996–7), 45.
27. Anatoly Dobrynin, *In Confidence* (Random House, New York, 1995), 403–4.
28. Piero Gleijeses, 'Havana's Policy in Africa', *CWIHP Bulletin*, 8–9 (Winter, 1996–7), 12.
29. Raymond Garthoff, *Détente and Confrontation* (rev. edn, Brookings Institute, Washington, 1994), 702.
30. Christopher Clapham, 'The Soviet Experience in the Horn of Africa', in E. J. Feuchtwanger and Peter Nailor (eds), *The Soviet Union and the Third World* (Macmillan, London, 1981), 218.
31. Paul B. Henze, 'Moscow, Mengistu and the Horn', *Cold War International History Project (CWIHP) Bulletin*, 8–9 (Winter 1996–7), 46.
32. Zbigniew Brzezinski, *Power and Principle: Memoirs of the National Security Adviser 1977–81* (Weidenfeld & Nicolson, London, 1983), 185.
33. *Time Magazine*, 15 January 1979.
34. Fred Halliday, *Threat from the East?* (rev. edn, Penguin, Harmondsworth, 1982), 129.
35. Zbigniew Brzezinski, *Power and Principle: Memoirs of the National Security Adviser 1977–81* (Weidenfeld & Nicolson, London, 1983), 189.
36. David McLellan, *Cyrus Vance* (Rowman & Allanheld, Totowa, 1985), 52.
37. Cyrus Vance, *Hard Choices* (Simon & Schuster, New York, 1983), 76.
38. Zbigniew Brzezinski, *Power and Principle: Memoirs of the National Security Adviser 1977–81* (Weidenfeld & Nicolson, London, 1983), 203–4.
39. Richard Thornton, *China: A Political History* (Westview Press, Boulder, 1982), 404.
40. Richard Thornton, *The Carter Years* (Paragon House, New York, 1991), 124–5.
41. Walter LaFeber, *The Clash: US–Japanese Relations* (W. W Norton & Co., New York, 1997), 369.
42. Christina Holmes, 'The Soviet Union and China', in Gerald Segal (ed.), *The Soviet Union in East Asia* (Heinemann, London, 1983), 25.
43. Rosemary Foot, *The Practice of Power* (Clarendon Press, Oxford, 1997), 228.
44. Robert Ross, *Negotiating Co-operation* (Stanford University Press, Stanford, 1995), 141.
45. Walter LaFeber, *America, Russia and the Cold War* (McGraw-Hill, New York, 1992), 293.
46. Roy Medvedev, *China and the Superpowers* (Blackwell, Oxford, 1986), 124.
47. Henry Kissinger, *Years of Renewal* (Simon & Schuster, New York, 1999), 342.
48. John Robert Greene, *The Presidency of Gerald R. Ford* (University of Kansas Press, Lawrence, 1995), 125.
49. Robert Strong, *Working in the World* (Louisiana State University Press, Baton Rouge, 2000), 38.
50. Andrei Gromyko, *Memories* (Hutchinson, London, 1987), 287.
51. Raymond Garthoff, *Détente and Confrontation* (rev. edn, Brookings Institute, Washington, 1994), 868.
52. It should always be remembered that there are significant problems related to any figures purporting to reveal relative weapons' strengths. Warheads may include bombs released from aircraft or they may not. Weapons can also refer to intercontinental, intermediate, medium, short-range, theatre, or battlefield weapons. It should also be noted that independent institutes generally try to factor in effectiveness by assessing the number of missiles likely to reach their targets (survivability and accuracy) and those capable of destroying hardened underground silos.
53. Cyrus Vance, *Hard Choices* (Simon & Schuster, New York, 1983), 102.
54. Anatoly Dobrynin, *In Confidence* (Random House, New York, 1995), 411.
55. Raymond Garthoff, *Détente and Confrontation* (rev. edn, Brookings Institute, Washington, 1994), 906; Strobe Talbott, *Endgame: The Story of SALT II* (Harper & Row, New York, 1979), 16.

15

The Return to Confrontation, 1979–80

Chapter contents

A. NATO's 'Dual-Track' Decision

The Nuclear Balance in Europe

However slow the progress of the SALT II talks, strategic weapons were at least subject to some efforts at control. Short-range and intermediate-range nuclear weapons, in contrast, continued to grow in number and sophistication, particularly in Europe, where NATO and Warsaw Pact forces still prepared for war against each other, despite détente. The failure to control theatre nuclear weapons led to a new twist in the European arms race at the end of the 1970s, which helped to undermine recent improvements in East–West relations.

In the late 1950s and early 1960s, the Kremlin had built up an arsenal of about 600 intermediate-range SS-4 and SS-5 missiles in Europe, but in the late 1960s, as the US deployed submarine-launched ballistic missiles (SLBMs) and nuclear-armed F-111 aircraft in the theatre, the Soviets had ceased their expansion. The deployment of the SS-20 missile in 1976–7 therefore seemed a 'new' departure and provoked concern in the West. The SS-20 marked a major advance on the older weapons systems it was to replace (SS-4s and SS-5s), being both solid fuelled (and therefore mobile, able to be launched quickly, and less vulnerable to attack) and multiple independent re-entry vehicled (MIRVed) (with several independently targeted warheads on each launcher). SS-20s were also deployed against the Chinese in Asia and were also intended as a match for the Chinese, British, and French nuclear arsenals. The Soviets described the SS-20s as a 'modernization' of their weaponry. The SS-4, for example, was a missile similar to the Thors, which the West had decommissioned in the 1960s. But to some in the West they marked an attempt by the Kremlin to win theatre nuclear superiority.

American critics of the SALT II negotiations saw the SS-20s as evidence that the Soviets wished to outmatch the US in more and more areas. At a time of apparent global nuclear balance, a combination of conventional and nuclear superiority in Europe might, it was argued, allow the Soviets to intimidate West European countries, inducing them to leave NATO. In extreme circumstances, it had been feared since the 1960s (when the Soviets acquired the ability to inflict enormous damage on the US after absorbing a first strike) that the Kremlin might launch an attack on Western Europe, confident that the US would not risk a strategic nuclear exchange. Now, it seemed, the Warsaw Pact's theatre nuclear weapons were also superior to the West's. The situation threatened to break the so-called 'chain of deterrence' (building from battlefield to intercontinental nuclear weapons) on which NATO's defence plans relied and it might also be intended to 'decouple' the US from European defence. Whatever the Soviets' main aim, it was soon clear that they had miscalculated the response. 'If the objective of the SS-20 deployment was to decouple Western Europe from the United States, it was . . . counterproductive; if the deployment was based . . . on military rationale, it was short-sighted, failing as it did to consider possible Western reactions.'[1]

The Carter administration was concerned about NATO defences on coming to office in January 1977, but mainly because of the conventional weapons situation. Carter immediately pressed his European allies to increase their defence budgets by 3 per cent per annum and this target was accepted at a summit meeting in May 1978. The move served as a boost to NATO morale and as a warning to Moscow, although not all West European governments met the target. At the same time, in 1977–8, American troop levels in Europe were increased by over 30,000. Carter's policy was therefore far from weak. He was determined to strengthen US capabilities to achieve a balanced SALT II deal and to attack the Kremlin on the human rights front. But he was not yet convinced that nuclear weapons deployed in Europe needed to be updated and this opened him up to criticism in Europe and America. Even those European leaders like West Germany's Helmut Schmidt, who welcomed détente and a SALT II treaty, were determined to preserve a secure military balance in Europe. They did not wish to see the superpowers negotiate a freeze on their strategic nuclear arsenals whilst there was uncertainty about a stable European balance. The Committee on the Present Danger shared such concerns, warning that the Soviets could also use the 'new Backfire' bomber in the European theatre and pointing out that, whilst SALT II would do nothing to limit SS-20s, it would limit America's deployment of Cruise missiles.

Confidence in Carter was further damaged in 1977–8 by the neutron bomb episode. The neutron bomb, or enhanced radiation weapon, had been developed by the US for 'battlefield' use, and was capable of killing enemy personnel without destroying buildings or other structures. It seemed the perfect weapon to use against Red Army tank divisions in Europe without causing large-scale and long-lasting physical destruction. The NATO Commander, Alexander Haig, was a strong supporter of it. After June 1977, when word of its production was leaked, however, the Soviets launched a propaganda campaign against it as a 'capitalist' weapon, which was designed to kill people while preserving property. It provoked moral concern in Europe too, especially among left-wing groups, including the ruling parties in Britain and West Germany. In January 1978, the US announced that it would be deployed in 1980 unless the USSR ceased deployment of its SS-20s, but European governments were increasingly divided on the decision. The Dutch Defence Minister resigned over it in March. The situation improved on 5 April when, controversially, Helmut Schmidt agreed to accept the weapon, but only two days later Carter decided to postpone production (which was revived in 1981 by his successor, Ronald Reagan). Schmidt felt snubbed, European governments lost faith in Carter, and his American critics renewed their attacks on his indecision.

The Cruise–Pershing Decision

In January 1979, Carter and Schmidt met with France's President Giscard d'Estaing and Britain's James Callaghan on the island of Guadeloupe. All the leaders were keen to maintain a stable nuclear balance in Europe. Thanks to the SS-20 deployment, Western European 'political elites had become increasingly sceptical of Soviet motives'.[2] Carter was anxious to silence his critics in Europe and at home, improving the chances of Congressional ratification of the SALT II treaty. But Schmidt was also determined to provide some concession to left-wingers in his Social Democratic Party and to the unilateral disarmament movement, which was reviving in numbers throughout Europe, after being in decline since the 1960s. The summit therefore agreed on a 'dual-track' approach to theatre nuclear forces. First, a NATO study was set up to decide on the types and numbers of new weapons to be deployed in order to maintain the 'chain of deterrence' (rather than trying to match the number of SS-20s, which would have demanded a large number of warheads). Second, NATO would propose arms control talks on theatre nuclear weapons with the USSR. At the same time, a propaganda effort was launched to convince European people that new systems were needed.

The NATO study was completed in time for the Atlantic Council meeting of mid-December 1979 when it was agreed to deploy 464 ground-launched Cruise missiles and 108 Pershing IIs, each with a single warhead, by 1983. NATO, like the Soviets, argued that this was simply a modernization but, as with the SS-20s, there were important qualitative differences between the old and the new weapons. The stockpile of US nuclear weapons in Europe would actually be cut by 1,000 to 6,000 when including battlefield and short-range weapons. And there was the offer of arms control talks on theatre systems to be negotiated by the superpowers in parallel with a planned SALT III treaty. European leaders saw superpower arms control as going hand in hand with controls on intermediate-range nuclear forces and 'SALT II played a part in European willingness to accept intermediate-range forces.'[3] A NATO communiqué stated that the 'dual-track' decision would 'promote stability and détente in Europe in consonance with . . . the Harmel Report'.[4]

Unfortunately, the 'dual-track' decision was made only two weeks before the Soviet intervention in Afghanistan, which put an end to détente and made meaningful US–Soviet talks impossible in the short term (see Chapter 15, C and D). But even without Afghanistan, the NATO decisions provoked problems, both within the Western alliance and for détente. While Britain, West Germany, and Italy agreed to accept the new missiles on their soil, Belgium and Holland put off a decision, and Denmark and Norway refused to accept them. It was partly because of the deployment that nuclear disarmament movements in Europe continued to expand in membership over the following years. The Soviets certainly did not see the NATO decision as making a limited 'modernization' of Western forces. Cruise missiles were difficult to detect, either on the ground or when fired, and the Pershing II, though limited in range, had a performance equivalent to a counterforce 'first-strike' weapon. It was fast, accurate, and could hit targets deep within the USSR, whereas no SS-20 could hit the US. From the Soviet point of view, the deployment of Pershing IIs appeared as first-strike weapons which could be used to try and win a nuclear war in Europe. Also, the commitment of NATO to arms control talks seemed insincere. Schmidt might genuinely want a deal but NATO military officials apparently supported the 'dual-track' approach, mainly as a way to minimize popular opposition to the deployment decision.

Apart from a visit by Schmidt to Moscow in June 1979, the Western powers made little attempt to explore Soviet reaction to the upcoming 'dual-track' decision, and in October Brezhnev began a public campaign against it, warning NATO not to deploy new missiles if it wanted to secure arms control. After the December Atlantic Council meeting, the Kremlin bluntly rejected the idea of talks. It persisted in this approach for six months as, in the wake of Afghanistan, superpower relations passed through one of their worst phases. Tentative conversations finally opened in Geneva in October 1980 but made only slow progress. The arguments over theatre weapons simply confirmed that each side in the Cold War could only see security issues from its own perspective. What one saw as a modernization of its forces the other saw as a new menace to the nuclear balance. Decisions were taken by each with little regard to the other side's reaction, helping to generate exaggerated fears about what 'real' intentions lay behind the other's move. In contrast to the advances détente made in the commercial and cultural spheres, therefore, military détente in Europe in the 1970s made little progress at all.

B. Origins of the Iranian Revolution

In the mid-1970s, Iran seemed a stable pro-American state set on a course of industrialization and Westernization. Despite the existence of a Marxist party, the Tudeh, and ethnic unrest from the country's Kurds, Arabs, and Azeris, the government's hold on the country appeared strong. The monarch or 'Shah', Mohammed Reza Pahlavi, had substantial modern armed forces and a ruthless, well-trained secret police, SAVAK. The Americans had built up the Shah's regime as a pro-Western bulwark in the region, with the close involvement of the Central Intelligence Agency (CIA) in the 1950s and early 1960s. As its growing oil wealth led to greater financial independence in the late 1960s, Iran developed a key regional role: 'with the British withdrawal [from east of Suez in 1968] looming . . . the US preoccupation with Vietnam, the continuing tide of Arab radicalism, and the fragility of Persian Gulf Arab states, Iran was the only regional country available to fill the vacuum'.[5] Massive arms sales to Iran formed part of the Nixon Doctrine to move the burdens of regional security problems from America to local powers, and Nixon first discussed Iran's role, as a US surrogate in the Middle East, when the Shah visited Washington in October 1969. Iran, being non-Arab, was prepared to supply oil from its massive reserves to America's other major ally in the Middle East, Israel. Nixon visited the country in 1972 and Jimmy Carter followed on New Year's Eve 1977, when he was effusive in his praise for the Shah and called Iran an 'island of stability in one of the more troubled areas of the world'. But, within months of Carter's visit, the Shah was facing widespread unrest and in little more than a year his government was replaced by what, to Westerners, seemed a frightening, alien regime based on Islamic law. This 'Iranian Revolution' sparked off years of instability in the Persian Gulf–Central Asian region, undermined US power in the area, and brought Islamic fundamentalism into play as a new force in world affairs. After decades in which religion had seemed in worldwide retreat before materialism, humanism, and secularism, the Islamic world was rocked by a new theological fervour. One of the victims was the Carter presidency which, ironically, had triumphed in the unpromising Camp David peace process only to see attention quickly shift in the Middle East to the Persian Gulf region, where American policy was soon in tatters.

The Regime of Mohammed Reza Pahlavi

On returning to power in 1953, with the help of MI6 and the CIA, Mohammed Reza Pahlavi followed his father in taking a determinedly anti-leftist line while trying to modernize Iran, using its oil wealth to finance changes and risking aristocratic opposition by adopting land reform. Although at times he allowed civilian cabinets to function, he sacked any prime minister who displeased him and at times relied on military rule (1953–7) or the suspension of the Parliament, the Majlis (1961–3). In 1973–5, the Shah was at the height of his success. To avoid being drawn itself into a security commitment in the Persian Gulf, the American government was happy to build Iran up as a 'regional superpower'. Larger than its neighbours, untroubled by the Arab–Israeli feud, and a proven ally of the West, the country seemed an ideal partner. Washington helped train SAVAK until the early 1960s and then willingly provided military hardware. In return, Iranian troops helped suppress a left-wing, Libyan-backed insurgency against the pro-Western ruler of Oman. The oil price rises which accompanied the 1973 Middle East War allowed the Shah both to finance military expansion and to press on with his hopes of creating a fully developed, industrialized Iran by 1990. The country's oil revenues leapt by eight times in 1973–5 and, between 1973 and 1978 defence spending grew about six times over. But such rapid expansion also brought high inflation and a move by millions of poor peasants into Tehran and other cities, where the infrastructure could not cope with them. The ill-advised dash to create industries, the wasteful concentration on defence expenditure, financial corruption, and autocratic rule made an unattractive mix for Western investors. In 1975, there was a withdrawal of capital, a balance of payments deficit, and a sudden depression. The economic boom had come to a precipitous end.

The Iranian Revolution

The Shah was a hard-working but uninspiring leader, isolated from most of his people and attracting little loyalty beyond the army, SAVAK, and the affluent, educated upper class that profited from his policies. Although he created a political party to mobilize popular support, his regime relied on arbitrary, personal rule, a ruthless secret police, and an absurd propaganda campaign to convince people that his reign marked a return to ancient Persian imperial might. There was no free press or freedom of assembly, the Majlis having been reduced to a rubber stamp. As economic conditions worsened after 1975, a diverse body of opposition grew up, ranging from the Tudeh and other left-wing groups, through middle-class liberals anxious to win political rights, to traditionalists who resented the rapid social changes in the country. The last group included Islamic religious leaders, who disliked both the Shah's long-running attempts to control them and such modern trends as women's equality. The Shah was initially disturbed when Jimmy Carter, with his emphasis on respect for human rights, entered the White House. But 'the Shah appears to have been desirous of placating the United States. He instituted a number of reforms in this area early in 1977.' It has even been argued that the President's human rights policy 'was a major, if inadvertent, factor' in leading to the revolution, because the Shah's rule relied in part on 'the belief of the Iranian people . . . that the US government was determined to maintain the royal dictatorship in power'.[6] Greater freedom of expression was allowed, a law was passed to end detention without trial, and an amnesty was announced for some political prisoners. But by the end of the year, upset that internal criticism of his regime simply became more vocal, the Shah launched another crackdown on his opponents. The US government avoided any condemnation of this, however, partly because Carter wanted the Shah's support for the Camp David peace process.

Serious disturbances in the universities revived in October 1977, with militant Islamic students in the forefront. The fundamentalists' leader was the Ayatollah Ruhollah Khomeini (see Box 15.1), who had left Iran in 1964 in the face of the Shah's attempts to suppress clerical independence. Khomeini, based in Iraq, then in France, had a deep personal hatred of the Shah and supported violent action as part of a determined campaign to destroy the current regime. In January 1978, government criticism of Khomeini led to large-scale riots in the holy city of Qom and sporadic violence continued for months, accompanied by left-wing terrorist activity and interspersed with periods of calm. Western observers long believed that the Shah could survive the troubles, and saw the Leftists as more dangerous opponents than the traditionalists. Washington had no desire to see a pro-Soviet Iran. But Iran's liberals and communists lacked a leader of the stature and ruthlessness of Khomeini. In August 1978, he called for the Shah's overthrow and even non-Islamic groups were willing to cooperate in the now-intensified campaign of opposition. The millions of uneducated poor living in the shanty-towns around Tehran were ready to demonstrate even in the face of the Shah's powerful military machine as discontent with the conditions under the Shah combined with traditional opposition to Westernization.

On 8 September, a declaration of martial law in the capital was followed by the deaths of hundreds of demonstrators at the hands of troops. Marches, clashes, and widespread strikes continued in late September and into October. The oil industry was virtually closed down. The Shah made some attempt to satisfy traditionalist opinion, closing the country's casinos and launching an anti-corruption drive. He also eased censorship. But it was too late. The US was anxious to see him retain power, seeing no acceptable alternative, but American support did him no good: such sophisticated equipment as the airborne warning and control system (AWACS), which Carter had provided, was no use against internal opposition; and the Islamic clergy saw America as representing the Godless materialism which they believed had created Iran's current problems. Furthermore, the policy machine in Washington 'was slow in seeing the seriousness of the crisis. Many of the Middle East experts were tied up with the . . . Camp David peace negotiations' and 'there was still strong resistance to any suggestion that the Shah might be slipping out of power', because his regime had appeared so stable for so long.[7] Carter himself has been criticized for being 'consistently baffled and frustrated by the . . . unpredictable nature of events' in Iran and for ignoring those who did warn of danger.[8]

In early December, religious festivals led to a new upsurge of violence, and a general strike was called. The Shah now tried to hand power to a civilian cabinet, whilst retaining personal control of the army which, since mid-November, had effectively become the government. But it took until 31 December before a well-known, moderate politician, Shapour Bakhtiar, agreed to serve as Prime Minister and he only took office on the understanding that the Shah would leave the country. Demoralized, though determined to retain some dignity, the Shah finally went into exile on 16 January 1979. Bakhtiar then hoped to restore order, but his attempts to deal with the Shah were condemned by Khomeini, and the army was unable to end the strikes and demonstrations.

On 1 February, Khomeini returned to Tehran and created his own government. Bakhtiar, his attempts to form a coalition virtually ignored by other politicians, resigned on the 11th, and the Shah's armed forces disintegrated over the following days. Fears of a left-wing takeover or a descent into complete anarchy ended as Khomeini became the leader of a theocratic, Islamic republic. Considerable turmoil and bloodshed ensued as Khomeini's followers took their revenge on those of the Shah, then turned against the liberal and leftist groups who had helped overthrow him. Khomeini retired to Qom, only occasionally making his views publicly known during religious ceremonies, but he retained ultimate religious and political power until his death in 1989. A prime minister, Mehdi Bazargan, was appointed to head the civilian government but Islamic reform was kept on course by a Revolutionary Council and local revolutionary committees, defended by a new military force, the Revolutionary Guards. As under the Shah, the government controlled the press, the right of assembly, and freedom of expression. It also continued to make money from oil exports. But in contrast to the old modernizing policies, the new order marked a return to religious observance, traditional dress codes, and financial honesty. The events of 1978–9 were compared to the French and Russian revolutions, inspiring a new emphasis on Islamic values throughout the Muslim world.

The Hostages Crisis

The Western powers were closely identified, in the eyes of the Shah's opponents, with his corrupt, arbitrary regime and in late 1978 foreign businesses had been attacked by demonstrators. In December, the US embassy was attacked by a mob, leading Washington to reduce the staff from over a thousand to fewer than a hundred. The Americans made some attempt to establish links to Khomeini's supporters, notably with a meeting between Cyrus Vance and the Iranian Foreign Minister, Ibrahim Yazdi, in September 1979. But President Carter also felt continuing loyalty to the Shah and, in late October 1979, after the latter became ill with cancer, decided to let him into the US for treatment on humanitarian grounds. Despite the danger signs, the Americans were surprised when on 4 November 1979, following two weeks of demonstrations outside, an Iranian mob seized control of the embassy and took 53 Americans hostage. Initial hopes that they would soon be released went unfulfilled. It became obvious that the Iranian government was happy to see the embassy occupied, partly as a way of maintaining enthusiasm for the revolution. Indeed, the occupation may have been planned well in advance, the Shah's entry to America merely providing the excuse for it to go forward, hence the argument that: 'Given the forces at work in Iran at the time, it is difficult to see what the United States could have done differently . . . that would have prevented the breach.'[9]

By Christmas, Carter and the American people were obsessed by the problem, and the President, though faced by an election campaign in 1980, decided that while the crisis lasted, he must remain in Washington. As he later admitted, 'The safety and well-being of the American hostages became a constant concern for me, no matter what other duties I was performing as President.'[10] He did not begin campaigning in the country until April, by which time the humiliation of the siege and America's apparent powerlessness had gravely harmed his chances of a second term. A rescue plan was considered, Iranian assets in the US were frozen, and purchases of Iranian oil were suspended, but Carter was reluctant to move beyond limited, economic sanctions for fear of endangering the hostages' lives. One possible solution, returning the Shah to Tehran to stand trial, as the Iranians demanded, was too distasteful to contemplate.

Although the Iranian militants threatened to put the hostages on trial, the Americans were actually treated well enough. Several black and female prisoners were quickly released and in February 1980 there were signs that Iran wanted a settlement. Abolhassan Bani-Sadr had now been elected as President and he seemed anxious to control the militants. The US believed him to be a 'moderate' who should be encouraged. There seemed good reasons why the Iranians should want to talk. Appalled by the seizure of an embassy and anxious to prevent the Americans from taking more extreme action, the West European and Japanese governments had joined Washington in taking economic sanctions against Iran. And tension was growing between Iran and its Arab neighbour, Iraq, which made it more urgent for Tehran to secure its oil revenues and overseas assets in case it needed to fight a war. Secret talks between Tehran and Washington led to a proposal for a UN-sponsored commission to investigate their differences, but the scheme floundered in the face of Iran's unpredictable politics. When a UN team arrived, Khomeini made a speech condemning US policy and the Revolutionary Council would not grant the team access to the hostages.

In the face of such confusion and failure, and despite the opposition of Cyrus Vance, the Secretary of State, Carter decided on 11 April to launch an armed rescue attempt. Vance 'was convinced that the decision . . . carried great risks for the hostages and for our national interests' and said he would resign if the President did not call it off.[11] Carter refused. The attempt, strongly backed by Zbigniew Brzezinski, went ahead on 24 April but was never likely to be easy. The hostages were held in the middle of a populous city, hundreds of miles from any American base. Hopes of a surprise rescue by helicopters were dashed when insufficient aircraft made it through dust storms to a remote airfield inside Iran; and as the mission was aborted a crash between aircraft on the ground killed eight Americans. Carter had to admit publicly to another failure and Vance resigned. Western allies were upset not to have been consulted about the American action in advance. The Iranians were elated and, despite the death of the Shah on 27 July, held on to the hostages (now dispersed around Tehran to prevent another rescue bid) until the US election was over. There were later claims that Carter's opponents, in Ronald Reagan's campaign team, had established links to Tehran and prevented an early hostage release: a 1992 Congressional investigation found these claims 'not proven' but did criticize the behaviour of the Reagan camp. Carter paid the price for his failure in Iran as it probably contributed to the scale of his electoral defeat, but in its closing phases he handled the hostage crisis well. Following Algerian mediation all were released in return for an unfreezing of Iranian assets, just as Carter left the presidency. But, meanwhile, the danger of regional instability was increased by events in neighbouring Afghanistan.

C. Soviet Intervention in Afghanistan

Debate over Soviet Motivation

Détente was clearly under threat well before 1979. Just as the Americans were increasingly disturbed by Soviet activity in the less developed world, especially because of events in Angola and the Ogaden War, so the Soviets—whilst keen to preserve détente if possible—were alienated by US activities in Latin America, Africa, and the Middle East and by criticism of their human rights policy, Carter's attempts to recast the SALT II treaty, and Brzezinski's 'playing the China card'. However, it was events in Afghanistan at Christmas 1979 which finally spelt the end of détente and the dawn of a new Cold War. On 25 December, in a well-executed operation and without any explanation to Washington, ground troops of the Red Army crossed into Afghanistan while airborne troops landed in the capital, Kabul. Within weeks, the Red Army presence numbered over 80,000. Some US and Western leaders feared the Soviet action to be a well-considered act of expansion, perhaps aimed at exploiting the current turmoil in Iran and extending Soviet influence towards the Indian Ocean and the oil-rich Persian Gulf. Zbigniew Brzezinski saw it as being the result of a US failure to demonstrate sufficient resolve on earlier occasions, noting in his diary that, 'Had we been tougher sooner, had we drawn the line more clearly . . . maybe the Soviets would not have engaged in this act of miscalculation.'[12]

However, Russian evidence on the intervention reveals a doubtful, divided leadership reluctantly acting to prop up communism in a neighbouring state which they believed to lie in their sphere of interest. Rather like Hungary in 1956 or Czechoslovakia in 1968, the Kremlin wished to replace a leader whose policies had become a menace to Soviet interests. They had no wider expansionist ambitions, hoped to withdraw their troops quickly, and even naively hoped that the West would quickly accept their action. 'Moscow did not envisage the long and costly guerrilla war which followed, nor did it see the Afghan

BOX 15.1

Biography: Ruhollah Khomeini (1902–89)

For the first 60 years of his life, Khomeini showed little active interest in politics. Born into a deeply religious family in the town of Khomein, as Ruhollah Hendi, he became a religious writer and scholar, rising to become an 'Ayatollah', a leading Shi'ite Muslim cleric. However, in 1962, the death of the leader of the Iranian Shi'ites, Ayatollah Boroujerdi, freed Khomeini to take a leading role in attacking the regime of the Shah. Khomeini resented the secularization of Iran, its links to America and Israel, and such reforms as votes for women. Exiled in 1963, he settled in neighbouring Iraq and made himself the best-known opponent of the Shah. In 1978, he was forced out of Iraq by Saddam Hussein and moved to Paris, but within months, mounting discontent in Iran forced the Shah out of office. In February 1979, Khomeini was able to return triumphantly to Tehran, was popularly acclaimed as leader of the Iranian Revolution, and, by the end of the year, had become Supreme Leader of an Islamic Revolution. He ruthlessly disposed of his opponents, and set up a theocratic state, putting the Shi'ite clergy in charge of all areas of life. Abroad, he hoped to spread the ideals of the Iranian revolution, he opposed both the US and USSR, and he was a reminder, as the Cold War decayed, that communism and liberal-capitalism were not the only ideological and political systems that could command loyalties. But the term 'fundamentalist', which the West used to describe his regime, was not one he ever used himself. From 1980, his energies became focused on the war with Iraq. Despite the costs of the conflict, he described his acceptance of peace in 1988 as 'more deadly than power' and died soon afterwards.

adventure as a stepping stone to the Indian Ocean and the oil of the Gulf States.'[13] The Politburo saw the threat to their position in Afghanistan as a 'special' case in the less developed world, different, for example, from the coups against nominally Marxist regimes in Africa since the 1960s that the Soviets had taken little action to prevent. Afghanistan was a neighbouring state, with numerous Soviet military advisers on its soil already and an area of Russian activity since the mid-nineteenth century, when the 'Great Game' had been played with the British Empire for influence in Central Asia. It would be easy to see the Soviet invasion as linked to broader international developments. After all, it was launched only days after NATO's 'dual-track' decision. However, the precise reasons for Soviet intervention can only be understood against the background of Afghan internal politics in the 1970s. The internal situation, 'too often omitted in evaluations of Soviet policy . . . acted as the main stimulus, if not complete explanation' for their actions.[14]

Marxist Rule in Afghanistan

Afghanistan, a poor, mountainous country, with a diversity of ethnic groups, had been recognized as fully independent by the British in 1919, after 40 years during which London controlled its external affairs. Two years later the Afghans made a friendship treaty with the USSR but did not, during the inter-war period, fall into the Soviet sphere. In 1955, the government of Prince Mohammed Daud Khan, a cousin of the King, took Afghanistan into the non-aligned movement. Daud, prime minister for a decade after 1953, accepted development aid from both Moscow and Washington. He returned to power in 1973 as president of a new republic, after overthrowing King Zahir, and continued to pursue a non-aligned role, resisting Soviet attempts to draw him closer to them. Increasingly, Daud fell out with the Afghan communists, who had formed the People's Democratic Party of Afghanistan (PDPA) in 1965, only to split into two broad factions soon afterwards. The Khalq faction, whose leading figure was Nur Mohammed Taraki and which also included Hafizullah Amin, drew most of its support from rural areas and was opposed to working with Daud. But the Parcham, led by Babrak Karmal, which drew its support from Kabul and other urban centres, was more moderate and ready to work with Daud and other groups to secure reform. By 1978, however, Prince Daud seemed bent on creating a one-party state with himself as life President. His attempt to exclude the Parcham from power led them to draw closer to the Khalq, whilst his decision to arrest the PDPA leaders in April 1978 led to a successful coup against him. The coup, which was apparently carried out by a communist group in the Afghan army without major Soviet involvement, brought the establishment of a 'Democratic Republic'. But it was significant that this was a coup by a narrow group, not a revolution backed by the Afghan masses. Afghanistan was now 'under the control of a small Communist movement . . . totally unprepared for the power that unexpectedly . . . fell into its hands. Its misuse of that power with a combination of idealistic reformism and brutal authoritarianism started the country on a downward spiral.'[15]

The new government continued to claim to be non-aligned and initially played down the Marxist elements in its policies, but it was dogged by the long-established Khalq–Parcham rivalry, inexperienced in government, and had little popular support. By September 1978, the Khalq were predominant and rapidly pushed on with a reform programme that was partly inspired by Marxist doctrine, and partly by a simple desire to modernize. 'Never before in Afghan history had there been such a ruthless attempt to push through so many basic reforms and fundamental changes in so short a period of time.'[16] The programme included land reform and educational improvements, but many elements, such as improved women's rights, offended Islamic opinion and disturbed the country's traditional social fabric. The use of a repressive secret police also alienated people and, despite the claim to non-alignment, the regime's reliance on the USSR offended the fiercely independent Afghan tribes. A Soviet–Afghan friendship treaty was signed on 5 December 1978 and the number of Soviet advisers in the country rapidly grew from 350 to 4,000. Such pro-Soviet leanings were emphasized in February 1979 when the American ambassador, Adolph Dubs, was kidnapped, only to be killed when the Afghans made a botched attempt to free him. This led the US, perhaps ill-advisedly, to give up its attempts to retain influence in Kabul.

The Kremlin was always doubtful about the wisdom of pressing Marxist reforms on Afghanistan but pleased that, 'for the first time [it] had achieved ideological congruence and de facto alliance with its strategically situated neighbour'.[17] Neither was Moscow over-concerned about the domestic situation in Afghanistan until March 1979. By then, a series of local uprisings had occurred against PDPA, and Afghan refugees began to stream across the long-contested south-eastern border with Pakistan. The Pakistani leader, General Zia ul-Haq, was sympathetic to the pro-Islamic, anti-communist feelings of the exiles and ready to give shelter and aid to groups which formed in opposition to the PDPA. The Afghan government's conscript army was reluctant to put down the uprisings and increasingly the Kabul government's authority was called into question. March 1979 was significant for the Soviets because it saw the worst uprising so far, in Herat, where some of the Afghan army mutinied and a team of Soviet advisers was massacred. This led to an intense debate in the Politburo and requests from the PDPA for Red Army combat troops to prop up the regime. For the moment, the Kremlin resisted such a course, preferring to increase the number of military advisers and the scale of arms supplies. In a sense, Brezhnev and his ministers were in a similar position to that faced by the Americans in South Vietnam in the early 1960s. They felt a moral obligation to a friendly government to which they had provided large-scale assistance already, and which seemed likely to fall from power, with great uncertainty about what might follow. But they had no categorical treaty commitment to assist it, they were well aware of its failings, and they had little desire to see their own forces locked into a prolonged campaign against local insurgents.

The Decision to Intervene

In the last three months of 1979, the Kremlin's reluctance to intervene was overcome largely because of violence and instability within the PDPA. The intervention has been described as 'an avoidable tragedy . . . in which the final script was ordained by perceptions, personalities and ideology far more than "interests" and "strategies"'. The Kremlin had gradually increased its commitment to the PDPA in 1978–9, despite clear problems in Afghanistan. There was an ideological confidence in Moscow that 'mass' support for Marxism would come in due course and this was accompanied by a belief that the USSR needed to secure its position because of the instability in Iran, which lay on Afghanistan's western border. The Soviets recognized the Iranian Revolution as a setback for Washington, but it did not necessarily help the Iranian communists. It could lead to an increasing sense of pan-Islamic feeling among the USSR's Muslim peoples. Within the Kremlin, decision-making was, as usual, confined to a narrow group, but this group was itself divided over policy options. Kosygin and the Chief of General Staff, Marshal Nikoloi Ogarkov, doubted the wisdom of intervention but the Defence Minister, Dimitri Ustinov, was keen to act. Brezhnev, old, suffering arteriosclerosis, and always cautious, was undecided on the course to follow but events in September–October tipped him in favour of intervention.[18]

In September, the Afghan President, Taraki, visited Moscow. Uprisings against the PDPA were now regular and widespread, a third of a million Afghans had fled to Pakistan, and the Soviets considered the wisdom of drawing non-communists into the Kabul government as a step to moderating its policies and so ending the rebellions. Taraki came with a proposal that the Khalq's leading hard-liner, the megalomaniac Amin, should be replaced before steps were taken to improve the government's popularity. The Soviets, keen to limit the power of the Khalq, agreed. 'It appears that the Soviets—quite correctly—placed the main blame for Kabul's unpopular policies on Amin.'[19] But, when Taraki returned to Kabul, he was arrested by Amin, who declared himself President. There were armed clashes in the capital between the PDPA factions and, in October, Taraki was executed. Brezhnev evidently felt personally responsible for Taraki's death and betrayed by Amin, whose behaviour seemed increasingly unstable. True, Amin tried to tone down the reform programme, but he also began to hold secret talks with US officials, leading the Soviets to fear his possible defection from the communist cause.

Ustinov began to plan actively for armed intervention, and to infiltrate special forces into Afghanistan in September. He soon won allies in the Foreign Minister, Andrei Gromyko and KGB Chief, Yuri Andropov. This trio increasingly dominated policy-making during the years of Brezhnev's physical decline. Gromyko was fearful of new US–Chinese links and aware that SALT II might not win Senate approval, so the need to retain US friendship was not high on the list of Soviet priorities. Later claims that the Kremlin was encouraged to act by Carter's supposed weakness of will, were apparently groundless. Andropov was evidently convinced of Amin's unreliability in November, when the latter demanded that the Soviet ambassador be replaced. Initially, Andropov believed the KGB could remove Amin without the large-scale use of the Red Army, but an attempt to assassinate him in mid-December failed.

The Politburo finally decided on military intervention, in Kosygin's absence, on 12 December, but hoped this would have a limited duration, requiring 75,000 troops at most. The action was designed to replace Amin with a more acceptable leader, deter meddling by Pakistan or Iran in Afghan politics, broaden the government, bolster the Afghan army, and end the uprisings. In a sense, it marked the continuation of established Soviet aims through new means. Increasingly, Brezhnev and most of his ministers were convinced that military action was needed if the PDPA government were not to collapse.

Ironically, when the Red Army arrived in force on Christmas Day, Amin welcomed them, believing they had come to prop up his regime. Two days later he was dead and the Soviet argument that they had been 'invited' into Afghanistan by its government, in fulfilment of the friendship treaty, seemed ridiculous. A major international crisis had begun and, for the Soviets, years of war. 'If the Soviet leadership had moved against Amin to exploit the hatred the Afghan people felt for his autocratic rule, then it had failed to realize that after the night of 27 December, this hatred would be transferred to the Soviet Union.'[20]

D. The Revival of Cold War

International Reaction to Afghanistan

Global reaction to the invasion of Afghanistan was far worse than the Kremlin feared. 'Because it involved Soviet troops rather than Cuban or Warsaw Pact forces, the attention of the world was focused directly on Soviet expansionist goals',[21] or what were assumed by some to be expansionist goals. The death of Amin made the Soviet action seem like blatant aggression against a neighbour, rather than an attempt to prop up a fellow communist regime. Western nations, China, and regional powers, like Pakistan and Iran, feared a general expansion of Soviet influence in the region, perhaps a drive towards the Persian Gulf, rather than the limited military operation which the Soviets actually planned. On 14 January 1980, the UN General Assembly voted by 104 to 18 to condemn the invasion and even friends of the USSR, such as India, were critical. On 29 January, 36 Muslim-majority states met in Islamabad, Pakistan to issue their own condemnation of the Kremlin. Some of these states quickly gave aid to the Mujaheddin opponents of the Soviets. Egypt and Saudi Arabia provided financial aid, Iran and Pakistan gave refuge to millions of refugees, and Pakistan allowed Mujaheddin guerrillas to operate from its soil. For Pakistan, indeed, there was a marked change in its standing with the West. General Zia ul-Haq, who had seized power in July 1977, had been widely criticized for the execution of his predecessor, Ali Bhutto, in early 1979. Concern over human rights had led the Carter administration to cut economic aid in April and US–Pakistan relations worsened in November, when a pro-Iranian mob burned the American embassy in Islamabad. But common concern over Soviet expansion now led America and Pakistan to become close partners in 1980 in aiding the Mujaheddin. The Chinese were predictably delighted by the end of Soviet–American détente and 'all Chinese doubts about the direction of US Soviet policy fell away after the invasion of Afghanistan'.[22]

Having launched their invasion hastily, the Soviets had clearly also bungled their propaganda campaign in defence of it. Claims that the Western powers and China had been destabilizing Afghanistan were simply not credible. Outside Eastern Europe, only a handful of states, such as Vietnam, supported Moscow's action. North Korea, Yugoslavia, and Romania now restored links to China, raising the old Soviet fear that Beijing could divide the Eastern bloc. The Soviets were also mistaken if they believed their difficulties over Afghanistan would soon recede. Even the experienced ambassador, Dobrynin, expressed surprise at the lasting strength of America's reaction, asking why it was 'so disproportionately strong when compared, for example, to the Warsaw Pact's invasion of Czechoslovakia'; and he wrote in his memoirs that it was not only the Soviet invasion but also 'the sharp response of the United States [that] proved a final turning point in Soviet–American relations', from which détente did not recover.[23] The summer 1980 Olympic Games held in Moscow, were boycotted by America, China, West Germany, Japan, and more than fifty other states. Then again, most West European states wished to maintain the personal, financial, and commercial links with Eastern Europe which had built up through the decade of détente. For them, Afghanistan was a remote concern and they considered some Soviet misbehaviour on the international stage to be inevitable. Once it became clear that the Soviets had no intention of launching an offensive against the Persian Gulf, it seemed better to concentrate on verbal criticism rather than to introduce sanctions. France's President Giscard d'Estaing and West

Germany's Helmut Schmidt were both resentful of the lack of American consultation over its response to the Afghan Crisis.

Carter's Cold War

In the weeks before Christmas 1979, American politics had been dominated by the Iran hostage crisis which, of course, ran on through 1980. During his last year in office, whatever his perceived weakness on Iran, Carter pursued a wide-ranging policy of toughness towards the USSR. Indeed, although Ronald Reagan became, in the eyes of the world, the personification of the New Cold War of the early 1980s, it was Carter who first adopted a confrontational stance, introducing economic sanctions, reducing high-level diplomatic contacts, and expanding America's nuclear arsenal. If anything, Carter overstated the extent of the Soviet menace in Afghanistan, perhaps in order to win domestic support. Yet the message was not received in the way he intended. His admission in the *New York Times* on 1 January 1980 that recent events had made 'a dramatic change in my own opinion of what the Soviets' ultimate goals are' seemed naive in one sense: it sounded like an admission that his critics on the Committee of the Present Danger had been correct all along, and that he had been too gullible and trusting of Moscow. The statement 'lent credence to the image of his naïvete', helped lead 'to a decline in his credibility and, ultimately, contributed to the election of Ronald Reagan'.[24]

On 4 January, the President announced a series of measures including financial assistance to Pakistan, a suspension of cultural exchanges, trade restrictions, and a grain embargo. Carter also suspended ratification of the SALT II treaty, which had been of such symbolic importance to the détente process. But the impact of the suspension was blunted by two points. First, SALT II had been in such trouble in Congress that it would probably not have been ratified anyway. Second, the State Department made clear the following day that the US would respect the terms of SALT II despite its non-ratification. The Soviets agreed to do the same and the two sides were actually able to hold exploratory talks in Geneva, on a SALT III treaty, before the end of the year. Indeed, there is a case that, in response to Afghanistan, Carter actually took 'no decisive action. That was because there was none to take that would not penalize the United States as much as the Soviet Union.'[25]

It has been argued that the invasion of Afghanistan 'did not validate the argument of people who argued that Soviet strategy [was] expansionist worldwide. It did no more than justify Vance's position that Soviet behaviour was . . . determined by security and status as a superpower.'[26] Yet, at the time, there was a genuine fear in Washington that the invasion of Afghanistan heralded Soviet expansionism, whether or not as a result of détente. There had been examples of Soviet activism in the less developed world throughout the 1970s, and the deployment of Cuban troops in Angola and Ethiopia had been detrimental to détente. Events in Afghanistan could be read as part of a continuing pattern of Soviet behaviour, designed to win influence in the less developed world whilst pursuing détente with America. But the use of the Red Army itself outside the Eastern bloc, for the first time since the Second World War, seemed novel and sinister. Also, the US specifically feared a 'pattern of Soviet expansion aimed at destabilizing core Western interests in the Gulf' because of the Iranian crisis, which had coincidentally 'heightened American sensitivity to events in the area'.[27] Before the Soviet invasion, few Americans knew anything about Afghanistan. Apart from Iran there were plenty of other pressing issues, such as the SALT II ratification and relations with China, and among leading figures only Brzezinski had been concerned by earlier Soviet interference in Afghanistan's internal affairs. The surprise, speed, and ruthlessness of the Red Army's action helped generate real fear. There was little attempt to understand the real Soviet motives for their action, which in any case would have been difficult, given the Kremlin's own confusion. Cyrus Vance, the strongest defender of détente in Washington, fully accepted that a firm stand must be taken. Already deeply 'affected by his experience of the Soviet record on human rights, the president jumped clearly in the direction of Brzezinski', taking the view that the 'Soviet regime was not only morally bankrupt it was expansionist as well'.[28] On 23 January, Carter therefore turned his State of the Union address into a declaration of America's determination to oppose further Soviet adventurism, especially in the Gulf. It has been described as 'an epitaph for détente, highlighting as it did the American reversion to traditional notions of containment'[29] (see Box 15.2).

In February, the US demanded that the Soviets must withdraw from Afghanistan, restoring it to non-aligned status if détente were to be saved. Alongside aid to the Mujaheddin, which was provided in secret from January onwards, this was part of a policy of making the war costly for the Soviets, keeping them 'on trial' in the court of world opinion while deterring them from further aggressive action. The demand was arguably unwise because, as months passed, it became clear that the USSR had no intention of abandoning Afghanistan and the Americans came to appreciate that their own direct interest in Afghanistan was minimal, compared to the need to deal with Moscow on international issues. 'The Carter administration . . . seem not to have learned . . . [that] it is self-defeating to term not acceptable a situation that cannot be changed.'[30] But, under Carter, any return to détente was unthinkable. Vance did suggest discussing Afghanistan with the Soviets but Brzezinski defeated the attempt. One result of Afghanistan in Washington was that Brzezinski's warnings about the USSR's mendacity seemed proven correct and his standing improved. Further evidence of the Carter administration's toughness were the measures taken at this time to improve America's 'war-fighting' capacity, building on the 1974 Schlesinger Doctrine (see Chapter 14, E). The basic idea was to strengthen America's ability to survive a nuclear attack, in particular by safeguarding command and communication centres, while developing the ability to hit such targets in the USSR. It was argued that if America could cripple the Soviet government while preserving its own decision-making intact it might be possible to win a nuclear war. Thus Presidential Directive (PD) number 57, of March 1980, concerned the mobilization of the US economy to fight a nuclear war; PD-58, of June, was directed at protecting key decision-makers in war; and most famously PD-59, of 25 July—parts of which were deliberately leaked to the press—concentrated on selective targeting of Soviet command centres and weapons sites, in various war scenarios. These frightening decisions, which became the basis of US nuclear doctrine throughout the presidencies of Reagan and George Bush, did not necessarily mean that the US was planning war: Brzezinski and the Defense Secretary, Harold Brown, believed they were responding to the USSR's own 'war-fighting' plans. But they helped fuel growing public concern, especially in Western Europe, over the dangers of a nuclear exchange.

In the short term at least, US policy did nothing to force the Soviets out of Afghanistan, even though some measures, especially the grain embargo, caused real harm. The Kremlin was dismayed by the US reaction to its invasion and did not properly understand it. Some Soviet leaders saw it as evidence that the Americans had been looking for an excuse to destroy détente all along and pointed to previous US actions, such as the slow ratification of SALT II and support for China's attack on Vietnam as evidence of this. Moscow never appreciated the adverse impact of its involvement in the less developed world and repeatedly stated its willingness to talk. Brezhnev and the Politburo had evidently always hoped that, after the initial shock of the invasion, détente would revive. There were particular attempts to sustain it in Europe, with a small reduction in the Red Army there. But the Soviets also gave a firm response to the Carter administration's revival of confrontation. Among a wide-ranging series of actions, Western broadcasts to the Eastern bloc were jammed once more, Jewish emigration was cut in 1980 below 100,000, and Soviet armed forces established new bases, notably at Cam Ranh Bay in Vietnam. The resignation of Vance in April was seen, in the Kremlin, as another nail in the coffin of détente and thereafter the sense of a renewed Cold War grew. The death in May of Yugoslavia's leader, Tito, growing domestic unrest in Poland, and the outbreak of war between Iran and Iraq in September all added to international unease and, as Carter's chances of re-election evaporated, there seemed no hope of a return to détente, especially given the anti-communist, strong-arm rhetoric of his Republican opponent, Ronald Reagan.

BOX 15.2

The 'Carter Doctrine', 23 January 1980

The Soviet invasion of Afghanistan at Christmas 1979 created a major challenge for Carter, who already had to face the embarrassing seizure of hostages in nearby Tehran. His prime public response to the situation was delivered during the annual 'State of the Union' address to Congress. The speech began with the assertion that 'it has never been more clear that the state of our Union depends on the state of the world', and it was international relations that took up most of the address. Carter was 'determined that the United States will remain the

BOX 15.2 (continued)

strongest of all nations' but he identified three factors that had created a new set of challenges: the steady growth and increased projection of Soviet military power beyond its own borders; the overwhelming dependence of the Western democracies on oil supplies from the Middle East; and 'the press of social . . . religious . . . economic and political change in . . . the developing world, exemplified by the revolution in Iran'. The Iranian occupation of the US embassy in 1979 had created one difficult problem, but the Soviet invasion of Afghanistan had added to America's difficulties enormously. After reviewing US policy during the Cold War, Carter accused the Kremlin of 'a radical and aggressive new step', which had to be resisted. He listed measures he had taken in response to the Soviet invasion of Afghanistan, including trade limits and an Olympic boycott, then he set out the strategic significance of the Persian Gulf area, which the USSR now seemed to menace: the Red Army was within 300 miles of the Straits of Hormuz, through which much of the West's oil was shipped. The heart of what became known as the Carter Doctrine was the statement that:

> An attempt by any outside force to gain control of the Persian Gulf region will be regarded as an assault on the vital interests of the United States . . . and . . . will be repelled by any means necessary, including military force.

The statement could be compared to the 1957 Eisenhower Doctrine (on the Middle East) or the 1965 Johnson Doctrine (on Latin America) in its determination to prevent communist expansion in a particular region. It was backed up by military preparations. Since 1977, the Carter administration had planned to establish a 'Rapid Deployment Force' for use in emergencies beyond the US and Europe. Now, as part of a substantial increase (5 per cent above inflation) in the defence budget a force of 100,000 men was created.

Visit the online resources that accompany this book to test your understanding and take your learning further: www.oup.com/he/young-kent3e

NOTES

1. Mike Bowker and Phil Williams, *Superpower Détente: A Reappraisal* (Sage, London, 1988), 220.
2. Odd Arne Westad (ed.), *The Fall of Détente* (Oslo University Press, Oslo, 1997), 11.
3. David McLellan, *Cyrus Vance* (Rowman and Allanheld, Totowa, 1985), 144.
4. Quoted in Raymond Garthoff, *Détente and Confrontation* (The Brookings Institution, Washington, 1995), 954.
5. Shireen Hunter, *Iran and the World* (Indiana University Press, Bloomington, 1990), 52.
6. Yonah Alexander and Allan Nanes, *The United States and Iran* (University Publications of America, Frederick, 1980), 435; Richard Cottam, *Iran and the United States: A Cold War Case* (University of Pittsburgh Press, Pittsburgh, 1988), 187.
7. Barry Rubin, *Paved with Good Intentions: The American Experience and Iran* (Oxford University Press, New York, 1990), 207–8.
8. James Bill, *The Eagle and the Lion* (Yale University Press, New Haven, 1988), 257.
9. Shireen Hunter, *Iran and the World* (Indiana University Press, Bloomington, 1990), 55.
10. Jimmy Carter, *Keeping Faith* (Collins, London, 1982), 459.
11. Cyrus Vance, *Hard Choices: Critical Years in American Foreign Policy* (Simon & Schuster, New York, 1983), 410.
12. Zbigniew Brzezinski, *Power and Principle: Memoirs of the National Security Adviser, 1977–81* (Farrar, Straus & Giroux, New York, 1985), 432.
13. Martin Walker, *The Waking Giant* (Joseph, London, 1986), 105.
14. Fred Halliday, 'Soviet Foreign Policy-Making and the Afghanistan War', *Review of International Studies*, 4 (October 1999), 678.
15. Henry Bradsher, *Afghanistan and the Soviet Union* (Duke University Press, Durham, 1983), 74.
16. Bhabani Sen Gupta, *Afghanistan* (Pinter, London, 1986), 55.

17. Alvin Rubinstein, *Soviet Policy toward Turkey, Iran and Afghanistan* (Praeger, New York, 1982), 162.
18. Odd Arne Westad, 'New Russian Evidence on the Soviet Intervention in Afghanistan', *Cold War International History Project Bulletin*, 8–9 (Winter 1996–7), quote from 129.
19. Thomas Hammond, *Red Flag over Afghanistan* (Westview Press, Boulder, 1984), 80.
20. Raja Anwar, *The Tragedy of Afghanistan* (Verso Books, London, 1989), 192.
21. William Watson, *The Collapse of Communism in the Soviet Union* (Greenwood Press, Westport, 1998), 33.
22. Robert Ross, *Negotiating Co-operation: The US and China, 1969–89* (Stanford University Press, Stanford, 1995), 171.
23. Alexander Dobrynin, *In Confidence* (Random House, New York, 1995), 444.
24. Richard Stevenson, *The Rise and Fall of Détente* (Macmillan Press, London, 1995), 204–5.
25. Richard Thornton, *The Carter Years* (Paragon House, New York, 1991), 467.
26. David McLellan, *Cyrus Vance* (Rowman and Allanheld, Totowa, 1985), 156.
27. Odd Arne Westad (ed.), *The Fall of Détente* (Oslo University Press, Oslo, 1997), 24.
28. John Dumbrell, *The Carter Presidency* (Manchester University Press, Manchester, 1995), 129.
29. Mike Bowker and Phil Williams, *Superpower Détente: A Reappraisal* (Sage, London, 1988), 235.
30. Raymond Garthoff, *Détente and Confrontation* (The Brookings Institution, Washington, 1995), 1066.

PART V

From Confrontation to Communist Collapse, 1981–9

The 1980s saw a remarkable change in international relations. The decade began in an atmosphere of revived Cold War confrontation with the Western economies in depression, an uncertain leadership in America, and a number of apparent communist advances in the less developed world. They ended with the collapse of Soviet communism in Eastern Europe, a resurgent US, a new approach to numerous long-running problems in the less developed world, and a relationship between Washington and Moscow which came close to friendship. In so doing, these changes produced a number of fundamental changes in the mainstream political and economic values that dominated the developed world. The economic and political order desired by the Right in the wake of the collapse of the consensus established by the Second World War was strengthened by the subsequent defeat of socialism. After the West's victory in the Cold War, the 1980s were to end with Western expectations of a completely new international order for the 1990s.

Reagan and Confrontation

In the West, the Reagan presidency that was deliberately promoted, if not manufactured, by the forces of the Right, such as the Committee on the Present Danger, marked for some the death of American liberalism. This death has been associated with the end of the Cold War by H. W. Brands, who claims that liberalism, a term increasingly used in a derisory way, was maintained by the Cold War. It may thus be possible to argue that the forces of conservatism, which were weakening liberalism within the US, triumphed because of winning the Cold War. For Brands, the Cold War consensus, which held liberal America together in the form of government intervention (such as Lyndon Johnson's Great Society programme of helping less well-off Americans) was an unusual Cold War feature of American history. Brands argues that the Cold War consensus within America was effectively broken by the Vietnam War and buried with the collapse of the Soviet Union.[1] By then, what was emerging was a distrust of government, the emergence of radical conservatism, born-again right-wing Christian fundamentalism, and the glorification of the individual liberated from society. In foreign policy terms, the question is how far the collapse of the Soviet Union was a result of global changes, of how far it was due to contradictions within communism itself, and of how far the resurgence of the radical Right in the West produced or reinforced it.

Reagan's reference to the Soviet Union as the 'evil Empire' was one feature of the renewed Soviet–American confrontation and antagonism in the early 1980s. Whether this was primarily influenced by the domestic climate or by international concerns is again a moot point, but the two are clearly linked, even if the causal connection appears difficult to find. Another issue is whether a division of the Cold War into two phases reflects all the changes that took place in the Cold War international system. If, for example, one sees the Cold War as a power-political struggle spiced with a large dose of ideology, did it really ever end? If the ideological battle was won by the Right, is the power-political battle centred on US attempts to shape the international system still taking place? If one regards the two rivals as seeking to maintain advantages in managing or changing the existing Cold War system, what are the implications of the Cold War's end? If part of the goal of managing the international system is to preserve the socio-economic status quo for the elites that benefit from it, the Cold War may have reflected different ways of attempting to do this as the global distribution of power was transformed. Unless one accepts a simplistic belief in a consistent Western 'containment' of the largely ill-defined ambitions of the other side, the idea of two Cold Wars sandwiching a period of precarious détente seems increasingly problematic.

The early years of the Reagan administration produced concern in Western Europe about the President's anti-communist rhetoric. Indications that his administration was prepared to fight a limited nuclear war in Europe, with an expectation that victory could be achieved in such a scenario, was especially worrying for many Europeans. The collapse of détente seemed to presage the Cold War becoming hot, as defence expenditure continued to rise. Reagan, astonished to discover that none of this could actually protect ordinary Americans, became convinced that what became known as the Strategic Defence Initiative (SDI) or Star Wars could provide protection by intercepting nuclear missiles before they reached their targets. This was unlikely to be feasible, but if it was, it threatened the whole concept of deterrence by rendering the Soviet nuclear arsenal obsolete. The only way out would be the building of yet more missiles to overwhelm the anti-missile defences, thereby contributing to another arms race.

In the Soviet Union, the early 1980s saw a procession of geriatric leaders who blamed the US for the breakdown of détente and who continued policies which maintained the atmosphere of confrontation. The Soviet intervention in Afghanistan became a full-scale guerrilla war; Poland was placed under martial law for a time; and it was the Soviets who, in late 1983, walked out of nuclear arms talks with the US. In pursuing this uncompromising policy, however, the Kremlin was matched by the Reagan White House. Reagan, a critic of détente and a life-long anti-communist, was more than ready to fight the Cold War which he inherited from the much-maligned Jimmy Carter. The expansion of American defence spending, which Carter had initiated, went on at an even greater pace, and in the less developed world he was determined to challenge the communists' supposed advances. In response to Soviet support for 'wars of national liberation', Reagan advocated support for 'freedom fighters' who took up arms against Marxist regimes. In particular, he supported the Mujaheddin in Afghanistan and the so-called 'Contras', who were seeking the overthrow of the leftist Sandinista regime in Nicaragua. Still fearful of another Vietnam-style imbroglio, yet paradoxically denying that the Vietnam War had been a mistake, the President also proved ready to use military force in limited operations, such as the invasion of Grenada (1987) and the intervention in Lebanon (1982–4).

The most common reason provided for a fundamental change in Cold War attitudes centres on the influence of Mikhail Gorbachev, who was elected as Soviet leader in March 1985. Six months beforehand, superpower relations were frozen in mutual suspicion, nuclear arms talks were in suspension, and each side accused the other of planning for war. Yet, only eight months after becoming General Secretary, Gorbachev was in Geneva, holding a surprisingly successful summit with President Reagan, the first such summit meeting since June 1979. Gorbachev went on to press for substantial cuts in nuclear arsenals, to pull the Red Army out of Afghanistan, to reduce the USSR's conventional forces without a quid pro quo from the West and, ultimately, to accept that the Soviet sphere of influence in Eastern Europe could not be upheld by force.

The End of the Cold War

Gorbachev undoubtedly provided a different approach to East–West relations as part of a reformist agenda, albeit aimed at the maintenance of communism in the Soviet Union. Yet, after 1985, it also became clear that Reagan was willing to change from confrontation to dialogue. That shift is difficult to explain but could be credited predominantly to Gorbachev: one heavily criticized feature of US policy in the late 1980s was that it seemed to react to Soviet behaviour rather than being proactive and taking initiatives. Yet there were other reasons for Reagan to be more positive himself and for contributing to the success of better US–Soviet relations. He had just secured a second term, with a convincing win over the Democrats' Walter Mondale in November 1984, and rather like Eisenhower, the last president to serve two full terms in office, wanted to make his reputation as a peacemaker. Also, those close to him in his first term knew that if the Soviets changed their policies Reagan was ready to talk to them. His suspicion of the Kremlin ran deep but was not based on a sophisticated, broad grasp of international realities. In the early 1980s, he was ready to put forward some dramatic proposals to reduce tension, notably the 'zero option' (to remove all intermediate-range nuclear force (INF) weapons) of November 1981; he genuinely saw his Star Wars anti-ballistic missile programme as the morally correct course; and he genuinely feared nuclear war.

The events that produced the end of the Cold War would not have unfolded in the precise way they did without Gorbachev's particular policies, but it is unhistorical to credit one individual with such a profound revolution in world affairs. There are a number of developments which may have had an important bearing on the end of the Cold War, irrespective of the influence of individuals. Before 1985, the USSR had agreed that nuclear arms talks must recommence and there were signs of reformist tendencies under Andropov. For a few years afterwards, there was intense debate in Western capitals about how far Gorbachev represented a real change in Soviet policy. Only in 1987–8, with the signature of a treaty abolishing INF and the settlement of the Afghan problem, was his true radicalism revealed. And even then, there were arguments in the US over how best to respond, partly because of a reluctance to believe the Cold War was ending.

Exactly when it was over has been the subject of intense academic debate, similar to that surrounding the question of when the Cold War began and how it developed over time. Unlike interstate hot wars, of course, there was no declaration by the protagonists as to when they were, or were not, engaged in Cold War, and how one chooses to date its end depends on what is seen as its key feature: a lack of regular,

BOX V.1

How Many Cold Wars were there?

It was suggested in Part I that the origins of the Cold War were related to the introduction of ideology into a power political dispute. Key elements of this dispute were the creation of regimes in Eastern Europe which would be answerable to Moscow (and thereby remove some of the threats and problems on the borders of the Soviet Union); the preservation of regimes in the Middle East which would be subject to British influence; and the establishment of American military dominance in Japan and the Western Pacific. These features of the prologue, as it might be called, to the Cold War were power-political disagreements about the way vital interests and spheres of influence would be reconciled in a new global order. The first Cold War might be said to have begun in 1946–7 as propaganda, ideological conflict, and fears over the preservation of the respective social and political orders became evident—with the West defining this as 'containing' Soviet power. By 1948, a new Cold War had begun, as the US sought to weaken and undermine communist control over Eastern Europe and the Soviet Union. Both leading powers seemed to believe that ultimately only one system would survive, with many in the US arguing that Soviet communism would have to be destroyed if the nature of the Soviet state were to change and the Cold War end. The communists under Stalin believed that the contradictions of capitalism would ultimately destroy it if communism in Eastern Europe and the Soviet Union could survive under the auspices of a powerful state.

The third Cold War arguably began after Stalin's death in 1953, when the contradictions of capitalism appeared less credible in the short term, the murderous nature of Stalin's regime less acceptable, and the idea of peaceful coexistence more desirable. By 1956, this had changed the Soviet approach and the Americans were questioning the prospect of destroying the Soviet satellite empire without resorting to hot war. The third Cold War was characterized by fears of a major hot war involving thermonuclear weapons, but a greater determination to fight the Cold War as the importance of the former colonial territories assumed greater importance. It took the Cuban Missile Crisis to convince both sides that Cold War competition could lead the two rivals to the brink of hot war outside Europe.

The fourth Cold War in the 1960s can perhaps be seen as the time of relative Soviet gains in military terms and of Moscow's attempt to close the gap with the US, whose capabilities had previously surpassed those of the Soviet Union. The Americans were caught up in a struggle in South-East Asia which had only partially developed as a battle between communist and non-communist forces, but which the US defined in those terms and tried and failed to resolve as part of the Cold War struggle. The relative strength of the two superpowers during the Cold War, highlighted by Soviet gains in this period, is another subject for debate and affects the description of the Cold War world as bipolar and between equals. Again, a more sophisticated analysis might reveal some subtle chronological differences and inequalities in a world generally deemed to be bipolar after 1945.

The fifth Cold War between the late 1960s and 1970s could be defined by the attempts at détente, and the realization that the world was more complex than a struggle between the US and the Soviet Union. The results of decolonization, with the emergence of newly independent states and conflicts in, and over, the less developed world and in the oil-rich Middle East were only partially linked to global rivalries. The emergence of China as a significant force accompanied this and led to ideas of a multipolar world appearing. The fifth Cold War, with its emphasis on détente, can be defined as an attempt to manage this new, more multipolar world in order to secure the same kind of advantages that were sought in the Cold War. Credibility and status as superpowers, as well as the adoption of particular ideologies with their contrasting ways of life, formed part of détente/Cold War and the attempt to preserve or change the global status quo in ideological and power-political terms.

The failure of both sides to achieve what they wanted from détente may have led to the sixth Cold War, from 1979 to 1985. This was characterized by a more proactive American policy with its renewed emphasis on confrontation and armaments, and a determination to avoid any possibility of the Soviets appearing as effective challengers to American power. Why this sixth Cold War ended so suddenly and unexpectedly is a vital question which depends to some extent on what the two powers were trying to achieve in the last phase of the Cold War.

high-level diplomatic contact between Moscow and Washington, the existence of an ideologically based propaganda contest over rival economic and political systems, military competition with preparations for hot war, the existence of two sets of alliances, and involvement by proxy in wars and conflicts might all be taken as important general features. More specific (and therefore easier to measure) would be the division of Europe by the Iron Curtain or the severing of Berlin between Soviet and Western sectors. Some might date the end of the Cold War as early as the INF treaty in 1987, some as late as the disintegration of the USSR in

1991, but a more plausible choice is the twelve months following December 1988. In that month, Gorbachev effectively ended the ideological war between capitalism and communism by denying, in a speech to the UN, that Marxism had a monopoly of the truth. This was when a majority of the American public came to believe the Cold War was over. But only in May 1989 did George Bush, now President, announce the end of the policies designed to prevent the spread of communism which had served as a general guide to US decision-makers since 1945. And the greatest symbol of the division of Germany and Europe, the Berlin Wall, was not breached until November 1989.

Reagan's Victory?

Right-wingers in the US and realists thinkers in international relations have always argued that as the Cold War ended with a victory for the West, it was thanks to Reagan rather than Gorbachev. This was not because the President had finally embraced the détente he once despised, but because his tough policies of the early 1980s, the arms spending, and the support for 'freedom fighters', were seen as having put such strains on the communist system in the USSR that it faced disintegration unless it attempted radical change. Thus, to the thesis which argued that Gorbachev had taken the initiative in ending confrontation, was opposed an alternative view that the Soviet leader only adopted 'new thinking' because he had to do so, and that this was thanks to Reagan.

A radically different view puts the emphasis not on Gorbachev moving away from confrontation but on a crucial change in Reagan's thinking. The opposite interpretation focuses on Reagan's conversion to a more cooperative and less confrontational position. The conversion was inspired by Reagan's concern for the vulnerability of Americans to nuclear war and his fears that confrontation might well bring it about almost by accident. The shooting down of KAL 007 and exercise Able Archer, a large-scale military exercise that produced a situation comparable to the command and communications procedures that would be used in a nuclear strike against the Eastern bloc, were other factors. When monitoring Able Archer through listening devices, the Soviets became alarmed, not least because NATO had always refused to agree to a no-first-use policy on nuclear weapons. Statements made by leading Soviet figures expressed the need for great vigilance and in private pointed to the possibility of an imminent attack and, if Soviet military doctrine had been followed, a nuclear strike would have been launched. It was on the day that the exercise ended, 11 November 1983, that Reagan made his first public call for the abolition of nuclear weapons. The turning point in this argument about Reagan's contribution was the President's January 1984 speech, calling for ways to reduce the fear of uncertainty and the possibility of misinterpretation over a surprise attack, while insisting that the US posed no threat to the Soviet Union. This line of seeking cooperation, as opposed to condemnation, was possibly the key moment leading to superpower rapprochement.[2]

Yet any intention to achieve this by confrontation or compromise hardly fits with the ideas of Reagan, Bush, and other conservative establishment figures. If Reagan was pressurizing the Soviets with a view to ending the Cold War, as had been hoped for in its early years, nobody realized it at the time. And Bush was slow to accept it after it had happened. Not only was he at pains to insist that the Cold War was not over in 1988, but he seemed to long to return to the confrontational deterrence which seemed to him to characterize the early 1960s. Yet Gorbachev's UN speech on 7 December 1988 had referred to the rights of the individual, to freedom, self-determination, and threats to the environment. When the Soviet leader embarked on unilateral disarmament in 1989, officials in the Bush administration accused him of trying to split the Western alliance, and the US began to modernize short-range NATO nuclear weapons in Germany. As Germans protested because the Soviets were removing their weapons, the Bush administration, members of Congress, and the media were outraged. The same Cold War message came from Washington as many times before. Failure to install the weapons would weaken resolve and damage the Western alliance. Answering why the Cold War ended has also to involve answering why no one predicted it and why some took so long to realize it had ended. Ultimately, this can only be explained by the enormous impact of the perceptions of actions of others previously defined and ingrained in human consciousness. Actions which differ markedly from expectations, and which are used to justify a way of life or the essence of a foreign policy, are initially ignored and events interpreted in order to fit preconceived ideas.

Explaining Gorbachev's Actions

Whatever the role of preconceptions, it is certainly essential, in explaining why the Cold War ended, to ask why Gorbachev chose the course he did. Why did he not continue the hard-line policies of his predecessors, insisting on the end of the Star Wars project before agreeing to nuclear arms control? Why did he not require an internal settlement in Afghanistan before pulling out the Red Army? But it is not necessary to accept that he decided on reform at home and dialogue abroad in reaction to Reagan's toughness, or even that international considerations were of prime importance to the 'new thinking'. Instead, it can be argued that Gorbachev was forced to make changes because of long-running problems within the Soviet Union itself, which would have reached critical proportions in the 1980s, with or without Reagan's policies. In that interpretation, the end of the Cold War was produced by Gorbachev acting in accordance with the constraints he was subject to as opposed to new ideas (ideational change) leading to new policies and changes in the international system.

The problems of the Soviet economy can be linked to defence expenditure and the war in Afghanistan, but the real problem was more fundamental and went back at least to the policies of industrialization favoured by Joseph Stalin. Central planning, a concentration on heavy industrial production, and the ruthless exploitation of agriculture all helped create a system which was incapable of meeting the demand for modern consumer goods. Bureaucratic controls and a lack of competition led to inefficiency and waste, made worse by production targets which were met on paper but never in reality. Nor did the Soviet system provide people with satisfactory housing or health care, even if it did control prices and guarantee employment. By the mid-1970s, Soviet economic growth was stagnant, defence spending was destructively high, and any idealism about Marxism-Leninism was being sapped by corruption, careerism, and cynicism.

Yet Gorbachev's predecessors never responded to economic difficulties in the way he did. Even if the problems had got worse, the attempt to solve them by the methods Gorbachev employed still requires explanation. He may have been attempting to imitate the comparative success of Western economies, believing, rightly or wrongly, that this was produced by market economics and political freedoms. If introduced to some extent in the Soviet Union, they could provide a panacea for the Soviet economy. In this scenario, it was necessary to end the Cold War in order to get the military to accept the results of Gorbachev's unilateral disarmament that would save the money to implement economic reform. Khrushchev had reduced Soviet forces to cut defence expenditure with no significant impact on the Cold War but the two could be seen as two sides of the same coin. It might even be suggested that the Soviet leader thought ending the Cold War could best be done by talking the same language as the West. If so, Gorbachev failed to realize what impact this would have on the communist political and economic system, which was based on Soviet control. More importantly, he forgot that the Cold War was a battle over which system would prevail, not just an expression of military and power political rivalries which, if negotiated away, would produce a more acceptable form of interstate relations.

Other arguments point to the way in which Gorbachev's policy of *glasnost* unleashed uncontrollable forces in the conditions of the 1980s. Even if more freedoms had not been granted, it would have been difficult to prevent access to greater knowledge about the benefits available to most people in the developed capitalist world. With access to computers and the internet and opportunities for travel opening up in Eastern Europe, repression was becoming an impossible solution to the challenges of high defence expenditure, economic inefficiency, and the need for reform. And the Soviet people had long been disillusioned with the careerism and corruption of communist officials, and cynical in their response to government propaganda. The average person increasingly believed little or nothing the government told them. They became more sceptical of the values of Marxist-Leninism and of the idea of containing the threat that the imperialist enemy allegedly posed. The situation was therefore ripe for pressure from below to play an important role in forcing the process of change and taking it further than Gorbachev had envisaged.

Realists deny the influence of internal forces on the making of foreign policy and cannot explain the end of the Cold War by pointing to ideological change in Soviet and American leaders. They are forced to explain events by pointing to the systemic effects of Reagan's confrontational policies and their emphasis on military strength, which the Soviet Union could not match. Gorbachev's achievements, if any, were to realize that the system of state-controlled socialism was on the way out and then to promote the changes that resulted in Western-style reforms and the collapse of the communist system wherever it was in place in Europe. The Soviet Union was thus destroyed by the introduction of market economics and political democracy and the failure to match the economic and military strength of the West. It was Reagan, pursuing in realist terms the traditional quest for greater military power, who brought this about and the world could look forward to a decade of peace and prosperity.

Again, like everyone else, realist theorists did not predict this outcome and at least part of the reason lies in the Western failure to accurately understand the nature of the Cold War, or to conceptualize it in ways in which peaceful change was seen as distinctly possible. The orthodox interpretation of the Cold War, based on a fundamentally expansionist Soviet Union deterred from pursuing its ambitious goals by Western containment, is one obvious conceptualization which, like realist ideas, prevents any prediction of developments leading to the Cold War's end. Described by John Lewis Gaddis in terms of its creation of a long peace, the alleged goal of Western policy was the prevention of war by vigilance and deterrence. The encouragement of change would not occur naturally with both sides locked into a process centred on Soviet expansion for a mixture of imperial and ideological reasons. The only thing that has to be explained is why war did not come about. The fact that the Soviets might have had no greater inclination to expand than the US is not considered and therefore the end of the Cold War is hard to conceive.[3]

The Less Developed World

The ideas as to why Gorbachev, the surprise hero in the West, acted as he did against all expectations and whether he was a prisoner of domestic or international events remain to be resolved. But Reagan deserves some credit for at least enabling the ending of the Cold War to be facilitated. Like Gorbachev, he may not have realized the full significance of what he was beginning, but from the American point of view relations with the Soviet Union were something of a triumph. Carter's refocusing on East–West relations rather than North–South ones were ultimately rewarded under Reagan, even if the price was paid in less developed world countries. The less developed world mattered to Reagan not because of the challenge of the lack of development, but because of its significance to Cold War rivalries, especially in such countries as Nicaragua, El Salvador, and Afghanistan. The Iran–Iraq war (the longest-running conventional war since 1945) was treated as a mere sideshow and Latin America, along with Africa, was left sunk in debt, with little attention paid to the poverty in which billions lived. Here, the moves towards reconciliation between Reagan and Gorbachev did not prevent the continuation of the struggle between advocates of revolution and supporters of the status quo.

In the early 1980s, Reagan took the advice of those who continued to put their trust in authoritarian dictators in the less developed world, dictators who were seen as more suitable than totalitarian ideologues. Murder, and the lack of political freedom, continued and for longer than some of the pro-American dictators, such as Marcos in the Philippines and Duvalier in Haiti, whose excesses helped modify US policy as poverty-stricken people resisted. In other countries, such as El Salvador and Nicaragua, resistance to American-backed groups continued. By the end of the decade, 40,000 people had died, as the US government, by fair and largely foul means, sought to overthrow the Sandinistas in Nicaragua. In El Salvador, a ten-year war had claimed the lives of around 70,000 people, most of whom were killed by right-wing death squads. Cold War conceptions continued in place at the end of the decade in parts of the non-European world. It was an open question as to whether this indicated a reluctance to take on board the post-Cold War world or whether the US was determined to pursue American interests by whatever means.

The losers were some of the people of the less developed world who found that the new liberal economic consensus on developmental progress merely brought them greater poverty. The debt trap was consuming an extremely large percentage of some of the poorer countries' GDP, but the remedy was now deemed to be more engagement with the world economy. The model countries were those in Asia who, by the end of the decade, had managed to achieve thriving industrial economies dominated by the export trade. There initial progress had, however, been made with the aid of government controls to foster successful industrial development. Those countries too poor to make the transition to industry now found themselves doubly penalized by the developed world. The structural adjustment programmes of the International Monetary Fund (IMF) were based on controls which maintained low government expenditure, and where welfare provision existed it suffered serious cut-backs. Yet, access to developed markets in agricultural produce remained difficult for producers in the less developed world because of the kind of protectionist policies maintained, for example, by the European Community. The 1980s saw the start of a process whereby the poorest countries, mostly in Africa, were more and more marginalized in the global economy, as they struggled with mountainous debts that the West had to reschedule or face the problems of default.

In the developed world, the end of the Cold War brought a sense of righteousness which ignored the problems facing many victims of capitalism in the less developed world. The sense of having been right all along was manifest, even if Western leaders tried not to humiliate Gorbachev by making the 'victory' too obvious. Socialism was deemed dead and the Soviet Union defeated. There was a sense of complacent satisfaction, but problems remained in the world and would eventually emerge to challenge the self-righteousness and rosy expectations that prevailed at the start of the 1990s. In a sense, they would show that, notwithstanding the indisputable superiority of the Western world in producing consumer goods and maintaining political freedoms, there were many problems, often ignored, which had little to do with the Cold War and the alleged ambitions of the Soviet Union.

Retrospect

In retrospect, the new Cold War of the early 1980s can be seen as the last phase in which the USSR tried to equal US might, not by addressing weaknesses at home, but by posing as a military giant. Or, it can be seen as the start of a new attempt by the American Right to dominate the exercise of global power in order to ensure that American interests prevailed. As the report of the British Foreign Office wartime inquiry into the attitudes of leading Americans put it, with reference to some US organizations and groups in 1944, their attitude was 'America first, the rest of the world nowhere.' The Soviet Union emerges as an empire in economic decline that was unable to maintain its levels of defence expenditure and its controls over everyday life. In the early 1980s, it was still able to uphold its allies in Eastern Europe, Cuba, and Vietnam while backing Marxists in civil wars in Afghanistan, Nicaragua, and Angola. However, even when Reagan came into office he was warned by the Central Intelligence Agency (CIA) of the poor state of the Soviet economy, a situation which continued to worsen. Around 1982, the USSR's oil production began to fall off and it was increasingly realized that the central planners could not provide raw materials to the country's industry 'free' of charge. It also became clear that Eastern Europe, whatever its military value had been as a defensive wall, was an economic liability that could no longer act as a barrier to ideas and culture. The post-Cold War was to emerge with a resurgent America on the rise and its main rival no longer able to provide a challenge.

To remedy this, Gorbachev initiated the policies of 'openness' and 'reconstruction'—*glasnost* and *perestroika*—which were intended to revitalize Soviet Communism but which actually unleashed the forces of nationalism, self-determination, and consumer culture that destroyed the Soviet Union. This process might not have occurred so quickly had the US not emerged from the doldrums of the 1970s with a new agenda. Moreover, after 1982, the success of Western capitalism contrasted starkly with the fortunes of the USSR and Eastern Europe much more so than in the previous decade. Rapid technological change was beginning to revolutionize the nature of communication, the media's impact was more encompassing, more money was spent on better Western propaganda, and more economic benefits were available as access to consumer goods was, for the most part, made instantaneous because of easier credit facilities. These were the things unavailable in the Soviet Union, where knowledge of Western culture and lifestyles began to cross the Iron Curtain on an extensive basis as Gorbachev entered the Kremlin.

The surprising thing was that many commentators continued to discuss not Soviet decline, but that of the US. When Gorbachev came to power, he was apparently able to seize the initiative in East–West relations for a time, but the US easily remained the predominant superpower, even if its relative strength, compared to the late 1940s, had fallen off. The shape of international relations after 1985 was set, not by the Kremlin, but by the fundamental weaknesses of the state over which it presided. By December 1989, it was clear that the new order that was emerging would have America as the only superpower. And if at the time there was insufficient understanding of the complex history of the Cold War (a battle to get nuclear superiority as defined primarily by the Committee on the Present Danger), it becomes easier to appreciate why no one predicted that it would end at all, let alone so dramatically.

Visit the online resources that accompany this book to test your understanding and take your learning further: www.oup.com/he/young-kent3e

NOTES

1. H. W. Brands, *The Strange Death of American Liberalism* (Yale University Press, New Haven, 2001), Chs 5 and 6.
2. Beth A. Fischer, *The Reagan Reversal* (University of Missouri Press, Colombia, 1997), 102–43.
3. On the predictive failures of Western theorists, see the introduction in Richard Ned Lebow and Thomas Risse-Kappento (eds), *International Relations Theory and the End of the Cold War* (Columbia University Press, New York, 1995).

PART V CHRONOLOGY

From Confrontation to Communist Collapse, 1981–9

1981

11 January	Martial law declared in El Salvador.
20 January	Iran releases US Embassy hostages, held since November 1978.
9 February	General Jaruzelski becomes Prime Minister of Poland.
17 June	First American arms deal with communist China.
23 September	US and USSR agree to open talks on intermediate-range nuclear forces (INF).
6 October	President Sadat of Egypt assassinated.
18 November	Reagan proposes the 'zero option', the complete destruction of INF weapons.
13 December	Jaruzelski declares martial law in Poland.

1982

2 April–14 June	Falklands War between UK and Argentina.
9 May	Reagan proposes Strategic Arms Reduction Talks (START).
6 June	Israeli invasion of Lebanon launched, to drive out the Palestine Liberation Organization (PLO).
29 June	START talks open in Geneva between the superpowers.
14 July	In the Iran–Iraq War, Iranians cross the Iraqi border for the first time.
21 August	PLO begins to pull out of Beirut; moves headquarters to Tunis.
10 November	Death of Soviet leader, Leonid Brezhnev; succeeded next day by Yuri Andropov.

1983

9 March	Reagan describes USSR as an 'evil Empire'.
23 March	Reagan launches 'Strategic Defense Initiative' (SDI) for space-based anti-nuclear systems.
21 July	Jaruzelski ends martial law in Poland.
1 September	South Korean Airlines Boeing 747, KAL 007 shot down by Soviets.
23 October	Over 300 US and French troops, from multinational peacekeeping force, killed in bombings in Beirut.
25 October	Invasion of Caribbean island of Grenada by US Marines.
15 November	Deployment of Cruise–Pershing missiles begins in Western Europe.
23 November	Soviets walk out of INF talks due to Cruise deployments; START talks suspended on 8 December.

(continued...)

PART V CHRONOLOGY (continued)

1984

9 February	Death of Andropov; succeeded on 13 February by Konstantin Chernenko.
26 April–2 May	Reagan visits China.
8 May	USSR says it will boycott forthcoming Los Angeles Olympics.
28 September	Reagan meets Soviet foreign minister, Andrei Gromyko, for the first time.
22 November	Reagan re-elected President.

1985

4 February	New Zealand refuses to let nuclear-capable US ships into its ports; leading to virtual breakdown of ANZUS Pact.
11 March	Mikhail Gorbachev succeeds Chernenko as leader of the Soviet Union.
12 March	INF and START talks reopen.
7 April	Gorbachev suspends new deployments of nuclear missiles and urges NATO to do the same.
26 April	Warsaw Pact renewed for twenty years.
1 May	US launches trade embargo against Nicaragua.
6 August	Gorbachev initiates a moratorium on nuclear tests (lasts until April 1986).
19–21 November	First summit meeting between Gorbachev and Reagan, in Geneva.

1986

15 January	Gorbachev accepts 'zero option' for destruction of INF systems.
25 February	In the Philippines, Ferdinand Marcos surrenders presidency to Corazon Aquino.
15 April	US air forces strike targets in Libya.
26 April	Chernobyl nuclear reactor melts down, near Kiev, USSR.
28 July	Gorbachev's Vladivostok speech urges improved relations with China.
23 August	Gennady Zakharov, a Soviet embassy official, is arrested for spying in US; on 30 August Soviets arrest Nicholas Daniloff, an American journalist.
30 September	Release of Zakharov and Daniloff.
11–12 October	Gorbachev and Reagan summit in Reykjavik breaks down over SDI.
3 November	The 'Irangate' scandal breaks: a Lebanese newspaper reveals a high-level US official visited Iran in May.

1987

10 April	Gorbachev's Prague speech advocates a 'common European home'.
20 July	UN passes Resolution 598 on an Iran–Iraq ceasefire and return to pre-war border.
7–10 December	Third Gorbachev–Reagan summit, in Washington. INF treaty signed on 8 December.

1988

8 February	Gorbachev announces Red Army will evacuate Afghanistan in March 1989 if a peace settlement is made.
23 March	Ceasefire in Nicaragua between the Contras and the government.
14 April	Geneva peace agreement on a settlement in Afghanistan.
29 May–2 June	Gorbachev–Reagan summit in Moscow.
30 June	Vietnam begins withdrawing its troops from neighbouring Kampuchea (Cambodia).
20 July	Ayatollah Khomeini agrees to end the war with Iraq.

PART V CHRONOLOGY (continued)

31 August	Lech Walesa meets a Polish government minister to discuss mounting internal unrest.
8 November	George Bush wins presidential election.
22 December	UN agreements on independence of Namibia and Cuban withdrawal from Angola.
1989	
11 January	Non-communist parties legalized in Hungary.
15 February	Last Red Army troops leave Afghanistan.
6 March	Talks on reducing 'Conventional Forces in Europe' open between Eastern and Western representatives.
26 March and 9 April	First elections for a 'Soviet Congress of People's Deputies'.
5 April	In Poland, the government agrees to recognize Solidarity and elect an assembly.
25 April	Soviets begin to pull troops out of Hungary.
7 May	In Panama, President Noriega annuls recent election results.
12 May	Bush's Texas A&M University speech effectively ends the policy of containment.
15–18 May	Gorbachev–Deng Xiaoping summit held in Beijing.
4 June	Chinese Red Army forcibly ends the occupation of Tiananmen Square, Beijing, by over 100,000 demonstrators.
4 and 18 June	Solidarity scores major successes in Polish elections.
23 August	Demonstrations in Estonia, Latvia, and Lithuania, in favour of independence from USSR.
26 September	Last Vietnamese troops leave Cambodia.
9–10 November	Opening of the Berlin Wall.
2–3 December	First Bush–Gorbachev summit in Malta.
20 December	US forces invade Panama, to overthrow Noriega.
29 December	Czechoslovakia chooses the dissident Václav Havel as its president.

Take your learning further by viewing the interactive version of this timeline:
www.oup.com/he/young-kent3e

16

The 'Second' Cold War, 1981–5

Chapter contents

A. US–Soviet Relations and the New Cold War

Reagan's International Outlook and 'Reaganomics'

Ronald Reagan, a former movie actor and Governor of California, had been a firm anti-communist since his post-war days as President of the Screen Actors' Guild, when he had denounced leftist influences in Hollywood. He had already been a critic of détente and the Strategic Arms Limitation Treaty (SALT) when seeking the Republican presidential nomination in 1976; in 1980 he triumphed over Carter and the divided Democratic camp by attacking the incumbent as a weak, indecisive figure whose economic policies had failed and who had lowered America's international reputation. Above all, Reagan promised a disheartened electorate strong leadership and he came to power on the back of a general rightwards shift in the political mood. He dismissed détente as 'a one-way street that the Soviet Union has used to pursue its aims'.[1] Many former Democrats (the so-called 'neo-conservatives'), dissatisfied with the SALT process and concerned by Soviet advances in the less developed world, had turned to the Right since 1976. In order to build a consensus behind its policies, the new administration promised 'to restore the domestic economy, reward the anti-communist friends of the United States abroad, halt the spread of Soviet influence and combat terrorism . . . without . . . risking another Vietnam-type conflict'.[2] In contrast to Carter, who was prepared to tackle complex issues like Middle Eastern peace, Reagan had little desire to master details whatever their importance, concentrated on a presentational role in government, and pursued a simple foreign policy. Neither intellectual nor particularly devious, he rejected détente as a communist trick, was initially determined to resist the spread of Soviet influence wherever it threatened and, going beyond that, wanted to carry the New Cold War into the Soviet camp.

In a sense, this was nothing new. Even under Truman, when the original idea of 'containment', appeared, American policy had soon developed a strong element of 'liberation', hoping to undermine the Eastern bloc through the use of covert action, economic pressures, and propaganda. Where Reagan differed from Truman was in his clear, public acknowledgement of the 'offensive' elements in the US arsenal. He wanted to force changes in Soviet policy by starving them of trade and technology in vital areas, by outspending them on defence, and by backing their opponents in less developed countries. The indigenous problems of the poorer regions of the world, the need to tackle poverty and local conflicts, were ignored as all foreign policy was interpreted in the light of Soviet–American confrontation. Under the 'Reagan Doctrine', the US promised support for so-called 'freedom fighters' in Afghanistan, Angola, and Central America. This strong-handed approach, underpinned by the President's public relations talents, went down well with the US public, which sensed that 'history had taken a U-turn. The United States . . . was reasserting its international hegemony [while the] Soviet Union was mired in a deeply unpopular war in Afghanistan.' Yet the appearance was deceptive. In fact, the current perception merely reversed 'a short period of [false] images of American weakness and Soviet strength'.[3] 'The Reagan administration . . . brought a new sense of dynamism and assertiveness to the Soviet–American relationship' perhaps, but the 'major changes . . . were in rhetoric rather than substance, and . . . it did little more than carry out the policies which had been formulated by Carter in . . . 1980'.[4]

In retrospect, even Andrei Gromyko shared the impression that a major change occurred in January 1981: 'On the coming to power of the Reagan administration, tension in Soviet–US relations increased . . . The new US government did everything it could to undo the work of its predecessors.'[5] Yet, at first, Reagan's outlook did not necessarily imply a more dangerous US–Soviet confrontation than in Carter's last year. Moscow had seen Carter, with his human rights crusade, as a difficult figure and had never shared the fantasies of the Committee of the Present Danger that the US was in cataclysmic decline, with the Soviets about to overhaul it in the nuclear arms race. American defence spending was already rising and, in talking of nuclear war-fighting doctrines, Reagan was largely building on Carter's Presidential Directive 59 (itself built on the 1974 Schlesinger Doctrine). Indeed, at the start of the new presidency, an astonished Alexander Haig, the incoming Secretary of State, was told by Soviet Ambassador Dobrynin that he 'failed to see any basic difference from the arrogant moralizing of the departed Carter administration'.[6] Some Soviet experts may have hoped that Reagan would prove as positive to deal with as Nixon, his Republican predecessor, who had also come to power as an outspoken anti-communist. And behind the blunt exterior, there were important nuances in Reagan's outlook: despite the fears of Western liberals, he did *not* want confrontation to lead to war; whilst advocating US strength, he was also ready to negotiate with the Soviets—if they respected US wishes; and he was capable of recognizing that the Cold War sometimes damaged American interests. Thus, in April 1981, three months after entering the White House, he both wrote to Brezhnev expressing a desire for peace and lifted the grain embargo on the USSR, which Carter had begun after the invasion of Afghanistan but which hit the profits of mid-West farmers. 'Perhaps', he wrote, 'this decision will contribute to creating the circumstances which will lead to the meaningful . . . dialogue which will assist us in our joint obligation to find lasting peace.'[7] He also quickly abandoned his earlier view that the Chinese communists were as bad as the Soviets, and visited Beijing in 1984.

Closely linked to his determination to fight the Cold War worldwide was Reagan's campaign to reduce inflation and bring growth to the US after the poor economic performance of the 1970s. During his first few years in office, in fact, the state of the economy took precedence over foreign policy on the administration's agenda. Again, Reagan had no sophisticated ideology to guide him. Once a Democrat himself, he had admired Franklin D. Roosevelt, the father of the New Deal, which many Republicans saw as the root of 'wasteful' social spending and a bloated federal government. Reagan, however, became closely associated with the ideas of a particular school of neo-liberal economists. Of those economists who in the 1970s had begun to challenge the post-war consensus of full employment and government intervention to counter other features of free-market capitalism that were seen as damaging to the social fabric, Milton Friedman, Friedrich Hayek, and the followers of the deceased

Leo Strauss came into their own under Reagan's presidency. The theories they held were nothing new: they had developed in the wake of the Second World War in opposition to the Keynesian consensus. They did, however, appear new to many who had become disillusioned with the failure of Bretton Woods in the 1970s and then with the troubles of the later years of the decade that emphasized social strife and continued inflation. In the 1980s, they took over from Keynesian ideas as the dominant force in Western economics in a changed political and economic climate. Reagan had emerged as a leader with an instinctive sympathy with their views and was prepared to assume a leadership role in popularizing them. Advocates of free market economics were united with philosophical libertarians and religious nationalists under the auspices of Leo Strauss, of the University of Chicago. Strauss, who saw connections between the interventionism of the Weimar Republic and the evils of the Nazis (the ultimate tragedy of market interference), was the precursor of the Christian religious Right, which was to become a powerful force in the US by the beginning of the 1990s. Individuals had to be responsible for their actions to become virtuous citizens while the market, based on individual self-interest, and self-regulating when free from state intervention, would rule society.

The work of another member of the Chicago school, Milton Friedman, seemed particularly relevant to the end of a decade characterized by stagflation because he offered a simple explanation of inflation. Friedman claimed that the inflationary pressures, which had grown so much in the 1970s, were caused directly by the growth in the money supply produced by the state that had a monopoly of producing money. If the state allowed too much money to circulate by setting interest rates too low or by high levels of public expenditure, then not only would the economy not respond to the market, but inflation would also result. The answer was to make sure the state did not print money; then inflation would come down, along with the money supply. In the event, such ideas were proved wrong, most notably in Britain, where the money supply increased but inflation came down nevertheless. Yet at the time they were extremely influential.

These ideas were popularized by right-wing think tanks in the US such as the American Enterprise Institute, the Hoover Institution, and the Heritage Foundation. This, in turn, was linked to the dissatisfaction with détente and the lack of American confidence, associated with the sense of perceived national decline and loss of US global dominance. Economic problems, as perceived by many on the American Right, required an approach which would liberate business from the constraints deemed to be at the root of American problems. As always, it was believed that the removal of such constraints and the resolution of US problems would be beneficial for the rest of the world, as well as America itself. The 'Washington Consensus' of tax cuts (especially for the rich), balanced budgets, deregulation, anti-trades union legislation, and tight money controls was central to Reagan's ideology and to some extent key aspects of his policies. It became associated with key international financial institutions, still largely controlled by the US, and then with the idea of 'globalization'. Reagan believed that reductions in marginal taxes and limits on state spending (as well as on economic aid to the less developed world) would encourage free enterprise. At first, his policy of high interest rates (necessary because of the effect of tax cuts and rising defence expenditure), though it drove down inflation, also deepened the depression inherited from Carter: unemployment reached 11 per cent in 1981 and the economy, stagnant in 1980, actually contracted by 2 per cent in 1982. But growth revived in 1983, peaking at 7 per cent in 1984 and averaging almost 4 per cent per annum in Reagan's second term. Such sustained expansion, linked to a fall in inflation below 2 per cent in 1986, boosted national confidence through a consumer boom but produced a remarkably high budget deficit and a serious imbalance within the US economy.

'Reaganomics' worked no real economic miracle for America and 1980s growth rates in countries such as Britain have been exaggerated by unfair comparisons with the sluggish late 1970s. Over the long term, on both sides of the Atlantic, the decade as a whole was no more successful in producing growth than past decades, with which it was broadly comparable. In the US, the 40 per cent increase in defence spending in 1981–6 kept interest rates high in the long term, pushed up the value of the dollar and, partly as a result, the trade deficit mushroomed, up from $25 billion in 1980 to over $140 billion in 1984. What was significant was the stagnation of blue-collar wages in the developed world as, particularly in America and Britain, successful enterprises were measured more and more by the value of the dividends paid to shareholders. And, of course, there was the reversal of the post-war trend in the developed world for the gap between the rich and the poor to narrow, with staggering increases in the incomes of the very rich. In the US, the 1980s saw the incomes of the top 1 per cent double while the bottom 20 per cent suffered a 10 per cent decline.[8] Nevertheless, it appeared that 'Reaganomics' and the arguments of the free deregulated marketers, with their tax cuts and reductions in social security, had won the day—even if Reagan, because of his defence spending, actually imposed high levels of expenditure on the public purse. In a sense, the apparent victory was not an economic one but a cultural one, embodied in an increasingly expansive and powerful global media, largely in the hands of the Right.

However, in the 1980s even the market could not refashion American dominance of the world economy alone. The trade deficit with Japan was particularly worrying, growing from $16 billion in 1981 to $46 billion in 1985, despite Japan's agreement to restrain sales of cars and other products. Reagan's tax cuts tended to foster spending on imported consumer goods, while his simultaneous insistence on an expanded defence budget pushed up the national debt, from less than $1 billion in 1981 to more than $2.5 trillion in 1989. In 1985, America became a debtor nation for the first time since 1914, a statistic which could support a view that the country was still in decline relative to the other industrial powers, despite Reagan's promises to reverse the trend. By the end of the presidency, America was the world's largest debtor, a statistic that caused problems for his successors in the White House. The conservative coalition was beginning to seem less secure when George Bush became President. The importance of right-wing Christian fundamentalism was increasing as the forces of the centre Right became more concerned about extremism.

It was the Japanese who exploited the opportunities offered by the economic situation most, buying up about a third of the expanded US deficit in Reagan's first term and becoming the world's largest creditor nation—but at the price of increasing American fear of Japan's burgeoning economic power. Japan, which imported all its oil but was a highly efficient producer of cars and electrical goods, continued to devote its wealth to investment rather than consumption. The Japanese trade surplus was partly offset by the nationalist Nakasone Yasuhiro's willingness to expand defence spending above the previous limit of one per cent of GDP. In particular, Yasuhiro proved ready to answer US calls for an expanded Japanese naval presence in the Pacific. There was also an attempt to rectify the trade imbalance by letting the yen rise in value against the dollar: in the eighteen months following the September 1985 Plaza agreement between finance ministers, the dollar fell by about 50 per cent against the yen (market interference to benefit the US economy). Yet, Japanese manufacturers simply compensated for the change by reducing their profit levels, and in 1988 Japan's surplus with America rose to $60 billion. The Japanese also continued to expand their investments in America, focusing on property purchases in the late 1980s, and their banks became some of the largest in the world.

By the end of the 1980s, many Americans were still concerned about the idea of decline, as seen in the popularity of Paul Kennedy's 1988 book, *The Rise and Fall of the Great Powers*, with its theme of military 'overstretch' draining the economic resources of even the mightiest states. The US was deemed to be making the sacrifices to fight the military battle against the real enemy of free enterprise while others gained the economic benefits of free-riding. Kennedy's theme was picked up by other works, who found striking statistics to prove their case. Thus, in 1950 the US had made nearly half the world's steel, but by 1990 only about a tenth, having been overtaken by both Japan and the European Community. As a result, one study argued, America 'found itself increasingly struggling to project power other than its military component'.[9]

By 1985, the US economy had left the age of 'stagflation' behind and helped pull other Western economies out of depression. Yet whether this marked a sound long-term future for the world economy and whether it signified the failure of state planning under communism or social democracy are difficult questions to answer. The decline of the US since 1960 relative to other industrial powers and its recovery in economic terms may both have been more imaginary than real, especially given the problems that appeared to blight the economic success of some Asian countries in the 1990s and the recession that struck the Western world after 2007. The US remained in a strong position, but its domination of the world economy was much reduced from the 1950s. The rise of Japan was of some concern, especially now that one-fifth of American national wealth relied on foreign trade. But talk of 'American decline' was certainly premature. The fact was that, under Reagan, the US retained its ability to pay for both strong defences and internal stability. It outmatched the Soviets in both economic and military power and easily remained the world's largest economy.

In the 1980s, West European countries could match neither America's nor Japan's performance, despite their high sales in the US, but they were seen as part of the threat to American economic power. In Britain, the Thatcher government cut taxes on the wealthy and placed tight controls on public spending while maintaining an overvalued pound which hit British manufacturing industry; unemployment of over 3 million was seen as the necessary cost to get inflation down below 5 per cent in 1983 and to secure several years of growth at over 2 per cent which, in the late 1980s, contributed to the economy overheating. In Germany after 1982, Helmut Kohl was rather less ideological in his approach but maintained the country's good record on growth, prior to the problems of reunification, while tolerating a higher level of unemployment than in the past. In Italy between 1984 and 1989, there was talk of another 'economic miracle' as growth averaged 3 per cent.

For much of the less developed world, the picture was a lot more worrying, and in some places verging on the catastrophic. In the US, Western Europe, and Japan, the 1980s economic expansion was accompanied by a desire not only to reduce government spending at home but also to restrict development aid abroad. America, in the era of Reaganomics and revitalized anti-communism, wanted to see the less developed countries embrace the free market, abandon state planning, and restrict government spending programmes. The threat to the provision of infrastructure, education, and health, all of which might help capitalism thrive, was seen as less damaging than state controls and high public expenditure. It is true that during Reagan's first term the US foreign aid budget expanded, but most of the increase was in the form of military assistance (which topped $7 billion in 1984, up from $3 billion in 1980) and even this fell off in the second term. Western countries now preferred the developing world to rely on private investment rather than foreign aid, and the US particularly pressed for the reduction of all forms of protectionism in order to boost global trade. Such aid as there was became conditional on the recipients accepting the need for 'structural adjustment'. The developing nations were thus required to emulate the free-enterprise policies now being embraced by the developed world and they had few weapons with which to fight back in the face of such pressure.

Moreover, they were increasingly hampered by the debt burden, which was a legacy of the oil price rise, and the ease with which Western banks lent money to poorer countries, whose terms of trade declined and whose available income was increasingly taken up with debt repayment. It was easy to point to corruption as a feature of many of the poorer— particularly African—nations, but whether this was more a cause than an effect of their economic plight is a controversial point. The last great call for a state-led transfer of resources from the North to the South (at $50 billion a year) was the 1980 Brandt Report, written by an international group under the former German Chancellor, Willy Brandt. The report argued that North and South had a vested interest in cooperation and that the alternative to tackling the problem was the creation of an ever more divided, insecure world. But these warnings caused little concern in northern capitals where Brandt's interventionist, social democratic outlook was already giving way to the free-enterprise doctrines of the New Right. In any case, the 1980s showed that the poverty-stricken South presented little menace to the North and therefore the poor could be quietly ignored, except when the publicity given to them by the well-known and the famous temporarily caught the attention of the Western public.

By the end of his second term, Reagan had helped create the impression that the US had beaten the USSR in the economic stakes. But, as the CIA told Reagan, the USSR in the early 1980s—far from being an all-powerful menace—was locked into a situation of stagnant growth, inefficient central planning, and corruption. The burdens of its own high defence spending and the need to prop up the equally inefficient economies of Eastern Europe, whilst also aiding 'wars of national liberation' in Angola and Central America, and fighting the war in Afghanistan, exacerbated Soviet economic problems. As the failings of the Soviet model became clearer, at least in the view of Reagan's supporters, Moscow was forced into radical reforms which ultimately destroyed the regime. The 1990s would see the US as the world's only economic and military superpower.

Years of Fear, 1981–3

It was said by one leading academic observer of the international scene in 1985 that, during the first Reagan term, 'all was actually quiet, save on the rhetorical front, in the central confrontation between the superpowers'.[10] Nonetheless, whatever the limits to his bellicosity, Reagan's first few years in office saw popular fears that the superpowers might go to war and there was some justification for this. In order to give US armed forces global mobility and also to put strains on the Soviet economy, Reagan expanded the already high levels of defence spending (especially on strategic nuclear weapons and the navy), whilst adopting a sceptical approach to arms control. His Defense Secretary, Caspar Weinberger, believed that US military strength was 'the only thing that could persuade the Soviets that they could not take actions such as they had taken in the 1970s in Angola and Afghanistan . . . Nicaragua, Ethiopia and elsewhere'.[11] The President reinvigorated the CIA, not least to tackle 'wars of national liberation' and support anti-communist 'freedom fighters' (its new director, Bill Casey, proving a keen advocate of covert operations), as well as launching a new psychological warfare campaign against communism and trying to tighten up on trade links with the Eastern bloc. Finally, Reagan engaged in the most extreme anti-communist rhetoric since Kennedy. In his most famous declaration of all, on 8 March 1983, at Orlando in Florida, Reagan denounced the USSR as an 'evil Empire' and predicted the end of communism. Fifteen days later he followed this up with the announcement of the Star Wars programme (more fully discussed in Chapter 16, C), designed to counter a Soviet nuclear strike and therefore seen as a threat to the concept of mutually assured destruction, whose logic of deterrence was seen by some as vital to superpower peace. This followed a series of what the Soviets saw as provocative decisions by Reagan: his March 1981 announcement of further aid to the Mujaheddin resistance in Afghanistan (see Chapter 16, D); his decision, three months later, to sell the first US arms to communist China; his accusation in October 1981 that the Soviets planned to fight and win a nuclear war; his aid to the Contra rebels fighting the leftist Nicaraguan government (see Chapter 18, B) and his support for the Solidarity trades union in Poland (see Chapter 16, B). Unwilling, like Eisenhower, to talk to the Soviets until they showed a readiness to make concessions, he refused even to see their high-level emissaries. The President did not meet Ambassador Anatoly Dobrynin until February 1983 and a first meeting with Foreign Minister Andrei Gromyko only came in September 1984, when: 'The conversation was edgy and . . . there was the inevitable confrontation' over Soviet aims in the world.[12]

For its part, the Kremlin was predictably unwilling to concede that it was guilty of any wrongdoing in world affairs. In Afghanistan, of course, as also in Eastern Europe, it saw itself as struggling to preserve socialism and stability, with no intention of offensive action beyond its own sphere. In Nicaragua and elsewhere in Central America, it still saw 'wars on national liberation' as an inevitable reaction to capitalist oppression. Where the military balance was concerned, Moscow insisted it was committed to nuclear parity and to the fulfilment of SALT II—claims which were probably correct, since the Soviets always recognized that they would lose a technological race with America, hence their enormous fear of the Star Wars programme. Ideas explored by the Soviet military for nuclear war-fighting simply mirrored those being discussed in the US, and Reagan himself caused consternation in Western Europe in November 1981, when he talked of localizing a nuclear exchange on the continent. At first, the Soviet Politburo 'decided to follow a course for détente in the hope that Reagan little by little would become more reasonable', but within months they felt they were dealing with 'a deeply disturbing figure . . . Once they reluctantly came to the conclusion détente could not be recovered . . . the inclination grew inside the Kremlin not to pacify him but to fight back.'[13] Moscow's interpretation of US policy—intervening in less developed world conflicts, undermining the nuclear balance, seeking to divide the Eastern bloc—was, ironically, a mirror image of Washington's view of Soviet designs. As so often in the Cold War, it was genuinely difficult to divorce reality from propaganda. Thus, when the Soviets tried to convince Europeans that Reagan was running the risk of war, the Americans dismissed the accusation as a Kremlin ploy to divide the West. But Brezhnev's statement on 3 February 1982 (a year into the Reagan presidency) that the international situation was at its worst since 1945, probably reflected genuine fear.

The situation was not helped by the instability and uncertainty of policy-making in Moscow. Even compared to the septuagenarian Reagan, the Soviet leadership seemed decrepit. Brezhnev, born in 1906, in power since 1964, and increasingly unwell since the mid-1970s, seemed the personal embodiment of the stagnation, corruption, and lack of idealism over which he presided. Even the KGB connived in scurrilous attacks on him before his death in November. He was succeeded by the KGB chief, Yuri Andropov, eight years younger, who seemed intelligent and decisive, who had served abroad and was reputed to have some liking for US culture, and who had strong support from Gromyko and Defence Minister Ustinov. But any hopes that Andropov would bring greater openness and imagination to superpower relations quickly faded. A loyal communist and strict disciplinarian, who hoped to root out the crime and corruption of the Brezhnev era, his initial vigour was soon sapped by kidney failure. His mind remained clear but from February 1983 he relied on a dialysis machine. Suspicious of Reagan, Andropov nonetheless agreed that an attempt must be made to work with him and even exchanged some private messages with the White House over the summer, in which both sides professed a readiness to talk and a desire for peace. But on 1 September one of the few crises of the new Cold War suddenly occurred, when a South Korean airliner, code named KAL 007, was shot down by a Soviet warplane, with 269 people on board, including a US congressman. The Boeing 747 was well off course and had crossed into Soviet airspace, but the incident was exploited by Washington to embarrass the Soviets, whose response was harsh and unapologetic. Such an isolated incident was never likely to lead to war, but it soured East–West relations once more. Most Western countries denied landing rights to the Soviet airline, Aeroflot, as a sanction. On 28 September, Andropov declared it was impossible to deal with the 'militarist' Reagan administration.

Early Signs of a Thaw, 1983–5

The US President too could seem blinkered in outlook and ready to risk nuclear war. In August 1984, he was heard joking about the subject. Easy-going in his approach to work, Reagan found it difficult to master complex issues and also found it difficult to deal with the idea that as President he should exercise a decisive influence on government. He often expected his staff to make policy and simply to tell him what required explaining to the people. His administration's decision-making process was therefore chaotic, leading his first Secretary of State, Alexander Haig, to resign after less than eighteen months, complaining 'there was no description of duty, no rules, no expression of the essential authority of the President to guide his subordinates'.[14] Reagan also surrounded himself with equally strong anti-communists like the Defense Secretary, Caspar Weinberger, the National Security Adviser (1982–3), William Clark, and the ambassador to the UN, Jeanne Kirkpatrick (see Box 16.1). The last was ready to assist virtually any anti-communist regime, however dictatorial and distasteful, on the grounds that they might one day evolve into democracies; whereas communists were beyond the pale and could never change into liberal states. But Haig's successor at the State Department, George Shultz, brought a calmer, more patient approach to foreign policy. In their first conversation, Dobrynin found that Shultz was at ease and did not use the sharp expressions characteristic of Haig. He conducted the conversation in a more businesslike manner.[15] Shultz favoured a more positive policy, emphasizing Reagan's desire for peace and displaying a greater readiness than his colleagues to seek negotiations with Moscow. In a meeting on 25 March, Reagan listened to an outline of Shultz's approach and declared: 'If Andropov is willing to do business then so am I.'[16] Two months later the Secretary of State argued before the Senate Foreign Relations Committee that it was possible to have a 'constructive dialogue' with Moscow on arms control, regional problems, even human rights, alongside a policy of firmness. This caused some confusion in the press and was very different from the 'linkages' approach of the 1970s, but it was little different to the old formula of 'negotiation from strength'. Shultz took the key element in his statement to be the declaration that 'strength and realism can deter war, but only direct dialogue and negotiation can open the path toward lasting peace'.[17] True, it proved difficult to execute. A new, $10 billion grain deal with the Soviets in July 1983 was followed by talk in Washington of a Reagan–Andropov summit, but then came the KAL 007 crisis, which left even Shultz livid at Soviet insensitivity, followed by the US invasion of Grenada (see Chapter 18, C), where the troubled left-wing regime had close links to Castro's Cuba. In November, the deployment of new, US intermediate-range, nuclear force missiles (INF) in Western Europe led the Soviets to break off talks on nuclear arms control, which had been underway in a desultory fashion for two years (see Chapter 16, C). And, at the same time, NATO carried out 'Exercise Able Archer', the largest ever 'war game'—so grand in scale that, as the spy Oleg Gordievsky reported to his British handlers, many Soviet experts feared it was a cover for an actual attack on the USSR. Elements of the Red defence forces were even placed on war standby. When provided with intelligence information of such Soviet fears, Reagan acknowledged 'it's something to think about' and the experience may have fuelled his desire to reduce nuclear arsenals.[18]

Yet, whatever the sense of tension in the closing months of 1983, there were signs that relations were

BOX 16.1

Ronald Reagan and his Key Advisers

For the first fifty years of his life, Ronald Reagan seemed an unlikely prospect for the presidency. Born in 1911 in Tampico, Illinois and educated at the little-known Eureka College, his first job was as a sports announcer on the radio before he entered film work. A well-known 'B-movie' actor, he made over fifty films between his debut in 1937 and his entry into full-time politics in 1964. His political interests first became obvious in 1947 when he became president of the Screen Actors' Guild, taking a leading role over the next few years in rooting out left-wing influences in Hollywood. In 1962, he switched from the Democrats to the Republicans, becoming a leading supporter of the extreme right-winger Barry Goldwater in the 1964 presidential election. Goldwater was crushingly defeated by Lyndon Johnson but the ever-resilient and confident Reagan went on to be elected Governor of California in 1966. His policies of tax cuts and restrictions on spending proved popular and he was re-elected Governor in 1970. Following unsuccessful bids for the Republican nomination in the 1968, 1972, and 1976 presidential elections, Reagan finally triumphed over the luckless Jimmy Carter in 1980, particularly by exploiting the state of the economy.

As President, Reagan's domestic policies echoed those he had followed in California, with tax reductions and limits on social spending. But his external policies included massive defence expenditure, which resulted in a growing budget deficit. In his first term, he pursued a determinedly anti-Soviet line, condemning the Kremlin's 'evil Empire' and providing aid to anti-communist 'freedom fighters' (under the 'Reagan Doctrine'). In his second term, he seemed to reach the early stages of senility and his administration was discredited by the 'Irangate' scandal. But he also had remarkable successes to claim in foreign policy, as a process of conciliation began with Gorbachev's USSR. By 1988, Reagan could even claim that the Cold War was reaching its end and that this military expenditure had helped to break the back of the Soviet economy, although others argued that deep-seated problems had existed in the Eastern bloc even before Reagan came into office and that it was Gorbachev's policies that did most to end the Cold War.

His first Secretary of State, Alexander Haig (b. 1924), a former army general, White House Chief of Staff during the Watergate scandal, and then Supreme Allied Commander in Europe, found it particularly difficult to adjust to the uncertainty of the Reagan White House. Haig's successor, George Shultz (b. 1920), however, adapted well to Reagan's work methods and survived until the end of the presidency. A former professor of industrial relations, Shultz had served under Nixon in several positions, most significantly as Secretary of the Treasury (1972–4). Known as the 'Buddha' for his cautious, thoughtful approach to policy-making, he was ready to support such tough actions as the 1982 deployment of a US force in Lebanon and the 1983 invasion of Grenada, but seemed more at home building up fruitful relations with the Soviets after 1985.

Shultz frequently differed with the equally long-lasting Secretary of Defense, Caspar Weinberger (b. 1917), a lawyer and business leader who had also served in the Nixon cabinet, but who had been Reagan's financial director in California in the late 1960s. More outspoken than Shultz, Weinberger was always personally close to Reagan, supervised military expansion with enthusiasm, and supported a strong policy against the Soviets. He finally retired in November 1987, being succeeded for the administration's last year by Frank Carlucci. The primacy of Shultz and Weinberger was helped by Reagan's failure to appoint any National Security Adviser (NSA) who survived in the post for long. Reagan's first NSA, Richard Allen, lasted less than a year because he was surrounded by allegations of financial misconduct. William Clark survived for longer but his lack of foreign policy experience drew ridicule and he was moved in October 1983 to be Secretary of the Interior. Robert McFarlane was then NSA until December 1985 but his influence was blunted by a feud with the White House Chief of Staff, Donald Regan. Admiral John Poindexter was forced to resign in December 1986, after only a year, because of involvement in the 'Irangate' scandal; Frank Carlucci then took up the post until November 1987; and that left only one year to serve for Reagan's last NSA, General Colin Powell, who later went on to be Chairman of the Joint Chiefs of Staff (1989–93) and, in 2001, Secretary of State.

about to improve. Shultz had never believed that a real change in superpower relations would be possible until the long-awaited INF deployment was completed. Once it was, Reagan could be persuaded that the West was in an excellent situation to pursue negotiation from strength. The President also recognized that a less bellicose policy could help him win a second term in the 1984 election and there was concern in Washington at the evidence—some of it from the Soviet spy, Oleg Gordievsky, who had defected to Britain—that Moscow really did expect an American attack. The death of Andropov, in February 1984, brought another ageing and sick leader to the general secretaryship: Konstantin Chernenko, a Brezhnev loyalist with no overseas experience, seemed, if anything, a step backwards. But Chernenko, who had fully supported détente in the 1970s, left foreign policy in the hands of the experienced Gromyko and was ready to enter into a new exchange of messages with Reagan. The Eastern bloc's decision to boycott the 1984 Los Angeles Olympics was not a serious setback because it was a predictable act of revenge for the US boycott of Moscow four years before. No great breakthroughs were likely in a presidential election year but the first Reagan–Gromyko meeting, on 28 September, was one of the most hopeful signs in superpower relations since 1979 and led to growing expectations of a new round of nuclear arms talks. Enraged as they were by America's INF deployment, the Soviets really needed such negotiations if they were to prevent Washington pulling ahead in the arms race. Reagan's landslide re-election was followed by two rounds of Shultz–Gromyko meetings, in November and January, which led to an agreement to resume negotiations in Geneva on both INF and strategic weapons. In retrospect, it was easy to forget that, although these talks began on 12 March, one day after Mikhail Gorbachev became the Soviet leader, they had actually been planned under the unfortunate, colourless Chernenko.

B. The Polish Crisis of 1980–2

The Emergence of Solidarity

The confrontation between the two blocs, which reappeared in earnest as Ronald Reagan became President, also featured difficulties within the Eastern bloc and indicated Moscow's initial determination to continue suppressing reform or dissent. In Poland, low growth, uncompetitive exports, and a desire to pave the way for economic reform, led the regime of Wladyslaw Gomulka, with its 'nationalist' brand of communism, to recommend price increases in December 1970. This sparked the already hard-pressed ship workers of the Baltic ports to riot and they attacked Communist Party offices and set up their own 'workers councils'. The shooting of strikers at Gdynia further inflamed the situation and led the Communist Party—as in 1956 (see Chapter 6, A)—to decide on a change of leader, partly to prevent any Soviet action. Edvard Gierek, a competent administrator, replaced Gomulka, withdrew the price increases, and promised to consult on reforms in future. The situation then eased, until another round of strikes in 1976, but the lesson was not forgotten: by organizing themselves, industrial workers (supposedly the backbone of any Marxist revolution) had forced a reversal of policy, and even a change of government.

At the end of the 1970s, Poland, a predominantly agricultural country, had run up debts to the West of nearly $20 billion. It even faced the humiliation of being a net food importer and its independent peasantry, unique in the Eastern bloc, were able to demand higher prices for their produce, so that the government was forced to hold down consumer costs by using substantial subsidies. In 1978, the election of the Polish Pope John Paul II stirred up nationalist sentiment and underlined the importance of Roman Catholicism in the supposedly atheist regime, a Papal visit in 1979 drawing huge crowds. The 'appropriation of national symbols . . . by the Church left the state in an unusually weak position . . . a competition that the party-state simply could not win', at least in the long term.[19]

The USSR had always feared serious trouble in Poland, a large state, strategically placed between itself and Germany, with a strong anti-Russian tradition in the eastern part of the country. And John Paul II's success helped inspire a KGB propaganda campaign, in Eastern Europe and the West, against Catholicism. It was against this economic and political background, and faced by negative growth rates, that Gierek, in 1980, reluctantly came to the same conclusion as Gomulka a decade before: if the Polish economy were ever to be reformed, price subsidies had to be removed. This also coincided with a growing sense of foreboding in Eastern Europe because of the death in May, of Yugoslavia's veteran leader, Marshal Tito. Washington had warned Moscow not to exploit the uncertainty in Yugoslavia and the Soviets were careful not to do so. Serious unrest in Yugoslavia was avoided but in Poland, on 3 May, a group of workers was arrested for trying to set up unofficial 'workers committees' to press for reform. It was a sign of what was to come.

In early July 1980, in a striking parallel to events in 1970, the introduction of meat price increases sparked off a new round of unrest, focused on the Baltic ports. On 14 August, the dismissal of a worker led to a strike being called in the Gdansk shipyard, where Lech Walesa soon emerged as a leading figure, and the strikes then began to spread, with the workers demanding free trades unions as well as better pay. At this point, the strikers 'made no claim to be attacking the mainsprings of the party's power. The lessons of 1968 had been learned.'[20] With the country paralysed and widespread food shortages, the government on

31 August again caved in to workers' demands, granting wage increases, a review of sentences on political prisoners, the broadcasting of religious services, and promising a free trades union, Solidarity. This agreement, 'although radical and a challenge to the system . . . fell within the accepted parameters of the Brezhnev doctrine' because it recognized 'the leading role of the party and . . . the established system of international alliances'.[21] But, in contrast to 1970 and 1976, these concessions were not followed by a return to calm. Instead, ten million Poles rushed to join Solidarity, which became an important political force in its own right, a workers' organization independent of the communist regime. Only when the government formally recognized Solidarity, in November did the strike wave recede. By then, Gierek had handed power (in September) to Stanislaw Kania, Solidarity was demanding liberal political reforms, and the Communist Party seemed to be disintegrating. As the Reagan administration entered office, many expected Soviet military intervention in Poland to restore communism on the lines of 1956 and 1968.

International Dimensions of the Crisis

'Martial law in Poland opened the 1980s with yet another demonstration of the limits to change in Eastern Europe.'[22] Once serious trouble broke out, the Soviets jammed Western broadcasts to the country, the Politburo set up a special commission to monitor the situation, and, as the CIA correctly deduced, contingency plans were made for a possible armed intervention with the aid of other 'fraternal' countries, namely East Germany and Czechoslovakia. Military manoeuvres began on the Polish border with the purpose of intimidating Solidarity. Solidarity, like the Roman Catholic Church, was seen as a 'counter-revolutionary' force in Moscow, an affront to the Brezhnev doctrine, exploiting Poland's economic malaise and national pride to threaten the communist system there and throughout the Soviet bloc, even inside the USSR itself. In October, Gromyko told the Politburo that the loss of Poland was unacceptable, in November, the East German government urged intervention, and on 3 December, in one of his last significant acts as President, Jimmy Carter sent a hot-line message to the Kremlin warning it to avoid military action. At a Warsaw Pact meeting two days later, even Ceauşescu expressed concern about developments in Poland, but Kania requested more time to deal with the situation, and Brezhnev decided to delay plans for an armed intervention. He realized that such a step would not only harm East–West relations, but could prove very costly in terms of money and lives if the Poles resisted and a long-term occupation were needed. There was an alternative way to restore order and that was by internal action, as with Gomulka in 1956, but this time using the Polish armed forces. The Polish police and army remained loyal to communism and even Kremlin hard-liners like Ustinov (Defence) and Andropov (KGB) believed internal action was preferable to the use of Soviet forces. To pave the way for this, on 10 February 1981 General Wojciech Jaruzelski, the former Defence Minister, was made Prime Minister. Eight months later he replaced Kania as General Secretary, further highlighting the fact that it was the military that now maintained communism in Poland. Indeed, 'Party leadership was barely evident in any real sense' and the regime was 'sustained by the influence of politically active generals'.[23]

After several strike-free weeks, Solidarity was surprised and concerned by Jaruzelski's appointment to the premiership. An outbreak of violence in March led to widespread expectation of martial law being introduced, but instead peace was restored—and a planned general strike avoided—when the government promised to punish those guilty of police brutality. While the Kremlin increasingly saw little alternative to martial law, Jaruzelski alternatively spoke of reconciliation and condemned Solidarity for provoking instability. In November 1981, he even tried to make peace with Walesa face to face. But the latter's demand for democracy and a share in power was difficult to meet and, having decided that direct Soviet intervention was all but impossible, Brezhnev demanded that Jaruzelski himself must act forcefully. It has been argued that Jaruzelski had been 'expecting Soviet troops to be sent' and that he suffered a 'lack of confidence that the martial law operation would succeed'. What would have happened if he had refused to act, or if he had acted and failed, is not clear because the Soviets were so reluctant to become embroiled in a Polish war that they refused even to guarantee him military aid if he ran up against strong opposition. But he later insisted, 'nobody can say that I lacked in decisiveness or self-control'; and it is certainly true that on 12–13 December he acted successfully.[24] Using the excuse that Solidarity had again considered a general strike, Jaruzelski took the union by surprise, introduced martial law, and arrested 200,000 Solidarity supporters, ruling Poland through a Military Council for National Reconciliation. Independent trades unions were banned, Solidarity was forced underground, and the Polish population was so fearful that substantial price increases were peacefully accepted.

The introduction of martial law in Poland 'achieved its immediate aims with tolerable success', even if the attempt to resolve the country's internal problems by force 'could only be transitional'.[25] The Soviets had avoided the grave risks of intervention and trouble was avoided elsewhere in the Eastern bloc. Indeed, in the rest of Eastern Europe there was remarkable political stability, despite the deep economic problems. Jaruzelski defended his action on the grounds that it avoided Soviet intervention and bloodshed, and that it did not prevent political change in Poland. Imprisoned Solidarity members were gradually released, including, in November 1982, Walesa. The following month martial law was suspended. The international costs were limited. The US and other Western powers condemned Jaruzelski's action and the Reagan administration was keen to restrict trade with the Eastern bloc. This was not only due to Polish events but also because, in contrast to the détente era, some Washington officials wished to end Soviet access to Western technology and put the USSR's economy under pressure. In December 1981, after months of argument, Reagan prohibited American firms from cooperating with a planned Siberian pipeline project, which would bring Soviet natural gas to Western Europe. The ban affected European firms manufacturing pipeline components under US licence. But this simply provoked a serious dispute in the Western alliance, especially after Reagan tried to apply the prohibition to US subsidiaries in Europe. Even Britain's Margaret Thatcher (see Box 16.2) objected to such domineering behaviour by her ally, and Reagan was forced to reverse his policy later in the year. One reason why he backed down was the need to reunite NATO ahead of its next challenge, the long-awaited introduction of new US INF weapons into Europe.

C. Nuclear Arms Control and the 'Year of the Missile'

Posturing and Propaganda in 1981

The Reagan administration inherited a complicated situation where nuclear arms talks were concerned. Although the SALT II treaty (Chapter 14, E) had not been ratified by Congress, both superpowers had undertaken to abide by its terms and Carter had entered exploratory talks with the Soviets on a SALT III agreement. At the same time, NATO was committed to its 1979 'dual-track' decision (Chapter 15, A) to seek talks on the reduction of INF whilst planning the deployment of US Cruise and Pershing II missiles in Europe, timetabling this for 1983. The last decision meant that meaningful talks on nuclear arms control could not be held before 1984 at the earliest. Many positions adopted by the superpowers on the subject before that were mere posturing, because the Kremlin could hope that the Cruise–Pershing decision would not be carried out: if it were not, then there was no need to limit Soviet forces through an INF treaty. In particular, Moscow hoped that anti-nuclear movements in Western Europe would persuade their governments not to make new missile deployments. Popular revulsion had already helped to defer production of the 'neutron bomb' in the late 1970s, and after 1979 nuclear disarmament groups grew in strength in West Germany, Britain, Holland, and elsewhere, fuelled by the new Cold War and by the fears raised over Reagan's anti-communist rhetoric. Exploratory talks on INF weapons, in October–November 1980, had suggested that the two sides were far apart, with NATO only anxious to control land-based weapons, but the Soviets keen to limit sea and air-based systems (which could more readily be deployed outside Europe) as well. These positions reflected the differing concerns of the two sides in a situation where SS-20s were already being deployed, whereas the Cruise and Pershing II missiles had yet to arrive in Europe, but NATO had British sea-launched missiles and the Soviets faced a threat from the French deterrent. For the Soviets, the increased fire-power stemming from the SS-20 replacing SS-4s and SS-5s equalized a European balance from which strategic US weapons were excluded. The West was keen to remove the threat from the land-based, mobile, and multi-warhead SS-20s if possible, without having to face the financial cost and unpopularity of a Cruise–Pershing deployment; but the Soviets, with superiority in land-based INF deployments, were keener to control Cruise missiles because these were a flexible weapon (either land, sea, or air based) that could escape radar detection once launched.

Reagan's earliest moves on the nuclear front were hardly calculated to reassure his European critics. In May 1981, he restated the fact that America was under no legal obligation to fulfil SALT II, in August he announced the stockpiling of neutron bombs (though only in the US), and in October his new armaments programme included a strategic bomber project, which Carter had earlier cancelled. Reagan's policy was, in part, predicated on the argument that the USSR might soon stride ahead in the nuclear arms race, despite the fact that, when he arrived in office, America actually outmatched the Soviets' total of 6,000 warheads by over 50 per cent: only two years later did the CIA admit that, since 1976, it had greatly overestimated Soviet military spending; and only in April 1983 did a commission under Brent Scowcroft report that US nuclear defences were quite adequate, ending fears of a 'window of vulnerability'. But the Reagan–Weinberger policy was also 'designed to give priority to autarkic reliance on American military power . . . rather than the pursuit of . . . arms control' and it was accompanied by claims of a 'decade of neglect' of US defences in the 1970s.[26]

In September 1981, Gromyko and Secretary of State Haig agreed to begin INF talks in Geneva within two months, but the posturing of both sides ahead of this date was clear. The Soviets, for example, notably in a speech by Gromyko to the UN on 22 September, pressed NATO to agree to a universal renunciation of the 'first use' of nuclear weapons in a conflict. This was a clever propaganda move which the Soviets knew the Western powers would reject: NATO was inferior to the Warsaw Pact in conventional weapons and had always planned to use nuclear arms in a response to any offensive from the East. But, on 20 October, Brezhnev repeated the call for a 'no first-use' commitment. For his part, Reagan attempted to steal the propaganda limelight on 18 November with a proposal for the complete destruction of INF weapons on both sides. This was the first time that the so-called 'zero option'—an idea that emerged from the German Social Democratic Party—had been officially adopted and it sounded a bold, imaginative initiative. But the Americans knew that the Soviets would never easily surrender their INF arsenal, the only nuclear area where they had a clear advantage over the West (if British and French weapons were excluded), especially ahead of the 1983 Cruise–Pershing deployment. Reagan had made his proposal knowing it would not be accepted, hence the argument that, while the zero option 'shored up political support in NATO countries for . . . deployment, the principal purpose of the administration, it also killed the prospect for serious negotiation'.[27]

Only in the late 1980s did the 'zero option' become a serious proposal when, to American surprise, the Kremlin came around to the idea. Yet there is evidence that, while being tough in negotiations, Reagan also had a hankering to control the arms race. Thus, Caspar Weinberger insisted that Reagan, 'contrary to virtually all the popular myths about him . . . had been very unhappy about the need to rely on nuclear weapons'.[28] Also, even if Reagan's proposal was no more than a propaganda, or time-buying, exercise, the Kremlin response was equally unconstructive. 'The Soviet negotiating position was designed to avoid . . . reductions in the SS-20s, while at the same time preventing NATO from acquiring a "unilateral advantage" with the Pershing IIs and Tomahawks.'[29] They now proposed a freeze on INF deployments (thus freezing their own SS-20 deployment) and wanted to count in the 'zero option' all nuclear systems 'intended for use' in Europe (a difficult concept to define, but including jet aircraft and the British and French deterrents). The US was never likely to negotiate on this basis.

INF and START, 1981–3

The INF talks got underway on schedule on 30 November 1981, and there were soon fears that the Americans would link them to the Polish crisis, a possibility which, however, Haig ruled out in late January. Shortly afterwards, the US rejected a proposal by Brezhnev to reduce INF numbers in Europe by two-thirds because the Soviets could deploy such systems in Asia: the mobile SS-20 could easily be redeployed to Europe in a crisis and the US had always been determined to restrict *total* INF figures, whether in Europe or beyond. Then, in March, Brezhnev tried another ploy to impress the West European peace movements and dissuade Washington from deploying the Cruises and Pershings. Of the 350 SS-20s deployed so far, about 240 were in Europe, but now he announced that no more would be sent to that theatre. Instead, the future build-up would take place against China. Again, however, the ability of the Soviets to redeploy the SS-20s *in future*, ensured a US rejection of the proposal. Exactly how far either side was genuinely interested in arms control is unclear. Nonetheless, it is significant that, in mid-1982, when the two chief arms control negotiators from each side (America's Paul Nitze and the USSR's Yuri Kvitsinsky) drew up a dramatic scheme for INF limits, it was quickly rejected. Their July 'walk in the woods' deal would basically have limited each superpower to only 75 INF weapons in Europe, but the US Department of Defense argued that this would still leave Moscow at an advantage because the mobile SS-20s were more powerful than slow-moving Cruise missiles and the US would have to cancel deployment of the Pershing II. Haig's successor Shultz was anxious to show the West Europeans that America took the INF talks seriously, but the failure of the 'walk in the woods' seemed to support Soviet claims that the opposite was true (though there was no guarantee that Moscow would have accepted the proposal either). Another offer to reduce SS-20 deployments, by the newly appointed Andropov in December, came to nothing and in 1983 both sides waited on the outcome of the Cruise–Pershing deployment.

Meanwhile, there had also been some movement on the strategic weapons front, where Reagan, despite his hard-line persona, had a real interest in reaching agreement. In May 1982, in a speech at Eureka College, he proposed that in future these should be 'Strategic Arms Reduction Talks' (START), an acronym designed to sound more positive than SALT. 'I decided that if we were to participate with the Russians in arms control talks, our goal should be to *reduce* nuclear weapons, not just limit their rate of increase, which is what past nuclear arms control agreements had done.'[30] Shortly afterwards, he reiterated that America would adhere to the SALT II limits as long as the USSR did, and he successfully pressed for the START talks to begin in June in Geneva. But the US found it extremely difficult to agree on a detailed negotiating position and the talks immediately fell victim to the same mutual distrust, posturing, and slow progress which marred the INF discussions. In October, shortly before his death, Brezhnev accused Reagan of wanting nuclear war and in December the Kremlin condemned the US President for his decision to proceed with the deployment of the 'heavy', strategic MX missile, originally planned under Carter. In 1983, the accusations and counter-accusations continued, with the US focusing attention on the Soviet decision to build a radar station at Krasnoyarsk, in Siberia, well away from the periphery of the USSR and therefore in contravention of the 1972 ABM treaty. Planned since 1979, there can be no doubt that this was a deliberate breach of the treaty, even if the Soviets saw it as a minor one.

The most celebrated step on the strategic arms front in 1983 was Reagan's 23 March announcement of the Strategic Defense Initiative (SDI), or Star Wars programme. Even Shultz, who only saw the announcement a day or two before, admitted: 'I had been surprised by the idea' and acknowledged 'the vision came from Ronald Reagan'.[31] SDI was designed to create a defensive shield against incoming nuclear missiles, perhaps with space-based laser or particle-beam weapons. In one sense, it was nothing new, since experiments on such weapons had already been carried out under Carter. In any case, many Western experts believed that the initiative would be expensive and fruitless; many dismissed the idea of space-based laser defences as pure science fiction, a fantastic product of the President's Hollywood past. The truth was probably more complex. Reagan did honestly believe it was morally right to seek protection from a nuclear attack, in which he feared that up to half the American population would be killed, and he even spoke of sharing a successful SDI system with the Kremlin. But he was certainly naive in not realizing that the initiative would revitalize Soviet fears of US technological prowess and undermine deterrence. In 1975, the US had scrapped its previous anti-ballistic missile (ABM) programme and the threat of 'Mutually Assured Destruction' (MAD) by second-strike forces remained. But a successful SDI—which, however unlikely, had now to be considered—could render the existing Soviet nuclear arsenal redundant, forcing them to invest in a costly, similar programme or vastly to expand their nuclear arsenal, in order to try and nullify the proposed US system by force of numbers. SDI could only add to the growing belief in Moscow that Reagan was determined to humiliate or defeat the USSR, possibly in a nuclear war, hence a Soviet general's warning to the Warsaw Pact in April that war was a real possibility. The Soviets criticized the initiative as a breach of the 1972 ABM treaty (which had forbidden development of new ABM systems) far worse than the Krasnoyarsk radar.

The 'Year of the Missile' and a Year without Talks

Whatever the ructions provoked by SDI, 1983 became the 'year of the missile' because of the INF debate, not because of strategic weapons developments. 'The most prominent struggle between Washington and Moscow in 1983 was over influence in Europe, specifically the battle over deployment of the new US intermediate-range missiles.'[32] As the deadline for the Cruise–Pershing deployment approached, the Soviets shifted their propaganda campaign from one of offering concessions to one of making threats. In April

1983, Gromyko rejected a fresh offer from Reagan to cancel the US deployment if the Soviets scrapped all their INF weapons, and warned that the arrival of the Cruise and Pershing IIs would lead them to walk out of the INF and START talks. The prospect of escalating international tension gave further impetus to the West European peace movements who, in late October, launched a series of large-scale demonstrations. Nevertheless, on 14–15 November the INF deployments went ahead in Britain, and a week later the West German Parliament also agreed to accept them. The first Pershing IIs arrived on 23 November, described by Shultz as 'D-Day': he feared that 'demonstrations could break the will of Allied governments' and 'undermine our resolve to stand up to the Soviets in future'. Indeed, overcoming the demonstrators had arguably become Washington's main concern, one far removed from 1979, when it had been hoped that deployment would 'reinforce deterrence . . . reassure the allies, and . . . enhance allied unity . . . All of these aims were, to some degree, casualties' by 1983.[33] So too was the hope that the threat of deployment would induce the Soviets to negotiate an INF treaty, for now the Soviets carried out their threat to leave the Geneva talks. They walked out of the INF sessions on 23 November and the START talks were adjourned on 8 December without setting a date for future meetings. The following week, the Vienna-based talks on conventional arms restriction, the Mutual Balanced Force Reduction (MBFR) talks, underway since the early 1970s, were also adjourned without the promise of further contacts. 'For the first time in nearly fifteen years, the Americans and the Soviets were no longer negotiating in any forum.'[34]

With the Soviets' simultaneous fear that NATO's 'Operation Able Archer' might be the cover for an actual attack, the situation for European security at the end of 1983 seemed bleak indeed. Furthermore, Moscow insisted in December on proceeding with new INF deployments of its own. This move upset the usually loyal Erich Honecker of East Germany, whose country became, along with Czechoslovakia, the base for the additional SS-20s. He, nonetheless, agreed to cancel a planned visit to West Germany but another, usually loyal ally, Todor Zhirkov of Bulgaria, underlined his own fear of the rising European tension by proceeding with a similar visit. Meanwhile NATO, with its deployments completed after so much doubt and tension, felt more confident about entering new INF talks from a position of strength. This situation, along with the forthcoming presidential election, gave Reagan a strong incentive to avoid further confrontation. In fact, 1984 proved an oddly quiescent year in superpower relations: with the Red Army bogged down in Afghanistan, the Polish crisis over, and other crises (the KAL 007 incident and invasion of Grenada) proving short-lived, there was no possible spark for an East–West conflagration. The Soviet refusal to talk

BOX 16.2

Biography: Margaret Thatcher (1925–2013)

The British Conservative Prime Minister was born in the provincial town of Grantham, the daughter of a grocer, but was educated at Oxford as a research chemist, married a wealthy businessman, and entered the House of Commons in 1959. She was little known abroad when, in 1975, she challenged the incumbent Edward Heath for the party leadership. Her readiness to step forward as a representative of the Right won her wide respect and she eventually secured the leadership race against several better-known figures. In May 1979, helped by considerable social discontent, which undermined the Labour government, she won the premiership. She was re-elected Prime Minister twice, in 1983 and 1987.

At home, Thatcher pursued similar policies to those of the Reagan administration: taxes were cut, social spending restrained, private enterprise rewarded, and state intervention in the economy reduced. Abroad she made her name as a firm anti-communist, America's most loyal ally in the 'New Cold War' of the early 1980s. But she was offended when Reagan invaded Grenada in 1983 because Britain had not been fully consulted on the invasion of this member of the Commonwealth and in 1985, she quickly embraced Gorbachev as 'someone we can do business with'. On other issues, she showed herself a strong defender of British national interests, opposing the extension of greater powers to the European Community (EC), and sending a force to reconquer the Falkland Islands when they were occupied by Argentina in 1982. However, in 1989–90, after ten years in power she seemed to many Conservative parliamentarians to be an electoral liability: she insisted on pursuing an unpopular reform of local taxation, she was opposed to German reunification, and she seemed increasingly unable to influence the course of EC debates. One of her last acts in office was to back a firm reaction to Saddam Hussein's invasion of Kuwait.

to the West increasingly appeared an empty gesture, especially since Reagan seemed set to return to office for another four years. The MBFR talks were actually revived in March 1984, though the INF and START talks did not recommence for another year.

D. The War in Afghanistan to 1985

From Intervention to Embroilment

When the Soviets invaded Afghanistan at Christmas 1979, they hoped that their intervention might be of a limited scale and duration. They were well aware of the dangers of being dragged into a guerrilla war in difficult terrain, in defence of an unpopular government, and in the face of a determined enemy. However, if a new, united government could be stabilized quickly under Babrak Karmal, and if the Afghan security forces remained loyal, then an early reduction in the Red Army presence might be possible. Despite Western fears of Soviet designs on the Persian Gulf, Moscow had no ambitions to advance beyond Afghanistan and believed that Washington simply manipulated the crisis in order to reignite the Cold War. For the first few months, after the shock of the invasion, there was limited active opposition in Afghanistan itself to what had occurred. 'The Soviet invasion met with no armed resistance in the first month because its target was not the countryside, which was in a state of rebellion, but the . . . government itself.'[35] But unrest grew as winter progressed, with demonstrations in Kabul itself in February. Foreign intervention, accompanied as it was by the murder of the former leader, Hafizullah Amin, simply made the Marxist government in Kabul even more unpopular and, despite conscription, the Afghan army was reduced by desertion from 150,000 in early 1979 to no more than 35,000 men a year later, too few to maintain order.

Soon, despite their original fears, the Red Army found itself having to take over the prosecution of the war. 'Conceived as a quick and decisive military operation, which would be followed by a rapid withdrawal of Soviet forces, the intervention in Afghanistan became the USSR's Vietnam.'[36] When the KGB chief, Andropov, visited Kabul in January 1980, it was clear that the Red Army would have to stay for some time. Andropov and Gromyko did study a possible political solution to the conflict, to pave the way for a Soviet withdrawal, but it was difficult to agree on what peace terms to offer to Afghan opposition groups. Global condemnation probably made it harder to consider retreat. The Soviets also hoped to negotiate from a position of strength, which simply did not exist at first. Besides, their opponents, the Mujaheddin, were both religiously inspired and divided among themselves, making negotiations doubly difficult. Indeed, when peace talks began in Geneva with a UN mediator, they were between the Soviet-backed Kabul regime and Pakistan, the Islamic state on whose territory the Mujaheddin leaderships were based. The talks did not begin until June 1982 and by the time of their fourth session, in August 1984, they had only just entered the 'proximity' stage—with the intermediary, Diego Cordovez, moving between the two delegations, who refused to meet face to face.

With the Afghan army so weak, the Soviets began to mount combat operations of their own against the Mujaheddin in February 1980, and the Red Army contingent of 50,000 men was soon increased to 80,000. Yet their 'presence spread and intensified the conflict from essentially a civil war among Afghans into primarily a national war of resistance to foreign invaders and their local puppets'.[37] Their generals did have contingency plans for a quick withdrawal and several realized that a political solution, based on a coalition government, was preferable to a long war that probably could not be won. However, the intervention soon assumed an air of permanency. Specialist counter-insurgency units were formed, but the Soviets at first relied heavily on 'sweep offensives' with tanks and ground troops to root out their opponents. 'Soviet armed forces had very little experience of dealing with insurgency . . . [They] had been trained for global war, not small war.'[38] Also, Soviet ideology was completely unprepared for war against a 'mass movement': the masses, after all, were supposed to be loyal to Marxism. But, rather like the US experience in Vietnam, conventional methods proved ill-suited to a war against lightly armed guerrillas, in mountainous regions of extreme temperatures, who could find shelter and supplies in a neighbouring country, Pakistan. In late 1981 and during 1982, the Red Army turned more, therefore, to the use of lightly armed troops, with helicopters to improve mobility. It is unclear what impact political instability in Moscow had on the war. With Brezhnev in physical decline and then two rapid changes of leader, there was presumably a lack of commitment to a vigorous prosecution of the Afghan campaign. In 1984–5, Chernenko, though ill himself, evidently had hopes of winning the war quickly, rather than seeing it drag on. He launched six large-scale offensives, accompanied by heavy aerial bombing and raids on refugee camps in order to break enemy morale, albeit at the cost of greater Soviet casualties. In 1983, when the war seemed to be deadlocked, the wisdom of pursuing it was increasingly questioned in Moscow and Andropov seemed genuinely interested in negotiations, partly to allow him to tackle the USSR's domestic problems. A peace policy received no support from Reagan, however, in the year of the 'evil Empire' speech, and it was opposed by Gromyko, Ustinov, and the Chief of Staff, Nikolai Ogarkov. With the Mujaheddin fighting on in 1985, the conflict seemed as intractable as ever.

Despite their internal wranglings and faulty tactics, it cannot be said that the Soviets were on the brink of defeat. Whatever the talk of a 'Soviet Vietnam', they were careful not to escalate on the scale of the Americans in the earlier conflict. At its largest, in 1985, the Red Army presence only reached 108,000 and during the worst year for casualties, in 1984, it suffered only about 2,000 deaths in combat. Despite the continued division within the Afghan Communists (between the elitist, urban Parcham faction, and the more extreme, rural Khalq), the Kabul government was not a complete liability. It was able to exploit differences among its opponents, to hold on to urban areas (where about 2 million of the 13 million Afghans lived), and to contribute to the war, not least through the expansion of the Afghan secret police (KHAD). The Soviets were determined that any peace settlement should leave the communists in power (though possibly in a coalition government) and they were helped by the fact that the Kabul regime was a UN member, with widespread international recognition, whose opponents were rebels. The Soviets were also helped by the divided nature of the Mujaheddin, whose factions sometimes fought each other. There was no Afghan 'nationalism' in such a divided country. The Mujaheddin was willing to unite against communism and foreign intervention, but Afghanistan was made up of various ethnic groups (about 40 per cent were Pathans, but there were also Turkomans, Tajiks, and others), who had a history of internal feuding and banditry, some of which reflected religious divisions between the majority Sunnis and minority Shi'ites, some of which involved tribal warlords. One observer noted that 'warring factions have portioned out Afghanistan into separate areas of influence sharing nothing in common but hatred and lack of trust'.[39] Only in early 1986 did seven factions unite to form a single government-in-exile, but even the US felt it unwise to recognize it, given the volatility of Mujaheddin politics. The guerrilla groups were resilient but ill-disciplined; experienced fighters but poorly armed. They were amateurish, lacking a united strategy, and without the heavy weapons, which might have threatened the Soviet hold on Afghanistan's towns and cities. The disparate nature of the opposition was 'in one sense a strength however: if the Soviets should succeed in destroying a few groups, many would be left. Like a bear attacked by a swarm of bees, the Soviet army [was] being hit from all directions.'[40]

External Involvement in the War

One advantage that the Mujaheddin had was in the scale of external assistance. In the face of the early Soviet offensives, between two and three million refugees fled Afghanistan, crossing the mountains to Iran and Pakistan. By 1985, their numbers had grown to about five million and Pakistan especially proved a protector, providing not only a refuge, but also guerrilla bases, arms, training, and military advice. 'The American-led support of the Mujaheddin was a multinational effort. Pakistan was the key, as the base for the rebels and as the conduit' for outside aid.[41] Some Pakistani troops were even sent into Afghanistan, though only as observers. Pakistan's leader, General Zia ul-Haq, used the Soviet threat in 1979–80—when some expected a Red Army advance across the Pakistani border or through Iran to the Gulf—to unite Pakistan under his dictatorial role. He also used his position as a 'front-line' state opposing the communist advance to improve relations with the West, having been criticized in 1979 for the execution of the former Prime Minister, Ali Bhutto. And Zia especially made Pakistan a close ally of the US. Already, after the fall of the Shah, Pakistan, a US ally mostly since 1954, had agreed to host electronic monitoring stations for the Americans, replacing those lost in Iran. The relationship had its opponents on both sides. Some in the State Department questioned the wisdom of relying on an oppressive regime which was trying to become a nuclear power, a development which would increase tensions with its neighbour, India. And the Pakistani Foreign Minister, Agha Shahi, resigned in February 1982 because he doubted the wisdom both of enraging the Soviet Union and relying on the Americans, whom he felt to be volatile and unreliable. Nevertheless, Zia and the army were convinced of the advantages of getting close to Washington and such thinking was encouraged by the White House, under both Carter and Reagan. Just as aid from the US, China, and Arab states was dependent on Pakistani goodwill, so Pakistan enjoyed 'prestige as a frontline state and substantial aid from Western states'.[42]

Zia was careful, however, not to provoke discontent in Afghanistan to the point that he actually risked Soviet invasion. He tried to control the Mujaheddin groups in exile, even breaking up an attempt by non-fundamentalist, Pathan factions to form a coalition in 1980 because he believed it was not in Pakistan's interest. Traditionally, the Pakistanis were suspicious of the Pathan predominance in Afghanistan, and Zia preferred to back the fundamentalists, who were strong among the minority ethnic groups, and who were ready to create a new kind of Afghan state, a centralized theocracy with ties to the wider Islamic world, including Pakistan. Of course, the fundamentalists were opposed to Western influences, as well as to communism, but this did not prevent Zia from steering American aid towards them. Zia was determined not to be treated as a US satellite. He wanted greater US assistance for Pakistan itself, as well as for the Mujaheddin, and he rejected an early offer of aid from Washington because it was not substantial enough. In June 1981, such tactics paid off, with a $3 billion package of economic and military aid over five years, including F-16 aircraft. As seen, when peace talks began in 1982, it was Pakistan, a UN-recognized government, which negotiated, effectively, for the Mujaheddin. But again, Zia pursued his own interests too, refusing to deal with the Kabul regime face to face, determined to remove Karmal, who was seen as a Soviet stooge, and equally determined at first to exclude the Afghan communists from power entirely, rather than accepting a coalition government with them.

Pakistan was not the only Islamic state to aid the Mujaheddin. Iran, Egypt, and Saudi Arabia were among the others providing assistance, the last with massive financial aid. Up to 2.5 million refugees were accommodated in Iran. The USSR's rival, China, another neighbouring state, also gave arms to the rebel groups. It was the Egyptians and Chinese who helped the CIA early in the war by sending some of their own Soviet-made weapons to the Mujaheddin. Once these arrived in Afghanistan, it was difficult for the Soviets to prove their source: the Mujaheddin could easily claim it had captured them from the Red Army. Given that the Kabul government was a legally recognized regime, it would have been embarrassing to Washington to have US-made weapons being used in these early stages because it could have seemed that America was equally responsible for the war.

It was the US, however, which remained the backbone of the external effort to arm the Mujaheddin and pin down the Red Army in an unwinnable war. In early 1980, Carter's National Security Adviser, Zbigniew Brzezinski, was especially keen to put the Soviets 'on trial' before the court of world opinion and he opposed suggestions from the Secretary of State, Cyrus Vance, that talks might be opened with Moscow on Afghanistan and wider security concerns in the region. US aid was markedly increased in October 1980, despite the reluctance of the CIA Director, Stansfield Turner. Such American behaviour made it less likely that the Soviets would talk peace: they had no desire in 1980 to be put 'on trial' or to admit defeat. Indeed, US policy did not seem so much to be aimed at ending aggression and pacifying Afghanistan, as causing maximum cost to the Kremlin. This continued under Reagan for whom, of course, anti-Sovietism was the prime motive behind his foreign policy. The new CIA director, William Casey, had none of Turner's qualms about aiding rebels and became the leading 'hawk' in Washington. He argued that if the Soviets were tied down in Afghanistan they were less likely to cause trouble elsewhere and he saw the 1982 opening of peace talks as a Kremlin ploy. Others were more cautious, ready to aid the Mujaheddin but reluctant to escalate the conflict. In 1981–3, Casey was unable to increase US aid to the Mujaheddin much beyond that planned under Carter (which was already considerable enough). There *were* substantial increases in 1984, but the continuation of the war and its intensification under Chernenko still led some in Congress to claim that the CIA was not doing enough. The result was a further increase in US aid in 1985 to $250 million, including anti-aircraft weapons, which might counter the Red Army's use of helicopters and thus reduce its mobility. The CIA also encouraged the Pakistani intelligence services to stir up fundamentalist discontent in the USSR's Central Asian republics, where most of the population was Muslim. In March 1985, as Mikhail Gorbachev came into power, the Afghan war raged as intensively as ever. That same month President Reagan, whose inaugural speech in January had confirmed his support for less developed world 'freedom fighters', decided that the aim should no longer simply be to make the war costly for Moscow, but to drive the Soviets out of Afghanistan.

Visit the online resources that accompany this book to test your understanding and take your learning further:
www.oup.com/he/young-kent3e

NOTES

1. Quoted in Raymond Garthoff, *The Great Transition* (Brookings Institution, Washington, DC, 1994), 8.
2. Richard A. Melanson, *American Foreign Policy since the Vietnam War* (2nd edn, Armonk, New York, 1996), 142.
3. Odd Arne Westad, *The Fall of Détente: Soviet–American Relations during the Carter Years* (Scandinavian University Press, Oslo, 1997), 1 and 14.
4. Mike Bowker and Phil Williams, *Superpower Détente: A Reappraisal* (Sage, London, 1988), 250.
5. Andrei Gromyko, *Memories* (Hutchinson, London, 1988), 296.
6. Alexander Dobrynin, *In Confidence: Moscow's Ambassador to America's Six Cold War Presidents (1962–1986)* (Random House, New York, 1995), 484.
7. Ronald Reagan, *An American Life* (Hutchinson, London, 1990), 273.
8. Will Hutton, *The World We're In* (Little, Brown, London, 2002), 106–10, citing Paul Krugman, *Peddling Prosperity* (Norton, New York, 1994), 135.
9. Thomas G. Patterson, *On Every Front: The Making and Unmaking of the Cold War* (W. W. Norton, New York, 1992 edn), 199.
10. Coral Bell, quoted in Richard A. Melanson, *American Foreign Policy since the Vietnam War* (2nd edn, Armonk, New York, 1996), 149.
11. Caspar Weinberger, *Fighting for Peace: Seven Critical Years at the Pentagon* (Joseph, London, 1990), 25.
12. Andrei Gromyko, *Memories* (Hutchinson, London, 1988), 305.
13. Alexander Dobrynin, *In Confidence: Moscow's Ambassador to America's Six Cold War Presidents (1962–1986)* (Random House, New York, 1995), 495.
14. Alexander Haig, *Caveat: Realism, Reagan and Foreign Policy* (Macmillan, New York, 1984), 355.
15. Alexander Dobrynin, *In Confidence: Moscow's Ambassador to America's Six Cold War Presidents (1962–1986)* (Random House, New York, 1995), 508.
16. George Shultz, *Turmoil and Triumph* (Macmillan, New York, 1993), 270–1.
17. ibid., 277.
18. Don Oberdorfer, *How the Cold War Came to an End: The US and the Soviet Union, 1983–90* (Jonathan Cape, London, 1992), 66–7.
19. George Schoplin, *Politics in Eastern Europe* (Blackwell, Oxford, 1993), 217.
20. Michael Waller, *The End of Communist Power Monopoly* (Manchester University Press, Manchester, 1993), 130.
21. Geoffrey and Nigel Swain, *Eastern Europe since 1945* (2nd edn, St Martin's Press, New York, 1998), 168–9.
22. David Mason, *Revolution and Transition in East-Central Europe* (2nd edn, Westview Press, Boulder, 1996), 41.
23. Paul Lewis, *Political Authority and Party Secretaries in Poland* (Cambridge University Press, Cambridge, 1989), 198.
24. For the debate, see Mark Kramer, 'Jaruzelski, the Soviet Union and the Imposition of Martial Law in Poland' and Jaruzelski's 'Commentary', in *Cold War International History Project Bulletin*, 11 (Winter, 1998), quotes from 9 and 32.
25. Robin Edmonds, *Soviet Foreign Policy: The Brezhnev Years* (Oxford University Press, Oxford, 1983), 202.
26. Raymond Garthoff, *The Great Transition* (Brookings Institution, Washington, DC, 1994), 505.
27. Ibid., 510.

28. Caspar Weinberger, *Fighting for Peace: Seven Critical Years at the Pentagon* (Joseph, London, 1990), 240; see also Alexander Haig, *Caveat: Realism, Reagan and Foreign Policy* (Macmillan, New York, 1984), 222.

29. Strobe Talbott, *Deadly Gambits* (Picador, London, 1984), 87.

30. Ronald Reagan, *An American Life* (Hutchinson, London, 1990), 549.

31. George Shultz, *Turmoil and Triumph* (Macmillan, New York, 1993), 261.

32. Don Oberdorfer, *How the Cold War Came to an End: The US and the Soviet Union, 1983–90* (Jonathan Cape, London, 1992), 34.

33. George Shultz, *Turmoil and Triumph* (Macmillan, New York, 1993), 373; Raymond Garthoff, *The Great Transition* (Brookings Institution, Washington, DC, 1994), 553.

34. Strobe Talbott, *Deadly Gambits* (Picador, London, 1984), 4.

35. Olivier Roy, *Islam and Resistance in Afghanistan* (Cambridge University Press, Cambridge, 1986), 118.

36. Geoffrey Roberts, *The Soviet Union in World Politics* (Routledge, New York, 1999), 81.

37. Henry Bradsher, *Afghanistan and the Soviet Union* (Duke University Press, Durham, 1983), 205.

38. Caroline Kennedy-Pipe, *Russia and the World* (Arnold, London, 1998), 165.

39. Raja Anwar, *The Tragedy of Afghanistan* (Verso, London, 1988), 238.

40. Thomas Hammond, *Red Flag over Afghanistan* (Westview, Boulder, 1984), 157.

41. Raymond Garthoff, *The Great Transition* (Brookings Institution, Washington, DC, 1994), 713.

42. Anthony Hyman, *Afghanistan under Soviet Domination* (3rd edn, Macmillan, London, 1992), 218.

17

Middle East Conflicts in the 1980s

Chapter contents

A. Lebanon and the Israeli Invasion

The Israeli Invasion and the Multinational Force, 1982–5

The Camp David settlement did not bring peace to the Middle East. An Egyptian–Israeli settlement could not resolve the conflict between Israel and the Arab states, let alone with the Palestinians, nor bring stability and peace to the region. Sadat and Begin had achieved a limited peace between Egypt and Israel. Egypt, for its part, had abandoned the myth of Arab unity between the competing states of the region and pursued national interests. However, other conflicts were being played out in the region, not least those arising from the Lebanese Civil War (see Chapter 14, B), which added to the fundamental failure to deal with the Palestinian Question. In fact, it could be argued that Camp David produced more regional instability and increased the level of conflict between Israel and the Palestinians. The Israelis could rightly point out that their statehood had only been accepted by Egypt, while the Palestinians could equally well point out that the problem of the refugees expelled from the homes and their right to a state had not been addressed.

In June 1981, Israeli–Palestinian tensions began to rise and were to culminate in the next Middle Eastern military conflict the following year—the Israeli invasion of Lebanon. The bombing of the Iraqi nuclear reactor, at Osirak near Baghdad, was followed later in the month by another Likud election victory in Israel and the appointment of Ariel Sharon as Minister of Defence. Prime Minister Begin now relied on several right-wing parties for his majority and the new coalition spelt out its determination to interpret the Camp David agreement in line with its own requirements. The government was determined that the Palestinians would never attain sovereignty over an independent state. Furthermore, settlement in the land of Israel was defined as a right and as essential for the nation's security. Tension continued to grow as the Likud government moved closer to full armed confrontation with the Palestinians in Lebanon. The installation of Syrian surface-to-air missiles in the Beka'a Valley and raids and shelling across the Lebanon–Israel border led to the 'Two Week War' in July 1981, which was only ended with the mediation of a ceasefire by a US envoy, Philip Habib. This in itself was a significant point, in that 'America had now become involved in Lebanon and Reagan was staking a considerable amount of prestige on Washington's "honest broker" role.'[1]

The Israeli Cabinet discussed two plans for the invasion of Lebanon. One called for the ejection of the Palestine Liberation Organization (PLO) from South Lebanon, the other for a drive to the Beirut–Damascus highway, the surrounding of Beirut after a seaborne landing, and the destruction of the PLO infrastructure throughout Lebanon in cooperation with the Phalange.[2] The attempted assassination, on 3 June 1982, of Israel's ambassador to London, Shlomo Argov, was used as the excuse to launch a full-scale invasion of Lebanon on 6 June. 'It was Israel's determination to clean out PLO strongholds in Southern Lebanon, rather than recent aggression by Arafat's (see Box 17.1) guerrillas, that provided the impetus for the invasion.'[3] The well-planned attack brought Israeli forces to Beirut in only three days, brushing aside both PLO and Syrian attempts at resistance. The driving force behind these operations was Ariel Sharon, who had grandiose plans for their ultimate objective. Once the PLO military position in Lebanon was destroyed and its political organization weakened, Sharon planned to work with his Maronite allies to establish a new political order in Lebanon. But this was only the first stage of the planned redrawing of the Middle East's political map. The next stage was the absorption of the West Bank into Greater Israel, leading those Palestinians fleeing from Lebanon and the West Bank to cross into Jordan, where they would ultimately bring down King Hussein and establish a Palestinian state on the East Bank of the Jordan.[4] The dilemma of having to give up the West Bank or absorb large numbers of Palestinians into Israel would then be ended.

The renewed danger of an Israeli–Syrian war brought Philip Habib back to the Middle East where, in early July 1982, he secured an outline agreement on a settlement of the crisis: the Israelis would begin a ceasefire without entering central Beirut, the PLO would leave the city, and a multinational force (MNF) would be deployed to ensure a peaceful PLO exit. Alexander Haig, at the end of his time as US Secretary of State, even hoped to seize the chance 'to move all foreign forces . . . out of Lebanon and return the country to the Lebanese'.[5] It proved an over-ambitious hope, quickly undermined by renewed fighting in Beirut, arguments over where the PLO might be sent, and public debate in the US about an American role in the MNF. Then again, after weeks of further tension, a peace deal was secured, and on 21 August the PLO exit began. Over the following days, 11,000 PLO personnel and fighters left by sea. Arafat himself went on 30 August, soon establishing a new headquarters in Tunis, far enough away from Israel for Begin to feel that the main aim of the invasion had been achieved. The PLO fighters were scattered around the Arab world: after the civil wars in Jordan and Lebanon, no Arab country wished to play host to them en masse. Begin now hoped to secure a peace treaty with Lebanon to ensure that it was never again used as a base by radical Muslim opponents of Israel.

However, the Israeli success soon turned sour. On 23 August, the Christian Phalangist leader, Bashir Gemayel, was elected Lebanon's President, apparently further emphasizing Israeli success: the Phalangists, never happy about accepting Syrian protection, now looked to Israel as the saviour of the Maronite cause, and some Israeli leaders saw Gemayel as their potential puppet. But barely three weeks later, on 14 September, Bashir, and dozens of his supporters, were killed by a huge bomb. Despite American and UN condemnation, the Israeli army then marched into central Beirut, supposedly to maintain order, but they effectively let the Phalangists take revenge on their enemies. The PLO may have left Beirut, but thousands of unarmed Palestinian refugees were left behind, huddled into the camps of Sabra and Shatila, and these the Phalangists proceeded to slaughter over a two-day period. When word leaked out, there was an international outcry. 'The Israelis had watched their allies massacre innocents and had done nothing to prevent the atrocity.'[6] The Begin government denied a direct hand in the massacres. Nevertheless, Israel's standing in Western countries suffered a major blow. 'Morally, and in terms of its influence on world opinion, the siege and bombardment of Beirut were a turning point' in this respect.[7] Even in Israel itself, there were calls for the Prime Minister to resign but an investigation into the massacres, published in

February 1983, claimed only one Cabinet victim, the Defence Minister, Ariel Sharon, and he would eventually return as Israeli Prime Minister.

Meanwhile, on 21 September 1982, the Israelis had begun to withdraw from Beirut, and the same day, Bashir Gemayel's brother, Amin, was elected President in his place. The Americans produced a peace plan known as the Reagan Plan, which proposed Palestinian self-government in association with Jordan. Both a Palestinian state and Israeli West Bank settlements were ruled out. In May 1983, Amin made a peace treaty with the Israelis which was designed, in part, to bring about a joint Israeli–Syrian withdrawal. But Assad, who in 1982 had survived both the Lebanese Crisis and an attempt to overthrow him at home, refused to pull his army out. The Israelis, faced by a war which was unpopular at home and a drain on their economy, were thus forced into a gradual, unilateral withdrawal back to southern Lebanon, which ended in June 1985. By then, it was evident that the 1982 invasion had only achieved mixed results at best. Arafat had gone but the cost to Israeli finances and reputation was considerable and much remained unchanged: the Lebanese government was as powerless as ever, Syrian influence remained strong, and Israel continued to sustain a Phalangist regime in the South, where Palestinian activity had revived. Furthermore, in the wake of the Israeli invasion, Iran had sent over 1,000 Revolutionary Guards to Lebanon, where they supported the 'Hezbollah' (Party of God) that had sprung up in reaction to the Israeli invasion. Their 'goal was to launch a war against Israeli occupation, which would eventually grow to embrace the task of ridding Lebanon . . . of western . . . influence'.[8] Moreover, the aim of Sharon and those seeking to reduce pressure on the Israelis to give up the West Bank had not been achieved and the Palestinian problem had grown.

To the costs of the invasion had also to be added the experience of the MNF, which had originally begun to arrive in Beirut in August 1982, spearheaded by a French contingent, though the Americans were the driving force behind it, and it also included Italian troops. The French, of course, had been the colonial power in Lebanon, the Italians had a strong interest in stabilizing the Mediterranean, and the Reagan administration believed it must contribute to pacifying Lebanon, partly because the Israeli and Lebanese governments both wanted this. Reagan acted despite the doubts of the Department of Defense, under Caspar Weinberger, who believed, in light of the Vietnam experience, that 'we should not commit American troops to any situation unless the objectives were so important for American interests that we had to fight, and that if those conditions were met, then we had to commit . . . enough forces to win'.[9] Israel preferred a US-led force to another UN operation, given the ineffectiveness of the latter in the past; the US were anxious that other countries should serve alongside them so that it appeared a genuinely international effort. At first, the MNF was only supposed to cover the PLO withdrawal, but the massacres at Sabra and Shatila led it to be immediately reconstituted, with the Americans, French, and Italians soon being joined by a small British contingent. Instead of contributing much to the long-term stability of Lebanon however, the MNF was soon the focus of Shi'ite attacks. On 18 April 1983, dozens were killed in a bomb attack by the pro-Iranian 'Islamic Jihad' group on the US embassy in Beirut; and on 23 October, 241 US marines and 58 French troops were killed in separate attacks, following the bombardment by US naval vessels of Muslim positions. Radical anti-Western groups were now becoming part of the increasingly problematic Middle Eastern scene. With an election year forthcoming and faced by a potentially intractable conflict if the MNF remained, Reagan led the way in withdrawing. On 7 February 1984, he announced the 'redeployment' of US forces. By the end of March, they had been 'redeployed' entirely out of the region.

The Search for a Settlement, 1985–92

In the wake of the withdrawal of Western forces and the Israeli retreat into south Lebanon, the lack of a stable government and army left the militias struggling for power. In the new situation, the Syrians and their 30,000-strong army, having fallen out with the Phalangists, at first supported the Druze (now led by Kamal Jumblatt's son, Walid) and the Shi'ite Amal militias (led by Nabih Berri). But later, notably in early 1987 and 1989–90, the Syrians tried to reach an internal settlement. Among the Shi'ites, pro-Iranian feeling remained important, notably in the shape of Hezbollah, which became active in South Lebanon and was eager, like the Palestinians, to launch attacks on Israel. Amal and Hezbollah fought each other for influence in the Shi'ite community, just as Maronite factions continued to vie with each other for Christian support. Between 1984 and 1987, Hezbollah and other Shi'ite groups also took 90 Westerners hostage, including the Central Intelligence Agency (CIA) station chief, William Buckley. The assassination by Maronites of the Sunni Prime Minister, Rashid Karawi, in 1987, was followed in 1988 by the formation of two separate governments, a Muslim one under Selim al-Hoss and a Christian one under General Michel Aoun, who had the unlikely ambition of expelling the Syrians and re-establishing Maronite predominance.

By 1989, however, many Lebanese groups realized that hopes of ultimate victory promised only an endless round of violence, and the country was physically, economically, and psychologically shattered. In October, the remaining members of the last Parliament, first elected back in 1972, met in Saudi Arabia to discuss a settlement. The Saudis had long been the strongest supporters of Assad's efforts to pacify the situation and had argued against Jordanian and Iraqi attempts to oppose Syrian intervention—attempts, driven by fears of a 'Greater Syria', which had even led the Iraqis to deny Syria oil exports. The latest attempt at peacemaking led to an agreement to restore stability with a renewed Muslim–Christian political balance, but at first it seemed likely to collapse. The newly elected, Maronite President, René Mouwad, was soon assassinated and General Aoun resisted attempts to sack him from command of what remained of the Lebanese army. But yet another president, Elias Hrawi, took Mouawad's place, and in late 1990 the Syrian army overwhelmed Aoun. The civil war then effectively ended, but South Lebanon remained in turmoil, with the Israeli-backed Phalangists, the Palestinians, and Hezbollah all active there and the UN force in the area virtually powerless. The Israelis did not withdraw their forces from the South until 2000. But, somehow, 'the Republic of Lebanon . . . had survived. Partition had been narrowly avoided. Assad had . . . managed to disarm the major Lebanese armed militias, previously thought to be an impossible task.'[10] Beirut was restored to stability and a massive rebuilding programme begun, with parliamentary elections being held in 1992. At around the same time, the Gulf War (see Chapter 21, B) brought the US and Syria closer together, and the new Iranian government, following Khomeini's death in 1989, was ready to see Hezbollah release its remaining Western hostages.

B. The Arab–Israeli Dispute and the Palestinian Question

The Failure to Find a Settlement

While Lebanon slipped into anarchy, for much of the 1980s the wider Arab–Israeli conflict rumbled on without any sign of a long-term resolution. There was no follow-up to the Camp David agreement (Chapter 14, B) and this has been blamed in part on the failings of Carter's successor: 'Reagan's disengaged style as president, his lack of curiosity, and his passivity on the Middle East were impediments to creative US peace diplomacy.'[11] Obsessed by the Soviet threat, Reagan's first instinct on becoming President was to hope—as Dulles had in the 1950s—that the Arabs and Israelis might be persuaded to settle their differences under the umbrella of a common opposition to communism. Egypt, Saudi Arabia, and Jordan seemed likely candidates for such cooperation, and, after the fall of the Shah, the Carter administration had already started the practice of joint exercises with friendly governments in the region. One early decision by the new administration was to sell state-of-the-art, early-warning aircraft with the airborne warning and control system (AWACS) to the Saudis so that they could contribute to the defence of the Middle East against the Soviets and their clients. The Saudis seemed a particularly good replacement for Iran as an American ally, and were well placed to act against socialist governments in South Yemen and across the Red Sea in Ethiopia. Furthermore, Carter had previously deployed AWACS aircraft in Saudi Arabia, even if he had not actually sold them to the Saudi government. The AWACS deal became an early indication of how difficult it was to reduce Arab and Israeli hostility when the Israelis, backed by the powerful Zionist lobby in Congress, tried to sabotage the arrangement. 'The Reagan administration, like its predecessor, laboured in vain to escape the dilemma of competing "special relationships". Neither Israel nor Saudi Arabia . . . could be convinced of the advantages . . . of joining together . . . against the Soviet Union.'[12] It took considerable efforts from the White House, supported by the business and trades union lobbies, to drive the sale through, with reassurances to Israel about the uses to which the aircraft could be put. This was not the only early setback in Israeli–American relations under Reagan. Washington was concerned not only by the July 1981 bombing raids on the PLO headquarters in Beirut, but also by an Israeli air attack the previous month on an Iraqi nuclear reactor at Osirak. Indeed, for a time, the US held back on promised financial aid and aircraft sales to Israel.

Such signs of animosity, however, quickly faded as Reagan recognized that Israel was likely to prove his most loyal and powerful ally in the Middle East against the Soviet Union. In November 1981, the two countries signed an agreement to oppose Soviet influence in the region and, across the Reagan presidency as a whole, the US supplied Israel with $23 billion in aid. The assassination of Anwar Sadat in October 1981 probably reinforced this pro-Israeli trend because, while Sadat's successor, Hosni Mubarak, maintained pacific relations with Israel, these were never warm and he took none of the diplomatic risks associated with Sadat. Instead, after securing Israel's final withdrawal from the Sinai in 1982, Mubarak concentrated on restoring Egypt's relations in the Arab world. Most of the Arab states had broken diplomatic relations with Egypt after the 1979 peace treaty with Israel, even though it was the most populous and militarily powerful Arab nation. In 1984, Mubarak took Egypt back into the Islamic Conference and five years later (following a decision by the November 1988 Amman summit) he rejoined the Arab League. This was a reward in part for his reaction to the Israeli invasion of Lebanon, where he had, at first, broken off talks (agreed in the 1979 treaty) on the Palestinian issue, and then, after the Sabra and Shatila massacres, recalled his ambassador to Tel Aviv. Mubarak also gave considerable assistance to his fellow Arab leader, Saddam Hussein, to help prosecute the latter's war against Iran. Indeed, the surprising thing is that Israeli–Egyptian relations did not break down completely in this period. But this could have destroyed Cairo's close relationship with Washington, carefully built up under Sadat, and for their part the Israelis acted with some restraint. Thus in 1989, after arbitration, Israel conceded certain changes to its border with Egypt.

Other Arab states continued to be offended by Israel's actions and refused to contemplate a peace treaty that would recognize its right to exist. Outside Lebanon, the Begin government declared Jerusalem the country's capital in 1980, despite its religious importance to Muslims. Until the 1967 Middle East War, East Jerusalem had been under Jordanian rule but, under the UN partition plan of 1948, Jerusalem was deemed sufficiently important to be excluded from the area to be divided between Israelis and Palestinians. In 1981, Begin embarked on more Israeli expansion after signing a strategic cooperation agreement with the Reagan government in November. Furthermore, Israel annexed the Golan Heights in December 1981. In so doing, Begin was in breach of international law, the May 1974 Israeli–Syrian disengagement agreement, UN Resolution 242, and the Camp David Accords. The Americans responded by temporarily suspending the strategic cooperation agreement. Such was the enormity of the act that some historians have speculated as to whether it was designed to stop the post-Camp David momentum for a comprehensive peace. The annexation 'put great strain on Israel's relations with Egypt . . . Syria reacted angrily'.[13] But it also confirmed Begin's credentials as a right-wing nationalist, pleasing his supporters at home.[14]

Meanwhile, Israel also continued to hold on to the West Bank and Gaza, where 1.5 million Palestinians lived and to which a similar number of refugees living in neighbouring Arab states hoped, one day, to return. Before they were broken off in 1982, the Israeli–Egyptian conversations on the Palestinian Question achieved nothing, not even an arrangement for limited autonomy. Sadat's earlier claims that the 1979 deal would lead over time to a wider settlement increasingly sounded hollow. Israeli policy in Lebanon, its continued refusal to recognize the PLO as the representative of the Palestinian people, and the extension of Jewish settlements in the West Bank all contributed to the lack of progress on the Palestinian question. Rather than settling the issue, Begin's Likud coalition, narrowly re-elected in 1981 (and more dependent thereafter on the support of small, extremist religious groups in Parliament) seemed determined to cripple the PLO and treat the West Bank as part of the 'Land of Israel'—as, according to the Old Testament of the Bible, it was.

The Israeli invasion of Lebanon led to another period of strain in US–Israeli relations and saw Reagan's only major attempt to resolve the Arab–Israeli conflict. The 'Reagan Plan', launched in a speech on 1 September 1982, followed Philip Habib's success in extracting the PLO from Beirut and was quite a bold step for any American president, since it tried to set out the specifics of a Palestinian settlement: there would be a freeze on Israeli settlements and a five-year period of Palestinian autonomy to show that such a situation was no threat to Israel's existence; the long-term future of the West Bank, Gaza, and Jerusalem would be decided by negotiation (but the US favoured a form of Palestinian autonomy in cooperation with Jordan in the West Bank and Gaza). However, although the Israelis and some Arab governments had been consulted in advance, the Reagan Plan satisfied neither side. The Begin government feared it offered the Palestinians too much and would weaken Israeli security just at the point when they had driven Arafat out of Beirut. King Hussein of Jordan showed some interest but later in September 1982 at the Arab League summit in Fez, he backed the consensus that there must be a fully independent Palestinian state with Jerusalem as its capital.

Significantly, 'although the Reagan Plan fell short of what the PLO could accept, Arafat and . . . the mainstream leadership did not reject it outright' but wished to discover whether 'limited self-government could lead in time to full self-determination',[15] an approach that would be revived a decade later, with better results. But over the following years the US strengthened relations with Israel once more, while neglecting the difficult Palestinian problems that the Reagan Plan had tried to address. Even the discovery of an Israeli spy, Jonathan Pollard, at the heart of the Pentagon in 1985, only upset these improved relations momentarily. With the Israeli retreat from most of Lebanon, attention was given again to a settlement based on Jordan and an association with the Palestinians that provided some form of autonomy for the latter, and could replace Israeli authority in the West Bank and Gaza. Since 1984, there had been a coalition government in Tel Aviv with Shimon Peres, the Labour leader, in favour of moves towards peace, whereas the Likud leader, Yitzhak Shamir, who alternated as Prime Minister with Peres, was instinctively averse to it. His famous and oft-repeated statement about Palestinian hostility to Israel's existence claimed that 'the Arabs are the same Arabs and the sea is the same sea'. Moreover, Shamir, like Begin a former terrorist, was committed to the retention of all of the 'Land of Israel'.[16]

The issues in the talks between Hussein and Shimon Peres were the role of the PLO in any moves to autonomy for the Palestinians and the process of reaching an international agreement on a comprehensive Arab–Israeli settlement. By 1986, an agreement between Israel and Jordan had been worked out on how negotiations would proceed, but the Palestinian role in the proposed international conference remained to be determined. Hussein had agreed with Arafat on their involvement but the Israelis remained adamant that they would not negotiate with the PLO. Only three months earlier, Israeli F-16s had attacked the PLO HQ in Tunis, killing 56 Palestinians and 15 Tunisians in response to an extremist Palestinian group, the Palestine Liberation Front, hijacking a cruise liner, the *Achille Lauro*, and killing one American passenger. On the other side, the PLO declared that they would recognize Israel's right to exist through recognition of Resolution 242 if the Americans guaranteed their participation at the international conference and recognize the Palestinians' right to self-determination. The first part was acceptable to Washington, but not the second; and Hussein failed to persuade Arafat of the importance of achieving a diplomatic breakthrough on that basis. The result of all these efforts was nothing but a split between Hussein and the PLO.

The years 1987 and 1988 were, however, crucial in the Israeli–Palestinian conflict. For decades, neither violence nor diplomacy had succeeded in making significant progress towards a settlement based on the rights of each side to live together in peace. Almost inevitably, the longer the stalemate persisted the more scope there would be for extremism, if it did not already predominate. Moreover, conditions for Palestinian refugees were steadily worsening and any solution to the problem of the occupied territories in the West Bank and Gaza would have to confront ever-more Israeli settlements—even though the construction of new settlements had slowed after 1984 the number of settlers was increasing. Under Begin, between 1977 and 1983 about 25,000 Jewish settlers moved into the area, a figure that excludes the thousands more who settled in East Jerusalem. Previously, there had only been 10,000 Jews in the West Bank; by 1992 there were about 100,000.

The Start of the Intifada

After two decades of international failure to make any progress on the Palestinian Question, it was the Arab population of the West Bank and Gaza who finally took matters into their own hands—though without at first producing new movement on the issue. On 9 December 1987, a traffic accident led to an outbreak of violence in Gaza. Previously, despite the presence of Israeli troops, the expansion of Jewish settlements, lack of economic development, and severe limits on their political rights, there had been only sporadic violence from the Palestinian people under Israeli rule. Despite the poverty of the densely populated Gaza strip, the

Israelis had always claimed that their rule was benign and that, despite PLO propaganda, most Palestinians were happy under Israeli rule. But, to the surprise of everyone, even the PLO, 9 December proved the beginning of a lengthy and widespread Intifada, or uprising, against Israeli rule. Demonstrations and marches were accompanied by stone-throwing at troops, who often overreacted, firing on the crowds and killing protestors. None of this helped Israel's international standing. As more and more Palestinians joined in the movement, Israeli rule was increasingly seen, even by US opinion, as oppressive. 'Palestinians, through the Intifada, [rejected] anything that represented Israeli rule . . . they were no longer willing to pay taxes without representation, to fund the military occupation of land which they perceived as their own.'[17] The PLO could hardly be said to have planned the uprising, and the benefits it may have gained came by chance rather than design. If world attention was now focused on Israel and the occupied territories, the PLO was losing its grip on the resistance to Israel. In November 1988, Arafat declared Palestine's independence and in 1989 established a government-in-exile to which many countries gave diplomatic recognition. Crucially, he restricted the boundaries of a Palestinian state to the West Bank and Gaza, and he acknowledged Israel's right to exist. It has been argued that the 'success of the Intifada gave Arafat and his followers the confidence they needed to moderate their political programme and so put Israel on the diplomatic defensive'.[18] At all events, the long-held Israeli claim to security and the threat of the Arab drive to the sea no longer formed a barrier to a settlement. The Israeli–Palestinian dispute had, with hindsight, reached a watershed.

It was the Intifada which finally induced the Reagan administration to renew its interest in the Palestinian–Israeli dispute. In March 1988, George Shultz, the US Secretary of State, was set to revive the peace process with the idea of Israeli talks with a Jordanian–PLO delegation on a transitional arrangement, followed by a long-term settlement, of the Palestinian issue. This again fell foul of Israeli opposition however, with Yitzhak Shamir, now Prime Minister for the whole term of the new Labour–Likud coalition government, unwilling to deal with the PLO or concede Palestinian autonomy. It was also difficult for the US to run risks for the sake of a settlement during a presidential election year. But, as the Intifada continued, the PLO was increasingly acknowledged as the only genuine representative of the Palestinian people and various indirect, secret links were established between the organization and Washington. Then, just before the Reagan administration ended, there was a significant advance. The President himself had always said he would only talk directly to the PLO if it renounced violence, and there had been no official talks between Arafat and the US since 1975, when Henry Kissinger had insisted that the PLO should recognize Israel. But, in addressing the UN on 13 December 1988, Arafat effectively renounced terrorism, at which point Shultz conceded that direct talks were possible once more. They began, in Tunis, on 16 December and continued into the Bush administration in 1989. In retrospect, this heralded a period in which US–Israeli relations would be much less warm. The general lack of progress on talks on a settlement (see Chapter 22, C) could now be ascribed to Israeli desires for settlement rather than their need for security. On the other hand, the number of hard-line opponents of Israel was exceeding the capacity of the PLO to control them.

If the talks failed, now that violence had been renounced and Israel's right to exist accepted, the Palestinian advocates of an agreement would have no more cards to play. With the benefit of hindsight, one can argue that from this moment the longer a settlement was delayed the more difficult it would be to reach agreement. As the arguments in 1986 over who should represent whom were raging at the highest levels, at the grass roots, ominous developments were taking place, some under the cover of the Intifada. Islamic Jihad emerged in 1986 and its influence was evident in the encouragement of participation in the Intifada the following year. One significant aspect of the Intifada was the creation of the Unified National Leadership of the Uprising (UNLU), which was composed of the most radical factions within the PLO and those outside its umbrella. The leaders of UNLU were no longer members of the bourgeoisie, who had previously characterized Palestinian political life, but were drawn from groups who had no connection with traditional Palestinian elites. Younger and more determined, many had a firm commitment to radical social change but remained within the PLO while increasingly denouncing the leadership in Tunis. There was cooperation between UNLU and Islamic Jihad, but the crucial difference was that the latter totally rejected the idea of a two-state solution and demanded the complete liberation of Palestine.

However, in January 1988 another Muslim extremist group emerged advocating, like Islamic Jihad, a more direct and confrontational challenge to Israel.

BOX 17.1

Biography: Yasser Arafat (1929–2004)

Arafat's origins are surrounded by mystery. Palestinian sources variously say that he was born in Jerusalem or the Gaza Strip, but it has also been claimed that he was born in Cairo. His father was evidently a merchant, who travelled between Palestine and Egypt, and Yasser was partly raised in Jerusalem. In 1948, with Israel established, he went to study civil engineering at the University of Cairo, but he also became a leading figure among Palestinian students in Egypt and in 1956, the year of the Suez Crisis, founded the radical Al Fatah movement. From 1965, Fatah launched small-scale attacks on Israeli territory, aiming to return Palestine to Arab control. The 1967 'Six Day War' made Arafat's violent resistance more popular among Arab leaders and in 1969 he became Chairman of the Palestine Liberation Organization (PLO), originally founded under more moderate leadership a few years before. Initially based in Amman, Jordan, he was forced to leave in 1970 after armed clashes with the royalist government, setting up new headquarters in Beirut, Lebanon. He was able to address the United Nations in 1974 but Israel condemned him as a terrorist and drove him from Beirut by force in 1982, after which he moved to Tunis.

In 1988, Arafat surprised the world by renouncing terrorism and offering to recognize Israel's right to exist, but he also declared an independent Palestinian state. Clandestine contacts with the Israeli government, backed by the popular uprising (Intifada) among Palestinian Arabs, helped bring about the 1993 Oslo Accords on the establishment of a Palestinian authority in the Gaza Strip and limited areas of the West Bank. For this achievement, Arafat shared the 1994 Nobel Peace Prize with two Israelis, Yitzhak Rabin and Shimon Peres. In January 1996, Arafat was overwhelmingly elected President of the Palestinian National Authority but, over the following years, his followers were increasingly discontented because of the failure to achieve real independence, while the Israelis resented the fact that he could not prevent Palestinian attacks on them. In 2001, with many Palestinians growing sympathetic to the radical Hamas movement, Israelis elected one of Arafat's bitterest enemies, Ariel Sharon, as prime minister. He broke off relations with the Palestinian Authority and left Arafat isolated, in the last years of his life, in a compound in Ramallah.

The Islamic Resistance Movement (Hamas) developed from the Muslim Brotherhood, but it was more militant, had no connection with the merchants and notables in the Brotherhood, and merged religious faith and Palestinian nationalism into a potent and violent political cocktail. And it helped extend the Intifada into a full-blown rebellion while rejecting any peace conferences, because it claimed the only solution lay in Jihad or holy war. James Baker, who had been Reagan's Chief of Staff during the ill-fated Lebanon intervention, felt 'there was no real evidence to believe the climate was ripe for generating any momentum' and 'frankly saw the Arab–Israeli dispute as a pitfall to be avoided rather than an opportunity to be exploited'.[19]

C. The Iran–Iraq War of 1980–8

Origins of the Conflict

The outbreak of war between the oil-rich states of Iran and Iraq in September 1980 was closely linked to the events surrounding the fall of the Shah the year before (see Chapter 15, B). In the 1970s, following the departure of British forces from the Persian Gulf, the Shah had been built up by the US as a regional strongman. Pro-Western and non-Arab, and leading a large, oil-rich country, he seemed the ideal candidate for the role, and his actions included helping the Sultan of Oman put down a rebellion (underway between 1965 and 1977) in Dhofar province. But, during this time the Shah also took the chance to press Iranian nationalist demands in the Gulf, seizing certain islands in the Straits of Hormuz (at the southern end of the Gulf) in 1971. In particular, he pursued a hard line against Iraq, with which there was a border dispute focused on the Shatt al-Arab waterway. In 1974–5, he encouraged a revolt by Iraq's oppressed Kurdish minority, then forced Baghdad to agree, during talks in Algiers, to a new definition of their border, down the middle of the Shatt al-Arab. There was little sympathy in the West for Iraq in all this because, since the Ba'ath coup in July 1968 and the emergence of Saddam Hussein, Iraq had opposed Resolution 242 and signed an agreement with the Soviets on oilfield development the same year. Partly in reaction to pressure from the Shah, Baghdad, having already broken off diplomatic relations with Tehran in 1971, then nationalized the Iraq Petroleum Company and signed a friendship treaty with the Soviets the following year. It used its enormous oil wealth to purchase military equipment from the Eastern bloc and also bought high-technology equipment from France and began to develop a nuclear capability—which the Israelis blunted in 1981 with their bombing raid on the Iraqi facility.

The fall of the Shah and the establishment of a theocratic regime in Iran after February 1979 revolutionized the situation in the Gulf. By the end of the year, Washington and Tehran were locked in bitter argument over the seizure of the US embassy staff as hostages and on 30 October the Iraqi leader, Saddam Hussein, grasped the opportunity to challenge the 1975 Algiers agreement. Saddam, a ruthless figure, even in the merciless world of Iraqi politics, had only recently made himself chairman of the country's Revolutionary Command Council, and then, in 1979, President. Like most other Arab leaders—the only exceptions being Syria and Libya—he was deeply concerned about Ayatollah Khomeini's Islamic Revolution, with its propaganda in favour of a united Islamic world under Iranian leadership, which threatened to stir up religious fervour among Iraq's Shi'ites—a majority of the population—and challenge the position of the secular, radical, and Sunni-dominated regime. Because of the threat he posed, Khomeini had been expelled from Iraq in 1978, having lived in exile there since 1965, and there was no love lost between him and the Iraqi leadership. In April 1980, he condemned Saddam as an 'enemy of Islam' and relations between the two continued to deteriorate. 'Baghdad was to argue later that by encouraging Islamic and Kurdish dissidents to overthrow the Ba'athist regime, Tehran's revolutionary leaders had effectively revoked the 1975 treaty which barred each country from provoking subversion in the other.'[20] But territorial wrangles also continued. On 4 September, following months of border tension, Iranian artillery shelled Iraqi positions and, on the 17th Saddam denounced the 1975 border treaty. With strong ideological fears of the neighbouring regime and a desire for revenge for the Shah's earlier humiliation of Iraq, Saddam seized the chance, five days later, to invade Iran. The Iraqis thereafter argued that the war had been started by Iran on the 4th but the Iranians always dated it from the Iraqi invasion on the 22nd.

Deadlocked War and the World Response, 1980–6

In launching his invasion, Saddam clearly hoped that the removal of US support from Iran (including the supply of American military equipment, on which the Iranian armed forces relied) and the upheaval caused by the Islamic Revolution would make the war a short, victorious one. His own forces were well prepared and Iraq was now the world's second largest oil exporter. At first, all this seemed a reasonable analysis, and within two days, on 24 September, his forces had seized the city of Khorramshahr. Soon the Iraqis occupied much of south-western Iran, an Arab-populated region and a centre of oil production, though they were never able to seize control of their main target, and the central city for the Iranian oil industry, Abadan. The UN called for a ceasefire but neither side wished to talk: Iran would not negotiate from a position of weakness and in any case Khomeini treated the conflict as a holy war; Saddam wanted to press home his advantage and faced little real pressure from the international community to make peace. As he expected, most Arab states verbally backed him for reasons of 'racial and religious solidarity', even if 'explicit support for Iraq [was] not . . . forthcoming, mainly because Saddam treated it as "his" war and had done nothing to consult his fellow Arabs before launching it'.[21] At the time the war broke out, the US had relations with neither Tehran nor Baghdad, but was happy at first to see the Iranians on the defensive. The Soviets were not entirely happy with Saddam, who had tried to destroy the Iraqi Communist Party, and they did not want to appear too anti-Iranian for fear of stirring up discontent among their own Muslims in Central Asia. Despite US fears of Kremlin involvement, the Soviets actually cut off arms to both sides in the war, joined the calls for a ceasefire and maintained diplomatic contacts with both Baghdad and Tehran. But, preoccupied with Afghanistan and committed to the 1972 Friendship Treaty, they too were not initially unhappy with the situation. Iraq was now one of their few allies in the Middle East, whereas one of the features of the Iranian revolution was its condemnation of Marxism.

A change in American policy might have been expected in early 1981 when the hostage crisis ended and Reagan came into office. However, lingering resentment over Iran's recent behaviour and Khomeini's continuing support for radical Islamic groups beyond Iran continued to drive Washington and Tehran apart, despite their shared anti-communism. Given its Cold War preoccupations, the Reagan administration found the situation very confusing because, whatever the ill-feeling towards Iran, Iraq was both pro-Soviet and an opponent of the Camp David peace process. Cold War rhetoric could not explain, still less resolve, the Iran–Iraq conflict. The US supported Khomeini's opponents yet had no desire to see the Soviets exploit an Iraqi triumph, especially following Moscow's intervention in nearby Afghanistan. The result was that America, while showing a preference for Iraq (largely because of a fear of Islamic radicalism spreading throughout the Middle East), wanted neither side to win, hoped to keep the conflict localized and tried to restrict arms sales to both sides. Therefore, for both superpowers in 1980–2, the Iran–Iraq War, however intensely it raged, became something of a sideshow in the new Cold War. Neither had much to gain from it and so 'for seven years America and the Soviet Union did no more than dabble, seeking rather . . . to contain the war than to bring it to an end, much less exploit global advantage'.[22]

During 1981, the war became deadlocked in south-western Iran, as the Iraqi offensive ground to a halt. Iran had not proved the weakened victim that Saddam originally hoped. Larger than Iraq in size and population, Iran retained sufficient industrial output to produce an adequate supply of arms, and its Revolutionary Guards were better motivated than the Iraqi army, helping to offset the latter's advantages in equipment. By 1982, the war seemed to move in Iran's favour. Khorramshahr was retaken in April and, three months later, the Revolutionary Guards drove the Iraqis back across the border. In June, Saddam's offer of a ceasefire was ignored: it simply underlined how anxious he had become. Instead, Khomeini demanded Saddam's replacement and the payment of reparations by the Iraqis. The following four years saw only a slow advance by the Iranians, however, as they tried to threaten the strategic city port of Basra and periodically bombarded Baghdad itself. It seemed that both sides would exhaust each other, as the struggle became the longest conventional conflict of the twentieth century, with long periods of trench warfare reminiscent of the First World War and substantial losses on both sides, but especially among the Revolutionary Guards. Saddam was consistently ready to end the war but, given his enemy's religious inspiration, decided he could only bring about a settlement by intensifying the conflict. In particular, aware that he could never win a conventional war on land, he came to rely on the superiority of his air force and on the use of unconventional weapons such as poison gas. He also hoped for growing international pressure on Tehran to make peace.

Iran's expulsion of the Iraqi invaders in 1982 provoked growing concern in Western countries, who continued in public to support UN peace efforts and an arms embargo but increasingly, and secretly, tried to arm Iraq. Arab states, such as Saudi Arabia and Kuwait, neither of them great friends of Iraq in the past, but both autocratic monarchies who felt threatened by the forces behind the Iranian Revolution, also gave aid to Iraq. Meanwhile, the policies of the Reagan administration were still very confused. Washington's essential aims remained that of avoiding outright victory for either side, whilst also preventing both the growth of Soviet influence in the region and the advance of Iranian fundamentalism. There were serious differences, however, over how to achieve these. The State and Defense departments preferred to build up Iraqi power to contain Iran; in 1983–4 they launched 'Operation Staunch', which effectively directed arms to Iraq while denying them to Iran; and in November 1984 supported the re-establishment of diplomatic relations with Baghdad, for the first time since 1967. But the CIA and key National Security Council staff felt that Iran's anti-communism might be exploited, and that a more moderate leadership could be encouraged in Tehran if American policy were more friendly. Such a policy might also help secure the release of Western hostages held by Shi'ite groups in Lebanon. In contrast, a pro-Iraq policy might, it was feared, drive the Iranians towards Moscow: after all, Tehran had taken economic aid from the Eastern bloc during the 1979–80 hostage crisis. It was thinking such as this which led to a highly secret attempt to ship arms to Iran and a visit by Reagan's then National Security Adviser, Robert McFarlane, to Tehran in May 1986. The policy was not, it seems, foredoomed to failure: Iranian leaders had one 'pressing motive' to improve relations and that was 'to obtain US arms . . . The Iraqi bombing of Iranian cities and economic installations was becoming increasingly effective, bringing tremendous psychological pressures to bear.'[23] But the revelation of the McFarlane visit by a Lebanese newspaper later in the year began the 'Contragate' scandal (discussed more fully in Chapter 18, B). Apart from the controversy this stirred up in America, the revelation also caused great confusion among US allies in the Middle East, not least Saudi Arabia and Kuwait, who had believed Washington was pursuing a pro-Iraqi policy.

The 'Tanker War' and a Settlement, 1986–8

In 1986, the Iranians seized control of the strategic Fao peninsula and over the following two years the war was at its worst, with the Iranians besieging Basra and the Iraqis making greater use of poison gas attacks.

In 1987–8, in the so-called 'war of the cities', bombs and missile attacks were directed by both sides on urban centres. At the same time, there were increasing attacks by the two sides on shipping in the Persian Gulf. These attacks became known as the 'tanker war' and, as Saddam seems to have intended, they both pushed up the price of oil (helping Iraq finance its war effort) and led to increased international efforts to resolve the conflict (which he now had little hope of winning). Saddam had first attacked the Iranian oil terminal at Kharg Island in August 1982 and by 1986 he was able to target all Iran's ports on the Gulf. This was a very worrying development for Tehran, which had to export all its oil—vital for foreign earnings—via tankers down the Gulf: Iraq, in contrast, could export oil westwards through pipelines. In response, rather than submit, Iran decided to intimidate Iraq's Gulf allies, especially Kuwait, by laying mines, threatening to close the 24-mile wide Straits of Hormuz, attacking ships of all countries which were bound for Kuwait, and, in October 1986, launching a missile strike on the major Kuwaiti oil terminal. They also broke off diplomatic relations with Kuwait and Saudi Arabia, who lacked the naval power to defend themselves.

Faced by such pressure the Kuwaiti government approached both the Soviet and US governments to try to secure protection. By now, Mikhail Gorbachev was in power in Moscow and simultaneously the 'Contragate' revelations made the Kuwaitis and Saudis suspicious of US intentions. Even so, Washington was taken aback by Gorbachev's offer in February 1987 to lease some Soviet-flagged tankers to Kuwait. Suspicious of his motives and anxious to reconfirm its trustworthiness, the US itself now agreed to reflag and escort Kuwaiti tankers in the Gulf. By the end of the year, a mixed armada of US, Soviet, and West European minesweepers was active in the area. Ironically it was an Iraqi attack on an American warship, the USS *Stark*, in May 1987, killing thirty-seven servicemen, which finally convinced the US people of the need to protect Gulf shipping. It has been said that, by 'agreeing that the Kuwaiti tanker fleet could sail under the American flag, the United States effectively joined, on the Iraqi side, the . . . tanker war in the Gulf'.[24] So anti-Iranian did Western policy now become that the US and West Europeans were willing to condone Iraqi attacks on any ships bound for Iran and even to overlook Saddam's use of poison gas. By early 1988, nearly 50 US vessels and 20 from Western Europe were on patrol. Yet attacks on neutral ships and the laying of mines by Iran actually increased, as did the dangers of a US–Iranian conflict. In April 1988, a clash between their forces led the Americans to sink half the Iranians' navy (admittedly small: it had only twelve ships in total). Then, three months later, on 3 July, a US warship, the USS *Vincennes* shot down an Iranian airliner, mistaking it for a military target. All 290 passengers and crew died. The incident shook Washington, which offered to pay compensation. It may also have influenced Tehran to end the war.

In the mid-1980s, the Western powers had tried to blame Iran entirely for lengthening the war and framed UN resolutions in a way which Iraq found easier to accept. But in July 1987, with relations between the superpowers beginning to improve, the US and USSR had both supported Resolution 598, calling for an immediate ceasefire and a withdrawal to the 1980 border, which could be seen as a neutral basis for a settlement. At first, the Iranians refused to respond to the proposal, either positively or negatively. But the hopelessness of securing a decisive victory was by now quite obvious. In early 1988, there was a new round of Iranian offensives but Saddam again responded, this time with gas and missile attacks, which included rocket attacks on Tehran itself. One gas attack was directed at the Kurdish village of Halabja, on Iraqi territory but a centre of resistance to Saddam's rule; it killed about 5,000 civilians, embarrassed Saddam's supporters, and led some to press peace on him more seriously. Such evidence of the Iraqi President's inhumanity reinforced the Western view that the best way for the war to end was as a stalemate. Meanwhile, the Halabja incident may have helped to demoralize the Iranians, who 'feared the use of chemicals against their cities. It became obvious to them that the cries of human rights organizations . . . mattered little in the face of American determination to help Saddam.'[25] The concern of Khomeini's advisers intensified still further when, in May 1988, a new Iraqi offensive threatened to cross Iran's borders once more. Khomeini himself declared that peace was 'worse than taking poison' but on 20 July 1988 he accepted Resolution 598. Neither side had gained any territory as a result of almost eight years of war. Both were economically shattered and faced the expensive challenge of reconstruction—the outcome that the US had hoped for when the war began.

It was partly in order to obtain the resources needed for such reconstruction that Saddam, in August 1990, invaded Kuwait, provoking another major conflict (see

BOX 17.2

The Revival of the United Nations?

The late 1980s and early 1990s saw a revival of fortunes for the UN, a new respect for the organization as a peace-making body, and a return to the original hopes, of 1945–6, that the Security Council might prove a forum for the great powers to work together. Certainly, Mikhail Gorbachev treated it more seriously than previous Soviet leaders. The successes of the UN included:

- the April 1988 Geneva Agreement between Afghanistan and Pakistan, guaranteed by the US and USSR, which paved the way for a Soviet withdrawal from Afghanistan—the agreement followed a series of talks since 1982, chaired by the UN's Diego Cordovez;
- the end of the Iran–Iraq War in July 1988 on the basis of Resolution 598 of twelve months earlier—the Resolution included a ceasefire, a return to the pre-war status quo, and an international commission to decide who was responsible for the war;
- the signature of agreements at the UN on 22 December 1988 on problems in southern Africa, following a series of talks since the previous January—the settlement provided for the independence of Namibia (previously the South African-administered mandate of South-West Africa) and for the withdrawal of Cuban troops from neighbouring Angola, where they had been since 1975;
- the liberation of Kuwait by a US-led force in early 1991, which might have gone less smoothly but for the UN's immediate condemnation of the original Iraqi invasion (Resolution 660 of 2 August 1990) and the agreement of the Security Council on subsequent steps (though China abstained on Resolution 678, authorizing members 'to use all necessary means' to remove Iraq);
- the restoration of Cambodian independence, after more than a decade of Vietnamese occupation, in the Paris agreements of 23 October 1991—these followed years of UN mediation attempts and put various responsibilities on the organization, including supervising the ceasefire, organizing elections, and repatriating refugees.

Such successes led to high hopes of a major UN role in world politics in the 1990s. But there were problems:

- On closer inspection, some of the settlements were seriously flawed. Resolution 598 produced no long-term settlement and Afghanistan continued to suffer internal turmoil.
- Many long-running international problems (Cyprus, Palestine, the division of Korea) continued without sign of imminent resolution.
- A number of conflicts in the 1990s (Somalia, Bosnia, Rwanda) harmed the UN's reputation and confirmed that it was at the mercy of the wishes of its members; a useful vehicle for talks when governments wanted this but with limited influence if they were unprepared to keep the peace.
- The UN Secretary General, Xavier Perez de Cuellar, admitted in his memoirs* that the successes of 1988–91 were largely dependent on the newfound cooperation of the US and USSR: 'It would have been self-defeating hubris to assume that the United Nations . . . could independently bring peace in any one of these cases.'

* *Pilgrimage for Peace* (Macmillan, London, 1997), 15–16.

Chapter 21, B). He initially tried to portray himself as the victor of the Iran–Iraq war, on the grounds that Iran had suffered far more casualties, but such claims were undermined by his decision, on 15 August 1990, to reaffirm the 1975 Algiers agreement on the Shatt al-Arab border: he was forced to do this, in order to concentrate on the Kuwait war. As to Iran–Iraq relations, they remained poor thereafter. There was no full exchange of prisoners and both countries continued to give assistance to the other's political opponents. The result was rather better for the US and the West, who had long favoured a stalemate and were happy to see both Iran and Iraq weakened and divided against each other. The only international actor to gain much was the UN, which could claim to have provided the diplomatic machinery for a settlement between two bitter enemies (see Box 17.2).

D. Libya and 'International Terrorism'

Despite the Vietnam syndrome, the Reagan administration was clearly not beyond limited military operations in the Middle East where these seemed to be in the US interest. The role of the US marines in the Lebanon Multinational Force in 1982–4 and the naval commitment in the Gulf in 1987–8 were obvious examples. But a much sharper, and no less dramatic intervention, took place in April 1986, when US aircraft bombed Libya. The reasons for this action lay in a growing exasperation with the behaviour of Libya's ruler, Colonel Muammar Gaddafi, especially his backing for what Washington condemned as 'international terrorism'.

Gaddafi, in power since a coup in 1969, was long known to provide support for organizations like the PLO and the Provisional IRA (Irish Republican Army). A dedicated opponent of post-1973 Middle East peace attempts, he was said to have plotted to assassinate Henry Kissinger and in 1974 secured a major arms deal with Moscow. In the early 1980s, he was credited with helping various rebel groups around Africa. He also aided opponents of the pro-French government in neighbouring Chad (France being the former colonial power) and, for a time, installed a friendly regime there. The Reagan administration despised Gaddafi from the start, as a paymaster of terrorists and because he was seen as a Soviet stooge. In May 1981, the Washington 'People's Bureau' was closed down and the US set out to isolate Libya diplomatically. Attention soon focused on the Gulf of Sidra, which Libya claimed to be entirely its own territorial waters, a claim the US denied. On 20 August 1981, two Libyan aircraft were shot down after firing on US airplanes over the Gulf. Seven months later, America introduced economic sanctions against Libya, but was unable to persuade NATO allies to follow suit. Rather than being cowed by this, Gaddafi, seen as a hero by Arab radicals, increased his support for anti-Western terrorist groups. Terrorist attacks were nothing new and Libya was not the only government accused of supporting them. Syria and Iran were both blamed for bombings in Lebanon. Iran was also responsible for a December 1983 attack on the American embassy in Kuwait and, exactly a year later, for the hijacking of a Kuwaiti airliner which led to two Americans being killed. Indeed, the CIA recognized Iran as the worst culprit in the scale of its backing for such actions. But it was also the hardest to attack in terms of its geographical position. It seemed likely to react strongly to any US countermeasures, there were persistent fears of driving it towards the Soviets, and, by the mid-1980s, the Reagan administration had hopes of moderating Iranian policy through clandestine contacts. Libya, in contrast, was geographically well placed for an attack and—given the way it alienated its neighbours—relatively easy to isolate. And Gaddafi continued to draw attention to himself: in mid-March 1984 there was a Libyan bombing raid on the Sudanese capital, Khartoum, and a month later a British policewoman was shot dead outside the Libyan 'People's Bureau' in London.

In 1985, international terrorism reached a new intensity, much of it linked to the Palestinian cause but with attacks sponsored by Iran, Syria, and Libya. The 'Islamic Jihad' group launched bomb attacks in Madrid and Riyadh in the spring; Frankfurt airport was bombed in June; October saw the seizure of the *Achille Lauro* cruise ship; in November sixty people died when an Egyptian aircraft was hijacked and on 27 December simultaneous attacks at Rome and Vienna airports killed twenty people. In response, Reagan was determined to act. There was some concern that retribution against Libya might lead Gaddafi to seize American hostages: about 1,000 US citizens were working for oil companies there. But contingency plans for a strike on Libya were laid. In January 1986, Reagan publicly accused Libya of aggression against the US and announced new economic sanctions, including severe travel restrictions and a freeze on Libyan assets. But, once again, America's NATO allies—who took 90 per cent of Libya's oil—refused to join in these steps, expressing doubts about their effectiveness. In January, the US navy also renewed its manoeuvres in the Gulf of Sidra, another provocative move, which won little NATO support. The Americans judged the Gulf to be an ideal place to challenge Gaddafi because it was easy for them to operate there and, though it was not tested, they believed they had a strong case in international law. 'No real effort was made, however, to disguise the fact that the operation was a warning signal about Libyan-inspired terrorism, rather than about maritime navigation rights.'[26] A few months later Gaddafi rose to the bait. On 24 March, the Libyans fired on US aircraft, and the Americans retaliated by sinking two patrol boats.

US–Libyan tension finally reached a crisis in April 1986. On 5 April, a bomb attack by Palestinians in West Berlin killed two American servicemen and injured others. Intercepted messages from the 'People's Bureau' in East Berlin linked the attack to Libya and a consensus was reached in Washington in favour of a retaliatory strike. On 14 April, US aircraft bombed Gaddafi's home and other targets, including barracks and airfields, in the Tripoli and Benghazi regions. The Secretary of State, George Shultz, had already publicly justified the action by insisting, 'There is substantial legal authority for the view that a state which supports terrorist . . . attacks against another state . . . is responsible for such attacks. Such conduct can amount to . . . armed aggression . . . under international law' and he later warned Gaddafi: 'You've had it, pal.'[27] But others doubted that America was justified in invoking the right of self-defence under Article 51. Furthermore, Gaddafi—despite the apparent hope of killing him in the attack—remained securely in power. In 1989, in another clash with the US in the Gulf of Sidra two Libyan aircraft were shot down; and Libyans were later implicated in the December 1989 bombing of a Pan-Am airliner over Scotland. The American action was not only criticized by the Eastern bloc and the non-aligned world, but also by moderate Arab countries like Egypt and Saudi Arabia, and by NATO governments. In contrast to the British, both Italy and Greece refused to allow their airbases to be used for the raids; France and Spain had refused to allow the American aircraft to overfly their territory. The attack seemed an act of frustration against a relatively easy target, and a reflection of America's inability to shape Middle East politics constructively. Then again, it boosted Reagan's popularity at home and evidently led to a lessening of terrorist sponsorship by a shaken Gaddafi.

Visit the online resources that accompany this book to test your understanding and take your learning further: www.oup.com/he/young-kent3e

NOTES

1. Robert Fisk, *Pity the Nation: Lebanon at War* (Deutsch, London, 1990), 193.
2. Avi Shlaim, *Iron Wall: Israel and the Arab World* (Allen Lane, London, 2000), 396–7.
3. Mark Tessler, *A History of the Israeli–Palestinian Conflict* (Indiana University Press, Bloomington, 1994), 571.
4. Avi Shlaim, *Iron Wall: Israel and the Arab World* (Allen Lane, London, 2000), 396.
5. Alexander Haig, *Caveat: Realism, Reagan and Foreign Policy* (Macmillan, New York, 1984), 342 and see 351.
6. Robert Fisk, *Pity the Nation: Lebanon at War* (Deutsch, London, 1990), 383.
7. Sasson Sofer, *Begin: An Anatomy of Leadership* (Blackwell, Oxford, 1988), 214.
8. Hala Jaber, *Hezbollah: Born with a Vengeance* (Columbia University Press, New York, 1997), 20–1.
9. Caspar Weinberger, *Fighting for Peace: Seven Critical Years at the Pentagon* (Joseph, London, 1990), 111.
10. Edgar O'Ballance, *Civil War in Lebanon, 1975–92* (Macmillan, London, 1998), 216–17.
11. William Quandt, *Peace Process; American Diplomacy and the Arab–Israeli Conflict* (Brookings Institution, Washington, DC, 1993), 378.
12. Seth Tillman, *The US in the Middle East* (Indiana University Press, Bloomington, 1982), 122.
13. Avi Shlaim, *Iron Wall: Israel and the Arab World* (Allen Lane, London, 2000), 394, citing Ilan Peleg, *Begin's Foreign Policy 1977–1983: Israel's Move to the Right* (Greenwood Press, New York, 1987), 190–5.
14. Avi Shlaim, *Iron Wall: Israel and the Arab World* (Allen Lane, London, 2000), 394.
15. Alan Hart, *Arafat* (Sidgwick & Jackson, London, 1984), 460.
16. Avi Shlaim, *Iron Wall: Israel and the Arab World* (Allen Lane, London, 2000), 426.
17. Beverley Milton-Edwards, *Contemporary Politics in the Middle East* (Blackwell, Polity Press, Cambridge, 2000), 102–3.
18. Avi Shlaim, *Iron Wall: Israel and the Arab World* (Allen Lane, London, 2000), 466.
19. James A. Baker, *The Politics of Diplomacy* (G. P. Putnam's Sons, New York, 1995), 115.
20. John Bulloch and Harvey Morris, *The Gulf War: Its Origins, History and Consequences* (Methuen, London, 1989), 38.

21. G. H. Hansen, 'The Attitudes of the Arab Governments', in M. S. El-Azhary (ed.), *The Iran–Iraq War: An Historical, Economic and Political Analysis* (Croom Helm, London, 1984), 81–2.

22. John Bulloch and Harvey Morris, *The Gulf War: Its Origins, History and Consequences* (Methuen, London, 1989), xvii.

23. Shireen Hunter, *Iran and the World: Continuity in a Revolutionary Decade* (Indiana University Press, Bloomington, 1990), 66.

24. Andrew and Patrick Cockburn, *Out of the Ashes: The Resurrection of Saddam Hussein* (HarperCollins, London, 1999), 81.

25. Said Aburish, *Saddam Hussein, the Politics of Revenge* (Bloomsbury, London, 2000), 250.

26. Coral Bell, *The Reagan Paradox* (Elgar, Aldershot, 1989), 86.

27. George Shultz, *Turmoil and Triumph* (Macmillan, New York, 1993), 678 and 688.

18

Instability in Latin America

Chapter contents

A. The Reagan Doctrine and El Salvador

Reagan's Policy towards Latin America

In the early 1970s, when the Nixon administration was obsessed by Vietnam and détente, Latin America had not figured prominently in Washington's world view. Apart from Chile, where the left-wing regime of Salvador Allende was toppled in 1973, the region seemed relatively stable, despite widespread poverty, illiteracy, and repressive government. Under the Nixon Doctrine, the US had relied on local governments to maintain authority and, although Cuba still existed as a Soviet ally in the western hemisphere, communism was virtually non-existent, and Castro was unable to promote revolution successfully. America's domination of the Latin American economies was in decline but still considerable; in the mid-1950s it absorbed about half their exports, twenty years later it took around a third. In the 1970s, the Latin American countries joined with other developing economies, in the G-77 group, to press for a 'new International Economic Order' that would redistribute wealth globally, but the US Trade Act of January 1975 put up greater barriers to Latin American exports. Economic changes in mid-decade had a profound impact on local societies. The oil crisis of 1973–4, followed as it was by trade deficits, depression, and high inflation, helped promote revolutionary ideas among the landless peasants and urban poor of many Latin American countries. In particular, the poverty-stricken 'banana republics' of Central America became prone to unrest, and this situation persisted through the next world economic depression in 1979–82.

Under Jimmy Carter, with his interest in promoting human rights, a more active and enlightened US policy towards Latin America might have been expected but in this region, as elsewhere, Carter's aims were inconsistent, as the moral cause of human rights clashed with local realities and other American interests. He did manage to cut military aid to Latin America by about a quarter in 1976–9 and one study found that, in 'several Latin American countries, the 1970s ended with a considerable increase in the level of respect for human rights related to the physical integrity of the person', with a reduction in torture and detention without trial.[1] But by the end of this period the Cold War with Moscow was reviving, leftist guerrillas were active in most Central American states, and 'the military governments affected by the arms restrictions lashed out at what they viewed as a new form of US intervention in their internal affairs'.[2] Rather than have Carter cut their military aid completely, several states—Argentina, Brazil, El Salvador, Guatemala, and Uruguay—declared that they no longer wanted US arms, and began to make purchases elsewhere. The military dictatorships of Argentina and Brazil, whose violent oppression caused Carter special concern, simply decided to pursue their own line regardless, jointly backing a military coup in Bolivia in 1980, developing links to right-wing regimes in other continents (such as South Africa), and encouraging other Latin American states to break free of US tutelage.

Any hopes that Carter could induce such regimes to democratize gradually, therefore proved naive. And any hope that America could use its wealth to launch a new effort at economic development in Latin America, given the failure of Kennedy's 'Alliance for Progress', was an illusion: American public opinion was shifting to the Right, as most people looked for state spending to be reduced. Carter's policy finally proved ineffective in July 1979, when he did little to prevent a leftist movement, the Sandinistas, toppling the long-standing Somoza dictatorship in Nicaragua (fully discussed in Chapter 18, B). In Carter's eyes, Somoza could be compared to other dictators, like Batista of Cuba, ousted in 1958, or Trujillo of the Dominican Republic, murdered in 1961, whose economically bankrupt police states had simply become an embarrassment to their foreign supporters. 'Administration spokesmen emphasized that here was an opportunity for the United States to demonstrate that it could respond positively to revolutionary change in the developing world.'[3] However, in 1980, with the new Cold War underway, it was easy for Republicans to accuse Carter of having made one more, grave error. In Nicaragua, a leftist regime, now allied to Fidel Castro, had been allowed into power and it might spread revolution to neighbouring Central American states, notably El Salvador. This was seen, by some, as an advance for Soviet interests in America's 'own back yard' and attributed to Washington's declining power, which Ronald Reagan was determined to reverse. Then again, as in US–Soviet relations, a 'change of policy . . . had been effected well before . . . Reagan entered the White House'. In Central America in 1980, Carter sought to 'erect a cordon sanitaire around Nicaragua, the Americans once again began to dispense generous military aid to the neighbouring countries [and] military advisers were sent to El Salvador'.[4]

In contrast to the Nixon period a decade before, the Reagan years saw Latin America, or more specifically Central America, assume primary importance in US foreign policy. 'For Reagan, Central America was the focal point of his tough new foreign policy . . . where Washington would draw the line against the spread of communism in the less developed world.'[5] Here was a testing ground for the Reagan Doctrine (see Box 18.1), with its promise of support for any 'freedom fighters' who were struggling to liberate their countries from communism. It was especially important too, after Carter's apparent retreats, to reassert US strength in an area long seen as its own sphere of influence and to reassure the region's right-wing governments that they could rely on Washington's leadership. 'We had already lost Cuba to Communism', Reagan later wrote. 'I was determined the Free World was not going to lose Central America or more of the Caribbean.'[6] As elsewhere, therefore, the main thrust of Reagan's policy was remarkably simple: previous ideas of support for human rights, encouraging democratization, and providing economic development aid were pushed aside more firmly than under Nixon by a determined anti-communism although, in January 1984, a commission under Henry Kissinger reported that economic aid should be a vital component of policy in Central America, alongside covert operations and assistance to anti-communists. The new policy *did* have an intellectual justification, provided by the ambassador to the UN, a former social science academic, Jeanne Kirkpatrick. In an article entitled 'Dictatorships and Double Standards', published in 1979, she argued that, although 'authoritarian' regimes might suppress freedom, they *were* pro-US, open to capitalism, protective of traditional values, and might be reformed over time; 'totalitarian' regimes on the other hand, such as those in the communist bloc, were anti-US, inimical to capitalism and (or so she argued) incapable of reform. In 1980, the recent examples of what had occurred in Iran and Nicaragua seemed to provide ample evidence in Kirkpatrick's favour and against Carter. In each case, she argued, 'the American effort to impose liberalization and democratization on a government confronted with violent internal opposition not only failed, but actually assisted the coming to power of new regimes in which ordinary people enjoy fewer freedoms . . . regimes, moreover, hostile to American interests'.[7] Reagan believed that the Kirkpatrick thesis 'provided . . . intellectual foundation for the argument he had been making . . . about the Carter policies . . . weakening US . . . influence . . . under the banner of advancing human rights'.[8]

Criticized at the time as being based on a poor grasp of history, it did not take many years for the flaws in the Kirkpatrick thesis to become apparent. Under Reagan, as in previous decades, the 'authoritarian' regimes which the US supported actually proved extremely unwilling to reform, they hardly provided the ideal, stable conditions for capitalism to thrive, and they frequently clashed with such traditional institutions as the Roman Catholic Church. Their violence and oppression remained an embarrassment to America and, in one case, foreign adventurism by the Argentinian dictatorship of General Leopoldo Galtieri provoked a major crisis. On 2 April, the Argentinians occupied the sparsely populated, British-ruled Falklands Islands in the South Atlantic to enforce a territorial claim; though the British had shown little interest in the islands in the recent past, the government of Margaret Thatcher would not tolerate such an affront to national dignity and sent a naval force to retake them (see Box 18.2). Ironically, given Kirkpatrick's lack of support for British action, it was the Argentinian defeat which led to a return to democracy in 1983, after years of dictatorship, during which around 6,000 opponents of the military had 'disappeared'. As the 1980s proceeded, two points became even more obvious. One, of course, was that 'totalitarian' states in the Eastern bloc, *were* capable of political and economic reform, as witnessed by the dramatic changes under Gorbachev after 1985: 'the final judgement on Kirkpatrick's theory occurred in Eastern Europe . . . when totalitarian regimes . . . were replaced by elected governments'.[9] The other was that there could be genuinely democratic uprisings against dictators, most obviously, not in Latin America but in the ex-US colony of the Philippines in early 1986. Here the corrupt but overconfident Ferdinand Marcos, President since 1966, agreed to hold elections only to be defeated by Corazon Aquino, the wife of a former opposition leader whom Marcos had murdered. Marcos tried to falsify the results but was faced by massive demonstrations and this 'people power' convinced Washington that he must be told to leave. Yet in the later 1980s the 'Kirkpatrick Formula'—that rightist dictatorships were capable of reform—did seem to find justification in one area, when several of Latin America's dictatorships held elections: Brazil, Uruguay, and Peru in 1985, Guatemala in 1986, Chile and Paraguay in 1989.

El Salvador

Whatever the lessons of events in the Philippines, in Central America the US government stuck doggedly to a policy of upholding right-wing governments, however vicious and unpopular, against left-wing guerrillas, supposedly backed by the Eastern bloc. 'American charges of Soviet and Cuban responsibility for revolution in Central America were . . . more convenient than acknowledging failures of reactionary regimes to provide for needed peaceful change.'[10] It was particularly important, in Reagan's view, both to prevent the Nicaraguan revolution from spreading beyond its own borders and to try to undermine the Sandinista regime. There were guerrilla movements in South America, notably the Maoist 'Tupac Amaru', who began to make advances in the Peruvian countryside in 1980. But US efforts concentrated on helping several Central American states resist the supposed attempt of Cuba and Nicaragua to export revolution. Those deemed most under threat included Honduras, Guatemala, and El Salvador. (Mexico, the largest Central American state, escaped serious internal dissent in this period; only in January 1994 did the Zapatista National Liberation Army become active in Chiapas province among the poor peasantry.) Honduras, the poorest country of the region, was heavily dependent economically on the US and seen by Washington as relatively secure. Guatemala, dominated by the military and wealthy landowners since 1954, was more troubled, having suffered an earthquake in 1976, which added to its economic problems. However, the government was ruthless in eliminating its opponents, not only leftists (who had begun a guerrilla campaign in 1962), but even Christian Democrats. By the time the leftist insurgency in Guatemala ended in December 1996, it was estimated that 200,000 had been killed, mostly by the army, making the process of national reconciliation very difficult. Carter had been so alienated by such repression that he cut off military aid to Guatemala, but Reagan used the country, like Honduras, as a base for covert operations against Nicaragua. Costa Rica was the only proper democracy in Latin America in 1980 but, paradoxically, something of a problem for Washington, because the Costa Rican government followed an independent line abroad, providing some economic aid to the Sandinistas and, especially after 1986 working for the reconciliation of the opposing forces in Nicaragua, rather than the destruction of the Sandinista regime.

'The most urgent visible crisis during the initial years of the Reagan period, however, was over El Salvador.'[11] Indeed, it was the need to prevent a leftist overthrow of the government in El Salvador which initially gave Reagan the justification to boost aid to those fighting the Nicaraguan Sandinistas. El Salvador, a major coffee exporter with a population of 5 million, was another country dominated by a landowning oligarchy, firmly supported by the military. About a third of the rural population owned no land; illiteracy, homelessness, and malnutrition were widespread. In 1969, the country won the short-lived 'Soccer War' (so-called because it was sparked by a football match) with neighbouring Honduras, but the triumph was financially costly and it also helped kill off lingering hopes for a Central American common market, a free trade zone, first proposed in the 1960 Managua Treaty. Support then increased in urban areas for the Christian Democratic Party, founded in 1960, with the support of the Roman Catholic Church, and led by José Napoleon Duarte. But when Duarte appeared likely to win the 1972 elections, the government cancelled them, drove Duarte into exile, and ruthlessly extinguished the ensuing signs of discontent. This experience meant that the regime's opponents then turned to non-democratic means to gain power. In 1977, General Humberto Romero was elected President amid violence and blatant corruption. Despite the opposition of the Catholic Church, the US decided it must supply him with more economic aid. One important feature of El Salvadorian politics was the degree to which the Church criticized repression and spoke out in favour of the poor. The opposition of an influential national, traditional institution was of grave concern to the military, who murdered several priests in the 1970s. Such actions were difficult to justify in terms of anti-communism.

In mid-1979, concerned at the fall of Somoza in Nicaragua and evidence that Cuba was training El Salvador's leftist insurgents, the Carter administration decided to press for a change of government. On 15 October, General Romero was duly overthrown by fellow officers, who established a junta with several civilian members and promised reform and, in January 1980, the Christian Democrats were brought into government. 'If the admittedly weak regime could be sustained by the United States in the short run, US officials believed, its programme of social reform would eventually attract support, rebuilding a political centre where none now existed.'[12] But the junta soon became divided, the landowners opposed even limited land reform, and there were no talks with the insurgents. Even when Duarte, with US encouragement, was installed as President, the violence continued. Events in Nicaragua also had a significant impact on El Salvador: 'The Sandinista victory . . . not only encouraged the Left, it had also galvanized the Right.'[13] The urban and rural poor were no longer impressed by Duarte's liberal credentials, whilst the army and police increasingly took decisions into their own hands, murdering their opponents. In March 1980, they even killed the country's religious leader, the outspoken Archbishop Oscar Romero, in his own cathedral. This, alongside the murder of three American nuns, caused an outcry in the US and led Carter to threaten a cut in aid. Leftist terrorism and army massacres seemed to be turning El Salvador towards anarchy, with about 10,000 dying through violence during 1980. Landowners, financiers, and military leaders began to move their money out of the country (thus provoking an investment collapse) and to connive in the activities of right-wing death squads. The most notorious of these was the 'White Warriors' led by a US-trained, ex-intelligence officer, Major Roberto d'Aubuisson. But in the face of the onslaught and ever-greater poverty, the leftists, hitherto very divided, became more united and determined. In October 1980, they formed the Farabundo Martí National Liberation Front (FMLN) and, though there were only a few thousand guerrillas, they took control of much of the countryside. A secret attempt by Duarte to talk to some of his opponents in November 1980 was ruined when the military discovered it and murdered the leftist delegates—making them reluctant to risk talks again.

Under Carter in 1980, the US was already providing El Salvador with considerable aid and even military advisers, and this trend inevitably continued under Reagan, urged on by Secretary of State Alexander Haig, who feared the country would be the next Latin

American 'domino' to fall to the Soviets and Cubans. It was also an excellent opportunity to prove that, notwithstanding Vietnam, 'national liberation' movements could be defeated. Haig had no doubt of Soviet and Cuban involvement and 'believed that our policy should . . . through the application of a full range of economic, political, and security measures, convince them to put an end to Havana's bloody activities'.[14] But there were several problems with this approach. First, despite the publication of a State Department paper on the subject in February 1981, it was very difficult to prove that the Soviets and Cubans were involved on any meaningful scale in El Salvador: the local support for the guerrillas was genuine and only a few Soviet arms were sent—arguably as a riposte to Central Intelligence Agency (CIA) activities in Afghanistan. The White Paper claimed to provide 'definite evidence of the clandestine military support given by the Soviet Union, Cuba and their allies to Marxist-Leninist guerrillas now fighting to overthrow the established government of El Salvador'.[15] But a number of press reports 'shredded the White paper's claim'.[16] Second, despite $200 million in military aid from the US in 1981–4, as well as schooling in counter-insurgency techniques, the Salvadorian army was unable to secure a decisive victory, or even to calm the situation. The US also had an embarrassing time trying to maintain Duarte. In March 1982, in elections which the leftists boycotted, he was defeated by the National Republic Alliance (ARENA), led by d'Aubuisson, who proved that there was a considerable body of genuine support for his extreme right-wing views, even among the smaller landowners. Washington poured over a million dollars into the Christian Democratic coffers ahead of the next election in May 1984, but Duarte won only narrowly and he was still unable to overcome the problems of poverty and corruption, or to control the activities of the death squads.

By 1989, ARENA was back in power, with their candidate Alfredo Cristiani, triumphing in that year's presidential election. By then, about 70,000 had been killed during ten years of trouble but the 50,000-strong army was no nearer to defeating the guerrillas, who probably numbered considerably less than 10,000. Outrages continued on both sides, the latest being the murder of six Jesuit priests by the army. US economic and military assistance had continued to flow into the country ($600 million in 1988 alone) but many Salvadorians turned against the American presence: 1986 saw widespread anti-US protests. With the Cold War over, a

BOX 18.1

The Reagan Doctrine

As with the Nixon Doctrine, the Reagan Doctrine was not included in a single statement but rather was explained by the President, and by other members of his administration, on several occasions. However, an important, early summary came in the February 1985 'State of the Union' address, where Reagan told Congress:

We must not break faith with those who are risking their lives, on every continent from Afghanistan to Nicaragua, to defy Soviet aggression . . . support for freedom fighters is self-defence.

In subsequent speeches, the Secretary of State, George Shultz, made clear that the Doctrine was meant to reverse the idea that the Soviets could expand their influence through 'wars of national liberation' and that the West was incapable of reversing the process. The Doctrine pleased the Republican Right. It seemed to go beyond the narrow defence of American interests that had characterized the Nixon Doctrine; and it marked a revival of 'roll-back' and 'liberation' ideas that had been advocated in Eisenhower's early years.

In actual fact, to the disappointment of some right-wingers, and despite the potential 'globalistic' nature of Reagan's rhetoric, the focus of US assistance was mainly on the Mujaheddin of Afghanistan and the Contras of Nicaragua (though there was diplomatic support for the opponents of pro-Soviet regimes in Angola, Mozambique, and Cambodia). Furthermore, Reagan had been helping these two causes since early in his first term, so that the Doctrine did not mark a new departure so much as a justification of existing practice. Opponents pointed out that some of those who received aid were hardly models of liberal-democratic ambition. In Cambodia in particular, the US was backing an alliance of forces that included the mass murderer, Pol Pot. In Nicaragua, some argued, it was the US rather than the USSR which was trying to curtail the country's independence. Yet despite the fears of his critics, Reagan avoided a serious, direct clash with the Soviets, partly because the Doctrine largely employed clandestine assistance to low-intensity conflicts. And over the following years the Soviets did retreat from less developed world involvement in Afghanistan, which the Reagan Doctrine targeted.

settlement achieved (in 1990) in Nicaragua and with both sides in El Salvador exhausted, a ceasefire was finally agreed in September 1991. A peace agreement was signed under UN auspices three months later, with both sides now ready to compromise. Cristiani 'pursued peace doggedly, despite resistance from the Right. The FMLN had given up its demands for powersharing . . . settling for changes in the armed forces.'[17] The death of d'Aubuisson, from cancer, in 1992, probably helped cement a settlement in which the leftists had a share in policing the country and a purge was carried out of those army officers who had participated in the death squads. But elections in 1994 confirmed that it was the Right, in the form of ARENA, which held the balance of popular support.

B. Nicaragua and the 'Contragate' Scandal

The Fall of Somoza

In Nicaragua, in contrast to El Salvador, the Reagan administration's aim was to topple a government rather than to maintain it. But the enemy, the radical Left, was the same and the conflict proved just as long-lasting and destructive. There was a long history of US involvement in Nicaraguan politics stretching back to the 1890s and it had been under virtual American occupation for two decades before 1933. Thereafter, it was dominated by the Somoza family, corrupt and oppressive but also trusted anti-communists who helped the CIA-backed operation to overthrow Guatemala's Jacobo Arbenz in 1954 (see Chapter 6, C) and whose dictatorship was the region's most stable and lasting. In 1967, Anastasio Debayle Somoza succeeded to the Nicaraguan leadership and, through the economic troubles of the 1970s, came increasingly to rely on the National Guard to maintain him in power. As in El Salvador, land ownership was concentrated in a few hands and there were large numbers of landless labourers. An earthquake (in 1972) devastated large areas and wealth was monopolized by the Somozas and their supporters, who also cornered much of the foreign aid that flowed in after the earthquake. Opposition was led by the Sandinistan National Liberation Front (FSLN), who were named after Augusto Sandina, an inter-war hero who had resisted American domination, before being murdered by Anastasio Somoza. The FSLN had been founded in 1961 and, while its main support came from rural areas, it launched attacks on urban centres after 1966. With a fragmented leadership, it had had limited success in fighting Somoza until the earthquake. Now things were different. The uprising was soon widespread and in January 1978 they began a mass uprising. A few months later, in their most daring operation so far, the Sandinistas seized control of the National Congress, releasing its members in return for concessions. But Somoza was unwilling to strike any lasting deal with the Left and, in late 1978, turned to ruthless suppression, murdering thousands and escalating the violence. In early 1979, Somoza's hold on power still seemed reasonably secure but events in Nicaragua were already of international concern, with some nearby governments sympathetic to the rebels. Costa Rica allowed the Sandinistas to establish a government in exile in 1978, and in May 1979, as a major rebel offensive was launched, Mexico decided to withdraw diplomatic recognition from Somoza, thus risking American displeasure.

Arguably the US shared the blame for the rising violence in Nicaragua. Carter's human rights policy had probably encouraged Somoza's opponents to seek reform in 1977 and it was partly to please the new President that the dictator himself had eased repression for a time, a move which simply made the opposition more vocal. Somoza himself even complained that Carter's pressure on human rights 'was his vehicle for the destruction of me'.[18] Yet on the other hand, a strong 'Somoza Lobby' in Congress ensured that America continued to provide arms for the National Guard into 1979. By then, Carter was caught in a difficult situation. 'On the one hand the Carter administration wanted to remain true to its human rights policy . . . but on the other hand the Sandinistas were leftists who would . . . take Nicaragua . . . toward Marxism.'[19] Ideally, he would have liked to find some moderate alternative (such as Duarte's Christian Democrats in El Salvador) to both Somoza and the Sandinistas. The latter, relying as they did on Cuban arms and training, were not a welcome replacement for the dictatorship in American eyes, yet Somoza's extreme oppression made it impossible for Carter to maintain him by force. In June 1979, when the CIA warned that the regime was in grave danger, the White House decided that nothing could be done to save him and instead continued to hope that a 'moderate', non-Sandinista replacement could be found who might pursue a gradual reform programme. A plan was devised whereby Somoza would resign in return for a

Sandinista ceasefire; the National Guard would remain intact to maintain order and this would buy time for a non-revolutionary government to be formed. 'The White House was especially eager to ensure the survival of the National Guard who . . . could provide a counterweight to the Cuban-trained Sandinista army in a post-Somoza Nicaragua.'[20] But such hopes were fanciful. It has been argued that if America had been 'willing to demand Somoza's resignation nine months earlier, a constitutional solution might have been feasible' but by late June 'even the most conservative Nicaraguan opposition groups had already endorsed the Sandinistas' provisional government'.[21] Somoza's regime was on the brink of collapse, a 'moderate' alternative did not exist, and the National Guard, which had killed up to 40,000 people in recent years, was hated. A scheme to send a peacekeeping force from the Organization of American States (OAS) was vetoed by Costa Rica, Mexico, and others. Even the US public turned against Somoza on 20 June, when National Guardsmen murdered a US journalist in front of film cameras.

Somoza was finally forced to leave the capital, Managua, on 17 July 1979, going into exile in Paraguay, a military dictatorship, where he was assassinated the following year. The National Guard disintegrated after his departure, though many of them too fled abroad, hoping to carry on their opposition to the new government, which the Sandinistas formed on 19 July. In some ways, their government, though radical, was not as extreme as the US feared. There were arrests and the use of censorship but violence quickly died down, justice was largely maintained (even in the case of judgments on former National Guardsmen) and, despite an ambitious programme of nationalization, many private businesses continued to flourish, not only those whose owners had turned against the corruption and arbitrary rule of the Somozas, but also some which were American-owned. The new government declared itself to be non-aligned and, in order to ensure the continuation of such moderation, Carter agreed to provide $20 million in economic aid. Congress agreed to provide further aid in 1980, but this was partly because of the desire of 'North American, European and Japanese banks to avoid a Nicaraguan default on the country's $1.5 billion debt',[22] and by then US–Sandinista relations were very poor. For even if Nicaragua claimed to be non-aligned, in effect it was close to the communist bloc, buying East European arms, and accepting several thousand Cuban advisers. The Sandinistas refused to condemn the Soviet invasion of Afghanistan and in May 1980 some of the more moderate members, including Violetta Chamarro, quit the government. The CIA was fearful that Nicaragua, backed by Cuba and the USSR, would aid leftist insurgents elsewhere, most obviously in El Salvador. And President Carter, accused by his opponents of having 'lost' Nicaragua to communism, began to approve limited covert operations against the Sandinistas.

Reagan and the 'Contras', 1981–6

In 1979–80, Carter effectively carried out a dual-edged policy towards the Sandinistas, establishing links to their opponents yet also using financial assistance to draw them away from Cuba. Under Reagan, there was a simpler policy of trying to destroy the Sandinistas, who were depicted as Soviet stooges, totalitarian and militaristic. The limited scale of Soviet aid and the fact that US companies could still operate in Nicaragua were ignored. Instead the country, like El Salvador, became a focus of American efforts to turn the communist tide in the less developed world and reverse the supposed defeats for the Western cause under Carter. Nicaragua eventually overtook El Salvador as the focus of US activity in the region, although in 1980 it was seen as a subsidiary issue, important mainly because it was a conduit for arms supplies to the El Salvadorean guerrillas. Alongside Afghanistan, Nicaragua also became the main focus of Reagan's ambition to support 'freedom fighters' in liberating their country from communist domination. To Washington, 'the Sandinistas were Marxist-Leninists. If they stayed in power, they would guide Nicaragua . . . toward a one-party . . . dictatorship, alliance with the Soviet Union and subversion of their neighbours.'[23]

By late 1981, the National Security Adviser, Robert McFarlane, was coordinating a wide range of activities to undermine the Sandinistas without provoking outright war or too much international outrage. These included diplomatic, psychological, economic, and military steps. On the diplomatic front, the Secretary of State, Alexander Haig, encouraged by Mexico, did make a secret attempt in November 1981 to persuade the Cubans to end their support for radical movements. But this failed: the Cubans argued that problems in Latin America were internally generated and that they were bound to help their fellow leftists. The US thereafter relied on isolating the Sandinistas diplomatically, especially in Latin America, and on trying to prevent them receiving foreign aid and conducting trade. In 1982, the US also used its influence to have the World Bank end its loans to Nicaragua. Securing the support of dictatorships like Honduras and Guatemala for such a policy was easy, but backing from others was more difficult to secure: in 1981 Mexico, keen to limit US domination of the region, provided Nicaragua with $200 million in aid. Reagan confirmed in April 1981 that all US aid to Nicaragua would end, pressure was put on companies to end ties, and eventually, in 1985, a full trade embargo was introduced. 'By the end of 1985, the United States . . . had effectively foreclosed any possibility of the Sandinistas obtaining loans from any of the major international lending agencies.'[24] On the psychological front, the State Department formed a new department, the Office of Public Diplomacy, to direct the propaganda effort against the Sandinistas. But this Office was put under the direction of a CIA official and it was the CIA which soon gained the leading role in trying to destroy the Sandinistas. The Agency's director, Bill Casey, became quite obsessed with the idea of Nicaragua as the main base for Soviet-Cuban activity in Central America.

Despite the above measures, it became clear that the 'most effective weapons in Washington's arsenal were political and military, namely the financing of right-wing opposition parties in Nicaragua and the . . . training of Nicaraguan exiles . . . into a guerrilla force'.[25] By 1982, the 'purpose of US activity was no longer just interdiction of arms shipments to neighbouring El Salvador. It became, first and foremost, an attempt to topple the Sandinista government.'[26] Although Ronald Reagan was one of the few leading Americans still to defend the Vietnam War, he recognized that the time had passed when US marines could be despatched to enforce order in the Central American states. Not only popular opinion, but also expert advice from the Department of Defense, was opposed to any action that risked 'another Vietnam'. So, given Reagan's determination nonetheless to put military pressure on the Sandinistas, the administration had to support a force of Nicaraguan-born 'freedom fighters' who would carry out a campaign of sabotage, assassination, economic disruption, and general harassment in their own country designed to demoralize the Sandinistas and drain their treasury. In fact, the CIA had virtually to create such a force because, despite Reagan's confidence that the Nicaraguan people were living under an unpopular oppressor, there was little active opposition to the government. The 'Contras', as the opposition became called, were often former members of the National Guard but, from April 1982, the CIA also funded a former Sandinista leader, Eden Pastora, who had gone into exile in Costa Rica. Since their existence soon became publicly known, the cover story was invented that they were operating only on the Nicaragua–El Salvador border, to try to stop the Sandinistas arming their fellow leftists in El Salvador; 'the Reagan administration vehemently insisted during 1982 and 1983 that it was not trying to overthrow the Sandinistas, despite mounting evidence to the contrary'.[27] In December 1981, only about 500 Contras were supported, with an initial fund of $19 million, and Argentina helped in their training. But by 1984, there were up to 12,000 of them, mainly operating from bases in Honduras, which became a virtual 'American Fortress' and the vital channel for financial aid to the Contras. They were engaged not only in murdering Sandinista officials and attacking military installations, but also in more general, poorly directed acts of terrorism, bombing workplaces, and ravaging villages. Such activities did nothing to win popular support; neither did their lack of an attractive political programme. According to McFarlane, the Contras became 'one of President Reagan's personal causes. In his eyes [they] were modern-day minutemen . . . whose struggle on behalf of liberty . . . deserved America's wholehearted . . . support.'[28] But in mid-1983, as it seemed increasingly unlikely that there would be an outright Contra victory, the President decided to supplement Contra pressure by intensifying naval exercises near the Nicaraguan coast: one feature of US policy was to keep the Sandinistas fearful of a full-scale invasion, forcing them to spend money on defence and creating a siege mentality. In September 1983, the CIA organized raids on Managua airport—which embarrassingly occurred just as two US senators were flying in. In 1984, there were some diplomatic talks with the Sandinistas, but these were largely to make Reagan appear moderate in election year, and at the same time Nicaraguan harbours were mined: incredibly, Congress, which had earlier objected to a naval blockade, was told but failed to grasp the significance of the step. In 1985, CIA-directed sabotage efforts focused on Managua itself.

The US-Contra campaign had a terrible impact on Nicaragua. By 1986, about 7,000 had been killed there, and an estimated $2.5 billion lost in physical destruction and reduced trade. Spending on infrastructure and reform programmes had to be cut, people were regularly drilled to prepare for a US invasion. 'Defence soaked up 40 per cent of the nation's budget by 1984 to pay for the now 75,000 active-duty army. Social programmes suffered. Polio, once eliminated by vaccination programmes, reappeared.'[29] Some 350,000 had become refugees. Ironically, the US trade embargo 'pushed the Sandinistas into greater dependence on Cuba and the Soviet Union'.[30] The latter provided $250 million in aid in 1984. Yet the Contras failed to take control of any areas of the country and the campaign was not without cost to the Reagan administration. There were internal divisions between those who favoured a tough military policy (Casey, Kirkpatrick, and, at Defense, Weinberger) and those who wanted a less violent, more diplomatic line (Haig and his successor, Shultz); there were also members of the CIA who disliked Casey's methods and, remembering the Congressional investigations of the 1970s, wanted to work in line with public opinion. The public were increasingly concerned about the anti-Sandinista campaign, with only about a third of people approving Reagan's policy; and the press outcry in 1984 over the mining of Nicaraguan harbours almost led the Democratic-dominated Congress to sever support to the Contras completely. In December 1982, the first Boland amendment (named after Congressman Edward Boland) had already tried to stop money being spent to 'overthrow' the Managua government, but Reagan skirted this by claiming that the Contras were ready to talk to the Sandinistas. In October 1984, in the midst of the US presidential election campaign, the Boland II amendment cut all *lethal* aid to the Contras. 'Any attempt to get money from Congress for the Contras in the near future would be fruitless', Shultz recognized, complaining that: 'As a result there was no chance that the Sandinistas would negotiate seriously.'[31] In fact, the administration was not able to restore aid until October 1986, when $100 million was provided.

American policy was also widely condemned abroad, being seen as no more than an attempt by one country to overthrow another government by force. In 1983, a number of Latin American states Mexico, Panama, Colombia, and Venezuela—met on Contadora island and discussed a peace plan: both sides should respect human rights, Contra subversion should end, the US should withdraw its advisers from El Salvador, and the Sandinistas should both end their support for the Salvadorian leftists and hold free elections. To Reagan's embarrassment, the OAS and most Central American States backed this scheme, and Nicaragua began to fulfil the Contadora Principles, holding an election in November 1984. But the President was determined to proceed with his military policy, refused to pull US advisers out of El Salvador, and actually bribed anti-Sandinista politicians to boycott the Nicaraguan elections. There was still a 75 per cent turnout, with several parties running, and the Sandinista leader, Daniel Ortega, only won the presidency with about 60 per cent of the vote. But since the Contras did not stand, Reagan could discount the result. In 1986, he also decided to ignore a judgment by the International Court that the US was guilty of supporting terrorism in Nicaragua (this in the same year that America punished Libya for its support of terrorism by bombing it). In late 1986, with lethal aid to the Contras restored, Reagan hoped that they might be able to launch a decisive campaign against Managua. But it was then that his administration paid its highest price for the Nicaraguan involvement, with the breaking of the so-called 'Contragate' scandal.

'Contragate' and a Nicaraguan Settlement

The 'Contragate' (or 'Irangate') scandal, which at one point threatened to topple Reagan as Watergate had toppled Nixon, and which overshadowed the remainder of the presidency, sprang directly from the administration's attempts to circumvent the Boland II amendment. If Congress would not provide sufficient aid to the Contras, then it might be possible to secure it from private donations and foreign sources. The National Security Council had actually approved such efforts in January 1984, but it was the Boland amendment nine months later which convinced Casey and the National Security Adviser, Robert McFarlane, to pursue the idea with determination. One of McFarlane's staff, Oliver North, helped obtain money from donors within the US and finance was also secured from Saudi Arabia, Taiwan, Brunei, and other strongly anti-communist governments, with about $37 million being raised in total, without the knowledge of Congress. In 1985, these activities became linked to secret US efforts to deal with Iran (Chapter 17, C). A complicated scheme was concocted whereby after November 1985 arms were secretly delivered (via Israel at first) to Iran (then fighting the war with Iraq) and the money earned was diverted to the Contras. It was also hoped that the Iranians would help secure the release of Western hostages in Lebanon. But in October 1986, the process began to unravel when a cargo aircraft was shot down in Nicaragua. One crewman survived and admitted that he was a CIA operative supplying arms to the Contras. Then, on 3 November, a Lebanese journalist reported that McFarlane had visited Tehran six months before and US press interest in the question became intense. Finally, on 25 November, Attorney-General Edwin Meese revealed the diversion of $4 million in arms earnings from Iran to the Contras.

Like Watergate, Contragate highlighted the fact that dishonesty, secrecy, and outright illegality were to be found at the top of the American body politic. 'Unelected and unaccountable military officers . . . worked with key State Department personnel to defy US laws.'[32] Some in government believed that they alone interpreted the national interest and that Congress and the public could be ignored. Reagan, who pleaded ignorance about the operation, avoided impeachment and insisted that, while he 'wanted the Contras maintained', it was 'only later . . . that I learned that some NSC staff had gone farther'.[33] The ensuing investigations focused on Oliver North, McFarlane, and the latter's successor, John Poindexter, though it was clear that many others knew about the Iran–Contra link. Poindexter was forced to resign as National Security Adviser in November 1986. North, who (like Poindexter) was found guilty of law-breaking only to have the conviction lost on a technicality, became a hero for the American Right. But the scandal seemed a fatal blow to the Contras, who in any case were suffering casualties at the rate of 400 per month. Congress was now unwilling to give them any money, despite requests from Reagan, and on 23 March 1988 the Contras were forced to agree to a ceasefire. In return, and partly due to pressure from Gorbachev, the Sandinistas offered an amnesty, a chance for their opponents to reintegrate into national life and a promise of new elections in 1991. Pressure for such a deal had been building among other Central American states, especially thanks to the efforts of Costa Rica's President, Oscar Arias, who in January 1987 launched a revised version of the Contadora Principles, including a ceasefire, amnesty, and elections. In effect, the Arias Plan 'furnished both the Sandinistas and the Reagan administration with one of their major desires: an end to support for the Contras, and pressure on the internal democratization process'.[34] A meeting of Central American leaders, including Ortega, at Esquipulas in Guatemala, accepted the 'Arias Plan' in August 1987. Arias went on to win the Nobel Peace Prize and the Sandinistas began to liberalize their regime, with a freer press and the release of political prisoners. The truth was that, whatever the troubles Reagan and the Contras faced, the Sandinistas were saddled with problems exacerbated by US subversion: high inflation, unemployment, falling wage levels, and financial weakness, especially as Gorbachev's increasingly troubled USSR now cut back on its aid programme—and ended all military assistance in 1988.

Although Reagan believed, to the end of his presidency, that the Sandinistas could be removed by force, his successor and former Vice-President, George Bush, all too aware of Congressional sensibilities, pursued a more pragmatic approach. 'To show his independence of Reagan and stress the non-ideological nature of his administration, he replaced confrontation with compromise.'[35] Furthermore, Bush did not give Central America the significance that Reagan had. The 'main priority was to get Central America off the foreign policy agenda so he could concentrate on important matters such as US–Soviet relations'.[36] The US economic stranglehold on Nicaragua was clearly having a profound effect on the country and Ortega's desire to be moderate was confirmed by his February 1989 offer to bring the election date forward to 1990. James Baker masterminded a policy that 'emphasized the promotion of democracy by diplomatic rather than military means', using trade and aid as pressure points on the Sandinistas, while urging the USSR and Cuba to stop aiding them.[37] He believed that the Arias Plan, with its 'call for democratic reforms, elections, and an end to regional subversion was politically unassailable', especially since 'it was an arrangement negotiated by the parties themselves, not something forced upon them' by America. This fitted in with Baker's wider approach to 'rolling back Soviet beachheads', which placed an emphasis on using 'elections as a tool to dislodge them', exploiting 'Gorbachev's own emphasis on *glasnost*'.[38]

There were still causes for concern: in July 1988 the US embassy in Managua, kept open throughout the Contra campaign, had been closed by the Sandinistas because of its links to their opponents; Nicaragua continued to help the leftists in El Salvador; and Cuba had boosted its arms supplies to the Sandinistas to make up for the Soviet withdrawal. But, unable to get more for the Contras from Congress than a limited amount of non-lethal assistance, Bush and Baker decided they must rely on Ortega's opponents winning the elections. In 1989, the US and USSR both undertook to respect the outcome of these. Bush then focused his efforts on building and supporting the National Opposition Union (UNO), a movement so broad-based that it included both conservatives and communists, and which was led by the ex-Sandinista Cabinet minister, Violeta Chamorro. Despite the scale of US support, there was still some surprise when the Sandinistas, with 41 per cent of the vote, lost the February 1990 election to the UNO coalition. Nicaraguan electors seemed keen to escape US opposition and the trade boycott, and to begin the task of reconstruction. Bush ended the trade embargo and provided $230 million in aid, but was aware that the Sandinistas remained a potent political force in Nicaraguan politics, with the largest number of seats in Parliament and an influential role in the trade unions and armed forces. His successful gamble on the elections had paid off and, with the resolution too of the El Salvador–Panama problems (on Panama see Chapter 18, C), US policy in Central America was in a better state that at any time since 1978. The settlement also helped heal the domestic wounds of the Iran–Contra scandal. 'By pursuing a policy of pragmatic accommodation and giving just enough to both supporters and foes of the Contras it had successfully resolved one of the most . . . divisive conflicts in US politics of the previous decade.'[39]

C. Two American Invasions: Grenada and Panama

In El Salvador and Nicaragua, the US lent economic, diplomatic, and covert support to those who opposed Marxism but avoided the open use of American armed forces. In two cases in the 1980s, however, Washington was prepared to use an actual invasion to remove governments. Grenada, in 1983, and Panama, six years later, were in many ways very different problems. In the first case, the Reagan administration acted swiftly to overthrow a regime on a small Caribbean island, which was seen as increasingly pro-Castro. In the second, the Bush administration resorted to armed force only after trying for several years to overthrow a volatile, oppressive dictator in a strategically important Central American state. Both invasions, however, were highly successful in terms of fulfilling the main US aims, even if the first in particular stirred international controversy, and both showed that the US was capable of taking military action, despite the 'Vietnam Syndrome'. The Syndrome made the Department of Defense reluctant to deploy conventional forces except in a narrow range of circumstances. Indeed, in October 1984 Casper Weinberger laid out several preconditions for any military action, including: the deployment of forces only in the defence of vital national interests, the assurance of popular and Congressional support, clear aims, continuous reassessments, and the ability to pull out of any commitment which went wrong. But to Secretary of State Shultz such conditions were too restrictive, undermining the effectiveness of US diplomacy, which 'could work . . . most effectively when force—or the threat of force—was a credible part of the equation'.[40] Reagan, too, was sometimes keen to use force in order to blunt any potential Soviet advance. In Lebanon (Chapter 17, A), the Defense Department's caution seemed justified, and the US was driven to withdraw rather than become embroiled in a complicated civil conflict. But in Grenada and Panama, the US began to recover its faith in its ability to deploy force successfully in limited operations.

Grenada, October 1983

Grenada, with a population of about 85,000, had been given its independence from Britain in 1974, under the leadership of Eric Gairy, a man obsessed with the paranormal, the occult, and UFOs, who soon proved oppressive and unpopular. On 13 March 1979, he was overthrown in a coup by the Marxist-influenced 'New Jewel Movement' led by Maurice Bishop, who set up a 'People's Revolutionary Government' and, whilst avoiding any extreme radicalism at home, soon started to import arms from the USSR and Cuba. In mid-1979, the Carter administration, concerned about the Latin American implications of Moscow's build-up of Cuban military power, had secretly made an approach to Castro: in a marked departure from the usual policy of isolating and harassing him, the US was ready to end its trade embargo on Cuba if it ended its interventionist policy in Angola, Ethiopia, and elsewhere. But Castro made no response. At the same time, Carter also hoped to use covert operations to undermine the New Jewel Movement in Grenada but, given the widespread suspicion of the CIA in America in the late 1970s, this proved difficult. Objections from the Senate's Intelligence Committee forced the CIA to end its operations in Grenada. So in late 1979, Bishop continued to develop his pro-Cuban policy and Castro took advantage of the opportunity to extend his influence. In September, Cuban troops arrived in Grenada on a training mission, and in December began to construct an airport with a long runway, which the US feared could become a staging post for Cuban intervention elsewhere—though its prime purpose at first was to help boost the island's tourist industry by allowing jet airliners to land.

On coming into office in January 1981, the Reagan administration ended all development aid to Grenada, including some which had gone to build the new airport. But real trouble between Washington and Grenada only blew up, quite suddenly, over two-and-a-half years later. The leaders of the New Jewel Movement had long been divided and on 13 October 1983 Premier Bishop was arrested by his deputy, Bernard Coard, and six days later executed—following an attempt by supporters to free him. A 'Revolutionary Military Council' was then formed. Several days of violence followed, which was of concern both to neighbouring Caribbean countries and to the US, the latter because nearly 500 American students were studying at a medical school on the island. Preparations for an invasion were made hastily. An appeal from the Organization of Eastern Caribbean States (possibly orchestrated by the US) helped give the impression that Washington was reacting to local concerns and on 22 October Grenada was suspended by another body, the Caribbean Community (CARICOM). Legitimacy was also given to the US action by the island's Governor, Sir Paul Scoon, who requested US aid. But, despite local fears and the vulnerability of American citizens, Reagan's decision on 24 October to approve armed intervention was undoubtedly primarily shaped by his anti-communism and his desire to teach Castro a lesson. On 25 October, 2,000 American troops landed on Grenada; 4,000 more followed over the next few days. They sustained only 19 losses but killed several dozen Grenadians and Cubans, many of them around the airport. The discovery of several Soviet advisers on the island was an unexpected bonus, which helped Reagan prove to the satisfaction of the US public that Grenada had fast been becoming a 'Soviet colony' and a centre for communist activity in the Caribbean. Others were less happy about such ruthless action. Apart from the predictable complaints of the Eastern bloc, the UN General Assembly and the OAS were both concerned about yet another example of the US tendency to bludgeon Caribbean and Latin American countries into line, colonial style, with little justification in international law. 'The action also conveyed the message that the United States opposed far-reaching economic and social reform in its own backyard.'[41] More unusually, Reagan's ally in London, Margaret Thatcher, was dismayed by the invasion, without proper consultation, of a Commonwealth country of which Queen Elizabeth II was Head of State. It should also be noted that the operation was less smooth than it appeared. As Colin Powell later conceded, 'it took most of a week to subdue all resistance' and the 'invasion was hardly a model of service cooperation'.[42] The protests, however, were soon forgotten, as Grenada held elections (in 1984) and US economic aid was provided. US troops left in December 1983. For Reagan, the invasion had been a low-risk, yet quick, triumphant, and high-profile operation, which boosted his popularity a year ahead of the next presidential election and helped to offset the ill effects, in public relations terms, of the Lebanon imbroglio. He could claim both to have restored order and democracy in one country and to have deterred the communists from acting against others. Whatever the lack of inter-service cooperation, the 'Pentagon's post-Vietnam skittishness about using military force in the less developed world receded a bit'.[43] The invasion, which the Soviets were powerless to oppose, also helped confirm 1983 as one of deep Cold War tensions.

Panama: The Noriega Regime

In contrast to Grenada, the invasion of Panama came at a time of much improved US–Soviet relations and, although the invasion was on a much grander scale, it did not stir up the same degree of international controversy. American intervention in Panamanian politics was well established. Even so, a large-scale invasion towards the end of the century was a remarkable and unexpected event, which the US government itself went to some lengths to avoid.

The last democratically elected Panamanian government had been overthrown in 1968 by General Omar Torrijos, who established a military dictatorship and made himself popular by pressing for the US to hand over the Panama Canal to Panamanian sovereignty. In 1978, Jimmy Carter agreed to do this at the end of the century (see Chapter 14, A), but in the interim, the US continued to have an interest in Panamanian stability and in maintaining their military base on the Canal. Arguably, the Canal was of limited strategic importance, with aircraft carriers too large to use it and nuclear submarines having to surface to pass through, but some US military leaders argued that, in the event of global war, it could prove vital once more. Indeed, one 1977 study warned that 'if the United States government were to relinquish control of canal operations, then it should be prepared for that day . . . when Washington would be forced to make a . . . landing . . . to regain control'.[44] Partly to please Carter, Torrijos claimed to be moving towards elections but was killed in an air crash in 1981. Presidential elections *were* held, in 1984, and won by Nicolas Barletta. But in effect the army continued to hold power, tolerated by the Reagan administration, which of course was determined to avoid a repetition of events in Nicaragua and El Salvador—especially given the strategic significance of the Panama Canal. The Panamanians proved a valuable channel for arms to the Contras and also gave diplomatic support to the US in its struggle with the Sandinistas. Particularly loyal to the Americans was General Manuel Noriega, Commander of the National Guard in 1983, who made himself dictator in 1986. Like El Salvador's right-wing leader d'Aubuisson, Noriega had partly been trained in counter-insurgency techniques at the US 'School of the Americas'; and he had close links to the CIA. Yet it did not take long for him to become an embarrassment to Washington, being involved in drug-trafficking, developing links to Castro, and murdering opponents. As elsewhere, the Americans tried to simplify a problem by personalizing it: Noriega was only one man and Panama had been unstable for years, but by mid-1987, his removal became a prime aim of Congress (despite its dislike of Reagan's meddling in Nicaragua). 'Noriega had supplanted Iran's Ayatollah Khomeini and Libya's Gaddafi at the top of American international demonology.'[45] On 26 June, only two senators voted against a motion calling for democracy to return to Panama.

The problem was that, unpopular as Noriega appeared to be in his own country, any US attempt to replace him was not guaranteed success and it could stimulate Panamanian nationalist feeling in an anti-American direction, perhaps threatening the security of the Canal zone. The US hoped that popular opposition might force him out of office, as it had done with Ferdinand Marcos in the Philippines; various plans were put forward for a transition to democracy and America sent diplomatic messages to the dictator suggesting he should go, with Reagan ready to barter Noriega's freedom from arrest for the end of his regime. US financial aid to the country was suspended in 1987 and other economic sanctions were introduced in March 1988, including the end of private bank loans. Panama, as a result, experienced bankruptcies and petrol shortages. In addition, the US sent covert aid to Noriega's opponents and encouraged the idea of a coup, but it was a Florida court—not the government in Washington—which, in February 1988, ignored the evidence of the Drug Enforcement Agency (which argued that he had helped break up drug rings) and indicted Noriega for drug-trafficking. The US government regretted the court's decision because, by threatening the dictator with up to 145 years in prison, it made him unlikely to strike a deal to secure his peaceful departure. 'The final break had come, but the indictment was unsuccessful to the extent that Noriega could not be brought into a US court without resorting to force in Panama.'[46] In fact, Noriega felt no need to resign, doubting that Americans would use force to remove him, despite the economic and psychological warfare techniques they employed. He secured foreign assistance from non-US sources and internal discontent remained at a manageable level, even when he annulled the result of the May 1989 elections, in which Washington had financed his opponents. With apparent American support, two coups were launched against Noriega, on 16 March 1988 and 3 October 1989, but both were failures.

'Operation Just Cause'

Whatever Noriega's resilience in the late 1980s, and however unpopular he became, the OAS (with its opposition to US colonialism) and the American military (ever fearful of 'another Vietnam') long resisted his armed overthrow. But as the 1990s approached, the US 'could not tolerate a drug-dealing dictator who, if left alone, would become responsible for the defence and operation of the Panama Canal'.[47] And in view of the lack of alternatives, after January 1989, the new administration of President George Bush began to consider military action. This was actively planned from October 1989 and on 15 December the Panamanian National Assembly declared a 'state of war' with Washington. The following day several American troops, one of whom was shot dead, were harassed by Panamanian troops and the day after that Bush approved 'Operation Just Cause', the invasion of Panama with the purpose of replacing Noriega—despite the danger that, if US policy did not alter, he might simply give way to another oppressive, unreliable dictator. The Operation went ahead, unexpected by the Panamanians, on 19 December, with 25,000 American troops, half of them coming from the Canal zone and half shipped in from beyond. The campaign also marked the first use of 'Stealth' aircraft, which could escape radar detection and which, at the end of the Cold War, underlined America's technological superiority over all other states.

The Americans lost only twenty-three in 'Operation Just Cause', a codename chosen (like later ones) for its propaganda value. In contrast to Grenada, the operation was based on extensive contingency planning and implemented very effectively. US forces seized key points throughout Panama, attacked military installations which remained loyal to Noriega, and quickly set up a government under those politicians who had been successful in the May 1989 elections, led by Guillermo Endara. Physical destruction was limited in the well-planned campaign and, despite several days of resistance by pro-Noriega forces, the Canal was reopened to shipping on 21 December. Noriega himself initially escaped, taking sanctuary in the Papal nuncio's residence, but he surrendered to the Americans on 4 January 1990 after they used loud rock music, which he hated, in an unusual demonstration of 'psychological warfare', to drive him out. For him, trial in Florida was preferable to a form of music he could not tolerate. (In 1992, claiming to be a 'political' prisoner, he was sentenced to forty years in prison.) Rather than opposing the Operation, some Panamanians demonstrated in America's favour, only complaining that the dictator had not been removed earlier. Later they also complained about the low level of American economic assistance to help them recover. It was not the first time that Panamanians had relied on the US to resolve their problems, refusing to risk death themselves in overthrowing an oppressor. The American public also praised Bush's action, giving him 85 per cent approval ratings. There were few ready, anywhere in fact, to defend Noriega. James Baker even wrote that, in Operation Just Cause, the US 'was simply enforcing the will of the Panamanians by restoring the legitimately elected government to authority'.[48] Moscow, of course, was currently preoccupied with events in Eastern Europe—on which, indeed, most world attention was focused.

But this did not mean that 'Just Cause' lacked disturbing elements. The operation was the largest-scale US military action since the Vietnam War, though soon overshadowed by the liberation of Kuwait in the Persian Gulf. It showed that Washington was ready

BOX 18.2

The 1982 Falklands War

The Falklands, known as the Malvinas in Spanish, are a group of islands about 300 miles from the South American coast, in the South Atlantic. The British were the first to land on them, in 1690, but the first settlement was built by the French in the 1760s and the islands subsequently sold to Spain. On winning its independence, Argentina inherited the Spanish claim to the islands but a British expedition expelled the Argentinians in 1833. Argentina revived its claim to the group in the twentieth century and took the issue to the UN in 1964, leading to years of fruitless talks. On 2 April 1982, an Argentinian force landed on the islands, seizing the capital, Port Stanley. Argentina was at that time ruled by a military junta, headed by General Leopoldo Galtieri, which was facing rising discontent due to political oppression and the effect of high inflation. The junta had hastily planned the invasion as a way to win popularity by exploiting nationalist feeling ahead of the 150th anniversary of the loss of the 'Malvinas'. They expected little resistance from the British government of Margaret Thatcher, which had just announced the withdrawal of its only naval vessel in the area, HMS *Endurance*. Thatcher proved unwilling to accept this affront to British prestige however, and a naval force was quickly put together to launch a re-invasion of the islands, 8,000 miles to the South. The European Community backed Britain with economic sanctions against Argentina, but most Latin American states strongly supported Galtieri's action and the US at first tried to play a mediatory role, reluctant to alienate either Britain or the Latin American states. Only on 30 April did President Reagan finally back Britain publicly, though the US military were already providing some assistance to Britain. Any chance of a peaceful settlement ended with the sinking of the Argentinian warship *General Belgrano*, on 2 May, with the loss of about 400 lives. An intermittent naval and air war then began, followed on 21 May by the first British landings on the islands. Port Stanley surrendered on 14 June. About 240 British servicemen died in the struggle for the islands, compared to over 650 Argentinians. Whereas the war helped Thatcher to secure re-election in 1983, the Galtieri junta collapsed, bringing a return to democracy in Argentina.

to overthrow Latin American regimes that it disliked even after the Soviet threat was removed and, in a sense, confirmed American contempt for, and desire for hegemony over, states in the region. 'One of the most striking facts about the whole episode was the extent to which questions about international law or Panamanian sovereignty were a non-issue in US policy-making circles.'[49] At another level, rather than demonstrating strength, it suggested limits to US power—the blunt weapon of intervention had only been used after covert action, economic warfare, and diplomatic pressure failed—and confusion in Washington's outlook—the Republicans had criticized Carter for allowing the fall of Somoza in Nicaragua, yet were as active as they could be in toppling Noriega, despite his anti-communism. It also showed the President acting without the need to consult Congress, in a way reminiscent of pre-Nixon days: 'On this occasion, as on others, President Bush effectively treated the War Powers Resolution of 1973 with contempt.'[50] As to the local impact, the OAS condemned the Operation as an imperialist venture, and in May 1994, Panamanian voters opted to replace the US-installed Endara with one of Noriega's deputies, Ernesto Peres Balladores. As in El Salvador, the extreme Right proved that it had some genuine popular appeal.

Visit the online resources that accompany this book to test your understanding and take your learning further: www.oup.com/he/young-kent3e

NOTES

1. Lars Schoultz, *Human Rights and US Policy towards Latin America* (Princeton University Press, Princeton, 1981), 346.
2. Michael Kryzanek, *US–Latin American Relations* (Praeger, New York, 1990), 76.
3. John Dumbrell, *The Carter Presidency: A Re-Evaluation* (Manchester University Press, Manchester, 1995), 159.
4. Frank Niess, *A Hemisphere to Itself: US–Latin American Relations* (Zed Books, London, 1990), 191–2.
5. William LeoGrande, *Our Own Backyard: The US in Central America, 1977–92* (University of North Carolina Press, Chapel Hill, 1998), 578.
6. Ronald Reagan, *An American Life* (Hutchinson, London, 1990), 239.
7. Quoted in Peter Smith, *Talons of the Eagle* (Oxford University Press, New York, 1996), 160.
8. Allan Gerson, *The Kirkpatrick Mission* (Free Press, New York, 1991), xv.
9. Walter LaFeber, *Inevitable Revolutions: The US in Latin America* (W. W. Norton, New York, 1993 edn), 277–8.
10. Raymond Garthoff, *Détente and Confrontation: American–Soviet Relations from Nixon to Reagan* (Brookings Institution, Washington, DC, 1995), 1140.
11. Coral Bell, *The Reagan Paradox* (Elgar, Aldershot, 1989), 113.
12. William LeoGrande, *Our Own Backyard: The US in Central America, 1977–92* (University of North Carolina Press, Chapel Hill, 1998), 43.
13. Richard Thornton, *The Carter Years* (Paragon House, New York, 1991), 511.
14. Alexander Haig, *Caveat* (Macmillan, New York, 1984), 122.
15. Quoted in Peter Smith, *Talons of the Eagle* (Oxford University Press, New York, 1996), 181.
16. Walter LaFeber, *Inevitable Revolutions: The US in Latin America* (W. W. Norton, New York, 1993 edn), 279.
17. William LeoGrande, *Our Own Backyard: The US in Central America, 1977–92* (University of North Carolina Press, Chapel Hill, 1998), 577.
18. Quoted in Robert A, Strong, *Working in the World: Jimmy Carter and the Making of American Foreign Policy* (Louisiana State University Press, Baton Rouge, 2000), 90.
19. Michael Kryzanek, *US–Latin American Relations* (Praeger, New York, 1990), 78.

20. John Dumbrell, *The Carter Presidency: A Re-Evaluation* (Manchester University Press, Manchester, 1995), 157.
21. William LeoGrande, *Our Own Backyard: The US in Central America, 1977–92* (University of North Carolina Press, Chapel Hill, 1998), 26.
22. Walter LaFeber, *Inevitable Revolutions: The US in Latin America* (W. W. Norton, New York, 1993 edn), 241.
23. William LeoGrande, *Our Own Backyard: The US in Central America, 1977–92* (University of North Carolina Press, Chapel Hill, 1998), 108.
24. Benjamin Keen and Keith Haynes, *A History of Latin America* (Houghton Mifflin, Boston, 2000), 570.
25. Frank Niess, *A Hemisphere to Itself: US–Latin American Relations* (Zed Books, London, 1990), 197.
26. Peter Smith, *Talons of the Eagle* (Oxford University Press, New York, 1996), 183.
27. William LeoGrande, *Our Own Backyard: The US in Central America, 1977–92* (University of North Carolina Press, Chapel Hill, 1998), 301.
28. Robert McFarlane and Zofia Smardz, *Special Trust* (Cadell & Davies National Book Network, New York, 1994), 67.
29. Walter LaFeber, *Inevitable Revolutions: The US in Latin America* (W. W. Norton, New York, 1993 edn), 307.
30. Thomas Skidmore and Peter Smith, *Modern Latin America* (Oxford University Press, Oxford, 1997), 343–4.
31. George Shultz, *Turmoil and Triumph* (Macmillan, New York, 1993), 426.
32. Walter LaFeber, *Inevitable Revolutions: The US in Latin America* (W. W. Norton, New York, 1993 edn), 338.
33. Ronald Reagan, *An American Life* (Hutchinson, London, 1990), 485.
34. David Ryan, *US–Sandinista Diplomatic Relations* (Macmillan, London, 1995), 135.
35. Raymond Moore, 'Foreign Policy', in Dilys Hill and Phil Williams (eds), *The Bush Presidency: Triumphs and Adversities* (Macmillan, London, 1994), 165.
36. William LeoGrande, *Our Own Backyard: The US in Central America, 1977–92* (University of North Carolina Press, Chapel Hill, 1998), 578.
37. David Mervin, *George Bush and the Guardianship Presidency* (Macmillan, Basingstoke, 1996), 165.
38. James A. Baker, *The Politics of Diplomacy* (G. P. Putnam's Sons, New York, 1995), 53 and 46.
39. Steven Hurst, *The Foreign Policy of the Bush Administration* (Cassell, New York, 1999), 23.
40. George Shultz, *Turmoil and Triumph* (Macmillan, New York, 1993), 650.
41. Benjamin Keen and Keith Haynes, *A History of Latin America* (Houghton Mifflin, Boston, 2000), 565.
42. Colin Powell, *My American Journey* (Ballantine Books, New York, 1995), 281.
43. William LeoGrande, *Our Own Backyard: The US in Central America, 1977–92* (University of North Carolina Press, Chapel Hill, 1998), 348.
44. Paul B. Ryan, *The Panama Canal Controversy* (Stanford University Press, Stanford, 1977), 155–6; but for a counter case see Walter LaFeber, *The Panama Canal: The Crisis in Historical Perspective* (Oxford University Press, New York, 1978), 222–3.
45. Larry Berman and Bruce Jentleson, 'Bush and the Post-Cold War World', in Colin Campbell and Bert Rockman (eds), *The Bush Presidency* (Chatham House Publishers, Chatham, 1991), 109–10.
46. William Drohin, 'The Development of US–Panamanian Relations', in Bruce Watson and Peter Tsouras (eds), *Operation Just Cause* (Westview Press, Boulder, 1991), 25.
47. Michael Hathaway, 'The Role of Drugs in the US–Panamanian Relationship', in Bruce Watson and Peter Tsouras (eds), *Operation Just Cause* (Westview Press, Boulder, 1991), 42.
48. James A. Baker, *The Politics of Diplomacy* (G. P. Putnam's Sons, New York, 1995), 193–4.
49. Steven Hurst, *The Foreign Policy of the Bush Administration* (Cassell, New York, 1999), 55.
50. David Mervin, *George Bush and the Guardianship Presidency* (Macmillan, Basingstoke, 1996), 168–9.

19

The Decline of the Cold War, 1985–9

Chapter contents

A. The Impact of Gorbachev, 1985–7

Gorbachev's 'New Diplomacy'

When Mikhail Gorbachev (see Box 19.1) became General Secretary of the Soviet Communist Party on 11 March 1985, he was, at 54 years of age, much younger than his two predecessors, Andropov and Chernenko, and he seemed destined to remain in power for some time. He was also twenty years younger than Reagan and soon proved able to match the US leader in the public relations field. Gorbachev's election as leader was no foregone conclusion: he had, after all, lost to Chernenko in 1984; there was, in the person of Moscow Party boss Victor Grishin, a hard-line alternative candidate; and much relied on good fortune, including the death of the conservative Defence Minister, Marshal Ustinov, in December 1984, and the unexpectedly firm support of the chair of the meeting, Andrei Gromyko, who used his casting vote in favour of Gorbachev. Thus, 'Gorbachev had won, but only by the slenderest and most artificial of margins.'[1] Then again, he was at the forefront of a body of opinion that had grown up within the USSR in the 1970s which was determined to break from the stagnation of the Brezhnev era, address the country's economic and political problems (the corruption and alcoholism, the careerism and cynicism in the Communist Party, the inadequate social provision, the inefficient industry), and adopt a more imaginative, less doctrinal foreign policy. 'Soviet economic growth in real terms had come to a complete halt', while 'the West . . . was conducting a . . . technologically sophisticated arms build-up', so the new leadership wanted to become competitive, in both military and economic terms.[2] Like many other leading economists, diplomats, and scientists, Gorbachev had lived most of his life in the post-Stalin era, was well educated, and had travelled abroad. He was a long-serving and loyal communist but also imaginative, ready to debate and explore new ideas, and confident too about pursuing new policies in a way no Soviet leader had been since Khrushchev.

Nonetheless, when the Politburo chose Gorbachev it did not expect him to pursue the radical course that he did. Gorbachev was expected to ease the stifling atmosphere of the Chernenko period, when would-be reformers had been dismissed from office, and he was expected to attack corruption, but he could easily have done this by his mentor Andropov's preferred method of tightening up the police state and introducing greater discipline into all walks of life. Why Gorbachev adopted his particular policies is not yet fully understood and interpreting his decisions is not helped by his enigmatic character, which made it difficult even for close colleagues to comprehend him. His early reforms were in fact quite cautious: in 1985–6 he '*talked* about technological innovation, about greater openness . . . about encouraging personal initiative . . . but made very little progress towards these goals'.[3] At first, he was probably genuinely uncertain about the direction to take at home and did show signs of using greater discipline: officials were executed for accepting bribes. He was also probably unaware of the exact scale of the USSR's economic inefficiencies. One of the features of the Brezhnev era had been the way figures on industrial output were massaged to suggest growth, when actually, under the central planning system, factories produced low-quality goods for which there was frequently no demand. It was a system that kept everyone employed, but it did not lead to competitiveness in world markets, and it was wasteful of raw materials (including Soviet oil reserves, which began to decrease in volume in the early 1980s). Two elements that Gorbachev did introduce quickly, however, were *glasnost*, a greater 'openness' about the problems of Soviet society, and *perestroika*, a determination to 'restructure' that society so that it became more disciplined and efficient. His aim was not to end communism, but to make it work better; and in 1985–6 his economic reforms involved little more than organizational changes and better incentives for workers. Political innovations were more far-reaching, with the replacement of many leading officials at the February 1986 Congress, the freeing of many dissidents, and suggestions of an increased respect for human rights. There were many hard-line opponents of these reforms and a reversal of policy was always possible, but in 1987 the pace of reform began to quicken and, arguably, to run out of control. It began, in June 1987, with the limited use of multi-candidate elections at local level, a reform that suggested alternatives to communist rule were now possible and that nationalist groups might challenge the unity of the USSR itself. Gorbachev then began to chart what has been called a 'path of well-meaning destruction', making him 'the Soviet Union's gravedigger'.[4]

In foreign policy, Gorbachev's first two years in power also saw mixed messages about his intentions, leading to uncertainties abroad, especially in the US, about whether a substantial change in East–West relations was possible. At Chernenko's funeral, Gorbachev called for an end to confrontation and progress on nuclear arms control, but even Chernenko had been a supporter of Brezhnev's détente policy and had presided over moves to restart arms control talks. Gorbachev inherited an ambitious defence programme, initially intensified the war in Afghanistan, and in 1985–7 continued to provide aid to Cuba, Vietnam, Nicaragua, and other less developed world allies (discussed in Chapter 19, C), all of which made Washington very suspicious. Britain's Margaret Thatcher met Gorbachev in December 1984 and declared, 'We can do business together.'[5] Her confidence that East–West relations could be improved had an important impact on both Washington and Moscow. After all, she was nothing if not a tough negotiator and an anti-communist, trusted by Reagan who, in his second term, was anxious to make his reputation as a peacemaker. At Chernenko's funeral, where Vice-President Bush represented America, Gorbachev was given an invitation from Reagan to visit the US for a summit. But many of Reagan's advisers were cautious about trusting the new Soviet leader and some were still determined to undermine Soviet power through a policy of relentless competition, especially in the nuclear arms area.

Gorbachev's early claims about wanting to improve the international atmosphere were good public relations, but on the surface little more. Thus, on 7 April 1985 he announced a temporary freeze on deployments of intermediate-range nuclear forces (INF) in Europe and offered to make this permanent if the US froze its deployments. He also suggested a freeze on strategic and space-based systems. But this was never likely to impress the US, since the Soviets already had superiority in INF systems in Europe and were trying, not only to maintain this, but also to forestall Reagan's 'Strategic Defense Initiative' (SDI) for a space-based nuclear shield. In his first letter to Reagan, Gorbachev emphasized the need to avoid nuclear war but wrote in terms reminiscent of 'peaceful coexistence': 'Each social system has the right to life, and it should prove its advantages not by . . . military means, but on the path of peaceful competition with the other system.'[6] Meanwhile, the USSR continued to devote a large proportion of its limited national resources to defence spending and deployed new types of nuclear missiles. Neither was the situation helped in Gorbachev's early months by the Red Army shooting, in late March 1985, of a US major, Arthur Nicolson, in East Germany or by the defection of a KGB officer, Oleg Gordievsky, to London in July.

After the collapse of the USSR, documents became available which showed that, behind the scenes, Gorbachev's early policy shifts were not mere presentational devices. He did wish to reduce arms spending, press on with nuclear arms control, and adopt a more flexible, less ideological foreign policy, the so-called 'new diplomacy'. He believed that 'a less confrontational stance towards the outside world would provide greater security than endless rearming'.[7] Even before he realized the full depths of his country's economic malaise, he hoped to end the confrontation with the West and reduce the danger of nuclear war. He also wanted to improve relations with China. It has been noted that, conceptually, changing foreign policy 'was much easier for Gorbachev than domestic change. It consisted of moving towards Western positions and hence it was easy to decide what the Soviet Union had to do.'[8] As time progressed, however, strong links developed between the new diplomacy and domestic reform. Gorbachev and his Foreign Minister, Eduard Shevardnadze (who replaced the veteran Gromyko when the latter became Soviet President in July 1985) realized that calm abroad would better help them restructure society at home. 'From the outset, it was clear . . . that the old methods of confrontation . . . were no longer suitable', wrote Shevardnadze. 'By remaining stuck in the old positions, we would not stop the arms race, which was bleeding our already anemic country.'[9] Also, an extension of links with the West, including greater trade, would encourage industrial competitiveness and bring injections of advanced technology. Yet there was always a danger in this: 'It also followed that if capitalism was no longer threatening, then Soviet society was no longer divided into . . . those who supported the Soviet system and "bourgeois subversives".'[10] Gorbachev and his aides were ready to concede that Soviet actions, not least in Afghanistan and the nuclear arms field, had contributed to worsening relations with the West and China; they knew that the USSR could not compete with the US in such areas as development aid and defence technology, and they doubted whether China and West Germany really posed a menace to Soviet security. Their new diplomacy was, as with domestic reform, uncertainly developed and was definitely not intended to lead to the USSR's demise. But it *was* intended to end the Cold War, to guarantee Soviet security via cooperation not confrontation, and to adapt to the realities of a multipolar, interdependent world.

Uncertain Steps to Engagement

Shevardnadze's succession to the foreign ministry brought a more human, if less experienced, figure to the forefront of Soviet policy abroad and one who rejected the logic of Khrushchev's 'peaceful coexistence' because it 'cannot remove the cornerstone of confrontation: the original premise that the victory of one socio-political system over the other is inevitable'.[11] His appointment was followed, in August, by the announcement of a moratorium on nuclear tests, which Gorbachev introduced despite the doubts of his military advisers. It had already been agreed in May 1985, after a wrangle over the venue, that a Gorbachev–Reagan summit should be held in November, in Geneva, and the run-up saw more, dramatic moves on the nuclear arms front by Moscow. On 27 September, Shevardnadze, during his first US visit, proposed the halving of the superpowers' nuclear arsenals, an idea publicly repeated by Gorbachev a week later. But the Soviets were always careful to make such a step conditional on Reagan's abandonment of SDI, which the President refused to do. In August, Gorbachev had insisted that SDI be controlled, declaring that without this, 'it will not be possible to reach an agreement on the . . . reduction of nuclear weapons either. The interrelationship between defensive and offensive arms is so obvious as to require no proof.'[12] Many US experts doubted the Star Wars project would come to much, and there was some public frustration that it seemed to stand in the way of a major step towards the reduction of nuclear tension. But, on 6 October, Reagan's National Security Adviser, Robert McFarlane, announced that the US now considered SDI legal under the 1972 Anti-Ballistic Missile (ABM) Treaty—a 'broad' interpretation which Moscow and even some of the US administration disputed. The arguments over SDI overshadowed the Geneva summit of 19–21 November, which saw no substantial progress. Reagan's offer to share Star Wars technology with Moscow, if it worked, was dismissed as naive. But the meeting was surprisingly friendly in atmosphere. It was the first such conference since Carter and Brezhnev had met in Vienna six years before, and the two agreed to meet again. Gorbachev noted that, 'our dialogue was very constructive and intensive, sometimes even emotional'. Soviet Ambassador Dobrynin felt this was a turning point because he sensed that 'changes appeared in the thinking of Reagan about the Soviet Union. He began to depart from unconditional confrontation and display some sense of realism toward negotiation.' However, Reagan merely felt that 'after almost five years I'd finally met a Soviet leader I could talk to'.[13]

By early 1986, the US government was deeply divided over whether Gorbachev's policy changes were substantial or merely rhetorical and what, if anything, was his international strategy. The CIA believed that he would have to make concessions on arms control in due course (as well as to embrace radical reform at home), because of his country's poor economic state. Gorbachev certainly proved able to retain the initiative in world affairs, offering, in a letter to Reagan of mid-January 1986, to eliminate all INF systems in Europe, followed by all other nuclear weapons by the end of the century. This effectively matched Reagan's 1981 offer of a 'zero option' on IMF. The price, however, was still the end of SDI, an insistence which only convinced Washington that the Soviets were terrified by the Star Wars project. Opinion about the Soviet leader was already beginning to fracture in Washington, however. Caspar Weinberger, Reagan's Defense Secretary, believed that 'Gorbachev is clearly adept at public relations in international politics. There is a great danger . . . that his approach will obscure the fundamental and unchanging nature of the Soviet system.' It was a view shared by CIA Director, Bill Casey, who still considered the USSR a serious military threat. But as early as May 1986 Secretary of State Shultz felt otherwise, telling a high-level meeting, 'My conclusion is radically different . . . The Soviets have lost the ideological battle. Their idea is receding; ours is moving forward.'[14] On 6 March, during the Communist Party Congress, Gorbachev had argued forcefully that nuclear defence was illogical and that the superpowers must agree to solve their differences on the basis of 'equal security'. This was another important statement because it suggested that, rather than the old doctrine of 'peaceful coexistence', Gorbachev now espoused genuine interaction with the West and China, no longer emphasizing competition but rather wanting to work with others to build security. Nonetheless, despite these positive signs, East–West relations worsened rather than improved over the following months. The date for another summit was pushed back because Gorbachev refused to meet Reagan if no concessions on SDI were on the table and hoped that the latter would be more likely to make concessions later in the year, as the Congressional elections approached. In March, the US demanded that the USSR's delegation to the UN be drastically reduced because so many officials were suspected of espionage; in April, Shevardnadze cancelled a visit to Washington because of the American bombing raids on Libya; and in May, the US accused the Soviets of being in breach of the SALT II treaty so that it too need no longer adhere to the limits. (The US actually breached the treaty in November.) The worst crisis, however, arose in late August, when the Americans arrested a KGB agent, Gennadi Zakharov, and the Soviets responded by seizing a US journalist, Nicholas Daniloff, who had unwittingly been used in CIA operations: the two were effectively 'swapped' in September, after which each superpower expelled numerous officials from the other.

Throughout these difficult months, there were, nonetheless, more positive signs. On 18 April, Gorbachev proposed deep cuts in conventional arms in Europe, and on 25 July, the US put forward a plan to eliminate all ballistic missiles—but since this did not offer anything on SDI, and since it would freeze US advantage in aircraft and short-range nuclear weapons, Gorbachev rejected it. The Soviet leader did, however, make progress on relations with China. In the early 1980s, Brezhnev had tried to reopen links to Beijing, at a time when Reagan was neglectful of Sino-US relations, but the Chinese were still concerned by the Soviet arms build-up, the Afghanistan War, and the Vietnamese presence in Cambodia. There were good reasons to expect an improvement in Sino-Soviet relations, however. Despite Reagan's visit to Beijing in 1984, the Chinese *were* disturbed by his anti-communism, the new US assertiveness in the world, and Washington's sympathy for Taiwan. On 28 July 1986, during a speech in Vladivostock, Gorbachev signalled a major shift of policy. He not only expressed a wish for improved relations with China, but also offered to reduce troop levels in Afghanistan and, on the Chinese border, Mongolia. This led to talks on the disputed Sino-Soviet border beginning in February 1987.

Superpower relations finally seemed to emerge from the doldrums on 30 September 1986, when Reagan unexpectedly announced that an 'interim' summit was to be held on 11–12 October, in the Icelandic capital, Reykjavik.

This was intended by the US as a brief, working meeting to prepare for a more substantial conference. Gorbachev had initiated the idea, hopeful that a personal meeting with Reagan could break the current deadlock in US–Soviet arms talks. Reagan hastily agreed in order to impress the public before the Congressional elections. But the Americans were again wrong-footed by Gorbachev, who arrived in Reykjavik with some unexpectedly far-reaching proposals. Now, he was not only ready to halve the superpowers' nuclear arsenals and to make an INF treaty, but to extend the ABM treaty for ten years (the US preferred five) and to make new concessions on the verification of these agreements. Previously, the Soviet's refusal to allow 'on-site' verification had always been a serious impediment to arms control. Once again, however, Gorbachev expected concessions on SDI and once again Reagan was not prepared to bargain. The earlier US offer to ban ballistic missiles was met by Gorbachev's demand that all categories of nuclear weapon should be destroyed. Despite an extension, the conference, hastily called and held in cramped conditions, ended in failure and recrimination, with the press generally blaming Reagan's SDI obsession for the breakdown. The President was typically unapologetic: when Gorbachev remarked, as they left the conference, 'I don't know what else I could have done', Reagan replied, 'You could have said yes.' But Gorbachev was determined to exploit his opponent's hard line, telling the Politburo, 'we have to score propaganda points, continue our offensive of enlightenment intended for the . . . public'.[15] Nor did relations improve over the following months. At the New Year, there was no exchange of messages between the White House and the Kremlin as there had been the year before. And in early February 1987, there was uproar in the US and European media when it was reported that Reagan was about to agree to SDI's deployment.

BOX 19.1

Gorbachev and Shevardnadze

The two men who dominated the foreign policy of the USSR in its closing years, were both identified as leading would-be reformers before 1985; loyal and long-serving members of the Communist Party of the Soviet Union (CPSU), but also firm opponents of inefficiency and corruption. Shevardnadze was born in Mamati, Georgia in 1928, joined the CPSU in 1948, and rose in the party hierarchy to become the First Secretary in Georgia by 1972. Gorbachev was slightly younger, having been born in 1931 in Privnolye, in the Stavropol region of southern Russia, joining the CPSU in 1952 and becoming head of agriculture in Stavropol region in the 1960s. But it was Gorbachev who came to national prominence first, being elected to the Central Committee of the USSR in 1971 and joining the Politburo in 1980. Shevardnadze only joined the Central Committee in 1976.

Between 1978 and 1985, Gorbachev was the Central Committee's Secretary for Agriculture, in which position he was critical of the inefficiencies of central planning and a close ally of Yuri Andropov who, as Soviet leader in 1982–4, launched an anti-corruption drive. Gorbachev failed to succeed Andropov in 1984, but did not have to wait long for another opportunity. In March 1985, he became General Secretary of the CPSU and rapidly began to promote other reformers. No appointment caused greater surprise than that of Shevardnadze to the Foreign Ministry, in succession to the veteran diplomat, Andrei Gromyko. But Shevardnadze had impressed Gorbachev in earlier encounters as a determined yet open-minded figure, and despite the Georgian's lack of experience overseas, they worked together closely over the following years to reduce Soviet involvement in conflicts in the less developed world and improve relations with the West. At home, Shevardnadze was a firm supporter of Gorbachev's policies of *glasnost* ('openness') and *perestroika* ('reconstruction').

In 1990, with the Eastern bloc breaking up, Gorbachev won the 1990 Nobel Peace Prize. But criticized at home for the 'loss' of Eastern Europe and concerned that the USSR might be heading back towards dictatorship, Shevardnadze resigned as Foreign Minister in December of that year. Gorbachev, who by then had become Executive President of the USSR, with an elected assembly, seemed increasingly uncertain about the pace of reform. In August 1991, an attempted coup by hard-line communists seemed to justify Shevardnadze's earlier fears. The coup, though defeated, effectively broke Gorbachev's hold on power and precipitated the disintegration of the USSR itself. Shevardnadze returned for a brief time as Foreign Minister in November–December 1991, but then focused his energies on the politics of Georgia, which now became independent. He was Georgia's head of state from 1992 onwards, being elected President in 1995 and re-elected in 2000, but popular protests led to his resignation in 2003. Gorbachev, in contrast, had very little political success in post-Soviet Russia. His attempt to run for the presidency in 1996 resulted in a paltry vote of less than one per cent and many Russians blamed him for their economic and political difficulties, even if he continued to be lauded in the West as a far-sighted reformer, who had done most to end the Cold War.

In retrospect, Reykjavik was not the disaster it seemed, for it evidently convinced Gorbachev that it was pointless to continue calling for the end of SDI. In fact, the US Ambassador to Moscow, Jack Matlock, believed that the summit had 'produced breakthroughs that cleared the way for subsequent treaties'; and even that it was 'just as well that no final agreement was reached at that time', because the eventual INF treaty was superior to anything that would have emerged from Reykjavik.[16] By now, Gorbachev was irretrievably set upon a course of decentralization and openness at home, alongside a freeze on defence spending and further steps to reduce tension abroad. His key initiative, on 28 February 1987, was to 'decouple' the INF talks from other issues and declare his readiness to sign an INF treaty regardless of what happened to Star Wars. This concession was publicly welcomed by Reagan on 6 March, but did not necessarily mean that the American was now in a dominant position: in November the Republicans had lost their majority in the Senate and, soon after, the administration was rocked by the Iran–Contragate revelations. Also, one of those leading figures who had doubted Gorbachev's sincerity, CIA Director Bill Casey, was forced to resign through illness on 30 January. The scene was set for the early conclusion of a major superpower arms deal and a general improvement in East–West relations which, within eighteen months, led some to conclude that the Cold War was over.

B. Is the Cold War Over? 1987–9

Gorbachev's Reforms Gather Pace

In 1987–8, although Western public opinion was very favourable to Gorbachev, Western capitals still feared that the USSR could revert to its old ways. It was still a centralized communist state and, under any 'realist' interpretation of international relations, it was unthinkable that Gorbachev would set out to retreat from positions of strength, weaken his country, and ultimately bring about his own fall. Such, indeed, was not his intention. But domestically and internationally, as he pressed on with new initiatives more vigorously after 1987, he began to lose control of events. His reforms at this time went far beyond his early, cautious experiments and have been called '*perestroika* mark 2'. They 'soon led him into uncharted territories, awakening suspicion . . . among some of those who had helped him come to power'.[17] At home, he finally introduced a major economic reform in early 1988 with the 'self-financing' system, under which state enterprises would become more profitable and efficient, making their own business plans, and facing closure if they did not succeed. Politically, following a special party conference in mid-1988, an element of choice was introduced into elections, held in March 1989, for a 'Congress of People's Deputies', which in turn elected the Supreme Soviet. Neither reform marked the abandonment of the command economy or the primary role of the Communist Party in Soviet life, but they were fiercely resisted in some quarters. The economic reforms, in particular, were modest and easy for opponents to undermine, yet provoked enough confusion for major shortages of certain goods to appear. Politically, the conservatives forced the removal of a leading reformer, Boris Yeltsin, from the Politburo in late 1987 but he was able to exploit the new openness to win election to the Supreme Soviet in 1989, where he continued to advocate a rapid move to market economics and pluralist politics. Others in the USSR wanted to divide up the country. The Union was actually composed of fifteen republics, in many of which nationalist feeling and dislike of Russian domination was strong. The danger, unthinkable since the 1920s civil war, that the USSR could break into several states, became very real by 1989. As early as December 1986, there had been nationalist violence in the Central Asian republic of Kazakhstan. The democratization process 'resulted not in a cleansing and strengthening of the Communist Party', as Gorbachev had hoped, 'but rather in a widespread defection from the Party's ranks', with anti-communist and nationalist movements emerging.[18] Whilst trying to reform communism, therefore, Gorbachev failed to foresee that *glasnost* and *perestroika* might simply provoke confusion, uncertainty, and opposition from various quarters from those who felt that changes went too far and those who wanted them to go much further.

In foreign policy, too, Gorbachev hoped for managed change rather than a revolution. His desire for economic reform was closely linked to his wish to match the West and continue to play a leading role in world affairs. But in the short term he needed to reduce the strains on the economy and pursue détente with the West. Also, he remained genuinely eager to promote peace and to remove the danger of nuclear war. In his book, *Perestroika*, he wrote that nuclear weapons placed 'an objective limit to class confrontation in the international arena' and argued that 'the backbone of the new way of thinking is the recognition of the priority of . . . humankind's survival'.[19] This implied that the expansion of communism worldwide was no longer a priority. When, in August–September 1987, there was a clash in the Politburo between Shevardnadze and the ideology chief, Yegar Ligachev, it was Ligachev, the proponent of class-based international relations, who was sacked. Shevardnadze's less ideological, non-confrontational, and non-militarist approach was now predominant. Gorbachev's and Shevardnadze's aims were to be achieved, however, by means which seemed to mark a retreat abroad and ultimately called into question the USSR's readiness to hold on to its long-standing sphere of influence in Eastern Europe. Gorbachev continued to restrain defence spending and used an embarrassing episode in May 1987—when a young German aviator, Matthias Rust, flew a small airplane through Soviet air defences and into Red Square—to purge the armed forces of his opponents, including the Defence Minister, Sergei Sokolov. Furthermore, on 30 May, the Warsaw Pact announced a new, defensive military doctrine, saying it would not start a war or be the first side to use nuclear weapons.

In the less developed world, the years 1987–9 saw important steps towards resolving the conflicts in Afghanistan, Angola, and Nicaragua, the most dramatic step being the Red Army's withdrawal from Afghanistan by mid-February 1989 (see Chapter 19, C). These moves in the less developed world were made without abandoning Moscow's clients: the communist government in Kabul eventually outlasted the USSR, the Popular Movement for the Liberation of Angola (MPLA) survived to win the country's first free elections in 1992, and though the Nicaraguan Sandinistas lost elections in 1990, they remained a leading force in the country's politics. But the general trend did suggest that, in order to pacify the West, Gorbachev was ready to goad his allies into compromise. And in Eastern Europe in 1989, when he was faced with the most serious crisis of all for Soviet power, he chose to abandon the Brezhnev Doctrine rather than rekindle the Cold War by using repression (Chapter 19, D). He hoped, perhaps, to replace the old division of Europe, between NATO and the Warsaw Pact, with a new united 'Common European Home', an idea first mooted in a speech in Paris in February 1986 and developed in Prague in April 1987. But, as with his domestic reforms, Gorbachev was not precise about what this meant and he tended, in practice, simply to press for the Conference on Security and Cooperation in Europe (CSCE) to be given a more significant role. By the end of 1989, though Washington deliberately avoided any overt triumphalism, it seemed that the Soviets had very definitely 'lost' the Cold War. They were out of Afghanistan, their days in Eastern Europe were approaching an end, and even the cohesion of the USSR itself was in doubt. It was inevitable that, popular as he was in the West, Gorbachev was blamed by his own people for his country's dwindling power.

Reagan, Gorbachev, and INF

In mid-April 1987, Secretary of State Shultz, the leading figure in Washington to believe that an arms deal was both possible and desirable, flew to Moscow to discuss the issue and propose a summit. Here Gorbachev continued his policy of offering concessions by saying the USSR would scrap its short-range SS-12 and SS-23 missiles, of which the West had no equivalent. Shultz was restrained by the doubts of others about the wisdom of a deal, but in May–June the Warsaw Pact and NATO alliances both approved an INF treaty in principle, and in August the German Chancellor, Helmut Kohl, agreed to dismantle his country's Pershing 1A missiles (with US-controlled warheads) as part of a deal. Gorbachev periodically raised SDI as a problem, and at one point threatened not to attend a summit without an SDI deal, but he also continued to make concessions, not least on his original desire to retain a substantial number of INF weapons on the border with China. The danger that SDI would produce a major technological breakthrough was reduced in late 1987 anyway, partly because of Congressional restrictions on its funding and partly because one of its key advocates, Weinberger, resigned in early November. The INF treaty, which virtually eliminated all nuclear weapons of an intermediate range, was signed during the Washington summit of 7–10 December, which also saw talks on regional problems, notably Afghanistan and Nicaragua, and led to expressions of hopes for a strategic arms reduction (START) treaty, despite the continuation of SDI. The INF treaty was especially important for reducing tensions in Europe, though there were some fears in NATO that it harmed the logic of escalated deterrence and flexible response. The Soviet leadership interpreted it as 'a major victory for the new thinking', but Weinberger described it as 'a monument to President Reagan's determination to regain our military strength', which had forced the Kremlin to strike a deal.[20]

BOX 19.2

The Intermediate Nuclear Forces Treaty

Signed in Washington on 8 December 1987, by Mikhail Gorbachev and Ronald Reagan, the treaty:

- eliminated all INF systems, mostly in Europe but also in Asia, these being missiles whose range was between 500 and 5,500 kilometres;
- included onsite verification and was to be carried out within three years;
- meant that the Soviets gave up about 1,750 nuclear missiles (some with multiple warheads) to the Americans' 850 (all single warhead);
- represented a real cut in nuclear arsenals and was therefore a true *disarmament* measure, in contrast to the SALT I and II treaties, which had merely established 'ceilings' on nuclear weapons and were thus *arms control* agreements; and
- ended almost a whole category of weapons, but only actually reduced total nuclear warhead numbers controlled by the superpowers by less than 7 per cent.

1988 was a difficult year for Gorbachev at home, as ethnic problems, conservative opposition, and shortages began to mount, but internationally it was one of great success, with US–Soviet relations almost approaching warmth. In the less developed world, there was a ceasefire in Nicaragua (23 March), an Afghan settlement was agreed (14 April), and accords were signed on Angola (22 December), while the Vietnamese began to withdraw from Cambodia. The steps in Afghanistan and Cambodia paved the way for a further improvement in Sino-Soviet relations, as did Gorbachev's readiness to eliminate INF weapons. Indeed, ironically, by the time Gorbachev visited Beijing for a summit meeting in May 1989, the Chinese were most concerned, not by the USSR's military power but by the danger which *perestroika* represented to communism everywhere. Diplomatic relations between the two were restored and Gorbachev undertook to reduce the Red Army on the border by 120,000 but the Soviet domestic reform programme had helped inspire dissidents in Beijing, who occupied Tiananmen Square during the summit. Meanwhile, the US and USSR had proceeded to ratify the INF treaty and another summit was arranged for Moscow, between 29 May and 2 June, to exchange the instruments of ratification. It was not possible to complete a START treaty before the conference because of the complexities involved. But the atmosphere at this, the fourth Gorbachev–Reagan meeting in three years, was the best yet and it had an important impact on Soviet domestic politics, as Ambassador Matlock understood: 'Gorbachev needed Reagan's endorsement and Reagan's visit to prove that his policy was bearing fruit. A successful summit would give him momentum for the Party conference, which, he hoped, would endorse a more radical course for reform.'[21]

Such a frequency of high-level contact had only been seen in the détente era of 1972–5 and, although Reagan himself would never use the much aligned term 'détente', he did walk through Red Square on 31 May and, when asked by a reporter about his 'evil Empire' speech, replied, 'I was talking about another time, another era.'[22] It was this remark which led Reagan's Vice-President and would-be successor, George Bush, to insist the following day that 'The Cold War's not over.' Five months later Bush was elected President and the key question was how he would deal with the Soviet leader when the Cold War, if perhaps 'not over', was clearly fading. This point was underlined by a remarkable speech from Gorbachev to the UN on 7 December, the first time a Soviet leader had addressed the organization since Khrushchev's embarrassing visit in 1960. Gorbachev's speech ranged from reflections on the way world affairs should now operate, including an appreciation of interdependence and a belief that freedom should be respected, to a specific proposal for conventional arms reductions, including a shrinking of the Red Army by half a million. It also included an important declaration that Marxist-Leninism was not an absolute truth, so that ideological conflict between East and West was no longer necessary. But later that day when Gorbachev met both Reagan and his successor-elect, Bush said very little. The Soviet leader was then forced to return home early because of a devastating earthquake in Armenia, and so was unable to fulfil his hope of winning Bush over to a hopeful, positive relationship.

Shultz, about to leave the State Department, was not without fear for the future: 'President Reagan and I were handing over real momentum. I hoped it would not be squandered.'[23]

Bush and Gorbachev in 1989

George Bush had been born into a political family and had considerable first-hand experience of national security policy, not only as Vice-President (1981–9), but also as ambassador to the UN (1971–2), envoy to China (1974–5), and Director of the CIA (1976–7). Cautious and pragmatic, he had doubted the wisdom both of Reagan's early anti-Sovietism and his later enthusiasm for embracing Gorbachev. As he had made clear in 1988, the new President doubted whether the Cold War had ended, and he preferred to keep the USSR under pressure while hoping that it would continue to change. 'The initial attitude of the incoming Bush administration towards the ongoing changes in the USSR was one of hope tempered by scepticism', with Bush later saying: 'I was probably less suspicious of Gorbachev than were others in my incoming team.'[24] His inaugural speech promised to maintain good relations with Moscow. In January, he gathered around him a group of old friends in key positions including James Baker, who had been Reagan's Chief of Staff in 1981–5 as Secretary of State, and Brent Scowcroft, back as National Security Adviser, a post he had last held under Gerald Ford. They kept their disagreements to themselves and appeared a coherent team, determined to improve on the hasty, ill-coordinated decision-making of the Reagan period. But to the press and public this did not necessarily seem an improvement. Rather than giving an active, welcoming response to Gorbachev, Bush set out on a three-month review of international issues, which was meant to clarify problems and allow for well-informed decisions, but which seemed simply to be wasting time. The 'impetus in Soviet–American relations was . . . lost as . . . Bush took time to reappraise his policy options.'[25] Baker did not make his first visit to Moscow until May and Scowcroft's first public statement claimed that Gorbachev was 'interested in making trouble within the Western alliance', adding: 'I think the Cold War is not over.' Scowcroft felt, for example, that in the less developed world, the 'few positive regional changes which had occurred . . . [stemmed] more from Soviet failures than from a general change of attitude about regional superpower competition'.[26] The review did not, as it transpired, produce any great change where US–Soviet relations were concerned. It concluded that Gorbachev *had* altered Soviet foreign policy and that he was the best leader to work with, but the future was uncertain and there were grave doubts about whether Gorbachev could stabilize and improve the Soviet economy.

Bush's policy review also meant that no progress was possible on the START treaty. Meanwhile, Gorbachev was upset that the 'Americans were apparently still influenced by obsolete stereotypes'[27] and he continued to win in the public relations stakes. He announced a major reduction of the Red Army in Mongolia in March and, in May, told Baker that there would be a large unilateral cut in Soviet theatre nuclear weapons in Europe. On 6 March 1989, NATO and the Warsaw Pact opened negotiations in Vienna on conventional arms reductions: these negotiations, which replaced the former Mutual Balanced Force Reduction talks, had been underway with little success since the early 1970s. They were renamed the 'Conventional Forces in Europe' (CFE) talks and it was clear that they would become part of a public relations battle, as Gorbachev would no doubt want to outbid Washington with concessions. Bush was determined to match his Soviet colleague on the CFE front, however, and by late May both sides were actually quite close in their proposals. Bush, with some trouble, persuaded a NATO summit on 29 May to offer a 10 per cent reduction in US forces, matched by cuts in other categories of weapons, all to be achieved by 1992. Meanwhile, in mid-April, the President had also begun a series of speeches in the US, to follow up the recent policy review. The most important of these, for superpower relations, was at the Texas A&M University on 12 May, where he revived Eisenhower's 'Open Skies' proposal to allow flights over each other's territory (see Chapter 5, B), offered to expand trade, and seemed to accept the waning of the Cold War by stating that America could move 'beyond containment', to a new policy, 'one that recognizes the full scope of change . . . around the world and in the Soviet Union itself . . . Ultimately, our objective is to welcome the Soviet Union back into the world order.'[28] Thus, despite 'the initial stumble of the policy review . . . by the end of 1989 the Bush administration had begun to develop a fairly coherent policy . . . based on the idea of "testing" Gorbachev and pushing him to translate his rhetorical commitment into concrete policies'.[29] As James Baker put it, 'Gorbachev was making powerful promises—and our job was to hold him to his word. The boldness . . . of Gorbachev's pronouncements made him vulnerable to being hoisted on his own petard.'[30]

The first Bush–Gorbachev summit was not discussed until July 1989, by which time there were already serious signs of difficulty for the Soviet-led system in Eastern Europe, which the US President toured that same month (Chapter 19, D). Bush wanted a conference, not to push the START treaty, which was still the subject of debate in Washington, but simply to re-establish relations on a private, informal basis. Some very friendly meetings between Baker and Shevardnadze in Washington and Wyoming in September gave encouragement to the idea. It was here that the Soviets finally gave up linking START to the scrapping of SDI. They also agreed to dismantle the Krasnoyarsk radar, the building of which had breached the ABM treaty. In October, Gorbachev agreed to a summit, and the date was brought forward to 2–3 December, partly because of the gathering pace of events in Eastern Europe. By now, Bush 'was convinced that he . . . should support *perestroika*'.[31] But it was hardly the most successful of superpower meetings. The venue, Malta, was as badly chosen as Reykjavik in 1986; storms in Valetta harbour made it difficult to travel between the US and Soviet ships which carried the two leaders. There were no substantive agreements, because none had been planned. But there was discussion of arms issues, trade, and regional problems, and another meeting was planned for June. By the time that was held, however, the political revolution in Europe was complete and few could doubt that, whatever the earlier doubts of Bush and Scowcroft, the Cold War had indeed ended.

C. Ending the Cold War in the Less Developed World: Afghanistan, Angola, Cambodia

One of the key features of international relations in the later 1980s, which stood in stark contrast to events of a decade before, was the retreat of the Soviets and their allies, Cuba and Vietnam, from the active policy they had adopted in the less developed world. In March 1983, Shultz had written to Reagan that a 'litmus test of Soviet seriousness in response to our concerns would be whether they are moving seriously toward a real pull-back from one of the positions gained in the 1970s'.[32] The Reagan Doctrine had been targeted at reversing the supposed communist advances in Afghanistan and Cambodia, Angola and Nicaragua. Under Gorbachev, the USSR was no longer willing or able to finance such commitments and the 'new diplomacy' called for tensions to be lowered with the West on a global scale. As early as October 1985, he told the Politburo, 'we should firmly adopt a course leading to our earliest withdrawal from Afghanistan', owing to the economic and political costs of the war there.[33] By the end of 1989, the Red Army had left Afghanistan and the Angolan and Cambodian problem seemed less acute. But this process of retreat was neither swift nor simple. Until 1987, when Reagan considered that 'we were at last seeing real deeds from Moscow',[34] important elements in the US government doubted whether Gorbachev was in fact ready to resolve Afghanistan and other less developed world problems; the US response to his moves has been described as 'reactive, cautiously encouraging, but wary';[35] and in all the places where a retreat occurred, the Soviets were able to secure some concessions to help their local clients.

Gorbachev and Afghanistan

Within six months of coming to power, Gorbachev looked at the option of withdrawing from Afghanistan and by the end of 1985 he had decided in principle to pursue this policy, hence his critical line on the war at the February 1986 Communist Party Congress. Here, as elsewhere, Gorbachev gave a new direction to policy after years of uncertain leadership. It has been noted that, 'One result of Gorbachev's reforms was to marginalize the issue and importance of less developed world revolutions . . . The 1986 party programme barely mentioned the less developed world.'[36] He had actually questioned the wisdom of the conflict under Brezhnev, when the high costs of the invasion were already apparent. It was a public relations disaster, upsetting not only the Western powers, but also China and the Non-aligned Movement. As an 'unwinnable' war, it demoralized an army whose conscripts already experienced low pay, poor training, and alcoholism: as with the US army in Vietnam, the Red Army's 'Afgantsy' troops—about 750,000 served some time in the war—generally came from poorer, less influential families and they soon felt both betrayed by their leaders and ostracized from society. Economically too the war, while (at 2 per cent of the budget) affordable, was an unwelcome burden on an already tottering economy. At home, the war became a symbol of communist failure and the need for reform. But Gorbachev did not want a withdrawal to appear as a defeat for the USSR. He needed to put the Kabul government in a strong position for talks with its adversaries on an internal settlement and he also had to consider the views of those Soviet hard-liners, including Gromyko and the Defence Ministry, who wanted to fight on. It was for these reasons that at first, in 1985–6, Gorbachev allowed some of the most destructive Red Army offensives of the war, with the use of special troops and aggressive new tactics, including the widespread laying of mines and the greater deployment of helicopter gunships, all of which caused high civilian casualties.

It was because of this intensification of the war that the CIA feared Gorbachev was determined to fight on and the US increased its aid to the Mujaheddin, up from $250 million in 1985 to $630 million in 1987, with similar amounts being provided by Saudi Arabia. One decision, taken by Reagan in early 1986, was to supply the Mujaheddin with advanced shoulder-held, anti-aircraft missiles, called 'Stingers'. Supported by Shultz, he did this despite their obvious US origin and Defense Department fears that the Soviets might capture, and copy, them. 'Unless we hurt the Soviets in Afghanistan', Shultz believed, 'they would have no interest in dealing with us to end the war there.'[37] The Stingers made it more dangerous to transport Soviet troops and supplies by air and proved a particular headache to Red Army commanders, but the idea that the missiles had a major impact on withdrawal is a myth: by the time the Stingers started to be used (after an essential period of training), around September 1986, Gorbachev was already preparing for withdrawal. In May, he had Babrak Karmal replaced with the more flexible Mohammad Najibullah who, though a former head of the KHAD secret police, had recognized that the communists could not win the war and was ready to attempt a 'national reconciliation' with their opponents. To this end, he offered a ceasefire, invited opponents to enter government, and in 1987 promulgated a new Constitution. There was now an 'Afghanization' of the war, with the Red Army lessening its involvement and handing areas over to the Afghan military or local militia. But the 'regime's wooing of the Afghan opposition had . . . only patchy results, in spite of war weariness and the toll of destruction'.[38] Meanwhile, there had been progress on the Geneva peace talks, which had been underway since 1982. In June 1985, both superpowers agreed to support the peace process, though the actual negotiations were in the hands of the Afghan and Pakistani governments. In December 1985, following the first Gorbachev–Reagan summit, the US agreed that it would guarantee a settlement so long as there was a timetable for Soviet withdrawal. And in May 1986, as Najibullah came to power, the seventh and last round of proximity talks between Afghanistan and Pakistan opened in Geneva.

Despite the apparent progress in 1986, it was only on 8 February 1988 that Gorbachev publicly stated his hope that Soviet troops would be out of Afghanistan in thirteen months' time and, even then, the moderate Soviet Foreign Minister, Shevardnadze, doubted the wisdom of such a declaration. For all sides, the peace process was surrounded by uncertainty. Hard-liners within Kabul and among the Mujaheddin did not want to talk at all, and the Afghan and Pakistani delegations in Geneva only met face to face on the day a peace agreement was signed on 14 April 1988 (see Box 19.2). Even Najibullah, who was told by Gorbachev in December 1986 about the planned withdrawal, hoped that the Red Army would actually stay to protect him. In Washington, the Reagan administration became divided between those who were ready to negotiate a settlement (and, until early 1988, even they had grave doubts about whether it could be achieved) and those who saw Afghanistan as a way to 'bleed' the USSR, forcing Gorbachev into ever more radical changes at home. The latter group doubted the wisdom of supporting a settlement and were determined to oust the communists from power in Kabul. A vital issue was whether, if peace was achieved, the US would end its assistance to the Mujaheddin: the danger that the US would continue such assistance was of concern to Gorbachev, provoking fears that he would not go ahead with a settlement; but the US Defense Secretary, Caspar Weinberger, was determined to resupply the Mujaheddin until the communists were ousted. In January 1988, Reagan said that America would only end aid to the Mujaheddin *if* the USSR ended aid to the Kabul government. The latter was a step Gorbachev would not take because the Kabul government—a legally recognized government fighting against rebels—would be placed in an impossibly weak position. If the USSR were not to appear a 'defeated' power, it was essential that Najibullah should survive. Shevardnadze acknowledged to Shultz that Najibullah might fall anyway, 'but nature must take its course after we leave and not be pushed by us beforehand'.[39]

Yet, in defiance of the views of Shevardnadze and the KGB chief, Vladimir Kryuchkov, Gorbachev *did* rule out the idea that the Red Army could return to Afghanistan if the Geneva settlement unravelled.

The Geneva agreement was only a partial settlement, which, to the benefit of the Soviets, kept Najibullah in power and eased the danger of Pakistani interference in Afghanistan, but which, on the negative side from Moscow's viewpoint, did nothing to end the civil war and committed the Red Army to withdrawal. It 'marked a major new stage in the Afghan struggle . . . Rather than guaranteeing peace . . . the agreement promised instability and indefinite warfare for the Afghan people.'[40] The fulfilment of the withdrawal promise, despite America's refusal to abandon the Mujaheddin, was one of Gorbachev's most remarkable decisions as Soviet leader. The last Soviet troops crossed the border at Friendship Bridge on 15 February 1989, having suffered 14,500 combat deaths in Afghanistan, 20,000 dead from other causes, and about 50,000 wounded. Just prior to this, anticipating a triumphant Mujaheddin advance on the capital, Western diplomats quit Kabul. But, to the annoyance of American right-wingers, the Najibullah regime did not collapse and it was the Mujaheddin who suffered setbacks in 1988–9, notably the death of their chief supporter, Pakistan's General Zia, in an air crash (July 1988) and the failure of their siege of Jalalabad (March 1989). Determined never to become directly involved in Afghanistan again, Gorbachev rejected pleas from the Kabul government to help them with air support during the siege, but he did resupply them with arms, just as the US and Pakistan resupplied the still-divided Mujaheddin. The Geneva agreement thus failed to prevent continued external interference in Afghanistan. Despite UN efforts and some desultory talks, it also failed to lead to an internal settlement. There was rather more success in resettling refugees: about four million, out of six million, returned in 1988–90.

Some progress was finally possible in September 1991, when the US and USSR agreed to cut off arms supplies to their clients, a policy which Pakistan, Iran, and Saudi Arabia also supported for a time. But the agreement only became effective in January 1992, by which time the Soviet Union had ceased to exist and the Mujaheddin were closing on Kabul. In April 1991, they had taken Khost, proving that the government could no longer protect its urban strongholds and, backed by the US, they continued to demand Najibullah's resignation. He finally offered to go in March 1992, on condition that a broad-based interim government was formed (as the UN had been working for), but in mid-April the Mujaheddin seized Kabul anyway, establishing an Islamic state amid chaos, violence, and continued tribal divisions, which made stable government impossible. Najibullah took refuge in the UN compound in Kabul, where he remained until September 1996 when a more united Islamic movement, the Taliban, seized the city and executed him. The Taliban had been backed since 1994 by Pakistan, which was increasingly frustrated by the failure of the Mujaheddin to work together. For a time, it seemed that the Taliban would unite the whole country but they met resistance in the north from one of Najibullah's former generals, Abdul Dostom, a champion of the Uzbeki minority, who defeated them in May 1997 at Mazar-e Sharif. In 1997–8, the US revived its efforts to end external interference in Afghanistan and form a coalition government. The Taliban's 'fundamentalism', their support for certain terrorist groups abroad,

BOX 19.3

The Geneva Accords on Afghanistan, 14 April 1988

The principal agreement was between the Afghan and Pakistani governments, who agreed the following:

1. They would respect each other's independence and integrity.
2. They would refrain from using force against the other.
3. They would not let their territory be used to violate the territory of the other or to encourage rebellion there.
4. There would be a voluntary repatriation of refugees.
5. There should be an internal settlement in Afghanistan between the Kabul government and other elements.
6. The Red Army would withdraw from Afghanistan within nine months. In addition, the USSR and US guaranteed the settlement but the US, in a verbal statement, reserved the right to resupply the Mujaheddin if the USSR continued to aid the Kabul government.

notably Osama bin Laden's al-Qaeda network, and Afghan drug production—all these continued to make the country of concern to Washington. Meanwhile, the civil war dragged on in a country which had already lost over a million dead since the communist coup of 1978, with the Taliban being resisted by an increasingly beleaguered 'Northern Alliance'.

Angola and Namibia

The situation in Angola differed from Afghanistan in that the Marxist government had armed support, not from the USSR, but from Cuba and about 40,000 of its troops. Also, in the 1980s the Angolan problem could not be tackled in isolation because, after 1981, the US and South Africa insisted on tying it to the neighbouring Namibian question. Namibia was the former German colony of South-West Africa which, after the Second World War, was never made a trust territory, and this led to controversy over whether its status as a League of Nations mandate under South African administration remained in force or not. In 1966, strong anti-apartheid feeling in the UN had led the General Assembly to terminate the mandate, thus theoretically placing South-West Africa under UN control. But in reality, the South Africans continued to occupy it and it was from there, after 1975, that they aided Jonas Savimbi's National Union for the Total Independence of Angola (UNITA) movement, which was fighting a guerrilla war against the Angolan government (see Chapter 13, E). After earlier hoping to annex South-West Africa, the South Africans accepted by 1975 that it ought to become independent, but they refused to deal with Sam Nujoma's South-West African People's Organization (SWAPO), which the UN accepted as the voice of the Namibian people. By 1978, UN-sponsored talks had led to a plan for a ceasefire between the South Africans and the SWAPO guerrillas (who operated from Angola), followed by elections and independence. But the South African government, under P. W. Botha, was unwilling to proceed while the communist threat existed in Angola and while SWAPO seemed at one with the Cubans and the Angolan government. Botha won predictable support in 1981 from the equally anti-communist Ronald Reagan and from then onwards the previously separate Angolan and Namibian questions tended to become linked in talks.

UN attempts to make progress on southern Africa failed in the early 1980s. In 1983–4, with UNITA in retreat and the US more active in exploring a settlement, the South Africans agreed to pull their own units out of Angola if SWAPO and Cuba did not exploit this: the Cubans should pull out of southern Angola and Angola should end its support for SWAPO attacks on Namibia. But this hopeful move failed to bring a settlement. The Reagan administration stepped in to support UNITA, the Cubans increased their troop numbers in Angola, and the Angolan government backed off from peace talks. At the same time, the South Africans offended SWAPO by setting up a puppet 'transitional government' in Namibia. For their part, the South Africans were offended when Reagan, under pressure from Congress on the apartheid issue, introduced economic sanctions against them, which undermined any US attempts to explore peace. Also important, however (and further evidence of the confused nature of American policy), was the UN Congress's August 1985 decision to repeal the decade-old Clark Amendment, which had previously prevented Reagan from providing aid to UNITA.

Among the lethal aid given by the CIA in 1986, using Zaire as a conduit, were Stinger anti-aircraft missiles. They helped UNITA to defeat a government offensive in southern Angola and helped convince the Angolan government of Eduardo dos Santos to talk to the US. US–Angolan talks began in 1987 and were joined by Cuba in January 1988. By then, of course, Gorbachev was anxious to reduce Cold War tensions and pressed the Cubans, whose presence in Angola he effectively bankrolled, to talk. In fact, Gorbachev's decision to pursue a settlement in 1987 was probably *more* significant than the military pressure now being exerted by UNITA and South Africa. In any case, in March 1988 the Cubans and Angolans scored an important victory, forcing UNITA to raise its siege of Cuita Cuanavale. Both the South Africans and the Angolan government were now keen to talk, not least to help their domestic economies. 'The warring parties mobilized ever greater resources . . . Yet they seemed to achieve less and less . . . In 1987–88, the . . . moment of maximum risk became converted into a magic moment of opportunity.'[41] As to the US, Shultz's strategy, geared as it was to dealing with a perceived 'Cold War' problem, was clear and simple: 'we tied Namibian independence to Cuban withdrawal from Angola'.[42]

The result was that, in May 1988, the US Assistant Secretary of State for African Affairs, Chester Crocker, along with the USSR's Anatoly Adamishin, helped broker a deal in talks in London, whereby the Cubans would leave Angola in return for a South African withdrawal from Namibia. By the end of August, all South Africa's troops were probably out of Angola, the Cubans agreed in principle to complete their withdrawal from Angola within three years, and a date for independence was set for 1990, following elections. A formal agreement on these lines was signed by South Africa, Cuba, and Angola at the UN on 22 December 1988, with Shultz and Shevardnadze attending to underline the superpowers' interest in a settlement. Both sides had gained from such a settlement: South Africa had secured the Cubans' departure from Angola, but Angola had the assurance that South African forces would leave Namibia.

In Namibia, at least, the settlement operated reasonably smoothly. Independence went ahead in March 1990. But an internal settlement proved more difficult to achieve in Angola. It has been argued that the incoming Bush administration, with its doubts as to whether the Cold War had ended, 'showed little interest in seizing the opportunity' for an Angolan peace, increased its aid to UNITA, and thereby 'ensured that Savimbi felt no need to go to the negotiating table'.[43] But James Baker has argued that he fully understood that 'by 1989 neither of the superpowers had overriding reasons for being involved in this conflict' and that the real cause of difficulty was the Angolan government's launch of a new offensive in December 1989.[44] Either way, by late 1989 civil war was raging once more. A UNITA government ceasefire in May 1991 was secured through the mediation of the former colonial power, Portugal. It was linked to a promise of elections and seemed likely to hold, partly because both sides had effectively lost key external supporters: the USSR was deeply troubled and South Africa was in the process of dismantling apartheid. But when the Marxist MPLA won the September 1992 elections, Savimbi refused to accept the result, and UNITA relaunched the civil war. By now, with the USSR gone, the US was committed to peace in Angola, and in May 1993 decided to give diplomatic recognition to the government, having withheld this since 1975. But an agreement on the formation of a government of national unity was only reached in March 1996 and it soon proved stillborn. In early 1999, the civil war renewed, but it finally ended after Savimbi was killed in 2002.

Cambodia

In Cambodia, or Kampuchea as it was then called, the Vietnamese continued to uphold the government of the Hun Sen with about 250,000 troops throughout the early 1980s, boycotting UN-sponsored peace talks and trying to extinguish Pol Pot's Khmer Rouge who, despite their genocidal policies in 1975–9, were still recognized as the legal government of Cambodia by China and the Western powers. About 300,000 Cambodian refugees had fled to Thailand, another government which backed the Khmer Rouge, seeing them as a barrier to Vietnamese expansion. By the mid-1980s, various intermediaries were at work trying to bring peace between the four factions in Cambodian politics, that is the Hun Sen regime, the Khmer Rouge, Prince Sihanouk (the former monarch), and another group led by Son Sann, who had joined with Sihanouk in 1982 to form a 'Coalition Government of Democratic Cambodia'. In 1984, the Vietnamese said that they would be ready to leave Cambodia (as the UN had demanded since 1979), but only on condition, first, that the Khmer Rouge were eliminated as a political force and, second, that China's borders with Vietnam and Laos were guaranteed. These conditions were not acceptable to China. But 1987–8, of course, saw key changes in Soviet policy towards Afghanistan, Angola, and Nicaragua, with a greater willingness to settle these issues and there was evidently pressure on Vietnam from Moscow to discuss withdrawal. Hanoi also found the occupation of Cambodia very costly and some Vietnamese troops began to leave in 1987. More withdrawals were announced in May 1988.

By July 1988, when the four Cambodian factions met in Jakarta, the general shape of a likely settlement was clear: the Vietnamese would announce their intention to leave completely, the internal factions would agree a ceasefire, a provisional government would be formed under Sihanouk, the factions would disarm, elections would be held, a UN peacekeeping force would be deployed, and refugees would return. But it took years to flesh out the details of this settlement. The key first move came in April 1989, when the Vietnamese, under Soviet pressure, announced that they would withdraw all their troops by September—a promise which helped ensure an improvement in Sino-Soviet relations at this time. In the middle of this withdrawal, in July, France (the former colonial power) and Indonesia began to co-chair an eighteen-nation peace conference in Paris. Here, the joint agreement of the five permanent members of the Security Council—something which would have seemed impossible four years before—was of vital importance. A framework document was completed by August 1990, in April 1991 all the internal factions agreed a ceasefire, and on 23 October 1991 agreements were signed which confirmed the ceasefire, the disarmament of the factions, the formation of a joint interim government, the election of a constituent assembly, the repatriation of refugees, and foreign aid programmes—all to be carried out under UN supervision. The settlement marked yet another boost to the UN during 1987–91, and the responsibilities given to the organization showed the respect in which it was now held. The Western powers would have liked to see the removal of the Hun Sen regime but it proved remarkably resilient, with a substantial army, and seemed the only barrier to the return of the murderous Pol Pot. Then again, as one study of Bush's policies noted, there had been 'Western victories' in Afghanistan, Angola, and Nicaragua; and of the four countries targeted by the Reagan Doctrine, 'only Cambodia remain[ed] under . . . a Communist government, and that conflict has been relegated to obscurity'.[45]

As with the Geneva Accords on Afghanistan and the Angola–Namibia settlement, the Cambodia agreements did not mark a complete victory for one side or the other. Hun Sen indeed proved better able to cooperate with Sihanouk (restored to this throne in September 1993) than did the Khmer Rouge, who—rather like Savimbi in Angola—refused to respect the results of the 1993 elections. For a time, a vicious civil war erupted once more, but by now there was little support for the Khmer Rouge and it was soon in steep decline. In mid-1997, Pol Pot was arrested by his own followers and sentenced to life imprisonment, after trying to eliminate some key deputies. The following year he died. There was a crisis in the new government, too, in 1997, after Hun Sen fell out with the royalist Prime Minister, Prince Ranariddh, forcing him into a short-lived exile. But Sihanouk, now King of Cambodia, remained in his position and Ranariddh was able to return in 1998. By then, too, relations had been normalized between the US and Vietnam and had greatly improved between the communists of Vietnam and Laos, on the one side, and the Association of South-East Asian States (previously seen as a pro-Western, capitalist organization) on the other. In South-East Asia, as in Central Asia and southern Africa, the decline of the Cold War had thus had a profound effect. The most astonishing effects of all, however, were in Eastern Europe.

D. The Demise of Soviet Communism in Eastern Europe

Eastern Europe and Perestroika

The resolution of the conflicts in Afghanistan, Angola, Nicaragua, and Cambodia could be seen as reversing the pattern of success for Soviet-backed left-wing forces in the less developed world, which had done much to bring about the new Cold War of the early 1980s. But the disintegration of the Soviet puppet governments of Eastern Europe in late 1989 removed a problem in East–West relations that had existed since the onset of the Cold War. Indeed, just as Stalin's imposition of communist control in areas of Eastern Europe occupied during the Second World War was central to original Cold War tensions, so Gorbachev's readiness to accept its removal was the most vivid evidence that the Cold War had ended. Yet when Gorbachev became General Secretary, the USSR's domination of Eastern Europe seemed as secure as ever, with the Warsaw Pact being renewed for twenty years on 26 April 1985, and the end, when it came, came quickly. Experienced diplomats and academic experts alike failed to predict the coming collapse even a few months beforehand, most adhering to the long-standing belief that any fundamental change in the communist system could only be effected gradually. As one leading analyst later admitted, 'I knew in the last months of 1988, that the communist regimes in Eastern Europe would have to change. But their swift collapse a year . . . later was impossible to predict.'[46] Bush's call in Mainz on 31 May 1989 for the Berlin Wall to come down—which merely echoed a similar plea by Reagan from June 1987—was timely in retrospect but not made with the expectation that it would fall within six months. Brent Scowcroft later candidly admitted, 'it would be gratifying to say that our Eastern European policy . . . had been among the catalysts of the changes' that came in 1989, 'It was not.'[47] Even Gorbachev's statement, in Strasbourg on 6 July, that force should never be used again in Eastern Europe, did not convince Western observers that the Red Army would avoid armed intervention to uphold Marxist-Leninism. Memories of Hungary in 1956 and Czechoslovakia in 1968 still carried great force. Yet by 25 October Gorbachev's press aide, Gennadi Gerasimov, had replaced the Brezhnev Doctrine of 'fraternal intervention' with the 'Sinatra Doctrine', whereby individual East European states 'did it their way'.[48] On 4 December 1989, a Warsaw Pact meeting condemned the 1968 invasion of Czechoslovakia, and the following day Gorbachev declared in *Pravda* that the Cold War had ended.

It is important to underline the point that it was only those communist states founded under Soviet domination which disappeared in Eastern Europe in late 1989. Two Marxist governments survived in the region who had long since distanced themselves from Moscow, and where communists had come to power in 1945 largely through their own exertions: in Yugoslavia, where Tito had shaped a particular brand of communism until his death in 1980, and in Albania, where the Stalinist Enver Hoxha had been succeeded by his loyal lieutenant, Ramiz Alia, in 1985. These communist systems would disintegrate over the following years. Also, even in the Soviet sphere, many representatives of the old regime survived, generally by turning themselves into 'socialist' parties (under various names). Sometimes they returned spectacularly to power, as in Poland in November 1995 when an ex-communist, Alexander Kwasniewski, was elected President. They may have been resented in the past, but that was partly because they symbolized domination by a foreign power: after the upheavals of the early 1990s they often came to symbolize stability and experience in office. In Bulgaria and Romania especially, some communists were astute enough to turn against the existing system in 1989 before genuine liberals gathered strength. Thus, one of Ceauşescu's ministers, Ion Iliescu, was able to be elected and survive as President until November 1996.

The reasons why communism was weak in Eastern Europe in terms of popular support are not difficult to fathom. As in the USSR itself, the system had never been legitimized through free elections; central economic planning in Eastern Europe had failed to deliver the same levels of wealth, health, education, and social provision which most people enjoyed in the West; and any idealism which once inspired the communists themselves had been dissipated by corruption and careerism. Unlike the USSR, communism in Eastern Europe had few local roots in the first place (except, arguably, among the heavy industrial towns of Czechoslovakia). It was imposed by Red Army bayonets and once it was clear that those bayonets would not be reintroduced it rapidly unravelled. A more interesting question therefore is why Gorbachev allowed the system to disintegrate by refusing to resort to armed force. But here, as elsewhere, the Soviet leader's exact motivations are difficult to comprehend. Indeed, where Eastern Europe was concerned (and in contrast to Afghanistan, for example), Gorbachev refused to turn his attention to the region's problems. Even before 1985, he was apparently a critic of Soviet domination of Eastern Europe, at least in its dictatorial form, and by 1989, he recognized that it placed a serious strain on Soviet resources, as well as embarrassing Moscow in its dealings with the West. During the critical year of 1981, Poland had cost Moscow $3 billion in support. 'Gorbachev regarded the Warsaw Pact as expendable because the strategic dividends that the USSR received from control of these countries were not worth the cost of the subsidies they received from the USSR in the era of *perestroika*.'[49] The USSR not only had to police and defend the region, it also provided cheap oil supplies and favourable trade deals. That Gorbachev had an interest in breaking down the barriers between East and West Europe was reflected in his talk about a 'Common European Home' in 1987, echoing as it did de Gaulle's ideas two decades before when European détente got underway in earnest (even if Gorbachev's ideas on European unity were never precisely explained).

But to the arguments that communism in Eastern Europe collapsed because it had no roots, or because the Soviet leader felt it a liability, must be added two other considerations. In the late 1980s, Eastern Europe saw both an intensification of its economic problems and a risky attempt at far-reaching reform of the communist system, a policy similar in fact to that which Gorbachev pursued in the USSR. Since the dawn of Soviet domination of the region in the 1940s, successive Soviet general secretaries had tried to mould it in their own image. Stalinization had been followed by Khrushchev's reforms, these in turn by Brezhnev's tolerance of divisions over economic practices. It was unsurprising, then, that Gorbachev should expect East European leaders to mirror his own policies of *glasnost* and *perestroika*. But, by now, the countries of the area were quite diverse in their economic and political practices, and reluctant to shift their own attitudes to suit Moscow. Gorbachev's policies simply provoked uncertainty and division. Would-be reformers were encouraged but, as in the USSR, they had their own agendas, geared to local considerations, and soon came to question the communist system itself. Communist leaders often tried to resist change but feared that Moscow would no longer back them and had no idea how to escape their economic and political sclerosis. In his memoirs, Gorbachev argued that Soviet intervention in the affairs of its 'satellites' had no place in his new thinking about world politics: 'Such procedures were against the principles of equality, independence . . . and full responsibility of the leadership of each country before its own people, all of which had been formally proclaimed even in Communist Party documents.'[50]

Finally, when the gathering crisis entered its decisive phase in the autumn of 1989, Gorbachev decided that he could not risk his improved relations with the West by turning to repression. 'If he sanctioned the use of force in Eastern Europe, it could terminate hopes of ending the Cold War.'[51] And if the Cold War was really ending there was no need to maintain a defensive glacis in Eastern Europe. Once the protection of the Red Army was effectively removed, most local communist leaders lost their nerve and then tried to come to terms with the new reality. 'The system expired and the empire fell apart because they had been drained of both legitimacy and power.'[52] Yet, while he won the Nobel Peace Prize in 1990, the results of events in Eastern Europe for the Soviet leader were mixed. 'The collapse of the Berlin Wall . . . strengthened Gorbachev's standing in the West, but it did nothing to help him at home', where hardliners blamed him for weakening the Soviet position in the world while reformers clamoured for greater change.[53]

The Soviet System Unravels

Ironically, liberalization in Eastern Europe took off with the greatest vigour in the same two countries which had been most affected by Khrushchev's 'deStalinization' process, Poland and Hungary. Poland had, of course, been the scene of intense anti-communist dissent in the early 1980s, centred on the Solidarity trades union. General Jaruzelski had restored order there by the use of martial law, but the Communist Party machine never recovered and Solidarity continued its activities underground. The country was, furthermore, heavily indebted to the West and its continued economic underperformance forced it, repeatedly, to reschedule repayments on its loans. Although he had successfully cowed the opposition, or at least dissuaded it from open revolt, Jaruzelski decided in 1987 to emulate Gorbachev and embrace reform. He not only advocated decentralized decision-making in industry but also multi-candidate (though not multi-party) elections and, in November, actually held a referendum on his proposals. This provided the ideal occasion for Solidarity to organize once more. Less than half the electorate backed the government in the referendum, and in spring and summer 1988, there were widespread strikes. In February 1989, after months of uncertainty, the government entered round-table discussions with the ever-influential Roman Catholic Church and, more controversially the Solidarity leader, Lech Walesa. This led to the dramatic decision in April to relegalize the free trades union and call elections for June, in which Solidarity did very well.

'The open, honest elections . . . proved to be a fiasco for the communists—a humiliating, definitive repudiation by the Polish people.'[54] Although many seats were 'reserved' for communists, by September, Jaruzelski had been forced to appoint a non-communist prime minister though, in Tadeusz Mazowiecki, a nervous and ineffective one. It was a key moment for all Eastern Europe, because it meant that the Warsaw Pact now included a non-communist government, the leading position of the Communist Party having ended. Yet Gorbachev accepted this with equanimity and from then on the pace of change in Poland was remarkable, with moves to a convertible currency, a market economy, and in December 1990 free presidential elections, won by Walesa. Poland remained reliant on Western financial aid and its people were so disheartened by the lack of economic progress that—as under Jaruzelski—less than half voted in the next general election in October 1991, but they had pointed the way for others to follow.

Events in Hungary moved hardly less quickly and had, if anything, a greater international impact. There were already signs of radical economic reform here in the early 1980s, before Gorbachev came to power, with reduced central planning, scope for private ownership of farms and small businesses, the closure of some particularly inefficient factories, and even the beginnings of a stock market. Yet this did not prevent growing indebtedness, inflation, and a growing 'underground' economy. There was also an experiment with political liberalization: a 1983 law allowed multi-candidate elections and in 1985 a number of independents entered Parliament—though they had to swear loyalty to the existing system. By 1987, Gorbachev had made it clear that he would accept further changes and the veteran communist leader, János Kádár, spoke of involving people more in decision-making. Opposition groups were soon openly tolerated and, as in 1956, the Communist Party itself became a centre of reform demands. The party replaced Kádár with Károly Grósz in October 1988. In January 1989, it was Hungary that became the first Eastern European state to promise free multi-party elections and to legalize organizations outside communist control. In June, Imre Nagy, the hero of 1956, was reburied, and over a quarter of a million Hungarians attended the funeral. By October, as in Poland, events were moving at a pace which was difficult to believe: elections had been set for March 1990, the communists had become the Socialist Party and Hungary ceased to be styled a 'People's Republic'. But Gorbachev signalled his approval of such developments by promising, in April 1989, to withdraw the Red Army from the country.

The liberalization of Hungary, which eventually led to a non-communist coalition being formed in April 1989, was doubly important because it was accompanied by the opening, in May, of the country's borders. This allowed thousands of East Germans to move into Hungary as the first step towards entering West Germany (via Austria). Until then, Erich Honecker's regime had been one of the most conservative in the communist bloc, resisting Gorbachev's reforms as irrelevant. East Germany was also the wealthiest communist state, in terms of income per head of population, but it had one decisive defect: its per capita income was less than half that of its neighbour, West Germany. 'The proximate cause of the . . . collapse of the GDR . . . was the Hungarian decision to allow German "tourists" . . . to emigrate over the borders with Austria. But there was an economic . . . frustration in the GDR which manifested itself . . . in the desire for foreign travel.'[55] In September, more than 10,000 people fled East Germany for the West. The gathering crisis provoked some concern in the US, where it was feared there could be a 'drawing of the line' by Gorbachev. 'Moscow had shown consistently during the Cold War that it would not tolerate a revived German threat', noted James Baker. 'This . . . made any change in East Germany potentially far more dangerous in terms of Soviet reactions than in any other country in eastern Europe.'[56] However, in early October, when visiting the country, Gorbachev—instead of urging a crackdown—accused Honecker of failing to respond to popular opinion. Opposition groups had already begun to form, mass demonstrations were being called in major cities, and faced by Soviet opposition to repression, the government belatedly began to reform. Honecker resigned in mid-October and on 9 November his successors decided to allow freedom of travel. For the rest of the world, this decision was the clearest indication yet of the collapse of Soviet domination in Eastern Europe, because it immediately led to the opening of the Berlin Wall, which had been the greatest symbol of communist repression since 1961. The opening was followed by serious consideration of German reunification.

In the wake of Honecker's departure, two other orthodox communist governments in the region also gave up hope, though in radically different ways. In Bulgaria, always very loyal to Moscow, there was a 'palace coup' against Todor Zhivkov, who had dominated the government since the mid-1960s. The new leader, Petar Mladenov, evidently had Gorbachev's support, promised reform, and easily won elections in June 1990 as head of the renamed 'Socialist Party'—though he was forced to resign soon after by revelations of how closely he had been associated in the repression of the Turkish minority and others in Zhivkov's last years. Bulgaria, like Hungary and Poland, has been described as a 'negotiated revolution' in 1989, because communist power had been surrendered with little struggle, in contrast to the 'last ditch' examples elsewhere.[57] In Czechoslovakia, meanwhile, another veteran leader, Gustáv Husák had initially tried to repress opposition in early 1989, only to face criticism from Gorbachev. Rather than a palace coup, the whole Politburo was forced to resign on 24 November, after days of mass demonstrations. But this did not prevent a general strike on 27 November, leading to the end of the communist monopoly of power two days later. Here there is 'thought to have been a KGB-approved attempt to provoke a minor crisis and install a reform communist regime', such as Gorbachev could cooperate with; but the pro-Gorbachev forces lost control of events.[58] The new party leader, Karel Urbanek, lasted barely a fortnight before giving way to a non-communist government. By the end of the year, Alexander Dubček, the reformist leader of 1968, had become the speaker of Parliament, and the best-known Czechoslovakian dissident, Václav Havel, had been made President.

The unravelling of the Soviet position took place without any superpower crisis. The CIA Director, Robert Gates, considered this was partly thanks to Bush's restrained response: 'He did not gloat. He did not make grandiose pronouncements. He did not declare victory.'[59] Remarkably, too, the only serious loss of life in these epochal developments occurred in Romania, a country which for three decades had tried to distance itself from Soviet control, under Nicolae

Ceauşescu, who posed as a defender of the country's distinct, Latin heritage. He had managed to repay the country's debt in the 1980s, but only at the cost of low growth, food shortages, and a dearth of consumer goods. He had also put down all political discontent, but only by vastly expanding the Securitate secret police and victimizing the Hungarian minority. It was this minority, in fact, which initiated unrest against Ceauşescu in mid-December, only weeks after he had been unanimously re-elected communist leader. Foreign allies, such as the Americans and British, who had previously lauded his resistance to Moscow, now clamoured for his removal, as did Gorbachev, whilst his colleagues among the Communist Party, as well as the army, decided to abandon him. Instead of being swept away like the leaders of Czechoslovakia and East Germany, some hoped for a transfer of power on the Bulgarian model. But, as the Securitate tried to repress the opposition, leading to bloodshed, 'Ceauşescu's overthrow could only be accomplished by force: the absence of a coherent opposition . . . the social and economic decay and the atrophy of . . . leadership …guaranteed this outcome.'[60] The army captured and (on Christmas Day, 1989) executed Ceauşescu, while his lieutenants formed a National Salvation Front. One leading ex-communist, Ion Iliescu, became President and at first violently repressed any opposition. However, when they won elections in May 1990, the National Salvation Front, despite their communist pedigree, emulated other East European governments by dismantling the centralized economy, embracing private enterprise, and accepting the costs of this in the form of inflation and unemployment, problems familiar to the West but novel in the former communist world.

Visit the online resources that accompany this book to test your understanding and take your learning further: www.oup.com/he/young-kent3e

NOTES

1. Mark Galeotti, *Gorbachev and his Revolution* (Macmillan, Basingstoke, 1997), 49.
2. John Dunlop, *The Rise of Russia and the Fall of the Soviet Empire* (Princeton University Press, Princeton, 1993), 4–5.
3. Geoffrey Hosking, *The Awakening of the Soviet Union* (Heinemann, London, 1990), 140.
4. Rachel Walker, *Six Years that Shook the World* (Manchester University Press, Manchester, 1993), vi.
5. Quoted in Martin McCauley, *Gorbachev* (Longman, London, 1998), 44.
6. Reproduced in Ronald Reagan, *An American Life* (Hutchinson, London, 1990), 613.
7. Geoffrey Hosking, *The Awakening of the Soviet Union* (Heinemann, London, 1990), 157.
8. Martin McCauley, *Gorbachev* (Longman, London, 1998), 77.
9. Eduard Shevardnadze, *The Future Belongs to Freedom* (Sinclair-Stevenson, London, 1991), xi.
10. Rachel Walker, *Six Years that Shook the World* (Manchester University Press, Manchester, 1993), 216.
11. Eduard Shevardnadze, *The Future Belongs to Freedom* (Sinclair-Stevenson, London, 1991), 48.
12. Quoted in Don Oberdorfer, *The Turn: How the Cold War Came to an End: The United States and the Soviet Union 1983–1990* (Jonathan Cape, London, 1992), 128.
13. Mikhail Gorbachev, *Memoirs* (Doubleday, London, 1996), 405; Alexander Dobrynin, *In Confidence* (Random House, New York, 1995), 564; Ronald Reagan, *An American Life* (Hutchinson, London, 1990), 641.
14. Caspar Weinberger, *Fighting for Peace* (Joseph, London, 1990), 233; George Shultz, *Turmoil and Triumph* (Maxwell Macmillan International, New York, 1993), 712.
15. Don Oberdorfer, *The Turn: How the Cold War Came to an End: The United States and the Soviet Union 1983–1990* (Jonathan Cape, London, 1992), 205; Martin McCauley, *Gorbachev* (Longman, London, 1998), 82.
16. Jack Matlock, *Autopsy on an Empire* (Random House, New York, 1995), 97.
17. Geoffrey Hosking, *The Awakening of the Soviet Union* (Heinemann, London, 1990), 141.

18. John Dunlop, *The Rise of Russia and the Fall of the Soviet Empire* (Princeton University Press, Princeton, 1993), 9–10.
19. Mikhail Gorbachev, *Perestroika* (Collins, London, 1986), 146.
20. Andrei Gromyko, *Memories* (Hutchinson, London, 1990), 343; Caspar Weinberger, *Fighting for Peace* (Joseph, London, 1990), 233; George Shultz, *Turmoil and Triumph* (Maxwell Macmillan International, New York, 1993), 246.
21. Jack Matlock, *Autopsy on an Empire* (Random House, New York, 1995), 123.
22. Quoted in Don Oberdorfer, *The Turn: How the Cold War Came to an End: The United States and the Soviet Union 1983–1990* (Jonathan Cape, London, 1992), 299.
23. George Shultz, *Turmoil and Triumph* (Maxwell Macmillan International, New York, 1993), 1138.
24. Steven Hurst, *The Foreign Policy of the Bush Administration* (Cassell, London, 1999), 23; George Bush and Brent Scowcroft, *A World Transformed* (Random House, New York, 1998), 9.
25. Martin McCauley, *Gorbachev* (Longman, London, 1998), 139.
26. Michael Beschloss and Strobe Talbott, *At the Highest Levels* (Little, Brown, Boston, 1993), 18; George Bush and Brent Scowcroft, *A World Transformed* (Random House, New York, 1998), 135.
27. Mikhail Gorbachev, *Perestroika* (Collins, London, 1986), 501.
28. *Public Papers of the Presidents of the United States, George Bush, 1989, Book I* (Washington, DC, 1990), 541.
29. Steven Hurst, *The Foreign Policy of the Bush Administration* (Cassell, London, 1999), 28–9.
30. James A. Baker, *The Politics of Diplomacy* (G. P. Putnam's Sons, New York, 1995), 69.
31. Jack Matlock, *Autopsy on an Empire* (Random House, New York, 1995), 271.
32. George Shultz, *Turmoil and Triumph* (Maxwell Macmillan International, New York, 1993), 266.
33. Alexander Dobrynin, *In Confidence* (Random House, New York, 1995), 442.
34. Ronald Reagan, *An American Life* (Hutchinson, London, 1990), 687.
35. Raymond Garthoff, *The Great Transition: American–Soviet Relations and the End of the Cold War* (Brookings Institution, Washington, DC, 1994), 748.
36. Caroline Kennedy-Pipe, *Russia and the World* (Arnold, London, 1998), 196.
37. George Shultz, *Turmoil and Triumph* (Maxwell Macmillan International, New York, 1993), 692.
38. Anthony Hyman, *Afghanistan under Soviet Domination* (3rd edn, Macmillan, London, 1992), 229.
39. George Shultz, *Turmoil and Triumph* (Maxwell Macmillan International, New York, 1993), 1086.
40. Anthony Hyman, *Afghanistan under Soviet Domination* (3rd edn, Macmillan, London, 1992), 256.
41. Chester Crocker, *High Noon in Southern Africa: Making Peace in a Rough Neighborhood* (W. W. Norton, New York, 1992), 464.
42. George Shultz, *Turmoil and Triumph* (Maxwell Macmillan International, New York, 1993), 1112.
43. Steven Hurst, *The Foreign Policy of the Bush Administration* (Cassell, London, 1999), 138.
44. James A. Baker, *The Politics of Diplomacy* (G. P. Putnam's Sons, New York, 1995), 599.
45. David Franklin and Robert Shepherd, 'Is Prudence a Policy?', in Ryan Barilleux and Mary Stuckey (eds), *Leadership and the Bush Presidency* (Praeger, Westport, 1992), 167.
46. Z. A. B. Zeman, *The Making and Breaking of Communist Europe* (Blackwell, Oxford, 1991), 312.
47. George Bush and Brent Scowcroft, *A World Transformed* (Random House, New York, 1998), 180.
48. He actually said 'had it my way': see Michael Waller, *The End of Communist Power Monopoly* (Manchester University Press, Manchester, 1993), 196–7.
49. William Watson, *The Collapse of Communism in the Soviet Union* (Greenwood Press, Westport, 1998), 13.
50. George Bush and Brent Scowcroft, *A World Transformed* (Random House, New York, 1998), 486.

51. Martin McCauley, *Gorbachev* (Longman, London, 1998), 135.
52. G. R. Urban, *End of Empire: The Demise of the Soviet Union* (American University Press, Washington, DC, 1993), xxxii.
53. Archie Brown, *The Gorbachev Factor* (Oxford University Press, Oxford, 1996), 239.
54. Joseph Rothschild and Nancy Wingfield, *Return to Diversity: A Political History of East Central Europe Since World War II* (3rd edn, Oxford University Press, Oxford, 2000), 230.
55. Geoffrey and Nigel Swain, *Eastern Europe since 1945* (2nd edn, St Martin's Press, London, 1998), 183.
56. James A. Baker, *The Politics of Diplomacy* (G. P. Putnam's Sons, New York, 1995), 161.
57. Michael Waller, *The End of Communist Power Monopoly* (Manchester University Press, Manchester, 1993), 220–6.
58. Geoffrey and Nigel Swain, *Eastern Europe since 1945* (2nd edn, St Martin's Press, London, 1998), 187.
59. Robert Gates, *From the Shadows* (Touchstone, New York, 1996), 449.
60. Jonathan Eyal, 'Why Romania Could not Avoid Bloodshed', in Gwyn Prins (ed.), *Spring in Winter: The 1989 Revolutions* (Manchester University Press, Manchester, 1990), 157.

PART VI

The Post-Cold War World, 1990–2000

The events of 1989 in Eastern Europe were not accompanied by an explosion of triumphalism in the West. From the point of view of the US and West European governments, this was deliberate, in that no one wished to humiliate the Soviet leadership for fear of undermining the position of Mikhail Gorbachev, who had seemed so essential to achieving the peaceful revolution in world affairs since March 1985. In order to move forward to a new era, it was important for the West to be seen as magnanimous and as the embodiment of a new conflict-free liberal international order. If international cooperation and broad-based government were now to be the norm, with less heed paid to the needs of individual states, it was important to attempt to integrate the Soviet Union into the new post-Cold War world. Moreover, the growing liberal perceptions of international problems, which no longer appeared to centre on power-political competition, required a more universal commitment to common (Western) values.

For a time, there was a belief, not least among certain US policy-makers, that the international environment was now guaranteed to evolve according to a Western agenda. The birth of democratic regimes in Eastern Europe, the continued reform of the USSR, and moves towards German reunification all pointed to a general realization of long-established Western aims in Europe. In a sense, the Cold War goals and what the US had tried to achieve by subversion had all been realized in a way which indicated, not just the superior attractions of Western commercialism and standards of living, but the superiority of Western ideas. State Department official, Francis Fukuyama, even boldly postulated 'the end of history'. He did not mean by this that there would no longer be an unfolding of events, or a cessation of international tension and conflict. But he did believe that the ideological struggles of the twentieth century had come to an end.

Bush and Clinton and the New World Order

The term 'new world order' actually began to be used in the summer of 1990, when Saddam Hussein's Iraq invaded the neighbouring oil-rich state of Kuwait, sparking the first major international crisis of the post-Cold War world. Significantly, the Bush administration did not rush to embrace the term and its exact meaning was never closely defined in any official US statement. But the President had pointed to certain features of a new world order in speeches he made during 1989, notably at the Texas A&M University in May when he accepted that the Cold War had ended and that the USSR was now a 'normal' part of global society. Bush therefore built on Reagan's success with arms control, by joining Moscow in pursuing the START process with greater vigour. This was one of the many factors in world politics from previous decades that continued after the Cold War ended, so that Bush's caution in modifying policy made sense: NATO and the European Community remained in existence and the problems of the less developed world were, if anything, more acute.

In political terms, the war to liberate Kuwait suggested the possibility of new elements in the picture: a renewed respect for, and greater unity within, the UN (where it was possible for the Security Council to approve the use of force against Saddam); an acceptance that the US held particular leadership responsibilities; and a readiness to respond forcefully to those who used aggression to challenge the new order. The routing of the Iraqis in February 1991 seemed to prove that such order could be successfully enforced, and future aggressors deterred from emulating Saddam. In a way, the agenda that America pursued in the wake of the Cold War was similar to that pursued at the end of the Second World War, when the Roosevelt administration had hoped to build future foreign policy around the UN, Great Power cooperation, and expanded world trade. The US would lead the world away from the old balance-of-power approach to international security and foster a 'universalist' alternative, with a reinvigorated UN and a new World Trade Organization. At the same time, again as at the end of the Second World War, it was possible to detect more ominous possibilities. In 1945, the US devoted a large amount of bureaucratic time to planning the precise nature of the post-war political and economic order it wanted to implement to best serve US interests—even to the extent of considering how the US might ensure that leaders agreeable to its interests might come to power in other countries.[1] Consequently, a lot would depend on whether the now undisputed hegemony would act in accordance with internationalist principles or with American interests, assuming the two did not mean the same thing. Many in the West, at the start of the 1990s, were too easily attracted by the idea that the world would be policed by the US, ignoring the fact that Washington might not be willing to bear the cost and the possibility that the exercise of American hegemony might not be universally welcomed.

In Europe, the fact that the Soviets accepted the incorporation of a reunited Germany into NATO further brought home the scale of the communist defeat. Europe was to be remade in the mould of political liberalism, linked to market economics. At a global level, poverty and exploitation would not only lead to their victims considering communism and socialism as impractical solutions, but also the 'revolutionary' factors in Soviet foreign policy would no longer be a concern. The origins and end of the Cold War were global, not European phenomena. Moscow's retreat from the Third World and the ideological 'victory' of the West promised a world in which both Western values and security interests were secure. 'Wars of National Liberation' would now be things of the past in India and Africa because, as in Eastern Europe, there was nothing meaningful in ideological or practical terms to liberate them from the values of Western capitalism.

The implications of all this were not sufficiently considered at the start of the 1990s. Just as the Cold War had often led those in the West to give insufficient weight to regional or territorial problems, so it had led them to ignore the practical problems of capitalism and to focus too much on its advantages, at least for those members of the developed world. It was now difficult for governments not to retreat from a reliance on economic planning, to embrace privatization, reduce state expenditure, and encourage free enterprise—as if these would automatically produce prosperity, now that markets were seen as all powerful and any form of state control was anathema. To a large extent, the collapse of communism and the embrace of free-market economics was seen as the way to enable the countries of the Soviet satellite empire to recover from the impact of stagnation induced by state controls, as if the only problems for the economies of Eastern Europe were government controls, and as if Stalinism was the same as the kind of mixed, but planned economy desired by social democratic governments in the West after 1945.

The problems of bringing the Eastern economies close to being able to provide similar living standards to the West were similar to bringing the war-torn economies of Europe up to the standard of living enjoyed by Americans in 1945. Except, fifty years later, there were two problems. First, the idealistic panacea of free-market economics had not been in vogue in 1945 and, second, massive aid from the US was made available to reconstruct Western Europe through the Marshall Plan which, while many governments would have liked to provide it in the early 1990s, important political constraints prevented them from doing so. Consequently, there was no Marshall Plan for the reconstruction of the former USSR or its satellites and the consequences have been at best mixed. The arrival of organized crime, significant unemployment, and greater inequality soon created dissatisfaction. In other words, the acquisition of greater political freedom and more consumer goods had come at a price. Arguably, this has also been paid in part by Western Europe, with the enormous resources West Germany had to provide for the East leading to a slowdown in overall German growth rates and the disinclination to use fiscal measures. As the German economy slowed, so did the rest of Europe and with inbuilt deflation, because of the reluctance to raise taxes or contemplate deficit spending. In a sense, incentives for cooperation were created when the Soviet threat was believed to exist, because taxpayers and national governments were more willing to consider making sacrifices for a greater cause than short-term self-interest. The future direction of Western Europe was uncertain in the early 1990s, as there was the possibility of the American connection being lost and the momentum for further integration was seemingly in the balance, partly because of the political need to incorporate the countries of the former Eastern bloc but at considerable economic cost.

US commentators hoped that capitalism would bring greater wealth and democracy would bring peace to Europe, with fascism, communism, and state controls assigned to the dustbin of history. Different forms of dictatorship might survive for a time, but they could not provide a long-term alternative to Western values, and it was arguable that the incidence of armed conflict would now be reduced, while 'general war' had become unthinkable. But while it was broadly true that democracies did not go to war against democracies, it was also the case that democratizing states were more unstable and warlike than dictatorships.[2] And, there was the all too obvious fact that, in parts of Eastern Europe, there were groups whose past suppression by the Soviets was not an unmitigated disaster from the point of view of peace and stability. Once the harsh communist controls were lifted, it was possible that groups previously associated with fascist or other extreme nationalists might come to power in former communist countries. The dangers of this, combined with the evidence that democratic states were war-prone, seemed nearest to realization in the former Yugoslavia. The moves under Tito towards decentralization encouraged the rapid acceleration of that process and the reduction of centralized Serbian power, which rapidly led to calls for independence from Belgrade. Led by the Croatians, and then the Slovenes, the march towards independence gathered pace and by the beginning of the 1990s had become a serious problem, focused on minority ethnic groups in those areas where secession had taken place or in Bosnia, where the complexities of the racial and religious mix made a simple political solution, linked to territorial division, problematic.

More significantly, events in Yugoslavia raised the question of nationalism and the relationship of society to the state. The idea that nationalism was a movement from below, which grew out of identity and consciousness of larger communities, was seriously challenged by the actions of Slobodan Milošović in Serbia and Franjo Tudjman in Croatia. The possibility that nationalism could be imposed from above by states, and the elites that controlled them, in order to build political support, was a concept which now had to be taken more seriously. The repeated reference to past Balkan conflicts appeared to divide communities that had lived together for hundreds of years and myths associated with identity, as laid down by elites, seemed potent even in a continent that had prided itself on the suppression of twentieth-century nationalism, which was interpreted as a negative and destructive force. The weakening of the state might not lead, as in Western Europe, to greater cooperation and prosperity on a transnational basis, but to violence and ethnic hatred, in which politicians could use nationalist myths and old experiences for political advantage.

By the mid-1990s, the feeling of satisfaction in the West had been dimmed and, instead of world order, many found it difficult to discern any pattern or system to international relations. Those who could discern a pattern were liable to be radically more pessimistic, and less 'universal' in their vision, than Fukuyama had been. Most celebrated of all, Samuel Huntington foresaw a coming 'clash of civilizations', in which groups of states would ally on the basis of cultural links, of religion or ethnicity perhaps, and would compete with other such groups for resources. This helped stir up fears for a time of a clash between the West and Islam, though this was as undesirable as it was unlikely, not least because Islam was itself a world of diversity and included some key American allies. The sense of confusion was not just generated by the lack of a central theme in world politics, such as the Cold War had provided, or by the bloody upheavals in the Balkans and Rwanda, but by concerns over the possible negative effects of what became known as 'globalization', and by doubts over the commitment of the new US administration to a just global order. After January 1993, the Clinton administration maintained some of the elements of the 'new world order' approach, even though Clinton initially seemed to have little personal interest in foreign or defence policy. In particular, America continued to seek the extension of liberal democracy and free enterprise ideals, whilst those who chose to oppose them were condemned as 'rogue states' and ostracized. This was seen most starkly in the Clinton administration's 'En-en' policy, which justified the continuing 'engagement' of the US in world affairs in order to pursue the 'enlargement' of areas under liberal, free enterprise regimes. Clinton recognized that, while the US was unique in its military strength, it could not contemplate isolationism because it needed to preserve access to global markets for its own economic good. The 'rogue states' that did not embrace liberalism included not just diehard Marxist-Leninists like Fidel Castro and Kim Il-Sung, but also countries like Iran, Iraq, and Libya, who were accused of backing international terrorism.

Even before Clinton came to office, however, there were signs that the American public were less interested in foreign affairs now that the Soviet menace had been removed. Clinton defeated Bush in the 1992 election by exploiting the slogan, 'It's the economy, stupid' against a president who focused on world politics while US living standards were stagnant. As to the New World Order and the 'end of history' idea, they were challenged by the start of vicious local conflicts in Bosnia, Somalia, and later Rwanda. These conflicts—especially Somalia, where a disastrous US intervention occurred—led some Americans to believe they should distance themselves from global affairs. There was no return to pre-war isolationism: it was recognized that US security could be threatened from outside, not least through the medium of international terrorism, which now touched America itself. Clinton repeatedly pointed out US reliance on exports, and the American people could still be motivated to act abroad in certain circumstances, not least by humanitarian concerns. But it proved impossible to develop coherent, consistent, determined US policies after the Cold War, especially when Congress battled with the White House for the control of policy. And Clinton himself soon began to see the economic difficulties of undertaking open-ended intervention, as in Somalia, on behalf of the world community, however humanitarian or altruistic such interventions might be. Any sustained, idealistic vision was potentially dangerous and military involvement had to be limited and given defined objectives. Clinton, in the wake of Somalia, laid down clear conditions relating to aims and an exit strategy for any future intervention on humanitarian grounds. Clinton was perhaps beginning the US move towards a more assertive, unilateral role in world affairs in which US interests would triumph over the idea of contributing to a new world order.

New World Order or Disorder in the Early 1990s?

The Cold War world has generally been seen as a battle, with weapons of mass destruction both threatening and keeping the peace. Power politics and ideology combined to heighten tensions which, if they escalated into war, would risk the future of the planet. In the West, fighting the Cold War was justified in the name of a way of life emphasizing political and economic freedom, and the importance of the individual. The end of the Cold War was expected to end the conflict between two contrasting ways of life, the confrontation of opposing blocs, and the emphasis on a bipolar world of competition. The post-Cold War world was anticipated in very different terms. Power politics and state-centric bipolarity would be superseded by a multipolar world, in which cooperative institutions of a governmental and non-governmental nature and organized more and more on inter-state lines would play key roles in a new international order. At the same time, the idea that America should take the lead in establishing a 'new world order' in 1990–1 became quite widely accepted, being reinforced by the continued difficulties of Gorbachev's USSR, which eventually disintegrated in December 1991, leaving what has commonly been perceived as a 'unipolar' world. By then, the Warsaw Pact and the Council for Mutual Economic Aid (COMECON), which had held the Eastern bloc together, militarily and economically, had also been wound down and a line had been drawn behind which old problems would disappear.

Such was the liberal desire to welcome this new order that the end of the 1980s and start of the 1990s have been seen as the start of a completely separate era, in which the study of contemporary history and international relations must be restarted afresh because of such a cataclysmic change in the nature of the international order. It is simply not viable to separate the Cold War world entirely from the 1990s and to assume that it needs to be analysed in new ways. There have been continuities as well as changes, and old problems, like poverty in the less developed world, how to achieve deeper integration in Europe, or how to control nuclear weapons, did not disappear. Yet the ideas of the liberal internationalists—in themselves far from new—seemed to have more scope for implementation, now that international cooperation was not constrained by the Cold War paralysis of the United Nations (UN). The acceptance of liberal capitalism was deemed to open new opportunities for a more prosperous world, with fewer resources wasted on armaments, and market forces being developed through international institutions and organizations working for the benefits of a global community. A globalized community was increasingly seen as an interdependent one, especially in economic terms, but also because of joint challenges like the environment. Conflict, so it was believed, would thus be less likely and greater prosperity would result from the acceptance of Western norms and political and economic values. The idea that such values were limited to the West, and had no relevance to many members of the post-Cold War world, was initially not much in evidence.

Nor was the possibility readily entertained that the loss of state power might have implications for stability and order. Values such as self-determination could be a double-edged sword. Eastern Europeans might embrace them, but there were many ethnic groups whose acceptance of controls and order had been the involuntary result of communist power. Now that it had evaporated, it was only natural that there would be competition and conflict over which group should inherit it, especially where racial or religious differences were present. In Europe, this was actually less of a problem than in areas like Nicaragua, Ethiopia, Afghanistan, Angola, Mozambique, or Vietnam. Capitalism, with or without colonialism, had done little for such areas in the past, and in the 1990s it began to look as if no easy solution would be provided by neo-liberal free-market economics. Yet liberalism and capitalism, led by America, held the field and appeared to offer the only viable model to which states would aspire. Those that did not, or did so without success, were increasingly marginalized. States may have helped increase inequality and exacerbate the problems of corruption, but the structural adjustment programmes of the International Monetary Fund (IMF) were seen by some as making a bad situation worse. In these circumstances, the struggle to gain advantage by seizing political power became more of an option and violence between groups competing for power became commonplace—hence the growing problems in Somalia and Rwanda, to name but two of the hardest hit countries. Even Europe was not immune from such conflicts in the 1990s.

There was also a sense that the very concept of security was changing as governments concerned themselves less with the military balance and territorial disputes, and more with such issues as trade, the environment, terrorism, and narcotics, challenges which were at once national and transnational. The communications revolution and growing economic interdependency appeared to challenge national sovereignty, leaving states at the mercy of global trends. Yet persuading the world's governments to tackle the pressing challenges of the 1990s in a cooperative way proved very difficult.

The UN, though it appeared better able to act now that the US–Soviet feud had ended, had always been at the mercy of its individual members, lacking strong, central institutions and primarily concerned with preventing recourse to war. It proved effective in supporting the war against Iraq in 1990–1, but largely because of the determination of the Americans and others to see the conflict through. In Bosnia, Somalia, and Rwanda, the story was very different. In the trade field, the General Agreement on Tariffs and Trade (GATT) was transformed into the World Trade Organization in 1994 but in some ways the world also became more fractured in commercial terms as, with US encouragement, a series of free trade areas was created. Partly inspired by the success of the European Community, but lacking that body's supranational elements, free trade schemes were pursued in North America, the western hemisphere, and the Asia-Pacific area. This was not the only way in which America's free enterprise approach, linked as it was by a desire to protect US interests, fostered certain trends in the global economy. Freed from the need to prevent Soviet advances in Asia, Africa, and Latin America, Washington also cut back even further on foreign aid programmes and demanded that the developing countries adopt liberal trade policies, privatization, and reduced government expenditure. Foreign aid declined consistently from a peak of $25 billion in 1985. By 1992, it had fallen by a third: US assistance to Africa was only about a dollar per person per year. Yet the free-enterprise approach worked no economic miracle. In 1997, Third World debt totalled about $2,200 billion (a 50 per cent rise on the 1990 figure), and one-third of the world's population lived on less than $400 per year.

The environmental challenges were faced at international gatherings in the 1990s, beginning with the vast Rio Summit of 1992, but the results, particularly in terms of cutting 'greenhouse' gases, fell short of what expert advice demanded. The major conflict centred on the differences between Washington and the less developed world. The latter was reluctant to constrain its development without compensation, given that the industrialized nations of the northern hemisphere had been able to industrialize without the environmental constraints that less developed nations were now being required to adopt. The split in the Western world was characterized in terms of the 'modernists' versus the 'eco-radicals'.[3] The 'modernists' foresaw environmental problems being overcome by technological advances that will avoid the destruction of the environment, while the eco-radicals saw the problems as insurmountable. Population growth and the needs of an increasingly consumer-orientated global society, they claimed, would ultimately exhaust the planet's natural resources unless the lifestyles prevalent in the developed world, and sought in many parts of the less developed world, were radically changed. Sustainable development that would enable greater harmony to exist between man and nature must become a goal. Yet the problems of how best to create any form of development in many areas of the world lacking significant industrialization remains unsolved. Those that did manage to achieve breakthroughs into modern industrial economies as in South Korea, Singapore, and Taiwan did so by state controls and going against the neo-liberal consensus. As soil erosion afflicts so many poorer countries and the production of agricultural surpluses becomes ever more difficult, the impact of new technology may be reduced significantly.

Globalization

Comprehending the post-Cold War world was made more difficult by the fact that globalization (which called into question the value of the nation state for the management of political, economic, and social life) moved to the fore just as ethnicity and nationalism seemed to find a new potency in areas like the former USSR, the former Yugoslavia, and Central Africa. Globalization is perhaps best defined as a 'significant shift in the spatial reach of social action and organisation'.[4] The obvious changes in technology and communication have reduced the distances between large areas of the globe. Consequently, the state has shrunk in comparison to the region and greater interregional flows of people, goods, and ideas have taken place. The market has been at the heart of this as old structures are replaced by new networks of power, and advocates of globalization's importance focus on the changes to the prevailing modes of socio-economic organization, the loss of power as embodied and exercised by the state, and the growing insignificance of the territorial state as the basis of international relations. This organizational base is thus being replaced by new social, economic, and political links and the role of the individual assumes new importance as the boundaries within which human activity was formerly contained disappear. Globalization for its advocates spells real change in the 'scale of modern social organization'.[5]

Others dispute the value of a term a such as globalization on the grounds that the nineteenth-century changes which brought in railways, the steamship, and the telegraph were more significant in reducing distance and bringing different parts of the globe closer together. To be able to travel from New York to Chicago in hours rather than days, for example, may have had a more dramatic impact on societal relations than even air travel. In addition, there remain parts of the earth where developments in technology such as the use of the internet and improved travel and communications have had little impact. Therefore, the global element of globalization is inaccurate with regard to place, if not time, critics of the concept argue, hence the claims that Westernization is a more apt description of the changes at the end of the twentieth century than globalization. The end of the Cold War simply ensured that the values and lifestyles of the victors would be diffused throughout the globe much more effectively.[6] Thus, globalization is seen as an ideological construct to carry forward neo-liberal ideas and explain the benefits of international capitalism in the post-Cold War world.

If this is the case, it follows that in the areas of media and communications there has been an expansion in the availability of information, but a reduction in its breadth and variety. The dominance of global media conglomerates, with narrowly based ownership, has developed an approach that claims to represent a consensus of a particular Western type. Consequently, knowledge may not have broadened, but narrowed, while being transmitted more widely in a way that justifies a particular view of society and international affairs. An appreciation of global diversity should not be assumed to accompany globalization. At the same time, it becomes possible to escape from reality more easily than to understand it. The lives of characters in soap operas and participants in game shows help to prevent the questioning of the neo-liberal consensus, whether or not history is assumed to have 'ended', as Fukuyama claimed.

In economic terms, the idea of a globalized economy had been taking root since the mid-1980s, not least because the volume of international production (companies based in one state producing goods in another state) had overtaken the volume of international trade. Multinational enterprises, cross-border banking services, information technology, and cultural diffusion were all part of a process that broke down national differences and trade barriers. They could be seen as the further development of liberal theories emphasizing the value of an interdependent world and the erosion of national forces with the increasing transnational focus of trade and finance.

Order and Disorder

Whatever the sense of disorder in the 1990s, the fact was that the post-Cold War world did have elements of stability and hope. For one thing, there was clearly only one superpower that at least aspired to uphold values other than state interest. Russia, though it could potentially cause problems for the US, in areas like the former Yugoslavia and the Middle East, was militarily and economically weak, a shadow of the old Soviet power. There were also signs, in certain regions, that the hopes of 1989–91 for a more peaceful, stable world were not mere illusions. Particular encouragement came from the end of apartheid in South Africa, the beginnings of an Israeli–Palestinian dialogue, and moves towards a settlement of Northern Ireland's inter-communal strife. Globalization offered new opportunities for greater knowledge, experience, and understanding. Yet such changes could be interpreted in both positive and negative ways, and could be seen as bringing advantages and disadvantages.

America's technological prowess, its economic wealth, and its military reach had never been greater and it *was* able to secure some of its aims in world affairs. But this might not be such an unmitigated benefit as was often assumed in the West. The crucial issues related to the extent and nature of American hegemony that provided the means to achieve this. The more dominant the US and the more generally beneficial its vision of world order based on American values, the more ordered and secure the world would become in comparison with the Cold War period. Yet, if this hegemony was threatened by countervailing forces, as in the Cold War, then instability might increase. In addition, as was shown after 2001, the US might decide to act unilaterally, to exploit its power in selfish and arrogant ways that sought to preserve America's significant economic and military advantages. The sources of opposition to the exercise of American power would then become more diverse than state-sponsored communism and less easy to contain through the exercise of state power.

The diverse nature of many intra-state conflicts and the loss of state control over some aspects of warfare, along with the problems of fighting so-called 'low-intensity conflicts' eventually imposed a heavy price on the US and its allies, in Iraq and Afghanistan. But danger signs were there in the 1990s. With conflicts becoming more difficult to control, especially in less developed parts of the world, it became more important to ensure that means were found to reduce their impact. Access to weapons of mass destruction, or to the nuclear technology of the former Soviet Union, added to the fears of increasing insecurity. Without the repression or discipline of the Cold War, new threats emerged. Even before 9/11, there were suicide bombs (in the Arab–Israeli conflict), the increasing commitment to mass killing by international terrorists (al-Qaeda already existed), important intra-state conflicts (as in Yugoslavia), and violent disputes over political power at local levels, too often with a strong ethnic element (as in Rwanda or Bosnia). Such problems did not appear so apocalyptic or simplistic as Huntington's clash of civilizations, but they may have been responses to a globalized world, where a sense of community based on shared experiences was replaced by new sources of identity, as well as by resentment at the lack of economic and political power. As old sources of identity were lost and new ones invented, they gave rise to greater economic and political expectations. In Serbia and Croatia, a sense of national identity could be invented and imposed by ruthless leaders out to seize political power in ways far more dangerous than those of the past.

In some ways, the new types of conflict and instability were related to the consequences both of globalization and liberalism. For many liberals, even those not of the 'neo' persuasion, the end of a world order based on state power was welcomed. Interdependence was seen as strengthening the bonds of the global community; wars would become even more disastrous irrespective of the role of nuclear weapons. Regional groups would erode nationalism as people developed transnational links in economic and political terms. Foreign policy-makers would focus less on narrow national interests, as they were continually required to work closely with their counterparts in regional or global organizations. A broader understanding of global problems would follow from such links as the world became a more closely interconnected and cooperative place. Regimes would develop as norms and customs became more widespread and worked for the general good. The influence of non-governmental organizations (NGOs) would add knowledge and experience to international discourse and work for the benefit of humanity, rather than for particular interests. International society would become more firmly established as power-political rivalries, ostensibly part of the Cold War, no longer troubled world peace. Americans would strive to bring a sense of unity and purpose to foreign affairs in a new world order and display a readiness to make sacrifices. Firm US action was self-evidently successful in the first part of the decade in the 1994 invasion of Haiti and the 1995 Dayton Accords, which settled the Bosnian conflict and might therefore form a key element in the twenty-first century.

Somalia, however, told a different story and could be seen as a precursor for the increasing collapse of so-called 'failed states', other examples being Sierra Leone and Liberia. The phenomenon of failed states could be tied to the neo-liberal global economy based on the Washington consensus of balanced budgets, low government expenditure, and conformity to the iron law of the market. The process of state collapse could be seen as the further extension and enforcement of Western domination, as expressed in the interests of multinational capital, and could constitute the latest manifestation of Western imperialism. The world's poorest countries continued to get poorer, in both relative and absolute terms, and in many parts of Africa death rates were rising, helped by the impact of incurable diseases, most noticeably Aids. Terms of trade showed little sign of moving in ways that benefited producers in poorer countries.

On the other hand, many were convinced that, by encouraging free trade agreements and ensuring that the IMF and World Bank support its free enterprise model of economic development with technological and scientific advances, prosperity would become more widespread. The Western world as a whole continued to hold together and saw its ideals develop in all continents. In some ways, in fact, the world was a more hopeful place for the Western powers in 2000 than had seemed likely when the Cold War ended. Then there had been predictions of trade wars between America and Japan, and between America and the European Community, but they had not yet broken out, despite some points of tension. Capitalism and democracy survived and were strengthened in much of Eastern Europe, despite predictions of poverty, anarchy, and a return to dictatorships. Liberal political ideals also seemed to gain new life in Latin America where, among others, the Pinochet dictatorship in Chile came to an end in 1991.

After 1991, one could look back on the Cold War as a period of certainty, in which the Western and Eastern blocs knew who their enemies were, with the tension between them creating a (supposedly) stable balance, and in which leaders in the less developed world had been able to play off Moscow and Washington in order to gain development aid. Much of the Cold War was a battle about ideas and rival social and economic orders, but sometimes conveniently forgotten were the elements of instability in the Cold War years. The power rivalries in Asia and Africa, which treated developing nations as pawns in a greater game, turned Korea, Indo-China, and Angola at various points into war zones. And there was frequent confusion in US and Western policy (Vietnam being only the worst example), oppression in the Eastern bloc, and the ever-present danger of nuclear Armageddon. The post-Cold War world may have seemed disorderly, unfamiliar, and frightening, But so too, to take just one example, had the mid-1970s, when the Middle East War threatened to drag in the superpowers and the ensuing oil price rises had thrown the international economy into the doldrums. Prospects looked somewhat less rosy when, in 1997–8, a new economic crisis, sparked by problems in East Asia, struck, which seemed to presage a worldwide depression and widespread political upheaval, including Russia, and there was a major crisis in South Asia when India and Pakistan, still at loggerheads over Kashmir, both tested nuclear bombs. But even the fears justified by these events proved short-lived. Economies recovered; there was no war in South Asia. Compared with the early decades of the twenty-first century, the 1990s may even be seen as a period of relative calm in global terms, when no major war threatened, international crises were kept localized and liberal ideals advanced in all continents. They seemed an era of calm, too, compared with the problems sparked by al-Qaeda's attacks on the US on 11 September 2001.

Visit the online resources that accompany this book to test your understanding and take your learning further: www.oup.com/he/young-kent3e

NOTES

1. Minutes of the Advisory Committee on Postwar Foreign Policy, 12 February 1942, Notter files, box 54. We are indebted to Chris O'Sullivan for this reference.
2. Edward D. Mansfield, Jack Snyder, and A. Wendt, 'Democratisation and the Danger of War', *International Security*, 201 (1995).
3. This is the idea of Robert Jackson and Georg Sorenson, in *Introduction to International Relations Theories and Approaches* (2nd edn, Oxford University Press, Oxford, 2003), 271.
4. D. Held and Anthony McGrew, 'The Great Globalisation Debate', in D. Held and Anthony McGrew (eds), *The Global Transformations Reader* (Polity Press, Cambridge, 2000), 3.
5. ibid., 6–8.
6. See D. Reynolds, *One World Divisible a Global History since 1945* (Allen Lane, Penguin Press, London, 2000), 3.

PART VI CHRONOLOGY

The Post-Cold War World, 1990–2000

1990

10 February	In Moscow, Gorbachev and Kohl agree to principle of German reunification.
26 February	Nicaraguan elections won by 'Uno' coalition of Violeta Chamorra.
11 March	Nationalists win elections in Lithuania, the first free elections ever in the USSR; Lithuania declares independence.
18 March	Christian Democratic 'Alliance for Germany' triumphs in East German elections.
30 May–4 June	Bush and Gorbachev meet in Washington.
29 June	Lithuania suspends its declaration of independence, following an economic blockade (since 17 April) by Moscow.
1 July	Economic and monetary union takes effect between the two Germanies.
2 August	Iraqi invasion of Kuwait; condemned by UN on 9 August.
12 September	US, USSR, Britain, France, and the two Germanies sign Moscow Treaty on a reunified Germany, which takes effect on 3 October.
19 November	Treaty on Conventional Forces in Europe signed in Paris.
29 November	UN Security Council resolution sanctions 'all means necessary' to remove Iraqis from Kuwait, if they do not leave by 15 January.
2 December	Helmut Kohl elected the first Chancellor of a reunified Germany.

1991

2 January	Lithuania revives its claim to independence.
17 January	US-led alliance begins air strikes in Iraq; start of Operation Desert Storm; Iraq launches Scud missiles against Israel.
24–28 February	Allied forces liberate Kuwait.
15–19 May	Jiang Zemin becomes first Chinese communist leader to visit Moscow since 1957.
21 May	Collapse of the Marxist regime of Colonel Mengistu in Somalia.
12 June	Popular vote in the Russian Federation elects Boris Yeltsin President.

PART VI CHRONOLOGY (continued)

13 June	End of communist domination of Albania, as a coalition government is formed.
23 June	Ceasefire agreed in Cambodia between Hun Sen government and Prince Sihanouk.
25–26 June	Yugoslav army attacks Croatia and Slovenia when they declare their independence.
1 July	Warsaw Pact is wound up.
29 July–1 August	Bush and Gorbachev finalize and sign START I treaty in Moscow.
18–21 August	A coup of hard-liners against Gorbachev is opposed in Moscow by Yeltsin and rapidly collapses.
9–11 December	Maastricht summit of European Community leaders signs a Treaty on European Union and plans a single currency.
25 December	Gorbachev resigns as President of the USSR, which breaks up into its fifteen constituent republics.
1992	
1 March	Bosnia-Herzegovina votes for independence from Yugoslavia.
27 March	Bosnian Serbs set up a separate government in Bosnia and fighting begins.
16 April	Fall of Marxist regime of Mohammad Najibullah in Afghanistan.
14 August	UN Human Rights Commission condemns Serb policy of 'ethnic cleansing' in Bosnia.
4 October	Treaty ends conflict between Mozambique government and RENAMO guerrillas.
9 October	UN Security Council introduces a 'no-fly' zone over Bosnia.
20 November	Macedonia declares its independence from Yugoslavia.
4 December	American forces land in Somalia to guarantee food supplies.
8 December	Serb siege of Sarajevo begins.
1993	
1 January	'Velvet divorce' separates Czech Republic and Slovakia.
3 January	Bush and Yeltsin sign START II treaty in Geneva.
15 January	Chemical Weapons Treaty signed by numerous UN members, banning manufacture of such weapons.
13 September	Palestinian leader Yasser Arafat and Israeli Premier Yitzhak Rabin sign a peace declaration in Washington.
3–4 October	Hundreds killed in clashes between US forces and Somali militia of General Aidid.
4 October	Russian forces storm the Congress of People's Deputies in Moscow.
7 November	President Clinton threatens force against North Korea if it obtains nuclear weapons.
17 December	US begins to withdraw forces from Somalia.
1994	
11 January	NATO launches 'Partnership for Peace' programme with ex-Eastern bloc states.
14 January	Ukraine agrees to destroy its nuclear arsenal (the third largest in the world).
28 February	In NATO's first military action, Yugoslav aircraft are shot down over Bosnia.
29 April	African National Congress wins first free elections in South Africa.
17 June	North Korea agrees to end its nuclear programme.
19 September	US forces land unopposed in Haiti to restore its elected President Aristide.
5–6 December	Summit of Conference on Security and Cooperation in Europe agrees to become a permanent Organization.

(continued...)

PART VI CHRONOLOGY (continued)

1995	
1 January	Austria, Finland, and Sweden join the European Union.
15 January	Russian forces capture Grozny, capital of Chechnya, from rebels.
11 July	UN 'safe haven' of Srebrenica is overrun by Serbs; Bosnian Muslims massacred.
30 August	NATO launches 'Operation Deliberate Force', with air attacks on Serbs in Bosnia.
31 October–21 November	Bosnian peace agreement brokered in Dayton, Ohio.
1996	
12 March	Clinton approves Helms-Burton Act, raising possibility of sanctions against any country trading with Cuba.
23 March	First free elections for a Taiwanese president; bitterly criticized by China.
30 June	Communists lose power after elections in Mongolia.
6 August	Chechen rebels seize control of Grozny.
29 August	Russia agrees to withdrawal from Chechnya.
27 September	Taliban movement seizes control of Afghan capital, Kabul.
1997	
17 April	Communist China and Taiwan open direct sea link for first time.
16–17 May	President Mobutu of Zaire overthrown by Laurent Kabila after months of civil war.
27 May	NATO–Russian Founding Act signed.
1 July	Hong Kong returns to Chinese sovereignty after British rule.
9 December	Geneva talks open between US, China, and the two Koreas to try to secure lasting Korean settlement.
1998	
4–24 February	Crisis in Gulf: US and British mass forces because of Iraq's refusal to allow arms inspectors to continue their work.
11–30 May	Series of nuclear tests by India, then by Pakistan.
7 August	Bomb attacks on US embassies in Kenya and Tanzania kill over 200; US launches retaliatory strikes on Sudan and Afghanistan on the 20th.
17 August	Economic crisis in Russia deepens, with value of rouble cut by a third.
September	Intensive fighting in Kosovo between Yugoslavian forces and local Albanians.
27 September	Following election defeat, Helmut Kohl loses power in Germany after sixteen years.
15–23 October	Clinton brokers Israeli–Palestinian peace deal at Wye Plantation, Maryland.
1999	
1 January	Introduction of the 'Euro' as a single currency between most European Union members.
12 February	US Senate throws out the impeachment charges against Clinton.
6–23 February	Rambouillet talks on Kosovo situation fail to secure a settlement.
12 March	The Czech Republic, Hungary, and Poland join NATO.
24 March	NATO begins air strikes against Yugoslavia over Kosovo.
7 May	US aircraft mistakenly bomb Chinese embassy in Belgrade.
10 June	NATO suspends its bombing campaign as Serb forces withdraw from Kosovo.
12 June	NATO ground forces begin deployment in Kosovo.

PART VI CHRONOLOGY (continued)

4 September	Israel and Palestinian leaders sign the Sharm el-Sheikh agreement, supposedly paving the way for a 'final' settlement in a year.
30 September	Following a month of tension, Russian ground forces invade Chechnya.
19 December	Portuguese-ruled Macao is handed over to Chinese sovereignty, ending the last European colonial possession in mainland Asia.
31 December	Panamanian sovereignty over Panama Canal takes effect.
	Sudden resignation of Yeltsin as President of Russia; Vladimir Putin becomes Acting President.
2000	
6 February	Putin announces the fall of Grozny, the Chechen capital, to Russian troops.
26 March	Putin is elected Russian President in his own right.
14 April	Russian Parliament ratifies the START II treaty (signed in 1993).
17 April	US and Russia open exploratory talks on a START III treaty in Geneva.
24 May	US Congress approves equal trading status for China.
17–19 July	Russian–Chinese (Putin–Jiang) summit condemns US plans for a 'National Missile Defence' system based on Star Wars research.
28 September	A visit by the right-wing Israel politician, Ariel Sharon, to the Dome at the Rock sparks the 'second Intifada'.
16–19 November	Bill Clinton becomes the first US president to visit a united Vietnam.

Take your learning further by viewing the interactive version of this timeline: www.oup.com/he/young-kent3e

20

Europe and the Former Soviet Union

Chapter contents

A. German Reunification

The collapse of communism brought about the greatest changes in the map of Europe since 1919, with the political disintegration of three Eurasian countries: the then USSR, with localized outbreaks of violence; Yugoslavia, with several years of bloody civil war; and Czechoslovakia, where the Czechs and Slovaks peacefully agreed to go their own way as of January 1993, in the so-called 'velvet divorce'. Elsewhere it led to profound political changes, notably in Italy, where the Christian Democratic Party, which had dominated government since 1947, lost its principal *raison d'être* and fell apart, leading to a new constellation of parties. But in one vital case, communism's demise brought reunification to a divided nation. The return of a single Germany was in many ways a natural result of Soviet retreat: the division of the country in 1945–9 was largely a result of the Cold War. The Western powers had always insisted that West Germany was the only legitimate German government, a point reiterated by Bush in a speech in Mainz as recently as May 1989. The West German Basic Law provided for easy accession by the Eastern provinces and in 1989–90 a clear majority of the German people wished to assert their national self-determination and have unity restored. In West Germany, nationalist opinion clamoured for this, with little attention to the potential financial cost of absorbing the East; in the East, the very desire to share in the West's wealth did much to undermine the Marxist state. Nevertheless, the process of reunification, though achieved in the space of a year, was far from simple. Given Germany's strategic position, industrial might, and historic importance, many European nations—not just the USSR, Poland, and Czechoslovakia, but also Britain, France, and other European Community members—were concerned about its return as a united power. Neither the Kohl administration in Bonn nor its main ally,

America, wished to alienate Gorbachev in the process, since this might risk a resurgence of Soviet militarism and imperial ambition. And many details of reunification, both inter-German and international, called for delicate judgement.

Reunification becomes Possible

The euphoria that accompanied the breaching of the Berlin Wall on 9 November 1989 was followed by confusion as to what would happen next. Reunification was immediately discussed in both West and East Germany but some East Germans hoped to reform their own state, while the Social Democrats and Greens in the West were fearful of a return to extreme nationalism and expansionism in a resurgent, single country. Even Chancellor Kohl had his doubts about how to proceed at first, but events on the ground demanded a response: polls soon showed that 70 per cent of West Germans favoured reunification and the East German state was obviously collapsing, its people threatening to move en masse to the West, now that the border was breached. It did not seem that international opinion would put up great resistance to reunification at this point. The US soon became enthusiastic, whilst Soviet policy appeared hopelessly confused. Bush believed West Germany was deeply committed to the Western alliance and that reunification 'would end the division of Europe on Western terms'.[1] On 28 November, reasonably certain that Washington was ready to exploit the fluidity in Europe to reshape the continent in Western interests, Kohl put forward a 'Ten Point Plan' for reunification. Vague on some key details, including the time frame, the plan proposed building cooperation with East Germany, transforming it into a liberal, capitalist regime and creating joint institutions, which would lead on to a single federation, while acting in line with the European Community and the 1975 Helsinki Accords. At this time, however, both France's president, François Mitterrand, and Britain's premier, Margaret Thatcher, became concerned about the potential dominance of German power in Europe in future. Mitterrand even talked to Gorbachev, in Moscow on 6 December, about how to halt the reunification process, which was troubling the Kremlin too. But Bush continued to support Kohl strongly, Gorbachev was divided in his own mind over what to do, and a Mitterrand–Thatcher axis failed to emerge. Whereas the former was determined on a course of containing the new Germany in stronger European Community (EC) institutions, the latter had no enthusiasm for European integration. An EC summit in Strasbourg in late December effectively accepted that reunification was likely. As to Gorbachev, his confusion was apparent at the Malta summit in early December, where he publicly called the division of Germany 'the decision of history' while privately telling Bush that he agreed with self-determination in principle and simply did not want 'to force issues'.[2]

Events within East Germany continued to force the pace. On 3 December, the communist leader of only six weeks, Egon Krenz, resigned with all the Politburo, leaving Premier Hans Modrow as the predominant leader, but one who was quite unable to control the situation. Hopes of reforming the existing system soon evaporated. The planned economy was in tatters, the currency worthless; opposition groups had been allowed to form, and in mid-January the Stasi secret police was disbanded. It was still felt, even in West Germany, that the full achievement of reunification could take several years, but the question now was how and when it would occur, not whether it would. A key point would be the first free East German elections, which Modrow conceded to the opposition groups in December. The original date set for these was May, but on 28 January, that target was brought forward to 18 March. On 28 January, Modrow also agreed to form a coalition government immediately. So it was that the communist cause in Germany evaporated, the Soviets were kept permanently off balance by their lack of means to control the situation, and Kohl pressed on determinedly towards the aim of reunification, the wisdom of which he never doubted. The German Chancellor was worried, however, that Gorbachev might successfully press for four-power talks, in which the former occupiers (the US, USSR, Britain, and France) would dictate a settlement, perhaps even reviving such questions as reparations. Modrow fed such fears by resuscitating the old Soviet aim of a reunited but neutralized Germany, detached from the North Atlantic Treaty Organization (NATO). As to Bush, he recognized that 'if we were to see progress on reunification, it would be our role to work with Moscow as an equal on the issue', so as to minimize Gorbachev's domestic problems.[3] But on 30 January Gorbachev publicly conceded that reunification was possible and, as elsewhere in Eastern Europe, it was quite plain that he was ready to compromise on the previous Soviet position in order to preserve peace and establish a stable, new balance of power.

It has been argued that three factors in particular led to the USSR's 'dramatic retreat' on Germany in 1990: 'the internal collapse' of East Germany; the Soviet Union's own economic problems; and the 'active policies of the West', with whom Gorbachev was desperate to build cooperation.[4] The West Germans did seem ready to offer some concessions to placate him: on 31 January their Foreign Minister, Hans Dietrich Genscher, proposed that alongside reunification Germany would remain in NATO but that former areas of East Germany would not be utilized by NATO armed forces. There was deep concern among some Soviet leaders about the situation. Even the liberal Alexander Yakovlev declared that 'the security of our borders must be firmly guaranteed. We must avoid the emergence of any kind of a new threat from the well-known direction.' But Foreign Minister Shevardnadze saw little alternative to moving towards agreement with the West: the 'alternative was to use our half-million troops in east Germany to block unification. We can imagine what that would have entailed.'[5]

A Settlement Takes Shape

In early February 1990, the machinery by which the German question would be settled took shape. First, on 6 February Kohl said there could be talks on economic and monetary union with East Germany, a step which would prevent the East's economic collapse but which would also effectively destroy its socio-economic system by absorbing it into the capitalist world. The likely political absorption of the East, via the adoption of the West German Basic Law, was already clear enough. Economic reunification was a difficult challenge, but the simplest method, and the way eventually adopted, despite its potential cost to the West, was to exchange the Deutschmark for the Eastern mark at the ratio of one-to-one. The second important organizational step was the US proposal, put to the Soviets by Secretary of State Baker on 8 February, after consultation with the other two Western powers, for the so-called 'two-plus-four' talks, through which the two Germanys would settle many (principally domestic) problems while the four ex-occupation powers would tackle the international dimensions of reunification. Baker saw this as 'a process that could steer the two Germanies to unification while also giving Gorbachev a place at the table, so he could explain to hardliners that Moscow was still in the game'.[6] The 'two-plus-four' approach, effectively a compromise between the German desire to dominate events and the Soviet–British–French wish to have a say, was confirmed by the breakthrough summit of NATO and Warsaw Pact nations in Ottawa on 13–14 February. Meanwhile, on 10 February, Kohl had travelled to Moscow and offered economic aid to the USSR in return for Bonn's role in setting the future pace of reunification. On 24–25 February, he was at Camp David, agreeing that a reunited Germany should stay in NATO, with its forces on its soil, although East Germany might have a 'special' status, free of NATO units for a time. It was the first time a German chancellor had been invited to the presidential retreat at Camp David. For the Bush administration, 'the key to future security and the development of East–West relations became German reunification, with Germany remaining in NATO, and Soviet acquiescence'—with all three of these having to be achieved together.[7]

The idea that East Germany could drive a hard bargain with the West on social and political concessions faded quickly after this, as did any Soviet hope of controlling the timetable of reunification. Modrow's government was already desperate for the West's financial support when, on 18 March, the East German elections resulted in a 48 per cent vote for the Christian Democrats and their allies. The Socialists won only 22 per cent and the communists, who had ruled the country for forty years, a mere 16 per cent. The election results were seen as a vote for reunification and specifically East German political movements did very badly. A new, Christian Democrat-dominated coalition was formed in mid-April, under Lothar de Mazière, who soon agreed that his country should be, in effect, swallowed up by the West. The only serious problem during these weeks was created by Kohl himself who, worryingly, questioned the validity of the German–Polish border. His reason for doing this, he said, was that he did not want to commit the government of a reunited Germany on the issue, but he inevitably stirred fears in Poland and elsewhere of a resurgence of German expansionism. This fear was only expunged in late June when the West and East German parliaments each confirmed the Polish border, with a chastened Kohl telling the Bundestag, 'Either we confirm the existing border or we gamble away the chance of German unity.'[8]

West Germany and the US hoped from the start that the 'two-plus-four' talks would achieve German reunification within NATO, but without offending the USSR or risking European stability. The USSR still hoped that the talks would adopt a broad approach and might be used both to delay the pace of progress and prevent German membership of NATO. But the US took a narrower view of the talks: Washington did not, for example, want them to embrace general European security or arms control issues, although they should discuss issues relating to Allied rights and German sovereignty. The US also wanted East Germany to be brought fully within NATO in future, even if it had some special status. Certainly, the US, supported by France and Britain, had no interest in a 'neutralized' East Germany. Scowcroft recognized that a 'Germany outside NATO would "gut" the alliance' and that, without Germany, the US 'military presence in NATO would be difficult if not impossible to maintain'.[9] As for the West Germans, they hoped for a rapid move to reunification, the withdrawal of the Red Army from the East, and the restoration of full sovereignty—including the right to remain in NATO. The 'two-plus-four' talks began, among officials, on 14 March but progressed slowly at first. A month later the USSR still hoped to avoid German membership of NATO, even if German reunification was inevitable. Some in the USSR felt that a compromise could be reached on the basis of German membership of both NATO *and* the Warsaw Pact, even though the latter organization had a doubtful future.

The first ministerial-level 'two-plus-four' talks took place on 5 May, by which time the US, Britain, and France had smoothed out their original differences on reunification. Mitterrand was happy with Kohl's continuing commitment to European integration, while Thatcher understood that reunification was unavoidable. The Soviets initially took a tough approach, hoping to 'decouple' the internal and external aspects of reunification, the main demand from Moscow still being that Germany should be neutralized. But, increasingly, it became evident that Kohl could hope to buy off the USSR with financial aid and a few concessions, including limits on the size of the German army. In mid-May, when he first began to hope that all-German elections might be held before the end of the year, he also secretly offered financial aid to Gorbachev in order to cover the costs of the Red Army's withdrawal from East Germany. From now until July, there were frequent, bilateral Soviet–German contacts to smooth the way to a deal. Furthermore, on 31 May the Washington summit between Bush and Gorbachev saw reassurances being given to the latter that German reunification would not be exploited to the USSR's detriment. By now, Gorbachev well knew that the 'question was not how to prevent the unification, but what the pace and conditions of this process should be'.[10] Even so, it was hard for the Soviets to accept the condition that Germany should remain in NATO. Before the summit, Kohl had encouraged the US to make concessions to the increasingly troubled Soviet leader, who was now facing both dire economic problems and severe unrest in Lithuania. Bush was able to give 'nine assurances' including reductions in the size of Germany's armed forces, recognition of Germany's established borders, German economic support for Moscow, and a more significant role for the all-European organization, the Conference on Security and Co-operation in Europe (CSCE), which Moscow hoped would play a leading role in continental security following the Cold War. After this meeting, Gorbachev seemed to accept that Germany could choose its own international future, including NATO membership, even if he still hoped that it might also enter the Warsaw Pact.

Germany Reunified

On 1 July, East and West Germany achieved the domestically popular aim of economic and monetary union. The danger of an East German economic collapse and mass emigration to the West was thereby removed, even if the financial cost to the West Germans would prove immense. The rest of the month was dominated by efforts to solve the international dimensions of the German problem and progress was now very rapid. The Soviet Foreign Minister, Shevardnadze, set the tone by telling the Communist Party Congress in Moscow of his own support for reunification; and it seems that Gorbachev was only waiting to get through the Congress in order to resolve the German problem for good, also accepting that NATO would include the reunited country. In return for this positive approach, he could expect further rewards.

On 5 July, a NATO summit in London took measures to make the organization appear less threatening to the USSR. Not only would the German army be reduced, but also the aims of the organization were altered to put greater emphasis on cooperation with Moscow and the role of the CSCE in developing pan-European security. On the economic front, the G-7 meeting in Houston on 9–12 July began a new study of Soviet needs, intending that an aid package should come later. This cautious policy reflected US and British doubts about the wisdom of pouring large sums into the ailing Soviet economy and it was much less than Kohl had wanted. But on 15–16 July the German Chancellor had his own bilateral talks with Gorbachev and promised large-scale technical and financial assistance to the USSR.

The German aid package was part of a more general deal between the two leaders that included several other significant aspects. Kohl confirmed the reduction of the Bundeswehr to 370,000, again undertook to pay for the staged withdrawal of the Red Army from East Germany (to be achieved by 1994), accepted the existing borders of Germany, and agreed to sign a friendship treaty with Moscow. He also said that, after 1994, only German troops (albeit under NATO command) would be based in the former East Germany and that no nuclear weapons would be based there. For his part, Gorbachev accepted the full restoration of German sovereignty, its membership of NATO, and the end of the USSR's occupation rights. There was some surprise, even in Western capitals, at the suddenness and scope of this agreement, which to some extent sidestepped the two-plus-four process. In effect, Kohl had exchanged financial and security guarantees in order to get the Red Army out of East Germany as soon as possible. It helped create the impression that this was no 'dictated peace . . . No other examples come to mind where . . . the occupation and indemnity were imposed by the vanquished on the victor.'[11]

The next three months saw a series of treaties to confirm the new German settlement, with several tracks moving in parallel. On the West–East German front, there was an agreement on 3 August to hold all-German elections by the end of the year and a Reunification Treaty was signed on 31 August, coming legally into force on 3 October, when the Eastern provinces effectively joined the Bonn Republic. On the German–Soviet front, a friendship treaty was signed on 13 September, and between Germany and Poland a border treaty was signed on 14 October. The two-plus-four negotiations ended on 12 September in Moscow, with a treaty recognizing Germany's borders, ending German territorial claims against others, restoring German sovereignty, and placing certain military limits on Germany, including confirmation of a promise, first made to the Western alliance in 1954, that it would not manufacture atomic, bacteriological, or chemical weapons. The treaty also embodied the special military status of the former East Germany, as agreed by Kohl and Gorbachev in mid-July. Four-power rights in Berlin and Germany were ended by an agreement of 1 October. This settlement was clearly better for the West than for Gorbachev, even if some Western nations were still concerned about the possible resurgence of an expansionist Germany. The USSR had had to retreat from its original hopes of delaying reunification and neutralizing Germany. Then again, the concessions on economic aid, the reform of NATO, and the strengthening of the CSCE showed that it was far from being a complete Soviet defeat. Washington, which had consistently backed and encouraged Kohl, could feel rather more satisfied, perhaps, than Paris or London, who were still concerned about their status in Europe compared to that of Germany. Clearly, it was Kohl who gained most, winning the first all-German elections since 1932, with 46 per cent of the vote going to his Christian Democrats on 2 December 1990. The Social Democrats came second, with 33 per cent, and the ex-communists fourth with 10 per cent, a shade behind the liberal Free Democrats. Kohl, hitherto an uninspiring chancellor, 'was saved from an unfavourable historical verdict by having the German question thrust upon him, and by seizing the opportunity with considerable astuteness and strength'.[12] Apart from his gaffe on the Polish border, he had resolved a highly complex problem with remarkable speed. But the economic price of such swift reunification had yet to be paid. The 1990s, which began with so much hope for Germany, became blighted by unemployment, which eventually rose to more than four million, as spending was restrained and interest rates increased to cope with the costs of modernizing the former East. In 1998, Kohl, the Chancellor for sixteen years, was roundly defeated at the polls, and he was later accused of financial corruption during his long years in office.

BOX 20.1

Biography: Helmut Kohl (1930–2017)

Kohl, who was born in the town of Ludwigshafen in the Rhineland, was just beginning military training when the Second World War ended and the Nazi regime collapsed. A Roman Catholic, who had seen at first hand the destruction that political extremism could bring about, he joined the new Christian Democratic Party (CDU) when only 16 and, like its leader Konrad Adenauer, became a firm believer in European unity. Educated at Frankfurt University and later obtaining a doctorate from Heidelberg, Kohl at first worked in industry before becoming a full-time politician in 1969. Already the chairman of the CDU in the Rhineland-Palatinate, he was elected that year to be Minister-President of West Germany's most wealthy and populous province. Four years later he was elected chair of the national CDU and ran for the Chancellorship for the first time in 1976. Much criticized as a lacklustre, undynamic figure, he nonetheless engineered the parliamentary overthrow of the Chancellor, Helmut Schmidt, in 1982, thus ending thirteen years of Social Democratic government. Re-elected West German Chancellor in 1987, Kohl showed great diplomatic skill in securing Germany's peaceful reunification in 1989–90 and then served two further terms as Chancellor, despite the economic problems that reunification brought. In 1998, the Social Democrats finally defeated him and, soon after, Kohl was beset by accusations of financial improprieties whilst in power. In January 2000, he resigned as the CDU's honorary chairman, his reputation tarnished.

B. The Break-Up of the USSR and the Wars of Succession

Gorbachev and the End of Soviet Power

By early 1990, after only five years as Soviet leader, Mikhail Gorbachev had transformed the country's political landscape and its foreign policy. To Western observers, he seemed an enlightened, intelligent leader who had recognized the failings of communism, adopted liberal values, and greatly reduced international tension, putting an end to the Cold War. But to many of his own people he had abandoned the certainties of the Brezhnev era for the uncertainties of free enterprise, with its bankruptcies, price rises, and unemployment; his political changes had encouraged regional independence in the republics, and so threatened the USSR's cohesion; and, by losing the country's grip of Eastern Europe, he had seriously compromised its security, wasting all that had been gained in the Second World War. In fact, the late 1980s revealed a great paradox: whilst no one individual could control the pace of change in the Soviet Union, it was equally difficult to see that things would have happened in the way they did without Gorbachev. His 'less-than-great personality shaped the end of the Cold War' because, even if he could not control events, 'many of the most extraordinary aspects of this remarkable' period could '*only* be understood by according primary importance to the Gorbachev *personality* factor'.[13] Gorbachev had decided that reform was essential, thanks to the corrupt and inefficient politico-economic system he inherited, and he was optimistic that the Soviet people could handle radical changes. But if anything, the pace of his reforms had been slow, undermined, especially on the economic side, by the conservatism of the Communist Party, and by his own uncertainty over precisely how to proceed. The growth of regionalism had largely been unexpected, as had the rate of decline in manufacturing output, and the two became linked, for the failure of reform to bring material benefits merely hardened support for secession.

Abroad, Gorbachev had taken a line no former Soviet leader had dared, engaging with the West and ending the USSR's reliance on force. But here too his optimism proved ill-founded, he failed to see difficulties, and he ended up reacting to events, rather than controlling them. He expected a gradual, mutual, and agreed reduction of tension, which would preserve Soviet security in a new international environment. But he was fundamentally weakened in 1985–9 by the USSR's poor economic and financial situation, at a time when the Western powers appeared politically stable and economically resurgent. Also, at first, many Western leaders saw his policies as a reaction to economic failure and did not accept, until 1989, that he was really ready to cooperate. In 1985–7, while the USSR compromised its position in Afghanistan, southern Africa, and South-East Asia, the developing world was ever more indebted to the West, and America—despite being wracked by doubts about its own 'decline'—was actually in an even stronger position. In 1989–90, while the Red Army prepared to leave Eastern Europe, NATO retained its unity and Germany was reunited on terms largely dictated by Washington and Bonn. Yet, none of this was as catastrophic as what would follow in 1990–1.

If Gorbachev failed to carry through his programme for more democratic institutions and free enterprise elements in the economy, then there seemed only two real alternatives by 1990. Either, as the Central Intelligence Agency (CIA) increasingly feared, the communist machine would strike back in an attempt to return to totalitarianism; or—and this seemed equally difficult to come to terms with—the USSR would dissolve and its fifteen republics would become independent, with their own constitutions and economic policies. Despite becoming Executive President in March 1990, Gorbachev seemed at a loss in how to deal with the unexpected, yet potent challenge of regionalism. In January 1990, he sought to prevent an immediate break-up of the USSR by promising a Law on Nationalities, including the right to secede, but he worked on this only slowly and, in March, he sent the Red Army into Lithuania when it precipitately declared itself independent under its recently elected President, Vytautas Landsbergis. Lithuania, along with Latvia and Estonia, was one of the three Baltic States, forcibly absorbed into the USSR by Stalin in 1940. They led the way among the constituent republics in pressing for autonomy. Estonia had actually issued a declaration of sovereignty (short of independence) in November 1988, followed by Latvia and Lithuania eight months later, after which Lithuania had declared the 1940 annexation illegal. In August 1989, a million people had joined hands across the Baltic States in a symbolic gesture of freedom. Gorbachev's action in March 1990 suggested that he might resist the USSR's break-up by force, provoking concern in the West and immediately putting at risk a proposed US–Soviet trade deal—a sign that the Cold War might not yet be over. Soviet troops disarmed the Lithuanian National Guard and arrested young Lithuanians who resisted conscription into the Red Army. Then, however, Gorbachev turned to an economic blockade, forcing Landsbergis to suspend independence in June, while the promised Law on Nationalities, now referred to as the 'Union Treaty', was completed. Once again, Gorbachev decided that force was not the answer: 'the chosen alternative was a war of nerves . . . to induce Lithuania to step back . . . and to show the secessionist forces in the . . . republics that pulling out of the USSR would not be painless'.[14]

The relaxation of tension allowed a highly successful summit, between Gorbachev and America's George Bush, to be held in Washington in May–June (see Chapter 21, C). Meanwhile, in May, Gorbachev's old rival and former minister, Boris Yeltsin, was elected President by the assembly of the USSR's largest constituent republic, the Russian Federation. He not only resigned from the Communist Party, but also set out to create an alternative power centre to the Kremlin, asserting the Russian Federation's right to sovereignty on 12 June. Within weeks, Moldova, Ukraine, and Belorussia had followed suit, all of them now with mass popular movements pressing for autonomy. 'From then on', Gorbachev later recalled, 'no major issue could be resolved outside the context of the relationship between the Union and the republics' and he admitted that he had simply 'underestimated the phenomenon of the election of Yeltsin in Moscow'.[15] Although Bush himself continued to hope for Gorbachev's survival, the CIA warned that 'like Moses, having brought his people out of bondage, it is increasingly evident that Gorbachev cannot lead them over into the Promised Land'.[16] Yeltsin increasingly seemed the man of the future.

By December 1990, the situation was ever more confused. With the beleaguered and uncertain Gorbachev promoting traditional communists back into the Politburo and taking new powers for himself, the reformist Foreign Minister, Eduard Shevardnadze, resigned, fearing a return to dictatorship. In January 1991, another reformist, Premier Nikolai Ryzhkov, was replaced by Valentin Pavlov, who accused the West of trying to destabilize the country by pressing it to adopt capitalism without providing adequate financial support. But then, just as the conservatives seemed back in the ascendant and with the Union Treaty still not completed, Landsbergis ended his suspension of Lithuanian independence, provoking another crisis over the regionalization issue. As the Red Army tried to seize key buildings in the Lithuanian capital, thirteen people were killed and five more died in clashes in neighbouring Latvia, where there was considerable sympathy for the Lithuanian case. 'If the forces of the centre can do this to the Balts', a worried Yeltsin told the US ambassador, 'they can do it to us.'[17] Though preoccupied by the Gulf War against Iraq (see Chapter 21, B) and anxious not to be seen advocating the USSR's disintegration, the US government expressed concern and a planned Gorbachev–Bush summit was postponed. Yeltsin also lent his rhetorical support to the Baltic States and Gorbachev again drew back from repression. On 7 March, he finally published the draft Union Treaty, which allowed the republics a wide degree of autonomy. A majority of Soviet votes approved this in a referendum ten days later, but this did not end Gorbachev's problems because six republics boycotted the poll. On 3 March, Latvia and Estonia had followed Lithuania by declaring independence. Soon afterwards the Caucasian republic of Georgia joined them. Furthermore, in June, Yeltsin reinforced his position by being popularly elected Russian President. The whole Soviet Union was now faced by permanent food shortages and widespread strikes, with little hope of large-scale Western aid: in late July the G-7 London summit had reluctantly decided that Gorbachev's economic reforms were too modest to deserve extra financial support.

The decisive crisis for the USSR came in mid-August 1991 when hard-line communists, many of them recently promoted by Gorbachev, launched a coup, hoping to forestall the signature of the Union Treaty. They imprisoned Gorbachev but were a group of little-known bureaucrats, lacking in confidence and unable to muster support. They could not command the loyalty of such an essential centre of power as the armed forces or even of the capital, Moscow, where Yeltsin held out against them. Within days, the coup collapsed and Gorbachev was freed. The coup failure was quickly followed by the abolition of the KGB and the suspension of the Communist Party itself. Yet the person who gained most from these events was not Gorbachev, who had been powerless throughout the coup, but Yeltsin, who was widely credited with defeating it. He now worked with other leaders of the constituent republics to destroy the USSR. He felt, perhaps, that he had little choice: after the August coup, 'we had a complete vacuum at the political centre. The centre—in the person of Gorbachev—was totally demoralized. The emerging national states had lost their faith in him.' But Gorbachev remembered things differently, believing that the 'Soviet Union really was a strong and solid multinational state. Its dissolution was by no means inevitable.' He claimed that Yeltsin and his entourage 'sacrificed the Union for the sake of realizing their ardent desire to reign in the Kremlin'.[18] Some republics opted for complete independence, but on 21 December eleven formed a loose confederation, named the 'Commonwealth of Independent States'. When Gorbachev resigned as Executive President on 25 December, the USSR ceased to exist. The attempt to democratize the country had only succeeded in dividing it against itself, giving power to ethnic majorities in the republics that wanted to be free of Russian control. Other than in Lithuania and parts of the Caucasus, this process had been achieved with remarkably little violence and, partly thanks to a lack of triumphalism in the West, no major international crisis. Apart from the Russian Federation, it left a series of new countries not only in Eastern Europe (the Baltic States, Ukraine, Belarus, Moldova) and the Caucasus (Georgia, Armenia, Azerbaijan), but also in Central Asia (Kazakhstan, Kyrgyzstan, Tajikistan, Uzbekistan, Turkmenistan). But all of these inherited social and economic problems from the former USSR and many also faced internal political divisions and foreign challenges which brought instability for many years afterwards.

Russian Policy and the Wars of Succession

The conflicts in the former Soviet republics took various forms, from ethnic tensions and ideological disputes that resulted in civil wars to border disputes between the newly independent states. There were numerous minor disputes of short duration and some potentially serious border claims (as between Russia and Kazakhstan, or Tajikistan and Uzbekistan), which failed to become critical. But some conflicts such as the attempt by ethnic Russians to establish an independent 'Transdniester Republic' in Moldova (1990–4) or the Tajikistan civil war (1992–7, fought between ex-communists and Islamic groups) lasted several years. And at least three were very intense, creating long-term instability in an especially complex region, the Caucasus: the Armenian–Azerbaijani war over the disputed region of Nagorno-Karabakh (1992–3, with renewed tension late in 1999); the ethnic Abkhazi revolt against Georgian rule (1992–3); and the Chechen bid to secede from the Russian Federation (post-1994). Most of these had their origins in much earlier periods. Nagorno-Karabakh, for example, though mostly populated by (Christian) Armenians, had been put under (Muslim) Azerbaijani administration in 1923, under Lenin. Violence had first broken out in the enclave in February 1988, with Armenia backing a secessionist movement opposed to Azerbaijani rule and leaders in both states exploiting the issue to win popular support. When war broke out between the two—now independent—republics in 1992, the Armenians, whose territory virtually surrounded the enclave, had a clear strategic advantage and soon captured all the urban centres, but Azerbaijan refused to accept its loss, and the danger of a renewed conflict persisted.

Despite the break-up of the USSR, Yeltsin's Russia was frequently active in trying to limit these conflicts, to make Russian borders secure, to protect the rights of ethnic Russians in the successor states, and to assert Moscow's continuing influence in most of the republics it previously ruled, areas which were now referred to as the 'near abroad'. In both Georgia in December 1993 and Tajikistan in June 1997, Russia played a leading role in brokering a peace settlement; and these settlements were both policed by forces from the Commonwealth of Independent States (CIS). There had been hopes in Moscow in early 1992, that the CIS might prove a vehicle for Russian predominance, even taking over the armed forces of the former USSR. This proved too ambitious and in March 1992 Yeltsin confirmed that Russia would create its own defence forces. Cooperation between Russia and the other republics tended to take the form of free trade agreements and friendship treaties, rather than political and defence cooperation, but was particularly close with the two Slav republics of Belarus and Ukraine—the original proponents, with Yeltsin, of the CIS in 1991. For much of 1992, Russia and Ukraine had been divided over the disposal of the Soviet Black Sea Fleet, before deciding to share it equally, and there was tension too over the treatment by Ukraine of ethnic Russians in Crimea (which had been part of Russia until 1954). But relations gradually improved. Both Ukraine and Belarus elected pro-Russian presidents in 1994; and May 1997 saw both a ten-year Russo-Ukraine cooperation agreement and a Russo-Belarus 'Charter of Union'. The latter was potentially far-reaching, but it was vague on detail and there was no timetable for its achievement. As to the CIS, it remained in being, held regular summits, and in its first five years of existence drew up about 800 agreements between its members. But many of these agreements were not signed by all the states and, after a few years, it was beginning to look insignificant, a focus for technical rather than substantive cooperation.

Russia was by far the largest of the former Soviet republics and Yeltsin's attempts to 'lead' the others and to protect ethnic Russians were designed to satisfy his nationalist and communist critics, who, though divided among themselves, tried to outbid the pro-reform lobby for popular support and posed as defenders of 'national' interests over the supposedly pro-Western policy of Yeltsin. In the December 1993 Russian parliamentary elections, there was a worrying success for an extreme nationalist party led by Vladimir Zhirinovsky, which won 23 per cent of votes; two years later, the communists emerged in first place in elections, with 22 per cent of the vote. Nationalists and communists might be divided on domestic and economic policy, and they were far from having an overall majority but, abroad, they both advocated cooperation with fellow Slavs (including Serbia), the assertion of Russian power in such former areas of influence as the Caucasus and Central Asia, and resistance to any sign of Western domination. A strong foreign policy was made difficult by the country's continuing economic weakness, by the poor quality and low morale of its armed forces, and by political divisions in Moscow, even among Yeltsin's supporters, over the pace and direction of reform. The political division reached its greatest crisis point in September–October 1993 when Yeltsin, criticized for months by the Congress of People's deputies, tried to dissolve it, only to have the deputies barricade themselves inside the Parliament building and try to seize control of the state television headquarters. Earlier, in April, he had silenced his opponents by winning a popular referendum on his leadership and market-based economic policies. But now he turned to brute strength, using tanks to bombard the Parliament and force the deputies to surrender. Over a hundred people were killed in the operation, and those who were arrested afterwards included a former vice-president, Alexander Rutskoi. 'From one perspective this was the end of the Soviet Empire', in that Yeltsin's old communist opponents had been signally defeated; but the bombardment also seemed reminiscent of Stalinist tactics and 'made an unpleasant and lasting impression in Russia and the West'.[19] Such firmness, and a lack of widely acceptable alternative leaders, helped Yeltsin win the mid-1996 presidential elections, but he was also, by then, troubled by ill-health and did not serve out his second term in full (see Chapter 21, C).

In Georgia, Yeltsin was pitted for a time against another reformer from the Gorbachev era, the ex-Foreign Minister, Eduard Shevardnadze. Shevardnadze was elected head of state at his home republic on 11 October 1992 after months of internal political uncertainty. By then, there was already a powerful secessionist movement in Abkhazia and a bid, too, from the Muslim-populated region of South Ossetia, for independence from Georgia. The Abkhazis are an ancient Black Sea people. They number only about 100,000 and are in a minority even in Abkhazia itself but, as elsewhere in the disintegrating USSR, they had been encouraged to work for increased national rights in 1988–9, had asserted the sovereignty of their own republic in August 1990, and even talked of joining the Russian Federation to escape Georgian domination, a move which generated some sympathy for the Abkhazis in Russia. Georgia was weakened in the face of this challenge by its own divisions: in early 1992 its then-President, Zviad Gamsakhurdia, had been overthrown and he subsequently tried to use Abkhazia as a base for revival. On 7 July, the Abkhazis declared independence, Georgian armed forces were sent to quell the rebellion, but Russia tried to bring about a ceasefire. In mid-1993, as the war continued, Yeltsin was blamed for helping the Abkhazis besiege Sukhumi, which Shevardnadze personally went to defend. When it fell, Shevardnadze faced personal humiliation, was forced to turn to Russia for help (agreeing a friendship treaty with them in February 1994 and joining the CIS), and had to accept a settlement in April 1994 which virtually gave Abkhazia independence. About 10,000 had died in the conflict, but many Georgians remained determined to reconquer Abkhazia and there were periodic outbreaks of violence, as in May 1998, when Abkhazi forces entered the neutral zone between the two sides, following attacks by Georgian partisans. Tensions in the region continued into the new millennium.

Chechnya

If Yeltsin managed to exploit Georgia's difficulties in order to assert Russian power, he had far less success a few years later within his own borders, in another area of the Caucasus, Chechnya. The Russian Federation, though it had been constituted as a single, united republic of the USSR, was itself a vast Eurasian country, with numerous ethnic and religious minorities and various types of regional government within it. Over twenty million people in the Federation lived under their own republican governments (twenty-one in number); others were part of autonomous 'Okrugs' (ten in number). The Russian republics all had a substantial non-Russian population, and many of the ethnic groups, such as the Tatars of Tatarstan, had a long history of resistance to rule from Moscow. In some of the autonomous areas, communists clung to power and undermined Yeltsin's reform programme; in others, constitutions were drawn up in the 1990s that violated the federal constitution by maximizing local autonomy. Chechnya became the principal test case of whether, in the wake of the USSR's demise, Russia itself would break up, and the outcome, for Yeltsin, was not hopeful.

Chechnya, as the republic of Chechen-Ingush became known, had a mixed population of 58 per cent Chechens, 23 per cent Russians, and 13 per cent Ingush, the last a Muslim people who tended to ally with the ethnic Russians to prevent local Chechen domination. The Chechens themselves were Sufi Muslims, who had resisted Tsarist conquest in the 1850s and were subjected to mass deportation under Stalin in the early 1940s. The republic first declared its independence of Russia on 1 November 1991 under its newly elected President, a former Soviet air-force officer, Dzhokar Dudayev, who had previously been seen as an ally of Yeltsin. Turkey, Iran, and other Muslim states gave diplomatic recognition to Chechnya and, at first, the Russian Parliament resisted Yeltsin's attempts to crush the secession, fearful that a military success for him in the Caucasus would strengthen his hand in dealing with opponents nearer home. Also, at least until 1994, there 'was simply . . . no pressing need for the Russian state to take action; there were few signs that the "Chechen infection" of radical nationalism . . . was spreading to other Russian autonomous republics'.[20] Moscow instead had to rely on an economic blockade and military manoeuvres on the border to intimidate Dudayev, whose increasingly authoritarian, personal rule stirred up civil war in early 1994, leaving the republic even more lawless. Thereafter, Russian policy became tougher, partly influenced by a need to meet the challenge from nationalists. For a time, Yeltsin hoped that Dudayev would be overthrown or assassinated by his domestic opponents. But in August 1994 the Chechens began to prepare for a Russian invasion, which seemed increasingly likely and for which the Russian army was clearly preparing. The invasion finally came on 11 December 1994, when three divisions marched on the capital, Grozny.

Few expected that the Chechens—poor, divided, and ill armed as they seemed—could resist the Russians for long. However, the invasion soon turned into embarrassment for Moscow. The army reached Grozny in five days, leading to some 200,000 refugees fleeing the city, yet despite repeated claims of victory from Yeltsin, the presidential palace was not taken until 15 January 1995, and the city was not declared clear of Chechen fighters until 8 February. Many Russians backed the invasion on patriotic grounds, keen to prevent a break-up of the Federation, but they also questioned the destructive scale of the operation and Yeltsin's approval rating dropped to 20 per cent. 'Buried in Grozny was Yeltsin's magic ability to read Russia's mind.'[21] The morale of the army was low and Russian generals bickered among themselves. After Afghanistan and the collapse of the USSR, the armed forces lacked the will to prosecute a war. Some soldiers were ready to sell their arms, even their tanks, to the enemy. Typically in guerrilla warfare, all Chechnya's urban centres fell into Russian hands in the spring of 1995 but the Chechens, though numbering only a few thousand fighters, held on in the countryside and hit back in a series of surprise operations: in May they again infiltrated Grozny; in June they seized hundreds of hostages in Budennovsk, on Russian soil, and only released them in return for a safe passage home; and in October, despite several preceding weeks of peace talks, they tried to assassinate the Russian commander, Lt General Anatoli Romanov. In January 1996, there were more successes for the guerrillas, with another hostage seizure at Kizylar and the capture of hostages on a Black Sea ferry. Yeltsin himself became involved in peace talks in March but would not concede to Chechen demands for a Russian withdrawal and independence. Dudayev was killed by a rocket attack in April 1996 but his successor, Aslan Maskhadov, maintained the independence demand and on 6 August the Russian military was embarrassed once more, as Chechen guerrillas again occupied the centre of Grozny.

Faced by what seemed an 'unwinnable' war, and one which had already cost about 50,000 lives, Yeltsin sent his national security adviser, General Alexander Lebed, to Grozny, with executive powers to negotiate a settlement. Lebed was a tough soldier-turned-politician, an ex-paratrooper, and veteran of Afghanistan, who had come third in the recent Russian presidential elections—though only with some help from the Yeltsin camp, which had used him to split the opposition vote. The General's solution to the Chechen problem was hardly calculated to please Russian nationalists but it was founded on his knowledge of the scale of the problems facing the Russian armed forces, and its manner confirmed his reputation for decisiveness. He quickly agreed to a ceasefire and, on 31 August, reached a settlement with Maskhadov based on a Russian military withdrawal, with a deferral of the independence issue until 2000–21. Until then, the exact fate of Chechnya was uncertain and not everything looked negative for Moscow. After the bloodshed there, other republics were reluctant to assert their own independence from Moscow just yet, so that a temporary settlement was not disastrous from Yeltsin's point of view. Also, there was some hope of working with Maskhadov who 'promised the restoration of internal . . . stability, and the reconstruction of the economy in cooperation with Russia'.[22] But the state of the Russian army was clearly terrible: the Defence Ministry admitted, in early 1997, that it was on the verge of disintegration. Furthermore, Maskhadov, who was popularly elected President of Chechnya in February 1997, seemed in a position to assert the republic's full independence in a few years' time, with Russian control largely nominal. Although Yeltsin sacked Lebed in October 1996, after accusing him of planning a mutiny, and thereby removed a potentially strong rival, there was always a danger that other opponents could exploit the failure to win a decisive victory over the Chechens. Neither would the Chechen problem disappear, given that a final decision on its future had merely been delayed.

By the summer of 1999, the situation appeared as difficult as ever. On 5 March, Russia's Deputy Minister of the Interior, Gennady Shpigun, had been kidnapped in Grozny. He was later murdered. In August and September, there was a series of bomb attacks in Russia by Chechen terrorists determined to secure their independence, and dozens of Russians were killed. Just as worrying for Moscow, Chechen guerrillas, under the warlord Shamil Basayev, had begun to operate in the neighbouring region of Dagestan, again raising the prospect that the Russian Federation could disintegrate. Meanwhile, the Chechen government seemed quite unable to establish order. But Yeltsin was increasingly unwell, the economy was in tatters, and a series of prime ministers had come and gone in rapid succession, none of which suggested that a reassertion of Russian control in Chechnya was likely (see Chapter 21, C). The latest prime minister to be appointed soon determined to show otherwise, however. Vladimir Putin, formerly a spy chief and head of Yeltsin's Security Council, believed that the regime might not survive the loss of Chechnya and that action had to be taken soon, both to preserve the federation and to prevent communists or extreme nationalists taking power if Yeltsin should die. Putin bluntly stated on 8 September, 'Russia is defending itself. We have been attacked. And therefore we must throw off the guilt syndrome.'[23]

Despite doubts about the fighting fitness of the armed forces, the Russians began large-scale air attacks on Chechen rebel forces on 23 September and launched a ground invasion of Chechnya one week later. By the end of October, the Russians had secured their position in the north of the region and had reached the outskirts of Grozny, which was then virtually razed to the ground, before being entered on 6 February. The ruthless campaign, which strongly contrasted with the confusion and ineptitude of 1994–6, created over 100,000 refugees and was widely criticized outside Russia because of reports of atrocities by its army. But at home it established Putin's reputation as a firm leader after years of weakness, it helped him secure the succession to Yeltsin when the latter resigned at the New Year, and it ensured a clear victory in the March 2000 presidential election—held only weeks after Grozny's fall. Sporadic violence continued, but Putin was unapologetic about the methods used, describing the rebels as 'terrorists', successfully controlling much of the news that came out of Chechnya, and resisting external involvement on the grounds that Chechnya was a domestic matter. In contrast to Lebed, Putin had been able to exploit the issue to secure himself in power, and he had done so by removing the possibility of Chechnya's independence that had earlier been conceded.

As President, Putin maintained his firm policy towards Chechnya and other parts of the north Caucasus. In May–June 2000, direct rule was enforced from Moscow in Chechnya, with the pro-Russian Ahmat Kadyrov installed as local leader. Fighting between Russian troops and separatists, led by the former Chechen President, Aslan Maskhadov, continued and rebels were sometimes able to strike at the heart of the Federation, most notably with the seizure of a Moscow theatre in October 2002, when over a hundred were killed. One of the worst outrages was a rebel attack on a school in Beslan, in neighbouring North Ossetia, two years later, when more than 300 were killed, many of them children. Such actions helped Putin to portray the separatists as part of an international terrorist challenge, linked to radical Islamist ideas, after the 9/11 attacks in America. Despite continued fighting, Moscow held a referendum in Chechnya in 2003 to endorse membership of the Russian Federation and then helped Kadyrov secure election as president of the Chechen republic. He was assassinated in a bomb attack the following year, but Putin persisted with his policy of marginalizing the rebels, while trying to set up a stable, pro-Russian government in Grozny. Russian forces had a success of their own when Maskhadov was killed by special forces in early 2005, after which the scale of violence receded. In 2009, Moscow declared that the situation in Chechnya had been 'normalized', although outbreaks of violence linked to the region persisted, with deadly bomb attacks on the Moscow underground in March 2010, and at Moscow airport in January 2011, both blamed on separatists from the north Caucasus.

C. Yugoslavia's Break-Up and the Bosnian War

The Break-Up of Yugoslavia

Although two East European communist states, Yugoslavia and Albania, had long been independent of Moscow's control, radical political changes occurred there in the wake of the collapse of the Soviet system. In Albania, the dictator Ramiz Alia, facing daily demonstrations in the capital, Tirana, was forced to concede free elections in late 1990. These were held in March 1991 and, though the communists did surprisingly well in rural areas, emerging in first place overall, there was continued unrest. A coalition government was formed three months later. Further elections, held in March 1992, were won by the Democratic Party, but they had only limited success in tackling the economic troubles of Europe's poorest country: in early 1997 a financial crisis, brought on by the collapse of so-called 'pyramid-selling' schemes, led to martial law, the fall of the government, and in April the deployment of an Italian-led peacekeeping force within the country. But, meanwhile, in Yugoslavia the end of the old order had proved far more divisive and violent. Indeed, the Yugoslav state, founded in 1918 through the union of several South Slav peoples, broke up amid the worst bloodshed seen on the continent since the Second World War, with the upheaval spreading to Albania at the end of the 1990s.

Although Yugoslavia seemed quite stable and united under both the inter-war monarchy (despite its pro-Serb policy) and between 1945 and 1980 under Marshal Tito (also repressive, but with the non-Serbs better treated), there were always deep ethnic tensions underlying the political order. 'To say that there [was] no Yugoslav nationalism is a euphemism. In 1919, the grouping of southern Slavs was brought about . . . by a will to escape' from German and Hungarian domination.[24] But the southern Slavs fell into several distinct ethnic groups and the Second World War had shown how quickly they could fall into vicious intercommunal conflict: particularly merciless at that time was the anti-Serb campaign of the Croatian 'Ustashas', which claimed around 400,000 victims. The Croats who, along with the Slovenes, populated northern Yugoslavia, had long been wealthier and better educated than the Serbs and the various other groups—Bosnians, Montenegrins, Albanians, and Macedonians—who lived to the south. There were also important religious divisions, the Serbs being Eastern Orthodox, while the Croats and Slovenes were Roman Catholic, and the Albanians and Bosnians included many Muslims. Indeed, under Tito, the Bosnian Muslims gained recognition as an ethnic group—not merely a religious group (as they had previously been seen)—in their own right. Tito tried to balance Yugoslavia's constituent republics against each other and, following serious unrest in Croatia, tried to strengthen their powers under the 1974 Constitution. But he could not prevent a growing sense of division before his death in 1980 and, indeed, this constitutional reform probably only encouraged hopes of greater autonomy from the centre. It 'became apparent that the effective power resting at the level of the republics was so strong that the parts were able to dictate the rules to the whole'.[25] Economic problems helped clinch the divide. The northern republics resented having to subsidize the poorer south; the Croats still felt that the Serbs, with control of the federal capital, Belgrade, and leading positions in the armed forces, were politically dominant; and the Serbs disliked Tito's attempts to curb their power, notably his decision to grant autonomy to the province of Kosovo which, though predominantly Albanian by population, had been part of Serbia for centuries.

Tito's successors, a collective group, at first not dominated by any one leader, inherited both inter-republican tension and economic problems of indebtedness to the West, a trade deficit, and poor growth. His attempt to marry central planning with free-market elements had only succeeded in combining the inefficiencies of the first with the unpleasant side effects of the second, such as inflation and unemployment. In 1983, the International Monetary Fund (IMF) had to step in to reschedule the country's debt and, in looking for a radical solution to their problems, the collective leadership, all members of which represented one Yugoslav republic or another, began to look both at greater free enterprise and at a regional solution to their problems. In 1987, this tendency took a new turn when Serbia's communists elected a crafty, outspoken nationalist, Slobodan Milošović, to lead them. In parallel with developments in the USSR, but with far bloodier results, 'What began as rivalry among the republics, communist parties turned into full-blown ethnic politics by the late 1980s.'[26] Milošović not only set out to reduce the autonomy of Kosovo, he also provoked fear in Croatia and Slovenia that, unless resisted, there would be a return to a Serb-dominated system in Yugoslavia. By 1990, there was strong support in Croatia and Slovenia for independence and virtual economic warfare had broken out between them and Serbia, with a severing of commercial links. A clear sign of Yugoslavia's political disintegration was the holding of free elections on different dates in the various republics, with the communists holding on to power firmly only in Serbia and Montenegro. These two, indeed, continued to function together as a federal republic in the 1990s, still calling itself Yugoslavia, while the other republics (not only Croatia and Slovenia, but also Bosnia-Herzegovina and Macedonia) sought independence. Everywhere leaders exploited fears that had been dormant in the early post-war decades, but 'the politicians could not have succeeded if there had been no embers to fan'.[27]

After vain attempts to negotiate a loose confederation, Croatia and Slovenia finally declared independence from Yugoslavia on 25 June 1991. A key influence on their decision was Serbia's refusal to accept a Croat as Yugoslav President in May, despite the fact that this should have occurred under the Constitution (which provided for the Federal presidency to 'rotate' between the republics). Milošović would not at first concede independence and the Serb-dominated Yugoslav Federal army invaded both republics. In a matter of weeks, he gave up on the attempt to suppress Slovenian independence, mainly because the Slovenes had prepared their defences well and captured several army units. But in Croatia fighting went on for many months, as there was a large Serbian minority, who made up a tenth of the population and hoped for the eventual formation a 'Greater Serbia' that would draw together all of Yugoslavia's ethnic Serbs under the rule of Belgrade. The Croats had elected their own extreme nationalist President, Franjo Tudjman, in May 1990 and were never likely to withdraw their declaration of independence. Faced by such determined resistance, Milošović's aims soon became more modest, involving support for the local autonomy of Croatia's Serbs, notably those living in Eastern Slovenia (on the border with Serbia itself) and Krajina (to the south-west, on the border with Bosnia). In September 1991, the UN introduced an arms embargo on all of former Yugoslavia in an attempt to arrest the drift to war. By the New Year, both Serbia and Croatia had agreed to the deployment of a UN 'Protection Force' to police the uneasy balance which had settled between their forces on the ground and which put almost a third of the country under Serb control. The force was formally established on 7 April 1992 but could not prevent several months of renewed fighting in early 1993.

Meanwhile, on 15 January 1992, following six months of urging by Germany, the European Community (EC) recognized Croatian and Slovenian independence, despite doubts both about their political stability and their respect for the human rights of minority groups. Recognition, though intended to stabilize the situation by forcing Milošović to come to terms with the end of the old Yugoslavia, proved a fateful decision because it gave international encouragement to the country's rapid break-up without sufficient attention being paid either to the problems that might follow or to the EC's ability to deal with them. In mid-1990, a majority of EC members had preferred to hold Yugoslavia together, but by October they had come to see its break-up as inevitable and, though they preferred to see this come about in an orderly way, had increasingly fallen out with Serbia. The US had followed a similar, reactive pattern, failing to heed warnings from its ambassador in Belgrade that the country was being torn apart by the demagoguery of Milošović and Tudjman. True, the EC did not recognize Macedonia's independence, but that was largely because one Community member, Greece, objected to the use of the name 'Macedonia', claiming that this should be reserved for the northern Greek province of the same name and fearing territorial claims by the former Yugoslav republic. Also, the EC did not at first recognize the independence of Bosnia-Herzegovina, but that was mainly because a referendum on the republic's independence had not yet been held. One was held on 29 February–1 March, followed by a formal declaration of independence on 3 March and recognition by both the EC and America on 6–7 April. The last date also marked the start of the Bosnian War.

War in Bosnia-Herzegovina

It had long been clear that the republic of Bosnia-Herzegovina presented a particularly difficult challenge for those bent on destroying Yugoslavia, because of its complex ethnic mix. About 45 per cent of the population were Muslims who, under President Alija Izetbegović, elected in November 1990, had increasingly wanted to emulate Croatia and Slovenia by seeking independence. The November elections were significant for being won by recently created nationalist parties, representing the Muslims, Serbs, and Croats. These parties 'were, in their anti-Communism and their championing of the market economy, very close in terms of programmes', and even formed a joint Cabinet, but they soon found it impossible to continue working together.[28] The Muslims had no wish to live under Serbian domination in a rump Yugoslav state and Izetbegović consistently argued that the partition of his republic—a course which Milošović and Tudjman discussed in early 1991—made no sense because the republic's ethnic groups were mixed together, so that drawing borders between them was a daunting problem. Yet about a third of the population were Serbs, many of who wished to remain tied to Serbia-proper, hence Milošović's interest in dividing Bosnia-Herzegovina and expanding his own republic's borders at its expense. In 1991, Bosnia's ethnic Serbs began to set up their own autonomous regions as well as, in October, their own parliament. They boycotted Izetbegović's referendum on Bosnian independence, held their own vote in favour of Yugoslav unity, and on 27 March 1992 declared their independence as the Bosnian Serb Republic. The other important ethnic group were the Croats, who made up about 18 per cent of the population. Many of these wished to be tied to Croatia-proper and, like the Serbs, they too began, in late 1991, to set up their own autonomous communes. Tudjman, who remained as keen on the partition of Bosnia-Herzegovina as Milošović (and with the same motive, of expanding his own area of control), backed the creation in December of a Bosnian Croat state, named Herzeg-Bosnia, under the leadership of Mate Boban.

In early 1992, therefore, Bosnia was on the brink not only of an ethnically based civil war but also of a war in which two other neighbouring republics, Serbia and Croatia, were closely involved. Despite their own animosity over the break-up of Yugoslavia, Milošović and Tudjman found a common cause, at some points, in advocating partition as preferable to Izetbegović's dream of a unitary state. In mid-March, the EC attempted to forestall bloodshed by devising a plan whereby Bosnia would remain a legal entity but be divided into three autonomous units on ethnic lines. It was the first of many similar schemes and it failed to prevent the outbreak of full-scale war in early April. From the start, little mercy was shown by any side. Although Muslims, Serbs, and Croats had lived together reasonably peacefully in the past (the Second World War being the exception rather than the rule), they soon took to driving each other from their homes, setting up internment camps, and massacring opponents. It was the Serb irregulars, however, backed by Milošović's Federal Army and air force, which proved most successful in grabbing territory and most ruthless in the policy of mass killing that they called 'ethnic cleansing'. They quickly seized about half of Bosnia and besieged the capital Sarajevo, whose population of 350,000 was threatened with starvation. At first, the Muslims and Bosnian Croats united against the Serb onslaught, which appeared to threaten the survival of them both; but by October there were serious clashes between them, focused on western Bosnia, with its substantial Croat population. By the end of 1992, millions of Bosnians had either been killed, interned, or become refugees, some of them fleeing to neighbouring states.

That such a vicious conflict could break out at the heart of Europe, after half a century of relative stability, put pressure on the EC in particular to find a solution to the problem. The US was anxious to limit its own overseas commitments and still fearful of 'another Vietnam', so that Secretary of State Baker publicly declared, 'we don't have a dog in this fight'.[29] Washington was keen to see the EC play a leading role in Bosnia and the Community's creation of a Common Foreign and Security Policy (CFSP) under the February 1992 Maastricht Treaty, led to real hopes of concerted action by the wealthy, well-armed West Europeans. Indeed, when the war began, the Luxembourg Foreign Minister, Jacques Poos, then chairing the EC Council of Ministers, stated that: 'If one problem can be solved by the Europeans it is the Yugoslav problem . . . It is not up to anyone else.'[30] The UN, with recent successes at peacemaking in Angola, Cambodia, and the Gulf War, was also pressed to act. In April–June, it agreed to extend its activities in Bosnia, sent 1,000 troops to protect food supplies to Sarajevo, and introduced far-reaching sanctions against Serbia, which soon caused shortages and encouraged hopes that Milošović would compromise on Bosnian independence, as he had already compromised over Croatia and Slovenia.

In August, the Security Council agreed to extend the UN's military presence in Bosnia, while the Human Rights Commission condemned the 'ethnic cleansing' policy. But such international efforts proved limited in their impact. The UN only gave protection to humanitarian aid supplies, it did not try forcibly to prevent the fighting, and at least one of its policies could be said to benefit the Serbs: forbidding arms supplies to all sides the UN, though it sought to be even-handed, made it difficult for the Muslims to secure advanced weapons, whereas Milošović helped supply the Bosnian Serbs with tanks, heavy artillery, and aircraft. 'Serb military superiority was an established fact. If the embargo was not lifted . . . the Bosnian government stood no chance of military success.'[31] The US began to criticize the arms embargo, but Britain and France argued that its removal would intensify the conflict and, perhaps, lead Russia to supply the Serbs, thus dragging the major powers in, on different sides. Izetbegović called for outside intervention to save Bosnia, and he secured some military aid from certain Islamic states, but the EC proved especially reluctant to be drawn into an intractable, ethnic conflict where a full-scale military intervention could prove long-lasting and costly, both in lives and money. The US too showed that there were limits to what it would do to maintain world order when there was no clear American interest at stake and the conflict was so complex. President Bush, who had recently claimed to have ended the 'Vietnam syndrome' through victory in the Gulf War, now said that he did 'not want to see the United States bogged down in any way into some guerrilla war. We lived through that once.'[32]

The US was more ready than the EC to condemn Serbia, and Britain and France were especially loath to escalate tension or even 'take sides', because they had troops on the ground in the UN 'protection force', which would bear the brunt of any fighting. They preferred instead to try to limit the conflict to Bosnia and to avoid intervention from outside the old Yugoslavia, while relying on economic pressures to control Serbia. EC governments made some dramatic gestures, notably with the visit to Sarajevo by France's President Mitterrand in June 1992; and the EC's peace envoy,

Lord Carrington, made various attempts to broker a ceasefire. But the August 1992 London Conference (which drew together not only the EC, but also the US, Russia, the former Yugoslav republics, and others, including some Muslim states), showed that, while outsiders were prepared to discuss the principles of peace in Bosnia they would do little concrete to achieve it. After this, Carrington gave way to another former British Foreign Secretary, Lord Owen who, along with the UN special envoy, the former US Secretary of State Cyrus Vance, chaired a permanent peace conference, set up in Geneva. In January 1993, this produced the Vance–Owen Plan, another bid to end the conflict on the basis of an ethnically divided Bosnia within a single, decentralized state. For a time, it seemed to win international support but it also, ironically, helped to intensify the scramble for territory between Muslims, Serbs, and Croats, and by May had run into the sand in its original form.

In May, the new Clinton administration talked of forcing a settlement with air strikes and a lifting of the arms embargo ('lift and strike'). It feared that the Vance–Owen Plan effectively rewarded Serb aggression, by giving the Bosnian Serbs autonomous control over a large area of the republic. Air strikes would have been the least costly method of US involvement, avoiding a commitment of ground troops, but whether Clinton (who had already raised the proposal in his election campaign) could have pushed the idea through against military doubts and public opposition in Washington was never tested. Britain and France, with Russian approval, predictably rejected 'lift and strike', a decision that led Clinton to back off from military involvement and rely on the UN to defend Muslims. The Bosnian Serbs formally rejected the Vance–Owen Plan and chose to fight on, controlling about 70 per cent of Bosnia by mid-1993. Another attempt by Milošović and Tudjman to partition the republic into three autonomous states was made soon afterwards but understandably rejected by the Muslims in August.

By early 1994, the war seemed endless, with Sarajevo still under siege and the Serbs predominant. But a Bosnian Serb mortar attack on a Sarajevo market place in early February provoked international outrage and led NATO to begin the enforcement of a 'no-fly zone' over Bosnia, thus neutralizing the Serbian air force. Such a 'no-fly zone' had first been declared by the UN in late 1992 but relied on the Western powers to be put into effect. NATO was also ready, now, to use its air power to protect UN Protection Force (UNPROFOR) troops and to force the withdrawal of Serb artillery units from around Sarajevo. Perhaps more valuable to the Muslims was the agreement by the Bosnian Croats—concerned by the scale of Serb advances—to form a single federation, with a single parliament and bureaucracy, following considerable diplomatic pressure on Tudjman from the US. This did not quite end local Muslim–Croat clashes but broadly it meant that from now on they would fight against the Serbs together. NATO and US action provoked concern in Russia, which had never recognized Bosnian independence and, encouraged by pan-Slavic feeling, posed as the defender of Serbia. But President Yeltsin was assuaged in April 1994 by the formation of a 'Contact Group' between Russia and the major Western powers (including America, Britain, France, and later Germany), which from now on played a major role in peace attempts. 'For Moscow, the group offered a way to confirm Russia's continuing international standing as a major power.'[33] In summer, the Group launched a plan for a two-fold partition of Bosnia, between the Bosnian Serbs and the Muslim-Croat Federation. This succeeded in dividing Milošović, who sensed a reasonable chance for agreement and supported the plan, from the Bosnian Serb leader, Radovan Karadžić, who wanted even more concessions and rejected it. The UN even agreed to ease sanctions on Serbia because of Milošović's stance, but this did not prevent an intensified period of conflict later in the year, which was only brought to an end by the onset of winter and a ceasefire brokered by the former US President Jimmy Carter. 'Indeed, even had the great powers set out to manufacture a state of permanent turmoil in the Balkans, it is unlikely they could have created a greater quagmire.'[34]

Achieving the Dayton Accords

Despite its unpromising beginning, 1995 proved the decisive year of the war, partly because of a military revival by the Muslims and Croats, partly because of mutual exhaustion, but also because of America's growing readiness to play an active role, backed by real force, in place of the ineffective EC and UN. In May, the UN suffered the humiliation of having hundreds of its soldiers held hostage by the Bosnian Serbs in retaliation for NATO air strikes; they were only released after several weeks, thanks to Milošović's help. Then, in July, the UN was powerless to prevent the Bosnian Serb commander, Radko Mladić, from overrunning Srebrenica, a Muslim enclave that had previously been designated a 'safe area' under UN protection. In the worst outrage of the war, Mladić's forces slaughtered about 8,000 of the male inhabitants, before overrunning another 'safe area', Zepa. It was because of these very events, however, which provoked such a strong response both locally and internationally, that determined action to thwart Serb ambitions was finally possible. In early August, the armed forces of Croatia, seeking to ease the pressure on their Bosnian allies, suddenly attacked the autonomous Croatian Serb region of Krajina, which was completely conquered in less than a week. In the US, Congress renewed its pressure to allow the Muslims arms and the government now backed tougher NATO action. The National Security Adviser, Anthony Lake, did much to press an active policy and the President was keen to resolve matters before the 1996 presidential campaign: 'Clinton's political fortunes could not be held hostage to events in the Balkans.'[35] He sent a special envoy, Richard Holbrooke, to try to achieve a diplomatic settlement. Holbrooke, a tough and experienced negotiator, recognized that the offensive in Krajina could mark a turning-point: 'we could not expect the Serbs to be conciliatory at the negotiating table as long as they had experienced nothing but success on the battlefield'.[36] With the Croats and Muslims now making major advances on the ground, NATO aircraft used air strikes in August–September to force the Bosnian Serbs back from Sarajevo, and in mid-October Holbrooke secured a ceasefire by all sides, to be followed by peace talks. Suddenly, 'the conditions were ripe for peace. Milošović might get . . . sanctions lifted. The Bosnian Serbs could head off further losses on the ground. The Croatians could consolidate their new territorial gains.' Ironically, it was the hard-pressed Muslims who were most sceptical about negotiation, though tempted by the prospect of getting firm Western backing for any settlement.[37]

The peace talks were held in Dayton, Ohio, further highlighting America's close involvement in a settlement, in contrast to the early years of the Clinton administration. The negotiations took the form of proximity talks, with US officials as the mediators between the presidents of Bosnia, Croatia, and Serbia: there was no place for the Bosnian Serb leader, Karadžić, who was effectively forced to accept the settlement by pressure from Belgrade. Milošović, having been powerless to save Krajina, could see no point in fighting a war where the Bosnian Serbs were in retreat and the UN could revive sanctions against Serbia. Nor could he rely on strong Russian backing: Yeltsin had been critical of NATO air strikes but, keen to assert Russia's standing in the world and desperate for Western financial aid, he also approved of the Dayton talks, being hopeful of taking part in a peacekeeping force. On 21 November 1995, the Dayton Peace Accords were finalized. Remarkably similar to earlier plans, the accords created a decentralized Bosnian government, with 51 per cent of the country in the Bosnian-Serb Federation, the rest under the Bosnian Serbs. This, of course, was far less an area of control than the Serbs might have hoped for a year earlier and it reflected the defeat of their attempt, in the spring of 1995, at complete victory. The settlement, which involved military withdrawals by all sides, a return of refugees to their homes, and free elections, was to be policed by a 60,000-strong NATO-led, 'Implementation Force' (IFOR). This would include not only 20,000 US troops but also, to Yeltsin's satisfaction, 2,000 Russian troops, who would be independent of NATO command.

Initially, the force was to remain in Bosnia only for a fixed period, but in late 1997 President Clinton, encouraged by European states, extended its mandate indefinitely. In its first few years, it did not experience any large-scale challenges, but the Muslims, Croats, and Serbs within Bosnia were far from agreeing joint policies (or even a 'national' flag) for their country, and the renewal of war was a permanent danger. In the first three-way elections for the rotating presidency, in September 1996, the communities voted on strongly ethnic lines and, while the Muslims confirmed support for Izetbegović, the Bosnian Serbs chose a suspected war criminal, Momčilo Krajišnik, as their leader. IFOR did periodically capture some of those accused of genocide, who were sent to face a war crimes tribunal in the Hague, and held its first trial in May–November 1996. But many of those who had led the way in ethnic cleansing, such as Karadžić and Mladić, though indicted, remained free.

The conflict had been successfully contained with the former Yugoslavia, and brought to an uneasy settlement, but it had exposed the limits to the powers of both the UN and the EC's common security policy, and had further highlighted the continent's continuing reliance on the US as a guarantee of stability. Washington was praised for the Dayton achievement but its very success in 1995 reinforced arguments that, if it had become active much earlier, perhaps backing the Vance–Owen Plan more forcefully, many thousands of lives might have been saved. Owen himself certainly believed this, arguing that, by failing to support the plan in 1993, the Clinton administration 'had decided that the price of putting US troops on the ground in order to reverse ethnic cleansing was too high . . .' and that the cost was two more years of carnage.[38] It is also arguable that, in the short term, 'the Dayton settlement had the general effect of strengthening Milošović's rule in Serbia', because he now seemed to be accepted as a negotiating partner by the West.[39] This was a background factor in the outbreak of violence in another Balkan troublespot, Kosovo, in 1998–9, which, however, was followed by the fall of Milošović and, later, his own appearance before the Hague tribunal.

The 1999 Kosovo Crisis

In the wake of the 1995 Dayton Accords on the future of Bosnia, several potential causes of tension still existed in the former Yugoslavia. The Dayton Accords themselves might have broken down; there was potential discontent among Serbia's Hungarian minority, mainly living in the Vojvodina region; and there was also the possibility of Montenegro, the only Yugoslav republic remaining in federation with Serbia, declaring independence. Some problems actually eased in the late 1990s: in 1998 the Serbs pulled out of Eastern Slavonia, their last enclave on Croatian territory. But serious trouble arose in the Serbian region of Kosovo. With a population of two million that was ethnically 90 per cent Albanian, Kosovo had lost its status as an autonomous province of Yugoslavia in 1989. Serbian national identity was closely wrapped up in possession of Kosovo, not least because of the battle of Kosovo, where a Serb army was defeated by the Turks in 1389. Until the seventeenth century, it had been at the heart of Serbian territory but there had then been an exodus of Serbs as they fled from Ottoman rule. In 1990, the Serbs also closed the local Kosovan assembly and during the 1990s Kosovo became a place where about 20,000 Serbs were resettled from elsewhere in the Balkans, especially from Krajina after it was conquered by Croats in 1995. But only in the first months of 1998 did Slobodan Milošović initiate a harshly oppressive policy in the region, which was condemned on 31 March by the UN Security Council. In May 1998, there was some hope of a negotiated settlement, thanks to a US-sponsored meeting between Milošović and the ethnic Albanian politician, Ibrahim Rugova. But some Kosovan Albanians already feared that Rugova was proving too moderate. A small Kosovan Liberation Army (KLA) had already been formed and had begun to target Serb officials.

Serious fighting erupted in Kosovo around September 1998, with Serb atrocities against the ethnic Albanians creating tens of thousands of refugees. It was in late September, with no desire to repeat the Bosnian experience and under mounting pressure from the public, that NATO began contingency plans for air strikes against the Serbs, a step which may have induced Milošović to attempt compromise. On 13 October, after days of talks with the US envoy, Richard Holbrooke, a ceasefire was agreed and a monitoring mission set up for Kosovo by the Organization of Security and Co-operation in Europe (OSCE). There was renewed violence in December, however, and international concern intensified with the discovery, in mid-January, of a massacre of Albanians in the village of Racak. NATO began a naval build-up in the Adriatic and Milošović was again urged to talk by the 'contract group' (already set up to deal with Bosnia) of America, Russia, Britain, France, Germany, and Italy. The British and French foreign ministers chaired 'proximity talks' between Serbian and KLA representatives in Rambouillet, France, in February and a second round in mid-March. The Albanians were ready to accept a deal on autonomy for three years, followed by talks on a permanent settlement but they would not accept Serb demands that the KLA be disarmed. The Serbs, determined to maintain their sovereign rights over Kosovo, refused demands for a NATO peacekeeping force to be deployed and for a referendum on Kosovan independence to be held in due course. One key problem was that Kosovo was constitutionally a part of Serbia and if it were broken off by force it would set an unwelcome precedent for conflicts elsewhere. Borders throughout the Balkans would be thrown into doubt. Indeed, during the whole 1999 crisis, NATO never questioned that Kosovo was part of Serbia. Paradoxically, however, NATO did feel it morally right to intervene in Kosovo by force to protect the Albanians, even though intervention in a 'civil' conflict was unjustified under international law. With the KLA limited in strength and a ground invasion by NATO forces likely to be costly in lives and money, it was decided to put pressure on Milošović by using air attacks. These were to be carried out by NATO, rather than a UN force, because UN action could have been impeded by Russia.

The failure of the Rambouillet talks was followed by a rapid escalation of violence. As Serb forces began large-scale attacks on the Albanians, the OSCE mission was withdrawn. Last-minute talks between Holbrooke and Milošović on 22–23 March failed to achieve anything. On 24 March, NATO began a series of bombing attacks, 'Operation Allied Force', against Serb military targets, communications systems, and fuel depots in Kosovo and in Serbia proper. Economic sanctions against Serbia were also strengthened, with an EU oil embargo enforced on 26 April. Yet rather than backing down, Milošović intensified the efforts at 'ethnic cleansing' and even tried to depopulate Kosovo by driving the ethnic Albanians out. There were about half a million refugees by the end of April, most of them fleeing into neighbouring Albania, itself poor and unprepared for such an influx. Over 100,000 fled south to Macedonia, which had its own Albanian minority. NATO's expectations of a swift victory were unfulfilled. The alliance's air campaign was blunted by poor weather, the Serb military's deployment of 'dummy' targets, and increasing concern over civilian deaths. Another problem for NATO was the potential support for Serbia from its fellow Slavs in Eastern Europe, not least Russia, as well as from other countries who were concerned about American-led military action, such as China. On 12 April, to raise the spectre of pan-Slavism, the Yugoslav Parliament voted in favour of a union with Russia and Belarus, whilst Sino-American relations were thrown into the crisis following the accidental bombing of the Chinese embassy in Belgrade by US jets on 7 May. Yugoslavia also tried to take NATO to the International Court over the legality of the bombing campaign. There was evidence of growing opposition to the campaign in some NATO countries, not least Italy, but the bombing was intensified in late May by attacks on Serbia's power and water supplies, and on 27 May Milošović was himself indicted for war crimes by the UN. In early June, Milošović showed signs of wanting a settlement and began to pull his army out of Kosovo, which led NATO to suspend its air campaign on 10 June.

The crisis, which cost perhaps 10,000 lives, was widely seen in the West as having been resolved, thanks to firm military action, with Serbia the defeated party. This impression was strengthened by the deployment of a NATO-controlled peacekeeping force, KFOR, and by the withdrawal of the last Serbian armed forces on 20 June. By early July, most ethnic Albanians had returned to a devastated Kosovo. But the eventual settlement was something of a compromise, with Kosovo remaining part of Serbia, no promise of a referendum on its future, and an undertaking by KFOR to protect Kosovan Serbs as well as Albanians. In addition to the military activity, there had also been considerable diplomatic endeavours to bring peace, notably, contact between the Russians and the Finnish President, who acted as a mediator with NATO. The Russians even deployed their own element in KFOR, initially beating British and French troops to the key town of Pristina, before accepting overall NATO command on 18 June. That Russian soldiers could serve in a NATO-led force was itself a remarkable development, ten years after the end of the Cold War.

Milošović clung on to power for barely a year after the Kosovo humiliation. He had survived mass demonstrations against him in Serbia in the winter of 1996–7 but in early October 2000 his regime collapsed in the face of renewed demonstrations, following his refusal to accept defeat in a general election held the previous month. Subsequently, he was sent to the Hague, to face war crimes charges before the international criminal court, but died in custody in 2006. His successor, Vojislav Kostunica, surrendered Milošović to the UN for trial in April 2001, improving Serbia's relations with the West in the process. At the same time, the KLA ceased to be valuable to the West as allies and, for some months, stirred up unrest among ethnic Albanians in Macedonia, leading to a NATO deployment in that country after August 2001, to help secure a peace settlement. The final break-up of Yugoslavia came in June 2006 when, following a closely fought referendum, Montenegro decided on independence. More humiliating for Serbia, was Kosovo's declaration of independence in February 2008. Although many states (including Russia) refused to recognize this, most of NATO and the EU did so. The former Yugoslavia remained a potential trouble spot. Aside from the inherent instability of the Bosnian settlement and bitter Serbian resentment over events in Kosovo, the 1990s had also seen the growth of organized crime, often linked to extreme nationalist groups and becoming deeply imbedded in government institutions. The newly independent states all had ambitions of eventually joining the EU, but they found it difficult to meet its pre-conditions of stable political institutions, fair judicial systems, and an end to corruption. Slovenia, which had largely escaped the violence of the 1990s, was able to join NATO (March 2004) and the EU (May 2004) at an early date. But only in June 2011 was a date set for Croatian membership. Around the same time, Serbia finally arrested the one, major remaining war criminal from the Bosnian War, Radko Mladić, and sent him for trial at the international criminal court in the Hague, where Karadžić had already gone on trial in October 2009, fifteen months after being captured.

D. NATO and European Security

NATO Outlives the Cold War

One of the most remarkable features of international relations in the wake of the Cold War was the survival of NATO. NATO had been created in 1949 as a means of strengthening Western Europe's resistance to Soviet influence (Chapter 4, B). Its military role soon became linked to the nuclear forces which would compensate for the West's numerical inferiority in conventional forces. In 1967, following the Harmel Report, it had taken on a second role as a participant in East–West détente. But by 1992 the military threat from the Eastern bloc had disappeared and relations with Moscow had moved beyond détente to normality. NATO therefore seemed to lack a *raison d'être*, and it seemed possible that the US and Western Europe would drift apart, divided by trade rivalry and differences in socio-political outlook. Yet the organization not only outlived the Cold War, it thrived in the new atmosphere, playing a more effective role in the Bosnian War (see Chapter 20, C) than did either the UN or the EC, and, by the end of the century, it was expanding its membership to former communist states. Declared by its own leaders in July 1990 to be 'the most successful defensive alliance in history', its resilience underlined the fact that, whatever the compromises on European security Gorbachev and Yeltsin hoped to secure, the Western powers did most to shape the post-Cold War world. This was not only true of the process of German reunification, which, albeit under limitations, brought the former East Germany into NATO in 1994; it was also seen in the end of the USSR's conventional superiority in Europe, the winding up (on 1 July 1991) of the Warsaw Pact, and the fact that Moscow's preferred security organization, the CSCE, was given only a subsidiary role in peacemaking.

In 1989, before the collapse of the Soviet position in Eastern Europe, large-scale cuts in conventional armaments on the continent had already been proposed by both alliance blocs. In March 1989, the 'Conventional Forces in Europe' (CFE) talks opened in Vienna and, in May, the Warsaw Pact accepted a NATO proposal for common ceilings on various categories of weapon. Around the same time, the Bush administration in Washington decided that it must match Gorbachev's long-established propensity to offer arms cuts, by proposing swingeing reductions in conventional forces. The National Security Adviser, Brent Scowcroft, even considered a mutual withdrawal of US and Soviet troops from Europe. By the end of the year, however, it was clear that NATO could expect more than an end to Soviet conventional superiority on the basis of equal ceilings and mutual concessions. Events in Eastern Europe included the beginnings of the Red Army's withdrawal from Czechoslovakia and Hungary and, whilst troops remained for the moment in Poland and East Germany, it was clear that the West was now in a commanding negotiating position. It was in order to realize its Cold War 'victory', not least in Germany, while keeping Moscow cooperative, that the US developed a policy known as the 'New Atlanticism'. In a speech on 4 May, Bush promised that the next NATO summit would give the alliance a greater political role and US officials put great effort into preparing this. A US-led NATO would be maintained, greater integration would be encouraged in the EC, and a reunited Germany would be treated as Washington's most important ally in both structures; NATO's role would be altered to allow it to deal with regional conflicts; and, to please the USSR, the role of the CSCE would also be expanded. Reliance on nuclear weapons would also be reduced, James Baker believing that 'a shift in nuclear strategy would do more than anything else to show the Soviets that the world had been transformed'.[40]

The 'New Atlanticism' created something of a crisis within the Western alliance, where Britain and France were concerned about Germany's increased standing. Thatcher especially was sceptical about reducing the role of nuclear weapons in European defence. Talks on the West's future defence doctrine led to a compromise at NATO's London summit of July 1990. Nuclear arms would still exist and might even be modernized, but they were to be fewer in number and treated as weapons of 'last resort': with the USSR's declining strength on the conventional side, NATO need no longer consider the 'first use' of such systems. There were also changes to conventional weapons doctrine, with a less 'forward' defence strategy and the creation of more multinational units. On the political side,

NATO welcomed the strengthening of the CSCE and also established closer military contacts with its former enemies by allowing Warsaw Pact members to set up liaison offices in Brussels. The London summit thus proved one of the most important in NATO history, maintaining the alliance's existence, altering its military doctrine, and opening the way to greater cooperation with the East. This was followed by the creation of a North Atlantic Cooperation Council in 1991, as an institutional link to the East Europeans.

Meanwhile, on 19–21 November 1990, a CSCE summit had been held in Paris, which was heralded by France's President Mitterrand as marking 'the end of the Cold War'. The most important document signed was the CFE treaty, which confirmed the end of Soviet armoured superiority and placed equal limits on types of military hardware. These limits were placed both on individual countries and alliance blocs as a whole: thus, the maximum number of tanks any county could have was 13,300, but there were only 20,000 in total for either NATO or the Warsaw Pact. Then again, within months, the end of the Warsaw Pact left the USSR in a much weakened position than envisaged at Paris: 'Moscow, which had controlled up to two-thirds of the conventional arms in Europe, would now control . . . only about a third.'[41] The Paris conference also included a declaration of democratic rights and individual freedom, emphasizing the ideological triumph of Western values, though there was no machinery to enforce this. And there was, for the first time, the creation of a formal institutional structure for the CSCE, with annual meetings of foreign ministers, two-yearly summits, and a 'conflict prevention centre', based in Vienna. But the last were modest steps, of uncertain significance, and over the following years it became clear that the West would only treat the CSCE with the minimum seriousness necessary to placate Moscow. The CFE treaty proved 'far from a panacea for the problems of European security' because in the 1990s crucial questions came to 'have less to do with force levels . . . than with broad political and security arrangements'.[42]

In July 1992, another conference, known as 'Helsinki II', agreed to turn the CSCE into a permanent body, to establish a parliamentary assembly, and set up a forum to discuss arms control and disarmament. The Russians still hoped that it might become the most significant security institution in Europe, outmatching NATO. After all, by including the US and Canada, the CSCE stretched in an easterly direction 'from Vancouver to Vladivostok' and there were doubts that NATO could outlive the Cold War. But the OSCE, with a Permanent Council in Vienna, was not launched until the December 1994 Budapest summit. Among other diplomatic tasks, it took on a role in peacekeeping (most notably on the disputed Armenian–Azerbaijani border in 1992–4), in conflict resolution (with little success in the case of the former Yugoslavia or Chechnya), and in democratization (it supervised elections in Bosnia and Albania in 1996 and in Chechnya in 1997). It set up an Office for Democratic Institutions and Human Rights, and it appointed a Commissioner for national minorities. But its potential as a pan-European body was undermined by the desire of East European states to join NATO, and by the fact that, with fifty-four members by 1995, it was too large and unwieldy to take rapid or effective action on international problems, especially since it had to work on the basis of unanimity, lacked a military force of its own, and could not make decisions binding on its members. The US and Britain were reluctant to rely on the OSCE, but even its key defender, Russia, was keen to prevent it meddling in Chechnya, which Moscow defined as a 'domestic' issue.

NATO Enlargement and the 'Partnership for Peace'

As it entered the post-Cold War era, NATO had both to satisfy its own members about its continued utility and to meet the demands of the former Warsaw Pact states—and even of some former Soviet republics—for entry to the organization. There were difficult challenges, which alternately threatened the Atlantic alliance with internal division and a revival of tension with Moscow. The threat from within came in the form of the Western European Union (WEU). Originally formed in the mid-1950s, but of little real significance in almost thirty years, the WEU was revived by Mitterrand in 1984 as a potential defence arm of the EC, with most members belonging to both. In 1990–1, the EC discussed the creation of a Common Foreign and Security Policy (CFSP), as included in the February 1992 Maastricht Treaty, and raised US concerns of a growing US–EC divide on defence matters as East–West tension receded. The US 'did not want to . . . kill off all further movement towards greater Western European defence cooperation', especially if this could remove some burdens from the back of the US, 'but nor did it want to let that movement be in directions it regarded as threatening to NATO'.[43] In November 1991, Bush even publicly warned that the EC must not try to push America out of its European security role, focused on NATO. Ideas for a Franco–German military grouping led to fears of 'a new European defence force wholly dependent on NATO . . . Such an arrangement could presage a future clash of interests', even within Europe, where the British and others would resent Franco–German dominance.[44] But by 1993 the incoming Clinton administration could afford to be more relaxed. The WEU and CFSP had remained separate entities, most West European states had no wish to compromise the US security guarantee, and CFSP had failed to prevent war in Bosnia, so that there seemed little chance of a coherent EC policy developing in the field of defence. Indeed, with the mounting difficulties in the Balkans and a desire to concentrate on its own domestic economic problems, Washington was actually eager to see the West Europeans take on a greater defence burden. A compromise position was effectively reached whereby the WEU was seen as reinforcing NATO and the US tolerated a strengthening of WEU activities, allowing the West Europeans to contemplate military operations independent of the US. Thus in 1994, France and Germany created the so-called 'Eurocorps' (first discussed in 1992) but committed it for use by NATO first of all. Also, in 1996 there was an agreement on 'Combined Joint Task Forces', under which the WEU might carry out operations of its own beyond the NATO area whilst using the NATO infrastructure. One result of this was that France, after thirty years of separation, became part of the alliance's military structure once more. Yet it was an exaggeration to claim that NATO's European members were somehow equal with Washington now, or that the West Europeans could really act without US approval. For only America had the long-range air transport facilities necessary for the Joint Task Forces to work, and in technological terms, US weaponry was becoming ever more advanced relative to its European allies.

If Washington had to temper its continuing military and political superiority in order to cooperate with West European governments, it was just as essential that it tread carefully in the East. Following the collapse of the Warsaw Pact, some of its former members looked to NATO members to provide them with military advice, armaments, and ultimately a security guarantee. Russia, however, was suspicious of Western attempts to enlarge their alliance eastwards and there was particular concern that the Baltic states on the Russian border were among those hoping to join NATO. The Atlantic Alliance had, therefore, to steer a delicate course between alienating Russia and disappointing the newly independent Eastern Europeans. 'The West must seek to move closer to Russia . . . while keeping NATO as a non-provocative insurance policy in case things go wrong', one study recommended.[45] The Bush administration was extremely cautious about upsetting Moscow and, for most of its first year in office, the Clinton administration seemed more focused on the Asia-Pacific region. Thus, the lines of a considered policy were only set in January 1994, when NATO's Brussels summit initiated the 'Partnership for Peace', itself rather tentative and disappointing to the Eastern Europeans. Under this programme, ex-Warsaw Pact members, ex-Soviet republics, and neutral countries could enter into military cooperation agreements with NATO, short of full membership. Enlargement might come in due course—and that possibility still disturbed Moscow—but for the moment, on offer were military consultations, joint exercises and the like, rather than any security guarantee. Despite disappointment with this in the East, countries subsequently signed up for the Partnership, beginning with Hungary in April. By June, it seemed that Russia would also join. But when the Russian Foreign Minister, Andrei Kozyrev, visited Brussels in December, he surprised his hosts by refusing to sign. Increasingly criticized by communists and nationalists at home for failing to protect Russian interests, he was determined to show that he was ready to risk a crisis with the West.

Kozyrev's resistance did not last long. As in other spheres, Russia was too weak, economically and politically, to stem the Western advance. On 31 May, the Foreign Minister was back in Brussels to sign a Partnership agreement. Yet the fear of a NATO–Russian crisis, which might also complicate attempts to resolve the Bosnian War, continued to hold back the process of actual NATO enlargement. There was a vigorous debate in Western capitals about the wisdom of admitting former communist states to alliance membership, with Germany tending to be more favourable than France or Britain. Germany was keen to stabilize the new democracies in the East and argued that NATO need not be seen as a threat to Russia. But critics countered that Russia was no longer a threat to Eastern Europe, so that NATO enlargement was unnecessary. At best, such enlargement would draw a collection of militarily weak and financially dependent states into the alliance; at worst it could provoke a new Cold War. In Washington, the debate finally favoured the East Europeans, and in 1996 the outgoing US Secretary of State, Warren Christopher, said that NATO enlargement could not be put off forever. Boris Yeltsin was facing a re-election campaign in June–July and, rather than put his presidency at risk by helping the communist opposition, Washington decided not to press the issue. But, in his second term, Clinton 'decided to adopt the enlargement of NATO as the emblem of his foreign policy'.[46]

Once the election was over, the US concentrated not on dealing with the East Europeans, but on negotiating an agreement with Russia that would set out the principles for her future relations with NATO. This gave Yeltsin the sense that he was being consulted as an equal, but the result of the talks, which included a Clinton–Yeltsin summit, was an agreement which confirmed that enlargement would take place without providing much succour to Moscow. The NATO–Russian 'Founding Act' of May 1997 created a permanent joint command to discuss security problems (including nuclear safety, peacekeeping operations, and counter-terrorism) but there was to be no Russian veto on NATO activities. It also included a statement that NATO had 'no intention' of deploying 'substantial' numbers of troops in any new member states, but the wording of this undertaking was much weaker than Moscow wanted. Statements that Russia and NATO did 'not consider each other adversaries', and would seek cooperation rather than confrontation, were backed up by Yeltsin with an announcement that Russia would no longer target NATO countries with nuclear missiles. Yet at the signature he also made clear that he was not happy about enlargement. Two months later a NATO summit in Madrid formally invited Poland, Hungary, and the Czech Republic to join with effect from April 1999, and others might follow later. In 1998, President Clinton confirmed that these might include former Soviet republics. The three new members took part in their first NATO gathering in Washington in March 1999, celebrating the fiftieth anniversary of the alliance. It was an occasion that confirmed that a Western agenda had dominated the post-Cold War security debate in Europe. The contrast with the situation ten years earlier was stark and underlined the diverging fortunes of Washington and Moscow: 'Former members of the Warsaw Pact have not simply defected from that alliance, but have joined what was once its opposition.'[47]

E. From European Community to European Union

The Single Market and Maastricht

The decade following the 'northern enlargement' of the European Community (EC) to Britain, Denmark, and Ireland in 1973 had been marked by disappointments for the organization. 'There were few new initiatives and no further successful integration.'[48] Stagflation had done much to destroy hopes of monetary union, though the 1979 Exchange Rate Mechanism (ERM) helped create some currency stability, especially in the mid-1980s. The years 1979–84 were dominated by arguments over Britain's budget contribution (see Chapter 13, C) and only after that was resolved did the fortunes of the Community begin to revive. In 1986, Spain and Portugal joined to complete the 'southern enlargement' of the EC: Greece had been a member since 1981. This not only increased the size of the EC to twelve states, but also forced greater spending on social and regional policies, through 'structural funds', to help the poorer Mediterranean states compete in the common market. It also encouraged consideration of institutional reform in order to strengthen the cohesion of the enlarged Community. At the same time, Western Europe's economies were growing strongly, making it easier to contemplate a new drive towards deeper integration, and there was widespread concern in Europe about the need to match US and Japanese competition, especially in the production of high-technology goods. In 1984–5, France's President, François Mitterrand, and West Germany's Chancellor, Helmut Kohl, both convinced 'pro-Europeans', worked together to support the establishment of an Intergovernmental Conference (IGC) on Community reform. The other original EC members—Italy, Belgium, the Netherlands, and Luxembourg—strongly supported this, as did Spain, Portugal, and Ireland, three countries who gained significantly from the structural funds. But Britain, Denmark, and Greece feared a loss of national power in the process.

The result of the 1985 IGC was the 'Single European Act'. This was something of a disappointment to keen 'federalist' states like Italy and Belgium. In many ways, it simply codified changes that had happened in the Community since its creation in 1957, such as the process by which, since 1974, the leaders had met in biannual summits. But it did include a number of institutional changes which made it easier in future to press on with integration, including greater powers for the European Parliament and, more importantly, the expanded use of 'qualified majority voting' (rather than unanimity between all the member governments) in the Council of Ministers. It extended the scope of the EC, to such areas as technological cooperation and the environment, and it included a commitment to Economic and Monetary Union (EMU), which would prove highly significant in future. Most important at the time, however, the Act included the undertaking to create, by January 1993, a genuine 'single market' not only in goods but also in services, capital, and people. 'The key motive behind the Single European Act was to resume the dynamic benefits of one large single market for European industry and commerce', following the growing protectionism of the 1970s.[49] It was mainly the last aspect which convinced the British government to support the reform programme, despite doubts about institutional reform and despite the fact that the process of creating the single market would strengthen the main supranational element in the Community, its executive body, the Commission. To the British, under Margaret Thatcher, the institutional changes seemed modest, whereas the single market promised to create a thriving European market, with a minimum of bureaucratic controls and maximum free enterprise, such as 'Thatcherite' policies aimed to achieve in Britain. An important factor was that, in order to force the British along, 'various items on the agenda of integration—completion of the common market . . . and the rather ambitious proposals for institutional reform—had been refined . . . in a single package', so that all had to be accepted together.[50]

Over the following years, three developments in the EC ran alongside each other. One was the preparation for the 'single market', which was achieved on schedule in 1993, but without quite the dramatic effect that had been hoped for, since by then the economic boom of the 1980s had ended. The second was the creation in mid-1988 of a committee under the Commission President, France's Jacques Delors, to study EMU. Britain and Denmark had little liking for this, believing that it could lead on to a full economic union and a major loss of national sovereignty. But the French were keen because EMU would fulfil their old aim of a European currency zone, in which German monetary power would be contained in a wider whole. EMU could also be seen as building on the single market, removing the cost of currency transactions from intra-EC trade and boosting growth. In April 1989, the Delors Plan was published, aiming to bring about a single currency in stages. Delors was in a strong position after successfully achieving the Single European Act and EMU was clearly his next aim. In October 1990, he openly declared that, 'we need a single currency before the year 2000'.[51] The third important development was also linked to the single market programme and backed by Delors. It was the proposal for a 'Social Charter', published in June 1989, which would guarantee minimum social welfare standards for the people of the Community and so protect them from the potential adverse impact of the free-enterprise Europe that the single market aimed to create.

Events at the end of 1989, with the collapse of Soviet Communism in the East, increased both Mitterrand's and Kohl's desire to strengthen EC institutions, primarily as a way to ensure that a reunited Germany remained committed to a European future, rather than the nationalism and militarism of the past. Indeed Kohl (like Adenauer in the 1950s) made it the central plank of his policy to tie Germany to its Western neighbours. In December 1989, EC leaders both expressed their support for German reunification and agreed that another IGC should meet to look at carrying the Delors Plan into effect. Later, it was agreed to set up two IGCs, the second to study a further round of institutional reforms. There was also, already at this time, talk of an 'eastern enlargement' of the Community to former communist states, though in the short term it was more realistic to think of bringing in countries like Austria, Finland, and Sweden, who had been neutral during the Cold War but who, with East–West tension in decline, could contemplate joining the EC.

The IGCs opened in late 1990 and the results of their work came before the European summit meeting at Maastricht, in the Netherlands, in December 1991. Here, changes were agreed which were embodied in a Treaty on European Union, signed at Maastricht in February 1992. 'The essence of the deal in Maastricht—like so much in the history of the EC—was a Franco–German bargain.'[52] The treaty had some similarities with the Single European Act in that it further strengthened the European Parliament, as Germany wanted, and expanded the use of qualified majority votes. But it also included the creation of a single European currency (the key French aim) by 1999 at the latest, it made the people of the EC citizens of a 'European Union', and it adopted the social charter. In all this, it seemed a great advance for advocates of integration, but there were problems. First, the British government, now under John Major, secured 'opt outs' from both EMU and the social protocol, believing Britain would be more competitive without them. Second, the supranational element in the Community was now only one 'pillar' among three. Other 'pillars' were created in the areas of a common foreign and security policy (CFSP) and of justice and home affairs (JHA), but here the greater coordination of European policy would be achieved by intergovernmental cooperation, on the basis of unanimity between the member states. The limits to supranationalism were further emphasized by the principle of 'subsidiarity', also part of the treaty, under which decisions were supposed to be taken at the lowest possible level, so that local, regional, and national governments retained wide responsibilities.

The Road to a Single Currency

Despite its complexities, the Maastricht Treaty proved to be a seminal point for the Community, the most important reform since the Treaty of Rome itself. Maastricht could not come into operation, however, until it had been ratified by all the members and this proved a difficult process, which for a time threatened to tear the Community apart. In all countries, there was debate over what the treaty really signified. Did it, as the British government claimed, mark the limits of integration, with the principle of subsidiarity a brake on the powers of the Commission once the single market was achieved? Or did it, as others argued, represent an important step forward, with strengthened central decision-making and the promise of a leap towards full economic union (with, perhaps, a common tax and spending system), thanks to EMU? In Denmark, one of the most 'sceptical' states where deeper integration was concerned, this debate was especially important because ratification was dependent on a referendum. Denmark, unlike Britain, had won no 'opt out' on the EMU, and on 2 June 1992 its people voted narrowly against the treaty.

The Danish referendum result threw the Community into turmoil, for two reasons. First, most obviously, it was not clear how to save the carefully framed Maastricht agreements, which required ratification by every member. An Irish referendum in mid-June in favour of the treaty could not prevent critics becoming more vocal elsewhere. In Britain, 'Eurosceptics' were euphoric and the government suspended the ratification process. Mitterrand tried to restore faith in the process of integration by calling a referendum in France, which, initially, he seemed likely to win easily; but by the time it was held, in September, it had become a vote of confidence in the President's leadership and he came within a whisker of losing. Meanwhile, the second problem created by the Danish 'no' vote, was currency instability. By threatening Maastricht, the Danes also questioned the likelihood of the single currency ever being achieved and deepened problems in the money markets, which were already troubled by the impact of low growth, rising unemployment, and, importantly, the economic costs of German reunification. By September, the exchange rate mechanism (ERM) was in crisis and several currencies were forced to leave it, including Britain (a member since 1992) and Italy (a founder member). Now, not only was the future of Maastricht in doubt, so also was that of a well-established body, the ERM.

The specific problem of Danish doubts was resolved in a second referendum in May 1993, which the 'yes' camp won because the government had now negotiated an exchange rate mechanism (ERM) 'opt out'. The Maastricht Treaty came fully into operation on 1 November, and at that point the EC became the European Union (EU). But by then there was little popular enthusiasm for integration, even in France (where the 1992 referendum had shown the potential strength of the Eurosceptic lobby) or Germany (where there was real concern over the loss of the Deutschmark, which had become the greatest symbol of national economic virility since 1949). With Europe back in the economic doldrums, the ERM was still unstable and, in early August 1993, became virtually meaningless when its remaining members decided to widen their possible fluctuations of exchange rates to a massive 15 per cent. Over the following years, it seemed that a single currency, the most significant promise of the Maastricht Treaty, might not come about or that, if it did, there would be few members. In order to join, countries had to achieve certain 'convergence' targets involving public debt, inflation, and budget deficits, and it seemed that even France and Germany might fail to meet these. Even as it became a 'Union', the EC seemed to be diversifying in ever more confusing ways. Britain and Denmark had their EMU opt outs. Seven countries, including France and Germany, joined together in the Schengen agreement (effective in 1995) to end passport controls on their shared borders, but the other members stood aside. Most countries were members of the WEU, which some saw as a potential defence wing for the EU, but Ireland was stubbornly neutral. Thanks to such diversity, the British government now advocated a 'multi-speed' Europe in which, instead of seeking integration of a common pace, members would pick and choose the areas in which they cooperated. In 1996–7, a review of the Maastricht Treaty was carried out by another IGC but the results, codified in the Amsterdam Treaty, were very modest: there was an extension of issues that could be decided by weighted majority voting; and the Union gained new powers over employment and immigration. Respect for the Commission in Brussels was marred by accusations of corruption and inefficiency, which led to all commissioners (including the President, Jacques Santer), submitting their resignations in 1999. In effect, Maastricht represented 'the high-water mark of the elite-driven reform agenda of the 1980's relaunch . . . provoking a popular backlash which subsequently strained the reform process'.[53]

Yet, however difficult the mid-1990s proved, the EU did continue to advance, and in January 1995 it was joined by Austria, Sweden, and Finland. This was soured somewhat in February 2000, when the ultra-right-wing Freedom Party entered Austria's coalition government, leading to seven months of sanctions by the EU. But agreement had already been reached, in the early 1990s, that there should be a further enlargement in future to include certain East European countries, including Poland, the Czech Republic, and Hungary. Talks on the eastern enlargement got underway in 1998 and, like the proposed expansion of NATO, showed that some key Western organizations, which had been created during the Cold War, could continue to thrive after it. In 1993–4, greater spending on 'structural funds' was agreed to help the poorer members with infrastructure projects in such areas as transport. There were further measures to create uniform practices across the EU, as in the field of health and safety at work and in 1997, when the Conservatives were voted out of office in Britain, the new Labour government signed up to the social protocol of the Maastricht Treaty. The most important, positive sign of all, however, was that, despite their economic difficulties, the single currency idea remained intact, and most members remained committed to it. The 1997 target date may have been missed, but in the spring of 1998, it was decided that, of those who wished to proceed, only Greece failed to meet the convergence criteria. The rest—minus Britain, Denmark, and Sweden, none of whom wished to be part of the 'first wave' of members—created the 'euro' in January 1999 as an accounting currency. Actual euro notes and coins began to circulate in January 2002.

Visit the online resources that accompany this book to test your understanding and take your learning further: www.oup.com/he/young-kent3e

NOTES

1. Steven Hurst, *The Foreign Policy of the Bush Administration* (Cassell, New York, 1999), 64.
2. Philip Zelikow and Condoleezza Rice, *Germany Unified and Europe Transformed* (Harvard University Press, Cambridge, 1995), 128–30.
3. George Bush and Brent Scowcroft, *A World Transformed* (Vintage Books, New York, 1998), 203–4.
4. Timothy Garton Ash, *In Europe's Name* (Random House, New York, 1993), 349–50.
5. Don Oberdorfer, *How the Cold War Came to an End: The US and the Soviet Union 1983–90* (Jonathan Cape, New York, 1992), 391; Eduard Shevardnadze, *The Future Belongs to Freedom* (Sinclair-Stevenson, London, 1991), 134.
6. James Baker, *The Politics of Diplomacy* (G. P. Putnam's Sons, New York, 1995), 198.

7. Raymond Garthoff, *The Great Transition: American–Soviet Relations and the End of the Cold War* (Brookings Institution, Washington, DC, 1994), 412.
8. Quoted in Stephen Szabo, *The Diplomacy of German Unification* (St Martin's Press, New York, 1992), 75.
9. George Bush and Brent Scowcroft, *A World Transformed* (Vintage Books, New York, 1998), 196–7.
10. Mikhail Gorbachev, *Memoirs* (Doubleday, London, 1996), 532.
11. Ian Clark, *The Post-Cold War Order: The Spoils of Peace* (Oxford University Press, Oxford, 2001), 92.
12. Mary Fulbrook, *Interpretations of the Two Germanies* (2nd edn, Macmillan, Basingstoke, 2000), 84.
13. Vladimir Zubok, 'Gorbachev and the End of the Cold War', *Cold War History*, 2 (2002), 62.
14. Don Oberdorfer, *How the Cold War Came to an End: The US and the Soviet Union 1983–90* (Jonathan Cape, New York, 1992), 402.
15. Mikhail Gorbachev, *Memoirs* (Doubleday, London, 1996), 372 and 346.
16. Robert M. Gates, *From the Shadows* (Touchstone, New York, 1997), 496.
17. Michael Beschloss and Strobe Talbott, *At the Highest Levels* (Little, Brown, Boston, 1993), 304.
18. Boris Yeltsin, *The View from the Kremlin* (HarperCollins, London, 1994), 105–6; Mikhail Gorbachev, *On My Country and the World* (Columbia University Press, New York, 2000), 83–4; Mikhail Gorbachev, *Memoirs* (Doubleday, London, 1996), 658.
19. G. D. G. Murrell, *Russia's Transition to Democracy* (Portland, Brighton, 1996), 184.
20. Anatol Lieven, *Chechnya: Tombstone of Russian Power* (Yale University Press, New Haven, 1998), 101.
21. Leon Aron, *Yeltsin, a Revolutionary Life* (HarperCollins, London, 2000), 570.
22. Anatol Lieven, *Chechnya: Tombstone of Russian Power* (Yale University Press, New Haven, 1998), 145.
23. Quoted in Boris Yeltsin, *Midnight Diaries* (Public Affairs Press, 2000), 335.
24. Michael Foucher, 'Western Europe and the Balkans', in F. W. Carter and H. T. Norris, (eds), *The Changing Shape of the Balkans* (University College London Press, London, 1996), 124–5.
25. 'Introduction' to D. A. Dyker and I. Vejvoda (eds), *Yugoslavia and After: A Study in Fragmentation, Despair and Rebirth* (Addison-Wesley Longman, New York, 1996), 19.
26. John Lampe, *Yugoslavia as History* (Cambridge University Press, Cambridge, 1996), 325.
27. Tim Judah, *The Serbs: History, Myth and the Destruction of Yugoslavia* (Yale University Press, New Haven, 1997), 309.
28. Xavier Bougarel, 'Bosnia and Hercegovina', in D. A. Dyker and I. Vejvoda (eds), *Yugoslavia and After: A Study in Fragmentation, Despair and Rebirth* (Addison-Wesley Longman, New York, 1996), 98.
29. Quoted in R. A. Melanson, *American Foreign Policy since the Vietnam War* (M. E. Sharpe, Armonk, 1996), 256.
30. Quoted in Mark Almond, *Europe's Backyard War* (Heinemann, London, 1994), 32.
31. John Hulsman, *A Paradigm for the New World Order* (Macmillan, Basingstoke, 1997), 129.
32. Quoted in Steven Hurst, *The Foreign Policy of the Bush Administration* (Cassell, New York, 1999), 217.
33. Ivo Daalder, *Getting to Dayton* (Brookings Institution, Washington, DC, 2000), 28.
34. Christopher Bennett, *Yugoslavia's Bloody Collapse* (Hurst, London, 1995), 236.
35. Ivo Daalder, *Getting to Dayton* (Brookings Institution, Washington, DC, 2000), 166.
36. Richard Holbrooke, *To End a War* (Modern Library, New York, 1998), 73.
37. William Hyland, *Clinton's World: Remaking American Foreign Policy* (Praeger, Westport, 1999), 41.
38. David Owen, *Balkan Odyssey* (Victor Gollancz, London, 1996), 196.
39. Noel Malcolm, *Kosovo: A Short History* (Macmillan, London, 1998), 353.
40. James Baker, *The Politics of Diplomacy* (G. P. Putnam's Sons, New York, 1995), 258.

41. Raymond Garthoff, *The Great Transition: American–Soviet Relations and the End of the Cold War* (Brookings Institution, Washington, DC, 1994), 535.
42. Phil Williams, 'CFE and the Future of NATO', in J. Philip Rogers (ed.), *The Future of European Security* (Macmillan, Basingstoke, 1993), 144.
43. Steven Hurst, *The Foreign Policy of the Bush Administration* (Cassell, New York, 1999), 211.
44. Peter Duignan and L. H. Gann, *The US and the New Europe* (Hoover Institution, PaloAlto, 1994), 257.
45. Trevor Taylor, *European Security and the Former Soviet Union* (Royal Institute of International Affairs, London, 1994), 137.
46. William Hyland, *Clinton's World: Remaking American Foreign Policy* (Praeger, Westport, 1999), 43.
47. Ian Clark, *The Post-Cold War Order: The Spoils of Peace* (2nd edn, Oxford University Press, Oxford, 2001), 92.
48. Martin Dedman, *The Origins and Development of the European Union* (Routledge, London, 1996), 123.
49. ibid., 126.
50. Paul Taylor, 'The New Dynamics of EC Integration in the 1980s', in Juliet Lodge (ed.), *The European Community and the Challenge of the Future* (Pinter, London, 1989), 8.
51. Quoted in Desmond Dinan, *Ever Closer Union?* (Macmillan, Basingstoke, 1994), 418.
52. Charles Grant, *Delors: Inside the House that Jacques Built* (Nicholas Brealey Publishing, London, 1994), 206.
53. Philip Lynch, Nanette Neuwahl, and Wyn Rees (eds), *Reforming the European Union: From Maastricht to Amsterdam* (Longman, London, 2000), 235.

21

US Predominance and the Search for a Post-Cold War Order

Chapter contents

A. US Foreign Policy in the 1990s: The Search for Direction

The Bush Administration

George Bush came to power in January 1989 with an uncertain political programme, but considerable experience in foreign policy-making behind him. In the 1970s, he had served as envoy to China and Director of the Central Intelligence Agency (CIA), whilst in the 1980s, as Vice-President under Reagan, he had held special responsibilities in the international field. As President, he very much concentrated on world affairs and drew an experienced, loyal team around him of old colleagues like the Secretary of State, James Baker, and National Security Adviser, Brent Scowcroft. Criticized at first for failing to define his policies promptly, and with some Republicans doubting the depth of his conservativism, he nonetheless had a series of foreign successes before the end of 1991 and was prepared to take tough, military action when he felt it justified. By then, he had overthrown General Noriega of Panama, successfully managed the collapse of communism in Eastern Europe, encouraged the peaceful replacement of the Sandinista regime in Nicaragua, backed Helmut Kohl in achieving the reunification of Germany, triumphantly dealt with Saddam Hussein's (see Box 21.1) invasion of Kuwait, made progress on Arab–Israeli talks, and witnessed the disintegration of the Soviet Union. His cautious, pragmatic, orderly approach carried both advantages and disadvantages. On the one hand, he escaped any major disasters abroad and avoided antagonizing the USSR or rekindling the Cold War. On the other hand, he seemed to be undynamic and at the mercy of events—he could hardly, for example, claim credit for the demise of the USSR—and he failed to provide a sense of overall direction to

US foreign policy once the Cold War ended. He did not appreciate early enough that, with the Cold War apparently 'won', the American people had become preoccupied with domestic concerns, notably the poor shape of the economy.

Here, arguably, Bush was a victim of his predecessor's policies: the high defence spending and tax reductions of 'Reaganomics' may, in some eyes, have resuscitated free enterprise and helped 'defeat' the Soviets, but they also left behind a massive budget deficit, which climbed to $230 billion in 1990. It was possible to reduce defence spending from the late 1980s onward but this did not come quickly enough to work any economic miracle and in 1991–2 there was a depression. Furthermore, the President failed to demonstrate how his concentration on foreign policy benefited the US and 'by late 1991 the public began to feel that Bush's international activities were actually hurting his ability to handle the economy'.[1] In 1992, his younger Democratic opponent, Bill Clinton, exploited concerns over lack of investment in the economy to achieve a victory in the presidential election that had seemed highly unlikely twelve months before. Bush also alienated the public by appearing to renege on his initial promise of 'no new taxes'. And, even in the foreign policy field there were criticisms, especially because 'Bush and his team were frequently intensely secretive, unaccountable and contemptuous of Congress.'[2]

For a time in 1990–1, it appeared that Bush might seek to build policy around the concept of a 'New World Order'. It was clear, even before the Kuwait crisis, that trying to secure old Cold War aims was no longer adequate. But what was now required remained far from clear. The USSR, even before it collapsed and even if it retained a huge nuclear arsenal, had ceased to be the ideological and security threat that it had been as recently as 1985. With the important exception of China—a country that continued to present its own special problems for Washington—very few Marxist-Leninist regimes had failed to collapse or come to terms with US predominance by 1992. Neither was the advance of democratic institutions only a product of communist retreat. In Chile, the Pinochet dictatorship came to an agreed end in March 1990, while in South Africa apartheid was being wound down. Yet, whatever the scale of hopeful changes, Bush believed the US must remain engaged in world affairs to ensure peaceful developments and remove new threats, and Saddam Hussein's invasion of Kuwait seemed to justify this. The decision to place the punishment of aggression at the centre of the 'new world order' concept 'accurately reflected the administration's conservative understanding of world politics, its preference for stability to reform, and its identification of stability with the status quo', notwithstanding all the changes going on around it.[3]

But the new world order was never defined very precisely by Bush. When he explained it to Congress on 11 September 1990, he spoke of 'a world where the rule of law supplants the rule of the jungle, a world in which nations recognize the shared responsibilities for freedom and justice', but this left much to be interpreted.[4] It has been said that 'many of the broader objectives sought by the United States since 1989 actually bear a strong resemblance to those it pursued before the end of the Cold War', including a rejection of isolationism, support for democracy, and a tendency to see the new order as coterminous with American national interests.[5] This had been equally true of the Truman Doctrine, though that had understandably emphasized anti-communism as well.

One sympathetic study of Bush's foreign policy argued that 'the New World Order was about much more than resistance to aggression: it did, in fact, represent a relatively coherent and plausible strategy for US foreign policy in the post-Cold War era'; in addition to 'order' it set out broad aims of peace, democracy, and free trade, which Bush hoped to achieve in cooperation with other countries and which had the sympathy of most Americans.[6] Another study accepts that a global, non-discriminatory trade system and a new 'system of collectivised security' were two vital aims for Bush, and adds, regarding the third, that 'liberalism was consciously . . . deployed at the end of the Cold War as an instrument for consolidating its . . . beneficial outcomes'. Liberalism became a vehicle for encouraging capitalism and democratic rights in former communist societies, for justifying 'humanitarian intervention' where states became anarchic, and for ostracizing those regimes that did not want to be part of the new order. In all areas, however, the US was actually highly selective in the way it interpreted Bush's principles.[7]

A major problem was that such objectives, like free trade, peaceful cooperation, and the fostering of liberal democracy, were more difficult to translate into precise strategic priorities when there was no single major power that presented a threat to them. US policy during the Cold War had hardly been flawless—Vietnam, above all, was testament to that—but it had a certain strategic direction, boosted presidential power, and at times (though less consistently after Vietnam) fostered bipartisanship in foreign affairs. Certainly, Bush wished to achieve some specific aims, such as strategic arms control agreements, the strengthening of the United Nations, and the punishment of Saddam Hussein's attack on Kuwait. There was a basic desire to secure the gains made from victory in the Cold War, not least by fostering US values of liberalism and free enterprise. But the very fact that US security no longer seemed to be menaced directly caused problems for those in power in Washington. Arms control agreements seemed less urgent after the Cold War; the powers of the UN were limited, as seen in its failure to deal with the conflict in Bosnia; and Saddam's Iraq, whatever its threat to the Middle East, was hardly a substitute for the Soviet Union as a rival to the US for global hegemony. There was also the old question of whether the US possessed the will and the resources to shape the world it wanted, especially when there was 'a more fragmented, and more politicized foreign policy process' than during the Cold War, with Congress very assertive and the press more active in whipping up public opinion.[8]

The ease of the military victory over Iraq, added to the demise of the USSR, led Americans to feel that they were safe from outside attack, with no major enemy to worry about, a view that would persist until the terrorist bombings of New York and Washington on 11 September 2001, which were reminiscent of the shock caused by Pearl Harbor. Such feelings were reinforced by the belief—which predated the end of the Cold War—that America's allies in Europe and Japan should bear more of the burden of their own defence. As to the UN, despite Bush's encouraging rhetoric, it was hardly a popular institution in the US, being seen as financially wasteful, dominated by a Third World agenda, and likely to draw America into problems that were none of its concern. The determination of the US to avoid any part in the Bosnian War in 1992 drew many of these elements together. Most Americans felt they had no security stake in the conflict, they wanted to leave its resolution to the European Community, and were baffled by the extreme hatreds of such ethnic conflict. Yet an important, paradoxical development in the outlook of the American public was that, while power-political motives for action had become less important, idealistic ones loomed larger, leading to the greater popularity of 'humanitarian intervention'. The desire to foster liberal values, linked to the lack of a major enemy, led the American media to demand action in Somalia in 1992, where the risks of involvement seemed few and the opportunity to end human suffering clear. This was despite the fact that the US, in the wake of Reagan, was unenthusiastic about huge-scale aid to the less developed world. The emotional and hasty decision to intervene in Somalia was arguably one of Bush's few foreign policy errors, but one taken in order to satisfy public and media opinion and done with the approval of President-elect Clinton, who soon inherited the problem.

New Agendas: The Narcotics Trade and Environmentalism

Apart from the 'new world order', before the 'war on terror' was declared by George Bush Jnr in 2001, there were several candidates for the issue that might provide a focus for American foreign policy after the Cold War. One was that Washington should treat so-called 'Islamic fundamentalism' as its chief ideological enemy following the communist retreat, and certainly the policies of Iran, the country most associated with 'fundamentalism' in US eyes, remained a key concern under Bush. But there was no major US–Iranian crisis and fundamentalism was an amorphous factor in world politics (even if a potent bogey in America). Furthermore, any attempt to treat 'fundamentalists' as enemies ran the risk of creating an unnecessary religious conflict between Christians and Muslims, when numerous Muslim states—Egypt and Jordan, Pakistan and Morocco—were US allies. A more promising focus for popular hatred was the drugs trade, which Bush in September 1989 described as the 'gravest domestic threat' to America. The issue was far from new: the US government had been trying to tackle the international commerce in narcotics since before the First World War. But, again, the end of the Cold War meant that the problem loomed larger. Already, under Reagan, the US has decided that it was easier to tackle the supply of drugs from traffickers and growers abroad rather than the demand from addicts at home. There was particular concern, from the mid-1980s, about cocaine production in the Andean nations of South America, where economic problems made the profits of the drugs trade tempting. Colombia was seen as the worst problem and here the US Drug Enforcement Agency, as well as some American military advisers, worked with the government to intercept shipments, seize the financial assets of known traffickers, and eradicate crops of coca leaf. For a time, Colombia also allowed the extradition of traffickers to the US. Yet many Colombian officials themselves became implicated in the trade and the scale of the local 'drugs war' soon threatened the country's political and social fabric, as well as taking the focus away from measures to relieve poverty. A presidential candidate was assassinated by the Medellin drugs cartel, headed by Pedro Escobar, in 1989; and in 1990 the government decided on a more moderate line which, among other things, meant that Escobar gave himself up, being imprisoned for only a year. By 1992, Bush was spending $10 billion per year on drug control but cocaine use in America continued to grow apace.

If the war on drugs failed to provide a successful centrepiece for foreign policy-making, another growing international concern—the state of the environment—was even more problematic. Like the concern over narcotics, fears for the environment were far from new in 1990. The UN had held its first environmental conference in Stockholm in 1972 and there had already been several attempts to secure international cooperation in the area, such as the 1983 London Convention to prevent the dumping of toxic and nuclear waste at sea. There were obvious problems with persuading all the world's countries to agree and pay for environmental protection measures, but the dangers of doing nothing were just as clear. As well as periodic environmental disasters, such as the meltdown of the Chernobyl nuclear reactor in the USSR in April 1986 and the massive oil spill from the tanker *Exxon Valdez* in Alaska in March 1989, there was growing scientific evidence of two types of damage to the earth's atmosphere. One was the erosion of the ozone layer (protecting the planet from ultraviolet radiation), due to the production of chlorofluorocarbons, or CFCs, a process which was likely to lead to increasing problems with skin cancer and which had first been recognized in the mid-1980s with the discovery of an ozone 'hole' over Antarctica. The other was 'global warming', or the 'greenhouse effect', which it was claimed was occurring because of a combination of the burning of fossil fuels and deforestation, and which was likely to lead to a rise in sea levels, threatening low-lying areas around the world. Concerns about environmental damage therefore grew, along with more awareness of the consequences of the earth's climate warming. Changing global weather patterns and the frequency of increased extreme weather events reinforced concerns about the potentially disastrous consequences of the continued production of 'greenhouse' gases.

In the early 1990s, the environment became an important area in which traditional interpretations of 'security' were challenged because, the 'threat is not seen . . . as being posed by weapons systems . . . and by one state against another, but by a range of environmental problems . . . that are threats to everyone'.[9] In fact, action had been taken at a conference in Montreal in 1987 to protect the ozone layer by reducing certain chemical substances that were harmful to it. One sign of the potential divisions that could arise between countries over the environment, however, was that whereas the developed countries wished to see an end to the destruction of tropical rainforests (especially the Amazon), the developing countries focused on the pollution coming from industry in the developed states. About a third of the world's CFC emissions, for example, were produced by the US. Other concerns included the production of 'acid rain' by industry, the growth of the world's population (it was 5.5 billion in 1990 and likely to double by 2070), the overworking of land in the less developed world, and the gradual exhaustion of non-renewable raw materials. In 1987, the UN's Brundtland Commission had called for policies of 'sustainable development' but it was not clear that this could be achieved.

One of the key international events of Bush's last year in office was the 'Earth Summit' in Rio de Janeiro. The largest conference ever held to that date, though it was surpassed as a gathering of world leaders by the September 2000 UN Millennium summit, it involved both governments and various international bodies. It led to a number of agreements, most importantly the Biodiversity Treaty, to protect plants and animals from extinction, and the Climate Change Convention, which established the principle of emission targets for 'greenhouse' gases in developed countries and obliged governments to report gas emissions. But the summit was just as noteworthy for the divisions it revealed between those present. Oil producers were reluctant to accept measures that limited oil use; small island states were preoccupied with the dangers of rising sea levels thanks to global warming; the Pope was opposed to population control; and the agreements reached represented a 'lowest common denominator approach' in which US leadership was scrupulously lacking. Washington not only refused to sign the Biodiversity Treaty, it only reluctantly accepted the

Climate Change Convention (its doubts being mainly due to the omission of developing countries from it). The Convention was, in any case, hardly radical. It allowed emissions to rise globally by 3 per cent by 1997. For America, it was clear that environmentalism was a complex area, in which national interests were to be protected and agreements should be negotiated grudgingly.

Indeed, environmental problems and narcotics simply served to highlight how confusing the world was, now that old, Cold War reference points had been stripped away, and this very fact made the US public less ready to seek involvement abroad. Yet there was one area where, despite the complexities of 'globalization', Americans could not wish themselves off the world scene. In finance and commerce, the world was ever more independent, with huge cross-border investments, a reliance on trade for ever larger proportions of national income and the possibility, thanks to the 'communications revolution', of moving large sums of money worldwide in an instant. The US itself relied on external trade for about one-fifth of its GNP and its share of world output in 1992 was about a quarter (a big reduction on the 40 per cent of 1950, but still formidable). It was partly to safeguard this position that Bush pursued a North American Free Trade Area. This proposal, signed in late 1992, only came to fruition under Clinton, for whom freer trade eventually provided something of the long-sought, central reference point in post-Cold War foreign policy.

The Clinton Administration and 'Enlargement'

Clinton beat Bush in the 1992 election mainly by concentrating on domestic economic concerns. The former Arkansas governor, accused of 'draft dodging' at the time of the Vietnam War, certainly did not share his predecessor's great experience in the field of national security. Clinton's priorities on entering office were ambitious but almost all focused on the domestic sphere: to reduce debt while using government policy to stimulate growth; to carry through welfare, health, and education reforms; and to deal with environmental threats. But he had made clear the need to protect US markets abroad, he had criticized Washington's alliances with dictatorial regimes, and he urged an active policy, not excluding military force, to back global democratization. Furthermore, as the Somali situation became desperate and the Bosnian war continued, it was soon clear that the new President could not ignore events overseas. Along with his Secretary of State, Warren Christopher, he was accused of lacking any direction abroad and Republicans liked to portray this as part of a general weakness in the President's make-up. One early academic study of his foreign policy was damning in its judgement: 'In 1993, Clinton was the leader of an unrivalled superpower; six years later he was a badly crippled lame duck . . . A magnificent opportunity to shape the international system had been missed.'[10] While he became mired in financial and sexual scandal at home, and was even impeached, a series of crises abroad, from Somalia and Rwanda to Bosnia and Kosovo, called into question the notion of a democratic world order. But Bush, for all his experience, had already shown how difficult it was to provide a sense of cohesion and direction to foreign policy after the Cold War and probably no one could have done so. The US was, apparently, 'secure' in terms of facing no imminent military threat from abroad. Talk of America's declining power vis-à-vis other states, a strong feature of political debate in the mid-1980s, no longer seemed relevant. Its economy was twice as large as Japan's, the world's second largest; its nuclear power and technological prowess were amply demonstrated by such developments as the Trident missile and Stealth bomber; and in the eyes of some it was to be feared as a potential hegemon, dictating its own values and policies to the rest of the world. This was especially the case in the economic sphere, where it insisted that developing countries adopt free-market policies that were interpreted by the countries themselves as a recipe for Western exploitation. On the other hand, some countries, as with Britain and Germany in the North Atlantic Treaty Organization (NATO), still welcomed US leadership and it could not escape its predominant position in the UN.

By 1993, it was evident that American power could not be turned into any consistent bid for hegemony. The world was too complex to interpret events reliably; the US people were too reluctant and emotional to act abroad with consistency; and Congress was too determined to assert itself against the White House, especially after the November 1994 elections, when the Republicans won control in both Houses for the first time since 1954. This was largely because of problems with Clinton's domestic policies but it had an impact on foreign policy because Republicans generally 'sought a more modest role for the United States since the Soviet threat had disappeared . . . In their view American policy should be based on tangible self-interests rather than ambiguous global concerns.'[11] Also, the policy-making machine through which American power was exercised—from the military and the intelligence services, to development aid and embassy staffs—suffered from spending cuts, because they appeared less necessary in the wake of the Cold War. In the case of the CIA, things were made worse by the exposure of two of its officials as Russian spies: Aldrich Ames in February 1994 and Harold Nicolson in November 1996. By the end of Clinton's first term of office, important decisions in American foreign policy sometimes seemed at the mercy of certain interest groups, minorities, or state governments (the last were entitled to introduce their own economic sanctions against foreign countries). Most notable was Clinton's decision to concede to pressure from Jesse Helms, right-wing chairman of the Senate Foreign Relations Committee, for sanctions against those foreign countries trading with Cuba. Such a step was of doubtful international legality and it provoked bitter condemnation abroad, even if it satisfied the Cuban community in Florida.

Yet Clinton's foreign policy could, nonetheless, claim some notable successes by the time he left the White House in January 2001 and he definitely had not shirked difficult decisions, including military commitments. The administration had supported the move to majority rule in South Africa (see Chapter 22, A), as well as the breakthrough Israeli–Palestinian agreement (see Chapter 22, C). It had maintained good relations with Russia while consolidating Bush's arms control agreements, had restored the elected President of Haiti, overseen a thaw in relations between North and South Korea, and taken an active role in moves towards a settlement of the 'troubles' in Northern Ireland, where there had been sectarian violence since 1968. The peace moves in Ireland stalled in early 1996 but revived in the summer of 1997 and reached a deal on creating a new Assembly, representative of all groups in the province, in April 1998. Even more remarkably, the Clinton administration had stepped in to achieve a Bosnian settlement (see Chapter 20, C). The strategic vision may have been difficult to see but, while 'Clinton got off to a rocky start, he eventually developed into an able practitioner of Band-Aid diplomacy', helping heal various wounds.[12] Furthermore, the closing months of 2000 saw the first foreign ministers-level talks with Iran for twenty years (at the UN in September) and Clinton's own visit to Vietnam, the first by a president since the war there. The only real disaster had come in Somalia but, of course, the original decision to intervene had been Bush's. Also, at home, the economy was much improved, with consistent growth, falling unemployment, and a move towards a balanced federal budget (finally achieved in 1998). It was largely thanks to the fulfilment of his economic promises that Clinton was re-elected in November 1996, defeating the lacklustre Bob Dole.

Despite the criticisms levelled at him by Republicans, Clinton was not lacking in ideas for a central direction for US foreign policy, even if these were developments of certain aspects of Bush's new world order. His first National Security Adviser, Anthony Lake, a former head of the State Department's Policy Planning Staff under Jimmy Carter, recognized the need to explain foreign policy not in terms of the balance of power but of 'enlarging' the regions of the world living under liberal democracy, the corollary of which was that opponents of the liberal order—such as Cuba, Iran, and Iraq—were to be isolated and condemned as 'rogue states'. It was in September 1993 that Lake said, 'the successor to a doctrine of containment, must be the strategy of enlargement—enlargement of the world's free community: we must counter the aggression—and support the liberalization—of states hostile to democracy'.[13] At first, it was hoped that the US would act in line with its allies and the United Nations (UN), but in his second term Clinton seemed more ready to act unilaterally (as in Haiti) and accepted the limitations of the UN (as in Bosnia). Apart from dealing, on the whole successfully, with regional problems, the Clinton administration also continued to devote considerable energy to arms control and non-proliferation, and tackled those 'new' security problems that had become important under Bush. Where the narcotics trade was concerned, the Drug Enforcement Agency had a major success in Colombia in 1995, by breaking up the Cali drug cartel, but lasting success proved as elusive as under Bush. The drugs traffic simply splintered among smaller groups and was, if anything, more difficult to control. Colombia, its independence undermined, was increasingly resentful of US policy, and in Washington sympathy grew for the argument that the drugs problem should be tackled by focusing on users in America itself, and not offloaded on the rest of the hemisphere. However, the Clinton administration continued to pour money into Colombia. In 2000, a new $1.5 billion aid package was agreed, mainly in the form of military assistance to tackle the drugs trade. By then, much of the trade was under the control of leftist guerrillas, who had been fighting against the government since the 1970s and whose popularity among the rural poor was, if anything, boosted by their opposition to American intervention.

On the environmental front, there was a series of meetings culminating in the ten-day Kyoto Conference of December 1997. But despite talking a great deal about its enthusiasm for environmentalism, not least through Vice-President Al Gore, the Clinton administration proved no more imaginative and responsive on this front than had Bush. Nor was the environmental cause helped by the Republicans' electoral successes in 1994. As the world's largest carbon emitter, the US was reluctant to accept radical cuts in 'greenhouse' gases by an early date. Agreement was eventually reached on a complex system of targets, aimed at reducing emissions by 5 per cent by 2012, but developing countries were not covered (it would have caused them difficult economic problems if they had been) and there was no agreement about how to punish those who exceeded their targets. There was also concern that the agreement allowed countries to 'trade' emission targets, so that if one did better than the target, another might do worse. Doubts were immediately raised about America's ability—and willingness—to meet the targets, though pressure to do so was particularly strong from its allies in Europe. In November 2000, a UN World Conference on Climate Change, made up of 180 states, broke down largely because the US and the European Union (EU) could not agree on ways to cut greenhouse gas emissions. However, a Biosafety Protocol was agreed that year, which allowed countries to protect themselves from 'genetically modified' products.

Economic Interdependence and Free Trade Areas

One essential point, of which Clinton was always aware, and which built on Bush's policies, was that the future health of the US economy was heavily dependent on the state of the world economy, so that, whatever some Americans might wish, the country could not retreat from global involvement: foreign and domestic policies could not be divorced. Since the mid-1980s, it had been recognized that the global economy was becoming more 'interdependent' as multinational companies, cross-border services, especially in the banking and insurance sector, and information technology broke down interstate boundaries. Companies with high export earnings were particularly likely to back free-trade zones. 'What engaged Clinton most . . . was the economy, and he and his advisers . . . appreciated the intimate relationship between the domestic and the international economy.'[14] The result was a series of initiatives designed to safeguard America's competitiveness in the market, which among other things made the Department of Commerce (under Commerce Secretary, Ron Brown, until his death in an air crash in 1995) a key factor in US foreign policy-making. The general theme was a reduction of trade barriers. There was some activity on a global level in 1994. The World Trade Organization (WTO) was created as a successor to the General Agreement on Tariffs and Trade (GATT) in setting rules for commercial exchange, resolving trade disputes, and carrying out trade talks. Meanwhile, GATT's latest comprehensive look at the reduction of trade barriers, the so-called Uruguay Round, had been completed and promised to cut tariffs by 38 per cent between 1995 and 1999. But the US could not guarantee that the WTO would achieve a more open global commercial system in future—it failed, for example, to agree in 2000 to negotiate a new round of reductions in trade barriers—and other moves by Clinton involved arrangements with regional economic groups. There was always a danger that such a policy might fragment the world economy, but such groups were forming anyway.

With the end of the Cold War, the significance of America's trade relations with Western Europe and, more especially, Japan became more significant relative to their political ones, placing emphasis on competitive rather than cooperative elements in relationships among the developed countries. Japan exported twice as much to the US, as it imported from there, but continuing pressure on Tokyo to rectify the situation had little effect and America's trade deficit proved difficult to reduce. Nonetheless, while being ruthless in protecting US interests, Clinton decided that the best route to preserve and expand trade opportunities was through multilateral action. In this, he built on the policies of his predecessor: Bush too had backed free trade in general but had also tried to build up specific trade links, especially to Latin America, in order to counter European and Japanese competition. Where the EU was concerned, there had been growing concern from American farmers over the Common Agricultural Policy as a discriminatory trade measure but, despite continuing arguments, Clinton felt the EU to be too important to European stability to risk a fully fledged trade war. Instead, a series of annual US–European summits was inaugurated in 1994; and in 1995 a 'New Transatlantic Agenda' was agreed, which aimed to boost the volume of transatlantic trade by, for example, establishing common safety regulations. Other measures to maintain healthy trade included the renewal of China's 'Most Favoured Nation' status (despite political differences and US complaints about Chinese trade practices) and Clinton's September 1994 announcement that the 1972 Jackson–Vanik Amendment (which had linked a trade deal with the USSR to its policy on Jewish emigration) need no longer hinder Russo-American commerce. The Clinton administration also tried to identify 'big emerging markets' in the developing world, in order to foster greater trade with them.

The most interesting developments in US trade policy in the 1990s concerned North America and Asia-Pacific. Although it was Clinton who focused most on commercial issues, it was Bush who signed the North American Free Trade Area (NAFTA) agreement, with Canada and Mexico, just before losing the 1992 election. This built on a US–Canadian trade treaty of 1988 and moves to liberalize the Mexican economy after the debt problem of the mid-1980s. Mexico had pressed strongly for such a deal since mid-1990 and the Bush administration took up the idea despite Canadian doubts. Other states in the western hemisphere were also showing an interest in free trade areas as a way to develop trade, if not to protect themselves from US competition and two other groupings slightly predated NAFTA: the Common Market of the South (MERCUSOR), dominated by Brazil and also including Argentina, Paraguay, and Uruguay, included two-thirds of South Americans; whilst twelve Caribbean islands formed another common market (CARICOM). Two other groups already existed in the Central American Common Market (Costa Rica, El Salvador, Guatemala, Honduras, and Nicaragua) and the Andean Group (Bolivia, Colombia, Ecuador, Peru, and Venezuela). NAFTA created a single trading zone of over 350 million people (rivalling the EU but without the latter's political integration), facilitated US investment in Mexico (a cheap source of labour), and was also intended to stabilize Mexican politics by boosting its economic performance. Mexico was responsible for half of Latin America's exports to the US and relied on America for two-thirds of its export sales. Bush had also had hopes of developing it into a western hemisphere free trade area and this proposal too came to fruition under Clinton. Following two summits of American countries, in Miami in December 1994 and Santiago in April 1998, from which Cuba was the only absentee, thirty-eight countries agreed to negotiate a 'Free Trade Area of the Americas' (FTAA) within ten years.

Yet, from the outset NAFTA was dogged by controversy. The free trade area, to be created by 2009, did not include the free movement of labour, for example, because of Congressional fears of large-scale Hispanic immigration from Mexico. Even then, it had a difficult path through Congress, where there were criticisms about Mexico's environmental record and the danger of cheap goods flooding into the US from its southern neighbour, putting US firms out of business. The public and labour organizations were also divided over the wisdom of the initiative. Once it came into effect on 1 January 1994, NAFTA fell foul of events in Mexico. That very day an uprising began among the Chiapas Indians, led by the 'Zapatista' resistance movement; and later in the year the troubled Mexican economy, already heavily in debt, required a large—$20 billion—reserve package from the International Monetary Fund (IMF) to stay afloat. By 2000, an uneasy peace had been reached with the Zapatistas, but Mexico was still barely able to cover its short-term debts. Meanwhile, the FTAA had also developed problems. Although Central and South American states recognized their reliance on US finance and markets, the MERCUSOR states in particular feared American domination and were keen to develop their own links to the EU and other trading blocs. Brazil, especially, demanded concessions from the US before signing up to the FTAA. Partly because of such difficulties, Clinton also focused on the Pacific.

The process of Asia-Pacific Economic Cooperation (APEC) also predated the Clinton administration, being launched, largely thanks to Australian and Japanese encouragement, in 1989. Until then, the expanding markets of the 'Pacific Rim' had lacked any regional forum for discussion. APEC was a modest body, principally an annual meeting of government representatives with consultative powers only, largely because South-East Asia nations were keen to safeguard the primacy of their own cooperation through ASEAN (see Chapter 22, E), A permanent Secretariat was only established in September 1992; based in Singapore, it studied ways to harmonize trade controls and improve mutual access to markets. But the organization had a wide membership: the inaugural conference in Canberra in November 1989 was attended by America, Japan, Australia, New Zealand, Canada, South Korea, and all the ASEAN members, and subsequently, it was joined by China, Taiwan, and Hong Kong (1991), Mexico and Papua New Guinea (1993), and Chile (1994). On coming into office, Clinton, who believed the Pacific Rim would prove an important area for economic growth in future, decided to make APEC more significant. At first, he even seemed likely to concentrate on Asian-Pacific matters to the detriment of transatlantic ones. At Seattle in November 1993, he presented his version of APEC as a vehicle to liberalize trade and open greater US–Asian commercial links. A year later, at Boyar, Indonesia, a resolution was passed in favour of a free trade area among APEC's industrialized states by 2010, drawing in the developing countries by 2020. Serious planning for the reduction of trade barriers began after another meeting at Subic in the Philippines in 1996.

But as with NAFTA, the story of APEC was a troubled one, with modest advances dogged by mutual suspicion. Whilst the US criticized some APEC members over human rights and the pirating of intellectual property, the developing Asian nations accused America of dictating its own moral and political values to them, and of placing selfish aims, such as trade liberalization and the protection of patent rights, above successful development policies. In the US itself, furthermore, Clinton's interest in free trade projects was greeted by most Americans with indifference and in 1997 he was forced to give up on an attempt to have Congress grant him the power to negotiate 'fast-track' trade deals. The tendency to set up trade groupings on a regional basis—NAFTA and APEC added to older groups like the EU and ASEAN—also threatened to fragment the management of the world economy, hardening the perception of the post-Cold War world as an increasingly divided place. Then, in 1997–8, the financial crisis in East Asia (see Chapter 22, E) threatened a new world recession and particularly undermined the efforts of liberalization through APEC.

BOX 21.1

George Bush and his Foreign Policy Team, 1989–93

George H. W. Bush Snr had enormous experience of foreign policy before becoming president. Born in 1924, his father was a New York banker who became Senator for Connecticut (1952–63). After wartime service as an air-force pilot, the President-to-be studied law at Yale but then distanced himself from his privileged, East Coast background by going to work in the oil industry in Texas. He made a fortune from an offshore drilling company that he founded, before going into politics. He became a Republican Congressman in 1966 and served under Nixon and Ford as ambassador to the UN (1971–2), envoy to China (1974–5), and Director of the CIA (1976–7). In 1980, he ran for the Republican presidential nomination, which was won by Ronald Reagan. Reagan, however, chose Bush as his running mate and he served as vice- president for two terms (1981–9), before being elected President in his own right. In 1991, with the end of the Cold War, and following the successes of the Gulf War and Panama, Bush was very popular, but he nonetheless lost the 1992 election owing to America's economic problems. The disappointment of being a one-term President was offset by the election of his son to the White House in 2000.

As President, Bush Snr gathered a close-knit group around him on foreign policy matters. His Secretary of State was James A. Baker (b. 1930), educated at Princeton and the University of Texas, who served in the Marines (1952–4) and practised law before becoming Secretary of Commerce under Ford in 1975. Baker managed Bush's presidential bid in 1980, then served as White House Chief of Staff (1981–5). He returned as Chief of Staff in August 1992, in a vain attempt to reinvigorate Bush's election campaign. As Secretary of State, he was criticized by some for arrogance, but paradoxically was also seen as mediator par excellence, helping to bring an end to the Cold War by building up a good working relationship with Moscow.

The National Security Adviser, Brent Scowcroft (b. 1925) had also served in the Ford administration in that position (1975–7). A US air force officer and West Point graduate, Scowcroft had gained a doctorate from Columbia University in 1967 and spent much of his military career in teaching and in planning, before serving as Deputy National Security Adviser to Henry Kissinger (1973–5). In contrast to Kissinger, Scowcroft did not take a high-profile public role but acted more as a coordinator of national security work.

(continued)

BOX 21.1 (continued)

Richard Cheney, the Defense Secretary for almost all the Bush presidency, the youngest of all the foreign policy team, was born in 1941. Educated at Yale and the University of Wyoming, he worked for Republican Congressman Donald Rumsfeld, who became Ford's Chief of Staff in the White House in 1974. When Rumsfeld moved to become Secretary of Defense in 1975, he recommended that Cheney succeed him. Cheney then became the youngest person to serve in the position and was thus in a high position in the Ford administration at the same time as Bush (CIA director), Baker (Commerce), and Scowcroft (National Security Adviser). After the Ford presidency, Cheney entered a political career of his own, being elected Congressman for Wyoming. As Secretary of Defense under Bush, Cheney's most important task was the organization of Operation Desert Storm. In 2000, his links to the Bush family helped him to become Vice- President to George Bush Jnr.

Another leading member of the 1989–93 administration was Colin Powell, the Chairman of the Joint Chiefs of Staff throughout the period. The son of Jamaican immigrants, Powell (b. 1937) had become a professional soldier, fought in Vietnam, and rose to command a brigade in the prestigious 101st Airborne Division. In contrast to the rest of the Bush team, he had no role in the Ford administration but was an adviser to the Defense Department under Reagan in 1983–6 and served as National Security Adviser in 1987–8. The youngest ever chairman of the Joint Chiefs, in 2000 he also became the first black Secretary of State.

B. Enforcing Order: The Gulf War of 1990–1

The Iraqi invasion of Kuwait on 2 August 1990 took the world by surprise and was rapidly seen as the first great 'test' of the international community's ability to maintain stability in the wake of the Cold War. Saddam Hussein's action threatened to create another oil crisis, driving up prices. It challenged the recent revival in status of the UN; and it raised questions about the readiness of the US and USSR to cooperate with one another, in a situation where Moscow had links to Iraq but Washington was determined to liberate Kuwait. When it became clear that the last aim could only be achieved through the use of military force, the crisis also raised questions about the unity of the Western alliance, the ability of the US to maintain good relations with other Arab states, and America's determination to prosecute a war when memories of Vietnam were still vivid. The war proved of central importance to the Bush administration because it forced the US to try to define a post-Cold War foreign policy and proved, on the whole, a major success. But there were criticisms of American policy too: 'that it failed to deter Iraq's initial invasion of Kuwait; that it refused to accept a negotiated settlement; that it resorted to force without determining whether . . . economic sanctions would achieve its goals; and that it ended the war too early, allowing Saddam Hussein to survive'.[15]

Saddam's Invasion and America's Reaction

With the end of the eight-year Iran–Iraq war in 1988 (Chapter 17, C), Saddam Hussein inevitably had to concentrate on rebuilding his country structurally and militarily. The last thing Iraq wanted, or so it seemed, was another major conflict. Yet the decision to invade Kuwait, a country that had aided Saddam during his war with Iran, was closely linked to Iraq's reconstruction needs. The country was about $80 billion in debt and could only realistically hope to pay this off by exporting oil. But oil prices had been drifting down since the early 1980s and attempts by the oil-exporting countries of the Organization of Petroleum Exporting Countries (OPEC) to reverse this trend by introducing quotas to limit production had little effect. To Saddam's annoyance, Kuwait was one country that broke the quota policy and so was blamed for pushing prices lower. For Iraq, the virtual halving of oil prices in the 1980s was a terrible blow and arguments with Kuwait on this issue alone had created enormous ill feeling by 1990. Saddam wanted Kuwait and Saudi Arabia, both oil-rich yet sparsely populated states with none of Iraq's economic problems, to demonstrate Arab solidarity by cancelling their wartime loans to Baghdad and handing over some of their oil production quotas to him. In February 1990, a series of talks began involving Iraqi and Kuwaiti representatives, and in July, Kuwait agreed that it would restrict its oil exports, an undertaking that would take effect in October. By then, Kuwait had been invaded and, on 8 August, annexed by Iraq, which now controlled one-fifth of OPEC oil production.

The need to obtain greater oil reserves was the primary, but not the only, reason for Saddam's action. Iraq also had a territorial claim on Kuwait from the days of the Ottoman Empire and had already threatened to invade it in 1961, when British troops had been rushed to its defence. The small sheikhdom, strategically placed at the top of the Persian Gulf, had been severed from the Ottoman Empire by Britain in 1899 and controlled as a protectorate from London. The Iraqis were therefore able to condemn it as a creation of British imperialism. But their own claim over it had severe flaws. Kuwait had had a separate existence under the Ottomans, being ruled by the Al-Sabah family since 1756; Iraq itself had been created by the British from several Ottoman provinces after the First World War; and Iraq had also recognized Kuwait's independence in 1963. There were, however, disputes over the exact line of the Iraq–Kuwait border and Saddam had pressed these, alongside the arguments over oil and loans, in the July 1990 talks. The demanding tone of the Iraqis in these negotiations and the fact that Saddam massed his army on the border provoked concern among Arab capitals and in the US. The fact that US–Iraqi relations had been strained since the end of the Iran–Iraq War reduced Washington's need of Saddam as an ally, and in April 1990 he threatened to attack Israel. It was well known that, despite Iraq's other problems, Saddam had continued to maintain substantial armed forces, had a capability in chemical and biological warfare, and was trying to develop both long-range weapons and a nuclear reactor. He had Soviet-supplied Scud missiles, which could strike as far as Israel, and he had been secretly armed by the Western powers during the war with Iran. Yet few expected he would actually invade his small, vulnerable neighbour and the US ambassador to Baghdad, April Glaspie, told him that Washington had no firm position on the border disputes with Kuwait.

Once the invasion took place, the main question was how America would react and whether it could persuade its allies, the Arab world, and the USSR to support its action. In America, there was little enthusiasm for war but plenty of reasons to contemplate it. Saddam had carried out a blatant act of aggression against a pro-Western state and, from his position in Kuwait, could now threaten a more important US ally and oil producer, Saudi Arabia. Whether an invasion of Saudi Arabia was likely did not matter: after Kuwait, Saddam seemed capable of anything and he had similar arguments with the Saudis, over oil and loans, as he had had with Kuwait. The US had helped build up the Saudis' military power since the early 1970s and they had become even more important to the defence of American interests in the Gulf since the fall of the Shah. If Saddam did overrun Saudi Arabia, he would control a huge proportion of the world's oil reserves and it would be very difficult to remove him. Liberating a small country like Kuwait would be an easier matter and President Bush soon decided that this must be done, ideally by diplomatic pressure backed by the threat of force, but if necessary, by the use of such force. In the past, the US had hoped that its local allies could maintain stability in the Gulf region, and in the 1980s it had been able to rely on the deadlocked Iran–Iraq War to check the ambitions of both Baghdad and Tehran. But now direct US intervention seemed essential to deter an invasion of Saudi Arabia, punish Iraq, and restore Kuwaiti independence. In deciding to make a stand, Bush personally seemed impressed by a most simple argument: 'we could not let aggression stand'. He told his children, 'I look at today's crisis as "good" versus "evil". Yes, it is that clear.'[16] But some critics pointed out that the US had been less than eager to punish some past acts of aggression—not least Saddam's invasion of Iran in 1980, which had also been designed to give him greater oil resources and better access to the Gulf, and which was launched on the pretext of a border claim. Then again, perhaps the President felt betrayed by the invasion of Kuwait, for: 'Bush had been a Saddam supporter, both under Reagan and after he became President.'[17] Another factor was that, with the Cold War over and Kuwait no democracy, Bush was forced to revert to 'World War II metaphors and referred to Kuwait as a victim of Nazi-like aggression',[18] when America's real motives for action had more to do with the fact that about half of America's energy needs were met by Middle East oil.

The Liberation of Kuwait

After invading Kuwait, Saddam portrayed himself as a hero to his fellow Arabs, hoping to win over allies in the region and make it difficult to remove him. He believed the Soviets would support him and doubted that the Western powers would have the necessary will and unity to fight. At first, he seized dozens of Westerners in Kuwait as hostages and, though these were later released, he made it clear that he would extract a heavy price if attacked, perhaps launching Scud missiles against Israel. Eventually, when the allies struck, he also set Kuwait's oil wells alight. But it was soon clear that, as in 1980, he had severely miscalculated the effects of military action, underestimating the resilience of his enemies and overestimating the strength of his position. He made a diplomatic settlement virtually impossible on 12 August when he made a withdrawal from Kuwait conditional on a US withdrawal from Saudi Arabia and an Israeli withdrawal from all the occupied territories. The Western powers were ready to fight, with Margaret Thatcher telling Bush on 21 August, 'this is no time to go wobbly'.[19] The Soviets did no more than try to postpone the US assault and few countries, even in the Arab world, offered Saddam much support. Indeed, only the Marxist government in Yemen, King Hussein of Jordan, and Yasser Arafat's Palestinian Liberation Organization (PLO) defended him. Some Arabs, notably the Egyptians, who had a centuries-old rivalry with Iraq for the leadership of the Arab world, were keen to condemn the annexation of Kuwait and welcomed US action, as of course did the Saudis. The UN, partly thanks to US–Soviet agreement, was quick to condemn the invasion and call for Iraq to leave Kuwait. With such strong support, it was unsurprising that Bush decided to rely on military force to deal with Saddam, rather than economic sanctions, which would take time to take effect and might not work. And America's 'Rapid Reaction Force', built up since the Carter Doctrine on Gulf security in 1980, and already used in joint operations with other powers, was deployed in Saudi Arabia at a remarkable rate. By the end of the year, about 400,000 US troops were there, alongside more than 100,000 from other Western states, including Britain and France.

Washington succeeded in creating a broad coalition against Saddam while preserving its own domination of the decision-making process on the war and minimizing differences with Moscow. When the Iraqi invasion took place, the US Secretary of State, James Baker, was actually in the Soviet Union for talks with Eduard Shevardnadze, and believed 'that we needed the Soviets more than anyone else'.[20] They immediately agreed to back a UN arms and trade embargo against Iraq. This included the end of oil exports from Iraq and Kuwait, thus cancelling one of the gains Saddam hoped to make from the invasion. Other OPEC countries, not least Saudi Arabia, raised their production levels to stabilize supplies and, though oil prices climbed steeply for a time, they soon fell back. Later, on 24 August, Shevardnadze supported another UN resolution, allowing military action to help enforce the sanctions policy; and on 8 September Bush and Gorbachev met in Helsinki, agreeing that force might be used to remove Saddam from Kuwait. This policy was not popular with everyone in the Soviet government and Gorbachev's special envoy, Yevgeny Primakov, travelled to Baghdad to press a diplomatic solution on Saddam. The Russian was only one of many emissaries to do so. But by late September it was clear to most observers that Saddam would not withdraw and that all-out war was inevitable. The argument that America must act quickly if it was to preserve the anti-Saddam coalition was highlighted by Arab outrage at the killing of twenty-one Palestinians on Temple Mount in Jerusalem in early October. There were also doubts in Congress in November about the rising number of troops in the Gulf and some support for a policy of economic sanctions. But US propaganda exploited Saddam's human rights record and supposed nuclear ambitions to maintain domestic and international support for the war preparations.

The most important UN resolution on Kuwait was that of 29 November, which authorized the use of 'all means necessary' to free the country and which set a deadline of 15 January for Iraqi's withdrawal. It was the first time since the outbreak of the Korean War in 1950 that the UN Security Council had approved military sanctions against an aggressor and, although China abstained on the vote, it revealed a remarkable and unprecedented sense of unity between the permanent members. A number of governments, apart from Kuwait and Saudi Arabia (who provided $15 billion each), helped pay for the war effort, including Germany and Japan (who provided about $20 billion between them). Eventually about three-quarters of American military costs were covered by its allies. There was still room for division: the French, whilst ready to liberate Kuwait, questioned the wisdom of restoring the authoritarian Al-Sabah family; Gorbachev subsequently tried to get the 15 January deadline pushed back; and efforts at a diplomatic solution continued, with last-minute trips to Baghdad by China's Foreign Minister, Qian Qichen and the UN Secretary-General, Perez de Cuellar. Talks were held in Geneva on 9 January between Baker and the Iraqi Foreign Minister, Tariq Aziz, but Saddam refused to withdraw from Kuwait. Bush then secured a Congressional vote in favour of war and on 16 January 1991 allied forces, led by the US, began air attacks on Iraq. The aim was to weaken Saddam's war machine and ensure a rapid victory for the allies when they eventually launched a land campaign. Although, in contrast to the Vietnam War, US media coverage of the conflict was closely controlled by the military, there was still a deep fear in the US of large casualties from the war, and the Senate had only approved the use of force by a majority of five. There were now 540,000 American troops in the Gulf, approximately the same number as had been in Vietnam at the height of that conflict. The air war lasted for six weeks and, despite some civilian deaths and a failure to destroy Saddam's chemical weapons production, it succeeded in 'softening up' the Iraqi military, while also demonstrating the allies' easy domination in the air and US technological virtuosity, with its Cruise missiles and Stealth aircraft. Saddam did fire over eighty Scud missiles at Israel and Saudi Arabia, but they were randomly targeted and some were brought down by US 'Patriot' missiles.

Finally, on 24 February the allies, under the US General Norman Schwarzkopf, launched Operation 'Desert Storm' to liberate Kuwait. Saddam had earlier promised his people 'the mother of all battles' but it proved a one-sided contest. The Iraqis were bundled out of Kuwait almost as quickly as they arrived, with allied forces also striking into southern Iraq. About 100,000 Iraqis were killed for the loss of only about 150 allied troops, many of these accidentally killed by their own side. Within four days, it was all over. On 27 February, Saddam agreed to comply with UN resolutions on Kuwaiti independence and the US military, as well as Bush, could congratulate themselves on a successful campaign, with Kuwait restored to freedom and none of the feared mass casualties among American troops.

The War's Impact

In the wake of victory, Bush declared that the US had 'kicked the Vietnam syndrome'.[21] But, while avoiding a repetition of Vietnam, the US arguably made new mistakes, allowing Saddam and most of his armed forces, including his elite troops, to survive. The Gulf War, as a conventional war against an undoubted aggressor, had little in common with Vietnam anyway and, as later seen in Somalia, it did not mean that America was now equipped to deal with civil conflicts. A closer parallel could be drawn with the Korean War in 1950, where the attempt to conquer the communist North, after liberating the South, had turned to disaster. A wholesale invasion of Iraq to depose Saddam could have tarnished the US claim to be liberating a victim of aggression, it would have threatened the carefully constructed relationship with Moscow, it might have stirred up ill feeling among other Arab countries, and, it might have led to a long-running, costly occupation of the country which the Iraqi people would have resisted and the US people would have come to oppose, and which would have gone beyond what UN resolutions allowed. An alternative leader might not actually prove better than Saddam, who for a time appeared cowed and humiliated. Nonetheless, the failure to remove Saddam carried its own costs. Allied forces had to remain in Kuwait and Saudi Arabia, and from time to time had to be strengthened because the Iraqi dictator again seemed to threaten, as happened in October 1994. Bush made plenty of remarks that suggested he wanted rid of the Iraqi leader. He evidently hoped Saddam might be toppled by a coup but all attempts to launch one ended in failure. Baker later admitted, 'we never really expected him to survive a defeat of that magnitude'.[22] But that is what Saddam did and he even became involved in an attempt to assassinate George Bush in 1993.

A particular problem was that, under the ceasefire agreement which ended the war, the UN was able to inspect Iraqi territory to check for chemical, bacteriological, and nuclear weapons, which were to be destroyed. This was confirmed by a UN resolution of 3 April 1991, which effectively dictated a settlement to Iraq and also included recognition of the existing Kuwait border, and a demilitarized zone between the two countries, the return of stolen Kuwaiti property from Iraq, and the fulfilment of Iraqi debt obligations to Kuwait. Meanwhile, the trade embargo stayed in place. But, periodically, Saddam would refuse to work with the UN inspectors or to comply with UN sanctions. 'Years before he had determined to build himself weapons that would force his neighbours . . . to acknowledge his power. Now the victorious allies made him accept a group of officially sanctioned spies, charged with rooting out the weapons.'[23] But when he resisted, the US was tough in its response. This happened in January 1993, when there were cruise missile attacks on Iraq; in October–November 1997, when Russian mediation defused the crisis; in January–February 1998 when the UN Secretary-General, Kofi Annan, persuaded the Iraqi leader to conform with UN inspections after a massive US and British force gathered in the Gulf; and again in December 1998, when US and

British air strikes took place over four days. Saddam also continued to offend the West by oppressing the Kurdish and Marsh Arab minorities in Iraq, a policy that led in April 1991 to the creation of 'no-fly' zones over the north and south of the country, enforced by allied aircraft. This attempt to provide some protection for the minorities had only a limited effect, however and, like the weapons inspections, it became another long-term commitment that carried its own dangers of violent confrontation: in August 2000 there were US and British air strikes on Iraqi anti-aircraft defences, which were threatening allied aircraft in the 'no-fly' zones. Despite their supposed sympathy for the Kurds, the Western powers were unwilling to contemplate a Kurdish state because this would offend Turkish and Iranian opinion: they too held land that was populated by Kurds and Turkey was a NATO ally.

The Gulf War, then, was undoubtedly a success for the US, but not untainted. Bush had asserted his country's leadership at the UN as the Cold War ended, had kept the USSR and China quiescent while punishing a Third World dictator, and had constructed a remarkable alliance, including European states, Japan (at least on the financial side), Israel, and Saudi Arabia. By adhering to the limited aim of liberating Kuwait, the US and its allies had kept the moral high ground, given the military a clear objective, and ultimately allowed the clear nature of their victory to emerge more starkly. Kuwait might be devastated and its oil wells in flames, but it had been liberated nonetheless, and in only a few days. The US had projected its power on the other side of the world, fully justifying the concept of the Rapid Reaction Force, and perhaps it did help, to some extent, to reverse the lack of faith in military power that had followed Vietnam. Yet Saddam remained in power, eventually outlasting most of the allied leaders—Bush, Thatcher, Mitterrand—who had fought against him. Sanctions on Iraq remained too, but with steadily lessening support in the UN, and the danger to Kuwait had not disappeared. The US carried more influence in the Persian Gulf but had to pay for this with a significant, continuing military presence. And, as events in Bosnia soon showed, Operation Desert Storm did not necessarily provide a model for resolving crises elsewhere. It was a unique war sparked by Saddam's miscalculation of the world's response. Other conflicts would look less clear-cut in moral terms and be less open to conventional military solutions.

C. Washington and Moscow in the 1990s

The Last Phase of US–Soviet Relations, 1990–1

By the beginning of 1990, it was clear that the Cold War was over and George Bush, who had initially been reluctant to rush into a policy of US–Soviet friendship,

BOX 21.2

Biography: Saddam Hussein (1937–2006)

Saddam Hussein came from a poor peasant background in Tikrit, Iraq and entered radical politics as a teenager, joining the secular Ba'ath Party. In 1958, he was imprisoned for his activities and in 1959 was involved in an attempt to assassinate the Prime Minister, Abdul Kassem. Wounded by one of Kassem's guards, Saddam fled into exile in Nasser's Egypt and was sentenced to death in absentia, but used his time abroad to study law at Cairo University. He was able to return to Iraq in 1963, when the Ba'ath briefly held power, but was imprisoned again for his part in an attempted coup the following year. Escaping from prison in 1967 he took part in yet another coup, this time successful, in July 1968, after which he became Vice- President of the 'Revolutionary Command Council' led by General Ahmed Bakr. During the 1970s, Saddam was particularly responsible for building up the regime's secret police force and in 1976 was promoted to a general in the army.

Saddam effectively overthrew Bakr in 1979, though nominally the latter retired. Promoted not only to the presidency, but also to the leadership of the Ba'ath Party and the rank of Field Marshal, Saddam exerted a strong grip on power. A veteran of coups, imprisonments, and exile himself, he proved ruthless at wiping out opponents and potential rivals. He even shot dead one of his own ministers during the course of a cabinet meeting. Despite the costly deadlock of the 1980–8 war with neighbouring Iran, he retained the loyalty of the military and the secret police. Defeat by a US-led coalition in the Gulf War of 1990–1 provoked some internal discontent and led both to isolation abroad and grave economic problems within Iraq. Yet Saddam clung on to power, only being ousted by a second invasion in 2003. He went into hiding, but was discovered by US troops, tried, and executed.

became more anxious to support the position of Mikhail Gorbachev, seeing him as the only hope for a stable, reformist USSR. The collapse of its position in Eastern Europe had confirmed that the Soviet regime had indeed fundamentally changed, although doubts about Gorbachev's ability to carry reform through persisted. The US Secretary of State, James Baker, had decided, even before the Berlin Wall fell, that: 'Any uncertainty about the fate of reform in the Soviet Union . . . is all the more reason, not less, for us to seize the present opportunity' and to 'lock in as much change as possible'.[24] In 1990–1, Bush continued to back this policy, even when others began to see Gorbachev's position as increasingly hopeless and, for a time, the US government proved none too enthusiastic about the break-up of the Soviet Union—even though this could be seen as final confirmation of America's 'victory' in the Cold War. Yet at the same time Bush was criticized for failing to provide the extensive financial aid that might have allowed the last Soviet leader to cling on to power. There were, in fact, good reasons to believe that Gorbachev's economic policies simply would not work, and Congress itself might not have approved larger sums than were provided. But as events continued to move at breakneck pace, the US president repeatedly seemed to be left behind by them, unable either to shore up Gorbachev's position or to contemplate a Soviet Union without him. Doubtful about Gorbachev's commitment to reform in the late 1980s and slow to develop a Soviet policy in 1989, Bush and his team continued to react to the revolutionary upheaval in the USSR in a pragmatic, cautious way that seemed inappropriate to critics. In contrast, his successor, Bill Clinton, was far keener to embrace Gorbachev's *bête noire*, Boris Yeltsin, to encourage reform in Moscow and to give advice to the Russian government.

Whatever the criticisms levelled at Bush, the years 1990–1 saw remarkable achievements in relations between Washington and Moscow. This was the period, of course, in which the democratization of Eastern Europe was consolidated and German reunification achieved, and both these processes were achieved without either humiliating Gorbachev or rekindling the Cold War (see Chapter 20, A). Bush himself wisely declared: 'I'm not going to dance on the [Berlin] Wall', because he did not want to humiliate Gorbachev and risk a Soviet backlash.[25] Furthermore, economic and political reform did continue in the USSR and there were major steps in arms control. Signs of a repressive Soviet policy in the Baltic States provoked concern in the US, especially over Lithuania in the early months of 1991: at the end of January the US postponed a summit meeting that had been planned for the following month. But at the same time the two countries worked tolerably well together over the Gulf War, progress was being made in arms control negotiations, and a high point of the Bush–Gorbachev relationship came with the Washington summit of 31 May–1 June 1990. Beforehand, the Soviet leader, despite his great popularity in the West, seemed to be in grave trouble at home, where a new economic reform programme was announced amid much scepticism on 24 May and where, on 29 May, Boris Yeltsin (see Box 21.4) strengthened his position as a potential alternative leader by winning a popular vote to confirm his position as President of the Russian Federation. This was also a key point in the process of German reunification, with the Soviets still reluctant to concede German membership of NATO.

The Washington summit confirmed, however, that Bush was anxious to prop up Gorbachev, just as the Soviet leader was ready to continue his retreat in the face of Western security demands. As well as agreements on cultural cooperation, educational exchanges, and nuclear tests, there was a grain deal; a long-awaited commercial agreement was signed, giving the USSR 'Most Favoured Nation' trading status, and conventional weapons reductions in Europe were discussed. Gorbachev conceded that a reunited Germany could be a NATO member and further progress was made on a Strategic Arms Reduction Treaty (START), despite the Bush team's initial doubts about the whole START process. Arguably most important, however, was an agreement by the two countries to destroy more than three-quarters of their chemical weapons stocks. As a public relations exercise, the summit was a great success, being followed up by more talks at Camp David, the presidential country retreat, and a visit by Gorbachev to California, where he once again met Ronald Reagan. In contrast to his scepticism about Gorbachev in mid-1989, Bush now acknowledged: 'We've come a long, long way from the depths of the Cold War', while Gorbachev 'was left with the impression of a growing understanding among Americans that the new Soviet Union . . . was consistent with the interests of the United States'.[26] Yet at home the Soviet leader's problems continued to mount, as food supplies faced serious disruption and Yeltsin's Russian Federation led the way in pressing for greater autonomy for the USSR's fifteen constituent republics. In October 1990 came the 'War of Laws', when the Russian and Ukrainian parliaments declared their legislation superior to Soviet law, only to have the Supreme Soviet insist that this could never be the case. Two months later Gorbachev proposed a period of executive rule, promoted hard-line communists back into top positions, and seemed ready to crack down forcefully on the separatist movements in the republics.

Yet again, however, Gorbachev backed off from any confrontation with the West and Bush avoided public criticism of the Soviet leader. By May 1991, with the situation in the Baltic States defused (see Chapter 20, B) and the West triumphant in the Gulf War, the State Department and CIA were primarily concerned with Gorbachev's weak domestic position. His promotion of hard-liners, with no personal loyalty to him, had made him vulnerable to a palace coup, and the previous weeks had seen a series of strikes, which further damaged industrial output. The most difficult problem facing Bush was whether to provide large amounts of financial aid to bail his Soviet counterpart out of the gathering crisis. The problem was that, however radical Gorbachev seemed in Soviet terms, Western experts were not convinced his economic reform programme would work. It tried to preserve too much central planning, was likely to be undermined by the unsympathetic Soviet bureaucracy, and had already absorbed a large amount of Western aid—much of it from Germany—with little effect. In late May, Gorbachev sent his foreign policy adviser, Yevgeny Primakov, to convince Washington that the reform programme *was* a meaningful one, but the US was reluctant to pour more money into a losing concern. Gorbachev himself attended the G-7 summit in London on 21 July to plead for large-scale assistance, but—despite some sympathy from Germany and France—could win little more than emergency humanitarian assistance. He consoled himself with the belief that he had 'achieved a fundamental political agreement about the integration of our country into the world economy', breaching another wall between East and West.[27]

A week later, Gorbachev and Bush met in Moscow for another summit. Though they were to meet once again (on 30 October, in Madrid, where multilateral talks on a Middle East peace settlement took place), this was to be the last ever US–Soviet summit, and it had one major arms control achievement to its credit. The START I treaty, under negotiation since the Reagan period, slashed strategic nuclear missile numbers on both sides by almost a third (see Box 21.3). By now, the US government was more than ever concerned about the possible break-up of the USSR, perhaps leading to a series of wars among its successor states. So, on a visit to Ukraine, Bush made a controversial speech saying that nationalist feeling must not become ethnic hatred (as was already the case in certain conflicts in the Caucasus) and warning that it was pointless to replace the old Soviet totalitarianism with a brand of nationalist despotism. The speech upset Ukrainian opinion, however, and within weeks Gorbachev's position was fatally undermined by the abortive August coup by hard-liners, which Yeltsin did most to defeat. For a time, in the wake of the coup, US–Soviet relations seemed as fruitful as ever, with statements from both about their determination to reduce nuclear forces. But a State Department memorandum of 25 October bluntly warned that, 'The Soviet Union as we know it no longer exists . . . Our aim should be to make the crash as peaceful as possible.'[28] By the end of the year, the US had to accept that, whatever the uncertainties this created, the USSR had ceased to exist.

The US and Yeltsin

Well before the USSR disintegrated, Bush had begun to establish links with the republican governments that became its successor states. Yeltsin and Bush had met in Washington on 20 June 1991, getting on better than expected, and in November–December the leaders of the USSR's republics were careful to keep Washington informed of their plans. Bush, in fact, was told of the intention of these leaders to dissolve the Soviet Union before the unfortunate Gorbachev. Bush was also keen to build on the success of the START treaty and to press on with nuclear arms reductions before any authoritarian regime returned to power in Moscow. Even START I would leave both sides with enormous destructive power and, now that the Cold War was definitely over, Congress was keen to make major defence savings. There were problems on both sides with the continuation of the START process, however. For one thing, America was determined to confirm its technological superiority and maintained, for example, research on the Strategic Defence Initiative. For another, the break-up of the USSR, however welcome to the US in other ways, created three new nuclear powers: as well as Russia, there were strategic weapons bases in Ukraine (for a time the world's third largest nuclear power), Belarus, and Kazakhstan. The destruction of those ex-Soviet nuclear warheads outside Russia became a priority for American and Russian arms control policy. Until this was achieved, it was impossible to carry START I into effect.

Despite these problems, and despite his reluctance to embrace Yeltsin as an alternative to Gorbachev, Bush pressed on towards a START II treaty with remarkable speed. The President's urgency was increased by the evidence of Gorbachev's last months about just how uncertain Russian politics had become; and the treaty was pursued despite serious doubts in the Department of Defense about reducing the US nuclear arsenal. Bush was helped by Yeltsin's equal determination to cut back on nuclear arms, not only because of the cost of maintaining these but also because Russian security seemed to rely, not on preparations for war with America, but on a continued relaxation of tension. The two leaders held their first US–Russian summit in February 1992, yet the START II treaty was signed only eleven months later. Not only was its negotiation far swifter than that of START I, but the new treaty also marked a more dramatic reduction of strategic nuclear arsenals by about two-thirds (see Box 21.3). In the interim in May 1992, the US and the relevant former Soviet republics had also signed a protocol to the START I agreement, aiming at the elimination of the Ukrainian, Belarussian, and Kazakh nuclear arsenals, which were of grave concern to the US. By the time he left office, Bush could claim to have negotiated two massive reductions in nuclear arms, and these within eighteen months of each other.

President-elect Clinton had criticized Bush earlier for backing Gorbachev for too long and not embracing Yeltsin soon enough, but the incoming President fully supported the START II signature and made arms control an important theme of his own relationship with Russia. In 1993, Belarus and Kazakhstan gave up their nuclear weapons; Ukraine followed in January 1994, signing an agreement with the US and Russia after being promised assistance with its nuclear energy programme by Clinton. This paved the way for the fulfilment of both START treaties, although the ratification of START II by the Russian Parliament proved a slow process because communists and nationalists were concerned not to reduce Russia's ability to defend itself. Meanwhile, the two governments were set on negotiating still more cuts in a START III treaty, and the US provided technical assistance, both to close down unsafe nuclear reactors and to destroy nuclear weapons in the former Soviet Union. There was a serious danger that these might fall into criminal or terrorist hands, or of a nuclear accident resulting from Russia's crumbling infrastructure and the poor state

BOX 21.3

The START Treaties: Principal Features

START I

- Signed in Moscow by Gorbachev and Bush on 31 July 1991.
- To be carried out over eight years with on-site inspections to verify its execution.
- Each side was to be restricted to 1,600 launchers (land-based and submarine-based intercontinental ballistic missiles, plus strategic bombers).
- Each side was to be restricted to 6,000 warheads of which up to 4,900 could be on ballistic missiles, 1,540 on 'heavy' missiles, and 1,100 on mobile, land-based missiles.
- The USSR was to halve its number of 'heavy' missiles.
- A separate agreement limited the number of submarine-launched cruise missiles to 880 each.

START II

- Signed in Moscow by Bush and Yeltsin on 3 January 1993.
- Cut strategic nuclear arsenals by about two-thirds, compared to START I's one-third reduction.
- Again, provided for on-site verification.
- By 2003, all 'heavy' missiles and multi-warhead intercontinental ballistic missiles were to be eliminated.
- By 2000, the total strategic nuclear systems on each side were to be no more than 4,250 and by 2003 were not to exceed 3,000.
- By 2003, the maximum number of submarine-launched ballistic missiles was to be 1,750.

of its armed forces. The possibility of disaster was underlined in 1995, when the Russians momentarily mistook the launch of a Norwegian rocket (of which they had been forewarned) for a nuclear assault; and again in 2000, when a Russian nuclear submarine, the *Kursk*, sank in the Barents Sea. It was not just Russian nuclear weapons that were of concern to America. There was also a determination to prevent any proliferation of nuclear know-how from the former USSR to non-nuclear powers. Thus, pressure was put on Moscow not to provide Iraq with help on a nuclear reactor, because this might lead on to a military programme by Saddam Hussein; and in 1995 America and Russia led the way in extending the nuclear Non-Proliferation Treaty (the NPT, originally signed in 1968) for an indefinite period. This was done despite the complaints of non-nuclear states that the nuclear powers were not doing enough to disarm themselves and that America condoned certain countries, notably Israel, which had developed a nuclear deterrent.

Certainly, as in so many other aspects of US policy after the Cold War, there was an element of hypocrisy in expecting other countries to adhere to the NPT while America—notwithstanding the START process—retained a large nuclear arsenal. There was an important alteration in US strategic planning under Clinton, away from a focus on war with Russia to the danger presented by 'rogue states', but the strategy continued to rely on the use of nuclear weapons. North Korea was successfully pressured, in 1994, into respecting the NPT but the difficulties of enforcing such a policy were highlighted in May 1998 when India, and then Pakistan, successfully tested nuclear weapons, raising the spectre of a nuclear confrontation in South Asia, where both countries continued to bicker over the fate of Kashmir. Despite a summit meeting between India's Atal Vajpayee and Pakistan's Nawaz Sharif in January, there was an upsurge of violence in Kashmir in the mid-1999, with India using air strikes for the first time since the 1971 Indo-Pakistani War. Clinton tried to deal with the crisis over nuclear proliferation, first by introducing sanctions against the two states at the time of the tests, then, in March 2000, by a visit to the region. But his brief stop in Pakistan was overshadowed by the recent military coup that had brought President Pervez Musharraf to power.

However, Clinton was not solely interested in the non-proliferation of nuclear arms. In fact, he was interested in preventing all weapons of mass destruction falling into the hands of 'rogue' states, and chemical weapons were a particular concern. Here too, he continued a policy begun under Bush, and supported by Moscow, of reducing the size of arsenals. In September 1991, at the Washington summit, Bush and Gorbachev had agreed to cut their chemical weapons stocks by more than three-quarters. In mid-January 1993, there was also a UN-sponsored Chemical Weapons Ban treaty designed to prevent the development, production, and use of such arms. But, whilst it was ratified by sufficient states (eighty of them) to come into force in April 1997, it was not signed by some of those states most likely to practise chemical warfare, especially Iraq. Therefore, even joint US–Russian leadership of a particular development could not guarantee its acceptance. Countries in the less developed world might no longer be able to play off Washington and Moscow against each other, but that did not mean that a US–Russian condominium existed in the world. Each state continued to look to its own security, well aware that the great powers did the same, and neither did the great powers always set the best example. It was significant in December 1997, for example, that whereas most of the world's nations were prepared to sign a treaty banning anti-personnel mines, the US and Russia were among the minority who refused.

Clinton's readiness to focus on relations with Russia even though the Cold War had ended was due to more than a desire for arms control and non-proliferation. 'For an administration routinely accused of foreign policy incoherence . . . its approach to Russia appeared quite consistent and even sophisticated.'[29] From the outset, he sought a 'strategic alliance' with Yeltsin, whom he first met at Vancouver in April 1993, and this alliance included support for reform in Russia. Moscow might only command a shadow of its former, global power but its stability was vital to the wider stability of all Eurasia, a new kind of Cold War was always a danger, and Russia could have created severe difficulties for American policy on such issues as the Bosnian War (see Chapter 20, C) or the 'dual containment' of Iraq and Iran. There was still considerable popular suspicion of the US in Russia and even reformers were disappointed at the scale of American aid. It was a particularly delicate matter to extend NATO into Eastern Europe, given Russia's historical and strategic interest in the region. American Republicans were often critical of Clinton for failing to press on with NATO enlargement, thereby tying Eastern Europe to the West, and for failing to oppose Russian predomination in areas formerly ruled by the USSR. But for the President it was pointless to antagonize Russia when it no longer represented an immediate security menace, and when Yeltsin's likely successors were either extreme nationalists and pan-Slavists, such as Vladimir Zhirinovsky (who emerged as an important figure in the December 1993 elections), or members of the Communist Party, which still commanded a fifth of the national vote.

The danger of collapse in Yeltsin's position was especially apparent at the start of the Clinton presidency: the months from March to October 1993 were ones of constant crisis in Russia, which was only brought to an end by Yeltsin's decision to bombard the parliament building to force opposition deputies into line. Despite such extreme action, and despite his ill health and drunkenness, the US still saw Yeltsin as the best hope for stability and democracy. Clinton's 'strong political and diplomatic support reached its peak during the failed 1993 coup . . . where the US found itself . . . endorsing the shelling of a parliament'.[30] On his visit to Moscow in January 1994—where both sides said they would no longer target each other with nuclear arms—Clinton described his Russian counterpart as an equal and a partner, and in March backed a large International Monetary Fund (IMF) loan to Russia. As to Yeltsin, he too felt a close partnership with Clinton: 'No other US president engaged in such intensive negotiations with the leaders of our country . . . Sometimes it seemed . . . that we were establishing . . . a new future for our planet.' Then again, even Yeltsin soon recognized that 'Russia and the United States viewed few conflicts in the world in the same way. We had different interests.'[31] And there was more to the sense of separation between Moscow and Washington than different interests on particular issues. In 1989, the two had been equals and in 1990–3 they worked quite closely together to prevent a return of the Cold War; but after 1994 the US felt more confident about pursuing its own agenda. The 'relationship with the West became more testing' and US policy amounted to 'a very substantial marginalization of Russia' in world affairs.[32]

The year 1994–5 proved a difficult one in US–Russian relations, however, with a more assertive Russian role in Bosnia, Yeltsin's opposition to NATO's 'Partnership for Peace' with Eastern Europe and the start of the war in Chechnya. But the Clinton policy, of a cautious approach to NATO enlargement while accepting Russian assertiveness in the former USSR, gradually brought results. In 1995–6, the Bosnian settlement, the prolongation of the NPT, and Russia's acceptance of the Partnership for Peace were accompanied by Yeltsin's—and Clinton's—successful re-election. Thereafter it was possible to begin the actual enlargement of NATO while rewarding Yeltsin with more financial aid, which was one main aim of his pragmatically pro-Western policy. A false note was the replacement of the Russian Foreign Minister, Andrei Kozyrev in January 1996 after long criticism in the Parliament of his pro-Western policies. Under Kozyrev's successor, Yevgeni Primakov, Russian policy was marked by a more nationalist tinge, notably in the attempts to prevent American attacks on Iraq when Saddam Hussein obstructed the work of UN weapons inspectors. But the continuing weakness of the Russian economy and the decrepit state of the armed forces—said by the Defence Minister in February 1997 to be on the verge of disintegration—pointed Yeltsin in the direction of cooperation with Moscow's former enemies. To this end, he signed a trade deal with the European Union (July 1995), began a series of annual conferences with the German and French leaders (1997), and held a series of summit conferences with China's Jiang Zemin, crowned in November 1997 by the settlement of their generation-old border dispute.

Not all of Yeltsin's policies were to the taste of the US, then, but their general direction was, and serious crises between Moscow and Washington seemed matters of the past. As to Clinton's policy, it may have been criticized by Republicans at home, and its caution may have seemed similar to that of Bush. But it did allow the US to keep its former arch-enemy quiescent, while other difficult problems were addressed, such as freer trade and the challenge of 'rogue states', at a time when the American public were reluctant to play an active overseas role in any case. The pay-off for supporting Yeltsin was that Russia continued on a capitalist, democratic course. In contrast to earlier decades, if Clinton's policy did have a fault in his second term, it was that he was too supportive of the Moscow regime for its own good. In particular, by backing Yeltsin in his attempts to maintain the value of the rouble in 1997–8, the US and the IMF probably drove the Russian economy deeper into depression. The country's economic and social problems were immense and included unemployment, growing inequalities of wealth, limited savings, low industrial production, a large public deficit, and an inadequate tax system. It is easy to see why Yeltsin's economic reforms were more to American taste than Gorbachev's had been.

BOX 21.4

Biography: Boris Yeltsin (1931–2007)

Born in the Sverdlovsk region, into a peasant family, in 1931, and trained as a construction engineer, Yeltsin joined the Communist Party in 1961 and rose to become the chief Party official in the city of Sverdlovsk by 1976, being recognized as one of the rising generation of reformers in the USSR. Promoted under Gorbachev in 1985 to be the Party boss in the capital, Moscow, he at first cooperated with the Soviet leader but then fell out with him, complaining about the slow pace of reform. Sacked from the Politburo in 1987, Yeltsin did what previous disgraced politicians in the USSR had been unable to do: he rebuilt his position by adopting a high public profile and by securing a key appointment outside the communist hierarchy, as President of the most important Soviet republic, the Russian Federation, in May 1990. The following year he greatly strengthened his position by winning a popular election to confirm his presidency. In contrast, Gorbachev was increasingly unpopular and could not risk a free vote on his leadership.

Yeltsin cemented his reputation as a democrat and strong-willed man of principle by resisting the August 1991 coup of communist hard-liners. In the following months, he worked for the destruction of the USSR, having already quit the Communist Party. Unpredictable, alcoholic, and increasingly dogged by ill health he, nonetheless, dominated Russian politics after December 1991. His radical reforms brought economic chaos, his democratic credentials were dented by his October 1993 attack on the Russian Parliament, and his foreign policy was criticized as betraying Russian interests to the West. But the pace of reform was maintained, cooperation with the West brought the rewards of peace and financial support, and he was successfully re-elected President in July 1996, beating the communist candidate, Gennady Zyuganov in a run-off. In November, he had complex heart by-pass surgery, from which his health never fully recovered, and he lost popularity thanks to continuing economic problems and the failure to deal effectively with Chechnya. In March 1998, he suddenly sacked his long-serving Prime Minister, Viktor Chernomyrdin, but did not find it easy to secure a successor: three more premiers were sacked over the next eighteen months before Yeltsin appointed the more successful Vladimir Putin on 9 August 1999. Meanwhile, in the year since August 1998, the rouble had lost about three-quarters of its value on international markets. Ill health forced him to hand power to Putin on 31 December 1999. Even the timing of this move caught the world by surprise, with Yeltsin making a television appearance in which he asked the Russian people to forgive his mistakes.

Yeltsin had embraced a more radical line in 1992, abandoning central planning as quickly as he could, privatizing industry, and (at the cost of high inflation) ending price controls. But he was forced to rely on the same civil servants who had served the communist regime, and the beneficial effects of the free market were further undermined by the failure to tackle growing corruption. Yeltsin was also increasingly unwell. A heavy drinker and workaholic, he spent several weeks in 1995 in hospital with heart problems and in late 1997 needed major by-pass surgery.

The 1997–8 world economic crisis, which began in South-East Asia, exposed the fragility of the Russian economy and of the man who, for all his flaws, Clinton backed as the best hope for capitalist reform and good US–Russian relations. In March 1998, Yeltsin, after another bout of heart trouble, decided on dramatic action, unexpectedly sacking Premier Viktor Chernomyrdin and replacing him with a young, inexperienced and little-known reformer, Sergei Kiriyenko, who was only reluctantly confirmed by the Russian Parliament. Two months later the government introduced a tough package to stabilize the currency, reduce tax evasion, tackle inflation, and press on with privatization. This impressed the IMF, which in July 1998 agreed a massive $22.6 billion loan, but it only propped up the rouble for another month and did nothing for Yeltsin's popularity. His decisions seemed increasingly desperate when, in late August, with widespread fears of a Russian economic collapse, he suddenly sacked Kiriyenko and brought back Chernomyrdin. A sense of stability was only restored in August 1999 when Vladimir Putin became the fifth Russian prime minister in seventeen months. Colourless but tough, efficient, and young (he was born in 1952), Putin's appointment led to renewed US concern about the future of Russian democracy because he was a former KGB officer and in 1998–9 head of the Russian intelligence service, the federal Security Bureau. He also renewed efforts to crush the separatist movement in Chechnya (see Chapter 20, B). Yet it was his success in the last operation that established his popularity and made him the natural successor to the increasingly decrepit Yeltsin, who gave one last surprise to the world with his sudden resignation on 31 December 1999. Initially appointed Acting President, Putin was elected into the position in his own right on 26 March 2000, with 52 per cent of the vote. He showed some readiness to stand up to Washington, not least in his criticism of the continued development of the Star Wars project, now nearing deployment as the 'National Missile Defence System'. Indeed, in a revival of an old, Cold War alliance, he joined with China in condemning this. Yet personal relations between Putin and Western leaders developed well at first and, as with Yeltsin before him, he was seen as far more preferable than the communist and ultranationalist alternatives. If, in Chechnya, he satisfied Russian nationalist opinion, he also persisted with a parliamentary system and economic reform.

D. The Clinton Administration and 'Rogue States'

The Concept of 'Rogue States'

One important way in which the Clinton administration tried to mobilize US and world opinion against its enemies, protect Western ideological values and create stability, was to press the concept of 'rogue' or 'backlash states'. Whilst trying to 'enlarge' the area of the world that was part of the American-led liberal order, it was also necessary, in the eyes of Clinton and his National Security Adviser, Anthony Lake, to isolate those states whose ideologies or support for terrorism made it impossible to deal with them on a normal basis. Thus, in spring 1994, Lake wrote of:

> [R]ecalcitrant and outlaw states that not only choose to remain outside the family but also assault its basic values . . . Ruled by cliques that control power through coercion, they . . . exhibit a chronic inability to engage constructively with the outside world . . . As the sole superpower, the US has a special responsibility . . . to neutralize, contain and . . . perhaps eventually transform these backlash states into constructive members of the international community.[33]

In November 1997, when making its first major change in nuclear targeting policy since 1980, the US retained a deterrent capacity against Russia and China, but widened its potential targets to include 'rogue states', on the grounds that they had access to weapons of mass destruction. Yet, as with roll-back during the Cold War, the concept of 'rogue states', though easy enough to explain in general terms, was difficult to execute in practice and surrounded by contradictions. The new doctrine was tolerant of any number of oppressive regimes so long as they were friendly to the US. Cynics charged that it also targeted small, isolated countries—like Cuba or Libya—which were no real threat to American interests, whilst a large, strategically significant country like China was dealt with through the alternative approach of 'constructive engagement'. Notwithstanding its communist ideology and questionable human rights record, Clinton decided that Beijing was too important as a trading partner, and too vital to East Asian security, to treat as an enemy (see Chapter 22, D). But it was not the case that US policy-makers victimized every small, Marxist state that had outlived the Cold War. The Marxist-led government of Angola, for example, was given recognition by Clinton in 1993 because it had shown a readiness to hold free elections, even if the 'pro-Western' opposition leader, Jonas Savimbi, did not respect the result and the civil war there continued until he was killed in 2002. More remarkably, Vietnam's willingness to engage with the West, introduce free-market elements into the economy, and provide information on those US troops reported missing-in-action during the Vietnam War, led to American diplomatic recognition in 1995. This was followed by a US–Vietnamese trade deal in July 2000 as well as by visits from Madeleine Albright in September 1999, and from Clinton himself at the very end of his presidency, so that his second term became a time of reconciliation with the most dogged of Cold War enemies. Cases where a continued adhesion to communist doctrine led to US economic sanctions and attempted diplomatic isolation were actually limited to two: Cuba and North Korea.

The concept of 'rogue states' was useful to the Clinton administration because of the fact that, after the collapse of the Soviet Union, it was so difficult to mobilize the US people in favour of an activist foreign policy. Under Bush, American policy had initially seemed successful in bringing a peaceful end to the Cold War, securing German reunification, and dealing with Third World dictators, Noriega in Panama and Saddam Hussein in the Gulf War. Indeed, Noriega and Saddam had already shown the value of pointing up certain distasteful regimes as primary threats to the New World Order. After 1991, American foreign policy, its 'victory' over the USSR complete, seemed more aimless, not helped by the ill-fated intervention in Somalia or the intractability of the Bosnian conflict. True, it was possible to focus on challenges such as the international drugs trade, 'global warming', and the interdependency of world trade, and Clinton did try to tackle these. A commitment to free trade areas in the western hemisphere and Asia-Pacific was central to his world outlook. But narcotics, environmentalism, and trade were all complex issues; they were difficult to make progress with and, especially in the case of the last two, they aroused controversy in the US about how best to tackle them. In contrast, it was quite easy to win support for attacks on those who were threatening their neighbours, developing chemical and nuclear weapons, or sponsoring international terrorism.

The last, of course, was an old problem, which had already led to US bombing raids in 1986 on Colonel Gaddafi's Libya (see Chapter 17, D). Libya was a leading candidate for the title 'rogue state' in the 1990s, not least because it refused to hand over two officials who were suspected of involvement in the 1988 bombing of an American Boeing 747 airliner over Lockerbie, Scotland, in which 270 people died. The US and Britain, backed by France—which blamed Gaddafi for the loss of a French airliner over West Africa in 1989—were able to secure UN sanctions against Libya in April 1992, and to maintain these despite the increasing doubts of the Organization of African Unity and the fact that Gaddafi ceased to be a high-profile sponsor of terrorism after 1986.

In May 1994, he also agreed to withdraw from the disputed Aozou strip on the border with Chad, which his forces had occupied since the 1970s. He continued to offend Washington, by offering to finance Louis Farrakhan's 'Nation of Islam' movement in the US, for example, and (apparently) trying to build a chemical weapons plant. But relations eased when he agreed to hand over, for trial in Holland, two Libyans who were suspected of involvement in the Lockerbie bombing. The trial opened in May 2000 and one Libyan was subsequently found guilty.

Neither was Libya the only Arab-led, Muslim, North African state accused of supporting terrorism. So, in August 1993, was Sudan, where the Islamic National Front had come to power in 1989, adopting the Sharia (holy law) and prosecuting more vigorously the civil war that had been underway since 1983 against the black, Christian south of the country. For a time, Sudan also provided a safe haven for the anti-American al-Qaeda terrorist network and its leader, the Saudi dissident, Osama bin Laden. Neighbouring countries like Uganda and Ethiopia were keen to see the Sudanese government replaced, foreign aid to it was cut back severely, and in November 1997 the US introduced economic sanctions against it. But al-Qaeda was not cowed: on 7 August 1998, it launched simultaneous bomb attacks on the US embassies in Kenya and Tanzania, killing more than two hundred people. The US responded two weeks later with cruise missile attacks on suspected terrorist bases in both Sudan and Afghanistan, which had also given facilities to al-Qaeda. Bin Laden was then forced to leave the Sudan but his terrorist network remained intact. By 2000, there was widespread famine in southern Sudan, and the next few years brought moves to end the war in the South.

One feature of the 'rogue states' concept, which was of concern to the US government itself, was that it could easily turn into an anti-Muslim policy. Apart from Libya and the Sudan, other key 'rogue states' were Iran and Iraq, and there were various reasons why Americans should have particular fears about what was termed 'Islamic fundamentalism'. As a doctrine, it seemed alien to core US values and, with the evident bankruptcy of communism, could be seen as the primary ideological competitor to liberal democracy. In Iran, of course, it had emerged as a threat to US interests as early as 1979, with the fall of the Shah and the seizure of the American embassy in Tehran. It was easy to ignore the ideals of mercy and tolerance in Islam, the deep divisions within the Islamic world—between, for example, the theocracy of Iran, the secularized Iraqi state, or the Saudi monarchy—and the genuine reasons for Muslim resentment of Western injustice and Christian enmity stretching back centuries. Muslims were critical of European imperialism, the creation of Israel, and more recently US attempts to foist its own political values and economic system on their own, well-established way of life. But the 1980s and 1990s saw many incidents of violence that Americans associated with Islamic radicalism, not only in Iran and the Sudan, but also in Algeria, Lebanon, at least in the 1980s, and Afghanistan, which gave refuge to Osama bin Laden when he was forced to flee the Sudan and which was subjected to limited US sanctions after November 1999. In Algeria, up to 100,000 people were killed during the 1990s in a vicious civil war between the military-dominated government and the main opposition party, the Islamic Salvation Front. Furthermore, the 'fundamentalists' seemed to be advancing in Central Asia, in Afghanistan, and the former Soviet republic of Tajikistan, and at times even seemed a threat to pro-Western governments in Egypt, Pakistan, and Turkey. Of the many terrorist incidents associated with Islamic groups, the most shocking was the bombing of the World Trade Center in New York in late February 1993, just after Clinton's election, though it was only a shadow of the attacks that would come in September 2001. But, as with Bush, the new administration could never entertain a crudely anti-Islamic policy, because too many of its friends and allies were Muslim states (Egypt, Saudi Arabia, and Indonesia to name just a few) and those like Turkey and Pakistan, who at times seemed likely to turn to fundamentalism, needed the firmest US support. As with the treatment of Marxist states, it was best to deal with those who would cooperate and isolate those who seemed the greatest threat.

Key Examples: Korea, Cuba, Iran, Iraq

Apart from Libya and the Sudan, the main 'rogue' states which the Clinton administration tried to isolate were the two Marxist regimes of Cuba and North Korea, and two Middle Eastern countries, Iran and Iraq. All, in fact, had been seen as opponents of US interests since before Clinton was elected. North Korea, indeed, had been an opponent since 1950. It still laid claim to South Korea and periodically tried to destabilize it, by stirring up border tension, infiltrating saboteurs, and carrying out assassinations. The worst incident was the murder of a seventeen-strong South Korean delegation to Burma in October 1983. But such intimidation failed to prevent South Korea's economy growing apace, while the North's stagnated, and the South was able to exploit the decline of the Cold War to host the Olympic Games (1988) and establish diplomatic relations with the North's former protectors, the USSR (1990) and China (1992). It seemed unlikely that the North would reopen the Korean War but it remained a centralized communist state, with substantial armed forces, under its 'Great Leader', Kim Il Sung. Attempts to turn the 1953 armistice agreement into a proper peace treaty had never advanced far and in 1991 it was feared that, in order to strengthen its position, the North might be building a nuclear weapon. If it succeeded, this would be of concern not only to South Korea, but to other pro-Western states in the region, like Japan, and to the South's key protector, America.

Initially, a crisis was avoided: the US was ready to withdraw any nuclear weapons it had based in the South, the North proved ready to fulfil the Non-Proliferation Treaty, and in December 1991 the South signed two agreements with the North to keep the peninsula nuclear-free. But, whilst the South now hoped for a gradual move to reunification, Kim Il Sung was determined to preserve its independent political development, and in March 1993 the nuclear agreements began to unravel, when the North started to block inspections on its soil by the International Atomic Energy Authority. By November, the Clinton White House was threatening to use force if the North obtained a nuclear weapon. In 1994, this dangerous crisis between the North and the US was only eased when, in July, Kim suddenly died, just as ex-President Jimmy Carter began to act a go-between for Clinton. In October, the North agreed to wind down its nuclear programme in return for help with energy supplies, trade, and investment, as well as an assurance that it would not be subjected to nuclear threats by the US. The years following this breakthrough were not easy, partly because the North was slow to carry out its promises. In April 1996, now under Kim Il Sung's son, Kim Jong Il, the North said it would no longer recognize the demilitarized zone; in September another group of Northern infiltrators landed in the South from a submarine. But the North was growing ever weaker in economic terms, facing widespread famine after 1997, and the Chinese pressed it to talk to the South. In May 1997, the South agreed to provide food aid to the North and, at the end of the year, talks opened between these two, alongside America and China, in Geneva to try to frame a permanent settlement of the Korean problem. Progress was fitful but June 2000 saw a summit meeting between Kim Jong Il and South Korea's Kim Dae Jung, cross-border reunions began in August between families that had been divided for decades, and the two countries competed at the Olympics that summer under a joint flag. But the following years would see a further deterioration in relations.

There was no similar relaxation of tension between Washington and another old enemy, Fidel Castro of Cuba. Castro's position, like Kim Il Sung's, was weakened by the end of the Cold War. In 1991, the USSR was still providing Cuba with about $2 billion in aid and 10,000 troops but Gorbachev, even before his downfall, announced this would end (the troops left in 1993) and meanwhile, in the Nicaraguan elections of February 1990, Castro had lost his only ally in the western hemisphere. 'Today we hear the breaking and crumbling of Castro's dictatorship', Bush announced.[34] Unable to trade on favourable terms with his former Council for Mutual Economic Aid (COMECON) partners, the Cuban leader decided to maintain his dictatorship but now allowed some free-market elements and foreign investment in the economy. He also showed, over the following years, that he was not completely isolated: the Russians kept a small presence in Cuba of signals intelligence experts, eavesdropping on the US; in August 1992, as part of a process of courting Latin American sympathy, he signed the Tlatelolco Treaty (the 1967 pact between Latin American and Caribbean countries, banning nuclear weapons in the region); in 1995, he was able to address the UN; and in 1998, Cuba was visited by Pope John Paul II. Castro even proved able to embarrass the mighty US in August 1994 when he ended the long-standing ban on emigration from Cuba. Not only did this seem an important act of liberalization, it also meant that tens of thousands of people now clamoured to leave Cuba and enter the US. This proved Washington's claim that many Cubans were unhappy living under communism, but it also stirred up ill feeling in America about high levels of Hispanic immigration. So great was the pressure that, in September, Clinton was forced to strike a deal with Castro on emigration levels.

Whatever the signs of political change in Cuba, the US was determined to maintain its pressure on Castro. Cuba might be small and lacking strong friends, but its leader had provoked a deep, personalized loathing in the US since the Bay of Pigs in 1961. Cuba was seen as an oppressive, totalitarian regime, and it had a wealthy, influential body of opponents in the Cuban-American community of Florida. The 'Cuban–American National Foundation' led the campaign against Castro, insisting that the trade embargo be maintained. US hatred of Latin American radicalism ran deep and Cuba lay on its very doorstep. The 1962 settlement of the Cuban Missile Crisis meant that force was ruled out as a way to topple Castro but a trade embargo had been introduced that same year and in the 1990s was tightened up, as economic warfare became America's principal weapon against him. The 1992 Torricelli Act extended the embargo to overseas subsidiaries of US companies, and more controversially, the March 1996 Helms–Burton Act allowed the prosecution of foreign-owned businesses that traded with Cuba. Clinton disliked the latter measure but 1996 was an election year, Florida was a key electoral battleground, the Republican-dominated Congress was firmly anti-Castro, and the Cubans had just (in February) shot down two aircraft carrying opponents of the regime off the island. It was questionable, however, whether America's toughness was not self-destructive. The European Union and Latin American states were offended by the Helms–Burton Act, claiming that it was illegal under the rules of the World Trade Organization. Arguably, it simply helped Castro to pose as the defender of Cuban independence against US imperialism. A policy of 'engagement' (as followed by Clinton with China) would have been a swifter way of ending the Castro regime. As it was, the campaign against Cuba seemed a telling example of America's determination to interpret general principles, like free trade and respect for human rights, in its own interests. It was a case of post-Cold War foreign policy being decided by domestic political considerations. Then again, a visit to Cuba by the Russian President, Vladimir Putin, in December 2000 served as a reminder that there was still some sympathy for Castro from his former Cold War allies.

Castro, while he survived in power, was an easier challenge with which to deal than Iran and Iraq. These countries, given their proximity and capacity for military action, had to be dealt with under a policy known as 'dual containment'. Saddam Hussein's decision to invade Kuwait in 1990 created a double dilemma for US policy: not only had he to be removed from Kuwait, but Iraq now became the second state in the Persian Gulf which threatened regional stability in the long term (Iran having been such a threat since 1979). In the 1980s, of course, Iraq and Iran had effectively 'contained' each other by fighting a long and bitter war, and one helpful factor in the 1990s, from the US viewpoint, was that they remained deeply suspicious of one another. There was always the danger that a hard-line American policy might drive them together and make each of them even more militant. But Washington felt it must take that risk. Both countries were opposed to the Israeli–Palestinian peace process, both supported international terrorist groups, both were known to be developing weapons of mass destruction, and both were seen as potentially aggressive against their neighbours. Also, 'Dual containment . . . built on policies that have long guided US Middle East policy . . . namely guaranteeing a continuing flow of oil . . . and keeping other powers from supplanting American dominance in the region.'[35] On several occasions after 1991, crises blew up over Saddam's threats to Kuwait and his refusal to allow UN inspections, whilst

Iran's attempts to build a nuclear weapon, linked to its support for terrorism, led Clinton to introduce a complete trade and investment embargo against it in June 1995. Meanwhile, the US still retained $11 billion of Iranian assets frozen in 1979, and the CIA was in contact with various opposition groups.

If anything, Iran, through its size and revolutionary fervour, seemed the more dangerous opponent, but there were indications that it might be possible to work with the regime. The death of the Ayatollah Khomeini in June 1989 had led to a strengthening of the political position of the President, as opposed to the supreme religious leadership, now held by Ayatollah Khamenei. After 1989, the President was Ali Akbar Rafsanjani, who adopted free-market reforms and helped secure the release of Western hostages in Lebanon. More dramatically, Rafsanjani's successor, Mohammed Khatami, seemed ready in December 1997 to offer improved individual rights within Iran and spoke of opening a 'dialogue' with the US. Iran had also been able to improve its relations with France and Russia, while fellow Islamic states like Saudi Arabia wanted to see better US–Iranian understanding. There were other reasons for Clinton to respond positively to Khatami: dual containment was costly and had failed to change the regime in either Iran or Iraq; and it was tempting to exploit Iran as an opponent of Saddam Hussein, in order to try to stabilize the Persian Gulf through an alternative policy. But Clinton was careful in evolving a policy. Thus in June 1998, the Secretary of State, Madeleine Albright, talked of breaking down barriers with Iran but, in return, wanted it to end its support for terrorism and its attempts to obtain weapons of mass destruction. Albright eventually met her Iranian opposite number in September 2000, but only on the neutral ground provided by the UN in New York and whilst relations showed signs of becoming more 'normal' they were still surrounded by mutual suspicion.

E. 'Humanitarian Intervention' in Somalia and Haiti

Dilemmas of Humanitarian Intervention

One way in which Western governments were pushed by their own media and public opinion to decide foreign policy priorities after the Cold War was on the basis of respect for human rights. In particular, in conflicts like Bosnia (see Chapter 20, C) and Rwanda (see Chapter 22, B), there was considerable pressure to intervene on humanitarian grounds, to end inter-ethnic violence, and guarantee both food and medical aid with the use of 'peacekeeping' missions. With about 20 million refugees in the world by the mid-1990s, the breakdown of order in so-called 'failed states' like Somalia, Liberia, and Sierra Leone, and vicious civil conflicts in the Sudan, Algeria, and elsewhere, it seemed essential to consider humanitarian intervention as a way to realize the promises of stability and plenty which had been generated by talk of a new world order. Furthermore, with the end of the Cold War, it seemed possible to intervene without raising the danger of superpower tension ensuing. The idea of humanitarian intervention was far from new and there had been many examples of mass murder in the twentieth century, not least the Holocaust, to support the argument that the world community should try to prevent such events occurring. A classic definition of such intervention emerged as the 'use of force by a state, or states, to protect citizens of the target state from large-scale human rights violations'.[36] But the 1945 UN Charter had respected both human rights *and* the national sovereignty of member states, with the latter generally winning out over the former. Since all states had a vested interest in preserving the sanctity of national sovereignty, few political leaders were genuinely prepared to entertain the idea of intervention in another country's affairs purely on humanitarian grounds. In any case, who was to judge when human rights violations became 'large-scale' enough to justify intervention?

Humanitarian intervention was, in any case, a far more complex moral issue than the Western media liked to pretend, and ethical questions were always tied up with issues of international law, self-interest, and political expediency. It could be argued that oppressive states forfeited legitimacy, so that their national sovereignty need not be respected but, given the number of oppressive regimes in the world and the fact that many were political allies and trading partners of the West, or else too strong and stable to allow intervention, it was difficult to decide at what point intervention was both opportune and possible. 'Domestic' and 'foreign' policy matters could become hopelessly confused in this debate, with universal values and national sovereignty also in the melting pot. At what point did judicial executions (a feature of legal life even in the US) or intercommunal violence (a feature of society in many Western states) justify external interference?

And who should make this decision? A majority vote in the UN General Assembly might be best for giving legitimacy to such a condemnation, and many states were ready to respect a decision to use force by the Security Council, but it was notoriously difficult to get the UN to act in unison and in practice it was left to individual states to decide on intervention, often for mixed motives. The Western definition of human rights was not necessarily shared in Asia or Africa; too often 'humanitarian' intervention seemed a disguise for what the non-aligned movement interpreted as 'imperialist' behaviour, 'to cover actions taken for other purposes', or even simply 'to justify continuing high military spending' after the Cold War;[37] and there was the basic dilemma of whether it could even be morally justifiable to use military force, with the inevitable civilian deaths that followed. Also, was intervention in the interests of those who carried it out? One critic accused Clinton of engaging in 'foreign policy as social work'.[38]

Many of these problems had in fact been seen during the Cold War when, despite the overwhelming tendency to treat any conflict as an extension of East–West rivalry, there had been various examples of 'humanitarian' action, or at least claims that states were motivated by humanitarian concern. The US had tried to use this argument to excuse its invasions of the Dominican Republic in 1965 and Grenada two decades later, but did not impress anyone. More seriously, the use of economic sanctions against South Africa and Rhodesia was defended as helping to put an end to racist oppression. Few objected to the overthrow of the dictator Idi Amin of Uganda by a Tanzanian-led invasion in 1979, or when the French toppled the equally oppressive 'Emperor' Bokassa of the Central African Republic the same year. But these were unusual examples of actions that were tolerated by both the Western and Soviet blocs, as well as the Non-Aligned Movement. South Africa and Rhodesia were guilty of a particular type of human rights abuse; other types went unchallenged by UN sanctions. Tanzania (backed by the West) had reasons of self-interest to overthrow a crazy dictator on their borders; there was no similar invasion to oust the equally cruel regime of Amin's eventual successor, Milton Obote. And the French only turned against Bokassa after building up his position in the first place. Elsewhere during the Cold War, even actions that self-evidently saved thousands of human lives were likely to be condemned if they offended one of the superpowers. Thus the US was critical of India's support for Bangladeshi independence in 1971 (because this represented a defeat for America's ally, Pakistan) and condemned the Vietnamese invasion of Cambodia in 1978 (because, although it put an end to the murderous Pol Pot regime, it represented an advance for 'pro-Soviet' interests).

Several examples of interventions after the Cold War were influenced by humanitarian pressures, some involving UN approval and some not. They included: Iraq, where Allied forces acted in April 1991 to provide protection for the Kurds and Marsh Arabs; Bosnia, where the UN acted after 1992 only with the Bosnian government's consent and had a limited impact; Liberia, where the Nigerians dominated attempts by fellow West African states to end the post-1990 civil war; and Rwanda, where the UN endorsed French intervention only to find that the Paris government took sides among the locals (see Chapter 22, B). However, there were two other examples of intervention, where the US took a leading role and where radically different outcomes showed both the perils and opportunities of humanitarian action. These were Somalia and Haiti, both of which fell into the category of so-called 'failed states'.

Somalia

Somalia, led since October 1969 by Siad Barré, had been of great significance in the breakdown of East–West détente in the late 1970s, thanks to the Ogaden War against Ethiopia (see Chapter 14, C). After suffering defeat in that conflict, various opposition groups became active against Barré and, as the Cold War wound down in the late 1980s, the fate of the Horn of Africa became less important to the superpowers. In the early 1990s, both Somalia and Ethiopia suffered deep internal traumas. In Ethiopia's case, this took the form of having to concede the independence of Eritrea in 1992 after decades of war, but at least the central government survived and was even able to fare well in a border conflict with Eritrea in 1999–2000. In Somalia's case, in contrast, there was a decline into virtual anarchy. Along with the rest of Africa, Somalia, never a wealthy country, received little Western aid or investment and by 1990 there was widespread famine. But there were enough weapons left over from the Ogaden War to keep the political factions well armed. On 27 January 1991, Barré was forced to flee into exile, having lost control of the capital, Mogadishu, to the forces of the United Somali Congress. Despite its impressive title, this was only one of several opposition groups, most of which relied on the support of particular Somali clans, and it was unable to agree with the rest. In the North, one group, the Somali National Movement, declared independence, basing its borders on those of the former colony of British Somaliland, which had been united with Italian Somaliland to form Somalia in 1960. By September 1991, the political divisions had grown worse, as the United Somali Congress split between the supporters of its Chairman, General Mohammed Aideed, and the President, Ali Mahdi. The UN tried to broker ceasefires and form a coalition government. In April 1992, it also set up the UN Operation in Somalia (UNOSOM) to help secure peace and humanitarian assistance. The force was deployed in August but was initially limited to about a thousand personnel.

Meanwhile, as images of starving Somalis filtered through to American television screens, there were calls for Bush to intervene on a large scale to protect food supplies. Since Aideed had earlier seemed to approve UNOSOM, there appeared little danger of US troops running into a Vietnam-style imbroglio. It was felt that American forces, fresh from their success in the Gulf War, could easily handle a famine relief mission in a poor country like Somalia. It would, however, be a marked departure from existing policy: in the wake of the Cold War, despite complaints from the Congressional Black Caucus and others, the US had run down aid to Africa. Aid to Somalia had been cut in July 1989. True, Bush had sent a force of marines to Liberia in West Africa in June 1990, but this was a limited operation to evacuate American citizens. 'That Bush, in so many ways a practitioner of Realpolitik, would have intervened in an area now devoid of strategic significance, appeared to expand considerably the meaning of his "New World Order".' Yet this is what happened. The intervention 'was justified purely on humanitarian grounds. There was no strategic, economic or narcotics interest that propelled the . . . US into action, nor foreign territory that had been invaded.'[39] Neither did the Somali authorities request external intervention.

In December 1992, the outgoing Bush administration, in full agreement with President-elect Clinton, launched 'Operation Restore Hope', sanctioned by the UN, with 20,000 American troops despatched to Somalia under US command. There was no opposition to their arrival but Somali politics remained anarchic and Aideed's attitude towards such a large-scale external intervention became more ambiguous. Coordination between the relief effort and the military command was poor and there was little attempt to consult the Somalis. In May 1993, the Americans still seemed likely to escape without loss, since they were due to be replaced by a substantial new 'UNOSOM II' presence. But, partly in order to make it safe for new UN deployments, in an example of 'mission creep', the US had moved beyond its narrow humanitarian action, to try to disarm the local militias. This could only provoke concern among warlords like Aideed. It was then, in early June, that Aideed's followers massacred twenty-three Pakistani UN soldiers, leading the UN to order his arrest. On 17 June, American forces had their first clash with Aideed's men and the date for withdrawal was pushed back, even though there was still no direct US economic and political interest in the conflict. Clinton later remarked that he did not want to 'pull out and have chaos, anarchy, starvation return'.[40] But the US mission had now become one of fighting Aideed. Eventually, on 3–4 October, the Americans launched a full-scale helicopter and troop attack on his headquarters in Mogadishu but they became trapped and shot their way out. Hundreds of Somalis were killed in the process but the US public were mainly concerned with the death of thirteen of their own men. Having clamoured for intervention in the first place, the public were suddenly unwilling to support the Somali operation. For Clinton, Operation Restore Hope had become the most disastrous failure of his first year in office. Between December 1993 and March 1994, the US troops were withdrawn, though UN forces remained to guard the harbour and airport of Mogadishu for another year. By then, Aideed's forces were in the ascendant in Somalia and they continued to expand their area of control without securing outright victory, until the General's death in August 1996. Ironically, his successor was his son who, in 1992, had been a member of the US marines. Meanwhile, in May 1994, Clinton had issued a presidential directive to the effect that future military interventions would be to defend vital interests and with clear aims of success. It was a directive, however, that would cripple America's response to the next humanitarian crisis in Africa, focused on Rwanda.

Haiti

Operation Restore Hope had unexpectedly turned from a humanitarian venture into a dangerous military embarrassment for the US, rekindling fears

BOX 21.5

Bill Clinton and his Secretaries of State

Clinton was born William Jefferson Blythe IV in Hope, Arkansas in 1946, but his father was killed in a car accident before he was born and he took a new surname when his mother married Roger Clinton. When aged 16, Clinton met President Kennedy and determined to become a politician himself. He studied international relations at Georgetown University, Washington; won a Rhodes Scholarship to the University of Oxford; then trained in law at Yale, where he met his wife, Hillary Rodham. Clinton became Attorney General of his home state in 1976, only three years after leaving Yale, and by 1978 was the youngest state governor in America. His liberal views cost him the 1980 election, however, and he then became more circumspect in his approach. Returning to the governorship in 1982, he held on to it for the next decade, slowly improving Arkansas's provision of schools and social welfare.

His bid for the presidency in 1992 was helped by the fact that most other leading Democrats decided not to run, having decided that the Republican, George Bush, was in an impregnable position. Clinton exploited difficulties in the US economy to overcome Bush, then became the first Democratic president since Roosevelt to serve out two full terms. This was despite the failure of his health reforms, the loss of both the House and Senate to Republican control in 1994, and questions surrounding his finances (the 'Whitewater Affair') and private life (the Lewinsky scandal, which even briefly led to an impeachment attempt). His greatest success at home was to reduce the government deficit and preside over healthy economic growth. In his foreign policy, he was often accused of lacking an overall direction, yet he encouraged the peace process in the Middle East and Northern Ireland, took firm action over Haiti and Somalia, and could even claim a belated success in Bosnia.

Clinton's Secretary of State in his first term was Warren Christopher. Born in 1925 in South Dakota, he had been educated in law at Stanford and, throughout his career, interspersed law practice with government service. He was Deputy Attorney General in 1967–9, under Lyndon Johnson, and Deputy Secretary of State from 1977 to 1981, under Jimmy Carter. In the latter post, he had a key role in dealing with the Iran hostage crisis. As Secretary of State, he again focused much of his time on Middle East issues and travelled over 750,000 miles, further than any of his predecessors. He died in March 2011.

In the second term (1997–2001), Clinton chose Madeleine Albright to succeed Christopher. Albright had been born Maria Jana Korbelova, in Prague in 1937, the daughter of a Czechoslovakian diplomat. Her family lived in England during the Second World War, after fleeing the Nazis, but settled in Denver, Colorado in 1948. The multilingual and academically gifted Albright received her PhD from Columbia University in 1976 and specialized in international relations, particularly Eastern Europe, working at the School of Foreign Service at the University of Georgetown in the 1980s. But she was also developing a political career, working for Senator Edmund Muskie (1976–8) and then on the staff of the National Security Council under Carter (1978–81). In 1993, she joined the Clinton administration as ambassador to the UN. As the first female Secretary of State, she proved outspoken and blunt but popular, taking a particularly firm approach when dealing with Serbia.

of 'another Vietnam'. But predicting the course of military action is never easy and in Haiti in 1994 the Clinton administration had almost the opposite experience to Somalia over another problem inherited from Bush: intervention was only decided with great reluctance yet, once underway, brought an easy victory—even if the internal politics of the country remained unsettled.

1994 was not the first time that the US had intervened in Haiti. The country had been under partial American occupation for two decades after 1915, but this had done nothing to help democratic ideals take hold. Instead, by the 1960s the Caribbean island was dominated by François ('Papa Doc') Duvalier and his son, and eventual successor, Jean Claude, known as 'Baby Doc'. Papa Doc had originally been elected leader in 1957, but soon became one of the most ruthless and eccentric of the western hemisphere's dictators, appointing himself President-for-life in 1964 and using the paramilitary 'Tontons Macoutes' to terrorize the population. This did not dissuade US governments from maintaining the Duvaliers in power for the sake of anti-communism and regional stability. But in 1986, the poverty and dissatisfaction of Haitians were such that there was widespread unrest, and Baby Doc was forced to flee. Even so, thanks partly to the opposition of the police and army, it took until December 1990 before free elections were held, and the winner, a Catholic ex-priest called Jean-Bertrand Aristide, proved a volatile leader. His reforms threatened the position of the landowners, the business community and the army, and in August 1991 he was overthrown in a military coup. The Americans, whilst critical of Aristide's performance, did not welcome his replacement. With the Cold War over and little to fear from Communism in the Caribbean, a repressive government in Haiti was an embarrassment. It was one case where the triumph of Western liberal values round 1989–91 seemed to go into reverse. The Organization of American States (OAS) opposed the military government from the outset and introduced a regional trade embargo against it. The UN followed suit and, with US approval that would have seemed unlikely in earlier decades, introduced economic sanctions, culminating in an oil embargo in 1993. Furthermore, the Bush administration soon found itself facing tens of thousands of would-be immigrants from Haiti. Both Bush, and in early 1993 Clinton, felt they had little alternative to the forced repatriation of these refugees, but it was an embarrassing policy for America to adopt. Black Americans in Congress took up the Haitian cause and one leading activist, Randall Robinson, went on hunger strike to force Clinton into action.

In July 1993, a UN-sponsored mediation effort led the Haitian military government, under General Raul Cédras, to agree to let Aristide resume power by the end of October, in return for an amnesty for his opponents. But when October came, partly encouraged by Clinton's current humiliation in Somalia, Cédras decided to renege on the agreement. A US warship was refused the right to dock in Haiti, Republicans questioned the need for military action, and Clinton felt powerless to respond. Yet, as the months passed, American public opinion became increasingly concerned about the plight of ordinary Haitians, which was not helped by the economic blockade and which still led many 'boat people' to risk escape to the US. In July 1994, a UN resolution approved 'all necessary means' to remove the military government and, as diplomatic pressure on Cédras mounted, the US openly prepared for an invasion. It was eventually timetabled for mid-September, under the code word Operation Uphold Democracy, and apart from backing the democratic cause, was intended to remove the refugee problem. But even as it was being launched Cédras was induced to stand down. In an eleventh-hour mission to Haiti, ex-President Jimmy Carter persuaded the military to allow Aristide's return. As a result, Operation Uphold Democracy, which Clinton had taken so long to launch, went ahead on 19 September without opposition. Even one critical account concedes that in Haiti, 'the combination of power and diplomacy that the administration had talked about . . . worked rather well'.[41]

Up to 20,000 troops, from other countries in the region, as well as the US, arrived to restore Aristide, and in March 1995 the UN then took over control of the peacekeeping mission. US–UN relations were much better than they had been in Somalia and only one American was killed. Not everything went smoothly. There was sporadic violence between pro- and anti-Aristide factions and, whilst UN troops were withdrawn in November 1997, a police presence had to remain. Years of low investment in Haiti meant there was widespread poverty, unemployment, and a lack of basic amenities or an adequate transport system, which in turn undermined social and political stability. A further blow struck in January 2010, with a massive earthquake. In contrast to 1915, the Americans had come and gone quickly, taking care that the UN and OAS approved their action, but the fact was that Haiti still needed external intervention to preserve the hope of a democratic future. 'Indeed, the operation can be seen as a typical case of "regional power projection" by the US government, in its own area of influence', the key contrast with some earlier interventions in the region being that 'there was a strong will amongst the local population in support of the intervention' and a legitimate government being restored.[42]

Visit the online resources that accompany this book to test your understanding and take your learning further: www.oup.com/he/young-kent3e

NOTES

1. Richard A. Melanson, *American Foreign Policy since the Vietnam War* (M. E. Sharpe, Armonk, 1996), 210.
2. John Dumbrell, *American Foreign Policy, Carter to Clinton* (Macmillan, Basingstoke, 1997), 171.
3. Richard A. Melanson, *American Foreign Policy since the Vietnam War* (M. E. Sharpe, Armonk, 1996), 220.
4. Quoted in John Dumbrell, *American Foreign Policy, Carter to Clinton* (Macmillan, Basingstoke, 1997), 168.
5. Michael Cox, *US Foreign Policy after the Cold War* (Pinter, London 1985), 5.
6. Steven Hurst, *The Foreign Policy of the Bush Administration* (Cassell, London, 1999), 134.
7. Ian Clark, *The Post-Cold War Order* (Oxford University Press, Oxford, 2001), 169, 202, and 217.
8. David Deese, *The New Politics of American Foreign Policy* (St Martin's Press, New York, 1994), xiv.
9. Thomas Homer-Dixon, 'Global Environmental Change and International Security', in David Haglund, John Kirton, and David DeWitt (eds), *Building a New Global Order* (Oxford University Press, Oxford, 1993), 186; Roger Cary, 'The Contemporary Nature of Security', in Trevor C. Salmon (ed.), *Issues in International Relations* (Routledge, London, 1999), 59.
10. William Hyland, *Clinton's World: Remaking American Foreign Policy* (Praeger, Westport, 1999), 204.
11. John Spanier and Steve Hook, *American Foreign Policy since World War II* (14th edn, CQ Press, Washington, 1998), 326.
12. Stephen Ambrose, *Rise to Globalism* (8th edn, Penguin Books, New York, 1997), 426.
13. Quoted in John Spanier and Steve Hook, *American Foreign Policy since World War II* (14th edn, CQ Press, Washington, 1998), 321.
14. Richard A. Melanson, *American Foreign Policy since the Vietnam War* (M. E. Sharpe, Armonk, 1996), 255.
15. Steven Hurst, *The Foreign Policy of the Bush Administration* (Cassell, London, 1999), 86.
16. George Bush and Brent Scowcroft, *A World Transformed* (Vintage Books, New York, 1998), 371, 435.
17. Said Aburish, *Saddam Hussein: The Politics of Revenge* (Bloomsbury, London, 2000), 296.
18. Richard A. Melanson, *American Foreign Policy since the Vietnam War* (M. E. Sharpe, Armonk, 1996), 220.
19. Quoted in Michael Beschloss and Strobe Talbott, *At the Highest Levels* (Little, Brown, Boston, 1993), 254.
20. James Baker, *The Politics of Diplomacy* (G. P. Putnam's Sons, New York, 1995), 281.
21. Quoted in Robert McMahon, 'Contested Memory: The Vietnam War and American Society', *Diplomatic History*, 2 (2002), 170.
22. James Baker, *The Politics of Diplomacy* (G. P. Putnam's Sons, New York, 1995), 42.
23. Andrew and Patrick Cockburn, *Out of the Ashes: The Resurrection of Saddam Hussein* (HarperCollins, New York, 1999), 85.
24. Quoted in Steven Hurst, *The Foreign Policy of the Bush Administration* (Cassell, London, 1999), 46.
25. Quoted in Michael Beschloss and Strobe Talbott, *At the Highest Levels* (Little, Brown, Boston, 1993), 135.
26. Don Oberdorfer, *The Turn: How the Cold War Came to an End: The United States and the Soviet Union 1983–1990* (Jonathan Cape, London, 1992), 428; Mikhail Gorbachev, *Memoirs* (Doubleday, London, 1996), 537.
27. Mikhail Gorbachev, *Memoirs* (Doubleday, London, 1996), 617.
28. James Baker, *The Politics of Diplomacy* (G. P. Putnam's Sons, New York, 1995), 558.
29. Richard A. Melanson, *American Foreign Policy since the Vietnam War* (M. E. Sharpe, Armonk, 1996), 270.
30. John Hulsman, *A Paradigm for the New World Order* (Macmillan, Basingstoke, 1997), 115.
31. Boris Yeltsin, *Midnight Diaries* (Public Affairs Press, New York, 2000), 135.

32. Ian Clark, *The Post-Cold War Order* (Oxford University Press, Oxford, 2001), 88, 150.

33. A. Lake 'Confronting the Backlash States', United States Information Service, 10 March 1994 (reprinted from *Foreign Affairs*, March–April 1994), 1–2.

34. Quoted in Thomas Paterson, *Contesting Castro* (Oxford University Press, New York, 1994), 263.

35. Charles Kegley and Eugene Wittkopf, *American Foreign Policy: Pattern and Process* (5th edn, Macmillan, Basingstoke, 1996), 77.

36. Simon Duke, 'The State of Human Rights', *International Relations*, XII(2) (1994), 27.

37. Mark Curtis, *The Great Deception: Anglo-American Power and World Order* (Pluto Press, Sterling, 1998), 204–6.

38. The title of an article by Michael Mandelbaum in *Foreign Affairs*, 1 (1996).

39. Richard A. Melanson, *American Foreign Policy since the Vietnam War* (M. E. Sharpe, Armonk, 1996), 259; Karin von Hippel, *Democracy by Force* (Cambridge University Press, Cambridge 2000), 55–6.

40. Quoted in Karin von Hippel, *Democracy by Force* (Cambridge University Press, Cambridge 2000), 76.

41. William Hyland, *Clinton's World: Remaking American Foreign Policy* (Praeger, Westport, 1999), 63–4.

42. Karin von Hippel, *Democracy by Force* (Cambridge University Press, Cambridge 2000), 117.

22

Stability and Instability in the Less Developed World

Chapter contents

A. Southern Africa: The End of Apartheid

South Africa's Growing Isolation

One of the signs, alongside the end of the Cold War, that old enmities were breaking down and that a more liberal-democratic world order might be emerging, was the end of the system of apartheid in South Africa. This development did have some links to the end of the Cold War, but it also followed a long period in which White supremacy had been in decline in southern Africa, leaving the home of apartheid exposed to strong external pressures. South Africa had, of course, been widely condemned by much of the international community, and especially the newly independent Black African states, since apartheid had been introduced by the Nationalist Party, which dominated the country's government after 1948. 'Apartheid stirred the international conscience as few other post-war issues had, in a sense making South Africa the world's favourite pariah.'[1] In the early 1960s, South Africa had been forced out of the Commonwealth and various UN bodies, despite arguments that a state's internal policies were no reason to ostracize it in external relations. In 1963, the UN General Assembly had voted for a voluntary arms embargo against South Africa, which most nations respected, including the US (despite its own segregationist policies in the southern states). But Pretoria did not retreat in the face of such pressure. It developed links to the other anti-communist states that felt threatened by the current international system, not least Israel, and it exploited its position as a major exporter of diamonds, gold, and other minerals. Britain and the US were anxious both to preserve their investments in South Africa and appreciated its value as a firm anti-communist state, the wealthiest, most powerful military force in sub-Saharan African, and the country which controlled the Cape of Good Hope, between the Atlantic and Indian Oceans. The importance of the last point was underlined in 1967–73 when, thanks to the Arab–Israeli War, the Suez Canal was closed to shipping and the Cape route was more extensively used.

In 1969, the Nixon administration decided it should try to work with South Africa in order to moderate and influence its policies, reasoning that an early collapse of apartheid was unlikely. A 1969 policy review argued that the 'whites are here to stay and the only way that constructive change can come about is through them. There is no hope for the Blacks to gain the political rights they seek through violence, which will only lead to chaos and increased opportunities for the Communists.'[2] At that time, South Africa's strategic position seemed very secure: it was occupying South-West Africa, a UN mandate since 1919, which had not been made into a trusteeship for South Africa in 1945 like the mandates of other countries; its northern neighbours included both Ian Smith's White supremacist regime in Rhodesia and the Portuguese colony of Mozambique; and the Black southern African states (such as Botswana, Swaziland, and Lesotho) were very weak, militarily and economically. South Africa could be considered a 'regional superpower' and the logic of the Nixon Doctrine was that the US should rely on such strong, local powers to maintain stability. As the 1970s progressed, however, the logic of this position was called into question and the trend, at global and regional level, was for South Africa to be isolated. In 1974, its spokesman was not allowed to address the General Assembly; in 1977, following the police murder of the Black activist, Steve Biko, a mandatory arms embargo was introduced; and at the same time remaining sports links with the outside world were cut.

Of more immediate worry to Pretoria were events in Angola and Mozambique in 1974–5, where Marxist governments came to power following the end of the Portuguese colonial empire, and in Rhodesia, where Ian Smith's regime was increasingly beleaguered. Lacking South Africa's size and mineral resources, Rhodesia was badly affected by UN sanctions and after 1975 two guerrilla armies led by Black nationalist politicians, Robert Mugabe and Joshua Nkomo, became a serious menace, using bases in Mozambique. Even Pretoria believed that Smith would have to compromise, and the election of Jimmy Carter, with his assertion of human rights, increased the pressures on Rhodesia. An attempt by Smith to install his own favoured Black Prime Minister, Bishop Abel Muzorewa, failed to impress world opinion, and in 1979 Britain—still the legal ruler of Rhodesia—brokered a settlement. Smith's 'Unilateral Declaration of Independence' was made void and, in December, a British governor returned, though only until March 1980, when Mugabe was elected Prime Minister. Rhodesia then became independent under the name of Zimbabwe. Mugabe and Nkomo fell out in 1982, leading to violence between the latter's Matabele people and the majority Shonas, but reasonable stability was maintained until the end of the millennium, when the oppressive nature of Mugabe's regime began to provoke increasing international concern.

Whilst the independence of Zimbabwe emphasized South Africa's lack of friends on its borders, Mugabe was no more a threat to South Africa's existence than were Botswana or the other former British colonies and protectorates in southern Africa. Zimbabwe needed to recover from the recent guerrilla war and was a poor, landlocked state, its external trade effectively controlled by South Africa. What happened to those who chose actively to oppose South Africa was revealed most starkly in Mozambique, where Ian Smith's intelligence service had already helped create an anti-government guerrilla movement, RENAMO (Mozambique National Resistance). In 1979–80, this was taken over by the South African intelligence service, BOSS, and began an ever more vicious campaign, terrorizing the countryside and helping reduce Mozambique to one of the poorest countries in Africa. Mozambique's crime was to act as a guerrilla base for the African National Congress (ANC), a long-standing Black South African political organization, which had decided in 1961 to use violent means to overthrow apartheid. By March 1984, Mozambique was in such turmoil that it offered, in the Nkomati Accord, to end ANC activities there if South Africa abandoned RENAMO. But Pretoria would not honour such a deal, and it was only in October 1992, after the demise of apartheid, that an internal peace agreement was reached in Mozambique, which led to elections under UN supervision in November 1994 (won by the government party). At times, notably in May 1986, the South Africans also launched attacks on ANC facilities in Botswana, Zambia, and Zimbabwe; and there were attempts to 'destabilize' these states through support for dissident groups, though never on the scale of Mozambique.

Meanwhile, in the late 1970s and early 1980s, the internal politics of South Africa seemed beyond peaceful change. The ANC leader, Nelson Mandela (see Box 22.1), remained in prison and other Black nationalists were exiled or murdered. The apartheid laws were maintained and the best reform that Pretoria could offer was to form small, autonomous administrative units in poorer areas (starting with Transkei in 1976) and claim that these were independent Black African nations. Other governments refused to recognize them. A series of school riots in 1976, in the country's largest Black township, Soweto, showed that the country was not quiescent in the face of continued discrimination, but the ANC guerrilla campaign had little impact on Pretoria. After 1978, a new president, P.W. Botha, initiated a few reforms, but of a limited nature, such as the legalization of non-White trade unions and of mixed marriages. Any modest extension of political rights, as in 1984, was restricted to two non-Black minorities, the Indians and mixed-race 'Coloureds'. From 1981, with the replacement of the moralistic Carter by the fiercely anti-communist Reagan, South Africa's international position improved somewhat. Reagan, in defiance of the UN view, insisted that Pretoria's occupation of South-West Africa could not end until Cuban troops left Angola (see Chapter 19, C). The influential Assistant Secretary of State, Chester Crocker, advocated a policy of 'constructive engagement', in a *Foreign Affairs* article of 1981, arguing that the best way to change South African policy was gradually, through cooperation and persuasion, not sanctions and isolation. Crocker himself insisted that this was 'not a formula for a love-in with apartheid . . . As a multiracial democracy, the United States cannot endorse a system that is racist in purpose or effect.' But some critics saw it differently: 'Crocker . . . ruled out economic sanctions, thus removing from consideration the one policy tool . . . viewed as the greatest threat by successive South African administrations.'[3] The Thatcher government in Britain, still South Africa's most important trading and investment partner, also argued that UN sanctions had harmed poor Blacks without bringing down apartheid.

From Botha to Mandela

In August 1984, a fresh outbreak of internal violence began to rock South Africa's Black townships. Eventually, on 25 July 1985, the government responded with a partial state of emergency. Young Blacks, frustrated by a system that kept wealth and political power in the hands of Whites, when they themselves faced poverty and unemployment, took part in months of riots and demonstrations. In the government crackdown that followed, about 2,000 were killed, and tens of thousands detained. Such violence, together with Botha's failure to embrace radical reform, led to the growing doubts in America about the policy of 'constructive engagement'. Congress at first forced Reagan to introduce limited sanctions in September 1985, then, in August 1986, passed a comprehensive Anti-Apartheid Act, with wide-ranging measures including a ban on new investments. Pressure for firmer sanctions also revived in the UN and the Commonwealth, backed by South Africa's church leader, the Nobel Prize winner, Archbishop Desmond Tutu. Thatcher resisted the change of policy and, together with Reagan, prevented the UN from adopting a mandatory embargo. But other Commonwealth and European Community states introduced their own extra sanctions. The state of emergency was suspended for a while, only to be re-imposed in June 1986, but the situation for the government was not yet critical. Over the years, it had built up its industries and had stockpiled oil and other resources, so that it could cope with isolation; it was still the regional superpower with little to fear from the 'front-line' Black African states to the North; diamonds and gold exports were strong; and some states, notably Germany and Japan, boosted their trade with South Africa at this time. Furthermore, there were divisions among Black South Africans, especially between the ANC and the Zulu political movement, 'Inkatha', led by Chief Mangosuthu Buthelezi. But there were serious problems of falling external investment in South Africa, a worsening balance of payments and currency instability, and a growing belief among some of the White elite that radical reform was inescapable.

In 1989, two major events occurred inside South Africa. First, in a general election, the National Party lost votes both to right-wingers, who rejected all change, and left-wingers, who wanted reform. Second, Botha suffered a stroke and was succeeded by F. W. de Klerk, who decided on a programme of change in preference to growing economic troubles and a potential bloodbath. At the same time, whilst disliking sanctions and still hoping for peaceful change, the Bush administration came to power in Washington with a more critical public line than Reagan on apartheid. The Angolan and Namibian disputes had now been settled (see Chapter 19, C). Despite widespread scepticism about de Klerk's intentions, Botha's successor not only spoke of a 'new' South Africa but also set out to create one. He was helped in this by the decline of communism in Europe and the Cuban withdrawal from Angola, which neutralized those—both inside and outside the country—who had always feared that reform would lead to a Marxist regime in Pretoria. De Klerk 'faced an entirely new set of political challenges within his own constituency base, as well as quite a different set . . . of international challenges', so that some shift in policy was unsurprising. But the scale of what followed surprised everyone: 'It is almost unprecedented in history for a government, enjoying the loyalty . . . of its security forces and bureaucracy, to begin a process which could imply the termination of its rule.'[4] In July 1989, de Klerk met Nelson Mandela, the greatest symbol of Black nationalism, for the first time, and on 2 February 1990, after further meetings, released him from prison. In the interim, the government moved from legalizing peaceful protests, to recognition of the ANC and other opposition groups, and then to the promise of constitutional talks. The state of emergency was lifted in stages after June 1990, coming to an end five months later. In August 1990, a deal was reached whereby the government issued an amnesty for political prisoners and let exiled opposition leaders return home while the ANC suspended its guerrilla campaign. Just as significant, in June 1991, the main laws that upheld apartheid were repealed, notably the Group Areas Act, which had segregated the races from one another.

In this process, the two sides had different goals. De Klerk's policy was to 'change the system sufficiently to restore social peace and normalize South Africa's relations with the rest of the world, but avoid a complete transfer of power to blacks'; while the ANC was 'confident it would take over after the demise of the white regime'.[5] As events unfolded, it was increasingly difficult to deny that de Klerk was seeking fundamental changes, and pressure grew to ease UN sanctions against South Africa. Britain led the way in this, relaxing some of its own sanctions in early 1990. The US was slower, ending all sanctions by mid-1991. At the same time, sports links to South Africa were reopened by international bodies. There was a continuing danger that the peace moves would be undermined by violence: indeed, especially in Natal, thousands of people died in the early 1990s in clashes between the ANC and Inkatha, with the latter receiving encouragement from the police and army—elements of which were opposed to de Klerk's policies. Also, sanctions were eased when Blacks were still without the vote: constitutional talks, through the 'Convention for a Democratic South Africa', only began in December

BOX 22.1

Biography: Nelson Mandela (1918–2013)

The first Black president of South Africa was born in 1918, the son of a chief of the Thembu tribe in Transkei. Trained as a lawyer, he gave up the position of Chief when he inherited it, preferring to pursue his political ambitions. Mandela joined the African National Congress (ANC), the main movement working for equal rights among the country's racial groups, in 1944. He was soon a leading figure among the radical, younger members of the party and became head of its youth league in 1951. Over the following years, he took part in non-violent resistance to the growth of the 'apartheid' system, introduced by the White supremacist National Party, and seen most notoriously in the Group Areas Act. In 1952, Mandela became a vice-president at the ANC and in 1956–61, along with other Congress leaders, successfully fought off government accusations of treason in a long-running court battle.

The Sharpeville massacre of 1960 led to a decision by the ANC to set up a paramilitary wing, the 'Spear of the Nation' in 1961, of which Nelson Mandela became head. But this shift to a readiness to use violent tactics made it easier for the government to resuscitate charges of treason against him. He was arrested in 1962 and sentenced to life imprisonment two years later. For the next eighteen years, Mandela was incarcerated on Robben Island, but in the process became the greatest symbol of resistance to apartheid and there was mounting pressure to release him. Despite government fears of his radicalism, he entered secret talks with them in 1986. In February 1990 Mandela was finally released from prison, in 1992 he was elected ANC president, and in 1993 he shared the Nobel Peace Prize with F. W. de Klerk. Old age meant that Mandela served only one term (1994–9) as President, being succeeded by his former deputy, Thabo Mbeki, who served as President until 2008. In 1996, after nearly forty years of marriage, Mandela divorced his second wife, Winnie, who had become identified with radical violence and been implicated in murder. On his eightieth birthday, he married Graca Machel, widow of a former president of neighbouring Mozambique.

1991 and White voters only approved reform in a (Whites-only) referendum in March 1992. But the international community felt it must act to encourage de Klerk by ending sanctions and the policy was justified by events. Within South Africa, the National Party, ANC, and other groups found it difficult to pull back from negotiations: 'despite the many differences between these parties on their ideal visions of a future state, there was among them . . . a considerable convergence on a post-apartheid democracy'.[6] Though troubled in 1992, and even suspended for several months, the constitutional talks resulted in agreement in February 1993, which led to equal political rights for all, free elections, and guarantees that the National Party might retain a share in power for five years.

The April 1994 elections, boycotted by Inkatha, were easily won by the ANC, which had effectively secured most from the negotiations with the National Party, at least on the political front. In 1996, feeling increasingly marginalized, the National Party quit the ruling coalition. By then, apartheid had disappeared as an international problem, the southern Africa region was at peace for the first time in a generation, and the new South African President, Mandela, was recognized as a statesman of global stature. For South Africa itself, however, notwithstanding its natural resources and its power in the region, the challenges of national reconciliation, boosting Black incomes and providing genuine equalities of opportunity were immense. There was a bold attempt to address the first problem by setting up a 'Truth and Reconciliation Commission', chaired by Archbishop Desmond Tutu, which held hearings from 1996, to investigate outrages carried out by all sides in the apartheid era. As to economic problems, there was some disappointment at the government's failure to redistribute wealth and a feeling that it had adopted a conservative approach to high finance. Even more than the rest of sub-Saharan Africa, the country was also increasingly blighted by infections from Aids. But such problems did not prevent the ANC winning the 1999, 2004, and 2009 general elections by clear margins.

B. Central Africa: Rwanda and Zaire

Poverty and Instability below the Sahara

If the peaceful transition to majority rule in South Africa was one of the most hopeful changes in international politics in the 1990s, it could not mask the fact that the continent south of the Sahara contained the world's poorest regions. In the mid-1990s, three-quarters of the countries designated by the World Bank as 'heavily indebted' were in sub-Saharan Africa, with total debts there of about $200 billion. Whereas Latin America's debts had fallen as a percentage of gross national product (GNP) since a long-running debt crisis in the 1980s, Africa's had continued to rise until many countries had debts in excess of their GNP. Many ordinary Africans lacked a basic education, health care, or even clean water, but their governments and Western aid agencies had no solution to the situation. There was simply no agreement on the root cause of African problems. The former colonial powers were variously blamed for dividing up the continent with little regard to local factors, either geographical or ethnic, and for abandoning the newly independent countries around 1960 with little preparation in economic or political terms. Subsequently, Western countries had shaped a global economy which let Africans run up huge debts but gave them paltry reward for their exports. In the 1980s, the International Monetary Fund (IMF) and World Bank became 'the most significant external influences on the political life of many African countries', acting in a way that some criticized as 'tantamount to a new form of colonialism'.[7]

African countries themselves had often adopted a centralized political model, based around strong leaders and socialist-style economic planning, which sometimes broke down into dictatorship, military coups, and financial corruption. Given sub-Saharan Africa's ethnic differences, military regimes, and economic problems, it is perhaps surprising that there was not more international conflict. Beyond southern Africa, and after the civil wars in the Congo and Nigeria in the 1960s, the number of conflicts was actually few. The Tanzanian-led invasion of Uganda in 1979 proved a unique example of one Black African state helping to overthrow the dictator of another by armed force. Here, once Idi Amin was replaced, the Tanzanians quickly withdrew. There was some interference from the former colonial powers, especially the French who, also in 1979, helped overthrow the dictator of the Central African Republic, Jean-Bédel Bokassa.

By the mid-1990s, however, there were a number of civil conflicts in sub-Saharan Africa which threatened to draw in outside states and which led, by 1994, to 7.5 million refugees on the continent. All of them involved questions of the future of the state. Two were in West Africa where Nigeria, despite being ruled by a military dictatorship, played a leading role in peacemaking efforts. In Liberia, a multinational force was sent by other West African countries after civil war broke out in 1990 between rebels of the regime of Samuel Doe (who had launched a military coup in 1980); and in Sierra Leone, there was a series of coups in the wake of the dictatorship of Siaka Stevens (1968–85), culminating in a Nigerian-led intervention in early 1998. On the latter occasion, the Nigerians themselves became enmeshed in the violence and there were further interventions by both the UN (1999–2005) and the former colonial power, Britain (2000–2), which helped restore stability. Across the continent, in the southern Sudan, there was long-running discontent with the Sudanese government, which burst into civil war in 1983, pitting the Black, Christian population against the Arab, Islamic regime in Khartoum. Here the rebels had the backing of neighbouring Uganda, but they faced an increasingly determined Sudanese army. Independence was only finally achieved—as South Sudan—in July 2011. From 2003, the Sudanese government was involved in an intractable conflict against rebels in its western province of Darfur, where the UN led a peacekeeping force after 2008. Small wonder that some experts considered that, of all Africa's problems, 'the crisis that is affecting the state is by far the most threatening for the future'.[8] The most bloody and dangerous conflicts of all arose in Central Africa, centred on the conflict between Tutsis and Hutus in Rwanda.

Civil War and Genocide in Rwanda and Burundi

Rwanda and its equally small neighbour, Burundi, had been given their independence by Belgium in 1962. Both were landlocked countries with a majority from the Hutu people but it was the minority Tutsis who had been favoured—at least until the 1950s, when they began to take a lead in anti-colonialism—under Belgian rule, as part of an apparent process of divide and rule. Both countries had also suffered political upheaval but seemed to be moving towards greater stability and a decentralization of government in the summer of 1993. Burundi, after military coups in 1976 and 1983, had returned to civilian rule in 1992 and held its first free elections in June 1993. Rwanda had been dominated by a Hutu-led military regime under Juvénal Habyarimana since 1993 and faced rebellion from the Ugandan-based Tutsi-led Rwandan Popular Front (FPR) after mid-1990, but in 1992 agreed to a ceasefire. In August 1993, at Arusha in Tanzania, a peace was agreed which promised a Tutsi share in power, a transitional government, and elections. A small UN-approved international force was sent to monitor this. But within months both countries were in turmoil. Burundi's President was killed in a failed coup in October, to be succeeded by Cyprien Ntaryamira who was unable to stem a rising tide of inter-ethnic violence. In Rwanda, fulfilment of the Arusha Accords was repeatedly delayed and the military were in fact planning to massacre the Tutsis. Then, on 6 April 1994, the presidents of both countries were killed in a rocket attack over Rwanda, while travelling together on an aircraft.

In Burundi, the violent death of the second president in six months, led to an intensification of the violence which already existed. Attempts were made to form a broad-based government in September 1994, but it proved unstable and by 1996 deaths were running at about 1,000 per month. In April of that year, the US and the European Union suspended aid to Burundi because of the government's failure to protect the Hutus from Tutsi attacks. Then, on 25 July the Tutsi military, under Major Pierre Buyoya, seized power, suspended parliament, and closed the country's borders. But the level of violence in Burundi was far less than that in Rwanda and, given what had happened to the latter, the international community was anxious to prevent the Burundi situation worsening. In Rwanda, the death of President Cyprien Ntaryamira in April 1994 was followed by the massacre of thousands of opponents of the military government, both Hutus and Tutsis. The victims included the Prime Minister, several other ministers, and some Belgian peace monitors. The government, now under Theodore Sindikubwabo, blamed the Tutsis for downing Habyarimana's aircraft. But it was not clear what the Tutsis hoped to gain from the assassination of a president who had negotiated the Arusha agreement with them. The FPR, which refused to recognize the Sindikubwabo regime, blamed the air crash on Hutu militants in the military, who, from the speed of reaction to it, had clearly been planning the massacres for a long time. Even the elite presidential guard joined the rank-and-file and Hutu youths in butchering Tutsis.

The Tutsis had been subjected to periodic bouts of victimization in the past, but the massacres of 1994 soon took the form of genocide. Within weeks, it was claimed that up to 200,000 had been killed, and a later UN report suggested that 500,000 people died in Rwanda, a country of only 8 million, by the end of June. Nothing had been seen in Africa on this scale, at least since the Nigerian civil war in the late 1960s. Many Tutsis also fled abroad to Tanzania, but the FPR was determined to strike back with its efficient and well-armed military. Meanwhile, the reaction of the international community to the Rwandan tragedy was hesitant, confused, and ineffectual. It would probably have been impossible to prevent many of the deaths that occurred, because the violence took off so quickly. But the Organization of African Unity (predecessor of the African Union) pointed out that the UN had been quick to send troops to Bosnia when ethnic conflict broke out among Europeans. Africa was treated differently. Here, the UN felt it had little choice other than to reduce the peace monitors in Rwanda, mainly because the Belgians, having helped to evacuate foreign nationals, were determined to leave. The UN Secretary-General, Boutros Boutros-Ghali, was appalled that the 'international community did little or nothing as the killing in Rwanda continued', but he was already running seventeen peacekeeping operations around the world and was entirely dependent on the UN member states to provide the resources to intervene in central Africa.[9] Help was given to refugees and there were attempts to broker a ceasefire, but only France showed much desire to intervene in the Rwandan bloodbath. The US had taken little interest in Africa since the Cold War, apart from Somalia—but what had occurred there helped ensure that President Clinton was unlikely to intervene in a second African country (see Chapter 21, E).

In June 1994, the Security Council approved 'Operation Turquoise', a supposed humanitarian intervention by 2,500 French troops to try to keep Hutus and Tutsis apart. But France proved the worst possible choice for such a force, because the FPR blamed Paris for having backed the Habyarimana regime. The French had helped to arm the Rwandan military since 1975 and had greatly intensified this aid after the FPR opened the civil war in 1990, even sending several hundred troops. There were some rumours that they were involved in the fateful air crash of 6 April and certainly the Rwandan military hoped for a continuation of support from Paris. This was in line with French policy elsewhere in French-speaking Africa: in 1990 the French had military advisers in twenty-six African countries. Without French backing, it could be argued, Hutu militants could never have hoped to begin their policy of genocide. Thus, 'although France was undoubtedly well placed to intervene from a technical point of view, politically and morally the situation was more ambiguous'.[10] Via Operation Turquoise, the French government hoped to recover from accusations at home that it had helped bring about the Rwandan crisis and, at the same time, it wanted to demonstrate to other African allies its ability to act militarily on the continent, even though the prime aim of the operation was to provide humanitarian aid.

By the time the French arrived, the FPR army was in control of most of Rwanda. Indeed, on 19 July, they claimed victory over the Hutu military and set out to fulfil the Arusha Accords, forming a coalition government which, while it was determined to track down those responsible for the recent genocide, included Hutus as well as Tutsis. There was a Hutu President, Pasteur Bizimungu, and Prime Minister. But such signs of a desire for reconciliation did not convince many Hutus who, encouraged by their own military leaders, began to flee over the western border, into Zaire. For a time, the French set up a 'safe zone' in part of Rwanda for the fleeing Hutus and, in an extraordinary twisting of their UN mandate, threatened to exclude the FPR from this by force. By late August, however, Operation Turquoise was brought to an end and the new Rwandan government could try to rebuild the country without direct external interference. There were cases of Hutus being killed but these were blamed on maverick elements, official policy being to put those individuals responsible for genocide on trial. In November, the UN set up its own International Criminal Tribunal in Rwanda and in December, after an investigation into the massacres, agreed with the FPR claim that the genocide, far from being the side effect of a lurch into anarchy after Habyarimana's sudden death, had been the premeditated action of the Hutu militants. And, for Rwanda, with a million Hutus based in refugee camps in neighbouring Zaire, the threat of violence had not ended.

Zaire: The Fall of Mobutu

As in Rwanda in April 1994, it proved impossible to create a sizeable UN force to police the refugee camps in Zaire. Instead, the responsibility for this task therefore fell on the regime of General Mobutu Sese Seko, who had held power in Zaire since 1965, backed by the West as the only strong figure who could hold his sprawling country together. He Africanized the running of former colonial companies and opposed the Marxist regime in Angola, on his south-western border but, in the wake of the Cold War, Mobutu's eccentricity and oppressiveness became increasingly embarrassing to the West. Inflation was high, the economic infrastructure was in tatters, and Mobutu's repeated promises to democratize had come to nothing. One aspect of his policy since the 1980s was the victimization of Zaire's own Tutsi minority, concentrated in the east of the country, in the very area to which a million Rwandan Hutus now fled. As with its support for France and Operation Turquoise, the UN's decision to let Mobutu police the situation in eastern Zaire was regrettable. It was, of course, impossible to deny a role to the Zaireans in keeping order within their own country, but an international force might have prevented what occurred in 1995–6 and—ironically—might have helped Mobutu's regime survive.

Hutu militants used the refugee camps as bases for a political and military revival of their cause. They not only planned to return to power in Rwanda, but also, with the connivance of some of Mobutu's troops, attacked the Zairean Tutsis. The latter, however, could now rely on help from the Rwandan government—which wanted the militants rooted out. In September 1996, fighting broke out in eastern Zaire while Mobutu was out of the country, receiving treatment for cancer in a Swiss hospital. While Hutu militants and Zairean troops attacked local Tutsis, the Rwandan government sent troops over the border to help a rebel force led by Laurent Kabila, a former Marxist revolutionary. Uganda, which also feared a spread of Hutu violence, supported the Rwandans, as did an old enemy of Mobutu, the Angolan government. By the end of October, the Zairean army, demoralized, underpaid, and ill-equipped, was in retreat. Ironically, most Hutus in the camps now decided that it was safer to return to Rwanda than stay in a war zone. In Zaire, Mobutu's support crumbled rapidly, as those with influence and wealth scrambled to come to terms with the new leader. Mobutu returned briefly, but on 16 May, he fled to Morocco, where he died four months later. Zaire was then renamed the Democratic Republic of the Congo. Until the end, Mobutu had hoped for support from his old allies abroad, but the Americans decided that Kabila—despite his Marxist past, his failure to democratize, and his slaying of opponents during his advance—was a preferred strong-man. As to his other main Western ally, France, it had already suffered a loss of face in Rwanda and could not hope to shore up such a corrupt regime.

Rwanda had done much to bring about a change of regime, but had not yet extinguished Hutu militancy. Late 1997 saw further inter-ethnic violence after Hutu rebels, still surviving in the Congo, attacked across the border. As to Kabila, he proved little more competent and democratic than Mobutu had been and soon fell out with the Rwandans and Ugandans, partly because he sought to restore good relations with his own Hutu minority. In August, in a virtual replay of the events of two years before, Rwanda and Uganda backed an anti-Kabila rebellion in eastern Congo. This time there was no irresistible advance on the capital, but Kabila was not in office for long, being assassinated in January 2001. He was succeeded by his son, Joseph, who maintained the war against Rwanda and its ally, Uganda. In the conflict, he received aid from several nearby states, including Angola, Namibia, and Sudan (the last also a supporter of rebel groups in Uganda), but with the most significant military aid coming from Zimbabwe, whose air force proved particularly effective against the Rwandans. In December 2002, the two sides struck a peace deal, which formally came into effect in July 2003: Rwanda withdrew its troops in return for a promise from DR Congo to disarm Hutu militants; and a transitional government was formed to reunite the Congo. By then, refugee agencies reckoned that more than two million people had been killed in the fighting. Kabila won free elections in 2006 and tension between the two states lessened for a time, although cross border incidents continued. In 2009, Rwandan troops crossed the border for several weeks in an anti-Hutu operation. There also remained serious problems in DR Congo associated with ethnic tensions (not only in the East), groups seeking regional autonomy (like the Mai-Mai movement in Katanga) and those disaffected with Joseph Kabila's regime (especially after he refused to stand down, after two terms as President, in 2016). The violence in the Congo in the twenty years after 1996 amounted to the greatest loss of life in any global conflict since the Second World War.

C. The Middle East: Progress and Retreat on Palestine

The Bush Presidency and the Washington Talks, 1989–93

After the neglect of the Arab–Israeli dispute under Ronald Reagan (see Chapter 17, B), the Bush presidency proved more determined in seeking a negotiated settlement, which would include security guarantees for Israel and progress on the main sticking point in previous talks—Palestinian rights. The US public was dismayed by Israel's killing of hundreds of Palestinian protestors in 1988 and, with the fading of the Cold War, it no longer seemed necessary to build Israel up as an anti-Soviet ally in the Middle East. Thus Bush, though personally well disposed to Israel, seemed to be in a position to pressure it to moderate its policies. Since December 1987, the Palestinian uprising, the Intifada, Yasser Arafat's Palestine Liberation Organization (PLO) had exploited the situation by condemning Israel's human rights record and pursuing a more sophisticated diplomatic and military strategy. Terrorist attacks by the Palestinian Liberation Front (PLF) were now concentrated on Israeli targets; a government-in-exile was created but it limited its territorial claim to the West Bank and Gaza, rather than the whole of Israel; and the PLO were prepared to recognize Israel's existence. By now, as one leading Palestinian intellectual put it, 'The central problem is the official Israeli refusal to recognize . . . the fact of Palestinian nationalism.'[11] Israel's attempt to undermine the PLO's popularity in the occupied territories by encouraging a rival organization, Hamas, turned to disaster. The fundamentalists of Hamas, set up in 1988 under Sheikh Ahmed Yassin, became tough and ruthless opponents. Ironically, in the 1990s, when Israel finally decided to deal with the PLO, Hamas was strong enough to threaten the peace process by a series of bomb attacks largely outside Arafat's control.

Israel's failure to contain the Intifada and its reliance on the Americans for $3 billion of military and economic aid each year did not, however, make it eager to rush into a settlement. Enmities and suspicion in the region were deep-seated, the right-wing Likud Party continued to dominate the government in Tel Aviv, and there was a strong Zionist lobby in Congress and outside which opposed Bush's attempts to use aid as a lever for concessions. Israelis remembered too many terrorist attacks in the past to deal with Arafat willingly. The Israeli Prime Minister, Yitzhak Shamir, was unwilling to make real concessions, himself believing that 'the only peace the PLO could produce in terms of Israel was the peace of the cemetery'.[12] Also, the contacts between Washington and the PLO, which had been taken up at the end of the Reagan presidency, proved tenuous. In June 1990, the US side severed them, following a PLF terrorist attack on an Israeli beach, and at the same time the Intifada assumed a new vigour. Only in late 1991 were Bush and Baker able to make progress on the Middle East and this thanks to two major developments. First, the continued weakening of the USSR, linked as it was to Gorbachev's willingness to discuss an Arab–Israeli settlement, showed hard-line Arab governments like Syria that they could no longer rely on Soviet backing in a crisis, that the US was now the only superpower with which to deal, and that negotiations were probably inevitable. A side effect of the USSR's retreat from Marxist-Leninism, however, was the increased flow of Soviet Jews to Israel: more than 350,000 in 1990–1. This helped Israeli–Soviet relations but it also increased the pressure to expand Jewish settlements on the West Bank, which in turn offended the Arabs, who did not see why refugees from far away should be settled on Palestinian land when so many Palestinian refugees were unable to return to their homes in Israel. The issue of new settlements also proved a running sore in Israeli–US relations and was the main justification for Bush's efforts to restrict aid to Israel in 1990 and 1991.

The second major development in 1990–1 was the Gulf War (see Chapter 21, B) which led to improved relations between America and Israel—especially after US missiles were deployed on Israeli soil to protect it from Iraqi missile attacks—and between America and those Arab states, including Egypt and Syria, who were opposed to Saddam Hussein. The war had a mixed effect on the Israeli–Palestinian issue. On the one hand, the Arabs were divided, a radical Arab leader, Saddam Hussein, was defeated, and Arafat alienated the US through his ill-judged support for Iraq. On the other hand, in order to keep his Arab allies happy, Bush agreed to work for a resumption of the Geneva Conference of Middle East states, which had first met after the 1973 war. Victory over Saddam gave the US even greater influence in the region, as well as bolstering Bush's position at home, and US officials were determined to exploit this to end, for good, the dangers of an Arab–Israeli conflict. The killing of 21 Palestinians on Temple Mount in October 1991 had helped maintain some sympathy in the West for their plight. Therefore in March 1991, the US Secretary of State, James Baker, began a series of visits to the Middle East in order to arrange a conference. Among others, on 12 March, he talked to Palestinian leaders in the occupied areas. The result was the Madrid conference, which opened on 30 October 1991. As with Geneva in 1973, the meeting was co-chaired by the US and USSR, both Bush and Gorbachev being present, and attended by Israeli and Arab delegations. Even

Syria attended, and, while Israel still refused to accept PLO representatives, there was a Palestinian group within the Jordanian delegation, and this was in contact with Arafat. But, hopeful as this was, the talks saw as many mutual recriminations (especially between Israel and Syria) as attempts at agreement, and broke up in less than a week.

Madrid showed that the US was more interested in bringing about negotiations than in pointing them in a particular direction. It made its general views on a settlement—Israeli security, Palestinian rights—clear enough but wanted the protagonists themselves to produce detailed ideas and had no wish to become involved in a long-term, complex process of mediation. Bush was also aware of his limited ability, because of the Jewish lobby, to press Israel for concessions, despite Arab hopes that he would do this. But, disappointing as Madrid was, it did not end American attempts to maintain Arab–Israeli contacts. Far from it. For a time, there seemed to be a 'reversal of the Palestinian and Israeli positions in relation to American policy in the Middle East', with one Israeli official describing his side as 'riddled with doubt, suspicion and even dread concerning what the future might bring'.[13] In December 1991, the US called more talks, this time in Washington, and these continued, with several rounds throughout 1992. There were both bilateral talks and multilateral ones (not all held in Washington), on a wide range of issues from the main political problems to general subjects like regional transport, health, and culture. But the key subject was the make-up and powers of any Palestinian authority in the West Bank and Gaza. On this, there were, predictably, wide differences, and when the government of Yitzhak Shamir began to discuss a possible form of interim self-government for Palestinians, its coalition supporters became divided.

The departure of two extremist groups forced an election which was won on 23 June by a Labour-led coalition under Yitzhak Rabin. This was welcome news to Bush. Rabin was better disposed than Shamir to a peace agreement and restricted the pace of new Jewish settlements on the West Bank. The new premier even talked of achieving peace within a year. His Foreign Minister, Shimon Peres, was influenced by the Bosnian crisis to 'believe in the need for political separation between Israelis and Palestinians' and now ready to place 'the future of Gaza in the hands of the people who lived there', even if he knew that the future of the West Bank would be more difficult to settle. Even more remarkably, in August 1992 he suggested 'that Israel should reconsider its position on negotiating with Arafat'.[14] But events in the second half of 1992 dampened such expectations. In America, Bush was preoccupied by his failing re-election campaign and in Israel the continuation of terrorist attacks, alongside the Intifada, made it difficult for Rabin to contemplate concessions. The year ended with Bush's election defeat in November, and the breakdown of the Washington talks in December. The Arabs walked out of the negotiations after Israel expelled over 400 suspected members of Hamas.

The 1993 Oslo Accords

The breakdown of the Washington talks and the election of Bill Clinton, a firm pro-Israeli, as US president hardly augured well for a Middle East settlement. But events were set in train in December 1992, in great secrecy and entirely without American involvement, which brought a surprise breakthrough more quickly than anyone had hoped. The 'benign neglect shown during the first months of the Clinton administration . . . created space for Norwegian mediation', which 'provided both sides with the possibility of exploring each other's position without recognition, commitment, or . . . violating Israel's law under which meetings with the PLO were illegal'.[15] A highly secret contact was established between a narrow group of Israeli and Palestinian academics, using Norwegian social scientist, Tarje Larsen, as a go-between. An initial contact in London was followed by months of talks in Oslo, with the Norwegian government becoming involved. Rabin, once informed of the contact, was concerned that the PLO might leak word of the fact, so as to embarrass Israel. He would have preferred to concentrate on the Washington talks, which were resumed in the spring, but these were too public to allow either side to discuss substantial concessions and Rabin was anxious to fulfil his promise of progress towards peace, ending the Intifada, and securing Labour's re-election. For his part, Arafat, far from wishing to embarrass Israel by leaking word of the talks, was anxious to challenge the popularity of Hamas in the occupied territories and show some results for the more realistic political strategy he had followed since 1988, so as to prevent moves being made to replace him. He also needed to recover, in the eyes of world opinion, from the costly mistake he had made in 1990–1 of backing Saddam Hussein's invasion of Kuwait.

During the Oslo talks, the Israelis were keen to defer discussion on difficult problems like the status of East Jerusalem (claimed by Israel, but part of the West Bank until 1967), which were impossible to settle in the foreseeable future, and to concentrate instead on the possible autonomy of Gaza, which was densely populated by Palestinians, though it did include some Jewish settlements. The Palestinians were divided about this approach to the problem: some wanted much more substantial gains, others were happy to accept any land. But Arafat decided to ask for both Gaza and the key West Bank city of Jericho, reasoning that this would give the Palestinians an autonomous foothold in the West Bank which could later be expanded. Behind the territorial issues was another question, of whether the creation of a Palestinian political entity would lead to full sovereignty. Arafat hoped it would, but the Israelis were ambiguous because their aims were rather different. As their negotiator, Uri Savir, put it, 'The Palestinians needed to know that autonomy could lead to a state, while we needed to know it would bring security.'[16] The PLO representatives, led by Abu Alaa, soon confirmed their seriousness in the talks by agreeing to concessions on such issues as self-government in the Israeli settlements and the right of Israeli troops to remain in areas of the West Bank. For a time in July, Arafat did toughen his demands, mainly it seems in an attempt to maximize the Israeli concessions, and with a breakdown looming, Israel did make a highly important offer: after twenty-nine years of refusal, they were ready to recognize the PLO officially. On 30 August, the talks were finally made public, provoking surprise everywhere, not least in the Washington talks (see Box 22.2), where even the Palestinian team had not been told of the Oslo contact. Ordinary Israelis and Palestinians were both concerned about what had been conceded, but two-thirds of Israelis soon claimed to support the Accords and Arafat was, for a time, able to carry the Palestinians with him. Although he had nothing to do with the negotiations, President Clinton was keen to steal some of the limelight and on 13 September hosted a meeting at the White House, where the Oslo 'Declaration of Principles' was signed and Arafat, previously condemned as a terrorist by the US and Israel, shook hands with a reluctant Rabin.

The Oslo agreement provided for a self-governing Palestinian Authority (most certainly not a proper government) under an elected council, which would

BOX 22.2

The 'Declaration of Principles on Interim Self-Government', 13 September 1993

The Declaration, signed in Washington in the presence of President Clinton, by Palestinian leader Yasser Arafat and Israeli Premier Yitzhak Rabin, was the basis of all future Israeli–Palestinian peace efforts. It had actually been negotiated via secret contacts in Oslo and opened with a statement that the two sides:

> agree that it is the time to put an end to decades of confrontation and conflict, recognize their mutual legitimate political rights . . . and achieve a just, lasting and comprehensive peace settlement.

Article One, set out the aim of their negotiations as being 'to establish a Palestinian Interim Self-Government Authority . . . for the Palestine people in the West Bank and Gaza Strip, for a transitional period not exceeding five years, leading to a permanent settlement based on Security Council Resolutions 242 and 338'. Article Three stated that elections for such an Authority would be held within nine months of the declaration entering into force.

Whilst Article Four made clear that the Authority should have jurisdiction over the West Bank and Gaza Strip, Article Five stated that 'the five-year' transitional period 'will begin upon the withdrawal from the Gaza Strip and Jericho area', so that the initial area controlled by the Palestinians in the West Bank was quite limited. Other issues, including Palestinian refugees, Jewish settlements on the West bank, and the future of Jerusalem—none of them easy to resolve—were to be the subject of negotiations which would open 'not later than the beginning of the third year of the interim period'. In fact, once such talks began, they proved very slow and difficult.

Article Eight of the Declaration covered the difficult issue of security in Palestinian areas. The Palestinian Authority, or Council, was to 'establish a strong police force, whilst Israel will continue to carry the responsibility for defence against external threats, as well as the responsibility for overall security of Israelis'. The Declaration, which ran to seventeen articles in all, and had a number of annexes, also dealt with economic and development programmes, the details of Israeli withdrawal, and ways of resolving future disputes (mainly via a Joint Liaison Committee, set up under Article Ten).

exist for a transitional period of five years (from the date of Israel's initial withdrawal) during which time a permanent settlement, including the status of Jerusalem and Jewish settlements, would be negotiated. The West Bank and Gaza were to be treated as one unit and Israel retained an overall responsibility for the defence and security of these areas, but the Palestinians would be able to govern and police Gaza and Jericho. Even in the short term, much was unclear, including the exact dates for executing parts of the agreements and the pace of future Israeli withdrawals. It set various deadlines for future talks but was deliberately ambiguous on some important issues of territory and transfer of powers to the Palestinian Authority. Also, opposition had immediately gathered on both sides, from Likud in Israel and Hamas in the occupied territories. But there was no doubting the significance of the breakthrough. While world attention had focused on the Washington talks, which proceeded slowly and uncertainly, the Oslo negotiations had produced an agreement which, however modest it appeared in detail, marked an unprecedented psychological breakthrough in Israeli–Palestinian relations, with the potential to produce a full agreement within a decade. It was 'intended as just a stepping stone along the road to peace, graduality being the guiding principle'.[17] Furthermore, it was followed by Israeli talks with both Jordan and Syria. Jordan was anxious to settle the problem of the West Bank, which it had ruled between 1949 and 1967, and to settle the future of the Palestinians for good. Rabin and King Hussein of Jordan signed an agreement in Washington in July 1994, agreeing to end the state of war between them and recognize one another, and this was followed by a peace treaty on 26 October, with Clinton present at the signature. By February 1995, it was even possible to hold a summit in Cairo between Rabin, Arafat, Hussein, and President Mubarak of Egypt, the first Arab country to make peace with Israel in 1979. An Israeli–Syrian deal proved elusive, however, despite strong US encouragement, which led Clinton to visit President Assad in Damascus in January 1994. The Israeli military were also keen on a settlement with Syria, recognizing that this would remove the danger of another Arab–Israeli war: some indeed would have preferred this to the Oslo deal with the PLO. But Assad's suspicion of Israel was such that, though talks were held, they proceeded only slowly, with Syria determined to win back all of the land on the Golan Heights seized by Israel in 1967.

The Stalling of the Oslo Accords

The gravest disappointment in the years after September 1993 was not the elusive Israeli–Syrian peace but the failure to realize the full promise of the Oslo principles. From the start, they were dogged by terrorist attacks, extremist opposition, and genuine disappointments between the Israelis and Palestinians. Arguments over border controls, for example, meant that the original date of 13 December 1993 for the start of Israeli withdrawals was missed. Then, on 25 February 1994 an Israeli fanatic killed nearly fifty Palestinian worshippers at a mosque in Hebron, leading the PLO to break off talks for several weeks. But there was a basic problem with the Accords that perhaps always made a comprehensive settlement unlikely: 'The arch-enemies . . . entered into short-term cooperation in order to build a lasting foundation for . . . their long-term interests', but, 'The parties' long-term objectives are still very much in conflict.'[18] Israelis hoped to end the Intifada and establish peace with their Arab neighbours, but to keep the Palestinians economically and politically subservient, with Arafat taking on the role of preventing Palestinian violence against Israel. Israel also hoped to maintain Jewish settlements in the West Bank and to retain all of Jerusalem. But Palestinians eventually hoped for a state in the whole of the West Bank and Gaza, free of Israeli domination, and with Arab refugees able to return to their ancestral homes inside Israel.

Given the scale of the differences of long-term vision, the surprising point is that, for a time, the peace process seemed to be advancing well. An agreement on Palestinian self-rule was finally signed by Rabin and Arafat in Cairo on 4 May, leading to Israel's military withdrawal from Gaza and Jericho in mid-month, the first meeting of the 'Palestinian National Authority' (PNA) on 26 June and Arafat's triumphant return to the Gaza strip on 1 July, after a quarter-century of exile. Despite clashes in Gaza between the PLO and Hamas, and the ill feeling created in late 1994 by new Jewish settlements in the West Bank, progress continued, albeit rather slowly. 'As Arafat lost more . . . of his support base, he grew less able to make concessions to Israel, making it that much more difficult for Rabin, himself harassed by . . . the Israeli Right, to proceed with the process.'[19] On 28 September 1995, the so-called 'Oslo B' agreement was concluded. Fourteen months later than scheduled, this provided for full PNA control of only 4 per cent of the West Bank but partial control (where Israel retained a security presence in another 23 per cent). Significantly, this included the most heavily populated areas with about two-thirds of West Bank Palestinians living in them. This agreement cleared the way for the first Palestinian elections in January 1996, predictably won by Arafat and his al-Fatah faction of the PLO.

By the time of Arafat's triumph, the peace process had suffered its worst setback so far. On 4 November 1995, Rabin, whose election had done so much to change Israeli policy, was assassinated by an opponent of the process. Though this further highlighted the fragmentation of Israeli society, it did not at first threaten the Oslo principles because Rabin was succeeded by another architect of dialogue with the PLO, Shimon Peres, who felt confident enough in February 1996 to call a general election. Within weeks, however, a series of three Hamas 'suicide bomb' attacks killed nearly sixty people and the opinion polls began to move against Peres, with some Israelis coming to believe that Oslo had merely encouraged Palestinian violence. The division between the 'pro' and 'anti' peace lobbies in Israel was such that on 29 May Peres lost the election to Likud's Benjamin Netanyahu by only 30,000 votes. Netanyahu's coalition government now included hard-line religious groups which made peace less likely. That the peace process was in serious trouble was obvious for, while 'Arafat has never deviated from his goal of establishing a Palestinian state . . . Netanyahu's policies preclude the creation of this.'[20] Netanyahu had criticized the Oslo agreement from the outset and, though he undertook to honour it, he minimized any concessions to Arafat, whom he at first refused even to meet. Relations with Syria became frozen. In January 1997, US mediation did help to secure the Hebron Accords, which showed that limited compromise was still possible, the Accords promising further Israeli withdrawals in three stages, though Israeli settlers would remain in the Hebron area. But, by March the new agreement had become deadlocked over the precise scale of the withdrawals, with the Israelis offering to pull back from only a few per cent of the West bank in the first phase, while the Palestinians had hoped for much more.

In March, July, and September 1997, there were further Hamas suicide bombings, making it increasingly difficult for Netanyahu to make concessions. Both 'Netanyahu and Arafat descended into mutual distrust . . . handicapped by extremist political constituencies', but with the Israelis easily continuing to hold the military advantage if it came to a showdown.[21] The Israelis condemned Arafat's failure to crack down on Hamas and increasingly tried to tackle the problems themselves. After all, one reason Israel had favoured the Oslo Accords was because it was hoped that Arafat would be able to control Palestinian attacks. But when in October 1997 two intelligence agents tries to assassinate a Hamas leader in Jordan, they were captured and had to be exchanged for numerous Palestinian prisoners, including Hamas's spiritual leader, Ahmed Yassin. Netanyahu, increasingly criticized for indecision, continued to resist major withdrawals from the West Bank and instead supported new Jewish settlements there. January 1998 saw the resignation of his Foreign Minister, David Levy, in frustration over the stalled peace process and the US and European Union both increased their pressure on Israel to compromise. But at talks in London and Washington in May 1998, attended by Netanyahu, Arafat, and the US Secretary of State, Madeleine Albright, agreement proved impossible, even though the main point of difference between the two sides seemed very narrow: the PNA would accept an initial Israeli withdrawal from 13 per cent of the West Bank but the most Netanyahu could accept was 9 per cent. There were much deeper differences on territory and political rights in the background: the Palestinians still hoped to rule 90 per cent of the West Bank in due course; Netanyahu was thinking of about half, and this without sovereign rights. For months after that, the Israeli premier refused to attend talks in Washington, and though in October, he made the Wye Accords with Clinton, which offered 17 per cent of the West Bank to the Palestinians, these too proved stillborn. Further upheaval was added to the situation by the death on 6 February 1999 of King Hussein of Jordan, long a source of stability in the region. He was succeeded by his son, Abdullah. For a time, Arafat even threatened to declare Palestinian statehood, a move that might have triggered full-scale war, but he agreed to defer such a step when Israeli elections were called for mid-May, raising the prospect of Netanyahu's removal.

Netanyahu did indeed lose the election but his opponent, Ehud Barak, leader of the Labour-dominated 'One Israel' movement, was without a clear majority and only able to form a government in July. Formerly the Commander-in-Chief of the Israeli armed forces, yet a firm supporter of the Oslo Accords, Barak seemed in a good position to pursue peace while reassuring Israelis that they were secure, and at first he showed energy and determination, even having a friendly exchange of messages with Assad of Syria. On 4 September, at a conference in Sharm-el-Sheikh in Egypt, Barak and Arafat reactivated the Wye Accords, leading to the release of Palestinian prisoners and paving the way for a 'final' agreement. The high point of this new period of hope came in early November, when the two leaders met Clinton in Oslo, quickly followed by the opening of 'final status' talks. But these talks failed to meet the February 2000 target date for a preliminary agreement and, although Barak agreed in May to pull Israeli troops out of southern Lebanon, the situation steadily worsened. In May, unrest was renewed in the West Bank and Gaza; in June, the death of Assad (succeeded by his son Bashar al-Assad) provided more instability; and in July, Barak's fragile coalition fell apart over his plans for concessions to the Palestinians.

Following a new peace effort by Clinton, there was a final attempt to save the situation in August through fresh peace talks, but they became deadlocked on the vexed question of East Jerusalem, one of the 'conquered territories' of the 1967 war but which the Israelis, partly for religious reasons, were reluctant to give up. Finally, in exasperation, ordinary Palestinians spontaneously began the so-called 'second Intifada'. Arafat had his autonomous 'Authority', he had been confirmed as Palestinian leader democratically, and he had won considerable international standing since his ill-judged support for Saddam Hussein. But he had full control of only a fraction of the West Bank, had failed to achieve the Oslo target of a permanent peace settlement by the end of the century, and he faced bitter condemnation from many Palestinians. As to the Israelis, they had secured peace with Jordan at least, but they had not fulfilled their hopes of ending Palestinian violence. The second Intifada was actually sparked off on 28 September by a visit from the right-wing Israeli politician, Ariel Sharon, to the Dome of the Rock, one of Islam's holy places. Yet in early 2001 it was Sharon, a determined enemy of Arafat, who won a clear electoral victory over the luckless Barak, becoming Israel's Prime Minister. With the second Intifada showing no sign of abating, Israeli–Palestinian relations seemed to be moving ever further from the hopes of Oslo.

D. East Asia's Changing Balance

The Decline of the Cold War in East Asia

Just as the Gorbachev era saw improved US–Soviet relations, lowered tensions in Europe, and a retreat from Soviet intervention in Afghanistan and Angola, so in East Asia there was an improvement in Moscow's relations with China and Japan, reduced tension on the Sino-Soviet border, and a retreat of Soviet-backed Vietnamese intervention in Cambodia. Yet whereas in Eastern Europe, and ultimately in the USSR itself, communism collapsed, in East Asia several Marxist regimes—most of those in the world now—remained in existence, including countries with which the US had fought bitter conflicts during the Cold War: China, North Korea, and Vietnam. The end of the Cold War led to some reduction in American force levels in the region, notably with the closure of the Philippines bases, though the US continued to use facilities in Japan. There was also a suspension of the Australian–New Zealand–US (ANZUS) Pact after August 1986 because of the New Zealand government's refusal to allow visits by nuclear-capable American warships. And, as elsewhere, the end of the Cold War raised questions about Washington's ability to remain involved in regional politics: without its previous anti-Soviet reference point, how could the US frame a coherent policy for an area as vast as East Asia? However, just as the US military presence seemed likely to follow the Soviets into retreat, so East Asia was growing in commercial and financial significance, partly because China's economy was now open to the West, and local capitalist governments were increasingly fearful of the rise of Chinese power. The retreat of Soviet power emphasized China's potential all the more.

In 1978–9, as the era of détente came to an end, China and the US had strengthened their relations in the face of the Vietnamese invasion of Cambodia and Soviet involvement in Afghanistan. But a decade later, Sino-American relations had cooled, whilst Sino-Soviet relations were improving. In the early 1980s, the Chinese, under Deng Xiaoping (see Box 22.2) had decided that, given Reagan's assertiveness and the USSR's troubled situation, it was better to steer a more independent line between the superpowers. But the Afghanistan and Cambodia problems, as well as the presence of substantial Soviet forces on the Chinese border, meant that China effectively remained closer to the US, with which there were few specific arguments, despite underlying ideological differences and American support for Taiwan. In January 1984, China's premier, Zhao Ziyang, visited Washington and a few months later Reagan made a week-long visit to China. Another factor was that Deng wanted to concentrate on economic development, so that an anti-American policy made no sense: it would simply drain Chinese resources into defence and deter Western investment. It was the advent of Gorbachev which allowed the real change in Sino-Soviet relations and the East Asian balance of power. The Soviet Red Army's withdrawal from Afghanistan, moves to settle the Cambodian question, and the reduction of Soviet forces on the Chinese border, as well as the destruction of SS-20s under the 1987 INF treaty, meant that Gorbachev had addressed all Deng's concerns. In 1988, Gorbachev had even made clear that he would not back Vietnam in its dispute with China over the Spratly Islands in the South China Sea and so encouraged Vietnam to improve its own relations with China.

Indeed, it was to crown these advances with a normalization of relations, that the Soviet leader visited Beijing in May 1989, only to see his visit overshadowed by the student occupation of Tiananmen Square at the heart of the city. Depicted in the West as 'pro-democracy' demonstrators, the students and the young workers who joined them, in fact had a range of concerns and their action had been sparked by the death of a leading modernizer, the former party secretary, Hu Yaobang. 'While centring on corruption and undefined notions of democracy . . . the student demands for freedom were essentially a protest against bureaucratic controls . . . which circumscribed their education, job prospects, right to travel.'[22] But they challenged the predominance of the ruling party and raised the danger that Chinese communism might accompany that in Eastern Europe into oblivion. Furthermore, the demonstrations began to spread to other major cities. On 4 June, once Gorbachev had departed, the demonstrations were ruthlessly crushed, with the loss of around a thousand lives, and the new party secretary, Zhao Ziyang, who had followed a more moderate policy, was sacked. His successor, Jiang Zemin, soon emerged as the likely predominant leader once Deng died.

Deng Xiaoping had eventually decided to back repression over conciliation and the price was a worsening in relations with America and Western Europe, most of whom cut their investments in China (harming growth rates for a time), severed military cooperation, and were unready to meet Chinese leaders for some years. But Deng's policies had been based on a mixture of economic modernization and the preservation of communist rule since he emerged as the predominant Chinese leader in 1978. Thus, in 1979, he had established the first special economic zones for foreign investment and thereby opened his country to greater outside contacts, but there were only four such zones at first and most industry remained under central control. In the 1980s, private ownership was extended, a market economy was created in agriculture, and healthy growth rates were achieved, albeit at the cost of inflation and growing corruption among officials. But the Western expectation that economic liberalization must be accompanied by greater political freedom proved false. The Chinese saw the one-party state as a guarantee of stability and effective rule over their huge population. Reform was focused on providing social welfare and rooting out corruption rather than improving human rights, and it was possible to be imprisoned without trial for several years. The events of 3–4 June 1989 were therefore predictable but, especially given the hopes raised by the decline of communism elsewhere, so was the Western reaction. James Baker noted that: 'The collapse of the Soviet Union had weakened the domestic consensus for engaging the Chinese as a counterweight to the Soviets' and, from June 1989 to the end of the Bush administration in January 1993, Sino-American relations 'essentially treaded water'.[23]

Then again, however shocked Western opinion might be, Tiananmen Square did not prove a foreign policy disaster. In its immediate aftermath, Deng, after criticizing the demonstrators, restated the need for economic growth. 'The second part of Deng's speech attracted little attention abroad. Yet it showed that an acute political mind was still at work.' He would not let Tiananmen throw the reform process into reverse and would pursue modernization and openness to external contacts, while maintaining the one-party state.[24] Many of China's pro-Western neighbours were anxious to preserve the improved relations of the 1970s and 1980s, not least Japan, which had massive trade and investment interests in China. In August 1991, the Japanese premier, Toshiki Kaifu, became the first major Western leader to visit Beijing since Tiananmen Square. Even South Korea and Taiwan had been improving relations with China in the late 1980s. South Korea, which established diplomatic relations with the USSR in 1990, did the same with China in August 1992. More remarkably, while Taiwan could not think in terms of mutual recognition of Beijing—both claimed to be the sole representative of a single China—the two governments were now able to sit in international organizations together. This began when Beijing accepted Taiwan as a member of the Asian Development Bank, not as an independent state, but under the title 'Taipei, China'. By then, there was considerable Taiwanese trade with the mainland and personal visits were allowed after 1987. The US government also recognized that Beijing was too significant a force in world politics to ignore and, despite some Congressional pressure for a policy of sanctions to force change in China, the Bush administration, while banning military exports, kept non-military trade flowing and maintained secret contacts. In 1990, Bush, who had been the first US envoy to communist China in the 1970s, also renewed China's 'Most Favoured Nation' trade status in the face of Congressional criticism. 'The administration's limited response was dictated by the belief that, if it was to exercise any leverage over Chinese actions, it had to remain "engaged".'[25] China's old enemy Vietnam also continued to improve relations, normalizing diplomatic relations with Beijing in November 1991. Indeed, since 1986, Vietnam had itself been pursuing a modernization programme, with greater private ownership and openness to foreign trade on lines similar to Deng's.

As with South Korea's friendlier policy to both the USSR and China, so Vietnam's move was part of a general reconciliation of old enmities, as the end of the Cold War altered everyone's security consideration in the region. In September 1990, the Vietnamese Foreign Minister, Nguyen Co Thach, even met America's James Baker on the neutral ground of the UN in New York. A month later Thach was in Tokyo, showing that Hanoi could now talk to America's leading ally in the Far East. It was a similar story for the Soviets. In May 1991, Gorbachev welcomed Jiang Zemin to Moscow, the first visit by a Chinese Party Secretary since Mao in 1957. The two of them not only stated that 'a new page is being opened in relations' bilaterally but also stated their readiness 'to make efforts together with all states of the world to institute a new world order', suggesting that this was no anti-American alliance that was being forged.[26] The previous month the Soviet leader had himself visited Tokyo, an important sign of improved relations which Gorbachev had wanted since at least his Vladivostok speech of 1986. In the late 1980s, in contrast to other Western countries, Japan had refused to join in the rush to make loans to the USSR because of the continuing dispute over the 'Northern Territories', the four Kuril Islands seized by the Red Army in August 1945. The dispute had prevented a peace treaty between the two countries being made after the Second World War but in 1989 a study group was set up on the issue. Gorbachev evidently had hopes of resolving it before his fall from power in December 1991. The break-up of the USSR came as a profound shock to the Chinese who, whatever their past differences with Moscow, found little joy in the collapse of the world's first communist state. Nonetheless, and notwithstanding the Tiananmen episode, the years 1985–91 could be seen to have benefited China more than most in East Asia. The Chinese Communist Party remained secure in power, Deng's modernization policies continued, and China faced no serious external security threat. China was 'more secure . . . than at any time under Communist rule, or indeed at any time in the several hundred years since the coming of Western imperialism to East Asia'.[27]

After the Cold War: China, America, and Japan

With the collapse of Soviet power, some events in East Asia could be seen in part as a consolidation of those trends evident before 1991. Chinese military and economic power were of concern to all other states in the region but, despite some critical moments, the prevailing policy was to work with Beijing in the hope of controlling its ambitions through cooperation. Moscow was still a player, though much reduced in significance. Yeltsin kept up the good relations with China achieved by Gorbachev, making visits to Beijing in 1992 and 1996, but Russian nationalist feeling prevented progress with Japan on the Northern Territories dispute. So, although Russia and China were able to end their thirty-year-old border dispute in 1997, and despite a visit by Yeltsin to Tokyo in 1998, a Russo-Japanese peace treaty remained unsigned.

In Cambodia, there was an internal settlement between the pro-Vietnamese regime of Hun Sen and his royalist opponents (see Chapter 19, C). Vietnam continued its emergence from isolation, most dramatically through improved relations with America. In April 1992, Bush eased the post-1975 economic embargo on Vietnam and in December, aware that other countries were taking advantage of the new investment and trade opportunities, allowed US companies to deal with the former enemy. The IMF and World Bank were able to resume their lending to Vietnam, and in February 1994, President Clinton ended the economic embargo altogether. Most important of all, however, on 11 July 1995, US–Vietnamese diplomatic relations were opened and, at the very end of his presidency, Clinton made a historic visit to Vietnam. The US continued to reduce its military forces in East Asia, while those of China continued to expand, but Washington remained a powerful force in the region, and in 1993 East Asia was probably the primary focus for the new Clinton administration. Most important was Clinton's own commitment to commercial involvement in the region, best seen in his support for Asia-Pacific Economic Cooperation (APEC) (see Chapter 21, A).

For the US, the three vital challenges in East Asia after the Cold War were: the protection of US trade and investment interests (worth about $350 billion in 1990); tackling the Japanese over their increasing trade surplus with America (up from $50 billion to $64 billion during the Bush presidency), while maintaining them as a military ally; and dealing with China, still a communist state with a poor human rights record, but ever more important in East Asia in economic and political terms. Despite its defeat in Vietnam, the US had emerged from the Cold War in a strong position in the Far East. It had preserved Taiwan and South Korea while improving relations with China, had fostered liberalism in Japan, and saw modern capitalist economies emerge in much of South-East Asia. But there were numerous difficulties, too. The end of the Cold War made Japan's importance as a political ally seem less vital than its commercial rivalry and there was persistent US pressure on Tokyo, going back to the 1970s, to deal with the trade imbalance—pressure which was resisted. Japan did take some action to reduce impediments to US exports, but Congress remained disappointed and even Bush, who felt good relations with Tokyo should be preserved, made commercial issues central to his visit there in January 1992. Clinton too found it popular in America to tackle Japan on trade but by the mid-1990s the Japanese economy was in the doldrums and the long post-war predominance of the Liberal Democrats was being replaced by political instability. As 'the American economy boomed and the Japanese economy weakened, the Clinton administration retreated from its confrontational trade policy'.[28] Among America's other allies, Taiwan and South Korea were democratizing but others, especially Thailand and Indonesia, were still authoritarian and, as seen in the latter in 1998, prone to internal discontent. Relations with Vietnam might be improving but those with another communist state, North Korea, became critical in 1994 (see Chapter 21, D). The Soviet menace might have ended, but the region's capitalist nations still saw America as a protector and the latent Chinese military threat meant that US forces could not be cut as much as originally hoped. Unlike in Europe, America lacked a multilateral alliance like NATO to help manage its relations, and deal with security problems in East Asia. Clinton evidently hoped that APEC would increase in significance as a multilateral organization, but it was only a trading organization, lacking a military-political rationale.

Washington might have been able to reduce its costs further if Japan had been ready to take on a greater defence burden. But instead, as in Western Europe, Tokyo continued even after the Cold War to restrict its own forces and rely on America for strategic defence. For years, this problem ran alongside that of trade in relations between the two countries. True, in the 1970s, partly because of trade tensions with Washington and the shock of Nixon's 'Opening to China', Japan had begun to play a fuller role in East Asian politics (see Chapter 12, A). But only in January 1983, at the depth of the New Cold War did Premier Nakasone Yasuhiro tell Reagan that the country's self-defence forces would have more than 1 per cent of GDP spent on them. Even then, with Japan set to take over much of the air defence of the Western Pacific, it took until 1987 before the 1 per cent limit was broken, and by 1990 it was back below it again. There was strong internal resistance to Nakasone's policy of greater international assertiveness in league with the US, most Japanese preferring both to avoid any resurgence of nationalism and to escape subservience to Washington. Rather than being translated into political and military power, Japan's position as the world's second largest economy bred a defense-mindedness not helped by the increased criticism it received from other Western powers. In 1989, the critics were answered on one point when Tokyo became the world's largest donor of development aid, but at the same time (Chapter 22, D) the Kuril Islands issue meant that Japan refused to give much financial help to Gorbachev's USSR. In 1990–1, Tokyo's refusal to send forces to expel Saddam Hussein from Kuwait—despite Japan's reliance on Middle East oil imports—provoked more criticism. The Japanese responded by providing $10 billion towards the costs of those who did fight, but this only further emphasized that the country was an economic giant unwilling to take any political risks. The 'impression of a free ride in the Gulf fed the Japan-bashers' in the US.[29]

After 1991, the political criticisms continued, the Japanese being attacked over the their failure to apologize to the Koreans, Chinese, and others over wartime atrocities, their restrictive immigration policy, and their failure to back Washington in the 1994 nuclear crisis with Korea—again, despite the fact that Japan was one of those most at risk if North Korea obtained nuclear weapons. In 1992, a new law allowed the self-defence forces to be deployed abroad, but only in UN peacekeeping operations and with a maximum of 2,000 personnel. Some troops were subsequently sent to police the Cambodian settlement, but this could be seen as a reflection of Japan's interest in good relations with South-East Asian states in general. South-East Asia was also one of the areas where Japan had become more diplomatically active since the 1970s (see below) and it was well aware that, after the experience of the Second World War, none of the states there really wanted to see a revival of Japanese military power. It was not that Tokyo was without international concerns or ambitions. Already part of the G-7 group of leading industrial states, it pressed after 1993 for a permanent seat on the UN Security Council. And, with the decline of Russian power and the rising Chinese profile, it was particularly concerned about the changing power balance in North-East Asia. The lowest point in relations with China after the Cold War came in 1995 because of a Chinese nuclear test. Yet, despite all the developments around them, the Japanese were reluctant to depart from the policy formula, first espoused by Premier Shigeru Yoshida in the 1950s, of limited armed forces, the US alliance, and a concentration on economic expansion. There was an internal debate in the 1990s over how involved Japan should be in world affairs, how its defence role might change, and what the future shape of relations with America should be, but it reached no firm consensus before 1998, when the dawn of economic recession emerged as a new frightening challenge.

Japan's reluctance to become a forthright military-political force in East Asia made developments in Sino-American relations even more significant, yet it was difficult to trace a particular pattern in these periods of crisis alternating with calm. Chinese economic growth was strong once again after 1991, with strong exports, healthy foreign reserves, and lower inflation. There seemed to be significant contradictions within their modernization process: what remained of state-owned industry was inefficient and unprofitable, but the shift towards free competition led to income inequalities and unemployment. Nonetheless, the communist leadership survived the death of Deng Xiaoping in February 1997, serious discontent was confined to Xinjiang province (where the Muslim Uighurs, China's largest ethnic minority, sought autonomy), and the government was able to use the return of Hong Kong to whip up popular support. The Chinese were sometimes disturbingly assertive abroad, as in the 1995 crisis with Thailand over the ownership of Mischief Reef in the South China Sea. More seriously, in March 1996, Beijing fired ballistic missiles during intimidating military exercises off the Taiwanese coast, ahead of the island's first presidential elections. The communists feared that the election winner, Lee Teng-hui, might declare Taiwan fully independent. By now, Taiwan had diplomatic relations with more than thirty countries and the US had revived large-scale arms sales to it in 1992, partly to match purchases from Russia. There was further tension during the next Taiwanese elections in March 2000. But generally, as over the Hong Kong negotiations with Britain, the Chinese relied on diplomacy rather than intimidation. Communist and Taiwanese officials had held their first bilateral meeting since the Civil War, in Singapore in April 1993. And in April 1997, a direct shipping link was opened between Taiwan and the mainland, also for the first time since 1949. Elsewhere, China helped to achieve a Cambodian settlement and to defuse the 1994 North Korean crisis (by providing the North with economic aid), improved relations with India and South-East Asian states, and joined in regional bodies like APEC. In 1996, China and Vietnam also resolved their long-running border dispute.

Yet, whatever the positive elements in Chinese policy, relations with America were dogged by a number of problems. It was clear that the end of the Cold War had not allowed a US retreat from East Asia any more than one from Europe and, 'China's economic dynamism, its growing military capability, its central role in the . . . resolution of regional tensions . . . underscored the long-term strategic significance of relations between China and the United States.'[30] One problem, as with US–Japanese relations, was trade rivalry. Although Bush and Clinton, under pressure from US business interests, annually renewed China's Most Favoured Nation status, the threat that it would not be renewed was ever present. China, like Japan, maintained a large trade surplus with the US and in 1993–5 there were particular arguments about China's pirating of US designs and patents. Although, in May 1994, Clinton said the US should 'delink' human rights and trade, America refused to support Chinese membership of the World Trade Organization (WTO) for most of the decade. Congress remained concerned about China's human rights record, especially its treatment of ethnic Tibetans. Another US concern was China's arms export policy and the fear that it would help Pakistan or Iran to build an atomic bomb. In 1991, the Chinese undertook to curb arms sales and respect the Non-Proliferation Treaty, but in August 1993, the US introduced certain economic sanctions because of Sino-Pakistani nuclear links. China's own nuclear tests also caused concern in America. Taiwan was another flashpoint, with Beijing upset that President Lee Teng-hui was allowed into the US on a 'private visit' in 1995 and the Americans deeply concerned by the March 1996 crisis. Jiang Zemin and Yeltsin also showed signs of working together against the US in the later 1990s, particularly criticizing the continuation of the Star Wars defence project. They not only ended their border dispute and expanded trade links but also, at a summit in Moscow in April 1997, rejected claims 'by any one country to the role of absolute leader'.[31]

Clinton's China policy appeared hopelessly confused both to his Congressional critics and the Chinese themselves. But after a difficult first term he became more confident in pursuit of a policy of 'constructive engagement', even if some saw this as freeing Beijing to abuse human rights and intimidate its neighbours. Like Bush, Clinton recognized that enmity with China could prove costly to America in terms of lost trade and military outlays, without any promise of reforming Beijing's approach to human rights, copyright law, or the Taiwan problem. Engagement on the other hand, while criticized by Republicans, might lead to mutual concessions and induce some change in Chinese policies, as had earlier occurred in the USSR. The US also had no desire to harass China when Deng was increasingly old and unwell, because such harassment might merely encourage an anti-American policy from his successor. As it was, Deng's death in February 1997 was overcome quite smoothly, and in October–November 1997, Jiang Zemin, who had already met Clinton at APEC summits in 1993 and 1996, visited the US and the framework of a Sino-American understanding became clear. Washington wanted China to support non-proliferation, peace in East Asia, and a free-market approach to economic problems in the developing world. In return, China wanted to be treated as an equal partner, to join the WTO, and to reduce US arms sales to Taiwan. A return visit by Clinton to Beijing in June 1998 showed that such an arrangement might work. Clinton spoke out on human rights, even on Tibet and Tiananmen Square, but he also said that Taiwan should not have independence. He and Jiang signed a trade deal and both criticized the recent nuclear tests by India and Pakistan. Ironically, however, such a friendly meeting between the region's most powerful actors provoked concern in other East Asian capitals: the summit might be reassuring, in the sense that it gave a promise of regional stability, but none of the smaller nations wished to be dictated to by a Sino-American agenda. Sino-American relations were soured in 1999 by the 'accidental' bombing of the Chinese embassy in Belgrade during the Kosovo crisis, but the Clinton administration was quick to

BOX 22.3

Biography: Deng Xiaoping (1905–97)

Born Deng Xixian, in the Sichuan province of China, Deng came from a land-owning family and was partly educated in France before joining the communists in 1924. Becoming a firm supporter of Mao Zedong, he took part in the Long March of 1934 and was elected to the Central Committee in 1945. His rise through the communist bureaucracy took him to the General Secretaryship of the Central Committee in 1954 but during the Cultural Revolution of the later 1960s he was condemned as a 'capitalist roader', losing all his official posts. He was rehabilitated, thanks to the support of Zhou Enlai and by 1975 was Chinese Vice Premier. Following the death of Mao Zedong and the defeat of the radical 'Gang of Four', Deng won a power struggle with Hua Guofeng to become China's paramount leader in 1978.

Deng maintained his primacy in Chinese politics for most of his remaining life despite old age, the onset of Parkinson's disease, and an increasing lack of formal positions: he resigned as Vice Premier in 1980 and quit his last official post in 1989. The key to his predominance was the loyalty of the armed forces and his promotion of trusted lieutenants, such as Zhao Ziyang, to key positions. Yet Deng was also ruthless enough to remove Zhao as Prime Minister in 1989 and crush the student demonstrations in Tiananmen Square, which had seemed to threaten communist rule. As leader, Deng was particularly identified with a modernization programme that allowed greater freedom for peasant farmers and 'Special Economic Zones', where there was foreign, capitalist investment. He criticized some elements of Maoism while maintaining one-party control and, as the Soviet Union collapsed, he shifted from close relations with the US to more circumspect ones.

offer compensation, and November saw China achieving one of its greatest international ambitions, when agreement was reached on its entry to the WTO. There were inevitable worries that Clinton's departure would spell the end of 'constructive engagement', however, especially when the Republican George Bush Junior, succeeded him.

E: ASEAN, the 'Tigers', and the Post-1997 Economic Crisis in Asia

The Rise of ASEAN and the 'Tigers'

The Association of South-East Nations (ASEAN) was founded at a meeting in Bangkok on 8 August 1967 between Indonesia (the largest member in terms of population), Malaysia, the Philippines, Thailand, and Singapore. All were capitalist, anti-communist, developing states, keen to maintain regional stability, improve their diplomatic weight in the world, and provide a healthy basis for economic development. It began as a modest but practical structure, whose main policy body was an annual meeting of foreign ministers. On the commercial front, preferential tariffs were established, but at first only on a voluntary basis, and on individual products. In the mid-1970s, with the US defeat in Vietnam, relations improved with China, while ASEAN summits began in 1976, with a conference in Bali. The 1980s saw progress with tariff reductions as member states industrialized and agriculture fell as a share of gross domestic product. The regimes of ASEAN were not free of internal upheaval, especially if they failed to deliver material rewards to their people, as seen with the fall of Ferdinand Marcos of the Philippines, who vainly tried to cling to power after an election defeat. But for most of ASEAN, the late 1980s and early 1990s were years of strong economic expansion. From 1989 to 1996, average growth rates across the association topped 7 per cent, with particularly good rates in Indonesia, Malaysia, Thailand, and the Philippines, the so-called 'ASEAN four'. Vietnam and Laos won observer status in the organization in 1992 and Brunei became a full member in 1995.

The economic success of ASEAN was part of a wider phenomenon in East Asia, where South Korea, Taiwan, and Hong Kong had average growth rates of more than 9 per cent in the 1980s. These three, together with Singapore, became known as the 'Asian tiger' economies because of their formidable expansion, sustained over many years. Explaining why some countries experience stronger economic growth than others is not easy, but ASEAN could offer skilled labour and relatively low costs to Western investors. Its members also had efficient bureaucracies that used government control to restrict international competition and achieve high levels of investment. Individual countries had particular strengths: Singapore, for example, became a centre for oil-refining, banking, and shipping, with one of the highest standards of living in the world. Furthermore, ASEAN and the 'tigers' were a significant part of a broader development around the Pacific Ocean, from Chile in South America, through California, round to Japan and China, and down to Australia—a vast area known as 'Pacific Rim'—of strong growth rates and greater commercial ties, which suggested that these countries may be able to outperform the 'Atlantic' economies of Western Europe and the United States in future. ASEAN leaders, such as Malaysia's Mohamad Mohathir, resisted Western pressure to define progress primarily in terms of the achievement of improved human rights and liberal democracy: it was up to Asian countries to find their own ways forward. The entry of three more states in 1997 emphasized this point. Burma, Cambodia, and Laos were all rural, less developed states with decades of authoritarian rule.

One political interest which members had in common was a fear of Chinese expansion, economic and political, a fear that intensified with the collapse of the Soviet Union. The Philippines and Vietnam had territorial disputes with China in the South China Sea and the Chinese navy was growing. ASEAN hoped to settle such disputes peacefully and, in July 1993, attempted to draw Beijing into dialogue through the creation of a Regional Forum, covering all East Asia. But it was a delicate relationship to manage. The formidable growth of the Chinese economy under Deng Xiaoping both reinforced East Asian growth in general and threatened to turn the South-East Asia states into economic satellites of Beijing. Yet ASEAN had only limited success in building up a regional trading bloc, along the lines of the European Union. In 1992, ASEAN did agree to create a free-trade area among its members, but it was limited to industrial goods and the target for achieving it was soon deferred for fifteen years. The majority of ASEAN members traded more with America and Japan than with each other, and pursued separate development strategies. Many, for example, were trying to create their own automobile manufacturers and to create high-technology industries, and they were all competing to attract outside investment. The enlargement to four new, agricultural members in the 1990s created a rather different challenge: how could countries like Vietnam and Burma hope to stand alongside 'tigers' like Malaysia if genuine integration were pursued?

1997–8: Asia's Economies in Crisis

In the mid-1990s, it seemed the future of the world economy was at its brightest on the Pacific Rim. Before 1997 ended, however, the prospects for ASEAN, now a generation old, had dimmed significantly. There were suddenly serious worries over the organization's economic future and concern spread around the region, leading stock market and currency values to fall. Falling currency values ought to have helped the East Asians export more, but it was difficult to do this when they were all trying to expand in an unfavourable market. By early 1998, it was clear that the gathering crisis had worsened Russia's economic problems and might even blunt China's economic miracle. Given the interdependent nature of the world economy, such a widespread malaise in the Far East also threatened to damage Western trade and investment. The situation was not helped by the close links between ASEAN and another suddenly troubled economy, Japan. Since the 1950s, growth there had helped the rest of East Asia to prosper, taking over a quarter of ASEAN's exports in the 1970s, for example. But in the later 1990s, a lack of liquidity at home, linked to low income from many investments in the US and Europe, led the Japanese to cut back their outward investment programmes and its banking system was troubled by bad debts, not least to ASEAN, Taiwan, and South Korea. In 1996–7, for the first time in more than twenty years, the Japanese economy contracted.

Yet, however sluggish Japan's performance had become, the depression would not have been so deep without the problems that became apparent within ASEAN itself. The growth rates it experienced in the early 1990s had fostered an excess of optimism and over-expansion resulting in high debts, balance-of-payments problems, a bloated property sector, and labour shortages. The realization that the bubble would burst first affected the stock market in Thailand, one of the weaker ASEAN economies, in July 1997. Thailand and Indonesia quickly turned to the IMF for massive loans, but they could not escape a large currency devaluation and there were fears that the restructuring demanded by the IMF could prove harmful in the long term. The Fund tended to favour an 'Anglo-Saxon' model of economic recovery based on privatization, reductions in government spending, free capital movement, and the end of price controls. This had been the IMF's recipe for tackling Western problems in the 1960s and 1970s, and was forced on South America during its 1980s debt crisis. But it was partly designed to tackle inflation (not a problem in ASEAN), it harmed growth and employment (thereby raising the danger of social discontent), and it tried to force developing states to accept a Western-dictated version of capitalism (which some criticized as a reworking of imperialist approaches). Countries needing IMF aid had little choice but to accept the price of restructuring, but Asian resentment at the IMF was one of the consequences of the crisis.

By late November 1997, the crisis had spread to South Korea, the most formidable of the Asian 'tigers' and the eleventh largest economy in the world, which had to ask the IMF for a $20 billion loan—the largest so far. South Korea had been one of the most remarkable economic successes in East Asia. As in Japan, its people had been happy to work hard and save assiduously, the reward being an increase in average income from less than $100 in 1960 to about $10,000 in 1995. But after borrowing in the years of plenty, many South Korean companies were indebted to several times their value and they now faced collapse. One result was serious unrest, with outbreaks of strikes and demonstrations. But the IMF, World Bank, and the other countries responded to Korea's predicament, in December, by producing a $35 billion rescue package in total, dwarfing any previous economic salvage operation. It was in the middle of these events that, on 24 November 1997, one of Japan's largest banks, Yamaichi Securities, collapsed, raising fears of a meltdown of the world's second largest economy. The total bad debt liabilities of Japanese banks were estimated at around $550 billion.

Before growth was restored in East Asia, the main political cost was borne by Indonesia. Indebted to a total of $120 billion and with the IMF demanding economic restructuring, Indonesians were faced, like South Koreans, by salary cuts, unemployment, and shortages. They reacted even more violently. For weeks in early 1998, there were protest marches calling for an end to the regime of General Suharto, the dictator since 1966. Condemned for corruption and nepotism, and no longer able to rely on the army to crush the opposition, he resigned on 21 May, leaving power in the hands of a former associate, Bacharuddin Habibie. Suharto was not the only political victim of the economic crisis. In Thailand, where the crisis had begun, Premier Chavalit Yongchaiyudh was forced to resign in November 1997. Premier Hashimoto of Japan followed in July 1998. But in most countries, governments weathered the storm. The impact of the crisis was, after all, uneven: while Indonesia's GNP tumbled by 80 per cent in 1997–8, that of Malaysia, and the Philippines fell by less than half that amount—although that was still bad enough. From 1999, there was a recovery in the East Asian economies but it was a slow process and, in general, they did not restore their per capita income levels until about 2006. Since Europe, America, and other regions had continued to grow throughout the period, the idea of an 'East Asian' miracle looked rather threadbare. Far more remarkable than the performance of the 'tigers' were those of India and, more particularly, China, which really did emerge as economic superpowers in the early twenty-first century.

Visit the online resources that accompany this book to test your understanding and take your learning further: www.oup.com/he/young-kent3e

NOTES

1. Dean Guldenhuys, 'International Involvement in South Africa's Political Transformation,' in Walter Carlsnaes and Marie Muller (eds), *Change and South Africa's External Relations* (International Thomson Publishers, Johannesburg, 1997), 47.
2. Quoted in Guy Arnold, *South Africa* (St Martin's Press, New York, 1992), 126.
3. Chester Crocker, *High Noon in Southern Africa: Making Peace in a Rough Neighbourhood* (W. W. Norton, New York, 1992), 77–8; Robert Scott Jaster, *The Defence of White Power* (Palgrave Macmillan, 1988), 111–12.
4. Lawrence Schlemmer, 'The Turn in the Road', in Robin Lee and Lawrence Schlemmer (eds), *Transition to Democracy: Policy Perspectives* (Oxford University Press, Cape Town, 1991), 14 and 20.
5. Marina Ottaway, *South Africa: The Struggle for a New Order* (Brookings Institute, Washington, 1993), 13–14.
6. Timothy Sisk, *Democratization in South Africa: The Elusive Social Contract* (Princeton University Press, Princeton, 1995), 199.
7. 'Introduction', to Phyllis Martin and Patrick O'Meara (eds), *Africa* (Indiana University Press, Bloomington, 1995), 7.
8. Tiebile Drame, 'The Crisis of the State', in Stephen Ellis (ed.), *Africa Now: People, Policies and Institutions* (J. Currey, London, 1996), 209.
9. Boutros Boutros-Ghali, *Unvanquished: A US–UN Saga* (Random House, New York 1999), 138 and 141.
10. Alain Destexhe, *Rwanda and Genocide in the Twentieth Century* (Pluto, London, 1995), 51.
11. Edward Said, *The Question of Palestine* (Routledge, London, 1980), 242.
12. Yitzhak Shamir, *Summing Up: An Autobiography* (Weidenfeld & Nicolson, London, 1994), 196.
13. Avi Shlaim, *The Iron Wall: Israel and the Arab World* (Allen Lane, London, 2000), 491; Eytan Bentsur, *Making Peace* (Praeger, Westport, 2001), 121.
14. Shimon Peres, *Battling for Peace* (Weidenfeld & Nicolson, London, 1995), 373 and 377–8.
15. Kirsten Schulze, *The Arab–Israeli Conflict* (Longman, New York, 1999), 85.
16. Quoted in David Makovsky, *Making Peace with the PLO* (Westview Press, Boulder, 1996), 47.
17. Andrew Buchanan, *Peace with Justice* (Macmillan, Basingstoke, 2000), 216.
18. Nils Butenschon, 'The Oslo Agreement', in George Giacaman and Dag Lanning (eds), *After Oslo* (Pluto Press, Chicago, 1998), 42.

19. Benny Morris, *Righteous Victims: A History of the Zionist–Arab Conflict* (Alfred A Knopf, New York, 1999), 626.
20. Said Aburish, *Arafat* (Bloomsbury, New York, 1999).
21. Andrew Buchanan, *Peace with Justice* (Macmillan, Basingstoke, 2000), 367–8.
22. Alan Lawrance, *China under Communism* (Routledge, London, 1998), 120.
23. James Baker, *The Politics of Diplomacy* (G. P. Putnam's Sons, New York, 1995), 112–13.
24. Richard Evans, *Deng Xiaoping and the Making of Modern China* (Hamish Hamilton, London, 1993), 300.
25. Steven Hurst, *The Foreign Policy of the Bush Administration* (Cassell, New York, 1999), 40.
26. Quoted in Raymond Garthoff, *The Great Transition: American–Soviet Relations and the End of the Cold War* (Brookings Institution, Washington, DC, 1994), 659.
27. Gerald Segal, 'Foreign Policy', in David Goodman and Gerald Segal (eds), *China in the Nineties* (Clarendon Press, Oxford, 1991), 160.
28. William Hyland, *Clinton's World* (Praeger, Westport, 1999), 134.
29. Dennis Smith, *Japan since 1945: The Rise of an Economic Superpower* (Macmillan, Basingstoke, 1995), 159.
30. Michel Oksenberg, 'The Asian Strategic Context', in Robert Zoellick and Philip Zelikow (eds), *America and the East Asian Crisis* (New York, 2000), 11.
31. Quoted in Alan Lawrance, *China under Communism* (Routledge, London, 1998), 135.

PART VII

The Age of Instability and Conflict: Terror, Economic Chaos, and Political Change, 2001–11

On the morning of 11 September 2011, a group of nineteen terrorists, linked to Osama bin Laden's al-Qaeda jihadist network, carefully coordinated the hijacking of four civilian airliners. The first of the airliners from Boston, an American Airlines flight, with 92 people on board, was flown by the hijackers into one of the twin towers of the World Trade Center in New York, a symbol of Western capitalism that had previously been the scene of a jihadist bombing in 1993. A little over a quarter of an hour later, a second Boston flight, with 65 people on board, was flown into the other tower. By 10.30 a.m., both towers, which previously dominated the New York skyline, had collapsed, killing over 2,600 people, including more than 400 fire-fighters, police, and paramedics. Meanwhile, a third aircraft, with 64 people on board, was flown to Washington DC and crashed into a wing of the Pentagon, killing 125 people there. A fourth flight, United Airlines 93, with 44 on board, crashed into a field in Pennsylvania after passengers tried to overthrow the hijackers. In all, almost 3,000 had been killed in the most destructive terrorist operation of all time.

The hijackers, mostly Saudis who had arrived in America since the start of 2000, were soon identified as having links to the al-Qaeda network. Its leader, Osama bin Laden, while he initially denied responsibility for the 9/11 operation, had already called on Muslims to attack the US, in a fatwa of February 1998, signed with three other jihadists, including the Egyptian Ayman al-Zawahiri. Bin Laden had also been involved in earlier, sophisticated, and merciless attacks, on US interests, such as the simultaneous bombings of the American embassies in Kenya and Tanzania, in August 1998, which killed more than 200 people. He was bitterly opposed to Washington's support for Israel and for the US presence in his homeland, Saudi Arabia, which was also the home of Islam's two holiest places. He had formed al-Qaeda (which means 'the Base'), a militant Sunni group that believed in adhering to sharia law, in the late 1980s, when he supported the Afghan Mujaheddin in their war against Soviet occupation. His capture or death and the destruction of al-Qaeda now became major aims of the US government and its allies. NATO members, who had generally lost lives on 9/11—there were 67 British victims, for example—accepted that the operation was an attack on them all. On 14 September, Congress approved military action against those responsible for 9/11 and, on 20 September, President Bush announced a 'war on terror' when addressing Congress.

The immediate result was a demand that the Taliban regime in Afghanistan hand over bin Laden, who was currently living there. After they prevaricated, the US and its allies, from 7 October, started air attacks on the capital, Kabul, and other targets. The War on Afghanistan had begun. In his January 2002 State of the Union address, Bush named North Korea and Iran, alongside Iraq, as elements in an 'axis of evil' that threatened world peace. Then in a speech of May 2002, the Under-Secretary of State added Cuba, Libya, and Syria to the list. The events of 9/11 and their consequences would prove a seminal moment for international relations in the twenty-first century, with widespread repercussions that went far beyond any focus on destroying al-Qaeda.

At the start of the Cold War in 1945–9, an ideological abstraction, the fear of communism, was quickly accompanied by an exaggerated belief in an aggressive Soviet military threat to the maintenance of US socio-economic values and power political interests. The effect, if not the aim, was to blur the vague abstractions of national security with concrete military threats, in order to protect ideological positions and the Western way of life, founded on the values of democratic capitalism. In 2001, the ideological threat was different and less existential, with no effective state power to support it. As in the ideological challenge of the Cold War, countering it required misrepresenting and exaggerating threats. Yet, because the events of 9/11 made threats to the US mainland appear much more tangible and immediate than in the late 1940s or the Cold War, al-Qaeda had to be countered by more than the abstraction of fighting terror. The implementation of tangible and specific responses in a concrete form were urgently required. Yet misrepresentation remained a key component of responses to ideological challenges and abstract threats; this was increasingly to become more evident in the war on terror. In both foreign and domestic affairs, the media failed, not simply to rely on honest investigative reporting, but to become fully engaged in the ideological battle through its misleading propaganda.

An important corollary was the reduction in expensive foreign correspondents, just as social media was facilitating the spread of instantly available information, however true or false it might be. For governments, foreign adventures became more likely to be undertaken without significant input from diplomats in embassies, who were best acquainted with the specifics of a particular, local problem. In the metropoles, the key factor increasingly became the presentation of policy rather than its substance, on a greater scale than previously seen. Thus, in the British Foreign Office, after Sir Christopher Meyer had been a visiting fellow at Harvard University's Centre for International Affairs and later Prime Minister John Major's press secretary, the process of blurring the distinction between those involved in the making of policy and those presenting it began. Developed by Major's successor, Tony Blair and his press secretary, Alistair Campbell, this process, now often resulting in what is called 'spin', made it much easier for people's emotive beliefs to be manipulated by companies and foreign governments. The ability to access to data, and use it through unregulated means of communication like social media, enabled significant numbers to be targeted with particular messages in order to influence their decisions in elections.

In America, the Bush administration's response to the new terrorist threats was set out in the September 2002 National Security Strategy. This was drawn up while preparations were being made to invade Saddam Hussein's Iraq and was sometimes referred to as the 'Bush Doctrine'. Confident of US power, and reflecting a deep belief in liberal principles, it argued that the Cold War struggle against totalitarianism was won and that:

> America is now threatened less by conquering states than we are by failing ones. We are menaced less by fleets and armies than by catastrophic technologies in the hands of an embittered few. We must defeat these threats.

Building on the idea of a 'war on terror' in the wake of 9/11, the document said:

> The struggle against global terrorism is different from any other war in our history. It will be fought on many fronts against a particularly elusive enemy over an extended period of time. Progress will come through the persistent accumulation of successes—some seen, some unseen.

But terrorists were not the only enemy. The strategy also claimed that Iraq and North Korea sought nuclear weapons, and argued that:

> The United States has long maintained the option of preemptive actions to counter a sufficient threat to our national security. The greater the threat, the greater is the risk of inaction—and the more compelling the case for taking anticipatory action to defend ourselves, even if uncertainty remains as to the time and place of the enemy's attack.[1]

The President and his advisers were guided, then, by a desire to pre-empt any supposed threats to the US forcefully, particularly from weapons of mass destruction (WMDs), which included nuclear, chemical, and bacteriological devices. Influenced by a generation of 'neo-conservative' thinking, the administration was ready to assert pro-actively its 'hard' (military) power, given the collapse of the Soviet Union, whatever the cost to the soft power (diplomacy, foreign aid and other non-coercive methods), which had been a key factor in winning the ideological battle with Moscow.

The US determination to act against threats before they materialized was a major factor in the 2003 war in Iraq, conducted on the basis of the suspicion of a threat from WMDs, without proof that the threat was real. Although the 2002 Strategy document talked of the need to 'strengthen alliances to defeat global terrorism' and 'work with others to defuse regional conflicts', the neo-conservatives around Bush were also prepared to act without paying too much attention to constraints posed by the UN and other international organizations, or even by allied states. The conflicts in Afghanistan and Iraq were both launched without unequivocal UN approval. They also marked the continuing transition in how war was being fought, or military force employed in conflicts. No longer were significant numbers of ground troops deployed by the more important military powers, who were increasingly averse to casualties amongst their soldiers. Spared the domestic consequences of returning body bags by relying on aerial warfare, casualties had to be damage of the increasing resort to drones or guided missiles.

Initial US aims of intervention and regime change in Afghanistan, Iraq, and elsewhere appeared to be the promotion of democracy (despite some key, non-democratic allies in the region) and hopes that 'a new era of global economic growth' would be ignited by 'free markets and free trade' in an increasingly interconnected, or globalized world. This built on the so-called 'Washington consensus', implemented at the end of the Cold War by the government and global economic institutions largely controlled and financed by US money, including the International Monetary Fund (IMF) and the World Bank. The aim was to shape economies worldwide according to 'free market' principles with domestic reforms and tax cuts accompanied by an openness to foreign trade and investment. At first, putting this into practice did create a renewed period of expansion and growth and strengthened the belief in a panacea of 'free markets', which were expected to cure most economic and social ills, even creating a classless society. But this soon proved to be an illusion. The boom in the consumer-dominated developed world was, in reality, driven by borrowing, encouraged in many countries by a property 'bubble'. The Washington consensus was accompanied by cuts in public expenditure and reduced state involvement in the economy and deregulated financial markets.

The 2007–8 Financial Crisis

All appeared to be going well until 2007–8; claims of ending the old 'boom-and-bust' economic cycle seemed justified. Unfortunately, the fact was that excessive lending, which included sub-prime loans (loans which brought high returns for investors, but carried a high risk), created conditions for borrowing and debt to spiral out of control. The problem lay in the burgeoning derivative markets, hedge funds, and short selling, which now operated free from most constraints. With securitization—that is, the combining of several debts into financial products which could be traded using loans as collateral—vast profits were generated while stock and bond markets prospered through the growing indebtedness of governments, companies, and individuals. The fall in US house prices, which began declining in 2006, was accompanied by growing worries over borrowers' ability to repay mortgages. But the real financial problems began with the 2007 failure of two Bear Steanes hedge funds, resulting in a fall in the values of Lehman Brothers shares. Lehman Brothers was a major investment bank highly leveraged because of securitization, and in 2007 it was underwriting more mortgage-backed securities than any other firm. Its shares fell in March 2008 by nearly 50 per cent as its large number of mortgage securities made it particularly vulnerable to deteriorating market conditions. An urgent bail-out was required, but this was refused by the Bush administration and, in September, Lehman declared bankruptcy. The stock market also collapsed, losing 30 per cent of its value. As the financial chaos spread, an international effort was made using state resources to increase capital flow and the capitalization of banks who, because of uncertainties about where debts lay, were increasingly reluctant to lend money to each other. These fears produced by securitization and unregulated borrowing (with credit default swaps allowing debts to be incurred with no prospect of the repayment of defaults) paralyzed the financial system. Interbank lending stalled, with businesses unable to borrow due to the perceived risk of lending in the climate of uncertainty produced by the inability to know the totality of given debts or where they lay.

Short-term profits had been accumulated by following the key capitalist principle of lending, which requires greater returns for greater risk, but which was no longer subject to adequate regulation or controls, as it was deemed simply that 'the market knows best'. States had to raise vast sums to keep the banking system afloat and ensure the whole capitalist system did not collapse, with disastrous consequences for the less well-off.

The countries in the European Union that were members of the single currency, or Euro, had their own particular economic problems that threatened Western Europe's political unity. There was a growing gap between those countries like Germany, running a large trade surplus, and those like Greece running a deficit, financed by borrowing. As the GDP difference between Germany and Greece increased by 50 per cent, in 2009 Greece faced a serious debt crisis. Far from bringing European countries together politically by strengthening economic ties, a single currency had the opposite effect.

Aside from the financial crises, the key threat to the world, that of global warming, had largely been ignored by the Bush administration of 2001–9, partly because policy-makers believed that limits on carbon emissions would damage the US economy to the benefit of competitors like China. One of Bush's first actions as President had been to pull out of the 1997 Kyoto Accords, a sign that his unilateralism pre-dated 9/11. The Kyoto Accords had come into effect in February 2005, with over 140 states having signed up to it, including all of America's NATO allies. But Bush persisted in standing aside. During the 2008 election campaign, Obama suggested that he would sign up to Kyoto despite sharing his predecessor's doubts over the impact on American jobs.

The War on Terror

Meanwhile, despite early successes in both Afghanistan and Iraq, with the toppling of the Taliban and Saddam Hussein, the US and its allies found it difficult to create viable, liberal regimes in either state. Stability and consensus were always going to be politically difficult to achieve in an environment where old animosities had been frequently suppressed by deposed authoritarian leaders. The problems were exacerbated, as in Vietnam a generation before, by an inadequate US understanding of different cultures and values and a failure to realize the importance of post-conflict reconstruction in those societies whose rulers were overthrown. In Iraq, the specific removal of members of the army and administration who were members of Saddam Hussein's Ba'ath Party had catastrophic effects on effective government. The US and its allies, facing widespread resentment from those opposed to the invasion of their country, soon became bogged down in ill-considered counter-insurgency operations. Sectarian differences had been kept at bay in Iraq by Saddam's brutal repression of the majority Shi'ite population. They now exploded in the wake of the invasion as the chaos and disorder brought by numerous armed groups helped facilitate the very terrorism that the invasion had claimed it would prevent. By 2006, American military intelligence noted that al-Qaeda, the terrorists carrying out the 9/11 attack, had become the effective government of Anbar province in western Iraq. Bush's decision not to withdraw, but to increase US ground forces in Iraq did mean, however, that US troops were able to withdraw without peace or honour, but a modicum of dignity, in 2011 and to hand the security task over to local forces.

The evident problems of exercising US power in the first decade of the new millennium led the post-2009 Democratic administration of Barack Obama to retreat from the unilateral use of military force. Obama, without developing a coherent doctrine of his own, was keen to pursue a foreign policy based on rebuilding the sympathy for America that had been dissipated by the war on Iraq:

> we have lost thousands of American lives, spent nearly a trillion dollars, alienated allies and neglected emerging threats—all in the cause of fighting a war for well over five years in a country that had absolutely nothing to do with the 9/11 attacks.[2]

But in many ways, he, too, lived under the cloud of 9/11 and continued to target terrorists in Afghanistan, Pakistan, Yemen, and elsewhere with the use of unmanned 'drones'. His greatest success against al-Qaeda was the US Special Forces' operation that killed Osama bin Laden, in Pakistan, in May 2011.

Economic problems in the West and conflict throughout the Middle East, alongside Obama's reluctance to flex American military muscles, opened the way to a more assertive policy by Vladimir Putin's Russia (although this only became clear after 2011, notably with Russian interventions in Crimea and Syria) and served to emphasize the growing significance of China. Following Obama's 'pivot' to the East and with the Chinese economy continuing to expand, each power hoped to produce stability through the peaceful adoption of its own values. In China, the key challenge was whether low wages and an undervalued currency could be superseded and growth extended to provide benefits more widely across Chinese society. Major difficulties had to be overcome, given the enormous population, and the government could always alleviate dissatisfaction with economic inequality and secure acceptance of the changes within China by playing the nationalist card, risking instability in East Asia and the Pacific. Aside from a more assertive Chinese policy in the South China Sea with disputes over various rocks and islands, there was the ever-present issue of Taiwan, seen as being of such fundamental importance to the territorial integrity of China that a 2005 law committed Beijing to take military action should the island unilaterally declare independence.[3] There was also a deepening US defence relationship with India, with the latter's often troubled past relations with China and the latter's historical links to Pakistan highlighting potential risks on that front. As China appeared set on developing a greater role that provided the prestige and status befitting the most important regional power, there was a danger that symbolism and perceptions would become entwined with concrete territorial clashes, however little might be at stake. The sense of Chinese humiliation at the hands of the West remains an important element influencing its leaders. Under Hu Jin Tao, however, the strategy of pursuing its international interests 'under the radar', originally adopted by Deng Xiao Ping, was largely maintained. Only with the coming to power of Xi Jinping, in 2012, would this self-effacing approach seem to end.

Visit the online resources that accompany this book to test your understanding and take your learning further: www.oup.com/he/young-kent3e

NOTES

1. The National Security Strategy 2002, at http://georgewbush-whitehouse.archives.gov/nsc/nss/2002/.
2. Barack Obama, 'A New Strategy for a New World', at www.huffingtonpost.com/2008/07/15/read-obamas-iraq-speech-a_n_112871.html.
3. Kerry Brown, *China's World: What Does China Want?* (I. B.Tauris, London, 2017), 110.

PART VII CHRONOLOGY

The Age of Instability and Conflict: Terror, Economic Chaos, and Political Change 2001–11

2001	
20 January	George W. Bush inaugurated as US President.
24 April	China protests against new US arms deal with Taiwan.
9 July	President Lee Teng-hui ends Taiwan's 'one China' policy; leads to weeks of tension with China.
11 September	Aircraft hijackings and attacks on the World Trade Center, New York and Pentagon, Washington kill more than 3,000.
6 November	Taiwan allows direct trade with China for first time since 1949.
13 November	Afghan Taliban abandon Kabul to US-backed Northern Alliance.
18–23 November	Al-Qaeda leader, Osama bin Laden, escapes from Kabul to mountains and caves of Tora Bora.
27 November	Bonn Conference of selected Afghan factions meets to agree on interim government and international peace-keeping force.
1 December	US Defense Secretary Rumsfeld orders General Tommy Franks to construct a plan for invasion of Iraq.
3 December	Israeli government breaks relations with Palestinian Authority.
5 December	Bonn Conference agrees on Hamid Karzai as interim head of Afghan government.
6 December	Mullah Omar, the Taliban leader, escapes from Kandahar.
11 December	China joins World Trade Organization.
2002	
1 January	'Eurozone' members issue their new Euro notes and coins.
3 January	CIA tells Vice-President Cheney only a military invasion, not covert operations, will overthrow Saddam.
11 January	Guantanamo base in Cuba is first used by US as a prison for al-Qaeda suspects captured in Afghanistan.
29 January	In State of the Union address, Bush describes Iraq, Iran, and North Korea as an 'axis of evil' and points to threat posed by regimes seeking weapons of mass destruction (WMD).
7 February	Bush signs executive order denying al-Qaeda suspects rights under the Geneva Convention; Taliban to be treated as unlawful combatants.
12 February	At UN tribunal in The Hague, trial begins of Slobodan Milošević, former Yugoslav president.
12 February	US Secretary of State Colin Powell testifies before a Senate Committee that US policy seeks regime change in Iraq but there are no imminent war plans.
20 February	CIA team enters Iraq to prepare for paramilitary deployment.
29 March–3 May	Israeli attacks on West Bank, following suicide bomb attacks in Israel; Yasser Arafat is isolated in his Ramallah compound.
24 May	Bush and Russian President, Vladimir Putin sign Strategic Offensive Reductions Treaty in Moscow.

PART VII CHRONOLOGY (continued)

7 September	With Bush alongside, British premier Tony Blair tells reporters Saddam has WMD; start of attempt to 'sell' war to Congress and public.
12 September	Bush speech to the UN in New York states the US will work with the Security Council to get the necessary resolutions to disarm Iraq.
1 October	US National Intelligence Board concludes Baghdad has chemical and biological weapons.
10–11 October	US Senate and House of Representatives pass resolutions authorizing President Bush to use force in Iraq.
12 October	Bomb attacks in Bali, by an al-Qaeda affiliate, kill over 200.
8 November	UN Security Council passes Resolution 1441 on Iraq, demanding access for UN arms inspectors, who had previously been expelled.
27 November	UN weapons inspectors under Hans Blix resume work in Iraq.
29 November	International Atomic Energy Authority requests inspections after North Korea says it has right to nuclear weapons.
7 December	Iraq submits detailed statement to UN inspectors to prove it had no weapons of mass destruction.
2003	
10 January	North Korea withdraws from the Non-Proliferation Treaty.
13 January	Bush tells Powell he has made up his mind to go to war.
20 January	Office of Reconstruction and Humanitarian Assistance established in the Pentagon to deploy to Iraq in the event of hostilities.
27 January	Blix reports ambiguously, that there is no evidence of a revived Iraqi WMD programme.
31 January	Bush and his main ally Blair meet at Camp David.
5 February	Powell presents 'evidence' in UN of supposed Iraqi WMDs.
10 February	French President Jacques Chirac says, 'nothing today justifies war'.
20 March	Iraq war begun by US-led coalition.
9 April	Fall of Baghdad to US forces.
1 May	Bush announces end of combat operations in Iraq.
11 May	Paul Bremer becomes head of the Coalition Provisional Authority (CPA) in Iraq.
16 May	CPA order number 1 removes about 30,000 Ba'ath party members from administrative posts.
24 June	Bush speech sets out 'road map' for Palestinian–Israeli peace, including a Palestinian state.
11 August	NATO mission in Afghanistan begins, leading the UN-approved International Security Assistance Force (ISAF).
19 August	Suicide bomb attack on UN office in Baghdad by Abu Musab al Zarqawi's men kills 22, including UN envoy.
29 August	Zarqawi's father-in-law uses truck bomb against Shi'ite mosque in Najaf, killing hundreds.
13 December	Saddam Hussein captured in Tikrit, Iraq.
2004	
11 March	Bomb attacks in Madrid, largely by Spanish and Moroccan members of 'leaderless jihad' kill over 200 people.
14 March	Socialist Party wins Spanish election after opposing the incumbent Popular Party's involvement in the Iraq war.

(continued...)

PART VII CHRONOLOGY (continued)

29 March	Seven eastern European states join NATO (Bulgaria, Romania, Slovakia, Slovenia, Lithuania, Latvia, and Estonia).
31 March	Four US security contractors killed in Fallujah. US retaliation in first battle of Fallujah kills hundreds.
4 April	Moqtada al-Sadr leads Shi'ite uprising in Najaf, which by 2006 has a force of 60,000—the largest Iraqi insurgent group.
29 April	Revelations of abuse of prisoners by US forces at Abu Ghraib prison in Iraq.
11 May	Video of the beheading of US businessman Nicholas Berg posted on internet.
28 June	Interim government under Ayad Allawi assumes power in Iraq, as a step away from coalition control.
September	Al-Qaeda formally establishes itself in Iraq.
1–3 September	Attack by Chechen separatists on a school in Beslan, Russia leaves nearly 350 dead.
7 October	CIA report concedes there were no WMD in Iraq when the 2003 war was launched.
17 October	Zarqawi issues statement pledging allegiance to bin Laden.
7 November	US marines begin 2nd battle of Fallujah, now controlled by insurgents.
11 November	Death of Palestinian leader Yasser Arafat in a Paris hospital.
21 November	Disputed presidential election sparks the beginning of Ukraine's 'Orange Revolution'.
26 December	A tsunami in the Indian Ocean, sparked by an earthquake off Indonesia, kills up to 220,000.
2005	
23 January	Victor Yushchenko is declared winner of new elections in Ukraine, ending the 'Orange Revolution'.
30 January	Shi'ite successes in elections to a provisional national assembly in Iraq deepen the divisions within the country.
28 February	Over 100 killed in a car bomb in Hilla, Iraq, heralding a major upsurge in violence.
29 April	Syrian military units withdraw from Lebanon after nearly thirty years.
30 May	French referendum rejects proposed European Union constitution, which is subsequently suspended.
24 June	Mahmoud Ahmadinejad elected President of Iran.
7 July	Bomb attacks in London by Islamic militants kill more than fifty people.
22 August	Israel completes removal of Jewish settlers from Gaza strip.
25 October	CIA report states Saddam's regime did not have a relationship with Zarqawi.
2006	
4 January	Israeli premier Sharon is incapacitated by a stroke.
25 January	Hamas wins Palestinian elections.
22 February	Al-Qaeda attack the Golden Mosque in Samarra, the world's most important Shi'ite shrine, effectively making the Iraq conflict a full-scale civil war.
11 April	Iranian President Ahmadinejad reveals his country has enriched uranium.
7 June	Abu Musab al-Zarqawi, head of al-Qaeda in Iraq, killed in US air strike.
12 July to 14 August	Israeli incursions into Lebanon following missile attacks by Hezbollah.
17 August	US Marine Intelligence report says al-Qaeda Iraq has become de facto government of Anbar province.
9 September	Creation of Sahwa, a movement of Sunni Anbar tribal sheiks opposed to al-Qaeda.
9 October	North Korea carries out a nuclear weapons test.
14 October	UN Resolution 1718 calls on North Korea to destroy its nuclear weapons.
26 December	UN Resolution 1737 introduces first sanctions against Iran over its nuclear programme.

PART VII CHRONOLOGY (continued)

30 December	Execution of Saddam Hussein.
2007	
1 January	Bulgaria and Romania join the European Union.
10 January	President Bush launches a 'surge' in troop numbers in Iraq to stem increasing violence.
2 April	US bank New Century files for bankruptcy due to problems with 'sub-prime' mortgages: first real sign of a potential global financial crisis.
7–15 June	Hamas takes control of Gaza strip, leading Palestinian President Abbas to sack the Hamas prime minister, Ishmail Haniya.
17 June	Thirty-five killed in Taliban suicide attack in Kabul, marking major upturn in violence in Afghanistan.
14 July	Russia suspends participation in 'Conventional Forces in Europe' treaty, in opposition to plans for a US missile shield.
9 August	French bank BNP Paribas reports liquidity problems; later seen as marking the start of the global financial crisis.
12 September	British bank Northern Rock asks for support from the Bank of England, deepening concern in global finance.
1 October	Swiss bank UBS reveals major losses thanks to exposure to US 'sub-prime' lending.
13 December	European Union leaders sign Lisbon Treaty, deepening integration.
2008	
17 February	Kosovo declares its independence from Serbia.
2 March	Dmitry Medvedev elected President of Russia; appoints his predecessor, Vladimir Putin, as Prime Minister.
11 March	US Federal Reserve launches $200 billion scheme to prop up the financial system.
21 July	Capture of the former Bosnian Serb leader, Radovan Karadžić, who faces trial for war crimes.
8–13 August	Russia launches invasion of Georgia, in support of separatists in its regions of South Ossetia and Abkhazia.
15 September	Lehman Brothers, US investment bank, files for bankruptcy.
3 October	House of Representatives approves a revised $700 billion financial rescue package.
7–8 October	Icelandic government takes over the country's three biggest banks after mounting financial crisis.
26 November	Over 150 people killed by a terrorist gang in Mumbai, India; subsequently blamed on a Pakistani-based Islamic group.
27 November	Iraqi Parliament approves agreement on the continued presence of US forces in Iraq; final withdrawal set for December 2011.
2009	
3 January	Israeli ground attacks begin on Gaza.
9 January	Susan Crawford, appointed to oversee military commission process at Guantanamo Bay, says methods used there meet the legal definition of torture.
17–18 January	Ceasefire in Gaza fighting.
20 January	Barack Obama succeeds Bush as US President.
4 June	Cairo speech by Obama seeks new relationship between Muslims and the US.
30 June	US troops complete withdrawal from Baghdad and other Iraqi cities.

(continued...)

PART VII CHRONOLOGY (continued)

20 August	Presidential election begins in Afghanistan amid claims of widespread corruption; leads to Karzai's re-election.
25 October	Suicide bombings in Baghdad kill over 150, marking worst violence since before US troop 'surge'.
1 December	Obama announces a 'surge' in Afghanistan, with 30,000 extra troops.
2010	
7 March	Iraqi elections are marred by violence and result in a deadlocked Parliament.
26 March	Sinking of the Cheonan, a South Korean warship by a torpedo; blamed on North Korea.
8 April	Presidents Obama and Medvedev sign the 'New Start' nuclear disarmament treaty in Prague.
23 April	Greece requests a financial bailout by the IMF and European Union after mounting government debt.
31 May	Israeli attack on Gaza-bound aid ships kills nine, provoking a crisis with Turkey.
29 June	China–Taiwan trade deal marks significant improvement in relations.
8 July	At Vienna airport, a ten-person Russian spy ring is 'swapped' for four American agents held by Russia.
21 November	Ireland requests a multi-billion Euro rescue package for its economy from IMF and European Union.
23 November	North Korean artillery attack on a South Korean island provokes weeks of tension.
2011	
14 February	Figures show that China has overtaken Japan as the world's second largest economy.
18 April	Portugal begins talks on an 80 billion Euro bail-out package with IMF and European Union.
2 May	Osama bin Laden is assassinated in Pakistan by US forces.

Take your learning further by viewing the interactive version of this timeline:
www.oup.com/he/young-kent3e

23

The 'War on Terror' and the War in Afghanistan

Chapter contents

A. Terrorism before 9/11

In the later years of the twentieth century, terrorist acts by Middle Eastern groups against Western targets had been strongly linked to the hijacking of airplanes for political purposes. They were not designed to inflict significant civilian casualties as an end in themselves but, by threatening to take innocent lives, force and intimidation were used to try to achieve political goals. The advent of suicide bombers and groups like al-Qaeda changed the relationships between means and ends in the use of terror. A new branch of the Central Intelligence Agency (CIA)—the Counter Terrorist Centre (CTC) had been created in 1986 in the wake of a glut of hijackings and bombings. The CTC was supposed to coordinate the many organizations, civilian and military, operating in the field of intelligence and thus provide centralized data on terrorism. It was thus thrown into the centre of the inter-agency 'turf wars', and the reluctance to share secret information of any kind, which has often characterized the workings of American governments.

As terrorist activities became more significant, some armed groups using force and intimidation were seen as Cold War allies of the US. Islamic groups, notably the Mujaheddin, attacking Soviet forces in Afghanistan after the 1979 invasion, had been seen as providing useful allies against 'godless communism' and the Soviet Union. From what has been gleaned from suicide bombers who survived the detonations of their bombs, the motives for causing havoc and destruction often combined a dissatisfaction about elements of the material world, whose conditions they were having to confront, with strong spiritual or religious beliefs. The harsh conditions in their daily lives, whether or not the direct result of political actions, such as the illegal Israeli occupation of the West Bank, provided a stark contrast with what their religious beliefs led them to expect awaited them after death.

The end of the Cold War had a dramatic, extremely adverse impact on the effectiveness of the CIA in gathering intelligence on terrorists. The lack of a powerful and threatening adversary in the form of the Soviet bloc helped reduce the CIA to a kind of bureaucratic inertia. The numbers of case officers stationed abroad were reduced, and the Directorate of Operations, responsible for covert operations and the recruiting of foreign agents, played a less important role. Even though the CTC received more money and manpower after the World Trade Center bombing of 1993, paperwork, 'procedure', and inter-agency rivalry remained dominant in Washington as the actions of terrorists began to have a bigger impact on US interests. The CIA was frequently in conflict with intergovernmental rivals, notably the National Security Agency, while the Federal Bureau of Investigation (FBI; focused on intelligence-gathering inside the US) continued to resist sharing data through its software systems, well before 9/11 fully exposed the problems.

Despite these glaring weaknesses, the Clinton administration developed measures to deal with the terrorist threat that was identified as emerging in the 1990s, including that from Osama bin Laden's (see Box 23.1) al-Qaeda. It was the World Trade Center bombing which produced the appointment of Richard Clarke, to coordinate security and counter-terrorism in response to the forty groups identified by the State Department as terrorist organizations (see Box 23.2). In the Middle East, groups like Black September, Muslim Jihad, Hamas, and, in Lebanon, Hezbollah were all then vehemently opposed to the existence of Israel. In 1995, terrorists bombed the Riyadh headquarters of the US military training mission and, in 1998, in the most sophisticated attacks so far, al-Qaeda simultaneously destroyed the US embassies in Kenya and Tanzania, killing twelve Americans and more than 200 local people. Clinton had signed Presidential Decision Directive (PDD) 39 in 1995, which instructed the CIA to conduct an aggressive programme of foreign intelligence-gathering and covert action. This could involve the capture of terrorists, by force if necessary, in countries which might be harbouring them, with or without the permission of the host government. Three years later Clinton signed a memorandum which changed the goal of capturing the leader of al-Qaeda, Osama bin Laden, to one authorizing his killing.

Al-Qaeda had no associations with Saddam Hussein. Iraq's secular state was opposed to the Islamic fundamentalism of bin Laden and was dominated by Sunnis, who differed from the Shi'ite Muslims and their interpretation of Islam. (Shi'ites assigned different positions to Mohammed's descendants than did the Sunni Muslims, who wielded political power in Saddam Hussein's Iraq.) Nonetheless, Iraq was very much in the minds of policy-makers in the Clinton administration, for a number of reasons. One was the treatment of Iraqi minorities. After the 1991 Gulf War, Saddam Hussein's use of poison gas against members of the Kurdish minority with separatist claims was a genocidal act, particularly unwelcome to Kuwait's liberators. Clinton had authorized a cruise missile attack on the Mukhabarat (Iraqi secret intelligence) headquarters in Baghdad, following an Iraqi attempt to kill former President George Bush Senior, on a visit to Kuwait in 1993. In addition, the US was concerned about Saddam's obstruction of the UN mission to inspect and dismantle Iraq's weapons of mass destruction (WMD) after the 1991 war. When Saddam suspended cooperation with the UN mission in 1998, Clinton retaliated with four days of air strikes in operation Desert Fox. Political reasons had influenced Bush Senior's decision not to impose regime change on Baghdad, by following up the military successes of the 1991 Gulf War. But it was clear that Saddam remained a thorn in America's side.

In 1998, Clinton also emphasized to the Joint Chiefs of the US Armed Services that he was concerned about Afghanistan, from which it was believed that al-Qaeda was operating, protected by the country's Taliban regime. The President even favoured the deployment of US ground forces to remove terrorist training camps and eliminate bin Laden from Afghanistan, where he had been based since his departure from Sudan in 1996. Such operations were opposed by the military for more than political reasons. The military argument was that it was not yet possible to locate bin Laden precisely and that any operation would lack support from US allies. Furthermore, any operation would require tens of thousand of troops, who would have to be deployed without a suitable staging area, since the US lacked bases close to Afghanistan. Al-Qaeda's attack on the US guided missile destroyer, the USS *Cole* off Aden, which killed seventeen sailors

Figure 23.1 Map of Afghanistan

Source: Bird and Marshall, 2011. Courtesy of Yale University Press.

BOX 23.1

Biography: Osama bin Laden (1957–2011)

Osama bin Laden was born in an upper middle-class neighbourhood of Jeddah, Saudi Arabia, to a Syrian mother Alia Ghanem. He was one of the younger of twenty-five sons of his billionaire father, Mohammed Awad bin Laden, who had acquired his wealth from public works made by renovating and expanding the holy sites of Mecca and Medina. Osama's father was killed in a plane crash when the boy was ten, an event that made the young bin Laden a millionaire in his own right. Inducted into the Muslim Brotherhood as a teenager, at the Al-Thagr High School in Jeddah, the young bin Laden was influenced by the writings of the Egyptian Sayid Qutb, who argued that the Westernized Middle East, after the 1967 Arab–Israeli war, was living in a state of pagan ignorance. Osama went on to study civil engineering at King Abdul Aziz University in Jeddah, but his life was transformed by the events of 1979, with the Iranian Revolution of Ayatollah Khomeini and the Soviet invasion of Afghanistan—the first time since the Second World War that a non-Muslim power had invaded and occupied a Muslim country. The latter propelled him from the comfortable greyness of Saudi middle-class domesticity to fighting the Soviets in Afghanistan. His mentor and ideological influence became the Palestinian cleric, Abdullah Azzam, with whom in 1984 he founded Maktab al-Khidamat, an organization based in Peshawar, Pakistan, to assist Arab volunteers fighting in Afghanistan. When Azzam issued a fatwa in the same year to expel foreign invaders from Islamic lands, it became the first global jihad call. Also in 1984, bin Laden crossed into Afghanistan for the first time and, two years later, established a base for Arab fighters in Jaji, in the east of the country. He used his own wealth to bankroll the various organizations in which he became involved.

Bin Laden's preoccupation with fighting the Soviets led him to distance himself from Azzam, from whom he split in 1988. Bin Laden then met Ayman al-Zawahiri (see Box 23.3) and discovered the Egyptian doctor's more radical views on jihad. It was an eagerness to play a more active role in the fighting which led him to create al-Qaeda from the group of Arab fighters in Afghanistan and Egyptian Islamic Jihad, probably around 1988.

During the 1980s, bin Laden's hatred for the US began to develop, although he had not found such feelings during his visit to the country in 1979. The change was essentially produced by American support of Israel and the rejection of his offer to deploy his forces in defence of Saudi Arabia after the 1990 Iraqi invasion of Kuwait. The Saudi royal family preferred to have

(*continued*)

BOX 23.1 (continued)

American troops deployed in their defence. In 1991, bin Laden left Saudi Arabia to return to Peshawar and, the following year, moved his men to Sudan, where he developed his first plans to attack American targets. Still outraged by the presence of American forces in Saudi Arabia, bin Laden spent the next five years planning attacks on US targets in Africa, resulting in the simultaneous attacks on the American embassies in Kenya and Tanzania in 1998, which killed 224 people and demonstrated the sophistication of the al-Qaeda machine. He was also implicated in the bombings of the World Trade Center in New York in 1993 and a US barracks in Saudi Arabia in 1996.

In May 1996, under pressure from the American government to expel him, the Sudanese government allowed bin Laden to leave for Afghanistan. In August, bin Laden issued his first public statement that he was at war with the US. By identifying the US as the main enemy (in contrast to al-Zawahiri's obsession with the overthrow of Mubarrak's Egyptian government), bin Laden was a key influence in directing jihad against the 'far enemy' as opposed to the 'near enemy' in the Middle East. When Zawahiri arrived in Afghanistan in 1997, bin Laden was much more the charismatic leader of global jihad with near-total control over al-Qaeda. He developed links to radical groups in Yemen, Somalia, and elsewhere, as far afield as Indonesia and the Philippines. Zawahiri's followers were assimilated into bin Laden's organization, whose members had to swear a religious oath of loyalty personally to him. Many of his followers were inspired by his abandonment of a life of luxury in a wealthy Saudi family for an austere and dangerous life devoid of material comforts. Bin Laden delighted in portraying himself as a heroic warrior monk, combining fearlessness with learning. One of his key messages was that the Islamic world had been collectively humiliated for decades by the West, but particularly the US and its policies in the Middle East, with its support for Israel and the regimes Osama believed to be the betrayers of Islam, from Cairo to Riyadh. This, and not American culture itself, was the focus of bin Laden's anti-American campaign. Even though he was willing to blame American citizens for the alleged crimes of their government, there was enough truth in his claims about US government actions, particularly their acceptance of the illegal occupation by the Israelis of land inhabited by Palestinians, for them to have some credibility in the Muslim world. Similarly, he was able to find some justification for his actions in the words of the Koran, even though he was not a religious scholar. In 1998, bin Laden held his first and only press conference to announce the formation of the 'World Islamic Front' to 'do jihad against the Crusaders and Jews'. A virulent anti-Semite, the Israeli–Palestinian conflict and the unflinching American support for Israel were always central to bin Laden's ideas. He saw himself as an instrument of God's will and a humble, even shy man in his dealings with other Muslims.

Bin Laden was in Afghanistan when the 9/11 attacks were launched on New York and Washington, killing nearly 3,000. Already on the FBI's most wanted list, he now became a prime target of the Bush administration for capture or assassination, with a $25 million bounty put on his head. Reports that he had died, either from US bombing raids or kidney failure, proved false. For almost a decade, he remained elusive, taunting the Americans with intermittent audio and, increasingly after 2004, voice tapes, which criticized Western actions and called on Muslims to rise against them. His deputy, Khalid Sheikh Mohammed, was captured in 2003; other senior al-Qaeda figures were located and killed; and Pakistani forces thought they came close to capturing bin Laden himself in 2004, the year in which he finally accepted responsibility for the 9/11 attacks. When the George W. Bush's term of office came to an end, bin Laden was still at large and intelligence leads to his whereabouts had gone dead. Partly to reduce the awe in which bin Laden was held, the next US President, Barack Obama, made few references to him. He was widely thought to be living a nomadic existence on the Pakistan–Afghanistan borders, but in August 2010 the CIA had a possible trace on bin Laden, living in a compound in Abbottabad, Pakistan, less than a mile from the Pakistan Military Academy, where he had been for a considerable time. He was assassinated in Abbottabad in the early hours of 2 May 2011 by US special forces. Questions and accusations immediately began about the role of Pakistan's military and security establishment in protecting him. After his killing, his body was taken out to sea for burial, to avoid a shrine being created for his followers.

in October 2000, did not lead to further attempts to assassinate bin Laden, partly because it could not immediately be proved that al-Qaeda was responsible. But, as Clinton left office, there were further warnings from Richard Clarke about attacks being planned by terrorist organizations and it could already be said that Washington was deeply concerned by the threats from Iraq and bin Laden's camps in Afghanistan.

B. Launching the 'War on Terror'

The bombing of the twin towers of the World Trade Center in New York City, and of the Pentagon in Washington DC, by al-Qaeda operatives using hijacked civilian aircraft, provided dramatic television footage that sent shock waves throughout the world. With three thousand innocent lives lost in a single terrorist operation, the American nation received near-universal sympathy in the immediate aftermath of this horrific and inhuman act. For the first time since 1814, the US was the victim of a significant attack on its home soil, the response to which, as it was developed prior to 2009 by George Bush Jnr's administration, became a vague and often ill-focused 'war on terror', which did much to dissipate that original sympathy. At the same time, the support from some sections of the Islamic world, from which the terrorists benefited by riding the waves of anti-Americanism, also decreased. As a result, the ill-considered US reactions in the 'war on terror' helped extend indiscriminate terrorist killings into different regions of the globe, despite the failure of al-Qaeda to build effectively on what it had carried out on 9/11.

In the initial response to 9/11, no specific measures were suggested, other than to retaliate against the perpetrators, their organization—al-Qaeda—and those who harboured and gave support to it. The nature of the response thus became absorbed into the general reassertion of US power, particularly through the use of 'hard' military power, more than the deployment of 'softer' US influence (using diplomacy, economic measures, and intelligence operations), against those states and groups whose ideologies did not conform to the dominant post-Cold War assumptions that had sprung from American political and economic interests. With the end of the Cold War, the world had increasingly taken for granted the benefits of 'free' market capitalism and liberal democracy, even as problems with some of these assumptions became more evident in the first decade of the twenty-first century, notably with the financial instability that resulted in the post-2008 recession.[1] The initial reaction, of using American military power to retaliate against those who had carried out the 9/11 atrocities had to be directed against the leadership of al-Qaeda, particularly Osama bin Laden and those states who provided him with support and shelter. It had to be implemented within a unilateral framework of US security and military action where allies had lost the importance to the US that the Cold War had earlier provided them. Yet, however necessary such a response may have been, it was never sufficient to translate the ideology of the Bush administration into the reality of an effective new American foreign policy. That would be the task of 'neo-conservative' thinkers within the administration. They soon argued that a combined threat was posed to the US by terrorist groups, the malignant influence of 'rogue' states that supported them, and the dangers of an uncontrolled spread of WMDs—though, ironically, WMDs, in the form of nuclear arsenals, had allegedly provided security and prevented major hostilities in the Cold War. These threats were incorporated and conflated into a 'threat triad' which, neo-conservatives argued, Washington had a duty to destroy.[2]

The idea of a tripartite threat was very much behind Secretary of Defense Donald Rumsfeld's initial encouragement of President Bush to think more broadly about an appropriate response to 9/11, one that went beyond al-Qaeda, about whom Richard Clarke, the National Coordinator for Security, Infrastructure Protection and Counterterrorism had long been sounding strident warnings. The threat presented by al-Qaeda, in the wake of a series of attacks around the world on US interests, was explicitly pointed out prior to the attacks on New York and Washington. As seen, these threats had produced bombings of US targets in the 1990s and, only a few months before Bush took office, the suicide attack on the USS *Cole*. For Rumsfeld, responsibility for these al-Qaeda attacks might be shared specifically by Iraq, Libya, Iran, and Sudan. Already, debate on responses that might help produce a world in which US security would be best enhanced was becoming diffuse and opaque—at least as far as a response to provide an international community less threatened by terrorism was concerned. On 12 September 2011, Richard Clarke was amongst the officials invited by the President to discuss any possible linkages between the 9/11 attacks and Saddam Hussein, when Clarke was only too aware that al-Qaeda—rather than Saddam—was clearly responsible. On the same day, the military director of operations for the Joint Chiefs of Staff was being told by Doug Feith, the Under-Secretary of Defense for policy, and a close ideological associate of Rumsfeld, that he should be looking into Iraq, not al-Qaeda's presence in Afghanistan.

The origins of the group which became known as the neo conservatives lay with the Vietnam War and the 'un-American' counter-culture, with which the 1960s became associated. The roots of this neo-conservatism, paradoxically, were liberal, and emerged from the shock produced by hippies and the counter-culture along with the violence on American streets, sparked by Vietnam, race relations, and poverty at the end of the 1960s. In foreign policy terms, the American defeat in the Vietnam War suggested that the exercise of US power was being limited by the humiliation experienced in Indo-China, the so-called 'Vietnam syndrome'. Overcoming such negative outcomes of the Vietnam War became a key part of the neo-conservative agenda for those who did not accept that the US had overreached the limits of its power. The Committee on the Present Danger, founded in 1976, brought together leading neo-conservatives, some of whom would have roles to play in the Ford and Reagan administrations and in opposing détente. To some extent, the Vietnam syndrome was challenged by the US success, under George Bush Snr, in leading a military coalition in the liberation of Kuwait from Saddam Hussein in 1990–1. But Saddam's continued survival as ruler of Iraq left a sense of unfinished business and his continued threat was highlighted by the Iraqi assassination attempt on Bush Snr in 1993, an event which may have given his son a personal motive for dealing with the problem. Certainly, the neo-conservatives believed in the 1990s that much more could be done to assert American power and shape world affairs in favour of American values. Men such as Donald Rumsfeld (who had already acted as President Ford's Secretary of Defense), Paul Wolfowitz, and Lewis ('Scooter') Libby participated in the Project for the New American Century established in 1997.

These neo-conservatives were to have prominent roles in Bush Jnr's administration and had particular contempt for ideas of 'nation building' and 'peacekeeping' which they regarded, based in part on Clinton's experiences in Somalia, Haiti, and Yugoslavia, as ill-advised and a waste of resources. They rebuked the Clinton administration for merely 'containing' Saddam Hussein rather than removing him and believed that US military power should be used to produce the maximum benefits for US political goals. In other words, the linkage between military and political affairs should be redefined, so that the appropriate use of significant and technically superior military force would, first and foremost, create of itself the desired political end. If the nature of war could be so changed and redefined in accordance with the technological advantages of US forces, then a successful show of strength would produce a more peaceful world. A revolution in warfare would thus lead to a neo-conservative revolution in political affairs, albeit through a bizarre surfeit of wishful thinking. Bush Jnr took power in January 2001, with Rumsfeld again in the Pentagon, determined to institute a significant transformation in the US approach to warfare and in the administrative practices of the Pentagon. 9/11 provided him and other neo-conservatives with

BOX 23.2

George W. Bush and his National Security Team

George W. Bush (b. 1946) was the son of George H. W. Bush, who had been US President from 1989 to 1993. Bush Jnr was born in Connecticut, but largely raised in Texas, where Bush Snr pursued a career in the oil industry. He was educated both at Yale, where he studied history, and at Harvard, where he gained a Masters degree in Business Administration. Critics claimed that his family connections helped him avoid service in Vietnam—instead, he served at home in the Air National Guard—and in 1976 he was found guilty of driving while under the influence of alcohol. He lost his first race for the House of Representatives in 1978 but then, like his father, proved a success in the Texas oil industry, helped run his father's presidential campaigns in 1988 and 1992, and in 1994 he was elected Governor of the state, by which time he had become a committed Christian. The governorship provided him with the base for his successful run as President in 2000, but he only won by a wafer-thin margin against Al Gore, Bill Clinton's Vice- President. The result hinged on voting in Florida, where George's brother, Jeb, was Governor. Bush was re-elected in 2004, again by quite a narrow margin, over John Kerry. As President, Bush sought to cut taxes, but failed to stimulate large-scale economic growth and, partly thanks to heavy defence spending, ran up a substantial government deficit. During his second term, he experienced a number of setbacks, including criticism over his handling of Hurricane Katrina (which devastated New Orleans in August 2005), loss of control in Congress to the Democrats in 2006 and, during his final year of office, the onset of economic recession. In foreign policy, his presidency was dominated by the wars in Iraq and Afghanistan that followed the 9/11 terrorist attacks on the US.

An unusual feature of foreign and defence policy under Bush was the leading role played by Vice-President Dick Cheney (b. 1941), a Nebraskan, educated at the University of Wyoming who, like the President, had avoided service in Vietnam. He came to prominence through working for Donald Rumsfeld in the Nixon–Ford years. Cheney rose to become Ford's Chief of Staff in 1975. Despite suffering several heart attacks, the first in 1978, he was a Congressman for Wyoming for ten years

BOX 23.2 (continued)

between 1979 and 1989. In March 1989, he became George Bush Snr's Secretary of Defense, a post he held until the end of the presidency. This, as well as his extensive knowledge of Washington, his quiet determination, and his reputation for good political judgement, helped make him Bush Jnr's running mate in 2000, although the choice was an unexpected one to political observers. Outwardly undemonstrative and lacking in charisma, as vice-president he took a leading role in shaping policy and was a hard-line supporter of war against Iraq, believing that Saddam Hussein was an ally of al-Qaeda. Cheney was keen to pursue an active foreign policy, unashamedly aimed at what he saw as the defence of American interests, on a unilateral basis if necessary. He also backed a firm response to North Korea's nuclear ambitions, defended the use of 'enhanced interrogation' of suspected terrorists and put the supposed needs of US business before measures to protect the environment.

The other key official for most of the period was Cheney's one-time mentor and close ally, Defense Secretary, Donald Rumsfeld (b. 1932). A graduate of Princeton and a naval officer, Rumsfeld had served as a Republican Congressman for his home state of Illinois in 1962–9 before resigning to take up a post in the Nixon administration. His international experience included time as US Ambassador to NATO in 1973–4, Secretary of Defense in 1975–7 and as President Reagan's special envoy to the Middle East in 1983–4, when he met Saddam Hussein. Rumsfeld, like Cheney was firm in prosecuting the wars in Iraq and Afghanistan. He was also sharp-tongued, sarcastic, and domineering in his defence of Bush's policy, including such controversial aspects as the imprisonment of suspected terrorists without trial at Guantanamo Bay. His position was harmed by the discovery of the abuse of prisoners at Abu Ghraib in 2004, but he only resigned in December 2006 in the face of strong criticisms of his strategy in Iraq from a number of generals. His successor was Robert Gates (b. 1943), who had been Director of the CIA in 1991–3 and who, unusually, remained as Secretary of Defense during the first years of the Obama administration.

Cheney and Rumsfeld did not always work easily with Bush's two Secretaries of State, Colin Powell (b. 1937), the first black candidate, who occupied the position during the first term, and Condoleezza Rice (b. 1954), the first black woman to be Secretary of State, who held it throughout the second. Powell came to the post with a formidable record behind him. He came from a humble background, the son of Jamaican immigrants to New York. Unlike Bush and Cheney, he had served in Vietnam, pursuing a military career and rising to the rank of General. After proving his value as an assistant to the Secretary of Defense, from November 1987 he was Reagan's last National Security Adviser and in 1989–93, under George Bush Snr, he was Chair of the Joint Chiefs of Staff. As Secretary of State, he emphasized the need to work with other countries in dealing with the aftermath of 9/11, but he helped publicly build the case for the invasion of Iraq. Rice, born in Alabama, became interested in international relations while studying at the University of Denver and went on to take a PhD, before pursuing an academic career at Stanford University. She was on the National Security Staff under Bush Snr, specializing in the Soviet bloc. In January 2001, she became the first woman to be appointed National Security Adviser (NSA). Although she faced accusations of having underestimated the danger of terrorist attacks before 9/11, she served as NSA throughout Bush Jnr's first term. The NSA in Bush's second term was Stephen Hadley (b. 1947), who had been on the National Security staff under President Ford, an Assistant Secretary of Defense under Bush Snr, and Deputy NSA to Rice in 2001–5.

the opportunity to translate their ideology into foreign policy, through actions under the auspices of a nebulous concept which was soon to be defined and accepted as the 'war on terror'.

C. The Defeat of the Taliban, 2001–3

In September 2001, after 9/11, the US gained universal sympathy and many willing allies, twenty-five of whom provided active support for the invasion of Afghanistan. The Secretary of State, Colin Powell, argued that allies would be important in any future war to demonstrate international acceptance of American goals. Unfortunately for Powell, the response to 9/11 had the ideological footprint of the neo-conservatives in the Pentagon more than that of external allies. As early as 13 September, Rumsfeld was noting that Saddam Hussein might give WMDs to terrorists, and by the time the President authorized an Afghanistan war plan, Rumsfeld and his civilian staff had been thinking for several months about how to deal with Saddam and Iraq. One week later, on 20 September, Bush, in a speech to Congress, referred publicly to the 'war on terror' for the first time.[3] However much the neo-conservatives focused on the practicalities and logistics of attacking Saddam, the response to 9/11 that was easiest to implement, and to justify, was to react to the refusal of the Taliban to hand over Osama bin Laden for interrogation. The Taliban, led by the cleric Mullah Omar—who had formed the government of Afghanistan since 1994, having won the power struggle following Soviet withdrawal—declined to surrender bin Laden to the Americans or to cease offering shelter to terrorists. Hence, on 27 September, US Special Forces were covertly inserted into Afghanistan to be followed, on 7 October, by American-led air strikes and, in November, by more inter-service special forces and small numbers of Marines.

Initially, the air strikes were against fixed installations, such as fuel depots and storage facilities, and it was not immediately clear whether the operation was to remove bin Laden or the government of the country that was prepared to tolerate his presence. The focus of US operations then changed to attacking the Taliban ground forces, as the US had the support of an indigenous group, the Northern Alliance within Afghanistan, who had long been fighting the Pashtun-dominated Taliban. Thus, overwhelming US air power could be used to support the ground forces of the non-Pashtun Northern Alliance, avoiding the need for significant numbers of US ground troops. This strategy seemed to pay off handsomely in mid-November, when the Northern Alliance seized control of the capital, Kabul. The city of Kandahar, supposedly a Taliban stronghold, fell in early December. The problem was that this saving of US casualties was achieved by relying on tribal warlords from different ethnic groups (such as Tajiks, Uzbeks, and Hazaras) opposed to the Pashtuns. Large amounts of CIA money provided the means to try and counter the impact of historically based tribal allegiances, self-interest, and ethnic divisions, which had long been evident within Afghanistan and the adjacent regions of Pakistan. The Pentagon was thus able successfully to transform US war fighting, from the army's reliance on overwhelming force of numbers, into a more mobile strategy linked to fewer US ground forces and precision air strikes. Initially successful in the Afghan campaign, this enabled US forces, supported by UK and Australian troops, to secure the surrender of what was left of Taliban fighters in December 2001. To the surprise of some, the US had achieved this in under three months, with the loss of only twelve American lives. It seemed an easy victory, one that might not easily be reversed.

Yet Osama bin Laden, on leaving Kabul, had holed up in a labyrinth of caves and tunnels in a remote, mountainous region near the border with Pakistan, called Tora Bora. The CIA chief on the ground was aware that the motley collection of Northern Alliance militias, whose leaders hated each other more than they did al-Qaeda, were unlikely to be able to deal with the hard core of fighters remaining with bin Laden in Tora Bora. His request for just under 1,000 elite US troops was not endorsed by General Franks and the ill-disciplined, lawless forces of different Afghan commanders were essentially relied upon to attack the Tora Bora complex, with the support of American air strikes. This almost certainly enabled the al-Qaeda leader to escape over the border into Pakistan. As 2002 progressed, Afghanistan then began to assume less importance for the US. After all, the defeat of the Taliban seemed complete and Washington's attention now focused on Saddam Hussein, as planning for the invasion of Iraq dominated US concerns.

Between the October 2001 invasion and the end of 2003, the US successes against terrorists implicated in 9/11 were significant. All were found, not in Afghanistan, nor mountainous border areas, but (like Osama bin Laden much later) in urban areas of Pakistan. The most important was Khalid Sheikh Mohammed (KSM), captured in Rawalpindi on 3 March 2003 who, according to the 9/11 report, was the principal mastermind behind the 9/11 attacks. The financer of the hijackers, Mustafa Ahmed al-Hawsawi, was also captured in this period, along with Walid bin Attash, who had played a leading role in the attack on the USS *Cole*, and Ahmed Khalfan Ghailani, who was involved in the 1998 bombing of the US embassies in East Africa. Thus, George Bush's claim in September 2002 that the US was hunting down the killers one by one had some real credibility and, at this point, US policy seemed to be making real progress.

The Limits of Victory

There were, nevertheless, significant qualifications to these 2002–3 successes in Afghanistan, even before the disastrous decision to attack Iraq began to increase the motivation, strength, and capability of terrorist groups operating against the US and its Western supporters. One was the position of Pakistan, clearly an ostensible American ally but deeply mired in a bitter, decades-old rivalry with neighbouring India over the border province of Kashmir, and whose largest intelligence service, the Inter-Services Intelligence

Directorate (ISI), certainly before 2001, had close links with the Taliban, to whom it provided support. The recent extent of its support, given the Pakistani need to be openly behind the US war on terror in order to continue to benefit from US financial largesse, is a matter of much dispute. In addition to the problems of terrorists inside Pakistani cities, the border areas adjacent to Afghanistan of the North West Frontier Province and the Federally Administered Tribal Areas (FATA), contain Pashtun tribes, as in Afghanistan, who have never been subject to effective central government control and who provide Taliban and al-Qaeda operatives and supporters. Thus the 1,519-mile Pakistan–Afghanistan border became a problem from the start of the conflict and later led the Obama administration to refer to the Af-Pak situation. After the flight from Afghanistan, much of al-Qaeda's remaining fighting force was north of Peshawar, in the district of Bajaur, which formed the northernmost part of the FATA, while the Taliban were centred to the south in Quetta, across the Afghan border from Kandahar. Sandwiched in between were the districts of Waziristan, where there was much tribal support for the Taliban from local Pashtuns.

Al-Qaeda was clearly not a terrorist organization sponsored by a state, which the Bush administration had tried to portray as the main danger from terrorism. At best, it was a parallel state to that operated by the Taliban. Initially, a highly centralized body, well versed in the controls that all bureaucracies are designed to promote, the loss of its base in Afghanistan helped begin its transformation into a more fragmented structure. With or without the war on terror, Osama bin Laden also certainly failed to achieve his goals of removing those Middle Eastern regimes who did not want to become religious states as part of a new Muslim caliphate. Even if he had not focused so much attention on the US as the distant enemy, and directed his efforts against the more vulnerable Middle Eastern regimes, bin Laden's global jihad through the use of terror would have been regarded as unjustifiable in the eyes of many Muslims. Yet, as new manifestations of terror became evident, the war on terror fought by the Bush administration was extended without proper consideration of its political impact on the world, even if the effectiveness of the operatives of some militant Islamic groups was reduced.

In January 2002, after its initial success against the Taliban, the US began withdrawing CIA agents and special forces from Afghanistan, allegedly to allow them to train for Iraq. In June 2002, the Bush Doctrine was expanded to include pre-emptive actions against possible threats and significantly shifted the emphasis of US defence and security policy. It was incorporated in the new National Security Strategy, made public in September 2002—a change which was accompanied by the fundamental shifts in policy on Iraq and Afghanistan. However, even the most ardent advocates of the already planned-for invasion of Iraq believed that the war would have to be sold carefully to the US public. Thus, the White House Iraq Group consisting of Karl Rove, Bush's long-time adviser; Condolezza Rice, the National Security Adviser; Andrew Card, the White House Chief of Staff; and 'Scooter' Libby was established, partly to do just that. Possession of nuclear weapons by Saddam Hussein was central to 'spinning' the Iraqi threat, and going into the November 2002 mid-term elections on a platform of national security against terrorism was central to Karl Rove's Republican political strategy. Maximizing the supposed extent of the threat to justify the war on terror was one part of the public relations equation. But US allies would need more convincing of the need for, or value of, exercising US power to produce regime change in Iraq when there appeared to be no connection between Saddam and al-Qaeda or the 9/11 attacks.

The growing focus on Iraq meant that constructing an Afghan nation free from the influence of the departing Taliban was not a central requirement for the Bush administration. Indeed, both the wars in Iraq and Afghanistan turned out to be object lessons in how military success can prepare the ground for political failure. In Washington, Rumsfeld in particular felt the same lack of enthusiasm that many Afghan fighters had for nation-building and peacekeeping. Having large military forces in place for war fighting was not his ideal, but then to tarnish them with such civilian tasks as peacekeeping and reconstruction was to be avoided at all costs. One of the aims and advantages of the new military strategy was to ensure that US troops were not in place to be dragged into such nation-building operations. Yet the situation created through the war on terror and the operations in Afghanistan soon became highly problematic. The first problem grew from the erosion, if not complete destruction, of important principles and agreements to which the US had previously subscribed and came with the dilemma of what to do with those Taliban fighters, or terrorists, captured in Afghanistan. American troops

Figure 23.2 Map of the North-West Frontier Province and Federally Administered Tribal Areas, Pakistan

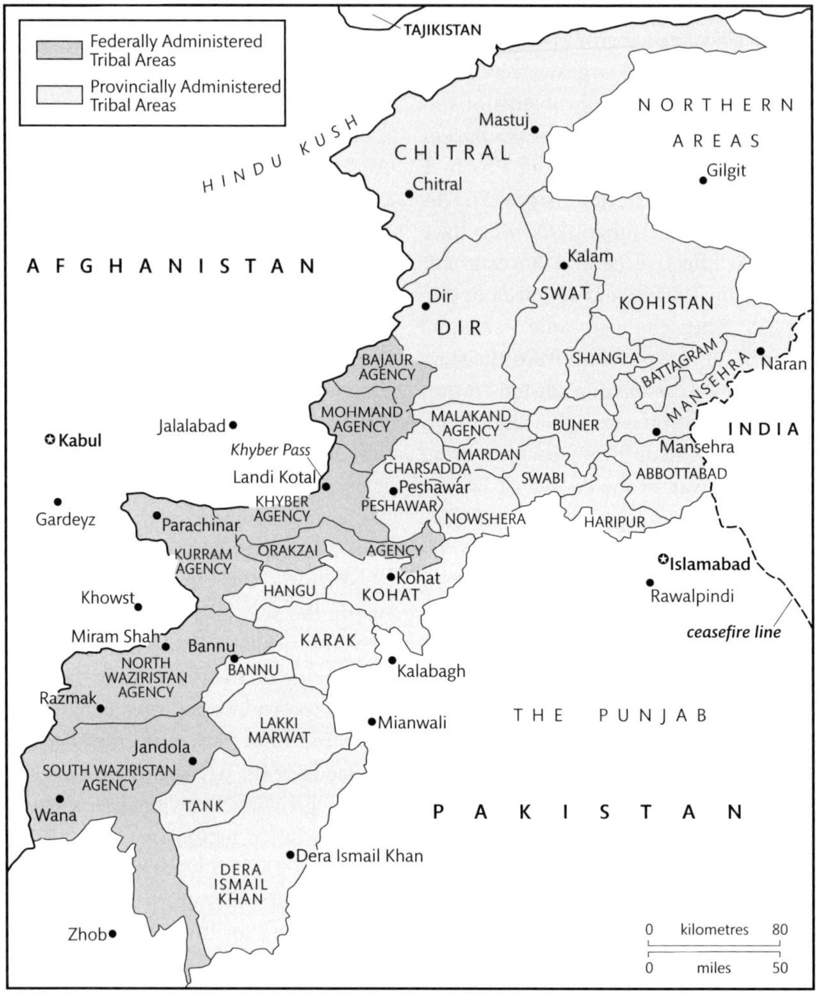

Source: Bird and Marshall, 2011. Courtesy of Yale University Press.

had captured hundreds of suspected terrorists and in November 2001 the President signed an executive order permitting the military to detain such captured 'enemy combatants', without access to the procedures of federal courts to determine if a prisoner had been legally detained.[4] The Bush administration also decided, in what has been seen as an attack on the rule of law—a long-held US value and practice—to detain such captors without the protection of the long-running Geneva Convention. Before any prisoners had arrived at the US military base in Guantanamo Bay, Cuba, the justifications for this were provided by the Office of Legal Counsel, in a memorandum by John Yoo. Yoo argued that al-Qaeda as a stateless entity was not protected by the Geneva Convention, and that the Taliban ran a failed state whose treaty rights could be ignored. In other words, their fighters were 'unlawful combatants'. On 2 February 2002, a presidential executive order gave effect to that view. Although the US was a signatory to the Geneva Convention giving rights to prisoners in any type of conflict, these combatants from Afghanistan would not be treated as prisoners of war and would thus be open to prosecution for any criminal acts. Yet the situation at Guantanamo was that, like prisoners of war, the Afghan prisoners were treated as persons who could be held indefinitely without charge and a court appearance. It took until 2006 before the Supreme Court reversed this and granted protection under the Geneva Convention to all captured 'enemy combatants' held in American custody. Meanwhile, the US government's behaviour attracted widespread criticism.

The second associated problem arose from the general threat to American values and its standing in the world, which the war on terror unleashed, and was contained in the new interrogation methods. These were justified by the supposed benefits of 'meeting terror with terror', through the use of 'coercive interrogations'. The practice soon developed of holding suspects abroad in foreign prisons or camps through a process of 'extraordinary rendition'. Coercive interrogations included sleep deprivation, extended nudity, waterboarding (the simulation of drowning), confinement in cramped boxes, face slapping, and dietary manipulation. Such practices, always regarded by some as torture, were justified by former Vice-President Dick Cheney in 2009 on the spurious grounds that, without a number of Bush administration actions, including enhanced interrogation techniques, the US would have been attacked again. Evidence suggests, however, that little valuable information was gained from such techniques and, in the past, the US had been quick to condemn other states who used torture. The treatment of prisoners in unacceptable ways culminated in the events at the Abu Ghraib prison in Iraq, some of which were filmed and posted online in 2004. An Army reserve unit, the 372nd Military Police Company, had abused naked prisoners. One was forced to crawl on his stomach as military police urinated and spat on him before a beating. In total, twenty prisoners died at Abu Ghraib. Eleven soldiers were subsequently court martialled, convicted, and given terms in military prison, and dishonourably discharged from service. As Admiral Dennis Blair pointed out in 2009, the tarnishing of the American image and the damage done to US global interests far outweighed any benefits obtained from such harsh treatment of prisoners.[5]

A third problem was that the Bush administration set aside national laws that prohibited warrantless surveillance on American citizens. One US citizen, later held at Guantanamo Bay, was denied his constitutional rights under the Fifth Amendment. Worse was to come before the end of the second year of the war in Iraq.

D. The Taliban Revival

In 2002–3, only about thirty US soldiers had been killed in Afghanistan, but the numbers trebled in 2005. This can essentially be explained by the increasing preoccupation in 2002 with planning the war on Iraq and the consequences of failing to plan effectively for anything other than military success. In Afghanistan, the aversion with which Rumsfeld and his supporters in the Pentagon felt for nation-building added to the difficulties that producing money to cover its costs always presented. The State Department and Colin Powell had a very different view from the Pentagon about the need for peacekeeping forces. Yet, with Rumsfeld having opposed any international peacekeeping force outside Kabul as unnecessary in February 2002, it was clear that Afghanistan was no longer going to be at the centre of a pro-active US strategy to deal with terrorists and their supporters. The winning of the war for American values, according to some in Washington, should have provided the Afghans with the required dose of much-needed reality. With the formal ending of operations against the Taliban in March 2002, some 18,000 members of the American-led military command and some 4,500 European members of the International Security and Assistance Force (ISAF, which had begun operations in January) were deployed in Afghanistan. ISAF eventually drew in contributions from forty-two different states, highlighting the extent of international sympathy for the war on terror after the events of 9/11. They included NATO members, long-standing US allies like Australia, New Zealand, and South Korea, and newer partners like Georgia and Azerbaijan, although most deployed fewer than a thousand troops. It was hoped in Washington that the Europeans and others would take the lead in assisting the Afghans to move forward in line with the Western model of constitutions and elections. But the victorious elements, within and without the Northern Alliance, had more interest in, and experience of, fighting each other than working together to build a nation. Even more significantly, a small number of troops, mainly US and British, were regarded as a necessary light touch in Afghanistan to avoid imposing a heavy external imprint on Afghan society, against which local feelings might react.[6]

Thus, with peacekeeping in theory provided by ISAF, America's allies were set institution-building tasks. The British were given the job of tackling the narcotics trade, in particular trying to reduce poppy production by Afghan peasants, which fed the demand for drugs in the West. The only roles for the US military would be in hunting down bin Laden and the Taliban, while training the Afghan National Army. This was itself problematic, as the Americans provided a plentiful supply of money, which eventually resulted in higher wages for Afghan forces than for those working for the government as civil servants. Stabilization was deemed to be the only real requirement, and in August 2003 NATO, in a major extension of its 'out-of-area' responsibilities after the Cold War, formally took over the leadership of ISAF and responsibility for security in the capital. The limited numbers of US soldiers meant that security effectively remained with the Afghan warlords, although in December 2001, during talks in Bonn, the US and its allies had helped set up a provisional government, under a Pashtun, Hamid Karzai. In November 2004, Karzai easily won a presidential election, which arguably marked the high point of Afghanistan's recovery, even if the economy was dominated by corruption and the opium trade. Thereafter, the rebuilding of Afghanistan continued to be neglected, as access to development money was restricted and the growing problems of the war in Iraq assumed more significance. The result was that Afghanistan got a mere fifth of the money being spent on Iraq. The Western input did not strengthen government institutions, or begin to establish a strong relationship between state and society. Instead, it opened the door to the kind of neo-liberal privatized enterprises operating in fiefdoms, where warlords were more in evidence than state bureaucrats. Between 2001 and 2005, the lack of a reconstruction programme increased the effects of economic liberalization in creating more instability in an already war-shattered country. During this time, the US spent eleven times more on military operations, however limited, than the combined amount it gave for reconstruction, humanitarian aid, and assistance, or even the training of Afghan soldiers. Also, 70 per cent of that aid was conditional upon US goods or services being purchased to encourage a 'thriving private sector' in Afghanistan.[7] In December 2005, as NATO agreed to an expanded role, Rumsfeld ordered 3,000 American troops, one-sixth of the force, out of the country. That same month, following elections a few months before, an elected Parliament met in Kabul for the first time in a generation, but it was a fractured body, largely composed of groups loyal to particular warlords.

From 2003, the growing weakness of the Afghan state and the apparent neglect by Western powers slowly facilitated a growing Taliban resurgence based on a hardcore of Pashtun fighters supplemented by foreign fighters, including Chechens and Arabs. It was based on a Pashtun village network expanding in the rural areas through local Islamic clergy. Mullah Omar, the Taliban leader, who had escaped from Afghanistan in December 2001, established a leadership council in 2003 in the Pakistani city of Quetta to provide an organizational structure at the top. The numbers of Taliban fighters grew to reach 17,000 in 2006, the year in which they became a real menace to Afghan stability. Alongside this revival, the Taliban also became divided for a number of reasons. One was the fractured nature of the Pakistani government. As noted above, elements in the Pakistani military, in particular, had had close ties with Afghanistan's Taliban government; but now some Pakistani leaders were determined to align themselves with the US in the war against terror. In 2002, the incursions of the Pakistani army into the FATA in the hunt for Osama bin Laden and al-Qaeda members helped produce Tehrik-i-Taliban Pakistan (TTP), a formally separate organization, which took up arms in 2004. The Taliban in Pakistan grew closer to al-Qaeda than their Afghan counterparts and by 2009 a split was developing between the two movements. Another divisive element was the return to south-eastern Afghanistan from Iran of Gulbuddin Hekmatyar, who was eventually involved in peace talks with the Karzai government in 2008. With the Taliban finding it difficult to establish an effective military operational force, as opposed to small bands of fighters, the US initially remained sanguine about their re-emergence.[8]

By 2006, as casualties began to mount, an optimistic view of Afghanistan was no longer sustainable. The extent of the Taliban revival since 2003 could no longer be concealed, nor could American delusions about the situation in Afghanistan be maintained. Despite attempts to blame the deteriorating situation on the inadequacies of ISAF, which took responsibility for security throughout Afghanistan from October 2006, the US did not seriously attempt to deal again with the Afghanistan problem until an improvement began in Iraq in 2008. By then, being in Afghanistan was more dangerous for American troops than a tour of duty in Iraq. The Karzai government was unsuitable for dealing with local problems, although the full scale of the difficulties did not become apparent until the British attempted to extend the government's authority into

Helmand province, in the south. The division between the hunt for terrorists on the one hand, and NATO's commitment to counter-insurgency, reconstruction, and stabilization on the other, became more of a problem with the Taliban's resurgence, which made stabilizing Afghanistan a remote and difficult prospect. Yet, for a long time Rumsfeld, faced with problems in Iraq, was determined to scale down the American military commitment in Afghanistan and have NATO forces play a larger role. For the British, also bogged down in the quagmire in Iraq, there was the incentive to solve that problem and keep on good terms with the Americans, by redeploying troops from Iraq to Afghanistan.

The key southern provinces were Kandahar and Helmand, the former the spiritual heart of the Taliban movement, the latter a complex mix of tribal rivalries and armed drug gangs. The Canadians asked to be responsible for Kandahar and the British ended up in Helmand, having given more thought to their position in NATO than to what would be required of them in the troublesome province. With limited intelligence and inadequate knowledge of the terrain or of the insurgency that faced them, the British initially had little idea of the tribal dynamics there or the connections to drug mafias and local militias. Their assumption was that the way forward was the extension of central government control and the creation of a more powerful state, so as to pacify the geographical space occupied by the insurgents. This failing was linked to inappropriate neo-liberal assumptions about the economic and political values of free markets and democracy. The latter, in a strong state, would be the answer to the problem of terrorism and the means to provide security, supplemented by the activities of non-governmental aid agencies. A strong democratic state in Afghanistan, complete with such elements as free elections and women's rights, was also seen as necessary, not just for the security of the region, but also as a prerequisite of Western security. Yet, confronted with the realities of the Afghan situation, the elected Karzai government pleaded for the rearmament of forces hostile to the Taliban to help provide security. How democracy and a strong state could be conjured up, let alone support Western economic values, was now increasingly unimaginable.[9]

The small British force in the vast province of Helmand had no choice but to work with the power realities, but was initially ill-disposed to do so. The failure of the West to appreciate that the Pashtuns of southern Afghanistan had hardly ever been effectively governed from Kabul in the twentieth century, but that they had a complex, if non-hierarchical, form of governance unrelated to Western concepts of 'good governance', formed a considerable obstacle. Pashtun society was based on social responsibility and justice, with individual conduct dominated by rigid codes of honour and revenge, and was particularly unsuited to externally imposed concepts of political order. To make matters worse, what little influence Kabul had in 2002 over the leaders of the quarrelling tribes who opposed the Taliban was reduced by the British insistence that corrupt provincial governors, even though they were loyal to Karzai, should be removed. It would have been more logical to send a larger force to fill the security gap this created, or to accept that a small force would have to work with the existing power structures on the ground. The British initially chose to do neither and the problem was compounded by the confusing command structure involving the Americans and NATO. Even worse, the British initially chose to deploy their small forces in pockets which became the focus of Taliban attacks, which then wreaked devastation on the surrounding area as the British relied on air attacks to try to regain control of the situation. It was a classic failure of counter-insurgency strategy that not only neglected the need to win over the local population, but was actually guaranteed to produce hostility.

Between 2006 and 2008, violence rose dramatically as the Taliban, now composed of a range of elements, not all of them jihadists, defied attempts at control, especially in the south, where the Pashtuns predominated. In early 2007, some attempts in Musa Qala, in the north of Helmand province, to broker a deal involving local leaders in contact with the Taliban, failed to break the US commitment to manufacturing effective central government by using Western military forces. In that year, insurgent attacks in Afghanistan rose by more than a quarter, with the most dramatic rise in violence in Helmand province. The Afghan conflict was now facing an increasingly effective insurgency focused on different Taliban elements. Some were tribesmen alienated by corrupt local officials or leaders; others had a central focus on the future of Afghanistan; others were criminal elements seeking material gain, while some were radical jihadists. Yet, whatever the contribution of Western failings following the American shift in priorities from Afghanistan to Iraq, the Taliban revival was fundamentally produced by forces emanating from Pakistan.[10]

The Problem of Pakistan

The war in Afghanistan against al-Qaeda had always been closely influenced by the actions of Pakistan. By the time the Taliban had returned in strength to Afghanistan in 2006, a key problem for the US in the war on terror was deciding whether Pakistan was attempting to defeat the terrorists, or whether its actions constituted an element of the actual terrorist problem in the region. The Pakistani army could sometimes act against its erstwhile Taliban allies, in order to convince the Americans that it was a useful ally in the war on terror. But some elements, notably in military intelligence, still retained links to the Taliban and continued to tolerate them in Pakistan. The difficulty in determining what role was being played by Islamabad, at which time, explains the oscillations in US policy to Pakistan. With Pakistan a long-standing ally of the US, going back to the Cold War, American policy ranged from an effusive supply of aid to be used by Islamabad in the fight against the Taliban and al-Qaeda, to condemnation of Pakistan's protection of the militant groups and perpetrators of terrorist attacks in the region.

After President Pervez Musharraf seized power in October 1999, through a bloodless military coup that overthrew the elected government of Nawaz Sharif (Prime Minister since 1997), the dilemma for Washington only increased. At that time, Pakistan's overriding priority was its power-political rivalry with India, primarily reflected in the dispute over Kashmir and both countries' possession of nuclear weapons. There were repeated war crises between the two neighbours: in December 2001, for example (after a suicide bombing of the Indian Parliament), and in May 2002 (when Pakistan carried out nuclear-capable missile tests). Pakistan had been more than willing to use radical Muslim groups to infiltrate Indian Kashmir, tying down large numbers of Indian soldiers. The presence of radical Islamists in Pakistan enormously increased after the US-led invasion of Afghanistan, when al-Qaeda and their Taliban allies simply moved across the border in the winter of 2001–2. Initially, the preference for those fleeing from Afghanistan was to seek refuge in Pakistan's teeming cities, rather than the remote and lawless FATA. For most Pakistani elites—civilian or military—the main external issue was the rivalry and open conflict that had been simmering for decades with their Indian neighbours. The role of US military and economic aid and assistance was always defined through that lens by Pakistan, with Afghanistan seen as a source of strategic depth against India. The Inter-Services Intelligence Agency (ISI) was thought to have links with militant groups connected to al-Qaeda.

In the years 2002–6, when, because of Iraq, Afghanistan had largely been under the radar, the Pakistani authorities handed over to the Americans nearly 400 suspected militants for millions of dollars. This followed Musharraf's decision, in the wake of 9/11, to support US action against Afghanistan—a step which also led the US to ease the sanctions that it had imposed on Pakistan in 1998, after the country tested a nuclear device. Pakistan also served as the main supply conduit for the Western forces in Afghanistan. By 2004, the US–Pakistani relationship seemed healthy. Despite Musharraf's concentration of power in his own hands, he initiated a ceasefire with India over Kashmir in December 2003 and finally launched military operations against al-Qaeda bases in Pakistan in mid-2004, supported by the American use of unmanned drones (small, guided cruise missiles) to target the terrorists. But it soon became clear that not all might be as it seemed. A number of unsuccessful military operations in the FATA took place and suspicions that Musharraf was merely giving the impression of being a staunch American ally were increased by these operations, which often coincided with the visits of important US officials. A series of Pakistani 'peace' agreements on a local basis with the Taliban, in 2005–6, gave credence to the idea of Musharraf being a master of rhetoric, rather than an implementer of anti-terrorist policy. There was a build-up of Taliban forces from 2003 in the FATA and the North-West Frontier Province and, as the Pakistani government continued to align itself publicly with the US, the ISI continued to maintain strong links with radical Islamist groups in Kashmir, whose members were recruited from the same Islamic schools or training camps as the Afghan supporters of Mullah Omar.

President Musharraf himself banned radical Islamist groups in Pakistan in early 2002, but he also had to balance opponents of military rule on the political left, in the form of Pakistan People's Party, led by Benazir Bhutto, who had been Prime Minister in 1988–90 and 1993–6, before leaving the country in the face of corruption charges. Musharraf founded his own, independent Muslim League in Pakistan in 2002, but political instability continued. In 2007, the bloody siege of Islamabad Red Mosque, occupied by supporters of the radical imam Abdul Rashid Ghazi, caused many of the militant jihadist groups in Pakistan to turn against the government. Led by the TTP, they mounted an offensive in the Swat valley against the Pakistani military, which evidently lost control of that region. Musharraf responded by tightening his authoritarian grip on power, culminating in a declaration of emergency rule in November 2007.

The Bush administration now believed that the US was being cheated with the millions of dollars it had used to underwrite the Musharraf regime, much of which had been spent on building up forces against India, rather than on fighting against al-Qaeda. In 2007, pressure from both domestic opposition groups and from Washington helped produce elections, which led to the end of Musharraf's dictatorial rule the following year. But the assassination of Benazir Bhutto, in a suicide bombing, during the December 2007 election campaign showed that instability was likely to continue, especially since the security forces were accused of failing to protect her. Pakistan, with its ambiguous and inconsistent response to Islamic militancy, was increasingly seen as the crux of the regional security problem, but also as a state in danger of collapse, not least because the global financial crisis of 2007–8 had a serious impact on the Pakistan economy, forcing it to borrow heavily from the IMF. Meanwhile, Pakistan continued to develop its nuclear capabilities and the fragility of relations with India was exposed in November 2008, when attacks in the Indian city of Mumbai were found to be the work of a Pakistan-trained terrorist group. To the ISI, the geopolitical advantages that the radical Islamists in Afghanistan provided in the struggle with India still exceeded the drawbacks they brought. Hence, the ongoing crisis in the Swat valley epitomized the conflictual dilemmas within Pakistani society and government. Thus, despite the removal of Musharraf in August 2008 and his replacement, as President, by Benazir Bhutto's widower, Asif Ali Zardari, by the end of the Bush administration Pakistan was a more unstable place than when the war on terror was launched.

Meanwhile, in the summer of 2008, the confusion in the West's command arrangements in Afghanistan was finally tackled with the appointment of General David McKiernan as commander of all US and NATO forces (apart from US special forces). For the first time, McKiernan changed the rules of engagement to emphasize the use of proportionate force when responding to Taliban attacks. The aim was to reduce the number of civilian casualties. McKiernan also began making contacts with the many Afghan tribes. He also requested 20,000 extra troops, reminiscent of the 'surge' idea that had recently been used with success in Iraq, to supplement the existing 32,000 on the ground. In his last weeks in office, President Bush agreed to send 10,000 troops. Moreover, the operations of al-Qaeda had generally been disrupted, and with the organization becoming more and more disjointed, its significant role in Iraq had ended by 2008. In the wake of 9/11, after which homeland security in the US was greatly tightened, groups associated with al-Qaeda had launched a number of suicide bomb attacks against American allies, notably in Bali (killing over 200 in October 2002), Madrid (where more than 200 died in March 2004), and London (with 50 killed in July 2005). But its capabilities had then declined as those of Western intelligence services grew. Yet these positive signs for the war on terror were countered by the growing cooperation between al-Qaeda and Taliban forces in the region bordering Afghanistan and Pakistan. The FATA became more important for both organizations, hence the crisis in the Swat valley, where the Pakistani government tried to bring about a ceasefire agreement in early 2009, before launching a large-scale military intervention in May.

E. Obama's War

When Barack Obama entered the White House in January 2009, the war in Afghanistan was rudderless and progress on the war on terror was going backwards. The President was also faced with defining a new approach in the wake of the improved, but far from stable, situation in Iraq. Obama was eager to define strategic goals and focus the objectives in Afghanistan and Pakistan on the disruption, dismantling, and defeat of al-Qaeda. As with the campaign against the Taliban, the issue was how best to achieve that goal through military means but, as under Bush, the rhetoric of lofty and vague objectives came first. Having begun by putting US forces in place on the ground, the Bush administration had then been keen to reduce their numbers but had gone back to supporting their value by the time Obama won the 2008 presidential election. How military force would produce effective and democratically accountable government, while removing corruption, was never stipulated. In Afghanistan, the need to create a viable economy to replace the links between the insurgents and the narcotics trade meant defining a form of capitalism which could somehow function within the difficult socio-economic and political environments existing in the region—hardly an easy task.

The Obama administration's review of the situation was led by Bruce Riedel, a veteran of the CIA who had formulated South Asian policy under Clinton. Another participant was General David Petraeus, whose strategy had earlier turned the tide in Iraq. The Taliban forces had roughly quadrupled in size between 2006 and 2009, and Petraeus made the point that the number of troops needed to stabilize the situation in Afghanistan would be nearer to 300,000 than the 30,000 now requested. Nevertheless, the consensus was in favour of deploying more counter-insurgency forces. The Secretary of Defense, Robert Gates, who defined Afghanistan rather than Iraq as the new administration's main challenge, replaced McKiernan with General Stanley McChrystal, as he was keen to see the latter apply his counter-insurgency skills in Afghanistan. However, Vice-President Joe Biden was a dissenter from the main view, advocating an alternative strategy which became known as counter-terrorism. Here the military emphasis, with a similar number of troops, was on improving the capability and training of Afghan forces to deal with the Taliban. This drew unfortunate memories of Richard Nixon's 'Vietnamization' policy after 1969, when the US had built up South Vietnamese forces to fight the communists, while American forces were reduced in size, a policy that had failed to prevent the collapse of South Vietnam in 1975. Counter-insurgency in Iraq provided a more positive comparison, given the apparent success of Petraeus's strategy there in 2008. Afghan society and culture was, however, very different from that of Iraq and Biden's strategy had certain advantages: it did not involve strengthening a central administration, nor providing additional US troops. In addition to building up the Afghan army, the aim was to prevent the Taliban from controlling cities and to deny training camps to al-Qaeda, while using drone attacks to eliminate key individual terrorists.

US drone attacks had their own difficulties, however. They had begun in the FATA on a significant scale in 2004 and the recorded attacks in 2008 had escalated to thirty-five, despite the criticism of the collateral damage and the deaths inflicted on innocent civilians. The Brookings Institution, based in Washington, estimated that at the start of the Obama administration ten civilians were killed in drone attacks for every militant suspect. There was also the issue of carrying out such attacks on the territory of a sovereign state, Pakistan, which was technically allied to the US, irrespective of the numbers of displaced persons in the FATA and North-Western province, which the UN now estimated to be around 6 million. It was no coincidence that the number of suicide bombings in Pakistan was six in 2006, but that this rose to fifty-six in 2008. The problems of large numbers of displaced, impoverished people in disease-ridden refugee camps was all part of the consequences of the war on terror being fought in Pakistan. Such was the situation in the newly defined 'Af-Pak' (Afghan-Pakistan) theatre in the early months of the Obama administration. Unsurprisingly, it did not take long before the administration began a search for an exit strategy.

Riedel's review of overall strategy for Afghanistan and the numbers of American troops needed to implement it was accompanied by the 2009 Afghan presidential election campaign, which was expected to provide Hamid Karzai with another term of office, but was disrupted by Taliban attacks. Karzai had his critics and was hardly a model candidate. In addition to the corruption surrounding his regime, which appeared likely to extend into the electoral process, there were his connections to the warlords, with whom he had initially played an important conciliatory role. Yet there was no more suitable candidate for the Americans and despite, or because of, the existence of fraudulent ballot papers, Karzai emerged as the electoral victor in November 2009, with a disappointingly low turnout.[11] Meanwhile, the US continued significantly to increase the numbers of drone attacks in the FATA, despite the civilian casualties they produced. A notable success was the killing of Baitullah Mehsud, the leader of TTP, in August 2009. The nature of the terrain, the regional dynamics, and the reluctance of the Bush administration to face up to the problems of nation-building, let alone pay for it, had handicapped any successful implementation of the war on terror on both sides of the lawless Afghan–Pakistan border. The success of counter-insurgency in Iraq ensured that Obama initially agreed to the extra troops desired by the military commander General McChrystal. These 30,000 extra troops were sent in November 2009, which, added to earlier expansions in February–March 2009, took the total of US troops to about 100,000. But this was accompanied by the caveat that their withdrawal would begin in 2011.

Biden's alternative strategy for the war on terror attached more regional importance to Pakistan and was based on the deployment of fewer US and NATO forces in Afghanistan. It also attached greater importance to specifically targeting al-Qaeda and emphasized that a violent, unstable Pakistan was the most important danger to guard against. As the debate progressed in Washington, in Afghanistan the impact of McChrystal's counter-insurgency 'clear, hold, build' on the ground was that Taliban forces were driven from the south of Afghanistan, but established a growing presence in the northern provinces of Kunduz and Faryab during 2009. In May of the same year, the major operation in the Swat valley carried out by Pakistani forces involved some 15,000 troops with air support and the use of drones. This added to the chaos and destruction brought about by the previous smaller and unsuccessful campaigns since 2008, with some 3 million displaced persons to accompany the successful elimination of Baitullah Mehsud.

Doubts were also cast over the likely success of counter-insurgency in Afghanistan by the fact that much Taliban success stemmed from being able to exploit local village grievances in rural areas, for which a strategy of controlling large urban population centres, as in Iraq, was unsuitable. Afghanistan had a much larger population than Iraq and the mountainous, sometimes impenetrable areas are more conducive to insurgents than Iraq. McChrystal asked for yet more troops in October 2009 to bring the additional US forces up to 40,000, and for more resources to build up Afghanistan security forces at a cost of around $10 billion per year for five years—virtually doubling the size of the army and police. For some in Washington, this was both unnecessary and impossible to achieve, given the limited effectiveness of existing Afghan forces and the doubts over their loyalty and capabilities.

December 2009 was the first month since the 2003 invasion without deaths of US soldiers in Iraq, and the commitment to withdraw from there was starting to be implemented. However, a renewed focus on the conflict in Afghanistan offered little or no prospect of a decisive outcome and continued to drain Western lives and resources. By now, the Taliban had expanded its operations into all but one province and the use of improvised explosive devices against Western troops (IEDs) had increased, with deadly effect. A year into the Obama administration, more questions were being asked about the ultimate goals in Afghanistan and their attainability. In the Swat valley, peace and prosperity were no nearer than the eradication of terrorism, despite, or because of, the Pakistani military campaigns. Far from it, Taliban strength and influence within Pakistan was continuing to grow, despite the blows suffered by the terrorists of the Swat valley. In addition, there was a dramatic increase in terrorist attacks within Pakistan as a whole (a suicide bomb in Peshawar in August 2009 killed more than a hundred), while in Afghanistan the long-term objective of defeating the Taliban still remained a distant goal. How vast the required outlay of American manpower and resources would be to achieve a viable Afghan state, free of the Taliban menace, had yet to be specified, let alone accepted by the US public. Some thought that, perhaps, McChrystal's requests were just the tip of the iceberg. After all, in parts of the country, the Taliban was now an integral part of Afghan society, so it might only be practical and desirable to prevent it taking control of Kabul and Kandahar, while negotiating an honourable US retreat—a process again eerily similar to Nixon's withdrawal from Vietnam. After McChrystal was fired by Obama for insubordination in an interview with the magazine *Rolling Stone* in June 2010, thinking in Washington seemed to be more focused on increasing the number of drone attacks and finding the exit door along the lines of Biden's thinking.

By 2010, Afghanistan was the second most corrupt country in the world according to Transparency International, being topped only by Somalia, a failed state. McChrystal's call for 'trainers' from NATO countries for the Afghan military and police was consistently not being met, as America's allies themselves sought an exit strategy from the quagmire. The Dutch announced their departure in August 2010 and the new French President, François Hollande, announced an early withdrawal of his nation's troops in May 2012. At best, the progress being made in 2010 was mixed, and, as David Petraeus succeeded McChrystal, another Obama policy review was scheduled for December. The only thing that was certain, given the divided views in Washington and the continued troubles in the Af-Pak region, was that a major offensive in Kandahar must be portrayed as a success. In the event, Petraeus's portrayal of success, as in Vietnam, had to resort to focusing on the numbers of Taliban fighters captured or killed. In the wake of the large amounts of US aid money that was now flowing into southern Afghanistan and assisting the corruption, the progress depicted by official US reports provided a marked contrast to the much bleaker pictures painted by international agencies. In September, the International Institute for Strategic Studies in London reported essentially in favour of Biden's strategy, now defined as containment and deterrence. In the US, the New American Foundation outlined an approach of peace and reconciliation, emphasizing the need to step back from counter-insurgency in Afghanistan and to concentrate more on fighting al-Qaeda and safeguarding homeland security in America.

One major success for Obama was Operation Neptune Spear, the assassination of Osama bin Laden, carried out by US special forces on 2 May 2011, in a residential compound in Abbottabad, Pakistan. By then, al-Qaeda was no longer the tight hierarchical organization it once had been, although the increased terrorist incidents in Pakistan were not unrelated to bin Laden's call in 2007 for attacks on the Pakistani state. But for some elements in Pakistan, bin Laden had always been, and might well remain, a hero. The fact that he was discovered hiding only a short distance from the Pakistan Military Academy fuelled American suspicions that elements within Pakistan had shielded him; while the fact that the US launched Operation Neptune Spear without consulting the Pakistani government ensured that relations between the two states reached their nadir. Any hope of an early improvement was dashed in November 2011, when a NATO air attack went astray, killing twenty-five Pakistani soldiers at a border checkpoint. In retaliation, Pakistan stopped NATO using its territory as a supply route. But the ability of Washington to pressure the Pakistanis was limited by signs that, in the event of further humiliations, the military might once again be prepared to launch a coup against the elected government.

While the Obama administration was able to identify the problems, and did at least narrow down America's political objectives, focusing on al-Qaeda and Af-Pak, discussions about the latter were immersed in the same old generalities of state-building and development. The successes of counter-insurgency in Iraq were unlikely to be repeated in Afghanistan, partly because there was no Sunni revolt to form a significant indigenous opposition to al-Qaeda. There remained a lack of strategic clarity about what the ultimate objective in Afghanistan should be, let alone the means needed to bring it about, given the failings of the corrupt Karzai government to act as an effective local partner. Thus, a reconstituted Taliban was present in parts of Afghanistan, the political situation had not been stabilized and yet, at a conference in Lisbon in November 2010, NATO had announced its intention to withdraw troops by the end of 2014. (Subsequently, bilateral security deals between the US, Britain, and Karzai suggested that a limited number of American and British troops would remain after 2014.)

Afghanistan, with its diverse ethnic and tribal patchworks and the strength of the local networks they provide, is inherently unsuited to modern nation-state concepts of centralized institutions, modelled on Western theories of global or good governance. Creating the capabilities for non-Western states or societies to function effectively in such a framework was always likely to be doomed. To make matters worse in Afghanistan, US policy was both disjointed and inconsistent, partly as a result of the application of neo-liberal economics and ideas of shrinking the role of the state. This produced an initial American reluctance to get involved in civilian affairs, at the very time when moulding them successfully (following the 2001 rout of the Taliban) was most likely. Instead, despite its proclaimed values, spending the necessary time and money on Afghanistan was never anything but a very remote possibility for the Bush administration, which in any case quickly shifted its focus to the war against Iraq. Even though the long-term costs of failure could be extremely high, understanding and responding to the confusing patchwork and violence of Afghan society proved to be impossible. It was not that there were no warnings. As far back as 1842, the British had lost an army of 16,000 in a retreat from Kabul, following a failed attempt to install a friendly regime in Afghanistan. The Soviet experience after 1979 was not much less stark. The preferred American strategy during the initial defeat of the Taliban was to rely on a number of local warlords, which enabled US policy to be implemented on the cheap. In the process, Osama bin Laden was allowed to escape. Then, while the security situation became worse as a direct consequence of the focus on Iraq, the US and its Western allies half-heartedly attempted to create a centralized state to stabilize Afghanistan. Pakistan always played an ambiguous role in the war on terror, but was itself eventually to succumb to the chaos and instability produced by the conflict in Afghanistan. In the wake of the bin Laden assassination, Pakistan still remained more favoured by al-Qaeda operatives precisely because the West and the US are not free to operate there as they wish.

BOX 23.3

Biography: Ayman al-Zawahiri (1951–)

The leader of al-Qaeda since June 2011, following bin Laden's assassination in May, Zawahiri was the son of a surgeon and medical professor at Cairo University. As a youngster, he was influenced by Sayid Qutb and his idea that a core of revolutionary activists was needed to restore 'pure' Islam. Zawahiri joined the Muslim Brotherhood when he was fourteen and later became one of the founders of the Egyptian Islamic Jihad. He married Azza Ahmed Nowari in 1978 and had a son and five daughters, including one with Down's syndrome, who was killed along with her mother and two of his other children in the US bombing of Gardez in West-Central Afghanistan in November 2001. He was arrested, tortured, and sentenced to three years imprisonment following President Sadat's assassination in 1981. Released from prison in 1984, Zawahiri became the leader of the Egyptian Islamic Jihad in 1991. In 1993, he visited the US and two years later was responsible for the bombing of the Egyptian Embassy in Islamabad. This alienated Pakistan and was denounced by Osama bin Laden. In 1996, Zawahiri visited Chechnya and his relations with the Russian Federation's Security Service (FSB), the main successor organization of the KGB, have been a matter for speculation. In 1998, he merged the Egyptian Islamic Jihad with al-Qaeda and became a leading figure in the organization, alongside bin Laden. In 2006, the US bombed a village on the Pakistan–Afghanistan border where Zawahiri was thought to be hiding, but failed to kill him. In April 2009, the State Department reported that Zawahiri, now regarded by some as the brains behind the organization, had already become al-Qaeda's operational and strategic commander. In a February 2012 video, Zawahiri called on Muslims in the states surrounding Syria to join the uprising against President Assad's 'pernicious and cancerous' regime.

Afghanistan was a state beset with a series of complex but interconnected dynamics provided by the opium trade, corruption, and the West's counter-insurgency measures, which were unsuited to the physical terrain and Pashtun society. By late 2011, a decade of conflict only reinforced what was always the likeliest outcome: the central government in Kabul was unable to impose control over the whole country or to prevent a Taliban resurgence. It seemed impossible that the insurgents in the south-east could ever be satisfactorily defeated, any more than that law and order could be fully imposed by Pakistan in the border areas with Afghanistan.

BOX 23.4

Afghanistan after 2011

In some ways, the situation in Afghanistan seemed to worsen further in early 2012. In February, reports that US officials had burnt copies of the Koran led to days of violent demonstrations; in March an American sergeant murdered sixteen villagers, triggering more anti-American violence; and in April the Taliban, who had already managed to assassinate Karzai's half-brother, the governor of Kandahar, launched an assault on Western embassies in the capital. By May, US deaths in the conflict stood at more than 1,800, while the British had lost more than 400. UN estimates suggested that about 14,000 Afghans had been killed since 2006, about two-thirds of them as a result of the Taliban. In this depressing situation, perhaps the only logical option was that local or regional arrangements, including with the Taliban, would have to be negotiated by the US and its allies. But the auguries for any successful negotiation were mixed. In January 2012, the Taliban did agree to open a political office in Dubai, with the intention of using this for diplomatic contacts with the West, but in May the figure selected by Kabul to talk to the Taliban, Arsala Rahmani, was assassinated.

During Obama's second term, 2013–17, Afghanistan remained an intractable problem. Plans to withdraw NATO forces went ahead, with the Afghan army assuming responsibility for security across the country in June 2013, but Western withdrawal was accompanied by a rising number of Taliban attacks. NATO formally ended its combat role in Afghanistan in December 2014, by which time Karzai had been succeeded (in September) as President by his former finance minister, Ashraf Ghani. But, despite Ghani's commitment to reducing poverty and improving the effectiveness of government, his administration continued to be marred by corruption and a reliance on local warlords. With Afghan government forces finding it difficult to deal with the Taliban resurgence, Western forces remained in training and counter-terrorist roles. The largest contingent by far came from the US, which still had over 10,000 troops there. From January 2015, the government was also faced by a growing ISIS

(continued)

BOX 23.4 (continued)

involvement in Afghanistan, but this also revitalized US interest in Afghan security. ISIS fighters also clashed with the Taliban, who were themselves plunged into a leadership crisis in 2015–16; yet, on the ground, Taliban advances continued in Helmand province and elsewhere. Against this confused background, Obama's hopes of peace talks proved impossible, but the Ghani administration did manage to strike a deal with one Taliban ally, the Hezb-i-Islami group, in September 2016.

By the end of the Obama Presidency, about a fifth of Afghanistan was reckoned to be under Taliban control. The new Trump administration showed no signs of abandoning Afghanistan, however. In April 2017, a Massive Ordnance Air Blast (MOAB) was used against an underground ISIS base in Nangarhar province. The US also targeted air attacks at drug-producing centres that were reckoned to provide millions of dollars for the Taliban. In September 2017, Trump increased US forces in Afghanistan by 3,000, to which the Taliban responded with an intensification of attacks in Kabul, including one on the Intercontinental Hotel in January 2018, which killed over 40 people. A further blow to US hopes of progress in the war came in August 2018, with a major Taliban offensive against the eastern city of Ghazni, just two months before a national election was due. But Trump's determination to continue the war was seen in his decision, on 3 September, to cut $300 million worth of military aid to Pakistan, the latest step in his efforts to force that country to co-operate in US efforts to eliminate militant groups. There seemed to be progress in secret US-Taliban peace talks after July 2018, but Trump broke such contacts off in September 2019, following a Taliban attack in Kabul.

Visit the online resources that accompany this book to test your understanding and take your learning further: www.oup.com/he/young-kent3e

NOTES

1. For the links between Iraq and the global economic crisis and the case for the radical nature of the Bush administration, see Paul Krugman, *The Great Unraveling* (WW Norton, New York and London, 2005).
2. The term is that used by Tim Bird and Alex Marshall in *Afghanistan: How the West Lost its Way* (Yale University Press, New Haven and London, 2011), 47.
3. Peter L. Bergen, *The Longest War: The Enduring Conflict between America and al-Qaeda* (Free Press, New York, 2011), 55–8.
4. Terry H. Anderson, *Bush's Wars* (Oxford University Press, New York, 2011), 88–9.
5. Peter L. Bergen, *The Longest War: The Enduring Conflict between America and al-Qaeda* (Free Press, New York, 2011), 157; Terry H. Anderson, *Bush's Wars* (Oxford University Press, New York, 2011), 176–8; Blair is quoted by Tim Bird and Alex Marshall in *Afghanistan: How the West Lost its Way* (Yale University Press, New Haven and London, 2011), 119.
6. Seth G. Jones, *In the Graveyard of Empires America's War in Afghanistan* (W. W. Norton, New York, 2010) Ch. 7; Peter L. Bergen, *The Longest War: The Enduring Conflict between America and al-Qaeda* (Free Press, New York, 2011), 175–82.
7. Tim Bird and Alex Marshall in *Afghanistan: How the West Lost its Way* (Yale University Press, New Haven and London, 2011), 130–4, 140.
8. ibid., 141–7.
9. These arguments are based on the analysis of Bird and Marshall, ibid., Ch. 5.
10. ibid., 168–82.
11. ibid., 205–26.

24

The War in Iraq

Chapter contents

A. The Decision to Invade Iraq, 2001–3

George Bush Junior's Vice-President, Dick Cheney, and neo-conservatives within the Department of Defense, led by Secretary Don Rumsfeld, had been considering an attack on Iraq well before the terrorist attacks of 9/11. At the same time, many experts within the government pointed to the lack of any evidence for Iraqi-sponsored terrorism directed against the US. The threats to US national security were outlined to the President in a briefing just prior to his inauguration, and these threats came from al-Qaeda's terrorism, the proliferation of nuclear arms and other weapons of mass destruction (WMDs), and the rise of China as a significant world power. Iraq did not figure in the list and the Cheney–Rumsfeld impetus came from an ideologically based assessment of the US, its values and role in the international system, rather than from a serious analysis of Iraq. The regime of Saddam Hussein, and its contribution to global terrorism, was perceived very differently by those who had studied its horrors within the administration and those fired by neo-conservative ideology.

Bush's Iraq Inheritance, 1991–2001

What the Bush administration was very much agreed on, and rightly so, was that the Iraqi regime, since the victory of the US-led coalition in liberating Kuwait in 1990–1, had been reluctant to comply with the disarmament measures being monitored by the UN weapons inspectorate (UNSCOM) and a team from the International Atomic Energy Authority. In April 1991, UN Security Council Resolution 687 had called for the destruction or removal from Iraq of all chemical and biological weapons and all production facilities, components for, and research and development, into ballistic missiles with a range of over 150 miles. At best, Saddam Hussein's relations with the UN weapons teams were uncooperative, and disputes arose over entitlement to papers detailing a nuclear programme and the refusal of the Iraqis to permit access to several sites. But, after Iraq agreed to accept Security Council Resolution 715 in 1991, demanding unconditional inspections, a steady flow of information had been provided by the Iraqis to UN inspectors on the destruction of chemical and biological weapons, which accompanied the continued obstructions.

To complicate matters still further, in 1992 'no-fly' zones were established over northern and southern Iraq and enforced by the Americans and British, to protect those groups, such as the Kurds in the north, who Saddam had attacked with chemical weapons. Furthermore, this air superiority was used by President Clinton to bomb Iraq on several occasions. A final source of resentment and mistrust came from the continuation of pre-war economic sanctions on Iraq, with some leeway for trade given in an Oil-for-Food programme. In such an atmosphere, Iraq continued to deny the weapons inspectors access to particular sites. There were repeated departures and recalls, which produced more condemnatory resolutions from the Security Council demanding complete unrestricted access. Finally, in October 1998 Iraq withdrew all cooperation with the weapons inspection teams and expelled them. At the end of December—days before Clinton implemented Operation Desert Fox, unleashing four days of bombing on Iraq for its non-compliance with UN resolutions on weapons inspections—the inspectors left Iraq with no prospect of return in the immediate future.

This history of obstructing the UN efforts to confirm the disarmament of Iraq, which had amounted to non-compliance with UN Resolutions regarding the weapons inspectors, was clearly in the minds of members of the Bush administration, when it produced its early assessments of Iraq. It was an important, but not the only, problem when considering the issue of the proliferation of WMDs in the world and

Figure 24.1 Map of Iraq

it became closely tied to the terrorist question before and after 9/11. After the 9/11 attacks, agencies and experts involved with US intelligence could find no evidence linking Iraq and al-Qaeda, yet as time passed after 9/11 this had less and less impact within the Bush administration.

Arguments for War, 2001–2

Iraq, the prime 'terrorist' threat, as perceived by some neo-conservatives, was ruled by a repressive, authoritarian, but secular, regime under Saddam Hussein and his Ba'athist party, who had nothing in common with al-Qaeda or militant Islamists. In fact, as was confirmed by investigations after 9/11, there was no causal connection between Iraq and Saddam and the attacks on New York and Washington, nor was he harbouring al-Qaeda. Rather the reverse; and none of the 9/11 attackers came from Iraq.

This did not prevent Rumsfeld investigating such links in the immediate aftermath of 9/11, while examining the existing Iraq war plans arising from the 1991 Gulf War. At the meeting of leading members of the administration on 15 September to discuss the measures to be taken in response to 9/11, he had abstained in the vote on invading Iraq. After the US bombing of Afghanistan began, Rumsfeld was horrified to discover that the existing plans in the Pentagon were still using the overwhelming force concept, from 1991, of Operation Desert Storm. The new thinking on a war against Iraq was tied into the development of a different form of military strategy, designed to wield American power in ways that would remove threats to the US more effectively and at lower cost.

As Kabul fell in November 2001, Bush, whose father had been the target of an Iraqi assassination attempt in 1993, decided it was time for the Pentagon to begin planning for a military operation against Iraq. On 1 December, Rumsfeld instructed General Tommy Franks, the Central Force Commander (responsible for an area that stretched from east Africa to central Asia), to begin estimating the rough requirements for a new outline war plan. The attempt to portray Saddam as the source of the terror threat, and to focus the source of the threat from al-Qaeda on Baghdad, rather than Afghanistan, was underway. If hard evidence was lacking on a link between Saddam and al-Qaeda, the withdrawal from Iraq of the UN weapons inspectors in 1998 and the previous lack of cooperation by the Iraqi authorities provided grounds for suspecting something was being hidden from the UN. If the desirability of removing Saddam had pre-dated the Bush administration, the best available means were now being actively considered, even though regime change through the use of force was against international law, unless it secured the authorization of the UN. Military means were only one possible option, once it seemed that UN sanctions against Iraq were failing to have a significant effect on the regime. The issue of subverting Saddam by covert operations was not a viable option, as opposition groups felt let down by the US after the 1991 Gulf War. The Kurds, in particular, now had little faith in promises of US support and assistance from the Central Intelligence Agency (CIA) against Saddam. The CIA was having difficulty even gathering human intelligence on Iraq in the new millennium, such was the terror that Saddam's intelligence services inspired among would-be opponents.

By January 2002, Bush had been briefed on why a CIA operation to overthrow the regime in Baghdad would not work. This made a military option more necessary if regime change were to be carried out. At the end of that month, Bush also delivered the State of the Union address and used it to outline the changes in American foreign policy and the wider world that were emerging in the wake of 9/11. The speech fused Bush's own high moral and religious certitudes with the creation of a better world, to be produced by the actions of unfettered US power deployed against the forces of terrorism. The apparent successes in Afghanistan at this point, with the overthrow of the Taliban, would reinforce the basic message of US power, and the speech detailed the progress allegedly being made around the world in the campaign against terror. The kernel of the speech, as of the Bush Doctrine more generally, was the elimination of the threat from those terrorist regimes seeking to possess WMDs, including a nuclear programme. Bush mentioned three states by name which, along with their terrorist allies, were said to constitute an axis of evil. Two such states were Iran and North Korea, to which Bush devoted a single sentence each in the speech, while devoting five sentences to Iraq.[1] Significantly, the speech ended by proclaiming that 'the US had been called to a unique role' in human events.

As February 2002 began, implementing this 'unique role' was looking more and more likely to involve regime change in Iraq and, on 16 February, Bush signed an intelligence order to that effect which instructed the CIA to support the US military in overthrowing

Saddam. Four days later a CIA survey team covertly slipped into Iraq to prepare for the deployment of paramilitary teams. The military plans were now at the fifth draft design stage and involved an attack that could be carried out without having to rely on any allies playing a support role, and which halved the preparatory deployment period before the fighting began from 180 to 90 days. Alongside this military planning, the Secretary of State, Colin Powell, told the Senate Budget Committee that since 1998 US policy had been regime change in Iraq, but that the President had no war plans on his desk at the moment.[2] If not strictly 100 per cent true, the question of how exactly this regime change was to be brought about was still very much an open one for Powell.

In contrast to the neo-conservatives, the Secretary of State found it difficult to believe in a connection between Iraq, terrorism, and the 9/11 attack and, therefore, it was the issue of WMDs and Iraqi disarmament which were the focus of his attention. There was thus a growing chasm between the divergent political rationales for the use of force in Iraq, between the Powell Doctrine on using overwhelming military force to secure a clear victory, and the fundamentally different military thinking on an Iraq campaign that Rumsfeld initiated in the Pentagon alongside General Franks. The divergence was made worse by Rumsfeld's determination to side-line the State Department in any planning of the operation, including dealing with its political consequences. This was to have a disastrous outcome following the formal creation in January 2003 of the Office of Reconstruction and Humanitarian Assistance (ORHA). Despite his considerable experience of war and government, Powell's influence was to remain severely handicapped by his lack of any real personal rapport with the President. This added to the tendency for the Pentagon to dominate the State Department in the key issues affecting even non-military aspects of planning a war against Iraq, which were an integral part of any military campaign, and increased the influence of Condoleeza Rice, the National Security Adviser, who was a Bush confidante more open to neo-conservative approaches.

It was not that neo-conservatives gave no thought to preparing world opinion for action against Iraq. The issue of finding potential US allies to back an attack was explored, in March, by Vice-President Cheney on a Middle East tour. But the visit was made essentially from the Pentagon's perspective of what support, in the form of military equipment, transit rights, staging facilities, and bases, would be promised for any future American action against Iraq. Most of the countries identified for Cheney's visit lay around the Persian Gulf, close to Iraq, and his message was to inform them about how seriously the US approached the prevention of WMDs falling into the hands of terrorists, or the states that supported them. For the Arab states, however, the priority was not terrorism but the Middle East peace process, designed to bring about a settlement to Israeli–Palestinian differences. This was also an important consideration for Bush's potentially most valuable North Atlantic Treaty Organization (NATO) ally, the British Prime Minister, Tony Blair, but he was won over surprisingly easily to the idea of action against Iraq. He visited the President at his ranch in Crawford, Texas in April, when Bush told reporters that Saddam had to go. This seemed to be endorsed by Blair, in a speech the following day. The outcome had evidently been decided, whether or not a more formal agreement had been reached in private by the two leaders. Considerable planning of the military means to realize that end had already taken place, and all that remained to be determined were the processes by which the military force would be unleashed and justified, within a framework that would strengthen those fighting the war against terror. But other NATO allies would be less easy to win over to military action than Blair had been.

Bush had already been a little disingenuous in stating there were no war plans on his desk, rather than stating that no final decision had yet been made as to the war plans, or the circumstances which might produce their implementation. He repeated his 'no war plans on my desk' assertion on his European tour in May, where he hoped to find further sympathy from NATO allies. Expectations were building in Europe and the Middle East that action by the Americans, against the 'evil' in Iraq, might be accompanied by steps to advance the Middle East peace process. Unfortunately, if this were to involve a more balanced approach to the Israeli–Palestinian question and serious differences with Israel, still America's most reliable ally in the region, the chances of real progress were remote.

Despite the neo-conservative ideal of wielding US power unilaterally, it was becoming clear, by the summer of 2002, that a successful, low-cost attack on Iraq could only be achieved, if it could be achieved at all, with a considerable diplomatic preparation to win over other members of the international community, who might have different priorities to Washington. Worse, there were the regional consequences of attacking Iraq to consider. The religious conviction of the American President, that his mission was to remove the evil of Saddam and replace it by a benevolent US-led system, based on liberal democratic values, whose innate benefits he believed to be self-evident, carried dangers within it. Whatever the actual effect of any US actions to impose its values on the Middle East, whether or not they removed Saddam and his oppressive regime, the result was not likely to bring automatic benefits to the region. Indeed, as the former National Security Adviser to Bush Snr, Brent Scowcroft, pointed out that summer, an attack on Iraq could well turn the entire Middle East into a cauldron, with detrimental consequences for the war on terror.[3]

In addition to the damaging consequences that an attack might have for the war on terror, the political legwork Powell was required to do with potential allies to persuade them of the terrorist threat presented by Iraq would be considerable. The case for getting UN support as the means of internationalizing the conflict, as in the 1991 war, remained a key aspect for many in Washington and American allies abroad. Regime change without such an endorsement from the UN, however undesirable and threatening Saddam's regime might be, would simply be illegal. The representations from the neo-conservatives about the value and benefits of the unilateral assertion of American power in the war against terror could not universally be regarded as an adequate justification for attacking Iraq. At the very least, efforts would be needed to 'spin' the story, presenting it in an appropriate way, with or without the UN.

Meanwhile, by August, the time frame for the planned military operations against Iraq had again been shortened because of the military preparations already underway. In what became the Hybrid Plan, the time for moving forces before offensive operations began was again reduced. Within sixteen days, the initial forces would have been transported to the region, with a similar time for air attacks before the decisive ground operations. These would take a further 125 days to complete if one division was in place at the time the ground attack began and another division arrived a week later. While Bush was on his August vacation, Rice chaired the deputies committee (with Richard Armitage of the State Department, Paul Wolfowitz from Defense, John McLaughlin of the CIA, and 'Scooter' Libby of the Vice-President's Office), in an attempt to define the goals, objectives, and strategy of an attack on Iraq. Eliminating Iraqi weapons of mass destruction, their means of delivery and the associated nuclear programmes, was an important part of the proclaimed goals of such a war. One final element noted was the need to demonstrate that America was prepared to play a significant role in the reconstruction of Iraq after Saddam's fall. However, such an idea flew in the face of neo-conservative ideology, which wanted to keep US expenditure low, and it was never to be translated into an effective policy.

In August, the search for a suitable justification for war was well underway, but so was the gathering of opposition to any attack on Iraq. Powell, dining at the White House with Rice, warned the President that Iraq was a fragile state and that an invasion could shatter it, leaving no government, but rather civil disorder, with adverse consequences for the Middle East, especially if this were done without approval of the UN.[4] Scowcroft, the former National Security Adviser, now suggested that the President should get the UN inspection teams (those expelled in 1998), back into Iraq for vigorous, no-notice inspections of its WMD facilities. Vice-President Cheney had never been at all enthusiastic about US involvement with international organizations, which he believed were far more likely to constrain US actions than to enable them. In a late August speech in Nashville, he referred to UN inspectors as unable to provide any assurance that Saddam was complying with UN resolutions. This was later to become the crux of the justification issue. Cheney had no doubt of its critical significance for dealing with his interpretation of the terrorist threat and its scale. He even went to the extent of issuing his own personal National Intelligence Estimate about the extent of the threat from Iraq. Its unequivocal conclusion was that there 'is no doubt that Saddam Hussein now has weapons of mass destruction' and that he intended to use them against the US and its allies.[5]

At the beginning of September, Andrew Card, the White House Chief of Staff, set up what became known as the White House Iraq Group, whose fundamental remit was to sell the justification for an attack on Iraq and the overthrow of Saddam Hussein.[6] Leaving aside their role in justifying an attack, the continued existence (or recent acquisition of) Iraqi biological and chemical weapons would have serious operational implications for the military assault. For both reasons—justification of action and the execution of an invasion—intelligence assessments of Iraqi capabilities became even more crucial. But in the absence of the UN inspection teams, and given the difficulty in gaining human intelligence about the situation in Iraq, putting watertight evidence together was far less easy than would normally be the case. The military could still find no hard evidence of the existence of Scud missiles with which Saddam might launch chemical or biological warheads. Yet Cheney had unequivocally asserted that Saddam had weapons of mass destruction and, at the end of the first week of September, when the President met Blair at Camp David, he repeated that assertion to reporters. Bush also made it clear that he was committed to ending the threat from Saddam once and for all, while Blair famously replied, 'I am with you.' It remains unclear just how far the British Prime Minister, who seemed determined to play the role of Washington's most loyal ally, was aware of the distance the President had already taken him in preparing for a likely war against Iraq.

The issue of justifying an invasion was now central. Powell continued to be supportive of involving the UN, to legalize action and maximize international support, while Cheney remained opposed, believing that the US must act unilaterally to defend its interests and must not be constrained by the UN. But there seemed a credible route to achieving the necessary justification by taking the course Scowcroft had indicated. If a Security Council resolution could be secured to bring the inspectors back into Iraq, and if Saddam continued to refuse to admit them or obstructed them on their visits, then that would provide adequate justification for the planned invasion. The important thing would be to get the UN to insist on the disarmament of Iraq and, if it was unable to carry this out, then Cheney and the neo-conservatives could be satisfied by a US determination to act unilaterally. Blair and Powell could both be appeased by the US acting through the UN and, ironically, Bush would get a plausible justification for war simply by attaching importance to the organization, even though it was denigrated by his own Vice-President.

Unfortunately, Scowcroft's proposal was not a complete solution. Importantly, it did not completely resolve the issue of what should be done by the UN to disarm Iraq. Getting it to 'act', by a Security Council resolution requiring the return of the inspectors, would leave the definition of 'non-cooperation' by Saddam unclear and it would not tackle the thorny question of what degree of non-compliance would justify war. Nevertheless, on 12 September 2002, when Bush spoke at the UN in New York, the rhetoric of 'soft' American values, such as the promotion of democracy and humanitarian rights, featured in the speech. Then again, while he was adamant that the US would work with the Security Council to get the necessary resolutions for the disarmament of Iraq, the tougher part of his message was that if the UN could not disarm him, then the US would. The importance of a justification, especially for key allies like Blair, was emphasized by the British release of intelligence on 24 September which suggested a real threat from Iraqi WMDs. Disputes over the extent to which this intelligence was 'spiced up' to exaggerate the threat should not conceal the fact that much of the intelligence on both sides of the Atlantic was dubious or flimsy. Even if the claim that Saddam was able to launch an attack in 45 minutes was largely a spin provided by the media, which the Prime Minister's office neglected to correct or qualify, there were, self-evidently, doubts as to its reliability.[7] Nevertheless, such unequivocal statements by some politicians and ideologues continued, while they were hotly disputed by others.

In the autumn of 2002, another key factor in the US was the campaign to convince Congress to support the war planned by the President. This would also fulfil a key element of coercive diplomacy against Saddam—a credible threat to employ force if necessary. In September, Bush had meetings with Congressional committee members, and Powell appeared before the House Committee on International Relations, supporting the need to have the threat of force as an important diplomatic weapon. But, while the head of the CIA, George Tenet, was prepared on occasion to support claims that Saddam possessed WMDs, the intelligence agencies were more equivocal in their assessments. According to Bob Woodward, the National Foreign Intelligence Board (the heads of all agencies involved in the National Intelligence Estimates), was inconsistent in its assertions about Saddam's possession of chemical and biological weapons. Furthermore, the State Department's Intelligence Bureau objected to the National Intelligence Estimates' claims about Saddam's nuclear programme, arguing that the evidence did not make a compelling argument.[8] Nevertheless, the case against Saddam was arranged so as to culminate in a prime-time television address by the President, from Cincinnati, Ohio on 7 October, and create the impression that Iraq was the most serious threat from terror that the US presently faced, perhaps only six months away from developing a nuclear weapon. Three days later, the House of Representatives voted to authorize the President's use of armed force in Iraq by 296 votes to 133 and, on 11 October, the Senate followed suit by 77 votes to 23. This was after the President had told them that, 'no terrorist state poses a greater threat or more immediate threat to the security of our people, and the stability of the world, than the regime of Saddam Hussein'.[9]

Thus, when the Security Council met in the first week of November, plans for war were already in place and Congress had authorized the need to use force against Iraq, despite the continuing controversies about regime change. Whether there were connections between Saddam and al-Qaeda was the first highly debatable issue; whether Iraq really possessed WMDs was the second. Yet such controversies hardly seemed to concern some key decision-makers or the US public. Rumsfeld stated, on 26 September, that 'you can't distinguish between al-Qaeda and Saddam Hussein when you talk about the war on terror'. The majority of the American public, according to the polls, believed Saddam Hussein was behind the 9/11 attacks, even though there was no evidence of that. The campaign to sell the Iraq war thus had a far greater success in the US than in Europe, where Saddam's role in 9/11 and the subsequent requirement to attack Iraq were much more in doubt.

Resolution 1441 and the Illusion of Peace, 2002–3

Washington had already discussed the wording of another possible UN resolution with the French (one of the most sceptical of America's allies), on the basis that Saddam on several occasions had been in material breach of past resolutions. Thus, the drafts of Resolution 1441, which finally emerged on 7 November, provided specific details of these previous breaches, going back to the victory of coalition forces over Iraq in 1991, before defining the new resolution as one final attempt get Iraq's compliance with UN disarmament demands. The question now would be not whether Iraq was in material breach of past UN resolutions, which it clearly had been, but whether it would now seize the final chance to comply with the disarmament demands and the verification process that had been aborted in 1998. The demands to readmit the inspectors were central, along with the specific conditions in Resolution 1441 pertaining to their 'full and free' inspections, which were laid out in detail, and Iraq was required to notify the Security Council of its total acceptance of such conditions. As part of this, Iraq was given thirty days to provide a complete documentary breakdown of the state of its nuclear, chemical, and biological programmes and those weapons which had been produced and destroyed, including those discovered by the previous UN weapons inspection teams. A false declaration would, in itself, constitute a material breach of 1441, justifying action.

The US was now following two increasingly divergent tracks in the fight against Iraqi terrorism. One of these was heading for war. It involved military planning and preparations, which would at some point require the deployment and pre-positioning of forces. The other track involved diplomatic efforts to preserve the peace by putting Iraq to the test of effective weapons inspections and justifying war if the test was failed. This was soon to provide a more formidable problem than convincing US opinion of the non-existent connection between Saddam and al-Qaeda terrorism. As the Iraqis accepted the conditions of Resolution 1441 and the inspectors resumed their work in late November, the day was not far away when irrevocable decisions would have to be made about war and the deployment of US forces. If Washington moved towards war, peace efforts through the UN would clearly be rendered irrelevant as a determining factor in the overall outcome. On 26 November, Franks informed Rumsfeld of the need to begin the mobilization deployments of some of the forces earmarked for the Iraqi attack. This recommendation was probably largely conditioned by the belief that war had to start by March 2003, given the weather in Iraq, especially if chemical or biological weapons were employed against US forces. Yet, in December, Bush did not want to be irrevocably tied in to a course of action that visible deployments would seem to imply.

The UN road seemed to be on track after the passing of Resolution 1441, but any progress soon proved to be illusory. Key US policy-makers had long been bent on a war with Iraq, whatever the circumstances, and were ill-disposed to the lengthy and somewhat murky processes that were often necessary at the UN. For them, Iraq constituted an ideal opportunity to implement the Bush Doctrine, and pre-empt threats from terrorists and those possessing WMDs, by unilateral American action if required. But there were additional reasons why the latest resolution on Iraq was to prove even more difficult. In order to get agreement on the wording of UN resolutions, to some extent, it is often necessary for some ambiguous leeway to be left, so that member states can justify different interpretations of an agreed text. This was true with 1441, although the ambiguity was to be most significant over whether Iraq was in material breach of that resolution based on Saddam's agreed disclosures to the UN, which allegedly proved the absence of WMDs. In one sense, Saddam Hussein was in a no-win situation when he provided several thousand pages of alleged proof that it had no WMDs. Given the assumptions by some US policy-makers that Iraq definitely did have WMDs, to them such claims were in themselves false and therefore self-evidently a material breach of 1441. If, on the other hand, Saddam admitted the possession of WMDs, he would have once again been lying to the world since agreeing to the latest inspections. Yet the amount of unaccounted material, arising from the apparent discrepancy between the numbers of weapons Iraq originally possessed and those recorded as destroyed in recent years, ensured there were plenty of questions to be answered. Some concerns arose about the components for biological and chemical weapons, others came from unaccounted material for makings shells. A lot would depend on what the inspectors would find if they were allowed unfettered access to Iraqi facilities, but Saddam continued to try to keep some buildings—notably his extensive palaces—out of bounds to the UN inspectors.

Bush himself had grave doubts about the ability of the UN inspectors to avoid being misled by the Iraqis. At the beginning of January 2003, after his Christmas break in Crawford, Bush told Rice that time was not on the Americans' side and 'we are probably going to have to go to war'.[10] A few days later, he had privately made up his mind and told Karl Rove that war was now the only option. As the President put it to Cheney on 10 January, since Saddam would not disarm and could not be made to change his mind, the US would remove him from power.[11] Thoughts then turned to the food relief efforts, to solve the humanitarian problems in Iraq which UN sanctions were producing. Before an invasion was launched, this issue would be in the hands of UN agencies and non-governmental organizations (NGOs), but there was a question of what to do after the invasion took place. A key aim for US policy-makers was that food relief should be controlled by the Pentagon which, after Saddam was defeated, would implement policy on the ground. The State Department, which had more experience in areas such as foreign aid, would be subordinate to the Department of Defense.

On 20 January, Bush set up the ORHA in the Pentagon, with detailed work being undertaken by the Under-Secretary of Defense for Policy, Doug Feith, a neo-conservative and close ally of Rumsfeld. The Office would have to deal with the full gamut of occupation issues in Iraq, from public utilities such as gas and electricity, to the dismantling of any WMDs, converting the Iraqi military into civilian armed forces, and reconstructing the economy on free-market lines. In effect, it would function as the administration of Iraq until an elected government could be put in its place. Feith had to work closely with the commander of US military forces, General Tommy Franks,[12] but the latter found little to admire in the Under-Secretary. Indeed, the head of the Executive Steering Group, which was charged with coordinating the various agencies within the US government on Iraq, soon found itself needing to bring cohesion to the different sections of the Pentagon. General Myers, the Chairman of the Joint Chiefs, Franks and his staff, and Feith's office, in reality all operated largely independently.[13] Rumsfeld chose retired Lieutenant-General Jay M. Garner, a Vice-Chief of Staff, to become Director of the ORHA. Garner, a Vietnam War veteran, had had supervision of Kurdish areas of Iraq after the 1991 Gulf War, in which he had also fought, and he was trusted by Rumsfeld. But, when Powell sent over the names of 75 Arab experts for possible inclusion in the team entering Iraq after the invasion, some immediately were declared unacceptable by Rumsfeld and Feith. It was a telling indication of the difficult, even obstructionist, relations between the two government departments.

General Franks, noting that initial deployments of troops would be 140,000 in the region by mid-February (including 78,000 ground forces), listed the final notification day for Bush to decide on the war as 22 February. In fact, of course, Bush had personally already made that decision and the issue was when rather than if. The White House Iraq Group had been making the case that Saddam possessed, but was concealing, nuclear weapons, even if, as 'Scooter' Libby tried to make a convincing case for this argument, the State Department considered it to be making too much out of too little. On 27 January and 7 March, two reports were delivered by the head of the UN inspection team in Iraq, Hans Blix, to the Security Council. Blix concluded that, after months of work, and hundreds of individual inspections, Iraqi cooperation with the process was, on the whole, good. But questions remained unanswered on chemical and biological weapons, and about Saddam's missile capability. So far, there was no evidence of any revival of Iraq's nuclear programme, which had been eliminated in the 1990s, but in the next months, rather than weeks or years, inspectors would be able to determine, with the implementation of the 'key remaining disarmament tasks', whether proscribed programmes of Iraqi WMDs had continued after 1998 or not. Thus, the concerns of intelligence services, who believed the programmes had been restarted, would be met. Unfortunately, the Pentagon war planners' chief concern was that war should begin before the post-March hot season began in Iraq.[14]

The Failed Search for a Second Resolution, January–March 2003

On 31 January, Britain's Tony Blair was again at the White House, to press the case for going back to the UN for another resolution. Blair needed this partly because of opposition to war from within his own government. Bush was naturally reluctant to upset his closest ally by ruling out diplomacy, even though his own decision for war had already effectively been made. It was, in essence, a question of justifying a war, for which planning and initial deployments were already underway, with Blair being told some 200,000 troops had already been ordered to deploy.[15] If the UN attempt should not succeed in disarming Iraq, the unilateralists in Washington would have a war without the UN. If the justification for war could be obtained, it would not just be Blair who would be gratified. The problem would be if the attempt at diplomacy failed and the US became bogged down in a lengthy diplomatic process, which threatened to jeopardize the execution of the military plans. The prospects of this occurring, and dividing those prepared to enlist in the war on terror, was soon increased.

In early February, shortly after the French President, Jacques Chirac, had called Bush to tell him war was not inevitable, Chirac, Putin (the Russian President), and Gerhard Schroeder (the German Chancellor) issued a joint statement that nothing *at present* justified war and that the three countries wanted everything possible to be done to disarm Iraq peacefully. This warning, intentionally or not, served as a riposte to Secretary of State Powell's dramatic speech, of 5 February, to the UN. This speech was designed to present the US case against Saddam and in particular to explain the 'facts', which in Powell's view proved that the Iraqi leader had, but was concealing, WMDs. Thus, Powell presented intercepts of a conversation between two senior officers from Saddam's elite military unit, the Republican Guard, about the 'evacuation of everything'. Powell interpreted this as meaning that everything was removed before UN inspectors could visit sites and find WMDs. The efforts at concealment, Powell noted, went back twelve years. Powell was constructing a case for Iraq being in material breach of Resolution 1441, including a failure to supply a complete list of the scientists involved with WMDs. As far as nuclear facilities went, Powell intended to convince the UN that Iraq still had a nuclear programme and was intent on bringing it to fruition by the acquisition of nuclear warheads, while also developing ballistic missiles that could send them over 1,000 kilometres.

Much of the intelligence on which Powell's claims were based, whether human or from intercepts, was subsequently proved to be false, or its interpretation wrong. Part of Powell's presentation focused on the connection of alleged Iraqi WMDs to the terrorist threat. In particular, he made claims about the presence of the Jordanian-born jihadist, Abu Musab al-Zarqawi's (see Box 24.1) presence in north-eastern Iraq and the links between other al-Qaeda affiliates in Baghdad and the network controlled by Zarqawi. The irony was that Saddam would have liked to remove Zarqawi as much as the Americans, and it was the invasion of Iraq that was to enable the rise of al-Zarqawi and the significant increase of al-Qaeda operatives in the country.[16] Powell made considerable efforts to link al-Qaeda and Iraq, despite noting the difference between secular and religious tyranny. Using human intelligence, which was suspect even at the time, the Secretary of State even claimed that Iraq was receiving requests from al-Qaeda training camps in Afghanistan for help in acquiring and manufacturing chemical and biological weapons. He also went as far as to refer to Saddam Hussein's cooperation with other Islamic terrorist movements and his provision of weapons to them.

One claim that Powell did make, which was supported by Blix when he made another report to the Security Council, on 15 February, concerned unaccounted-for numbers of munitions of a biological or chemical nature which were previously known to be in Iraq. Blix was clear that the problems in accounting for them did not mean they still existed, but he also said that such a possibility should not be ruled out. However, Blix criticized Powell's claim that Iraq was preparing sites prior to the inspections, by clearing out damaging evidence about WMDs. Blix's conclusion was that, if Iraq were to cooperate more fully, being able to guarantee disarmament through a peaceful process of inspections would not take long. This was not good news for the military planners in Washington, who envisaged serious problems if the attack could not begin in March, which was now only a couple of weeks away. It was also not good news for Powell, as the main point of his UN speech was to demonstrate that, in Iraq's case, disarmament through inspections was not possible and that the Iraqi dictator was clearly in breach of Resolution 1441. The issue was now one of whether the Security Council would decide for Powell or for Blix. Should there be war immediately or should war be delayed until the final confirmation by the UN inspection team that Saddam did, or did not, have WMD? Unfortunately, in Washington, this ran counter to the views of those inherently ill-disposed to delays occasioned by the UN and its processes, and who were already convinced of the threat posed by Saddam. There was also the enormous difficulty of postponing the invasion, which would require keeping thousands of troops on hold. The prospects of a peaceful outcome looked bleak.

The twin pressures to prepare for war and yet give the appearance of seeking a diplomatic solution now led to the attempt to get a second UN resolution on the consequences of a material breach of 1441 by Saddam. Such a resolution would provide an unequivocal justification for war, which Bush had promised to Blair. The President, in a prime-time televised conference on 6 March, set out his commitment to seek another resolution, and he was careful to say that no decision for war had yet been taken. Three days later, Powell publicly expressed confidence in the chances of obtaining the new resolution, even though only Spain and Bulgaria had so far committed themselves to supporting a draft resolution put forward by Britain and the US. Bush was four votes short of the nine votes needed, irrespective of any veto from France or Russia, two permanent members of the Security Council who were already on record, of course, as being sceptical about military action. On 12 March, Bush called Blair, who pleaded with the President to contact two Latin American members of the Security Council that he might be able to persuade—Chile and Mexico—but

BOX 24.1

Biography: Abu Musab al-Zarqawi (1966–2006)

Born in the Jordanian town of Zarqa, into a poor Bedouin family, Abu Musab grew up as a street child, dropping out of school and joining gangs, where he was heavily involved with alcohol. He volunteered to fight with the Mujaheddin against the communist Afghan regime in 1989, having met Osama bin Laden. In 1993, having returned to Jordan, he was jailed for conspiring against the government and became a ruthless leader of his fellow convicts. On being granted an amnesty in 1999, he returned to Afghanistan with his followers in al-Tawhid wal-Jihad, but he was soon also plotting to blow up the Radisson Hotel in Amman. He established a training camp for his Arab followers in western Afghanistan, near the Iranian border. Independent of al-Qaeda when the US war against the Taliban began in 2001, Zarqawi took part in the defence of Kandahar and, when the city fell, he fled to Iran. In 2002, several months before the US invasion, he decided to cross into Kurdish Iraq to join the militant group, Ansar al-Islam, in attacking American targets.

In August 2003, following the US-led invasion of Iraq, Zarqawi's group bombed the UN Headquarters in Baghdad, killing twenty-two people. Further attacks on police and diplomats followed. Zarqawi's unique contribution to the horrors of the insurgency was to videotape his operations, from the use of Improvised Explosive Devices (IEDs) to kidnappings and suicide bombings. Zarqawi uploaded the records of gruesome scenes onto the internet, becoming the most feared insurgency leader after he recorded the beheading of a US hostage, Nicholas Berg. Zarqawi's strategy was to provoke a civil war in Iraq by killing Shi'ite Muslims and creating a vicious circle of violence. In October 2004, Zarqawi joined forces with al-Qaeda and his pledge of loyalty to Osama bin Laden resulted in him becoming de facto head of al-Qaeda Iraq (AQI). The culmination of his terrorist success was the bombing of the Golden Mosque at Samarra, one of the holiest Shi'ite sites, in February 2006, marking the final stage of the conflict's development into a civil war. AQI was able to pay its operatives from smuggling, extortion schemes, and ransoms earned from kidnapping. It was at the peak of its success when, on 7 June 2006, Zarqawi was killed by two large US F-16 bombs in a remote village compound in Baqubah, just north of Baghdad. His vicious campaign of terror, particularly against the Shi'ites, rather than infidels, meant that even bin Laden may not have been too sorry to learn of his death.

Bush's entreaties to them proved unsuccessful. As the two leaders acknowledged later that day, the attempt to get a second resolution had failed. The only ploy left was to transfer the blame for this failure on to the French, who had been the firmest opponents of a military solution before the UN inspectors had definitely concluded that Saddam's uncooperative actions and possession of WMDs were a material breach of Resolution 1441.

In early March, Feith finalized a paper on the aims and objectives of the forthcoming war in Iraq. Like many such formulations, it often piled abstraction on abstraction. It laid out the objectives of maintaining Iraq's territorial integrity and improving the quality of life of its people, while moving the country towards democratic institutions, which would serve as a model for the whole region. The US intended to continue the unfettered pursuit of the war on terror and its eradication of WMDs, and to obtain international participation in the Iraqi reconstruction effort. The support of the Iraqi people would be secured, along with the political support of the international community, preferably through Security Council resolutions. This was clearly intended to reduce the burdens carried by the US, as was the hope that Iraqis could be placed in positions of authority as quickly as possible. The possible costs of the Iraqi operations did not feature in this paper, but the Deputy Secretary of Defense, Paul Wolfowitz, was adamant that the risks of long-term complications were low because not only did Iraq have abundant oil supplies as a base for economic revival, but also there was no record of ethnic militias fighting each other. In contrast, Lawrence Lindsey, the Special Assistant to the President for Economic Policy, had estimated that the war would cost $200 billion and, as a result, had been forced to leave his job in December 2002. The administration's estimate was much lower, at $50–60 billion. In fact, even Lindsey's estimate proved to be a small fraction of the actual, eventual cost.[17]

The practical requirements of dealing with officials in Saddam's administration and essential government departments, which would be needed to run any post-invasion regime, were tackled later on 12 March, when Feith briefed the National Security Council on the plans. The Iraqi intelligence services were to be completely dismantled, to enable the US to show ordinary Iraqis that a clean break was being made with Saddam's regime. Similarly, the Republican Guard would be disbanded and the foreign service dealt with by asking host governments to expel senior diplomatic staff. The ultimate aim was to remove all vestiges of the Ba'ath party, as was planned for the Nazis in Germany at the end of the Second World War. It was seen as particularly important to depoliticize the armed forces and place them under civilian control. Feith had some notion of managing the demobilized military units as a reconstruction force. But how this was to be achieved, and who would pay for it, was left up in the air. The obvious probability—that thousands of soldiers would vanish with their weapons and provide the basis for future militias—was not considered.[18]

While these optimistic plans were being finalized, the diplomatic preparations for war were proving far from smooth. With the failure to justify regime change through a second resolution at the UN, it was far from certain that Blair would win the parliamentary vote for war in Britain, raising the danger that the US would have to fight without its key ally. At the UN, the US now had to argue that Resolution 1441 justified war without the inspectors reporting a material breach of it. But Bush remained eager to help Blair and found another way of encouraging potential allies to support Washington, by encouraging the myth that an invasion would open new doors to peace and democracy throughout the Middle East. On 14 March, the President announced a 'road map for peace'. The following day, CIA forces, which had been infiltrated into northern Iraq to encourage Kurdish resistance, carried out their first acts of sabotage.

B. The War in Iraq, 2003–11

Operation Iraqi Freedom: From Liberation to Quagmire, 2003–6

By 19 March, despite the failure to secure a second UN resolution, Blair won his parliamentary vote, while at least thirty-one teams of US Special Forces entered Iraq from the west and north. That evening, the first air strikes began. By the end of the day, General Franks could report that US Special Forces now controlled a large area and 241,516 US military personnel were in the region, plus 41,000 UK personnel and 2,000 each from Australia and Poland. At 10.16 p.m., the President addressed the nation on television to inform them that the campaign had begun. The war would test Rumsfeld's commitment to a new military doctrine that no longer involved overwhelming force. It would be a particularly demanding test, once the military campaign was over, and the administrative occupation of Iraq had to begin with the limited numbers on the ground. At first, the military campaign appeared to go remarkably smoothly. By 3 April, the outskirts of Baghdad had been reached with a mere third of the troops used in the 1991 invasion. However, US post-war planning, through Feith's office and OHRA, for running the Iraqi capital after it fell, was conspicuous by the absence of practical measures. The US involvement in the tearing down of a statue of Saddam Hussein in Baghdad, amongst much cheering and flag waving, symbolized the short-term victory over Saddam's conventional army, but it did nothing for the reconstruction of Iraq for the benefits of its citizens, now freed from the tyranny of a ruthless dictator. The removal of Ba'athist officials from civilian and military positions, without any consideration of the likely consequences, simply created a power vacuum that the US and its allies were unprepared to fill. The destructive use of military force was well planned, but reconstruction after the war was conspicuous by its absence in the planning process.

Almost before celebrations over the fall of Saddam ended, Iraq began to disintegrate. Bush had announced the end of combat operations on 1 May, but an insurgency against the US-led coalition forces was already beginning. Yet it was partly because he did not seem intent on destroying the Ba'athist machine swiftly enough, that Jay Garner, the first Director of the OHRA, now transposed into a Coalition Provisional Authority (CPA) was sacked on 6 May, to be replaced by Paul 'Jerry' Bremer. Bremer, a Yale graduate with an MBA from Harvard, was an ardent Christian Republican who, despite considerable experience in diplomacy and counter-terrorism, had no experience of reconstruction work, had never been to Iraq, and could not speak Arabic. The CPA was dominated by the ideology of turning Iraq into a free-market economy and a liberal democracy. It began privatizing publicly owned companies and firing their employees, while in its first four months it only spent $23 million on reconstruction projects.[19] The first thing the CPA did through its order number 1, on 16 May, was to order the removal of several thousand Ba'athists from government offices, hospitals, and educational institutes. CPA order number 2 dissolved the Iraqi military, their intelligence units, and their bureaucracies, as part of a process of bringing the armed forces under civilian authority. Nearly half a million people lost their jobs at a time when opponents of the US occupation were already beginning to act against it. By such actions, the CPA created a pool of discontent almost overnight, making hundreds of thousands of men, with access to weapons, redundant in a country where unemployment was around 50 per cent. As the weeks went by, the liberation of Iraq was rapidly transformed into an unpopular occupation, with growing numbers of armed insurgents hostile to it.[20]

The US tried to find Iraqis to help in reconstruction and the Bush administration sought, with equal desperation and an even greater lack of success, for the WMDs, with which Saddam had allegedly threatened the world—and which had justified the war in the first place. Considerable efforts and resources were devoted to what turned out to be a wild goose chase: Saddam had destroyed all his chemical and bacteriological weapons after all. Bush soon backtracked from his original assertion that finding the weapons would only be a matter of time, now referring to Saddam's supposed programme for nuclear weapons, while Blair shifted to arguing that it had been morally right to bring down Saddam's oppressive dictatorship. Considerable efforts were also put into rounding up key figures from the Ba'athist regime and putting them on trial. Saddam's sons, Uday and Qusai, were killed in a gun battle with US troops in July 2003, while the dictator himself was captured, without a struggle, in December. He was subsequently tried, found guilty of ordering the killing of his own people and, in December 2006, executed. But, by then, any hope that such an action would mark a break from a horrific past had gone. For many Iraqis, life had only become worse since 2003.[21]

The antipathy to Kennedy-style 'nation building', which emanated from Rumsfeld and neo-conservatives in the Pentagon, meant that the US tried to rely on local groups, a process that included building links with traditional tribal authorities in parts of the country and encouraging the Kurds to create a semi-autonomous administration in the north-east. But such steps served to fracture the country, while anti-coalition groups sought to disrupt the occupation. In May 2003, Iraq's electrical power grid had thirteen downed transmission towers; by September this number had climbed steeply to 623. Looting became rife as the Iraqi police abandoned their posts. Law and order disappeared along with the pay of officials, while effective reconstruction could hardly take place amidst all the violence. The US, while vainly searching for WMDs, was failing to provide basic services and to encourage the development of any respect for the invading power. By November 2003, six months after Bush had announced the termination of hostilities, US fatalities in the conflict had exceeded 400 and one CIA (overly optimistic) forecast predicted them rising to 2,000. The Iraqi casualties were astronomical by comparison, as the insurgency developed. By 2006, refugees from Iraq formed the largest number in Middle East history—some 4.7 million in total—and, at the height of the conflict that year, 3,000 civilians were dying every month. By the end of 2008, suicide attacks had killed more than 10,000 Iraqis and in the four years after the invasion more attacks occurred in Iraq than in the whole of the rest of the world combined since 1981.[22] In 2004, Wolfowitz still denied in public that the failure to plan effectively for the functioning of Iraq after the invasion had become a problem. In June, he told TV viewers, 'it's not an insurgency'. Yet, other reports suggested that Sunni support for the insurgency had risen from 14 per cent in 2003 to 75 per cent by 2006. By mid-2005, a majority of Americans believed the Bush administration 'had intentionally misled' them into war.

In 2004, in particular, armed groups and suicide bombings provided opportunities for terrorists, including representatives of al-Qaeda, to become established in Iraq. In Fallujah, a predominantly Sunni city some forty miles from Baghdad, the insurgency had initially been encouraged, in April 2003, by American soldiers firing into a crowd of demonstrators and killing seventeen. Less than a year later, in March 2004, a convoy carrying private US security contractors was ambushed. Four Americans were killed and two of their bodies strung up from a bridge. In retaliation, a major operation in Fallujah was carried out by American forces in April, killing hundreds of insurgents but also many ordinary civilians. By then, Americans were attempting to groom suitable Iraqis for government, mostly non-Sunni, but the deaths aroused considerable protest from such collaborators and led Bremer to call off what became known as 'the first battle of Fallujah'. The ceasefire seemed to provide a partial victory for the insurgents, including al-Qaeda members. As a result, many Iraqi Sunnis who had not previously been active in opposing the US, began to fear they would be marginalized in the future Iraq, and as a consequence, Sunni-dominated areas of Iraq, not just Fallujah, exploded into violence. In November 2004, the Marines went back into Fallujah for a second round, by which time there were far more jihadist insurgents in the city. At enormous cost in terms of lives lost, buildings destroyed, and refugees, American forces ensured that Sunni insurgents would never again significantly resist US authority in Fallujah. They also drove out al-Qaeda members and al Zarqawi who, in October, had pledged allegiance to Osama bin Laden, soon becoming the leader of al-Qaeda in Iraq. Notwithstanding US plans for elections and the re-establishment of Iraqi governmental authority, a civil war, as one senior military commander pointed out, was taking place in Iraq that was of US making.[23]

The CPA lasted until June 2004, when it was replaced by the Iraqi Interim Government, under a moderate Shi'ite, Ayad Allawi, who had spent much of his life in exile. The Interim Government, in turn, was replaced by the Iraqi Transitional Government in May 2005, following elections in January. Allawi then handed the premiership to Ibrahim al-Jaafari, of the Islamic Dawa Party. Far from providing the basis for a stable, Western-style democracy, however, the elections made a bad situation worse. Voting was almost entirely on sectarian lines and most Sunnis boycotted the election. By then, corruption was endemic in Iraq; reconstruction remained slow or non-existent; Sunnis and Shi'ites continued to kill each other without much sign of central authority. Al-Jaafari survived in office barely a year, before dissatisfaction from Sunnis, Kurds, and even President Bush forced him from office.

Furthermore, by late 2004, the al-Qaeda jihadist group, which had carried out the 9/11 attacks on the US, was among those trying to exploit the chaos in Iraq that the Americans had been instrumental in creating. A Marine intelligence report, in August 2006, noted that al-Qaeda had even become the de facto government of the western province of Anbar, bordering on Saudi Arabia, Syria, and Jordan, concluding that al-Qaeda Iraq had become 'an integral part of the social structure of Western Iraq'. It controlled territory larger than New England and exerted considerable influence over the Sunni population there.[24] The ideologues of the Bush administration had encountered Middle Eastern reality and helped create exactly what their illusions had convinced them they were destroying. Nor was al-Qaeda the only powerful, well-organized, and motivated group opposed to the coalition. The Sadr City area of Baghdad fell under the domination of a Shi'ite cleric, Moqtada al-Sadr, who also wanted to create an Islamic state, and had his own paramilitary force, the Mahdi Army, to help achieve it. With support from the Shi'ite poor, he created a virtual state within a state, and led a propaganda campaign against the occupation, with sporadic outbursts of violence between his followers and the Coalition forces. There were open battles with the Americans over the city of Najaf in the spring of 2004 and the size of the Mahdi Army reached 60,000 by 2006. That some Shi'ites, as well as Sunnis and al-Qaeda, were opposed to the coalition, emphasized the extent to which the US and its allies had failed to create the foundations of a post-Ba'athist state.

The escalating sectarian Iraqi violence in 2005 produced 1,800 bomb attacks per month, with over a hundred insurgent groups claiming responsibility for attacking Americans, while the US Army failed to meet its recruitment targets. Yet, the extent of the ideologues' illusions was further revealed by Cheney's statement, in May 2005, that the violence was in decline.[25] The war on Iraq also made it more difficult to fight Bush's wider war on terror. In March 2004, a group of Moroccan Spanish exploded multiple bombs on Madrid's transport system, killing 191, as a protest against Spanish participation in the war in Iraq. On 7 July 2005, in London, four home-grown English terrorists, two of whom had made trips to Pakistan where they linked up with militant groups, detonated bombs on tube trains and a bus, killing themselves and 52 others. Once again, the reason made clear from the videos left behind was British involvement in the attack on Iraq. A study at New York University, which compared the number of deadly attacks by jihadist terrorists between 9/11 and the attack on Iraq with the number of deadly attacks after the start of the war until September 2006, found that in the latter period attacks had increased seven-fold. Excluding the attacks in Iraq and Afghanistan, fatal terrorist attacks by jihadists in the rest of the world had trebled.[26]

'Surge' and Withdrawal, 2006–11

In Washington, the departure from the Pentagon in 2006 of Feith and Wolfowitz, key architects of the disaster that the invasion had been instrumental in bringing about, at least offered the opportunity for rethinking. In Iraq, the Americans increasingly realized that counter-insurgency did not simply mean killing insurgents, but also involved winning the confidence and trust of the local population. The new military commanders, generals George Casey (commander of coalition forces in 2004–7) and John Abizaid (who had succeeded Tommy Franks as commander of the Central Command in 2003), and even Rumsfeld himself, were all in favour of a phased run-down of US troop numbers. On the lines of the 'Vietnamization' a generation before, they wanted to see Iraqis trained up to take over the main security role in their own country. In the summer of 2006, Casey recommended the withdrawal of up to 10,000 soldiers. Yet, amidst the appalling levels of disorder in Baghdad, two joint efforts by the US and the Iraqi army and police, to suppress fighting between Sunnis and Shi'ites, both failed. This strengthened the hands of those who argued that more troops on the ground were needed, not fewer. Their ideas were based on a lengthy, new Counterinsurgency Field Manual, produced that year under the direction of General David Petraeus. Where Iraq was concerned, the emphasis of this alternative strategy was on making ordinary civilians more secure through a 'surge' in American troop numbers, by 30,000.

In early November 2006, the President, still smarting from a significant Republican setback in the midterm elections, launched a formal review of the war. At the same time, Rumsfeld resigned as secretary of defense in the face of criticism from many military professionals, being replaced by Robert Gates. The White House was now seriously considering a 'surge' and, in January 2007, Bush publicly acknowledged that Iraq was wracked by violence and disorder, while announcing some 20,000 extra soldiers. As the extra troops began arriving in Iraq in February 2007, so did General Petraeus, replacing Casey, the American commander. The US Army patrols, which had hitherto been designed to kill insurgents before returning to large, fortified bases, now began to be reduced and replaced by smaller groups operating from smaller, local command posts—eventually throughout Baghdad, as the surge reached 30,000 troops. Petraeus told his troops that living amongst the people, and patrolling on foot while engaging with them, was essential to defeating the insurgents. But attention also continued to be given to building up Iraqi security forces, so that they could eventually play the prime security role.

The effect of the surge, which lasted until June 2008, was not instantaneous. The policy change initially increased the attacks on US troops and the recreated Iraqi forces, as insurgents tried to show that the new tactics could not succeed. Yet, while May 2007 brought 120 dead US soldiers, the worst month for two years, security in Baghdad began to improve significantly in the second half of 2007, and the Iraqi government began paying Shi'ite men to work in public service jobs. In November 2008, a contentious and lengthy process of negotiating a Status of Forces agreement between the Bush administration and the al-Maliki government finally ended, with the Iraqi Parliament approving the withdrawal of American troops from Iraqi cities by June 2009. All US forces would leave by the end of 2011. But there were signs that the Iraq they left behind was far from stable and might not even be particularly friendly to Washington. The parliamentary elections of April 2010 were closely fought, with al-Maliki's followers narrowly outnumbered by the National Movement of former premier Ayad Allawi, so that it was not possible to form a government, which included Allawi as head of national security, until December. The American invasion had not offered real prospects of future stability, rather the reverse, and there seemed little prospect of the latest government reconciling the man ethnic and religious divisions in Iraq that Saddam's cruel dictatorship had kept a lid on. Pandora's box was opened by the Americans, but with little idea what to do with the contents. And there were new and ominous threats to a future stable Iraq that had emerged by October after Zaqarwi's assassination.

C. The Israeli–Palestinian Dispute

The 'Two-State' Solution and Divided Palestine, 2001–8

The election of Ariel Sharon as Israeli premier in February 2001 ended any lingering hopes of quickly reviving the Israeli–Palestinian peace process (see Chapter 22, C). With Palestinian Arabs engaged in the second Intifada against Israeli occupation, Sharon ended talks with the Palestinian Authority and its head, Yasser Arafat. The Hamas movement, Arafat's main rivals for leadership of the Palestinians, continued their attacks on Israeli targets including, among many smaller scale actions, the suicide bombing of a nightclub in June, which killed twenty-one. Another group, the Popular Front for the Liberation of Palestine (PFLP), had a rare success in targeting Israeli leaders, when they assassinated a Cabinet minister in October. Finally, in late March 2002, another suicide bomb attack, at a hotel, which killed thirty, was followed by a large-scale Israeli invasion of the West Bank, leading to weeks of intense violence. In June, Israel also began to construct a defensive wall along its border with the West Bank. This wall, which often ran across Arab land, was seen by some as another land-grabbing exercise, relentlessly pushing forward areas of Israeli control. Its building was declared illegal by the International Court of Justice in July 2004. But Israel argued that it was vital to stop terrorists crossing onto its territory and, as evidence, could point to the sharp fall in suicide bomb attacks within Israel. The violence certainly eased after July 2002, although there was a further revival in August 2003, when militant Palestinians tried to disrupt efforts at a peace settlement (details of which are discussed later). Meanwhile, Yasser Arafat, who seemed unable or unwilling to control Palestinian violence, and in any case was utterly distrusted by Sharon, was confined by the Israelis to his compound in Ramallah. In 2004, he was allowed to leave the compound for medical treatment in Paris, where he died in November.

Against this depressing background, there were continuing diplomatic attempts to resolve Israeli–Palestinian differences. In the short term, they had little success. In May 2001, a commission headed by US Senator George Mitchell, who had previously helped secure a settlement of inter-communal differences in Northern Ireland, called on the two sides to bring the violence to an end and resume negotiations, but the violence continued. More significant, on 12 March 2002, as Israeli–Palestinian violence reached its height, the UN Security Council passed Resolution 1397 calling for an end to violence and the resumption of peace talks, raising the 'vision of a region where two states, Israel and Palestine, live side by side within secure and recognized borders'. This was the first time the UN had supported a 'two-state' solution to the long-running problem, with Israel and the Palestinian Authority negotiating a settlement of their differences, culminating in the creation of an independent Palestinian state. The alternatives to such a course were hardly attractive. It seemed impossible that the two peoples could ever live in a single political entity; continuation of the current situation clearly offered no long-term solution; while the destruction of the Israeli state, or Israeli absorption of the whole of Palestine, could only lead to a drawn-out, bitter conflict with an uncertain outcome. Furthermore, there was increasing evidence that the two-state solution was acceptable, not only to the international community, but also to at least some Israelis and Palestinians.

An important factor was that the Bush administration in Washington backed the Resolution, thereby committing itself to the creation of a Palestinian state. Just as surprising perhaps, Israel welcomed it. Then again, while Resolution 1397 was a step forward, it can be argued that the 'two-state' solution had been implicit in Israeli–Palestinian talks since the Oslo Accords, and that the US and Israel already recognized this fact. Also, the US may only have decided to act at this point because it was trying to muster support in the Middle East for action against Saddam Hussein: the second Intifada complicated relations with Arab allies and made it difficult to form a coalition to fight in Iraq. Meanwhile, through a peace plan recently launched by the Saudi Crown Prince, Abdullah, the Arab side had shown its willingness to recognize Israel's right to exist, if the Palestinian problem was resolved. The Saudi plan was endorsed by the Arab League at a meeting in Beirut in late March. Much depended on the precise way that talks on Resolution 1397 were carried out. For Israel and the US, it was important that the Palestinians could only achieve statehood if they previously negotiated—from a position of weakness—with Israel over such complex issues as borders, the status of East Jerusalem, Arab refugees from Israel and the position of existing Jewish settlements in the West Bank.

Another noteworthy development was that, in April 2002, at a meeting in Madrid, the so-called 'Quartet' was formed, of representatives from the US, UN, European Union, and Russia—the key states and international organizations interested in brokering a Middle East settlement. In effect, the US was the key player, pushing initiatives forward and able to carry weight with Israel, but the involvement of the other players helped sustain their support for peace efforts and win Arab support, as well as support in the wider world. The Quartet usually met several times a year over the next decade, but one of its most important steps came early in its history when, on 16 July 2002, it launched the idea of a 'road map' to peace based on Resolution 1397. With neither Israel nor the US willing to work with Arafat, the latter was forced to appoint a more moderate figure, Mahmoud Abbas, as Palestinian prime minister in March 2003. Only then were full details of the road map released. It was based on US ideas for a phased move towards a settlement, beginning in phase one with an end to violence, Palestinian elections, and a freeze on new Israeli settlements. An immediate problem, however, was that Sharon rejected the last proposal and issued a number of conditions for a settlement, including the demilitarization of any Palestinian state and denying Arab refugees the right to return to Israel. As a sign of goodwill, however, to help kick-start talks he released a number of imprisoned Palestinians. President Bush visited the region in early June to meet local leaders and press for the road map to be implemented. A summit with Sharon and Abbas was held in Aqaba on 4 June, and those two leaders also met together on 1 July. But this was followed by a revival of violence on the ground and the road map ran into the sand, unable to achieve even phase one: for while Israel argued that one precondition for talks—an end to Palestinian violence—was not being met, the Palestinians could complain that new Israeli settlements continued to be built.

Arafat's death led to hopes that the peace process might revive. Mahmoud Abbas, who had been Palestinian prime minister in March–October 2003 and who wanted to end the second Intifada, was elected President of the Palestinian Authority in January 2005, although his victory was helped by the fact that Hamas boycotted the poll. But real signs of an improvement in relations came only slowly. The most hopeful step was the Israeli removal of Jewish settlements from the Gaza Strip in August–September 2005, at which time Israel also ended its military occupation of the area. Israeli politics were disrupted early the following year, when Sharon—barely a year after the demise of his old enemy Arafat—was permanently incapacitated by a stroke. But his successor, Ehud Olmert, met Abbas in Jordan, in June 2006, when there was speculation that the 'road map' might revive. In the interim, however, a major shock had hit hopes of peace, with the results of the January 2006 Palestinian legislative elections. Hamas not only took part on this occasion but won, with almost 50 per cent of the vote. As the Oslo Accords stalled and Arafat was humiliated at Israeli hands, so many Palestinians had begun to feel that Hamas's criticisms of the peace process were justified. Hamas was also able to attack the corruption of the Palestine Liberation Organization (PLO) government and to appeal to Islamic values, at a time when secularist movements, like Ba'ath and Fatah, were on the ideological defensive in the Middle East. Just as the first Intifada had tended to benefit the PLO, so the second tended to benefit Hamas. Now it had emphatically shown that the hold of the PLO and its leading component, Fatah, on the Palestinian political leadership could be broken. In late March, after some resistance from Fatah, one of Hamas's leaders, Ismail Haniyeh, became Prime Minister. But the Hamas victory was not total. Abbas was still President of the Palestinian Authority and Fatah, which had the second highest number of seats in the legislature, still held on to the machinery of power. In particular, a deep divide was created by the fact that Hamas was at its strongest in the Gaza Strip, while Fatah was popular on the West Bank. Qatar and Saudi Arabia both tried to mediate between the PLO and Hamas, to try to keep the Palestinian political leadership together, but a serious split seemed increasingly likely.

The January 2006 elections could only prove a further setback to the stalled peace process, for Hamas was blamed for many of the suicide bomb attacks on Israel, it was committed to a violent struggle against the occupation, and it did not recognize Israel's right to exist. Even some moderate Arab regimes, including a pro-Western sheikhdom like Qatar, believed that Hamas deserved respect as the elected representatives of the Palestinian people. But, as in other situations (like Allende's Chile in the Nixon years) where elections had brought unwelcome movements into power, the US government showed that its own supposed interests (and those of its allies, in this case Israel) trumped any respect for a democratic verdict. The US and the European Union suspended their aid programmes to the Palestinians. Certainly, there were serious barriers to treating Hamas as a 'normal' actor in the international field. Its belief that the whole of Palestine was inalienable Islamic territory made it quite unwilling to deal with Israel or, indeed, with anyone who wished to mediate in the dispute. Hamas also had links to Iran and Syria, which were hardly calculated to appeal to the Bush administration. Instead of seeing moves towards a settlement, 2006 was remembered for new problems opening up, with tension between Israel and Hamas, focused on the Gaza Strip, and all-out war between Israel and another radical Islamist movement, Hezbollah, on Israel's northern border with Lebanon.

Israel had long been subjected to sporadic rocket attacks from Gaza, on its south-western border. Gaza is a small area of land, less than 400 square kilometres, bounded by Israel to the east and south, Egypt to the south-west and the Mediterranean Sea. But it was densely populated with one-and-a-half million Palestinians, many of them poor, refugee families who had fled there during the war of 1948. This history made it a stronghold for militant movements like Islamic Jihad and, of course, Hamas. In retribution for the rocket attacks, Israel had launched a large-scale military incursion into the territory in mid-October 2004, when more than a hundred Palestinians were killed. But rocket attacks increased markedly after the withdrawal of Jewish settlers and the Israeli army from the Strip in October 2005, leading Israel to respond with artillery shelling. The rocket attacks intensified following the January 2006 Hamas election victory, and in June 2006 an Israeli soldier, Gilad Shalit, was captured and taken to Gaza (eventually being exchanged in 2011 for a thousand Palestinians held by the Israelis). His capture triggered a sustained Israeli incursion, which included the detention of numerous Hamas officials, a blockade of the territory by land and sea, and the death of several hundred Palestinians. The operation was weakened by Israel's war with Hezbollah in the north and, after a renewed Israeli push in November, ended with a ceasefire. But it did not take long for rocket attacks on Israel to revive, along with some limited punitive Israeli raids on the territory, while Hamas still rejected any idea of negotiation.

Meanwhile, there were growing differences in Palestinian ranks, especially in Gaza, where violence broke out between Hamas and Fatah supporters. In June 2007, Hamas moved militarily against Fatah in Gaza, quickly driving them out. As a result, on 14 June, Abbas sacked Haniyeh as Prime Minister. The Palestinians now divided territorially and politically in two, with Hamas holding the monopoly of power in its Gaza stronghold, where Haniyeh remained as premier, while Fatah dominated the West Bank, where Abbas (with doubtful legality) appointed an alternative premier, Salam Fayed. Israel quickly tightened its control over the Gaza border, leading to further hardship in the Strip, but failing to prevent arms supplies being smuggled into the territory through tunnels, dug across the border into Egypt. For a time, Israel effectively relied on an economic stranglehold, including (from September 2007) limits on oil supplies, to ensure Hamas's good behaviour, but the Palestinians continued to fire rockets—many of them crude, home-made weapons with only a short-range—into Israel, bringing air strikes and limited military incursions in reply. Israel also proved ready to reopen peace talks with Abbas in November 2007, a move that helped keep Fatah and Hamas divided. During a large-scale international conference at Annapolis, in the US, in November, Abbas and Olmert both supported the idea of a two-state solution and expressed hopes of a settlement the following year.

The Gaza Crisis of 2008–9 and its Aftermath

In 2008, far from seeing peace, the Israeli–Palestinian situation settled into deadlock: Hamas and Fatah remained bitterly divided; Israeli premier Olmert was increasingly beleaguered by accusations of corruption and criticized for considering concessions to Fatah; his talks with Abbas, which Hamas condemned, made no real progress. Then, in November, several months of uneasy ceasefire between Israel and Hamas broke down, and Israel decided to cripple its opponents in Gaza. Beginning on 27 December 2008, Israel launched air attacks, focused on the Hamas police force and government buildings, but also targeting the tunnels from the Gaza Strip into Egypt, through which Hamas smuggled weapons and supplies. Hundreds of civilians were killed or wounded. An Israeli ground invasion followed on 3 January 2009, while air strikes continued, some hitting the homes of Hamas officials. A number of Hamas leaders were killed, including their interior minister, Said Siyyam. By around 11–12 January, the Israeli army was in heavily populated parts of Gaza City itself, and international concern was mounting. Despite this, Gaza remained effectively sealed off, and the inhabitants paid a high price for the Israeli actions against Hamas, which did not discriminate between armed militants and ordinary civilians. Some schools, businesses, and buildings housing international workers were destroyed by Israeli military action. In addition, the Israelis were accused of illegally using white phosphorous and suffered a further blow to their international image. When Israel unilaterally ended the attacks on 17 January, well over a thousand Gazans had been killed, the infrastructure of the Hamas government had been wrecked, and Israel had secured an agreement from Egypt to close off the supply tunnels into Gaza. Hamas continued to fire hundreds of rockets into southern Israel throughout the invasion, but they had tended to lessen in number and caused limited damage.

By the time the Israeli offensive into Gaza was called off, Israel's close ally George Bush had given way to a new US President, Barack Obama. As part of his move away from the unilateralist foreign policy of his predecessor, he not only announced that US combat troops would be out of Baghdad and other cities in June and withdraw from Iraq by the end of 2011, but sought to improve US relations with the Islamic world, notably in a much heralded speech at Cairo University on 4 June. The desire for improved engagement with Islam seemed genuine enough but, with US influence threatened by economic depression and a reluctance to risk foreign wars, and with Washington's continued commitment to Israeli security, as well as its abiding suspicion of Iran, the ambition proved difficult to fulfil. During Obama's early months in office, talk of better relations with the Arabs was balanced by closer military ties to Israel, including further arms supplies. The 'Quartet' continued to back the 'road map' to peace, including the eventual creation of a Palestinian state, but in February 2009 Israeli voters elected a new government under the Likud leader, Benjamin Netanyahu, who was known for his tough approach to negotiations and almost immediately differed with the new American president. Obama's Cairo speech had included criticism of Israeli settlements in Palestinian territory, but, speaking at Bar-Ilan University, Netanyahu set out his peace terms as being recognition of a Palestinian state only if it had no armed forces, left Jerusalem entirely under Israeli control, and gave up hopes that Palestinian refugees might return to lands their families had owned in Israel before 1948. Like Sharon before him, he continued to reject an important element of the road map, a freeze on Israeli settlements, although in November 2009 he did prove ready to introduce a temporary, ten-month freeze. Talks followed between the two sides under US and Egyptian auspices, but they stalled in September 2010, when Netanyahu's freeze on settlements came to an end. Although Obama shared in the general criticism of the Israeli action, there were limits to how far he would distance himself from Washington's commitment to its major Middle East ally and, in February 2011, the US vetoed a UN resolution that condemned the Israeli settlements.

Meanwhile, the Palestinian position seemed to strengthen in some ways. For one thing, Israel effectively lost the sympathy of one of its few friends in the region, Turkey. This was partly due to a reorientation of Turkish policy to improving relations with other Islamic powers, but it was also because of the death of several Turks when Israel attacked a ship carrying aid to Gaza in May 2010, and subsequently refused to apologize. More importantly, in late April 2011 a reconciliation deal was finally achieved between Hamas and Fatah, which promised to pave the way to a united Palestine. This paved the way for a call from the Egyptian foreign minister, Nabil al-Arabyi,

BOX 24.2

Gaza after 2011

Gaza remained the key flashpoint for Israeli–Palestinian tension in the following years. In mid-November 2012, following an upsurge in rocket attacks over the border, there was another Israeli incursion into the Gaza Strip, over a week, which left five Israelis and about 140 Palestinians dead. Eighteen months of relative calm followed, until the murder of three Israeli teenagers in June 2014 sparked yet another invasion of Gaza, this time preceded by a week of missile strikes and lasting for several weeks. While Israel justified it as a defensive action against Hamas rocket attacks (hence the codename of the operation, 'Protective Edge'), it was a large-scale, sustained invasion that killed over 2,000 Palestinians and about 70 Israelis, as well as leaving much of Gaza devastated. It confirmed Netanyahu's readiness to take extreme unilateral action, further set back any long-term settlement of Palestine's future, and left the Israeli blockade in place. Despite widespread criticism of Israeli tactics, Hamas found little meaningful diplomatic support and Palestinians turned to new tactics, such as a series of knife attacks that began in late 2015. The continuing sense of threat arguably helped Netanyahu retain power: in 2013 he was elected to his third term in office as Prime Minister and, in 2015, to a fourth, the first person to achieve this since Ben-Gurion. Meanwhile, relations between Netanyahu and Obama remained poor. In addressing Congress on 3 March 2015, the Israeli premier criticized the President's readiness to enter into the upcoming Iran nuclear deal, while on 23 December 2016, to Israeli fury, Obama refused to veto UN Security Council Resolution 2334, which condemned Israeli settlements in occupied Palestinian territories. But by then Obama's days in office were numbered and it should be emphasized that he always remained committed to Israeli security. In September 2016, he had agreed a massive, $38 billion deal on arms deliveries to Israel over the next ten years. Meanwhile, the situation of the two million Palestinians isolated in Gaza continued to deteriorate. In July 2017, ten years after Hamas took over the enclave, a UN report detailed the impact of the Israeli blockade on the 'wretched' population, including inadequate water and electricity supplies, poor health facilities, and declining economic growth, with only limited reconstruction since the Israeli invasion of 2014. The election of the strongly pro-Israel Donald Trump allowed Netanyahu to ignore Resolution 2334 and announce, in January 2017, the building of almost 600 new settler homes in East Jerusalem. The two leaders had a friendly summit in May 2017 and Trump recognized Jerusalem as Israel's capital in December, whilst also claiming to remain committed to a two-state solution. The act of recognition sparked outrage across the Arab world and led the Palestinians to say that the US could no longer mediate a settlement between them and Israel. There was another upsurge of violence on the Gaza border, beginning in April, as Palestinians began protests to mark the seventieth anniversary of the creation of Israel.

on 2 May, for the US to support the creation of a Palestinian state, and for President Obama's initiative in May for a peace based on the 1967 borders. Netanyahu was negative in his response. On a visit to Washington over the following days, he declared the 1967 borders to be 'indefensible' and spoke of demographic changes (that is, the Jewish settlements that Israel continued to expand on the West Bank) having altered realities on the ground. But the Palestinian Authority, under Abbas, now developed a strategy of forcing the issue onto the international agenda by asking the UN to recognize the existence of a Palestinian state. Of course, this would undermine the US–Israeli strategy of having the Palestinians, while in a weakened, stateless situation, negotiate on their differences with the Israeli state. Abbas's speech to the UN, on 23 September 2011, appealing for recognition, included a statement of the Palestinian readiness to accept Israel's existence and resolve differences peacefully. But in a reply, Netanyahu argued that it was the Palestinians who were currently unwilling to talk.

D. The Israeli Invasion of Lebanon, 2006

Israel's continuing readiness to use military force against its enemies was not only seen in Gaza in this period. 2006 also saw a short-lived invasion of Lebanon, but one that had a profound effect on that country's politics and suggested that, even for Israel, military force could be a blunt weapon. Problems on the Israel–Lebanon border went back decades. There had been clashes between Hezbollah (the 'party of God') and Israel even after the supposed end of the Lebanese civil war in 1990 (see Chapter 17, A). An Israeli incursion into southern Lebanon in July 1993 failed to deter cross-border attacks on Israeli settlements, so another, larger-scale incursion was launched in spring 1996, which ended after Hezbollah and other pro-Palestinian groups agreed to end their cross-border attacks on civilians. But when Israel finally pulled its troops out of its southern Lebanon 'security zone' in mid-2000, after a presence lasting eighteen years, it was done unilaterally, attempts to secure a peace agreement with the Lebanese government having failed. As the Israelis left, replaced by a small UN force, Hezbollah celebrated it as a victory. Having originally been seen in the 1980s as an extremist, Shi'ite group in Lebanon, backed by a foreign power, Iran, Hezbollah had grown in popularity, helped by its appeal to Islamic values, its support networks for many poorer Lebanese, and its determination to stand up to Israel. Differences between Israel and Lebanon were further stirred in 2000–2 by renewed differences over exploiting the waters of the River Jordan. Meanwhile, Syria, which had maintained its own forces in eastern areas of the country since 1976, continued to exert significant influence over Lebanese politics and, indeed, clung to a belief that the two countries were a unit. Syria was Israel's most hard-line opponent among the Arab states, willing to deal with Iran and, like Iran, to support two radical anti-Israeli groups, Hamas in Gaza and Hezbollah in Lebanon. A resolution by the UN Security Council, in 2004, for Syrian troops (numbering up to about 15,000) to withdraw and for militias, like Hezbollah's, to be disbanded was ignored.

Then, in February 2005, Syria was accused of being behind the murder of its key Lebanese critic, the (twice) Prime Minister, Rafiq Hariri. This led to a renewed threat of civil conflict in Lebanon, as pro- and anti-Syrian elements held mass rallies. In the complex sectarian mix of Lebanese politics, some (mainly Sunni and Christian groups) wanted to remove Syria's influence, but many (especially Shi'ite groups, including Hezbollah) saw it as a protector. Other key anti-Syrian figures were assassinated over the following years, but mounting international criticism led Syria to withdraw its remaining troops in April. Furthermore, anti-Syrian elements who won June's parliamentary elections, helped by the fact that the electoral system (reformed in 1989, but still dividing seats on confessional lines) worked against the Shi'ites, guaranteeing half the seats to Christians and most of the rest to the Sunnis and Druzes. But it was at this same point that Hezbollah, perhaps to bolster its support, revived its cross-border attacks on Israel, firing rockets at civilian settlements and attempting to capture Israeli soldiers. The Bush administration, which already considered Syria to be a supporter of international terrorism, withdrew its ambassador from Damascus after the Hariri assassination and later helped secure a UN Security Council demand that the main suspects, four Lebanese generals, be brought before an international tribunal.

Tensions between Israel and Hezbollah finally came to a head in mid-2006 when, amid rocket and missile attacks on civilian targets in northern Israel, Hezbollah ambushed an Israeli military patrol, killing a number of soldiers. This triggered an Israeli invasion of Lebanon in July–August 2006, with air strikes across the country, a naval blockade and a land invasion of the south. Aside from any motivation of retribution, Israeli leaders may have hoped to force the Lebanese government to act against Hezbollah. A swathe of destruction was cut across the area, a major refugee problem, involving perhaps a million people, was created, and about a thousand Lebanese were killed. On the other side, about 160 Israelis died and Jewish refugees, numbering hundreds of thousands, fled the border region. A UN-initiated ceasefire came in mid-August after nearly seven weeks of fighting. The UN peacekeeping force on the border was much enlarged, with the Lebanese army—which had rarely appeared there for decades and which had largely stood aside during the Israeli invasion—also now moving up to the border. Israeli troops then pulled back and the naval blockade was lifted, but it proved impossible to disarm the Hezbollah militias, who had continued to fire thousands of rockets into Israel's towns and cities during the invasion.

Both sides could claim successes. Israel had destroyed many of Hezbollah's weapons stocks, inflicted hundreds of casualties on the militia and could now hope that UN and Lebanese government forces would deter further Hezbollah military operations. But Hezbollah had both sustained its campaign against Israel and showed it could fight the Israeli army on the ground and avoid defeat. Other groups, including Shi'ite Amal militias and the PFLP, helped resist the Israelis, but it was Hezbollah that bore the brunt of the fighting, suffered by far the heaviest losses, and proved that the Israeli Defence Force could no longer guarantee a military victory. Even Israelis felt that the government of Ehud Olmert had, effectively, lost the war because of Hezbollah's survival. An inquiry, headed by a judge, Elijah Winograd, concluded in 2008 that the invasion was poorly executed and had failed to destroy Hezbollah despite Israel having massive military advantages. There were calls for

Olmert to resign, but he clung to office until early the following year. The Winograd Commission may have been too negative, however, because while stockpiling weapons and maintaining its organization, Hezbollah desisted from further rocket attacks on Israel. Indeed, the following years were remarkably calm on Lebanon's southern border.

Arguably, the outcome of the invasion in Lebanon was, from an Israeli perspective, most disappointing because of its impact within Lebanon. Hezbollah, which many saw as having defended the country from foreign invasion, now solidified its popularity in Lebanon, even winning the respect of Sunnis and Christians, just as it also won respect among other Arab countries. It objected to attempts to bring the suspected assassins of Rafiq Hariri to trial, encouraged demonstrations against the government in 2007, and engaged in armed clashes with its opponents in Beirut in the spring of 2008, when renewed civil war again seemed possible. But, after several months without a stable government, Lebanon stepped back from a return to the 1980s, with a national unity administration being formed in July, under Fouad Siniora, followed by an attempt to improve relations with Syria. The Syrians even agreed to exchange ambassadors with Lebanon for the first time, thereby conceding that the two states were separate political entities. The national unity government was sustained after elections in June 2009, when a Hezbollah-led alliance came second to an opposing one. But a renewed political crisis in the first half of 2011 saw a new government formed in which Hezbollah and its allies held many Cabinet posts.

Israel had, perhaps, secured a period of relative security on its northern border, but there was always the danger that violence could break out there again. There was renewed border tension in October 2010, for example, when the Iranian President, Mahmoud Ahmadinejad, visited Lebanon, underlining Iranian influence there. Such influence was sustained over the following years. Lebanon did not see a major internal upheaval during the 2011 Arab Spring, but *was* seriously affected by the ensuing civil war in neighbouring Syria. More than a million refugees fled over the border to Lebanon, where the fear of success for Assad's Sunni opponents led Hezbollah to lend support to President Assad. Hezbollah fighters probably began to cross the border in 2011, receiving support from Iran, and even fighting as part of Syrian army units. Lebanon remained one of the few democracies in the region but, worryingly for Israel, in the general election of May 2018 (the first since 2009), Hezbollah and its allies again emerged in strong position.

E. The Post-War Consequences of the War in Iraq

The Tribal Revolt

In May 2006, as the violence in Iraq was reaching its zenith, another government was finally formed, following further elections in December 2005. Al-Jaafari was succeeded by another Dawa Party leader, Nouri al-Maliki, and thereafter significant changes began to occur, especially after the US assassination of Zarqawi in June 2006. Al-Qaeda in Iraq's position began to change, essentially because of the growing opposition of local tribal sheikhs to it in Anbar province. They began a covert campaign of killing al-Qaeda members and, in the autumn, named their movement publicly as Sahwa (the Awakening). The leader of Sahwa was killed by al-Qaeda in 2007, but the movement had facilitated a link between the US 'surge' in troop numbers and Iraqi Sunnis, which eventually helped bring about an improvement in the security situation in the country.

With the significant reductions in the attacks on US and Iraqi forces in late 2007, businesses began to operate normally, and electricity supplies reached pre-war levels. In 2008, the decline in violence was considerable and Iraqi security services were becoming more effective, while the Iraqi police appeared more in control of the streets of Baghdad than did the Shi'ite militias. Outside Baghdad, Moqtada al-Sadr and his army of militia forces remained a key figure, with close links to Iran (where he lived in exile after 2007), a considerable body of support in Parliament, and no liking for the Americans or their Israeli allies. He initially opposed the surge, but his weakening position, apparently because of fracturing among his own supporters, had led him to announce a six-month ceasefire in August 2007. In 2008, the Iraqi government, still under Nouri al-Maliki, successfully launched operations against Moqtada's followers in Baghdad and Basra, and in August the cleric agreed to disarm much of the Mahdi Army. The weakening grip of al-Qaeda contributed to an improved security situation, as did the decision of Moqtada al-Sadr, but there were also disturbing developments, and waves of bombings in both August 2011 and again in January 2012.

The Growing Links to Syria

Links that developed between Iraq and Syria through the porous border helped to expand the Middle East conflict, as it was to enter a more devastating phase. The overnight removal of Iraq's 35,000 border guards by the American authorities had already produced an almost open border between Iraq and Syria, across which the movement of terrorists and jihadists might freely occur. Helped by Syrian President Bashar Assad, and his intelligence services, who were eager to promote the departure of elements opposed to the regime, jihadi fighters were encouraged to cross into Iraq from Syria, to join the fight against Western 'infidels'. The Syrian conflict was also to grow from ground first fertilized by that key source of Middle Eastern turmoil, the 2003 American invasion of Iraq. The attack produced a desire among Ba'ath party members in Syria to cross the border, from the eastern governorates of Hasakah and Deir ez-Zur, to defend Iraq.

The rapid internationalization of the war in Iraq, spearheaded by Palestinian 'Arab Liberation Front' fighters from Lebanon, led to a large migration of Arabs, which the Assad government either encouraged or did little to prevent. As the Iraqi insurgency developed, Syrian military intelligence, led by Assad's brother-in-law, had an interest in exporting Salafi jihadists and Chechen fighters across the border, to join Zarqawi and al-Qaeda in Iraq. With Syria's withdrawal from Lebanon in April 2005, the Iraqi border could have been more effectively protected, but a lucrative trade in smuggling fighters was already in place and, while there was some decrease in traffic in 2006, there were still many eager recruits for jihadism. By the time of Bush's 'surge', US intelligence reports suggested that nearly 90 per cent of foreign fighters in Iraq had come through Syria.[27]

There was a watershed in 2007 in the development of terrorism in the Middle East because it exposed the connections, not only between the two countries of Iraq and Syria, but also between them and other longstanding Middle Eastern problems. On one side of the conflict was the US surge, and its links to the Sawha movement, that had the short-term effect of weakening al-Qaeda in Iraq, just as much of it was being transformed into another jihadist movement; on the other side were the seeds sown along the porous Syria–Iraq border, fertilized by the US-favoured Maliki regime in Baghdad and the Alawite regime in Damascus, that were both beginning to bear their poisonous fruits which had been growing on the American tree planted by the invasion of Iraq.

The Origins of the Islamic State in Iraq (ISI)

One fear of those opposed to sending Western military forces to Iraq after 2003 was that it would increase the scale of terror threats and deepen instability in the Middle East. The actions of the US-imposed Coalition Provisional Authority in dismantling the military and administrative elements of Saddam Hussein's regime certainly increased these dangers. Nonetheless, few envisaged the awful consequences that arose from the ashes of the Iraqi state, as US forces departed in late 2011. Al-Qaeda in Iraq had been significantly weakened with the US assassination of its leader, al-Zarqawi, and the revolt of Sunni tribal leaders aided by the extra troops deployed in Bush's 2007 'surge'. Yet a weakened al-Qaeda in Iraq gave birth to a new and more horrific force, which the new Iraqi state, in the aftermath of the American departure, had great difficulty in containing, and had an especially profound impact on events in Syria. This movement emerged from a splinter group in al-Qaeda in Iraq as Zarqawi's most significant successor, which by October 2006, formed a new jihadist movement, the Islamic State in Iraq (ISI) under Omar al-Baghdadi. Moreover, by late September 2007, some 29 senior ISI figures had been killed, and although the group's leader, Omar al-Baghdadi, survived attempts to kill him until April 2010, it is possible that the weakened movement was only kept alive by Palestinian refugee fighters and links to Syria, as well as by the recruitment network that was being established there. In early 2008, as ISI was retreating north to a relatively safe, Sunni-dominated zone around Mosul, it was weakened like al-Qaeda by the changes in Iraq. Hence the cross-border connections to Syria, in May 2008, enabled ISI to launch a daring cross-border raid from Syria into the Iraqi town of al-Qaim, in Anbar province, demonstrating the importance of Syria to continued jihadist operations in Iraq.

The ISI leader, Omar al-Baghdadi, initially hoped to maintain the links to al-Qaeda while wanting the new organization to be seen more as a state than a jihadist terrorist movement. Somewhat ambivalently, he announced at the end of 2006 that al-Qaeda was but one of the groups in the Islamic State and that AQI was no more. Although bin Laden refused to denounce the Islamic state in Iraq, the leadership of al-Qaeda believed it was too soon for the establishment of an Islamic state and the leadership battle over the direction of the global jihadist movement had begun. Things looked far from promising in Iraq though, especially with Omar Baghdadi's assassination, along with other ISI leaders in April 2010. But with the departure of American troops in 2011 the difficulties facing ISI were reduced as the invasion's legacy with its increased violence and conflict soon resurfaced. The divisions between Sunni and Shi'ite remained, as Maliki and his government appeared to have little interest in reducing the recently exacerbated divisions between Sunnis and Shi'ite produced by the war and its aftermath. The adoption of democratic elections in a majority Shi'ite country, whose population had suffered at the hands of Saddam Hussein's Sunni regime, meant that politics offered easy opportunities to win support by favouring the Shi'ites. The leading Shi'ite power in the region was, of course, Iran and with ISI, like Zarqawi but unlike al-Qaeda, keen to condemn Shi'ites in the same way as infidels, the stage was set for conflict at several levels that would threaten the stability of Iraqi politics and society.

This post-US situation would play into the hands of ISI, who could exploit both the disturbing failures and successes left by the American occupation. Renewal, for Iraq Sunnis who were attracted to the narrow religious dogma and the violent and distorted view of Islam, could come through religious fulfilment. At the same time, the possibility of an Islamic state offered an escape from the despair of poverty and lack of opportunity that had dominated much of the new millennium for many poorer people. Crucially, the American invasion by eroding the things holding Iraqi society together, soon promoted militias and the sectarian violence by which further destruction was implemented. In the second half of the noughties when ISI emerged, the role of special forces, often American and British ones working together with significant short-term success, became a significant Western element of the war. One Task Force (TF145), with sophisticated equipment, consisted of three groups of American special forces and one British group, and at one stage was conducting 300 night raids per month. It was behind the air strike that killed Zarqawi, and the general tactics brought in large numbers of prisoners (one estimate is more than 100,000) to be held without trial in special camps. Such camps like the one where Omar al-Baghdadi's May 2010 ISI successor, Abu Bakr al-Baghdadi, had been held, were hotbeds of jihadist proselytizing. When the regular American forces left, most of the detainees were released, including the future leader of ISI and the eventual caliph of the Islamic State. In addition to the thousands of contacts that were made, many of the insurgents came into ISI from the recruiting ground of the American camps and were fighters with long experience of engaging well-equipped sophisticated forces, as well as militia fighters. The war on terror had certainly encouraged terrorism in Iraq and helped ensure that the proficiency of its fighters was soon to be a key factor in the rapid advance of ISI and Islamic State in Iraq and al-Sham (ISIS).

Curiously, the exact reasons why the war on Iraq was embarked upon remain unclear, despite the Senate Report on pre-war intelligence on Iraq and the 9/11 Report. Important influences and motives were Bush's personal convictions linked to faith, gut feelings, and the Iraqi assassination attempt of 1993 on his father; the twin aims of the Bush Doctrine to act against terror and those supporting terrorism or possessing WMDs—linked to faulty intelligence over Iraqi weapons and the absurd idea that Saddam and bin Laden were allies; a US desire to secure supplies of Middle East oil; and ideological hopes of democratizing the Middle East through the exercise of US power—all of these possible reasons have to be considered. The consequences of the administration's actions in Iraq are clearer, and more disturbing, than the reasons for them. As some genuine Middle Eastern experts had predicted, Christian US troops invading the Islamic Middle East helped to inspire jihad and militant Islam, rather than to prevent it, as seen in the fact that terrorist attacks worldwide increased markedly after the attack on Iraq.

That the outcome for America was ultimately much better than might have been expected around 2005, was partly due to Bush rejecting advice from some key military and civilian sources and allowing a temporary increase in force levels, under the 'surge', accompanied as this was by a new counter-insurgency strategy. Bush must take credit for that decision, made against the advice of most military leaders and foreign policy advisers, in the same way that he must take the blame for the failures the war left behind. Al-Qaeda's strong, if temporary, role within Iraq by 2006 had been created by the conflict that was portrayed as destroying the links between Saddam and al-Qaeda, which had never actually existed. The threat from Saddam and his WMDs was not prevented, because in 2003 it had not existed, but what did emerge from the conflict was a Shi'ite-dominated state with closer links to Iran and its nuclear programme. The costs of all this included about 100,000 Iraqi dead, a burden on US taxpayers in excess of a trillion dollars, 30,000 US soldiers wounded and 4,500 dead, as well as the damaged international reputation and prestige of both the military and civilian arms of the US government, who once, in the wake of 9/11, had commanded global sympathy.[28]

Visit the online resources that accompany this book to test your understanding and take your learning further: www.oup.com/he/young-kent3e

NOTES

1. Much of the detail in the preceding paragraphs is taken from Bob Woodward, *Plan of Attack* (Simon & Schuster, London, 2004), 52–106.
2. Ibid., 108–9, 96–7, 103.
3. Ibid., supplies the details on the basis of interviews.
4. Terry H. Anderson, *Bush's Wars* (Oxford University Press, New York, 2011), 103.
5. The quote is from Bob Woodward, *Plan of Attack* (Simon & Schuster, London, 2004), 164.
6. Two weeks after 9/11 a CBS poll found only six per cent of Americans believing Saddam Hussein was behind the attacks, but by the time of the invasion in March 2003, fifty-three per cent believed this to be the case.
7. We are indebted to James Strong, then an LSE PhD student, for pointing this out.
8. Bob Woodward, *Plan of Attack* (Simon & Schuster, London, 2004), Chs 17 and 18, 197–9 in particular; Terry H. Anderson, *Bush's Wars* (Oxford University Press, New York, 2011), 112.
9. Terry H. Anderson, *Bush's Wars* (Oxford University Press, New York, 2011), 106.
10. Terry Anderson dates the decision to July 2002: ibid., 101.
11. Bob Woodward, *Plan of Attack* (Simon & Schuster, London, 2004), 254, 256, 258.
12. For the difficulties produced by the clash between the ideological paper-pushing approach of Feith and those like Franks, with greater practical awareness of the reality on the ground, see ibid., 281–3.
13. ibid., 281 and Chs 27–9.
14. Transcript of the oral introduction to the 12th UNMOVIC quarterly report, www.un.org/Depts/unmovic/SC7asdelivered.htm.
15. Terry H. Anderson, *Bush's Wars* (Oxford University Press, New York, 2011), 122.
16. Bob Woodward, *Plan of Attack* (Simon & Schuster, London, 2004), Chs 27–9.
17. Terry H. Anderson, *Bush's Wars* (Oxford University Press, New York, 2011), 128.
18. Bob Woodward, *Plan of Attack* (Simon & Schuster, London, 2004), Chs 30–1.
19. Terry H. Anderson, *Bush's Wars* (Oxford University Press, New York, 2011), 159.
20. Terry H. Anderson, *Bush's Wars* (Oxford University Press, New York, 2011), 151–6; the Bush administration 'tended to gloss over' the fact that al-Qaeda established itself in Iraq eighteen months after the US invasion.
21. The scale of the disaster inflicted on Iraq can be gauged from Ivy League Research at Brown University that put the number of known Iraqi civilian deaths from direct war related violence at 182,000. As all such deaths were not recorded accurately, the actual figure is much higher. Several times as many Iraqi civilians may have died as an indirect result of the war, due to damage to the systems that provide food, health care and clean drinking water, and as a

result, illness, infectious diseases, and malnutrition that could otherwise have been avoided or treated. https://watson.brown.edu/costsofwar/costs/human/civilians/iraqi.

22. Peter L.Bergen, *The Longest War* (Free Press, New York, 2011) 167.

23. Ibid., Ch. 10.

24. Ibid., 158, 171 quoting US Marines, 'State of the Insurgency in al-Anbar'.

25. Terry H. Anderson, *Bush's Wars* (Oxford University Press, New York, 2011), 189–91.

26. Peter L.Bergen, *The Longest War* (Free Press, New York, 2011) 172.

27. Charles R. Lister, *The Syrian Jihad* (Hurst, London, 2015), 41.

28. Peter L.Bergen, *The Longest War* (Free Press, New York, 2011) Ch. 16, especially 278–96.

25

Economic Problems in the West and the Economic Rise of China in the East

Chapter contents

A. The 2008 Economic Crisis

Origins of the Crisis

Countries of the developed world and, particularly those in Europe, had seemed to enjoy prosperity as consumerism blossomed in the late 1990s and early Noughties, notwithstanding the creation of the Euro in 1999, while in Asia economies were recovering from the 1997 crisis. In Latin America, even Argentina, which had suffered the worst from the debt problems of the previous decades, achieved a trade surplus and a growth rate of 9 per cent that year. Three years later the problems flowing from Europe and the US were so big, and were becoming so difficult to resolve quickly, that the future of capitalism itself was being questioned. The starting point for the doubts was the self-evident assumption (at least for those able to face the implications) that the 'credit crunch had destroyed faith in the free market ideology that dominated Western economic thinking for a decade. But what can—and should—replace it?' It was as if the Cold War had been fought to produce a highly successful failure. The next day, the London *Financial Times* quoted a banker, lamenting that he did not know what could replace it—an indication that it might have to continue.[1]

The end of the post-war economic consensus and the reduction of inequality in the developed world had heralded a period of lower growth, which, when the Cold War ended, had contributed to the Washington Consensus on economic growth. The ten principles of the Washington Consensus (see Chapter 16, A) were accompanied by the rise of neoliberal economics with its emphasis on cutting public expenditure and reducing state involvement in the economy. These had begun before the Cold War triumph of democratic capitalism and were to continue as the belief in market-enabling individualism began to weaken the state and its perceived role of helping the 'undeserving poor' to be sustained by the services and provisions paid for out of 'excessive' taxation on the rich. (In reality, the rate of basic direct taxation in the UK has declined from 34p in the pound to 20p since the 1960s.) For a considerable time before the 2008 crisis in the US and most European states, high levels of public and private expenditure had only been sustained by increasing levels of national and personal debt. The effects of this had been exacerbated by the faith invested in 'free' market changes to the globalized financial world since the 1980s, and the accompanying loss of national government power over an increasingly deregulated economy. Widespread distrust of the state, despite its provision of benefits for many individuals, especially the poor and the disadvantaged, was increasingly evident as the consumption boom, funded more and more by debt, continued to expand. Manufacturing in the developed West, and its provision of secure jobs for many workers, was undermined by the new economic environment of globalization, as well as the growth of cheaper manufacturing in China and the other BRIC countries (Brazil, Russia, and India). A new epoch of financial capitalism, which had emerged since the 1980s, was in full swing by the start of the Noughties. In the new millennium, it was particularly aided by new regulations that allowed commercial banks to operate as investment banks in a world which already allowed cross-border flows of capital in a globalized international financial system.

In some of the developed world, revenue came less from manufacturing and production, but more from service industries, and borrowing achieved at ever-higher levels of risk. In addition, increased oil prices were the result of the 2003 Iraq war, when the US spent hundreds of millions of dollars importing oil, at a time when demand for energy from expanding economies like China and India was rising significantly. Financially, the iron law of capitalism, which states that the greater the return on the use of capital the greater the risk in such a use, could no longer be regulated by the realities of repayment or governance. Hence, the increased role of derivatives, hedge funds, collateralized debt obligations (CDOs) (known, without any hint of irony as 'securitization' in much the same way as 'securitization' was introduced into the military world of strategy), credit default swaps (CDSs), and short-term selling, in a high-risk world often referred to as 'casino capitalism'. As paper financial transactions became increasingly subject to the charging of high fees, to boost the profits of banks and the financial services industry, new priorities and incentives were provided by more complex financial schemes to make money from debt. The false premises of this new financial world were soon to be dramatically exposed. The catalyst of the crash producing the changes was the huge amount of 'sub-prime' mortgage debt in the US and its contribution to 'securitization'. Just as the medieval alchemists attempted to transform base metal into gold, so the modern sorcerers aimed to 'securitize' high-risk loans which were unlikely to be paid back. In essence, this modern alchemy meant packaging debts with other debts, thereby transforming them into products with high credit ratings. Thus began the failure of the regulators to counter the opportunities and incentives presented to the bankers, in order to encourage them to make greater profits from castles built on the sands of debt.

For small businesses and householders in particular, the debt obligations were underwritten by dramatic increases in property prices. This was the bubble that burst in a US-dominated globalized economy, where international movements of capital were unregulated. In the UK, the property bubble was helped by the shortage of new houses, which followed the failure of governments to see that housing provision was a key part of social policy. Consumerism and material gain were replacing values of social responsibility, not just internationally but within nation states. The main aim of the financial sector was no longer to provide the monetary means for entrepreneurs to achieve profits out of the 'real' economy; it was to maximize the revenue from financial transactions. As the property bubble of casino capitalism burst in many parts of the developed world, individuals were also trapped with credit card debts in states whose own indebtedness from wars and social security payments was to increase dramatically with the expansion of the financial sector.

Casino capitalism was the effect, rather than the cause, of the crisis of capitalism. It was significantly aided, especially during the 1990s, by concerted efforts of governments to deregulate the financial markets—measures favoured widely by financiers in the US, from the chairman of the Federal Reserve downwards. 'Big bang' deregulatory reforms in the City of London had begun in 1986. Deregulation meant the removal of controls which had forced the banks to follow strict capital reserve and liquidity ratios as part of a set of rules to limit risk-taking. The provision of unsecured high-risk loans, particularly on sub-prime mortgages,

BOX 25.1

Financial Glossary

Bail-out The financial rescue of a struggling borrower (e.g. banks that are the main borrowers and lenders in any financial system). A bail-out can be achieved in various ways:

- providing loans to a borrower that markets will no longer lend to
- guaranteeing a borrower's debts
- guaranteeing the value of a borrower's risky assets
- providing help to absorb potential losses, such as in a bank recapitalization

Bearer bonds Like bonds, a fixed income security with a maturity date and coupons attached to enable interest to be paid. They do not have registered owners, as the ownership is vested in the bearer of the paper bond. They can thus ensure anonymity and facilitate tax evasion.

Bond A debt security, or more simply, an IOU. The bond states when a loan must be repaid and what interest the borrower (issuer) must pay to the holder. They can be issued by companies, banks, or governments to raise money. Banks and investors buy and trade bonds.

Collateralized debt obligations (CDOs) A financial structure combining individual loans, bonds, or other assets in a portfolio, which can then be traded. In theory, CDOs attract a stronger credit rating than individual assets, owing to the risk being more diversified (securitization). But as the performance of many assets fell during the post-2007 financial crisis, the trading value of many CDOs was also reduced. (See www.investopedia.com/terms/c/cdo.asp especially for tranches, and for the important contribution of CDOs to the financial crash.)

Credit crunch A situation where banks and other lenders all cut back their lending at the same time, because of widespread fears about the ability of borrowers to repay. If heavily indebted borrowers are cut off from new lending, they may find it impossible to repay existing debts. Reduced lending also slows down economic growth, which thus makes it harder for all businesses to repay their debts.

Credit Default Swap (CDS) A financial contract that provides insurance-like protection against the risk of a third-party borrower defaulting on its debts. For example, a bank providing loans to Greece may choose to hedge the loan (see **Hedge fund**) by buying CDS protection on Greece. The bank makes periodic payments to the CDS seller. If Greece defaults on its debts, the CDS seller must buy the loans from the bank at their full face value. CDSs are not just used for hedging—they are used by investors to speculate on whether a borrower such as Greece will default.

Derivative A financial contract which provides a way of investing in a particular product without having to purchase it. For example, a stock market futures contract allows investors to make bets on the value of a stock market index such as London's 'FTSE 100' increasing by so many points or not. If the bet is successful, interest on the cost of the contract (i.e. the amount invested) is paid to the investor without the individual or bank having to buy or sell any shares. The value of a derivative can depend on anything from the price of coffee to interest rates or the weather, as well as stock market values. Derivatives allow investors and banks to hedge their risks or to speculate on markets. Futures, forwards, swaps, and options are all types of derivative.

Dodd–Frank Act Legislation enacted by the US in 2011 to regulate the banks and other financial services. It includes:

- restrictions on banks' riskier activities (see **Volcker rule**)
- a new agency responsible for protecting consumers against predatory lending and other unfair practices
- regulation of the enormous derivatives market
- a leading role for the central bank, the Federal Reserve, in overseeing regulation
- higher bank capital requirements
- new powers for regulators to seize and wind up large banks that get into trouble

EFSF The European Financial Stability Facility, a temporary fund worth up to €440 billion, set up by the Eurozone countries in May 2010. Following a previous bail-out of Greece, the EFSF was originally intended to help other struggling Eurozone governments, and has since provided rescue loans to the Irish Republic and Portugal.

Eurobond A common, jointly guaranteed bond issued by the Eurozone governments. Eurobonds are bonds issued or traded in a country using currency other than that in which the bond is denominated. A bond denominated in dollars sold in Europe by a US company is a Eurobond. Eurobonds were seen as a solution to the Eurozone debt crisis, as they would prevent markets differentiating between the creditworthiness of different government borrowers in the Eurozone. The Germans, until June 2012, resisted the idea.

Fiscal policy The government's borrowing, spending, and taxation decisions. If a government fears it is borrowing too much, it can raise taxes and/or cut spending. Alternatively, if a government wants to avoid the economy going into recession, it

BOX 25.1 (continued)

can engage in fiscal stimulus, which can include cutting taxes, increasing public spending, and/or borrowing more.

Freddie Mac, Fannie Mae Nicknames for two US Government Sponsored Enterprises (GSEs), respectively, the Federal Home Loans Mortgage Corporation and the Federal National Mortgage Association, established to make credit available to consumers. They never provided mortgages directly to home-buyers, but obtained a large part of the money that is lent out as mortgages in the US from the international financial markets. Both privately owned, they now operate as agents of the US federal government. As a result of the financial crisis, the government put them into 'conservatorship', guaranteeing to provide them with any new capital needed to ensure they would not go bust.

G8 The seven major industrialized economies of the world: US, UK, France, Germany, Italy, Canada, and Japan (the old G7), plus Russia.

G20 The G8 plus developing countries that play an important role in the global economy, such as China, India, Brazil, and Saudi Arabia. It gained in significance after leaders agreed how to tackle the 2008–9 financial crisis and the recession at G20 gatherings.

Glass–Steagall A US inter-war law separating ordinary commercial banking from investment banking. The commercial high street banks, which lend to consumers and businesses, are deemed vital to the 'real' US economy. The law was designed to protect their depositors from the risky speculation of investment banks. The law was repealed in 1999, enabling the creation of the banking giant, Citigroup, a move that many commentators say was part of the deregulation that contributed to the 2008 financial crisis. (See also **Volcker Rule**.)

Hedge fund A private investment fund that uses a range of sophisticated strategies to maximize returns including hedging, leveraging, and derivatives trading.

Hedging Making an investment to reduce the risk of price fluctuations in the value of an asset. For example, airlines often hedge against rising oil prices by agreeing in advance to buy their fuel at a set price. In this case, a rise in price would not harm them—but nor would they benefit from any falls.

Investment bank Investment banks provide financial services for governments, companies, or extremely wealthy individuals. They differ from commercial banks, where you have your savings. Traditionally, investment banks provided underwriting, and financial advice on mergers and acquisitions, and how to raise money in the financial markets. They and commercial banks now engage in the riskier activities, often referred to as 'casino capitalism', including trading directly in financial markets for their own account.

Leverage Leverage, or gearing, means using debt to supplement investment. The more you borrow on top of the funds (or equity) you already have, the more highly leveraged you are. Leverage can increase both gains and losses. 'Deleveraging' means reducing the ratio of what you are borrowing to the value of ordinary share capital (equity).

Liquidity crisis A situation in which it suddenly becomes much more difficult for banks and businesses to obtain cash, owing to a general loss of confidence in the financial system. Investors (and, in the case of a bank run, even ordinary depositors) may withdraw their cash from banks, while banks may stop lending to each other, if they fear that some banks could go bust. Because most of a bank's money is tied up in loans, even a healthy bank can run out of cash and collapse in a liquidity crisis. Central banks usually respond to a liquidity crisis by acting as 'lender of last resort', providing emergency cash loans to the banks.

Loan-to-deposit ratio For financial institutions, the sum of their loans divided by the sum of their deposits. It measures a bank's vulnerability to the loss of confidence during a liquidity crisis. Deposits are usually guaranteed by the bank's government and are therefore considered a safer source of funding for the bank. Before the 2008 financial crisis, many banks became very reliant on other sources of funding—meaning that they had very high loan-to-deposit ratios. When these other sources of funding suddenly evaporated, the banks were left critically short of cash.

Mortgage-backed securities (MBS) Banks repackage debts from a number of mortgages into MBS, which can be bought and traded by investors. By selling off their mortgages in the form of MBS, it frees the banks up to lend to more homeowners.

Securities lending When one broker or dealer lends a security (such as a bond or a share) to another for a fee. This is the process that allows short selling.

Securitization Turning something into a security. For example, taking the debt from a number of mortgages and combining them to make a financial product, which can then be traded (see **Mortgage-backed securities**). Investors who buy these securities receive income when the original home-buyers make their mortgage payments.

Security A contract, or something deposited or pledged for the fulfilment of an undertaking, that can be assigned a value for the repayment of a loan and traded. It could be a share, a bond, or a mortgage-backed security. When the term 'security' is used

(continued)

BOX 25.1 (continued)

to pledge the borrower's home when taking out a loan, as is usually done to secure mortgages in the UK, this means that if the borrower cannot repay, the lender can seize the security—the home—and sell it in order to help repay the outstanding debt.

Shadow banking A global financial system—including investment banks, securitization, Special Purpose Vehicles (SPVs), CDOs, and monoline insurers—that provides a similar borrowing and lending function to banks, but is not regulated like banks. Prior to the financial crisis, the shadow banking system had grown to play as big a role as the banks in providing loans. However, much of shadow banking system collapsed during the credit crunch that began in 2007, and in the 2008 financial crisis.

Shell companies Non-traded companies—i.e. not listed on the stock exchange—that do not own assets or conduct business operations. They exist only as registered financial entities, often with nothing more than a mailing address. Functioning to facilitate financial transactions, they often serve to conceal the actual owners of assets and to get more favourable tax treatment. They can be used to obtain finance or maintain control of companies, and can be vehicles for the illegal activity of money laundering. Transparency International said the UK has insufficient controls and 'there are practically no barriers to UK companies being incorporated by money launderers' and 'companies are being set up under our noses, with the sole purpose of laundering illicit wealth; money very often stolen from some of the poorest populations in the world, starving them of vital resources'. (Source: www.ft.com/content/11d83f24-c496-11e7-a1d2-6786f39ef675)

Short selling A technique used by investors who think the price of an asset, such as shares or oil contracts, will fall. They borrow the asset from another investor and then sell it in the relevant market. The aim is to buy back the asset at a lower price and return it to its owner, pocketing the difference. Also known as 'shorting'.

Spread The difference in the yield (see below) of two different bonds of approximately the same maturity, usually in the same currency. The spread is used as a measure of the market's perception of the difference in creditworthiness of two borrowers.

SPV A Special Purpose Vehicle (also Special Purpose Entity or Company) is a legal entity created by a bank or investment bank solely for the purpose of fulfilling a particular function, e.g. a subsidiary company to protect the parent company from high-risk investments. Before the financial crisis, SPVs were regularly used by banks to offload loans that they owned, freeing the banks up to lend more. SPVs were a major part of the shadow banking system and were used in securitization and CDOs.

Stability pact A set of rules demanded by Germany to limit the borrowing of governments inside the Euro to 3 per cent of their GDP, with fines to be imposed on miscreants. The original stability pact was abandoned after Germany itself broke the rules with impunity in 2002–5.

Sub-prime mortgages These carry a higher risk to the lender (and therefore tend to be at higher interest rates) because they are offered to people who have had financial problems or who have low or unpredictable incomes and thus face difficulties in maintaining repayments.

Swap A derivative that involves an exchange of cash flows between two parties. For example, a bank may swap out of a fixed long-term interest rate into a variable short-term interest rate, or a company may swap a flow of income out of a foreign currency into their own currency.

TARP The Troubled Asset Relief Program(s), a $700 billion rescue fund set up by the US government in response to the 2008 financial crisis. Originally, the TARP was intended to buy up or guarantee toxic debts owned by the US banks, hence its name. However, shortly after its creation, the US Treasury announced a series of initiatives on 14 October 2008 to strengthen market stability, improve the strength of financial institutions, and enhance market liquidity. Under TARP's Capital Purchase Program, US financial institutions were encouraged to build capital to increase the flow of financing to US businesses and consumers, and to support the US economy. Under that program, the Treasury would purchase up to $250 billion of preferred shares and assisted recapitalization of the entire US banking system. (Source: www.federalreserve.gov)

Tobin tax A tax on financial transactions, originally proposed by Nobel prize-winning economist James Tobin as a levy on currency conversions. The tax was intended to discourage market speculators by penalizing short term currency speculation, and in this way increase stability in financial markets following the 1971 collapse of the Bretton Woods system and the introduction of flexible exchange rates. It has been formally proposed by the European Commission and opposed by the post-2010 UK coalition government unless it was applied globally.

Toxic debts Debts that are highly unlikely to be recovered from borrowers. Toxic debt describes a whole package of loans, through securitization, that are unlikely to be repaid. During the financial crisis, toxic debts were very hard to value or to sell, as the markets for them ceased to function, with the banks unwilling to lend to each other. This greatly increased uncertainty about the financial health of the banks that owned much of these debts.

BOX 25.1 (continued)

Volcker Rule Section 619 of the Dodds Frank Reform Act, commonly named after US Federal Reserve chairman, Paul Volcker, is a federal rule that bans US commercial banks and their affiliates from engaging in risky activities, such as proprietary trading (taking speculative risks on the markets with their own money contrary to depositors' money) or owning or investing in hedge funds or private equity funds. (Source: www.federalreserve.gov)

Yield The percentage return to the owner of a security embodied in the interest or dividend received from it. It can indicate a bond's current market price and also the current cost of borrowing in the market for the bond issuer. As a bond's market price falls, its yield goes up, and vice versa. Yields for all bonds in a particular currency will rise if markets think that the central bank in that currency will raise short-term interest rates owing to stronger growth or higher inflation.

Additional sources: dummies.com, economicsonline.co.uk, financial-dictionary.info, investopedia.com, myaccountingcourse.com, thebalance.com, thefreedictionary.com, uwsa.com, wikipedia.org

was accompanied by a naive faith in the infallibility of the market, and in the new technological methods and smart accounting procedures having ironed out any problems with the money-making capacity of the banking system. The idea that 'securitization' virtually eliminated risk became the gospel, spread by Alan Greenspan, chairman of the Federal Reserve Bank. As investors, particularly pension fund managers, demanded higher returns on lending, the tsunami of 2007–8 was created, which quickly threatened to sweep away important elements of the banking system.

The actions of some bankers were helped by a belief, which turned out to be correct, that the mismanagement of risk and the misallocation of funds would not produce disastrous losses for themselves. Either by the time any losses happened their particular profits would have been made, or else governments would not allow financial companies that got into difficulties to collapse. Instead, the system would be bailed out with taxpayers' money: the implications of not helping extract bankers from the mess they had got into would be disastrous for all those involved in the real economy. Two important accompaniments to deregulation were the importance of fees in providing incentives for more financial transactions (without adequate management of the longer-term risks) and the need to drive up stock market prices by deceptive (or 'creative') accounting. This was to produce the final obfuscation of who owned what debt. However much or little banks might know about their own debts, they were unable to accurately evaluate that of others or to estimate the consequences of a price fall. The result was that, as soon as the crisis broke, banks were unwilling to lend to other banks and all economic activity was under threat.

In April 2007, the New Century bank in the US became the first to file for bankruptcy. In July, the New York investment bank Bear Stearns shut down its $42 million hedge funds, after massive losses on mortgage-backed securities, and announced that its CDSs were worthless. In Europe, it was the French bank BNP Paribas that announced liquidity problems in August. Then, in September, problems at the Northern Rock bank in Britain led to a request for help from the Bank of England, the country's central bank. As the government dithered, the request produced a 'run' on deposits, with account holders withdrawing large amounts of money, which put the government under pressure to step in and prop it up. If the government did not act, then the consequences for everyone involved, including ordinary people who might be unable to access their money, in what were once purely commercial banks, would be very severe. The traditional role of banks in making money from providing loans to businesses, many of them in the local community, was fast disappearing. In February 2008, the cash assets of Bear Stearns in the US had fallen from $18 billion to $2 billion within days, and its shares, which began the year at $173, were now only worth a few dollars. It became an early candidate for a bail-out.

The failure of the two Bear Stearns hedge funds had resulted in a fall in the values of Lehman Brothers shares. Lehman Brothers was a major investment bank highly leveraged because of securitization, and in 2007 it was underwriting more mortgage-backed securities than any other firm. With an $85 billion portfolio of four times its shareholders' equity, its shares fell in March 2008 by nearly 50 per cent, despite raising $6 billion from investors and a $4 billion dollar preferred shares issue. With short-term creditors cutting the supply of credit and hedge fund clients pulling out, an urgent bail-out was refused by the Bush administration, and on 15 September, Lehman declared bankruptcy with only $1 billion left in cash.

The stock market also collapsed, losing 30 per cent of its value, and the crisis was made worse because of the fall in US house prices that had begun in 2006. The failure to regulate the mortgage market meant there was no stringent requirement to be able to repay the loan, and this sub-prime housing market, which had been growing since 1990s was accompanied by adjustable rate mortgages (ARMs), which meant repayments would start low and then increase. Such borrowers were particularly vulnerable to house prices collapsing. More significantly, the lack of financial regulation meant there was no requirement on credit default swappers to have an ability to fulfil the contract and repay the loan, should it be necessary. Days before Lehman's bankruptcy, the two US Government Sponsored Enterprises (GSEs)[2] were taken into conservatorship, the Federal National Mortgage Association (Fannie Mae) and the Federal Home Loans Mortgage Corporation (Freddie Mac). These organizations dealt with property lending, and were therefore badly affected by sub-prime lending and their massive mortgage backed securities.[3] Placing them under the Federal Housing Finance Agency was the only way US Treasury Secretary Henry Paulson could justify using taxpayers' money to invest $200 billion in preferred shares and to extend credit to 2009 in order to keep the publicly chartered private companies operating with their trillions of dollars in loans.

In July 2008, Indy Mac became the third largest bank to fail in US history and this was followed, in September, by the disintegration of Fannie Mae and Freddie Mac, the world's largest mortgage lenders, whose $200 billion debts, as we have seen, had to be taken over by the US government. The crisis was rapidly spreading because of the global nature of the international financial system. Central to this was the post-2000 expansion of financial mechanisms[4] pertaining to loans, securities, and derivatives (see the Glossary for CDOs and CDSs) with the combination of globalization and neoliberalism. Globally, the notional values of derivatives contracted without an intermediary grew from $72 trillion in 2005 to $684 trillion in June 2008, while those traded within organized exchanges rose from $14 trillion in 2000 to $100 trillion in 2007. Hence the growing gross debt of the US financial sector with 'securitization' had risen from 3 per cent of GDP in 1952 to 119 per cent of GDP in 2008. Sparked by the crisis in property debt in the US, which in direct terms was less than one-third of the debt from 'securities', losses from 'securities' almost trebled between April and October 2008 and were reflected in the simultaneous fall of stock prices on the European and Korean stock exchanges as well as in Tokyo, New York, and San Paulo.[5]

State Financial Assistance in Reaction to the Crash

The extent of the crisis was emphasized when after the collapse of Lehman Brothers, the largest bankruptcy in US history, at $635 billion, the following day the US government bailed out American International Group (AIG), the world's largest insurance company. Wall Street investment banks Goldman Sachs and Morgan Stanley were turned into holding companies to get some government protection and, in Europe, several banks failed, while governments began to pour money into others facing collapse. In Britain, two major banks were almost completely nationalized, in that the government now owned over three-quarters of their shares. The Prime Minister, Gordon Brown, shrank from the final, if logical, step of nationalization and this was to become a significant moment for the way in which the problems were subsequently tackled.

In Washington, the incoming Obama administration was already deeply troubled by high spending on the wars in Iraq and Afghanistan, launched under President Bush, and the US entered recession from mid-2008 to late 2009, its worst performance since the 1930s depression. Despite grave doubts from Republicans, Congress passed a $700 million rescue package, in October 2008, which helped to stabilize the banking sector. This amount, known as the Troubled Asset Relief Program or TARP, was already looking grossly inadequate. Vast amounts went into propping up vehicle manufacturers, but the world's largest, General Motors, still had to seek bankruptcy protection in June 2009. Led by Gordon Brown, world leaders, meeting at the G-20 summit in London, in April 2009, did try to coordinate their actions. For the moment, Brown's chairmanship prevented 1930s-style protectionism (when states put up tariff barriers against each other) taking hold and important elements of international cooperation were maintained. The International Monetary Fund (IMF) stepped in with money for

Ukraine, and there was G-20 help for less developed countries. The US introduced some stricter banking regulation, while avoiding a major change in the operation of financial capital, and Obama increased federal spending, linked to tax cuts, at the beginning of 2009. Yet some states, like Germany, were critical of the government investment strategy favoured by Obama and Brown. Despite the formal end of the recession in the US, still the world's largest economy, during 2009, that year saw the lowest growth in the world economy since 1945. Furthermore, with debt emerging as a new threat to financial confidence, it was soon clear that there would be no rapid recovery from the 2008 downturn.

World governments had long run up debts to pay for social security, wars, and expensive defence equipment, as well as health and education but, with an ageing population leading to higher pension payments and increased pressures on health services, even more money had to be found. With unemployment higher, thanks to the recession (which was now turning into another depression), expenditure was rising at a time when income from taxation was falling, both because of decreasing numbers of earners and significant reductions in taxation in many countries. Even servicing debt—that is, paying the interest on what had been borrowed—was becoming a major liability for some states before the 2008 crisis required trillions of dollars of debt to be incurred through the bail-out of banks. There were other problems, which soon added to the sense of economic woe. After some falls in energy prices with the improved situation in Iraq in 2009, there were renewed price rises in 2011 because of the instability in Libya. Also, the mushrooming world population and severe climatic problems, such as those that led to a disastrous Russian harvest in 2010, brought about a general increase in food prices. In Japan, problems were intensified by the earthquake and tsunami that struck the north-east in March 2011, leading to a fall in manufacturing output and exports.

However, in general, concern on the money markets focused on levels of state indebtedness and, specifically, worries about the ability of governments in Europe to finance these loans, especially when refinancing them would be subject to abnormally high interest rates. This, of course, offered large profits to bondholders willing to take the risk. The mostly right-of-centre European governments sought a reduction of their, now, massive debts by austerity measures that would cut public services and benefits. Countries outside Europe and North America were not immune to the crisis. In the 'real' economy, one of the earliest confirmations of the globalization of capital movements and debt problems was in Dubai, in the Persian Gulf, in November 2009; but Dubai was rescued at that point by one of its oil-rich neighbours, Abu Dhabi. Attention continued to be focused over the following years on Europe, in the hitherto successful Eurozone, where the future of the common currency, the Euro, was called into question by those states with the highest levels of debt relative to their GDP and the problems proved persistent over several years (see Chapter 25, C).

Post-Crisis Problems

As a direct result of the state bail-outs of private Western financial institutions, several advanced economies acquired what was regarded as unsustainable levels of borrowing. The risks of sustaining those levels (ironically, given the markets' previous behaviour) now appeared to be excessive. There was a political benefit in trying to put the entire blame on the public borrowing of past governments, a misleading accusation that, despite the events of 2008, also served to justify continuing faith in free-market capitalism. Nonetheless, the real issue now was how to revive economic growth in a climate no longer conducive to the easy borrowing of money. It was important for recovery that the rescued banks should lend their bail-out money to businesses in the 'real' economy rather than improve their own financial positions. For governments, raising direct taxation had long been politically unacceptable, and it was, in part therefore, an ideological choice in the UK between the devil, of cutting expenditure, and the deep blue sea, of borrowing money, for example to finance much needed low-cost housing by capital expenditure on public-sector infrastructure projects, which would increase public debt levels in the short term. Moreover, directly cutting government expenditure would not reduce the debt as rapidly as expected, because of its deflationary consequences. Unemployment was likely to increase, pushing up social security expenditure and reducing household spending: all these would serve to increase government spending and reduce the revenue from taxation. Thus, economic growth and recovery would become more difficult.

In the US, the government debt from the bail-outs was used by some as a reason for reducing the scale of

Obama's health-care reform. This was an example of how Western societies have polarized, in a zero-sum game, the difference between public (bad) and private (good) rather than, as was the case until the 1970s, believing that individual and social benefits should be reconciled and balanced for the benefit of all. The Obama administration chose not to restructure the banks (meaning reorganizing their liabilities with losses for shareholders and owners of capital). Instead, the federal government continued to give bail-outs to the banks. The initial money in TARP was provided without conditions and, in 2009, the administration announced a new programme, the Public–Private Investment Program, to buy toxic assets from banks, and so remove debt that was unlikely to be repaid from their balance sheets. Like all off-balance sheet transactions this did not mean that the debt disappeared, just that it was redistributed to someone else's balance sheet, in this case the cost to the US taxpayer. By 2012, all the bail-outs and guarantees provided by the federal government (though not all of the guarantees will necessarily have to be met) totalled nearly 80 per cent of US GDP—a staggering $12 trillion.[6]

One key question was how best to restore some degree of regulation to prevent a reoccurrence of a financial crisis. The other more immediate task was how best to repair the damage done to the real economy by the 2008 financial crash. In the UK, which returned to recession in the first quarter of 2012, greater liquidity from increased public expenditure was deemed undesirable and thus 'quantitative easing' (effectively printing money and using it via bond issues and the banks channelling it into the 'real' economy to stimulate economic activity) was adopted. Yet, unless the banks were to be nationalized, there was no way of guaranteeing money would reach the real economy. Bizarrely, on both sides of the Atlantic, governments expected that giving money to the very institutions that had demonstrated such incompetence in risk and credit assessment in the past would now ensure that credit flowed to those sectors of the economy best able to use it to deliver growth. Unfortunately, there was nothing to prevent the banks using the extra money to improve their own balance sheets by reducing liabilities ('deleveraging') as opposed to providing loans to businesses. This prevented many smaller businesses from getting access to the loans which they required to make a positive contribution to growth. After the 'credit crunch', therefore, the same problems of banks being reluctant to lend remained, and small businesses were still less able to access loans from banks to promote new initiatives. Instead, governments in North America and Europe cut public expenditure, which provides most benefit to those less well off, sometimes misleadingly in the name of debt reduction, even as it increased, without creating significant economic growth for a more long-term reduction of the deficit problem. Most advanced economies therefore stagnated, with no clear indication of how, or when, a significant recovery would occur.

Keynesian economists claim that a greater role for government is required in the disruption of the market, by directing money into areas, such as infrastructure, which provide jobs and social benefits for the majority, while alleviating the impact of depression. The Right, however, sees the solution in removing expensive social provisions, such as free health care, in the continuing belief that the market can operate most effectively without any form of government intervention. When the market failed to operate perfectly in the advanced economies, the US government chose not to help those losing their homes, but to introduce a corporate welfare system. The consequence was the largest market intervention by governments in history.[7] The impact of this contributed much to creating the new age of globalized uncertainty. The social consequences of the economic changes and their effects on the international system, now less subject to the power of nation states, remain to be determined. Surprisingly, the financial crisis initially showed little effect on the faith of Western governments in free-market capitalism. This may increase the speed of the shift in production to China and other developing countries. On the other hand, the continuing crisis of capitalism, in a globalized system, still dominated by the US, may yet severely damage the developing states as well. Nonetheless, the free-market mantra that has dominated the world since the 1980s, suffered a near-mortal blow. Western capitalism was no longer a fixed point around which the turbulent winds of democracy can flow freely. Thus, while the end of the Cold War may have removed the utopian illusions of Soviet-led communism and its horrors, it may be said that the West clung to an opposing set of utopian fallacies, similarly detrimental to the weaker members of society, which were exposed after 2008. The future of the West in managing its flawed economic dominance remains problematic and unclear. It is now time to turn to look in more detail at events in the European Union, before reviewing key developments in the international role played by America and Russia, then turning to the rise of a major competitor for the US, communist China.

B. The European Union in the Twenty-First Century

From Nice to Lisbon

After some difficult years in the late 1990s, the successful introduction of the single currency, the Euro, in twelve of the member states in January 2002 led to a revival of confidence in the European Union (EU). The Euro became the most important trading currency after the dollar and, for several years, under the guidance of the European Central Bank, it seemed to guarantee members of the 'Eurozone' sustained growth and low inflation. The major challenge of the early twenty-first century was to expand the Union eastwards, to states that had formerly been part of the Soviet bloc. As with previous enlargements, it was felt necessary to strengthen the cohesion of the Union through bureaucratic reforms to compensate for any centrifugal forces that an expanded membership might bring. Already, in February 2001, a treaty had been signed in Nice which, among other steps, altered voting arrangements, reduced the number of European Commissioners appointed by each member, and expanded the size of the European Parliament. But the process of reform did not prove easy. There were bitter arguments about the voting rights that should be apportioned to particular states and the complicated, compromise treaty was initially rejected by Irish voters in a referendum of June 2001. Some concessions (including an assurance about Ireland's continuing neutrality, notwithstanding the EU's move towards cooperation on security) helped reverse the vote in October 2002, paving the way to it entering into force the following year. But it was a warning of problems to come.

Meanwhile, in December 2001, a Convention was set up in Brussels under the chairmanship of former French President, Valéry Giscard d'Estaing, to draw up a Constitution for the EU. This was designed both to supersede all previous treaties and to push the process of integration further forward. It was also supposed to make the organization easier to understand and more genuinely democratic, with a number of principles set out to guide future integration, including the principle of 'subsidiarity', by which decisions were to be taken at the lowest appropriate level. This was calculated to reassure those who feared the creation of some impersonal European super-state. The Convention produced a draft document in July 2003 and symbolically, after considerable wrangling between the member governments, the Constitution was signed in October 2004 in Rome—the same place where the original European Economic Community (EEC) treaty had been signed forty-nine years earlier. The EU also continued to expand, with an unprecedented number of countries joining in May 2004—the ten included eight East European states (Poland, Hungary, Czech Republic, Slovakia, Slovenia, Estonia, Latvia, and Lithuania) and two Mediterranean ones (Cyprus and Malta)—with two more East European states, Romania and Bulgaria, following in January 2007. By then, however, the sense of progress had been marred by the defeat of the Constitutional Treaty. In mid-2005, it had to be abandoned because voters in two key states, France and the Netherlands, both founder members of the European Community, had rejected it. The French vote, by a decisive 55 per cent on a high turn-out, was especially shocking, though it could be blamed on it having been turned into a vote on the performance of President Jacques Chirac, rather than as reflecting a fundamental French turn away from the dream of European unity.

The situation was salvaged by drafting yet another treaty, signed in Lisbon on 13 December 2007, after only six months' work by an intergovernmental conference, which effectively included many proposals from the Constitution. The Lisbon Treaty simplified the workings of the EU by ending the existence of three separate 'pillars' (including one on justice and home affairs, and one on foreign and security policy) that had figured in the Maastricht Treaty. It strengthened the powers of the European Parliament, further extended the use of weighted majority voting by the Council of Ministers, and sought to raise the profile of the organization as an international actor by creating the positions of President of the European Council and a 'High Representative' for foreign affairs. It included a Charter of Fundamental Rights for EU citizens, a document that had first been published in 2000, but had hitherto lacked full legal force. It also declared the Euro to be the EU currency, even though member states could continue to opt out from using it. Another 'no' vote in Ireland ensured delays in the ratification progress, but the Treaty finally came into force in December 2009, when Belgium's Herman van Rompuy became the first President of the European Council and another little-known figure, Britain's Catherine Ashton, became High Representative. By then, the organization was being buffeted by the global financial crisis which, by leading to severe economic problems in Greece, Ireland, and Portugal, called into question the stability of the Euro.

Problems in the Eurozone

High levels of public expenditure and increased consumerism continued after the creation of the Eurozone in 1999. Ironically, the Eurozone was designed to bring further growth in Europe, stabilizing exchange rates and giving confidence for trade, but its intrinsic flaws soon produced serious economic instability. The political requirements of the leading European states might be met by a single currency, but all their economic needs could not, unless fiscal policies were coordinated to offset the lack of competitiveness of some European economies. The process would resemble the incorporation of the economic backwater of East Germany into the reunified German state after 1990, which brought considerable costs. Otherwise, the single currency would prevent the less competitive southern European countries being able to offset this disadvantage through devaluation of their currencies. Just as the other element of Keynesianism, higher taxes in times of boom, had been ruled out by consumer-driven liberal democracy, so the balance-of-payments problem could no longer be resolved by devaluation once a single currency was created. Not all countries could emulate the economic successes of German industry, nor could they always guarantee to run similar trade surpluses to Germany's within Europe.

The initial crisis struck in Greece, where the Socialist government, elected in October 2009, announced a few months later that debt had reached more than 110 per cent of GDP (the true statistics having been hidden previously). This was well above the level that was supposed to be allowed by Eurozone rules and led to fears that Greece might have to leave the zone, and maybe even default on its debts. In February 2010, the introduction of an austerity package sparked the first of many street protests in Athens; in May, the Eurozone and IMF, rather than see Greece collapse, put together a rescue package of €110 billion. Action in Greece, however, only focused attention on similar problems in another Eurozone member, Ireland, where government debt had been increased by the need to bail out one of its largest banks, Anglo-Irish, back in January 2009. In November 2010, the Eurozone and IMF had to put together a rescue package for Ireland, too, this time totalling €85 billion linked, as in Greece, to a swingeing austerity package. Similar measures were required in Portugal in May 2011, when a €78 billion bail-out fund was created. The Eurozone's leaders eventually hoped that the creation of a €500 billion 'European Stability Mechanism' would prevent any further problems on the money markets. But, instead, problems persisted. Greece was still saddled with enormous debts, its people were demoralized, and there seemed little chance of a quick recovery. By mid-2011, there were renewed fears that it could default on its debts and yet another round of austerity measures had to be introduced before a second rescue package, almost as large as the first, was put in place. All of this, however, added to the indebtedness of the rest of the Eurozone and there were now fears that the next crisis would occur in one of the big economies, like Italy or Spain. Italy's economy was larger than those of Greece, Ireland, and Portugal combined.

In August 2011, the European Central Bank took steps to ease the debt burden on both Italy and Spain, but there were doubts about the long-term ability of the Eurozone to continue shoring up economies in this way. There were also doubts about the willingness of voters in Germany to continue paying most of the costs. Germany had good reasons to sustain the Eurozone, where its largest export market lay and which had helped guarantee low inflation over the past decade. The Euro also provided a highly competitive currency so far as German exporters to non-Eurozone states were concerned: if Germany had retained its own currency, this would have risen in value on the exchange markets, thanks to the country's buoyant circumstances; this in turn would have made German exports more expensive and acted as a brake on its growth. But, despite such advantages, Berlin was not happy to throw money at the weaker economies. Germany had come through the 2008–9 recession better than most, its manufacturing output remained strong, and voters were frustrated by what they saw as the failure of other members to keep their houses in order, while expecting the Germans to pay for their consumption and living standards acquired through borrowing rather than earnings. In other words, rather like the bankers, the weaker Eurozone members were expecting ordinary German people to pay the costs of their misguided decisions. A fundamental difficulty became the German refusal to allow the European Central Bank and German money to guarantee debts of the weaker Eurozone members, at least until a savage programme of cuts in public expenditure had been implemented.

C. The Economic Rise of China and its Impact, 2001–11

After the death of Mao Zedong in 1976, China had embarked on a gradual economic restructuring which took the Asian giant down a successful economic path, merging strong elements of private enterprise with a much-reduced degree of state regulation. The resulting positive impact on economic growth accompanied by greater access to foreign capital, a more open interaction with the outside world, and increased opportunities for individual gain, had far-reaching consequences for many millions of Chinese and a major impact on international relations. There was still a big gulf between China, now an apparently successful capitalist state experiencing high economic growth rates of over 9 per cent, and the capitalist, democratic states of North America, Europe, and Japan, who had enjoyed economic growth for much of the post-war period based on state-influenced market economies and a liberal political ideology.

The transformation produced by Deng Xiaoping's economic reforms, which attempted to combine a strong Chinese state with Western-style free enterprise elements, raised a series of questions about China's role in the world, which has been evolving as a direct consequence of the reforms. With the acceptance of something akin to the Western economic system and the delivery of dramatic economic growth rates, the establishment of capitalist norms and the increasing involvement with international institutions—including, since late 2001, the World Trade Organization (WTO)—have to be reconciled with Chinese culture, society, and its values. If it were simply to supersede Chinese culture, trampling over tradition and history, then the country's positive participation in the international system will face more Chinese questioning. This threat to internal stability and to China's external involvement with the international world, both politically and economically, will grow more acute should economic expansion falter. Indeed, there are arguments that the growing inequality, and consequent resentment, that capitalism engenders when freed from economic state controls and social responsibilities, has already produced significant unrest in parts of China. Equally ominously, there are those who claim that China, as with former economically expanding powers, will demand greater international respect and influence. Thus, it should be assumed, according to these traditional 'realist' thinkers, that China will challenge the status quo which will require other powers, especially the US and Japan, to contain and balance it, before China is tempted to embark on more threatening policies. In short, China's economic rise had power-political implications which had to be considered in both reginal and international terms.

Economic Transformation

China's economic rise was dramatic and substantial. GDP increased tenfold between 2003 and 2012, with a limited state-controlled economy accompanied by an expanding and increasingly important private sector. Its annual economic growth in GDP terms averaged 9.7 per cent; by comparison, its neighbour Japan grew at an average rate of only 1.2 per cent over the same period. In qualitative terms, the World Bank estimated that, between 1978 and 2005, 402 million Chinese people were lifted out of poverty, meaning that they were now living on more than the equivalent of a dollar per day. There are, however, real problems with measuring wealth, given the different currencies' purchasing power, with the cost comparisons between states purchasing the same product only working for those products that are traded internationally. There is an equally tricky problem when translating economic statistics into economic 'power' even within a narrow framework of purchasing power, which in turn raises the vexed question of the contribution of economic strength to a state's 'power' more generally. Yet there is little doubt that China's economy in the new millennium overtook Japan's in its share of world consumption. It became the leading exporter in Asia, and the result has been that, in February 2011, China overtook Japan as the world's second largest economy. The vast size of the Chinese population, which the 2010 census put at 1,340 million, is recognized as both an opportunity and a drawback, providing a huge workforce and market, but also many mouths to feed and individuals to rule over. But, if it ever achieved a per-capita GNP of just a quarter of that of the US, it would have a total GNP greater than the US.[8]

Collectivized agriculture was phased out in rural China and a more diversified banking system has also been put in place. With the establishment of stock markets and a dramatic rise in foreign investment, the march of financial capital began. China has already established itself as the world's largest manufacturer of a significant number of goods. While these were initially in the areas of cheaply produced clothing, toys, and footwear, China now began manufacturing large numbers of advanced electronic and computer goods. Its technological potential was emphasized by the launch of its first manned spacecraft in October 2003. Most importantly, state enterprises were given more autonomy in developing, producing, and marketing goods, while at the same time the government has increased its financial support for the more important state-owned enterprises. In other words, the economic changes have not simply incorporated 'free' market reforms but, in contrast to the West, the Chinese have attempted to build more effective links between the still-vital public sector and the emerging private one, as Chinese foreign exchange reserves exceeded $2.3 trillion in 2010.

Moreover, its economic rise and consequent demands for more resources, in the form of oil, minerals, and finite natural resources, cannot be ignored. This was part of a broader challenge to the pre-eminence of North American and European capitalism by the so-called BRIC powers (Brazil, Russia, India, and China), to whom could be added other rising economies, especially South Africa, although China was unique amongst the so-called BRICs in achieving consistent and substantial economic growth. The challenge became more marked after 2007 when the international economic order, with its features of high wages and social benefits for employees in the developed world, came to the brink of financial collapse—although, by the end of 2011, there were signs that the continuing economic problems in 'the West' were having a knock-on effect among the BRIC countries (BRICS with South Africa included) and that Chinese growth rates were suffering. Increasingly after the 1980s, high levels of wealth for employees in the West were focused on the financial services sector, as opposed to the manufacturing one which, in essence, only prospered significantly in low-volume luxury goods in much of the developed world. As China supplied more and more manufactured goods as a percentage of international trade, these momentous changes were accompanied by the virtual collapse of the Western-dominated global financial system, which was increasingly 'liberated' from government-imposed controls after the 1980s in the belief that freer markets were the best way to deliver growth. The 2007–8 financial crisis was bigger and longer-lasting than any since the 1930s Depression. As shown, in contrast to the post-1997 crisis, which was largely confined to Asia and a few other less-developed economies (notably Argentina), the 2008 crisis centred on the US and Europe, where high levels of debt, notably in the Eurozone, where the financial system became threatened by large defaults on debt, making it unsustainable without massive state and international intervention. The concern at the resulting uncertainty for employment, pensions, and average wage levels in the West was more palpable than the uncertain outcomes of Chinese attempts to contain domestic social unrest, created by the growing inequality produced by unconstrained market forces.

China's Peaceful Rise?—East Asian Reactions to China's Growing Economic Strength

The initial reaction to China's increasing economic power and defence expenditure, which doubled in size between 1998 and 2003, was not one of counter-measures. South Korea and Japan, despite past hostilities with China, only slightly increased defence expenditure between 1998 and 2003, like the Philippines and Indonesia, while others (Taiwan and Thailand) reduced their defence expenditure in these years. The Japanese also reduced their defence budget in 2005.[9] This is despite the fact that, since the 1990s, Japan has tried to become less reliant on the US to deter aggressors and has shown some willingness to send forces overseas. While China was named as a potential threat in the 2004 National Defense Program Outline, the document emphasized economic interdependence, ruled out the idea of becoming a major military power, and showed no desire for a leadership role in East Asia. What changed was the economic role of Japan in the region since the 1997 financial crisis. By 2001, Japan's share of Asian trade had dropped from 45 per cent in 1992 to 30 per cent, with a relatively stagnating economy. By contrast, China's share over the same period grew from 6 per cent to 15 per cent, and this with considerable foreign direct investment (FDI) from Japan. Japan's economy has shown a turn to Asia, reinforcing the increasingly Sino-Centric Asian economic order.

Sino-Japanese relations were marred by some heated rhetoric, including diplomatic exchanges in 2005 over the content of Japanese historical textbooks on the Second World War. Yet relations had recovered by the time Wen Jiabao made the first visit of a Chinese premier to Japan, in April 2007. Economic relations grew closer, and Japan may even have accepted that China will eventually dominate the region. In 2004, Japan became China's largest trading partner and commerce between the two has continued to grow throughout the decade—faster than US trade with China. Thus, as with the South-East Asian states, the rising economic influence of China offered prospects of encouraging new opportunities.

For some of these East Asian states, particularly South Korea, for decades now a capitalist state closely allied to the US, China's trading potential was initially not seen as a threat. Whatever the increase in China's economic and military strength, concerns seem still to have been focused more on a revival of Japanese militarism. Korea, after all, was subjected to Japanese occupation between 1895 and 1945, and the treatment of its people still rankles. Apart from Japan itself, it had the most reasons to be concerned about its giant communist neighbour, given the military conflict that began in 1950 and still lacks a peace settlement. True, Beijing's close relations with North Korea have continued to encourage South Korea's military alliance with the US. The military umbrella provided by America and the importance South Korea attached to the future reunification of the peninsula could be seen as challenges to China. Yet economic trends were aligning South Korea more with China. In 2003, China surpassed the US as the largest export market for South Korean goods (a position America had held since 1965). Over 25,000 South Korean enterprises developed production facilities in China and, since 2004, all major South Korean banks have had branches there. South Korean opinion seems to support these closer ties as polls indicated that China, not the US, is the most important country with which South Korea should have good relations. For other local powers, there was no desire to embrace the US even more closely, especially since there seemed to be little to fear from increasing Chinese strength. Economic benefits from improved relations with China and increasing economic interdependence in the region offered more attractive ways forward.

This prediction of an uncertain and unstable international future was accompanied by concerns arising from the experiences of China's unfortunate past, which had brought division and subjugation at the hands of the imperialist powers. The humiliation experienced by China at the hands of the imperialist powers in the nineteenth and twentieth centuries, including the Japanese and the US as well as the European powers, provided the historical context in which China's search for identity and development were located. The conflicts imperialism produced in the twentieth century continued to resonate strongly in China. The elements of nationalism and territorial sovereignty had long been present at a number of levels amongst the Chinese population, both during and after Mao's dictatorship. In future, this nationalism might manifest itself in positive and peaceful forms, or in harmful and threatening ways. Some issues, such as the British hold on Hong Kong, or the Portuguese enclave at Macao, were peacefully resolved in China's favour, and they reverted to Chinese sovereignty in 1997 and 1999 respectively. Neither, despite protests from some of the indigenous population, did the Chinese hold on Tibet, which Mao's forces invaded in 1950, seem in doubt. However, a key focus of past nationalism and Chinese unity was the position of Taiwan following the creation of two Chinas after the Chinese Civil War (the People's Republic of China on the mainland and the nationalist government on Taiwan).

Taiwan

For Chinese elites in the early twenty-first century, economic development and increasing access to wealth formed part of a bargain with which to legitimize, and gain acceptance for, reforms and the changing political and economic roles of the communist government. But, if economic growth were to falter or produce major challenges to the social and political order, then one way of dealing with this would be to 'play the nationalist card' which has always been hovering over Taiwan. Whereas much of the world regards Taiwan as an important East Asian issue, for the mainland Chinese it has always been purely a domestic issue bound up with territorial unity and national identity. As such, Taiwan has remained the most likely source of a spark that could produce war in the region. Since the 1980s, relations across the Taiwan Strait have been volatile between the 'two Chinas'.

Visits between the island and the mainland began in 1986 and, during the early 1990s, the two governments were able to communicate using two supposedly non-government bodies as cover, thus avoiding the vexed question of official recognition. But the same decade saw Taiwanese leaders increasingly think in terms of independence, abandoning their previous belief that China and Taiwan could be reunited under nationalist control. Relations worsened significantly when a pro-independence politician, Chen Shui-Bian, was elected President in 2000. In mid-2001, both sides seemed to be preparing for a possible war. Chen's re-election in 2004 made the situation even worse, with Beijing again showing signs of contemplating an invasion. Yet, even in these difficult years, the attractions of economic cooperation could outmatch the political suspicions: in 2001, Chen allowed Taiwanese businesses to trade directly with the mainland, and 2005 saw the first commercial airline flights across the strait. The Nationalist Party's return to power in 2008 led to an improved atmosphere and the revival of talks via supposedly non-government bodies (which were actually official talks in disguise). Tensions persist, even though Taiwan had no great strategic significance and constituted a question of identity and status, rather than power, for both sides. Whatever the views on what Taiwan is, the crux of the question was whether it is, or is not, a nation state: if it is not, the implication is that it is part of China. For the moment, both protagonists accept the practicalities arising from Taiwan *not* being formally recognized as an independent state, but in practice it was continuing to behave like one.

The majority of Taiwanese, especially from the business community, accepted the present uneasy compromise and the increased economic contacts with mainland China which had been established. In May 2009, Taiwan began to allow Chinese investment on the island and, in June 2010, the two sides made an Economic Cooperation Framework agreement to reduce trade barriers further. By then, their bilateral trade already topped the $100 billion figure annually. Yet, while China rejected force as a means of settling territorial disputes in the case of the South China Sea, it refused to do so over Taiwan and it was openly increasing its military capability to invade, should Taiwan declare independence.

The development of Chinese nationalism is the key internal factor which may impact on the present government policy of trying to preserve both past rhetoric and mutually beneficial economic relations. In 2005, Japan also issued a statement calling on the two parties to resolve the problem in a peaceful manner, and many Asian states generally tended to favour the Chinese line of Taiwan being an internal issue. But, even alone, the US is a major military player in East Asia and, in January 2010, despite Chinese outrage, the Obama administration agreed on arms supplies to Taiwan worth over $6 billion. The military balance has definitely been shifting towards China and the issue remains, as it has done since 1949, whether the US would commit forces to protect Taiwan. However, it was difficult to see how the US could have constructed a 'coalition of the willing' to defend Taiwan. Moreover, on the other economic side of the coin, the main deterrent to Taiwan actually declaring independence was that this was seen as the action most likely to trigger a Chinese invasion.

China's 'Peaceful Rise'?—The Importance of Maintaining Chinese Economic Growth

There were economic advantages and benefits from increased trade and wealth for elites on both sides of the Straits of Taiwan in maintaining the two-China compromise and the existing status quo, however fragile or imperfect it might be. Yet the contribution to stability that China's economic rise could continue to provide extends well beyond Taiwan. Benefits provided for all, domestically and internationally, by Chinese economic growth in the context of Western capitalism have only increased the interconnectedness of China and the West, particularly the US and, so the argument goes, have created mutual interests rather than antagonism and rivalries. The large trade surplus and currency reserves produced by the economic expansion served to reinforce the mutual interests of the Chinese creditors financing the American debtors, through bond purchases. At the same time, economic development brought mutual benefits to China and its trading and financial partners by enabling good returns to be gained from trade and the reinvestment of financial surpluses. Thus, the common economic interest produced by the operations of a stable, profitable trading and monetary system will prevent any rocking of political boats. Moreover, China's acceptance of many of the existing international economic norms reflected and reinforced a strategy of 'peaceful rise'. Yet, this interpretation of Chinese economic policy does beg the question of exactly how high China will rise in the world—could it eventually achieve global economic hegemony—and whether the policy is a means to an (as yet undefined) end or an end in itself. The bigger question is whether the idea that a policy of 'peaceful rise' was being pursued in the new millennium by the PRC government in Beijing.

Significantly, the signs of economic cooperation and integration superseding East Asian politics became clearer under Hu Jintao who became General Secretary of the Communist Party (CCP) in 2002. Supporters of the idea that China has used constructive diplomacy with regional issues point to the way China's increased economic power has been perceived and reacted to by its Asian neighbours. Due to benefits and advantages for all East Asian powers being seen as stemming from China's rise, which has boosted economic growth, that rise was welcomed and readily accommodated in the East Asian region. The signs of opposition and a perceived need to build alliances or take measures against China were simply not there in the new millennium's first decade. Moreover, this optimistic position reflected not only the economic growth that capitalism was providing, but also the peaceful quest for a new and modern Chinese identity through successful nation-building within China. The continuation of the concomitant construction of world power status seemed initially to have been built on better, more cooperative relations with its regional partners, rather than threats and bullying, but this may well come to depend on economic growth continuing.

One example was the cooperation between China, the Philippines, and Vietnam over oil exploration in the contested Spratly Islands. Certainly, China's regional interests had, so far, predominated over global ones in the form of defining maritime boundaries and developing regional economic interests. Yet the question remains about the extent to which political relations will be influenced by favourable economic ones, whether or not the latter continue. There was also concern about whether the Chinese emphasis on forging its new identity peacefully and without territorial ambition, despite the Taiwan issue, will become a long-term objective or give way to some less palatable alternative. Balancing nationalist pressures for a more assertive foreign policy with friendly external relations (some of which may be beyond China's control) may not be so easy to maintain. The emphasis that China has placed on sovereignty through control over its own internal affairs, free from external interference, may not ultimately be so easy to reconcile with the economics of globalization and the free movement of capital across national boundaries, as well as with the cross-border flow of liberal political ideas. Unless the huge market for goods that China provides can continue to persuade others to cooperate willingly in its economic expansion, without arousing fears of Chinese military power and political domination, problems are likely to arise.

China's Integration into the International Economic System

At the start of the new millennium, the tendency of events to produce an acceptance of China's rise were reinforced by the apparent willingness of China to participate in existing international institutions and their rules, which were originally put in place by the West. After the start of the internal reform process begun by Deng in the 1980s, the Chinese emphasis on sovereignty and non-interference in internal affairs was accompanied by a preference for bilateral rather than multilateral relationships. In the twenty-first century, however, China, as well as joining the WTO after fifteen years of negotiation, has also cooperated closely with the Association of South-East Asian Nations (ASEAN). China's positive approach to international organizations was influenced, of course, by self-interest, ultimately including a potential desire to influence the Western rules and norms that dominate them. Beijing has not restricted its policy of cooperation to the West and South-East Asia and helped establish the 'Shanghai Five' group in 1996. Along with Russia and the central Asian republics of Kazakhstan, Kyrgyzstan, and Tajikstan, it was extended to Uzbekistan and renamed the Shanghai Cooperation Organisation in 2001. The organization began with a security focus, designed to reduce cross-border tensions, but it later developed cultural and economic projects. Despite some problems, such as respect for copyright law, China generally complies with international norms, and has adapted to the requirements of institutions based on Western values. It has also clearly moved from favouring bilateral relations to accepting multilateral ones. China's formal links with ASEAN, beginning in 1991, have included Chinese adherence to the Association's Treaty of Amity and Cooperation in 2003, agreement on an Investment Cooperation Fund in 2009, and the launch, in January 2010, of a free trade area, all of which indicate a deepening commitment to regional cooperation. In some organizations, China's respect for the rules has led to real advantages. For example, China has been a member of the IMF and the World Bank since 1980, after taking over the seat from nationalist China (whose regime had been a founder member of both organizations in 1945). In 2008, a Chinese academic, Yifu Lin, became the Chief Economist at the World Bank and, in 2010, China was given an increase in its weighted vote, making it the third most significant member after the US and Japan. In 2001, it was given an increase in its quota shares in the IMF, and a further increase in 2011 made it the third largest member of that organization.

But it is doubtful whether its overall commitment to stability and acceptance of important Western values will lead China to move closer to, or ally with, the US. China could hardly accept the degree of insubordination to Washington that this would entail. Then again, China could enlarge the areas of common interest it has with America. Relations may always be based on a mix of cooperation and confrontation, with the common acceptance of economic values preventing any escalation into serious threats or challenges to the stability provided by the existing international system.[10]

Political Change

At the political level, the pattern of a government dominated by a single individual leader, exercising power through the Communist Party machine and the role of the People's Liberation Army (PLA), was changing. The governmental structures and involvement of more elements of the Communist Party had broadened the base of decision-making, which in part reflected efforts to separate the state from the Communist Party. While Deng Xiaoping's position as supreme leader in terms of decision-making was achieved by complex political manoeuvring after 1976, he never held the top position of General Secretary of the Chinese Communist Party. Between 1989, in the aftermath of the Tiananmen Square unrest, and 2002, that post was held by Jiang Zemin, who had helped push the policies of market economics and export-led growth, especially in coastal cities, while maintaining the firm political control of the Communist Party under a privileged elite. Hu Jintao, the party leader from November 2002 (and President after 2003), inherited a more fluid situation in which the assumptions of a 'Mandate from Heaven', epitomized by Maoism, were increasingly filtered through the influence of important interest groups. These reflected the more open and diverse roles that the Chinese state fulfilled after Deng's reforms and the meteoric growth of the Chinese economy. As an aspiring member of the international community, with growing contacts in the Western world, the effect was to unleash new forces in Chinese society. For the moment, their political dimensions stayed beneath the surface and were still contained. One adverse consequence of the growing economy was the temptation of senior officials to use their political position for financial advantage, otherwise known as 'graft', which has led to a number of anti-corruption drives since 2000.

With no strong memories of life before the communist revolution (he was born in 1942), Hu Jintao formed a close alliance with his close contemporary, Wen Jiabao, who became Prime Minister in 2003. Cautious, thin on charisma, and lacking any radical, ideological drive, together they shifted China's policy from a focus on growth in major coastal cities to one which benefited the rest of the country, and they tried to protect the position of Chinese agriculture. They thus sought a stable, broad-based economic development that minimized the dangers of social division and maintained the Communist Party's firm hold on power. They were also responsible for China's moderation abroad, focusing their international efforts on the development of trade and investment, the success of which served both to justify their policy choices and strengthen their hold on power. There were problems, including those already mentioned, of growing inequalities and high-level corruption. But there was no serious political challenge to the communist system such as had occurred in 1989. There were individual dissidents, such as the artist Ai Weiwei, the blind lawyer, Chen Guangchen, and Chen Wei, who had helped organize the Tiananmen Square protests. There was also a wave of protests in several cities in February 2011, apparently inspired by the uprisings of the so-called 'Arab Spring'. But such threats were ruthlessly dealt with by the police. Ai Weiwei, who had helped design the main stadium for the 2008 Olympics—which was turned into a celebration of China's growing international status—was accused by the authorities of tax evasion in April 2011. Chen Guangchen was imprisoned for several years, before being allowed to leave for the US in April 2012. Chen Wei was imprisoned on a number of occasions. There were also outbursts of regional, ethnic-based discontent, including periodic unrest (in 1997, 2000, and 2009) in Xinjiang province, in north-west China, involving clashes between Uighurs and ethnic Chinese, as well as continuing opposition to Chinese rule by Tibetan Buddhists, with particular problems in March–April 2008. But these were kept easily under control, with no serious threat to communist authority. The problem, rather, was the international embarrassment that dissidence and regional unrest could cause. The Tibetan violence of 2008, for example, came in the build-up to the Beijing Olympics and, in 2010, the dissident Liu Xiaobo won the Nobel Peace Prize.

On the positive side, the involvement of more individuals in political life, even if only through better provision of information, might sow the seeds for a less-centralized Communist Party. On the other hand, the rise of various coordinating groups which wield power over the party, state, and military organs might increase confusion. China still lacked a well-defined bureaucratic hierarchy and the Politburo's Standing Committee had to rely on a complicated array of civil and military bureaucracies to implement policy, which is itself frequently shifting. The Foreign Affairs Leading Small Group (FALSG), concerned with defining China's role in international affairs, and chaired by Hu Jintao, is an example of a group that has grown in importance since the 1990s. Partly thanks to the growth of rival bodies, the influence of the People's Liberation Army (PLA) over the party and government, particularly in external affairs and defence policy, was no longer as absolute as it once had been, whatever continuity there had been in the strategic principles underlying Chinese security policy since Deng's death. The reduction of the PLA's power and the strengthening position of FALSG could be interpreted as an attempt to bring together the Party and the state government bureaucracies, including the Ministry of Foreign Affairs, involved in the formulation and implementation of international policy. But the precise aim, if there was one, is uncertain. This is of some concern because the PLA's role is highly relevant to any analysis of the long-term goals of Chinese foreign policy. There also remains inherent tension between the role of the Politburo's Standing Committee and the informal, personal relationships that still characterize the post-Mao leadership system, which makes who succeeds Hu and Wen enormously important.

Of course, for many Western observers, the problem remained China's lack of real progress towards basic freedoms, liberal democracy, and human rights. As long as people in China remained at risk of imprisonment for their political views, the possibility of a worsening of relations with the West would be there. Both sides may have to restrain their rhetoric on such sensitive issues to preserve better relations. The dilemma for China was that, by allowing greater political freedom, including such simple steps as greater access to the internet, it might weaken the degree of government control necessary to avoid the more negative repercussions of the dramatic economic change.

Military Change

The development of China's military strength, alongside its remarkable economic growth, increased the intensity of the debate about whether China's power could be reconciled with the existing international order, or whether significant revisions of the latter would be required. One military element that has been relatively constant since before the communists even took power, had been the importance of the PLA, which included all the branches of Chinese armed forces. In 2005, China had 2.3 million members in the armed services: 1.7 million in the army, 220,000 in the navy, and 420,000 in the air force. But since the end of the Mao era in the 1970s, the PLA had been subject to greater civilian influence. Alongside increases in the production of consumer goods had also come the greater production of arms for export. Although China had yet to match the West and Russia in this field, it found particular markets in some less developed states, including Sudan and Zimbabwe, which had drawn criticism because of the authoritarian nature of the countries involved. China also helped arm Pakistan and Iran. Some of its weapons found their way to Iraq and Afghanistan, giving the impression of some anti-Western design, but the weapons may have passed via the black market, and the Chinese government introduced tighter controls on such exports.

Progress in the development of the air force was significant, even if China has had only limited success in producing cutting-edge supersonic aircraft and has thus relied on Russian technology. Of particular importance is the Russian Sukhoi SU-27, which is their major fighter aircraft. China initially received 50 planes in the 1990s and planned to assemble 150 more. Before that, it had an air force of antiquated aircraft, including 450 MiG-19 and even some Korean War-era fighters. Chinese strike aircraft carried unguided bombs or missiles, which could be operated only within visual range. It was thus unable to carry out effective air-to-ground attacks, as it lacked the modern weapons necessary. The primacy given to holding air superiority over China and defending attacks on the country made the PLA air force an essentially defensive force. It had no long-range strategic bombers and its bomber force was small. Since 2000, not only has more advanced equipment arrived, but also Chinese armed forces have become more 'professional', with a drop in numbers accompanied by improved training. The number of advanced 'fourth-generation' aircraft, similar to those operated by the US, has quadrupled. These include China's own advanced fighter jet, the Jian-10, deployed since 2002 and comparable in performance to the US F-16. The Chinese have now tested their own air-to-air missile, the PiLi-12, and in 2007 they even test-fired a missile into space, successfully hitting a redundant satellite. In part, all this may simply be a natural 'modernization' of equipment, but advances in the air force also provide greater offensive capabilities. A greater proportion of fighters are now capable of attacking ground forces.

Any increase in offensive capabilities obviously has significance for any future attack on Taiwan. Yet a key element in any invasion would be airlift capability, to carry troops to the island, and there has been no significant development of such a capacity, even if the 2008 National Defence Review talked of improving its 'strategic force delivery'. Meanwhile, the lack of a mid-air refuelling capability limited China's ability to project air power on a global scale. The obvious conclusion is that China remained a long way from challenging the US in terms of air power, but its military strength from projecting that air power on a *regional* basis can no longer be dismissed. After the modernization of the air force began in the 1990s, by 2005 China had added nearly 400 fighter aircraft to its forces, giving it vastly superior numbers than the Japanese. In December 2010, the first pictures appeared of an advanced Stealth fighter, which the Chinese government later confirmed had undergone test flights and which could propel China into the front rank of the world's air forces.

Turning to naval strength, in July 2011, China acknowledged it had an aircraft carrier programme to enhance its capabilities. The first carrier was actually built from a former Soviet vessel, acquired from Ukraine, and had its first sea trials in August 2011. With only one carrier, the projection of Chinese naval power is clearly subject to considerable constraints and China effectively relies on US naval power to protect its shipping lanes. Cooperation with the US is so vital that Chinese ships docked in the US navy base at Guam in 2003, a month after US ships docked in the port of Zhanjian, in Guangdong province. But China also began construction of its first fully domestically built carrier, in Shanghai. At the beginning of the new millennium, China already had 149 surface combat ships compared to Indonesia's 51, giving it regional naval dominance within South East Asia. Again, as with the air force, questions have to be asked as to the purpose of these developments, not least by the Taiwanese. In a future limited conflict with Taiwan, the Chinese navy might be able to blockade the island long enough for its ground forces to overwhelm the island's defences. China also had 67 submarines, a number of which are nuclear-powered vessels armed with ballistic missiles, even if the boats were unreliable and rarely ventured out to sea. Once again, since 2000, a number of these have been bought from Russia. But in 2004 China launched a new, Shang class of nuclear submarine and in 2005 it successfully tested the Jilang 2 intercontinental nuclear missile with a range of nearly 10,000 kilometres. Yet none of this made it anything like a global force able to come close to air or naval parity with the US in East Asia and the Pacific.

Visit the online resources that accompany this book to test your understanding and take your learning further: www.oup.com/he/young-kent3e

NOTES

1. In March 2009, *The Financial Times* ran a series of articles on 'The Future of Capitalism'. The quotes are from 9 March 2009, reproduced in David McNally, *Global Slump: The Economics and Politics of Crisis and Resistance* (PM Press, Oakland CA, 2011).
2. GSEs are a type of financial services business which were first established by Congress in the early twentieth century to enhance the flow of credit to certain sectors of the economy, including agriculture and homes, and to reduce the risk to investors purchasing their securities. Fannie Mae and Freddie Mac were private companies, but with an 'implicit guarantee' from the federal government.
3. Conservatorship is a US legal term roughly equivalent to power of attorney and means something less than nationalization.
4. Figures are those of the Bank of International Settlement found in Gérard Dumenil and Dominique Lévy, *The Crisis of Neoliberalism* (Harvard University Press, Cambridge MA, 2013), 187.
5. Figures provided by the Bank of England printed in ibid., 254.
6. Joseph Stiglitz, *Freefall: Free Markets and the Shrinking of the Global Economy* (Norton,New York, 2009), 110. See also Ch. 5.
7. ibid., 153–4.
8. David C. Kang, *China Rising* (Columbia University Press, New York and Chichester, 2007), 12–15.
9. These figures come from the Stockholm International Peace Research Institute (SIPRI) in constant (2016) US dollars.
10. As put forward by Ze Zicheng, *Inside China's Grand Strategy the Perspective from the People's Republic* (University Press of Kentucky, KY, 2011), 3–5.

PART VIII

The Age of Uncertainty: Chaos and Confusion in a Globalized World, 2011–18

In 2007–8, the unregulated market had taken the global economy to the brink of an unprecedented depression and faith in so-called 'free markets' proved to be misplaced. Yet, despite the crash, neoliberal economics survived into the second decade of the new millennium. The Left in North America and Europe proved unable to overcome right-wing media dominance and convince the public that it could alleviate the hardships of post-financial crash austerity, which the Right often emotively blamed on immigrants. War and poverty combined with a greater knowledge of the external world to make migration the frequently chosen escape route for those with nothing to lose. Desperation or alienation in the less developed world, enhanced by growing inequality, added to the desires for a better life in those areas of the world that apparently offered better opportunities. Financial transactions remained far from transparent, especially without a broader range of media interest. Elites throughout the world were able to retain vast sums of money because of the increasing wealth that the unregulated financial sector made available. With fewer people benefitting, inequality has grown, along with the collapse of social and communal values that the commitment to individualism and unregulated capitalism tend to produce.

The financial crash contributed to a structural shift in the global economy eastward and away from the West. The reduction in manufacturing jobs in the West was accompanied by threats to Europe's social welfare systems. With the decline of the state and its influence over national economies, and the increasing reluctance of democratic politicians facing re-election to increase direct taxation, expenditure on public services in the developed world has been increasingly under pressure. Nowhere was this more evident than in the US, where Barack Obama inherited significant tax cuts for the rich that had constituted a key strategy of the Bush administration. While avoiding a swingeing austerity package and eventually achieving a return to economic growth, the new President accepted the continuation of the US financial system, without restoring effective regulation to correct the flaws in corporate governance and investment risks that had brought the 2008 crash. In the 2016 presidential election, Donald Trump campaigned successfully on ending the decline of US industries and preventing further damage to the living standards of US workers, which he regarded as linked to unfair trade practices, notably by China. Once in power, he imposed new tariffs on some goods entering the US, re-negotiated the terms of the North American Free Trade Area with Mexico and Canada (which became the 'US–Mexico–Canada Agreement', or USMCA in October 2018), but also implemented tax cuts, with particular benefits for the wealthier members of society. This, the surest way of uniting an increasingly divided Republican party, was one electoral promise he was able to deliver on in his first year, but also created renewed concerns over income inequality, rising national debt, and another downturn in world trade.

The Resurgence of Populism

Manufacturing jobs were transferred from the West to the developing world, with its lower labour costs, including the BRIC countries (Brazil, Russia, India, and China). China had become the second largest global economy by about 2011 and the BRIC countries had already begun to hold annual summits in 2009, being joined in 2011, at the third summit, by South Africa (to become BRICS). Other less developed countries increasingly grew in economic weight, including Indonesia and Turkey. In simplified terms, the owners of capital in the developed world have been able to invest more freely in those less developed areas where labour costs are less, thus satisfying an important capitalist goal of greater profitability. Some successes in manufacturing and technology companies may allow for increased wages in the less developed world, as in parts of China, but the downside in the developed world is that the wages of many workers have dropped or stagnated because of new competition. Many areas in Europe and America are being decimated by industrial decline, with the key elements of wealth production dramatically transformed. Social disintegration results from the human cost of old skills no longer being needed or valued, and there has been a dramatic decline in trade union membership, accompanied by the growth in zero-hour contracts, which suppress wages and increase alienation. Governments have increasingly facilitated these changes to the international economy, which have resulted in massive gains for the owners of capital, while wages stagnate and inequality rises.[1] One major political result in the US and Europe has been the rise of 'populism', often directed against immigrants, and seen not only in Trump's election victory, but also in the 2016 British vote to exit the European Union, the rise of the far-right in Germany's 2017 election, and the triumph of two populist parties in the 2018 Italian general election.

The difficulties facing the environment because of global warming were worsening because of the resource demands of the expanding Asian economies, who wished to use natural resources in the same, wasteful ways that developed economies had in the past. Hence in 2015, at the Paris Conference on Climate Change, developed countries were committed to 'mobilizing' $200 billion per year by 2020, to help less developed nations with the costs of reducing global warming, and an 'intention' was agreed to continue this through 2025. Obama, leader of the world's second biggest emitter of greenhouse gases—an important cause of global warming—agreed to limit the rise in global average temperatures to 1.5 degrees centigrade. Intended Nationally Determined Conditions (INDCs) targets for limiting the emission of greenhouse gases, were also agreed, though none were legally binding. The agreement, signed by 195 countries, lacked real teeth; instead, 'pledges' were welcomed as an important advance on previous climate change conferences in dealing with a key threat to the world that could only be dealt with internationally. Yet even this proved too much for Trump, who did not accept that global warming, now an indisputable fact, was produced by human activity rather than by a natural cycle of change. In June 2017, he therefore announced US withdrawal from the Paris agreement, although this did not prevent the UN holding a conference in Katowice, Poland in November–December 2018 to decide on measures to meet the Paris goals.

Continued US Involvement in Global Conflict

Meanwhile, in many ways, international affairs continue to be overshadowed by the chaos and uncertainty arising from the US attempt to apply its 2002 National Security Strategy, launched in the wake of the 9/11 attacks. Expenditures on armaments for 'national security' and, after 2001, the war on terror, have never significantly been reduced. In trying to impose Western values and political systems on Middle Eastern and North African states, socially, culturally, and economically ill-prepared to receive them, the US and its allies have produced conflict and considerable loss of life without much positive benefit. This was especially the case in states subject to Western intervention. Despite withdrawing combat troops from Iraq, in 2011, the country's future remained deeply uncertain. Similarly, in Afghanistan, combat operations ended in 2014 but, as Obama's presidency ended, nearly 10,000 US troops remained there to train Afghan forces and conduct 'anti-terrorist' operations following another Taliban revival. But the effects of Western policy were felt much more widely. After the 2008 financial crash, the pain of austerity was experienced in much of the developed world as neoliberal economics contributed to the growing sense of powerlessness and alienation amongst those failing to reap any rewards from Western capitalism. While the contemporary world appears to deny all prospect of attaining such benefits, the attractions of extreme religious ideologies, which include the comforting benefits of an after-life for the faithful, become very powerful for the poorer elements of society, especially in the Middle East.

During his second term, Obama faced new and unprecedented challenges to Western capitalism's international order from both state and non-state actors in the Middle East. Ironically, what initially erupted in the Middle East did so under the banner of democracy unfurled by the 2011 Arab uprisings. The political optimism and hope of reform soon came up against the social and economic barriers and grievances that no political system could easily resolve and, feeding on religious differences, the instability unleashed by the ill-advised American invasion of Iraq spread through the region. The international community was faced with the growing violence of the conflicts in Syria, Iraq, and Yemen, to which a generous wringing of hands often seemed the only practical international response. True, the American pursuit of democracy in the Middle East at the time of the so-called 'Arab Spring' seemed to bring some limited success. Helped by North Atlantic Treaty Organization (NATO) allies, particularly France and Britain, the domestic opponents of General Gaddafi in Libya were able to remove him. There was also democratic political change in Tunisia. But, aside from Tunisia, the long-term results were characterized by political turmoil. In some ways, Washington had tried to resist change in this most sensitive region of the world, initially being reluctant to abandon Egypt's

Hosni Mubarak, whose removal did lead to a short lived democratically elected government. The fact that democracy seemed to encourage radical religious elements soon ensured that the old Egyptian military elites, who had long dominated Egyptian society, were restored to predominance. Even more concerning was the situation in Yemen, with a Sunni–Shi'ite civil war and intervention by a Saudi-led coalition, and in Libya, where Gaddafi's overthrow and ensuing anarchy had a significant impact on Moscow's decision to intervene in Syria, where another bitter civil war broke out, accompanied by external intervention.

The chaos in Syria fed off the problems in Iraq, as the US departure did not heal sectarian divisions there. Despite Iraqi elections in 2010, the government of Nouri al-Maliki favoured the majority Shi'ite population, influenced by its fellow Shi'ites governing Iran. The growing regional influence of Iran developed from the Iraqi situation, but the challenge it presented was exacerbated by the developing conflict in neighbouring Syria. The precarious balance of Syrian society with its mix of important economic, religious, and ethnic elements, was even less conducive to simple regime change or political reform than Iraq. The main financial and military support for the Assad regime was provided, from 2012, by Tehran and its non-state Shi'ite ally Hezbollah, based in Lebanon. The violence was also linked to extreme forms of religion, whose leaders appealed to the dispossessed, poorer elements of their societies and employed indiscriminate violence and terror. The most effective was initially known as the Islamic State in Iraq (ISI), with its effective organization and strict religious dogma. This new threat actually originated from al-Qaeda in Iraq and was linked to the chaos created by the US-led invasion. When ISI extended its operations into Syria, becoming ISIS in 2013, it not only added a new dimension to the idea of terror, but changed the ultimate goal of al-Qaeda's jihadism. ISIS did not simply use religion to fight the secular West and other infidels, in order to create a society based on Sharia law, but to establish a viable territorial state. As ISIS again rebranded itself as the Islamic State (IS), its leader Abu Bakr al-Baghdadi declared a caliphate in June 2014 and won control of a substantial amount of territory in both Iraq—where Baghdad itself seemed threatened for a time—and Syria. But this alerted many external powers to its threat. Obama, although reluctant to wield US military strength and fearful that supplying American arms would result in them falling into the hands of jihadis, was sufficiently aroused by the rise of IS to use American air power in late 2014.

Foreign Policy in Trump's White House

By now, there was a complex variety of jihadis and non-jihadist groups in Syria, who never formed an effective national or cohesive force. Rather, as casualties climbed into the hundreds of thousands and many more became refugees, there was a series of battles in different areas of Syria, involving different combatants. Half the entire population had been displaced or become refugees by 2015.[2] With intervention by Vladimir Putin's Russia after September 2015, President Bashar Assad's position became more secure, but without him being able to assert his authority over the whole of the now fragmented country. As Assad's forces, with Russian support, began a brutal siege of rebel-held Eastern Aleppo in 2016, the Iraqi army also made advances against IS. Yet, while the US and Russia were in theory fighting on the same side against IS, they were engaged in two separate wars and, in Syria, took opposing sides, for and against Assad. In fact, the Syrian civil war had become a Middle Eastern melée of many international actors with their own specific goals. Not only were Russia, Iran, and Hezbollah directly involved, but Israel and Turkey were also drawn in, while Saudi Arabia backed certain groups from outside. The conflict even moderated old enmities. For example, the Saudis and Israel were more concerned about limiting Iranian influence than with pursuing old animosities. But the Turks, keen to ensure that events on their border with Syria did not increase the power of Kurdish separatists seeking independence, were upset at US support for the Kurdish peshmerga and drew closer to Russia and Iran, with a joint attempt by the three powers in 2017–18 to establish 'de-escalation zones'. There were few certainties left in the state of flux that the increasingly violent Middle East experienced and uncertainty only increased with Donald Trump's advent in power since, ever-eager to reverse Obama's policies, he showed strong support for Israel (controversially moving the US embassy there to Jerusalem) and, in May 2018, reneged on a 2015 deal to prevent Iran developing nuclear weapons and returned to a policy of confrontation with Tehran.

Another key aspect of Trump's foreign policy was his launch of a trade war against China, by now the world's second largest economy. Before he took office, Sino-American relations already had an ambivalent nature that combined mutual admiration with fear and growing rivalry. This relationship is at the heart of questions about prospects for China's peaceful rise continuing and whether tension with America will lead to growing conflict, rather than a partnership. Since the start of the millennium, China's economy had quadrupled in size, with a significant increase in military capacity. Although growing military strength is nowhere near being able to challenge the US as a global power, it does raise questions about China's ultimate goal. With the advent of Xi Jinping as President in 2012, the issue of whether China will continue as a 'status quo power' had to be re-evaluated by the US to take account of the changes he has brought to foreign policy and governance by the Communist Party. In a 2011 speech to the Australian parliament, Barack Obama stated that as 'a Pacific nation, the US will play a larger and long term role in shaping this region and its future, by upholding core principles . . . We will allocate the resources necessary to maintain our strong military presence in this region.'[3] In future, US concern may only deepen, born out of resentment at the loss of primacy. The disapproval of China resorting to cyber warfare, the one area of technology where it can fight the US on equal terms, could be an indicator of future conflict. Similarly, the establishment of the Asian Investment Bank (AIIB) could be seen as a challenge to the US-dominated financial order.

It is still possible that the US will, like many Asian powers, see more of an opportunity than a threat in China's growing importance. Yet, Xi appears to want China's role to be at the centre of the world stage and some Western ideologues portray China as a threat which must be contained, just as the Soviet Union was contained during the Cold War. This is despite the fact that the US has 600 military installations in 120 countries, whereas China has only one similar facility, a naval refitting yard in Djibouti.[4] However, one measures the continued, but lessening, disparity between the power of the US and China, it is the *perceptions* of the implications of that shift which will determine its impact as much as its actual effects. Negative perceptions, based on American fear and resentment of the passing of more economic and political influence in the international system to the Chinese may well, as with the 'war on terror', help create the very problem the US sought to prevent. Donald Trump's determination to reduce America's massive trade deficit with China by beginning a trade war may prove to be a significant step in a lengthy contest.

The Destabilization of Western Powers

The predominance of US power and values in a more unipolar world in the twenty-first century has, as they begin to be questioned, produced less uniformity within the international system, partly because the centripetal forces no longer operate within the opposing blocs, as they did during the Cold War. Since 2001, wars in Afghanistan and Iraq, initially justified by the events of 9/11, but also derived from the mantra of liberal interventionism under the aegis of US power, have proved extremely damaging and undermined the confidence and reputation of America itself. It would be a mistake to take too pessimistic a view of a world in which extreme poverty is declining, education widening, and health improving, but political developments in the new millennium certainly leave cause for concern. The ties that now bind states and communities together are becoming weaker, despite some continued efforts at regional integration, partly thanks to the decline of the state, the rise of individualism, the survival of neoliberal economics beyond its apparent failure in 2008, and resentment that the most vulnerable should look to migration as the only means of escape. In Europe, the creation of a single currency has fostered inequalities and the rise of populism, putting integration at risk, even if 'Brexit'—the British withdrawal from the European Union, which followed a 2016 referendum—looks likelier to damage Britain than the EU. In Russia, liberal hopes have retreated in the face of oligarchy and authoritarianism under Putin, who was ready to risk the anger of the West with his invasion of Crimea in 2014 and subsequently intervened in Syria. In the Middle East, where the hopes of reform brought by the Arab Spring have been dashed, civil wars continue to rage in Syria and Yemen, the Israeli–Palestinian conflict remains intractable, and there is now a deep power-political conflict between Saudi Arabia and Iran, which builds on the religious divide between Sunni and Shi'ite. America, under Trump, has become more unilateralist and protectionist than at any time since the 1930s, even if the President did prove able to shift, in 2017–18, from a policy of threats to one of the diplomatic engagement with North Korea over its nuclear ambitions. As international reality becomes more disturbing and difficult to shape, it is evident that the end of the Cold War, far from leading to the global triumph of Western values, has been followed by considerable fragmentation, violence, and uncertainty in an increasingly interconnected world.

Visit the online resources that accompany this book to test your understanding and take your learning further: www.oup.com/he/young-kent3e

NOTES

1. Thomas Piketty, *Capital in the Twenty-First Century* (Harvard University Press, Cambridge, 2014), 166–8 and 571.
2. Charles R. Lister, *The Syrian Jihad: Al-Qaeda, the Islamic State and the Evolution of an Insurgency* (Hurst, London, 2015), 384.
3. Remarks at www.whitehouse.gov/the-press-office/2011/11/17/remarks-president-obama-australian-parliament.
4. Kerry Brown, *China's World* (I.B. Tauris, London, 2018), 96.

PART VIII CHRONOLOGY

The Age of Uncertainty: Chaos and Confusion in a Globalized World, 2011–18

2011

14 January	President Zine Ben-Ali flees Tunisia in the face of widespread popular protests.
11 February	Following two weeks of popular demonstrations, Egyptian President Hosni Mubarak, in power since 1981, resigns.
17 February	Serious unrest begins against President Gaddafi in Libya, focused on eastern city of Benghazi.
14 March	Following weeks of unrest in Bahrain, Saudi Arabia sends in troops to support the royal government.
17 March	UN authorizes 'all means necessary', short of an occupation, to protect Libyan civilians; leads to Western-led 'no-fly zone'.
29 March	After two weeks of unrest, President Assad of Syria sacks his whole cabinet in an attempt to placate protestors.
2 May	Osama bin Laden is killed in Pakistan by US forces.
1 August	Congress agrees to increase US debt ceiling in return for government spending cuts; world stock markets fall in value.
22–23 August	Anti-Gaddafi forces largely take control of the capital, Tripoli.
20 October	Gaddafi is killed while trying to flee.
4 December	Parliamentary elections in Russia are won by Putin's United Russia party, amid accusations of poll-rigging.
19 December	Death of North Korea's Kim Jong-Il is announced; succeeded by his son, Kim Jong-Un.

2012

23 January	European Union agrees on oil embargo against Iran, over its nuclear programme and development of ballistic missiles.

PART VIII CHRONOLOGY (continued)

4 February	Russia and China veto a UN Resolution to end growing violence in Syria.
12 February	Under EU pressure, Greek Parliament passes a tough austerity programme.
6 May	Greek elections result in major advances for parties opposed to austerity, sparking renewed economic uncertainty in the Eurozone.
9 June	Spanish financial bail-out by the Eurozone.
22 August	Mohammed Morsi wins Egypt's first free presidential election.
11 September	US Ambassador to Libya killed in militant attack.
9 October	Taliban try to assassinate Malala Yousefzai, campaigner for female education; she later wins Nobel Peace Prize.
14–21 November	Major Israeli incursion into Gaza Strip.
2013	
8 March	UN agrees new sanctions against North Korea after its third nuclear test.
6 June	Edward Snowden reveals US surveillance operations; escapes to Russia on 23rd.
18 June	Afghan forces take over security from NATO in remaining areas of country.
1 July	Croatia becomes 28th member of European Union.
3 July	After days of unrest, Egyptian army overthrows President Morsi.
16 September	UN report says Syrian government used chemical weapons against rebels.
21 September	Seventy killed by Somalia-based Al-Shabab militants in Nairobi, Kenya.
1–16 October	US government shuts down after Congress fails to agree budget.
1 November	US drone strike kills Hakimullah Massud, Taliban leader in Pakistan.
November–December	Protests in Ukraine after President Yanukovich's refuses to sign agreement with EU.
2014	
23 February	Ukraine's parliament replaces pro-Russian Yanukovich with Aleksander Turchynov; unrest follows in Crimea and eastern Ukraine.
1–3 March	Russian army seizes control of Crimea.
6 March	US introduces first sanctions against Russia over Crimea.
24 March	Other members suspend Russian membership of G-8.
11 June	Advances by ISIS (Islamic State in Iraq and Syria) in Iraq culminate in capture of Mosul.
30 June	ISIS declares Caliphate and renames itself 'Islamic State'.
17 July	Malaysian Airlines flight is shot down over Ukraine, killing 298 people.
July–August	Sustained Israeli incursion into Gaza.
7 August	US air strikes begin against ISIS in Iraq.
September	Shi'ite Houthi rebels take over Sana'a, the capital of Yemen.
5 September	Ceasefire between Ukrainian government and pro-Russian rebels in border areas.
16 December	Taliban attack on school in Pakistan kills about 150 people.
28 December	NATO formally ends combat role in Afghanistan.
2015	
7 January	Islamic militants attack offices of *Charlie Hebdo* magazine in Paris.

(continued...)

PART VIII CHRONOLOGY (continued)

25 January	Left-wing Syriza party wins Greek election with anti-austerity promises.
26 March	Saudi-led coalition begins military intervention in Yemen against Houthis.
April	About 1,200 refugees drown while trying to reach Europe across the Mediterranean.
2 April	Al-Shabab militants kill 150 at a college in Garissa, Kenya.
25–26 June	Series of ISIS attacks in Kuwait, Syria, and Tunisia kill almost 300 people.
5 July	Greek referendum rejects international financial rescue plan.
14 July	Vienna nuclear deal signed between Iran and the six-power liaison group.
20 July	US and Cuba restore diplomatic relations for first time since 1961.
20 July	Over 30 killed in ISIS bombing in Suruc, Turkey.
23 July	Turkey begins air strikes on ISIS in Syria.
14 August	Greek parliament endorses new financial bail-out.
30 September	Russia begins air strikes in support of Assad regime in Syria.
5 October	Trans-Pacific Partnership trade agreement between US and eleven other states.
31 October	Russian airliner blown up over Sinai by ISIS bomb.
7 November	First-ever meeting between Chinese and Taiwanese presidents, in Singapore.
13 November	ISIS bomb attacks in Paris kill 130 people.
24 November	Turkey shoots down Russian air force plane operating in Syria.
12 December	Deal reached at UN climate change conference, Paris.
2016	
3 January	Iran severs diplomatic relations with Saudi Arabia.
22 March	ISIS bomb attacks in Brussels, Belgium kill over 30 people.
27 March	Islamic militants in Lahore, Pakistan kill over 70 people.
31 March	UN-backed unity government set up in Tripoli; fails to win broad support.
23 June	Referendum in the United Kingdom votes to leave the EU.
12 July	Permanent Court of Arbitration sides with Philippines against Chinese claims in the South China Sea.
15 July	Failed military coup in Turkey.
15 November	Russian aircraft carrier begins air strikes in support of Syrian government.
22 December	Syrian government retakes control of Aleppo.
23 December	Security Council Resolution condemns Israeli settlements in occupied Palestinian territories.
2017	
27 January	New US President, Donald Trump, issues Executive Order limiting travel from seven predominantly Muslim states.
28 February	Trump's annual message to Congress includes 10 per cent increase in defence budget.
4 April	Chemical attack on rebel-held Khan Sheikhoun, Syria.
7 April	US cruise missile attack on Syrian air base in response to Khan Sheikhoun.
1 June	Trump withdraws from Paris climate accord.
3 August	Further US sanctions against Russia over alleged interference in 2016 election.
14 October	Over 500 killed in militant bomb attack in Mogadishu, Somalia.
20 October	ISIS driven out of Raqqa, their self-proclaimed capital in Syria.

PART VIII CHRONOLOGY (continued)

24 November	Over 300 killed in militant attack on Sufi mosque in al-Rawda, Egypt.
28 November	North Korea tests ballistic missile that could reach the US.
6 December	Trump recognizes Jerusalem as capital of Israel.
8 December	UK and EU reach deal on first stage of Brexit deal.
22 December	UN tightens sanctions against North Korea, including oil supplies.
31 December	Kim offers to open talks with South Korea.
2018	
February	Winter Olympics includes joint team from North and South Korea.
7 March	Trump increases US tariffs on steel and aluminium imports.
8 March	Announcement that Trump and Kim are to meet.
11 March	Chinese Congress ends ten-year limit on presidential terms.
12 April	Syrian government completes re-conquest of eastern Ghoutta, near Damascus.
14 April	US, UK, and France bomb Syrian targets after suspected government chemical attack.
21 April	Kim Jong-un announces suspension of North Korea nuclear and missile tests.
8 May	Trump withdraws the US from the 2015 Iran nuclear deal.
12 June	Singapore summit between Trump and Kim Jong-un.
15 June	Trump imposes 25 per cent tariffs on $50 billion worth of Chinese goods.
7 July	British Cabinet defines its preferred Brexit deal.
16 July	First bilateral Trump–Putin summit, in Helsinki.
3 September	Trump cuts $300 million in military aid to Pakistan.
16 September	Trump announces tariffs on another $200 billion of Chinese goods.
1 October	New trade deal agreed between the US, Mexico, and Canada.
25 November	European Union summit in Brussels reaches Brexit agreement.
15 December	Katowice meeting agrees steps to follow the 2015 Paris climate deal.
19 December	Trump says IS has been defeated in Syria and US troops will be withdrawn; leads Defense Secretary Mattis to resign.
2019	
15 January	UK parliament rejects premier May's 'Brexit' deal by a large majority.
26 January	Reported breakthrough in US–Taliban talks on peace in Afghanistan, including a US troop withdrawal.
1 February	US formally suspends its commitments under the 1987 INF Treaty, raising dangers of a new arms race with Russia.
26–27 February	Cross-border violence between India and Pakistan over Kashmir.
27–28 February	Second Trump–Kim summit, in Hanoi, breaks up in disagreement.
21 March	EU summit agrees to extend Brexit talks beyond the original deadline.
23 March	Fall of the last territory held in Syria by the so-called Islamic State.
3 April	Trump recognizes Israeli sovereignty over the Golan Heights.

Take your learning further by viewing the interactive version of this timeline:
www.oup.com/he/young-kent3e

26

Conflict and Chaos in the Middle East

Chapter contents

A. The Syrian Conflict and the Rise and Fall of IS[1]

In the wake of the 2010–11 uprisings elsewhere in the Middle East (see Chapter 26, C), the situation in Syria was changing. Feeding on the so-called 'Arab Spring' and enabled by the ease with which the social media could spread news, protests against President Assad's authoritarian rule quickly grew. Illusions that a democratic political system would establish a new era—empowering the many people excluded from significant status and economic benefits in Syrian society—gained momentum, one intention being to shatter the privileges of the Alawites, a Shi'ite sect who dominated the army officer corps and intelligence services. But, fuelled by the deadly cocktail of economic neo-liberalism and religious identity, many of Assad's original opponents were to be superseded by those, often from outside Syria, who embraced radical Islamist and Salafist ideology[2] that promoted jihad against both the invading infidel and the corrupt Islamic or secular regimes in the region.

The Roots of the Syrian Uprising

The unrest in Syria that exploded in 2011 was driven by the policies of Bashar Assad who, in the decade since his father's death, used the ideology of economic neo-liberalism to supersede the secular Arab nationalism that previously defined Ba'ath party ideology. As in Europe, the consequences of neo-liberalism were similar, in that the less well off were severely disadvantaged by increasing inequality. In Syria, the divisions between rural inhabitants and those in more affluent, urban areas had grown dramatically. While neo-liberalism exposed farming communities and many small manufacturers to cheap imports, the Alawite elites enjoyed a more affluent lifestyle. Agricultural producers were further hit between 2006 and 2010 by drought and the removal of state subsidies for fuel and fertilizer; these resulted in a significant rural–urban migration. Some 460,000 stopped working in the agricultural sector between 2001 and 2007, leading to a decline of 33 per cent in Syria's agricultural labour force. The Raqqa governorate in the north-east became one of the hardest hit provinces, where the divide between the pro-government elite and the rural poor, who were now arriving in the cities in increasing numbers, was particularly acute.[3]

Assad's use of external actors to distract attention from the defects of his regime soon began to unleash uncontrollable forces within Syria.[4] His neo-liberal economic policies had a particularly detrimental economic impact in eastern regions, where contemporary ideologies were more extreme: around this time, the UN estimated that, in the Hasakah and Deir ez-Zur governorates, some 60 to 70 per cent of the villages were entirely deserted.[5] Assad belatedly began the next decade by attempting to integrate Sunnis and minority groups, like the Kurds and the Druze, into Syrian society but, by the end of 2011, the situation was ripe for the development of an alternative society, based on the assertion of Islamic values and the rejection more than the promotion of Western democracy, which was associated with the failure of capitalism to provide economic benefits for significant segments of the population.

Syria, from Anti-Assad Protests to Civil War

In early 2011, protests swept through Syria, particularly after demonstrators were shot, in March, in the southern city of Deraa, and children there detained by the security forces for writing graffiti. This was the first serious unrest in Syria since 1982, when then-President Hafez al-Assad ruthlessly put down a Sunni uprising in the city of Hama. Ominously for the regime, anti-government protests rapidly spread to several cities, including Homs, the country's third largest, which became the 'capital of the revolution', though it never fully fell into opposition hands. The initial demands of Assad's critics centred on political and social reform rather than regime change, but their economic grievances were significant and exacerbated by the political frustrations arising from life in a one-party state, governed by one family and its loyal cliques. However much the protests were inspired by events elsewhere in the Arab world, economic and social conditions in Syria itself were crucial. Even without the growth of jihadism that had been flourishing in Iraq, cultivated by al-Qaeda and Islamic State in Iraq (ISI), trouble was brewing in Syria. After a weakened ISI was helped to survive the first decade of the twenty-first century by its links to Syria, the events of the second decade were to witness the jihadist boot very firmly on the other foot.

As protests grew, Assad made no effort to introduce significant reforms and he probably made the situation worse by attempting to appease the protestors with an amnesty for political opponents under detention and the end of a state of emergency that had been in force since 1963. In Assad's favour, there were very few mass defections by whole military units—in contrast to contemporary events in Egypt, most of the army remained loyal to the President—and thus his opponents faced the challenge of uniting into a cohesive force that could take on the armed forces. He also retained important support from sections of society produced by what have been termed 'buy ins'. These included the urban population, made more affluent by his economic policies, and those who benefitted from his sectarian favouritism in the security forces and tribal favouritism in eastern Syria. Particularly significant, of course, were the Alawite-dominated officer corps and intelligence services, which made his regime more difficult to overthrow.[6] Nevertheless, with the growing importance of armed resistance, some soldiers who were disillusioned with the regime formed a group, initially free from jihadist ideology, known as the Free Syrian Army (FSA). Assad's reliance, after April 2011, on brutal repression led to more opponents taking up arms, not least to defend their local communities but the formation of Local Co-ordination Committees (LCCs) made it difficult to establish a broader-based opposition movement, simply because of the emphasis on local initiatives. FSA actions, too, tended to be driven by local-organized groups. Also, as armed resistance began to supersede the demands for political reform, demands for regime change came more to the fore, but this provoked debate over what kind of government should succeed Assad. It also led to growing concern on the international stage, where outsiders were often unable to understand the Syrian situation. Westerners especially failed to grasp the nature and strength of support for Assad, while Russia and China, already concerned by the disastrous consequences of the US war in Iraq, feared that the use of force against another authoritarian leader would result in Syria falling under Western domination.

In February 2012, Russia and China vetoed a UN Resolution critical of Assad, who sought to bolster his own position by holding a referendum that month, which opposition groups boycotted.

In 2012, the Western belief that the Assad dictatorship must be replaced, with the idealistic dream of a liberal democracy, was one factor that contributed to continued violence and a failure to agree on peace talks. The US Secretary of State, Hillary Clinton, was keen to see regime change, but she was opposed by US officials on the ground, who were in the best position to understand the situation. Robert Ford, the US ambassador to Syria, advised against Clinton's stance, because the US was in no position to bring it about.[7] Despite this, there was an expectation by many rebels that, sooner or later, the US would intervene militarily, leading to the dictator's removal. This misperception was born of a failure to appreciate the reduced willingness of Barack Obama to assert US power in the Middle East after the mess created by Bush in Iraq; and Obama's caution only deepened as the situation in Libya worsened, following the Gaddafi regime's overthrow in late 2011. Syria's rebel fighters, believing in ultimate victory, saw little incentive to negotiate peace, but they also faced a crippling lack of unity. Some opposition groups came together to establish the Syrian National Council (SNC), in November 2011, with the original aim of overthrowing Assad in six months, but its leadership was dominated by political exiles, out of touch with events in Syria, rather than those opposing Assad on the ground, who were already divided into many different armed groups. Crucially, a short-lived effort to stop the fighting through an Arab League peace mission, in December 2011–January 2012, failed completely as both sides saw prospects of victory, with help coming to them from beyond Syria. A UN peace mission, deployed in April 2012, similarly failed, but by then the Syrian conflict was beginning to affect the regional and international power dynamics.

By the autumn of 2011, as the final US regular troops prepared to leave Iraq, ISI decided to expand from Mosul, its main centre of power, into an increasingly violent and disturbed Syria. October saw the establishment, in Syria, of Jabhat al-Nusra, led by Abu Mohammed al-Jolani, formerly close to al-Zarqawi and the ISI emir in the Nineveh governorate, in which Mosul is situated. Al-Nusra (sometimes referred to as al-Qaeda in Syria) delayed announcing its establishment until January 2012, when it released a video declaring war on the Assad regime and calling for the *Sharia,* or Islamic law, to be established throughout Greater Syria (Syria, Lebanon, Jordan, and—before the creation of Israel—Palestine). Al-Nusra did not acknowledge its links to ISI until the Spring of 2013. Throughout 2012, the role of Assad's radical Islamic opponents was much enhanced. Between September and December 2012, jihadist insurgent groups were established in Damascus and northern Syria, gaining some military successes against Assad's forces. Indeed, jihadist insurgents increasingly played the key role in fighting against government forces, with al-Nusra soon particularly prominent. Yet, while external aid to the rebels was offered by Assad's Arab opponents in the region, particularly Saudi Arabia and Qatar, translating it into successful military action proved difficult, especially for moderate non-jihadist groups. As the external funding was not co-ordinated—and it was provided by the suppliers in the hope of gaining support from and influence over the broader Sunni Middle Eastern communities—it only encouraged the recipients to compete for external funding. But the Americans, if not always the Saudis and Qataris, were particularly concerned to avoid money going to, or falling into the hands of, groups like al-Nusra, with its links to al-Qaeda. This was a grave risk for any Middle East government thinking about funding rebel groups; such governments always had one eye on their own domestic stability and its connection to a particular Islamist creed.

Two large groups of Islamic forces emerged in 2012. The first and less hard-line was the Syrian Islamic Liberation Front (SILF), formed of some twenty organizations, some of whom had representatives on the Supreme Military Council (the coordinating body for military commanders in the FSA), and who were prepared to retain links with the West. The second was the Syrian Islamic Front (SIF), comprising around a dozen Salafist organizations, hard-line and anti-Western. By late 2012, the Syrian National Coalition of Syrian Revolution and Opposition Forces (ETILAF) had also been formed, with links to many local rebel groups. Although jihadist groups were now partially integrated into the rebel movement, differences between jihadist and non-jihadist forces handicapped the effective allocation and distribution of aid and weapons. Moreover, the close relationship between some FSA members and jihadis often made it difficult to distinguish non-jihadist fighters and thus guarantee that weapons would not fall into the hands of those whom Washington labelled 'terrorists'. In

August 2012, Obama explained the reluctance of the US to become involved in the conflict, but in the context of a 'red line' which would be crossed if chemical weapons were ever used by the Syrian government, the clear implication being that crossing the 'red line' would lead to greater American assistance for Assad's opponents. But, when it became clear, the following year that chemical weapons had been used in the Damascus suburb of Ghouta, there was no change in Washington's policy. This only hastened the already declining influence of the moderate, non-jihadist members of the FSA over the fighting. The Obama administration, which defined the al-Nusra as a terrorist group in December 2012, held back from providing significant weapons to the fragmented and overlapping insurgent groups. This arguably only benefitted the more successful fighters with radical ideologies and recent experience of war zones in Afghanistan, Iraq, and Chechnya.

Growing Divisions and Increasing Violence in Syria

By the end of 2012, the civil war had become a conflict between a myriad of different armed groups, internal and external to Syria, and their religious ideologies. These forces—manifestations of globalization and changing Middle Eastern dynamics—metamorphosed the war into a complex mix of regional, religious and ethnic, state and non-state conflicts, with disastrous implications for Syria's inhabitants and the already unstable Middle East. Hezbollah, the Lebanese Shi'ite movement, which had benefitted from co-operation with Assad before the war, was one of the significant external, but non-state actors in Syria. It helped with the training of government forces from June, as was confirmed in September 2012 by a US government report. In fact, both Hezbollah and its Shi'ite allies in Iran may have begun their involvement in the fighting a year earlier. Assad's need for more forces increased as the insurgency and the casualties it inflicted on the Syrian army grew. By early 2013, Iranian Revolutionary Guard officers were assigned to Syrian army units. Partly as a result, Sunnis and Shi'ites increasingly saw the growing conflict as a sectarian war against their rival branch of Islam. This sectarian divide, alongside Iranian and Hezbollah intervention, meant that the unbroken, if unspectacular successes rebel forces had against Assad could no longer be taken for granted. January 2013 saw the formation of the volunteer Shi'ite and Alawite-dominated National Defence Force (NDF), with some Iranian Revolutionary Guards attached to it, loyal to the regime. Signs of a change in the balance of power between government forces and their opponents were beginning to appear.

By the end of 2012, another divisive element in the Syrian situation was the Syrian Kurds' armed wing, *Yekîneyên Parastina Gel* (YPG), which strengthened its hold over the northern part of the Aleppo governorate. Whilst not an Islamist movement, the YPG again indicated the variety of competing rebel groups and their links to external forces, in this case other Kurdish nationalist groups in Iraq, Iran, and Turkey, who had long dreamt of establishing a Kurdish state or autonomous regions. The increasingly complex situation made it more difficult to move towards a resolution of the conflict, because the insurgents themselves were so divided in their aims. Largely thanks to the impact of the more experienced fighters, however, there was a growth in the power and influence of jihadist elements on the anti-government side. The influence of the FSA and ETILAF declined as sectarianism became more evident and militants gained some notable successes: Jabhat al-Nusra, for example, began to focus its operations on oilfields, capturing three in the Deir ez-Zur governorate by December, as control of natural resources became a key goal. The early months of 2013 also bore witness to the growing importance of the Salafist movement among Sunni members of the insurgency.

The Growth of Jihadism and the Establishment of ISIS

By March 2013, the number of insurgents in Syria was estimated to be 75,000, of whom 3,000 were foreign fighters.[8] A number of Salafist groups had merged to form Ahrar al-Sham, under Hassan Abboud. Now the largest insurgent force, with about 15,000 fighters, Ahrar al-Sham, which was especially strong in the Idlib, Aleppo, and Hama governates, also contained within its leadership several with links to al-Qaeda. That same month a coalition of insurgents, containing FSA units, came together with Islamist fighters from al-Nusra and Ahrar al-Sham to launch a successful offensive against Aleppo city. March also saw Sunni insurgents capture the town of Raqqa, the first provincial capital lost by Assad. Although Assad's forces, strengthened by Hezbollah and Iranian para-militaries, regained or consolidated their hold over central and western Syria, the northern part of the country was now dominated by the opposition. In fact, the conflict was creating numerous, separate 'war zones', involving different coalitions of participants.

A highly significant development was the March involvement of ISI fighters in the Syrian border town of al-Yaroubiya on the frontier with North East Iraq, in which al-Nusra was also involved. The recovery of ISI had been aided by the sectarianism of the Iraqi government after the American withdrawal. Nouri al-Maliki, the Prime Minister from 2006 to 2014, had tended, especially after 2010, to strengthen the political power of Iraq's Shi'ites and, while pressing on with the US withdrawal, developed links to neighbouring Iran. Against this background, the ISI could pose as leaders of Sunni resistance to the increasingly dominant Shi'ites, while also increasing involvement across the border in Syria. As the numbers of foreign fighters entering Syria grew, in April 2013 ISI announced the extension of its operations into Syria and renamed itself the 'Islamic State in Iraq and al-Sham', or ISIS (often referred to in the Middle East as Daesh). By now, reports of the mass killings of civilians for their religious or political leanings were becoming more common. Such brutality became entrenched and divisions between Assad's opponents widened once ISIS began using displays of brutality as a propaganda tool, promoting acceptance of its presence by using fear.

The leader of ISIS was Abu Bakr al-Baghdadi, whose rise had begun, according to those who knew him, with the American invasion of Iraq in 2003.[9] Born in 1971 to a lower middle-class Sunni family in Samarra, north of Baghdad, he helped found an insurgent group as part of the broader Sunni revolt. Called *Jamaat aish Ahl al-Sunni wal Jamaa,* it was not part of Zarqawi's al-Qaeda network. Baghdadi was captured in early 2004, in Fallujah, by US forces searching for Sunni militants and detained in the notorious Camp Bucca, but only as a 'low- level' threat. The camp was regarded as a production line for the manufacture of radical Salafi jihadists: the Iraqi government later judged that 17 of the 25 most important ISIS leaders of the conflicts in Syria and Iraq spent time in US detention centres between 2004 and 2011.[10]

In 2006, Baghdadi had joined AQI and begun making contacts amongst the 24,000 men incarcerated in Bucca, many of them former Ba'athist officers under Saddam Hussein. Zarqawi had always been suspicious of these elements but, after his assassination in 2006 and the temporary weakening of ISI, the process of incorporating Ba'athists began and was intensified under his eventual successor, Baghdadi. This proved an important contributory factor to the subsequent battlefield success of ISI and later ISIS fighters.

When ISIS was launched in April 2013, however, it also created jihadist divisions as some al-Nusra fighters joined ISIS over the following weeks, but their leader, Abu Mohammed al-Jolani, decided to resist Baghdadi's attempt to incorporate his movement into ISIS and proclaimed loyalty to al-Zawahiri and al-Qaeda central. Thus began the conflict between al-Qaeda and ISIS over the leadership of the global jihadist movement, which predated Baghdadi's controversial announcement of a caliphate in 2014. ISIS became an important player in the bitter Syrian conflict and was soon especially strong in the governorates of Aleppo and Raqqa, but the conflict between the Islamic groups diverted attention from the anti-Assad campaign. The chances of the FSA continuing operational cooperation with jihadists also became less likely, which in turn boosted the chances of Assad staging a military recovery. One success for him came in May–June 2013 when, after Hezbollah admitted its fighters were in Syria, it helped the army win a bloody battle with the FSA over the town of al-Qusayr, which lay in a strategic position between Damascus and the coast.

The number of conflicts within the Syrian civil war continued to increase; eventually there were nearly a hundred different groups engaged in the ever-more complex conflict. By July 2013, the *Partiya Yekitiya Demokrat* (PYD), the non-military wing of the YPG, had announced a constitution for a self-proclaimed Kurdish state in Syria. While there were victories for pro-Assad fighters in the south and west, these were accompanied by the eruption of sustained inter-rebel fighting in the north between the YPG and Islamist forces, including ISIS, al-Nusra, and al-Sham, which were opposed to the creation of a Kurdish state. Al-Nusra was weakened by the loss of defectors to ISIS, but it was also the only jihadist group still operating in southern Syria, where its contacts with the Palestinians in Lebanon (formerly in Fatah al-Islam), became closer. Many in the Islamist forces became concerned about the extreme brutality of ISIS, and members of SILF and SIF discussed forming a new alliance. Other jihadist groups emphasized the dominance of Salafism in the increasing religious orientation of the rebels as they received support and financial help particularly from Qatar and Turkey. In the summer of 2013, seven groups began talks on closer cooperation, and the Islamic Front was created in November. Its 55,000 fighters rejected straightforward political opposition and sought 'a just Islamic state'. Despite the formation of the Syrian Revolutionaries Front in December, under the moderate leadership of Jamal Maroof and with strong links to Saudi Arabia, the position of the more secular FSA continued to deteriorate.

Meanwhile, the wealth and fighting expertise of ISIS continued to attract recruits to its side, as did its use of social media. Heaping praise on the mujahidin and the value of martyrdom, its campaign reaped benefits because it fed on feelings of inequality and alienation, in Syria and far beyond, in the face of a dominant Western neo-liberalism. As winter approached, the numbers of foreign fighters entering Syria increased and ISIS, for several months, concentrated its forces on the northern border with the recruitment of foreign fighters very much in mind. One Turkish smuggler claimed to have moved 400 such recruits across the border in a few months, with the long northern border being the preferred route into Syria for would-be ISIS recruits. The numbers crossing trebled following the Syrian government's August 2013 chemical attack in Damascus (whereas the Western powers were satisfied with a Syrian government undertaking to destroy its chemical weapon stocks).[11] Hundreds were killed in the attack, which UN weapons inspectors confirmed was due to Sarin nerve gas. By the beginning of 2014, there were 11,000 fighters from outside Syria, most of whom had arrived over the course of the previous year.

Meanwhile, efforts at peace talks failed to make any real progress. After the initial failure of the Arab League's peace efforts in 2011–12, a UN special envoy, the former Secretary-General Kofi Annan, had got an international peace conference, including the US, Russia, and China, to discuss the creation of a transitional Syrian government in Geneva in June 2012 (known as the Geneva I talks). However, in these talks US Secretary of State Hillary Clinton clashed with the Russian Foreign Minister, Sergei Lavrov, over whether Assad should remain in power, a key issue that would continue to divide Washington and Moscow over the following years. Subsequent attempts at peace talks, including the Geneva II talks of January 2014, also quickly broke down. The international community may have been concerned about the rising civilian death toll and the refugee crisis created by the war, but it seemed unable or unwilling to do anything to end it. In any case, the more militant groups involved in the civil war no longer welcomed intervention by outside powers: when eleven Islamist groups issued a joint statement renouncing any links to the Western-backed ETILAF, this was followed by SILF, on behalf of nineteen Islamist factions, rejecting the proposed Geneva peace talks as part of a viable peace process.

Although the human costs of the war cannot accurately be established, almost half of Syria's population had either been killed or has fled by the end of 2013, with 6.5 million displaced people within Syria. It was not just ISIS that used deliberate brutality as a tactic: Assad's daily targeting of civilians in Aleppo with barrel bombs was designed to destroy the facilities needed by the civilian population to live, in order that the high level of urban destruction and the deaths of non-combatants would force the insurgents to surrender. Central to ISIS objectives was the effort to establish a firmer territorial grip on its conquered areas and the human and material resources they contained. Hence the removal of Assad became a secondary issue, just as for Assad the toleration of ISIS now became a useful option. As long as ISIS presented no existential threat to his regime, and instead concentrated on creating the ideological and administrative trappings of an embryonic state in rebel-held regions, it served to weaken and divide the anti-Assad forces.

Key to the growth of ISIS was the provision of services and local government for the inhabitants of areas it controlled, which accompanied the imposition of Sharia law. The exercise of influence through the control of basic needs, like water, electricity, and refuse collection, arguably made ISIS rule welcome in some areas, alongside the kudos and power that successful fighters provided, but these were accompanied by the use of bestial acts to intimidate Sunni populations into co-operation. Financial resources were built up by the development of a taxation system and the marketing of oil and gas, which were sold, at attractively low prices, to supposed opponents of the government, but also to the Assad regime itself. Former government personnel from Saddam Hussein's regime, cast adrift by the American occupation authorities in Iraq, helped ISIS operate administrative departments in areas it controlled, such as security and education, and bolstered its support amongst the Sunni populations in Syria and Iraq. The transfer of captured weapons, many of them American, from Iraq to Eastern Syria, also induced some tribes there to pledge allegiance to ISIS.

ISIS successes drew a response from its rivals, however. The early months of 2014 saw jihadist and Salafist groups opposed to ISIS launch a coordinated offensive against it in alliance with FSA-aligned fighters. One element of the forces attacking ISIS consisted of Islamist groups that had formed Jaish al-Mujahaddin and Jaish al-Islam. The dynamics of the Syrian insurgency were changing once again, with ISIS helping to unite other jihadist groups and 'moderates' in violent opposition to it, although differences between the moderate Islamists, including the Muslim Brotherhood, and the jihadists remained. It is likely that some of this coalescence of forces against ISIS was assisted by America's Central Intelligence Agency (CIA) and pressure from the Saudis. Certainly, the supply of more advanced American arms to moderate anti-ISIS insurgents was one result, albeit that the arms were supplied not directly, but via the Saudis. Saudi Arabia and Qatar also supplied arms of their own to the insurgents, channelled through Jordan and Turkey.[12] Al-Nusra and the Islamic Front not only fought against ISIS, but also supported al-Qaeda in a war of words with it over doctrine. This civil war between Islamists within the civil war in Syria had its absurd dimension in early 2014, with Zawahiri and al-Qaeda Central adopting the role of peacemakers, calling for an immediate ceasefire. By then, some 1,400 fighters had lost their lives in inter-factional jihadist conflicts. But it proved difficult for the anti-ISIS forces to create a lasting cohesion or make decisive advances. Instead, in mid-January, ISIS drove al-Nusra and Ahrar al-Sham out of Raqqa city and took full control there, then made it their de facto capital.

Such clashes between his opponents helped Assad recover from earlier losses: the regime conducted successful operations with Russian-supplied weapons in the Latakia region of North Western Syria, while continuing the sustained bombing of Aleppo city and advancing in the Aleppo governorate. Also, hopes that political tensions would also be eased by the Islamic Front releasing a 'Revolutionary Covenant' in May 2014 proved ill-founded. The idea of a Covenant, detailing the aims of the revolution (including condemnation of the regime, ISIS, and external intervention in the war), may have been influenced by a wish to win Western sympathy and broaden the anti-ISIS movement. But, when the Islamic Front, now the largest insurgent group, dominated by Ahrar al-Sham, stated that an Islamic state was no longer one of its political goals, (the Covenant, which emphasized a 'state of law' and respect for Syria's multi-ethnicity, but excluded al-Nusra), Salafist political unity against ISIS was made more problematic.

The Announcement of the Caliphate and its Impact

By May 2014, intense fighting had begun in the Deir ez-Zur governorate, where both al-Nusra and Ahrar al-Sham were targeted by ISIS, and around 60,000 people fled their homes. The following month, as the West faced its first Syrian-linked terrorist attack, on a Jewish museum in Brussels, ISIS launched a major new offensive in Iraq. In January, the group had already established a foothold in Fallujah, barely forty miles from Baghdad, but now, in its most stunning success so far, it captured Mosul, Iraq's second largest city. In only six days, about 1,500 fighters defeated Iraqi army units numbering twenty times that figure. In the process, ISIS seized significant quantities of military vehicles and armaments. This was followed by simultaneous ISIS attacks across the four other provinces of North Eastern Iraq. Often using suicide bombers in the initial phases of their attacks, ISIS forces not only learnt how to defeat the security forces deployed against them through terror tactics, but also how to use conventional land warfare methods, using captured tanks, artillery, and other heavy weaponry. Their advances were so extraordinary and unexpected that, with ISIS approaching Baghdad itself, Obama informed Congress on 16 June that he would send military personnel to Iraq to protect US Embassy staff. ISIS had exposed both the ineffectiveness of the Iraqi army and the utter failure of the Maliki government to produce stability through the acceptance of Iraqi Sunnis—many of whom now looked to ISIS as protectors from the government in Baghdad. As the scale of the ISIS advance in Iraq and Syria became obvious to the world, its leader, Baghdadi, made a rare public appearance in Mosul to proclaim the establishment of a Caliphate, with himself as the Caliph. The first Caliphate had been established soon after the death of the Prophet Muhammed, to provide a leader for all Muslims, but the last major Caliphate, based at Istanbul, had been abolished in 1924. The re-establishment of the Caliphate gave jihadist theology concrete, human form, with rule over a territory based on Sharia law by a Caliph. The Caliphate meant the abolition of ISIS, which now assumed the title of the so-called 'Islamic State' (IS).

Following the announcement of the Caliphate, to which all Muslims were traditionally expected to pledge *bay'ah* (oath of allegiance), IS focused more on its English language propaganda campaign, designed to recruit followers globally, using films and videos made to a professional standard. It received pledges of *bay'ah* from a range of groups beyond Iraq and Syria, including jihadists from several Arab states, Indonesia, Pakistan, the Philippines. On the ground, the group had control of territory from Al Bab, in the north of Syria's Aleppo governorate, nearly 700 kilometres southwards to Iraq's Salah ad Din province.[13] The Iraq–Syria international border had largely been rendered meaningless, with border posts overrun and the guards slaughtered. By July, IS also dominated the resource-rich Syrian governorate of Deir ez-Zur, defeating rival insurgents and securing tribal allegiances there, using the stick of brutal executions and the carrot of distributing money estimated at two mlllion dollars.[14] After that, IS was ready to resume its attacks on Assad, which had been absent for over a year, with continued advances in the north. In Iraq, IS fighters captured the town of Sinjar, in August, killing or enslaving thousands of Yazidis, a Kurdish minority, and forcing thousands more to flee into the mountains, without food or water. The Iraqi government began air drops of food to tackle this humanitarian disaster, while IS continued to capture more towns in northern Iraq and threatened the Iraqi Kurdish capital of Erbil.

By now, IS was clearly far more than a terrorist group and did, indeed, have some of the trappings of a state. It was no longer significantly dependent on external donations, but was largely financially self-sufficient. By using taxes and extortion in the territory it controlled, and the resources of oil and gas that they provided, its monthly income was already estimated in 2013 at between one and three million dollars, with less than 10 per cent coming from external contributions.[15] With such a sizable income, it was easily able to pay its fighters, buy tribal loyalties, and provide social services, especially in areas of Iraq and Syria, where such fundamentals had been lacking. Transport, power, infrastructure repair, policing, and religious education in accordance with IS's ideology were provided, along with food subsidies. The price of bread in Deir ez-Zur, for example, was fixed, and local bakeries were required to provide a specified sum of *zakat* (charity) for the poor. Accompanying these elements was the strict enforcement of behavioural codes, with disobedience being met by such punishments as whipping, stoning, and beheading. Forced conversions were carried out among Christians, Shi'ites, and other non-Sunni religious groups.

The stunning IS advance in Iraq drew an international response. On 8 August, the US launched its first air strikes against IS in Iraq, with F-18s bombing positions in the north, which helped the Iraqi Kurds' military forces, the Peshmerga, to halt the IS advance there. In September, Obama announced that the US would target IS in both Syria and Iraq, and he sent extra advisers to Iraq, bringing the numbers of US personnel up to 1,600. Having launched two invasions, of Afghanistan and Iraq, supposedly to hit back at al-Qaeda after 9/11, Americans were about to assist jihadis—and, in Syria, even an al-Qaeda affiliate—against an even worse adversary that the original Iraq war had helped to create.

Attempts to Build a Unified Resistance, 2014

In September 2014, Secretary of State John Kerry met representatives of Arab states in Jeddah, Saudi Arabia, and announced a coalition of ten Arab states to join the struggle against IS.[16] Iran had already begun to provide weapons and military advice to Shi'ite militias in Iraq, and with the US (separately, given the deep suspicions between them) sought to bolster the Iraqi army. This helped prevent any IS advance on Baghdad and, by November, anti-IS forces were able to recover territory, including oil wells. IS had responded to the renewal of US military action in Iraq by beheading several Western captives and displaying videos of its brutality online, while demanding that the air attacks should cease. This only hardened Western determination to destroy the group. Meanwhile, the Syrian regime also increased its air strikes on IS, using Russian-supplied aircraft, and anti-IS insurgent groups continued to seek greater unity.

On 3 August, the Wa'tasimo ('hold fast') Initiative was launched, in Idlib, with the aim of uniting eighteen groups, some now armed with American anti-tank weapons, into a Revolutionary Command Council (RCC), the hope being that this would gain greater legitimacy and support than ETILAF. Four months later the RCC included 72 insurgent groups, including all seven members of the Islamic Front. It brought together Salafists and the SRF coalition backed by the US, and it had a 73-member general command, divided geographically. It also managed to issue a Political Charter and a Unified Arab Code largely based on the *Sharia*. Tensions became evident almost immediately, not least over who should be members of the executive council, and ideological divisions remained among the anti-IS insurgents, with al-Nusra seeking to create

Islamic emirates in the Idlib, Aleppo, and Deraa governorates. On 9 September, Ahrar al-Sham was seriously weakened when many of its senior leaders were killed in an explosion in Idlib, just as it was discussing membership of the RCC. It was unclear who was responsible. The victims included the group's leader, Hassan Abboud, who favoured reconciliation with more moderate Islamic elements. Yet, it was now clear that the jihadists were much the stronger and more effective opposition to Assad, despite there sometimes being open conflict between them. Their campaign against the regime was clearly separate from the battle IS was waging (against both them and Assad). They also received financial support from Saudi Arabia and Qatar, even if the Saudis were becoming concerned about the threat posed to the region's stability.

One ethnic group in the region initially without external support was the Kurds. Split between the four states of Turkey, Iran, Iraq, and Syria, the Kurdish quest for an independent state had effectively been nullified by government opposition in Turkey and Iran, while autonomy had been achieved by the Iraqi Kurds after 2003. Different political parties and their ideologies existed within each Kurdish region. The Syrian Kurds formed the smallest group, inhabiting three different regions or 'cantons' bordering the frontier with Turkey, which were separated by Sunni Arab areas, and also interlaced with other minority groups, such as the Turkomans, Assyrians, and Armenians. Leaving aside the animosities between the various groups in the separate states, the uneasy relations between the different Kurdish groups, like much else in the Syrian conflict, were complicated by the changes that external powers and non-state participants produced.

Increased Bombing and its Destructive Impact

The US bombing campaign in Syria began on 22 September with strikes on the town of Kobane, on the Syrian–Turkish border, against which IS had launched an offensive on 16 September. Such air strikes were, however, far from popular with the Syrian rebels, especially the jihadists, who were infuriated by the American failure to attack Assad. Since Washington labelled al-Nusra a terrorist organization, and because US strikes were also directed against it, this caused bitter resentment amongst Assad's jihadist opponents and did little to promote unity against IS. Ironically, al-Nusra now developed a leading role in the north, courtesy of the American air strikes. The Islamic Front was critical of US bombing and the idea that America sought a 'war on Islam' gained ground. Indeed, for some rebels, the US seemed an agent of the Syrian government in attempting to eliminate al-Nusra. Meanwhile, the government continued to make advances: by October, its forces controlled most of Damascus, as well as the strategic road north through Homs and west into Latakia, and Assad looked increasingly safe. Assad's forces also intensified their bombing of Aleppo city in the wake of the US air strikes, and government troops were increasingly assisted by Hezbollah in the struggle over the wider Aleppo governorate. On the other hand, in a demonstration of the value of co-operation, FSA and al-Nusra had a notable success in capturing a joint Syrian–Russian signals intelligence and electronic warfare facility in Deraa.

By December 2014, despite the US air strikes, IS was in control of about a third of Syrian territory, with some of the bitterest fighting focused on Kobane, which for several months became the crucial urban battlefield in the north. Despite the arrival of an additional 1,000 Kurdish fighters, IS captured the YPG's headquarters and controlled almost half the town. As well as bombing, the US dropped aid and weapons to the anti-IS forces, while the Kurdish Peshmerga from Iraq provided reinforcements. Slowly, the advantage shifted in favour of the Kurdish forces. IS continued to pour new recruits into the town in January, but defeat came by the end of the month and marked a watershed for the war against IS, although it took several months to remove its fighters from the surrounding villages.

The key urban destruction was now produced through Assad's intense barrel-bombing of Aleppo city. There was a deepening sense of stalemate as neither the government nor its opponents showed any prospect of achieving a decisive victory. The Syrian Observatory for Human Rights noted that the numbers killed in the Syrian conflict since March 2011 was 210,000 with probably at least 85,000 more fatalities.[17] Less than two years later, the estimate had risen to 350,000, which was three times the total deaths in the 70 years of the Arab–Israeli conflict and double the deaths in the 2003–11 Iraq War.[18] About half of the Syrian population had also become refugees abroad or were internally displaced within the country, the latest mass exodus being from Kobane. This created a significant problem for neighbouring Turkey, Lebanon, and

Jordan which, by the end of 2015, had about 6 million Syrian refugees between them.

The Growing International Dimensions of the Conflict

The success of IS had produced direct US intervention in Syria and promoted the further coalescence of anti-IS opposition jihadist forces and Assad's few remaining moderate opponents. Unfortunately for those seeking to defeat Assad, any cooperation against IS was inevitably a diversion of manpower and other resources from the struggle against government forces, but some compensation was had in the easing of conditions attached to the supply of US weaponry, which was no longer made conditional on the approved recipients not sharing them with jihadist groups. As neither government nor opposition forces could sustain military operations across the whole country, the conflict varied in intensity in different regions, with different combinations of actors operating in different geographical areas. Assad's regime, despite Hezbollah and Iranian support, continued to struggle for manpower, hence its tactic of destroying cities (with their housing and public services) in order to make them uninhabitable for the rebels. The government had avoided collapse and was now able to regain strategically important areas: in 2015, backed by 5,000 Hezbollah and other Shi'ite militia fighters, the regime gradually re-took full control of Homs and launched an offensive in the south, including the Quneitra governorate adjacent to Israel. Israel was deeply disturbed by having its sworn enemies, Iran and Hezbollah, close to the border and periodically launched air attacks to disrupt their operations. The Quneitra offensive indicated the growing influence of Hezbollah on the Syrian government, as its fighters, along with Iranians, assumed leading roles in the most important battles. The strengthening of the YPG and al-Nusra in the North led IS to pay more attention to the strategically important Homs governorate. It captured Palmyra, with its UNESCO World Heritage Site, and the oil-producing centre of al-Sukhna in Homs in May 2015. Meanwhile, al-Nusra strengthened its own position in the North by defeating both SRF forces in Idlib and the Western-backed Harakat Hazm in the Aleppo governorate. Al-Nusra also joined with Ahrar al-Sham, which had absorbed some smaller groups in the Islamic Front, in March–April 2015, to form an 'Army of Conquest'—Jaish al-Fatah—to capture Idlib. On 28 March, it became the second provincial capital (after Raqqa) lost by Assad. Despite their degree of coordination in Idlib, Jabhat al-Nusra and Ahrar al Sham remained separate organizations and ideological rivals but, faced by Assad's recovery in the South, Zawahiri had instructed Jolani to integrate al-Nusra more closely with the Syrian opposition.

The international dimensions of the Syrian civil war had become an ever more important and complicating factor since 2011, as was apparent from American, Iranian, and Hezbollah involvement, and the backing some groups received from Arab states and Turkey. IS may have lost the battle for Kobane, but it continued to develop as a global movement and to recruit foreign adherents, some of whom found targets nearer home: January 2015 saw a murderous attack on the offices of *Charlie Hebdo* in Paris, which heralded a series of attacks outside the Levant that year—the deadliest being bombings in Tunisia and Kuwait in June and gun and bomb attacks in Paris in November.

Another important shift occurred with the Turkish government's decision to provide increased support to the insurgency against Assad. Recep Erdogan, Turkish President from 2014, was concerned about the refugee problem and worried that Kurdish successes in northern Syria could create problems with Turkey's substantial Kurdish minority by encouraging the separatist ambitions of the Kurdistan Workers' Party (PKK), which had pursued an armed struggle against Ankara since the 1980s in pursuit of Kurdish autonomy in eastern Turkey. With the US increasingly focused on IS rather than the rebellion in Syria, there was greater scope for Turkey to influence, if not control, Assad's jihadist opponents in the RCC and ensure an effective counter to Kurdish separatists. The events of 2014 had reset some of the dynamics of the Syrian War, as became clearer the following year. Although Turkey was supposedly fighting on the same side as the Kurds, the PYD/PKK's relations with Turkey changed as more substantial links grew between the Syrian and Iraqi Kurds. The possibility of autonomy for a Kurdish-controlled area of Syria along its southern border was of growing concern to the Turkish government, not least because it would set a dangerous precedent for the PKK. When, in June 2015, two of the three Kurdish cantons in northern Syria were united geographically by the Kurdish seizure of Tell Abyad from IS, Ankara became even more aware of the potential PYD threat. January 2015 also saw the death of Saudi King Abdullah, whose successor,

Salman, was more willing to work with Qatar and Turkey and accept Sunni jihadists in Syria. Salman also intervened in Yemen, in what was seen as part of a resistance movement to growing Shi'ite influence in the Middle East, apparently orchestrated by Iran. By this point, the original Syrian political differences had long been superseded by ethnic and religious divisions and the increasing international involvement brought diverse power-political aims, making an already complex situation even murkier and less amenable to solution. The stronger links to Turkey, Qatar, and Saudi Arabia influenced Ahrar al-Sham, the most significant rebel fighting force, to pay more attention to political alliances, and rebel operations were linked more directly to the wishes of external actors. It was becoming ever more difficult to conceive of a single Syrian war or to judge the meaning of victory. Hence UN peace efforts, which revived in February–May 2015, still found no success. The UN special envoy, Staffan de Mistura, was unable even to achieve a ceasefire.

Turning the IS Tide

Despite the IS retreat in the North, it remained a significant force in Syria and Iraq, and in July–August 2015 it began attacking opposition-held areas of the Aleppo governorate. On 20 July, over a hundred people were killed or injured in a suicide bomb attack in Suruc, just over the Turkish border, by a Kurdish suicide bomber with links to IS. This was the signal for Turkey to embark on a more interventionist policy in Syria, albeit with a significant focus on fighting Kurdish separatists. Turkey sent troops over the border to fight IS, while air sorties began against both the PKK in northern Iraq and IS in northern Syria. In retrospect, it became clear that IS had passed its high point by the summer of 2015, when Turkey also granted the US permission to use the air base at Incirlik for anti-IS operations. Some argue that the opposition to IS was effectively used as cover for specific Turkish aims in the region, focused more on preventing the creation of a Kurdish state, or any significant Kurdish authority over the border in Syria.

Turkey's increased role brought it into closer contact with the fragile coalition of Islamist groups, in which Ahrar al-Sham became the most pro-Turkish element and the keenest to pay heed to the politics of the situation. Differences with the more hard-line jihadist al-Nusra grew as Ahrar al-Sham also sought contact with the West. In a *Washington Post* article of July 2015, Ahrar al-Sham announced a new commitment to dialogue, so as to find a way to replace Assad with a more representative government and defeat IS. As the Obama administration considered whether to talk to Ahrar al-Sham and its new leadership, in July US Special Forces began implementing a 'train-and-equip' mission to integrate trained recruits into some of the factions in northern Syria. This almost immediately ran into problems with armed opposition from al-Nusra.

Turkey's growing influence was accompanied by Iranian encouragement of Shi'ite militias from outside Syria, especially from Iraq, to join in the fighting. Shi'ite militias had been an important element in Iraq for years and, in 2014, Nouri al-Maliki's Iranian backers were instrumental in organizing these into a more coherent military unit, the Popular Mobilisation Force (PMF), able to confront IS and fight alongside the Kurdish Peshmerga, to which Iran also supplied arms. After the victory over IS at Kobane, the Iranians saw the need to give the militias a new focus, buttressing Assad's regime in Syria. Not all Iraqi Shi'ites were happy with such a role: the Shi'ite supporters of Moqtada al-Sadr and Grand Ayatollah Ali al-Sistani declined to answer the call to fight in Syria.[19] But Iranian and Iraqi Shi'ite forces now played a key role in recovering territory for the Assad regime, led by the highly successful Major General Qassem Suleimani, head of the 'Quds Force' of Revolutionary Guards, who specialized in operations outside Iran. But Iran was also willing to use negotiation to achieve its aims. A substantive six-month cease fire was announced in September by Hezbollah, which was applied to a rebel-held town near Damascus and two Shi'ite-held towns in North West Syria. Although only lasting a short time, the negotiations were facilitated by Iran and confirmed the influence Tehran and Hezbollah had gained over the Assad government.

The Beginning of Russian Intervention

In July 2015, another vital step in the internationalization of the war was reached when Assad, faced with stalemate on the ground, external diplomatic pressure, and delicate relations with his Shi'ite allies, made a formal request to the Russian government for air strikes to help combat 'terrorism'.[20] One of Assad's concerns was the attempt by IS, after suffering losses in the North, to advance in southern Syria and parts of Damascus. In August, an agreement on Russian use of Syrian facilities, notably the Khmeimim air base, was signed and Russian pilots, tanks, and artillery, along with troops, were stationed in them. Then, on 30 September, at Assad's request, Russia intervened directly in the conflict with air strikes against Assad's jihadist opponents, including IS and al-Nusra. By participating in the war against the 'terrorism' of IS, a smokescreen was provided for Russia to help weaken Assad's opponents and further its own aims as an important, non-Western power in the Middle East. The immediate Russian impact on the fighting was not that decisive in terms of the overall war's direction, but it did make it more likely that the military stalemate would continue and Assad would survive, albeit with the growing significance of jihadist groups in the anti-Assad rebels.[21]

For Russian President Vladimir Putin, the important issue was the prestige and status to be gained from overcoming the international isolation that followed the initial 2014 events in Ukraine. From the first Russian–Chinese veto of a UN Security Council resolution, Putin was keen to ensure there were no more regime changes, either in Europe or the Middle East, brought about by the adoption of Western values and backed by the West's greater economic muscle. The extension of Western socio-economic or political influence would detract from Putin's overall goal, similar to that of the Soviets in much of the Cold War, of asserting a leading position on the global stage. The Syrian conflict offered the prospect not only of ending the series of losses of Russian influence following the collapse of the Soviet Union, but also of enhancing Russia's international role and its influence in the Middle East. By preventing another Western-sponsored regime change and ending a dangerous conflict, it could reverse the situation in the 1970s, when Kissinger had denied the Soviets a peacemaking role after the 1973 Arab–Israeli war.

Russian intervention was, however, a risky strategy because of the volatile nature of the situation and the danger of being dragged piecemeal into a lasting war, like US forces in Vietnam in the 1960s. Straightforward military success was unlikely to occur and even less likely to restore stability in Syria. Putin's move may have been prompted by increased Turkish and American aid to the rebels. The Russian President may also have disliked the increasingly important Iranian role in preserving the Syrian dictator: Russia had no interest in allowing Iran to develop greater regional status or outshine its own much-desired influence in the Middle East. A more immediate explanation may have been Assad's surprising public acknowledgement, in June 2015, that the regime could not now defend all its positions. Its survival might have seemed to depend on Russian assistance.[22]

The Russians were not alone in using air power in Syria, of course. The US and Turkey had already done so. French air strikes against IS began in November 2015 and similar British strikes were approved in December. There were also 'special forces' operating in Syria from a number of other countries, all of which added to the image of an international conflict that could no longer simply be described as a civil war and where the combatants had a bewildering array of aims and objectives, which it would be difficult to reconcile even on a short-term basis. They bore little resemblance or connection to the demands for political reform born of the Arab Spring. The castles of democratic sand had been destroyed by the economic forces that had given rise to them and by the ideological storms of religion and ethnicity whose winds were whipped up by external intervention.

The role of IS as an expanding territorial force with increasing military power and access to economic resources did, however, come to an end after the summer of 2015. With the number of state and non-state forces ranged against it, the area it controlled began to shrink. It had taken on too many enemies with too little attention to allies in Syria or Iraq. After the intensified bombardment of western Iraq and eastern Syria in 2015, the PMF engaged with IS in Iraq along with government forces in the autumn of 2015. Ramadi, the capital of Anbar province, was recaptured by February 2016, after nine months of IS rule. In Syria, however, Russian air strikes were initially directed more against the threat to Assad from rebel jihadist forces than against IS. The aim was to consolidate the regime's control of key areas using sophisticated Russian military hardware. Constraining the expansion of the rebels in Idlib governorate, following IS's defeat there, was very much a secondary concern.

The Expanded Peace Efforts

But for Putin to pose as a peacemaker, it was also important to try to bring the warring parties together to gain the prestige and status Russia's important role as a successful peacemaker would incur. Only weeks after the Russian air strikes began, John Kerry, Sergei Lavrov, and other foreign ministers, including

Figure 26.1 Map of Syria, Iraq, and the spread of 'Islamic State', 2014

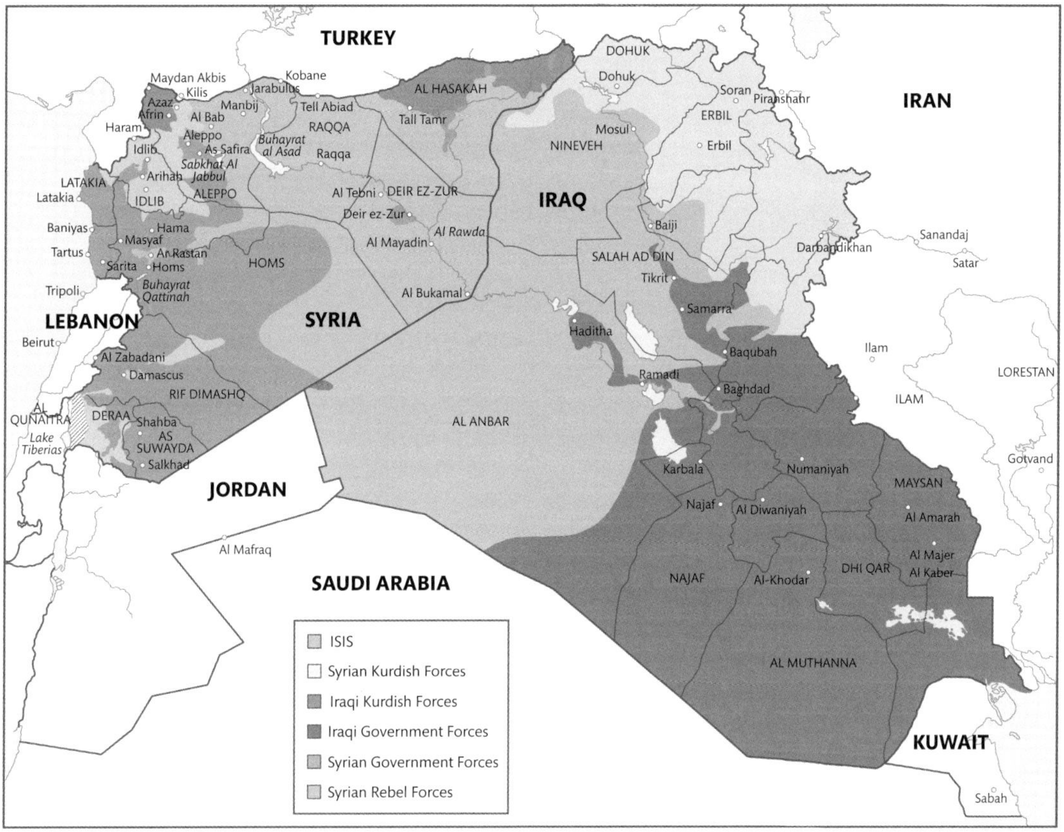

those of Iran and Saudi Arabia, met in Vienna and by mid-November reached agreement on the need for the Syrian government and the rebels to begin formal talks. Twenty states also set up an International Syria Support Group (ISSG), chaired by the US and Russia, to work for a settlement, but Assad refused to negotiate with what he termed 'foreign terrorists'. After a US–Russian foreign ministers' meeting, the UN Security Council unanimously passed Resolution 2254 on 18 December, endorsing an ISSG plan for formal talks and a unity government within six months. Meanwhile, at a meeting in Riyadh, 34 opposition groups, excluding Jabhat al-Nusra, agreed on a High Negotiations Committee (HNC) to decide on 15 representatives for the Syrian opposition at another UN Peace Conference (Geneva III) under the UN special envoy, de Mistura. On the opening day, representatives of the government and the rebels refused to sit in the same room and de Mistura suspended the talks.

At this point, Putin seemed averse to allowing Assad to reject peace overtures, especially since the US and Russia were equally involved in the diplomatic process. He even told *Das Bild,* in January 2016, that the Syrian leader 'had done much wrong over the course of the conflict'.[23] The gains in Russian international credibility, which the peace process was supposed to bring, were thereby undermined by the repeated failures of the participants to engage effectively in negotiations. Thus, international efforts began to focus on the more limited aim of a ceasefire to end the civilian carnage that was facilitated by the crude, but extensive, use of barrel bombs dropped from helicopters. After another Kerry–Lavrov meeting, a UN-sponsored ceasefire was scheduled to begin on 27 February. It went ahead but crucially excluded operations against 'terrorist' organizations, a point which was used by the Syrian government and their Russian backers to justify attacks on the rebels in general. Neither Syria nor Russia was

Figure 26.2 Map of Syria showing the occupation of various forces in 2016

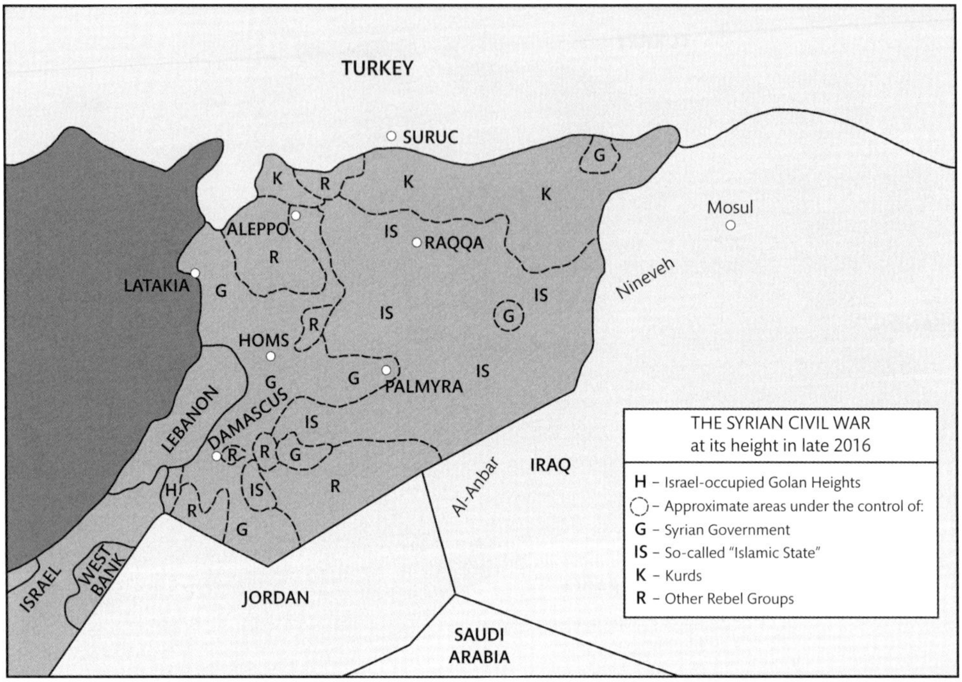

willing to accept the Western argument that 'terrorist' groups like al-Nusra were fundamentally different from 'moderate' Islamic opponents of the regime. It was the first of many repeated failures to produce effective ceasefires.

The Syrian Regime, Russia, the US, and Iran in Both Peace and War Making

Instead, Putin announced on 14 March, that in view of what had been achieved he would start to draw down the Russian air forces. He spoke in terms of Russia having successfully completed its mission. But if this was designed to put pressure on Assad to implement a settlement which preserved him as a stooge of Putin, it failed: Assad responded two days later by declaring that Iran had been the 'chief supporter' of his regime since 2011. There was little trust between Tehran and Moscow, but Putin's attempts to manage the conflict and Assad were weakened, while the Russian and Syrian air forces' need for ground support from Iran and its Shi'ite supporters remained crucial.[24] Assad was effectively able to play off Putin and Iran as they competed for influence in the region, and he thus ensured that both his allies focused on improving his military position in the conflict.

While Russia may have wished to target IS to justify its intervention under the guise of fighting jihadist terrorists, Assad's priority remained fighting other rebels—jihadists or not—especially those who occupied half of Syria's second city, Aleppo. The horrific 2016 destruction of Eastern Aleppo was almost beyond comprehension, as Assad sought to make it uninhabitable. Then the rebel fighters and the tens of thousands of innocent civilians would be forced to surrender, or more civilians would keep dying. Hospitals were specifically targeted, as were water and power supplies. For his part, Putin—whatever his hopes of achieving a settlement—did not discourage the sustained bombing of Eastern Aleppo, which began in April. Russian air power facilitated the blockade and destruction of the rebel enclave, aided, from July 2016, by 2,000 Shi'ite militia fighters from Iraq, while in November Russia's only aircraft carrier, *The Admiral Kuznetsov* arrived in the Mediterranean. Despite its lack of modern equipment and repeated engine failures, the ship joined in the air assault. It was an attempt to demonstrate Russia's alleged power and importance in preventing regime change in Syria. International disapproval of the wanton killing undermined Putin's hopes of winning the international community around to accepting an improved situation for the Assad regime in a Russian-facilitated peace process. With the West unable to stop the bloodshed, the US focused almost entirely on its bombing campaign against IS, with various local allies on the ground.

There remained the complication of US–Russian relations when fighting a war on opposing sides, each with its different friends and enemies, while working together in attempts to stop it. Obama had made great efforts to avoid US actions which threatened to repeat the mistakes of 2003: eliminating one problem at the cost of creating many more. By moving from the massive use of military force in Iraq to a limited involvement in Syria, he still failed to prevent similar chaos and destruction. The bloody siege of Aleppo dragged on until the end of December, when Assad's 'victory' amounted to no more than control of destroyed buildings in largely uninhabitable streets. The brutality against civilians was almost unprecedented. According to the UN, 300,000 people had lived in Eastern Aleppo at the start of 2016, but only 110,000 registered for the January 2017 evacuation. Between June and December, about 3,500 people, mostly civilians, had died there.

The Battle against IS in Iraq

Meanwhile, in Iraq, the campaign against IS continued to progress in 2016 and, with the reduction in the territory it controlled went a significant loss of revenue. But the Iraqi government had its own problems, not least the rivalry between Maliki, now a vice-president, and the new Prime Minister (since September 2014), Haidar al-Abadi, which spilled over into a contest to control the Shi'ite Dawa party. These internal differences harmed the fight against IS, especially when it was planned to end its control of Fallujah, west of Baghdad. This city had to be taken before the assault on IS could advance northwards. It was initially intended that the Golden Division, the elite Iraqi counter-terrorist unit, would carry out the task, supported by US air power and the Shi'ite militias of the PMF, which Abadi wanted to incorporate into the Iraqi army. However, this was resisted by pro-Iranian Iraqis, conscious not just of the implications for Iraq, but of a need to use the PMF in Syria. Following a compromise in February 2016, in which the PMF was incorporated into the attack as an 'independent military formation', the recapture of Fallujah was finally achieved in July 2016.[25]

The next major goal was Mosul, a city of more than a million people, but here the problem was that neither the Kurds nor the Sunni Arabs of Nineveh province were keen to see Shi'ite Arabs fighting in the north. Iran, however, insisted that the PMF had to be involved in the north, alongside 50,000 Iraqi troops, Sunni militias, and Kurdish Peshmerga forces. Once again, the advance proved a slow one. As anti-IS forces approached the suburbs east of the River Tigris in October, the Peshmerga seized the Turkomen town of Tel Afar and its air base. With the main road from Mosul to Syria cut, so that IS could no longer draw in reinforcements, the eastern part of the city was entered in November. Its residents in the west then faced bombing by US-led coalition aircraft. It was only in July 2017, some seven months later, that Western Mosul and its old city, where IS was entrenched, were retaken. Like Eastern Aleppo, Western Mosul had been reduced to rubble. One monitoring group noted that, in defeating IS in Mosul, 5,805 civilians had died as a result of US and Iraqi government actions.[26]

The way was now open to drive IS out of the rest of Iraq and to re-establish the border with Syria. The border town of Rawa fell in November 2017 and on 9 December 2017 the Iraqi army announced that it had 'fully liberated' Iraq from IS and US forces. This still left plenty of questions about whether the Iraqi government could create national unity. An early challenge was a September 2017 referendum in favour of independence by the Kurdish-controlled region of Kurdistan, whose Peshmerga fighters had been so valuable in the struggle against IS. Iraqi elections in May 2018 proved a major setback for Nouri al-Maliki, with the largest parliamentary group being supporters of Moqtada al-Sadr, the Shi'ite cleric and long-standing critic of American policy.

No Peace and More Destruction: Assad Recovers Ground

A resolution of the Syrian situation could never easily be achieved, though the position of IS collapsed there too, following Assad's army's advance through central Syria, which re-took Palmyra in March and al-Suknah in August. The IS 'capital', Raqqa, had fallen in November to US-backed 'Syrian Democratic Forces', a Kurdish-dominated group formed in late 2015, which included various minorities opposed to jihadism. By November, with IS collapsing, the main emphasis was back on the contest between Assad and other opposition groups.

In September 2016, Russia and the US, with Assad and opposition groups in the HNC agreed on a ceasefire, but it collapsed after a week. On the day Assad resumed control of Aleppo in December 2016, representatives from twelve rebel factions met a Syrian government delegation for indirect talks in Astana, Kazakhstan. These talks, now only sponsored by Russia, Turkey, and Iran because of the hiatus between the Obama and Trump administrations, were heralded as the 'International Meeting on a Syrian Settlement'. It was agreed that the Astana delegates should meet again in January 2017 under the framework of UN Security Council Resolution 2254, with Iran, Russia, and Turkey agreeing to work on forming a joint monitoring body to enforce yet another ceasefire. The 'Astanization' of the peace process in a former Soviet republic retained a link to the UN, and the talks were arguably more successful than previous efforts. The main problem was the exclusion of Kurdish representatives from the rebel HNC, as Turkey would have no truck with the YPG or YPD. That there was no single representative of the various rebel fighters on the ground made any ceasefire agreement likely to be ineffective, so no lasting ceasefire was achieved. Instead, more Astana meetings were held in March and May 2017, with Turkey, Iran, and Russia becoming guarantor states of four 'de-escalation zones', where combat operations were to cease. Inevitably, some rebel groups rejected this plan, which they saw as 'dividing Syria' and taking the pressure off Assad.

The most striking feature of the Astana process was the US exclusion as a major player, even if it continued to arm some groups on the ground. Turkey, despite being a NATO member, helped Putin to side-line the Americans, arguably because of growing differences over their support for Kurdish forces in northern Syria, while US distaste for the increasingly authoritarian government of President Erdogan did not make US–Turkish relations easy. Earlier Turkish opposition to Russian involvement in Syria, which had reached its height when Turkey shot down a Russian jet in November 2015, now seemed to melt away. Erdogan saw Kurdish separatism as a greater threat and criticized Washington for harbouring his political rival, Fethulleh Gulen, who was said to be behind the recent botched military coup in Turkey. The advent of the Trump administration in January 2017 showed little sign of bringing America back into a leading role. Trump used cruise missiles against the Assad regime in April 2017, in retaliation for a poison gas attack on Khan Shaykun, but this was seen as little more than a knee-jerk reaction and probably designed to underline Trump's difference from Obama, who had so signally failed to enforce the 'red line' against the use of chemical weapons.

One difference in the latest round of Astana peace talks was the desire to create four 'de-escalation zones' in Syria to act as eventual ceasefires. One zone would be in the Idlib governorate and parts of the adjacent governorates of Aleppo and Latakia, one in the rebel enclaves of northern Homs, one in Eastern Ghouta and one in the rebel-held south west bordering Jordan. Apart from the Damascus suburb of Eastern Ghouta, there was a decrease in the fighting in the rest of 2017, but there was a problem in that the exact delineation of the zones had not been precisely determined. Hence the prospect of a lasting ceasefire remained as far away as ever, and Assad was particularly eager to continue his military operations, with his erstwhile military allies now posing as the guarantors of de-escalation.

In early 2018, the significant areas of conflict in the south centred on the Damascus suburb of Eastern Ghouta and further to the west, in rebel-held areas bordering Jordan. Eastern Ghouta—besieged by the government since 2013—was subjected to massive Syrian and Russian air attacks from November 2017. It became what Eastern Aleppo had been earlier: a beleaguered rebel enclave, its infrastructure and hospitals bombed, its buildings reduced to rubble, and its people killed or forced to flee. In February, the UN Security Council unanimously passed a ceasefire resolution (not vetoed by the Russians) to enable relief to be provided to the beleaguered civilian population of 400,000 in Eastern Ghouta. However, this proved to be of no avail as the fighting continued and Russia was accused of delaying its implementation.

If anything, the divisions amongst the Kurds had grown, while the possibility of escalation in the international sphere had become more likely. IS fighters had only a very limited presence in Idlib and Eastern Syria, and the military conflict within Syria itself was moving in favour of Assad. On the ground, the Syrian army was assisted by significant numbers of Iranian troops and Shi'ite militias, along with the battle-hardened fighters of Hezbollah. The end for Eastern Ghouta came in April 2018, and so Assad's Syrian Army could successfully occupy another destroyed suburban town. As in other devastated parts of Syria, there was no money available to repair the destruction.

Meanwhile, in Idlib governorate in the north, fierce fighting was taking place between the Syrian Army and the rebel Islamist forces, with most of the leading groups combined in Tahrir al-Sham. Led by former leaders from Ahrar al-Sham and containing many former al-Nusra militants as well as eleven other Salafist groups, the rebels—also engaging the last remaining pockets of IS fighters—were being pushed northwards by Iranian troops and Hezbollah fighters, under heavy Russia bombardment. On 18 February, another merger between hard-line Islamic groups, also containing elements from Ahrar al-Sham, established the Syrian Liberation Front (SLF) as a rival to Tahrir al-Sham, thus continuing rebel disunity. Turkey sought either to create an effective buffer zone between itself and the Syrian conflict or to establish an area held by Arab and Turkoman forces under its influence, thereby avoiding support for the US-backed Kurds, who had been significant in the battle against IS. It thus combined Erdogan's dislike of Assad with ensuring that the PKK, and its offshoots, did not benefit from the forces opposing the Syrian regime.

Turkey's main desire was to deal with the Kurds. This desire was behind its 2016 military actions within Syria to prevent the maintenance of a unified corridor between the three Kurdish enclaves across the border. In January 2018, Erdogan announced another military incursion into the northern part of Aleppo province, not to assist the Islamist rebels in Idlib, but to capture the town of Afrin, and later Manbij, from the YPG Kurds—but ostensibly to establish a 'safe zone' on both sides of the Syria–Turkey border. The US special forces in Manbij supporting the Kurds were warned by the Turkish Foreign Minister to leave, while further to the east pro-Assad forces attacked the YPG/SDF Kurds and were subjected to US coalition air strikes. In the even more conflicting patchwork of fighting in the north, pro-Syrian government militia arrived to help the Kurds resist the Turkish invaders in February, while the YPG called on Assad's Syrian army to help drive out the Turks. The animosity and distrust between Turkey and Assad was underlined in March 2018 when Turkish forces captured the border town of Afrin from the Kurdish fighters, but refused to hand it over to Syrian government control.

With the Syrian Army's success in taking the remains of Eastern Ghouta in April, other than the Idlib governorate and the Kurdish-controlled areas along the border with Turkey, the rebels' only remaining stronghold was in Deraa, in the south west. In July 2018, the Syrian Army began an assault on Quneitra, in the western part of the Deraa governorate, bordering the Golan Heights and Jordan. The initial week of fighting led more than 250,000 people to flee their homes in what was ostensibly a de-escalation zone guaranteed by Russia and Iran. Both supported the Assad offensive, while trying to negotiate a deal with the rebels, who were mostly members of moderate groups. Unfortunately for those refugees fleeing towards Jordan, that border was closed, with Amman refusing to add to the one million displaced Syrian people it already had. The Israeli border was protected by a fence and minefield, but the fleeing refugees tried to get as close to it as possible, in the hope that the regime and its allies would want to avoid stray fire on Israeli territory.

The Golan Heights were a particularly sensitive area, where Iran might be keen to pressurize Israel, which had already engaged in bombing raids on Iranian positions, with one plane shot down. Looking forward, Israeli–Iranian tension is part of the uncertainty affecting the two major external, and three significant regional, powers whose military forces are engaged in the conflict within Syria. With IS essentially no longer of territorial significance, there is now more scope for power-political and ideological rivalries to be unhampered by the threadbare cloak of cooperation. Assad looked likely to succeed in retaking the south west, but in the north east there remained the Kurdish-dominated 'state' of Rojava and the presence of their external supporters in the form of US Special Forces. Turkey occupied two enclaves on the Syrian side of the border and, given Erdogan's dislike of the Assad regime and desire for a safe zone in Syria, accompanied by his intense aversion to Syrian Kurds with their PKK links, there was considerable uncertainty about the future of the north east and north west of Syria.

Further south was rebel-held Idlib, a refuge not only for fighters fleeing from the growing advances of the Syrian Army in the south, but also for two million displaced civilians. If Assad and his allies turn to Idlib after a success in the south west, and repeat the Aleppo and East Ghouta scenarios, the scale of the carnage could be so much worse. Idlib contains many extreme jihadists, unlikely to accept the surrender that some of the more moderate opponents of the regime in the south west entertained. The prospect of barrel bombing and a repeat of the deliberate targeting of civilians had already alarmed the UN and aid agencies at the time of writing. Moreover, Assad, despite his dependency on Russia and particularly Iran, has been reluctant to follow the wishes of either of those allies and embark on a peace process by accepting ceasefires.

Putin may have assumed that standing up for Assad in the face of American determination to remove him would result in the Syrian leader assisting Russia in ending the conflict. Russia's peacemaking status could thus be enhanced, in contrast to the US, simply in return for Assad staying in power. Iran, on the other hand, arguably saw Assad and Syria as pawns in its long-standing rivalry over Middle Eastern influence with Saudi Arabia, made more intense by their conflicting Islamist ideologies.

Apart from the Syrian people, Iran is in danger of becoming the major loser in the conflict, ironically along with the US, whose power and credibility in the Arab world had been significantly damaged even before Donald Trump's close co-operation with Netanyahu's Israel. A subservient Syria under Assad was ideally placed to provide Iran with territorial influence from Tehran to Lebanon, bringing it close to its arch enemy, Israel. Yet Iranian ambitions may be severely curtailed by its growing domestic crisis, arising from economic difficulties which will be exacerbated by Trump's re-imposition of sanctions after his reneging on the 2015 Joint Comprehensive Plan of Action. Alternatively, Hassan Rouhani may be replaced as president by less moderate leaders and a greater risk of instability, with or without any Iranian commitment to produce nuclear weapons, may result.

Israeli interests probably lie in preserving an independent Assad, rather than seeing Syria act as an Iranian puppet or become a jihadist regime. If Iran were to come close to acquiring weapons-grade plutonium, then Israel taking pre-emptive action, with air strikes on the nuclear facilities, cannot be ruled out. There also remains the bizarre possibility that Iranian ambitions may yet lead, overtly or covertly, to an Israeli–Saudi alliance; that would reveal just how much the Middle Eastern dynamics have been altered by the conflict in Syria. The Saudi intervention in Yemen has shown a new Saudi desire to act without the cover of paid proxies or the shelter provided by US friendship, but it has produced more failure than success in terms of increased influence in a changing region.

At the heart of this new dynamic is the Russia of Vladimir Putin, who appears to be the main beneficiary of the conflict, with his role both as a military player and political arbiter having been enhanced. That said, the unreliability of Assad as an ally and the lack of important shared interests with either Iran or Turkey could still prove to be significant drawbacks for Russia; and Putin cannot welcome the danger of instability on the Syrian–Israeli border which the conflict has made possible. Yet, no longer do Middle Eastern states (other than Israel) look first and foremost to the US for support, and the relative disparity between American and Russian influence in the region has been reduced. More importantly, Putin's key goal of preserving Assad and ending the run of American-sponsored regime changes (like that in Libya) looks likely to be achieved. With Assad and his allies now having to be involved in any future plans for what was once a united country, this marks a defeat for US aims under the tenure of Hillary Clinton (the arch-enemy of both Putin and Trump) as Secretary of State, with the Trump administration showing a desire to escape the Syrian imbroglio as quickly as possible. As for Syria itself, with its hundreds of thousands of deaths and half of its population displaced, it must confront vast swathes of destruction in its increasingly deserted towns and villages, which are unlikely to be swiftly or painlessly rebuilt.

B. Iran: The 2015 Nuclear Deal and Rivalry with Saudi Arabia

One of the many impacts of the war in Syria was to help Iran secure a more prominent role in the Middle East region, which in turn aroused the suspicions of the United States, Israel, and Saudi Arabia. These suspicions also complicated long-running attempts to prevent Iran developing a nuclear weapon. Washington was persistently concerned with the danger of Iran building atomic weapons, but Iran, which for many years had kept its nuclear experiments secret, argued that it had as much right as any power to develop a peaceful nuclear power industry. In the wake of the 'axis of evil' speech, Russia proved ready to help it to develop the nuclear reactor at Bushehr (first begun under the Shah). As there was always a danger that this could lead on to weapons, EU and UN concerns led them also to attempt to induce Tehran to drop its nuclear programme.

When the 2005 Iranian presidential election was won by a conservative, Mahmoud Ahmadinejad, he ignored international criticism, and in April 2006 Iran announced it had successfully enriched uranium—a key step to building an atomic bomb. The UN Security Council called on Tehran to suspend the programme and, in December, introduced limited sanctions against it (including a ban on exporting nuclear materials to Iran), but by spring 2007 it was clear that Tehran might be able to make nuclear fuel on a substantial scale and in March the UN approved an arms embargo against it. By 2008, the Bush administration and the UN had introduced a new range of sanctions, and Iran had tested a rocket, the Shahab-3, that could hit Israel, while developing its own space programme. In the future, Iran might develop the capability to equip it with nuclear warheads, but with Russia opposed to new sanctions there was little the UN could do to induce Tehran to alter its policies. Moreover, as Tehran showed little interest in Western offers of concessions (on trade, for example) in return for ending the nuclear programme, at times it seemed that US President Bush might be ready to contemplate an attack on Iran.

The fact that the US was so deeply embroiled in Iraq could only help deter any such plans, New presidents in Washington and Tehran offered hope for improved relations and both Ahmadinejad and Barack Obama made statements suggesting that they wanted such an improvement. Unfortunately, in June 2009 the re-election of Ahmadinejad as President, in a closely contested poll, in which the government was accused of rigging the result, produced sustained demonstrations against the regime, which responded in ways which raised more concern over the limited human and political rights in Iran. The prospects of increased and more dangerous instability seemed more likely with the announcement by Iran, in September 2009, that it had built a second uranium enrichment facility, hidden underground at Qom, which was followed by condemnation from the International Atomic Energy Agency (IAEA). Tehran simply said it would build more and continued to insist that its nuclear programme was for the peaceful use of nuclear energy, but the climate was not conducive to concessions and compromise. In June 2010, more UN sanctions were agreed, and while sanctions still did not include oil (Iran's major export), they did include items that could contribute to nuclear missiles and sophisticated weapons development. It was also open to states to introduce additional measures: the US and EU both had additional sanctions, including ones aimed at financial investment.

The EU tightened sanctions further in January 2012, with the intention of ending oil imports from Iran in July, but Iran was clearly not willing to bow easily to intimidation. It was also clear that, while Iran wanted to be treated as an equal, Washington was above all determined to end Iran's nuclear ambitions. Meanwhile, rather than waiting for the EU to impose sanctions, Iran itself announced an end of oil supplies to Britain and France. There were also concerns that Iran might try to blockade the Straits of Hormuz, at the base of the Persian Gulf, through which a considerable amount of oil was exported. Some experts believed that it could build a nuclear weapon within a few years if it wanted and Israel, which had nuclear weapons of its own, was particularly concerned about a possible Iranian attack. Others, such as the IAEA's former head, Mohamed El Baredei, felt that the dangers were exaggerated. There were realistic fears that Israel might launch a military strike on Iranian nuclear sites, to prevent Tehran building a nuclear weapon. But a long-range operation against such a large country was hazardous; the Iranians could easily disperse their nuclear efforts and Western powers, already faced by deep-seated problems in Afghanistan, could hardly welcome an extension of conflict to Iran.

In this fraught situation, it seems that sanctions, and perhaps the use of computer virus attacks, as well as the targeted assassination of several Iranian nuclear scientists (which Iran blamed on Israel), may have impeded Iran's programme. Yet if progress were to be made in reducing tensions, the emphasis had to be placed on diplomacy, albeit diplomacy backed by the threat posed to Iran by sanctions. The five permanent members of the Security Council (the US, Russia, China, the UK, and France), plus Germany, had already formed a liaison group to handle the issue. Diplomatic progress finally proved possible after a more moderate president, Hassan Rouhani, was elected in 2013, and an interim agreement was rapidly negotiated, under which Iran suspended elements of its programme. Months of complex talks followed, leading on 14 July 2015 to a deal, officially known as the 'Joint Comprehensive Plan of Action', signed in Vienna between Iran and the six-power liaison group. The basis of the deal was that UN, US, and EU sanctions would be removed in return for Iran undertaking to limit severely its uranium enrichment activities and, with international co-operation, modify its research reactor, with an effective monitoring system by the IAEA. The deal was widely welcomed around the world and, in January 2016 and again in May 2018, the IAEA confirmed that no evidence had been found of nuclear weapons activity after 2009. But there was heavy criticism from Israel's premier, Benjamin Netanyahu, who still feared that Iran would develop nuclear weapons in the long term and was concerned by Iran's growing influence in Iraq, and particularly Syria, which bordered on Israel. Also, the deal did not prevent Iran from returning to a nuclear arms programme in future, nor did it end the country's ballistic missile programme; arguably, therefore, it was a threat to efforts at non-proliferation.

Iran, a majority Shi'ite country, was a key supporter of President Assad in the Syrian civil war, as was its Lebanese ally, Hezbollah. Tehran also backed the Houthi militias fighting in the Yemeni civil war and it improved relations with the government in Iraq, aiding it in the fight against ISIS. By the end of 2015, serious rivalry had developed for influence in the region between Iran and another oil-rich state: Sunni-dominated, pro-Western Saudi Arabia. In fact, tension had existed between the two for decades, but it worsened after 2010, partly due to the political upheaval brought by the crises in Iraq and Syria (see Chapters 24, B and 26, A), which brought increased Iranian influence in both. Saudis were long-standing critics of Assad, were concerned over possible Shi'ite predominance in Iraq (their neighbour to the north), and launched military intervention in Yemen (their neighbour to the south) after March 2015 to prevent a Houthi takeover. Tension on these three issues was deepened by the death of hundreds of Iranian pilgrims during a stampede at the Hajj in Saudi-controlled Mecca in September 2015, and the Saudi execution of a senior Shi'ite cleric, Nimr al-Nimr on 2 January 2016, which led a mob to attack the Saudi embassy in Tehran. On 4 January 2016, Saudi Arabia broke off diplomatic relations with Iran. Behind these regional actors and reflecting 'new Cold War' tensions, the US backed Saudi Arabia with arms supplies and (in Yemen) some active military support, while Russia drew closer to Tehran, helped by their joint sympathy for Assad and the fact that the 2015 nuclear deal paved the way for Russian arms supplies to Iran, including a missile defence system.

The advent of Donald Trump as US President in January 2017 raised the prospect of a renewed crisis over Iran's nuclear programme because he condemned the July 2015 Plan of Action as inadequate to control Iranian ambitions. Following frequent criticism of Iranian policies in the Middle East and concern over Iran's ballistic missile programme, in mid-October 2017, Trump refused to certify Tehran's compliance with the nuclear deal and, in May 2018, he withdrew the US from it. This was welcome to Israel, which at the same time launched a series of air attacks on Iranian forces and facilities in Syria, but it was criticized by Washington's key European allies—Britain, France, and Germany—who remained signatories to the agreement. Their feeling was that, whatever the limitations of the Plan of Action, it was the best deal available, Iran was fulfilling its side of the bargain, and that any alternative would be difficult to negotiate.

Meanwhile, tensions between Iran and Saudi Arabia continued to simmer. In Yemen, Saudi air strikes in support of the government failed to defeat the Houthi rebels who, aided by Iran, even developed the ability to launch a ballistic missile attack near Riyadh in November 2017. Meanwhile, the war brought both famine and disease on a considerable scale. In Lebanon, the continuing strength of Iran's Hezbollah allies and the sudden resignation of the Saudi-backed prime minister, Saad Harir, also provoked a political crisis that November. Further regional instability was created by Iran's support of the Iraq government against the latest threat to its stability, an attempt to create a break-away state in the Kurdish north east; while months of pressure, including an economic blockade, were directed by Saudi Arabia and other neighbours against Qatar, the most liberal Gulf state and home of the influential news channel al-Jazeera. The heir to the Saudi throne, Mohammed bin Salman, was determined to resist the spread of sympathy for Iran around his country's borders, including Yemen to the south and, in the north, a tract of influence through Iraq and Syria to the Mediterranean Sea. Widespread criticism of the Saudi campaign in Yemen, alongside discontent in Iran in December 2017 and January 2018 (sparked by rising prices and youth unemployment) showed that both sides might have good reason to wind down their antagonism. Iran's economic position was further threatened when Trump, having withdrawn from the Iran nuclear deal, also set an August 2018 date for the re-imposition of economic sanctions, threatening sanctions against any companies trading with Iran, including those based in the EU. There was widespread Western criticism of Saudi Arabia in October 2018, following its murder of a dissident, American-based journalist, Jamal Kashoggi, but Trump insisted that US economic and political interests continued to be best served by close relations with the kingdom.

C. The Arab Uprisings

Tunisia

In early 2011, a wave of popular unrest, which became known as the 'Arab Spring', passed across the Islamic Middle East and North Africa, leading to significant changes of regime and, in some countries, fuelling years of intense instability. There had been some signs of trouble the previous year, but nobody predicted that this would lead to major upheaval. In June 2010, the murder of a young political activist, Khaled Said, by the Egyptian police, had sparked protests in his home city of Alexandria, which spread for a while to Cairo, before fizzling out in the face of repression. In December, sporadic protests began in Jordan over the rising prices of basic commodities. Then, in mid-December in Tunisia, a street vendor named Mohamed Bouazizi, burned himself to death in protest after being harassed by the police. This proved the trigger for widespread disturbances in the country, where the oppressive regime of President Zine al-Abidine Ben-Ali had held power for twenty-four years, but where the younger generation were now less willing to accept the situation, especially in the face of inflation and high unemployment. This mix of economic discontent and a desire for political change, especially among the young, proved a common element in the unrest that now spread around the region. In the Arab world as a whole, about 60 per cent of the population was under 30 years of age.

In Tunisia, as elsewhere, the internet and mobile phones allowed the protestors to organize themselves and evade state controls. On 13 January 2011, the President made a belated offer of political reforms and said he would retire in three years' time, but this did nothing to quell the discontent. The following day, 14 January, after declaring a state of emergency, Ben-Ali and his much-hated wife, Leila, fled to Saudi Arabia in the face of the protests, taking as much gold as they could carry. An interim committee took over. Despite promises of a transition to liberal institutions, including elections (set for July), the protestors complained that too many representatives of the former regime remained in office. The new Acting President was Mohamed Ghannouchi, who had been Ben-Ali's prime minister since 1999. It took a renewal of popular protests to secure his resignation on 27 February. Then, on 7 March, all members of the former regime were removed from the Cabinet. Parliamentary elections were eventually held in October 2011, with a moderate Islamist party, Ennahda, emerging in first place. The new national assembly then began work on a constitution, while in December Moncef Marzouki, formerly a leading opponent of the Ben-Ali regime and a member of the secular Congress party, became President.

The Arab world had been rocked by the events in Tunisia at the start of the year and leaders of some states rapidly made concessions to buy off their opponents. On 1 February, as popular protests spread in the Arab world, Abdullah II of Jordan appointed a new prime minister, while President Ali Abdullah Saleh of Yemen, who had been in power for thirty-two years, promised to step down at the end of his current term of office in 2013. For a few days, there were disturbances across the Arab world, from Mauritania to Oman, though most were limited in scale. Across the region there were common problems with oppressive, corrupt governments, rising prices, youth unemployment, and a desire for greater personal freedom. But the real focus was on Egypt, the most populous Arab state, likely to serve as an example to others.

Egypt

In Egypt, there were strikingly similar reasons for discontent as in Tunisia. After a military coup, Egypt had been under authoritarian regimes the latest of which under Hosni Mubarak, a former general, had held power with a 'state of emergency' in place which was used to justify widespread repression. For a generation, Mubarak relied on strict censorship, the secret police, imprisonment of opponents, and the daily use of torture to keep Egypt quiescent. He presided over a system marked by corruption, nepotism, and reliance on the secret police. As late as November 2010, rigged elections had been held for a Parliament dominated by his supporters. There were periodic, localized signs of discontent but it was possible to elect independent members of Parliament even under the rigged voting system. Yet the events in Tunisia gave Mubarak's opponents hope that he too might be overthrown by a widespread, determined campaign.

As in Tunisia, it was the younger generation that spearheaded the 2011 discontent, proving that they could use new technologies to outwit the police apparatus. They began by calling for a 'day of revolution', set for 25 January. Simultaneous protests were held in numerous locations, which the police found impossible to control, so that the general population could see that the state was not all-powerful. The key step was to occupy Tahrir Square, a vast space in the centre of the capital, Cairo, on which the attention of the world's media could then focus. Soon, the police had abandoned large areas of Cairo, where local vigilante groups formed to keep order. As confidence in the possibility of protest began to grow, so did the numbers and on 1 February it was possible to mobilize one million people on the streets of Egypt's major cities. The protests drew together a broad coalition of Mubarak's opponents, including the Muslim Brotherhood, human rights activists, individuals who simply wanted greater freedom of expression, and some well-known figures like Mohamed El-Baradei, a former UN weapons inspector, who had won the Nobel Peace Prize. He had been living in exile but returned to the country on 27 January 2011, by which time the government seemed bent on intimidation, arrests and attempts to block communications over the internet. The determination of crowds to remain in occupation of Tahrir Square, in the centre of Cairo, under the gaze of the world's media, was at first matched by Mubarak's determination to cling to office. A curfew was introduced; the state-controlled media attacked the demonstrators as being under 'foreign' control; and in speeches to the people, the 82-year-old dictator insisted that he would stay in office to oversee reform. The President had some supporters among state-controlled enterprises, the police apparatus, and paid gangs of thugs. But, as the demonstrations continued and strike action threatened to cripple the economy, concessions were wrung from him, including the appointment of a Vice-President, Omar Suleiman, who offered to talk to the protestors.

The key player, however, was the army, which had provided all Egypt's leaders—including Mubarak—since the overthrow of the monarchy in 1952. The decision of army leaders not to use force against the protesters, and the readiness of the crowds to welcome the army when it moved peacefully into Tahrir Square ensured there was no bloodbath. Instead, the soldiers simply sat and watched the demonstrations taking place. Indeed, despite the deaths of more than 250 protestors—deaths that helped keep the protests alive—a striking feature of the Egyptian revolution was its lack of open, widespread violence. The crowds continued to wave the republican flag, sang the national anthem, and even chanted, 'the army and people are one'. There was tension in this approach. The army had supported Mubarak loyally. The new Vice-President, Suleiman, was a former intelligence chief, responsible for state repression. And when Mubarak supporters invaded Tahrir Square on 3 February, soldiers at the scene simply sat and watched. Nonetheless, the army provided Egypt with a widely respected institution that could provide stability during the transition to a democratic constitution. More importantly, as Egypt's businesses historically had had a much lower level of foreign ownership than in other Middle Eastern states, in the years after the military coup, the army had emerged as owning important elements of the Egyptian economy. It was a military council that took over power from Mubarak on 11 February, when he finally resigned. The military promised to move towards a democratic state, with an elected civilian government, but was reluctant to establish an interim civilian government. As a result, demonstrators were initially reluctant to give up the occupation of Tahrir Square.

Despite the calls for democracy from Arab demonstrators, Western states were initially cautious about the changes in Tunisia and only gave them a belated welcome. The French foreign minister, Michelle Alliot-Marie, was forced to resign in February over criticisms of her close support for Ben-Ali. To the US and its European allies, Arab dictators seemed preferential to the possible alternatives, who might include radical Islamists and regimes anxious to support the Palestinians' cause. Unrest in North Africa also created a refugee problem, with many trying to flee across the Mediterranean to Italy or France. The US was in a particularly difficult position where Egypt was concerned: the Obama administration wanted to see a transition to liberal democracy, but it also saw Mubarak as a loyal ally and one who had assisted the US in its support of Israel. Mubarak had held a successful, friendly summit meeting with Obama only months before and as the protests began in Cairo, the initial US reaction was to praise their ally. Washington also had to respect the views of its other allies in the region, such as Saudi Arabia, which was deeply concerned about Mubarak's possible overthrow and readier to see him use force to retain power. But the sight of repression on the streets of Cairo could hardly be welcome to Obama, who also publicly urged Mubarak, on 28 January, not to use violence against the opposition. American policy was hesitant and sometimes confused, especially on the question of whether Mubarak should remain in power while a transition to democracy took place.

In early February, the US envoy Frank Wisner publicly declared that Mubarak should stay in office, but the administration soon changed its view, working for a peaceful transition to some kind of democratic system, without the octogenarian President. Such a transition to 'democracy' was never likely to be easy. Egypt lacked a constitutional tradition and political parties. Another concern was that the revolution might somehow fall under the influence of radical Islamists. Despite a substantial Coptic Christian minority, the vast majority of the population was Muslim and one of the oldest political groups was the Muslim Brotherhood. But the US evidently believed that Omar Suleiman could bring about a transition in an orderly way, while remaining loyal to Egypt's established friendships. Sure enough, on 12 February, the new Egyptian government promised to respect international agreements, including peace with Israel. Over the following weeks, there were mixed signals about the direction of the revolution. Protestors continued to be arrested, but on 3 March the reformist Essam Sharaf became premier. One of the first signs of the new political freedom was a referendum, held on 19 March, in which an overwhelming majority backed constitutional changes, including a limit on presidential terms of office in future. The army dissolved the pro-Mubarak Parliament and took steps to arrest members of the previous regime who had engaged in corruption. In April, Mubarak himself was detained and later put on trial, accused of ordering deadly attacks on demonstrators. But there were persistent concerns about the army's attitude towards human rights, heightened in December 2011 by its tough response to a renewed occupation of Tahrir Square and by raids on the Cairo offices of several non-governmental organizations. Political instability led to the virtual collapse of the tourist industry, which in turn contributed to Egypt's growing economic problems. There were also signs that the turmoil might worsen religious differences, with serious violence between the army and Coptic Christians in Cairo in October.

A complex election process, over three stages, resulted in January 2012 in success for the Muslim Brotherhood. This was repeated in presidential elections, which were won in June by the Brotherhood's candidate, Mohammed Morsi. He tried to limit the power of the army, removing several key generals from office in August but, in November, the wider presidential powers that he sought and his evident support for Islam over other religions, provoked concern from many reformers and sparked renewed protests in Tahrir Square. A new constitution was drawn up by a constituent assembly and approved by an almost two-thirds majority in a national referendum in December 2012, before being signed by Morsi. The constitution put limits on presidential terms (to a maximum of eight years), strengthened the powers of parliament, and included protection for basic rights like freedom from arbitrary arrest, but it aroused some controversy because it seemed contradictory on key points (arrest was still possible on the order of a judge), the link it maintained between the law and Sunni interpretations of Islam, and the powers it granted to the military. Only a third of electors voted on the referendum. The political uncertainty also deepened the country's economic problems, which left people facing power shortages and rising unemployment. Rising discontent peaked in June 2013, with mass protests across the country, and on 3 July, Morsi was toppled in a military coup, led by the defence minister, Abdul Fatah al-Sisi.

Morsi's downfall may be variously blamed on his own unpopular decisions, economic mismanagement, and failure to protect minorities, or on the difficult position he faced, with a disloyal military and civil service, and a dire economic inheritance. The coup had the approval of some opposition politicians and religious leaders, but provoked criticism from abroad—given that Morsi was an elected leader—and outraged the Muslim Brotherhood. It was followed by weeks of violence, peaking in the deaths of hundreds of his followers in mid-August, when their protest camps were attacked. In September, the Brotherhood, most of whose leaders—along with thousands of their followers—had already been arrested, was outlawed. Over the following years, many were sentenced to death, including more than 500 at a single sentencing in March 2014. Morsi himself was sentenced to death in May 2015, which provoked international outrage until the sentence was overturned eighteen months later. Some Islamists turned to terrorism, with regular attacks on police and army targets. One of the most successful groups, Ansar Bayt al-Maqdis, based in Sinai, predated the Morsi presidency, but became more active with his overthrow and, in late 2014, many of its members pledged loyalty to ISIS. Meanwhile, new presidential elections were held in Egypt in May 2014 and won, predictably and easily, by al-Sisi, who had given up his military post to run. He weathered international criticism, partly by using improved relations with Russia to limit American criticism of the 2013 military coup. After overcoming grave problems with energy supplies, he also had some success in stabilising the economy and seemed reasonably popular in winning re-election in March 2018. But his dependence on military support and the repression of the Muslim Brotherhood suggested that the Arab Spring had brought little change to Egypt since the Mubarak days.

Arab Uprisings and External Conflict in Yemen

The uprisings in the Middle East, or Arab Spring, largely failed to realize their early hopes, with the only example of genuine, stable political change being Tunisia. Among the monarchical states, serious unrest in Oman, with demands for political reform, was met by force while, in Saudi Arabia, where stirrings of discontent began in early March, the government quickly placed a ban on protests. In the Gulf island-sheikhdom of Bahrain, there was a religious element to the discontent, with a Sunni monarchy ruling over a Shi'ite majority population. Emulating the Egyptians, Bahraini protestors gathered, in February, in the main square of the capital, Manama, under the eyes of the world's media, while the regime at first tried to break up the demonstrations by force, then offered dialogue, then shifted back to force. On 14 March, neighbouring Saudi Arabia sent 1,000 troops in to support the government, followed by a declaration of martial law and a police clampdown on the opposition. Among less Islam-dominated Arab republics, the picture was rather less certain. In Algeria, in mid-February, the authorities clamped down quickly on the popular unrest. But in Yemen, Libya, and Syria, discontent proved more persistent and all three states faced years of internal division and external intervention.

In Yemen, demonstrators were not intimidated by the government's use of force and President Saleh became increasingly desperate. On 20 March, he sacked the whole Cabinet, but leading officials and generals defected to the opposition and he claimed to be ready to stand down. For months, the uncertainty persisted, with sporadic outbursts of violence and different signals from Saleh about whether, and on what terms, he might stand down. He only finally left the country in January 2012, in return for a promise of immunity from prosecution. A complicating factor was that, for more than a decade, Yemen had been a centre of al-Qaeda activity. However undemocratic Saleh was, he had declared himself an American ally in the war on terror since 2001 and, in September 2011, Washington had a key success against al-Qaeda in Yemen, when a drone attack killed the US-born jihadist, Anwar al Awlaki. Saleh's departure was followed by a period of stability, with elections later in February 2012 that confirmed Abd Rabbu Mansur Hadi, the only candidate to run, as President. While he promised political reforms and national reconciliation, he was closely identified with the old regime, under which he had been a soldier, minister, and Acting President. But he was acceptable to Western powers because he maintained strong opposition to al-Qaeda. Initially elected for only two years, he extended his term in 2014, but he was unpopular even within his own party, the General People's Congress, and soon faced a widespread rebellion in the north from the Shi'ite minority Houthis.

The clerically inspired Houthi rebellion had actually begun against Saleh back in 2004, but it now gathered pace, apparently with support from the Shi'ite regime in Iran. In September 2014, the Houthis entered the capital, Sana'a, and in January 2015 seized the presidential palace. Hadi, effectively a prisoner in his own capital, resigned under Houthi pressure, but then escaped to Aden and denounced them for an unconstitutional takeover. As the Houthis advanced on Aden, Hadi fled to Saudi Arabia, which was Sunni dominated and deeply concerned about the spread of Iranian influence in the region. In March, the Saudis—who, as seen above, had already successfully intervened in Bahrain—began an armed intervention against Houthis and in support of Hadi. The Saudis led a coalition of forces from the Gulf states and further afield, including Bahrain, Egypt, Morocco, and Sudan, with US and other Western powers providing additional support. But the Houthis proved difficult to dislodge, attempts at peace talks came to nothing, and the coalition's reliance on bombing from the air brought severe damage to Yemen's infrastructure, including hospitals, and the threat of starvation, with over two million internal refugees. The threat of starvation only worsened after the key port of Hodeidah became the focus of fighting in mid-2018. Some foresaw a split in the country between the north west, where the Houthis were strongest, and the south, where secessionists formed an independence council in Aden, in May 2017. Such a radical step would have returned the situation to one which prevailed before 1990, the year that the old North and South Yemen were united under Saleh's rule. The seriousness of that threat was highlighted in January 2018, when southern separatists took over much of Aden, surrounding the presidential palace where the Saudi-backed government was based. Meanwhile, to US dismay, swathes of central Yemen also effectively fell under the control of al-Qaeda and its local affiliate, Ansar al-Sharia. In November 2018, the US intensified the pressures for a settlement of the civil war but peace negotiations, under UN auspices, made only slow progress.

Libya: The Fall of Gaddafi

Libya, too, saw the downfall of an established president and a drift towards anarchy after 2011. When violence first flared in the north-eastern city of Benghazi on 17 February, the 42-year old regime of Colonel Muammar Gaddafi chose to meet the protests with tough police action, supported by foreign mercenaries. But, as in Egypt, state suppression only seemed to strengthen the opposition's resolve and, in this case, the security forces began to fracture, with a few military units joining in the rebellion. Eastern Libya had long been less loyal to Gaddafi, partly for tribal reasons, and he had left it underdeveloped. Now the whole region turned against him and he was soon left holding on to areas around the capital, Tripoli, and his home city, Sirte. Even government ministers defected. The wider world was at first reluctant to become involved and Western nations initially focused on safely removing their own nationals from the oil-rich state. But on 26 February the UN approved sanctions against the Gaddafi regime and there was already discussion of enforcing a 'no-fly' zone over the country, to prevent him using aerial bombardment against the rebels. An arms embargo was also introduced. The French government, much criticized at home for its links to oppression in the Arab world, now took the lead against Gaddafi, even taking the dramatic step of recognizing the rebel regime in Benghazi as the government of Libya. But in early March Gaddafi's forces began to strike back against the rebels. By the middle of the month, he seemed secure in the west, and his forces were advancing eastwards against the rebels, who were poorly trained, badly organized, and had few aircraft. Soon, the only rebel enclave in western Libya was the port of Misrata, which became both a focus of Gaddafi's attacks and a symbol of resistance to him.

By the time the UN Security Council passed Resolution 1973 authorizing action to protect civilians by 'all necessary means' (short of any occupation of Libyan territory), on 17 March, Gaddafi's forces were approaching Benghazi. There were serious doubts about the wisdom of the resolution. Even the rebels believed it had come too late, with many citizens fleeing Benghazi, while some governments feared a long war in which, as in Iraq, predominantly Western forces would become lodged in an unpopular war in an Arab state. As soon as the resolution was passed, Gaddafi declared a ceasefire, but it was soon clear that this was a mere ploy to allow his forces to strike into Benghazi, where it would be more difficult for aircraft to attack. Within a few days, a coalition, initially led by the US, but also including France, Britain, Italy, and Canada, began military action, ostensibly to use a 'no-fly' zone to protect civilians as provided for by the Security Council Resolution. While French aircraft bombed Libyan units close to Benghazi, the US and Britain began cruise missile strikes to neutralize Gaddafi's air defences. His claims of civilian casualties led to criticism of the NATO action from Russia and the Arab League, but the rebels in Benghazi, who had successfully held on to the city, were exuberant. With Gaddafi's air force unable to operate, the rebels began to advance one more. But he was not going to go easily. He still had the loyalty of most people in Tripoli and he was able to portray the Western powers as 'crusaders'. Although, after some days, Qatar sent some aircraft to help enforce Resolution 1973, the coalition was predominantly Western. There were also tensions within the allied coalition. Initially, it was led by the US, which bore the greatest military burden in the attacks on Gaddafi. But, after Iraq and Afghanistan, Washington was reluctant to play the primary role in yet another intervention in an Islamic state. So, as US combat aircraft withdrew, other NATO members took charge of the operation, but whereas some NATO members, such as Germany and Turkey, wanted to focus on protecting civilians with a 'no-fly' zone, others, such as France and Britain, wanted to take a more active role in attacking Gaddafi's forces. It seemed clear that the badly organized Libyan rebels would be unable to oust the dictator without active coalition help.

Differences within the alliance were discussed at a conference in London on 29 March, when ideas were mooted for arming the rebels—this despite the UN's arms embargo. In effect, Resolution 1973 was now interpreted in a way that, rather than saving lives, aimed at regime change. There were ways to achieve this other than relying on the eastern rebellion. There were indications that continuing defections might lead Gaddafi's regime to collapse from within. On 31 March, Libyan Foreign Minister, Moussa Koussa, flew to London and announced that he no longer wished to serve the dictator. But during April, the situation on the ground settled into a stalemate, which persisted for three months. NATO air strikes gradually wore down Gaddafi's defences, but only in late July did Gaddafi's position begin to disintegrate, with a rapid rebel advance on Tripoli in August, which fell late in the month. The National Transitional Council, which had increasingly been recognized by other states as Libya's legitimate government, then moved to the capital. Some of Gaddafi's family fled abroad, but he sought refuge in his home city of Sirte, finally being killed as he tried to escape on 20 October. NATO's military operation ended on 31 October and Western banks, which had frozen the dictator's assets, now released them to the new government.

The challenge now was to create a new, stable regime but with tribal differences, armed militias, damage to the country's infrastructure, and the survival of some Gaddafi loyalists, this process would not be easy. The National Transitional Council did succeed in holding elections in July 2012, which led to the formation of a National Congress the following month, but there were deep divisions over such questions as the influence of religion and the extent of civil liberties. The Congress was unable to make progress on a constitution over the following two years. Meanwhile, armed militias and jihadi groups exploited the confusion to carve out their own areas of influence. Kidnapping and assassination were frequent, as were attacks on Congress members. In September 2012, US Ambassador to Libya, Chris Stevens, was killed alongside three other Americans in Benghazi during an attack by a jihadist group. The decision of the Congress to cling onto power after its mandate expired in January 2014 generated more unrest and led the army commander, Field Marshal Khalifa Haftar, to turn against it. In May, Haftar began a campaign against jihadist groups and successfully pressed the Congress to hold elections in June. But less than a fifth of electors turned out to vote and the new Council of Deputies, though it assumed power in August, had only limited authority. Supporters of the old Congress, who now formed a 'New National Congress', continued to dominate Tripoli, forcing the new Council to move east, to Tobruk. The New National Congress had the support of Islamist and other western paramilitary groups, who drew together in the 'Libyan Dawn' movement. Libya was then effectively in a state of civil war, with two rival governments claiming power, but both having limited authority. In December 2015, the UN gave its support to a unity government that included politicians from eastern and western Libya; this was formally established in March 2016, in Tripoli, but it too failed to secure widespread loyalty, being seen by many Libyans as imposed by outsiders. It did not, for example, have the support of Haftar, now the head of the so-called 'Libyan National Army' but effectively an independent warlord, who controlled much of the East. In November 2018, the UN acknowledged that hopes of holding elections before the end of the year were unrealistic but hoped they might prove possible in 2019.

Visit the online resources that accompany this book to test your understanding and take your learning further: www.oup.com/he/young-kent3e

NOTES

1. We are particularly indebted to Charles Lister, on whose detailed work the information in the following section, especially pre-2015, is primarily based. Charles R. Lister, *The Syrian Jihad* (Hurst, London, 2015).
2. Salafists are followers of a conservative ideology within Islam named after the salaf as-salih (pious forefathers) of Mohammed and his early followers, whose lives and customs they believe should be emulated. They often used the same language as jihadists but did not wish to extend the holy war beyond Syria, once a religious state was established there.
3. Report by the Special Rapporteur on the Right to Food, on his mission to Syria, Addendum, 27 January 2011, UN Office for the Coordination of Humanitarian Affairs, New York. Cited in Charles R. Lister, *The Syrian Jihad* (Hurst, London, 2015), 9.

4. For details of Syrian officials encouraging jihadist participation in the conflicts in Iraq and Lebanon, see Peter Neumann, 'Suspects into Collaborators', London Review of Books, 28 March 2014, using leaked State Department documents.
5. Charles R. Lister, *The Syrian Jihad* (Hurst, London, 2015), 24.
6. Christopher Phillips, *The Battle for Syria: International Rivalry in the New Middle East* (Yale University Press, CT, 2016), 51–3.
7. Ibid., 79.
8. Charles R. Lister, *The Syrian Jihad* (Hurst, London, 2015),111.
9. Details in Fawaz Gerges, *ISIS: A History* (Princeton University Press, NJ, 2016), Ch. 4; Jessica Stern and J. M. Berger, *ISIS: The State of Terror* (Harper Collins, New York, 2015), Ch. 2; and William McCants, *The Isis Apocalypse* (St Martin's Press, New York, 2015), Ch. 4.
10. Fawaz Gerges, *ISIS: A History* (Princeton University Press, NJ, 2016), 122
11. Nick Paton Walsh, 'The Secret Jihadi Smuggling Route through Turkey', CNN, 5 November 2013. Cited in Charles R. Lister, *The Syrian Jihad* (Hurst, London, 2015), 175.
12. Charles R. Lister, *The Syrian Jihad* (Hurst, London, 2015), 89.
13. Charles Lister, 'ISIS: What Will the Militant Group Do Next?', BBC News, 27 June 2014.
14. Charles R. Lister, *The Syrian Jihad* (Hurst, London, 2015), 242.
15. Ibid., 272.
16. Bahrain, Egypt, Iraq, Jordan, Kuwait, Lebanon, Oman, Qatar, Saudi Arabia, and UAE.
17. Reuters, 7 February 2015. Cited in Charles R. Lister, *The Syrian Jihad* (Hurst, London, 2015), 330.
18. William Harris, *Quicksilver War* (Hurst & Co., New York, 2018), 6–7.
19. Ibid., 64, 81–2.
20. Ibid., 380–2.
21. Ibid., 385.
22. Ibid., 76.
23. Ibid., 80, citing interview with Putin, 12 January 2016.
24. Ibid., 85; Christopher Phillips, *The Battle for Syria: International Rivalry in the New Middle East* (Yale University Press, CT, 2016), 229–30.
25. William Harris, *Quicksilver War* (Hurst & Co., New York, 2018), 90–2.
26. Ibid., 93.

27

Threats to the Existing Global Order: Instability in the West

Chapter contents

A. The US under Obama and Trump

Obama's Foreign Policy

Barack Hussein Obama, the first Black American President, defeated Hillary Clinton, wife of former President Bill Clinton, for the Democratic presidential nomination in 2008, largely because of his oratorical skills. He went on to beat the Republican candidate, John McCain, by a healthy margin; then he appointed Hillary Clinton to be his first Secretary of State. Obama inherited a difficult situation, with a brittle economy at home in the wake of the banking crisis and two major wars—in Iraq and Afghanistan—abroad. His major domestic political success in extending health care, and his attempts to meet the banking crisis by pumping money into the US economy, only contributed to a worsening of the government's debt. In turn, this contributed to renewed economic uncertainty and helped to ensure heavy Democratic losses in the November 2010 Congressional elections. Abroad, Obama sought a less unilateralist foreign policy than his predecessor, including improved relations with the Islamic world, signalled by his 2009 Cairo speech, which emphasized the need for dialogue and bridge-building. He had some successes. In April 2010, he signed a Strategic Arms Reduction Treaty with Russia, in August 2010 he was able to announce an end to the US combat mission in Iraq, and in May 2011 US Special Forces finally killed Osama bin Laden. In Libya in 2011, he was able to rely on North Atlantic Treaty Organization (NATO) allies to carry much of the burden in toppling the Gaddafi regime. But he decided to deploy additional troops to Afghanistan in 2009, where the war against the Taliban proved increasingly intractable (see Chapter 23, E).

Obama beat the Republicans' Mitt Romney in 2012 to secure a second term in office, now with John Kerry as Secretary of State. Kerry, a navy veteran who had opposed the Vietnam War, was previously chair of the Senate Foreign Relations Committee, had been Democratic presidential candidate in 2004, and shared Obama's preference for both diplomacy over military force and multilateralism over unilateral action. Whereas Obama's first term had been dominated by retreating from the massive use of military power in the 'war on terror', his second was overshadowed by his reaction to growing Middle Eastern conflicts after the 'Arab Spring' in the Levant (Al-Sham), particularly the rise of Islamic State (ISIS) in Syria and Iraq (see Chapter 24, E). The President was blamed by some for failing to intervene in Syria earlier to replace the Assad regime and for backing a predominantly Shi'ite regime in Iraq that alienated many Sunnis. Other setbacks included the lack of progress on an Israeli–Palestinian settlement, the continued failure to close Guantanamo Bay, and increasing tensions with Russia. Obama had a distinctly frosty relationship with both Putin and Israel's Benjamin Netanyahu, without exerting much influence over either. Despite his liberal credentials, continued involvement in the Middle East and Afghanistan meant he maintained high defence spending and a global military presence, provided arms to authoritarian regimes, and—in a new development that reflected a determination to minimize US casualties—relied far more than Bush on pilotless 'drones' to strike at America's enemies in Pakistan and elsewhere. These caused thousands of civilian casualties and the terror they generated helped aid recruitment for militant groups. Looking back on his record in 2016, the President deemed his backing for military intervention in Libya to be his 'worst mistake', because of the failure to plan for political stability once Colonel Gaddafi was toppled. Nonetheless, Obama had some diplomatic successes in his second term, notably with the 2015 deal limiting Iran's nuclear programme, progress towards the Trans-Pacific Partnership on trade and, in another success for patient multilateral negotiation, the Paris climate deal. In July 2015, he also restored diplomatic relations with Cuba, broken since 1961, and visited the island in March 2016, the first sitting president to do so since the 1920s.

Obama's time as President generated widely differing interpretations of his foreign policy. To some extent, he fulfilled his original intention, set out in 2008, to reduce America's dependence on military power, rely more on diplomatic action and, as a corollary, to engage in multilateral negotiations, as with his acceptance of climate controls, support for trade deals, and backing NATO action in Libya. But he could hardly be said to have made the world more committed to human rights and the rule of law. Critics questioned whether he had a strategy at all or, if he did have certain aims, how seriously he pursued them. His emphasis on diplomacy rather than force, for example, may have provided a laudable general aim but, in practice, he oscillated between the use of force—as in Libya or with the use of drones—and a reluctance to intervene—as in Syria, where Russia and Iran (two of America's long-standing rivals) were able to fill the vacuum. His policy could seem incoherent to the point of endangering well-established aims, like the maintenance of US primacy and the promotion of free market, democratic regimes, which had characterized Washington's global rhetoric through the Cold War and after. More sympathetic voices, however, argued that he was a pragmatist, whose caution reflected a recognition that America could no longer shape the world in its own image. The Bush years had exposed the limits of military power, rather like Vietnam a generation before, and the US people themselves were sceptical about paying the price of a leading role in world affairs.[1]

The Trump Administration, 2017–18

In a widely unexpected turn of events, the 2016 presidential election was won by Donald Trump, who adopted Ronald Reagan's promise to 'Make America Great Again'. Democratic candidate Hillary Clinton secured more popular votes, but Trump had a majority in the Electoral College; a similar situation had allowed Bush to win in 2000. In January 2017, Trump became the first president with no previous experience of government or military service; rather, he was a billionaire property tycoon and reality television star. At 70, he was also the oldest president ever inaugurated, one year older than Reagan had been. Trump had alienated sections of his own Republican party with his crude campaigning style; he also caused concern among America's allies, with criticisms of the Paris climate accords, free trade agreements, the nuclear deal with Iran, his scepticism about the value of NATO (which, at one point, he dismissed as 'obsolete'), his praise of Brexit, and his desire for a close relationship with Vladimir Putin. Much of this was aimed at undoing policies pursued by Obama. Also disturbing to established diplomatic norms was his tendency to express his opinions forthrightly on Twitter. An early example was his accusation, tweeted on 2 January 2017, that

'China has been taking out massive amounts of money and wealth from the US in totally one-sided trade but won't help with North Korea'.[2] Another early diplomatic step certain to upset Beijing was the suggestion that he might recognize the independence of Taiwan, after he accepted a telephone call from its President.

Among his most controversial plans, Trump declared that he would have Mexico pay for a wall along the US–Mexican border as a way of tackling illegal immigration and drug trafficking; while, as part of his firm support for Israel, he intended to move the US embassy from Tel Aviv to Jerusalem, a step he carried out in December 2017. His criticisms of the Washington 'establishment' included bitter remarks about the Central Intelligence Agency (CIA)—which, in the wake of the election result, reported that Russia had helped to undermine Clinton's presidential bid. Trump, upon entering office, made a series of controversial appointments to key posts, for example, Scott Pruitt, a prominent climate-change sceptic, to head the Environmental Protection Agency.

Trump seemed determined to pursue an American-centred foreign policy, including trade protectionism, threats to cut overseas aid, and defence based on nuclear deterrence. In policies reminiscent of 1980s 'Reaganomics', he also believed that high defence spending and domestic job creation through infrastructure projects could be accompanied by substantial tax cuts, designed to boost growth and encourage business. This fitted the populist message of his election campaign, based around patriotism, support for blue-collar workers, and resentment of the impact of globalization on the United States. It also reflected a development already evident under Obama: many Americans wished to withdraw from a leading role in world affairs and focus on problems nearer home. Yet, as it transpired, this did not prevent Trump from pursuing a highly active, if changeable and inconsistent, foreign policy in many respects.

Once in the White House, key decisions disappointed those who presumed that office would moderate Trump's approach. Within a few days, he restated his determination to make Mexico pay for the proposed border wall, expressed support for the use of torture against suspected terrorists (although he later backtracked on these proposals, saying he would defer to Defense Secretary James Mattis on interrogation matters), and withdrew from the Trans-Pacific Partnership. Obama had signed the Partnership agreement in February 2016, after years of complex negotiations with eleven other countries in East Asia (Japan, Vietnam, Malaysia, Brunei, and Singapore), Australasia (Australia and New Zealand), and the Americas (Canada, Mexico, Peru, and Chile), who together controlled a third of world economic output. As well as boosting trade by ending a range of tariffs, it was intended to rein in China's growing influence. It had already been criticized, however, for benefitting big business rather than workers and Trump believed it would harm employment in the US, as firms shifted investment to other members of the group. After his withdrawal from the Partnership, the other members negotiated a new deal, without the US, in March 2018.

Another of Trump's early executive orders introduced a ninety-day travel ban on immigrants from seven countries with Muslim majorities—Iran, Iraq, Libya, Somalia, Sudan, Syria, and Yemen—provoking accusations of Islamophobia and legal challenges within the US (until the Supreme Court narrowly endorsed Trump's action in June 2018). The move also threatened to undermine US policy in Iraq, driving its Shi'ite-dominated regime closer to Iran.

Trump himself had no diplomatic experience, nor did any of his original national security team or White House staff. The new Secretary of State was Rex Tillerson who, like Trump, had a successful commercial background, becoming Chief Executive Officer of ExxonMobil in 2006. In the late 1990s, Tillerson had headed Exxon operations in Russia and was seen as likely to seek better relations with Vladimir Putin. But he had also backed a US military build-up in Eastern Europe, was more open to multilateral trade deals than Trump, and his suitability for the State Department role had been pressed by senior Republicans, like former National Security Adviser Condoleezza Rice. Trump's first (and short-lived) National Security Adviser was a former general, Michael Flynn, who had served in Afghanistan and Iraq and became head of Obama's Defence Intelligence Agency in 2012, but retired after differences with the administration over its Syria policy, which he feared was increasing support for radical Islam. Flynn, too, was sympathetic to improving relations with Russia. The new Secretary of Defence, James Mattis, was another retired general, appointed by Obama to head the US Central Command (with responsibility for operations in Afghanistan and Iraq) in 2010–13, but critical of the Iran nuclear deal. He was, however, a believer in NATO, in which he held a Command in 2007–9, and was concerned about the Russian threat in Eastern Europe.

One unusual, short-lived step by Trump was to appoint to the National Security Council (NSC) his chief strategist, Steve Bannon, a controversial representative of the 'alternative right' news media. In February 2017, Bannon set out the administration's key aims as including not only stronger defence and economic nationalism, but also the 'deconstruction of the administrative state'[3], which seemed to explain why so many Cabinet members had been critical of government in the very areas they now controlled. Bannon was removed from the list of principal figures on the NSC in April and, in August, agreed to leave the White House. He was one of several key staff to quit in the administration's first year and his departure reflected the growing power of John Kelly, yet another former general, who became White House Chief of Staff in July 2017.

In February 2017, there were signs Trump might moderate some of his intentions. He now expressed support for NATO, while still arguing that European allies should pay more towards defence, if only to fulfil NATO's aim of spending 2 per cent of GDP on defence. This target was currently met by only 5 of the alliance's 28 members, while the US was spending over 3.5 per cent. Mattis made an early visit to allies in East Asia, to reassure them of Washington's support. In the Middle East, Trump himself visited Saudi Arabia, despite having criticized it in his 2016 campaign. The new US Ambassador to the UN, Nikki Haley, was critical of Russia after an upsurge of violence in eastern Ukraine, while Flynn was forced to resign after less than a month in post (the shortest term ever served by a national security advisor) for misleading Vice-President Pence over talks with the Russian ambassador about possibly lifting sanctions against Russia. The new advisor was Lieutenant General Herbert McMaster. With service in the Gulf War, Iraq, and Afghanistan, he was known as an intellectual general, having written a book critical of American policy in the Vietnam War. But, in what became a regular pattern, the President's volatility ensured that an apparent step forward was followed by renewed concern over his intentions.

Concern over Russian meddling in the 2016 election persisted, and suspicions over the Trump links to Moscow were only fuelled when, in May, he suddenly sacked Federal Bureau of Investigation (FBI) Director James Comey. The FBI had been investigating Russian electoral interference since late 2016, but Comey's firing led to the appointment of a special prosecutor, former FBI Director Robert Mueller, to look into any possible illegality in the connections between the Trump campaign and Russian interference in the presidential election. Concerns over relations with US allies were rekindled when, in one of his most controversial steps, on 1 June 2017, Trump announced that America would as promised, quit the Paris climate agreement. In the wake of a divisive G-7 meeting, the German Chancellor, Angela Merkel, even said that the days in which Europeans 'could rely fully on others' were passed, suggesting that Washington was now seen as an erratic rather than reliable partner.

While Trump upset his European allies, his relations with Russia could hardly be said to have improved. His wish to spend more on nuclear weapons sat uneasily alongside his initial desire for improved relations with Putin and this threatened to upset negotiations on the next Strategic Arms Reduction Treaty (START) treaty, scheduled to be completed between the US and Russia in 2018. The negotiations already faced problems because, while Washington tended to rely on missiles developed during the Cold War, Putin had been modernizing the Russian arsenal. Both powers still had total numbers of missiles that exceeded the limits set in the last START treaty in 2010. On 27 February 2017, Trump announced a $54 billion increase in defence spending, to over $600 billion per year. This was despite America's massive budget deficit and it was to be paid for by cuts elsewhere, including on the State Department and foreign aid budgets, thus endangering American soft power capabilities. The increased spending went hand in hand with a more muscular defence policy abroad, including increased involvement in Yemen, mainly in the form of air strikes against al-Qaeda; the deployment of hundreds of Marines and Special Forces, supported by artillery, to fight ISIS in Syria; and, in quick succession in April 2017, the despatch of an aircraft carrier to Korea, the use of a massive 'MOAB' bomb against an ISIS base in Afghanistan, and a cruise missile strike against a Syrian air base following a government chemical weapons attack on rebels.

The latter marked a further downturn in relations with Moscow, an important ally of the Assad regime in the Syrian civil war, and this was compounded in July by an expulsion of diplomats reminiscent of the Cold War: in response to US sanctions, pushed by Congress rather than the White House, against Russian interference in the 2016 presidential election, Putin told Washington to reduce its diplomatic staff by no less than 755. This was a large figure, one designed to match the number of Russian diplomats in America. There was a further mutual expulsion of diplomats, which also involved other members of NATO—28 countries in all, with more than 150 Russians expelled—in March 2018, following the attempted murder of a former Russian intelligence officer in Britain, using a nerve agent.

Meanwhile, Trump was unhappy with Robert Mueller looking into links between Russia and his White House staff, including his family members, associated with his presidential campaign. But the President's insistence that there was no case to answer did not prevent some former aides facing accusations of wrongdoing: in December 2017, former National Security Adviser Flynn pleaded guilty to making false statements to the FBI. All this made steps towards improved relations with Russia difficult. Besides, whatever Trump's hopes for such an improvement, in mid-December Flynn's successor, McMaster, publicly condemned what he called Moscow's 'campaign of subversion' against the West. Introducing a new national security policy, McMaster accused Russia and China of being 'revisionist' powers and, by implication, accepted that the US should maintain the existing world order. Neither was Putin intimidated by Trump's nuclear spending: on 1 March 2018, shortly before his re-election to a fourth presidential term, the Russian announced his country had a cruise missile that could fly around the world, illustrating his speech with a video of an apparent missile attack on America. In April 2018, there were even fears of a US–Russian military clash in Syria, when the US, France, and Britain bombed chemical weapon sites there. But there were signs that Trump himself still hankered after a rapprochement with Russia, not least in June 2018, when he urged that it should re-join the G-7 powers, and he announced plans for a summit with Putin.

Trump's first State of the Union address in January 2018, delivered in the wake of a raft of tax cuts, promised to maintain the war against Islamic State (IS), condemned the 'depraved' regime in North Korea, and criticized 'bad trade deals', but also talked of 'rivals like China and Russia that challenge our interests'. Yet, rather than heralding a more consistent policy, it was followed by more volatility in both foreign policy-making and foreign policy personnel. In March, Tillerson and McMaster were both replaced in quick succession. Each had tried to moderate the President's behaviour. The new Secretary of State was a right-wing Republican, Mike Pompeo, previously Director of the CIA, a critic of both the Iran nuclear deal and—a point that might divide him from Trump—Putin's Russia. McMaster's successor was John Bolton: a former Ambassador to the UN under Bush, he continued to defend the 2003 invasion of Iraq, was known for hawkish views on Iran and North Korea, but was another Putin critic. An editorial in the *New York Times* feared that the two appointments showed 'the degree to which Mr. Trump is indulging his worst nationalistic instincts'.[4]

These instincts had just been seen in the President's sudden decision to introduce additional tariffs, of 25 per cent on steel and 10 per cent on aluminium imports. This was in line with his promises to protect US jobs and reduce the trade deficit with China (though China only accounted for about 3 per cent of US steel imports); and the need to preserve steel production could also be justified on national security grounds. But Trump's method of protecting US steel production, using unilateral action rather than seeking negotiation via the World Trade Organization, threatened to begin a global trade war. The President's focus seemed mainly on China against which, in mid-June, he confirmed another $50 billion worth of tariffs, after accusing it of intellectual property theft. At that point, the US trade deficit with China was about $500 billion which, as Trump pointed out, was the largest ever between two countries. With the EU, the deficit was about $40 billion. The tariffs meant a volatile time for the financial markets, who did not accept the President's tweeted opinion that, 'trade wars are good, and easy to win'. The EU and China both introduced tariffs on a raft of US goods in response. The issue helped make June's G-7 summit in Quebec one of the most divisive in history, pitting Trump—who departed early—against the other Western leaders. But, at a Washington meeting with the EU Commission President, Jean-Claude Juncker, in July, Trump seemed more conciliatory, hoping to bring trade barriers down. He showed no signs of backing down against China, however, against which he announced further tariffs that month.

The appointment of Pompeo and Bolton was also followed, on 8 May, with Trump finally withdrawing from the 2015 Iran nuclear deal, despite Tehran fulfilling its terms. As with his earlier policy towards North Korea, this was followed over the next few months by both escalating rhetoric and, in late July, an offer to meet Iranian leaders. On 14 May, the new US embassy opened in Jerusalem, accompanied by Palestinian protests, in which about 60 were killed by Israeli forces.

Trump also kept up his pressure for higher NATO defence spending, even telling a summit in July that Europeans should increase this to 4 per cent of GDP. Meanwhile, Trump's tough policy towards North Korea, even threatening war, seemed to pay off, with Kim Jong-un's announcement that he would suspend nuclear tests. A meeting between the two men—the first between a North Korean leader and an American president—in Singapore on 12 June proved a major media event and saw a mutual commitment to 'denuclearize' the Korean peninsula, although it was thin on details of how this would be achieved.

Whatever the volatility and unpredictability of his short-term decision-making, Trump's first eighteen months in office had shown a certain consistency on such questions as opposition to the nuclear ambitions of Iran and North Korea, support for Israel, disdain for multilateral organizations, an emphasis on trade protectionism, and a more confident use of American military and economic power. Neither could observers be surprised any longer by his immunity to criticism. Trump could only provoke concern, however, with his willingness to damage international talks on pressing issues like climate change, or his readiness to ride roughshod over the feelings of traditional US allies in NATO, while hoping for a better relationship with Moscow. There was always room for uncertainty about how seriously some of his declarations should be taken. His sudden cancellation of the summit with Kim Jong-un in May 2018, only to go ahead with it a few days later, was a case in point. It was also unclear how far he would go in pursuit of aims he was determined upon. But if his apparent success with Kim gave him greater confidence, might this lead to damaging actions? Would he sustain a full-scale trade war with China and maybe even the EU, for example? Might his policies change, following the Democrats' capture of control of the House of Representatives after the mid-term elections of November 2018? And, one might ask, why would anyone make an agreement with Trump, say, on new international trade arrangements, given his readiness to abandon agreements to which he took a dislike?

Seventy years after President Harry Truman had begun delivering Marshall Aid to Europe and rebuilding Japan, Trump appeared set on a very different course, characterized by unilateralism and protectionism. At the same time, the political values initially provided by democratic capitalism's opposition to totalitarian communism seemed compromised by a readiness to work with authoritarian leaders, like Kim and Putin, while criticizing America's allies. Yet, when faced by sufficient criticism Trump seemed quite capable of backing off, as seen most starkly in the wake of his first bilateral summit with Putin, held in Helsinki on 15 July. Trump went into the summit after a divisive NATO summit and after even describing the EU as a 'foe' on trade; yet he not only avoided criticism of Putin, but even seemed to support the latter's denials of intervention in the 2016 US elections. Then, faced by a hostile reaction in the US, the President claimed to have been misquoted and stepped back from any early invitation for Putin to visit America.

B. The Consequences of the 2008 Financial Crash and the Problems of Neo-Liberalism

In the short term, the financial crash produced some essentially conservative consequences protecting the status quo. First, although pension funds and small enterprises, along with corporate owners of capital and the small percentage of the population with enormous individual wealth, all faced problems left by the crisis, the main burden would be shouldered by individual taxpayers. The immediate reaction had been for governments to pursue policies which injected taxpayers' money into the undercapitalized banks and prevented significant losses to investors' money. Thus, shareholders and bondholders gained some protection, reversing the normal operation of capitalism that penalizes unsuccessful risk takers. Shareholders of manufacturing companies, or corporations faced with liquidation, would normally expect to lose their money if their decisions misfired, but now they found themselves protected by governments and taxpayers despite management mistakes.

Thus, while the economic failure of communism had eventually produced the reforms of Mikhail Gorbachev in an attempt to rectify the failures, the failed neo-liberal economic system produced no such reactions. Western elites were intent on preserving the essence of neo-liberalism, with failed banks, like the Royal Bank of Scotland, limiting the loss to shareholders with the provision of government money, but eager to preserve the bonus culture and the benefits it gave to bankers who had overseen the losses in the first place. The consequence was, therefore, that nothing of major significance was done to reform the system that had allowed the financial crisis to happen.

Perhaps the greatest irony, though, was that massive state intervention had been necessary to save many of the self-same ideologues who had, for decades, decried state involvement in the economy. In effect, banks were 'feather-bedded' by states and protected from collapse, just as nationalized industries had been protected by government funding before 'privatization' took hold. One might have expected a return of adequate regulations—this seemed necessary, not just desirable—but it was done only in a half-hearted fashion and there was a new bout of evidence of bankers breaking the rules in 2012, when crisis engulfed another major operator, Barclays in the UK. Thus, the system has been criticized as 'corporate socialism' or 'socialism for the rich'.

Be that as it may, there is no doubt that a de facto alliance between far right-wing and centre right political groups and the richest members of a globalized society had developed, which accepted an economic ideology that had contributed to the crash and influenced the reaction to it. With the growth of the alt-right, to use US terminology, with its rejection of mainstream politics, and the emergence of populism in Europe, it is based on ensuring that the form that capitalism takes benefits the owners of capital more than the less well off citizens in paid employment. Built on the myth of 'markets know best', which has beguiled neo-classical economists and the new Keynesians, it has revealed the significance of the political economy of neo-liberalism in justifying the relationship of financial transactions to the real world.

Neo-Liberalism and Explanations of the Crash and its Impact

Stagnation after the financial crisis was a reflexion of the redistribution of wealth, and the global influence of neo-liberal economics, that produced similar problems to those capitalism had faced during the 1930s, but now with significant gains for the owners of capital. One new phenomenon facilitating this was the globalization of capital movements that, beginning even before the collapse of Bretton Woods, was enabling capital to move more freely across international borders. When this international element was added to by the deregulation of important financial sectors, 'casino capitalism' was allowed to develop. Moreover—and epitomized by the City of London's *laissez-faire* emergence at the heart of international finance and money laundering—it was allowing criminals and other significant owners of capital increasingly to earn and use money acquired by both legal and illegal means. Since the 1970s, it has no longer been necessary to hide money away in Swiss bank accounts to retain anonymous ownership. Finally, an extensive global system of tax havens has developed initially dominated by those under British control from Jersey to Crown Colonies,[5] until the latter were renamed dependent territories in 1981. After 2002, the 14 territories still under the sovereignty of the British Crown were then called UK overseas territories, but their operations did not decrease.[6] This enabled the very rich, using the deregulated financial sector to retain more of their earnings by reducing their tax liabilities legally (tax avoidance) or illegally (tax evasion) through the establishment of shell companies registered in the jurisdictions without income tax.

All these long-term processes had been developing since the reaction against the constraints produced by the post-war reductions in economic inequality and their effective replacement by the Washington Consensus, which was justified by the alleged benefits of 'free markets'. The growth of free market economics had been assisting the delivery of changes in the international economy that affected its agents and institutions and altered the distribution of income between states and the individuals within them. This was particularly significant in the wake of the 2008 financial crash and the inadequate, or limited, recovery from it, despite the indications that neo-liberal capitalism had embedded inequality on an increasing and damaging scale. What was uncertain was the impact of this on social cohesion and stability in both the developed and less developed worlds, as the nature and location of these changes in international capitalism developed.

The workings of the financial world have always largely been unknown, even to the better educated, but as the tax incentives and the ease by which shell companies could be established and set up in tax havens have increased, the earnings ratio of capital to labour has changed to the benefit of the former. The impact of globalization exposed high-earning workers in the developed world to low-wage competition from the less developed world, and—with capital and production facilities flowing more freely across the globe—enabled owners of capital to earn and retain greater profits. At the same time, media campaigns against trade unions in the developed world helped reduce workers' bargaining power. This became politically significant, as many wage earners felt left behind by the wealthier owners of capital, especially with the rise of private equity companies. Manufacturers came under increased pressures to be more competitive, and as their managers and shareholders faced these pressures on profits and credit after the financial crash, labour costs tended to be reduced. As little or no real increase in wages therefore occurred in many countries in the developed world, lower levels of spending power helped produce the stagnation after the financial crash. It became more of an accepted economic feature, along with the growing disparity in incomes and assets, even as the richest 1 per cent in particular continued to benefit significantly. With the richest 5 per cent in the developed world also enjoying large income gains, the gig economy grew, with zero-hours contracts keeping employment up and wages down, while the austerity measures reduced public services and social welfare provisions. Hence important economic factors were influencing the rise of developed world populism, with more extreme right-wing political movements across Europe from Hungary to Germany and Italy to Sweden. The connection to the success of Trump in the US and the European far right is embodied by Steve Bannon, the former White House chief strategist and NSC member, who, since ceasing to advise Trump, is now devoting time to cultivating links with the leading lights of such movements in Europe.

After the financial crash, the forces of globalization, active since the nineteenth-century revolutions in communication and transport, have helped to preserve a social order, which in the twenty- first century enables the richest few to increase their wealth significantly. Although changes in technology have made the spread of ideas and ideologies more pervasive, including 'fake news', this has been aided by the international free movement of capital. In the 1960s, when access to foreign cash was strictly controlled and limited by governments,[7] Sigmund Warburg began the issuing of bonds (which became known as Eurobonds after Eurodollars) to ensure money could move freely across borders without any controls or taxes, and without paying Swiss bankers to look after any suspect money. Issued in one country (initially at Schipol Airport to avoid tax, as if issued in the City of London they faced a 4 per cent tax) and with interest paid in another country (Luxembourg, again to avoid tax), ownership of such bonds would eventually be concealed through bearer bonds. Warburg persuaded the London Stock Exchange to list the bonds, not issued or redeemed there, and the pattern was set of freeing up money, previously subject to a charge in Swiss banks, to earn interest and avoid paying tax. The highway to tax havens was opened.[8]

As establishing shell companies was both cheap and easy, with neo-liberal ideology portraying the state in negative terms, money would increasingly leak offshore to these tax havens, as long as one country (originally the UK with the City of London) tolerated it.[9] By the late 1970s and early 1980s, this new era of 'financialization'[10] was taking hold, leading to the essentially unregulated movement of capital across international boundaries, often with little or no taxation being paid.[11] Despite the financial crash and the widening gulf between—and within—countries and their citizens that neo-liberalism had enhanced, the expanded financial sector was effectively obscured under a cloud of austerity. Ostensibly needed to reduce debt from excessive spending, democracy was powerless to prevent such misleading information frequently being accepted, and uncertainty surrounds the extent to which politics in much of the West will fall prey to extreme political movements of the right. As in the 1930s, when economic benefits could not be provided more generally throughout the developed world, there is now a danger of similar political movements gaining power.

A range of explanations can be provided for why capitalism in general, and its development within particular states, facilitated the financial crash and the subsequent survival of neo-liberalism during a period of stagnation. Although the decline in economic growth rates has been a global phenomenon, the explanations of the crisis and stagnation go beyond the vague and disputed idea of globalization. Thomas Piketty, after surveying vast amounts of statistical data in different countries (notably US, France, and the UK) over the period since the eighteenth century, has argued that without state intervention, for example the New Deal and the socialism of the Attlee Government, the development of uncontrolled capitalism will result in the returns on capital exceeding the rate of return provided by economic growth and income and output. Hence, reduced growth rates, except in those states catching up with more advanced economies, in the long term will average out at less than 2 per cent. Consequently, inequality is an inbuilt structural feature of capitalism made worse by its global scale, which enables wealth to avoid taxation more easily.[12] Those who advocate different phases of capitalism, like Marx, believe that one such phase is 'diminishing profit rates', which produces slow accumulation, increased stability, and financial turmoil.[13] Hence why the development of neo-liberalism and the restoration of the profit rate leading up to the financial crash occurred. On the other hand, those concerned with phases of 'boom and bust' like Minsky, while accepting the important role of debt in capitalist success,[14] maintain that periods of stable, 'tranquil' growth in capitalism create heightened expectations and the desire to increase leverage, and as in 2008, produce instability and the 'bust' phase.

Further explanation is required for why, despite the limited changes it has produced in the politics of many developed countries, the political choice of austerity has generally been accepted. The control of the media and significant misrepresentation, including in the UK by an allegedly neutral news organization keen to avoid further antagonizing the government, may have played a part. Moreover, after the Cold War had led the West—and its ideological opponents—to engage in all forms of manipulation and covert practices, lessons have been learnt as we enter the new ideological era of 'fake news'. A parliamentary committee, and similar bodies in the US have been looking into the increasing difficulty of determining the truth from 'facts' and 'alternative facts'. Advances in technology have facilitated this process and the trivialization of social media has prepared the ground for the receipt of 'fake news'. As the leader of the Western world displays an unprecedented capacity for disseminating untruths, foreign governments have been found, by US intelligence agencies, for example, to use IT to disseminate untruthful information to influence political voting.

Debt and the Deficit: The Case of the UK

By 2012, it was clear in Britain, a non-Eurozone state, where external bail-outs did not require the imposition of strict austerity, that simply relying only on cuts would restrict economic growth and recovery. The Conservative-led government of David Cameron had planned to achieve debt reduction predominantly through cuts in public expenditure, as opposed to increases in taxation. While some economists are keen to point to a high level of government debt to GDP as unsustainable, despite such levels of debt—including Greece's—being much less than that incurred in the immediate post-war years, changes in the exponential levels of private debt are generally ignored by mainstream economists, especially as much less data on it is available. Academics and researchers such as Bezemer, Hudson, and Keen however, argue that private debt levels are important because of their exponential post-war rises which first produced a bubble in Japan that burst in the 1990s. In the US, and to a lesser extent in Europe, it was the noughties before such bubbles burst, having reached unsustainable levels of growth, and thus caused recessions and stagnation. In other words, it is debt deflation, as first argued by Fisher,[15] in the private sector, including finance, that is more likely to produce recessions and stagnation (the level of demand being determined by debt and the money in circulation) than high levels of government debt.

The policies of Cameron and George Osborne had simply led to growth rates again becoming negative after the crash. In the US, more thought was given in 2012, a presidential election year, to allowing for a mild economic stimulus, although the economy still faced a slow-down, not helped by the knock-on effects of problems in the Eurozone. In both the US and Britain, the burden of any required deficit reduction would, to a greater or lesser extent, fall on ordinary taxpayers because, if public expenditure was significantly reduced, it is they who depend most on public services. UK debt reduction, often portrayed as necessary, as for households, to live within what is affordable, first requires a reduction in the deficit (the gap between the money raised by the government and public expenditure). Much less important than the deficit, given the very much higher levels of debt in the past, Cameron was prepared to aid the public confusion between debt (on which the banking system has always been based) and the deficit. In February 2013, he stated incorrectly that 'the government was paying down Britain's debts', when they were actually trying to reduce the deficit as the amount of debt increased. Rather than with contributions from the high earners in the banks and financial service industries, who had been primarily responsible for the reckless lending in the financial sector, or owners of capital who would have been hit by partial defaults, the deficit was to be reduced by the imposition of what was deemed necessary austerity on the 'real' economy. Public sector workers, in particular, have paid a high price in redundancies and wage restrictions.

The Spread of Economic Problems in the Eurozone

In 2012, the Spanish banks had reached crisis point following the bursting of the country's property bubble and rising mortgage debts. As there had only previously been attempts to put patches on the Eurozone's problems, in the summer of that year what many termed (not for the first time) the 'last chance' for the Eurozone was being faced. As the latest crisis engulfed Spain, the German Chancellor, Angela Merkel, softened her hard-line stance on debt reduction and European bail-out money. Merkel, for the first time, agreed to remove the requirement that preferred creditor status be given to governments over private creditors on a proposed €100 billion rescue package for Spanish banks. In other words, the latter would not play second fiddle to governments if the debt had to be rescheduled, thus making Eurozone taxpayers, including Germans, as much at risk as private creditors. Another concession was to make the bail-out funds directly available to the banks for recapitalization, instead of going through governments and thus adding to national debt levels. Finally, the most significant development was the agreement to set up a supervisory system for European banks that could form the first step towards a full banking union, and would mark a significant new step for European integration. As a result, the interest rates earned by lenders and paid by the Spanish government on ten-year Spanish bonds, which had risen to an unsustainable 7 per cent, began to fall, although the spending cuts that accompanied the rescue deal helped push unemployment in Spain over 25 per cent.

A smaller bail-out was also given to Cyprus in March 2013, after a crisis of confidence triggered by loans the country's banks had made to the property sector, which led the government to propose a tax on bank deposits. In this case, the Eurozone, EU, and International Monetary Fund (IMF) agreed a 10 billion Euro rescue package in return for banking reforms. But Greece remained the most serious and persistent concern for the Eurozone, with continuing popular unrest against the spending cuts, tax increases, and measures to reduce tax evasion that the IMF, EU, and Eurozone (the so-called 'troika') insisted upon. The initial 2010 bail-out was followed by a second bail-out offer of 130 billion Euros, in October 2011, but the conditions of this were so harsh that there was a change of government in Athens before it was finally accepted. The situations in Portugal and Ireland improved, allowing them to manage without bail-out support from mid-2014, but the last quarter of the year saw another downturn in Greece, where there was a renewed sense of deepening crisis. A general election in January 2015 was won by Syriza, a left-wing, anti-austerity party led by Alexis Tsipras, who formed an uneasy coalition with a right-wing anti-austerity party, the Independent Greeks. His administration sought to renegotiate the terms of the existing bail-out, before breaking off talks in June and holding a referendum, which rejected further new bail-out terms that had been offered. Meanwhile, on 1 July 2015, Greece had the distinction of becoming the first developed country ever to miss an IMF debt repayment, deepening the sense of crisis. The country's banks had intermittently been closed for weeks, there seemed a real chance of a Greek exit—or 'Grexit'—from the Eurozone and there was renewed instability on global financial markets. But Greece and its EU partners all baulked at the prospect of Grexit and the situation was eased by a third rescue bail-out, worth about 85 billion Euros over three years. This was put together in August, despite the opposition of many Syriza MPs over the spending cuts and tax increases that accompanied it. The discontent led Tsipras to call a snap election, which returned him as Prime Minister, and allowed him to fulfil the latest bail-out deal, even though its terms seemed to be at odds with his coalition government's supposedly anti-austerity credentials.

Over the following few years, the problems of the Eurozone seemed to ease and its GDP growth rate improved from 1.7 per cent in 2016 to 2.8 per cent in 2017. Fears of a Greek exit—or 'Grexit' from the currency zone receded. But in 2018 more uncertainty struck, thanks to the results of a general election in Italy. In the wake of the previous election, back in 2013, few could have predicted such a crisis. In February 2014, a coalition government had been formed under the Democratic Party's Matteo Renzi, who promised government reforms and improved growth. But the dynamic Renzi was undermined by Italy becoming the focus of large-scale immigration from across the Mediterranean Sea. His proposals to reform the Senate were defeated in a referendum in December 2016, leading him to resign and paving the way for a major political realignment, accompanied by criticism of immigration, divisions over Italy's future in the Eurozone, and the growth of two populist parties. The March 2018 election saw the Democratic Party lose almost 200 seats, with the main winners being the left-wing Five Star Movement (227 seats) and the right-wing Lega (125 seats). It then took two months before the two populist groups, the Movement and Lega, were able to put together a coalition government, committed to a mixture of tax cuts and higher welfare spending. (President Sergio Mattarella refused to endorse their first proposed list of ministers because he feared it might pull Italy out of the Eurozone.)

The crisis provoked a general fall in European stock markets, pushed up the cost of financing Italian national debt, and raised new doubts about the future of the Eurozone, whose operation seemed to benefit northern Europe—especially Germany, which had the dual benefits of a highly industrialized economy and the ability to keep export prices low, thanks to its membership of the Euro—at the cost of increased surpluses in trade within the Eurozone and deficits and low economic growth for its Mediterranean members. The key question here was whether the problem would be allowed to drag on, risking more financial crises, or whether some realignment could be achieved to aid the Mediterranean economies. In November 2018, the populist Italian government showed that it was determined to take a radical stance, when it pressed forward with budget plans for increased welfare spending and public infrastructure projects that would increase the deficit beyond the levels permitted by the EU. Meanwhile, however, financial instability was matched as a challenge for the EU by the decision of its second largest economy to quit the bloc altogether.

C. The Brexit Challenge

While not a founder-member of the old European Economic Community, Britain was part of the first enlargement of January 1973 and approved continued membership in a 1975 referendum with a clear two-thirds majority. Membership provided access to a large market that might help boost growth rates, which had lagged behind the UK's continental competitors in the 1960s, as well as providing a basis for the projection of British power as its Empire wound down. However, as an industrialized state which drew relatively low payments back under the Common Agricultural Policy, the country was always a heavy net contributor to the Community budget. Into the twenty-first century, most political leaders in London remained favourable to membership, fearing economic costs and a loss of global influence if the country left the European Union. That said, few were interested in a deepening of political integration and there were increasing doubts about the very idea of membership from some right-wing Conservatives. They were influenced not just by a patriotic desire for independence and exaggerated fears of a European 'super-state', but also by a belief that the policies and practices of the European Union (as it became in 1993) were damaging to Britain. They were concerned over business regulations, Britain's large net budget contribution to the EU, the activities of the European Court of Justice, and—because it boosted immigration numbers into Britain, especially from Eastern Europe—the free movement of people within the single market. Conservatives in particular were also worried over a loss of votes to the UK Independence Party (UKIP), founded in 1991, which grew in popularity to the point that, in the 2014 elections to the European Parliament, it won the largest share of the UK vote, at 28 per cent.

For David Cameron, the Conservative Prime Minister from 2010 to 2016, who supported continued EU membership, a referendum seemed a possible way to end the Conservative party's internal divisions, deflate UKIP support, and allow the country to focus on other issues. A Referendum Act was passed in 2015 and the campaign was launched in February 2016, but despite Cameron's personal popularity, support from other major parties (Labour, the Liberal Democrats, and the Scottish National Party), and a well-funded campaign that included a pro-EU leaflet being delivered by the government to every home, the result was not the one that was expected. Instead, on 23 June, there was a 51.9 per cent majority for a British exit, or 'Brexit', from the EU. A combination of factors combined to deliver this narrow defeat for Cameron. He had failed to secure any dramatic concessions from other EU members when he had sought a better deal for Britain in talks during late 2014–16, although there were some limits placed on child benefit payments to EU immigrants. Then again, he had not asked for much in the first place, since extensive changes would have demanded amendments to the EU treaties, which would have meant long and difficult talks, with an uncertain outcome. Eastern European members were unwilling to make changes that damaged their citizens residing in Britain.

During the referendum campaign, the 'Remain' effort arguably revolved too much around scare tactics, dubbed 'Project Fear' by the 'Brexiteers', including claims (not borne out by later events) that there would be an immediate, significant downturn in the economy in the event of a 'Leave' victory. The leader of the Opposition, Jeremy Corbyn, a left-winger, never well disposed to the EU, failed to drive home the message in traditional Labour heartlands that, in the long term, 'Brexit' could bring higher unemployment, as firms re-located into the much larger EU market. For its part, the 'Leave' campaign made false promises of shifting expenditure from EU membership to health care and cuts in immigration on the back of quitting the single market. Most major newspapers backed Brexit, some of them playing on fears of EU workers 'taking' British jobs. The referendum also coincided with the worst refugee crisis in Europe since the Second World War, which heightened the feeling against immigration—already associated in some minds with the EU's free movement of labour. In addition, the economy was still only slowly recovering from the 2008 crash, Cameron being identified with a policy of swingeing expenditure cuts.

A vote to leave the EU seemed to go against all recent history. In July 2013, after a decade of negotiation, Croatia had become the 28th member of the Union while, despite current problems, the Eurozone had also continued to expand, with seven new members between 2007 and Lithuania's accession in 2015, bringing its total to nineteen. In the immediate wake of the UK vote, there was considerable consternation and confusion. Global stock values fell sharply on this surprise decision by voters in the world's fifth largest economy (and the EU's second largest) and, while the markets soon recovered, the fall in the value of the pound was longer lasting. Partly to minimize the uncertainty, EU leaders were initially keen to see Britain initiate exit negotiations quickly, but under Article 50 of the Lisbon Treaty this process could take two years (longer, if all parties agreed) and it was up to the member affected to initiate the process. It soon became clear that, so confident was the British government of the referendum resulting in a remain vote, no serious preparations had been made for any exit talks, so that the process of defining a negotiating position would take several months. Meanwhile, Cameron immediately stood down as Prime Minister, to be succeeded by his former Home Secretary, Theresa May, who had only taken a limited role in the Remain campaign. She soon appointed a leading member of Leave, Boris Johnson, as Foreign Secretary.

There was then a debate over whether to seek a 'soft' Brexit, under which Britain might remain in a close trading arrangement with the EU, while leaving such elements as the Common Agricultural Policy and Common Fisheries Policy, or a 'hard' Brexit, where it might cut itself off from the EU altogether and make its own trade deals with the rest of the world. Those from the old Remain camp, including large companies, argued that a 'soft' deal would minimize the costs to the economy. But if Britain stayed in the single market, the EU was bound to insist on continuing the free movement of people, as one of the four binding freedoms of the single market (free movement of capital, goods, services, and people), which was seen by the Leave camp as the cause of high immigration into Britain and the most popular plank in their recent campaign. Complications were caused by the fact that most voters in Scotland and Northern Ireland had voted in favour of continued membership. Scotland, where the Scottish National Party won almost all seats in the 2015 general election, had only recently, in September 2014, held its own referendum, when 45 per cent voted for independence from the UK. It was possible that another independence referendum might be called to forestall departure from the EU. Relations with Ireland, an EU member, might also become difficult after Britain left, though May said she was keen to maintain the 'common travel area' between the two states, who benefitted from the free movement of people and goods within the island of Ireland.

Going into the Brexit negotiations, Britain was not in a strong position. True, as May and others underlined, it represented a substantial export market for the EU, not least for German car manufacturers, and the City of London was by far the biggest provider of financial services in Europe. But the EU was unlikely to grant Britain a generous deal, simply because this might encourage others to leave. The talks were likely to be difficult because of their technical nature, the number of countries involved and (given the difficulty of unanimously agreeing to any extension of it) the two-year time limit. There was basic initial difference between the two sides in that, while Britain hoped to negotiate a future trade deal simultaneously with arranging the 'divorce' terms, the EU wanted to keep these processes separate, dealing with the 'divorce' first (including a large 'exit bill', covering expenditure to which London had already committed itself).

The Lisbon Treaty meant that a final deal had to be approved, not only by government leaders meeting in the European Council, but also by the European Parliament. Failure to secure approval from even one member state might leave London trading with the EU on normal WTO conditions, without any special trading arrangements with a market of 450 million people on its doorstep. Only after leaving the EU customs union could Britain finalize trade deals with states outside the bloc.

In October 2016, May said she intended to invoke Article 50 by the end of March 2017, but only in January 2017 did she announce that she would seek a compromise deal, in which Britain would leave the customs union and single market, but seek some kind of 'bespoke' free trade agreement with the EU. The Supreme Court decided that Brexit talks could only open after an Act of Parliament was passed and, since Britain was a parliamentary democracy, the Westminster parliament could have overruled the result of what was a non-binding referendum. In the event, most MPs did not feel they could reject the narrow referendum result. The talks were then disrupted by elections in the two leading EU states, France (won by a pro-EU centrist, Emmanuel Macron, in May) and Germany (where Angela Merkel's Christian Democrats were unable to achieve a decisive victory and faced months of talks—until March 2018—on creating a coalition government), but most of all by a 'snap' election called by Theresa May in June 2017. This proved an ill-advised step that further complicated Britain's position. Against a background of favourable opinion polls, she had hoped to strengthen her majority in parliament on her 'hard Brexit' stance but instead, after running a lacklustre campaign against a resurgent Labour Party, saw it lost altogether. The Conservatives were still the largest party in parliament, but without an overall majority and with a leader whose stature was seriously tarnished, just as formal exit talks began. May was forced to rely on support in parliament from Democratic Unionist MPs, who wanted any deal to safeguard Northern Ireland's place in the UK.

Progress on the revived Brexit talks was slow at first, with the May government still divided over its tactics—including, now, whether to seek transitional arrangements after 2019, before a full withdrawal—and the EU disappointed over the British position on the 'exit bill', the rights of EU citizens in the UK, and the Irish-Ulster border. Far from resolving divisions in the Conservative party over Britain's relations with the EU, the referendum simply led them to be re-formed on new ground, focused on the 'hard' and 'soft' options for Brexit. The election result made May vulnerable to rebellions from Conservative MPs on either side of the debate and made it more difficult to achieve an exit deal that satisfied both the EU and the Conservative party. On 22 September, speaking in Florence, May proposed a transitional period of up to two years, during which Britain would continue to contribute to the EU budget, but was weak on other details, though she did hint at a lasting role for the European Court of Justice in protecting EU citizens in the UK. An important step forward was an agreement, in December, on the principles that EU citizens could remain in the UK after Brexit; there would be no 'hard' border between Northern Ireland (part of the UK) and the Irish Republic; and Britain would pay a 'divorce bill' of about £37 billion. It was still unclear how some of these principles would be carried out, but the EU Council agreed sufficient progress had been achieved for the talks to proceed to their second stage, defining a post-Brexit deal with the UK.

Talks on the post-Brexit deal began in February 2018, with the ambitious aim of completing a deal by October. There was also general agreement that Britain's departure from the EU in March 2019 would be followed, down to the end of 2021, by a 'transitional' period, in which Britain would still be subject to EU regulations, to allow economies to adjust to the changes. But as the talks intensified, divisions between 'Brexiteers' and former 'Remainers' in the Conservatives party intensified, making it difficult for May to maintain authority over her ministers, some of whom were openly critical of her attempts at compromise. Meanwhile, many large UK businesses, some foreign governments (notably Japan, a major source of overseas investment), and even studies by the government itself, believed that Brexit would condemn the economy to lower growth in future.

In the spring of 2018, the key issue became Britain's relationship with the customs union, a debate which focused on differences within the Conservative party, rather than between London and the EU. Previously, May had rejected continuing membership of the customs union or even of a free trade area, yet one of these options might prove the best way to safeguard growth and investment, as well as allowing a 'frictionless' border with Ireland. Various compromises were discussed, including Britain extending its membership of the customs union beyond 2019, to allow the Irish border question to be resolved, or keeping Northern Ireland—but not the rest of the UK—in the customs union. But the last was an option likely to be opposed by May's Democratic Unionist allies, who could hardly welcome the re-imposition of any border within the island of Ireland at odds with The Good Friday Agreement bringing peace to the province. Nor, as Unionists, could they accept new customs controls, giving the impression of differences between Northern Ireland and the rest of the UK, while 'hard' Brexiteers were determined to avoid any customs union. A customs union with the EU would prevent the country making its own trade deals with the rest of the world, independently from the EU. By mid-2018, the EU was increasingly frustrated with Britain's inability to decide what it really wanted from the talks and a number of major manufacturers, including the aircraft maker Airbus and car maker BMW, warned of the danger to future investment if the indecision continued.

Only at a special Cabinet meeting on 6 July 2018 did May persuade her ministers to agree their aims on Brexit, the aim being to create a free trade area, in which Britain would collect tariffs for the EU in a 'facilitated customs arrangement'. This at least seemed to offer a frictionless border with Ireland, but it was almost immediately attacked from both sides of the Brexit debate. Pro-EU businesses were concerned over the likely costs of collecting tariffs under the customs arrangement (some doubted that it was even technically feasible) and felt it easier to remain in a customs union. Also, the proposed free trade area would be one of industrial and agricultural goods only, omitting the service sector that was so central to the British economy: the City of London could gradually lose business to Frankfurt and Paris if barriers were thrown up between Britain's financial services and the EU. For their part, Brexiteers feared the proposed deal would continue to submit Britain to EU regulations, especially since the free trade area would need a common 'rule-book', and maybe make it harder to strike trade deals beyond Europe. Neither did ministerial unity last long: one leading Brexiteer, David Davies, who had been leading negotiations with the EU, resigned the following evening, quickly followed by Boris Johnson, who claimed that May's compromise deal would make Britain a 'colony' of the EU. Once negotiations re-started, it was clear that the EU also had doubts about the British plan, with particular scepticism about the idea London might collect EU tariffs (which was rejected by the EU negotiator Michel Barnier as inappropriate for a non-member state), even if it did hold better hope for a deal on the Irish border. All this raised the real prospect that Britain might exit without a deal and be left to trade with the EU on World Trade Organization (WTO) terms, a situation that might induce some businesses to leave the UK.

It proved impossible to achieve a UK–EU withdrawal deal by the original October deadline, but one was finally signed off, at a special summit in Brussels, on 25 November 2018, a bare four months before Brexit was set to occur (on 29 March 2019). The withdrawal deal, a legally binding document that ran to almost 600 pages in length, confirmed the £39 billion 'divorce bill', guaranteed the rights of EU citizens living in the UK (and UK citizens in the EU), included a 'backstop' position on the Irish border that might yet leave Northern Ireland in a special customs relationship with the EU and established a transition period down to the end of 2020, to allow both sides to adapt to the changes before they came into effect. The withdrawal agreement was designed only to settle short-term arrangements surrounding Britain's departure from the Union. But it was accompanied by a non-binding political declaration, which set out the two sides' aspirations for their long-term relationship. This had yet to be negotiated in detail, but it was intended to include close co-operation on security, crime-fighting and foreign policy, as well as trade and economics. Mention of a 'single customs territory' worried Brexiteers, however, who feared becoming committed to a customs union, which would prevent the UK pursuing trade deals without common EU tariffs. There were also concerns from Brexiteers about, for example, the continuing power of the European Court of Justice in future arrangements, a new form of common fisheries policy and the danger that the Irish 'backstop', instead of being replaced by some more acceptable deal, could become permanent. Such gains as ending the free movement of people between the UK and EU did not seem to compensate for such dangers for Brexiteers. On the other side of the political spectrum, Remainers asked if it was worth leaving the EU at all, given how close the future relationship looked likely to be, but also given that Brexit would remove the UK's ability to shape future Union policies.

With Ulster Unionists particularly troubled by the future status of Northern Ireland, Liberal Democrats and Scottish Nationalists critical of Brexit, and Labour—the main opposition party—hopeful of bringing about a general election, May's chances of pushing the deal through the British Parliament were doubtful, even before the Brexiteers within her own party—boosted by more ministerial resignations—were added to the mix. If the deal was voted down in the UK, the future was highly uncertain, with options ranging from a 'no-deal' Brexit, through a general election and/or a renegotiated withdrawal deal, to a further referendum, with the last three options leading to months of uncertainty that might prove seriously damaging to the economy. With the EU stating that negotiations were over, even if the withdrawal deal was passed by London and the 27 members of the EU, there remained years of talks ahead on their future relationship.

The EU was Britain's largest trading partner and the substance of their future trading relationship was something the EU refused to discuss in detail until the withdrawal agreement had been settled, although they were prepared to make changes to the political declaration that accompanied it and which sketched out their future relationship. May remained committed to the withdrawal deal as the best precursor to any future economic arrangement talks, but the problem was getting it accepted by her parliamentary allies, the DUP, and the right-wing pro-Brexit elements in her own party, who formed the 'European Research Group'. Its chairman, Jacob Rees-Mogg, an Eton/Oxford educated multi-millionaire, who established Somerset Capital Management in 2007, was notable amongst the right-wing elements who made her position in a 'hung' parliament far from strong or stable. Yet, opposition to the withdrawal agreement came from all sides of the House of Commons, including some junior ministers in May's own government. Those who rejected the deal had very different reasons for so doing, with some desiring to maintain close economic ties with the EU and avoid the damage likely to be caused by Britain no longer having similar economic relations with its largest trading partner. Others were concerned that the break with the EU was not decisive enough. With the breadth of parliamentary opinion against her deal, the vote on it was lost in January 2019, in the biggest-ever defeat of a government bill in British history.

A key sticking point was the agreement on the British-Irish border in Northern Ireland, known as the Irish 'backstop'. With the importance of the peace enshrined in the 1998 Good Friday Agreement, which had ended three decades of 'troubles' in Northern Ireland, the 'backstop' was designed to ensure that the free movement of goods and people within the island would continue, until an alternative arrangement had been agreed. With the defeat of the Withdrawal Agreement Bill by 290 votes and the resignation of more junior ministers (to add to the two Brexit Secretaries who had resigned in 2018), in February 2019 May headed for Brussels to attempt to change the 'backstop'. Although it was part of the legally-binding deal agreed with the EU, the 'backstop' was opposed by Unionists primarily because of the emotive issue of the different treatment of Northern Ireland threatening the preservation of the Union between Northern Ireland and Great Britain. In Brussels, May was unable to get the withdrawal agreement altered by the EU, and the assurances the latter provided could not satisfy the Attorney-General that the legal position arising from the 'backstop' had changed. Hence, many Tory opponents of the original deal voted against it again. With only a handful of Labour MPs prepared to support it, the Withdrawal Bill suffered another crushing defeat, by 148 votes, on 12 March 2019.

There then began a frenetic period of unprecedented parliamentary turmoil over the increasingly chaotic Brexit circumstances. On 14 March, May again went to Brussels and secured an extension to Article 50. Its implementation—and Britain's departure from the EU—had originally been scheduled for 29 March, but was now put back to 12 April if the withdrawal agreement was approved. That agreement was immediately rejected again, if only by 58 votes. Then, on 27 March, the House of Commons rejected all eight proposals designed to determine if there were any form of departure from the EU which MPs could agree on. Thus, the ever-deepening split in the country was replicated in a paralysing parliamentary stalemate over Brexit. The only point that the Commons could agree upon was that to leave the EU without a deal would be unacceptable and seriously damaging to the UK. Britain's departure had again to be delayed, with the EU eventually fixing it for 31 October. The divisions and problems present in British society, still gripped by austerity, and the failure to move forward with implementing the result of the referendum had made Brexit an ever more dominant and highly toxic issue in the country. The difficulty of reconciling the result of the 2016 referendum with a withdrawal deal that avoided serious economic damage to both the EU and UK was now more evident. Furthermore, rather than Cameron's referendum gamble healing the long-standing rift over EU membership in the Conservative party, it now had the opposite effect, tearing the Tories apart, as the debate became entangled with emotive questions of British identity and status. The whole country was now infected with the 'Europe' virus and desperate for the illness to be over.

May's complex compromise agreement with the EU remained the only option on the table, but since it had been rejected by parliament, it meant that leaving without a deal had become a real possibility, with the risk of economic chaos. Out of desperation, May finally decided to reach out to the opposition in a search for an acceptable way forward, but her talks with the supposed 'Marxist' leader of the Labour Party, Corbyn, only created more dissatisfaction with her leadership among Conservatives. On 24 May, under intense pressure from her own side, she agreed to stand down as party leader and Prime Minister. On 25 July, Boris Johnson, the former Brussels correspondent of the right-wing *Daily Telegraph* and leading figure in the 2016 Brexit campaign, succeeded her, hailed as someone who could deliver 'the will of the people' and persuade the EU to renegotiate the withdrawal agreement, or at least the Irish 'backstop', even though EU representatives insisted that the only issue open for discussion remained the non-legally-binding political declaration.

Visit the online resources that accompany this book to test your understanding and take your learning further: www.oup.com/he/young-kent3e

NOTES

1. For discussion of these various views of Obama's foreign policy, see Michael Clarke and Anthony Ricketts, 'Did Obama Have a Grand Strategy?', *Journal of Strategic Studies*, 40 (2017).
2. https://twitter.com/realdonaldtrump/status/816068355555815424.
3. See, for example, *Washington Post*, 23 February 2017.
4. *New York Times*, 23 March 2018.
5. For details on how the system worked in Jersey, see Oliver Bullough, *Moneyland: Why the Thieves and Crooks Rule the World and How to Take it Back* (London, Profile Books, 2018), 60–4 and for its international development driven by secrecy and Manafort's role, see the extent of their international impact at 16–21, 44–8.
6. Jersey, Guernsey, and the Isle of Man, under the sovereignty of the Crown, have different constitutional arrangements with the UK and are 'Crown Dependencies'.
7. UK tourists were limited to £50 in foreign currency given over bank counters in 1964.
8. Oliver Bullough, *Moneyland: Why the Thieves and Crooks Rule the World and How to Take it Back* (London, Profile Books, 2018), 34–5, for how the City used dollars deposited there from outside the US to provide dollar loans outside US government control. There was no limit on the interest to be paid on loans, unlike in the US, where banks, immediately after the collapse of Bretton Woods, were also restricted in the amount they could lend by a Required Reserve Ratio (RRR). Examples of the restraints on the use of capital requiring removal to maximize earnings.
9. Details on how these tax havens worked to protect the owners of capital from tax and conceal their accounts were leaked and published in 2016: Bastian Obermayer and Frederik Obermaier, *The Panama Papers* (London, One World Publications, 2016).
10. Financialization refers to Hilferding's old terminology of financial capital (Rudolf Hilferding, *Finance Capital: A Study of the Latest Phase of Capitalist Development* (London, Routledge, 1910)) combined with the addition of the new and highly sophisticated methods by which debt and assets are related and used by the managers of financial institutions and funds to achieve enormous incomes, for some of these mechanisms. See Glossary.

11. Oliver Bullough, *Moneyland: Why the Thieves and Crooks Rule the World and How to Take it Back* (London, Profile Books, 2018), 36–9.
12. Thomas Piketty, *Capital* (Cambridge MA, Belknap Press of Harvard University Press, 2014), 571–2.
13. Karl Marx, *Capital, Volume 3, 1894* (New York, Vintage Books, 1981).
14. 'Debt is an essential component of a capitalist economy': H. P. Minsky, 'The Financial Instability Hypothesis: An Interpretation of Keynes and an Alternative to "Standard Theory",' *Nebraska Journal of Economics and Business*, 16 (1977), 10. Cited in Steve Keen, *Can We Avoid Another Financial Crisis?* (Cambridge, Polity Press, 2017), 16–17.
15. Irving Fisher, 'The Debt-Deflation Theory of Great Depressions', *Econometrica*, 1(4) (1933).

28

Threats to the Existing Global Order: Challenges from the East

Chapter contents

A. Putin and the Reassertion of Russia: A New Cold War?

When the Russian President, Boris Yeltsin, made Vladimir Putin prime minister in August 1999, Putin was little known abroad and had some better-known rivals for leadership at home. However, he soon proved a highly able political operator, exploiting the rising violence in Chechnya to make himself the natural successor to his ailing leader (see Chapter 20, B). Born in 1952, in the last months of Stalinism, Putin had studied law at university, served in the Soviet intelligence service, the KGB, and became head of the Federal Security Service (the main successor to the KGB in Russian domestic politics) in 1998. His efficiency and toughness marked a major step away from Yeltsin's volatile, even embarrassing leadership and, helped by growing oil revenues, he soon gave Russians more hopeful economic prospects. To strengthen his hold on power, he established a semi-authoritarian regime, marked by control of the media, manipulation of election results in favour of the United Russia party, and the intimidation of opposition figures. Putin won his second four-year term as President in March 2004 by an overwhelming margin of 70 per cent. Critics believed the government was involved in the death of key opponents of the regime, including Anna Politkovskaya, a journalist who was shot in Moscow, and Alexander Litvinenko, a former intelligence official who was poisoned in London, both in 2006.

Some opponents remained active, but they were a disunited mix of liberals, nationalists, and former communists. The nationalists found some of their appeal stolen by a president who reasserted central power in the regions; communists found it difficult to compete with a former KGB officer; while the liberals who had been brought into power by Yeltsin were now gradually pushed aside in favour of Putin loyalists. The Russian constitution would not allow Putin to serve a third consecutive term as President, but he was able to persuade a close ally, Dmitri Medvedev, to stand for the post instead. Medvedev, born in 1965, was a fellow native of St Petersburg, a lawyer who had met Putin after entering the city's politics. He helped run Putin's 2000 election campaign and became a deputy Prime Minister five years later. In May 2008, after winning the presidential elections, he made Putin his Prime Minister but, with the latter continuing to play the dominant role in Russian political life, it seemed to many that Medvedev was little more than puppet. Putin's predominance was confirmed when he decided to run for the presidency once more in 2012. His popularity was called into question by large-scale demonstrations against supposed irregularities in December 2011 parliamentary elections, which were again won by United Russia—but with its share of votes falling below 50 per cent. He easily won the March 2012 presidential election, with almost two-thirds of the votes cast. Some irregularities were reported again, sparking further demonstrations against him, but his hold on power seemed secure enough.

Putin not only maintained the firm policy towards Chechnya that had helped secure his succession to Yeltsin, but was also prepared to be tough in relations with the states of the former Soviet Union. The most serious differences arose with Georgia, which steered a pro-Western policy, but was weakened by the continuation of separatist movements in Abkhazia and South Ossetia. In August 2008, after Georgian troops entered South Ossetia, Russian forces launched a week-long invasion of Georgia, after which Moscow recognized the independence of both the rebel regions. One element in Russian policy was the use of its privileged position in terms of energy reserves, as one of the world's richest sources of oil and the largest potential supplier of natural gas. Putin's government played an increasing, direct role in the energy industry. The state-controlled oil company, Rosneft, was able to take over part of the operations of the imprisoned Khodorovsky and in 2005 the Kremlin took a majority stake in the gas company Gazprom, which then expanded its operations and struck major deals with foreign firms to develop gas fields and pipelines. Gas was supplied to much of Europe and to China. Control over huge gas reserves allowed Russia to flex its muscles against uncooperative neighbours, as in January 2006, when it cut supplies to Ukraine during a dispute over prices, and in January 2007, when an argument about a transit tax led it to cut supplies through Belarus, a step which temporarily halted supplies to the rest of Europe. A similar, but more serious dispute blew up two years later, when renewed differences with Ukraine cast uncertainty over gas supplies to parts of Europe for a month.

In foreign policy, Putin at first seemed to maintain Boris Yeltsin's policy of cooperation with the West and China. He was sympathetic to American efforts in the 'war on terror', given continuing problems in Chechnya. Participating in climate change talks and the G-8 (which Yeltsin joined in 1998) in May 2002 Russia, under Putin, helped establish the NATO–Russia Council (NRC). While its practical results were limited, it fostered some practical co-operation, including Russian supplies to NATO forces in Afghanistan. Elements of the multilateral policy could still be seen in 2012, when Russia joined the World Trade Organization (WTO), cementing its role in the global economy, where it was now perceived as a promising site for investment, part of the so-called 'BRICS' group, alongside Brazil, India, China, and—since 2012—South Africa.

But Putin had also begun to show a preparedness to reassert Russian power and influence and risk tension with the West, especially when it seemed to flout Russian sensitivities by ignoring their interest. Nuclear disarmament talks seemed seriously troubled as early as the Bush administration and the very fact that Washington prioritized the logic of the 'Bush Doctrine' over relations with Russia could be seen to reflect how far American Cold War concerns had slipped into a triumphalism that involved reduced attention to former Soviet Union republics. In 2007, Putin became highly critical of US President Bush's attempt to create a new missile shield in east-central Europe, including Poland and the Czech Republic. Washington said the shield was to defend NATO against the possible development of an Iranian threat, but the Kremlin was not persuaded by American arguments and Putin accused the US of starting a missile race with Russia. The rhetoric on both sides was soon reminiscent of the Cold War, but the reality was that Russian Cold War concerns and a desire for greater recognition were being replaced by a more assertive nationalism and resentment of the West.

Tensions with Washington eased during 2009 when the new President, Barack Obama, ended his predecessor's plans for missiles to be deployed in Poland and the Czech Republic, in favour of a scheme for missiles largely based on US navy vessels in the Black Sea (though with some based in Romania). In April 2010, it was even possible for Medvedev and Obama to sign a new Strategic Arms Reduction Treaty, in Prague, reducing their strategic arsenals by almost a third (limiting each side to 1,550 nuclear warheads). Even the arrest of ten Russian spies in the US soon afterwards did not disrupt relations for long before, in 2011, Putin criticized NATO action against Libya's Gaddafi regime. Medvedev—in a unique personal difference with his Prime Minister—publicly rebuked him. When Putin was elected to a third presidential term in 2012, however, the situation was rather different, with the implications of more Western-sponsored regime changes in the Middle East having to be faced. Along with China, Russia resisted Western pressure for strong UN action against Syria, as it slipped into civil war.

Moscow often felt the relationship with the West was one-sided, with a distinct difference between, on the one hand, the West's economic and strategic expansion into areas that had been of particular interest to the former Soviet Union, and on the other increased Russian influence in areas beyond Europe of particular interest to the West. The West saw increased tension created by Putin's support for Venezuela's leftist President, Hugo Chavez; in improved relations between Russia and Iran; in America's improved relations with India; and in revived Russian use of its old base at Cam Ranh Bay in Vietnam. For Putin, as for Gorbachev, the expansion of NATO westwards to include even former Soviet republics (when Estonia, Latvia, and Lithuania joined in 2004), planned new NATO missile deployments in Eastern Europe, and the recognition by most NATO members (including the US), of Kosovo's 2008 declaration of independence from Serbia were even more alarming. In turn, NATO was concerned about the revival, in 2007, of long-range Russian bomber patrols and a planned naval exercise in the Mediterranean. The alliance also condemned Russia's August 2008 invasion of Georgia and Putin's recognition of the independence of Abkhazia and South Ossetia (from Georgia). Meetings of the NRC were suspended for a time. Then, in 2009, came a proposal to hold NATO military manoeuvres in Georgia, another move condemned by Moscow, which increasingly feared the Atlantic military alliance might be extended to Georgia and Ukraine; and NATO's intervention in Libya in 2011 and the ensuing death of Colonel Gaddafi, both of which Putin condemned. Ideologically, Putin's regime, based on a mixture of Russian nationalism (which increasingly sought to protect Russian minorities in neighbouring countries), and religious conservativism (with gay rights one point of contention), appeared very different to liberal democratic ideals, even if it was also a marked departure from Soviet communism.

The mix had more in common with China, where another authoritarian regime mixed state controls and capitalism to achieve economic growth. Putin had been careful to build good relations with China and building up the so-called 'Shanghai Group', originally formed in 1996 by Russia, China, Kazakhstan, Kyrgyzstan, and Tajikistan, which was joined by Uzbekistan in 2001 and included annual summits, with co-operation on counter-terrorism and energy security. In 2015, the Group agreed to membership bids from India and Pakistan which, among other gains (for example, it would now include about half the world's population), promised to make it look less of an authoritarian club.

The new 'Cold War' included propaganda campaigns, with the television broadcaster *Russia Today* proving especially successful in the West, as the Kremlin took steps to close off Western media outlets, like *Voice of America*. Washington was also offended, in June 2013, when Moscow gave refuge to Edward Snowden, a Central Intelligence Agency (CIA) officer who had leaked information on Western intelligence agencies' mass surveillance programmes. The decision to grant Snowden asylum led, on 7 August, to Obama cancelling an upcoming summit meeting with Putin, in Moscow, highlighting personal differences at the highest level and raising memories of the cancellation of the Paris summit back in 1960, in the depths of the Cold War. But the Russian economy suffered serious blows when the invasion of Crimea was followed by Western economic sanctions that coincided with a major downturn in global oil prices. When Putin tried to place the blame for Russia's economic hardships on the West, this only deepened the divisions between the two sides.

The Russian–Western split grew significantly in 2014–16 by events in Ukraine and Syria. In Ukraine, the 2010 presidential election was won by the pro Russian Viktor Yanukovich, who defeated former premier Yulia Tymoshenko. The narrow result—there were only 3 per cent of votes dividing the candidates—reflected the country's deep division between ethnic Russians and Ukrainians. These were deepened further when Tymoshenko was put on trial for embezzlement and, in October 2011, imprisoned, a step which also complicated the negotiations for association with the

European Union. Increasingly, ethnic differences inside Ukraine were reflected in divisions over whether the country should align itself, in foreign policy and trade, with either Russia or the EU. Putin, too, wanted to see a delay in preparations for a Ukraine–EU deal. In November 2013, Yanukovich backed away from plans to sign an EU association deal and talked instead of creating a trade deal that included Ukraine, the EU, and Russia, but this sparked mass protests on the streets of Kiev. While EU leaders criticized Russian behaviour, Putin spoke of a threat to Russian security, and unrest in Ukraine spread, with protests against ministerial corruption and a lack of civil rights. Violent clashes between protestors and the police in mid-February were followed by Yanukovich fleeing to Russia, after which the parliament removed him as President and released Tymoshenko. New presidential elections were held in May, resulting in a win for Petro Proshenko, a billionaire businessman, former foreign minister, and ally of ex-President Yushchenko. A Ukraine–EU association agreement was signed in June 2014, but by then there were questions over whether Ukraine might not break up, because of its ethnic differences and Putin's response to the divisions they reflected.

On 23 February 2014, immediately following the deposition of Yanukovich by the Ukrainian parliament, pro-Russian protests broke out in Sevastopol, capital of Crimea, in the south-east of the country. Putin saw a chance to re-assert Russian control over this strategic area, with its long Black Sea coast and naval bases. Under Soviet rule, Crimea had been administratively part of Ukraine since 1954, but had been part of the Russian Federal Socialist Republic before that and was largely Russian in ethnicity. On 27–28 February, armed men posing as pro-Russian separatists began to take over key government buildings in Sevastopol; it was soon clear they were actually the first elements of an invasion force. On 1–3 March, facing only limited resistance from local Ukrainian forces and with remarkably few casualties, the Russian army seized control of Crimea, expelled Ukrainian forces, and quickly arranged a referendum, on 16 March, that approved merger with the Russian Federation.

But, however smooth the operation, it drew an angry response from the West. Sanctions by the US, EU, and others included suspension of Russia's membership of the G-8, economic measures (notably a ban on food imports), travel bans on certain individuals, and suspension of the NRC. Concern was also created by Russian support for separatists in eastern Ukraine, especially in the Donbass region, where the Donetsk *oblast* declared independence on 7 April and a Luhansk 'People's Republic' was declared on 27 April. Months of sporadic violence and diplomatic activity culminated in an agreement, signed in Minsk on 11 February 2015, between Putin, Poroshenko, Angela Merkel of Germany and François Hollande of France, which brought about a ceasefire and mutual withdrawal of heavy weapons, to be followed by steps towards a political settlement. But, while the violence receded for a time, no long-term solution was reached and there was sporadic tension in border areas thereafter as well as dangers of a clash over Crimea, where tensions grew in November 2018 after a naval clash between Russian and Ukrainian vessels.

Russia's military intervention in Syria, from September 2015, was something of a surprise to the world. Russia did not have a history of military or significant diplomatic intervention in the Middle East; it seemed preoccupied with events in Ukraine, its economy was in a poor state, and the Syrian civil war was a messy conflict that looked extremely difficult to resolve. The costs of being dragged into such an imbroglio could easily outweigh any benefits. On the other hand, Syria had been the Kremlin's main ally in the Middle East since the 1970s and a Soviet naval facility was established at Tartus in 1971. Before intervention, Putin had made Russia Syria's main arms supplier, written off substantial Syrian debts, and vetoed attempts to enforce UN sanctions on the Assad regime.

By 2015, it was clear that the Obama administration and other Western governments were unlikely to intervene with ground troops (other than limited numbers of special forces) in the four-year-old civil war, but Assad was struggling to hold ground and his position might deteriorate if Russia did nothing, leading to another Western-sponsored regime change and the use of Syria as a base by militant groups. Military action could be justified as responding to an appeal from an ally and directed at 'terrorists'. The focus of Russian military action was on air strikes, including cruise missiles, so that Russian losses could be minimized, although Russian special forces were deployed. Putin was also keen to negotiate some political settlement while ensuring the survival of the regime. The dangers of being drawn into a regional conflict were very real, despite Assad's forces being in the ascendant by mid-2018. The intervention helped expunge memories of failure in 1980s Afghanistan and bolstered Putin's ambitions for Russia to be treated as a global power, more like the former Soviet Union. He had put Assad in a stronger position, cemented better relations with Iran (Assad's other key international ally), and even largely side-lined the US diplomatically. Indeed, partly by making himself a key player in trying to achieve peace in Syria, Putin was able to improve relations with Turkey, a NATO member, despite their very different aims in the conflict, as its increasingly authoritarian President Erdogan was facing criticism from the alliance.

Excluded from multilateral ties with the West, via the G-8 and NRC, Putin focused more on his ambitions for 'Eurasian' co-operation, exploiting Russia's geographic position between the two continents. He made particular progress in building co-operation, on a Eurasian basis, with friendly former members of the USSR, especially Belarus, Kazakhstan, and Kyrgyzstan. Since the mid-1990s, these states, sometimes joined by Tajikistan, had aimed to create a customs union. The five of them created a 'common market' in 2000 and a customs union was created between Russia, Belarus and Kazakhstan in 2010. In May 2014, the three agreed to create a full-scale economic union and by August 2015 this had been joined by Armenia and Kyrgyzstan, with a total population of about 180 million. This was both far smaller and far poorer than the European Union and it did not include political integration, but it was seen by some Western commentators as a step towards recreating a Russian-dominated Eurasian bloc. In Moldova, too, in the wake of the Crimean crisis, Putin could be content that pro-EU parties lost popularity in the November 2014 elections, while the pro-Moscow Socialists became the largest party. Yet, President Obama used his last presidential news conference, in December 2016, to ridicule Putin's great power ambitions, declaring, 'They are a smaller country, they are a weaker country, their country doesn't produce anything that anyone wants to buy, except oil and gas and arms.'[1] Whatever his successes in Syria and despite re-election as President, in 2018 Putin's Russia had dropped out of the top ten world economies. In economic terms, China was much more significant.

B. North Korea's Nuclear Ambitions

When President Bush originally talked of an 'axis of evil' in his 2002 State of the Union address, formed of Iran, Saddam's Iraq, and North Korea, he was referring to the nuclear ambitions of a diverse group of states, with different political systems and ideologies. They did not coordinate their policies, but were bound together by suspicion of the US and by a desire for weapons of mass destruction (WMDs), which might threaten their regions with war. North Korea had already been defined as a 'rogue state' under Clinton in the 1990s, and as a hard-line communist state, had been an opponent of the US since the Korean War of 1950–3. Laying claim to South Korea, it showed signs in the early 1990s of developing a nuclear capacity, with which it might intimidate or attack its neighbour. The US maintained over 30,000 troops as evidence of its determination to defend South Korea. However, the North, under the dictator Kim Jong-Il, was weakened by economic stagnation.

Nevertheless, the North began to reactivate its nuclear facility at Yeongban and, in January 2003, also withdrew from the Non-Proliferation Treaty. In April 2003, the UN Security Council expressed concern over the situation, but that same month US–North Korean talks opened in China, which were expanded in August to include South Korea and the three major East Asian powers—China, Russia, and Japan. In mid-2005, there were signs that mounting economic problems in the North might give South Korea bargaining counters, including food aid and electricity supplies. Only a year later in October 2006, the North successfully tested a nuclear device, leading to UN sanctions, but also to an intensification of diplomatic talks. This produced an apparent settlement, with the Yeongban reactor shutting down in return for energy supplies.

As the Bush presidency ended, there were signs that the nuclear programme was being reinvigorated and the US suspended its energy supplies to the North. Tensions continued into the Obama years, with intermittent threats against the South, alternating with an apparent readiness to talk, until in March 2010, a South Korean warship was sunk. Evidence later suggested that the North was responsible. The US tightened up sanctions but this time, despites economic weaknesses, the North did not back off. Instead, in November, North Korea shelled the island of Yeonpyeong, killing several, which led the South to reply with its own bombardment. The death of Kim Jong-Il in December 2011 was followed by the testing of a ballistic missile, further increasing tension as the long-term direction of North Korean policy remained unpredictable.

Under Kim Jong-un, who was only 26 when he succeeded his father, North Korea remained a highly secretive police state on Stalinist lines, with a personality cult around the leader and the ruthless elimination of any dissident opinion, including numerous government officials and family members who might challenge his power. A UN report in February 2014 suggested there were around 100,000 political prisoners in the North, who faced brutal treatment.

For North Korea's neighbours, however, the key issue remained its nuclear ambitions, especially as it developed the capability to deliver weapons by long-range missiles, with a successful test in December 2012. The North also had hundreds of shorter-range missiles, developed since the 1980s, that could strike American allies like South Korea and Japan. Its third nuclear test, in February 2013, was followed by more UN sanctions, this time with the North's neighbour and sometime protector, China, playing a leading role. An undaunted Kim responded by threatening a nuclear strike on America. Claims he had a hydrogen bomb were generally dismissed in January 2016, but he launched another rocket into space that month.

Further missile firings in March 2017 led the new Trump administration to deploy a missile defence system in South Korea, though this risked antagonising China. While Trump had been critical of China during the 2016 election over the trade imbalance between their two countries, he soon showed an interest, like presidents before him, in encouraging Beijing to pressurize North Korea to give up its nuclear ambitions. A summit meeting between Trump and China's Xi Jinping, in April 2017, proved friendlier than anticipated, but Beijing was unlikely to welcome an American military build-up. While the North depended on China for trade and (in recent famines) emergency food supplies, Kim knew that Beijing was unlikely to relish the collapse of his hard-line communist regime. Such a collapse was most likely to result, either in the unification of all Korea as a pro-Western, capitalist state, or a breakdown of order, perhaps leading to a refugee crisis on China's border. Neither option was desirable to China.

Amid rising tensions and fears there might even be war, on 1 May 2017, Trump announced he would be willing to meet Kim, even though Washington had never recognized North Korea's existence. At this point, South Koreans also elected a new President, Moon Jae-in, who was keen to reduce tension with the North. Kim again showed little desire to compromise, however, launching an intercontinental ballistic missile (ICBM) on 4 July, provocatively timed to coincide with America's Independence Day. Trump, having promised to prevent such a development, then faced some unpalatable options, ranging from further condemnation of the North (a tactic that had achieved nothing in the past) to a war that might cost millions of lives. In early August, following a second ICBM launch, Secretary of State Rex Tillerson made clear that the State Department preferred diplomacy to force, and China proved ready to allow new economic sanctions against North Korea, affecting about a third of its exports. When the North made a massive sixth nuclear test in early September 2017 (large enough to be its long-feared hydrogen bomb) and test-fired two missiles across Japan, the UN toughened sanctions even further. In mid-September, Trump ridiculed Kim as a 'rocket man . . . on a suicide mission' and threatened 'to totally destroy North Korea'; in turn, the North Korean leader dismissed Trump as 'mentally deranged'.[2]

Then, in a surprise move, Kim suddenly offered to open talks with South Korea, and following a summit with the South's President Moon, announced that he was ready to suspend missile tests and meet Trump. This suggested that Kim was trying to do more than drive a wedge between South Korea and the US, but it left open the question of whether sanctions and Chinese diplomatic pressure had finally made him ready to enter meaningful talks or whether he was seeking a propaganda coup. In April 2018, he announced a suspension of nuclear and long-range missile tests, though sceptics pointed out that this could be linked to a reported roof collapse at the North's main nuclear test site. He also met Moon for a summit, even briefly stepping across into South Korea, then released three US citizens imprisoned in the North in more conciliatory moves. But, from the start, there were doubts about whether Kim would really be prepared to 'denuclearize' North Korea unilaterally, as the US hoped, or whether he would seek a mutual military de-escalation on the Korean peninsula, which also affected American forces.

In May 2018, perhaps feeling that his recent concessions had been too one-sided, Kim criticized joint US–South Korean military exercises, and this was used by Trump as an excuse to cancel the proposed summit. However, that same day, North Korea blew up its nuclear test site as a further gesture of goodwill and Moon hastily met Kim for another summit, all of which helped put plans for the summit back on track. The summit duly went ahead on 12 June, in Singapore, and seemed a success, at least as a media event. It was the first time that US and North Korean leaders had met, as such drawing global media attention, and also led to talk of Kim visiting Washington. But the only agreement signed was a vague one, which committed the two sides 'to build a lasting and stable peace regime on the Korean peninsula' and committed North Korea 'to work toward complete denuclearisation of the Korean peninsula'. No timetable for this was provided and no means of verification were agreed, although economic sanctions against the North would remain in place. After the meeting, to the concern of America's other regional allies, Trump said there would be no further joint US–South Korean exercises of the sort that had recently upset Kim. Neither was Kim pressed on his human rights record. Indeed, the North Koreans arguably seemed to get the better deal, being recognized as an equal by the American President in return for making vague promises that went no further than previous, unfulfilled North Korean commitments on nuclear weapons going back to the 1990s. Another winner was China, which had avoided any renewed Korean War on its border and could hope North Korea would remain stable for years to come. South Korea could be happy that Trump and Kim were talking, but not about the American President's concession on military exercises, about which Moon had not been consulted. But, the true significance of Singapore could only be judged by whether it was followed by a real advance towards ending North Korea's nuclear ambitions. Further summits between Trump and Kim in 2019 suggested that progress towards this aim would be slow: a conference in Hanoi, in February, ended prematurely in disagreement; while a further meeting, on the border between North and South Korea, in June, was only brief and could achieve nothing substantial—though it did show that both leaders wished to maintain a dialogue.

C. The Continuing Rise of China: Xi Jinping and Future Prospects

The positive impact on economic growth in the early twenty-first century, under Hu Jintao, with greater access to foreign capital, a more open interaction with the outside world, and increased opportunities for individual gain, had far-reaching consequences for many millions of Chinese and a major impact on international relations. China remained a communist state in social and political terms, with the Chinese Communist Party continuing to exert enough political control to prevent Western ideological values of democracy, freedom of speech, and information being fully accepted by Chinese elites and absorbed into Chinese society. With the advent of Xi, it soon became clear that the new leader intended to ensure that the social and economic forces produced by elements of capitalism would not escape from Communist Party control. While keeping control over domestic opportunities that were posing a challenge for China, it seemed that external opportunities were also arising for a leading Chinese economic role following the financial crisis in the West and the subsequent slow growth and economic recovery. Xi could champion China as the economic leader of globalization in the new interconnected world and consider the values and historical achievements of China in a more assertive international role. Yet despite greater political control there are problems to be faced, not so much in the lack of political freedom, but in the impact of the economic success.

Prime Minister Li was eager to assert closer control over economic policy and ensure that local governments, the main source of fiscal spending, began to aim for lower but more sustainable growth by more environmentally friendly expansion. Yet although this might help overcome the key Chinese challenge of reducing inequality, one main driver of inequality, as in the West, has been the growing financial sector and its liberalization with the 2013 abolition of all restrictions on lending rates. The financial system in China may have been an important contributor to economic growth, but Hu Jintao had been criticized for a hands-off approach, which, by failing to rely on the central organizing role of the Party, opened the door to deregulation and the uncontrolled expansion of credit. Not only did Chinese income per head rise from \$1,293 to \$7,080, or in purchasing power parity terms, from \$3,940 to \$12,205 under Hu, but China's car sales were now one-third of global car sales. Construction of highways, airports, and high-speed rail links also grew along with the doubling of health and education expenditure from 2 per cent of GDP to 4 per cent.[3] One of the problems facing China and Xi is dealing with the consequences of the extent to which this growth has been driven and financed through debt.

There was also still a big gulf between Chinese society, now part of an apparently successful capitalist state experiencing high economic growth rates, and its Western counterparts. These capitalist, democratic societies of North America, Europe, and Japan had enjoyed post-war economic growth until the start of the eighties based on state-influenced market economies and a liberal political ideology. There would be some adaptions required domestically by the Chinese government, given the impact of rapid economic growth on Chinese society, just as the international consequences raised questions, fears, and economic opportunities for the countries of East Asia and the wider world. At stake was the compatibility of an increasingly open economic system operating within a firmly closed political one.

Table 28.1 Top twelve economies in GDP, 2017, in $ trillion (World Bank figures)

USA	$19.39
China	$12.24
Japan	$4.87
Germany	$3.67
UK	$2.62
India	$2.60
France	$2.58
Brazil	$2.06
Italy	$1.93
Canada	$1.65
Russia	$1.58
South Korea	$1.53

Source: World Bank Data 2017, http://databank.worldbank.org/data/download/GDP.pdf.

China's New International Economic Roles

When Xi Jinping succeeded Hu Jintao as General Secretary of the Chinese Communist Party at the end of 2012, he seemed committed to making China an integral part of the world economy, and his embrace of 'globalization' included signing the Paris climate change accords, meeting with leaders of the other BRICS members, developing the 'silk road' initiatives and the Belt and Road Initiative (BRI) first launched in September 2013 as One Belt One Road (OBOR). Xi claimed that the aim for investment and infrastructure projects across Eurasia and beyond, including rail projects, sea routes, and 'economic corridors' was to encourage a process of regional integration. Projects that do not have a rhetorical impact as part of contributing to the grandiose display of Chinese economic influence in Eurasia are intended to impact Asian reality at home. They include high-speed rail links from China to Laos, which has been started with plans to continue via Thailand and Malaysia to Singapore, and rail links in Indonesia from Jakarta to the textile hub of Bandung in Java.

Economic power is always likely to be accompanied by the acquisition of greater international political influence. One key indication of whether or not China intends to use its economic power to challenge and replace the Western-dominated international economic system is its role in international organizations. To some extent, China's success has been based on adopting the values and practices of Western capitalism and its maintenance of that success, which has experienced reduced growth rates of 6 per cent since 2015, depends on accepting its norms, including increasing involvement with international economic institutions. Or China may be seeking to adapt or replace such norms by using economic influence to enhance its prestige and impact in the international economic order.

The BRI has become a headline initiative for incorporating all manner of infrastructure projects financed by direct investment from China and may be the economic project to produce the most grandiose political effects. The scale of it is vast enough to warrant serious consideration, and it has been estimated at between $1 and 5 trillion, compared to the value of the Marshall Plan, which in today's money amounted to $130 billion. The newly created Asian Infrastructure Investment Bank (AIIB) now has 86 member states since it began operating in late 2015 on China's initiative. The UK was a founder member, perhaps in order that the City of London could become the first clearing house for the Yuan[4] outside Asia, and the bank has a registered capital of $100 billion, allowing China to play a greater role in the financing of Asian infrastructure projects. As an addition to the older Asian Development Bank, also involving China, but dominated in capitalization and voting rights by the US and Japan, the AIIB provided another means to assert more Chinese soft power in international finance. These regional actions were designed to invigorate Asian trade and begin developing western areas of China, while extending the country's political influence, especially in Central Asia, as China's economy threatened to overtake that of the United States.

By also accepting that something has to be done at local and international levels to deal with the dramatically poor air quality in major Chinese cities, more self-interested motives indicate a further willingness to work within the Western-dominated international order to solve domestic problems. In addressing the nineteenth Party Congress, Xi announced his attention to focus on pollution and environmental degradation, and China has made the commitment to greenhouse gas reduction and clean energy development targets. Moreover, in 2016 China invested over $78 billion in renewable energy, which was more than the US or the EU, but another area in which the key will be the implementation.

With the increasing contacts with the outside world that were part of the continuing development of global trade links, especially after China joined the WTO in 2001, and with the undervalued exchange rate of the Renminbi, China's balance of payments surplus jumped dramatically, but by 2017 had fallen back from 10 per cent of GDP to 1.4 per cent. While ending its isolation from the rest of the international community, China began to play a more important role in many areas of the less developed world, especially Africa. Other less developed states are also looking to Chinese investors, both public and private, for the first time. The Chinese government has created a large and very significant sovereign wealth fund with the potential to become an important player in international financial markets. All these developments bear witness to the developmental process of Chinese economic growth as China moves from its original role as a low-cost exporter of cheaper manufactures in textiles, toys, and shoes, which now come more from Bangladesh, Vietnam, and Cambodia, to exporting more electrical and mechanical goods. The labour-intensive manufactures, like clothing, formed a mere 16 per cent of Chinese exports in 2016, whereas more advanced technological products constituted some 20 per cent of exports, and less technologically advanced electrical and mechanical goods another 40 per cent of exports.[5] A key environmental threat to continued economic growth, which is specific to China, is the water shortage in the northern regions. The water-intensive coal industry and the leading agricultural centres are predominantly in areas short of water, with most of China's water located in the south. The regions around Beijing contain 120 million people who have less water per head than the inhabitants of Saudi Arabia and, while this in itself is a problem, the key water constraint is the inadequate distribution system, made worse by the large levels of pollution in underground sources.

The consequences of China's greater involvement in international economic affairs have had some important domestic consequences, not least in the realm of governance, with the total control exercised by the Chinese Communist Party (CCP). At the same time, a growing number of businessmen have become involved in informal government roles because of the vital national economic interests that the Communist Party and its institutions have had to take account of. Moreover, new economically important regions of China, with a variety of economic needs, have sought a greater input into national policy.

Political Developments and Governance Changes

The pattern of Chinese government dominated by a single individual leader, exercising power through the Communist Party machine and the role of the People's Liberation Army (PLA) have been changing since the last decade of the twentieth century. The Communist Party has had to confront many more informal contacts with the academic and business communities which have broadened the base of consultation, which in part reflects efforts to alter the state's relationship with the Party as they develop. Under Xi, there have been some important institutional changes, along with the social effects of tighter political controls and the centralization of the operations of the Communist Party.

The future social and institutional challenges became clearer as the Communist Party began strengthening its political control, while economic development was partially freed from the party's shackles. Accommodating the political requirements of the new and rapidly emerging economic elites might fail to maintain the cooperation constructed from the mutual economic benefits acquired by the more affluent members of Chinese and Taiwanese society. Their acceptance of Communist Party controls, as they were integrated into a different Chinese society entering the twenty-first century, had to involve a reconciliation between the traditional elements of Chinese culture and values and the forces of modernization emanating from the West, in both domestic and foreign relations terms.

Of course, many Western observers see the key problem being China's continued lack of real progress towards basic freedoms, liberal democracy, and human rights. As long as Chinese people remain at risk of imprisonment for their political views, the possibility of worsening relations with the West will be present. Both sides may have to restrain their rhetoric on such sensitive issues as human rights to preserve better relations. The dilemma for China is that allowing greater political freedom, including such simple steps as greater access to the internet, may weaken the degree of government control necessary to avoid the more negative repercussions of the dramatic economic change. These concerns may have influenced Hu Jintao's 'Harmonious World' statement of a Chinese vision of the future comprising cooperation to achieve sustainable development, peace, and prosperity. Whether this was more policy than rhetoric is a moot point, but it does point a clear way to cooperation internally, but also more specifically in the external world of foreign relations. The emphasis on a multilateral approach to common security needs, the mutual benefits of economic cooperation on the route to prosperity, the importance of a reformed and more efficient United Nations, and the acceptance of the coexistence of all civilizations, whatever their differences, have not been cast aside by Xi Jinping, rhetoric or not.

Xi Jinping, whose father had been an early member of the Communist Party in the 1920s, but later purged by Mao, had made a steady rise through Chinese government to become a provincial governor, central secretariat member and then, in 2008, Vice-President. He succeeded Hu Jintao as Party General-Secretary late in 2012 and as President in March 2013, and quickly began to tackle one adverse consequence of the growing economy: corruption. Influenced by the importance of bureaucracy under communism, the temptation of senior officials was to use their political positions for financial advantage, otherwise known as graft. Xi's anti-corruption drive led to government inspections targeting corruption among tens of thousands of low-level bureaucrats, but also some high-level figures, including a former potential rival for the presidency, Ling Jinua, who was sentenced to life imprisonment in 2016. Xi, with an emphasis on revived party discipline, also claimed to stand for the rule of law, and along with opening more state-controlled enterprises to competition, took some popular initiatives (such as replacing the 'one-child policy' with a 'two-child policy', making efforts to end poverty, and introducing anti-pollution measures). He also began to change the institutional way Communist Party governance was adapting to a broader range of issues and challenges, which involved a shift away from Hu's preference for collective leadership in favour of a more personal form of rule and a greater degree of central control directed by himself.

A key challenge for Xi Jinping to overcome has been the growing complexity of China's rapidly extending overseas contacts at business and diplomatic levels.[6] Increasing strains are being felt by the Ministry of Foreign Affairs and its relatively small numbers of diplomats. China has fewer diplomats than Australia, a country with less than one-twentieth of the Chinese population and a budget comparable to the western region of China.[7] On the one hand, more engagement with the world of international capitalism had produced an expanded scope of economic interests. On the other hand, despite the business expertise and intellectual awareness that the Communist Party needed to use and develop, there was the requirement to retain control and manage the more mixed economy. Pressures to confront the expanding horizons therefore clashed with the need to narrow the management base embodied in Communist Party governance.

Although much is opaque and uncertain regarding Chinese government structures, in both domestic and foreign policy terms, Xi seems to have tried to distinguish important decisions on strategy and policy and channel them more through himself. While the Ministry of Foreign Affairs was not represented in the crucial seven-member Standing Committee of the Politburo, nor in the full membership of the latter body, Xi (like his predecessor) chairs the Leading Small Group on Foreign Affairs. This Communist Party body, between the Standing Committee and the Ministry of Foreign Affairs, exists alongside the Leading Small Group on Taiwanese Affairs and the Leading Small Group on Military Products Exports, and is a way of centralizing Communist Party power and influence through Xi. More significantly, in November 2013 Xi established the National Security Commission, which seems to have reduced the active roles of the Leading Small Groups. It was designed to coordinate intelligence and security with foreign policy and provide a clearer path through an increasingly fragmented bureaucracy, where decision-making was more difficult in an increasingly complex world.

In March 2018, as the end of Xi's first presidential term approached, China's party-controlled National

People's Congress agreed to abolish the two-term limits on the President that Deng Xiaoping had introduced, allowing Xi to remain in power beyond 2023 and potentially for life. This was criticized by some Western commentators as reflecting a move to greater authoritarianism, accompanied by a Mao-style personality cult. Xi has tightened party discipline and censorship (especially against the projection of Western liberal values) and taken key roles for himself in the foreign policy and military spheres. Security for China primarily involves social control and the maintenance of internal cohesion, an aspect of security policy normally erased from view in Western societies. Xi may be using the vague and non-specific concept of national security, as it is used in the West, but adapted to the Chinese situation with its National Security Commission, to reduce the influence of the Central Military Commission of the Chinese Communist Party and the more hard-line Peoples Liberation Army (PLA), whose influence had already been declining under Hu Jintao. The National Security Commission also represents Xi's continuing development of his personal authority in the party, and a desire to move beyond Hu Jintao and pursue a more assertive foreign policy in the East and South China Seas, while enabling China to project a more active presence onto the world stage.

Military Developments

The recent increase in China's military strength, alongside its remarkable economic growth, has raised the issue of the ultimate goal of increased hard power. Even though China's military power was still, in 2012, much less than that of the US, it could no longer be dismissed, insignificant, as it was in the 1980s. Since Xi Jinping, the increased military capability has increased the advantages China had enjoyed over its East Asian neighbours and reduced the still considerable disparities between its military strength and that of the US. In the early twenty-first century, it was possible to downplay the hard power issues, including the importance of military strength, by arguing that Chinese growth in expenditure and equipment was insignificant in global terms, but this is less plausible under Xi. Yet China's power could still be reconciled with the existing international order without significant revisions of the latter being required, but this is now increasingly questionable. One significant consideration in 2017 was the Chinese unveiling their extremely advanced fifth-generation J20 aircraft, based on the advanced US Stealth aircraft. Technology has become an ever more important component of military strength, and the Chinese have begun to make up the considerable technological gap with the West, and the US in particular. China is now deploying modern advanced aircraft but has a lot of catching up to do before it can achieve parity with the US in acquiring technologically advanced armaments. Significant increases in China's defence budget, however, have also meant a greater proportion of fighters now being capable of attacking ground forces, but China is still some way behind the US in terms of defence expenditure. Meanwhile, the lack of a mid-air refuelling capability limits China's ability to project air power on a global scale. The obvious conclusion is that China remains a long way from challenging the US in terms of air power, but the increased power from projecting that increased military strength in the air on a *regional* basis can no longer be dismissed.

The projection of Chinese naval power, with only one carrier constructed in the former Soviet Union, was clearly limited and China effectively relied on cooperating with US naval power to protect its shipping lanes. But it has now constructed its first fully domestically built carrier, in Shanghai. Completed in 2017, this second Chinese aircraft carrier will bolster the regional significance of Chinese military power, but pales into insignificance by comparison with the eleven operational aircraft carriers of the US navy. As a regional naval power, China has significantly more surface combat ships than Indonesia, giving it regional naval dominance within South East Asia. Again, as with the air force, questions have to be asked as to the purpose of these developments, not least by the Taiwanese. In a future limited conflict with Taiwan, the Chinese navy might be able to blockade the island long enough to give greater credibility to a political confrontation.

The navy has received most attention from the increased defence expenditure and technologically advanced new equipment. In the military field, Chinese benefits originally accrued from its vast population size, but as equipment became less labour-intensive and more dependent on advanced technology, these were reduced. In 2015, as Xi issued a new policy document stating that 'the traditional mentality that land outweighs the sea must be abandoned', the Dongfeng-21 and -26 missiles were unveiled. Obviously directed against the US, these are the world's only anti-ship cruise missiles. Short-range ballistic missiles now form part of China's expanding naval power and also allow China to target US bases on Pacific islands.

Foreign Policy Developments

Historically, foreign humiliations contain possible present dangers with past resentments spilling over into domestic affairs and a dislike of foreigners. They might also influence China's stance on particular disputes and may undermine Hu Jintao's stated 'Harmonious World' goals. Xi's reforms to the structure of communist governance especially with regard to the making of foreign policy may well indicate an important difference between the two leaders of China in the twenty-first century. While this may not mean less emphasis on Hu Jintao's harmonious co-existence of distinct cultures and practices within the common acceptance of capitalist economic values, for some the signs of Xi's desire for a more assertive and controlling role within the Chinese Communist Party inevitably presages a more assertive foreign policy.

With the number of states having diplomatic relations with the People's Republic of China (PRC) trebling since it gained its seat at the UN in 1971, from the outset there were plenty of opportunities for Xi to pursue an active foreign policy, including early visits to Putin in Moscow, in March 2013, and to Obama in California, in June of the same year. The close relationship between the Chinese and Russian presidents was reinforced by strong trade links between them, and a desire to assert their own unique political brands against Western attacks. Putin has his own Eurasian Economic Union of former Soviet republics but has welcomed Xi's BRI initiative and seems willing to play a cooperative economic role in which Russia will play second fiddle to China's greater economic power. At the same time, Xi has avoided any criticism of Putin's assertive policies in Ukraine and Syria. Like Hu Jintao, Xi also seemed to believe that Chinese interests were better served by a positive engagement with America. But relations there have been marred by US complaints of a one-sided trading relationship and accusations of Chinese cyber-attacks and theft of intellectual property; while Xi pressed other Asian states to work together, without relying on other powers (like the US) for defence. Xi's attentions went far beyond the major powers and, in his first two years in office, included trips to Africa, South America, South Asia, and Europe. He also co-operated with US-led economic sanctions against North Korea when these were tightened under President Trump.

This internationalist role on the world stage was matched by interest in a growing regional presence. At the same plenary session of the Central Committee that led to the National Security Commission, China announced the creation of an 'Air Defence Identification Zone' (ADIZ) around areas it claimed in the East China Sea. An ADIZ itself was not unusual: the first had been introduced by America at the time of the Korean War in 1950 and was designed to force aircraft to identify themselves, to show they posed no security threat. Japan, South Korea, and Taiwan also had them. But China's was controversial because it embraced islands that were disputed by South Korea and Japan. South Korea, which disputed Socotra Rock and other islets, expanded its own ADIZ in response to the Chinese action. Differences with Japan focused on the uninhabited island group known as the Senkaku to Japan, which annexed them in 1895, and Diaoyutai to China, which claimed it had ruled them prior to 1895 and that Japan had given up control in 1945. The Chinese ADIZ was criticized by America and other Western powers, but most airlines decided to respect it. In 2016, Japan also complained about Chinese vessels infringing the territorial waters around the islands.

In the South China Sea, Xi followed a rather different line, avoiding the creation of an ADIZ and speaking, in November 2014, of the need to negotiate differences. But he also continued to assert Chinese territorial claims to most of the Sea. Apart from Taiwan, China's claims clashed with Vietnam, Malaysia, Brunei, and the Philippines. The simmering dispute with Vietnam, the Philippines, and Malaysia over the Spratly Islands in the South China Sea, was initially reduced, thanks to a 2002 agreement by the parties to seek a peaceful settlement and the Chinese renunciation of force in 2005. There was also an oil-gas exploration agreement with Vietnam and the Philippines, covering an area of 140,000 square kilometres, another indication of the importance attached to economic development in the region. Then again, the dispute over the scattered Spratly Islands remained unresolved, and there were harsh words between Vietnam and China in mid-2010, with Vietnam—ironically—looking to Washington for support. On this issue, at least, China showed a preference for bilateral talks, presumably because it could exert pressure more easily on this basis. In May 2012, there was a stand-off between Chinese and Philippine naval vessels off Scarborough Shoal, north of the

Spratly Islands and, with a continued Chinese presence in the Shoals, tension there has continued to mount.

Other states beyond the region believed the South China Sea should be treated as international waters, and America regularly sent aircraft and ships there in order to assert the right to freedom of navigation. Part of the problem was that states laid claim not only to what were widely agreed to be islands, but also to outcrops that might be defined as rocks and reefs, but where such a definition could be contested. There were disputes about where traditional fishing grounds lay and competition was intensified by the belief that huge oil and gas reserves lay beneath the Sea. The 1982 UN Convention on the Law of the Sea, which entered into force in 1994, was of limited use in settling these disputes because, apart from the fact that some states (including the US) refused to sign it, it focused on defining rights and responsibilities with regard to recognized territorial waters. The Convention did provide for a tribunal to settle disputes, but when, in 2016, this decided in favour of the Philippines against China, regarding the exploitation of the sea around the Spratly Islands, China refused to recognize the decision. China argued that the question concerned ownership of the islands (on which the UN tribunal refused to adjudicate) rather than sea use, and that it should be settled in bilateral talks with the Philippines.

This dispute drew out all the complexities of attempts to settle maritime disputes: parts of the Philippines case revolved around defining 'rocks' and 'low tide elevations' (as opposed to islands) and to the inexact nature of traditional fishing grounds; while three other governments—Malaysia, Indonesia, Brunei, along with Taiwan—also had a direct stake in the issues. But, China emphasized that it wanted a peaceful settlement of the dispute and the tribunal's decision coincided with the election of a new Philippines President, Rodrigo Duterte, who focused on tackling drugs crime rates at home and wanted to distance his country from its traditional reliance on the US, so that he proved amenable to talks with China. Elsewhere in the South China Sea was more potential for violent clashes: between Taiwan and the Philippines over fishing rights in 2013, between Chinese and Vietnamese vessels over oil drilling near the Paracel Islands in 2014 and, after 2015, between several states (including China) and Indonesia, after the latter introduced a policy of destroying any foreign fishing boats found in its territorial waters. Furthermore, China was accused of taking the lead in militarizing the dispute, because of its decision to build three air bases, by creating concrete islands on reefs in the disputed Spratly Islands, and developing another base (with cruise missiles, as well as fighter aircraft) on Woody Island in the Paracels. The potential for a clash between China and America over the disputed waters was emphasized when, in March 2018, a US aircraft carrier visited Vietnam for the first time since the Vietnam War.

There is no doubt that Xi is keen to defend China's own political system, based around loyalty to the Communist Party, while seeming to want to build mutually beneficial co-operation abroad, but the tensions between the nationalist and internationalist elements of this vision in a more assertive 'new era' are not easy to resolve. The rhetoric of his version of the 'China Dream' and the 'Harmonious World' have to be converted into policies which can be implemented, but they might not easily translate into a peaceful and prosperous global community recognizing, if not embodying, Chinese values. The tension between a conflict-free integration, or a clash of Western and Chinese history and culture is becoming more acute. It is not simply the refusal to undermine the ubiquitous political dominance of the Communist Party's presence in Chinese society which sits uneasily with traditional forms of liberal and neo-liberal capitalism. Nor is there just a simple and straightforward set of options for China between accepting an international position as a status quo power or overthrowing the existing international order. The relationship between the impact of modernity on both the external and internal worlds that China has to continue adapting to is becoming more complex.

Domestic Threats

The rapid economic growth and the partial integration of a Western capitalist system into communist China has led, as in the West, to a considerable expansion of debt, the life blood of any banking system, but in a dramatically expanded financial sector. Yet this is a very recent phenomenon of the past ten years in China, which has seen a rapid rise and increase in the scale of the financial transactions dependent on some form of debt. While debt in China in particular has been a more long-term driver of investment and economic growth, there has been a recent and dramatic increase in the banks' loans to deposit ratios. In sum, China's financial assets and liabilities are now more than five times its GDP, and predictably much of this has occurred away from the four main Chinese banks and in the lightly regulated 'shadow banking' system. Although the debt has arisen not from excessive foreign currency borrowing abroad but from domestic factors, these smaller financial institutions (shadow banks), along with smaller banks, are much more exposed to liquidity risks. As in the West, it is not the size of the debt that is the crux of the problem as much as the ability to bear its burden, which becomes a crisis when more short-term borrowing is prevented by the reluctance of other banks and financial institutions to lend more money to a debtor when the measurement and exact location of the debt become tricky.

The involvement of more individuals in political life, even if only through better provision of, or less limited access to, information, may sow the seeds for a less centralized Communist Party to grow from. On the other hand, the rise of various coordinating groups which wield influence over the party, state, and military organs may increase confusion. China still lacks a well-defined bureaucratic hierarchy and the Politburo's Standing Committee has to rely on a complicated array of civil and military bureaucracies to implement policy, which is itself frequently shifting. Tension also remains between the role of the Politburo's Standing Committee and the informal personal relationships that were becoming more difficult and which Xi's reforms may only partially address. Living standards generally continue to rise, but too much inequality could damage social and political cohesion. In the western provinces, per capita income is only half that of the coastal regions, and in Shanghai in 2016, income was four times as great as in Gansu in north west China. Another problem is the significant exploitation of resources by Chinese industry, which has already produced severe environmental degradation. The limited availability of Chinese skilled labour is becoming more significant as the economy expands and diversifies, and China's huge population size remains a problem. Large numbers of people, many of them still rural dwellers (only in 2012 did statistics suggest that these had become a minority), meant that China's per capita income at the end of the first decade of the twenty-first century was still significantly less than Japan's. If economic growth should stall, problems already evident in the corruption and lack of a social security system that properly protects the sick and those unable to benefit from economic growth are likely to become worse.

The preservation of internal stability within the different ethnic groups in important regions of China has generally been facilitated by maintaining the economic growth able to satisfy increasing numbers of aspiring middle-class Chinese. The bargain between greater access to wealth and limited political freedom may well have to be extended from the extremely wealthy Chinese and the emerging middle classes to more of the rising numbers of urban workers arriving in China's rapidly expanding and increasingly polluted cities. If this economic transformation cannot be achieved, then internal stability may depend on how China's role in East Asia—and its links to the global community—play out. In a worst-case scenario, external historical animosities (between states, nations, individuals, ethnicities, religions, ideologies, or cultures) might be encouraged by the government on the back of economic difficulties at home, or on signs of possible weakness or humiliation abroad, in order to promote a more strident nationalist reaction and provide an alternative focus and justification for more aggressive actions. Less dramatically, if it were perceived that Chinese culture and its place in the world was not being accorded the respect that China's newfound economic strength was deemed to deserve, or that Chinese traditions and history were being trampled over, then the country's positive participation in the international system would face more Chinese questioning. If this is linked to any further conflicts with its regional neighbours, or even eventually with the US, the more China's hard power capabilities catch up with its economic strength, the more the danger will increase.

Even if growth continues, the key internal danger may lie in the combination of growing inequalities of wealth with the failure to extend political freedom. In short, the question is whether gradually rising living standards for the many can compensate for the growing gulf between them and the more successful, privileged few, when political freedom is denied, rather than manipulated, without promoting xenophobic nationalism to act as an alternative focus of attention.

Future Prospects: Regional Stability and Chinese Cooperation with the Western International System?

There are economic advantages and benefits for East Asian elites from increased trade with China and the wealth it produces, especially for those elites facing each other across the Straits of Taiwan. So far, the maintenance of the two-China compromise and acceptance of the existing status quo, in reality if not in rhetoric, however fragile or imperfect it might be, has prevented conflict. This provides support for the bigger, more general argument made especially by those in the PRC, that cooperation will provide benefits for all, domestically and internationally, as China grows. Its adoption of Western capitalism initially helped US imports from East Asia to grow to $263 billion in the decade before 2005, of which China contributed $200 billion. Although this has now led to US measures being taken to try and mitigate this, for the optimists and believers in free trade, the opportunities for peaceful change and growing economic prosperity will eventually resume, and China's integration into the international community will continue to be strengthened.

The idea of an economically powerful China bringing stability, or the idea that a policy of economic integration, regionally and internationally, is being pursued by the PRC government in Beijing, has strong advocates in East Asia. Supporters of the idea focus not only on the constructive and diplomatic way in which China has acted, particularly with regard to regional issues, but also on how China's rise has been perceived and reacted to by its Asian neighbours. The signs of opposition may be starting to appear in the second decade of the millennium, but the remaining positive East Asian acceptance of the economic advantages increased Chinese power brings is likely to have important consequences. Any concomitant association with the gaining of world power status through compromise and cooperation with its regional partners could also assist the successful establishment of better international relations outside East and South East Asia.

For some of these states within the region, especially South Korea, for decades now a capitalist state closely allied to the US, whatever the increase in China's military strength, concerns seem still to be focused more on a revival of Japanese militarism. Korea, after all, was subjected to Japanese occupation between 1895 and 1945, and the treatment of its people still rankles. For other local powers, there is no desire to embrace the US even more closely, especially while there seems little fear of increasing Chinese strength. Economic benefits from improved relations with China and increasing economic interdependence in the region arguably offer more attractive ways forward. A long-term objective of peace and stability may successfully be realized even if there is a risk of it perhaps giving way to some less palatable alternative goals.[8] The prospects may hinge on balancing nationalist pressures with friendly external relations (some of which may be beyond China's control). Preserving tight political control over its own internal affairs, free from external interference, may be reconcilable with a more open and less regulated economy in a globalized financial world. The free movement of capital across national boundaries in such circumstances may coexist with the restricted cross-border flow of information and political ideas. The economic strength of the huge market for goods that China can provide has been a mythological and holy grail for many Westerners at different times in the past, but now it is reachable it should provide encouragement to accept Chinese growth without arousing fears of Chinese military power.

Any tendency to accept a peaceful rise for China has so far been reinforced by its participation in existing international institutions such as the WTO, and both new and existing regional ones. A strategy of upholding regional security and stability as a necessary component of economic development appeared very much on track in 2012, an impression strengthened by its attempts to promote a peaceful resolution of the North Korean nuclear issue (see Chapter 28, B). Under Xi Jinping, China seems determined to avoid any degree of subordination to Washington and to gain recognition of specifically Chinese values and achievements as befitting a civilization now of global economic importance. There are areas of common interest with America to build on, even if relations may have to be based on a mix of cooperation and confrontation. Prior to President Trump there appeared to be key common economic values which would help prevent any escalation into serious threats or challenges to the stability of the existing international system.[9] Moreover, another power political option for stability is the so-called denial strategy,[10] essentially by using demilitarized zones to avoid challenges that China's increased status is now more capable of posing to the US.[11] Tensions could be reduced, even if China still lacks the military capability to successfully respond if there is a reaction to any such challenges and escalation follows. Reducing the risk of conflict in a more neutral area of the South China Sea could enhance Chinese prestige and status by denying the world's leading military power unrestrained access to waterways and air space close to the Chinese border. By such means, the assertion of Chinese power would be replaced by actions reflecting a greater commitment to peace and cooperation that could be interpreted as damaging to Chinese prestige. In so doing, it would also involve the US in accepting a greater reduction of the ability to use or project its military power.

Future External Prospects: Regional Conflict and Alienation from the Western International System?

Aside from Taiwan, the other main problem in successfully implementing China's peaceful integration into the international community stems from the impact of change on Chinese foreign policy. Major social and economic challenges inherent in China's population size could be translated into an aggressive nationalist policy if economic growth falters or is inadequately distributed within Chinese society. In addition, the short-term US reactions to increasing Chinese power and influence could be a critical concern. So far, US policy has been ambiguous, with some in Washington cautiously welcoming the success of Chinese capitalism, while others have remained suspicious and resentful. The scale of further Chinese military acquisitions could be crucial in determining US policy, as could the way China builds up cooperation with potential allies, like Russia (with which joint military exercises were held in 2005). Whether such actions flow from a Chinese desire for greater recognition or from an intention to use force to back more threatening diplomacy, is less important than the perception in Washington of their ultimate aim.

The advent of President Trump and his obsession with trade deficits, particularly with China, along with his protectionist commitment to 'America First' had, by the start of 2018, produced the threat of a tariff war led by an extraordinarily conflictual White House. The resignation of Gary Cohn, the former Chief Operating Officer of Goldman Sachs, who was appointed to be the head of the White House National Economic Council and Trump's Economic Advisor in March 2018, and whose advice on Chinese economic matters was rejected by Trump, opened the door to the tariffs which Cohn and his White House allies had fought to prevent. In August 2018, the first tariffs were imposed on some imported Chinese goods, and a trade war has already escalated as the Chinese have responded, with little or no benefit to either party.

Another source of external danger may lie in US reactions to Xi Jinping's economic initiatives towards Central and South East Asia, the so-called Belt and Road Initiative (BRI). The Central Asian Silk Road (One Belt One Road) is an attempt to tie Central Asia to China's rich industrial East Coast through the building of new transportation links that would enhance the economic integration of the region. It was a response to US Deputy Under-Secretary of State Robert Zoellick's 2005 call for China to become more involved in the region; it was also designed to challenge and supersede Secretary of State Hillary Clinton's wish for a New Silk Road Initiative to boost Afghanistan's regional trade and transportation links. On a visit to Indonesia, Xi followed up his Central Asian initiative by proclaiming a Maritime Silk Road to enhance China's economic ties to its South China Sea neighbours with new ports and fibre-optic communications. In short, the two Belt and Road Initiatives were a bid, using a $40 billion fund and other future Chinese investments, to create a new China-centred economic order in Asia. The BRI was seen as an alternative to the twelve-state Trans Pacific Partnership, originally proposed by Barak Obama, but which Donald Trump later refused to ratify. It was an assertion of China's economic power and increased regional status that required recognition of a distinctive Chinese role, reflecting a greater degree of equality with the US, and one which did not involve hitching the Chinese economy to the US Asia-Pacific bandwagon. The initial reaction of President Trump to Xi's more economically assertive China, may prove to be the major threat to East Asian stability. It seems unlikely that the Trump administration will acquire the necessary sophistication to understand the nature and importance of the economic issues; or have the political inclination to accord China a greater degree of equality in any international sphere recently dominated by the US. It is far more likely they will see China and the US engaged in a zero-sum contest, with a winner and loser in the competition for a single 'Harmonious Asia-Pacific World'.

There are other pitfalls, arising from the relative scarcity of crucial resources in China, notably oil, gas, and water. China has only a quarter of the world's average water resources by country; a 2006 drought affected around 20 million people; and its percentage per capita average oil and gas resources is only just into double figures. The shortage of resources in the country was compounded by the government's initial focus on exports and urbanization, leading to a relative neglect of the domestic market. So far, the Chinese have followed policies which involved the peaceful acquisition of such resources from as far afield as Africa and Australia. China has also recently become a key donor of development aid, and at the end of 2016 the Development Bank and Export Import Bank of China reported making together $675 billion in loans in Asia, Latin America, and Africa.[12] There has been a particular drive to build up relations with Africa since 2006–7. But these efforts seemed to be linked to gaining natural resources, including purchases of agricultural land, and further afield also involve oil deals with Venezuela and Brazil that could amount to a protected trade bloc anathema to the US.

It is easy to portray the significance of East Asian countries financing almost $2 trillion dollars of US debt by 2012 as interdependence that removes any potential problems arising from foreign policy differences. But the future could point in very different directions. As China's hard, military power continues to develop, it may breed opposition from the US and other states. The Pentagon may be suspicious of China's naval and military expansion as keeping at bay those US aircraft carriers that serve as potent symbols of unchallenged US power. Not only do the latest Chinese short-range ballistic missiles carry a threat, but the US can point to the installation of high-frequency radio towers on some of the artificial Chinese islands in the Spratlys,in 2015, and the 2016, positioning of anti-aircraft barriers and fighter aircraft in the Paracels. According to the Centre for Strategic and International Studies, China is on the verge of turning the South China Sea into a Chinese lake. The head of the US Pacific Command commented that one would 'have to believe in a flat Earth' not to grasp that China's goal was to 'achieve hegemony in East Asia'.[13]

In this respect, a problem for the US in a stable East Asia may be the need to accept more Chinese power stemming from different cultural values and approaches to such key political concepts as human rights. But it should also be borne in mind that some of the challenges for the future are shared ones. The question of how to maintain an appropriate balance between the individual benefits provided by capitalism and state-influenced social obligations necessary for political stability may have to be successfully answered both in the liberal democratic America and in communist China for positive connections between the two states to be made. At the time of writing, it seems unlikely that President Trump will be prepared to accept the equality of two different societies with their different political values and traditions, which would be necessary to build on the joined-up economic relationship embodied in the common membership of economic institutions and the large amounts of Chinese investment in US debt. The idea of accepting China as an economically friendly nation has already been rejected by Trump, notwithstanding what he regards as his great personal relationship with Xi, so that arguably the best that can be hoped for in American policy is to avoid increasing economic hostility. Moreover, there is a risk that US leaders will see the question of the growth of Chinese economic and military power and influence in the Asia-Pacific not merely as threatening, but as something too demeaning for the US to accept. It may be that a more multipolar world, if it includes continuing American hegemony in the Asia-Pacific, will ultimately be incompatible with China's peaceful rise.

There are still enormous problems for China to confront. The coordination of economic, military, and maritime affairs may fail, however authoritarian the efforts to overcome the bureaucratic fragmentation become. There is much scope for the growing competition between different bureaucracies and trading interests involving Chinese multilateral corporations eager to escape party control. Or Xi may fall victim to the revenge of the many Chinese officials he has offended with his anti-corruption drive and bureaucratic reforms; or he may fail to ensure that the internet and social media in China are controlled in the same ways that were possible under Hu Jintao. With the increasingly important role of media and communications that enabled Chinese citizens with virtual private networks (VPNs) to access blocked web sites, there are now more efforts to control the flow of information. For the Chinese, the important ability to compete on equal terms with the US in information technology offers opportunities for hackers to gain access to restricted Westerns sites and to be able, should the need arise, to impose considerable damage on important Western systems, affecting such things as power and hospitals. Moreover, ensuring some element of control over accessing information on the internet is a vital part of maintaining the controlling role of the CCP in communist society. Xi's government has invested in technological upgrades to monitor and censor content, and passed laws to punish those who defy the new restrictions. This will do nothing to appease US resentment and suspicion of Chinese government-sponsored cyber-attacks. Xi's attendance at the second World Internet Conference in December 2015 enabled him to emphasize the overriding importance for China of international respect for the rights of individual countries to choose their own path of cyber development.

For Xi, the main security issue is the general maintenance of internal stability and one key future threat is the acute Chinese problem of an aging population, which by 2050 is likely to give it 329 million people over 65 (equal to the entire current population of France, Germany, the UK and Japan combined). By 2050, nearly 37 per cent of the population will be over 60. As young men of working age decline, the Chinese problem of 'getting old before you get rich'[14] will become acute due to the social security system being flooded with pensioners.[15] Although the numbers covered by health care and pensions have significantly increased,apart from migrant workers, the amount of GDP spent in these two areas remains roughly half that spent on average in the West. The consequences of this and the distortions of the 1979–2015 one-child policy will be exacerbated by the reduction in household savings from more elderly people and the decline in the numbers of the working age population to support the elderly, which can only be compensated by increased immigration. Thus, the rate of investment and tax revenues will decline as the demands on public expenditure increase, with a significant impact on the rate of economic growth, which is already slowing down. China's eagerness to play a role in international organizations may therefore be linked to the limited time available to Xi to benefit from rapid Chinese economic growth before decline and social crises begin. Attempting to play a strong, but cooperative international economic role from a crumbling social base does not augur well for the future.

In a society still influenced by traditional non-Western values, there is additionally Xi's growing aspiration to compensate for China's inadequate past status and secure more international recognition, through greater acceptance of the distinctive achievements of Chinese civilization and its past mistreatment by the West. His political thoughts[16] include the promise of a 'Chinese approach to solving the problems of mankind', meaning it will be incumbent for those seeking global peace and prosperity to adopt more Chinese values as they accept a less modest role for China in international affairs. More than for other countries, the complexity of the interplay in China between the domestic and the international, epitomized by the emotive issue of Taiwan, remains a key challenge for the changing communist bureaucracy to overcome. The traditional context of hierarchy and control in Chinese society has to be brought into the modern world without destroying it. This new China contains the similar ambivalence between rhetoric and the reality which will be influenced by how China responds to regional events and confronts the increasingly erratic international policies of the US.

D. Conclusion: The Uncertain International Future and Economics and Geopolitics in the Rise of Asia

In the twenty-first century dominated by the increasing economic strength and geo-political influence of a capitalist China controlled by its Communist Party, the old-world order dominated by the US, and once challenged by a Soviet Union, which itself disintegrated a quarter of a century ago, has disappeared. With the leaders of both China and the US proclaiming pivots or tilts to Asia and the East, the predominance of Europe and its Atlantic links to a hegemonic US are over. The fault lines in the Eurozone, and the stresses of the European Union, exacerbated by the emotive decision of a majority of the British people to leave the Union behind, have cleared the way to a future with a more important place for Asia in general, and China in particular. It may be that neither cooperation nor conflict will be the clear outcomes of future Chinese policy, which remains clouded in obscurity and ambiguity. The consequences of the economic rise of China are, therefore, likely to remain a key component of the age of uncertainty which the new millennium has produced.

There are signs that the changing balance of global economic power contains positive elements of stability from Chinese economic growth in developing a more Asian-based international economic order that will modify and stabilize capitalism. But there are also indications that implementing the prevalent ideological form of capitalism favoured in the West will help spread disorder and conflict much further afield than the areas bordering Europe. China itself contains a variety of economic and political contradictions and weaknesses that have been made worse by the speed of economic growth. China is now the world's largest exporting nation, with 15 per cent of the world's exports, and the hub of a global and regional system that provides the imports of energy, raw materials, and food that it depends on. As in the West, the older, less innovative industries like coal and steel have had problems adapting to the new modernity and led to a build-up of excess capacity. The BRI might alleviate the problem of 'dumping' steel in international markets, which is an important component of President Trump's condemnation of China's unfair practices. This has already begun a Sino-US tariff war and even if the other geopolitical corollaries of economic power do not begin to play decisive roles in the BRI, or compete more directly with the US in the Asia-Pacific region, there are some disturbing possibilities.

Rivalry with India, the only power refusing to attend the 2017 Belt and Road Forum in Beijing, has historical roots, and the sense of mistrust has pervaded discussions with the US, Japan, and Australia on a four-way foreign economic policy strategy as an alternative to the BRI. The danger is the development of economic rivalry extending into geopolitical hostility and US steel tariffs have already been extended beyond China, while after Chinese retaliation more imported Chinese goods are subject to them. Obama's 2013 pivot to Asia, according to Michael Green a former national security official, was driven by a 'reluctance to tolerate any other power establishing exclusive hegemonic control over Asia or the Pacific'.[17] A major concern therefore about the impact of China's rise on international relations is how growing Chinese economic power is perceived as affecting geopolitics in Asia, and the prestige of the existing regional hegemon. If an ill-informed and emotive maverick were to be at the helm in the White House, the concerns about stability or escalating conflict would be all the greater.

The uncertainty about the future of a changing international system, and the unprecedented nature of many of its unstable and rapidly changing economic components, is perhaps epitomized by Xi's China. The precise nature of his apparently more assertive regime is impossible to determine accurately, even for mandarin speakers, but it symbolizes the two sides of a coin embodying the rhetoric and the realities of global power. There are some clear and positive possibilities inherent in China's rise and the global tilt to the East. Yet there are equally some negative and ominous signs arising from such unprecedented changes. As the focus of attention shifts eastwards, the economically and politically successful developed nations of the northern hemisphere, which form the West on both sides of the Atlantic, appear to be facing difficulties and decline.

It all began in a Eurasian context with the collapse of the Soviet Union, which then led to the West almost snatching ideological defeat out of the jaws of victory with the near collapse of global capitalism's entire financial system. In the wake of the crash, unlike communism, the failed neo-liberal economic system has stumbled through a troubled period of austerity without significant changes. In this altered American and European world, the old ideological pillars have crumbled. Much of the European Left embraced neo-liberalism as many workers in the old heavy industries of raw material production and manufactures faced an uncertain future devoid of opportunities for a better material life and facing increased impoverishment. Both in America and Europe, increased economic and social divisions were developing out of the heightened inequality and opening the doors to a new form of politics in which the ideological certainties of the Cold War that had dominated political life were disappearing. A new form of populism was now emerging over much of Europe which pointed the blame at foreigners, or those from different ethnic or religious groups, and even those generally outside the boxes of ideological conformity which the right-wing media deemed acceptable to reside in.

Internationally, the forces of globalization, technological advance, and new electronic means of communication provided windows of opportunity with which to view a greater variety of different cultures and experiences, but they were increasingly only viewed through the lenses of sound bites and superficiality that social media provides for a manipulative media to exploit. Meanwhile, the West struggles to maintain democratic capitalist societies, which now reserve most of their vast economic benefits for a small, privileged minority. At the individual and international levels, the values which underpinned the dominance of the West and its hegemonic national power are waning. International law fails to be respected and the international society of states as proclaimed by the English School of International Relations can no longer restrict the horrific scale of the violence and humanitarian crises in the Middle East. As the West's soft power wanes, it nevertheless has opportunities far more attractive than the destruction, alienation, and poverty produced by the developmental failures of capitalist societies in much of the less developed world. Both Europe and North America are faced with the problems of mass migration from the South in the more interconnected world.

At the same time, a new economic power is rising on a tide of shifting economic currents in the East with greater self-confidence and a different political ideology, partly encouraged by the international economic failures in the West. The new China is full of contradictions and potential internal conflicts, as its involvement with the international system increases. Still lacking in Joseph Nye's soft power, its full international impact, with a strange blend of economic capitalism and political totalitarianism, remains uncertain. Given the fall of Soviet communism and the emaciation of the Left in its European heartlands by the economic forces of neo-liberalism, the socio-economic landscape in which states and individuals define their international relations cannot remain unaffected,by the growth of uncertainty.

The decades that followed the end of the Cold War and the collapse of Soviet power witnessed the removal of all the checks and constraints preventing the excesses of individualism and economic exploitation in the West. The ideological victory of democratic capitalism ended the hopes and fears that had given impetus to the unity achieved across international borders in order to protect values, however flawed, that were under threat and met more universal human needs. The fear of something more harmful to the elites in the capitalist democracies of the West had contributed to the maintenance of a form of capitalism with more generous social and economic provision for the less fortunate. This had been the political cost of social unity in the West paid for through accepting the portrayal of a militaristic, expansionist Soviet Union, threatening the use of force against the West rather than the actual threat of social and political change offered by left-wing ideas. The first challenges to this legacy of World War II in the West were quickly followed in the next decade by Gorbachev's ideological *volte face* and the ill-considered economic triumphalism of the ideologues of democratic capitalism. During the final years of the last millennium, the arrogant overestimation of the transformative power of capitalism, if freed of all constraints and allied only with democracy, ensured individuals and states witnessed international armed conflicts and genocide in several continents through a haze of rhetoric often referred to as 'liberal interventionism'. As the rhetoric began to obscure the reality, and emboldened, but increasingly blinded, by ideology, the US and its allies began to apply military force to international relations. With scant attention to international law, invasions and military force were aimed at creating internationally what appeared as the only remaining socio-political system viable in all national circumstances. Opponents deemed 'bad', dangerous, or unworthy were to be eliminated as terrorists or supporters of terrorism, as a small minority in reality became all three. Meanwhile, 'free markets' were sold as providing all the economic answers and resolving the urgent social questions without the millstones of government to contend with. National and international agencies of states, so the argument goes, would increasingly stand aside in line with neo-liberal ideology and enable market forces to do their benign work through the skills and entrepreneurship of private non-state actors.

The scale of these illusions has now been revealed by the damage, some of it irreparable in the foreseeable future, that the application of these forces has produced. The lack of understanding of the circumstances in which they could possibly be applied, or the likely consequences of their application, has destabilized areas of the globe, especially in the Middle East, to a catastrophic extent. One effect has been that the West, and the US in particular, has been much less willing to attempt to mould the international system, or any of its members, through armed interventions. In keeping with the mistaken ideology that in economic and political terms only views the state through the lens of negativity, the importance of non-state actors especially in the conduct of terrorist activities, which ironically the leading ideologues in the West initially sought to eliminate through armed force, significantly increased in the twenty-first century's second decade.

Yet the consequences of a flawed Western ideology have run much deeper than the flaws of communism, whose leading state once sought equality more than hegemony within an international framework. The scale of the genocide in Myanmar, the enormous humanitarian crisis caused by Saudi Arabia and the Houthi rebels in Yemen, and the systematic killing of thousands of civilians in Syria, including through the extensive and repeated use of chemical weapons (particularly chlorine gas) to drive out those living in rebel areas (resulting in almost 1,000 Syrian towns and villages now being devoid of people) has intensified, producing a mass exodus of people. The West's leading role in the international system was under threat, morally and ideologically, whilst the economic success of China brings a blend of a political and economic ideology incorporating one valued component of Western life and one that was completely anathema to it.

As the comparative decline of the West continues and the international system has to deal with more of its failures, the need for ideological justifications to be provided increases. As in the Cold War, there is again the need to sell the values and benefits of the West's socio-economic system internationally, albeit no longer amongst newly emerging independent states, while strengthening domestic support for a much-changed form of capitalism. In such difficult circumstances, we are already seeing ideology driving the importance of rhetoric and spin as it supersedes reality in the West. This development is clear, not just in foreign policy and the portrayal of its implementation, but in many aspects of domestic life from education to building regulations.

In the East, while it appears that the international importance of China and Asia can only increase, a more in-depth study reveals dangers that may well be more significant than the opportunities, both domestically and internationally for China. Questions and uncertainties arise as to whether its continued military growth can maintain the regional acceptance of a peaceful China as the dominant East Asian force. Problems could easily arise over Taiwan and Japanese acceptance of a more important China. But the major questions concern a potential Chinese global role, rather than an enhanced regional one, which runs the risk of undermining the prestige of the US under a president unable or unwilling to acquire knowledge of China or East Asia, and distinctly averse to accepting advice on such matters. Already displaying a readiness to challenge China economically, the dangers of confrontation over trade, intellectual property, and information technology escalating are real.

Like in the West, the dominance of rhetoric over reality is also becoming clearer in China. The outcomes that might result are more difficult to predict, as would be expected in any less open society, but there are enormous contradictions to overcome in the goals of Chinese economic policy, in addition to the limited nature of the domestic political arena in which it operates. Moreover, the problems of Chinese capitalism may develop in the same way as its Western counterpart did, despite the efforts of the state to prevent the removal of all the regulations that limit the excesses of financial capital. Or problems could arise from either the failure or the success of the Renminbi in becoming a reserve currency. In both the political and economic dimensions of the international system, a new alignment of forces has emerged, and while the precise nature of some remains obscure, what is very clear is the increased uncertainty surrounding their possible consequences.

Visit the online resources that accompany this book to test your understanding and take your learning further: www.oup.com/he/young-kent3e

NOTES

1. https://obamawhitehouse.archives.gov/the-press-office/2016/12/16/press-conference-president
2. www.theguardian.com/us-news/2017/sep/19/donald-trump-threatens-totally-destroy-north-korea-un-speech www.theguardian.com/world/2017/sep/22/a-rogue-and-a-gangster-kim-jong-uns-statement-on-trump-in-full
3. George Magnus, *Red Flags: Why Xi's China is in Jeopardy* (Yale University Press, New Haven CT, 2018), 51.
4. The Yuan and the Renminbi are the equivalent in currency terms of pounds and sterling.
5. George Magnus, *Red Flags: Why Xi's China is in Jeopardy* (Yale University Press, New Haven CT, 2018), 54, 98–9.
6. The number of counties China has diplomatic relations with has tripled in size since it gained the 'China seat' in the UN in 1971: Miles Lampton, 'Xi Jinping and the National Security Commission', *Journal of Contemporary China*, 24 (2015), 762.
7. Kerry Brown *China's World* (I. B. Tauris, London, 2017), 43.
8. For example, using force to settle a dispute in the South China Sea, using force against Taiwan, detaining Western agents or businessmen, carrying out cyber-attacks, which it is now able to do in order to paralyse important service providers in the west.

9. As put forward by Ze Zicheng, *Inside China's Grand Strategy: The Perspective from the People's Republic* (University Press of Kentucky, KY, 2011), 3–5.
10. See Steven Brooks and William Wolforth, *America Abroad: The United States Role in the 21st Century* (Oxford University Press, New York 2016), for a modification of Michael Caine's suggestion of making the South China Sea a buffer and preventing US aircraft and ships using it to project power.
11. The challenges might be to a US navy ship in international waters or waters claimed by the Chinese; buzzing of US planes; diplomatic challenges to avoid particular actions; holding of US agents/diplomats as spies.
12. www.brookings.edu/blog/order-from-chaos/2017/05/08/yes-china-is-investing-globally-but-not-so-much-in-its-belt-and-road-initiative as cited in George Magnus, *Red Flags: Why Xi's China is in Jeopardy* (Yale University Press, New Haven CT, 2018), 177.
13. Karen Young, 'Beijing's Actions in South China Sea Aimed at Hegemony US Admiral Says', *Washington Post*, 23 February 2016.
14. In Western countries, the numbers of people over 60 roughly doubled to 24 per cent of the population in the 60 years ending in 2015, when per capita income was $41,000. In China, that doubling to 25 per cent is likely to take place over the 20 years to 2030 (because of past birth rates), but per capita income in 2015 was less than one-third, hence the getting old before you become rich.
15. See 'China's Achilles Heel: A Comparison with America Reveals a Deep Flaw in China's Model of Growth', *Economist*, 21 April 2012; Mark Haas 'A Geriatric Power: The Future of US Power in a World of Aging Populations', *International Security*, 32(1) (2007); all cited in Howard W. French, *Everything under the Heavens: How the Past Helps Shape China's Push for Global Power* (Vintage Books, New York, 2017), 274–81.
16. Xi Jinping, *The Governance of China* (Foreign Language Press, Beijing, 2014) contains his main statements on foreign policy issues.
17. Michael Green, *By More than Providence: Grand Strategy and American Power in the Asia Pacific since 1783* (Columbia University Press, New York, 2017).

Bibliography

The aim of this bibliography is to enable wider reading in a way that covers interpretation and introduces new material, rather than to provide an in-depth list of books containing basic information. There is no intention of making this a comprehensive bibliography.

General Works

For overall analyses of the period see:

Antony Best, Jussi Hanhimaki, Joseph Maiolo, and Kirsten Schulze, *International History of the Twentieth Century and Beyond* (Routledge, London, 2008).

David Reynolds, *One World Divisible: A Global History since 1945* (Allen Lane, Penguin Press, London, 2001).

And for a comprehensive discussion of the Cold War:

Melvyn Leffler and Odd Arne Westad (eds), *The Cambridge History of the Cold War* (three volumes, Cambridge University Press, 2010).

On theories of the Cold War:

Allen Hunter (ed.), *Rethinking the Cold War* (Temple University Press, Philadelphia, 1998).

Richard N. Lebow and Thomas Risse-Kappen (eds), *International Relations Theory and the End of the Cold War* (Columbia University Press, New York, 1995).

Odd Arne Westad (ed.), *Reviewing the Cold War: Approaches, Interpretations, Theory* (Frank Cass, London, 2000).

For general Cold War surveys:

Simon J. Ball, *The Cold War: An International History 1947–1999* (Arnold, London, 1998).

Michael Dockrill and Michael Hopkins, *The Cold War, 1945–91* (Palgrave Macmillan, Basingstoke, 2005).

John L. Gaddis, *The Cold War* (Penguin, London, 2007).

Walter LaFeber, *America, Russia and the Cold War, 1945–2000* (9th edn, McGraw-Hill, New York, 2002).

Melvyn Leffler, *For the Soul of Mankind: The US, the Soviet Union and the Cold War* (Hill and Wang, New York, 2007).

Wilfried Loth, *Overcoming the Cold War: A History of Détente, 1950–91* (Palgrave, London, 2002).

Mike Sewell, *The Cold War* (Cambridge University Press, 2002).

Odd Arne Westad, *The Cold War: A World History* (Allen Lane, London, 2017)

On Vietnam:

Mark Lawrence, *The Vietnam War: A Concise International History* (Oxford University Press, Oxford, 2010).

Robert McMahon (ed.), *Major Problems in the History of the Vietnam War* (2nd edn, D. C. Heath, Lexington, 1995).

James S. Olson and Randy Roberts, *Where the Domino Fell: America and Vietnam, 1945–95* (2nd edn, St Martin's Press, New York, 1996).

Kevin Ruane, *War and Revolution in Vietnam, 1930–75* (University College London, London, 1998).

Vivienne Sanders, *The USA and Vietnam, 1945–75* (Hodder, London, 2007).

On armaments and military strategy:

J. D. Boutwell (ed.), *The Nuclear Confrontation in Europe* (Croom Helm, London, 1983).

Nathan Busch, *No End in Sight: The Continuing Menace of Nuclear Proliferation* (University of Kentucky Press, Lexington, 2004).

David Ford, *The Button: The Pentagon's Strategic Command and Control System* (Simon & Schuster, London, 1985).

Jonathan Haslam, *The Soviet Union and the Politics of Nuclear Weapons in Europe, 1969–1987* (Macmillan, Basingstoke, 1989).

David Holloway, *The Soviet Union and the Arms Race* (Yale University Press, New Haven, 1984).

Nina Tannenwald, *The Nuclear Taboo: The US and the Non-Use of Nuclear Weapons since 1945* (Cambridge University Press, Cambridge, 2007).

Marc Trachtenberg, *History and Strategy* (Princeton University Press, Princeton, 1991).

On the Eastern bloc:

A. Kemp-Welch, *Poland under Communism* (Cambridge University Press, Cambridge, 2008).

Vojtech Mastny and Malcolm Byrne (eds), *Cardboard Castle? An Inside History of the Warsaw Pact* (Central European University Press, Budapest, 2005).

Kevin McDermott and Matthew Stibbe (eds), *Revolution and Resistance in Eastern Europe: Challenges to Communist Rule* (Berg, Oxford, 2006).

Robert Service, *Comrades: Communism, a World History* (Pan, London, 2008).

Geoffrey and Nigel Swain, *Eastern Europe since 1945* (2nd edn, Macmillan, Basingstoke, 1995).

Z. A. B. Zeman, *The Making and Breaking of Communist Europe* (2nd edn, Basil Blackwell, Oxford, 1991).

On China:

Jonathan Fenby, *The Penguin History of Modern China: The Fall and Rise of a Great Power, 1850–2009* (Penguin, London, 2009).

Chen Jian, *Mao's China and the Cold War* (University of North Carolina Press, Chapel Hill, 2001).

John Keay, *China: A History* (Harper, London, 2009).

Rana Mitter, *A Bitter Revolution: China's Struggle with the Modern World* (Oxford University Press, Oxford, 2004).

And on its key political leaders in the Cold War:

Jung Chang and Jon Haliday, *Mao: The Unknown Story* (Cape, London, 2005).

Maurice Meisner, *Mao Zedong* (Polity Press, London, 2007).

Kuo-Kang Shao, *Zhou Enlai and the Foundations of Chinese Foreign Policy* (St Martin's Press, New York, 1996).

Gao Wenqian, *Zhou Enlai* (Public Affairs, New York, 2007).

On European integration:

Desmond Dinan (ed.), *Origins and Evolution of the European Union* (Oxford University Press, 2006).

Geir Lundestad, *Empire by Integration: The US and European Integration, 1945–97* (Oxford University Press, Oxford, 1997).

John W. Young, *Britain and European Unity, 1945–99* (Macmillan, London, 2000).

On Europe as a whole:

Tony Judt, *Postwar: A History of Europe since 1945* (Vintage, London, 2010).

John W. Young, *Cold War Europe, 1945–91* (Edward Arnold, London, 1996).

On the Arab–Israeli Conflict and the Middle East:

Peter Mansfield and Nicholas Pelham, *A History of the Middle East* (Penguin, London, 2004).

Adeed Dawisha, *Arab Nationalism in the Twentieth Century* (Princeton University Press, Princeton, 2003).

Rashid Khalidi, *The Iron Cage: The Palestinian Struggle for Statehood* (Beacon, Boston, 2006).

Douglas Little, *American Orientalism: The US and the Middle East since 1945* (University of North Carolina Press, New Haven, 2002).

Benny Morris, *Righteous Victims: A History of the Zionist–Arab Conflict* (John Murray, London, 1999).

Avi Shlaim, *The Iron Wall: Israel and the Arab World* (Allen Lane, London, 2000).

Mark A. Tessler, *A History of the Israeli–Palestinian Conflict* (Indiana University Press, Bloomington, 1994).

On Latin America in general:

Leslie Bethell (ed.), *The Cambridge History of Latin America* (Cambridge University Press, Cambridge, 1994).

Peter Calvert, *The International Politics of Latin America* (Manchester University Press, Manchester, 1994).

Benjamin Keen and Keith Haynes, *A History of Latin America* (6th edn, Houghton Mifflin, Boston, 2000).

More specifically on US policy towards Latin America:

Greg Grandin, *Empire's Workshop: Latin America, the US and the Rise of the New Imperialism* (Metropolitan Books, New York, 2005).

Henry Raymont, *Troubled Neighbours: The Story of US–Latin American Relations from FDR to the Present* (Westview, Boulder, 2005).

Peter Smith, *Talons of the Eagle: Dynamics of US–Latin American Relations* (Oxford University Press, Oxford, 2000).

On international economic issues:

Robert Brenner, *The Economics of Global Turbulence, 1945–2005* (Verso, London, 2006).

Barry Eichengreen, *The European Economy since 1945* (Princeton University Press, Princeton, 2007).

Derek K. Fieldhouse, *The West and the Third World* (Blackwell, Oxford, 1999).

James Foreman-Peck, *A History of the World Economy* (Harvester Wheatsheaf, London, 1995).

J. A. Frieden, *Global Capitalism: Its Fall and Rise in the Twentieth Century* (Norton, New York, 2006).

On the end of Empire:

British Documents on the End of Empire, Series A, vol. 2, R. Hyam (ed.), *The Labour Government and the End of Empire* (Stationery Office, London, 1992).

British Documents on the End of Empire, Series A, vol. 3, D. Goldsworthy (ed.), The Conservative *Government and the End of Empire, 1951–1957* (Stationery Office, London, 1994).

British Documents on the End of Empire, Series A, vol 4, Ronald Hyam and W. Roger Louis (eds), *The Conservative Government and the End of Empire, 1957–1964* (Stationery Office, London, 2000).

British Documents on the End of Empire, Series B, vol. 1, R. Rathbone (ed.), *Ghana* (Stationery Office, London, 1992).

British Documents on the End of Empire, Series B. vol. 4, John Kent (ed.), Egypt and the Defence of the *Middle East, 1945–1956* (Stationery Office, London, 1998).

John Darwin, *Britain and Decolonisation* (Macmillan, Basingstoke, 1988).

John D. Hargreaves, *African Decolonisation* (Longman, London, 1996).

Robert F. Holland, *European Decolonization 1918–1981* (Macmillan, Basingstoke, 1985).

Ronald Hyam, *Britain's Declining Empire: The Road to Decolonization, 1918–1968* (Cambridge University Press, Cambridge, 2006).

On the US, the Cold War, and the less developed world:

Mark Berger, *The Battle for Asia: From Decolonization to Globalization* (Routledge, London, 2005).

Peter Hahn and Mary Ann Heiss (eds), *Empire and Revolution: The United States and the Third World since 1945* (Ohio State University Press, Colombus, 2001).

Robert J. McMahon, *The Limits of Empire: The US and South-East Asia since World War II* (Columbia University Press, New York, 1999).

Odd Arne Westad, *The Global Cold War: Third World Interventions and the Making of our Times* (Cambridge University Press, Cambridge, 2005).

On US foreign policy:

Stephen Ambrose and Douglas Brinkley, *Rise to Globalism: American Foreign Policy since 1938* (9th edn, Penguin, London, 2010).

John Dumbrell, *American Foreign Policy: Carter to Clinton* (Palgrave Macmillan, Basingstoke, 2003).

John L. Gaddis, *Strategies of Containment: A Critical Appraisal of American National Security Policy during the Cold War* (2nd edn, Oxford University Press, 2005).

Steven Hook and John Spanier, *American Foreign Policy since World War II* (19th edn, Congressional Quarterly, Washington, 2012).

Richard A. Melanson, *American Foreign Policy since the Vietnam War: The Search for Consensus from Richard Nixon to George W. Bush* (4th edn, M. E. Sharpe, Armonk, 2005).

On Soviet foreign policy:

Sven Holtsmark, Iver B. Neumann, and Odd Arne Westad (eds), *The Soviet Union and Europe in the Cold War 1945–1989* (Macmillan, Basingstoke, 1994).

Caroline Kennedy-Pipe, *Russia and the World, 1917–91* (Arnold, London, 1998).

Vladimir M. Zubok, *The Failed Empire: The Soviet Union in the Cold War from Stalin to Gorbachev* (University of North Carolina Press, Chapel Hill, 2007).

On Japan and the US occupation and reconstruction:

W. LaFeber, *The Clash: A History of US–Japan Relations* (W. W. Norton & Co., New York, 1997).

Ray Moore and Donald Robinson, *Partners for Democracy: Crafting the Japanese State under MacArthur* (Oxford University Press, Oxford, 2002).

M. Schaller, *The American Occupation of Japan: The Origins of the Cold War in Asia* (Oxford University Press, Oxford, 1985).

And, on the Arab–Israeli conflict:

Avi Shlaim, *The Iron Wall: Israel and the Arab World* (Penguin, London, 2001).

Charles D. Smith, *Palestine and the Arab–Israeli Conflict: A History with Documents* (7th edn, Palgrave Macmillan, Basingstoke, 2010).

Mark A. Tessler, *A History of the Israeli–Palestinian Conflict* (2nd edn, Indiana University Press, Bloomington, 2009).

Part I, 1945–53

Students who wish to read a general account of the origins of the Cold War from an orthodox or traditional post-revisionist perspective should sample one of the following:

John L. Gaddis, *The United States and the Origins of the Cold War 1941–1947* (Columbia University Press, New York, 1972).

Randall B. Woods and H. Jones, *Dawning of the Cold War: The United States Quest for Order* (University of Georgia Press, Athens; London, 1991).

Those wishing to evaluate revisionist or non-orthodox post-revisionist works should look at:

Melvyn P. Leffler, *A Preponderance of Power. National Security, the Truman Administration and the Origins of the Cold War* (Stanford University Press, Stanford, 1992).

T. McCormick, *America's Half Century: US Foreign Policy in the Cold War and After* (2nd edn, Johns Hopkins University Press, Baltimore, 1995).

Thomas G. Paterson, *On Every Front: The Making and Unmaking of the Cold War* (W. W. Norton, New York, 1992).

On the issue of whether the Cold War was primarily about power or about ideology and culture:

John L. Gaddis, 'The Emerging Post-Revisionist Synthesis on the Origins of the Cold War', and Responses to Gaddis, *Diplomatic History*, 7(3) (1983).

Michael Hunt, *Ideology and Foreign Policy* (Yale University Press, New Haven, 1987).

Howard Jones, Randall B. Woods et al., 'The Origins of the Cold War: A Symposium', *Diplomatic History*, 17(2) (1993), and the commentaries by E. Rosenburg, A. Stephanson, and B. Bernstein.

Cold War writing in the West has often been confined to a set of assumptions such as an expansionist Soviet Union, the idea of containment, or the influence of communism as a crusading ideology, and has assessed the Cold War in terms of who was most to blame. In terms of these standard parameters three books deserve particular mention for challenging them:

Sarah Jane Corke, *US Covert Operations in the Cold War Strategy: Truman, Secret Warfare and the CIA* (Routledge, London, 2007).

Scott Lucas, *Freedom's War: The US Crusade against the Soviet Union, 1945–1956* (Manchester University Press, Manchester, 1999).

Gregory Mitrovich, *Undermining the Kremlin: America's Strategy to Subvert the Soviet Bloc 1947–1956* (Cornell University Press, Ithaca, 2000).

On the tensions in the Grand Alliance that developed in 1945 and early 1946:

J. L. Gormly, *The Collapse of the Grand Alliance 1945–1948* (Louisiana State University Press, Baton Rouge, 1987).

John Kent, *British Imperial Strategy and the Origins of the Cold War 1944–1949* (Leicester University Press, Leicester; New York, 1993).

Robert L. Messer, *The End of an Alliance* (University of North Carolina Press, Chapel Hill, 1982).

On Cold War economic policy:

Michael J. Hogan, *The Marshall Plan: America, Britain, and the Reconstruction of Western Europe, 1947–1952* (Cambridge University Press, Cambridge, 1987).

Ian Jackson, *The Economic Cold War: America, Britain and East–West Trade, 1948–63* (Palgrave, Basingstoke, 2001).

R. A. Pollard, *Economic Security and the Origins of the Cold War 1945–1950* (Columbia University Press, New York, 1985).

On post-war atomic issues:

Gregg Herken, *The Winning Weapon: The Atomic Bomb in the Cold War 1945–1950* (Knopf, New York, 1980).

David Holloway, *Stalin and the Bomb: The Soviet Union and Atomic Energy 1939–1956* (Yale University Press, New Haven, 1994).

Frank Kaplan, *The Wizards of Armageddon* (Simon & Schuster, New York, 1983).

Specifically on the dropping of the first atom bombs:

Gar Alperowitz, *The Decision to Use the Atomic Bomb* (Fontana, London, 1996).

Tsuyoshi Hasegawa, *Racing the Enemy: Stalin, Truman and the Surrender of Japan* (Harvard University Press, Cambridge, 2005).

Samuel Walker, *Prompt and Utter Destruction: Truman and the Use of the Atomic Bombs against Japan* (University of North Carolina Press, Chapel Hill, 2004).

On NATO and militarization:

John Kent and John W. Young, 'Britain the Third Force and the Origin of NATO: In Search of a New Perspective', in B. Heuser and R. O'Neill (eds), *Securing Peace in Europe* (Macmillan, London, 1992).

John Kent and John W. Young, 'The Western Union Concept and British Defence Planning 1947–48', in Richard J. Aldrich (ed.), *British Intelligence Strategy and the Cold War* (Routledge, London, 1992).

Timothy P. Ireland, *Creating the Entangling Alliance* (Aldwych Press, London, 1981).

Ernest R. May (ed.), *American Cold War Strategy; Interpreting NSC-68* (Bedford Books of St Martin's Press, Boston, 1993).

On the crises in the Middle East and the Mediterranean:

Jamil Hasanli, *At the Dawn of the Cold War: The Soviet–American Crisis over Iranian Azerbaijan* (Rowman & Littlefield, Lanham, 2006).

John Kent, *British Imperial Strategy and the Origins of the Cold War 1944–1949* (Leicester University Press, Leicester; New York, 1993).

Bruce Kuniholm, *The Origins of the Cold War in the Near East* (Princeton University Press, Princeton, 1980).

L. L'Estrange Fawcett, *Iran and the Cold War: the Azerbaijan Crisis of 1946* (Cambridge University Press, Cambridge; New York, 1992).

E. Mark, 'The War Scare of 1946 and its Consequences', *Diplomatic History*, 21(3) (1997).

On the Soviet actions in Eastern Europe:

Caroline Kennedy-Pipe, *Russia and the World 1917–1991* (Arnold, London, 1998).

Vojtech Mastny, *Russia's Road to the Cold War* (Columbia University Press, New York, 1979).

Vojtech Mastny, *The Cold War and Soviet Insecurity: The Stalin Years* (Oxford University Press, New York, 1996).

N. Naimark and L. Gibianskii (eds), *The Establishment of Communist Regimes in Eastern Europe 1944–1949* (Westview, Oxford, 1997).

Vladimir Zubok and Konstantin Pleshakov, *Inside the Kremlin's Cold War from Stalin to Khrushchev* (Harvard University Press, Cambridge, 1996).

Specifically, on the personality of Stalin:

Simon Sebag Montefiore, *Stalin: The Court of the Red Tsar* (Phoenix, London, 2007).

Robert Service, *Stalin: A Biography* (Pan, London, 2010).

On Western Europe:

William Hitchcock, *France Restored, 1944–54* (University of North Carolina Press, Chapel Hill, 1998).

Alan Milward, *The European Rescue of the Nation-State* (2nd edn, Routledge, New York, 1992).

Alan Milward, *The Reconstruction of Western Europe, 1945–1951* (Methuen, London, 1984).

John W. Young, *France, the Cold War and the Western Alliance 1944–1949* (Leicester University Press, Leicester, 1990).

On the German question:

Carolyn Eisenberg, *Drawing the Line: The American Decision to Divide Germany 1944–1949* (Cambridge University Press, New York, 1996).

Spencer Mawby, *Containing Germany: Britain and the Arming of the Federal Republic* (St Martin's Press, New York, 1997).

On Palestine and the Middle East:

William Roger Louis, *The British Empire in the Middle East 1945–1951: Arab Nationalism, the United States, and Postwar Imperialism* (Clarendon, Oxford, 1984).

Mark A. Tessler, *A History of the Israeli–Palestinian Conflict* (Indiana University Press, Bloomington, 1994).

On the Iranian crisis:

J. A. Bill, *The Eagle and the Lion: The Tragedy of American–Iranian Relations* (Yale University Press, New Haven, 1989).

M. J. Gasiorowski, *Mohammad Mossadeq and the 1953 Coup in Iran* (Syracuse University Press, Syracuse, 2004).

For US intelligence and subversion:

Richard J. Aldrich, *The Hidden Hand: Britain, America and Cold War Secret Intelligence* (John Murray, London, 2001).

Christopher Andrew, *For the President's Eyes Only: Secret Intelligence and the American Presidency from Washington to Bush* (HarperCollins, New York, 1995).

Rhodri Jeffreys-Jones, *The CIA and American Democracy* (2nd edn, Yale University Press, New Haven, 1999).

Tim Weiner, *Legacy of Ashes: The History of the CIA* (Doubleday, New York, 2007).

For Soviet intelligence and subversion:

Christopher M. Andrew and O. Gordievsky, *KGB: The Inside Story* (Hodder & Stoughton, London, 1990).

Christopher M. Andrew and Vasily Mitrokhin, *The Mitrokhin Archive: The KGB in Europe and the West* (Allen Lane, London, 1999).

J. T. Richelson, *Sword and Shield: Soviet Intelligence and Security Service Operations* (Ballinger, Cambridge, 1986).

On China and Korea and the nature of East Asian problems not defined in terms of a Soviet–US global confrontation:

S. N. Goncharov, J. W. Lewis, and Xue Litai, *Uncertain Partners. Stalin, Mao and the Korean War* (Stanford University Press, Stanford, 1993).

Chen Jian, *China's Road to the Korean War* (Colombia University Press, New York, 1994).

Chen Jian, 'The Myth of America's "Lost Chance" in China', *Diplomatic History*, 21(1) (1997).

William Stueck, *The Korean War: An International History* (Princeton University Press, Princeton, 1995).

William Stueck, *Rethinking the Korean War* (Princeton University Press, Princeton, 2002).

Odd Arne Westad, 'Losses, Chances and Myths: The United States and the Creation of the Sino-Soviet Alliance, 1945–1950', *Diplomatic History*, 21(1) (1997).

Shen Zhihua, 'Sino-Soviet Relations and the Origins of the Korean War: Stalin's Strategic Goals in the Far East', *Journal of Cold War Studies*, 2(2) (2000).

Part II, 1953–63

On Eisenhower:

Stephen E. Ambrose, *Eisenhower, vol. 2, The President, 1952–1969* (Allen & Unwin, London, 1984).

Robert R. Bowie and Richard Immerman, *Waging Peace: How Eisenhower Shaped an Enduring Cold War Strategy* (Oxford University Press, Oxford, 1998).

Robert Divine, *Eisenhower and the Cold War* (Oxford University Press, New York, 1981).

Saki Dockrill, *Eisenhower's New Look National Security Policy* (Macmillan, London, 1996).

Kenneth Osgood, *Total Cold War: Eisenhower's Secret Propaganda Battle at Home and Abroad* (University of Kansas Press, Lawrence, 2006).

On Churchill and early ideas of détente:

Klaus Larres, *Churchill's Cold War* (Yale University Press, New Haven, 2002).

John W. Young, *Winston Churchill's Last Campaign: Britain and the Cold War, 1951–5* (Clarendon Press, Oxford, 1996).

On Khrushchev:

Aleksandr Fursenko and Timothy Naftali, *Khrushchev's Cold War* (Norton, New York, 2006).

William Taubman, *Nikita Khrushchev: The Man and his Era* (Norton, New York, 2003).

W. J. Thompson, *Khrushchev: A Political Life* (Macmillan, Basingstoke, 1995).

Vladimir Zubok and Konstantin Pleshakov, *Inside the Kremlin's Cold War from Stalin to Khrushchev* (Harvard University Press, Cambridge, 1996).

On Kennedy, with important material on the crises he faced:

Nigel Ashton, *Kennedy, Macmillan and the Cold War* (Palgrave Macmillan, Basingstoke, 2002).

Michael Beschloss, *Kennedy v. Khrushchev: The Crisis Years, 1960–1963* (Faber & Faber, London, 1991).

Robert Dallek, *An Unfinished Life: John F. Kennedy* (Little, Brown, Boston, 2003).

Lawrence Freedman, *Kennedy's Wars* (Oxford University Press, Oxford, 2000).

James Giglio, *The Presidency of John F. Kennedy* (University of Kansas Press, Lawrence, 2006).

There are some interesting articles on the Kennedy years in:

Diane B. Kunz (ed.), *The Diplomacy of the Crucial Decade American Foreign Relations during the 1960s* (Columbia University Press, New York, 1994).

Thomas G. Paterson (ed.), *Kennedy's Quest for Victory* (Oxford University Press, New York, 1989).

Mark White (ed.), *Kennedy: The New Frontier Revisited* (Macmillan, Basingstoke, 1998).

A crucial element when studying the Cold War period is to ensure that works are read that base their analyses on distinguishing between Cold War and hot war. The campaign against the Soviet Union and communism on the one hand, and communism's support for and involvement in revolutionary movements on the other, were different from the attempts to avoid the catastrophe of hot war and to resolve US–Soviet disputes. For material relevant to this:

Kenneth A. Osgood, 'Form before Substance: Eisenhower's Commitment to Psychological Warfare and Negotiations with the Enemy', *Diplomatic History*, 24(3) (2000).

David Tal, 'Eisenhower's Disarmament Dilemma: From Chance for Peace to Open Skies Proposal' in *Diplomacy & Statecraft*, 12(2) (2001).

On European issues between the two protagonists:

Andreas Daum, *Kennedy in Berlin* (Cambridge University Press, Cambridge, 2007).

John Lewis Gaddis, *We Now Know: Rethinking Cold War History* (Clarendon Press, Oxford, 1997).

Jeffrey Giauque, *Grand Designs and Visions of Unity: The Atlantic Powers and the Reorganization of Western Europe, 1955–63* (University of North Carolina Press, Chapel Hill, 2002).

Erin Mahan, *Kennedy, de Gaulle and Western Europe* (Palgrave, New York, 2002).

M. Trachtenberg, *A Constructed Peace: The Making of the Europe Settlement 1945–1963* (Princeton University Press, Princeton, 1999).

Pascaline Winand, *Eisenhower, Kennedy and the United States of Europe* (Macmillan, Basingstoke, 1993).

On Eastern European problems:

Charles Gati, *Failed Illusions: Moscow, Washington and the 1956 Hungarian Revolt* (Stanford University Press, Redwood City, 2006).

Mark Kramer, 'The Soviet Union and the 1956 Crises in Hungary and Poland: Reassessments and New Findings', *Journal of Contemporary History*, 33(2) (1998).

Mark Kramer, 'The Early Post-Stalin Succession Struggle and Upheavals in East-Central Europe: Internal–External Influences in Soviet Policy Making', *Journal of Cold War Studies*, 1(1–3) (1999).

Christian F. Ostermann, 'The United States, the East German Uprising of 1953 and the Limits of Rollback', Working Paper 11, CWIHP (1994).

Alexsandr Stykalin, 'The Hungarian Crisis of 1956: The Soviet Role in the Light of New Archival Documents', *Cold War History*, 2(1) (2001).

On armaments:

F. Kaplan, *The Wizards of Armageddon* (Simon & Schuster, New York, 1983).

Andreas Wenger, *Living with Peril Eisenhower: Kennedy and Nuclear Weapons* (Rowman & Littlefield, Lanham, 1997).

On the Suez Crisis and the Middle East:

British Documents on the End of Empire, Series A, vol. 4, R. Hyam and Wm. Roger Louis (eds), *The Conservative Governments 1957–1964* (Stationery Office, London, 1998).

British Documents on the End of Empire, Series B, vol. 4, J. Kent (ed.), *Egypt and the Defence of the Middle East, 1945–1956* (Stationery Office, London, 1998).

Keith Kyle, *Suez* (Weidenfeld & Nicolson, London, 1991).

W. S. Lucas, *Divided We Stand: Britain, the US and the Suez Crisis* (Hodder & Stoughton, London, 1991).

On US policy towards the Middle East:

Warren Bass, *Support any Friend: Kennedy's Middle East and the Making of the US–Israeli Alliance* (Oxford University Press, 2002).

Salim Yaqub, *Containing Arab Nationalism: The Eisenhower Doctrine and the Middle East* (University of North Carolina Press, New Haven, 2004).

On Latin America for the contrasts and similarities between the policies of Eisenhower and Kennedy:

Stephen G. Rabe, *Eisenhower and Latin America: The Foreign Policy of Anti-Communism* (University of North Carolina Press, Chapel Hill, 1988).

Stephen G. Rabe, 'Controlling Revolutions: Latin America the Alliance for Progress and Cold War Anti-Communism', in T. G. Paterson (ed.), *Kennedy's Quest for Victory* (Oxford University Press, New York, 1989).

Stephen G. Rabe, *The Most Dangerous Area in the World. John F. Kennedy Confronts Communist Revolution in Latin America* (University of North Carolina Press, Chapel Hill, 1999).

For details of the CIA coup in Guatemala:

Richard H. Immermann, *The CIA in Guatemala: The Foreign Policy of Intervention* (University of Texas Press, Austin, 1982).

E. Kinzer and S. Schlesinger, *Bitter Fruit: The Untold Story of the American Coup in Guatemala* (Doubleday, Garden City, 1982).

On the Berlin crises:

H. M. Catudal, *Kennedy and the Berlin Crisis* (Berlin Verlag, Berlin, 1980).

David G. Coleman, 'Eisenhower and the Berlin Problem 1953–1954', *Journal of Cold War Studies*, 2(1) (2000).

On China, the Sino-Soviet split, and the offshore islands:

G. H. Chang, *Friends and Enemies: The US, China, and the Soviet Union, 1948–72* (Stanford University Press, Stanford, 1990).

Lorenz Luthi, *The Sino-Soviet Split* (Princeton University Press, Princeton, 2008).

Sergey Radchenko, *Two Suns in the Heavens: The Sino-Soviet Struggle for Supremacy* (Woodrow Wilson Centre, Washington, 2009).

Robert S. Ross and Jiang Changbin (eds), *Re-Examining the Cold War. US–China Diplomacy 1954–1973* (Harvard University Press, Cambridge, 2001).

Odd Arne Westad (ed.), *Brothers in Arms: The Rise and Fall of the Sino-Soviet Alliance 1945–1963* (Woodrow Wilson Center Press, Stanford, 1998).

In general, on the struggle in the so-called 'third world':

Kathryn Statler and Andrew Johns (eds), *The Eisenhower Administration, the Third World and the Globalization of the Cold War* (Rowman & Littlefield, Lanham, 2006).

On the Cuban Missile Crisis:

Graham Allison and Philip D. Zelikov, *Essence of Decision* (2nd edn, Longman, New York, 1999).

Michael Dobbs, *One Minute to Midnight* (Knopf, New York, 2008).

Max Frankel, *High Noon in the Cold War* (Presidio, New York, 2004).

Ernest R. May and Philip D. Zelikov, *The Kennedy Tapes inside the White House during the Cuban Missile Crisis* (Harvard University Press, Cambridge, 1997).

Sheldon Stern, *The Week the World Stood Still* (Stanford University Press, Redwood City, 2004).

For a focus on Cuba and the Soviet perspective:

Bruce J. Allyn, J. G. Blight, and David A. Welch, 'Essence of Revision: Moscow, Havana and the Cuban Missile Crisis', *International Security*, 14(3), 136 (1989/90).

Barton J. Bernstein, 'Reconsidering Khrushchev's Gambit—Defending the Soviet Union and Cuba', *Diplomatic History*, 14(2) (1990).

P. Brenner, 'Thirteen Months: Cuba's Perspective on the Missile Crisis', in James A. Nathan (ed.), *The Cuban Missile Crisis Revisited* (St Martin's Press, New York, 1992).

Alexsandr Furschenko and Timothy Natfali, *'One Hell of a Gamble': Khrushchev, Castro and Kennedy 1958–1964* (Norton, New York, 1992).

For details and debate:

B. J. Bernstein, 'The Cuban Missile Crisis: Trading the Jupiters in Turkey?', *Political Science Quarterly*, 95(1) (1980).

James G. Hershberg, 'Before the "Missiles of October": Did Kennedy Plan a Military Strike against Cuba?', *Diplomatic History*, 14(2) (1990).

R. N. Lebow, 'Domestic Politics and the Cuban Missile Crisis', *Diplomatic History*, 14(4) (1990).

For details of the early years of the Vietnam conflict:

David L. Anderson, *Trapped by Success: The Eisenhower Administration and Vietnam, 1953–1961* (Columbia University Press, New York, 1991).

Cheng Guan Ang, *Vietnamese Communists' Relations with China and the Second Indochina Conflict, 1957–1962* (McFarland, Jefferson, 1997).

Mark Lawrence and Fredrik Logevall (eds), *The First Vietnam War* (Harvard University Press, Cambridge, 2007).

John M. Newman, *JFK and Vietnam: Deception. Intrigue, and the Struggle for Power* (Warner, New York, 1992).

Stein Tonnesson, *Vietnam 1946: How the War Began* (University of California Press, Los Angeles, 2011).

James Waite, *The End of the First Indochina War: An International History* (Routledge, London, 2012).

On the US attitudes to the end of the European Empires and the African crises, which were important under Kennedy:

C. Fraser, 'Understanding American Policy Towards the Decolonization of European Empires, 1945–64', *Diplomacy & Statecraft*, 3(1) (1992).

M. Kalb, *The Congo Cables: The Cold War in Africa—from Eisenhower to Kennedy* (Macmillan, New York, 1982).

John Kent, *America, the UN and Decolonisation Cold War Conflict in the Congo* (Routledge, London, 2010).

R. D. Mahoney, *JFK: Ordeal in Africa* (Oxford University Press, New York, 1983).

Part III, 1963–71

For archive-based books on the Johnson administration:

H. W. Brands, *The Wages of Globalism: Lyndon Johnson and the Limits of American Power* (Oxford University Press, New York, 1995).

W. I. Cohen and Nancy B. Tucker (eds), *Lyndon Johnson Confronts the World American Foreign Policy 1963–1968* (Cambridge University Press, New York, 1994).

Thomas Schwartz, *Lyndon Johnson and Europe* (Harvard University Press, Cambridge, 2003).

Much of this period is dominated by the escalation of the Vietnam War and subsequent US defeat:

David M. Barrett, *Uncertain Warriors: Lyndon Johnson and his Vietnam Advisers* (University Press of Kansas, Lawrence, 1993).

Larry Berman, *Lyndon Johnson's War* (Norton, New York, 1989).

Larry Cable, *Unholy Grail: The US and the Wars in Vietnam, 1965–8* (Routledge, New York, 1991).

Lloyd C. Gardner, *Pay any Price: Lyndon Johnson and the Wars for Vietnam* (Ivan R. Dee, Chicago, 1995).

Gerard J.de Groot, *A Noble Cause? America and the Vietnam War* (Pearson, Harlow, 2000).

George C. Herring, *LBJ and Vietnam: A Different Kind of War* (University of Texas Press, Austin, 1994).

Michael H. Hunt, *Lyndon Johnson's War: America's Cold War Crusade in Vietnam, 1945–1965* (Hill & Wang, New York, 1996).

David Kaiser, *American Tragedy: Kennedy, Johnson, and the Origins of the Vietnam War* (Harvard University Press, Cambridge, 2000).

Fredrick Logevall, *Choosing War* (University of California Press, Berkeley, 1999).

Robert S. McNamara, *In Retrospect* (Times Books, New York, 1995).

Marilyn B. Young, *The Vietnam Wars, 1945–90* (HarperCollins, New York, 1991).

On the Chinese and Soviet sides:

Ilya Gaiduk, *The Soviet Union and the Vietnam War* (Ivan R. Dee, Chicago, 1996).

Ilya Gaiduk, *Confronting Vietnam* (Stanford University Press, Redwood City, 2003).

Qiang Zhai, *China and the Vietnam Wars, 1950–75* (University of North Carolina Press, Chapel Hill, 2000).

On Nixon and Vietnam:

Jeffrey Kimball, *Nixon's Vietnam War* (University of Kansas Press, Kansas, 1999).

William Shawcross, *Sideshow: Kissinger, Nixon and the Destruction of Cambodia*. (1st edn, Simon & Schuster, New York, 1987, 1979).

For the increasing involvement of the superpowers in the Middle East and how this interacted with the regional and domestic situations:

Nigel Ashton (ed.), *The Cold War in the Middle East: Regional Conflict and the Superpowers, 1967–73* (Routledge, London, 2007).

M. N. Barnett and J. S. Levy, 'Domestic Sources of Alliances and Alignments: The Case of Egypt, 1962–73', *International Organization*, 45(3) (1991).

G. Golan, *Soviet Policies in the Middle East: From World War II to Gorbachev* (Cambridge University Press, Cambridge, 1990).

Laura James, *Nasser at War* (Palgrave, Basingstoke, 2006).

Michael Oren, *Six Days of War: June 1967 and the Making of the Modern Middle East* (Oxford University Press, Oxford, 2002).

William B. Quandt, *Decade of Decisions: American Policy towards the Arab–Israeli Conflict, 1967–76* (University of California Press, Berkeley, 1977).

Yezid Sayigh and Avi Shlaim (eds), *The Cold War and the Middle East* (Clarendon Press, Oxford, 1997).

For details of how participants saw the nature of Soviet–US relations:

Anatoly Dobrynin, *In Confidence* (Random House, New York, 1995).

Dean Rusk, *As I Saw It* (Norton, New York, 1990).

For an overview:

Peter G. Boyle, *American–Soviet Relations* (Routledge, London, 1993).

For the US opening to China and its background:

Chen Jian and David Wilson, 'New Evidence on the Sino-American Opening', *Cold War International History Project Bulletin*, 11 (Winter 1998).

Yang Kuisong, 'The Sino-Soviet Border Clash of 1969', *Cold War History*, 1(1) (August 2000).

On Latin America:

Walter LaFeber, *Inevitable Revolutions: The US in Central America* (2nd edn, Norton, New York, 1993).

Abraham Lowenthal, *The Dominican Intervention* (Johns Hopkins University Press, Baltimore, 1995).

On the Cold War in other parts of the less developed world:

Matthew Jones, *Conflict and Confrontation in South East Asia, 1961–1965: Britain, the United States, Indonesia and the Creation of Malaysia* (Cambridge University Press, Cambridge, 2002).

On the Prague Spring in 1968:

James G. McGinn, 'The Politics of Collective Inaction: NATO's Response to the Prague Spring', *Journal of Cold War Studies*, 1(3) (Fall, 1999).

William Shawcross, *Dubček* (Hogarth Press, London, 1990).

Kenneth K. Skoug, *Czechoslovakia's Lost Fight for Freedom* (Praeger, Westport, 1999).

On transatlantic relations, détente, and integration in Europe:

Stephen R. Ashton, *In Search of Détente* (Macmillan, Basingstoke, 1989).

F. Bozo, *Two Strategies for Europe: de Gaulle, the United States and the Atlantic Alliance* (Rowman & Littlefield, Lanham, 2001).

James Ellison, *The US, Britain and the Crises in Tansatlantic Relations, 1963–68* (Palgrave, Basingstoke, 2007).

Pieres Ludlow, *The European Community and the Crises of the 1960s* (Routledge, London, 2006).

Piers Ludlow (ed.), *European Integration and the Cold War: Ostpolitik–Westpolitik, 1965–73* (Routledge, London, 2007).

Jan van der Harst, *Beyond the Customs Union: The European Community's Quest for Completion, 1969–75* (Nomos, Baden, 2008).

Part IV, 1972–80

The essential text for these years is still:

Raymond Garthoff, *Détente and Confrontation: American–Soviet Relations from Nixon to Reagan* (2nd edn, Brookings, Washington, 1994).

Memoirs from some key US players are particularly rich in this period. On the Nixon–Ford administrations:

Henry Kissinger, *The White House Years* (Little, Brown, Boston, 1979).

Henry Kissinger, *Years of Upheaval* (Little, Brown, Boston, 1982).

Henry Kissinger, *Years of Renewal* (Simon & Schuster, New York, 1989).

Richard Nixon, *RN: The Memoirs of Richard Nixon* (Grosset & Dunlap, New York, 1978).

And on the Carter years:

Zbigniew Brzezinski, *Power and Principle: Memoirs of the National Security Adviser, 1977–81* (Farrar, Strauss & Giroux, New York, 1983).

Jimmy Carter, *Keeping Faith: Memoirs of a President* (Collins, London, 1982).

Cyrus Vance, *Hard Choices: Critical Years in American Foreign Policy* (Simon & Schuster, New York, 1983).

On the Soviet side, the essential memoirs are:

Anatoly Dobrynin, *In Confidence: Moscow's Ambassador to Six Cold War Presidents, 1962–86* (Times Books, New York, 1995).

Andrei Gromyko, *Memories* (Hutchinson, London, 1989).

There are also a number of good, detailed studies on the Nixon–Kissinger years:

Jonathan Aitken, *Nixon: A Life* (Weidenfeld & Nicolson, London, 1995).

William Bundy, *A Tangled Web: The Making of Foreign Policy in the Nixon Presidency* (I. B. Tauris, New York, 1998).

Jussi Hanhimaki, *The Flawed Architect: Henry Kissinger and American Foreign Policy* (Oxford University Press, Oxford, 2004).

Walter Isaacson, *Kissinger: A Biography* (Faber & Faber, London, 1992).

Jeremy Suri, *Henry Kissinger and the American Century* (Harvard University Press, Cambridge, MA, 2007).

Richard Thornton, *The Nixon–Kissinger Years* (Paragon, New York, 1989).

On the Carter administration see especially:

John Dumbrell, *The Carter Presidency* (Manchester University Press, Manchester, 1993).

Burton I. and Scott Kaufman, *The Presidency of James Earl Carter* (2nd edn, University of Kansas Press, Lawrence, 2006).

Gaddis Smith, *Morality, Reason and Power: American Diplomacy in the Carter Years* (Hill and Wang, New York, 1986).

Robert Strong, *Working in the World: Jimmy Carter and the Making of American Foreign Policy* (Louisiana State University Press, Baton Rouge, 2000).

Richard Thornton, *The Carter Years: Towards a New Global Order* (Pentagon, New York, 1991).

Valuable studies of Soviet foreign policy include:

Richard Anderson, *Public Politics in an Authoritarian State: Making Foreign Policy during the Brezhnev Years* (Cornell University Press, Ithaca, 1993).

Edwin Bacon and Mark Sandle (eds), *Brezhnev Reconsidered* (Palgrave, Basingstoke, 2002).

Robin Edmonds, *Soviet Foreign Policy: The Brezhnev Years* (Oxford University Press, Oxford, 1983).

Harry Gelman, *The Brezhnev Politburo and the Decline of Détente* (Cornell University Press, Ithaca, 1984).

Adam B. Ulam, *Dangerous Relations: The Soviet Union in World Politics, 1970–82* (Oxford University Press, Oxford, 1983).

On the theme of détente, its rise, and decline:

Mike Bowker and Phil Williams, *Superpower Détente: A Reappraisal* (Sage, London, 1988).

Robert Litwak, *Détente and the Nixon Doctrine* (Cambridge University Press, Cambridge, 1984).

Richard Pipes, *US–Soviet Relations in the Era of Détente* (Westview Press, Boulder, 1981).

Richard Stevenson, *The Rise and Fall of Détente* (Macmillan, London, 1985).

Jeremy Suri, *Power and Protest: Global Revolution and the Rise of Détente* (Harvard University Press, Cambridge, 2003).

John van Oudenaren, *Détente in Europe* (Duke University Press, Durham, 1991).

Odd Arne Westad, *The Fall of Détente* (Oslo University Press, Oslo, 1997).

But for a focus on European détente:

Kenneth Dyson (ed.), *European Détente: Case Studies in the Politics of East–West Relations* (Pinter, London, 1986).

Vojtech Mastny, *Helsinki, Human Rights and European Security* (Duke University Press, Durham, 1986).

Daniel Thomas, *The Helsinki Effect: International Norms, Human Rights and the Demise of Communism* (Princeton University Press, 2001).

And the continuing Sino-American rapprochement is analysed in:

Evelyn Goh, *Constructing the US Rapprochement with China* (Cambridge University Press, Cambridge, 2005).

William Kirby et al. (eds), *The Normalization of US–China Relations* (Harvard University Press, Cambridge, 2005).

Robert Ross, *Negotiating Co-Operation: The US and China, 1969–89* (Stanford University Press, Stanford, 1995).

On the continuing problems of Indochina:

Ben Kiernan, *The Pol Pot Regime: Race, Power and Genocide in Cambodia* (Yale University Press, New Haven, 1996).

Jeffrey Kimball, *Nixon's Vietnam War* (Kansas University Press, Lawrence, 1998).

Odd Arne Westad and Sophie Quinn-Judge (eds), *The Third Indochina War: Conflict between China, Vietnam and Cambodia, 1972–79* (Cass, London, 2006).

On the 1973 war and its aftermath in the Middle East:

Anwar el-Sadat, *In Search of Identity* (Collins, London, 1978).

William Quandt, *Camp David: Peacemaking and Politics* (Brookings, Washington, 1986).

Kenneth Stein, *Heroic Diplomacy: Sadat, Kissinger, Carter, Begin and the Quest for Arab–Israeli Peace* (Routledge, New York, 1999).

On the Civil War in Lebanon:

Farid el-Khazen, *The Breakdown of the State in Lebanon* (Harvard University Press, Cambridge, 2000).

Robert Fisk, *Pity the Nation* (Deutsch, London, 1990).

While, on the Iranian revolution and its impact:

James Bill, *The Eagle and the Lion* (Yale University Press, New Haven, 1988).

Richard Cottam, *Iran and the United States: A Cold War Case Study* (University of Pittsburgh Press, Pittsburgh, 1988).

Shireen Hunter, *Iran and the World* (Indiana University Press, Bloomington, 1990).

Nikki Keddie, *Modern Iran* (Yale University Press, New Haven, 2003).

Charles Kurzman, *The Unthinkable Revolution in Iran* (Harvard University Press, Cambridge, 2004).

Kenneth Pollack, *The Persian Puzzle: The Struggle between Iran and America* (Random House, New York, 2004).

Barry Rubin, *Paved with Good Intentions: The American Experience and Iran* (Oxford University Press, New York, 1990).

And on the Cold War's impact on Africa in the 1970s:

Piero Gleijeses, *Conflicting Missions: Havana, Washington and Africa* (University of North Carolina Press, Chapel Hill, 2002).

Donna Jackson, *Jimmy Carter and the Horn of Africa* (McFarland, Jefferson, 2007).

Norrie McQueen, *The Decolonisation of Portuguese Africa* (Longman, London, 1997).

Robert Patman, *The Soviet Union in the Horn of Africa* (Cambridge University Press, Cambridge, 1990).

On the advances in strategic arms control in these years:

John Newhouse, *Cold Dawn: The Story of SALT* (Holt, Rinehart & Winston, New York, 1973).

Strobe Talbott, *Endgame: The Inside Story of SALT II* (Harper & Row, New York, 1979).

Part V, 1981–9

Essential memoirs for these years are:

Mikhail Gorbachev, *Memoirs* (Doubleday, New York, 1996).

Ronald Reagan, *An American Life* (Hutchinson, London, 1991).

Eduard Shevardnadze, *The Future Belongs to Freedom* (Sinclair-Stevenson, London, 1991).

George Shultz, *Turmoil and Triumph* (Scribners, New York, 1993).

Margaret Thatcher, *The Downing Street Years* (HarperCollins, London, 1993).

In general, on the Cold War in the 1980s:

Olav Njolstad (ed.), *The Last Decade of the Cold War* (Cass, London, 2004).

The period of the so-called 'Second Cold War' of 1980–5 is discussed in:

Noam Chomsky, Jonathan Steele, and John Gittings, *Superpowers in Collision: The New Cold War of the 1980s* (Penguin, Harmondsworth, 1984).

Fred Halliday, *The Making of the Second Cold War* (Verso, London, 1986).

William G. Hyland, *Mortal Rivals: Superpower Relations from Nixon to Reagan* (Random House, New York, 1987).

Strobe Talbott, *Deadly Gambits: The Reagan Administration and the Stalemate in Arms Control* (Pan, London, 1985).

An essential, contemporary work that fuelled ideas of relative US decline was:

Paul Kennedy, *The Rise and Fall of the Great Powers* (Fontana, London, 1989).

While, on the end of the Cold War in 1985–90, see especially:

Michael Beschloss and Strobe Talbott, *At the Highest Levels: The Inside Story of the End of the Cold War* (Little, Brown, Boston, 1993).

Saki Dockrill, *The End of the Cold War Era* (Bloomsbury Academic, London, 2005).

John L. Gaddis, *The United States and the End of the Cold War* (Oxford University Press, Oxford, 1992).

Raymond Garthoff, *The Great Transition: American–Soviet Relations and the End of the Cold War* (Brookings Institution, Washington, 1994).

Mark Kramer, 'The Collapse of East European Communism and the Repercussions within the Soviet Union' (Part 1), *Journal of Cold War Studies*, 5(4) (2003).

Mark Kramer, 'The Collapse of East European Communism and the Repercussions within the Soviet Union' (Part 2), *Journal of Cold War Studies*, 6(4) (2004).

Mark Kramer, 'The Collapse of East European Communism and the Repercussions within the Soviet Union' (Part 3), *Journal of Cold War Studies*, 7(1) (2005).

Richard Ned Lebow and Richard Herrmann (eds), *Ending the Cold War* (Palgrave, Basingstoke, 2004).

Don Oberdorfer, *The Turn: How the Cold War Came to an End* (Jonathan Cape, London, 1992).

Silvio Pons and Federico Romero (eds), *Reinterpreting the End of the Cold War* (Cass, London, 2005).

On the war in Afghanistan:

George Arney, *Afghanistan* (Mandarin, London, 1990).

Rodric Braithwaite, *Afgantsy: The Russians in Afghanistan, 1979–89* (Profile Books, London, 2011).

Theo Farrell, *Unwinnable: Britain's War in Afghanistan, 2001–14* (London: Bodley Head, 2017).

Gregory Feifer, *The Great Gamble: The Soviet War in Afghanistan* (Harper, London, 2010).

Mark Galeotti, *Afghanistan: The Soviet Union's Last War* (Frank Cass, London, 1994).

Anthony Hyman, *Afghanistan under Soviet Domination* (Macmillan, London, 1992).

The collapse of communism has generated an enormous literature and remains the centre of intense debate, but on Soviet policy see especially:

Archie Brown, *Seven Years that Changed the World* (Oxford University Press, Oxford, 2007).

Archie Brown, *The Rise and Fall of Communism* (Vintage, London, 2010).

Mark Galeotti, *Gorbachev and his Revolution* (Macmillan, Basingstoke, 1997).

Geoffrey Hosking, *The Awakening of the Soviet Union* (Harvard University Press, Cambridge, 1991).

Mark Kramer, 'The Collapse of the Soviet Union' (Part 1), *Journal of Cold War Studies*, 5(4) (2003).

Mark Kramer, 'The Collapse of the Soviet Union' (Part 2), *Journal of Cold War Studies*, 6(4) (2004).

William Taubman, *Gorbachev* (Simon & Schuster, New York, 2017).

William Watson, *The Collapse of Communism in the Soviet Union* (Greenwood Press, Westport, 1998).

Vladimir Zubok, 'Gorbachev and the End of the Cold War', *Cold War History*, 2(2) (2002).

While on events in Eastern Europe:

Frederic Bozo, Marie-Pierre Rey, N. Piers Ludlow, and Leopoldo Nuti (eds), *Europe and the End of the Cold War: A Reappraisal* (Routledge, London, 2008).

Jacqueline Hayden, *The Collapse of Communist Power in Poland* (Routledge, London, 2006).

Charles S. Maier, *Dissolution: The Crisis of Communism and the End of East Germany* (Princeton University Press, Princeton, 1997).

David Mason, *Revolution and Transition in East-Central Europe* (2nd edn, Westview Press, Boulder, 1996).

Renée de Nevers, *Comrades No More: The Seeds of Political Change in Eastern Europe* (MIT Press, Cambridge, 2003).

Elise Sarotte, *1989: The Struggle to Create Post-Cold War Europe* (Princeton University Press, Princeton, 2011).

Viktor Sebestyen, *Revolution 1989: The Fall of the Soviet Empire* (Phoenix Books, London, 2010).

Michael Waller, *The End of Communist Power Monopoly* (Manchester University Press, Manchester, 1993).

And on the Iran–Iraq War:

John Bulloch and Harvey Morris, *The Gulf War: Its Origins, History and Consequences* (Methuen, London, 1989).

Stephen Pelletiere, *The Iran–Iraq War* (Praeger, New York, 1992).

For the strides taken in European integration in the 1980s, down to the Maastricht Treaty:

Alasdair Blair, *Dealing with Europe: Britain and the Negotiation of the Maastricht Treaty* (Ashgate, Aldershot, 1999).

Juliet Lodge (ed.), *The European Community and the Challenge of the Future* (Pinter, London, 1989).

Peter Ludlow, *The Making of the European Monetary System* (Butterworths, London, 1982).

George Ross, *Jacques Delors and European Integration* (Oxford University Press, New York, 1995).

For discussions of Reagan's role in ending the Cold War:

John P. Diggins, *Ronald Reagan* (Norton, New York, 2007).

Paul Lettow, *Ronald Reagan and his Quest to Abolish Nuclear Weapons* (Random House, New York, 2005).

Richard Reeves, *President Reagan* (Simon & Schuster, New York, 2005).

And on Central America:

William LeoGrande, *Our Own Backyard: The US in Central America, 1977–92* (University of North Carolina Press, New Haven, 1998).

Part VI, 1990–2000

A fascinating overall interpretation of the period is:

Ian Clark, *The Post-Cold War Order* (Oxford University Press, Oxford, 2001).

And on globalization:

D. Held and Anthony McGrew (eds), *The Global Transformations Reader* (Polity Press, Oxford, 2000).

In general, on the US policy in the Post-Cold War years:

Lester Brune, *The United States and Post-Cold War Interventions: Bush and Clinton in Somalia, Haiti and Bosnia* (Regina Books, Claremont, 1998).

Derek Chollet and James Goldgeier, *America between the Wars: From 11/9 to 9/11* (Public Affairs, New York, 2009).

Michael Cox, *US Foreign Policy after the Cold War* (Pinter, London, 1995).

John Dumbrell, *Clinton's Foreign Policy* (Routledge, London, 2009).

Jeffrey Engel, *When the World Seemed New: George H.W. Bush and the End of the Cold War* (Houghton Mifflin, Boston, 2017).

James Goldgeier and Michael McFaul, *Power and Purpose: US Policy towards Russia after the Cold War* (Brookings, Washington, 2003).

John C. Hulsman, *A Paradigm for the New World Order* (Macmillan, Basingstoke, 1997).

Steven Hurst, *The Foreign Policy of the Bush Administration* (Cassell, London, 1999).

Robert Hutchings (ed.), *At the End of the American Century: America's Role in the Post-Cold War World* (Johns Hopkins University Press, Baltimore, 1998).

William Hyland, *Clinton's World* (Greenwood Press, Westport, 1999).

John Ikenberry, *American Unrivalled: The Future of the Balance of Power* (Cornell University Press, Ithaca, 2002).

For controversial, yet sometimes influential discussions of the implications of the end of the Cold War and how future US policy might develop:

Francis Fukuyama, *The End of History and the Last Man* (Penguin, London, 1993).

Anthony Lake, 'Confronting Backlash States', *Foreign Affairs*, 73(2) (March–April 1994).

Samuel P. Huntington, 'The Clash of Civilizations?', *Foreign Affairs*, 72(3) (Summer 1993).

The last was later expanded into:

Samuel P. Huntington, *The Clash of Civilizations and the Remaking of World Order* (Free Press, New York, 2002).

For a seminal critique of the tendency of Western policy-makers to misread Asian and Middle Eastern questions:

Edward W. Said, *Orientalism* (3rd edn, Penguin, London, 2003).

On Russia and the problems of the former USSR:

Leon Aron, *Yeltsin: A Revolutionary Life* (HarperCollins, London, 2000).

Timothy Colton, *Yeltsin: A Political Life* (Basic Books, New York, 2008).

John Dunlop, *The Rise of Russia and the Fall of the Soviet Empire* (Princeton University Press, Princeton, 1993).

Stasys Knezys and Romanas Sedlickas, *The War in Chechnya* (Texas A&M University, College Station, 1999).

Anatol Lieven, *Chechnya: Tombstone of Russian Power* (Yale University Press, New Haven, 1998).

Peter Shearman, *Russian Foreign Policy since 1990* (Westview, Boulder, 1995).

Memoirs by key US policy-makers include:

Madeleine Albright, *Madam Secretary: A Memoir* (Pan, London, 2004).

James A. Baker, *The Politics of Diplomacy* (Putnam, New York, 1995).

George Bush and Brent Scowcoft, *A World Transformed* (Knopf, New York, 1998).

Warren Christopher, *Chances of a Lifetime* (Simon & Schuster, New York, 2001).

Bill Clinton, *My Life* (Arrow, London, 2005).

While, from Russia:

Boris Yeltsin, *The View from the Kremlin* (HarperCollins, London, 1994).

On South Africa:

F. W. de Klerk, *The Autobiography: The Last Trek, a New Beginning* (Macmillan, London, 1999).

Nelson Mandela, *Long Walk to Freedom* (Little, Brown, Chicago, 1994).

German reunification at the start of the decade is the focus of a number of works, but see especially:

Stephen Szabo, *The Diplomacy of German Unification* (New York, 1992).

Philip Zelikow and Condoleeza Rice, *German Unified and Europe Transformed* (Harvard University Press, Cambridge, 1995).

On the Balkans conflicts:

Christopher Bennett, *Yugoslavia's Bloody Collapse* (Hurst, London, 1995).

Ivo Daalder, *Getting to Dayton: The Making of America's Bosnia Policy* (Brookings Institution, Washington, DC, 2000).

Misha Glenny, *The Fall of Yugoslavia* (Penguin, London, 1996).

Tim Judah, *The Serbs* (Yale University Press, New Haven, 1997).

Noel Malcolm, *Bosnia: A Short History* (2nd edn, Macmillan, London, 1996).

Noel Malcolm, *Kosovo: A Short History* (Macmillan, London, 1998).

Jeffrey Morton, Paul Forage, Stefano Bianchini, and R. Craig Nation (eds), *Reflections on the Balkan Wars: Ten Years after the Break-Up of Yugoslavia* (Palgrave, Basingstoke, 2004).

While two memoirs on the attempts to settle the Bosnian conflict are:

Richard Holbrooke, *To End a War* (Modern Library, New York, 1999).

David Owen, *Balkan Odyssey* (Victor Gollancz, London, 1996).

On European security:

Clay Clemens, *NATO and the Quest for Post-Cold War Security* (Macmillan, Basingstoke, 1997).

Andrew Dorman, *European Security: An Introduction to Security Issues in Post-Cold War Europe* (Dartmouth, Aldershot, 1995).

William Park and Wyn Rees, *Rethinking Security in Post-Cold War Europe* (Longman, London, 1998).

Trevor Taylor, *European Security and the Former Soviet Union* (Royal Institute of International Affairs, London, 1994).

On East Asia:

Samuel Kim, *North Korean Foreign Relations in the Post-Cold War Era* (Oxford University Press, New York, 1998).

Russell Ong, *China's Security Interests in the Post-Cold War Era* (Curzon, Richmond, 2001).

Li Xiaobang, *Interpreting US–China–Taiwan Relations: China in the Post-Cold War Era* (University Press of America, Lanham, 1998).

Suisheng Zhao, *Power Competition in East Asia* (St Martin's Press, New York, 1997).

In the Middle East, on the Oslo peace process and its difficulties:

Andrew Buchanan, *Peace with Justice* (Macmillan, London, 2000).

Robert O. Freedman, *The Middle East and the Peace Process* (University Press of Florida, Gainesville, 1998).

Ahmed Qurie, *Beyond Oslo: The Struggle for Palestine* (I. B. Tauris, London, 2008).

Ofira Seliktar, *Doomed to Failure? The Politics of the Oslo Peace Process* (Greenwood Press, London, 2009).

Graham Usher, *Dispatches from Palestine: The Rise and Fall of the Oslo Peace Process* (Pluto Press, London, 1999).

On conflict in the Gulf:

Said Aburish, *Saddam Hussein* (Bloomsbury, London, 2000).

Andrew and Patrick Cockburn, *Out of the Ashes: The Resurrection of Saddam Hussein* (HarperCollins, New York, 1999).

Lawrence Freedman and Efraim Karsh, *The Gulf Conflict* (Faber & Faber, London, 1993).

Dilip Hiro, *Desert Shield to Desert Storm: The Second Gulf War* (HarperCollins, London, 1992).

And on the changes in southern Africa that accompanied the demise of apartheid:

Walter Carlsnaes and Marie Muller (eds), *Change and South Africa's External Relations* (Thomson, Johannesburg, 1997).

Chester Crocker, *High Noon in Southern Africa* (Norton, New York, 1992).

Timothy Sisk, *Democratization in South Africa* (Princeton University Press, Princeton, 1995).

Patti Waldmeir, *Anatomy of a Miracle: The End of Apartheid and the Birth of the New South Africa* (Norton, New York, 1997).

Parts VII and VIII, 2001–19

Substantial memoirs by Western policy-makers include:

Tony Blair, *A Journey* (Arrow, London, 2011).

George W. Bush, *Decision Points* (Virgin Books, London, 2011).

Dick Cheney, *In My Time: A Personal and Political Memoir* (Threshold Editions, New York, 2011).

Condoleezza Rice, *No Higher Honor* (Simon & Schuster, New York, 2011).

Donald Rumsfeld, *Known and Unknown: A Memoir* (Sentinel, New York, 2011).

For valuable retrospective discussions of Bush's foreign policy:

Peter Baker, *Days of Fire: Bush and Cheney in the White House* (Doubleday, New York, 2013).

Hal Brands and Peter Feaver, 'The Case for Bush Revisionism: Re-Evaluating the Legacy of America's 43rd President', *Journal of Strategic Studies*, 41(1-2) (2017).

Melvyn Leffler, 'The Foreign Policies of the George W. Bush Administration', *Diplomatic History*, 37(2) (2013).

Jean Edward Smith, *Bush* (Simon & Schuster, New York, 2016).

On the events of 9/11 and their background:

Steve Coll, *Ghost Wars: The Secret History of the CIA, Afghanistan and bin Laden from the Soviet Invasion to September 10, 2001* (Penguin, London, 2005).

National Commission on Terrorist Attacks upon the United States, *The 9/11 Commission Report* (W. W. Norton and Co., New York, 2004).

Lawrence Wright, *The Looming Tower: Al-Qaeda's Road to 9/11* (Penguin, London, 2007).

Bob Woodward wrote a series of highly important and well-informed books on policy-making under George Bush Junior (all published by Pocket Books, New York):

Bush at War, Part I (2003).

Plan of Attack (2004), on the invasion of Iraq.

State of Denial: Bush at War, Part III (2007).

The War Within: A Secret White House History, 2006–8 (2009).

Early attempts to interpret the Obama administration during his first term included:

Stephen Carter, *The Violence of Peace: America's Wars in the Age of Obama* (Beast Books, New York, 2011).

James Mann, *The Obamians: The Struggle inside the White House to Redefine American Power* (Penguin, New York, 2013).

David Sanger, *Confront and Conceal: Obama's Secret Wars and Surprising Use of American Power* (Broadway Books, New York, 2013).

Bob Woodward, *Obama's Wars* (Simon & Schuster, New York, 2010).

Fuller discussions, covering both terms, now include:

Derek Chollet, *The Long Game: How Obama Defied Washington and Redefined America's role in the World* (Public Affairs, New York, 2016).

Colin Dueck, *The Obama Doctrine* (Oxford University Press, 2015).

Robert Kaufman, *Dangerous Doctrine: How Obama's Grand Strategy Weakened America* (Kentucky University Press, Lexington, 2016).

Chollet is positive about the President, Dueck and Kaufman more critical. For a balanced, short discussion:

Michael Clarke and Anthony Ricketts, 'Did Obama Have a Grand Strategy?', *Journal of Strategic Studies*, 40(1-2) (2017).

In general, on the War on Terror:

Richard A. Clarke, *Against all Enemies: Inside America's War on Terror* (Free Press, New York, 2004).

Peter L. Bergen, *The Longest War: America and Al-Qaeda since 9/11* (Free Press, New York, 2011).

Peter Bergen, *Manhunt: from 9/11 to Abbottabad—The Ten Year Search for Osama bin Laden* (Bodley Head, London, 2011).

Jason Burke, *The 9/11 Wars* (Allen Lane, London, 2007).

Fawaz A. Gerges, *The Rise and Fall of Al-Qaeda* (Oxford University Press, New York, 2011).

Bruce Riedel, *Deadly Embrace: Pakistan, America and the Future of Global Jihad* (Brookings Institution, Washington, 2011).

Syed Saleem Shahzad, *Inside Al-Qaeda and the Taliban* (Pluto Press, London, 2011).

Specifically, on Afghanistan:

Tim Bird and Alex Marshall, *Afghanistan: How the West Lost its Way* (Yale University Press, New Haven, 2011).

Sherard Cowper-Coles, *Cables from Kabul: The Inside Story of the West's Afghanistan Campaign* (Harper Press, London, 2011).

Seth G. Jones, *In the Graveyard of Empires: America's War in Afghanistan* (W. W. Norton, New York, 2010).

Ahmed Rashid, *Taliban: The Power of Militant Islam in Afghanistan* (I. B. Tauris, London, 2010).

Peter Tomsen, *Wars of Afghanistan* (Public Affairs, New York, 2011) (which puts US policy in the broad perspective of Afghan history).

And on different aspects of the Iraq conflict:

Ali A. Allawi, *The Occupation of Iraq: Winning the War, Losing the Peace* (Yale University Press, New Haven, 2008).

Terry H. Anderson, *Bush's Wars* (Oxford University Press, New York, 2011).

Patrick Cockburn, *The Occupation: War and Resistance in Iraq* (Verso, London, 2007).

Patrick Cockburn, *Muqtada al-Sadr and the Shia Insurgency in Iraq* (Faber & Faber, London, 2008).

Con Coughlin, *Saddam: The Secret Life* (Pan, London, 2007).

Brian Jones, *Failing Intelligence: How We were Fooled into Going to War in Iraq* (Dialogue, London, 2010).

Thomas E. Ricks, *Fiasco: The American Military Adventure in Iraq* (Penguin, London, 2007).

On the British role in these conflicts:

John Chilcot et al., *Chilcot Report: Executive Summary* (Canbury Press, London, 2017).

Jack Fairweather, *A War of Choice: The British in Iraq 2003–9* (Jonathan Cape, London, 2011).

Frank Ledwidge, *Losing Small Wars: British Military Failure in Iraq and Afghanistan* (Yale University Press, New Haven, 2011).

Richard North, *Ministry of Defeat: The British War in Iraq 2003–2009* (Continuum, New York, 2009).

A work that tries to understand why Britain voted to leave the European Union in 2016 is:

Harold Clarke, Matthew Goodwin, and Paul Whiteley, *Brexit* (Cambridge University Press, Cambridge, 2017)

The perspective of a Downing Street official:

Craig Oliver, *Unleashing Demons: The Inside Story of Brexit* (Hodder, London, 2017).

And on the troubles of the Euro:

Joseph Stiglitz, *The Euro and its Threat to the Future of Europe* (Allen Lane, London, 2016).

Among the many books that attempt to understand Russia under Vladimir Putin, and his impact on world affairs, some balanced and insightful accounts are:

Peter Conradi, *Who Lost Russia? How the World Entered a New Cold War* (Oneworld Publications, London, 2017).

Masha Gessen, *The Man without a Face: The Unlikely Rise of Vladimir Putin* (Granta Books, London, 2012).

Bobo Lo, *Russia and the New World Disorder* (Brookings Institution, Washington, 2015).

Kimberly Marten, 'Putin's Choices: Explaining Russian Foreign Policy and Intervention in Ukraine', *Washington Quarterly*, 38(2) (2015).

Richard Sakwa, *Russia against the Rest: The Post-Cold War Crisis of World Order* (Cambridge University Press, Cambridge, 2017).

Michael Stuermer, *Putin and the Rise of Russia* (Phoenix Books, London, 2009).

Shaun Walker, *The Long Hangover: Putin's New Russia and the Ghosts of the Past* (Oxford University Press, Oxford, 2018).

On the implications of the continuing rise of Chinese power:

William Callahan, 'China's Strategic Futures: Debating the Post-American World Order', *Asian Survey*, 52(4) (2012).

Yong Deng, *China's Struggle for Status: The Realignment of International Relations* (Cambridge University Press, New York, 2008).

Yong Deng and Feiling Wang, *In the Eyes of the Dragon: China Views the World* (Rowman & Littlefield, Lanham, 1999).

Christopher R. Hughes *Chinese Nationalism in the Global Era* (Routledge, London, 2006).

Linda Jakobson and Dean Knox, 'New Foreign Policy Actors in China', *SIPRI Policy Paper*, no. 26 (2010).

David Kang, *China Rising: Peace, Power and Order in East Asia* (Columbia University Press, New York, 2007).

James Kynge, *China Shakes the World* (Phoenix Books, London, 2009).

Richard McGregor, *The Party: The Secret World of China's Communist Rulers* (Penguin, London, 2011).

Jisi Wang, 'China's Search for Stability with America', *Foreign Affairs*, 84(5) (Sept/Oct 2005).

Jeffrey N. Wasserstrom, *China in the Twenty-First Century* (Oxford University Press, Oxford, 2010).

Ye Zicheng, *Inside China's Grand Strategy* (University Press of Kentucky, Lexington, 2011).

Insightful works on China under Xi Jinping include:

Kerry Brown, *CEO, China: The Rise of Xi Jinping* (I. B. Tauris, New York, 2016).

Kerry Brown, *China's World* (I. B. Tauris, New York, 2017).

Howard French, *Everything under the Heavens: How the Past Shapes China's Push for Global Power* (Alfred Knopf, New York, 2017).

David Lampton, 'Xi Jinping and the National Security Commission: Policy Coordination and Political Power', *Journal of Contemporary China*, 24(95) (2015).

On the South China Sea controversies and the Law of the Sea:

Sarah Raine and Christian Le Mière, *Regional Disorder: The South China Sea Disputes* (Routledge, Abingdon, 2013).

Ian Storey and Lin Cheng-yi (eds), *The South China Sea Dispute: Navigating Diplomatic and Strategic Tensions* (ISEAS, Singapore, 2016).

Accessible works on the post-2008 economic depression:

Alistair Darling, *Back from the Brink: 1000 Days at Number 11* (Atlantic Books, London, 2011) (by Britain's Chancellor of the Exchequer).

Paul Krugman, *The Return of Depression Economics and the Crisis of 2008* (Allen Lane, London, 2008).

Nouriel Roubini, *Crisis Economics* (Penguin, London, 2011).

Joseph Stiglitz, *Freefall: Free Market and the Sinking of the Global Economy* (Penguin, London, 2010).

Initial attempts to understand the 'Arab Spring' included:

Hamid Dabashi, *The Arab Spring: The End of Post-Colonialism* (Zed Books, London, 2012).

Jean-Pierre Filiu, *The Arab Revolution: Ten Lessons from the Democratic Uprising* (C. Hurst and Co., London, 2011).

Toby Manhire, *The Arab Spring: Rebellion, Revolution and a New World Order* (Guardian Books, London, 2012).

Tariq Ramadan, *The Arab Awakening: Islam and the New Middle East* (Allen Lane, London, 2012).

For the conflict in Syria, the most detailed book up to 2016 is:

Charles Lister, *The Syrian Jihad: Al-Qaeda, the Islamic State and the Evolution of an Insurgency* (Oxford University Press, New York, 2015).

Other valuable works are:

Patrick Cockburn, Robert Fisk, and Kim Sengupta, *Syria: Descent into the Abyss* (Mango Media, London, 2016) (which provides a blow-by-blow account).

William Harris, *Quicksilver War: Syria, Iraq and the Spiral of Conflict* (Oxford University Press, New York, 2018) (which lists some useful internet sources).

Christopher Phillips, *The Battle for Syria: International Rivalry in the Middle East* (Yale University Press, New Haven, 2016) (useful for understanding how the Syrian civil war developed into a broader conflict).

On the so-called Islamic State (IS / ISIS) see:

Fawaz Gerges, *ISIS: A History* (Princeton University Press, Princeton, 2016).

William McCants, *The ISIS Apocalypse: The History, Strategy, and Doomsday Vision of the Islamic State* (St Martin's Press, New York, 2015).

Useful broader context on IS is provided by:

Patrick Cockburn, *The Rise of Islamic State: ISIS and the New Sunni Revolution* (Verso, London, 2015).

Paul Rogers, *Irregular War: ISIS and the New Threat from the Margins* (I. B. Tauris, London, 2016).

Jessica Stern and J. M. Berger, *ISIS: The State of Terror* (HarperCollins, New York, 2015).

Index

A

B

C

H

J

K

L

N

O

Q

R

S

V

W

X

Y

Z